INVESTIGATION OF
THE ASSASSINATION OF PRESIDENT JOHN F. KENNEDY

HEARINGS

Before the President's Commission on the Assassination of President Kennedy

PURSUANT TO EXECUTIVE ORDER 11130, an Executive order creating a Commission to ascertain, evaluate, and report upon the facts relating to the assassination of the late President John F. Kennedy and the subsequent violent death of the man charged with the assassination and S.J. RES. 137, 88TH CONGRESS, a concurrent resolution conferring upon the Commission the power to administer oaths and affirmations, examine witnesses, receive evidence, and issue subpenas

EXHIBITS
2190 TO 2651

Volume
XXV

25

UNITED STATES GOVERNMENT PRINTING OFFICE
WASHINGTON, D.C.

U.S. GOVERNMENT PRINTING OFFICE, WASHINGTON: 1964

For sale in complete sets by the Superintendent of Documents, U.S. Government Printing Office
Washington, D.C., 20402

PRESIDENT'S COMMISSION ON THE ASSASSINATION OF PRESIDENT KENNEDY

CHIEF JUSTICE EARL WARREN, *Chairman*

SENATOR RICHARD B. RUSSELL
SENATOR JOHN SHERMAN COOPER
REPRESENTATIVE HALE BOGGS
REPRESENTATIVE GERALD R. FORD
MR. ALLEN W. DULLES
MR. JOHN J. MCCLOY

J. LEE RANKIN, *General Counsel*

Assistant Counsel

FRANCIS W. H. ADAMS
JOSEPH A. BALL
DAVID W. BELIN
WILLIAM T. COLEMAN, Jr.
MELVIN ARON EISENBERG
BURT W. GRIFFIN
LEON D. HUBERT, Jr.
ALBERT E. JENNER, Jr.
WESLEY J. LIEBELER
NORMAN REDLICH
W. DAVID SLAWSON
ARLEN SPECTER
SAMUEL A. STERN
HOWARD P. WILLENS*

Staff Members

PHILLIP BARSON
EDWARD A. CONROY
JOHN HART ELY
ALFRED GOLDBERG
MURRAY J. LAULICHT
ARTHUR MARMOR
RICHARD M. MOSK
JOHN J. O'BRIEN
STUART POLLAK
ALFREDDA SCOBEY
CHARLES N. SHAFFER, Jr.

Biographical information on the Commissioners and the staff can be found in the Commission's *Report*.

*Mr. Willens also acted as liaison between the Commission and the Department of Justice.

Contents

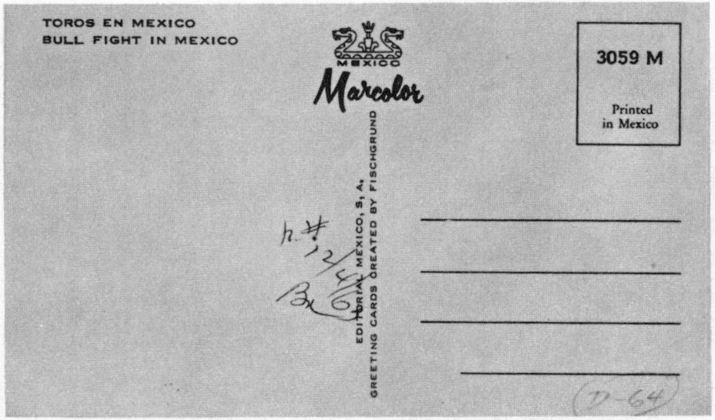

Commission Exhibit No. 2190

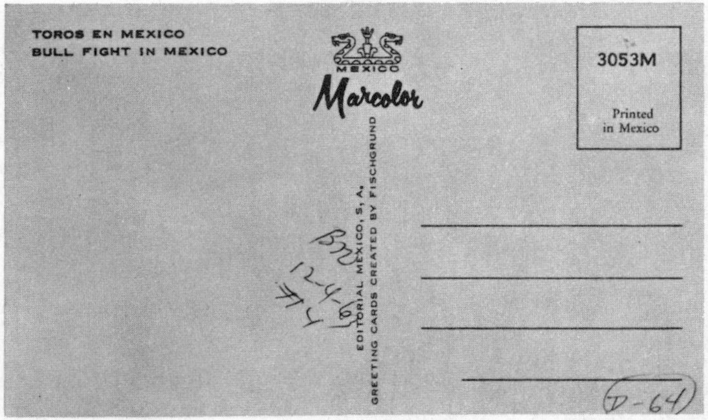

Commission Exhibit No. 2190—Continued

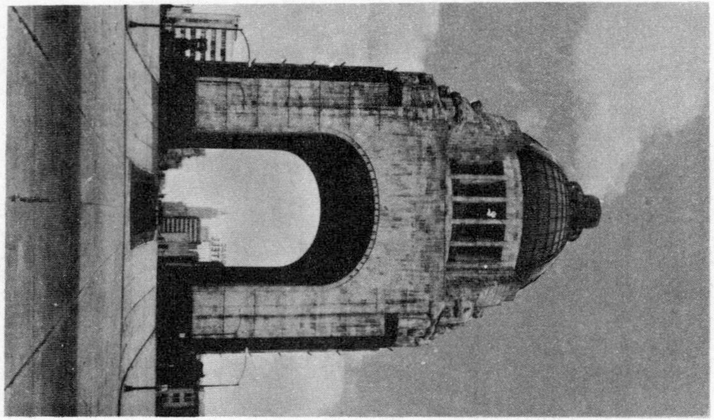

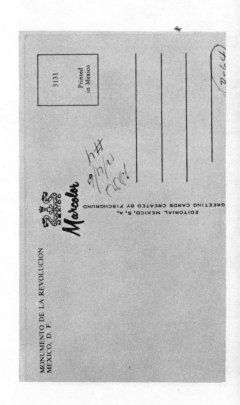

MONUMENTO DE LA REVOLUCION
MEXICO, D. F.

MEXICO
Marcolor

EDITORIAL MEXICO, S. A.
GREETING CARDS CREATED BY FISCHGRUND

3131

Printed
in Mexico

#4

D-64

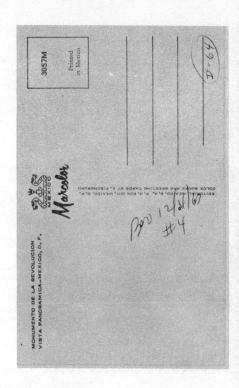

MONUMENTO DE LA REVOLUCION
VISTA PANORAMICA–MEXICO, D. F.

MEXICO
Marcolor

EDITORIAL MEXICO, S. A. P. O. BOX 2071, MEXICO, D. F.
COLOR BOOKS AND GREETING CARDS BY E. FISCHGRUND

3057M

Printed
in Mexico

#4

D-64

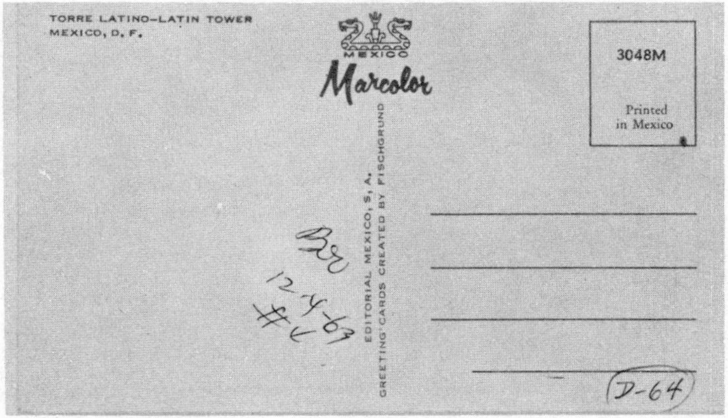

COMMISSION EXHIBIT No. 2190—Continued

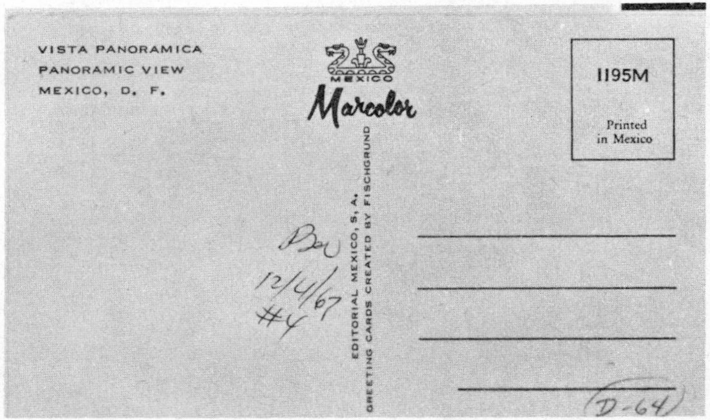

COMMISSION EXHIBIT No. 2190—Continued

UNITED STATES DEPARTMENT OF JUSTICE
FEDERAL BUREAU OF INVESTIGATION

Copy to:

Report of: SA EDWIN DALRYMPLE   Office: Houston
Date: 2/20/64

Field Office File #: Houston 105-1291   Bureau File #: 105-82555

Title: LEE HARVEY OSWALD

Character: INTERNAL SECURITY - R - CUBA

Synopsis:

No record located at Houston of air travel by OSWALD from Houston to Austin, Texas, on 9/25/63. Pan American World Airways unable to locate any record that OSWALD inquired regarding flights from Houston to Mexico City. E. P. HAMMETT, Continental Trailways ticket agent at Houston, identified ticket stub of ticket sold on 9/25/63 at Houston for travel to Laredo, Texas, as ticket he sold. HAMMETT went on duty at 10:30 PM on 9/25/63. HAMMETT viewed photographs of OSWALD and stated he believes he recalled selling a ticket to OSWALD in approximately September, 1963. HAMMETT stated person in question inquired as to price of tickets to Mexico City and had difficulty making up mind regarding travel. Other employees of Continental Trailways Bus Terminal on duty at above period unable to recall seeing OSWALD. Mrs. LOLA E. HOLIMAN, operator of employment service at Houston, reportedly had conversation with OSWALD in approximately October, 1963, but upon interview unable to positively identify him.

\- P -

— Commission Exhibit No. 2191 —

DETAILS: AT HOUSTON, TEXAS:

The following investigation was conducted concerning OSWALD's reported travel and movements between New Orleans, Louisiana, and Mexico City, Mexico, during the period September 25 - 26, 1963. Previous investigation

established OSWALD cashed a check at New Orleans, Louisiana, after 8:00 AM on September 25, 1963. He was reported to have telephoned Mrs. HORACE TWIFORD at Houston on the evening of September 25, 1963, at a time she believed was between 7 and 9:00 PM. In the interim, an employee at Selective Service. Headquarters, Austin, Texas, reported she believed she was contacted by OSWALD at Austin on September 25, 1963, at approximately 1:00 PM. When OSWALD talked to Mrs. TWIFORD at Houston, he indicated he was considering flying to Mexico. Other witnesses have reported OSWALD boarded a Continental Trailways bus at Houston, Texas, at approximately 2:00 AM on September 26, 1963, on which bus he traveled to Laredo, Texas, and thereafter traveled to Mexico City. Investigation was conducted to determine if OSWALD might have flown from New Orleans to Houston and thence to Austin, Texas, on September 25, 1963.

On January 16, 1964, DON RODGERS, Continental Airlines, Inc., Houston International Airport, stated that in September, 1963, Continental had the only air schedules between Austin and Houston, although these routes were subsequently taken over by Trans-Texas Airways in November, 1963. RODGERS checked his records and schedules and reported that on September 25, 1963, Continental Airlines had no flights to Austin from Houston between 6:50 AM and 12:20 PM. A person could have left Houston on Continental Flight 215 at 12:20 PM and would have arrived at Austin at 1:10 PM on that date. RODGERS located the manifest for Flight 215 on September 25, 1963, and the passenger list was examined. Neither OSWALD's name nor any of his known aliases appeared on this manifest.

RODGERS reported that a passenger could have left Austin on Continental Flight 212 at approximately 2:30 PM on September 25, 1963, arriving at Houston at approximately 3:20 PM. There were no more scheduled flights from Austin to Houston from 2:30 PM until 10:00 AM on September 26, 1963. RODGERS pointed out the identities of passengers on flights from Austin to Houston would not be available in the records maintained at Houston, Texas.

In view of the possibility that OSWALD, after arriving at Houston from New Orleans, actually considered flying to Mexico City, JAMES D. GIBSON, Station Manager,

Pan American World Airways (PAA), Houston International Airport, was interviewed on January 16, 1964. GIBSON made available copies of PAA flight releases for September 24, 25,26, 1963. These are lists of the persons who requested space on PAA Flight 501 from Houston to Mexico City on those dates. OSWALD's name was not on these lists nor was any of his known aliases. GIBSON pointed out that persons who fail to appear at flight time, who cancelled previous reservations, or who appeared at the last minute without reservations are also recorded on these lists, sometimes in ink by the employees on duty. These flight release lists are actually prepared by the PAA Central Reservations Department at Miami, Florida, and are furnished interested offices by teletype. GIBSON pointed out that the PAA Central Reservations Office at Miami had previously been carefully checked in connection with this investigation without locating OSWALD's name. GIBSON stated his office had no record of any request or inquiry on the part of OSWALD in connection with possible air travel to Mexico City.

On January 17, 1964, DAVID R. TAYLOR, District Sales Manager, PAA, 1210 South Main Street, checked all available records in an effort to find a file card or other data indicating that OSWALD may have made an exploratory inquiry concerning possible travel to Mexico City without actually making a reservation. Mr. TAYLOR stated he could find no such record and his records had been searched thoroughly at an earlier date without locating any record pertaining to OSWALD. Mr. TAYLOR pointed out that PAA has the only direct air travel to Mexico City from Houston.

On January 24, 1964, S. R. COBB, Station Manager, Continental Trailways Bus Terminal, 1114 McKinney, made a thorough review of personnel and payroll records to identify all employees of his company who were physically present at the Continental Trailways Bus Terminal on the evening of September 25, 1963, and up to 2:30 AM on September 26, 1963. It was determined that the following twelve employees, consisting of six ticket agents, one information clerk, three porters, and two snackbar attendants were on duty at that time and could conceivably have observed OSWALD. Each of the listed employees was interviewed on the dates indicated and photographs of OSWALD and of his baggage were

19 part 5 (1) 22 my

displayed to them. With the exception of E. P. HAMMETT, mentioned below, none of these employees could recall having seen OSWALD in the Continental Trailways Bus Terminal:

Ticket Agents

Name	Date Interviewed
ROBERT STEPHENSON 10:30 PM - 6:30 AM	January 21, 1964
MORGAN LAIRD, JR. 12:15 PM - 9:15 PM	January 21, 1964
RAY DYAL 2:15 PM - 11:00 PM	January 21, 1964
J. D. MOSS 2:15 PM - 11:00 PM	January 27, 1964
THOMAS MARSHALL 4:00 PM - 1:00 AM	January 27, 1964

Information Clerk

MARTHA OATES 4:00 PM - 1:00 AM	January 27, 1964

Porters

THEODORE GREEN 9:30 PM - 6:30 AM	January 28, 1964
JIMMY HOLLINS 11:15 PM - 8:15 AM	January 28, 1964
EDWARD ARCHIE 2:45 PM - 10:45 PM	January 27, 1964

Snackbar Attendants

LUCILLE LAUGHLIN 10:30 PM - 6:30 AM	January 28, 1964
VIRGINIA HUGHES 2:30 PM - 10:30 PM	February 4, 1964

On January 21, 1964, GEORGE PRATT, Manager, Continental Trailways Cafeteria, advised the cafeteria closes at 7:20 PM and between that time and 7:00 AM the only employees on duty in connection with his facility are the snackbar attendants who were identified and interviewed as set out above.

Previous investigation at the Continental Trailways Bus Terminal, Houston, Texas, revealed that for the period September 24, 1963, through September 26, 1963, only one ticket, bearing number 112230, was sold from Houston to Laredo, Texas, the price being $10.60. It was indicated the stubs of all such tickets were permanently filed at Dallas, Texas.

On January 17, 1964, CONNIE WALTERS, Continental Trailways Bus Company, 2805 Logan, Dallas, Texas, made available a copy of auditor's stub for Continental Trailways bus ticket number 112230. A rubber stamp impression on this stub indicated the ticket was issued on September 25, 1963, at Houston, Texas, for travel from Houston, Texas, to Laredo, Texas, at a price of $10.60. This rubber stamp impression carried "die number" 12, which Mr. WALTERS pointed out would identify the ticket agent at Houston who made this sale.

On January 21, 1964, E. P. HAMMETT, 8603 Detroit Street, Houston, Texas, employed as a ticket agent by Continental Trailways Bus Company, observed this copy of the above ticket stub and identified this as a ticket which he had sold on September 25, 1963. Photographs of LEE HARVEY OSWALD and of a small zipper bag used by OSWALD were exhibited to HAMMETT. HAMMETT furnished the following information:

There are very few tickets sold for travel between Houston and Laredo, Texas, and HAMMETT sometimes will not sell more than one in a week. He stated for this reason any sales or inquiries about tickets to Laredo and/or Mexico are unusual and he usually remembers them. On September 25, 1963, HAMMETT went on duty at 10:30 PM and was the only ticket agent on duty from 10:30 PM until 6:30 AM on September 26, 1963.

HAMMETT stated he could recall a man strongly resembling the photograph of OSWALD coming to his counter at some time which would have been approximately in late September, 1963, and making inquiry concerning travel to Laredo and to Mexico City. HAMMETT believes this man came to his counter at approximately midnight. The man HAMMETT recalls was wearing a pull-over sweater which he believes was brown and white, white dungarees, and dirty white canvas shoes. This man inquired as to prices of tickets directly to Mexico City and also to Laredo. HAMMETT stated this man seemed to be very undecided and could not make up his mind and after considerable discussion he left the counter and was not observed for a short period. There was no discussion of visas or Mexican tourist cards, these matters normally being handled when passengers arrive at Laredo, Texas. This man did not give HAMMETT his name, and normally there is no occasion for ticket agents to learn passengers' names.

HAMMETT stated after leaving his counter for some time, the above man finally returned and stated he decided to buy a ticket to Laredo, which HAMMETT sold him. This man was alone at the time and HAMMETT did not observe how he arrived at the bus terminal. HAMMETT noted that he believes it was about 1:30 AM or possibly 2:00 AM before this man finally purchased a ticket for use on a Continental Trailways bus which left Houston at 2:35 AM on September 26, 1963, for Laredo.

HAMMETT stated that the date stamp which he uses at the ticket counter is not changed at exactly midnight but is normally changed at 2 or 3 AM. He stated the date September 25, 1963, appearing on the ticket in question would not establish that it was necessarily purchased prior to midnight but could have been purchased as late as 2:30 AM.

After further study of the photograph of OSWALD, HAMMETT stated this photograph was definitely familiar to him and he believes he can associate OSWALD with the person who discussed with him travel from Houston to Laredo and Mexico City several months ago.

HAMMETT stated that between mdinight and 2:00 AM there is only one ticket agent at the counter, two porters work in the driveways, and normally one person is on duty in the snackbar operated in the lobby. The restaurant opening onto the lobby closes every night at 7:20 PM.

On January 29, 1964, Mrs. MARINA OSWALD, widow of LEE HARVEY OSWALD, was interviewed at Dallas, Texas, and advised that to the best of her knowledge LEE HARVEY OSWALD had not owned a brown and white pull-over sweater or white dungarees or white canvas shoes.

On January 25, 1964, JOHNNY W. JACKSON, 1111 West 26th Street, Houston, Texas, advised that he had recently applied for a job at the Spring Branch Employment Service on Long Point Road, which was operated by a woman approximately 55 years of age who conducted this business alone. JACKSON related that while talking with this woman she mentioned that she believed LEE HARVEY OSWALD had been in her agency to seek employment on or about October 24, 1963. This woman allegedly told JACKSON the man she believed to be OSWALD had told her his wife was in Dallas and was expecting a baby and that he was staying with friends while visiting in Houston. This woman also stated the man referred to remained in Houston for about four days before returning to Dallas. JACKSON stated this woman indicated she had not reported this matter to the FBI because she "did not want to become involved."

On January 28, 1964, Mrs. LOLA E. HOLIMAN, owner, Spring Branch Employment Service, 7511 Long Point Road, advised that she is the sole employee of her company and that she deals mainly in office and technical personnel. She stated occasionally a transient "wanderer" will come to her office from the Texas Employment Commission located directly across the street.

Mrs. HOLIMAN related she could recall that one afternoon in late October a young man came in who stated he was looking for a job and would take any kind of work. She recalled this man was wearing a white shirt and stated he had been selling books but was not making any money. This man had a slight accent, stated his wife was expecting a baby and that he needed a job badly. Mrs. HOLIMAN asked this man if he was a local man and he replied he had been working in New Orleans. Mrs. HOLIMAN commented that she had formerly lived in New Orleans and this caused a short conversation. This man commented that "things were rough" in New Orleans and he was trying to get back to Texas. He stated his mother resided at Fort Worth. Mrs. HOLIMAN asked this man if he was from Fort Worth and he said he

COMMISSION EXHIBIT No. 2191—Continued

had lived there a long time and went to school there. Mrs. HOLIMAN did not obtain this man's name and did not take an application from him, but suggested that he go across the street to the Texas Employment Commission.

Mrs. HOLIMAN stated when she later saw photographs of LEE HARVEY OSWALD in the newspapers she immediately thought that this man may have been OSWALD. At that time she recalled that the man mentioned above had visited her about one month before the assassination of President KENNEDY. She recalled that this man was about 25 years of age, approximately 5'7" in height, wore no hat and had a very soft voice with a definite accent. He was wearing some type of jacket rather than a suit.

Photographs of LEE HARVEY OSWALD were exhibited to Mrs. HOLIMAN, and she stated she now feels very uncertain as to whether the man she spoke to was OSWALD, although the photograph did look familiar. Mrs. HOLIMAN stated she had mentioned this matter to several of her customers but she denied having said to anyone that she knew this to be OSWALD or that the man in question had made any statements about staying with friends in Houston or how long he had been in Houston. Mrs. HOLIMAN stated she may have associated this man with OSWALD because of the published accounts that OSWALD was from Fort Worth and had been in New Orleans, although she believed she associated OSWALD with this man because of the similarity in appearance.

On January 27, 1964, BOYD A. LARSEN, Manager, Northwest Office, Texas Employment Commission, 1806 Woodvine, made a thorough check of all records maintained by his office and stated there was no record of LEE HARVEY OSWALD having applied for work through his agency at any time. Mr. LARSEN telephonically checked with the downtown offices of the Texas Employment Commission and was advised that records of those offices had previously been thoroughly checked and no information pertaining to OSWALD had been located.

It is noted the Northwest Office of the Texas Employment Commission is located directly across Long Point Road from the Spring Branch Employment Service.

COMMISSION EXHIBIT No. 2191—Continued

FD-204 (Rev. 3-3-59)

UNITED STATES DEPARTMENT OF JUSTICE
FEDERAL BUREAU OF INVESTIGATION

Copy to:

Report of: SA STEPHEN M. CALLENDER Office: NEW ORLEANS
Date: December 16, 1963

Field Office File No.: NO 100-16601 Bureau File No.: 105-82555

Title: LEE HARVEY OSWALD

Character: INTERNAL SECURITY - R

Synopsis: Greyhound Bus Co., New Orleans, La., officials advised one way bus tickets to Mexico City from New Orleans are prepared in three sections, first section for travel from New Orleans to Lake Charles, La., second section for travel from Lake Charles, La., to Laredo, Texas, and third section from Laredo, Texas, to Mexico City. Third section can not be used on Mexican bus lines for travel from Laredo, Texas, to Mexico City, but must be turned in at Laredo, where traveler is issued ticket on Mexican bus line. Greyhound Bus drivers who left New Orleans 2:45 p.m., 9/25/63, en route Laredo, Texas, via Lake Charles, La., do not recall observing any passenger resembling LEE HARVEY OSWALD on their buses. Continental Trailways **Bus leaves** New Orleans daily for Laredo, Texas, at 4:40 p.m., arriving Laredo at 1:20 p.m. following day. Another Continental Trailways Bus leaves New Orleans daily at 8:15 p.m., arriving next day Laredo, Texas, 7:35 p.m. Bus drivers for these Continental Trailways Buses leaving New Orleans, 9/25/63, for Laredo and drivers of buses connecting with these Laredo bound buses unable to recall any one possibly identical with LEE HARVEY OSWALD on their buses. Photo of OSWALD displayed to Canal Streetcar employees and Tulane Avenue bus operators employed on 9/24/63, but they were unable to recall seeing OSWALD on their streetcars or buses on 9/24/63. Subscribers of telephone numbers called from telephone of Mrs. CHARLES F. MURRET identified and no pertinent information

COMMISSION EXHIBIT No. 2192

NO 100-16601
SMC:gas

obtained. OSWALD donated to New Orleans Public Library an unidentified item and acknowledgement sent him on 10/9/63. ARTHUR ALBERT HEBERT vaguely recalls OSWALD as student in art class at Beauregard Junior High School. No record of any contact by OSWALD with Radio Station WSMB, New Orleans, La.

DETAILS:

COMMISSION EXHIBIT No. 2192—Continued

NO 100-16601/bap

CONTACT AT GREYHOUND BUS COMPANY,

NEW ORLEANS, LOUISIANA

3

COMMISSION EXHIBIT No. 2192—Continued

FD-302 (Rev. 1-25-60) FEDERAL BUREAU OF INVESTIGATION

1 Date 12/13/63

Mr. E. A. REIMHERR, Terminal Manager, Greyhound Bus Terminal, 1710 Tulane Avenue, furnished the following information relative to the purchasing and handling of tickets sold by his company at New Orleans.

He informed that when a traveler buys a ticket that this ticket may come in one or more sections depending upon the travelers destination.

For example if a traveler purchased a one way ticket from New Orleans, Louisiana to Mexico City, this ticket would come in three sections. This ticket is known as Greyhound form number three. The first section of this ticket is for travel from New Orleans, Louisiana to Lake Charles, Louisiana via Southern Greyhound Lines. Section number two is designated for travel from Lake Charles, Louisiana to Laredo Texas via Central Lines. Section number three of this ticket is for travel from Laredo, Texas to Mexico City, Mexico.

As far as Mr. REIMHERR knows, travelers who have purchased Greyhound tickets to Mexico City use the Mexican bus line called Transportes Del Norte.

Then if a round trip ticket is purchased from New Orleans, Louisiana to Mexico City, Mexico the ticket would consist of a total of six sections and this ticket is known as Greyhound form number six. The first three sections are the same as previously enumerated and the last three sections for travel are as follows:

Section number four designates travel from Mexico City, Mexico to Laredo, Texas. Section number five designates travel from Laredo, Texas to Lake Charles, Louisiana via Central Greyhound Lines. Section number six designates travel from Lake Charles, Louisiana to New Orleans, Louisiana via Southern Greyhound Bus Lines.

Mr. REIMHERR said the value of a one way from New Orleans to Mexico City costs $30.25. A round trip ticket from New Orleans to Mexico City and return costs $54.45.

On 12/13/63 at New Orleans, Louisiana File # NO 100-16601

by SA STEPHEN M. CALLENDER/bda Date dictated 12/13/63

4

This document contains neither recommendations nor conclusions of the FBI. It is the property of the FBI and is loaned to your agency; it and its contents are not to be distributed outside your agency.

COMMISSION EXHIBIT No. 2192—Continued

2-

NO 100-16601

Mr. REIMHERR said that the following is the administrative handling of the various sections of the travelers' tickets from New Orleans, Louisiana to Mexico City on a one way fare.

The first section of the ticket is kept by the bus driver who travels from New Orleans to Lake Charles, Louisiana. At Lake Charles, Louisiana the driver turns in the ticket to the terminal manager at Lake Charles, Louisiana, who in turn, forwards this ticket to the accounting division of the Southern Greyhound Lines at Lexington, Kentucky.

The second section of the ticket remains with the traveler from Lake Charles, Louisiana until the bus driver who drives the bus to Laredo, Texas takes this ticket. This bus driver then turns the second section of the ticket into the Greyhound terminal manager at Laredo who in turn forwards this second section to Central Greyhound Lines accounting office in San Francisco, California. The third section of the ticket cannot be used on Mexican bus lines, therefore, the holder of the ticket turns in this third section and in place of this section he is issued a ticket on the Mexican line. The third section of the ticket is then forwarded to the accounting section of Central Greyhound Bus Lines, San Francisco, California by the Mexican ticket agent. Mr. REIMHERR advised that all Greyhound bus tickets are numerically sequenced and have to be accounted for by his office. He pointed out that at the end of each week or whenever an excessive amount of copies of tickets sold accumulate, he then forwards these copies to the Southern Greyhound Accounting Division, in Lexington, Kentucky for accounting purposes.

5

FD-302 (Rev. 1-25-60)

FEDERAL BUREAU OF INVESTIGATION

Date 12/5/63

1

Mr. V. H. HOLSHOUSER, Superintendent, Southern Greyhound Lines Regional Office, 720 South Galvez Street, furnished the following information upon reviewing Photocopy of the sixth part of Greyhound ticket #185273 date issued August 31, 1963 :

This part of ticket #185273 is the sixth part of the ticket showing transportation from Lake Charles, Louisiana, to New Orleans, Louisiana. There is no record available in the Regional Office, Southern Greyhound, which will show the date of travel from Lake Charles to New Orleans. He pointed out the t h r e e punch marks in the endorsement space on this part of the ticket represents a cancellation of this portion of the ticket by the driver. The large punch mark near the word "GREYHOUND" is probably a punch mark of the baggage section, as it is too large to represent a driver's punch mark.

From a review of the Coach Operator Punch Card Record, he i d e n t i f i e d the punch mark shown on the sixth part of this ticket to be those of either Driver CECIL MAYFIELD or E. J. BERGERON, as the punch record of these drivers is similar to the punch marks on the sixth part of ticket #185273.

The drivers daily log for MAYFIELD, Badge #1258, dated September 24, 1963, shows MAYFIELD left Lake Charles, Louisiana, 12:30 PM September 24, 1963, and arrived at New Orleans 7:15 PM, September 24, 1963, and it was possible that the sixth portion of ticket #185273 was handled by MAYFIELD on this return trip to New Orleans.

The drivers daily log for BERGERON, Badge #1291, dated September 24, 1963, disclosed that BERGERON was off-duty on this date; however, the log for September 25, 1963, shows BERGERON left New Orleans driving a bus to Baton Rouge, Louisiana, at 10:30 PM and continued driving to Lake Charles, Louisiana, arriving at 3:45 AM, September 26, 1963. Mr. HOLSHOUSER pointed out that he was of the opinion that driver BERGERON did not handle the sixth part of ticket #185273.

On 12/5/63 at New Orleans, Louisiana File # NO 89-69

by SA JAMES E. SCHMIDT, JR. /jm Date dictated 12/5/63

6

He pointed out that if the first part of ticket #185273 was used at New Orleans on September 24, 1963, it was not possible for either MAYFIELD or BERGERON to have handled the first part of this ticket. He believed perhaps the date of September 24, 1963, may have been the date of return by the holder of this ticket, #185273, since the punch marks on the sixth portion of this ticket seems to match BERGERON's punch record.

Mr. HOLSHOUSER advised that he possibly could identify the driver handling the first part of ticket #185273 if same would be made available to him, and that the second and fifth parts of this ticket should be reviewed for identification of driver by the Superintendent of General Greyhound Lines in Houston, Texas.

Mr. HOLSHOUSER pointed out that the date of issuance was August 31, 1963, and that he was of the opinion that this ticket was probably used shortly after i s s u i n g date, and that the date of September 24, 1963, was probably the date on which the last portion of this ticket, #185273, was turned in when used by the holder of this ticket.

The drivers daily log identifies the bus driver and time of run but this log does not identify tickets by number for any trip, nor does it show the total number of passengers that were aboard the bus when it began its run. However, he pointed out that the register record or trip sheet submitted by the driver will disclose the date, time, driver and the number of passengers aboard the bus when leaving the bus station and also the bus destination. He advised that the tickets which are collected by the bus driver are placed in a separate envelope and forwarded to the accounting section of Southern Greyhound for further handling and that no entry is made by the bus driver on this register to identify tickets by ticket number.

7

Therefore, it is not possible to identify a passenger by the ticket number which may have been issued to the passenger.

He advised that on September 24, 1963, the bus leaving New Orleans for Lake Charles at 5:45 PM was driven by Operator #1190, EDWARD G. CONRAD, who resides at 20 Soniat Place, New Orleans. He pointed out that Operator CONRAD has changed assignments since September 24 and that he is presently on his run and will not return to New Orleans until December 7 or 8, 1963. A review of the register submitted by CONRAD for September 24, shows he left New Orleans at 5:45 PM with 26 passengers aboard, en route to Lake Charles, Louisiana. This record further disclosed that upon arriving at Lake Charles there were a total of 10 passengers continuing on beyond Lake Charles. He pointed out there was no way to identify the numbered tickets collected by the bus driver as these tickets are placed in an envelope by the driver without any identification except the total number of tickets enclosed and forwarded to the accounting section, Lexington, Kentucky.

8

NO 100-16601
JES/bap
1

The following investigation was conducted by SA (A) JAMES E. SCHMIDT on December 11, 1963:

Mr. V. H. HOLSHOUSER, Superintendent, Regional Office, Southern Greyhound Bus Lines, New Orleans, advised that Bus Number 1198 was driven by operator WILLIAM E. LEE, on run from New Orleans at 2:45 PM, September 25, 1963, for Lake Charles, Louisiana.

He advised there was not a "Double Header" out of New Orleans on September 25, 1963, however, there are two buses leaving at the same time, 2:45 PM, for Lake Charles, Louisiana. One bus is considered a through bus originating in Miami, Florida, continuing through New Orleans, and the other is a local bus originating at New Orleans. The local bus Number 1249 was driven by Operator Number 1177, F. A. McLAUGHLIN, 420 Deckbar Street, New Orleans.

Mr. HOLSHOUSER advised that any passenger holding a ticket from New Orleans to Laredo, Texas, would not be permitted to board the local bus, but would be directed by the driver of the local to the through bus at the time of boarding. He advised that the "Schedule" number assigned to a bus is for accounting purposes and no other reason.

9

FD-302 (Rev. 1-25-60)

F[EDE]RAL BUREAU OF INVESTIGATION

1

Date 12/12/63

Mr. WILLIAM E. LEE, 648 Claiborne Towers, New Orleans, advised he is employed as a Bus Operator for Southern Greyhound Bus Lines, New Orleans, and he furnished the following information regarding his driving Bus Number 1198 leaving New Orleans at 2:45 PM on September 25, 1963, for Lake Charles, Louisiana:

Bus Number 1198 is a bus through New Orleans originating at Miami, Florida, and arrived in New Orleans with 20 passengers continuing past New Orleans. This run from New Orleans to Lake Charles is not his regular run and was handled by him as an extra and he does not recall much of the details. He advised the dispatcher's records show he left New Orleans with 42 passengers aboard, indicating that 22 passengers boarded at New Orleans. Upon viewing a photograph of LEE HARVEY OSWALD, he was not able to state specifically that OSWALD was not on his bus. There is a possibility that OSWALD may have boarded this 2:45 PM bus on September 25, 1963, however, he does not pay any particular attention to the passengers, other than to make sure they are on the right bus according to the bus ticket in their possession. His only responsibility is to make sure the total number of passengers is correctly recorded showing how many passengers continue on past Lake Charles, Louisiana, which is the change point between Southern Greyhound and Central Greyhound.

LEE said there was another local bus for Lake Charles, Louisiana, leaving New Orleans at the same time which was driven by operator McLAUGHLIN, but he is not able to give any details on this bus. He does not specifically recall any other bus leaving New Orleans at 2:45 PM on September 25, 1963, nor does he recall any transfers to his bus from any other bus at Baton Rouge, Louisiana, on this run.

On 12/12/63 at New Orleans, Louisiana File # NO 100-16601

by SA(A) JAMES E. SCHMIDT, JR./bap Date dictated 12/12/63

10

1

Date 12/12/63

Mr. F. A. McLAUGHLIN, 420 Deckbar Street, Metairie, Louisiana, advised that he is employed as a Bus Operator for Southern Greyhound Bus Lines, New Orleans, and he furnished the following information regarding his driving Greyhound Bus Number 1249 leaving New Orleans 2:45 PM on September 25, 1963:

McLAUGHLIN related he drove the local Bus Number 1249 from New Orleans to Lake Charles on September 25, 1963, as there are two buses which leave at the same time each day, 2:45 PM. The other bus is considered a through Bus which originates in Miami, Florida. This through bus handles all the passengers going west past Lake Charles, Louisiana, and his bus would accept such passengers only when the through bus was over loaded. He referred to the dispatchers sheet for September 25, 1963, which disclosed the following:

Bus Number 1249 left New Orleans at 2:45 PM, Driver Number 1177 (McLAUGHLIN) with 35 passengers aboard, one by Baton Rouge and none by Lake Charles. Bus Number 1198 left New Orleans at 2:45 PM, Driver Number 1342 (LEE) with 42 passengers aboard, with 36 by Lake Charles. Bus Number 1597 left New Orleans at 2:45 PM, Driver Number 1368 (A. C. LANGFORD) with 8 passengers aboard with one by Lake Charles.

McLAUGHLIN advised that he does not recall observing anyone resembling LEE HARVEY OSWALD having boarded Bus Number 1249 on September 25, 1963, and pointed out that according to the dispatcher's records, he did not carry any passenger who boarded his bus at New Orleans past Lake Charles, therefore, he does not believe OSWALD was on his bus. He advised that the through bus, Number 1198, driven by operator WILLIAM E. LEE, arrived in New Orleans from Miami with 20 through passengers and left New Orleans with 42 passengers, which indicates this bus loaded twenty-two new passengers and of these 42 passengers, 36 continued past Lake Charles, Louisiana.

He pointed out that if a passenger attempted to board his bus with a ticket for passage past Lake Charles he would send this passenger to the through bus, which is usually parked next to his bus for loading purposes.

Regarding Bus Number 1597, which left New Orleans at

On 12/12/63 at New Orleans, Louisiana File # NO 100-16601

by SA(A) JAMES E. SCHMIDT, JR./bap Date dictated 12/12/63

11

the same time as the other two busses, 2:45 PM, September 25, 1963, Mr. McLAUGHLIN advised this was a Western Greyhound bus and was being returned September 25, 1963 to Western. Bus 1597 carried only 8 passengers when leaving New Orleans with only one past Lake Charles, however, the records disclosed this bus was taken off the run at Baton Rouge, Louisiana, and the only passenger shown as past Lake Charles must have been transferred to through Bus Number 1198 at Baton Rouge, Louisiana.

McLAUGHLIN advised that he was relieved at Lake Charles by F. O. LEONARD, driver for Central Greyhound Bus Lines and he further recalls that on the evening of September 25, 1963, after arriving in Lake Charles, Louisiana, he had his evening meal with operator WILLIAM E. LEE, who drove Bus Number 1198 that evening as an extra driver.

McLAUGHLIN advised that he can be contacted through his wife, Mrs. EVELYN McLAUGHLIN, 619 South Carrollton Avenue, telephone UN 6-7620.

Mr. McLAUGHLIN explained that when he used either the word "by" or "past" before the name of a city it meant the passenger or passengers would continue travel beyond the city mentioned.

12

NO 100-16601 /lyc

The following investigation was conducted by SA (A) JAMES E. SCHMIDT, JR., on December 12, 1963:

Mrs. A. C. LANGFORD, 305 North Pierce Street, Jefferson Parish, advised her husband is employed by Southern Greyhound Bus Lines, New Orleans, however, he is presently on vacation at the home of his parents in the country area near West Point, Mississippi.

Mrs. LANGFORD produced a copy of her husband's Driver's Payroll Report for September 25, 1963. This report listed A. C. LANGFORD, #1368, as operator of bus under schedule #4875 (bus number not shown) from New Orleans to Baton Rouge, Louisiana, departing from New Orleans 2:55 p.m. and arriving Baton Rouge, Louisiana at 4:50 p.m. It also shows LANGFORD returned to New Orleans via another bus as a rider. This form does not list disposition of bus driven by LANGFORD to Baton Rouge nor does it list the number of passengers from New Orleans to Baton Rouge.

Mrs. LANGFORD advised that she expects her husband to return to New Orleans on Monday, December 16, 1963. She advised that if it is necessary to contact him prior to his return, he can be contacted at the home of his parents, A. C.. LANGFORD, SR., Route 2, Montee, Mississippi. LANGFORD, SR. owns a farm in a rural area out of Mantee, Mississippi located about 30 miles out of West Point, Mississippi on Highway #15 toward Memphis, Tennessee. She said if the farm cannot be located, her brother-in-law, THURMAN LANGFORD resides in West Point, Mississippi, address unknown, West Point telephone 1629, and he can give better directions to the LANGFORD's farm.

13

FD-302 (Rev. 1-25-60)

FEDERAL BUREAU OF INVESTIGATION

Date December 13, 1963

1

Mr. A. C. LANGFORD, 305 North Pierce Street, Jefferson Parish, telephonically furnished the following information from his parents' home near West Point, Mississippi:

He advised he is an operator for Southern Greyhound Bus Lines, New Orleans, Louisiana. He recalls that on September 25, 1963 he did make a short run to Baton Rouge, Louisiana, but does not recall the exact time he left New Orleans. His Driver's Payroll Report will list the exact time, but he believes it was about 2:45 p.m. He returned to New Orleans from Baton Rouge, Louisiana the same afternoon on another bus as a rider.

LANGFORD does not recall LEE HARVEY OSWALD being a passenger on his bus to Baton Rouge on the afternoon of September 25, 1963, but remembers there were only a few passengers on his bus when he left New Orleans. He believes one of these passengers was listed as "by" Baton Rouge, Louisiana. This "by" passenger was a white male, of average size and shape with light colored thinning hair on the front of his head. He has no information regarding possible luggage in possession of this white male passenger and he does not recall handling any luggage on this trip.

LANGFORD advised he could give no details as to the transfer of this passenger to another bus at Baton Rouge, nor does he know what disposition was made of the bus he drove from New Orleans. He believes this bus was cut out at Baton Rouge, which can be verified at the Baton Rouge Greyhound Bus Terminal.

LANGFORD advised he will return to New Orleans on December 16, 1963, at which time he desired to view a photograph of OSWALD to determine if OSWALD could be the white male passenger who was listed as a "by" passenger at Baton Rouge on September 24, 1963.

On 12/12/63 at New Orleans, Louisiana File # NO 100-16601

by SA (A) JAMES E. SCHMIDT, JR. /lyc Date dictated 12/12/63

14

The following investigation was conducted by SA MCINNIS L. WARD at Lake Charles, Louisiana:

On December 11, 1963, EUGENE SANDERS, Terminal Manager, Greyhound Bus Lines, 404 Broad Street, advised records of his company reflect the following information:

Greyhound Bus #1198, Schedule #637, departed New Orleans, Louisiana, at 2:45 PM September 25, 1963, and arrived at Lake Charles, Louisiana, on time, at 8:05 PM the same day. This bus left New Orleans with 39 passengers and arrived at Lake Charles with 37 passengers. The other two passengers departed from the bus between New Orleans and Lake Charles. The driver of this bus was W. E. LEE, who operates out of the New Orleans terminal. LEE was relieved at Lake Charles by J. D. KENNEDY, a driver who operates out of the Houston terminal.

Bus #1198 departed Lake Charles on time at 8:40 PM September 25, 1963, with 35 passengers and with KENNEDY as driver. Of the 35 persons, six were destined North of Houston, Texas, and 24 by Houston and West of that city. Mr. KENNEDY was scheduled to drive the bus to the Houston terminal where he was to be relieved by another driver, identity not reflected in these records.

Bus #1198 is the regular express bus from Miami, Florida, to Los Angeles, California, and as such, would have carried passengers from New Orleans to San Antonio, Texas, without change. On this date, however, a "double" was dispatched at New Orleans. The other bus, #1249, Schedule #4875, also departed New Orleans at 2:45 PM, September 25, 1963, and arrived at the Lake Charles terminal on time, at 8:05 PM the same date. This bus left New Orleans with eight passengers and arrived at Lake Charles with five passengers. The other three

15

passengers departed from the bus between New Orleans and Lake Charles. The driver of Bus #1249 from New Orleans to Lake Charles, was F. A. MC LAUGHLIN, who operates out of the New Orleans terminal. MC LAUGHLIN was relieved at Lake Charles by F. O. LEONARD, a driver who operates out of the Beaumont, Texas, terminal.

Bus #1249 also departed Lake Charles on time, at 8:40 PM, September 25, 1963, with nine passengers and with LEONARD as driver. Of the 9 passengers, three were destined by Houston and West of that city and none were destined North of Houston. Mr. LEONARD was scheduled to drive the bus to the Houston terminal where he was to be relieved by another driver, identity not reflected in these records.

Mr. SANDERS explained that when he used the word "by" before the name of a city it meant the passenger or passengers would continue to travel beyond the city mentioned.

16

FD-302 (Rev. 1-25-60) FEDERAL BUREAU OF INVESTIGATION

Date 12/12/63

1

Mr. A. J. PROVOST, Operating and Terminal Supervisor, Southern Greyhound Lines, 220 St. Phillip Street, advised that Greyhound Bus #1597 from New Orleans to Baton Rouge on September 25, 1963, arrived at 4:50 PM and this bus was cut off at Baton Rouge. Four persons were on this bus on arrival with one scheduled to go by Lake Charles.

Mr. PROVOST advised that this person who was scheduled to go by Lake Charles could have gotten Bus #1249 to Lake Charles which left Baton Rouge at 5:00 PM on September 25, 1963. He advised when Bus #1249 left Baton Rouge it had seven persons on it and five of these persons were to go by Lake Charles. This bus was scheduled from New Orleans to Lake Charles and the driver was F. A. MC LAUGHLIN, #1177, from New Orleans.

Mr. PROVOST advised the person on this bus #1597 may have left Baton Rouge on Bus 1198, which left Baton Rouge at 5:00 PM. This bus originated at Miami, Florida, destination Los Angeles, California. Upon departing Baton Rouge, there were 39 persons on this bus with 37 to go by Lake Charles. The driver of this bus was W. E. LEE, #1342, an extra driver from New Orleans, Louisiana.

Mr. PROVOST explained that when he used the word "by" before the name of a city he meant the passenger or passengers would continue to travel beyond the city mentioned.

On 12/12/63 at Baton Rouge, Louisiana File # NO 100-16601

by SA ELMER B. LITCHFIELD /jm Date dictated 12/12/63

17

UNITED STATES DEPARTMENT OF JUSTICE

FEDERAL BUREAU OF INVESTIGATION

In Reply, Please Refer to
File No.

March 16, 1964

LEE HARVEY OSWALD

On March 9, 1964, a confidential source abroad made available a copy of a report prepared by Mexican Immigration Inspector JOSE MARIO DEL VALLE and submitted to the Mexican Ministry of "Gobernacion" (Interior) under date of November 30, 1963, with respect to investigation conducted by him concerning LEE HARVEY OSWALD. A translation from Spanish of that report is recorded hereinunder:

"In accordance with the orders which I received to proceed to the city of Nuevo Laredo, Tamaulipas, for the purpose of conducting investigation regarding the alien of North American nationality, LEE HARVEY OSWALD, I am pleased to furnish to you the following report:

"REPORT DATA: The alien in question entered the country (Mexico) at Nuevo Laredo, Tamaulipas, documented with FM-8 No. 24085 on September 26, 1963. The Immigration Inspector who received him, HELIO TUEXI MAYDON, failed to record three essential items of information: the time he entered, his means of transportation, and his nationality. Interrogated in this connection, he admitted those errors and added that he was unable to furnish any further data which might assist in this investigation because of the lapse of time. He was unable to remember anything whatsoever with respect to the alien, OSWALD.

"It was possible to determine with certainty he was received in the Immigration Office between 6:00 a.m. and 2:00 p.m. on that day, since the personnel records reflect that Agent TUEXI MAYDON was on duty during that shift.

"DEPARTURE: The above-mentioned alien left the country on October 3, 1963, having been handled by Immigration Agent ALBERTO ARZAMENDI CHAPA at Kilometer 26 of the highway. When he left, said Agent noticed the omissions on the immigration form and corrected in his handwriting the one relating to nationality by writing the word 'American.'

"Agent ARZAMENDI has two Assistants named LUIS DE LA PENA and LIBRADO GARCIA, but as was the case with the former (ARZAMENDI), they were unable to furnish any information.

"It was also possible to ascertain that said alien passed Kilometer 26 between midnight and 8:00 a.m. of the day in question.

"STAY IN NUEVO LAREDO, TAMAULIPAS: Several hotels were checked in the foregoing locality without determining that he had stayed at any of them on September 26, 1963. However, taking into account that on the following day, September 27, 1963, he registered at the Hotel del Comercio in the Federal District, it must be assumed that he initiated his travel immediately without delaying in Nuevo Laredo, Tamaulipas.

"METHOD OF TRAVEL: Passenger lists of the Mexican Aviation Company were reviewed, and it does not appear that the above-mentioned OSWALD made the trip by that means. Furthermore, since the 27th of September was a Friday, he would not have been able to travel by plane in view of the fact that during that month the company was not making daily flights to Mexico (city).

"It was not possible to determine whether or not he traveled on the bus line Transportes del Norte, since they do not prepare passenger lists. In addition, despite the fact that said line makes connections with 'Greyhound,' it also was not possible to verify if he traveled thereon, as the latter merely makes the notation 'occupied' on its passenger manifest.

"It appears most likely that OSWALD traveled by autobus, which would have allowed him to register at the hotel in Mexico on the day following his entry to the country, and railroad travel does not leave any record whatsoever of its passengers. The possibility exists that he might have made the trip by automobile, but this would only be reasonable if acquaintances had allowed him to ride with them, since, as will be seen later, he did not enter the country with a personal automobile.

"OSWALD'S DIVORCE: There are rumors in the city of Nuevo Laredo, Tamaulipas, to the effect that said foreigner had been there previously for the purpose of obtaining a divorce. In this connection, it was determined at the First Court of Nuevo Laredo under Attorney PINTO that it was another foreigner named HARVEY LARRY HUDSON who applied for and obtained a divorce there in 1960 from his wife, JUNE MARIE HUBER HUDSON. From a review of the file it was concluded that it was not related to the foreigner OSWALD.

"In a nearby town called Colombia, Nuevo Leon, divorces are also handled for North American citizens with a minimum of red tape. In view of the rains which were sweeping the area, it was not possible to travel by highway, which is the only means of access to that town, to determine whether or not any record could be located concerning the divorce in question. For that reason, an urgent telegram was sent to CIRO MANUEL RIOJAS, head of the Civil Registry in that locality, requesting the information, and up to 29th of the current month, no reply had been received. The Chief of the Immigration Office at Nuevo Laredo, Tamaulipas,

"Mr. GILBERTO CAZARES PEREZ, volunteered to advise immediately in the event a reply was received.

"At the same time, in this connection, Attorneys JOSE TONONE RAMON and MARCOS TRINIDAD SALINAS, as well as the Tourist Guide, MATEO REYES, were interviewed, and they advised that they had not assisted the foreigner, OSWALD, in any judgment of this nature.

"ENTRY OF RELATIVES: A careful check was made for the purpose of determining whether or not the wife of OSWALD, MARINA NIKOLAEVNA OSWALD, had entered the country without any positive results. Also, with respect to his mother, named MARGUERITE CLAVIRE OSWALD, (a check was made) with the same results with respect to the border at Nuevo Laredo, Tamaulipas.

"AUTOMOBILE IMPORT PERMITS: According to what appears on the FM-11 Lists of departures, the alien OSWALD left the country on October 3, 1963, at Nuevo Laredo, Tamaulipas, by automobile. Nevertheless, this data constitutes another error, this time by Miss SOLALINDE, typist charged with making up said lists, who admitted that she had made a mistake, since the FM-8 which she had in view with respect to the alien OSWALD does not have any place thereon the appropriate notation to the effect that he traveled by automobile.

"On the other hand, there is annexed hereto a list of the Automobile Temporary Import Permits issued on September 26, 1963, by the Customs authorities at Nuevo Laredo, Tamaulipas, together with the Immigration data of each person. A study of this list reveals nothing that would be identifiable with the alien OSWALD.

"FM-8 CARDS LOCATED: A search was conducted and the FM-8 Nos. 24086 and 24087, which are the two following that of the alien OSWALD, were located and record the following data:

"FLORENCE PARSON DE MEN, 38 years of age, married, housewife, resident of New Orleans, Louisiana, of

- 4 -

COMMISSION EXHIBIT No. 2193—Continued

"North American nationality, having entered the country at Ciudad Miguel Aleman, Tamaulipas, with destination of Monterrey, Nuevo Leon.

"GEORGE HENRY DE MEN, 42 years of age, married, laborer, resident of New Orleans, Louisiana, with destination as Monterrey, Nuevo Leon, and the same place of entry and nationality as the foregoing.

"As did OSWALD, they applied for their cards (tourist) in New Orleans, Louisiana, and the importance of this information rests in the fact that since they obtained their immigration form(s) on the same day, they might be able to furnish some information, as their turn at the Mexican Consulate would have been immediately following that of the alien in question. In order to obtain additional data concerning both persons, the Automobile Temporary Importation Permit at Ciudad Miguel Aleman, Tamaulipas, should be checked.

"Also, the FM-8 No. 24082 and No. 24083 were located for SAMUEL THOMAS NORTH and JUDITH MARIE MUTH NORTH, both North Americans and domiciled in New Orleans, Louisiana, who entered with an automobile at Ciudad Miguel Aleman, Tamaulipas. For the purpose of obtaining further data concerning both of them, the respective Importation Permit (automobile) should be reviewed.

Respectfully,

Mexico, D. F., November 30, 1963

/s/ JOSE MARIO DEL VALLE"

- 5 -

COMMISSION EXHIBIT No. 2193—Continued

INTERVIEW OF INSPECTOR JOSE MARIO DEL VALLE

On March 12, 1964, Immigration Inspector JOSE MARIO DEL VALLE advised that "Kilometer 26" is the Mexican Immigration and Customs checking station which is located on Mexican Federal Highway No. 85 twenty-six kilometers (16 miles) south of Laredo, Texas, and Nuevo Laredo, Tamaulipas.

DEL VALLE related that subsequent to his submission of the report recorded above, he had been advised by Mr. GILBERTO CAZARES PEREZ, Chief of the Mexican Immigration Office at Nuevo Laredo, that a report had been received from the Chief of the Civil Registry at Colombia, Nuevo Leon, to the effect that no information identifiable with OSWALD had been located in the divorce records of that locality.

With respect to the method utilized by Inspectors of the Mexican Immigration Department in handling departure data concerning aliens who have entered Mexico with tourist cards valid for a limited time, DEL VALLE stated that he had made the following observations during the course of his investigations in the area of Nuevo Laredo:

In connection with aliens entering the country, reasonable care is exercised by personnel of the Immigration Department to record information concerning method of travel and the exact hour of entry, as this can become a matter of interest to the Mexican Government in the event the traveler fails to leave Mexico within the period of time permitted by his tourist card, or should a person who has entered as the owner of an automobile attempt to leave the country without removing that vehicle. He pointed out that a late departure usually occasions the assessment of a fine against the individual guilty of this violation, and both Mexican Customs and Immigration are constantly alert for the possibility that a traveler by automobile may illegally have disposed of the vehicle in Mexico despite warnings against this procedure which appear on the Automobile Temporary Importation Permit.

In regard to departure records, however, he had determined that although the Immigration Inspectors are charged with obtaining accurate data for completing the FM-11 forms (separate lists of persons entering Mexico and departing from

COMMISSION EXHIBIT No. 2193—Continued

the country which are submitted semimonthly by each Mexican port of entry and departure Immigration Station and record basic data which appears on the tourist cards or travel documents of each traveler), in actual practice very little attention is given to ascertaining actual "destination" and "means of travel," as this information is not of primary interest to the Mexican Immigration Department other than as a means of identifying the traveler and verifying his departure in the event any question of investigative interest should arise. He had found that it is the usual practice for the typist who prepares the FM-11 forms for "departures" merely to copy from the cancelled tourist card the "destination" as the place where the card was issued and as "means of travel" the same as that reflected on the card at the time the traveler entered the country. He also had verified that when an automobile or bus stops at the Kilometer 26 checking station traveling toward the border, the Immigration Agent merely collects the tourist cards of the passengers who are identified as aliens, places his personal cancellation and date stamp on the tourist cards he has handled, and subsequently delivers them to the desk of the typist who is to organize them in alphabetical order by date and copy from them the data which is required on the FM-11.

Inspector DEL VALLE expressed his personal conviction that the recording of "auto" as OSWALD's means of departure from Mexico had been merely a mental lapse on the part of the typist, although his having departed through the Kilometer 26 checking station does indicate with certainty that he left the country in a motor vehicle of some type.

COMMISSION EXHIBIT No. 2193—Continued

OFFICE OF THE DIRECTOR

UNITED STATES DEPARTMENT OF JUSTICE

FEDERAL BUREAU OF INVESTIGATION

WASHINGTON 25, D.C.

March 26, 1964

BY COURIER SERVICE

Honorable J. Lee Rankin
General Counsel
The President's Commission
200 Maryland Avenue, N. E.
Washington, D. C.

Dear Mr. Rankin:

Reference is made to your letter dated March 18, 1964, dealing with the Mexican aspect of this investigation.

In this connection, there are enclosed two copies each of two memoranda dated March 16, 1964. Our investigation into Oswald's trip to Mexico is continuing.

Upon detachment from the enclosures, this letter may be regarded as unclassified.

Sincerely yours,

J. Edgar Hoover

Enclosures - 4

COMMISSION EXHIBIT No. 2193—Continued

FD-204 (Rev. 3-3-59)

UNITED STATES DEPARTMENT OF JUSTICE
FEDERAL BUREAU OF INVESTIGATION

Copy to:

Report of: CHESTER C. ORTON   Office: Los Angeles, California
Date: 12/18/63
Field Office File #: 105-15823   Bureau File #: 105-82555
Title: LEE HARVEY OSWALD

Character: INTERNAL SECURITY-R - CUBA

Synopsis:

PATRICIA WINSTON and PAMELA MUMFORD rode in bus with OSWALD from Monterey, Mexico, departing at 7:30 p.m. on 9/26/63, to Mexico City, arriving at 10:00 a.m. on 9/27/63. On the bus, was an Englishman who had lived in Mexico for 30 years. He sat next to OSWALD and a young English couple, who were destined for Yucatan, to study the Indians. All the other passengers on the bus were Mexicans, who spoke no English. OSWALD introduced himself, exhibited his American passport, showing his travel in the U.S.S.R. He said that he had lived in Russia for two years, and had a hard time getting out. OSWALD recommended they stay at the Hotel Cuba, Mexico City, as he had stayed there several times. He said he was not staying there this time. OSWALD acted friendly, made no comment concerning Russia, Cuba, or communism. OSWALD did not indicate why he was in Mexico, where he was going in Mexico, his occupation or future plans. OSWALD was last observed by the girls standing in the bus station in Mexico City. OSWALD was traveling alone and had one piece of luggage, a small zipper bag.

\- P -

DETAILS:

COMMISSION EXHIBIT No. 2194

Date 12/18/63

Miss PATRICIA CLARE RASHLEIGH WINSTON, Jacqueline Apartments, #206, at 153 North New Hampshire Avenue, Los Angeles, furnished the following information:

Miss WINSTON and PAMELA LILLIAN MUMFORD were both born in the Fiji Islands. The parents of both of these girls represented a British company in the Fiji's. They subsequently moved to Australia. Miss WINSTON is an occupational therapist, and Miss MUMFORD is a legal stenographer. Two years ago, they set out to tour the world, and worked their way as they traveled. From Australia, they went to Great Britain and the continent. This took over a year. They then immigrated to the United States as permanent residents under the Fiji Islands quota. They were in New York for about six months, and then toured the United States, including a trip to Mexico. Miss WINSTON is presently unemployed. When the girls were in Texas, they took a trip by bus to Mexico City. They were traveling on what was known as the "See Mexico on $5 a Day."

On September 25, 1963, WINSTON and MUMFORD purchased bus tickets at the Trailways Bus Depot in Laredo, Texas. These tickets were to Mexico City, with a stopover at Monterey, Mexico. They departed the bus depot at 10:00 a.m. on September 25, 1963, and arrived in Monterey, Mexico at 6:00 p.m. on the same day.

On September 26, 1963, WINSTON and MUMFORD boarded a bus at Monterey at 7:30 p.m. This bus arrived in Mexico City at about 10:00 a.m. on September 27, 1963.

When the girls boarded the bus at Monterey, Mexico, a man who later introduced himself to them as OSWALD, was sitting in the first seat of the bus next to the window. Next to him in the first seat was an Englishman in his late 60's. He was about 6' tall, weighed about 200 pounds, had a paunchy stomach, was slightly bald, his hair was gray, he was clean shaven, and he wore no glasses. He had lived in Mexico for

On 12/17/63 at Los Angeles, California File # Los Angeles 105-15823

by SA HOWARD H. DAVIS
SA CHESTER C. ORTON:gcw Date dictated 12/18/63

about 30 years. He had a definite English accent. He spoke excellent English; the accent appeared to be that of a Londoner. Miss WINSTON indicated that she was familiar with the various accents in the various parts of Great Britain, and it was her opinion that this man was or had been a Londoner.

Behind OSWALD and this Londoner, were a young English couple, man and wife, in their 30's, who apparently had done extensive traveling in the United States, and were en route to Yucatan to study the Indians. The girls were desirous of sitting in the front seat on the other side of the bus, but it and all the other seats in the front of the bus, as well as the other seats in the bus, were occupied by Mexicans, crying babies, and small animals. None of these Mexicans spoke English. The bus was loaded. There were about 39 passengers. The only vacant seats were in the middle of the bus, and this is where WINSTON and MUMFORD sat. As they attempted to sit down in these two vacant seats, the Englishman came to them and asked if he could be of assistance. He spoke in Spanish to the Mexicanssitting nearby to clean up the area so the two girls could sit down.

The bus stopped every two hours at a rest and eating station. Practically every time the bus stopped, OSWALD would go in and eat the Mexican food, which he said he enjoyed.

At these various stops, and also while traveling, the girls had conversation with the four persons on the bus who spoke English. On one occasion, the man sitting next to the Englishman came back to the girls and asked them where they had been traveling, and they told him of their world tour. He said that he had done considerable traveling also. He said he had been to Japan, and he asked them if they had been to the Soviet Union. They said "No", but that they had known a girl who had visited Moscow a year or so ago, and they told OSWALD that this girl had said that all the tours that she had in Moscow were "guided" tours, and that the only thing that the Soviets let you see in Moscow is what they want you to see, and that they only tell you what they want you to know. They also told OSWALD that this girl friend had said that if you asked a question, and they did not want to give you the answer, they would either ignore the question completely or else tell you that they would answer the question at a later date. At this,

OSWALD said nothing, however, he did at that point jump up and say, "Oh, I've been to Russia. Let me show you." He then went to the front of the bus, where he had a small zipper bag. He opened it up and brought out a passport which he presented to the girls. When he first introduced himself to the girls, he said his name was LEE. They examined the passport and saw his last name was OSWALD. He also pointed out to them a stamp in the passport which indicated that he had traveled in the Soviet Union. OSWALD told them he had lived in Moscow for two years and that he had had quite a hard time getting out of Russia and back to the United States.

OSWALD did not indicate that he was married, however, he was wearing a gold wedding ring.

OSWALD made no comment concerning Russia, Cuba, or communism. He did not discuss the international situation, no mention was made of politics, no controversial issues were discussed, and nothing was said of Socialism or any type of ism or ideology.

OSWALD recommended that the girls stay at the Hotel Cuba in Mexico. He told them he had stayed there several times before while in Mexico City, as it was an inexpensive hotel. He told them that he was not staying there this time. They stayed at the Hotel Calvin because it was the hotel which their taxi driver recommended to them.

During their conversation with him, Miss WINSTON recalled that OSWALD said he came from Dallas, Texas.

OSWALD did not say why he was in Mexico, where he was going in Mexico, or what his future plans were, or what his occupation was.

At one of the stops that the bus made for rest and eating, the Englishman said to the girls, "I gather the young man sitting with me has been to Mexico City before." Miss WINSTON assumed from this statement that the Englishman had not been acquainted with OSWALD prior to boarding the bus. In talking with the English couple who were going to Yucatan, she concluded that this couple had never heretofore seen OSWALD.

It was Miss WINSTON's opinion that OSWALD was traveling alone, that he had had no previous contact with any of the English speaking people on the bus prior to that time. When they arrived in Mexico City, the girls left the bus and took a taxi cab to the Hotel Calvin. When they last saw OSWALD, he was standing in the bus depot with one piece of luggage in his hand. OSWALD was always the first one off the bus at each rest point, and immediately went into the restaurant. He was not observed to talk to anyone at these restaurants. He always ate alone, except for breakfast on the morning of September 27, 1963, when he ate with the English couple in their 30's. OSWALD was wearing light gray pants, a pale green jersey, open shirt with a collar, and from time to time, would wear a charcoal gray sweater with a collar.

After first talking with OSWALD on the bus, the girls gave him the nickname of "Texas", and they referred to him in conversations between themselves thereafter as "Texas."

On the weekend of the assassination, Miss WINSTON and Miss MUMFORD were on a weekend vacation in Las Vegas, Nevada, and in the hotel in which they stayed, there was a television which had on it pictures dealing with the assassination of President JOHN F. KENNEDY. During that weekend, they observed pictures of the person who had been arrested for the assassination. They also observed pictures of OSWALD as he was being taken out of the jail, at which time he was killed by RUBY. As soon as they saw the first pictures, WINSTON and MUMFORD said to each other, "Oh, there's Texas." Miss WINSTON stated that she and Miss MUMFORD both immediately identified the pictures of this person as LEE OSWALD, who had been on the bus with them from Monterey,Mexico to Mexico City.

Date 12/18/63

1

Miss PAMELA LILLIAN MUMFORD was interviewed at her place of business, 611 Wilshire Boulevard, Los Angeles, California, Room 700. She is employed there as a legal stenographer for Dillavou and Cox, Attorneys. She resides at the Jacqueline Apartments, Apartment 206, 153 North New Hampshire Avenue, Los Angeles. She furnished the following information:

Miss MUMFORD was born in the Fiji Islands. Her father was a representative of a British company operating in the Fiji's. Subsequent to her birth, her family moved to Australia. Two years ago she set out in company with PATRICIA WINSTON to travel around the world. She went to Great Britain and the European continent. She then immigrated to the United States as a permanent resident and worked in New York for about six months. She then toured the United States and took a trip to Mexico.

On September 25, 1963, Miss MUMFORD said that she and Miss WINSTON purchased tickets at the Trailways Bus Depot in Laredo, Texas. They departed from Laredo on September 25, 1963, in the morning and arrived at Monterey, Mexico on the same day at 6:00 p.m.

On the following day, September 26, 1963, Miss MUMFORD in company with WINSTON boarded a bus in Monterey at 7:30 p.m. and arrived at 10:00 a.m. on September 27, 1963 in Mexico City.

When MUMFORD boarded the bus with WINSTON at Monterey, Mexico, a man who later introduced himself to her as OSWALD, was sitting in the first seat of the bus. Next to him was an Englishman in his late 50's, approximately 5' 7" height, 160 pounds, short plump with white hair, balding.

This Englishman told her that he had been in Mexico for about 30 years. He still retained an English accent. The accent appeared to be that of a Londoner.

Behind OSWALD and the Londoner sat an English couple in their late 30's. They apparently had done extensive traveling in the United States. They indicated that they had been aboard the bus for approximately 36 hours prior to their

On 12/17/63 at Los Angeles, California File # Los Angeles 105-15823

by SA HOWARD H. DAVIS and SA CHESTER C. ORTON/vl AK Date dictated 12/18/63

2
LA 105-15823

arrival at Laredo. They indicated they had come from Washington, D. C. They said that they were going to Yucatan to study Indian culture.

MUMFORD recalled that there were approximately 39 people aboard the bus and that the only people that spoke English besides herself and WINSTON, were OSWALD, the Londoner, and the British couple. When they made an attempt to get seats in the bus, the only ones vacant were midway back in the bus and that the Londoner came back and talked in Spanish to the Mexicans so that the two girls could sit down.

The bus made a stop every two hours at a rest station, and at each one of these stations there was a cafe. MUMFORD recalled that OSWALD got off at every bus stop and would go in and eat some food.

At one of these stops the Londoner, sitting next to OSWALD, came over to MUMFORD and WINSTON and they engaged in conversation. MUMFORD said that she and WINSTON told him of their world tour. MUMFORD recalled that the Londoner indicated that he was retired and had lived in Mexico about 30 years and was very fond of the country and its people. MUMFORD recalled that the Londoner said during one of these conversations "I gather the young man sitting with me has been to Mexico before". Miss MUMFORD assumed from this statement that the Londoner had not been acquainted with OSWALD prior to boarding the bus. At one of these stops MUMFORD and WINSTON talked to the English couple going to the Yucatan and MUMFORD concluded from their conversation that this couple had never had any contact with OSWALD prior to boarding the bus.

While traveling on the bus the man sitting next to the Londoner came back to where they were sitting and engaged in conversation. They told him of their world tour and he said that he, too, had done considerable traveling having been to Japan and also to the Soviet Union.

He asked MUMFORD and WINSTON if they had ever been to the Soviet Union and they said no. MUMFORD said at this point that she and WINSTON told the man that a friend of theirs, a girl, had been to Moscow on a "guided" tour and that the only thing that she had seen was what the Soviets wanted her to see. Furthermore, that the Soviets would not answer questions freely. This man made no comment to this story.

At this point in their conversation with the man, he said "I have been to Russia" and he went to the front of the bus and got his passport which he showed to MUMFORD. He introduced himself as LEE and she recalled in examining the passport that his last name was OSWALD. He pointed out to her in his passport a stamp which indicated that he had traveled in the Soviet Union. OSWALD said that he had lived in Moscow for two years and he had had quite a hard time in getting back into the United States.

OSWALD was wearing a gold wedding ring, however, he made no mention of a wife or family. OSWALD made no comment concerning Russia, Cuba or communism. He did not discuss the international situation and no mention was made of politics and no controversial issues were discussed between MUMFORD and OSWALD.

MUMFORD recalled that OSWALD recommended staying at the Hotel Cuba, in Mexico City. He indicated that he had stayed there several times before while in Mexico City. He pointed out that it was an inexpensive hotel. He added, however, that he was not going to stay at the Hotel Cuba on this visit.

MUMFORD recalled that OSWALD said he came from Fort Worth, Texas, He did not indicate to her why he was making this trip to Mexico City, how long he was going to remain, what his future plans were, or what his occupation was.

Upon their arrival in Mexico City, MUMFORD said that she and WINSTON took a taxi cab to the Hotel Calvin. The last time she saw OSWALD he was standing in the bus depot with one piece of luggage in his hand. Miss MUMFORD believed that the bus line on which they traveled from Monterey Mexico, to Mexico City, was called Auto Buses Estrella. She also believed that the bus depot in Mexico City where she last saw OSWALD was called the Estrella Bus Depot.

Miss MUMFORD said that OSWALD was wearing a charcoal colored sweater with a crew neck, a colored, possibly checkered shirt. His luggage appeared to be zippered over-night bag.

After first talking with OSWALD on the bus, Miss MUMFORD pointed out that she and WINSTON gave him the nickname of "TEXAS". On the weekend of the assassination of President KENNEDY, Miss MUMFORD was with Miss WINSTON in a vacation in Las Vegas, Nevada. While there, they observed on television pictures of the person who had been arrested for the assassination of the President. They also observed pictures of OSWALD on television when he was being taken out of the jail at which time he was killed by RUBY. Miss MUMFORD said as soon as she and WINSTON observed these pictures, they said to each other, "Oh, there's TEXAS". Miss MUMFORD advised that she immediately identified the television pictures of OSWALD to be identical with the LEE OSWALD who had been on the bus with her and Miss WINSTON from Monterey, Mexico to Mexico City, on September 26 and 27, 1963.

FD-204 (Rev. 3-3-59)

UNITED STATES DEPARTMENT OF JUSTICE
FEDERAL BUREAU OF INVESTIGATION

— Commission Exhibit No. 2195 —

Copy to:

Report of: SA EMORY E. HORTON
Date: March 11, 1964
Office: DALLAS

Field Office File No.: DL 100-10461
Bureau File No.: 105-82555

Title: LEE HARVEY OSWALD

Character: INTERNAL SECURITY-RUSSIA-CUBA

Synopsis:

Investigation disclosed LEE HARVEY OSWALD made a trip on Flecha Roja Bus leaving Nuevo Laredo, Mexico, 9/26/63 and arrived Mexico City, Mexico, 9/27/63. OSWALD reportedly sat beside an elderly white male on this bus trip. The elderly white male has been identified by other English speaking passengers that were on the bus as ALBERT OSBORNE who is also known as JOHN HOWARD BOWEN. ALBERT OSBORNE was interviewed 1/7/64 at which time he described JOHN HOWARD BOWEN as an acquaintance but said he had no way of communicating with BOWEN. He was interviewed as BOWEN on 2/8 and 17/64 at which times he denied being identical to OSBORNE, but said he was acquainted with OSBORNE, and furnished considerable information regarding OSBORNE and himself. On 3/3/64 OSBORNE was again interviewed at which time he admitted that he is also known as JOHN HOWARD BOWEN, having used that name since soon after World War I. During latter 3 interviews, OSBORNE admitted making a trip from Nuevo Laredo, Mexico, to Mexico City, Mexico, on September 26-27, 1963, but does not identify photographs of LEE HARVEY OSWALD as person he sat beside on trip. He states he sat beside a young man that appeared to be Mexican or Puerto Rican and claims he, OSBORNE, was only English speaking passenger on bus. OSBORNE is reputed and claims to be a missionary in Mexico for many years and he receives financial assistance from churches and individuals throughout the United States for this work. OSBORNE has not furnished any detailed information as to his movements and/or activities, claiming he is unable to supply such data. OSBORNE is 75 years of age, born in England, reportedly served in the British Army and migrated to the United States in 1914. Thereafter, he claims he has lived in Washington, D. C. and

COMMISSION EXHIBIT No. 2195

Philadelphia, Pennsylvania, served in the Canadian Army during World War II, returned to the United States and has traveled throughout the United States and Mexico, being employed as an itinerant rug cleaner, gardener, boys' camp operator, and minister. States he is not a naturalized citizen of the United States.

- P -

COMMISSION EXHIBIT No. 2195—Continued

TABLE OF CONTENTS

COMMISSION EXHIBIT No. 2195—Continued

ENCLOSURES

Enclosed herewith and attached are the following exhibits for the President's Commission that is investigating the assassination of the late President John Fitzgerald Kennedy on November 22, 1963.

EXHIBIT NUMBER	DESCRIPTION	WHERE RESULTS OF INVESTIGATION REPORTED
D-141	Photograph of letter addressed to Central YMCA, Montreal, Canada, signed ALBERT OSBORNE with an address in the upper, right hand corner of "EMILIO CARRANZA 4-a Texmelucan Pue. Mexico".	Instant Report, Pages 14-15
D-142	Photograph of certified copy of entry of birth, Application No. 514371, reflecting birth of a boy, name ALBERT, born November 12, 1888 to JAMES OSBORNE and EMILY OSBORNE-formerly COLE	Instant Report Page 37

DETAILS:

ALBERT OSBORNE - JOHN HOWARD BOWEN

The following investigation has been conducted incidental to identifying, locating and interviewing the man who sat beside LEE HARVEY OSWALD on a bus trip from Nuevo Laredo, Mexico to Mexico City, Mexico, on September 26 - 27, 1963. Much of the investigation hereinafter set out has been previously reported, but is again being set out for the sake of clarity, continuity and completeness:

INVESTIGATION TO IDENTIFY AND LOCATE THE PERSON THAT SAT BESIDE LEE HARVEY OSWALD ON THE BUS TRIP FROM NUEVO LAREDO, MEXICO TO MEXICO CITY, MEXICO, ON SEPTEMBER 26 - 27, 1963, AND INTERVIEWS WITH THE INDIVIDUAL IDENTIFIED

On December 2, 1963, Mr. HARVEY CASH, American Consul, Nuevo Laredo, Mexico, furnished a list of persons who entered Mexico at Nuevo Laredo, Mexico, on September 26, 1963. The list was obtained from a check of the Mexican Immigration records and the Mexican Customs records at Nuevo Laredo.

On December 2, 1963, Confidential Informants Dallas T-1 and T-2, confidential sources abroad, reviewed the list prepared and advised that it was a complete list of persons entering Mexico at Nuevo Laredo on September 26, 1963. The address of the persons entering Mexico was available only in those cases where the individual entered by automobile and was the owner or person entering the automobile into Mexico. Appearing on the list is the name JOHN H. BOWEN, Houston, Texas, type of transportation - unknown, destination - Mexico, D. F., and tourist card type FM5. Data on the tourist card issued to BOWEN reflects he was married, age 60 years, born America, employed and a resident of Houston, Texas.

Confidential Informant Dallas T-3, a confidential source abroad, advised on December 6, 1963, that a review of the records of Flecha Roja (Red Arrow) Bus Lines, Nuevo Laredo, Mexico, revealed the name LEE H. OSWALD appears on the bus lines

COMMISSION EXHIBIT No. 2195—Continued

manifest of September 26, 1963, as having entered Mexico at Nuevo Laredo, Mexico, en route to Mexico, D. F. The person using the name OSWALD was on the 2:00 PM Flecha Roja bus and had one bag. The bus was No. 516 with the driver being listed as ROBERTO MORALES. A total of eighteen passengers boarded this bus at Nuevo Laredo, twelve of whom were en route to Monterey, Nuevo Leon, Mexico. Passengers en route to Mexico City were listed as PABLO VASQUEZ and possibly his wife, since he is listed as a party of two, S. MORAN, ALFREDO BRESENO, ROIG SORQUIS, T. GONZALEZ, (FNU) ROWEN, LEE OSWALD, (FNU) BOWEN - possibly JOHN H. BOWEN, Houston, Texas, JOHN MC FARLAND and two other persons for a party of three.

Passengers en route Monterey, Nuevo Leon, Mexico, were ANDRES MORALES and one other person for a party of two, APE MARTINEZ, HARRY J. MITCHELL with two for a party of three.

On December 24, 1963, Confidential Informant Dallas T-4 furnished the following information concerning efforts to locate JOHN H. BOWEN, a passenger with OSWALD on a southbound bus from Nuevo Laredo, on September 26, 1963.

Informant advised that investigation discloses BOWEN departed Mexico City, October 1, 1963, on Flecha Roja bus, bound for Nuevo Laredo. Mexican Immigration records reflect BOWEN departed Mexico, at Nuevo Laredo, on October 2, 1963, but no information concerning his home address was available.

Informant advised that Flecha Roja bus records reflect BOWEN and one WILLIAM S. SHIVELY purchased consecutive tickets for Flecha Roja bus trip from Mexico City to Nuevo Laredo, although they did not occupy adjacent seats. Mexican Immigration records reflect SHIVELY was issued a tourist card at Nuevo Laredo, September 22, 1963, and entered Mexico at that location on the same date. SHIVELY departed Mexico at Nuevo Laredo on October 2, 1963, with BOWEN and him being checked out by the same Mexican Immigration Service employee.

The Mexican tourist card described SHIVELY as an American citizen, 22 years of age, and a student. He presented

COMMISSION EXHIBIT No. 2195—Continued

a birth certificate as proof of identity and his home address was given as Cincinnati, Ohio, no street address.

The following investigation was conducted by SA TERENCE D. DINAN, between December 5 - 9, 1963, in an effort to identify and locate JOHN H. BOWEN:

AT HOUSTON, TEXAS

The below listed persons advised that their records failed to reflect any information identifiable with a JOHN H. BOWEN:

ALLIE FUTRELL
Credit Bureau of Greater Houston

CAROL STELLEY
Houston Police Department, Identification Division

ROBERT ANTHONY
Harris County Sheriff's Office

SUE ROGERS
Houston Lighting and Power Company

JEAN WARD
Texas Employment Commission

JOHNNIE FRY
Southwestern Bell Telephone Company

STERLING BAKER
Security Officer
University of Houston

MICHAEL MC ENANY
Registrar
Rice University

COMMISSION EXHIBIT No. 2195—Continued

W. PAUL HARRIS
Chief Deputy Clerk
U. S. District Court, Southern
District of Texas

J. D. HARPOLE
Immigration & Naturalization Service

A. R. SPINDOLA
Mexican Consul

M. GAXIOLA
Mexican Government Tourist Department

Captain ALLEN LASTER
Pasadena, Texas, Police Department
Identification Division

In addition to the above, all of the persons in Houston, Texas, with the name JOHN BOWEN, regardless of middle name and initial, were contacted, and all advised that they did not travel to Mexico on September 26, 1963.

The current telephone and city directories for Houston, Texas, fail to reflect the names JOHN H. or J. H. BOWEN. Telephonic inquiries were made of all the persons named BOWEN listed in the Houston Telephone Directory, but they were unable to furnish any information concerning a Houston resident named JOHN H. BOWEN.

JOHN R. EATON, Superintendent of Census and Attendance, Houston Independent School District, advised that his records from 1926 to date fail to reflect any person named JOHN H. BOWEN, as ever having attended a Houston Independent School from 1926 to 1963.

Confidential Informant Dallas T-5, a confidential source abroad, reported Doctor and Mrs. JOHN BRYAN MC FARLAND, 10 Fulwood Park, Liverpool, England, were interviewed December 12, 1963, at which time they furnished certain information, part of which follows:

The MC FARLANDS remembered LEE HARVEY OSWALD as they got into conversation with him on the trip from Nuevo Laredo to Mexico City, Mexico, on September 26 - 27, 1963. They recalled that OSWALD traveled alone, but also spoke to two Australian girls who were in their mid-twenties that boarded the bus in Monterey and left the bus in Mexico City. They stated OSWALD sat behind them, the MC FARLANDS, and next

to an eighty-year-old United States citizen who looked to be about sixty years of age who lives in Cuernavaca and the State of Tennessee. The individual that sat beside OSWALD was allegedly a retired schoolteacher who taught in India and Arabia and is currently writing a book on the Lisbon Earthquake of 1775.

A review of FBI files reflects one JOHN HOWARD BOWEN, born January 14, 1887, at Chester, Pennsylvania, once resided in Houston, Texas.

On June 4, 1942, CHARLES M. PICKEL, Rural Route 7, Henderson Springs, Tennessee, Sevier County, advised an Agent of the FBI, Knoxville, that one J. H. BOWEN, whom he believed to be an Italian, had resided in the vicinity of Henderson Springs for the past two years. He stated that BOWEN operates a camp for boys known as the "Campfire Council." According to PICKEL, one of the boys at the camp told GEORGE SHARP, of Route 7, Henderson Springs, Tennessee, that he had seen BOWEN tear down an American Flag and stomp it into the ground. PICKEL said that BOWEN had three large police dogs at his home, which were very dangerous. PICKEL complained that the boys at the camp were committing some acts of thievery and property damage in the neighborhood. PICKEL stated that BOWEN spends time traveling over the country roads in and around Henderson Springs and that he knew for a fact that BOWEN had once traveled to Mexico City.

At the request of the FBI, PAUL LILLY, Patrolman, Tennessee Highway Patrol, made an investigation of the above allegation. On August 21, 1942, Patrolman LILLY, by letter, advised the FBI, Knoxville, that he had contacted Mr. GEORGE SHARP, Mr. CHARLES M. PICKEL, and others, and all of these persons had told him that the main trouble concerning BOWEN was on account of some vicious dogs which BOWEN had at his camp. LILLY stated that the neighbors told him they were deathly afraid of these dogs and that something had to be done about them. LILLY reported that he talked to some workers at the camp and they told him they had never seen or heard of any activities that would lead them to believe that BOWEN was or had been disrespectful to the United States.

The news article referred to by HAL C. STEPHENS of the Boys' Club regarding BOWEN's reported departure for Europe appeared in the November 14, 1963, issue of the Knoxville Journal; however, an examination of the records of the morgue on December 30, 1963, did not disclose any correspondence relative to this particular article. The morgue did reflect a news article dated December 5, 1953, in the Knoxville Journal, which reported that JOHN HOWARD BOWEN resided in Laredo, Texas, and had established a missionary station and a Baptist Church in Mexico. He was reported to be the first protestant missionary in the land of the Mixtecas Indians. His address was listed as Box 308, Laredo, Texas. The source of this item appeared to be a letter addressed to the Journal from BOWEN.

The newspaper file contained a postal card from BOWEN bearing an illegible postmark of Tampa (Florida?), November ?, 1954. On this postal card BOWEN advised the Knoxville Journal that he was mailing some photographs to the Journal. He stated that last Christmas he announced he was retiring but after a trip to England, where he spoke at a missionary conference, he decided to return to Mexico.

The news file contained a letter dated April 7, 1958, from a Dr. MARTIN HILDAGO, Oaxaca, Oax, Mexico. He wrote that BOWEN, a missionary, had saved two schoolchildren from being struck by a truck. In dashing in front of the truck to sweep the children from the path, BOWEN was slightly injured on his left side when he came in contact with the truck. The writer stated that this was the same missionary who had saved three children from a burning hut about eight years previously.

A short article in the Knoxville Journal dated April 12, 1958, described this incident, based on the above letter.

The newspaper file also contained a letter dated September 11, 1961, from an ALBERTO OSBORNE, which was postmarked at Texmelucan, Pue, Mexico. This letter reported that BOWEN was injured when he fell on a bus between Mexico

City and Publea, and it reported that BOWEN had been doing missionary work in Mexico since he left Knoxville in April, 1943. The letter set forth that BOWEN was invited to Mexico by the late Dr. C. E. LACEY, a missionary of the Southern Baptist Convention. The letter reported that BOWEN would be eighty-two in January (1962), but that he could easily pass for a man in his middle 50's. This letter went on to relate that BOWEN, prior to coming to Knoxville, had served as a missionary in India and had been active in missionary work since 1910 except the time he spent in Knoxville.

The Knoxville Journal published a short news article on September 15, 1961, based on the above letter.

On December 20, 1963, Mrs. CLARA BULL, Knoxville Credit Bureau, advised that a search of her files reflected no credit record for JOHN HOWARD BOWEN.

On December 20, 1963, Mrs. CHARLES DAVIS, Records Department, Knoxville Police Department, advised she found no arrest record in the files of her office for JOHN HOWARD BOWEN.

The newspaper files also contained two photographs that purport to be pictures of J. H. BOWEN. One photograph depicts a white male wearing a waist length zippered jacket and a sun helmet. The other photograph depicts a white male wearing a double-breasted business suit, no hat, standing before a castle-like edifice. Copies of these photographs were obtained.

PATRICIA WINSTON and PAMELA MUMFORD, 153 North New Hampshire Avenue, Los Angeles, California, were interviewed on January 8, 1964, by SA'S CHESTER C. ORTON and JOSEPH DOYLE POWELL.

WINSTON and MUMFORD viewed photographs of BOWEN that were obtained from the files of the Knoxville Journal and stated the photograph of BOWEN wearing the sun helmet was not familiar to them. They said that the picture taken in 1954 of BOWEN standing in front of a castle was familiar and possibly could have been the man who sat next to OSWALD on the bus trip from Laredo to Mexico City, on September 26 - 27, 1963.

DL 100-10461/eah

In this regard, it is pointed out that both WINSTON and MUMFORD had previously stated that they made a trip from Nuevo Laredo to Mexico City on a Flecha Roja bus on September 26 - 27, 1963, and identified LEE HARVEY OSWALD as a passenger on that bus with whom they conversed.

On December 20 & 27, 1963, reviews were made of birth records, school board records, credit bureau records, city directories, newspaper morgues and death records at Chester, Pennsylvania, with no information being developed to identify JOHN HOWARD BOWEN, born January 14, 1887, at Chester, Pennsylvania.

On January 7, 1964, Confidential Informant Dallas T-4, supra, advised that JOHN HOWARD BOWEN had not been located in Mexico.

Dallas T-4 reported the interview, on January 7, 1964, of Reverend ALBERT OSBORNE, an elderly Canadian missionary, residing at 4-A Emilio Carranza Street, San Martin De Texmelucan, State of Pueblo, who disclosed the following information:

JOHN HOWARD BOWEN is an ordained Baptist Minister who, over the years, has collected funds for construction of several churches in Mexico. BOWEN has not been in Mexico since late September or early October, 1963, at which time he advised OSBORNE he was thinking of giving up his missionary work because many of his contributors who helped him financially over the years are now deceased. OSBORNE suggested that BOWEN could be located through the Hotel Jong or Jung, New Orleans, Louisiana, where he was recently employed and was making efforts to qualify for Social Security benefits. OSBORNE also opined BOWEN might be located through Hotel St. Anthony, Laredo, Texas.

OSBORNE claimed he has no way of communicating with BOWEN and does not know his exact address in the United States, although he believed BOWEN was in the United States at that time. He said BOWEN never lived at 4-A Emilio Carranza Street, San Martin De Texmelucan, Pueblo, but did pick up his mail there during his visit to Mexico in September - October, 1963.

-11-

COMMISSION EXHIBIT No. 2195—Continued

DL 100-10461/eah

The following investigation was conducted on January 13, 1964, by SA MILTON R. KAACK:

HARWOOD HOLT, Auditor, Jung Hotel, 1500 Canal Street, New Orleans, Louisiana, checked his records and advised that JOHN HOWARD BOWEN is not presently employed by the Jung Hotel and has not been employed during the past two years.

Mrs. MAXINE MATTHEWS, Secretary to GEORGE DAWSON, Manager, Hotel New Orleans, 1300 Canal Street, New Orleans, checked the records and advised that JOHN HOWARD BOWEN is not employed at the present time by the Hotel New Orleans, nor has he been employed during the past two years.

Reverend O. S. CHIOCCHIO, Pastor, Canal Boulevard Baptist Church, 5320 Canal Boulevard, New Orleans, advised that JOHN HOWARD BOWEN is unknown to him. Reverend CHIOCCHIO stated that he would know BOWEN if BOWEN was living and working in the New Orleans area and was engaged in missionary work for the Baptist Church.

Miss DOROTHY PATERSON, Secretary to Reverend JOHN GILBERT, New Orleans Baptist Association, 3939 Gentilly Boulevard, New Orleans, advised that she could find no record in her files of JOHN HOWARD BOWEN. Miss PATERSON stated that if BOWEN was engaged in missionary work for the Baptist Church in the New Orleans area he would be listed in her files.

On January 21, 1964, Dallas T-4, supra, reported that the photographs (2) of JOHN HOWARD BOWEN, one wearing a sun helmet and zipper jacket, the other with him standing before a castle-like edifice, were identified on that date, January 21, 1964, by a servant at the residence of ALBERTO OSBORNE, in Texmelucan, Mexico, and by a Mexican minister in the same community as being identical with OSBORNE.

Dallas T-4 further reported that when ALBERTO OSBORNE was interviewed on January 7, 1964, he was in possession of a Canadian Passport, No. 5-605377, and claimed residence of 4114 Drummond Street, Montreal, Canada. Correspondence was

-12-

COMMISSION EXHIBIT No. 2195—Continued

located at the residence of 4-A Emilio Carranza Street, San Martin De Texmelucan, Pueblo, bearing a return address of WALTER OSBORNE, Old Folks Home, Grimsby, Lincolnshire, England.

The servant at the Texmelucan, Mexico, address stated OSBORNE was then on a trip to an unknown part of the United States and indicated he may return to Mexico within the next two or three weeks.

Dallas T-4 reported that inquiry at the American Express Office, Mexico City, Mexico, revealed ALBERT OSBORNE was known there as JOHN H. BOWEN and last visited that office about two weeks prior to January 21, 1964.

Further, on November 15, 1963, BOWEN requested that letters to him be forwarded to American Express, 649 5th Avenue, New York City, New York, and American Express has no other address for him, but reported that BOWEN frequently travels to Laredo and San Antonio, Texas.

On January 27, 1964, Dallas T-4 reported that a Canadian missionary, ALBERT OSBORNE, was known to the Mexican Immigration authorities in 1958 as a missionary in Mexico and inquiries then conducted failed to develop any background information of value through investigation by the Royal Canadian Mounted Police in Canada. The Canadian address for OSBORNE then in possession of the Mexican Immigration authorities was found to be non-existent. A photograph of OSBORNE obtained at that time appears to be the same person interviewed as ALBERT OSBORNE on January 7, 1964.

Dallas T-4 reported that several officials of the Baptist Church in Mexico City had reported they have no knowledge of JOHN H. BOWEN or ALBERT OSBORNE.

T-4 reported that OSBORNE normally resides in a native mud wall dwelling in Texmelucan, where the only person having knowledge of his movements is the teen-age caretaker who, himself, frequently visits his family in Oaxaca, Mexico, when OSBORNE is not there.

On January 16, 1964, the caretaker disclosed that a wedding announcement had been received from Mrs. LOLA

LOVING, Milsboro, Oregon, announcing the wedding of her daughter, SHARON RUTH LOVING, on October 20, 1963.

Dallas T-4 reported that on January 21, 1964, letters addressed to BOWEN had been received at the Texmelucan, Mexico, address from Osteghus Publishing Company, Minneapolis, Minnesota, and from "The Beam", 6248 Camp Bowie Boulevard, Fort Worth, Texas.

On January 27, 1964, Confidential Informant Dallas T-6, a confidential source abroad, reported that a check of the passport files, Department of External Affairs, Ottawa, Ontario, indicates an ALBERT OSBORNE was issued Passport No. 5-605377, on October 10, 1963, through the office of the Canadian Consul, New Orleans, Louisiana. At that time, OSBORNE indicated his mailing address as "Will Call" and his permanent address since 1917 as 1441 Drummond Street, Montreal, Quebec. OSBORNE reflected his date of birth as October 22, 1888, in Grimsley, England, 5'10", 200 lbs., blue eyes, dark brown hair - slightly gray, single, and indicates he is a member of the clergy.

Attached to his passport is an affidavit in lieu of guarantor indicating he was at the time in New Orelans and was "presently in transit." The passport contained a photograph of ALBERT OSBORNE having been taken in October, 1963. Copies of the photograph were obtained.

On January 28, 1964, Dallas T-6 reported 1441 Drummond, Montreal, Quebec, is a YMCA and ALBERT OSBORNE is not known there. The YMCA received a letter from an ALBERT OSBORNE, dated January 13, 1964, with return address of Emilio Carranza Street, San Martin de Texmelucan, Pueblo, Mexico, indicating that he, OSBORNE, would not come to Montreal as planned, but instead was going to Alberta and any mail should be forwarded in care of General Delivery, Detroit, Michigan. The original of this letter which bears the signature of ALBERT OSBORNE was obtained.

Dallas T-6 reported on February 6, 1964, that Passport No. 4-34736 issued to ALBERT OSBORNE by Canadian Authorities on June 8, 1953, at Ottawa, Canada, and was valid until June 8, 1958. It was not revalidated at the time and, therefore, expired on that date. Further, OSBORNE could have retained possession of the passport until June, 1963, but it would not have been a valid document.

DL 100-10461/eah

Under date of February 19, 1964, the FBI Laboratory furnished the following information concerning a document examination requested by Confidential Informant Dallas T-6 on February 11, 1964:

Specimens received 2/17/64

Q493 One page typewritten letter bearing heading "Emilio Carranza 4-A Texmelucan Pue. M E X I C O." addressed to "Central Y.M.C.A. Montreal, Canada," beginning "Dear Sir - If you have ...." and signed "Albert Osborne"

Result of examination:

The typewriting on Q493 matches most closely the Laboratory standard for an Underwood pica style of type spaced ten letters per inch. This typewriting was not identified in the Anonymous Letter File and a photograph of the typewriting will be added to this file.

The typewriting on Q493 was not identified with any of the previous typewriting in this case.

On February 14, 1964, extensive investigation, which has previously been reported, and is not being repeated in detail, was made at the General Delivery, U. S. Post Office; Special Investigations Squad, Detroit Police Department; Better Business Bureau; Board of Commerce; Council of Churches; Catholic Missions Office, all Detroit, Michigan, with negative results concerning ALBERT OSBORNE's present location.

FD-302 (Rev. 1-25-60)

FE RAL BUREAU OF INVESTIGATION

Date 2/3/64

1

GEORGE E. BLACKSTOCK, Canadian Consul, Suite 1710, 225 Baronne Building, produced an application for a Canadian Passport which was signed by Reverend ALBERT ALEXANDER OSBORNE at the office of the Canadian Consulate General, New Orleans, Louisiana. This application was dated October 10, 1963, at which time OSBORNE furnished his residence address as 1441 Drummond Street, Montreal, Canada. The application contained the following descriptive data concerning OSBORNE: Born November 12, 1888; sex - male; place of birth - Grimsley, Linco, England; height - 5'10"; weight - 200 pounds; blue eyes; brown and gray hair; marital status single; no visible scars and marks; occupation - minister (clergy).

OSBORNE claimed that he resided in Canada from August 21, 1917, to the present time and is a naturalized citizen of Canada because of his services in the Canadian Armed Forces. OSBORNE's Canadian Passport #4-347367, which was issued in June, 1953, was cancelled and Canadian Passport #5-605377, dated October 10, 1963, was issued to him by Chief Clerk PERCY WHATMOUGH, of the Canadian Consulate General's Office. This passport is valid until October 10, 1968, and was delivered to OSBORNE personally on October 10, 1963. At the time OSBORNE applied for a new passport, he exhibited his birth certificate and a record of service in the Canadian Armed Forces. In addition, he signed an affidavit claiming that no one knew him in New Orleans well enough to act as a guarantor because he was "in transit." OSBORNE's file contained a letter from OSBORNE dated October 16, 1963, at Mexico, D. F., which was received at the Canadian Consulate General's Office on October 18, 1963. This letter thanked the office employees for their kindness and enclosed $5.00 with the instructions that BLACKSTOCK purchase a little present for the clerical employees at the Canadian Consulate General's Office. The $5.00 was returned to OSBORNE by letter dated October 18, 1963, explaining that the employees of the Consulate General's Office could not accept any gifts, which letter was addressed to "Reverend ALBERT OSBORNE, care of American Express Company, Niza 22 Mexico, D. F."

On 1/31/64 at New Orleans, La. File # NO100-16601 DL 100-10461

by SA MILTON R. KAACK:lav:eah Date dictated 2/3/64

1

Date 2/3/64

PERCY WHATMOUGH, Chief Clerk, Canadian Consulate General's Office, Suite 1710, 225 Baronne Building, advised that he examined OSBORNE's application for a passport, cancelled his old passport, which was issued in June, 1953, and issued his new passport, No. 5-605377, to OSBORNE on October 10, 1963. WHATMOUGH recalled that OSBORNE told him that he, OSBORNE, had come to New Orleans from his residence in Montreal, Canada, by bus and that he was on his way to Mexico City by bus and that he was making this trip as part of his vacation.

OSBORNE did not tell WHATMOUGH what bus route he had taken from Montreal to New Orleans, nor did he tell him his intended route from New Orleans to Mexico.

On 1/31/64 at New Orleans, La. File # NO 100-16601 DL 100-10461

by SA MILTON R. KAACK:lav:eah Date dictated 2/3/64

AT NEW ORLEANS, LOUISIANA

The following investigation was conducted by SA MILTON R. KAACK on January 31, 1964:

JOHN A. DONALD, Canadian Consul, Canadian Consulate General's Office, Suite 1710, 225 Baronne Building, advised that in many instances natives of Great Britain who are naturalized citizens of Canada, claim dual citizenship and therefore continue to carry a British passport in addition to their passport issued by Canada.

HARWOOD HOLT, Auditor, Jung Hotel, 1500 Canal Street, advised that he had no record of ALBERT OSBORNE as an employee of the Jung Hotel during the past two years.

GEORGE DAWSON, Manager, Hotel New Orleans, 1300 Canal Street, advised that ALBERT OSBORNE has not been employed by the Hotel New Orleans during the past two years.

Reverend O. S. CHIOCCHIO, Pastor, Canal Boulevard Baptist Church, 5320 Canal Boulevard, advised that the Reverend ALBERT OSBORNE is not known to him. Reverend CHIOCCHIO stated that if OSBORNE was engaged in missionary work for the Baptist Church in the New Orleans area he would most certainly know him.

Miss DOROTHY PATERSON, Secretary to Reverend JOHN GILBERT, Executive Secretary, New Orleans Baptist Association, 3939 Gentilly Boulevard, advised that there was no record in her files concerning Reverend ALBERT OSBORNE. Miss PATERSON said that if OSBORNE were engaged in missionary work in the New Orleans area he would be listed in her files.

On February 10, 1964, Dallas T-4, supra, advised that OSBORNE had not called for his mail at the American Express Company, Mexico City, Mexico, since that office was previously contacted and additional letters had been received addressed to JOHN HOWARD BOWEN from GEORGE FULLER CUIDLIN, Jonesville, Virginia, postmarked January 29, 1964; from P. O. Box 517, Eagle Pass, Texas, postmarked January 31, 1964, and from Pisgah Home Movement, Pikeville, Tennessee, postmarked February 5, 1964.

T-4 further reported that JOHN HOWARD BOWEN was known to the Senior Cashier, American Express Company, for the past eight years and has cashed numerous U. S. Postal Money Orders in amounts of $25 - $30 each. The cashier does not know ALBERT OSBORNE and is unable to substantiate the claim that the American Express Company, Mexico City, had agreed to honor payments for OSBORNE in the name of BOWEN because BOWEN had died and OSBORNE was carrying on BOWEN's missionary work. This individual is only known at American Express Company as BOWEN and as being connected with some type of religious activities in Mexico.

T-4 reported that inquiries at Texmelucan, Mexico, on February 8, 1964, revealed OSBORNE had not been seen there since about January 15, 1964, but the caretaker reported that he had received post cards from ALBERT OSBORNE postmarked February 3, 1964, with a return address of General Delivery, Birmingham, Alabama; postmarked January 22, 1964, at Chattanooga, Tennessee, with return address of General Delivery, Atlanta, Georgia, and postmarked January 21, 1964, at Chattanooga, Tennessee, contained in the envelope of the William Len Hotel of Memphis, Tennessee. Caretaker claimed he was unaware of the present whereabouts of OSBORNE, but believed he was still in the United States.

T-4 quoted the caretaker as stating that he had not mailed any letter to LOLA LOVING of Forest Grove, Oregon, in late January, 1964, but pointed out that OSBORNE may have mailed such letter before departing Texmelucan.

T-4 reported that Mexican Immigration authorities, Mexico City, are interested in detaining OSBORNE if he returns

to Mexico as he was ordered to leave Mexico in 1958 as an undesirable alien and at that time exited Mexico at Laredo, Texas, April 5, 1958. The Mexican Immigration files show BOWEN to also be known as JOHN H. OWEN.

FD-302 (Rev. 1-25-60)

FEDERAL BUREAU OF INVESTIGATION

Date 2/11/64

1

JOHN HOWARD BOWEN was interviewed February 8, 1964, and he furnished the following information:

BOWEN advised that he has been in the Russellville, Alabama, area, speaking at various rural Baptist Churches, and has been residing at the residence of WYLIE UPTAIN, Rural Route, Russellville, Alabama. He stated he intended leaving the Russellville, Alabama, area February 11, 1964, en route back to Laredo, Texas, by way of New Orleans, Louisiana.

BOWEN stated to the best of his knowledge he was born at Chester, Pennsylvania, on January 12, 1885, and his father's name was JAMES A. BOWEN, and his mother was EMILY BOWEN. He did not know his parents, but he was reared in an orphanage in Philadelphia, Pennsylvania. His grandmother, SARAH HALL, participated to a limited extent in giving him guidance and shelter during the early years of his life. His grandmother and relatives are all deceased, and he has no known relatives of any kind.

BOWEN attended elementary school intermittently in the Philadelphia, Pennsylvania, area, but took correspondence courses and has completed the equivalent of about two years of college. He also took a correspondence course in theology, which he completed in about 1914. About fifty years ago, he was ordained as a minister by the Plymouth Brethren Church, in Trenton, New Jersey, and about forty-five years ago he was ordained as a minister by the Northern Baptist Convention at Binghamton, New York. He also is recognized as an ordained minister by the Missionary Baptist Convention and he currently considers himself associated with that church body.

BOWEN stated he considers himself an itinerant gardener and preacher. He was formerly a member of the First Baptist Church at Knoxville, Tennessee, and more recently was a member of the First Baptist Church at Laredo, Texas. He has visited and worshiped at the latter church intermittently for the past twenty years.

About thirty years ago, BOWEN applied for a job as a juvenile counselor, with the Tennessee Valley Authority at Knoxville, Tennessee, and recalled that he was fingerprinted on that occasion. From about 1929 to about 1934, BOWEN worked

-21-

On 2/8/64 at Florence, Alabama File # BH 105-908 DL 100-10461

by SA ERVIN B. BRUNINGA:ela:eah Date dictated 2/10/64

COMMISSION EXHIBIT No. 2195—Continued

BH 105-908
DL 100-10461

2

with juvenile delinquents for the City of Knoxville, Tennessee. While doing this work, he became well acquainted with Doctor A. D. MUELLER, who is now associated with the Veterans Hospital in Memphis, Tennessee, and lives at 4035 Tutwiler Road, Memphis, Tennessee. He also became well acquainted with Miss MARY ELLIOTT, who is a prominent social worker in the Knoxville, Tennessee, area.

BOWEN states since becoming ordained about fifty years ago he has traveled extensively in the United States, particularly in the Stanton, Virginia, area, and in the southern part of the United States as an itinerant Baptist Minister. During the past twenty years, he has also made numerous trips as an itinerant Baptist Minister throughout Mexico. He stated he has never been to Canada or England or any other foreign country, except in about 1939, he once visited Bermuda. On these itinerant preaching tours, he resides in the homes of the host pastor, and he moves from place to place frequently. He considers his home to be the St. Anthony Hotel, Laredo, Texas, and he is well known there by the manager, OSCAR FERRINA. He has been residing at that hotel intermittently for the past twenty years, and has made trips to Mexico for the past twenty years as an itinerant preacher.

BOWEN stated he has no passport, but carries for identification purposes the following items:

Social Security Card in the name of JOHN HOWARD BOWEN, Social Security No. 449-36-9745.

Texaco Company Credit Card #T-11372, in the name of J. H. BOWEN, P. O. Box 3042, Knoxville, Tennessee.

-22-

COMMISSION EXHIBIT No. 2195—Continued

BH 105-908
DL 100-10461

3

Gold Star Insurance Company Card,
Policy No. N3176,

Card from Laredo National Bank, in the name of JOHN HOWARD BOWEN, 920 Salinas Avenue, Box 308, Laredo, Texas, Account No. 10-7400-1.

BOWEN stated that in 1956 he contacted an unrecalled attorney in Philadelphia to apply for Social Security. This attorney experienced great difficulty in obtaining a date of birth for him. The attorney was not able to completely verify his birth, but furnished him with a card reflecting the following data:

Name:	JOHN HOWARD BOWEN
Born:	1/14/1880
Father:	JAMES A. BOWEN
Mother:	EDITH MONTGOMERY
Place of birth:	Chester, Pennsylvania
File No.:	D-869-1880
Filed:	March 6, 1956

The above card bore the signature of a person which appeared to be BERWIN F. WATKINS as the person who executed the birth data form. BOWEN stated he doubted if the above was exactly correct, but it was the best birth data which the attorney could obtain through unknown sources. He could not recall the name of this attorney and was not certain if WATKINS was his name or not. BOWEN stated he had been unable to obtain Social Security benefits because of his inability to obtain correct birth data.

BOWEN states that in about 1958 he was residing at the Reece Hotel, Oaxaco, Mexico, and also residing in that same hotel was ALBERT OSBORNE, who was a retired itinerant Baptist Minister from Canada. OSBORNE was about 70 years of age, 5'8" tall, 190 pounds, hair gray and balding, and had an

BH 105-908
DL 100-10461

4

English or Scottish accent. BOWEN acknowledged that OSBORNE was about his same size and age.

A census of some type was then being taken by Mexican authorities, and BOWEN was unable to locate his identification papers. He, therefore, borrowed the identification papers of OSBORNE on that occasion, and exhibited them to the Mexican authorities. He thereafter returned these papers to OSBORNE. He later found his own identification papers, and states he has never before or since claimed to be anyone other than JOHN HOWARD BOWEN.

BOWEN stated he next saw OSBORNE in about the Spring of 1961 or 1962, at the Railway Express Company Office in Mexico City, Mexico. He pointed out he corresponds occasionally with OSBORNE, but has not seen him since the above occasion. He recalled having heard through friends in Mexico that OSBORNE was traveling in Mexico as an itinerant Baptist preacher in December, 1963, and January, 1964, but he was planning on returning to Canada, and possibly taking up residence in the vicinity of Vancouver, Canada.

BOWEN observed a photograph of a man standing in front of a castle-like building, holding what appeared to be a camera, and he identified that person as being ALBERT OSBORNE. BOWEN explained that he has a copy of that same photograph, which was sent to him by OSBORNE, and it apparently was taken during a trip to England or Scotland.

BOWEN also observed a photograph of a man in a zippered jacket and a helmet, and identified that as being a photograph of himself, which had been taken about twenty years ago at Veracruz, Mexico. BOWEN stated that ALBERT OSBORNE has traveled in the same areas in Mexico as an itinerant Baptist preacher, and OSBORNE has stayed at the two independent churches in Texmelucan, Mexico, where the churches maintain a home for ministers. These churches also distribute food for children from destitute families. He explained that it was entirely possible persons might confuse him with OSBORNE, because they are both itinerant Baptist preachers, are about the same size and age, and both travel extensively in Mexico.

BOWEN stated he was not interviewed in Mexico at Texmelucan or anywhere else, by the FBI, regarding OSBORNE or OSWALD. He pointed out when he came to Laredo, Texas, recently he learned that the FBI had been making inquiries there regarding his recent trip to Mexico. He stated that he thereafter looked through his papers and files at Laredo and learned that he had made a trip by bus from Nuevo Laredo, Mexico to Mexico City, on September 26-27, 1963.

BOWEN explained that at the bus station in Nuevo Laredo, Mexico, at about 3:30 PM, September 26, 1963, he boarded a bus en route to Mexico City, and signed his own name, JOHN HOWARD BOWEN, to the roster of passengers. He sat in the third seat from the front on the right side. A young man who apparently boarded the bus at the same time sat in the seat adjacent to him. He described this person as follows:

Sex:	Male
Race:	White
Age:	29
Height:	5'8"
Weight:	150 lbs.
Hair:	Blond and thin
Complexion:	Dark

He explained this passenger had a small zipper bag which he placed in the rack above his feet. He did not talk to this person or hear him speak to anyone else on the bus. He presumed this person was Mexican or Puerto Rican, because he was dark complected and did not appear to be an American. He recalled that directly in front of him was a man and a woman who were about sixty years of age. The man was retired from the Bermuda Police Department, and he apparently had been traveling extensively since his retirement. BOWEN recalled that two Mexican women and a small child occupied the seat directly behind him. He could not recall who the other passengers might have been on the bus. He did recall that the bus was fully occupied when it left Nuevo Laredo.

BOWEN stated the young man sitting next to him went to sleep shortly after getting on the bus, and did not converse with him or anyone else. At about 4:30 or 5:00 PM, on September 26, 1964, the bus stopped for a lunch stop at Sabinas Hidalgo, Mexico. This young man went to the restroom and ate a lunch at the bus station. When he returned to the bus, he went to the rear of the bus where he reclined on a rear seat and went to sleep.

BOWEN stated he did not recall seeing the above person again during the trip to Mexico City, and has not seen him before or since that time. He did not know where the above person got off the bus. BOWEN stated he does not recall having specifically seen a particular photograph of subject LEE HARVEY OSWALD, but is rather certain he had seen some newspaper photographs of him. He stated he does not feel that the above person was identical to LEE HARVEY OSWALD, because the above person was quite dark complected and appeared to be a Mexican or Puerto Rican.

BOWEN stated he arrived in Mexico City on the above bus about 9:30 AM, September 27, 1963. He thereafter boarded another bus in Mexico City and went to Puebla, Mexico, where he resided at the St. Augustine Hotel. The next day, he boarded a night train at Puebla and traveled to the Railroad Hotel in Jesus Carranga, which is north of Juchitan, Mexico. He remained in this area for about one week, contacting various native ministers, and delivering Bibles to them. He preached some in Juchitan and Tehuantepec, area. He then returned to the area of Puebla, Mexico, where he resided with various persons connected with Baptist churches in that vicinity. He then traveled back to Laredo, Texas, in about the middle of November, 1963. While in Mexico City, he usually resides at the Canada Hotel Annex, which is on Cinco De Mayo Street. BOWEN stated at no time on this trip did he again see the above-mentioned person who had been on the bus with him from Nuevo Laredo.

BH 105-908
DL 100-10461

7

BOWEN stated he intends to travel from the Russellville, Alabama, area to Laredo, Texas, by way of New Orleans, and expects to be at the St. Anthony Hotel, Laredo, Texas, about February 15 - 17, 1964, where he will remain indefinitely. He stated that, at Laredo, he could locate the bus ticket which would verify the date of the above-mentioned trip into Mexico in September, 1963. He stated he may also have there correspondence from ALBERT OSBORNE.

BOWEN stated he has never taught school, has never been to any foreign countries, other than Mexico and Bermuda. He stated he has never written a book, knew nothing about the Lisbon earthquake of 1775. He could not recall seeing any American girls on instant bus, and knew of no one on the bus who might have talked to the young man sitting in the seat adjacent to him.

BOWEN stated he definitely is not identical to ALBERT OSBORNE and, with the one exception, he has never posed as ALBERT OSBORNE. BOWEN stated he would cooperate fully in this matter. He volunteered to have his photograph and fingerprints taken on this occasion.

BOWEN furnished the following descriptive data regarding himself:

Name:	JOHN HOWARD BOWEN
Sex:	Male
Race:	White
Birth data:	1/12/1885, Chester, Pa.
Height:	5'8"
Weight:	190 lbs.
Hair:	Gray and thin
Eyes:	Blue
Build:	Heavy
Complexion:	Medium
Scars & marks:	Small round sore or scar on right temple
Characteristics:	Wears heavy, dark-rimmed glasses for reading
Occupation:	Itinerant Baptist Preacher

COMMISSION EXHIBIT No. 2195—Continued

FD-302 (Rev. 3-3-59)

FEDERAL BUREAU OF INVESTIGATION

Date February 24, 1964.

OSCAR FERRINO, owner of St. Anthony Hotel, Laredo, Texas, viewed photographs of JOHN HOWARD BOWEN, one taken with pith helmet and other in business suit in front of what appears to be old English castle, and stated that both photographs appeared to be photographs of the JOHN HOWARD BOWEN that has been staying periodically at the St. Anthony Hotel, P. O. Box 308, for several years.

FERRINO stated that BOWEN usually stays at the St. Anthony when he is passing through Laredo, Texas, en route to Mexico.

FERRINO stated that when BOWEN is not at the St. Anthony Hotel he, FERRINO, holds BOWEN's mail until he receives instructions from BOWEN on where to send the mail or until BOWEN returns for the mail.

FERRINO stated that the name of ALBERT OSBORNE sounds familiar and he was of opinion that mail has come for BOWEN with name of ALBERT OSBORNE on it, but he said that he could not be certain of this, but that BOWEN has always been known around the hotel as BOWEN and has not, to FERRINO's knowledge, used the name of ALBERT OSBORNE in Laredo.

on 2/14/64 at Laredo, Texas File # SA 105-2909

by Special Agent SA ROBERT L. CHAPMAN/cbl/les Date dictated 2/20/64

COMMISSION EXHIBIT No. 2195—Continued

FD-302 (Rev. 3-3-59)

FEDERAL BUREAU OF INVESTIGATION

Date February 20, 1964

JOHN HOWARD BOWEN was interviewed at the St. Anthony Hotel, Room 105, Laredo, Texas, at which time he related the following information.

He made available two ticket stubs from the "Flecha Roja" (Red Arrow) Bus Lines, one purchased at Nuevo Laredo, Mexico, bearing number 0921, dated September 26, 1963, reflecting fare of $71.40 pesos, from Nuevo Laredo, Mexico, the other purchased in Mexico bearing number 1142 and dated October 1, 1963, reflecting fare of $71.40 pesos from Mexico-Nuevo Laredo.

BOWEN stated he departed Nuevo Laredo, Mexico, approximately 2:00 p.m., September 26, 1963, on a Flecha Roja Bus and arrived in Mexico City around 10:00 a.m., September 27, 1963. He stated there were no other Americans or English speaking persons on this bus and to his knowledge, none of the Mexican passengers spoke English. He sat near the front of the bus next to the window and there was a young man sitting next to him.

This man appeared to be Mexican, about 29 years of age, dark brown hair, had Spanish look, about 5'8", 150 pounds. He was shabbily dressed, wearing khaki pants and was carrying a brown zippered traveling bag which he placed on the top rack of the bus.

BOWEN stated he did not talk to this man, nor did this man speak to him, or anyone else on the bus. He stated that upon leaving Sabinas Hidalgo, after stopping there for lunch, this person went to the rear of the bus and went to sleep. He stated he does not know where this man got off the bus.

A photograph of LEE HARVEY OSWALD was exhibited to BOWEN, and after viewing it carefully, stated that he could not identify this photograph as being identical to the man who sat next to him on the Flecha Roja Bus September 26, 1963. He viewed the photograph of OSWALD again and stated that he has never seen that person at any time.

on 2/16/64 at Laredo, Texas File # SA 105-2909

by Special Agent LEOPOLDO E. ARMIJO/mkd/les Date dictated 2/18/64

-29-

COMMISSION EXHIBIT No. 2195—Continued

SA 105-2909
LEA/mkd/les
2

BOWEN stated that this bus arrived in Mexico City about 10:00 a.m., September 27, 1963, and he boarded another bus on the afternoon of the 27th and went to Puebla, Mexico, where he stayed at the Teresa Hotel overnight. From there he boarded a train and went to JESUS CARANZAS, Mexico, and stayed at the Railroad Hotel about two nights, and returned to Laredo, Texas, on October 2, 1963.

When queried about his activities since September 1, 1963, he became indignant, and wanted to know why the FBI was interested in his itinerary, adding that this was a free country and he could travel whenever and wherever he pleased.

Under further interrogation, BOWEN stated that during the month of September, 1963, he stayed at the St. Anthony Hotel, Laredo, Texas, until his trip to Mexico on September 26, 1963. After returning from Mexico on October 2, 1963, he remained in Laredo at the St. Anthony Hotel until the latter part of October when he went on a lengthy trip in the United States, visiting churches and collecting religious books. He added that the records at the St. Anthony Hotel would not reflect that he stayed there in September or October inasmuch as the owner of the hotel owed him money from a typewriter that was stolen from his room and did not charge him for use of the room and, therefore, did not sign his name on the hotel register.

Referring to the lengthy trip he took in the United States the latter part of October, November, and most of December, he stated that he first went to Houston, Texas, where he stayed two nights at the Spur Hotel near the Greyhound Station having left Laredo, Texas, in mid-October. From Houston, he went to Memphis, Tennessee, to see Dr. A. D. MULA; however, did not see him as he arrived there at night. He stayed in Memphis two nights at the William Len Hotel. From there, he went to Charlotte, North Carolina, where he stayed at the YMCA and then went on to Columbia, South Carolina, and back to Laredo, Texas, just before Christmas. After Christmas, he went on another trip and visited Houston, Texas; Lake Charles and Baton Rouge, Louisiana, and returned to Laredo, Texas. He added that this occurred in January, and in February, he made a trip to Birmingham, Alabama.

-30-

COMMISSION EXHIBIT No. 2195—Continued

SA 105-2909
LEA/mkd/les
3

BOWEN stated that he has never stayed in Texmelucan, Mexico, adding that he has only been through there on his way to Mexico City. He denied being interviewed in Mexico by anyone, and denied ever using a dual identity or ever having been in any other foreign country. He further stated that he has never used the name of ALBERT OSBORNE. He knows a man by that name who is also a preacher and missionary in Mexico. He last saw OSBORNE in Mexico City in mid-summer of 1963, and he and OSBORNE were last together in Oaxaca, Mexico, in 1959. He added that he and OSBORNE look very much alike and were often mistaken for each other in Mexico.

BOWEN stated that during his travels in Mexico, he always stays with pastors and Christian people and sometimes does the same thing in the United States. He could not furnish names of people in the United States with whom he has stayed, explaining that he just could not remember their names. He stated that he is well known in Mexico, particularly Vera Cruz, and Oaxaca, and mentioned the following names of persons who know him and with whom he has stayed in the past: MOSIS NAUM, pastor in Vera Cruz; LEONARD INGRAM and PERCY COX, both preachers in Mexico City; JOHN HARRIS, preacher in Arizaba, Vera Cruz. He added that COX and INGRAM are both listed in the directory, Mexico City. He also knows the man in charge of the Bible Society in Mexico City, however, cannot recall his name. He stated that he visits other cities in Mexico, however, could not recall all the names.

BOWEN was again exhibited photograph of OSWALD and reiterated that he could not identify OSWALD as being on the same bus with him on September 26, 1963, and has never seen him at any time. When confronted with the fact that three other people on the same bus identified him and OSWALD as being seated in the same seat, he stated that he was saying only what he knew, and that possibly other people are not being truthful.

When queried about his background, BOWEN stated that he organized the Boys Club in Knoxville, Tennessee, in 1934, now known as the Boys Club of America. At this point,

SA 105-2909
LEA/mkd/les
4

BOWEN was pressed for his full background, specific details regarding his activities since September 1, 1963, names of friends, relatives, and people he has visited, etc., and he became very indignant. He stated that he had furnished all of this information to the Birmingham FBI Office and did not have to furnish it again. He stated that he did not understand why the FBI was interviewing him everywhere he went, and wanted to know what he was being charged with as he might get a lawyer. He was advised that he was not charged with anything and was not under arrest. At this point, he stated that he did not want to make any further statements. When asked where he intended to go from Laredo, Texas, he stated he did not know, and refused to say where he was going.

FD 302 (Rev. 3-3-59)

FEDERAL BUREAU OF INVESTIGATION

Date 2/20/64

OSCAR FERRINO, owner, St. Anthony Hotel, Laredo, Texas, advised that he recalls JOHN HOWARD BOWEN staying at this hotel in October and November, 1963; however, did not recall the dates and his records would not show inasmuch as a typewriter belonging to BOWEN was stolen from his room and he, FERRINO, paid BOWEN $30.00 for the loss of this typewriter. He did not actually give BOWEN $30.00, but let him stay in the room free, which would be about fifteen days for that amount of money.

In view of this, he did not record BOWEN's name on the register. In checking his records further, he noted that BOWEN stayed at the St. Anthony Hotel three nights in December, 1963, commencing on December 29.

FERRINO added that BOWEN checked out of the hotel at 7:00 a.m., February 17, 1964, and did not say where he was going.

on 2/17/64 at Laredo, Texas File # SA 105-2909

by Special Agent LEOPOLDO E. ARMIJO/ldb/les Date dictated 2/18/64

33

SA 105-2909
1
FTL/cbl

The following investigation was conducted by SA FRED T. LEE, JR., at Eagle Pass, Texas.

On February 18, 1964, Reverend WALTER L. HLUCHAN, Minister, Pentecostal Church of God, advised that on about February 8, 1964, he had received an undated letter from ALBERT OSBORNE whom he knows as JOHN HOWARD BOWEN. Return address on the letter was ALBERT OSBORNE, Emilio Carranza-4-8, Texmelucan, Pue., Mexico. In this letter OSBORNE indicated that on about December 20, 1963, he had returned to Texmelucan after preaching for some time in England, Spain, Northern France, and Northern Africa. OSBORNE did not indicate in his letter the length of time he had spent in Europe, but did indicate he expected to remain in Texmelucan for some time. Reverend HLUCHAN advised he could not furnish any additional information concerning the whereabouts or travel plan of OSBORNE.

On February 19, 1964, Reverend JAMES TIMMONS, Baptist Minister, advised he has known OSBORNE since about 1944. TIMMONS advised he has not seen OSBORNE for some two years and does not know anything concerning his present whereabouts or activities. TIMMONS indicated that he recently sent a letter to OSBORNE with a return address Eagle Pass, Post Office Box 517, but that he has not received any reply to this letter. TIMMONS continued by stating that in the past OSBORNE had frequently visited Reverend JOE AMARINE, Mission Secretary, Southern Baptist Convention, Alice, Texas.

Further, Mr. TIMMONS described OSBORNE as a person who "acted mysteriously and secretively" and that to his knowledge had not attended any ministerial school and his only affiliation with any religious group was the "Plymouth Brothers" which he described as an English non-denomination sect.

34

DL 100-10461
EEH/les

Dallas T-5, supra, reported the following information:

Dr. and Mrs. JOHN MC FARLAND, 7A Riversdale Road, Liverpool, England were contacted by Detective Inspector WILLIAM BESTALL of the Liverpool City Constabulary on February 12, 1964.

The MC FARLANDs viewed the photos of ALBERT OSBORNE and JOHN HOWARD BOWEN. They definitely identified the photo of OSBORNE taken October, 1963, as being identical with the man they previously described who sat next to OSWALD on the bus trip into Mexico on September 26, 27, 1963. They were not that positive in identifying the other photos, however.

Mrs. MC FARLAND stated that she remembered OSBORNE as speaking with a slight North England accent and when she questioned OSBORNE if he had ever been in England he replied in the negative, stating that his mother was English. She was led to believe by OSBORNE that he was an American Citizen and had traveled in Mexico extensively as he appeared to know intimately the countryside they were passing through while on the bus trip from Nuevo Laredo to Mexico City.

Both the MC FARLANDs were specifically questioned as to whether they had any knowledge of previous trips OSWALD had made to Mexico and they replied they were under the impression OSWALD had never been to Mexico before because he appeared to be completely ignorant about the country and language.

The Hotel Cuba never came into their conversation with either OSWALD or OSBORNE. Mrs. MC FARLAND stated OSBORNE was carrying a haversack-type bag containing canned food and she was under the impression he was returning to some sort of school or mission in Mexico and she believed it was at Cuernavaca.

On February 15, 1964, Detective Sergeant J. STANDISH, Grimsby Police, England, conducted investigation and interviewed relatives of ALBERT OSBORNE in the Grimsby area. The persons

DL 100-10461
EEH/les

interviewed were WALTER OSBORNE, who resides in an old people's home in Grimsby and is ALBERT OSBORNE's brother. The other individual interviewed was a Mrs. LILLIE FEATHERSTONE, sister to ALBERT OSBORNE who resided at Station Road, Greatcoates, Lincolnshire and is a rural district outside Grimsby.

Both WALTER OSBORNE and Mrs. FEATHERSTONE immediately identified all photos as being that of their brother, ALBERT. They stated that ALBERT was born in Grimsby and left England as a young man with a Lincolnshire Army Regiment for Gibraltar and Bermuda. This was some time prior to World War I as by that time he was in Canada and studied for the ministry and served as a chaplain in the Canadian Army during the period 1914-1918.

They stated it was almost 40 years before ALBERT returned to England and that very little was actually known of his life. He corresponded infrequently with them and they have heard that he was married and had a son but have no idea of the present whereabouts of them.

They did state, however, that for approximately the last five years they have used the address in corresponding with him as ALBERT OSBORNE, care of JOHN H. BOWEN, Box 308, Laredo, Texas, and they continued to use that address until ALBERT suddenly appeared in Grimsby in early November, 1963. According to WALTER OSBORNE, ALBERT traveled to Prestwick, Scotland in the company of a group of scientists who were going to Iceland to photograph a volcano which has emerged there from the ocean. It is not known whether he got off the plane in Prestwick before or after the expedition did the photographing in Iceland, however, he traveled over night by train from Prestwick and arrived early in the morning at Mrs. FEATHERSTONE's home. He remained there four or five days and left for London stating he was going on to Spain.

Mrs. FEATHERSTONE then received a letter dated December 14, 1963, postmarked New York City, in which ALBERT stated he had arrived back in the United States at New York on December 5, 1963.

WALTER stated he heard from ALBERT by letter postmarked Mexico, January 8, 1963, in which ALBERT used the following return address: Emilio Corranza 4A, Texmelucan, Pue, Mexico. He said that he had destroyed the envelope so that it was not possible for Sergeant STANDISH to determine from where the letter had been sent.

Neither WALTER OSBORNE nor Mrs. FEATHERSTONE was able to shed any light on the name JOHN H. BOWEN except that ALBERT had told them in the past to write to him care of that name in Laredo. They had never heard him mention BOWEN in any of his letters or in conversation with him.

Mrs. FEATHERSTONE advised, however, that she has a sister, a Mrs. ADA AMOS, who resides on Manchester Street, Gary, Indiana, and it is the only other relative she has who resides in the United States. She added she does not think Mrs. AMOS and ALBERT have been in close contact over the years as Mrs. AMOS visited them in Grimsby a few years ago and at that time advised she had seen or heard very little from her brother, ALBERT, even though they were in the same country.

Dallas T-5 also furnished photographs of certified copy of an entry of birth given at the General Register Office, Somerset House, London, Application No. 514371. This document reflects a birth in the District of Caistor, Sub-District of Great Grimsby in the County of Lincoln, England, on the 12th day of November, 1888, at 106 Oxford Street, New Clee, England. The baby is reflected as a boy, name-ALBERT, father-JAMES OSBORNE, mother-EMILY OSBORNE, formerly COLE, with the birth having been recorded December, 1888.

On February 26, 1964, Mrs. ADA AMOS, 353 Marshall Street, Gary, Indiana, advised ALBERT OSBORNE, her brother, was born November 12, 1889, Grimsby, England, parents JAMES and EMILY COLE OSBORNE, both deceased.

Mrs. AMOS said ALBERT OSBORNE attended primary schools in Grimsby, England, was subsequently employed by Grimsby Grocery Store and enlisted in British Army in 1908 and served most of his enlistment in India. She said he bought himself out of the Army in 1914 and migrated to the U. S. during the same year. He settled in the South living most of the time in unrecalled areas of Tennessee.

She stated her brother was occupied as a preacher, church affiliation not known, and was also engaged as an

actor and lecturer involving places and speeches on India. She stated ALBERT married, wife's name and whereabouts being unknown, had one son, reportedly killed in action in the U. S. Armed Forces during World War II, has a daughter-in-law and grandson in the United States, whose names and whereabouts unknown.

She stated ALBERT once lived in Laredo, Texas, address and occupation not recalled. She has some vague knowledge that he was affiliated with some Christian Association and fulfilled engagements making talks on India. She stated that at one time, he was affiliated with an unrecalled boys camp in the South, possibly Tennessee. She remembered in ALBERT's infrequent correspondence and letters that he frequently traveled to Mexico, crossing at Laredo and El Paso, Texas, but recalled no information regarding possible travel to Canada, Spain, or Scotland.

Mrs. AMOS recalls ALBERT formerly lived in New York City and Washington, D. C., addresses unknown, and does not know whether ALBERT is a naturalized United States Citizen. Mrs. AMOS was unable to supply any information regarding ALBERT having lived in Canada or about possible Canadian citizenship.

Mrs. AMOS has not seen ALBERT in over 20 years at which time he visited her home in Gary, Indiana, for one night, this being the only occasion she has seen him in 55 years. She recalled that at that time he was involved preaching and lecturing. She said she has not been in close contact with him because of a minor disagreement regarding his borrowing money from her. She recalled that he wrote her during the 1920s requesting funds at which time she sent him some money in care of JOHN HOWARD BOWEN in New York City. She has no knowledge of ALBERT OSBORNE using the dual identity of BOWEN or ever utilizing any name other than his true name.

Mrs. AMOS said she has never heard of ALBERT having any scientific or technical skills or being involved in oceanography or other scientific projects. She recalled that in earlier years he did manifest some talent as an artist and spent time sketching.

DL 100-10461
EEH/les

Mrs. AMOS stated ALBERT has brothers, ARTHUR OSBORNE, date of birth April 9, 1882, residing Horncastle, Hope Castle, England; WALTER OSBORNE, born March 28, 1868, residing Old Peoples Home, Scather Road, Scather, England, and sisters, ROSETTA GELL, born May 19, 1886, residing 87 Sthellers Road, Cleethorpes, Lincolnshire, England; Mrs. FLORRY BOND, born July 9, 1864, residing 32 Ownit Street, Abbeywood, London, SE2, England. Other sister and brothers are RHODA, WILL, JIM, FRANK, and ABBOTT, deceased.

Mrs. AMOS related that sisters ROSETTA GELL, FLORY BOND, and EMILY FEATHERSTONE have been in closer contact with ALBERT and might be able to furnish more recent information regarding his activities.

On February 17, 1964, Special Agent ERVIN B. BRUNINGA, Birmingham, Alabama, viewed photograph of ALBERT OSBORNE taken October, 1963, and reported that in his opinion, that person is identical with JOHN HOWARD BOWEN whom he, BRUNINGA, interviewed at Florence, Alabama, February 8, 1964.

FD-302 (Rev. 1-25-60)

FEDERAL BUREAU OF INVESTIGATION

Date 2/25/64

Miss PAMELA LILLIAN MUMFORD furnished the following information:

She continues to be employed as a legal stenographer at Dillavou and Cox, Attorneys, 611 Wilshire Boulevard, Room 700, Los Angeles. She resides at the Jaqueline Apartments, 153 North New Hampshire Avenue, Apartment No. 212.

Miss PATRICIA WINSTON, who was her former roommate and with whom she was traveling around the world, departed Los Angeles on January 21, 1964, and is presently residing with her parents in Flat 4, #8 Wood Street, Manly, Sidney, Australia.

Three photographs of ALBERT OSBORNE, also known as JOHN HOWARD BOWEN, were displayed to Miss MUMFORD. The first photograph was taken in October, 1963, in connection with his passport application and shows his head and shoulders. He is wearing a white shirt. The second and third photograhs were taken on February 8, 1964, and he is wearing a dark suit, white shirt, and striped tie, and is holding a pipe in his right hand. These are stand-up, full face and profile photos.

Upon viewing these photographs, Miss MUMFORD advised that she was positive that this individual was identical to the man whom she had seen and who sat next to LEE HARVEY OSWALD on the bus which had come from Nuevo Laredo, and which she and Miss WINSTON had boarded at Monterey, Mexico, on September 26, 1963, and which arrived in Mexico City on September 27, 1963. During the time that Miss MUMFORD was on the bus, OSWALD sat next to this man, whom she had previously described as "the Englishman".

On 2/24/64 at Los Angeles, California File # Los Angeles 105-15823

by SA CHESTER C. ORTON:jab:les Date dictated 2/25/64

FD-302 (Rev. 1-25-60) FEDERAL BUREAU OF INVESTIGATION

Date 3/5/64

1

ALBERT OSBORNE, whose permanent address is 920 Salinas, Box 308, Laredo, Texas, was interviewed at his temporary place of residence at the Central YMCA, Nashville, Tennessee, where he is registered under the name JOHN H. BOWEN.

At the outset of the interview, OSBORNE denied his true identity and claimed that his name was JOHN H. BOWEN; however, he later admitted that his correct name is ALBERT OSBORNE and he furnished the following background information concerning himself:

OSBORNE indicated that he was born November 12, 1888, at Grimsby, England, to JAMES OSBORNE and EMILY COLE OSBORNE, both of whom are deceased. He identified his brothers as WALTER OSBORNE, Grimsby, England; ARTHUR OSBORNE, Grimsby, England; WILLIAM OSBORNE, deceased, and FRANK OSBORNE, deceased. He identified his sisters as EMILY FEATHERSTONE, Grimsby, England; FLORE BOND, London, England; ROSETTA GELL, Lincolnshire, England, and ADA AMOS, Gary, Indiana. He stated that he was educated at St. James Academy at Grimsby, England, until the eighth grade. OSBORNE stated that he joined the British Army in 1908, serving in India, Arabia, and Bermuda. He purchased his discharge from the British Army in 1914 while in Bermuda and thereafter came directly to the United States and proceeded to Washington, D. C., where he obtained employment in several grocery stores under his correct name, ALBERT OSBORNE. While in Washington, D. C., he took a correspondence course in Religion from the University of Chicago. Thereafter, he went to Philadelphia, Pennsylvania, where he attended the Philadelphia Bible College for approximately one year while living and working as a janitor at the YMCA in Philadelphia. In 1916, he proceeded to Canada, where he joined the Canadian Army as OSBORNE and remained in the Canadian Army until the cessation of hostilities in World War I. Thereafter, he returned to Washington, D. C., where he met a Syrian, whose name he does not recall, and went into the rug cleaning business with this individual.

OSBORNE indicated that the rug cleaning business was of an itinerant nature and he and the Syrian traveled throughout the United States in this venture. During this period and at the suggestion of the Syrian, he adopted the name JOHN H. BOWEN, in order to obtain a more Americanized name and for the purpose of eventually obtaining American citizenship and an American

41

On 3/3/64 at Nashville, Tennessee File # ME 105-891 DL 100-10461

by SA EDWARD T. STEELE and SA JOHN E. RODGERS:mvd:eah Date dictated 3/5/64

This document contains neither recommendations nor conclusions of the FBI. It is the property of the FBI and is loaned to your agency; it and its contents are not to be distributed outside your agency.

COMMISSION EXHIBIT No. 2195—Continued

ME 105-891
DL 100-10461
2

passport in order that he might accompany the Syrian to the latter's native country. He indicated, however, that he did not thereafter take any steps to obtain American citizenship or to obtain an American passport. He stated that he took no steps to have his name changed legally but merely adopted the name BOWEN. After leaving the rug cleaning business, he worked for several years as an itinerant gardener primarily in the States of Virginia and North Carolina. In 1929, he went to Knoxville, Tennessee, where he became affiliated with the YMCA in that city in boys' work and indicated that he organized the organization which subsequently became known as the Boys Club of America.

OSBORNE indicated that he remained in Knoxville, Tennessee, until about 1943 when he became an itinerant Baptist preacher throughout the south, having been ordained as a Baptist Minister in the Bethany Baptist Church, Philadelphia, Pennsylvania, in 1916 after he attended the Philadelphia Baptist College.

OSBORNE stated that he first visited Mexico in 1939 as a tourist and became interested in missionary work and has been in and out of Mexico numerous times since then.

He indicated that for the past twenty years he has maintained occasional residence and a permanent mailing address at 920 Salinas, Box 308, Laredo, Texas. In this connection, OSBORNE denied that he had ever received correspondence from relatives addressed as "Albert Osborne, care of John H. Bowen, Box 308, Laredo." He said he was well known at Laredo, Texas, as JOHN H. BOWEN and was a member of the First Baptist Church in that city.

OSBORNE stated that he got in trouble in Mexico in about 1956 when the Mexican authorities were conducting sort of a census in order to identify Americans residing in Mexico. He stated that when he was questioned by Mexican authorities he was required to produce identification documents and the only documents he had were his birth certificate and Canadian Army enlistment papers in the name of ALBERT OSBORNE, which he produced, stating, "This mixed my name up with people in Oaxaco," and indicated that he was known in Mexico by the names OSBORNE and BOWEN.

42

COMMISSION EXHIBIT No. 2195—Continued

ME 105-891
DL 100-10461
3

He indicated that he had used the name JOHN H. BOWEN in the United States since about 1916 except when he applied for and received a Canadian passport at New Orleans, Louisiana, on October 10, 1963, in the name OSBORNE, using the above-mentioned OSBORNE identification documents. He indicated that after obtaining the passport he visited his sisters and brothers in England and a Baptist Church in Madrid on a 21-day trip ending in New York, December 5, 1963. He traveled to Europe and returned to the United States as a passenger on the Icelandic Airlines.

OSBORNE was questioned concerning his missionary work in Mexico. He indicated that he had visited various evangelical churches in Mexico City and other places in Mexico providing books and financial assistance to these churches. He was questioned concerning his source of funds to provide the financial assistance and books and he stated that these funds came from various independent Baptist Churches and members of Baptist Churches with whom he was in contact. He was questioned concerning the identity of others who knew of his work in Mexico and he mentioned he was well known to PERCY COX, who is well known in Baptist missionary circles in Mexico City, and whose name is listed in the Directory of Americans Residing in Mexico City. He also indicated LEONARD INGRAM, who operates a publishing house of religious materials in Mexico City, could provide information concerning his work as a missionary in Mexico. He indicated he was well known to the Bible Society known as the Mexicana Bible Society in Mexico City.

Regarding churches from whom he has received financial support, he indicated that the First Baptist Church, Roanoke, Virginia; Isabell Baptist Church, Leighton, Alabama, and several other churches in that area as well as some churches in Florida, the identity of which he was unable to provide, assisted him financially. He indicated that EARL KIRBY, who is postmaster at Leighton, Alabama, was a person who had rendered considerable financial assistance to him. OSBORNE emphasized that he did not solicit these funds but that these churches and individuals knew of his work and voluntarily sent contributions from time to time.

43

COMMISSION EXHIBIT No. 2195—Continued

ME 105-891
DL 100-10461
4

OSBORNE was specifically questioned concerning specific activities since June, 1962. In this connection, he indicated that in June, 1962, he was at Laredo, Texas. He stated that since that time he has been traveling around considerably. When questioned for specific places he had been in his activities, he indicated he had spent some time in New Orleans and Baton Rouge, Louisiana, and other Louisiana towns and cities looking for old, rare books which he collected and was able to sell for a profit. He indicated that he stayed in rooming houses and cheap hotels, none of which he was able to identify. He was questioned concerning his contacts during that period but was unable to provide specifics.

OSBORNE was questioned specifically concerning his trip to Mexico City on September 26, 27, 1963. OSBORNE indicated that he was a passenger on the Red Arrow Bus Lines from Laredo, Texas to Mexico City, on September 25, 26, 1963. When reminded that he had previously furnished bus ticket stubs of the Red Arrow Bus Lines indicating that he journeyed to Mexico City from Laredo on September 26, 1963, OSBORNE indicated that it was possible that the date of the beginning of his journey was September 26, 1963, but that it was his first recollection that he left on September 25, 1962. He maintained that on the trip to Mexico City there were no other English-speaking people who were fellow passengers and specifically denied that LEE HARVEY OSWALD, whose picture he had viewed on several occasions, was a fellow passenger. He stated he was seated on the bus with a young Mexican or Spanish-appearing person who apparently spoke no English. He stated that this person boarded the bus on the Mexican side of Laredo. He said this person was wearing khaki pants, colored shirt and no hat, and he indicated this person tended to be bald-headed and had a sallow complexion. He got off the bus at the first coffee break at Sabino Hilidgo. His seat mate re-entered the bus after the coffee break, but proceeded to the rear of the bus where he slept. OSBORNE indicated that the only conversation he had with any person on the bus was with two elderly Mexican women who were holding a young baby.

44

COMMISSION EXHIBIT No. 2195—Continued

He stated that the nature of his conversation with these elderly women was to apologize to them for any inconvenience he may have caused them in pushing his seat back since they were seated behind him. He stated he did not know where the boy who was his seat mate at first left the bus, indicating he may have left the bus at Monterey, Mexico. He denied seeing and talking to an English couple and denied seeing and talking to two Australian girls who boarded the bus at Monterey. It is his present recollection that he arrived at Mexico City September 26, 1963, at 9:30 P.M. and took a bus to Puebla where he stayed at the Teresa Hotel.

He indicated that he remained there two or three days and then picked up some religious books at the Evangelical Book Store and proceeded to Texmelucan and went to a residence maintained by missionaries who are native preachers who come and go from that residence. He indicated that he returned to Laredo on October 1, 1963 by Vera Cruz and thereafter went to New Orleans, Louisiana, where he obtained his Canadian passport on October 10, 1963. He remained in New Orleans about three days and returned to Laredo, where he remained a few days and then went to New York City via bus leaving New York City for London as mentioned above. He indicated he was in New York City approximately two days staying at the William Sloan on 34th Street under the name OSBORNE.

OSBORNE admitted he had been untruthful in three previous interviews concerning his own identity and had furnished false information concerning JOHN H. BOWEN, whom he had previously indicated was an acquaintance for whom he, OSBORNE, has been frequently mistaken. He indicated that his reason for his untruthfulness was that he had been caught up in his own web of furnishing false information years ago to the Mexican authorities which established his dual identity as OSBORNE and BOWEN.

It is noted that OSBORNE had in his possession at the time of the interview Canadian Passport No. 5-605377 in the name of Reverend ALBERT OSBORNE, occupation - Clergyman. His place of birth was listed as Grimsby, Lincoln, England, November 12, 1888. This passport is valid until October 10, 1968. It was issued at New Orleans, Louisiana, by G. F. BLACKSTOCK, Consul of Canada.

contained with the Canadian passport was an International Certificate of Vaccination in the name of ALBERT OSBORNE, 1441 Drummond Street, Montreal, Canada, which was issued at the U. S. Quarantine Station, Laredo, Texas. A notation contained in this document indicated he was vaccinated on September 24, 1963, at the above mentioned Quarantine Station. It was also noted that OSBORNE had in his possession Social Security Card No. 449-36-9745 in the name JOHN HOWARD BOWEN. It was also noted he had in his possession a Texas Company Gasoline Credit Card, T11372, in the name JOHN H. BOWEN. Typed on this card is the above Social Security Number. The expiration date or the date of issuance on this gas credit card was obliterated.

OSBORNE was questioned concerning his means of livelihood in the past several years. He indicated that he was an expert gardener and when funds became low he obtained jobs at various places as an itinerant gardener. When questioned for names of persons or concerns for whom employed, he was able to furnish only the name of Tyler Nursery Company, Tyler, Texas, as a place where he worked during the summer of 1963. However, he indicated that he had worked at various homes in other Texas cities including Austin, but maintained that he could not recall names of such employers nor was he able to furnish identities of other cities where he had worked as a gardener.

OSBORNE was advised that his photograph had been positively identified by other English speaking people on the Red Arrow Bus from Laredo, Texas, to Mexico City on September 26, 27, 1963. OSBORNE again denied that he was on a bus with any other English speaking people and that he himself spoke no English to anyone on the bus.

He stated that since he had finally revealed his true identity that he would have no purpose in being further untruthful, and that if he were a passenger on the bus with LEE HARVEY OSWALD and other English speaking people, he would freely admit same now, but he continued to maintain that he had never seen OSWALD or been a fellow passenger with him on the bus or the above-mentioned English couple and Australian girls.

DL 100-10461

TRAVEL OF ALBERT OSBORNE-
JOHN HOWARD BOWEN

FD-302 (Rev. 1-25-60)

FEDERAL BUREAU OF INVESTIGATION

Date December 24, 1963

OSCAR FERRINO, owner of the St. Anthony Hotel, Laredo, Texas, advised that JOHN HOWARD BOWEN has been staying at the St. Anthony Hotel in Laredo for many many years as he travels to and from Mexico. FERRINO stated that BOWEN is a Baptist Missionary who teaches the Baptist Religion in Puebla, Mexico, and at present is operating a school for approximately 25 to 30 boys. FERRINO advised that he has no records for BOWEN at the hotel for the past two or three months inasmuch as a typewriter belonging to BOWEN was stolen at the hotel and that he gave BOWEN free rent at the rate of $8.00 per week for Room 108 which is the room BOWEN always occupies until typewriter is paid for and, therefore, did not enter his appearance at the hotel in the registry book. FERRINO stated that BOWEN is approximately 80 years old, but appears to be around 60 or 70 years, is heavy set, bald headed, and is approximately 5'9" tall.

FERRINO stated that he forwards BOWEN his mail each Friday to the address of "JOHN HOWARD BOWEN, Emilio Carranza 4-A Texmelucan, Puebla, Mexico".

On 12/24/63 at Laredo, Texas File # SA 105-2909

by SA ROBERT L. CHAPMAN/dte/les Date dictated 12/24/63

DL 100-10461
EEH/les

On January 15, 1964, OSCAR FERRINO, St. Anthony Hotel, Laredo, Texas, advised Special Agent ROBERT L. CHAPMAN that approximately two weeks prior to that date, JOHN HOWARD BOWEN had passed through Laredo from Mexico. He stated that BOWEN told him that BOWEN had been interviewed in Mexico by the Federal Bureau of Investigation and he was then en route to Austin, Texas, for interview by the Federal Bureau of Investigation in Austin. He said BOWEN did not leave any forwarding address, but stated he was en route to Kansas City to straighten out his Social Security and said he, BOWEN, would write to FERRINO and tell him where to forward his, BOWEN's, mail. BOWEN did not state what the FBI had interviewed him about in Mexico.

On February 14, 1964, Miss NANCY DAVIS, Secretary to K. W. NEWMAN, Manager, William Len Hotel, Memphis, Tennessee, advised Special Agent WILLIAM H. LAWRENCE from records that one ALBERT OSBORN , listing his home (no number) at Drummond Street, Montreal, Canada, William Len Hotel, Folio No. 90193, checked into this hotel on January 17, 1964, stayed in Room 205, at the rate of $4.68 and checked out January 18, 1964, leaving no forwarding address, made no telephone calls, and occupied the room by himself.

On February 14, 1964, Mrs. SUE HOWARD, Room Clerk, who checked OSBORNE into the hotel, and Mrs. MARTHA BRENNAN, cashier, who checked him out, and Bellman RAYNER DANNER, who took his bags to Room No. 2D5, all advised Special Agent WILLIAM H. LAWRENCE, after viewing photographs of ALBERT OSBORNE, that they did not recall him and had no idea as to his purpose in being at Memphis, Tennessee.

FEDERAL BUREAU OF INVESTIGATION

Date February 17, 1964

On February 16, 1964, WILLIAM S. SHIVELY, JR., 6650 North Clippinger Drive, Cincinnati 43, Ohio, advised he was unacquainted with any ALBERT OSBORNE or any JOHN HOWARD BOWEN.

He said he is a third-year student at the University of Cincinnati and had hitchhiked from Cincinnati to Laredo, Texas, during September, 1963, and bought a railroad ticket from there to Mexico City, Mexico, on September 22, 1963. He said he lived at the Royal Prince Hotel while in Mexico City and had also visited Veracruz, Mexico, for several days, staying at the Emporio Hotel. On October 2, 1963, he left Mexico City for Laredo, Texas, via a bus line, name unrecalled, since he failed to make train connections. At Nuevo Laredo, Mexico, Mexican authorities checked out the passengers on the bus by taking their tourist cards that were issued upon entering Mexico. He said his tourist card was taken also.

Upon being shown the photograph of ALBERT OSBORNE, he said he merely recalled seeing someone who looked like that person either at the bus station in Mexico City or on his bus ride from Mexico City to Laredo, Texas, on October 2, 1963. SHIVELY said he had no conversation with OSBORNE who was not recalled as traveling with anyone else. Also, SHIVELY stated he was unacquainted with the other passengers on the bus, which had about thirty passengers. He stated he could not remember where OSBORNE departed the bus and did not know his destination or whereabouts. Also, he said he was unable to recall what luggage, if any, OSBORNE had, or the type of clothing he wore.

SHIVELY advised he was unable to recall ALBERT OSBORNE's height, weight, color of eyes, color of hair other than greying, or any peculiarities. He said that had he had any conversation with OSBORNE, SHIVELY would have been able to furnish more information.

On 2/16/64 at Cincinnati, Ohio File # 105-2505

by SA JOHN W. SHINDOLER/ked/les Date dictated 2/17/64

CI 105-2505
2

SHIVELY volunteered that he had read newspaper accounts that LEE HARVEY OSWALD had been in Mexico at about the same time as SHIVELY visited that country. SHIVELY stated that he had not seen OSWALD in Mexico, was unacquainted with OSWALD, and had no information about OSWALD.

DL 100-10461
EEH:vm

Dallas T-7, a confidential source abroad, advised on February 7, 1964, that under that date the Spanish police reported their records fail to reflect entry into Spain of ALBERT OSBORNE or JOHN HOWARD BOWEN, elderly white male. Further, no record of OSBORNE was located in the Embassy records, Paris, France.

Dallas T-6, supra, reported under date of February 4, 1964, that efforts by the Royal Canadian Mounted Police Headquarters, Ottawa, Canada, had developed no additional information regarding ALBERT OSBORNE than that previously reported but efforts were continuing.

Little Rock T-1 reported on February 3, 1964, that JOHN HOWARD BOWEN left a forwarding address at the Hot Springs, Arkansas, U. S. Post Office, on January 29, 1964, of General Delivery, Russellville, Alabama.

The following investigation was conducted by SA HORACE H. WILLIS:

Mrs. WILEY UPTAIN, Route 2, Leighton, Alabama, advised February 13, 1964, JOHN HOWARD BOWEN lived at her home during most of approximately two weeks he visited North Alabama, in late January and early February, 1964. She advised she did not know details of BOWEN's itinerary en route back to his home in Mexico, however, she said she transported BOWEN to Russellville, Alabama, on February 10, 1964, where he said he planned to board a Greyhound Bus at 11:32 a.m., February 10, 1964, en route to Mexico, the exact place she did not know, stating she understood BOWEN conducted much of his business at Laredo, Texas. She said BOWEN indicated he intended to contact friends at Birmingham, Alabama, and at New Orleans, Louisiana, en route. He never identified these friends by name or address. She stated she expected BOWEN to reach Mexico on or before February 17, 1964.

Birmingham T-1 reported on February 13, 1964, that the Post Office, Russellville, Alabama, received a postcard postmarked Birmingham, Alabama, February 10, 1964, advising the Russellville Post Office to forward mail for BOWEN to JOHN HOWARD BOWEN, General Delivery, Corpus Christi, Texas.

<u>INTERVIEWS WITH ACQUAINTANCES AND CONTACTS OF ALBERT OSBORNE - JOHN HOWARD BOWEN</u>

FD-302 (Rev. 3-3-59)

FEDERAL BUREAU OF INVESTIGATION

Date January 29, 1964

1

Mrs. VIRGIL (WILMA) DYKES, 1038 South Whitcomb, Indianapolis, Indiana, advised that she is a contributor to the Baptist mission in Mexico. She stated that approximately two years ago, someone submitted her name to this particular mission run by JOHN HOWARD BOWEN and she has been contributing to this mission ever since that time. She stated her last contribution was mailed in the middle of January, 1964, to BOWEN at Niza 22, Mexico.

Mrs. DYKES personally never met BOWEN, but has received a number of thank you notes from BOWEN and Christmas cards with some informative comments concerning the mission and himself. She stated the last thank you card contained information that he had hurt his back and was going to Hot Springs, Arkansas in January, 1964, and that for any reason, could be located through General Delivery in that city.

Mrs. DYKES was exhibited two photographs of BOWEN, which she was unable to identify. She further advised she never heard of the name ALBERTO OSBORNE.

Mrs. DYKES made available a group photograph of BOWEN along with some of his parishioners, which was apparently taken in December, 1961, and it was sent to her by BOWEN as a Christmas card.

Mrs. DYKES advised she had no other information available pertaining to BOWEN other than it was her impression that he was running a bona fide Baptist mission in Mexico.

on 1/28/64 at Indianapolis, Indiana File # DL 100-10461 / IP 105-3399

by Special Agent KENNETH P. PETTIJOHN and PATRICK J. FLETCHER:kam:vm Date dictated 1/27/64

53

COMMISSION EXHIBIT No. 2195—Continued

DL 100-10461

Mrs. EUGENE (LOLA) LOVING, 2617 Seventeenth Street, Forest Grove, Oregon, said on January 31, 1964, that her husband is no longer living but that prior to his death, both he and she had been active missionaries for the Pentecostal Church of God, serving for a number of years in Indonesia.

In the early 1950's, they returned from Indonesia, and in about 1956 they and their daughter, SHARON, went to Mexico City, where they opened a Bible School for the Pentecostal Church of God. Not long after beginning their work, they met another missionary by the name of ALBERT OSBORNE. This man, whom she believed to be a Baptist, had a mission at Texmelucan, not far from Mexico City. His mission consisted of his own large home where he gathered in young men who appeared to have no homes or ties, trained them and then sent them out on their own as missionaries.

It was not long before the LOVINGs found that OSBORNE was using two names. His second was JOHN HOWARD BOWEN. In fact, OSBORNE readily admitted the use of both names and voluntarily explained that JOHN HOWARD BOWEN, at one time, had been an associate of his in the mission at Texmelucan but had died. Monetary contributions for the mission, which is dependent upon such donations, kept coming in to Texmelucan in BOWEN's name, and rather than lose this money, OSBORNE had gone to banking officials and explained the situation. Specifically mentioned by OSBORNE were American Express authorities in Mexico City, who had agreed to honor the contributions and make the payments to OSBORNE, using BOWEN's name. Consequently, over the years since that time, OSBORNE had assumed the dual identity.

Mrs. LOVING continued that she and her husband and daughter were in Mexico City until about 1958 and that during that time and over the years since, OSBORNE has used both names indiscriminately. She pointed out that he continues to correspond with her and that she never knows, from letter to letter, which name he will be using. She usually writes to him, however, in the name of ALBERT OSBORNE.

Mrs. LOVING went on to say that she had received a letter only a week ago from OSBORNE. The return address, which she had torn from the letter, was ALBERT OSBORN, Emilio Carranza 4-A, Texmelucan, Pue. Mexico, which, she said, was the address of his mission. She expressed the belief that OSBORNE would be at that address at the present time, having only recently returned from Europe. She recalled that in recent weeks, possibly in the past month or two, she had received a letter from OSBORNE in Spain.

54

COMMISSION EXHIBIT No. 2195—Continued

Mrs. LOVING readily and without hesitation identified two photographs of JOHN HOWARD BOWEN and one of ALBERT OSBORNE as being those of the same person, ALBERT OSBORNE, the man she had known in Mexico. She frequently referred to OSBORNE as a "fine old man" and indicated that she regarded him highly. At one period in his life he supposedly served for twenty years as a missionary in India. Mrs. LOVING believed him to be an American citizen but said she knew of no connections of OSBORNE in the United States except some friends in Texas, whom he visits from time to time. She identified one of his friends as the Reverend WALTER L. HLUCHAN, Post Office Box 1343, Eagle Pass, Texas, who operates a mission near Eagle Pass. Mrs. LOVING said that it had been Reverend HLUCHAN who had introduced OSBORNE to her and her husband and that Reverend HLUCHAN knew OSBORNE well and possessed detailed information concerning him.

Mrs. EUGENE (LOLA) LOVING, 2617 7th Street, Forest Grove, Oregon, advised on February 11, 1964, that she had destroyed the last letter which she had received from ALBERT OSBORNE. This was the letter which bore the return address of ALBERT OSBORN, Emilio Carranza 4-A, Texmelucan, Pue. Mexico. Mrs. LOVING went on to say that she felt that the letter was written from Texmelucan although this may have been only because she was aware that that was his normal address. She recalled definitely that the letter had come from Mexico because it bore Mexican postage stamps which she had removed and saved for a friend.

Mrs. LOVING further advised that every month she sends a financial contribution to OSBORNE, always sending the contribution to him at Texmelucan. The contributions are usually by check, the checks being cashed at American Express in Mexico City.

Mrs. LOVING added that she was currently preparing a contribution of clothing which was to be sent to OSBORNE. She pointed out, however, that regulations prevent shipment of such clothing into Mexico and consequently such clothing contributions are picked up by OSBORNE when he comes to the United States for visits. He normally informs her as to what point she should mail such clothing. These locations are usually in Texas, Mrs. LOVING said, since that is where he usually visits.

Mrs. LOVING recalled that in the last letter received from OSBORNE, the one which had been destroyed, he had told her that the

clothing this time should be sent to him in either name, ALBERT OSBORNE or JOHN HOWARD BOWEN, Post Office Box 308, Laredo, Texas. Mrs. LOVING said that this was the address of a friend of OSBORNE's but that she had never known the name of this individual. She commented that she presumed, in view of his mailing instructions to her, that OSBORNE might be at this Laredo, Texas address either at present or soon if he is not currently in Texmelucan.

FD-302 (Rev. 3-3-59)

FEDERAL BUREAU OF INVESTIGATION

Date February 28, 1964

1

Reverend WALTER LADDIE HLUCHAN, Pentecostal Church of Christ, 711 Madison, Eagle Pass, Texas, advised as follows:

In 1939 he was assigned by the Pentecostal Church of Christ to do missionary type work at Vera Cruz, Vera Cruz, Mexico. In the latter part of this year, 1939, he met a person who was introduced to him as JOHN HOWARD BOWEN at the residence of Reverend A. C. HORSTMAN, then a missionary for the Pentecostal Church of Christ at Vera Cruz. At this time the person he met as JOHN HOWARD BOWEN, but whose true name he now knows to be ALBERT OSBORNE, was living at Nocheslan, Oaxaca, Mexico, which location is between Oaxaca City, Oaxaca, Mexico, and Puebla City, Puebla, Mexico. OSBORNE had suffered financial losses due to a flood in Oaxaca and at that time he (HLUCHAN) bought a Remington portable typewriter from him (OSBORNE) for 150 pesos ($30.00 in United States money). OSBORNE was at this time selling Bibles and distributing religious literature but was apparently not connected with any specific church or religious denomination.

After this he did not see OSBORNE for approximately eight months but during the following twelve months, 1940-41, he visited OSBORNE several times at Nocheslan, Oaxaca, Mexico, when he (HLUCHAN) chanced to be in Nocheslan on duties connected with his missionary work.

In 1941 he (HLUCHAN) became extremely ill from fever and because of ill health left Mexico for about nine years. During this period he did not see OSBORNE and did not receive any information concerning him. In late 1949 or early 1950 he (HLUCHAN) returned to Mexico City to continue his missionary work. During the next eight or nine years, 1950-58, he saw OSBORNE on about four or five occasions, most of which were at the Mexico City, Mexico, home of Mrs. LOLA LOVING, wife of a now deceased missionary who now resides at 2223 A Street, Forest Grove, Oregon, and that at some unrecalled date between 1950 and 1958 OSBORNE changed his residence from Nocheslan, Oaxaca, Mexico, to Texmelucan, Puebla, Mexico, which location is also known as San Martine, Puebla, Mexico.

In about 1958 OSBORNE was in some difficulty with the Mexican Immigration authorities at Mexico City concerning his residence in Mexico and his using the name JOHN HOWARD BOWEN.

on 2/27/64 at Eagle Pass, Texas File # SA 105-2909

by Special Agent FRED T. LEE, JR./cbl:vm Date dictated 2/28/64

57

COMMISSION EXHIBIT No. 2195—Continued

2
SA 105-2909

On one occasion during this period he (HLUCHAN) was at the residence of Mrs. LOLA LOVING in Mexico City and OSBORNE, who was also at the residence, was discussing his problems with the Mexican Immigration authorities. At this time OSBORNE explained in his (HLUCHAN's) presence that many years ago (HLUCHAN did not recall if OSBORNE indicated a specific number of years) he, OSBORNE, had come to Mexico with one JOHN HOWARD BOWEN to do missionary type work. A short time later he lost or misplaced his Mexican Tourist Card which permitted him to live legally in Mexico and it happened that BOWEN, with whom he had come to Mexico and with whom he was doing missionary work, was leaving Mexico and did not need his Mexican Tourist Card. OSBORNE explained that for this reason BOWEN gave him his Mexican Tourist Card to use for identification as a tourist legally in Mexico. OSBORNE explained that subsequent to this he (OSBORNE) was known to persons whom he met as JOHN HOWARD BOWEN and among all his acquaintances he used only this name.

Reverend HLUCHAN stated that he positively does not know any reason other than the above as to why OSBORNE used the name JOHN HOWARD BOWEN. Reverend HLUCHAN stated although he met OSBORNE in 1939 he has probably seen him less than a dozen times, has never been closely associated with him and has not seen him since sometime in 1961. Reverend HLUCHAN stated he does not know of any ministerial training OSBORNE may have had, OSBORNE has indicated that prior to going to Mexico he had done missionary work in India for many years; he has never heard OSBORNE called anything but "Mr."; he has never known OSBORNE to have an associate or to organize a church in Mexico; he has never known the religious faith of OSBORNE; as to his knowledge OSBORNE has distributed literature of the Methodist, Baptist, and other churches and had at times indicated a connection with an unknown church in England. Reverend HLUCHAN stated OSBORNE has for many years given religious instruction to Mexican boys who resided at his residence and has distributed religious type literature in Mexico. Reverend HLUCHAN pointed out that during the time he has known OSBORNE since 1939, the only letter he recalls receiving from him was one he received in early February, 1964, indicating a return address of EMILIO CARRANZA 4A, Texmelucan, Puebla, Mexico, which letter was signed ALBERT OSBORN , and including information that OSBORNE had apparently returned to Texmelucan shortly before Christmas, 1963, after participating in evangelistic services in England, Spain, Northern France and Northern Africa.

58

COMMISSION EXHIBIT No. 2195—Continued

Reverend HLUCHAN pointed out that he was vague on some dates regarding his contacts with OSBORNE as he was unable to recall clearly the details of these contacts. Reverend HLUCHAN stated that he has never known OSBORNE to be connected with any occupation or activity other than missionary type work in Mexico and does not know anything unfavorable concerning him. Reverend Hluchan concluded by stating that he could not give any additional information or reason why OSBORNE had used the name JOHN HOWARD BOWEN when his true name was ALBERT OSBORNE.

The following investigation was conducted by Special Agent DEAN W. GASTEIGER:

AT JONESVILLE, VIRGINIA

On February 17, 1964, GEORGE FULLER CRIDLIN, age 16, Jonesville, Virginia, son of JOE CRIDLIN, Judge, Circuit Court, Lee County, Virginia, and a student at Jonesville, Virginia, High School, advised that he had met a JOHN HOWARD BOWEN a couple of years ago, when he was in Appalachia, Virginia, for a church meeting. He said as a result of this, and influence of his mother, he became interested in the missionary work that BOWEN was reported to be doing in Mexico, and therefore, sent him some money to be used in the missionary work. He recalled that about January, 1964, he sent about $14.00 to him in Mexico, but he could not recall the address. He mentioned his mother, Mrs. JOE CRIDLIN, would be able to furnish more information concerning BOWEN. He was shown the photograph of ALBERT OSBORNE and he said he could not be sure if this person is identical with BOWEN.

On February 18, 1964, Mrs. JOE CRIDLIN, Jonesville, Virginia, advised that she knew a JOHN HOWARD BOWEN, and a photograph of ALBERT OSBORNE was shown to her. She said that this photograph resembles the person she had met as BOWEN. She recalled she first heard about BOWEN through her sister, Mrs. LOUISE FULLER FRALEY, Appalachia, Virginia, when he first came to Appalachia, Virginia, about 20 years ago and spoke to a group in Appalachia, Virginia, about his missionary work. She did not see BOWEN until about two years ago when he returned to Appalachia, Virginia, and stayed with her sister, Mrs. FRALEY, for a night, and while in Appalachia, he spoke before a group at the Baptist Church. She said that about six years ago she decided to send some money to BOWEN to help out in the missionary work he had said he was doing in Mexico. She stated since then she has been receiving correspondence from BOWEN and presently has numerous letters that he has written. She said that the last letter she received from him was postmarked Chattanooga, Tennessee, January 22, 1964, which had a return address of JOHN HOWARD BOWEN, Niza 22, Mexico, D. F., and this letter mentioned that in December, 1963, he had a back injury and went to Hot Springs, Arkansas, for treatment, but when he got there the pain went away and he returned to the Mexican border and he still did not have any pain. Also in this letter was a receipt for $50.00, dated December 31, 1963, signed JOHN HOWARD BOWEN, on a

RH 105-3777
DWG/pgh:ds:vm
- 2 -

receipt form of the Mixteca Baptist Church, Number 151. Mrs. CRIDLIN explained she had sent BOWEN $50.00 to be used in his missionary work. She said that when she would send clothes for use in the missionary work they would always be sent to Box 308, Laredo, Texas, at BOWEN's request.

She related that her son had sent a Cashier's Check for $14.00 to him recently and it was sent to JOHN HOWARD BOWEN, Niza 22, Mexico, D. F., but he has not received any indication that BOWEN received this money.

She received a letter dated January 6, 1964, from JOHN HOWARD BOWEN which mentioned that he was going to Hot Springs, Arkansas, for treatment for a sprained back. Also this letter contained a report of the gifts he had received from Americans and Mexicans to be used in the mission. She also received a letter in October, 1963, which indicated that BOWEN was going to Spain to talk regarding his mission. A letter postmarked November 28, 1963, Madrid, with return address of JOHN HOWARD BOWEN, Plaza de las Cortes 2, Madsia, Espana, indicated that he was returning the next week. Also, at one time, BOWEN had given his address as JOHN HOWARD BOWEN, Av. Juarez 8, Mexico, D. F.

AT APPALACHIA, VIRGINIA

On February 18, 1964, Mrs. LOUISE FULLER FRALEY, Appalachia, Virginia, said she first met JOHN HOWARD BOWEN about 20 years ago when he came to the First Baptist Church, Appalachia, Virginia, and spoke in the church. She related she had not seen him again until about one and one-half years ago, when she received a message from him that he was in Knoxville, Tennessee, and wanted to come to Appalachia, Virginia, to speak at the church. She arranged for him to speak on one occasion and he stayed that evening in her home. She said she knew very little about BOWEN except what he has written in his letters. She ascertained from these letters and conversations with him that BOWEN reportedly was 82 in January, 1963, his wife had been killed in 1963; and his children had died in India where he reportedly had been a missionary for the Baptist Church. He had, in September, 1962, mentioned that a Deacon in the First Baptist Church, Knoxville, Tennessee, had given him enough money to finance his mission for three years. He was also well acquainted with

RH 105-3777
DWG/pgh:ds:vm
- 3 -

Mr. and Mrs. FRED ALLEN, 1400 North 4th, Knoxville, Tennessee. He mentioned he had been checked by the Internal Revenue but when they found he operated a mission they discontinued their investigation.

He is not sponsored by the Baptist Church in his mission work, but reportedly is doing the missionary work on his own. She said on occasions she has contributed money to BOWEN's mission.

She said she does not know anything about BOWEN except what he has written or told her. The photograph of ALBERT OSBORNE was exhibited to her and she advised that OSBORNE's photograph appears to be identical with the person she knows as JOHN HOWARD BOWEN who visited in her home about one and one-half years ago.

DL 100-10461
EEH:vm

The following Baptist ministers advised SA ROBERT LEE MORRISON on February 20, 1964, that ARTHUR OSBORNE and/or JOHN HOWARD BOWEN is unknown to them. They said that in the event they learn of this individual's being in the area they will immediately notify the FBI:

Reverend ORTIE E. BRADSHAW, Grandview Avenue, Jonesboro, Tennessee

Reverend HARVEY SEYMORE, Pine Street, Jonesboro

Reverend W. PAUL HALL, Superintendent of Missions, Holston Baptist Association, 2310 Nave Drive, Johnson City, Tennessee.

FD-302 (Rev. 3-3-59)

FEDERAL BUREAU OF INVESTIGATION

1

Date February 25, 1964

Reverend FRED B. ALLEN, Jr., 505 Oklahoma Avenue, advised he is pastor of the North Glenwood Baptist Church, Knoxville. He advised he and his parents, Mr. and Mrs. FRED B. ALLEN, Sr., 1400 North 4th Avenue, Knoxville, are long-time friends of JOHN HOWARD BOWEN, whom he described as an 84 year old missionary. Reverend ALLEN stated that BOWEN has worked as a missionary in Mexico for the past 22 years.

Reverend ALLEN advised he has not seen BOWEN for quite some time, but advised he had recently received a post card from BOWEN postmarked 2/18/62 at San Antonio, Texas. He advised this was an airmail postcard of the type purchased at U. S. Post Offices. He said the only message on the card was BOWEN's new mailing address and that BOWEN hoped to hear from him soon. Reverend ALLEN stated the new address furnished by BOWEN was Niza 22, Mexico D. F.

Reverend ALLEN advised he had absolutely no idea as to BOWEN's present whereabouts, but advised he would immediately notify the Knoxville FBI Office if he or his parents heard anything further from BOWEN.

on 2/21/64 at Knoxville, Tennessee File # KX 105-528

by Special Agent JACK K. MURPHREE - mlc:vm Date dictated 2/21/64

FEDERAL BUREAU OF INVESTIGATION

Date February 25, 1964

1

Mrs. BESSIE WHITE, Vice President, Pisgah Home Movement, Pikeville, Tennessee, advised she has known of JOHN HOWARD BOWEN for about the past four years. She stated she received information through some source, unrecalled at the present time, that BOWEN was a supervisor of a mission in Mexico, and she has been making contributions to be used to support one of the Evangelists. She said that BOWEN is a representative of the Pentecostal or Full Gospel Church and that he reportedly has several Evangelists working under him at this mission that he operates. She said that the Evangelists are reportedly Mexicans and are working throughout Mexico.

She indicated that she contributes $35.00 per month at the present time but originally only contributed $25.00 per month. This money is supposed to be used to support one of the Evangelists and she receives a receipt each month from the person who received the money. The money is sent to BOWEN, who, in turn, makes the money available to the Evangelists. BOWEN also furnishes a receipt indicating that he receives the money that she contributes. She stated that she makes the contribution in the form of bank drafts, which are drawn on the First National Bank of Pikeville, Pikeville, Tennessee, and these drafts are made payable to BOWEN. She said that these cancelled bank drafts, as well as the receipts, are presently in her possession. She said that she has received information that other persons were contributing to this same cause, but she did not know the identity of any of these persons. She said that BOWEN has never solicited any contributions from her, however, he did notify her that the cost of supporting one of the Evangelists had increased from $25.00 to $35.00 per month. She has never seen BOWEN and her only contact has been through the United States mails by letter.

She said that she knew very little about BOWEN, but he has advised her in his letters that he is originally from Knoxville, Tennessee. She does not know anything about his background but understands that he has been in Mexico for about 18 years doing missionary work. In addition to the money sent each month, the Pisgah Home Mission occasionally sends used clothing and other articles to BOWEN to be distributed to the needy.

She said that the only name she ever knew this person by was JOHN HOWARD BOWEN and his last address was Niza 22, Mexico, D.F., as of about two weeks previously. She said that the name of the Evangelist that she was supporting was a ZENNEN MIGUEL CRUZ, Niza 22,

on 2/17/64 at Pikeville, Tennessee File # KX 105-528

by Special Agent WILLIAM B. HUDSON cyp:vm Date dictated 2/18/64

2
KX 105-528

Mexico. She has never seen this person but does receive receipts from him indicating that he received the money which was furnished by her.

She said that the name of ALBERT OSBORNE was not familiar to her. She said the Pisgah Home Movement is an independent, non-profit and non-denominational organization established to aid and assist any needy person, and to do the work of the Lord.

DL 100-10461

MISCELLANEOUS INVESTIGATION
RE OSBORNE - BOWEN

FD-302 (Rev. 3-3-59)

FEDERAL BUREAU OF INVESTIGATION

Date December 4, 1963

1

MYRA SILVER, Secretary, Jones Printing Company, 422 Girod Street, New Orleans, Louisiana, was interviewed at her place of employment and advised that her records reflect the following information:

She stated that on May 29, 1963, a person who she understood gave his name as OSBORNE appeared at the Jones Printing Company and placed an order for 1,000 copies of a handbill, a rough draft of which he submitted on a 8 x 10 looseleaf paper. She stated that the handbill read as follows:

"HANDS
OFF
CUBA!

"Join the Fair Play for
Cuba Committee

"NEW ORLEANS CHARTER
MEMBER BRANCH

"Free Literature, Lectures

"LOCATION:

"EVERYONE WELCOME!"

She advised that the order was placed on job ticket # D-7548 and promised the completed product on June 4, 1963. She advised that the business relationship was strictly cash, due to the fact that her company had never done business with OSBORNE before.

She advised that her records show that OSBORNE appeared on May 31, 1963, and placed a $4.00 down payment on his order. She stated that the handbills were made up on June 1, and locked up on June 3, 1963. She advised that OSBORNE probably appeared on June 4, 1963, picked up his handbills and paid the balance of $5.89 in cash. The total cost for the handbills was $9.89.

on 12/3/63 at New Orleans, Louisiana File # NO 89-69

by Special Agent JOHN M. McCARTHY /dmm:vm Date dictated 12/4/63

COMMISSION EXHIBIT No. 2195—Continued

NO 89-69/dmm:vm

2

Mrs. SILVER was shown a photograph of LEE HARVEY OSWALD, at which time she stated she could not recognize the person repressented in the picture as the person who placed the order for the handbills.

MYRA SILVER furnished the following items to SA McCARTHY:

1) Original rough draft layout for the above mentioned handbills.

2) Jones Printing Company job ticket # D-7548.

3) Three copies of finished handbill beginning, "Hands Off Cuba," which handbills were being retained as file copies by the Jones Printing Company.

COMMISSION EXHIBIT No. 2195—Continued

FD-302 (Rev. 1-25-60)

FEDERAL BUREAU OF INVESTIGATION

1

Date 3/4/64

MYRA SILVER, Secretary, Jones Printing Company, 422 Girod Street, observed photographs of ALBERT OSBORNE and JOHN HOWARD BOWEN, and advised that neither OSBORNE nor BOWEN was identical with the individual who contacted her on May 31, 1963 and placed an order for some handbills. She stated that the individaul who placed the order was a young man and that she recalls that although he gave her the name of OSBORNE, she may have been mistaken and understood that the name he gave was OSBORNE whereas he gave her the name of OSWALD. She stated that she repeated the name OSBORNE and that he did not correct her so that she assumed that that was his name.

On 3/2/64 at New Orleans, Louisiana File # DL 100-10461 NO 100-16601

by SA MILTON R. KAACK/gml Date dictated 3/4/64

COMMISSION EXHIBIT No. 2195—Continued

FD-302 (Rev. 1-25-60)

FE.-RAL BUREAU OF INVESTIGATION

1

Date 3/4/64

DOUGLAS JONES, Jones Printing Company, 422 Girod Street, observed photographs of JOHN HOWARD BOWEN and ALBERT OSBORNE, and advised that the individual, who ordered handbills during the latter part of May, 1963, was not identical with these photographs.

On 3/2/64 at New Orleans, Louisiana File # DL 100-10461 NO 100-16601

by SA MILTON R. KAACK/gml Date dictated 3/4/64

This document contains neither recommendations nor conclusions of the FBI. It is the property of the FBI and is loaned to your agency; it and its contents are not to be distributed outside your agency.

-70A-

COMMISSION EXHIBIT No. 2195—Continued

FD-302 (Rev. 1-25-60)

FEL-RAL BUREAU OF INVESTIGATION

1

Date 3/4/64

ARTHUR B. NUESSLY, Printer, Jones Printing Company, 422 Girod Street, advised that he had no contact with the individual who placed the order for handbills in the latter part of May, 1963. He observed photographs of JOHN HOWARD BOWEN, ALBERT OSBORNE, and LEE HARVEY OSWALD and advised that he could not identify either one of the photographs.

On 3/2/64 at New Orleans, Louisiana File # DL 100-10461 NO 100-16601

by SA MILTON R. KAACK/gml Date dictated 3/4/64

This document contains neither recommendations nor conclusions of the FBI. It is the property of the FBI and is loaned to your agency; it and its contents are not to be distributed outside your agency.

-70B-

COMMISSION EXHIBIT No. 2195—Continued

DL 100-10461
EEH:vm

On February 25, 1964, the FBI Identification Division reported that the fingerprints of the individual interviewed February 8, 1964, at Florence, Alabama, as JOHN HOWARD BOWEN had been identified with the prints of one JOHN HOWARD BOWEN, fingerprinted December 18, 1953, by the Houston, Texas Police Department under their Identification No. 64246.

On February 25, 1964, a review of the Houston Police Department records under Identification No. 64246 reflect individual giving name JOHN HOWARD BOWEN was arrested 5:05 a.m., December 11, 1953, at 412 Travis, Houston, Texas, which is the location of the Woods Hotel. BOWEN was held for "investigation in connection with mattress fire" and gave his date of birth as January 14, 1887, Chester, Pennsylvania, being described as a white male, 5'10", 220 pounds, heavy build, brown hair - thinning, blue eyes, ruddy complexion, being employed by and residing at the Woods Hotel.

Detective J. D. ROLLINS, Houston Police Department, advised on February 25, 1964, that no charge was actually filed against BOWEN and he was apparently released the same day as arrested. ROLLINS made available a copy of the Houston Police Department Identification Record and photograph taken of BOWEN on December 11, 1953.

NEGATIVE INVESTIGATION
RE OSBORNE - BOWEN

71

COMMISSION EXHIBIT No. 2195—Continued

FD-302 (Rev. 3-3-59)

FEDERAL BUREAU OF INVESTIGATION

Date December 17, 1963

1

Mr. ARTURO GARZA CANTU, Deputy Consul, Mexican Consul General's Office, 127 Navarro Street, San Antonio, advised that a check of all applications for tourist cards for travel in Mexico on file in his office for the months of August and September, 1963, does not reflect that an application was received or Mexican tourist card issued during that period of time in the names of JOHN H. BOWEN or LEE HARVEY OSWALD.

Mr. CANTU stated his office has no way to determine the place of issuance of Mexican tourist card bearing number 4329926.

on 12/13/63 at San Antonio, Texas File # SA 105-2909

by Special Agent BRUNO F. DREYER/mjb:vm Date dictated 12/13/63

72

COMMISSION EXHIBIT No. 2195—Continued

FD-302 (Rev. 3-3-59)

FEDERAL BUREAU OF INVESTIGATION

Date December 17, 1963

1

GILBERTO CAZARES GARZA, Chief of Mexican Immigration, Nuevo Laredo, Mexico, advised that according to his records, JOHN H. BOWEN, 60 years of age, married, from Houston, Texas, obtained a tourist FM-5 card from his office numbered 4329926 on September 26, 1963.

BOWEN departed Mexico through Nuevo Laredo, Mexico, on October 1, 1963.

Mr. CAZARES stated that his records did not reflect any address for BOWEN or any other information.

on 12/13/63 at Nuevo Laredo, Mexico File # SA 105-2909

by Special Agent LEOPOLDO E. ARMIJO/mjb:vm Date dictated 12/13/63

73

FD-302 (Rev. 3-3-59)

FEDERAL BUREAU OF INVESTIGATION

Date December 26, 1963

1

Mr. IVAN D. MARICLE advised he is the Associate Registrar of the Baptist Annuity Board, Southern Baptist Convention (SBC), Room 202, 511 North Akard Street, Dallas, Texas. He said he had no record of JOHN HOWARD BOWEN in the files of that office and that he doubted BOWEN had ever been a Baptist minister or a regular appointed missionary from the information concerning BOWEN's background and history of employment.

He said that a record might be located in the files of the Foreign Mission Board, Southern Baptist Convention, 3806 Monument Avenue, Richmond, Virginia, if BOWEN served for any length of time under one of their appointments. He said the records of the Baptist Annuity Board at Dallas only cover members of the retirement plan of the Southern Baptist Comvention in this area, and would not necessarily cover all persons listed in the Richmond Office of the SBC.

on 12/26/63 at Dallas, Texas File # DL 100-10461

by Special Agent ARTHUR E. CARTER:mvs:vm Date dictated 12/26/63

74

DL 100-10461
EEH:vm

On February 27, 1964, Reverend REUBEN J. CANAS, Pastor, First Mexican Southern Baptist Church, 801 W. 23rd Street, Kansas City, Missouri, advised he has made numerous contacts with people of Mexican extraction and people associated with the Baptist Church without developing information concerning JOHN HOWARD BOWEN or ALBERT OSBORNE. Reverend CANAS recommended contact with the following two organizations in the order they are set forth since these organizations would have a record of any Baptist missionary working in, or who has worked in, Mexico:

1. Baptist General Convention of Texas, Reverend DALLAS LEE, Co-ordinator, Language Mission Department, Baptist Building, Dallas, Texas.

2. Reverend ROBERTO BARRAS MAYNES, Executive Secretary of the Condencion Nacional Bautista, Mexico City D.F., Mexico.

Reverend CANAS advised that whereas there were numerous conventions within the Baptist Church in the United States, the missionary work in Mexico approximately the past twenty years has been consolidated into one organization.

75

COMMISSION EXHIBIT No. 2195—Continued

FD-302 (Rev. 3-3-59)

FEDERAL BUREAU OF INVESTIGATION

Date 3/2/64

1

Rev. DALLAS LEE advised he is the co-ordinator, Language Department, Baptist General Convention, Baptist Building, 703 N. Ervay, telephone No. RIverside 1-1991, Dallas, Texas. He said he resides at 3125 Damascus Way in Dallas, Texas.

Rev. LEE said he checked the records of the Baptist General Convention Language Department and was unable to locate any information concerning ALBERT OSBORNE or JOHN HOWARD BOWEN.

He said he contacted the following individuals:

LOYD CORDER, Secretary of the Baptist Home Mission Board, Language Department, Atlanta, Georgia;

R. G. VAN ROYEN, Retired Missionary, Southern Baptist Convention of Panama;

OSCAR ROMO, Latin-American Associate of South Baptist Convention in Dallas.

Rev. LEE advised that each of these persons assured him that they had never heard of a missionary in Mexico whose name was ALBERT OSBORNE or JOHN HOWARD BOWEN.

He said he would keep this request of the Dallas Office in mind and if information concerning OSBORNE or BOWEN came to his attention he would immediately notify the Dallas Office.

on 3/2/64 at Dallas, Texas File # DL 100-10461

by Special Agent ARTHUR E. CARTER:vm Date dictated 3/2/64

-76-

COMMISSION EXHIBIT No. 2195—Continued

DL 100-10461
EEH:vm

On January 24, 1964, Mrs. MAZIE SCOGIN, Receptionist, Baptist Home Mission Board, 161 Spring Street, Atlanta, Georgia, checked all departments of her organization and could find no record of Reverend JOHN HOWARD BOWEN.

On February 4, 1964, Mrs. SCOGIN checked all departments of her organization for a record of Reverend ALBERT OSBORNE and could locate no record.

Exhaustive efforts at the Passport Office, U. S. Department of State, Washington, D. C., on December 23, 1963, failed to locate any information regarding JOHN HOWARD BOWEN based on descriptive data then available.

On January 24, 1964, IC THOMAS WHITE was advised that Immigration and Naturalization Service, Washington, D. C., records were negative concerning ALBERT OSBORNE.

On January 28, 1964, SA KENNETH J. HASER was advised the records of the Office of State, Security and Visa, U. S. Department of State, Washington, D. C., contain no record identifiable with ALBERT OSBORNE.

The following investigation was conducted by SA WILLIAM F. MARTIN:

At New York City

On December 23, 1963, SIDNEY A. DAVIS, Assistant Chief, Records Administration and Information Section, Immigration and Naturalization Service (INS), 20 West Broadway, New York City, that a review of airline and steamship records located at INS failed to disclose any identifiable information regarding one JOHN HOWARD BOWEN and his alleged departure from New York on November 13, 1963. DAVIS stated, however, that INS files did reveal that on November 13, 1963, one GEORGE F. BOWEN, Passport Number B584700, 18 Plymouth Road, Westfield, New Jersey, departed New York via Pan American Airways (PAA) Flight 100 for London. On the same date, the files also disclosed that CHARLES H. BOWEN, Passport Number 11248841, 58 Oakley Avenue, Lawrenceburg, Indiana, departed New York via PAA Flight 114 for Paris.

77

COMMISSION EXHIBIT No. 2195—Continued

DL 100-10461
EEH:vm

Mrs. BETTY P. LAMBERT, Assistant Office Manager, and Mrs. MAVIS LEHMAN, Clerk, American Express Company, 649 5th Avenue, New York City, advised SA J. WILLIAM LOVE on January 27, 1964, that records of Visitors Mail Service, American Express Company, reflected no information regarding the names JOHN HOWARD BOWEN or ALBERT OSBORNE.

78

COMMISSION EXHIBIT No. 2195—Continued

FD-302 (Rev. 3-3-59)

FEDERAL BUREAU OF INVESTIGATION

Date 2/25/64

1

MARINA OSWALD was interviewed at the home of Mr. and Mrs. DECLAN P. FORD, 14057 Brookcrest, Dallas, Texas. Mr. HENRY BAER, law partner of Mr. WILLIAM A. McKENZIE, Attorney for MARINA, was present during this interview.

MARINA was asked if she or her husband, LEE HARVEY OSWALD, had known an individual by the name of ALBERT OSBORNE or JOHN HOWARD BOWEN. She advised she did not know any persons by these names. She said she had never heard him mention the names. She was asked if OSWALD had mentioned making an acquaintance on his trip to Mexico in September-October, 1963. MARINA said she cannot recall that OSWALD said he made any such acquaintances. She said OSWALD took the trip to Mexico alone and returned alone.

MARINA was exhibited a photograph of one JOHN HOWARD BOWEN which depicts him standing on a grassy lawn before a castle-like edifice. She said she could not identify this person. She was exhibited a mug type photograph of one ALBERT OSBORNE taken October, 1963, and she advised she had never seen this person to her knowledge.

on 2/24/64 at Dallas, Texas File # DL 100-10461

by Special Agent WALLACE R. HEITMAN and ANATOLE A. BOGUSLAV:vm Date dictated 2/25/64

-79-

This document contains neither recommendations nor conclusions of the FBI. It is the property of the FBI and is loaned to your agency; it and its contents are not to be distributed outside your agency.

COMMISSION EXHIBIT No. 2195—Continued

DL 100-10461
EEH:vm

On February 10, 1964, Mrs. RUTH PAINE, 2515 W. 5th Street, Irving, Texas, examined photographs of ALBERT OSBORNE, also known as John Howard Bowen, after which she advised she has never seen the person depicted in those photographs and has never heard either name to the best of her recollection.

It will be noted that Mrs. MARINA OSWALD was residing with Mrs. PAINE as of November 22, 1963, and had been an acquaintance of Mrs. PAINE for some months prior to that date.

During the investigation of captioned matter it was determined that at the time LEE HARVEY OSWALD was employed by Jaggars-Chiles-Stovall, Dallas, Texas, October 12, 1962, to April 6, 1963, he had a fellow employee known as JACK LESLIE BOWEN.

In an effort to determine if JACK LESLIE BOWEN was identical to or connected with JOHN HOWARD BOWEN, alleged missionary in Mexico, who was a fellow passenger with OSWALD on a bus trip to Mexico City on September 26-27, 1963, the following investigation was conducted:

A photograph of JOHN CAESAR GROSSI, also known as JACK LESLIE BOWEN, Federal Bureau of Investigation, Identification Number 3,967,794, was obtained from Wheat Photo Studios, Bryan Street at Peak, Dallas, Texas, on June 21, 1956, by SA NAT A. PINKSTON, the photograph having been made in April, 1956.

On interview July 6, 1956, the following description of JOHN CAESAR GROSSI was obtained from observation and questioning:

Name	JOHN CAESAR GROSSI, also known as Jack Leslie Bowen
Age	30
Born	8/5/25, Paterson, New Jersey
Height	6'
Weight	168-170 (normally over 200)
Build	Medium
Hair	Dark brown, wavy, thick
Teeth	Good
Complexion	Tan (normally medium), clean shaven
Eyes	Blue, no glasses
Military Service	None

80

COMMISSION EXHIBIT No. 2195—Continued

DL 100-10461

Education	1 year high school, Paterson, New Jersey, high school diploma obtained while serving time at El Reno, and equivalent 2 years college at other penitentiaries
Peculiarities	Accomplished artist, caricaturist
Father	JOHN GROSSI, whereabouts unknown
Mother	ROSE GROSSI, believed to reside at Paterson, New Jersey
Sister	JEAN GROSSI (married name unknown)
Brother	ALBERT GROSSI, believed to reside in Paterson, New Jersey
Wife	LUCILLE RYDER BOWEN (now pregnant).

81

COMMISSION EXHIBIT No. 2195—Continued

FD-302 (Rev. 3-3-59)

FEDERAL BUREAU OF INVESTIGATION

Date 2/21/64

1

GARY EUGENE LAWLER advised he resides at 3235 Seevers, Dallas, Texas, and is employed by the Prior Products, Inc., at 4828 Recoll in Dallas. He said his residence telephone number is FR 4-5305 and his business telephone number is HA 8-7411. He observed a photograph of JOHN CAESAR GROSSI, FBI No. 3 967 794, and advised he is identical with a person whom he knew as JACK BOWEN who formerly lived in the Oak Cliff area of Dallas at an apartment on Stevens Forest Drive. He said he last saw BOWEN about three weeks prior to February 15, 1964, when BOWEN was residing at the Executive Inn and told him he was leaving the following day on a trip to Mexico and New York. BOWEN told him on that occasion he could be reached through MAX CHERRY, c/o Mrs. M. M. CHERRY, at 3542 Purdue, Dallas, telephone EM 3-1246. He said that BOWEN told him he and CHERRY planned to go into the import-export business at El Paso, Texas, and Chihuahua, Mexico. BOWEN told him about a deal he had with a Mr. McCOLLOM who was in the insurance business in Dallas which had fallen through so he was going into business with MAX CHERRY.

He said BOWEN married a Canadian whose name is PATRICIA GERVAN BOWEN about three or four years ago and she lives with her mother, MABLE GERVAN, at 50 Ragland North, Renfrew, Ontario, Canada, and BOWEN is occasionally in contact with his wife's sister, EDNA ELIOTT, who resides at 39 Lorne Street South in Renfrew, Ontario, Canada. LAWLER said he was employed at Jaggars-Chiles-Stovall until about November, 1963, and BOWEN was there for some time leaving about August. He said he recalled that LEE HARVEY OSWALD, the accused assassin of President JOHN FITZGERALD KENNEDY, was employed at this same firm for a very short time while BOWEN was there.

He said BOWEN had never discussed anything about the import-export business until after August of 1963. LAWLER said he was barely acquainted with LEE HARVEY OSWALD and only saw him when he went into the department where OSWALD was employed at Jaggars-Chiles-Stovall. He said he, LAWLER, was in the production office and BOWEN and OSWALD were in the camera department. He said that BOWEN set up a form of type called "Headliner" and produced miscellaneous art work, cartoons, etc.

LAWLER said he never discussed any political beliefs or anything except the production work with LEE HARVEY OSWALD while OSWALD was employed at the Jaggars-Chiles-Stovall plant in Dallas.

LAWLER said he did not know JACK RUBY, however, he had

on 2/15/64 at Dallas, Texas File # DL 100-10461

by Special Agent ARTHUR E. CARTER:vm Date dictated 2/19/64

82

visited the Carousel and Vegas Clubs when they were operated by RUBY at Dallas. He said he had no personal knowledge of any association between LEE HARVEY OSWALD and RUBY and he felt certain that BOWEN had not discussed any import-export business with OSWALD because LEE OSWALD left his job with Jaggars-Chiles-Stovall long before JACK BOWEN first began to talk about the import-export business.

He said he never heard JACK BOWEN mention Texas Import-Export Company and never heard of or knew a person whose name is ALEXANDER KLEINLERER.

He advised he knew of no other associates of JACK L. BOWEN and he would immediately notify the FBI if he determined BOWEN's current location and/or address.

During the efforts to identify and locate ALBERT OSBORNE, it was determined that the individual known as OSBORNE had received at his residence in Texmelucan, Mexico, on January 21, 1964, a communication from "The Beam", 6248 Camp Bowie, Fort Worth, Texas.

FD-302 (Rev. 1-25-60) FE RAL BUREAU OF INVESTIGATION

Date February 22, 1964

1

Mr. JIM JOHNS, Southern Baptist Radio & Television, 6248 Camp Bowie Boulevard, furnished the following information:

"The Beam" is a monthly religious magazine published by this organization. It is distributed mainly in the Southern and Southwestern part of the United States. Mr. JOHNS caused a search to be made of all mailing lists of this organization. This search failed to find any record of ALBERT OSBORNE. The following names were listed among their various mailing lists:

Mrs. JOHN H. BOWEN
335 West Earle Street
Greenville, South Carolina

Mrs. JOHN BOWEN
75 Neron Place
New Orleans, Louisiana

On 2/18/64 at Fort Worth, Texas File # DL 100-10461

by EARLE HALEY - gj Date dictated 2/20/64

85

DL 100-10461
EEH:vm

On February 26, 1964, Mrs. JOHNBOWEN, 75 Neron Place, New Orleans, Louisiana, was unavailable for interview but her husband, JOHN WARD BOWEN, Director of Personnel, Texas Pacific-Missouri Pacific Railroad, advised that JOHN HOWARD BOWEN was unknown to him and is not related to him. JOHN WARD BOWEN stated he does not know ALBERT OSBORNE.

On February 26, 1964, Mrs. JOHN HOLCOMBE BOWEN, 335 W. Earle Street, Greenville, South Carolina, advised her husband, JOHN HOLCOMBE BOWEN, has been deceased for 32 years. She said she does not know any other JOHN H. BOWEN.

86

FD-302 (Rev. 1-25-60)

FEDERAL BUREAU OF INVESTIGATION

Date 3/5/64

1

Mr. JIM JOHNS, Southern Baptist Radio and Television, 6248 Camp Bowie Blvd., furnished the following information:

JOHNS was furnished the list of customers on March 3, 1964, whose subscription had expired to "The Beam" Magazine, in February of 1964. Among the names on this list was that of H. H. BOWEN, Emilio Carranza, 4A, Texmelucan, Puebla, Mexico. He further advised his office sends out about three letters to subscribers advising the expiration date of their subscription and asking them to renew their subscription. Their records do not indicate BOWEN has renewed his subscription.

On 3/3/64 at Fort Worth, Texas File # DL 100-10461

by EARLE HALEY:vm:les Date dictated 3/3/64

87

This document contains neither recommendations nor conclusions of the FBI. It is the property of the FBI and is loaned to your agency; it and its contents are not to be distributed outside your agency.

COMMISSION EXHIBIT No. 2195—Continued

DL 100-10461

- 88 -

COMMISSION EXHIBIT No. 2195—Continued

B (cont'd)

C

D

E

F

G

G (cont'd)

COMMISSION EXHIBIT No. 2195—Continued

K

COMMISSION EXHIBIT No. 2195—Continued

DL 100-10461

- 95* -

COMMISSION EXHIBIT No. 2195—Continued

Emilio Carranza 4-a
Texmelucan, Pue.
M E X I C O.

Central Y.M.C.A.
Montreal, Canada.

Dear Sir-

If you have any mail for me, will you kindly forward the same to-

General Delivery,

Detroit, Mich. U.S.A.

As I am going to Alberta, instead of coming to Montreal. as anticipated.

Yours sincerely
Albert Osborne
Albert Osborne

13/1/64

COMMISSION EXHIBIT No. 2195—Continued

CERTIFIED COPY OF AN ENTRY OF BIRTH

The statutory fee for this certificate is 3s. 9d. Where a search is necessary to find the entry, a search fee is payable in addition.

GIVEN AT THE GENERAL REGISTER OFFICE, SOMERSET HOUSE, LONDON.

Application Number 514371

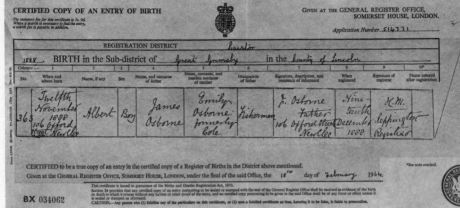

REGISTRATION DISTRICT Caistor

1888. BIRTH in the Sub-district of Great Grimsby in the County of Lincoln

Columns:— 1	1	2	3	4	5	6	7	8	9	10*
No.	When and where born	Name, if any	Sex	Name, and surname of father	Name, surname, and maiden surname of mother	Occupation of father	Signature, description, and residence of informant	When registered	Signature of registrar	Name entered after registration
363	Twelfth November 1888 106 Offord Street New Clee	Albert	Boy	James Osborne	Emily Osborne formerly Cole	Fisherman	J. Osborne Father 106 Offord Street New Clee	Nineteenth December 1888	H. M. Leppington Registrar	

CERTIFIED to be a true copy of an entry in the certified copy of a Register of Births in the District above mentioned.

Given at the GENERAL REGISTER OFFICE, SOMERSET HOUSE, LONDON, under the Seal of the said Office, the 18th day of February 1964.

*See note overleaf.

This certificate is issued in pursuance of the Births and Deaths Registration Act, 1953.

Section 34 provides that any certified copy of an entry purporting to be sealed or stamped with the seal of the General Register Office shall be received as evidence of the birth or death to which it relates without any further or other proof of the entry, and no certified copy purporting to be given in the said Office shall be of any force or effect unless it is sealed or stamped as aforesaid.

CAUTION.—Any person who (1) falsifies any of the particulars on this certificate, or (2) uses a falsified certificate as true, knowing it to be false, is liable to prosecution.

BX 034062

GENERAL REGISTER OFFICE ENGLAND

LAL 6/7

Form A502X (S.10474) Wt.23848/324 120m 8/63 Hw.-RE-30

COMMISSION EXHIBIT No. 2195—Continued

A name given to a child (whether in baptism or otherwise) before the expiration of twelve months from the date of registration of its birth, may be inserted in Column 10 of the birth entry under the procedure provided by Section 13 of the Births and Deaths Registration Act, 1953. If the parents or guardians wish to avail themselves of this facility at any time, they must deliver a certificate of baptism or of naming to the registrar or superintendent registrar having the custody of the register in which the birth was registered. This certificate must be in the prescribed form which can be obtained on application to any registrar.

COMMISSION EXHIBIT No. 2195—Continued

FD-302 (Rev. 1-25-60)

FEDERAL BUREAU OF INVESTIGATION

Date 2/3/64

1

GEORGE E. BLACKSTOCK, Canadian Consul, Suite 1710 225 Baronne Building, produced an application for a Canadian Passport which was signed by Reverend ALBERT ALEXANDER OSBORNE at the office of the Canadian Consulate General, New Orleans, Louisiana. This application was dated October 10, 1963 at which time OSBORNE furnished his residence address as 1441 Doummond Street, Montreal, Canada. The application contained the following descriptive data concerning OSBORNE: Born November 12, 1888; Sex Male; Place of birth Grimsley, Linco, England; height 5'10"; weight 200 pounds; blue eyes; brown and gray hair; marital status single; no visible scars and marks; occupation minister (clergy).

OSBORNE claimed that he resided in Canada from August 21, 1917 to the present time and is a naturalized citizen of Canada because of his services in the Canadian Armed Forces. OSBORNE's Canadian Passport #4-347367 which was issued in June, 1953, was cancelled and Canadian Passport #5-605377 dated October 10, 1963 was issued to him by Chief Clerk PERCY WHATMOUGH of the Canadian Consulate General's Office. This passport is valid until October 10, 1968 and was delivered to OSBORNE personally on October 10, 1963. At the time OSBORNE applied for a new passport, he exhibited his birth certificate and a record of service in the Canadian Armed Forces. In addition, he signed an affidavit claiming that no one knew him in New Orleans well enough to act as a guarantor because he was "in transit". OSBORNE's file contained a letter from OSBORNE dated October 16, 1963 at Mexico D.F., which was received at the Canadian Consulate General's Office on October 18, 1963. This letter thanked the office employees for their kindness and enclosed $5.00 with the instructions that BLACKSTOCK purchase a little present for the clerical employees at the Canadian Consulate General's Office. The $5.00 was returned to OSBORNE by letter dated October 18, 1963, explaining that the employees of the Consulate General's Office could not accept any gifts, which letter was addressed to "Reverend Albert Osborne, care of American Express Company, Niza 22 Mexico D.F.

On 1/31/64 at New Orleans, Louisiana File # 100-16601

by SA MILTON R. KAACK :lav Date dictated 2/3/64

3

This document contains neither recommendations nor conclusions of the FBI. It is the property of the FBI and is loaned to your agency; it and its contents are not to be distributed outside your agency.

COMMISSION EXHIBIT No. 2196

FD-302 (Rev. 1-25-60)

FEDERAL BUREAU OF INVESTIGATION

Date 2/3/64

1

PERCY WHATMOUGH, Chief Clerk, Canadian Consulate General's Office, Suite 1710, 225 Baronne Building, advised that he examined OSBORNE's application for a passport, cancelled his old passport, which was issued in June, 1953 and issued his new passport, number 5-605377, to OSBORNE on October 10, 1963. WHATMOUGH recalled that OSBORNE told him that he, OSBORNE, had come to New Orleans from his residence in Montreal, Canada by bus and that he was on his way to Mexico City by bus and that he was making this trip as part of his vacation.

OSBORNE did not tell WHATMOUGH what bus route he had taken from Montreal to New Orleans, nor did he tell him his intended route from New Orleans to Mexico.

On 1/31/64 at New Orleans File # 100-16601

by SA MILTON R. KAACK :lav Date dictated 2/3/64

4

This document contains neither recommendations nor conclusions of the FBI. It is the property of the FBI and is loaned to your agency; it and its contents are not to be distributed outside your agency.

COMMISSION EXHIBIT No. 2196—Continued

FD-302 (Rev. 1-25-60)

FEDERAL BUREAU OF INVESTIGATION

1

Date 12/10/63

The records of the Conveyance Office, Parish of Orleans, located in the basement of the Civil District Court Building, Loyola and Poydras Street, New Orleans, reflect ROBERT LEE OSWALD, SR., on July 26, 1938, purchased from the First Homestead and Savings Association, property and improvement located on the block bound by Alvar, North Galvez, Bartholomew and North Miro, property fronting 45 feet on Alvar, running to a depth of 119'4", within parallel lines. This property begins 32 ft. from the corner of Alvar and North Galvez. The property was listed as $3900 and is recorded in Book 499, Folio 696.

On January 21, 1944, a judgment of possession was granted, placing Mrs. MARGUERITE CLAVERIE, divorced wife of EDWARD J. PIC and now widow of ROBERT LEE OSWALD, SR., individual and as natural tutrix of minor ROBERT L. OSWALD, JR., and LEE HARVEY OSWALD, in possession of property located in the square bound by Alvar, Galvez, Bartholomew and Miro Streets. The property was described as fronting 45 feet on Alvar, running in parallel lines 119'4", from Alvar and being 32 feet from the corner of Alvar and North Galvez. This judgment of possession is recorded in Book 531, Folio 376.

On January 28, 1944, Mrs. MARGUERITE CLAVERIE, divorced wife of EDWARD J. PIC and widow of ROBERT LEE OSWALD, SR., sold to the First Homestead and Savings Association, New Orleans, the property acquired by judgment of possession, January 21, 1944. The sale price of this property was $6,500 and it is recorded in Book 530, Folio 357.

Dr. BRUNO F. MANCUSO was reflected in the next entry as the purchaser of this property from the First Homestead and Savings Association.

The records of the Conveyance Office reflect under Book 513, Folio 451, Mrs. MARGUERITE CLAVERIE, divorced wife of EDWARD J. PIC, and now widow of ROBERT LEE OSWALD, SR., purchased from the Third District Homestead Association on March 5, 1941 for a price of $1300, and terms, a property

— Commission Exhibit No. 2197 —

On 12/9/63 at New Orleans, Louisiana File # NO 100-16601

by SA REGIS L. KENNEDY /mh Date dictated 12/9/63

79

COMMISSION EXHIBIT No. 2197

NO 100-16601/mh
2

at 1010 Bartholomew Street, New Orleans.

On January 16, 1942, this property was sold for a price of $2100 to the Third District Homestead Association. The sale is recorded in Book 522, Folio 26, Conveyance Office, Parish of Orleans.

80

COMMISSION EXHIBIT No. 2197—Continued

FD-302 (Rev. 1-25-60) FEDERAL BUREAU OF INVESTIGATION

Date 12/6/63

1

Mrs. ALBERTA LEGNON, 2133 Alvar Street, New Orleans, Louisiana, advised that she has lived at her present address since May, 1939 and she recalls that Mrs. MARGUERITE OSWALD was living in the block when she moved into her present address. She further stated that she recognized Mrs. OSWALD to be the same person when she saw her picture in the newspaper and on TV in connection with the assassination of the President.

She stated that she believes Mr. and Mrs. LEE OSWALD lived at 2109 Alvar with their two sons, JOHN and ROBERT. She stated that she believed JOHN was by a prior marriage.

She advised that after the death of Mr. OSWALD, who was an insurance salesman, that Mrs. OSWALD had her baby, LEE HARVEY OSWALD, and shortly thereafter moved from the neighborhood.

Commission Exhibit No. 2198

On 12/6/63 at New Orleans, Louisiana File # NO 100-16601

by SA JOHN W. MILLER/lrs Date dictated 12/6/63

65

This document contains neither recommendations nor conclusions of the FBI. It is the property of the FBI and is loaned to your agency; it and its contents are not to be distributed outside your agency.

COMMISSION EXHIBIT No. 2198

FD-302 (Rev. 1-25-60) FEDERAL BUREAU OF INVESTIGATION

Date 12/6/63

1

Mrs. BESSIE VILLARS, 2137 Alvar Street, New Orleans, Louisiana, advised she has lived at her present address since 1938 and stated she did recall a family by the name of OSWALD who lived in the 2100 block of Alvar (exact number unknown) for a short period of time. She stated she can recall that this woman by the name of OSWALD was pregnant and that prior to her termination of pregnancy, her husband died in the early morning hours of a heart attack. She stated that she could not recall what month this may have been, but that it was not too long after she moved into her present home in November, 1938.

She further stated that as best she could recall, that this OSWALD woman had two other boys which she believes to have been by a prior marriage. She further stated she could not recall if this OSWALD woman was living on Alvar Street when she delivered her child. She stated that she believed the OSWALDS were buying the home in which they were living.

On 12/6/63 at New Orleans, Louisiana File # NO 100-16601

by SA JOHN W. MILLER/lrs Date dictated 12/6/63

66

This document contains neither recommendations nor conclusions of the FBI. It is the property of the FBI and is loaned to your agency; it and its contents are not to be distributed outside your agency.

COMMISSION EXHIBIT No. 2198—Continued

FD-302 (Rev. 1-25-60)

FEDERAL BUREAU OF INVESTIGATION

Date 12/9/63

1

Mrs. BERNARD CHATELAIN, 1744 Tennessee Street, New Orleans, Louisiana, furnished the following information:

She stated that she was acquainted with Mrs. MARGUERITE OSWALD during the time that Mrs. OSWALD lived in the 2100 block of Alvar Street. She said that the OSWALD's moved into the neighborhood in 1939, prior to the birth of LEE HARVEY OSWALD. She stated that distinctly she remembered Mrs. OSWALD living in the 2100 block of Alvar, as LEE HARVEY OSWALD was born three days after her, Mrs. CHATELAIN's, son was born. She stated that the OSWALD's were good neighbors.

Mrs. CHATELAIN advised that the OSWALD's moved from the 2100 block of Alvar Street, when LEE HARVEY OSWALD was approximately one year old. She stated that she has not had any contact with the OSWALD family since they moved from the Alvar Street address.

On 12/7/63 at New Orleans, Louisiana File # NO 100-16601

by SA EMIL HENRY BECKER/cay Date dictated 12/9/63

67

FD-302 (Rev. 1-25-60)

FEDERAL BUREAU OF INVESTIGATION

1

Date 12/9/63

Mrs. F. CARLETON LA BICHE, 2125 Alvar Street, New Orleans, Louisiana, advised that she resided at her present address since October 19, 1938. She stated that the OSWALD family was already residing at 2109 Alvar when they moved in, and she believes they were purchasing their home. She stated that shortly after they moved in, MR. LEE OSWALD died of a heart attack, and shortly after this, LEE HARVEY OSWALD was born. She was unable to recall an exact date as to when the OSWALDS moved from 2109 Alvar, but she stated that LEE HARVEY OSWALD was still a baby and was unable to walk as yet.

Mrs. LA BICHE advised that she has heard from Mrs. OSWALD once since she moved from 2109 Alvar and recalls it to be about two years after the OSWALDs had moved from 2109 Alvar. She stated that Mrs. MARGUERITE OSWALD called her and stated that she was only visiting New Orleans, but was residing somewhere in Texas. (Place not recalled). She further stated that she was unable to recognize Mrs. MARGUERITE OSWALD from her pictures on television and in the newspapers.

She further stated that there never has been a 2123 Alvar and that she cannot recall the OSWALDs ever residing at 2205 Alvar.

On 12/7/63 at New Orleans, Louisiana File # NO 100-16601

by SA J. W. MILLER /mrk Date dictated 12/9/63

69

FD-302 (Rev. 1-25-60)

FEDERAL BUREAU OF INVESTIGATION

Date 12/9/63

DAVID LUTENBACHER, Principal, William Frantz School, 3811 North Galvez, New Orleans, Louisiana, advised that the school records contained the following information regarding ROBERT LEE OSWALD, JR., AND JOHN EDWARD PIC:

ROBERT LEE OSWALD, JR.

Place of birth:	New Orleans, Louisiana
Date of Birth:	April 7, 1934
Parent:	ROBERT LEE OSWALD
Parent's occupation:	Agent-Metropolitan Insurance
Residences	2109 Alvar, 914 Hennessey,
	2109 Alvar, 1242 Congress
Dates of admission:	September 8, 1938
	January 30, 1939
	September 7, 1939
	September 18, 1939
	November 6, 1939
	January 29, 1940
	September 5, 1940
Dates of discharge:	September 15, 1939
	January 2, 1940
	November 12, 1940

JOHN EDWARD PIC

Place of birth:	New Orleans, Louisiana
Date of birth:	January 17, 1932
Parent	Mrs. LEE OSWALD
Occupation of Parent:	Insurance
Residences	1661 Paul Morphy
	2132 Gallier Street
	1917 Gallier Street
	2109 Alvar
	1242 Congress
Dates of admission:	September 16, 1936
	February 1, 1937
	September 9, 1937
	January 28, 1938
	September 8, 1938
	January 3, 1939
	September 7, 1939
	September 5, 1940
	November 1, 1940

On 12/6/63 at New Orleans, Louisiana File # New Orleans 100-16601

by SA CLAUDE L. SCHLAGER/gml Date dictated 12/9/63

57

COMMISSION EXHIBIT No. 2199

2
NO 100-16601

Dates of discharge:	January 4, 1937
	January 2, 1940
	November 12, 1940

Record indicated a transfer to George Washington Elementary School.

58

COMMISSION EXHIBIT No. 2199—Continued

FD-302 (Rev. 1-25-60) FEDERAL BUREAU OF INV

Commission Exhibit No. 2200

1

Date 12/10/63

Dr. BRUNO F. MANCUSO, 2001 Alvar Street, New Orleans, Louisiana, furnished the following information:

He advised that he first met MARGUERITE OSWALD sometime in 1938 or 1939. After the death of her husband LEE OSWALD, she came to him and asked him to deliver her child, and Dr. MANCUSO stated that he agreed to do so, and he did deliver the baby around the end of 1939. He stated that the baby was born at the Old French Hospital, Orleans Avenue, New Orleans, Louisiana.

Dr. MANCUSO said that a couple of months after the birth of the baby, Mrs. OSWALD told him that she could not continue to finance the house she was living in at 2109 Alvar Street, and that she was moving out. Dr. MANCUSO told her that he was interested in renting or buying her house. He stated that he rented the house at 2109 Alvar from the early part of 1940 to the early part of 1944, when he bought the property at that address. Dr. MANCUSO stated that he cannot recall where he sent the rent checks, and that all of his cancelled checks for that period have been destroyed. He stated that he had no other information regarding MARGUERITE OSWALD or her son LEE HARVEY OSWALD.

On 12/9/63 at New Orleans, Louisiana File # NO 100-16601

by SA WILLIAM F. MC DONALD/bap Date dictated 12/9/63

69A

COMMISSION EXHIBIT No. 2200

FD-302 (Rev. 1-25-60) FEDERAL BUREAU OF IN

Commission Exhibit No. 2201

1

Date 12/6/63

The records of the New Orleans Retail Credit Bureau, 333 St. Charles, regarding MARGUERITE OSWALD were made available by BETTY ENGELBRACHT which reflect the following information:

RESIDENCES	DATE OF RESIDENCE
2132 Gallier	March, 1937
805 Greenwood	Unknown
808 Taft Place	Unknown
220 North Telemachus	Unknown
123 South Cortez	Unknown
1917 Gallier	October 29, 1937
2205 Alvar	October, 1938
2123 Alvar	April, 1939
2109 Alvar	July 11, 1940
1242 Congress	September 28, 1940
813 Pauline 831 Pauline (?)	January, 1942
1454 St. Mary	May 17, 1954

EMPLOYMENT	DATE OF EMPLOYMENT
Burts Shoe Store 1117 Canal	March, 1954
Lady Oris Hosiery New York City Saleslady	July, 1953

On 12/6/63 at New Orleans, Louisiana File # NO 100-16601

by SA JOHN WILLIAM MILLER/bap Date dictated 12/6/63

63

COMMISSION EXHIBIT No. 2201

NO 100-16601
GMA:jab
2

It could not be determined from a review of the records of the New Orleans Retailers' Credit Bureau what dates Mrs. MARGUERITE OSWALD resided at 805 Greenwood, 808 Taft Place, 220 North Telemachus and 123 South Cortez. These addresses were written on a card and were listed between the dates of March, 1937 and October 29, 1937. The address of 813 Pauline was listed on the front of the card, however, on the reverse side of the card was listed the address of 831 Pauline.

The records did not contain any inquiry from credit bureaus located in any other city.

64

COMMISSION EXHIBIT No. 2201—Continued

FD-302 (Rev. 1-25-60)

FEDERAL BUREAU OF IN

Date 12/9/63

1

Mrs. CLARA C. HESSLER, 1241 Congress Street, New Orleans, Louisiana, advised that she has lived at this address for approximately 30 years. She stated that during this time she has seen numerous families move in and out of the residence located at 1242 Congress Street.

Mrs. HESSLER stated that she vaguely recalled a Mrs. OSWALD, with her two or three sons, residing at 1242 Congress Street during 1940. She advised that she was unable to furnish even an approximate date for the period that Mrs. OSWALD lived at this address. She stated that the only persons who might have information on this matter would be Mrs. F. E. VALLEY, 1644 Tennessee Street and Mrs. BERNARD CHATELAIN, 1744 Tennessee Street.

Mrs. HESSLER advised that in 1940 the property at 1242 Congress Street was owned by FRED C. HUFF, 1740 Alvar Street. She stated that Mr. HUFF is deceased, but that she believed that Mrs. HUFF is still living and still lives at 1740 Alvar Street.

On 12/6/63 at New Orleans, Louisiana File # NO 100-16601

by SA EMIL HENRY BECKER/cay Date dictated 12/7/63

70

COMMISSION EXHIBIT No. 2202

FD-302 (Rev. 1-25-60)

FEDERAL BUREAU OF INVESTIGATION

Date 12/9/63

1

Mrs. F. E. VALLEY, 1644 Tennessee Street, New Orleans, Louisiana, furnished the following information:

She advised that she resided next door to Mrs. MARGUERITE OSWALD, during the time that Mrs. OSWALD lived at 1242 Congress Street. She stated that Mrs. OSWALD, and her family, which consisted of two or three boys, resided at 1242 Congress Street from the middle part of 1940 to sometime in 1941, when they moved to a residence on Bartholomew Street. She stated that she was unable to furnish any exact dates for the period that Mrs. OSWALD resided next door to her on Congress Street.

On 12/7/63 at New Orleans, Louisiana File # NO 100-16601

by SA EMIL HENRY BECKER/cay Date dictated 12/9/63

71

COMMISSION EXHIBIT No. 2202—Continued

FD-302 (Rev. 1-25-60)

FEDERAL BUREAU OF INVESTIGATION

1

Date 12/10/63

Mrs. FRED C. HUFF, 1740 Alvar Street, New Orleans, Louisiana, furnished the following information:

She advised that in 1940 the property at 1242 Congress Street was owned by her husband, who is now deceased. This property is presently owned by her.

Mrs. HUFF advised that her records for rental of the property at 1242 Congress Street during 1940 are not complete. She stated that her records do indicate that the residence at 1242 Congress Street was rented to Mrs. L. OSWALD from November 10, 1940, to March 9, 1941. She stated that the records would indicate that the rent had been paid up to March 9, 1941, however, she could not recall the exact date that Mrs. OSWALD moved out of the house at 1242 Congress Street. She also stated that it was possible that Mrs. OSWALD moved into these premises prior to November 10, 1940, however, her records for the period prior to that date have been destroyed, and she has no way of telling the exact date that Mrs. OSWALD moved into the house at 1242 Congress Street.

On 12/9/63 at New Orleans, Louisiana File # NO 100-16601

by SA WILLIAM F. MC DONALD/bap Date dictated 12/9/63

72

COMMISSION EXHIBIT No. 2202—Continued

FD-302 (Rev. 1-25-60) FEDERAL BUREAU OF IN

Date 12/9/63

VERNON E. KAPPEL, Principal, George Washington Elementary School, 3819 St. Claude, New Orleans, Louisiana, advised that the school records contained the following information regarding ROBERT LEE OSWALD, JR., AND JOHN EDWARD PIC:

ROBERT LEE OSWALD, JR.

Place of birth:	New Orleans, Louisiana
Date of birth:	April 7, 1934
Parent:	Mrs. ROBERT LEE OSWALD
Parent's occupation:	Saleslady
Residences:	2109 Alvar 914 Hennessey 2109 Alvar 1242 Congress 1010 Bartholomew Street Bethlehem Orphanage
Dates of admission:	September 8, 1938 January 30, 1939 September 7, 1939 September 18, 1939 November 6, 1939 January 29, 1940 September 5, 1940 November 12, 1940 January 27, 1941 September 4, 1941
Dates of discharge:	September 15, 1939 January 2, 1940 November 12, 1940 January 5, 1942

JOHN EDWARD PIC

Place of Birth	New Orleans, Louisiana
Date of Birth	January 17, 1932
Parent:	Mrs. LEE OSWALD
Parent's occupation:	Insurance
Residences	1661 Paul Morphy 2132 Gallier 1917 Gallier 2109 Alvar

On 12/6/63 at New Orleans, Louisiana File # New Orleans 100-16601

by SA CLAUDE L. SCHLAGER/gml Date dictated 12/9/63

53

COMMISSION EXHIBIT No. 2203

2
NO 100-16601

Residences, cont'd.	1242 Congress Bethlehem Orphanage
Dates of admission:	September 16, 1936 February 1, 1937 September 9, 1937 January 28, 1938 September 9, 1938 January 30, 1939 September 7, 1939 January 29, 1940 September 5, 1930 November 1, 1940 January 27, 1941 September 4, 1941
Dates of discharge	January 4, 1938 January 2, 1940 November 12, 1940 May 13, 1941 January 6, 1942

KAPPEL also furnished copies of the above records.

54

COMMISSION EXHIBIT No. 2203—Continued

FD-302 (Rev. 1-25-60) FEDERAL BUREAU OF IN\

1

Date 12/10/63

Mrs. LILLIAN BOUTERIE, 1911 Schnell Drive, Arabi, Louisiana, was interviewed and she advised as follows:

Mr. and Mrs. THOMAS M. ROACH were her mother and father. They lived in a house in the 800 block of Pauline Street, in about 1942 for a short period of time. Mrs. BOUTERIE could recall having rented the house for her mother herself. Her mother at that time wanted to get away from the children and the house on Lesseps Street for a little while and try living alone with her husband. Mrs. BOUTERIE said that her mother, Mrs. ROACH, was a very soft-hearted woman and was often helping friends and neighbors and even strangers when there was sickness or trouble. She would take them into her home and take care of them or would go to their homes and help out. Mrs. BOUTERIE could not, however, recall the name OSWALD as being familiar to her. She said it was possible though that she had never met them even if her mother had known or lived with them at that time.

Mr. and Mrs. THOMAS M. ROACH lived at the house in the 700 block of Lesseps Street for a long time before 1942. When they moved to the Pauline Street address, there was no other occupant of the house at that time. When they moved in, the house was empty. Mrs. BOUTERIE recalled that her parents, Mr. and Mrs. ROACH, did not live at the house on Pauline Street very long. She said that it was only for a month or so. They moved in in about the first week in May and moved out about the first week in June. If the OSWALDS ever lived there, it must have been between those times.

Mrs. BOUTERIE stated that her brother's name is THOMAS J. ROACH, and that recently he has been very ill.

Mrs. BOUTERIE could not recall anything more about the time when her mother and father lived on Pauline Street.

On 12/7/63 at New Orleans, Louisiana File # NO 100-16601

by SA LAWRENCE F. FOLSE/bap Date dictated 12/9/63

77

DL 100-10461
HJO:mam
1

On December 16, 1963, Mr. JOHN OSORIO, National Bankers Life Insurance Company, Austin, Texas, telephonically advised SAC J. GORDON SHANKLIN, Dallas, Texas, that his company has a file regarding MARGUERITE C. OSWALD, who has a life insurance policy with this company. He advised that Mr. SAMUEL GILBERT, of the Dallas Office, would make available this file.

Mr. SAMUEL GILBERT, Executive Vice President, National Bankers Life Insurance Company, National Bankers Life Building, Dallas, Texas, on December 16, 1963, advised that he had made a complete review of their files regarding MARGUERITE C. OSWALD, and that he had prepared a memorandum showing all information in this file. Mr. GILBERT made available a copy of this memorandum which is set out below:

"Marguerite C. Oswald Hospital Policy #128664-H and Life Policy #148813.

"The above subject was licensed as an agent through the Joseph Luker Agency in 1950 with this Company. She worked directly under Mr. Eddie Ohel and Mr. S. S. Bjornson who were managers in Fort Worth, Texas under the direction of the Luker Agency in Dallas, Texas. She voluntarily terminated her agents contract to represent this Company on March 6, 1952. Mr. Luker advises me that during the period the above represented this Company, she wrote between twenty (20) and fifty (50) applications per month. He further advised that she was an excellent agent, and the business she submitted to this Company was a good quality of business. He stated that she serviced her policyholders very well, and she never gave them any trouble whatsoever in connections with the business she wrote.

"Mrs. Oswald purchased a Hospital policy #128664-H on October 9, 1950 in this Company. The benefits were $6.00 per day room coverage together with the usual surgical schedule. This was a family Hospital Policy covering Mrs. Oswald and her two sons

DL 100-10461
HJO:mam
2

"Robert E. Oswald and Lee H. Oswald. At the time she purchased this coverage, our records give her age as 43, Robert's age as 16 and Lee Oswald's age as 11 years. The premium for this coverage, at the time of purchase, was $5.00 per month. On July 25, 1952, Mrs. Oswald requested that we delete Robert E. Oswald from this policy stating that he had entered the U. S. Marine Corp_. With the deletion of Robert E. Oswald the premium was then lowered to $3.50 per month. On July 25, 1954, this Company had an overall rate increase on all Hospital policy-holders raising Mrs. Oswald's premium to $4.50 per month. On January 5, 1961, Mrs. Oswald came into the Home Office in Dallas and visited with Mr. Leo Good, Jr._ manager of Policy-holder Service Department, and at that time stated to him that her son_ Lee H. Oswald_ had entered the U. S. Marine Corp_ on October 31, 1956. She further stated that he was not in the United States at that time, and that the State Department was attempting to locate him, and she further stated that she belived that he was in Russia. At that time, she requested that her son_ Lee H. Oswald_ be deleted from this same Hospital Policy. The Company of course honored her request and refunded to her that portion of the premium that had been paid for Lee H. Oswald's coverage under her policy since the date he entered the Marine Corp_ which was October 31, 1956 to January 5, 1961. As there was no coverage afforded under the Hospital policy during the time he was in the service, this was the Companies practice. The amount of the refund was $75.00. As she was the only insured left under that Hospital policy at that point, her premium was then reduced to $3.25 per month which was the premium for a female at her age then. In August 1961, the Company has another overall rate increase, and at that time Mrs. Oswald's premium became $3.75 per month which is the current premium she is now paying as her Hospital policy is paid to December 25, 1963 and as of this writing is still in force.

"In addition to the above mentioned Hospital policy, Mrs. Oswald purchased a Life Insurance policy on her life on March 11, 1951

569

COMMISSION EXHIBIT No. 2205—Continued

DL 100-10461
HJO:mam
3

"with this Company, the policy number being #148813. When purchased, the annual premium on this Life policy was $31.21 per year. The premium on this type policy she purchased doubles starting the sixth (6th) year. On March 11, 1956, her' premium doubled to $42.62 annual premium. She has been paying that premium since that date with her policy now being paid to March 11, 1964. She changed the beneficiary on the above Life policy on January 5, 1961 from her Estate to her son_ Robert Oswald_ who is still the beneficiary. On January 5, 1961, Mrs. Oswald made a loan on her Life policy in the net amount of $120.88. She repaid this loan in full on March 21, 1963.

"On the same date of March 11, 1961, Mrs. Oswald also purchased the same type as hers on the life of her son, Robert Oswald_ who was then age 17. The policy was #148814; however, on March 11, 1953 she allowed this policy to lapse from non-payment of premium. So the policy on her son is not in force.

"Following is a list of all change of addresses taken from our premium cards that we have on Mrs. Oswald since she bought her first insurance from this Company in 1950 to the present time.

"October 9, 1950 - 7408 Ewing
Fort Worth, Texas

"March 11, 1951 - 7408 Ewing
Fort Worth, Texas

"September 26, 1952 - 325 East 92nd Street
New York, New York

"October 28, 1952 - 1455 Sheridan
Apt. #F
Bronx, New York

570

COMMISSION EXHIBIT No. 2205—Continued

DL 100-10461
HJO:mam
4

"February 9, 1953 - 825 East 179th Street
Apt. #3 C
Bronx, New York

"March 9, 1954 - 1454 St. Mary
New Orleans, Louisiana

"March 16, 1955 - 126 Exchange
New Orleans, Louisiana

"July 25, 1956 - 4936 Collinwood
Fort Worth, Texas

"May 28, 1957 - 3830 West 6th Street
Fort Worth, Texas

"May 27, 1958 - 3006 Bristol Road
Fort Worth, Texas

"November 20, 1958 - 2006 Bristol Road
Fort Worth, Texas (Mrs. Oswald corrected this address from 3006 Bristol Road.)

"March 24, 1959 - 313 Templeton Drive
Fort Worth, Texas

"January 27, 1960 - 1605 8th Avenue
Fort Worth, Texas

"April 26, 1960 - 1111 Herring Avenue
Waco, Texas

"May 27, 1960 - 1410 Hurley
Fort Worth, Texas

472

COMMISSION EXHIBIT No. 2205—Continued

DL 100-10461
HJO:mam
5

"July 21, 1960 - 1407 8th Avenue
Fort Worth, Texas

"September 12, 1960 - Box 305
Boyd, Texas

"March 27, 1961 - 1612 Hurley
Fort Worth, Texas

"June 14, 1961 - Box 608
Crowell, Texas

"August 25, 1961 - 1808 Eagle Street
Apt. #3
Vernon, Texas

"December 11, 1961 - Box 982
Vernon, Texas

"August 29, 1962 - 808 Summit
Apt. #301
Fort Worth, Texas

"December 28, 1962 - 1013 5th Avenue
Fort Worth, Texas

"September 25, 1963 - 2220 Thomas Place
Fort Worth, Texas (This address shown on Hospital Policy at this date.)

"1013 5th Avenue
Fort Worth, Texas (This address shown on Life Policy #148813 at this date.)"

472

COMMISSION EXHIBIT No. 2205—Continued

Commission Exhibit No. 2206

FD-302 (Rev. 3-3-59)

FEDERAL BUREAU OI

Date December 13, 1963

1

Mr. HARRY BODOUR, 4204 Ridgehaven Road, stated that he formerly resided at 1509 8th Avenue and resided at that address for a number of years. He stated about 1947 or 1948, Mrs. OSWALD and her small son, LEE, who was then about 7 years of age, moved into the upstairs of the residence at 1505 8th Avenue. Mrs. OSWALD lived there for about six months to a year. BODOUR stated that on several occasions, he had occasion to talk with Mrs. OSWALD when he was out in his yard, and from these conversations, he learned that she had two older sons who were off in a military school and that LEE was attending the first or second grade at the Lily B. Clayton Elementary School which is nearby. Mrs. OSWALD had a job, but BODOUR does not recall where she worked.

He stated that he did not recall anything else about Mrs. OSWALD or her son, LEE.

on 12/11/63 at Fort Worth, Texas File # DL 100-10461

by Special Agent B. TOM CARTER/rms Date dictated 12/13/63

COMMISSION EXHIBIT NO. 2206

Commission Exhibit No. 2207

FD-302 (Rev. 1-25-60)

FEDERAL BUREAU OF IN...

1

Date 12/24/63

CLEM H. SEHRT, Attorney, Pere Marquette Building, New Orleans, Louisiana, advised that when he was a youth, his father operated a bakery at 934 North Claiborne Avenue, New Orleans, Louisiana. SEHRT stated he worked in this bakery and one of the bakery's customers was the CLAVERIE family who resided in the neighborhood, and through his employment at the bakery he became acquainted with the CLAVERIE family.

SEHRT recalled that the father of MARGUERITE CLAVERIE was employed as a motorman by the New Orleans Public Service. Mr. SEHRT advised that he recalled that Mr. CLAVERIE's photograph was published in one of the New Orleans newspapers when he retired because of the many years he had worked as a streetcar motorman. Mr. SEHRT stated he did not remember the year of Mr. CLAVERIE's retirement.

Mr. SEHRT recalled that there were at least two other children in the CLAVERIE family, one an older son whose name he did not recall who died of tuberculosis many years ago and a daughter named PEARL who married and subsequently died in the Louisiana State Mental Hospital, Jackson, Louisiana. Mr. SEHRT could not recall the identity of the individual that PEARL CLAVERIE married.

Mr. SEHRT particularly recalled MARGUERITE CLAVERIE. He stated she was a very beautiful girl approximately two years older than he. He stated that she married an EDDIE PIC with whom he was well acquainted and shortly after their marriage, EDDIE PIC divorced MARGUERITE CLAVERIE. SEHRT recalled that MARGUERITE CLAVERIE was unfaithful to her husband and was consorting with an individual by the name of V. J. KNOBLOCK (PH) who for years was an automobile salesman in New Orleans. Mr. SEHRT stated he has not seen KNOBLOCK in years and does not know whether he is still alive.

SEHRT stated he was a close friend of EDDIE PIC's as a youth inasmuch as they both attended the S.J. Peters High School in New Orleans and both played on a local basketball team. They were both members of the New Orleans Athletic Club (NOAC) and played on the NOAC teams. SEHRT stated that EDDIE PIC was struck in the eye with a loose lace on a basketball and from this accident he lost the use of one eye and gave up sports. SEHRT stated that his friendship was with EDDIE PIC,

On 12/23/63 at New Orleans, Louisiana File # NO 100-16601

by SA REGIS L. KENNEDY /bal Date dictated 12/24/63

50

COMMISSION EXHIBIT NO. 2207

2 NO 100-16601
RLK:bal

but nevertheless, he had known EDDIE PIC's wife, MARGUERITE CLAVERIE for many years from the time he was a young boy until after EDDIE PIC's divorce from her.

SEHRT advised that EDDIE PIC is now an official with T. Smith and Son, Stevedoring Company, New Orleans, Louisiana.

Mr. SEHRT stated that over twenty years ago, MARGUERITE CLAVERIE came to him and requested that he handle the settling of an estate which involved a piece of property. Mr. SEHRT stated that he recalled that one of the attorneys in the office handled the case and placed MARGUERITE CLAVERIE in possession of the property. SEHRT recalled that at this time, MARGUERITE CLAVERIE was the widow of a man named OSWALD. Mr. SEHRT stated that he has not seen or heard of MARGUERITE CLAVERIE in over twenty years and it was not until he saw her photograph in a magazine that he recognized her as the person he had known in his youth and as a young, practicing attorney.

Mr. SEHRT advised that he has never seen MARGUERITE CLAVERIE's son, LEE HARVEY OSWALD and has no knowledge of LEE HARVEY OSWALD's activities or associates. Mr. SEHRT advised that he did not know JACK RUBY and had no knowledge of JACK RUBY or of his associates.

51

COMMISSION EXHIBIT No. 2207—Continued

Commission Exhibit No. 2208

FD-302 (Rev. 1-25-60)

F EDERAL BUREAU OF INVE...

Date 4/1/64

Reverend A. J. SCHERER, 152 Hollywood Drive, New Orleans, Pastor of the Trinity Evangelical Church, advised that although he had no recollection of the OSWALD boys or the PIC boy, his records revealed the following information:

In a book of Baptisms, Marriages, and Deaths, on page 3, the record indicates that JOHN EDWARD PIC was baptized on January 31, 1932. The record shows that PIC was born January 17, 1932, and the sponsors for the bapism were LILLIAN and CHARLES MURET (no address).

On page 4, the record indicates that ROBERT EDWARD LEE OSWALD, JR. was baptized April 29, 1934, and was born April 7, 1934. The sponsors were listed as ARTHUR PRESTON BARRIE and ALICE OSWALD BARRIE.

On page 8, the record contains information that ROBERT EDWARD LEE OSWALD and MARGUERITE FRANCES CLAVEIRE were united in marriage July 20, 1933. Mrs. OLGA TILDEN and HARRY F. OSWALD were witnesses.

Reverend SCHERER advised that he did not bury Mr. PIC or Mr. OSWALD when they died and did not know them. He said he did not recall anything specific about Mrs. OSWALD, except that she had faced some very trying times as a result of losing two husbands and thereafter trying to take care of her children.

On 3/30/64 at New Orleans File # NO 100-16601

by SA DONALD C. STEINMEYER/ush Date dictated 4/1/64

37

[redacted]

DL 100-10461
BDO:cv
1

The following investigation was conducted by SA BARDWELL D. ODUM at Irving, Texas, on December 16, 1963, in an effort to identify a fourteen year old boy reportedly present with OSWALD on one occasion at Clifford's Barber Shop, Irving, Texas.

CLIFFORD M. SHASTEEN, 1321 South Story Road, operator of Clifford's Barber Shop at that address, advised that he has not been able to identify the fourteen year old boy who was in his shop on one occasion about two months ago with LEE HARVEY OSWALD. He stated that as he recalls this boy and OSWALD were in the shop on a Wednesday or Thursday at which time OSWALD had his hair cut by BERT GLOVER. GLOVER on a later date, possibly the next Monday or Tuesday, cut the hair of the fourteen year old boy, and at this time OSWALD was not in the shop but someone else had brought this boy to the shop and waited outside in a car.

On this occasion, SHASTEEN recalls that someone was complaining about high taxes, and the unidentified boy said that there would be no peace until all people had the same amount of possessions and that most of our trouble now was caused because the poor people had so little and the rich so much. This boy indicated that "peace" would come when all people had the same amount of wealth.

SHASTEEN stated that he has not seen this boy since this time and has not been able to determine who he is.

BERT GLOVER, barber in Clifford's Barber Shop, advised that he recalls cutting this boy's hair but has not been able to identify him in the neighborhood and does not know where he lives at this time. He stated that if he determines the identity of this boy he will immediately notify the Dallas Office of the FBI.

Mrs. RUTH PAINE, 2515 West Fifth, Irving, Texas, advised that she has no child even as old as school age and knows of no boy of about fourteen with whom OSWALD was ever associated in the neighborhood. She further repeated

COMMISSION EXHIBIT NO. 2209

DL 100-10461
BDO:cv
2

that she had never allowed OSWALD to take her car by himself anywhere.

COMMISSION EXHIBIT NO. 2209—Continued

FD-302 (Rev. 1-25-60)

FEDERAL BUREAU OF INVE

Commission Exhibit No. 2210

1

Date 12/6/63

CELSO MACARIO HERNANDEZ, 519 Adele Street, Apartment E, New Orleans was interviewed in the Spanish language by Special Agent RICHARD E. LOGAN.

Mr. HERNANDEZ advised that on August 9, 1963, he left his home to see a complainant in the business district of New Orleans and as he was passing the International Trade Mart he noticed an individual whom he learned later was LEE HARVEY OSWALD distributing hand bills and was wearing a placard around his waist on which was written "Viva Fidel". He said he was unable to read the hand bills because they were printed in the English language but he got the idea that they had something to do with communism and were no doubt pro Castro. HERNANDEZ said he became quite angry and went to a clothing store operated by his friend CARLOS BRINGUIER and told him of this. HERNANDEZ said that BRINGUIER is able to read English and he wanted BRINGUIER to see one of these pamphlets. While in the store he encountered another friend of his MIGUEL CRUZ and the three of them left the store to return to the spot where OSWALD was passing out pamphlets. At this point HERNANDEZ and his friends took some of the pamphlets and tore them in shreds. Subsequently a struggle ensued between OSWALD and these three men. HERNANDEZ said that by this time many persons had gathered on the street and were encouraging the three men to kill OSWALD. At this point the New Orleans police arrived and four men were taken into custody and the crowd disbursed.

HERNANDEZ stated that he had never seen OSWALD prior to this time nor had he ever heard of him. He last saw OSWALD at the time all four were charged for creating a disturbance by New Orleans police. HERNANDEZ stated that inasmuch as he could not speak English, he had no intelligible conversation with OSWALD.

part 1

On 12/6/63 at New Orleans, Louisiana File # NO 89-69

45

by SA ROBERT M. WHOMSLEY and SA RICHARD E. LOGAN/bda Date dictated 12/6/63

COMMISSION EXHIBIT NO. 2210

Commission Exhibit No. 2211

Form No. 1588 (Revised) Memorandum Report (7-1-50)

UNITED STATES SECRET SERVICE
TREASURY DEPARTMENT

ORIGIN Field (Dallas) OFFICE Dallas, Texas FILE NO. CO-2-34030

TYPE OF CASE	STATUS	TITLE OR CAPTION
Protective Research	Continued	Assassination of President Kennedy Lee Harvey Oswald
INVESTIGATION MADE AT Dallas and Fort Worth, Texas	PERIOD COVERED 11/28/63 - 12/11/63	
INVESTIGATION MADE BY Special Agent Gary R. Seale		

DETAILS

SYNOPSIS

This report sets out background information on Lee Harvey Oswald from birth up until the time of his return to the United States from Russia.

DETAILS OF INVESTIGATION

Please refer to previous reports submitted in this case.

The material contained in this report was compiled from school and military records; from personal interview with Marguerite Oswald; and from a review of letters written by Lee Harvey Oswald from Russia.

Lee Harvey Oswald's parents, Marguerite Oswald, and Robert Edward Lee Oswald, were married in New Orleans, Louisiana on July 20, 1933. Mrs. Oswald had previously been married to Edward J. Pic, a Certified Public Accountant. She and Mr. Pic were divorced on July 15, 1933.

Robert Edward Lee Oswald, an insurance salesman for the Metropolitan Life Insurance Company, died on August 19, 1939, two months before Lee Harvey Oswald's birth on October 18, 1939, in New Orleans, Louisiana.

Lee Harvey Oswald has a half-brother, John Edward Pic, born January 17, 1932 in New Orleans. Pic is presently a Sergeant on active duty with the U. S. Air Force, stationed at Lackland Air Force Base, Texas. Oswald's brother, Robert Lee Oswald, was born in 1934 in New Orleans. He resides in Denton, Texas, and he is a sales co-ordinator for the Acme Brick Company, Denton, Texas.

When Lee Harvey Oswald was three years old, his mother placed him in the Bethlehem Lutheran Home, New Orleans, Louisiana. He remained in the Home until his mother married an electrical engineer, Edwin Eckdahl, on May 7, 1945.

DISTRIBUTION	COPIES	REPORT MADE BY	DATE
Chief Dallas	Orig.&2cc 2 cc's	Gary R. Seale SPECIAL AGENT Gary R. Seale	12-13-63
		618 SPECIAL AGENT IN CHARGE	12-13-63

(CONTINUE ON PLAIN PAPER)

U. S. GOVERNMENT PRINTING OFFICE 16—61906-1

COMMISSION EXHIBIT NO. 2211

The family then moved to Benbrook, a suburb of Fort Worth, Texas. Lee Harvey Oswald's mother lived with Eckdahl only a short while, less than a year, she said. She said she divorced Eckdahl in 1947.

School records documenting Lee Harvey Oswald's first year in the Fort Worth School system are incomplete. Mrs. Oswald said she thinks he began the first grade at the Benbrook Elementary School, located in Benbrook.

School records show that Oswald entered the Lillie B. Clayton Elementary School, 2000 Park Place, Fort Worth, Texas, on January 27, 1947. He completed the first grade there on May 30, 1947.

Oswald began the second grade at the Lillie B. Clayton Elementary School on September 9, 1947. On March 18, 1948, he transferred to the George C. Clark Elementary School, 3300 S. Henderson Street, Fort Worth, where he completed the second grade on June 2, 1948.

From September 8, 1948 until June 3, 1949, Oswald attended the Arlington Heights Elementary School, 5100 El Campo Street, Fort Worth, completing the third grade there.

From September 7, 1949 until May 29, 1952, Oswald attended the Ridglea West Elementary School, 7325 Kermit, Fort Worth, completing the fourth, fifth, and sixth grades there.

Mrs. Luella Murrett, principal of the Ridglea West School, stated that at the time Oswald attended school there the pupils were graded by an "A" - above average; "B" - average; "C" - below average; "D" - failing. Oswald's grades indicate that he was average and below average on most of his subjects.

On January 16, 1950, when Oswald was eleven years old, he was given an I.Q. test at Ridglea West School. He scored 103. Mrs. Murrett stated that this score indicated that, when Oswald was eleven years old, he had the I.Q. of a child eleven years and three months old.

In September 1952, Mrs. Oswald and Lee Harvey Oswald moved to New York City. Mrs. Oswald stated that, up until this time, she always worked, and that Lee Harvey Oswald was cared for at home by his older brothers, John Pic and Robert Oswald.

(Oswald's residence in New York from September 1952 until January 1954 is being developed by the New York office.)

Mrs. Oswald and Lee Harvey Oswald moved back to New Orleans, Louisiana, in January 1954. Oswald graduated from P. G. Beauregard Junior High School in the summer of 1955. He attended Warren Easton High School, New Orleans, from

618

COMMISSION EXHIBIT No. 2211—Continued

September 8, 1955 until October 10, 1955. He quit school at this time and started working as an office boy for Gerard F. Tujaque, Inc., Steamship Lines. He worked for this firm for about four months and then, for about four months, he worked as a delivery boy for a dental laboratory.

(Oswald's residence in New Orleans from 1954 until 1956 is being developed by the New Orleans office.)

Lee Harvey Oswald and his mother moved back to Fort Worth on July 1, 1956. On September 5, 1956, Oswald enrolled at A lington Heights High School, 4501 W. Rosedale. He withdrew from this high school on September 28, 1956 to join the U. S. Marines. He received no academic credit at Arlington Heights High School.

On October 24, 1956, Oswald joined the U. S. Marine Corps at Dallas, Texas. His serial number was #1653230. This was just six days after his seventeenth birthday. Mrs. Oswald stated that Oswald attempted to join the Marines in New Orleans after his sixteenth birthday; that she even filed an affadavit stating that he was seventeen years old. She said he was not accepted by the Marines at that time because of his age.

(Oswald's military records are being checked by the St. Louis office.)

On 3-4-59 Oswald made application to Albert Schweitzer College, Switzerland. He was accepted for enrollment but never attended there.

In July 1959, Oswald wrote a letter to his mother telling her what steps she should take in helping him to obtain a hardship discharge.

Oswald was honorably separated from the U. S. Marine Corps on September 11, 1959. On 8-17-60, after defection to Russia, Oswald received an undesirable discharge. He arrived at his mother's home in Fort Worth, Texas, on September 14, 1959. He spent three days with his mother and on September 19, 1959 she received a letter from him postmarked New Orleans, in which he stated that he had booked passage on a ship to Europe.

(The New Orleans office is attempting to determine the name of the ship.)

On October 31, 1959, Oswald appeared at the American Embassy, Moscow, and attempted to renounce his American citizenship. He resided at the Metropole Hotel during his stay in Moscow. In December 1959, Oswald moved from Moscow to Minsk, Russia, where he worked as a metalsmith in a radio-television plant.

On April 30, 1961, Lee Harvey Oswald married Marina Nikolaelva in Minsk. Marina was born July 17, 1941 in Molotsk. She was a Russian citizen and was a registered pharmacist in Russia.

618

COMMISSION EXHIBIT No. 2211—Continued

CO-2-34030
12-13-63
Page 4.

On February 15, 1962, Marina Oswald had her first child, a daughter, June Lee Oswald.

Lee Harvey Oswald, his wife Marina, and daughter June Lee lived in Minsk, Russia, until May 1962 when they appeared in Moscow on their way to the United States. On June 4, 1962 they boarded the SS Maasdam in Rotterdam, Holland. They arrived in New York on June 13, 1962.

<u>ATTACHMENTS</u>: (For Chief)

Copy of Cumulative Record from Lillie B. Clayton, School #19
" " " " " George C. Clark, School #18
" " " " " Arlington Heights Elementary, School #28
" " " " " Ridgelea West Elementary, School #48
Photostats (2) of application form dated 10-2-45.
Photostats (2) of application form dated 9-6-56.
Photostat of Arlington Heights High School Permanent Record #266.

GRS:mla

618

COMMISSION EXHIBIT No. 2211—Continued

Copy (obtained from George C. Clark).

NAME Oswald, Lee (Last) (First) (Middle) BIRTH: YEAR 1939 MONTH Oct. DAY 18 SEX: MALE FEMALE
ADDRESS 1505 - 8th Ave
FATHER'S NAME Edwin Ekdall GUARDIAN'S NAME
MOTHER'S NAME ORIGINAL RECORD SENT TO DATE

DATE OF ENTRY	School	Grade	Days Present	Days Absent	Tardy	Dismissed Early	Citizenship	Reading	Spelling	Handwriting	English	Spanish	Soc. Sci. St. Soc. Studies	Arithmetic	Art	Music	Instrumental Music	Health Sci.-Health	Speech	Industrial Arts	Homemaking	Band Orchestra		Phys. Ed.		Reading Level	Date of With-drawal	Destination	Home Room Teacher
1-27-47	19	1	87	1			B	B		B	B		B	B	B	B		a						a			5-30-47	2nd	Lowrimore
9-9-47	19	2	120	5	2																						3-18-48	#18	Murphy
3-19-48	18	2	40	6			B	C	D	B	B		A	A	B	A								A			6-2-48	3	Pressa

618

(Residual Copy—Cumulative Record—Grades K-9—Fort Worth Public Schools)

COMMISSION EXHIBIT No. 2211—Continued

(COPY) from Ridglea West

1.Q. 123
1-16-50

NAME Oswald (Last) Lee (First) (Middle) BIRTH: YEAR 39 MONTH Oct DAY 18 SEX: MALE / FEMALE
ADDRESS 1505 8th Avenue 7408 Ewing
FATHER'S NAME Edwin Ekdall (Deceased) GUARDIAN'S NAME
MOTHER'S NAME Mrs. Marguerite Oswald ORIGINAL RECORD SENT TO DATE

DATE OF ENTRY	School	Grade	Days Present	Days Absent	Tardy	Dismissed Early	Citizenship	Reading	Spelling	Handwriting	English	Spanish	Soc. Sci. St. Soc. Studies	Arithmetic	Art	Music	Instrumental Music	Health Sci.-Health	Speech	Industrial Arts	Homemaking	Band Orchestra		Phys. Ed.		Reading Level	Date of Withdrawal	Destination	Home Room Teacher
-27-47	19	1	87	1			B	B		B	B		B	B	B	B		a						a			5-30-47	2	Lowrimore
-x-48	22	3	154	23	2		a	C	D	C	C		a	B	a	a		B						B			6-3-49	Gr 4	R Hailey
-7-49	48	4	163	10	1		B	B	C	B	B		B	B	B	B		B						B			6-2-50	Gr 5	Livingston
-6-50	43	5	165	17			B	C	D	B	C		B	D	B	B		B						B			6-1-51	Gr 6	Dabsey
-5-51	48	6	170	5			B	B	D	C	D		C	D	B	B		a						a			5-29-52	Gr 7	Bratton

618

Begun at W B Clayton

(Residual Copy—Cumulative Record—Grades K-9—Fort Worth Public Schools)

COMMISSION EXHIBIT No. 2211—Continued

COPY

NAME Oswald (Last) Lee (First) (Middle) BIRTH: YEAR 1939 MONTH Oct. DAY 18 SEX: MALE / FEMALE
ADDRESS 1505 - 8th Ave.
FATHER'S NAME Edwin Ekdall GUARDIAN'S NAME
MOTHER'S NAME ORIGINAL RECORD SENT TO #28 DATE 5-9-49

DATE OF ENTRY	School	Grade	Days Present	Days Absent	Tardy	Dismissed Early	Citizenship	Reading	Spelling	Handwriting	English	~~Spanish~~ El. Science	Soc. Sci. St. Soc. Studies	Arithmetic	Art	Music	Instrumental Music	Health Sci.-Health	Speech	Industrial Arts	Homemaking	Band Orchestra		Phys. Ed.		Reading Level	Date of Withdrawal	Destination	Home Room Teacher
-27-47	19	1	87	1			B	B		B	B	B	B	B	B	B		a						a			5-30-47	2	Lowrimore
							3-18-48 Destination #18																						

618

(Residual Copy—Cumulative Record—Grades K-9—Fort Worth Public Schools)

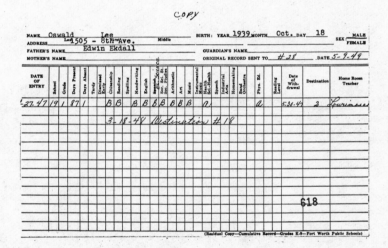

COMMISSION EXHIBIT No. 2211—Continued

Pupil's name Oswald, Lee Harvey Address 740 Ewing ~~Worth Hotel~~ 4936 [illegible] School No. 266 48 28

Last Name First Name Middle Name

Date of birth 7 19 39 Age last birthday

Month Day Year

Father's full name Oswald Address

Mother's full name Ekdahl, Marguerite Address same

Name of person with whom child lives if not with parent Relationship

What was the child's address last March

Name of school attended last year

List below the names of all brothers and sisters under 18 years of age.

LAST NAME	FIRST NAME	MIDDLE NAME	DATE OF BIRTH MO.	DAY	YEAR	AGE BOY	GIRL	SCHOOL ATTENDING	SCHOOL CHANGED TO
Oswald	Robert	Lee Ed.	4	7	34			~~62~~ 66	
								—	

Change of Address		Change of School	
10-2-[illegible]			

618

Commission Exhibit No. 2211—Continued

APPLICATION FOR REGISTRATION

FORT WORTH PUBLIC SCHOOLS

R K U T N

SCHOOL NUMBER DATE SEPT. 6 1956

NAME OF PUPIL Oswald LEE HARVEY TELEPHONE [illegible]

LAST FIRST MIDDLE

DATE OF BIRTH Oct 18 39 AGE 16 SEX M PRESENT GRADE 10

MONTH DAY YEAR

AUTHORITY GIVEN IN ESTABLISHING BIRTH DATE

TO BE FILLED IN FOR FIRST GRADE OR KINDERGARTEN PUPILS ONLY

RESIDENCE OF PUPIL 4936 Collinwood BIRTHPLACE NEW ORLEANS, LA.

NUMBER STREET CITY COUNTY STATE

NAME OF PERSON WITH WHOM CHILD LIVES IF NOT WITH PARENTS

SCHOOL ATTENDED LAST YEAR WARREN EASTERN, NEW ORLEANS, LA.

NAME CITY STATE

CHILD'S ADDRESS WHEN ENUMERATED IN SCHOLASTIC CENSUS LAST JANUARY

FATHER'S NAME Dead ADDRESS

LAST FIRST NUMBER STREET CITY STATE

MOTHER'S NAME Oswald MARGARET ADDRESS 4936 Collinwood Ft. Worth, Tex

LAST FIRST NUMBER STREET CITY STATE

FATHER'S OCCUPATION — MOTHER'S OCCUPATION SALESLADIE

DATE PUPIL MOVED TO FORT WORTH July 1st 1956

MONTH DAY YEAR

618

IS THIS PUPIL A MEMBER OF ANY HIGH SCHOOL FRATERNITY OR SORORITY?* YES NO ✓

*Members of high school fraternities and sororities are banned from attendance in public schools by act of the Texas Legislature, October, 1969.

FORM 8

OVER

Commission Exhibit No. 2211—Continued

CUMULATIVE RECORD

NAME Oswald, Lee (SURNAME) (CHRISTIAN NAME)
BIRTH 39 (YEAR) Oct. (MONTH) 18 (DAY)
PARENT Edwin Ekdall (Deceased)
or Guardian Mrs. Marguerite Oswald

ADDRESS 1505 8th Ave. PHONE none
ADDRESS 7408 Ewing PHONE PE-7995
ADDRESS PHONE
VACCINATION EXPIRES 1951 - #19

M. A.
C. A.
I.Q. 103
DATE 1-16-50

Date of Entry	School	Grade	Room	Days Present	Days Absent	Tardy	Dis. Early	LANGUAGE ARTS Reading	Spelling	H'Writing	English	Spanish	S. Studies	El. Science	Arithmetic	FINE ARTS Art	Music		Phys. Ed.	Health		Citizenship		Date of Withdrawal	Destination	Teacher
1-27-47	19	1	103	87	1			B		B	B		B	B	B	B	B		a	a		B		5-30-47	2	Lowrimore
3-18-48 Destination #18																										
9-8-48	28	3	34	154	23	2		C	D	C	C		a	a	B	a	a		B	B		a		6-3-49	Gr. 4	R. Hailey
9-7-49	19	4	108	163	10	1	1	B	C	B	B	C	B	B	B	B	B		B	B		B		6-2-50	Gr. 5	Livingston
9-6-50	48	5	105	157½	17½	3	-	C	D	B	C		B	B	D	B	B		B	B		B		6-1-51	Gr. 6	Darsey
9-5-51	48	6	113	170½	5½			B	D	C	D	C	C	C	D	B	B		a	a		B		5-29-52	Gr. 7	Brattan

		Date	Norm	Gr. Eq.	High Score		Low Score	
Met. Ach.	Form	2-8-50	4.5	4.0	Read.	4.7	Spell.	3.3
Stanford.	Ach.	2-13-51	5.5	4.0	Read.	4.9	Elem. Sci.	3.0
"	"	2-11-52	6.5	7.4	Word M.	8.6	Spell	4.4

School Lily B. Clayton Millicent Keeble Principal

FORM B

COMMISSION EXHIBIT No. 2211—Continued

Form H.S.—S

SCHOOL HONORS
(Give Activity and Year)

1. ....
2. ....
3. ....
4. ....
5. ....
6. ....
7. ....

PERMANENT HIGH SCHOOL RECORD
FORT WORTH PUBLIC SCHOOLS

Arlington Heights HIGH SCHOOL NO. 266

Vaccination Expires ....
Recorded in School No. ....

Date of Graduation ....
No. in Class .... Rank ....
Transcripts Sent — Date
1. Secret Service (Mr. Searle) 12-11-63
2. ....
3. ....

Name Oswald, Lee Harvey
Address 4936 Collinwood Parent Marguerite C. Oswald
Date of Birth October 18, 1939 Place of Birth New Orleans, La.
Date Entered Sept. 5, 1956 School Last Attended ....
Date Withdrawn 9-28-56 Reason Marines Destination ....
I. Q. .... Test Given .... Date of Test ....

		19 54 F S			19 55 S S			19 55 F S			19 56 S S			19 56 F S			19 S			19 S			19 S			19 S			19 S			Total	
	DAYS ATTENDED / CITIZENSHIP	Beauregard New Orleans La.						Warren Easton H.S. New Orleans La.																									DAYS ATTENDED / CITIZENSHIP
		Div.	Gr.	Cr.	Div.	Gr.	Cr.	Div.	Gr.	Cr.	Div.	Gr.	Cr.	Div.	Gr.	Cr.	Div.	Gr.	Cr.	Div.	Gr.	Cr.	Div.	Gr.	Cr.	Div.	Gr.	Cr.	Div.	Gr.	Cr.		
LANGUAGE ARTS—	English	1	D	1/2	2	D	1/2	Attended from 9-8-55 to 10-10-55 No Credits						No credits																			English
	Journalism																																Journalism
	Speech																																Speech
MATHEMATICS—	Gen. Mathematics	1	D	1/2	2	D	1/2																										Gen. Mathematics
	Algebra																																Algebra
	Plane Geometry																																Plane Geometry
	Solid Geometry																																Solid Geometry
	Plane Trigonometry																																Plane Trigonometry
	Adv. Arithmetic																																Adv. Arithmetic
SOCIAL STUDIES—	Jr. Social Studies																																Jr. Social Studies
	Anc.-World History																																Anc.-World History
	Modern History																									CONSTITUTION							Modern History
	American History																																American History
	Texas History																																Texas History
	Civics	1	C	1/2	2	C	1/2																										Civics
	Economics																																Economics
SCIENCE—	General Science	1	D	1/2	2	D	1/2																										General Science
	Biology-Botany																																Biology-Botany
	Health Education																																Health Education
	Chemistry																																Chemistry
	Physics																																Physics
LANGUAGES—	Latin																																Latin
	French																																French
	Spanish																																Spanish
VOCATIONAL—	Mech. Drawing																																Mech. Drawing
	Shop																																Shop
	Foods																																Foods
	Clothing																																Clothing
	Home Management																																Home Management
COMMERCIAL—	Com. Arithmetic																																Com. Arithmetic
	Com. Law																																Com. Law
	Shorthand																																Shorthand
	Typewriting																																Typewriting
	Bookkeeping																																Bookkeeping
	Salesmanship																																Salesmanship
MISCELLANEOUS—	Art	1	D	1/2	2	D	1/2																										Art
	Bible																																Bible
	Distrib. Education																																Distrib. Education
	Driver Education																																Driver Education
MUSIC—	Music Orientation																																Music Orientation
	Music History																																Music History
	Band																																Band
	Orchestra																																Orchestra
	Chorus																																Chorus
PHYSICAL EDUCATION—	R.O.T.C.																																R.O.T.C.
	Physical Education	1	D	1/9	2	D	1/8																										Physical Education
	TOTAL						5¼																										TOTAL

FD-302 (Rev. 3-3-59) FEDERAL BUREAU O Commission Exhibit No. 2212

1

Date 12/16/63

Mr. W. M. YOUNG, Identification Officer, Sheriff's Department, Fort Worth, Texas, stated that he resided at 3233 Willing in Fort Worth from approximately 1941 until 1960. He stated that in about 1948 he recalled some people living at 3300 Willing whom he now believes was Mrs. OSWALD and her son, LEE HARVEY OSWALD. He explained that the house at 3300 Willing was a rent house, and the tenants moved frequently. He stated at this time he does not recall anything definite about either Mrs. OSWALD or her son, LEE. As he recalls, the OSWALDs only lived in this house for a few months. He stated that there was no one in that neighborhood at the present time who would possibly remember the OSWALD family.

on 12/16/63 at Fort Worth, Texas File # DL 100-10461

by Special Agent B. TOM CARTER: mam Date dictated 12/16/63

COMMISSION EXHIBIT No. 2212

FD-204 (Rev. 3-3-59) Commission Exhibit No. 2213

UNITED STATES DEPARTMENT OF JUSTICE
FEDERAL BUREAU OF INVESTIGATION

Copy to:

Report of: JOHN JAMES O'FLAHERTY Office: New York, New York
Date: 12/13/63

Field Office File No.: 105-38431 Bureau File No.: 105-82555

Title: LEE HARVEY OSWALD

Character: INTERNAL SECURITY - R

Synopsis:

On 12/4/63, NY T-1 advised that during a meeting of the NY Local - Socialist Workers Party (SWP) on 11/27/63, discussion held re subject's subscription to SWP publication "The Militant." Information re subject as contained in files of American Civil Liberties Union set forth. NY T-2 advised that on 12/6/63 information received from a source to the effect that the assassination of KENNEDY was the result of a plot prepared and executed jointly by Chinese Communists and FIDEL CASTRO. Records of Community Service Society (CSS), Salvation Army and Welfare Department, all NYC, set out. Information contained herein reflecting previous employment of subject's mother. Former co-employees of subject's mother interviewed and same set out. Investigation conducted re MICHAEL PAINE, associate of subject, and same set forth.

- P -

COMMISSION EXHIBIT No. 2213

DETAILS:

On December 4, 1963, NY T-1 advised that a closed membership meeting of the New York Local - Socialist Workers Party (SWP) was held on November 27, 1963, at 116 University Place, New York City. FARRELL DOBBS, National Secretary of the SWP, related that the party was recently very upset over the fact that LEE OSWALD, accused assassin of President KENNEDY, reportedly was in possession of a copy of the SWP publication "The Militant."

According to DOBBS, the subscription files of SWP headquarters, New York City, reflected that OSWALD had a subscription to this publication which expired during September, 1963, however, he was still receiving copies of this paper at the time of the assassination. Informant advised that it is the policy of the paper to continue sending issues of this publication subsequent to the expiration of subscriptions in anticipation that the subscription will be renewed.

Source related that, according to DOBBS, the party was thus very upset over the fact that it possessed information possibly pertinent to the current inquiries being conducted by the government concerning the assassination. The party could not, without embarrassment, furnish this information to the Federal Bureau of Investigation (FBI). DOBBS related that therefore, this information was made available to the "New York Times" in the person of a reporter named PETER KHISS (phonetic), which reporter usually writes articles concerning the activities of all radical parties in the New York City area. DOBBS added that the above information was made available to the "New York Times" through counsel which was obtained by the party.

DOBBS further related that the party was afraid the FBI would eventually find out the above information concerning OSWALD's subscription and utilize this information as a method of harrassment to the party as to why the party had not brought this information forward. Thus the above action taken to the "New York Times" was an attempt to get the party "off the hook".

DOBBS felt compelled to also report in regard to this incident that the above reporter was very sympathetic to the party, not politically, and indicated that he would report this information in a way that the party would not be persecuted by the United States (US) Government. DOBBS stated that he was personally elated that a capitalist newspaper, such as the "New York Times" could possibly take such a stand as this.

According to DOBBS, KHISS recently wrote an article for the "New York Times" on the radical party activities toward the assassination of President KENNEDY.

Additional information concerning the SWP is contained in the Appendix of this report.

FD-302 (Rev. 1-25-60)

FEDERAL BUREAU OF INVESTIGAT I

Date 12/11/63

1.

Ernest Angell, Chairman, Board of Directors, American Civil Liberties Union (ACLU), 156 5th Avenue, New York, New York, was interviewed at his office at 1 East 44th Street. He furnished the following information:

He advised that on November 23, 1963, it was revealed in the press that Lee Harvey Oswald, the alleged killer of President Kennedy, was a member of the ACLU. The national office of the ACLU in New York received a telephone call from the President of the ACLU in Dallas, Texas, and Alan Reitman, Associate Director in Charge of Public Relations, received the telephone call. He immediately conducted an inquiry to determine if Oswald was a member of their organization. A record check was made and no membership record could be located at the National Headquarters at 156 5th Avenue, and a news release was then issued to the press on Sunday, November 24, 1963, setting forth that Oswald was not a member.

On November 26, 1963, a clerk discovered Oswald's application at the National Headquarters, and the application, along with an incoming letter, was stamped received by their office on November 4, 1963. This application was put in a safe, along with other contributors. His application was found with $2.00 in cash attached. Their Headquarters then immediately submitted a news release to the press on Tuesday, November 26, 1963, setting forth that Oswald's application had been received and how his application was discovered.

Angell pointed out the original application with Oswald's handwritten letter was forwarded to the Attorney General of the United States, Department of Justice, for their assistance in the matter.

He pointed out that Reitman has in his possession the two news releases and information concerning the application of the handwritten letter. He said that Oswald's application was received with $2.00 contribution and the money was deposited, but his application was not

On 12/9/63 at 1. East 44th St., NY, NY File # NY 105-38431

by SA JAMES O. INGRAM/vmm Date dictated 12/11/63

This document contains neither recommendations nor conclusions of the FBI. It is the property of the FBI and is loaned to your agency; it and its contents are not to be distributed outside your agency.

COMMISSION EXHIBIT No. 2213—Continued

2.

NY 105-38431

processed. Therefore, he had not been entered on the membership rolls of the ACLU.

He is not acquainted with Lee Harvey Oswald and said Reitman could furnish pertinent information.

- 5 -

COMMISSION EXHIBIT No. 2213—Continued

FD-302 (Rev. 1-25-60) FEDERAL BUREAU OF INVESTIGAT

1. Date 12/11/63

Alan Reitman, Associate Director in Charge of Public Relations, American Civil Liberties Union (ACLU), 156 5th Avenue, New York, New York, was interviewed at 1 East 44th Street, New York, New York, and he furnished the following information:

He said he received a telephone call from Greg Olds, President, ACLU Affiliate, Dallas, Texas, on November 23, 1963, inquiring if Lee Harvey Oswald, the alleged killer of President Kennedy, was a member of the ACLU. He understood that Oswald had been contacted by a Mr. Nichols, President of the Dallas Bar Association, where Oswald was being held by the Dallas Police Department. During the interview with Nichols, he understood Oswald related to Nichols that Oswald wanted John Abt, an attorney in New York City, or an attorney from ACLU, to defend him, since he was a member of ACLU.

He said he told Olds by telephone that he, Reitman, had the files of the ACLU Headquarters reviewed and no membership record could be located for Oswald. After the records had been reviewed, the following news release was issued to the press:

"FOR IMMEDIATE RELEASE "Sunday November 24, 1963

"The following statement was issued tonight by Ernest Angell, Chairman of the Board of the American Civil Liberties Union, concerning Lee Harvey Oswald, the alleged killer of President Kennedy.

"'The press has reported that Lee Harvey Oswald, the alleged killer of President Kennedy, was a member of the American Civil Liberties Union. This statement is false. A careful check of the membership files of the ACLU reveals no record whatsoever of Oswald's name.

"'Since Oswald has been slain, there is now no way of determining the basis of the statement attributed to Oswald concerning his purported connection with the ACLU. But we want explicitly to make clear that there was no

On 12/9/63 at 1 East 44th St., NYC File # NY 105-38431

by SA JAMES O. INGRAM/vmm Date dictated 12/11/63

COMMISSION EXHIBIT No. 2213—Continued

2.

NY 105-38431

"relationship between Oswald and the ACLU.

"'Any implication that Oswald's political views accorded with the ACLU's is likewise incorrect. The ACLU is a wholly non-partisan organization concerned solely with defense of the Bill of Rights, the freedoms guaranteed by the Constitution. We believe in free speech, advocacy of opinion, reason and open debate.

"'As civil libertarians we are deeply concerned at the effect of the successive acts of violence that have occurred upon the atmosphere in the Dallas community and the country. In such an atmosphere it may become increasingly difficult for reason and due process and justice to prevail.

"'With other Americans, members of the ACLU are shocked by the terrible killing of the President, and with the country, mourn his death.'"

On November 26, 1963, a Finance Department clerk was reviewing the November receipts and found an application under the name of Lee H. Oswald, Post Office Box 6225, Dallas, Texas. The application enclosed a membership contribution in the amount of $2.00 cash, and the application, which is very brief, with a statement: "Please enroll as a new member of the ACLU". He said this application was stamped received on November 4, 1963, and was placed in the safe along with 351 other contributions received during the same date. He said this is normal procedure. Oswald's application also had a short handwritten letter attached to the application, which is as follows:

"Pleas_ enroll me as an associate member at $2.00

"Also please notifie me as to how I may contact ACLU Groups in my area

"Thank You.

"Lee H. Oswald

COMMISSION EXHIBIT No. 2213—Continued

3.

NY 105-38431

Upon locating the application, the ACLU immediately submitted the following news release to the press:

"FOR IMMEDIATE RELEASE: TUESDAY, NOVEMBER 26, 1963

"The following statement was issued today by the American Civil Liberties Union concerning the Lee H. Oswald case.

"'On November 24 the American Civil Liberties Union issued a public statement concerning the reports in the press that Lee H. Oswald, the alleged killer of President Kennedy, was a member of the ACLU. We said then that "A careful check of the membership files of the ACLU reveals no record whatsoever of Oswald's name."

"'We learn today that on November 4 a $2 cash contribution was received from Oswald, along with a filled-out membership application. This contribution was placed in the safe along with 351 other contributions received the same day, which is our normal procedure.

"'These envelopes were opened and the contributions contained therein tabulated and deposited in the bank on November 15.

"'On November 26 a finance department clerk who was checking the November 4 receipts against the existing membership file found Lee H. Oswald's application. The name of Oswald, as those of the 351 other contributors, had not been entered on our membership list.

"'Because of the continuing governmental investigation, as announced by President Johnson, the Department of Justice has been informed of these facts and the original application of Oswald, as received in our office, has been sent to the Department.'"

Olds (He) said the membership application was in the possession of the National Headquarters, but had not been processed, and therefore, he had not been entered on the membership rolls.

- 8 -

COMMISSION EXHIBIT No. 2213—Continued

4.

NY 105-38431

He pointed out he has had several conversations with Olds on this matter, and Olds has conducted an inquiry regarding Oswald in the Dallas area. Olds related to him that Oswald may have attended an ACLU meeting in Dallas October 25, 1963. One Michael Paine of Dallas, Texas, according to Olds, was quoted as having taken Oswald to the meeting. Olds also mentioned to Reitman there has been an allegation made that Oswald may have spoken out at a discussion group meeting on October 23, 1963, in Dallas, regarding Major General Edwin Walker. He stated Olds would have background information concerning the above. He may be contacted at his home address, 1316 Timberlake Circle, Richardson, Texas, home telephone ADams 1-0841.

- 9 -

COMMISSION EXHIBIT No. 2213—Continued

NY 105-38431

On December 7, 1963, NY T-2 advised the Miami Office of the FBI that on December 6, 1963, NY T-2 had received information from a source alleging that the assassination of President KENNEDY was the result of a plot prepared and executed jointly by the Chinese Communists and FIDEL CASTRO through intermediaries. It was indicated that the source obtained his information from an unidentified individual described by the source as very good. It was alleged that one (FNU) SAAVEDRA, an alleged close friend of CELIA SANCHEZ, who is the secretary of FIDEL CASTRO, had uttered indiscretions in Cuba which pointed to the complicity of the Chinese Communists and CASTRO in the assassination. It was also alleged that intermediaries in the plot, located in Dallas, Texas, were RAMON B. CORTES, identified as half Mexican and half American, and (FNU) FERNANDEZ FEITO, identified as a Cuban. It was reported that these men were financed through an unidentified bank at 14 Wall Street, New York City.

In connection with the above information the following investigation was conducted by the New York Office of the FBI.

FD-302 (Rev. 1-25-60)

FEDERAL BUREAU OF INVESTIGA

1

Date 12/12/63

A confidential source advised that a review of the files of the Bankers Trust Company, 14-16 Wall Street, New York City, failed to reflect any bank accounts maintained by Ramon B. Cortes or First Name Unknown (FNU) FERNANDEZ FEITO. Source further advised that a search of the records at the above bank, based on identifiable information available, failed to disclose any information concerning the above individuals.

Source advised that under the name of Saavedra a special checking account appeared for one Miguel Saavedra at the main office of the bank, 14 Wall Street, New York City. This individual's address was listed as in care of Braden Copper Company, Rancágua, Chile. Source further advised that he also had a special checking account for one Alfred Saavedra, 1332 Bronx River Avenue, Bronx, New York, which account is located at the Claremont Parkway Branch of the above bank.

On 12/9/63 at 14-16 Wall Street New York City File # NY 105-38431

by SA BOYD B. HENRY:rkh Date dictated 12/12/63

The foregoing information regarding a check of the records at the Bankers Trust Company, 14-16 Wall Street, New York City, is not to be made public except in the usual proceeding following the issuance of a subpoena duces tecum. Such a subpoena should be directed to any officer, Bankers Trust Company, 14-16 Wall Street, New York, New York.

1

Date 12/12/63

Peter M. Brown, Esq., General Counsel for Community Service Society (CSS), made available for review at his office, Cadwalader, Wickersham and Taft, 14 Wall Street, New York, the file of the CSS pertaining to Marguerite Claverie - [illegible], Case Number 219055. The file indicated that the case had been referred to CSS from the Federation of Protestant Welfare Agencies. The file reflects an address for Marguerite Claverie as 825 East 179th Street and indicated that she had three children, one Lee born October 19, 1939, and two boys with the notation "in service". The file contained the following information:

"1-16-53 Mrs. O phoned and sounded rather upset as she went on to ask for an appt. 'as soon as possible.' She mentioned that the problem is with her only boy Lee, 13 yrs. of age. Mrs. O is a widow and along with boy came to N.Y. from Texas in this past October. Ever since the boy has been in N.Y. he has been refusing to go to school. There has been frequent truancy and in recent hearing before the school Attendance Board of JHS 117, Mrs. O was warned that she would have to do something about the boy or else the school would take authoratative action, just what kind of action, Mrs. O would not say. I was able to clarify that suspension was not specifically threatened. Mrs. O said she felt the problem was probably due to the change in environment and the problems that Lee was having in adapting himself to the new surroundings. At present, the boy hasn't been back to school since the hearing, and it is 'nearly driving her crazy.' To complicate things further, Mrs. O said she had to move and this will mean Lee will have to be transferred to a new school because she is now out of the district which is covered by JHS 117. Mrs. O mentioned that she had learned of us as a result of a phone call to the Federation of Protestant Wel. Agency who in turn had suggested she call us. Mrs. O was quite uncertain as to the kind of services we have here and although I suggested perhaps we could give some fuller clarification of this in an interview which I would be glad to give her, she went to a good deal of questioning as to the type of services which I tried to clear up for her to some extent.

On 12/10/63 at 14 Wall Street New York City File # NY 105-38431

by SA JOHN D. HURLEY, JR.:rkh Date dictated 12/12/63

2

NY 105-38431

"When it came to the question of giving an appt., there was not one available before the 30th and Mrs. O expressed disapproval of this, felt that she would need to be seen sooner because she was a busy woman, worked and it was difficult for her to keep getting time off. However, accepted rather reluctantly my explanation as to how interviews are based on appts. and unfortunately we do have a bit of a waiting list in relation to this. Wondered what to do immediately about Lee's not going to school, wondered if she should discuss this with the principal and I said that she certainly might do this if she wished and that I would like to be able to clear with the school as to understanding L's problem there a little more clearly. This was permissible with Mrs. O who finally accepted an appt. for Friday, Jan. 30th at 2 PM with MVR.

"Near end of day, Mrs. Neill of Federation of Protestant Wel. Agencies, SP 7-4800, phoned to inquire as to whether Mrs. O had called for an appt. Mrs. N confirmed that Mrs. O had called her to engage Federation in helping out with the problem with Lee. Mrs. O wanted a worker to come to the home and talk with the boy, something which incidentally I neglected to record above was a request which Mrs. O had made when she called me. At any rate, what Mrs. N gave me was substantially along the lines of what Mrs. O had discussed in her phone covnersation earlier with me. It was made clear to her that the Federation only has a referral service and suggestion was made that she try CSS. Mrs. Neill requested that we be in touch with her in relation to disposition in the case which I promised would be done.

"Denham:mb

"1-23-53 Called JHS 117, TR 8-6211, to find out boy's new school. Talked with Miss Kahn, assistant principal. And explained that she was not able to give much in the way of impressions about the boy because she has only seen him once or twice and actually he only came to school while he was in 117 a total of 15 days, being absent 47½, during the period 9-30 thru 12-31-52. Lee arrived in N.Y. in Sept. and initially attended the Trinity Lutheran School in the Bronx from 9-8-to-9-26-52, where the record indicates he was present 9 days, absent 6 days. Miss Kahn felt that the boy seemed rather withdrawn, was rather difficult to reach him on the one instance she spoke with him. Miss Kahn thought that PS 44 was the new school, but suggest I call the attendance office for this information.

- 14 -

COMMISSION EXHIBIT No. 2213—Continued

3

NY 105-38431

"Spoke with Mr. Keating of the Attendance Bureau, LU 3-2470. Mr. Keating explained that he is not currently assigned to case, rather Mr. Brennan is working with the boy. However, in Mr. Brennan's absence, Mr. K was able to give me some background on the contact of Attendance Bureau with the family. Mr. Keating advised that he has actually, before case was transferred to Mr. Brennan, spoken once with the mother. Mrs. O complained at the time she simply couldn't handle Lee, that he was stubborn and refused to go to school and kept expressing wish to return to Texas where he said he felt more at home. On the other hand, mother later admitted that she does nag the boy quite a bit and that she would try easing up on him to see whether he would go to school. L is now attending JHS 44, but apparently has only been in school there for about 2 days, since the first of Jan. School dispatched a visiting teacher to the home who spoke with the boy, trying to persuade him to come to school. Lee is alleged to have replied that he would think about it and hadn't made up his mind, etc. To the hearing, this was held on 1-13-53 and the District Superintendent's recommendation was that the boy be placed on probation to Mr. Brennan until June. Mr. Keating said that it seemed there was a question of possible suspension here and agreed at my suggestion that this might be something that ECH JBG should be involved in rather than CSS at this point. He, however, promised to have Mr. Brennan phone me for further discussion on this.

Denham:mb

"1-30-53 Appt. failed. Case closed. Russell:fs

"4-23-53 Miss Strickman, Youth House (AL. 4-1350) telephoned for summary which was given. Lee is with them on account of truancy. He seems pretty 'schizy'.Hallett:RH

"4-29-53 Request for Information from DRC.

- 15 -

COMMISSION EXHIBIT No. 2213—Continued

NY 105-38431

"5-7-53 Telephone inquiry from Mr. Carro, Children's Court, LU 8-5000 ext. 30. Lee, 13, a serious truancy problem, came with mother from Texas in 8-52. Problem seems to have evolved around difficulty of adjustment to new environment, relationship with mother. Father died when Lee was in infancy.

"Complete study made by Youth House indicated 'Personality pattern distrubance with schizoid features, passive aggressive tendencies, rejection by a self-involved, conflicted mother.' While Mrs. O denies any problem, there was consensus in the study that both Lee and Mrs. O needed help. It was felt that a child guidance clinic or family service agency would be preferable, with a male therapist for Lee, as he 'can be reached by a male, shown at Youth House.' Mother works; Lee has isolated himself, preferring to stay home and watch TV. He in intelligent, has an I.Q. of 118. Family is Lutheran and therefore a non-sectarian agency was considered first. It is known at this time that Catholic Charities has closed their intake for a month; Salvation Army intake situation is similar to ours. Mr. Carro has spoken with supervisor, Miss Corning, and they were in agreement that while Lee had been paroled until September, it was inadvisable to consider letting the boy wait so long for any kind of individual attention. The alternative if therapy cannot be found, is a placement away from the mother.

"Mr. Carro said that he would be glad to talk with Salvation Army and at the same time pleaded for further consideration. I indicated that I felt in view of the difficulties presented, the skill required in treating such a disturbed boy, that there was little likelihood of our being able to take on the case. Nevertheless I would take it up with the intake supervisor while Mr. Carro in the meantime talked with Salvation Army. It was agreed therefore that I would get in touch with him either the following day or early the next week to advise whether there was any greater likelihood of our taking responsibility for such a case at this time.

"Application pending. Benjamin:bb

NY 105-38431

"5-13-53 Following discussion with Intake Supervisor on 5-13, telephoned Mr. Carro and indicated that due to our intake situation and waiting list we could not give this situation the proper attention it appeared to require. Mr. Carro was appreciative of this, said that he was planning to call Salvation Army, was anxious to get the matter attended to, as he is going on vacation at the end of this week.

"Mr. O accepted report of our previous contact in answer to form inquiry which we had received. Agreed that we would not need to send written report. Benjamin:cp

"5-31-53 Case closed."

The foregoing information contained in the files of the CSS, as reflected above, cannot be made public except in the usual proceeding following the issuance of a subpoena duces tecum and such subpoena may be directed to PETER M. BROWN, General Counsel, Cadwalader, Wickersham and Taft, 14 Wall Street, New York.

On December 10, 1963, Miss C. ELIZABETH CHICHESTER, Director of Family Service, Salvation Army, 546 Sixth Avenue, telephonically advised SA JOHN D. HURLEY, JR. that the only information pertaining to LEE HARVEY OSWALD was notations on a card. One notation indicated that a Court Probation Officer made a telephone call to Salvation Army on September 3, 1963, requesting that the Salvation Army assist LEE HARVEY OSWALD. The only other notation indicated that on September 8, 1963, a letter from the Salvation Army was directed to the Court stating that the Salvation Army was unable to offer any assistance in this case, as it appeared that LEE HARVEY OSWALD was in need of psychiatric treatment and the Salvation Army does not offer such services.

A review of the files of the New York City Department of Welfare reflected the following information concerning subject and his activities upon his arrival in the United States from Russia in June, 1962:

A Department of Welfare form captioned "Application For Public Assistance Or Request For Care" indicated that the applicant, LEE OSWALD, born October 18, 1939, Louisiana, and accompanied by his wife MARINA and child JUNE, arrived in New York City June 13, 1962, aboard the "SS Maasdam" from Rotterdam. The following is also set forth in the above form:

"Repatriated by the State Department from Minsk, Russia. Money & transportation furnished by the State Dept. Arrived in NYC with $63. Now has $58 left.

"Honorably discharged from Marine Corps on 9/59. Went to Russia in 10/59. Was employed as a metal worker in a TV and Radio factory in Russia. Was receiving 60 rubbles or about $52 a month. Rent is free and so is medical expenses.

"Because he is a foreigner he was allowed one room by himself. Russian families usually share one room. 2 families in one room.

"Last night spent $10 for room rent and $18 to ship luggage out to Fort Worth, Texas."

The Welfare file also contained a letter dated June 14, 1962, concerning subject sent by LULA JEAN ELLIOTT, Senior Welfare Consultant, to Mrs. JANET RUSCOLL, Administrative Supervisor, Special Services Welfare Center, and disclosed the following:

"Thank you for bringing the above repatriation case to our attention in your telephone call of June 13, 1962 to the effect that Miss Norman of the Travelers Aid Society had referred the family to you for possible assistance and possible removal to Texas.

"This will confirm the subsequent information we relayed to you by telephone the same afternoon following our clearance with the regional office of the U. S. Department of Health, Education and Welfare. Miss Choda of that office was able to advise us that the Oswald family was expected on June 13 from Russia via Rotterdam on the SS Maasdan of the Holland American line. We understand Mr. Oswald had been in the U.S.S.R. for the last two and one-half years and that his wife is Russian. The family, if they need help, will be eligible under the repatriation program according to the information given us. The family was considered destitute although they had paid part of their passage home, but may need help in going to Texas if the relatives are unable to pay passage. The address for Mr. Oswald's mother, Mrs. Margurette Oswald, is Box 473, 316 East Donnell, Crowell, Texas. She is said to be interested but the extend of her help and interest is unknown. There are some brothers living in the same town.

"P.S. Since the above was dictated, we understand that a brother, Robert, 7313 Davenport, Fort Worth, Texas, forwarded $200 (to supplement the $60 Mr. O had on arrival) and that the family left for Fort Worth on Delta Flight #821 on 6/14/62."

In addition the above Welfare file contained a "History Sheet" regarding LEE OSWALD which set forth the following:

"6/13/62 Mr. Oswald and his wife are a repatriation case whose fare to the United States from Russia was paid for by our State Department. They arrived on the S.S. Maasdom on 6/13/62. They had $63 upon their arrival. They were brought to our office upon their arrival by a worker from Travelers Aid. They were referred overnight to the Times Square Hotel and Mr. Oswald returned to our office the following morning.

Before leaving our office on 6/13, a long distance call was placed to client's brother, Robert Oswald, 7313 Davenport St., Ft. Wroth, Texas. Mr. Oswald informed us that he would take out a mortgage on his car for $200 and send this money to us the following day.

"6/14/62 On 6/14, client was seen in this office, and at first balked at using the money sent by his brother. He preferred that this money be returned to his brother, and that we advance the money for transportation expenses, and he would repay us when he is able. (See interview of administrator on 6/14/62)

"6/14/62 In accordance with Mr. Oswald's request to see the Administrator, he was interviewed in the reception room.

Mr. Oswald urgently requested that the $200 sent here by his brother for his transportation expenses be returned to his brother. He stated that his brother is a dairy deliveryman and that it had been a great hardship upon his brother to advance the money.

Mr. Oswald said that he telephoned his brother this morning and was informed by his brother, Robert, that the money was raised by placing a mortgage on the car. Mr. Lee Oswald said his brother would be obligated to make an immediate repayment of this loan. Mr. Oswald would prefer that the $200 be returned to the brother, that we advance the money for the transportation expenses, and he would then repay us when he was able.

Mr. Oswald said that his brother had told him that the family would meet him on arrival and that local newspapermen would also meet him as they had been informed of his return home. Mr. Oswald said that he anticipated that he would have difficulty in obtaining employment in a large organization. He was most concerned about the possibility that he might need to apply for some public assistance prior to obtaining employment because he sponsored his wife's entry and he wanted to avoid her having any difficulties with the Immigration Department.

Mr. Oswald spent three years in the Marines, was stationed in Japan and the Phillipines, and said that he received an honorable discharge.

Mr. Oswald was so anxious that he not use the money sent by his brother that he stated he was considering returning the money and using the "small portion of his own funds remaining to carry the family as far as these monies would permit, and then requesting the local authorities to transport him the balance of the way to Texas. We discussed with Mr. Oswald that that would be poor planning on his part, that it was urgent that he reach his destination in Texas for the benefit of his family group, that any locality in which he stopped off might contact us and that it would be obligatory for us to report about the fact he had the funds available to him here for his return to Texas.

In view of Mr. Oswald's extreme anxiety to not use the money sent him by his brother, we telephoned Miss Elliott of the State Department and informed her of Mr. Oswald's request.

Miss Elliott told us that she would discuss the matter with the New York City office of the Department of Health, Education and Welfare and call back.

She called back later and requested additional information regarding the man's relatives. She was informed that Mr. Oswald has told us that Robert is his only full sibling. He has one half-brother, who is a sergeant stationed in Japan, who has a wife and two children. His only other relative is his widowed mother who has no home establishment of her own and who makes her home with the persons for whom she works, moving from job to job as a practical nurse for elderly patients.

"6/14/62 (contd.) We gave Miss Elliott the information regarding the flight and departure time, and arrival time in Texas, obtained from the Unit.

Miss Elliott said that the Health, Education and Welfare office is wiring ahead to the local public assistance agency informing them that shoul

"Mr. Oswald apply for assistance any funds expended in his care are federally reimbursable under the Repatriation Program. Any assistance extended will not create difficulties for his wife with the Immigration authorities.

It will be necessary for Mr. Oswald to use his brother's funds for his return transportation.

This information was shared with Mr. Oswald. He was not completely satisfied with the decision but accepted it and accepted the fact that at this point the wisest course he could pursue was to prepare himself and his family for the return flight today.

Janet F. Ruscoll
Janet F. Ruscoll, Administrator

After client agreed to use his brother's money for his fare, we went to the office manager and picked up the money order received made out to Lee Oswald.

We escorted Mr. Oswald to the Western Union office 428 Broadway, who issued $150 and gave client a check made out for $50, to be cashed at the 1st national bank on Broadway and Canal. We then escorted client to the 1st National Bank, where after first being told that they could not cash the check eventually agreed at the bank manager's insistence that they could cash it. Client was issued $50.

Worker then went with client to the West Side Airlines Terminal and borught two tickets previously reserved for flight 821, Delta Airlines, to Ft. Wroth Texas. We were informed that the plane would land in Dallas, which is right next to Ft. Worth.

Worker and client then went to Times Square Hotel where client paid his bill, went to his room to pick up his wife and baggage and infant, and met "worker in the lobby. At this point he had 5 pieces of luggage. Worker, who had seen client with 7 pieces the day before, asked client what had happened to the other two pieces, and he informed us that he had sent them on ahead, railway express. We helped client and his family and his baggage to the street where we took a taxi to the ESAL, and checked client's luggage and then escorted cleint to the Delta Airlines building at Idlewild, remaining with Mr. Oswald until he boarded his plane at 4:15 PM. Worker then returned to New York City.

"6/26/62 On this date a summary was preapred to be sent to State Department of Social Welfare. A memo was submitted to Misc. Aud. requesting reimbursement for $3.50 inc. expenses expended on this case by worker who escorted client to the airport.

"6/27/62 We recommend that this case be closed, client was transported to his home on 6/14/62.

(Signature appears to be) Lehrman, FCT

FA"

On December 10, 1963, Miss PATRICIA AARONS, Personnel Clerk, Lerner Shops, 354 Park Avenue South, New York City, advised SA ROGER H. LEE their records reflect that MARGUERITE OSWALD, Social Security Number 435-22-5686, was employed by their firm, as Assistant Store Manager, from July, 1949 to October, 1949, at the Lerner Store, Fort Worth, Texas. The file indicated that from October 13, 1952 to February 7, 1953, Mrs. OSWALD was employed at the Lerner Store, 45 East 42nd Street, New York City. Miss AARONS stated that when Mrs. OSWALD applied for work at the Fort Worth store she listed the following employers:

Texas Prudential Insurance, city unknown, November, 1948 to January, 1949; W. C. Stribling Company, city unknown, July, 1948 to August, 1948; Leonard Brothers, city unknown, June, 1948 to July 1948; and Princess Hosiery Shop, city unknown, March, 1944 to November, 1945.

She advised that Mrs. OSWALD also listed the following personal references on her 1949 application:

ANICE B. NEILL, 7420 Ewing, Fort Worth, and PRESTON ALLEN BENBROOK, Texas. It was indicated that Mrs. OSWALD's address as of February 10, 1949, was 7428 Ewing, Fort Worth. The application form dated October 13, 1952, and submitted by Mrs. OSWALD reflected the following previous employers:

Evans and Associates, Fort Worth, January to August, 1952; National Bankers Trust, city unknown, 1950 to 1952; Literary Guild, Rockefeller Plaza, New York City, November, 1949 to May, 1950. It was also indicated that on her 1952 application she listed the following personal references:

DOROTHY BROCKHORN, 1455 Sheridan, Bronx, and ALFRIEDA LOPEZ, 1455 Sheridan, Bronx. Mrs. OSWALD's address as of October 13, 1952, was Apartment F, 1455 Sheridan, Bronx.

The file reflected that Mrs. OSWALD was rated as a satisfactory employee on both occasions that she was employed by Lerner's. It was also noted that Mrs. OSWALD's supervisor was MADELINE GROSS, 77 West 85th Street, New York City, who retired in 1947.

On December 10, 1963, Miss CLARA NAGEL, Personnel Supervisor, Literary Guild, 575 Madison Avenue, New York City, advised SA ROGER H. LEE that Mrs. OSWALD was employed as a sales representative from November 22, 1949 to May 25, 1950. Mrs. NAGEL stated that she worked under the supervision of Mrs. LOWELL HOPKINS at the R. E. Cox Department Store, Fort Worth, Texas. She stated that Mrs. OSWALD was dismissed at the request of the store management and that she has no additional information concerning Mrs. OSWALD.

Mrs. MADELINE GROSS, 77 West 85th Street, New York City, advised SA ROGER H. LEE that during 1952 and 1953 she was employed as the Manager of Lerner Shops, 45 East 42nd Street, New York City. She recalls that a Mrs. MARGUERITE OSWALD was employed there for a short time over the Christmas season of 1952. Mrs. GROSS did not get to know Mrs. OSWALD well, never saw her outside of the store, and knew nothing about her family. Mrs. GROSS had no further contact with Mrs. OSWALD after she terminated her employment.

EDWARD AIZER, Owner, Lady Oris Hosiery, 443 Park Avenue South, New York, New York, advised SA JAMES O. INGRAM on December 9, 1963, his records show an Employees Withholding Exemption Certificate dated July 9, 1943, in the name of MARGUERITE FRANCES OSWALD, 2136 Broadway, New Orleans, Louisiana, with Social Security Number 435-22-5686. The Certificate was signed by Mrs. MARGUERITE OSWALD, and the Certificate indicated she had three dependents as of July 9, 1943.

AIZER stated that he opened a hosiery store in New Orleans in July, 1943, and he hired Mrs. OSWALD as Manager of the small store. He described her as a woman who was neat in appearance, rather attractive, and a hardworking woman. He also remembered that she was a very aggressive individual, and he believed she would make a good manager. To the best of his recollection, Mrs. OSWALD was employed for approximately two months; however, she was very poor with figures and could not add and subtract; therefore, she was fired by him after approximately two months employment. He recalled Mrs. OSWALD was upset at being released from her employment, but he had no other alternative at that time. He said at the time he employed Mrs. OSWALD she was dating a gentleman from New Orleans who had a heart condition, and reportedly was well-to-do in New Orleans. He could not furnish the name of this individual or any additional information concerning him or if Mrs. OSWALD eventually married this man.

He further advised that during the Spring of 1953, Mrs. OSWALD came to his New York City office and contacted him regarding employment. She advised him she had recently moved to New York and was seeking employment. He did not have an opening for her, but he recommended her to his brother, JOSEPH AIZER, who hired her as a saleslady. She confided to him, at that time, she was having trouble with her son, name not recalled at that time, but she did not explain to him her difficulties. He never saw her again after the meeting in the Spring of 1953.

AIZER said he was not acquainted with LEE HARVEY OSWALD or other members of the OSWALD family. The only individual who would recall Mrs. OSWALD, to his knowledge, would be Mrs. ORIS DUANE, Manager, Lady Oris Hosiery, 929 Canal Street, New Orleans, Louisiana.

JOSEPH AIZER, Owner, Lady Orva Hosiery, 404 Park Avenue South, New York, New York, advised SA INGRAM on December 9, 1963, his records show an Employees Withholding Exemption Certificate dated May 9, 1953, in the name of MARGUERITE OSWALD, 825 East 179th Street, Apartment 3C, with Social Security Number 435-22-5686. The Certificate indicated two exemptions. A forwarding address was also listed on this Certificate as 809 French Street, New Orleans, Louisiana.

AIZER advised that he hired Mrs. OSWALD in May, 1953, as a saleslady for his company on the recommendation of his brother, EDWARD AIZER. After he hired her he had no further contacts with her and he could furnish no information concerning her friends, associates, or her family. He does not know LEE HARVEY OSWALD.

A review of his records indicate Mrs. OSWALD was employed as a saleslady from the week ending May 10, 1953 through the week ending December 26, 1953. He was not sure, but believes she resigned her position to return to her home in the South. The records show she was employed as a saleslady at the three hosiery shops owned by AIZER during 1953, as follows:

184 Broadway
358 5th Avenue
545 5th Avenue

A review of the records indicates that three employees, Mrs. ANITA SHASHA, Mrs. ANN SOLOMON, and Mrs. GERRI KOCH, worked with Mrs. OSWALD.

COMMISSION EXHIBIT No. 2213—Continued

FEDERAL BUREAU OF INVESTIGATION

1.

Date 12/11/63

Mrs. Anita Shasha, 2132 69th Street, Brooklyn, New York, advised she knew Mrs. Marguerite Oswald in 1953, when they were both employed by Lady Oris Hosiery at 184 Broadway, New York City. She said she, Mrs. Shasha, was the Manager of the shop at 184 Broadway, and Mrs. Oswald was a saleslady. Mrs. Shasha was approximately 20 years of age at the time, and Mrs. Oswald was about 40 years of age at that time. She believes they worked together for approximately three months.

She described Mrs. Oswald as a person who had a grudge against the world. Her husband had died when her son was a small baby and evidently her son, whom she now knows to be Lee Harvey Oswald, was constantly giving her trouble. She recalled that in 1953, Mrs. Oswald, while at work, received several telephone calls from school authorities inquiring about her son, who was missing from school. She recalls that during one of the conversations about the boy, at work, Mrs. Oswald stated: "You Northerners and your kids make fun of my boy because he wears bluejeans and can't dress in suits". She wanted to point out she has never met Lee Harvey Oswald and she has never met any member of the Oswald family; however, she recalls having a telephone conversation with one of Mrs. Oswald's sons, whom she believes was Robert, who was in the military service at the time. He called one day inquiring about his mother, since he was visiting her on furlough.

In her opinion, Mrs. Oswald was very disillusioned about life in general, but she could furnish no additional information concerning this. She said she never associated with Mrs. Oswald outside of the hosiery shop and after she left her employment, she never had any contact with her again.

On 12/10/63 at 2132 69th Street Brooklyn, New York File # NY 105-38431

by SA JAMES O. INGRAM/vmm Date dictated 12/11/63

COMMISSION EXHIBIT No. 2213—Continued

FD-302 (Rev. 1-25-60) FEDERAL BUREAU OF INVESTIGATION

1. Date 12/11/63

Mrs. Ann Solomon, 353 Ocean Avenue, Brooklyn, New York, advised that in 1953, she and Mrs. Marguerite Oswald were co-workers at a small hosiery shop at 184 Broadway, New York City. To the best of her knowledge, she believes she worked with Mrs. Oswald for approximately two months during the fall of 1953. They were employed by Lady Orva Hosiery.

She described Mrs. Oswald as a miserable person to work with and a person who had a very nasty attitude towards life in general. She was uncomfortable to work with and although she never used profanity she would let a person know, in her own way, she did not like them. She believes that she had a grudge against the world and hated people in general. Mrs. Solomon said she is Jewish, and therefore, in her conversations with Mrs. Oswald, Mrs. Oswald would make anti-Semitic statements, knowing this would hurt her feelings. She also, from general conversation, had the impression that Mrs. Oswald did not like Negro people and felt they were below her. She could not recall the exact statements made by Mrs. Oswald, but again reiterated she had a grudge against the world.

Mrs. Solomon said she did not know Lee Harvey Oswald, but evidently she was having difficulty with her son in 1953, because she would receive telephone calls from persons, whom she would later relate to her were authorities, who would insist that Mrs. Oswald send her son back to school. She recalls on at least two occasions, she left her work during her lunch hour to travel to her home in the Bronx, address not recalled, to attempt to persuade her son to go back to school. She could furnish no additional pertinent information, and said with the exception of Mrs. Anita Shasha and Mrs. Gerri Koch, there would be no one in their organization who would know her.

She added she never questioned the loyalty of Mrs. Oswald to the United States.

On 12/10/63 at 353 Ocean Avenue Brooklyn, New York File # NY 105-38431

by SA JAMES O. INGRAM/vmm Date dictated 12/11/63

This document contains neither recommendations nor conclusions of the FBI. It is the property of the FBI and is loaned to your agency; it and its contents are not to be distributed outside your agency.

FD-302 (Rev. 1-25-60) FEDERAL BUREAU OF INVESTIGATION

1. Date 12/11/63

Mrs. Gerri Koch, 6960 108th Street, Forest Hills, New York, advised she met Mrs. Marguerite Oswald during the Summer or early Fall of 1953. She and Mrs. Oswald were co-workers for the Lady Orva Hosiery Company, as salesladies, at a small shop located at 34th Street and 5th Avenue. She believes that Mrs. Oswald worked at all three stores for Joseph Aizer, the owner of the company, and Mrs. Anita Shasha and Mrs. Ann Solomon would know Mrs. Oswald.

Mrs. Koch advised that she was not acquainted with Lee Harvey Oswald and could furnish no information concerning him. Mrs. Oswald never discussed her personal problems with her; however, she mentioned she did have a son named Lee.

She recalled that Mrs. Oswald was a very jealous individual who appeared to dislike Northerners in general. She based this statement upon the fact that Mrs. Oswald would make general statements in her presence, on occasions, downgrading the Jewish and the Negro peoples. She could not recall any specific statements made by her and she indicated she could furnish no additional information regarding Mrs. Oswald.

On 12/10/63 at 6960 108th Street Forest Hills, New York File # NY 105-38431

by SA JAMES O. INGRAM/vmm Date dictated 12/11/63

This document contains neither recommendations nor conclusions of the FBI. It is the property of the FBI and is loaned to your agency; it and its contents are not to be distributed outside your agency.

Residence

825 East 179th Street
Bronx, New York

It is noted the above address was previously set forth as the residence address of Mrs. MARGUERITE and LEE HARVEY OSWALD during 1953.

Mrs. GUSSIE KELLER, first floor, 821 East 179th Street, Bronx, New York, advised SA JAMES O. INGRAM on December 10, 1963, that she has been away from her residence since the Thanksgiving holidays; however, she wanted to state that she recalled the OSWALD family residing in Apartment 3C at 825 East 179th Street, during 1953. She said MARGUERITE OSWALD resided at the address with her one son, LEE, for approximately a year, before they moved in the latter part of 1953, or early 1954, to return to one of the southern states.

She was not personally acquainted with Mrs. OSWALD, and she only talked with her on two occasions. Mrs. OSWALD was employed as a saleslady in mid Manhattan for a hosiery company, and her son, LEE, who was approximately eleven years of age, attended school. She recalled, however, that LEE did not attend school too often and was home by himself on many occasions.

She said due to her limited contact with Mrs. OSWALD, she could furnish no additional information, but the landlord, PHILLIP JACOBS, and Mrs. MAY ZARENBACH, might recall the OSWALDs.

PHILLIP JACOBS, 1401 Carroll Street, Brooklyn, New York, advised SA INGRAM on December 10, 1963, he was the landlord of the building at 825 East 179th Street, Bronx, during 1953, but he could not personally recall Mrs. OSWALD. He said the tenants mailed in their rents and he had no contact with the tenants. He has no records and the person

who might recall the OSWALD family would be Mrs. GUSSIE KELLER, who resides in the above neighborhood.

Mrs. MAY ZARENBACH, 1871 Schieffelin Place, Bronx, New York, advised SA INGRAM on December 10, 1963, she formerly resided at 825 East 179th Street, in 1953. She said she lived in Apartment 2C, and Mrs. OSWALD resided in Apartment 3C. Mrs. OSWALD was employed by a hosiery shop on 5th Avenue, and she resided at the address for approximately eight or nine months.

She wanted to point out she was not a close associate of Mrs. OSWALD since she considered she and her son to be "loners", and usually the only contact she had with Mrs. OSWALD was when Mrs. OSWALD asked to use her telephone. She did not know the associates or relatives of Mrs. OSWALD, but in 1953, she had a boy in military service.

She recalled that before Mrs. OSWALD moved away to return to her home in one of the southern states, she bitterly criticized the school system in New York over the treatment of her son. She could furnish no details, but she remembered that Mrs. OSWALD had difficulty with her son over school problems and, on many occasions, she would notice the boy at home and not in school.

She has had no contact with Mrs. OSWALD since the latter part of 1953 or early part of 1954, and she has received no communications.

Records of the Bureau of Vital Statistics, New York City, reviewed by IC ANTHONY AMOROSO, JR. on December 9, 1963, reflected under Certificate Number 21698 that MICHAEL RALPH PAINE was born June 25, 1928, in New York City. His father was listed as LYMAN, age 26, born in New York, and residing at 39 West 67th Street, New York City. The father's occupation was recorded as an architect. Above records reflected that MICHAEL RALPH PAINE's mother was RUTH FORBES, age 24, born in Massachusetts.

Selective Service records of Local Board 8, 321 West 44th Street, New York City, made available by DOROTHEA WECKBECKER, Clerk, were reviewed by SA TIMOTHY B. LAGRONE on December 9, 1963. Above records reflected that MICHAEL RALPH PAINE had registered for Selective Service September 15, 1948, with Local Board 17, Cambridge, Massachusetts, listing his residence address as 35 East 75th Street, New York City, and his mailing address as 1314 Grays Hall, Cambridge, Massachusetts. The person listed as always knowing his address was RUTH FORBES YOUNG, 35 East 75th Street, New York City. PAINE listed his date of birth as June 25, 1928, New York, New York, his occupation as student, Harvard University, and his description was noted as: eyes - brown; hair - brown; complexion - fair; height - 6'2"; weight - 165 pounds; and race - white. Local Board 8 was designated as the Local Board of jurisdiction as determined by the residence address furnished by PAINE at the time of his registration.

A Classification Questionnaire executed by PAINE September 25, 1950, reflected his address at that time as Swarthmore College, Swarthmore, Pennsylvania. The records also reflected that PAINE had received student deferment and later an occupational deferment as an employee of Bartol Research Foundation, Swarthmore, Pennsylvania.

COMMISSION EXHIBIT No. 2213—Continued

He was inducted and entered on active duty with the United States Army on July 15, 1952 at New York City, and was assigned Army Serial Number US51169740. He received an honorable discharge April 28, 1954, at Camp Kilmer, New Jersey.

By letter dated June 22, 1956, PAINE furnished a change of address from 35 East 75th Street, New York City, to Rural Delivery #1, Malvern, Pennsylvania.

By letter dated March 7, 1960, he advised Local Board 8 he was married on January 28, 1957 and had a daughter born November 17, 1959. He also advised by above letter that he was, at that time, employed as an engineer at Bell Helicopter Corporation, Fort Worth, Texas, and was residing at 2515 West 5th Street, Irving, Texas.

COMMISSION EXHIBIT No. 2213—Continued

1. APPENDIX

SOCIALIST WORKERS PARTY - NEW YORK LOCAL

A source stated on August 25, 1960, that the New York Local of the Socialist Workers Party (SWP) was founded during January, 1938, in New York City.

A second confidential source stated on May 6, 1963, that the New York Local of the SWP is affiliated with and follows the aims and purposes of the National SWP.

The SWP has been designated pursuant to Executive Order 10450.

COMMISSION EXHIBIT No. 2213—Continued

VIEW FROM TRIPLE UNDERPASS, DALLAS, TEXAS

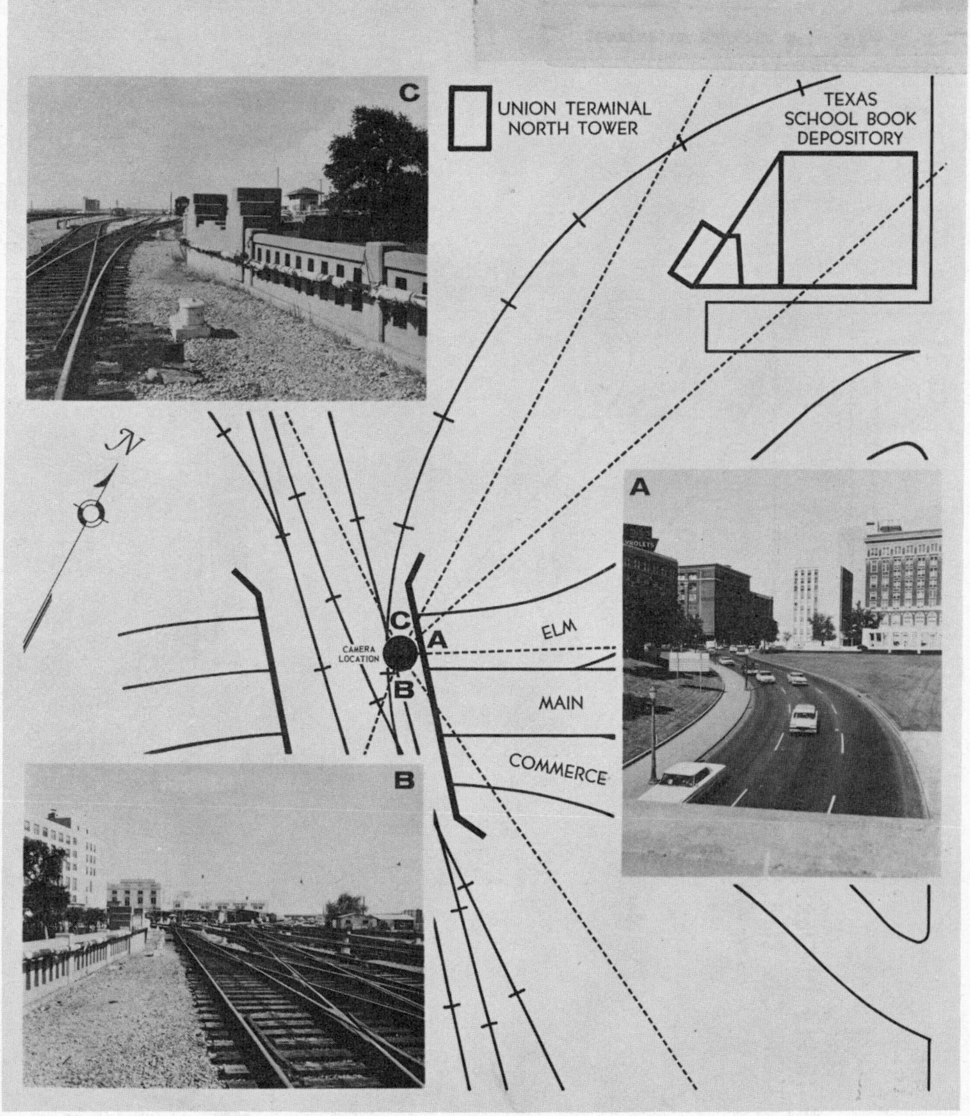

COMMISSION EXHIBIT No. 2214

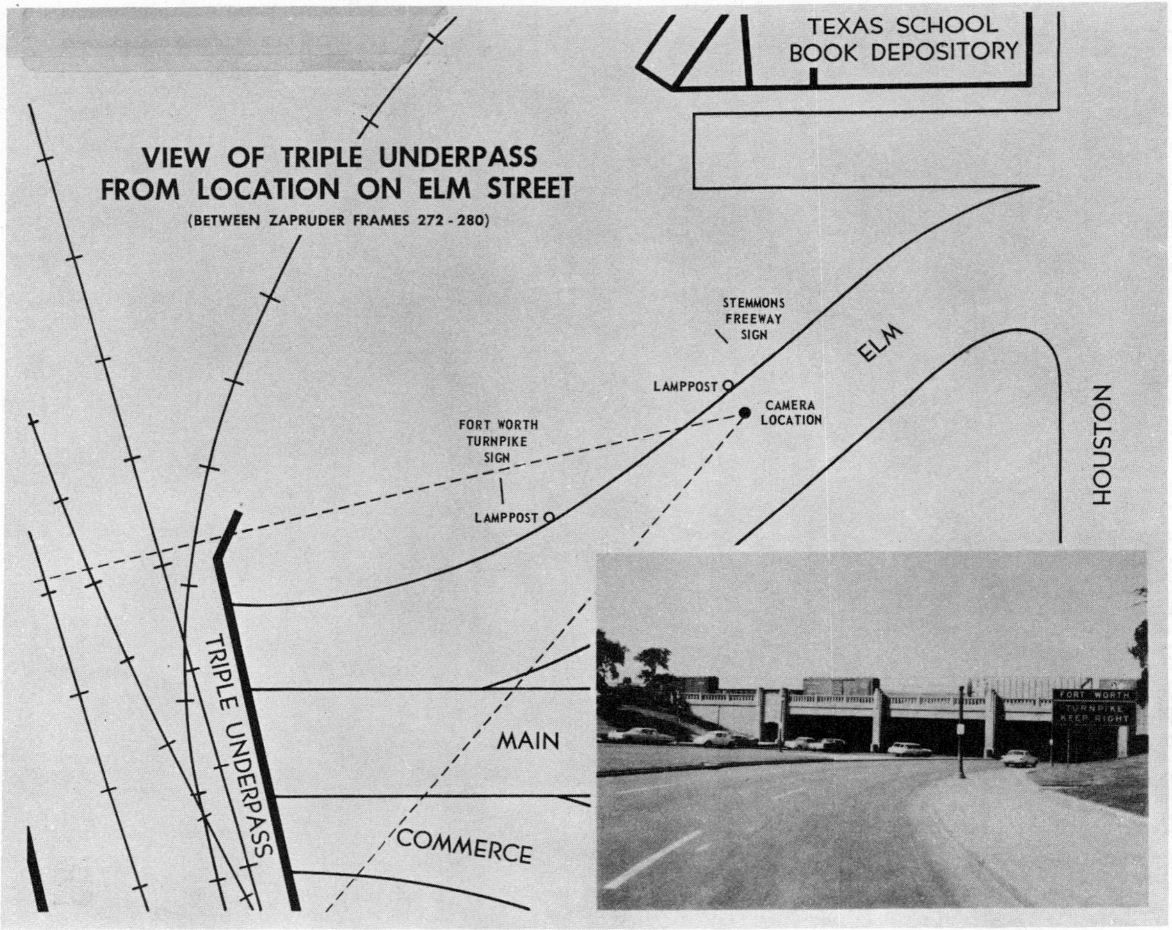
VIEW OF TRIPLE UNDERPASS
FROM LOCATION ON ELM STREET
(BETWEEN ZAPRUDER FRAMES 272 - 280)
TEXAS SCHOOL
BOOK DEPOSITORY
STEMMONS
FREEWAY
SIGN
ELM
LAMPPOST
CAMERA
LOCATION
FORT WORTH
TURNPIKE
SIGN
LAMPPOST
HOUSTON
TRIPLE UNDERPASS
MAIN
COMMERCE
FORT WORTH
TURNPIKE
KEEP RIGHT

Commission Exhibit No. 2215

Commission Exhibit No. 2216

FD-302 (Rev. 1-25-60)

FEDERAL BUREAU OF INVESTIGATION

1

Date December 4, 1963

Mrs. BILLIE GILMORE, Docket Clerk, Second Municipal Court, Section B, 501 North Rampart Street, advised that her records reflected that on August 12, 1963, LEE HARVEY OSWALD appeared before Municipal Court Judge EDWIN A. BABYLON and pleaded guilty to a charge of violation of Ordinance 828 of Mayor Council Series, Section 42-22, relative to disturbing the peace by creating a scene. Mrs. GILMORE stated Judge BABYLON sentenced OSWALD to pay a $10 fine or serve 10 days in jail. Mrs. GILMORE said that her records revealed OSWALD paid a $10 cash fine.

Mrs. GILMORE stated the Municipal Court record on OSWALD disclosed that on August 9, 1963, he was arrested and charged as indicated above, and at 5:20 p.m., August 10, 1963, he was paroled for a Mr. A. HECKMAN, a Jury Commissioner, State of Louisiana, Orleans Parish, New Orleans, Louisiana.

Mrs. GILMORE advised that the Municipal Court records further disclosed that CARLOS J. BRINGUIER, CELSO M. HERNANDEZ and MIGUEL M. CRUZ had also been arrested on August 9, 1963 with OSWALD and charged with violation of the same Ordinance and Section. On August 12, 1963, these individuals appeared in court at the same time as OSWALD, however, they pled not guilty. The record shows that the charge against these three individuals was dismissed.

On 12/4/63 at New Orleans, Louisiana File # NO 89-69

by SA JOHN L. QUIGLEY /sw Date dictated 12/4/63

This document contains neither recommendations nor conclusions of the FBI. It is the property of the FBI and is loaned to your agency; it and its contents are not to be distributed outside your agency.

COMMISSION EXHIBIT No. 2216

FD-302 (Rev. 3-3-59)

FEDERAL BUREAU OF INVESTIGATION

1

Date 12/2/63

Mrs. A. LOGAN MAGRUDER, 321 N. Vermont Street, formerly 311 Vermont Street, advised that for many years she has rented apartments at this residence and as such, recalled renting an apartment about 17 years ago to a MARGUERITE OSWALD of New Orleans, Louisiana, and her young son, LEE OSWALD, whom she stated was about six or seven years old at the time. She stated that the OSWALD's rented this apartment for about a year, during which time Mrs. OSWALD was a seamstress and apparently supported her sons, of which there were three, in this fashion. She stated that the other two boys whose names she did not recall, were a little older and went to some type of military school in Mississippi, and only came home to the mother periodically.

She stated that she believed that the OSWALD's had previously lived in an apartment or house belonging to Mrs. BENNY COMMENGE of Covington, Louisiana, but that this apartment was, as she recalled, too small for her and the boy, and for that reason she, Mrs. OSWALD, moved to her apartment.

She stated that she recalled nothing about these people, other than the fact that Mrs. OSWALD seemed to be a respectable woman, and LEE OSWALD seemed to be a nice young boy.

She informed that she had seen MARGUERITE OSWALD only once since they moved from Covington 16 years ago, and this was about three years ago when she saw her in Kriegers Department Store in New Orleans, where she was working in the Ladies Lingerie Department. They spoke only briefly, she stated.

on 12/2/63 at Covington, Louisiana 50 File # NO 89-69

by Special Agents FRANK A. SASS, JR. & SA EUGENE E. BJORN/jas Date dictated 12/2/63

This document contains neither recommendations nor conclusions of the FBI. It is the property of the FBI and is loaned to your agency; it and its contents are not to be distributed outside your agency.

COMMISSION EXHIBIT No. 2217

FD-302 (Rev. 3-3-59) FEDERAL BUREAU OF — Commission Exhibit No. 2218

Date 12/3/63

1

MARY LOU LAUTENSLAGER, Assistant Medical Records Librarian, Harris Hospital, 1300 W. Cannon Street, Fort Worth, Texas, stated her records, No. G1375, identified by the name LEE OSWALD, Grandbury Road, Route No. 45, Benbrook, Texas; birth place Louisiana; religion Lutheran, reflects the following information: Admitted: February 8, 1946, Discharged: February 12, 1946.

Relatives	Mother - Mrs. MARGUERITE EKDAHL (address same as above)
	Stepfather - Mr. E. A. EKDAHL (address same as above)
Diagnosis	Acute Mastoiditis - Left
Operation	Simple Mastoidectomy
Attending Physician	Dr. C. E. BALL
Intern	J. C. RILEY

Page headed "History and Physical Examination" dated February 8, 1946, and signed RILEY, bears the following notation: "6 year old admitted with acute mastoiditis, left. Simple mastoidectomy performed, no complications."

Page entitled "Operative Record" bears the following notation: "A simple mastoidectomy was done. The wound was closed with dermal. A rubber dam drain was used."

Miss LAUTENSLAGER further stated her records contain Outpatient file No. 8554, identified as Master LEE OSWALD, Benbrook, Texas; Mother Mrs. MARGARET OSWALD, Benbrook, Texas, appeared in Outpatient Clinic July 19, 1948, was treated "Puncture Wound, Right Heel," and discharged same date. The record indicates OSWALD was brought to Harris Hospital by a Mr. (first name unknown) ALLEN, in private automobile. Attending physician was G. O. HUTCHESON, Jr.

on 12/3/63 at Fort Worth, Texas File # DL 89-43

by Special Agent BENJAMIN O. KEUTZER:vm Date dictated 12/3/63

234

COMMISSION EXHIBIT NO. 2218

FD-302 (Rev. 3-3-59) FEDERAL BUREAU OF I — Commission Exhibit No. 2219

Date December 13, 1963

1

Mrs. W. H. BELL, 100 San Saba, on December 11, 1963, stated that Mrs. MARGUERITE OSWALD, a widow, and her three sons lived across the street from her in the house at 101 San Saba. She stated that she recalled Mrs. OSWALD lived at 101 San Saba for about three months during the summer of 1948. Mrs. OSWALD was a practical nurse. Mrs. OSWALD was continually complaining that she was very poor, she was very talkative and was continually talking about her family and stating that society was against her and how hard it was for a widow to provide for a family.

She stated that LEE was the youngest of the three boys and at that time, she noted that he was a boy who liked to be alone and as she recalled, he was a boy who did not like to be disciplined. She stated that the two older brothers appeared to be of a different personality and seemed to get along better with the other children than did LEE.

She stated that this is about all the information she remembers concerning the OSWALD family, and that she has never seen or heard of them after they moved away up until the time the assassination took place in Dallas.

on 12/11/63 at Benbrook, Texas File # DL 100-10461

by Special Agent B. TOM CARTER/rms Date dictated 12/13/63

COMMISSION EXHIBIT NO. 2219

FD-302 (Rev. 3-3-59) FEDERAL BUREAU OF I[illegible] Commission Exhibit No. 2220

Date 6/4/64

1

Mrs. CLYDE I. LIVINGSTON, 7304 Pensacola, furnished the following information:

During the period of 1949 through 1951, she was a teacher at the Ridglea West Elementary School in Fort Worth, Texas. She was the home room teacher for the fourth grade during the school year of 1949-1950. During this time, LEE HARVEY OSWALD was a student in the fourth grade and was in her home room. She also taught music to the fifth grade during the term of 1950-1951 and believes she did teach music to LEE HARVEY OSWALD while he was in the fifth grade but she does not recall anything concerning OSWALD while he was in the fifth grade.

At the beginning of the school term in September, 1949, LEE HARVEY OSWALD entered this school with a group of all new students as this was the first year this elementary school was in operation. He was a quiet and rather shy type of student, did not know any of the other students, and it took him a long time to get acquainted with the other students. She also recalled that LEE HARVEY OSWALD was a very poor student in the beginning of the fourth grade as he could not read and his spelling was very poor. Mrs. LIVINGSTON spent a great deal of her spare time in helping LEE HARVEY OSWALD with his spelling. He did not mind the extra work and his attitude was good in learning to spell. He became a fairly good student while in the fourth grade and never gave her any trouble. At times he was very quiet and was not an aggressive type in making friends with the other students in the school.

At Christmas of 1949, LEE HARVEY OSWALD gave Mrs. LIVINGSTON a puppy as a Christmas present. After that he would drop by the home of Mrs. LIVINGSTON to see this puppy and talk with Mrs. LIVINGSTON and her family. He usually stayed for only a short period of time. She recalled that LEE HARVEY OSWALD appeared to be a lonely type of boy and that his mother was employed while he was in the fourth grade of this school. He remarked one day that he had to fix his own lunch and she asked him if there was anyone at home to help him prepare his lunch or his meals. He told her there was no one at home and he could open a can of soup as well as anyone else. She stated to the best of

241

on 6/4/64 at Fort Worth, Texas File # DL 100-10461

by Special Agent EARLE HALEY and RICHARD T. RABIDEAU:vm Date dictated 6/4/64

This document contains neither recommendations nor conclusions of the FBI. It is the property of the FBI and is loaned to your agency; it and its contents are not to be distributed outside your agency.

COMMISSION EXHIBIT No. 2220

2
DL 100-10461

her knowledge she never saw Mrs. OSWALD at this school and did not meet any other members of the family although she knew LEE did have two brothers. She stated LEE HARVEY OSWALD never gave her any serious trouble while he was a student in her room.

242

COMMISSION EXHIBIT No. 2220—Continued

[redacted]

FD-302 (Rev. 3-3-59) FEDERAL BUREAU OF IN Commission Exhibit No. 2221

Date 6/5/64

1

RICHARD WARREN GARRETT, 4928 Penrose, furnished the following information:

GARRETT attended Ridglea West Elementary School during the fourth, fifth and sixth grades. He recalled being in a room at this school with LEE HARVEY OSWALD, but he does not recall whether it was in the fourth or fifth grade. He stated they were about ten or eleven years of age. During this school year, he played with LEE HARVEY OSWALD a great deal at the school and sometimes they would walk home from school and play together. He only knew OSWALD during the fall and spring semester of this one school year. LEE HARVEY OSWALD was easy to get along with at that time and he considered him a perfectly normal boy. He recalls on one occasion they did have a disagreement on some matter and he believed they had a short fight, but he does not remember what this was all about. He was in the home of OSWALD on one occasion, but does not recall ever meeting Mrs. OSWALD or the brothers of LEE HARVEY OSWALD. He stated that LEE OSWALD acted like the other students in school at that time and he did not recall anything particularly different about him when compared with the other boys in the school.

GARRETT did not see LEE OSWALD during junior high school and the next time he saw LEE OSWALD was at Arlington Heights High School in Fort Worth. He talked to him for a few minutes between classes as they were both surprised to see each other at this high school. He recalled that LEE OSWALD seemed to be a little more hesitant, a little more quiet, and did not talk too much during this conversation. GARRETT never saw him anymore in high school and did not run around with him and was unable to furnish any further information on LEE HARVEY OSWALD.

243

on 6/5/64 at Fort Worth, Texas File # DL 100-10461

by Special Agent EARLE HALEY/eah Date dictated 6/5/64

This document contains neither recommendations nor conclusions of the FBI. It is the property of the FBI and is loaned to your agency; it and its contents are not to be distributed outside your agency.

COMMISSION EXHIBIT NO. 2221

FD-302 (Rev. 1-25-60) FEDERAL BUREAU OF INVESTIGATION

Date 12/17/63

Mrs. DOROTHY BOCKHORN, 490 Bleecker Avenue, Mamaroneck, New York, advised that she and her husband, HARRY BOCKHORN, had been superintendent at 1455 Sheridan Avenue, Bronx, New York, for a period of approximately nine (9) years, commencing in 1946.

Mrs. BOCKHORN stated that she recalled MARGUERITE OSWALD and her young son lived at the Bronx address for a period of about four to six weeks. Mrs. BOCKHORN stated that they lived in a one room apartment and no lease was required since these apartments were rented on a temporary basis due to the housing shortage on a month to month tenancy.

She recalled that Mrs. OSWALD worked in a department store somewhere in the Bronx, New York area. She also recalled that her son went to school but spent most of his free time in their apartment.

Mrs. BOCKHORN could furnish no information regarding the OSWALDs which would indicate any friends or associates in the area. Due to the temporary tenancy, no request was made of Mrs. OSWALD for any references or business address. Mrs. BOCKHORN stated that to her knowledge and recollection she was never requested by any concern to comment upon Mrs. OSWALD's reliability or character.

[redacted]

Commission Exhibit No. 2222

On 12/17/63 at Mamaroneck, New York File # NY 105-38431

by SA MICHAEL R. CARRANO/Dad Date dictated 12/17/63

- 11 -

This document contains neither recommendations nor conclusions of the FBI. It is the property of the FBI and is loaned to your agency; it and its contents are not to be distributed outside your agency.

COMMISSION EXHIBIT NO. 2222

Big Brothers Inc., 223 East 30th Street, New York 16, N. Y.

MUrray Hill 0-2042

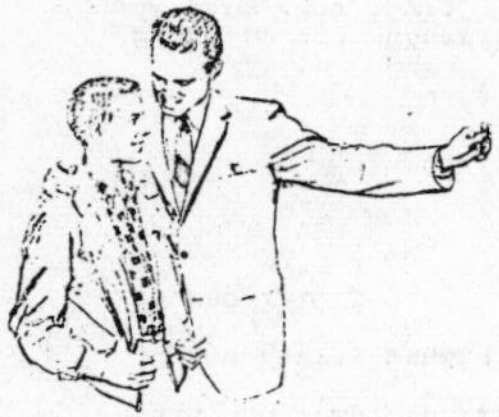

One Man - One Boy

May 22, 1964

Commission Exhibit No. 2223

Mr. J. Lee Rankin,
General Counsel
President's Commission on the
Assassination of President Kennedy
200 Maryland Avenue, N.E.
Washington, D. C. 20002

Dear Mr. Rankin:

In accordance with my letter of May 4th, I am forwarding herewith a complete record of our Agency file on Lee Harvey Oswald. Said file covers the period from December, 1953 to January, 1954.

Included herein are the following items:

a) A letter from Mr. John Carro, Probation Officer in the Bronx Domestic Relations Court, dated December 2, 1953, together with the probation report of that Court, which I assume was prepared for the guidance of the Justices of the Court.

b) A "face sheet" on Lee Harvey Oswald indicating that this is our case No. 12335. It is our practice to prepare such a "face sheet" on every client who is accepted for service by the Agency.

c) A two-page record carrying a summary of all our contacts with Lee Harvey Oswald and/or his mother, and/or the appropriate officers of the Court. Said contacts are dated

Serving Manhattan, Bronx, Brooklyn and Queens • Affiliated with Community Council of Greater New York and Big Brothers of America

COMMISSION EXHIBIT No. 2223

12/1, 12/15, 12/17, 12/23/53, and 1/4, 1/5, 1/6 and 1/10/54.

Please be advised that Item C above was also forwarded, under date of December 3, 1963, to Mr. Hugo Winteroad at the office of the Federal Bureau of Investigation, 201 East 69th Street, New York 21, N.Y.

You will find attached herewith an affidavit, properly executed, to the effect that the material enclosed herewith represents the full and complete file in this office on the case of Lee Harvey Oswald.

Please excuse the delay in transmitting this material to you.

Respectfully,

Howard A. Kieval

HOWARD A. KIEVAL
Executive Director

HAK/b
Enc.

P.S.

I should have mentioned that the caseworker whose initials you find on the record ("W.E.G.") is William E. Grote, who retired from this agency in 1956. His present age is approximately 75 years. In my conversations with him after the assassination of President Kennedy, I had the feeling that his memory was distinctly hazy and that I was prodding his recollections rather than that he was independently supplying me with information above and beyond what he recorded at the time of his very brief association with young Oswald and with Mrs. Oswald. If, for any reason, however, the Commission should wish to communicate with Mr. Grote directly, his present address is 99 Metropolitan Oval, Bronx, New York.

HAK

COMMISSION EXHIBIT No. 2223—Continued

Big Brothers Inc., 223 East 30th Street, New York 16, N. Y.

MUrray Hill 6-2012

One Man - One Boy

May 22, 1964

A F F I D A V I T

STATE OF NEW YORK }
COUNTY OF NEW YORK } SS.:

I, Howard A. Kieval, the undersigned, Executive Director of Big Brothers, Inc., 223 East 30th Street, New York 16, New York, do hereby swear and affirm that I have caused a thorough search to be made of the case record files of Big Brothers, Inc. of New York, and that the materials forwarded herewith to the President's Commission on the Assassination of President Kennedy represent the full and complete file of data available at this office on the case of Lee Harvey Oswald (our Case No. 12355, opened 12/1/53 and closed 1/10/54).

Howard A. Kieval

HOWARD A. KIEVAL
Executive Director,
Big Brothers, Inc. of New York

Sworn to and subscribed before
me this 22nd day of May, 1964

Russell J. Fornwalt

RUSSELL J. FORNWALT
Notary Public, State of New York
No. 31-1276600
Qualified in New York County
Commission Expires March 30, 1965

Serving Manhattan, Bronx, Brooklyn and Queens • Affiliated ... New York and Big Brothers of America

TRUE COPY

OSWALD, LEE 12335

REFERRED: Bronx Children's Court - 12/1/53. See court papers for details.

12/1/53 Received telephone call from Mr. Carro, probation officer, referring Lee Oswald of 825 East 179th Street for Big Brother supervision. Requested that Mr. Carro send us a copy of the court papers. WEG.

12/15/53 (delayed due to illness) Called at the home of Lee Oswald. Not finding anyone there, left card in door. WEG.

12/17/53 Received telephone call from Mrs. Oswald who stated that she found our card on returning home from work and wished to know the reason for our contact. Explained to her that Mr. Carro, probation officer of the Children's Court had asked that become interested in her son Lee. She seemed quite disturbed stating something to the effect that how long was this thing going to last because since the boy had returned from Youth House, he had been attending school each day and from all accounts was doing well. Could sense that Mrs. Oswald was rather disturbed about this matter and tried to give her an idea of what the Big Brother program was. She seemed to calm down considerably and suggested that Lee stop in at the office some time during the Christmas holidays. She did not take too kindly to this idea and advised that we would stop in at the home some evening as soon as possible. WEG.

12/23/53 Called at the home of Lee Oswald but no one was at home. Will call again. WEG.

1/4/54 This evening about 7:30 called at the home. Met Mrs. Oswald and Lee. Was cordially received by both the mother and boy. Mrs. Oswald stated that inasmuch as Lee was attending school and doing well and had been so ever since his return from Youth House, she could see no reason why there should be so much investigation. Again explained to Mrs. Oswald the nature of Big Brother work and learned that, as suggested by the probation officer, she had taken out a membership for Lee at the West Side Y.M.C.A. and he spent every Saturday there. She also stated that he was not the type of boy who cared for group activities preferring to remain at home watching TV, working on his stamp collection, etc. Lee was friendly allthough it was apparent that he was also displeased with the idea of being forced to joing various "Y" organizations about which he cared little. During the conversation, Mrs. Oswald stated that she had quit her job and planned to return to her former home down in New Orleans. Advised Mrs. Oswald that before she took this step, that she contact Mr. Carro by phone the following morning to get his advice as to what she should do about getting a release from the Children's Court. She said that Mr. Carro had agreed that she could move to New Jersey and she could see no difference betweeing moving to New Jersey or New Orleans. Explained to Mrs. Oswald that that there was a right way and a wrong way of doing things and that under existing circumstances, felt that she should notify Mr. Carro at once of her decision to move. WEG.

1/5/54 Received telephone call from Mrs. Oswald who stated that she had

OSWALD, LEE 12335

1/5/54 Cont'd contacted the Children's Court as suggested and that Mr. Carro was on vacation and she talked with Mr. Dunn who was handling Mr. Carro's cases while he was away. She stated that Mr. Dunn advised her that the court had supervision over the boy and that she should bring the boy to the court on Monday morning 1/11 when Mr. Carro was expected to be back in his office. She stated that she would be glad to go down there alone, but hesitated to take Lee with her because she felt that if she did they would probably remand him or in some way not allow him to return home and inasmuch as her rent is paid up to the 15th of the month, she wanted to move some day before that time. Later on in the day talked with Mr. Dunn about this and he stated that the boy must appear before the Court before permission is granted for him to leave the city.
WEG.

1/6/54 Called at the home of Mrs. Oswald. Explained again to her what Mr. Dunn had advised should be done but she was most sceptical about taking Lee before the Children's Court. Suggested to her that inasmuch as she felt this way, that she contact Mr. Carro upon his return as the boy was on parole to Mr. Carro and be guided by what suggestions he made. Suggested to Mrs. Oswald that we would be happy to hear from her if she wished to write when she got located and settled in New Orleans.
WEG.

1/10/54 Learned from Mr. Carro, Probation Officer, of the Bronx Children's Court that he had written to Mrs. Oswald so that the boy could be brought in for a hearing and that the letter was returned to him marked "moved - left no address." This evidently means that Mrs. Oswald carried out her intentions which were told to the writer on 1/5. At that time she said that she would not report to Mr. Carro because he might take Lee away from here and all her plans would be up-set. Please close.
WEG.

Commission Exhibit No. 2223—Continued

Commission Exhibit No. 2224

Cadwalader, Wickersham & Taft

14 Wall Street
New York 5

Telephone, Rector 2-5100
Cable address, Labellum

Washington Office
1725 Eye Street, N.W.
Washington 6, D. C.
Telephone (202) 296-5087

Cornelius W. Wickersham
R. Keith Kane
Charles W. McConaughy
John J. Redfield
Jacquelin A. Swords
Catherine Noyes Lee
H. Lee White
Richard N. Crockett
H. Gilmer Wells
Henry Allen Mark
J. Franklin Van Deren
John A. Sullivan
Richard J. Taylor
Harold W. Conroy
William N. Clarke
William J. Moss
Peter Megargee Brown
Peter Van Dyk Berg
Daniel Clay Draper
Ernie P. Stevens
George D. Roycraft
Jerome Shelby

Merrill M. Manning
(Inactive)

May 13, 1964

Honorable J. Lee Rankin
General Counsel
President's Commission on the
Assassination of President Kennedy
200 Maryland Ave. N.E.
Washington, D. C. 20002

Dear Mr. Rankin:

Pursuant to your letter of May 12 and the subpoena addressed to the Community Service Society and its counsel we enclose my affidavit to which are attached clear photostatic copies of all materials relating to Lee Harvey Oswald in the possession or control of the Community Service Society or its counsel.

We trust this complies with your request and that the subpoena for our appearance on May 18 is accordingly withdrawn.

Very truly yours,

Peter Megargee Brown

Enclosures
Via Air Mail

Commission Exhibit No. 2224

WASHINGTON, D. C.

--------------------------------x
PRESIDENT'S COMMISSION :
ON THE : **AFFIDAVIT**
ASSASSINATION OF :
PRESIDENT KENNEDY :
--------------------------------x

STATE OF NEW YORK)
: ss.:
COUNTY OF NEW YORK)

PETER MEGARGEE BROWN, being duly sworn, says:

I am a member of the firm of Cadwalader, Wickersham & Taft, counsel for the Community Service Society and am familiar with the papers and records in the possession of the Society relating to Lee Harvey Oswald.

This firm has caused a search of the files of Community Service Society under my supervision which reveals one file entitled "Marguerite Claverie Oswald #219055". The foregoing file is now in the possession of the deponent. To the best of my knowledge this file contains the only papers relating to Lee Harvey Oswald in the possession or control of the Community Service Society. Accordingly under my supervision photostatic copies have been made of this entire file, such copies being attached to this affidavit.

On information and belief the attached photostatic copies are of the entire file and comprise all the papers

COMMISSION EXHIBIT No. 2224—Continued

relating to Lee Harvey Oswald in the possession and control of the Community Service Society or its counsel.

Peter Megargee Brown
Peter Megargee Brown

Sworn to before me
this 13th day of May, 1964.

Teresa M. Cofone
Notary Public

TERESA M. COFONE
Notary Public, State of New York
No. 24-0676950
Qualified in Kings County
Certificate filed in New York County
Commission Expires March 30, 1965

-2-

COMMISSION EXHIBIT No. 2224—Continued

OSWALD James or John Marguerite Claverie 219055

ADDRESS: 825 East 179 St. | DATE: 1-16-53, 5-7-53 | DISTRICT: Bronx

MAN: (dec.)

WOMAN: RELIGION: P. | CASEWORKER: WD, OB

NAMES OF SINGLE CHILDREN: Lee 10-19-39; 2 boys in service

PERSONAL APPLICATION; HEARD OF AGENCY THRU: Federation of Protestant Welfare Agencies

REPORT FROM REGISTRATION BUREAU AND SOCIAL SERVICE EXCHANGE: 1-16-53 No record

SURNAME OSWALD WOMAN'S FIRST NAME & MAIDEN NAME Marguerite Claverie MAN'S FIRST NAME James or John (d) CROSS REFERENCE CASE NO. 219055

1-16-53 Mrs. O phoned and sounded rather upset as she went on to ask for an appt. "as soon as possible." She mentioned that the problem is with her only boy Lee, 13 yrs. of age. Mrs. O is a widow and along with boy came to N.Y. from Texas in this past October. Ever since the boy has been in N.Y. he has been refusing to go to school. There has been frequent truancy and in recent hearing before the school Attendance Board of JHS 117, Mrs. O was warned that she would have to do something about the boy or else the school would take authoratative action, just what kind of action, Mrs. O would not say. I was able to clarify that suspension was not specifically threatened. Mrs. O said she felt the problem was probably due to the change in environment and the problems that Lee was having in adapting himself to the new surroundings. At present, the boy hasn't been back to school since the hearing, and it is "nearly driving her crazy." To complicate things further, Mrs. O said she had to move and this will mean Lee will have to be transferred to a new school because she is now out of the district which is covered by JHS 117. Mrs. O mentioned that she had learned of us as a result of a phone call to the Federation of Protestant Wel. Agency who in turn had suggested she call us. Mrs. O was quite uncertain as to the kind of services we have here and although I suggested perhaps we could give some fuller clarification of this in an interview which I would be glad to give her, she went to a good deal of questioning as to the type of services which I tried to clear up for her to some extent.

When it came to the question of giving an appt., there was not one available before the 30th and Mrs. O expressed dis/approval of this, felt that she would need to be seen sooner because she was a busy woman, worked and it was difficult for her to keep getting time off. However, accepted rather reluctantly my explanation as to how interviews are based on appts. and unfortunately we do have a bit of a waiting list in relation to this. Wondered what to do immediately about Lee's not going to school, wondered if she should discuss this with the principal and I said that she certainly might do this if she wished and that I would like to be able to clear with the school as to understanding L's problem there a little more clearly. This was

CSS FAMILY SERVICE FACE SHEET: FORM 7

COMMISSION EXHIBIT No. 2224—Continued

1-16-53 contd. permissible with Mrs. O who finally accepted an appt. for Friday, Jan. 30th at 2 PM with MVR.

Near end of day, Mrs. Neill of Federation of Protestant Wel. Agencies, SP 7-4800, phoned to inquire as to whether Mrs. O had called for an appt. Mrs. N confirmed that Mrs. O had called her to engage Federation in helping out with the problem with Lee. Mrs. O wanted a worker to come to the home and talk with the boy, something which incidentally I neglected to record above was a request which Mrs. O had made when she called me. At any rate, what Mrs. N gave me was substantially along the lines of what Mrs. O had discussed in her phone covnersation earlier with me. It was made clear to her that the Federation only has a referral service and suggestion was made that she try CSS. Mrs. Neill requested that we be in touch with her in relation to disposition in the case which I promised would be done.

Denham:mb

1-23-53 Called JHS 117, TR 8-6211, to find out boy's new school. Talked with Miss Kahn, assistant principal. And explained that she was not able to give much in the way of impressions about the boy because she has only seen him once or twice and actually he only came to school while he was in 117 a total of 15 days, being absent 47½, during the period 9-30 thru 12-31-52. Lee arrived in N.Y. in Sept. and initially attended the Trinity Lutheran School in the Bronx from 9-8-to-9-26-52, where the record indicates he was present 9 days, absent 6 days. Miss Kahn felt that the boy seemed rather withdrawn, was rather difficult to reach him on the one instance she spoke with him. Miss Kahn thought that PS 44 was the new school, but suggest I call the attendance office for this information.

Spoke with Mr. Keating of the Attendance Bureau, LU 3-2470. Mr. Keating explained that he is not currently assigned to case, rather Mr. Brennan is working with the boy. However, in Mr. Brennan's absence, Mr. K was able to give me some background on the contact of Attendance Bureau with the family. Mr. Keating advised that he has actually, before case was transferred to Mr. Brennan, spoken once with the mother. Mrs. O complained at the time she simply couldn't handle Lee, that he was stubborn and refused to go to school and kept expressing wish to return to Texas where he said he felt more at home. On the other hand, mother later admitted that she does nag the boy quite a bit and that she would try easing up on him to see whether he would go to school. L is now attending JHS 44, but apparently has only been in school there for about 2 days, since the first of Jan. School dispatched a visiting teacher to the home who spoke with the boy, trying to persuade him to come to school. Lee is alleged to have replied that he would think about it and hadn't made up his mind, etc. To the hearing, this was held on 1-13-53 and the District Superintendent's recommendation was that the boy be placed on probation to Mr. Brennan until June. Mr. Keating said that it seemed there was a question of possible suspension here and agreed at my suggestion that this might be something that ~~JBG~~ should be involved in rather than CSS at this point. He, however, promised to have Mr. Brennan phone me for further discussion on this.

Denham:mb

1-30-53 Appt. failed. Case closed. Russell:fs

CASEWORK UNIT 12 DATE CLOSED 1/31/53

BRIEF-SERVICE ✓ CONTINUED-SERVICE ______

4-23-53 Miss Strickman, Youth House (AL 4-1350) telephoned for summary which was given. Lee is with them on account of truancy. He seems pretty "schizy". Hallett:RH

REPORT ONLY - CENTRAL SERVICES

4-29-53 Request for Information from DRC.

COMMISSION EXHIBIT No. 2224—Continued

Oswald -2- 219055

5-7-53 Telephone inquiry from Mr. Carro, Children's Court, LU8-5000 ext. 30. Lee, 13, a serious truancy problem, came with mother from Texas in 8-52. Problem seems to have evolved around difficulty of adjustment to new environment, relationship with mother. Father died when Lee was in infancy.

Complete study made by Youth House indicated "Personality pattern disturbance with schizoid features, passive aggressive tendencies, ~~lot of space for thought~~, rejection by a self-involved, conflicted mother." While Mrs. O denies any problem, there was consensus in the study that both Lee and Mrs. O needed help. It was felt that a child guidance clinic or family service agency would be preferable, with a male therapist for Lee, as he "can be reached by a male, shown at Youth House." Mother works; Lee has isolated himself, preferring to stay home and watch TV. He in intelligent, has an I.Q. of 118. Family is Lutheran and therefore a non-sectarian agency was considered first. It is known at this time that Catholic Charities has closed their intake for a month; Salvation Army intake situation is similar to ours. Mr. Carro has spoken with supervisor, Miss Corning, and they were in agreement that while Lee had been paroled until September, it was inadvisable to consider letting the boy wait so long for any kind of individual attention. The alternative if therapy cannot be found, is a placement away from the mother.

Mr. Carro said that he would be glad to talk with Salvation Army and at the same time pleaded for further consideration. I indicated that I felt in view of the difficulties presented, the skill required in treating such a disturbed boy, that there was little likelihood of our being able to take on the case. Nevertheless I would take it up with the intake supervisor while Mr. Carro in the meantime talked with Salvation Army. It was agreed therefore that I would get in touch with him either the following day or early the next week to advise whether there was any greater likelihood of our taking responsibility for such a case at this time.

Benjamin:bb

Application pending.

5-13-53 Following discussion with Intake Supervisor on 5-13, telephoned Mr. Carro and indicated that due to our intake situation and waiting list we could not give this situation the proper attention it appeared to require. Mr. Carro was appreciative of this, said that he was planning to call Salvation Army, was anxious to get the matter attended to, as he is going on vacation at the end of this week.

Mr. O accepted report of our previous contact in answer to form inquiry which we had received. Agreed that we would not need to send written report. Benjamin:cp

5-31-53 Case closed.

CASEWORK UNIT 121 DATE CLOSED 5/31/53
BRIEF-SERVICE ______ CONTINUED-SERVICE ______ Ck 7-17-53

COMMISSION EXHIBIT No. 2224—Continued

FORM CF-101-40

DOMESTIC RELATIONS COURT
CITY OF NEW YORK

1118 GRAND CONCOURSE
Bronx, N. Y.

APR 29 1953

PROBATION BUREAU

Date 4/28/53

To the Registrar

Community Serv.Soc.
Family Div.
105 E. 22 St.
N.Y., N.Y.

Re: Lee H. Oswald

Dear Sir:

Father's name Robert or Jas.John
Mother's maiden name Clavorie, Marguerite
Children ______
Address 825 E. 179 St.

The Social Service Exchange reports the above family known to you under date of 1/16/53, your Case No. 219055

We are interested in Lee H., B. 10/19/39 This case is scheduled for hearing in Court on 5/8, and we should appreciate a summary of your contact with the family and any special information you may have regarding this family (if possible) before that date.

Thanking you for your cooperation, I am

Very truly yours,

J.Carro

Probation Officer.

5/13 Tel. report accepted by Mr. Carro in conjunction with completion of intake inquiry—

COMMISSION EXHIBIT No. 2224—Continued

FD-302 (Rev. 1-25-60)

FEDERAL BUREAU OF INVESTIGATION

Date 12/18/63

VICTOR J. CONNELL, Attendance Officer, Bureau of Attendance, School District 22, 2424 Jerome Avenue, Bronx, New York, advised that during the spring of 1953, he recalls while working in the Bronx Zoo he observed a young boy approximately 13 years of age in the zoo. He described the boy as very clean and very well dressed. He approached the boy and determined that his name was LEE OSWALD and he was a truant. He described him as surly and referred to CONNELL as a "damned Yankee".

CONNELL stated he apprehended OSWALD and returned him to the school district and escorted him to the school. CONNELL advised he is sure he had no other contact with the OSWALD boy but he may have telephonically contacted OSWALD's mother at the time.

He could furnish no additional information.

Commission Exhibit No. 2225

- 8 -

On 12/16/63 at New York, New York File # NY 105-38431

by SA JAMES O. INGRAM:pmg Date dictated 12/17/63

This document contains neither recommendations nor conclusions of the FBI. It is the property of the FBI and is loaned to your agency; it and its contents are not to be distributed outside your agency.

COMMISSION EXHIBIT NO. 2225

FD-302 (Rev. 1-25-60)

FEDERAL BUREAU OF INVESTIGATION

Date 12/18/63

ARTHUR CLINTON, Director of Attendance, Board of Education, City of New York, advised his records contain information concerning LEE HARVEY OSWALD. He stated his records show OSWALD attended Public Schools 117 and 44 in the Bronx, New York, during 1953, however, his records did not reveal the exact dates of OSWALD's attendance at these schools. CLINTON advised that he is the Director of the Attendance Bureau, therefore all attendance officers are under his jurisdiction. He said any violation by a truant is usually handled by their office.

His records show that LEE HARVEY OSWALD resided at 1455 Sheridan Avenue, Bronx, and 825 East 179th Street, Bronx, during 1953, however, his records did not indicate any dates of their residence at these addresses. OSWALD's parents were listed as ROBERT LEE OSWALD and MARGUERITE CLAVERIE. The children in the family were listed as JOHN, born January 19, 1932; ROBERT, born April 7, 1934; and LEE, born October 9, 1939.

Their records show that a Board of Education Calendar of Bureau Hearings was conducted by the Bureau of Attendance on January 13, 1953, in District 24, Hearing Number 60, concerning LEE HARVEY OSWALD, 1455 Sheridan Avenue, and the Attendance Officer was Mr. BRENNAN. The disposition was listed as adjourned until January 20, 1953 for appearance.

On January 20, 1953, Hearing Number 60, in the matter concerning LEE H. OSWALD, same address, was held before the Bureau of Attendance and Officer BRENNAN was the Attendance Officer. The disposition was listed as probation to June 30 and a resummons would be issued.

Commission Exhibit No. 2226

On 12/16/63 at 110 Livingston Street Brooklyn, New York File # NY 105-38431

by SA JAMES O. INGRAM:pmg Date dictated 12/17/63

- 6 -

This document contains neither recommendations nor conclusions of the FBI. It is the property of the FBI and is loaned to your agency; it and its contents are not to be distributed outside your agency.

COMMISSION EXHIBIT NO. 2226

NY 105-38431

On January 27, 1953, a hearing was held in District 24 on Case Number 60 for OSWALD and his address was then listed as 825 East 179th Street, Apartment 3 C. The Attendance Officer was J.F. BRENNAN. The disposition was listed as probation to June 20, 1953 and would prosecute the child on the next violation.

CLINTON said their records also show the Board of Education Calendar of Court Prosecutions in District 24 by the Bureau of Attendance. This record indicates LEE H. OSWALD had a hearing on March 12, 1953, before Magistrate DELANEY. The Attendance Officer was J.F. BRENNAN and OSWALD's address was listed as 825 East 179th Street. The disposition was only listed as March 19, 1953.

The records show that on March 19, 1963, the LEE H. OSWALD case was again before Magistrate DELANEY and the records indicate that the Warrant Officer was unable to execute the warrant concerning OSWALD.

The records show that on May 7, 1953, LEE H. OSWALD, 825 East 179th Street was again brought before the court before Magistrate MC CLANCY. OSWALD was accompanied by his mother, MARGUERITE and the Attendance Officer was listed as J. F. BRENNAN. The disposition was listed as case adjourned to September 24, 1953, and the latter was referred to the Community Service Society.

CLINTON stated he has no additional records concerning OSWALD, however, he understood that only one Attendance Officer actually recalls having any personal contact with OSWALD and this was VICTOR J. CONNELL, an Attendance Officer in the 22nd District.

COMMISSION EXHIBIT No. 2226—Continued

Commission Exhibit No. 2227

FD-302 (Rev. 1-25-60)

FEDERAL BUREAU OF INVESTIGATION

1

Date 11/25/63

GERARD F. TUJAGUE, owner and operator of Gerard F. Tujague Inc., 442 Canal Street, Third Floor, New Orleans, Louisiana, advised that LEE HARVEY OSWALD was employed by his company as a messenger boy beginning November 10, 1955 until January 14, 1956. He advised that OSWALD's specific duties were strictly messenger type, that he would deliver official papers dealing with the forwarding company business. OSWALD's contacts would be such locations as other forwarding companies, the U. S. Customhouse Export Office, steamship lines and in some cases foreign counsel offices which may have to do with the export or import business. Mr. TUJAGUE was not able to specifically enumerate these foreign counsel offices and there is no definite record to disclose these particular contacts.

Mr. TUJAGUE advised that OSWALD's official duty time was 8:30 AM to 4:30 PM on Tuesday, Wednesday and Friday and 8:30 AM to 5:30 PM on Monday and Thursday. He also worked on Saturday from 8:30 AM to 12:30 PM. Mr. TUJAGUE stated OSWALD's normal lunch hour was between 12:00 and 1:00 PM and he has determined from various employees that OSWALD was a non-social, in that he did not at any time associate with any of the employees either during his lunch hour or after hours. He was a rather quiet type of individual and did not have very much contact or conversation with any of the other employees. He also determined that normally OSWALD would go to his home during the lunch hour to be with his mother which was 126 Exchange Place and is a very short distance from the business office of TUJAGUE. He advised that OSWALD's work hours were usually by time card and that his pay at the end of each period was by check, however, at this time he does not have available either OSWALD's time cards or cancelled checks, however, he advised he will make a diligent search for this material and will advise Agents and make these available.

Mr. TUJAGUE made available the only records he had available at this time on OSWALD which are payroll employee records beginning November 10, 1955 through January 14, 1956 which disclose the name LEE HARVEY OSWALD, 126

On 11/25/63 at New Orleans, Louisiana File # NO 89-69

by SA JAMES E. SCHMIDT, JR. and SA THEODORE R. VIATER/jab Date dictated 11/25/63

4

COMMISSION EXHIBIT No. 2227

Exchange Place, Social Security Number 433-54-3937, listing position as office boy at a rate of $130 per month. This record also listed OSWALD as single. The other available record was the W-4 form, employee withholding exemption certificate. This certificate shows the name of LEE HARVEY OSWALD, 126 Exchange Place, Social Security Number 433-54-3937 dated November 12, 1955 signed in pencil LEE OSWALD. Mr. TUJAGUE advised that this form was prepared in the handwriting of LEE OSWALD and that this was the only document he has at this time which was prepared by OSWALD.

Mr. TUJAGUE advised that to the best of his knowledge he believed LEE OSWALD was recommended to him by one of several employment agencies, enumerating the Louisiana Unemployment Bureau, Apex Employment Service and Bee Robertson's Employment Service. Mr. TUJAGUE advised that he is not sure as to the reason for OSWALD resigning, however, he believes it may have been due to the fact that he was either drafted or joined the armed forces or possibly to obtain a better job as he does recall OSWALD complaining about the fact that this type of work was too strenuous.

Mr. TUJAGUE advised that he will search his records for possible cancelled checks as well as time cards and would contact Agents if same are located. Mr. TUJAGUE requested that the payroll sheets and withholding form be returned to him when no longer needed by the FBI.

Mr. TUJAGUE further advised that he has contacted each of his employees and determined that none of these individuals were friendly with OSWALD either during office hours or after work. He advised that each of them told him they were not able to give any specific details as to the personal life of OSWALD nor were they acquainted with any of OSWALD's friends or associates since they themselves did not associate with OSWALD during this short period of employment of three months either in the office or after office hours.

Mr. TUJAGUE advised he would make available the names of all of these employees and their home addresses so they might be interviewed. Concerning the check of his records for time cards and cancelled checks he will make these available if they can be located.

5

COMMISSION EXHIBIT No. 2227—Continued

FD-302 (Rev. 1-25-60)

FEDERAL BUREAU OF INVESTIGATION

Date 11/27/63

1

Mr. NICK MAZZA, Office Manager, J. R. Michels, Inc., 442 Canal Street, New Orleans, Louisiana, stated that he had no personal recollection of LEE HARVEY OSWALD and has made inquiry among the current employees of his company and has no one who has the slightest recollection of OSWALD.

MAZZA stated that he has searched the records of his firm and was only able to locate a U. S. Treasury form W4 which lists the following information:

Employee's Name	LEE HARVEY OSWALD
Employee's Residence	126 Exchange Place
Social Security No.	433-54-3937
Exemptions	1
Date	January 17, 1956

Mr. MAZZA stated that OSWALD worked there for two weeks as an office boy and runner. The records contain no additional information and the reason for OSWALD's termination of employment is not recorded or known.

[redacted]

Commission Exhibit No. 2228

On 11/26/63 at New Orleans, Louisiana File # NO 89-69

by SA MERRIMAN D. DIVEN/lrs Date dictated 11/26/63

COMMISSION EXHIBIT No. 2228

FD-302 (Rev. 1-25-60)

FEDERAL BUREAU OF INVESTIGATION

Date 11/25/63

1

PAUL ANTHONY FIORELLO, residence address 204 Marais Street, telephone 522-7746, employed as a dental technician by Pfisterer Dental Laboratory Company, 227 Dauphine Street, furnished the following information:

He recalled that LEE OSWALD worked as a messenger for Pfisterer in about 1956 for a period of not more than a few months. He recalled that OSWALD used to talk a lot with PALMER MC BRIDE and is of the opinion OSWALD used to go to MC BRIDE's home to listen to a hi-fi set and look through MC BRIDE's telescopes, as MC BRIDE was interested in astronomy. He recalled that OSWALD used to talk to MC BRIDE about Russia but FIORELLO did not know what was said about Russia. FIORELLO did not know where OSWALD lived in New Orleans. When OSWALD quit he told FIORELLO he was going to Texas where he had a job selling shoes. FIORELLO did not recall that any city in Texas was mentioned. FIORELLO knew of no friends of OSWALD other than MC BRIDE.

FIORELLO advised he was employed as a messenger at Pfisterer during the time OSWALD was a messenger there. He recalled the other messengers at this time as being LIONEL SLATER, JR., JOHN ULMER and PALMER MC BRIDE.

[redacted]

Commission Exhibit No. 2229

On 11/25/63 at New Orleans, Louisiana File # NO 89-69

by SA JOSEPH G. ENGELHARDT /jm Date dictated 11/25/63

17

This document contains neither recommendations nor conclusions of the FBI. It is the property of the FBI and is loaned to your agency; it and its contents are not to be distributed outside your agency.

COMMISSION EXHIBIT NO. 2229

FD-302 (Rev. 1-25-60)

FEDERAL BUREAU OF INVESTIGATION

1

Date November 25, 1963

LIONEL SLATER, JR., residence address 1411 France Street, employed as a messenger by Pfisterer Dental Laboratory Company, 227 Dauphine Street, furnished the following information:

He recognized the photograph of LEE HARVEY OSWALD as a messenger who worked at Pfisterer for several weeks in about 1956 during the time PALMER MC BRIDE worked there. He did not know the boy's last name but did recall his first name was LEE. This LEE was a friend of MC BRIDE and SLATER is of the opinion he visited MC BRIDE's home several times. He knows nothing concerning OSWALD and does not recall OSWALD ever discussing any political matters.

[redacted]

Commission Exhibit No. 2230

On 11/24/63 at New Orleans, Louisiana File # NO 89-69

by SA JOSEPH G. ENGELHARDT :gas Date dictated 11/25/63

18

This document contains neither recommendations nor conclusions of the FBI. It is the property of the FBI and is loaned to your agency; it and its contents are not to be distributed outside your agency.

COMMISSION EXHIBIT NO. 2230

FD-302 (Rev. 1-25-60)

FEDERAL BUREAU OF INVESTIGATION

1

Date 11/27/63

Mrs. MILDRED SAWYER, 126 Exchange Place, New Orleans, Louisiana furnished the following information:

Mrs. SAWYER advised that she is the widow of JOSEPH S. SAWYER, and that she was residing at 126 Exchange Place in the latter part of 1955, and has continued to reside at that address since that time. She stated that she recalled a Mrs. OSWALD and her young son living there at that time. She stated that the boy was only about 14 or 15 years old and attended school during the day. She did not know of any jobs that he might have had, either after school or on the week ends.

Mrs. SAWYER advised that Mrs. OSWALD was a saleslady and worked for one of the large department stores on Canal Street. The son would always arrive home prior to his mother, and was always very quiet. He seemed to read a lot and was seen on several occasions bringing library books home to read. Mrs. SAWYER stated that at that time the son appeared to be an average, normal teenage boy, dressed neatly, and was not boisterous in any way. As far as she could recall she never heard him being reprimanded by his mother. Both Mrs. OSWALD and her son seemed to have few friends, and very few people visited them in their apartment. She believed that on a few occasions some teenage boys did come home with the OSWALD boy after school, however, they were always very quiet, and did not stay long.

Mrs. SAWYER stated that she never saw the OSWALD boy with any kind of gun, and never heard Mrs. OSWALD mention that he had any gun, or was interested in guns.

Mrs. SAWYER advised that she believed sometime in the Spring of 1956, Mrs. OSWALD told her that she was leaving New Orleans with her son, and that she was going to Fort Worth, Texas where she had another son. Mrs. SAWYER could not recall if Mrs. OSWALD quit her job voluntarily or whether she was terminated by the department store where she was employed

Commission Exhibit No. 2231

On 11/27/63 at New Orleans, Louisiana File # NO 89-69

by SA G. MYRYWIN ALDERSON /bda Date dictated 11/27/63

127

This document contains neither recommendations nor conclusions of the FBI. It is the property of the FBI and is loaned to your agency; it and its contents are not to be distributed outside your agency.

COMMISSION EXHIBIT No. 2231

FD-302 (Rev. 1-25-60)

FEDERAL BUREAU OF INVESTIGATION

1

Date November 27, 1963

JOHN NEUMEYER, Sans Lounge, 801 Jefferson Highway, (residence, 1541 Franklin Avenue, New Orleans) furnished the following information.

NEUMEYER advised that he attended Beauregard Junior High School in New Orleans approximately 10 years ago. He recalls LEE HARVEY OSWALD being a student in that high school at the same time, however, OSWALD was one year ahead of NEUMEYER and NEUMEYER advised that he had no contact whatsoever with OSWALD except on one occasion. NEUMEYER explained that when he was either in the 7th or 8th grade he got into a fight with OSWALD because OSWALD was picking on his, NEUMEYER's, brother, MICHAEL. NEUMEYER recalls that OSWALD struck him a few times and that ended the fight. NEUMEYER advised that he did not know OSWALD personally, could not recall any former students OSWALD may have associated with, and could recall no background information concerning OSWALD. He noted however that OSWALD went by the nickname of "Yankee" and did not seem to get along with other students as he, NEUMEYER, had heard OSWALD often became involved in fights.

NEUMEYER further advised that the last time he saw OSWALD was in Junior High School and he has not seen or heard about OSWALD until reading about him in the newspapers a few days ago.

Commission Exhibit No. 2232

On 11/27/63 at New Orleans, Louisiana File # NO 89-69

by SAs KEVIN J. HARRIGAN and WILLIAM L. NEWBROUGH :sms Date dictated 11/27/63

197

This document contains neither recommendations nor conclusions of the FBI. It is the property of the FBI and is loaned to your agency; it and its contents are not to be distributed outside your agency.

COMMISSION EXHIBIT No. 2232

FD-302 (Rev. 1-25-60)

FEDERAL BUREAU OF INVESTIGATION

1

Date 11/25/63

Mrs. PEGGY ZIMMERMAN, 832 Avenue G, Marrero, Louisiana, advised that she attended Beauregard Junior High School in New Orleans for three years and recalled that LEE HARVEY OSWALD also attended during the 1954-55 school year. She said she did not know him well enough to even speak to him but seems to recall that he may have been in her home room as the tenth grade was set up alphabetically. She does not recall having any classes with him. She did state, however that he was always alone and did not appear to have any friends. She said she never saw him with ED VOEBEL although she was acquainted with VOEBEL during this time. She said she never heard him make any statements nor saw him do anything, nor did she ever hear anything about him which would indicate that he had any bitter feelings toward the United States or the President nor did she ever hear of him discussing Marxism or Communism. She stated she had no personal contact with him and did not know where he lived. She said the only thing she was able to recall was that he wore an old vest-type sweater all the time and she noted that she could never remember seeing him smile.

Mrs. ZIMMERMAN said he did not appear to be close to any teacher and did not participate in any athletics, clubs or any activities.

She stated that JOHNNY NEWMEYER was also in her room at Beauregard Junior High School. She said that the last she heard NEWMEYER was the operator of the Sands Lounge which is located on Jefferson Highway near the approach to the Huey P. Long Bridge. She said she has had no contact or information concerning OSWALD since she remembered seeing him at Beauregard Junior High School in 1955.

[redacted]

Commission Exhibit No. 2233

On 11/25/63 at Marrero, Louisiana File # NO 89-69

by SA NATHAN O. BROWN and SA KEVIN J. HARRIGAN/jab Date dictated 11/25/63

277

This document contains neither recommendations nor conclusions of the FBI. It is the property of the FBI and is loaned to your agency; it and its contents are not to be distributed outside your agency.

COMMISSION EXHIBIT No. 2233

FD-302 (Rev. 1-25-60)

FEDERAL BUREAU OF INVESTIGATION

Date 11/26/63

1

MICHAEL PATRICK NEUMEYER, 1541 Franklin Avenue, New Orleans, advised that he vaguely recalls LEE HARVEY OSWALD from Beauregard Junior High School. NEUMEYER advised that he is about three years younger than OSWALD and was probably in the sixth grade at the time OSWALD was in the ninth grade at Beauregard Junior High School. NEUMEYER knew nothing regarding OSWALD's friends, interests, or other pertinent background data. The only incident he could recall which ever involved him and OSWALD was a fight between his brother, JOHN NEUMEYER and OSWALD, which occurred while both his brother and OSWALD were in either the eighth or ninth grade. MICHAEL NEUMEYER recalls that one day OSWALD began picking on him at which time his brother JOHN had a fight with OSWALD. MICHAEL could only recall that JOHN won the fight and could not remember any further details.

MICHAEL NEUMEYER stated that his brother JOHN who was in OSWALD's homeroom, might possibly recall OSWALD and be able to furnish more information than he could. He advised that JOHN owned The Sands Motel, 801 Jefferson Highway and resided at 1541 Franklin.

[redacted]

Commission Exhibit No. 2234

On 11/26/63 at New Orleans, Louisiana File # 89-69

by SA's KEVIN J. HARRIGAN and WILLIAM L. NEWBROUGH :lav Date dictated 11/26/63

344

This document contains neither recommendations nor conclusions of the FBI. It is the property of the FBI and is loaned to your agency; it and its contents are not to be distributed outside your agency.

COMMISSION EXHIBIT No. 2234

Mr. Jack Loyakano, 737 Brockenbraugh, Metairie, Louisiana, advised on April 1, 1964 that he recalled Lee Harvey Oswald when they both attended Beauregard Junior High School, New Orleans, Louisiana, during the school year 1954 - 1955.

Mr. Loyakano stated he believed that he was one year ahead of Oswald in school but recalled seeing Oswald in the various hallways, classrooms and on the playground at the school.

He informed that he did not associate with Oswald and therefore he did not consider himself an acquaintance. He said that Oswald kept to himself and the only person who seemed to associate with Oswald during this time was Edward Voebel.

Mr. Loyakano said he did not recall Oswald participating in any school activities and therefore he considered Oswald to be a "loner". He informed that Oswald did not seem to be able to get along with fellow students because Oswald would get into fights with other boys, however, he could not recall the identities of the boys who had fights with Oswald.

Mr. Loyakano said he could recall no additional information regarding Oswald and that he did not know Robert Lee Oswald, Jr. or John Edward PIC.

Carrol A. Battistella, 917 Cougar, Arabi, Louisiana, advised on April 2, 1963 that he attended Beauregard Junior High School, New Orleans, Louisiana during the school year 1954 - 1955 at the same time as Lee Harvey Oswald.

He stated that he vaguely recalls Oswald, did not consider himself an acquaintance and did not associate with Oswald. Battistella stated that he would see Oswald in various classes and speak to Oswald and this was the extent of any association. He stated he knew that Oswald did not participate in any school activities or athletics because Battistella was active in such programs and would have been aware of any such participation by Oswald.

Battistella stated that from his recollection of Oswald he would consider Oswald to be a "loner" as Oswald

21

COMMISSION EXHIBIT No. 2235

did not appear to have any friends and kept to himself most of the time. He stated he recalled that Edward Voebel associated with Oswald on occasions.

Battistella informed that he could recall no other information about Oswald and that he did not know anyone by the name of Robert Lee Oswald, Jr. or John Edward Pic.

Joan Burgard, 2000 Illinois, Kenner, Louisiana, advised on April 2, 1964 that she formerly attended Beauregard Junior High School, New Orleans, Louisiana, at the same time as Lee Harvey Oswald in 1954 - 1955.

She informed that she vaguely recalls Oswald as a fellow student and that to her knowledge Oswald did not participate in school activities nor did he belong to the various groups of students that associated with each other. She informed that on some unrecalled date Oswald became involved in a fight with John Neumeyer on the school grounds. She was unable to recall any additional information in this regard or anything further regarding Oswald, and she did not know Robert Lee Oswald, Jr. or John Edward Pic.

Steve Cohen, 8405 Dixon, advised on April 2, 1964 that he and his wife Marilyn Cohen, nee Reilly had formerly attended Beauregard Junior High School, New Orleans, Louisiana, at the same time as Lee Harvey Oswald. He advised that he vaguely recalled Oswald attending the school but that he did not associate with Oswald.

Mr. Cohen said that as far as he knew the only person that Oswald associated with was Ed Voebel, and Oswald did not participate in school activities.

Mr. Cohen said that after Oswald had been arrested in connection with the assassination of President KENNEDY, he and his wife MARILYN, had attempted to recall what kind of a person OSWALD was during OSWALD's attendance at Beauregard and his wife informed him that she could only vaguely recall Oswald at the school and nothing else.

Mr. Cohen said that neither he nor his wife knew Robert Lee Oswald, Jr. or John Edward Pic and that he could furnish no additional information.

Mr. Cohen said his wife was unavailable for interview.

22

COMMISSION EXHIBIT No. 2235—Continued

Don Ferrara, 125 Conrad advised April 2, 1964 that he had attended Beauregard Junior High School, New Orleans, Louisiana at the same time as Lee Harvey Oswald. He advised that his recollections of Oswald were that Oswald appeared to be an introvert in that he did not mix with the other students and kept mostly to himself.

Mr. Ferrara advised that he engaged Oswald in conversation on a few occasions and in these conversations Oswald professed that he did not believe in God and that religion was a waste of time.

Ferrara stated that Oswald did not participate in school activities and the only student who associated with Oswald was Ed Voebel. Ferrara said he recalled Oswald had some fights with other students but that he did not know what these fights were about or the identities of the students with whom Oswald fought.

Ferrara said he did not know Robert Lee Oswald, Jr. or Robert Edward Pic and that he could recall no additional information regarding Lee Harvey Oswald.

Dimitri Bouzon, 523 Dumaine Street, advised April 2, 1964 that he attended Beauregard Junior High School, New Orleans, Louisian at the same time as Lee Harvey Oswald.

Bouzon stated that he did not associate with Oswald, that Oswald kept to himself and did not mix with the other students. He informed that Oswald did get into fights with some of the other boys, that on one occasion Oswald got into a fight with a student by the name of Robin Reilly and that Reilly gave Oswald a bloody lip. Bouzon advised he did not know what this fight was about. He stated that some of the other students would taunt Oswald by calling Oswald "Yankee" which appeared to upset Oswald but did not know if this was the basis for the fight.

Bouzon said that Oswald did not appear to have any friends at the school and did not participate in school activities.

Bouzon stated that he does not know Robert Lee Oswald, Jr., or John Edward Pic and that he could recall no additional information regarding Lee Harvey Oswald.

Huey Ricks, 4116 North Roman Street, advised on April 2, 1964, that he had formerly attended Beauregard Junior High School, New Orleans, Louisiana, at the same time as Lee Harvey Oswald.

Mr. Ricks stated that he did not associate with Oswald, but believed that he may have had a gym class with Oswald. Mr. Ricks stated that from his recollection of Oswald, Oswald appeared to be quiet and introverted. He said that Oswald did not join in the various activities in gym class but for the most part would stand to the side and watch the activity.

Mr. Ricks stated that his only contact with Oswald was to say hello and that to his knowledge, Oswald did not date any girls nor participate in school functions. He said that during his limited contact with Oswald, he found Oswald to be pleasant. Mr. Ricks said that there was another schoolmate by the name of Don Boos who had limited contact with Oswald, inasmuch as Boos was on the school track team and Oswald came to Boos on one occasion and expressed an interest in track. Mr. Ricks said that Boos is deceased having been killed in an automobile accident.

Mr. Ricks said that he could recall no additional information regarding Oswald and that he does not know Robert Lee Oswald, Jr. or John Edward Pic.

Billy Dean, 209 South St. Patrick, informed on April 2, 1964, that he formerly attended Beauregard Junior High School, New Orleans, Louisiana, at the same time as Lee Harvey Oswald.

He informed that his only recollection of Oswald was that Oswald kept to himself and did not enter into school activities or mix with the students. Dean stated that he did not associate with Oswald but recalled that on occasions he may have conversed with Oswald. His recollections were that these conversations pertained to school work.

Dean said that to his knowledge, Oswald did not have any friends at the school, although Oswald did associate from time to time with another student by the name of Ed Voebel.

Dean informed that he does not know Robert Lee Oswald, Jr. or John Edward Pic and that he could recall no additional information about Lee Harvey Oswald.

Myra Darouse, 3116 Prytania, Apartment 29, informed on April 2, 1964, that she was the home room teacher for Lee Harvey Oswald during Oswald's attendance at Beauregard Junior High School, New Orleans, Louisiana.

She said that she recalled Oswald as being a physically small boy who did not associate very much with the other students. Mrs. Darouse said she recalled that generally during the school lunch period, Oswald would be by himself and quietly eat his lunch, and after finishing his lunch would then begin to read from various unrecalled books while the other students would usually be engaged in conversation or other activity.

She advised that she did not consider Oswald to be a trouble maker at the school, but recalled on one occasion that Oswald did get into a fight with another student. She could not recall the name of the other student Oswald was fighting with, but did recall that other students were holding Oswald on the ground during which time Oswald was being punched.

Mrs. Darouse said that she came out on the school ground and observed blood on Oswald's face and thereafter wiped the blood from his face and put some band-aids on the bruises. She said she could not recall the identities of the other students who were holding Oswald nor did she know why they were fighting.

Mrs. Darouse said that she could recall nothing else about Oswald and that she does not know Robert Lee Oswald, Jr. or John Edward Pic.

27

COMMISSION EXHIBIT No. 2236

UNITED STATES DEPARTMENT OF JUSTICE

FEDERAL BUREAU OF INVESTIGATION

In Reply, Please Refer to File No.

Dallas, Texas
February 28, 1964

LEE HARVEY OSWALD

Exhibit D-113 is two employee's record sheets (front and back each) in the name LEE HARVEY OSWALD in connection with his employment at Gerald F. Tujague, Inc., 422 Canal Street, New Orleans, Louisiana.

This exhibit was obtained on November 25, 1963, from Mr. GERALD F. TUJAGUE, owner and president of Gerald F. Tujague, Inc.

The results of investigation pertaining to this exhibit are reflected on page 5 of the report of Special Agent WARREN C. deBRUEYS dated December 2, 1963, at Dallas, Texas.

COMMISSION EXHIBIT No. 2237

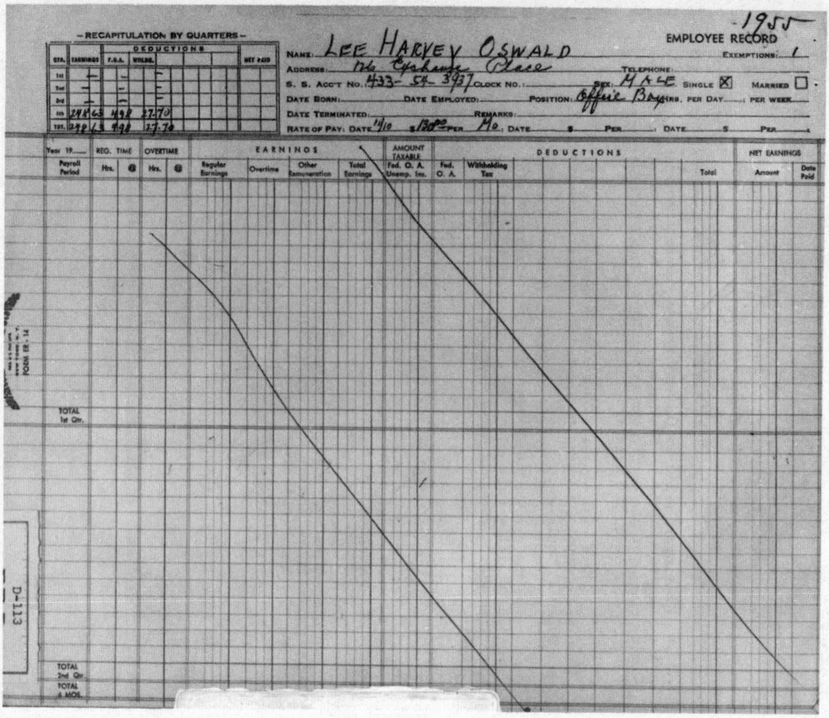

-1955

EMPLOYEE RECORD

— RECAPITULATION BY QUARTERS —

QTR.	EARNINGS	DEDUCTIONS F.O.A.	DEDUCTIONS WHLDG.				NET PAID
1st	—	—	—				
2nd	—	—	—				
3rd	—	—	—				
4th	248 63	4 98	27 70				
TOT.	248 63	4 98	27 70				

NAME: LEE HARVEY OSWALD EXEMPTIONS: 1
ADDRESS: 126 Exchange Place TELEPHONE:
S. S. ACC'T NO. 433-54-3937 CLOCK NO.: SEX: MALE SINGLE [X] MARRIED [ ]
DATE BORN: DATE EMPLOYED: POSITION: Office Boy HRS. PER DAY: ; PER WEEK:
DATE TERMINATED: REMARKS:
RATE OF PAY: DATE 11/10 $130.00 PER Mo.; DATE $ PER ; DATE $ PER

Year 19— Payroll Period	REG. TIME Hrs.	REG. TIME @	OVERTIME Hrs.	OVERTIME @	EARNINGS Regular Earnings	EARNINGS Overtime	EARNINGS Other Remuneration	EARNINGS Total Earnings	AMOUNT TAXABLE Fed. O. A. Unemp. Ins.	DEDUCTIONS Fed. O. A.	DEDUCTIONS Withholding Tax	DEDUCTIONS Total	NET EARNINGS Amount	NET EARNINGS Date Paid
TOTAL 1st Qtr.														
TOTAL 2nd Qtr.														
TOTAL 6 MOS.														

D-113

Commission Exhibit No. 2237—Continued

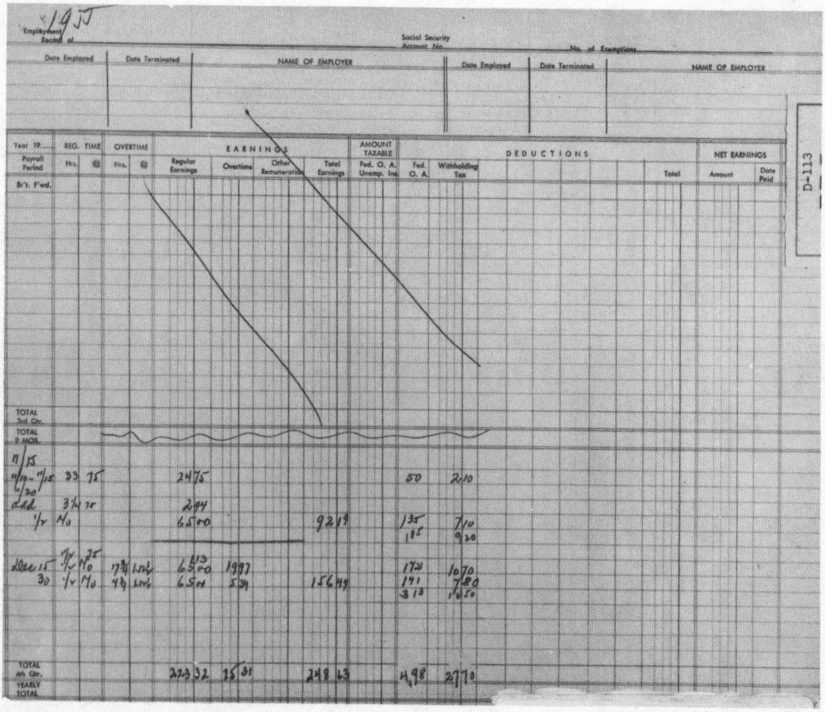

1955

Employment Record of — Social Security Account No. — No. of Exemptions —

Date Employed	Date Terminated	NAME OF EMPLOYER	Date Employed	Date Terminated	NAME OF EMPLOYER

Year 19— Payroll Period	REG. TIME Hrs.	REG. TIME @	OVERTIME Hrs.	OVERTIME @	EARNINGS Regular Earnings	EARNINGS Overtime	EARNINGS Other Remuneration	EARNINGS Total Earnings	AMOUNT TAXABLE Fed. O. A. Unemp. Ins.	DEDUCTIONS Fed. O. A.	DEDUCTIONS Withholding Tax	DEDUCTIONS Total	NET EARNINGS Amount	NET EARNINGS Date Paid
Br't. F'wd.														
TOTAL 3rd Qtr.														
TOTAL 9 MOS.														
11/15 11/10-11/15 11/20	33	75			24 75					50	2 10			
add	3 1/4	75			2 44									
	1/2	Mo			65 00			92 19		1 35 / 1 85	7 10 / 9 20			
Dec 15	1/2	Mo 75	17 3/4	1.12 1/2	65 00 13	19 97				1 72	10 70			
30	1/2	Mo	4 3/4	1.12 1/2	65 00	5 34		156 44		1 41 / 3 13	7 80 / 18 50			
TOTAL 4th Qtr. YEARLY TOTAL					223 32	25 31		248 63		4 98	27 70			

D-113

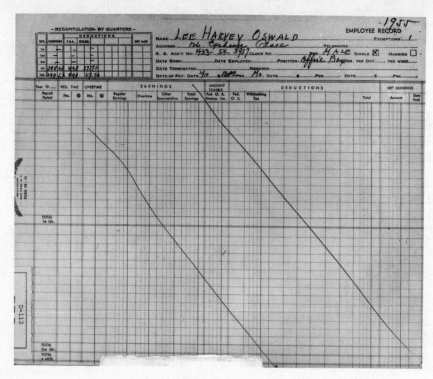

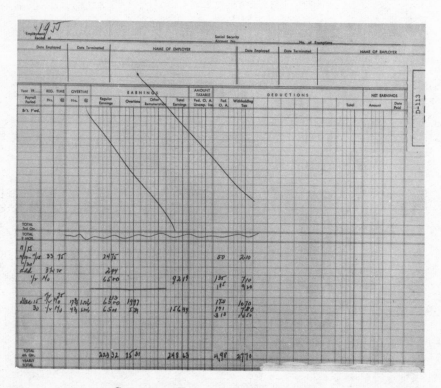

Commission Exhibit No. 2237—Continued

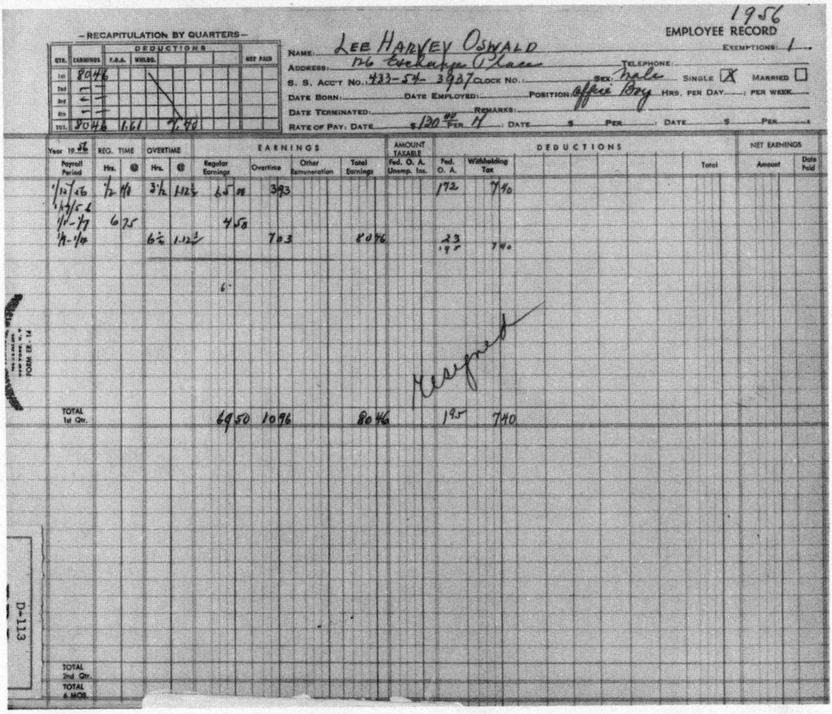

1956

EMPLOYEE RECORD

—RECAPITULATION BY QUARTERS—

QTR.	EARNINGS	F.O.A.	WHLDG.				NET PAID
1st	80 46						
2nd	—						
3rd	—						
4th	—						
TOT.	80 46	1.61	7.40				

NAME: LEE HARVEY OSWALD EXEMPTIONS: 1

ADDRESS: 126 Exchange Place TELEPHONE:

S. S. ACC'T NO. 433-54-3937 CLOCK NO.: SEX: Male SINGLE [X] MARRIED [ ]

DATE BORN: DATE EMPLOYED: POSITION: Office Boy HRS. PER DAY: PER WEEK:

DATE TERMINATED: REMARKS:

RATE OF PAY: DATE $120.00 PER M. DATE $ PER DATE $ PER

Year 1956 Payroll Period	REG. TIME Hrs.	@	OVERTIME Hrs.	@	EARNINGS Regular Earnings	Overtime	Other Remuneration	Total Earnings	AMOUNT TAXABLE Fed. O. A. Unemp. Ins.	DEDUCTIONS Fed. O. A.	Withholding Tax	Total	NET EARNINGS Amount	Date Paid
1/12/56	½	4/0	3½	1.12½	65 08	3 93				1 72	7 40			
1/13/56														
1/1–1/7	6	75			4 50									
1/9–1/14			6½	1.12½		7 03		80 46		23 / 1 95	7 40			
TOTAL 1st Qtr.					69 50	10 96		80 46		1 95	7 40			
TOTAL 2nd Qtr.														
TOTAL 6 MOS.														

Resigned

D-113

Commission Exhibit No. 2237—Continued

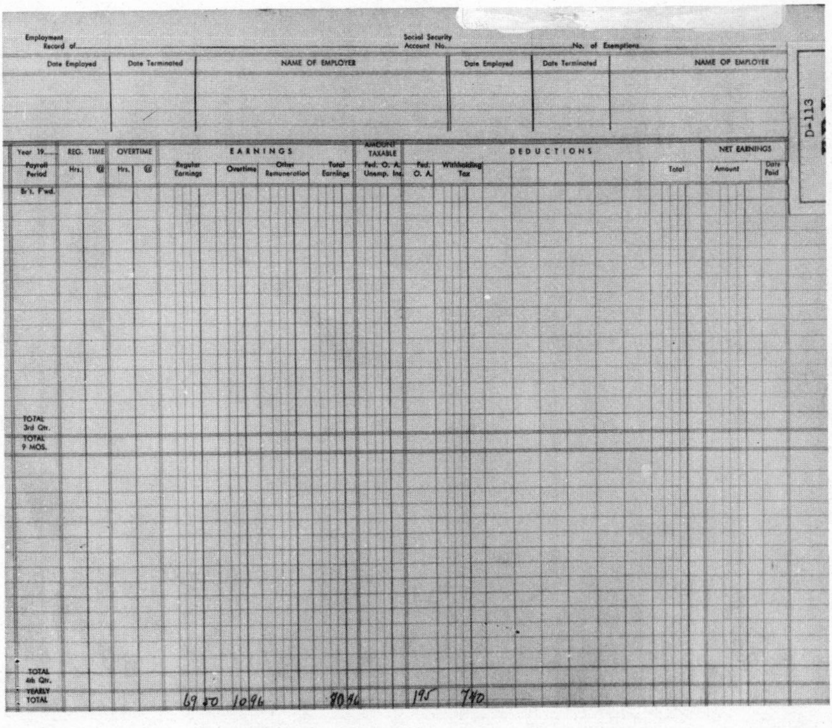

Employment Record of ________ Social Security Account No. ________ No. of Exemptions ________

Date Employed	Date Terminated	NAME OF EMPLOYER	Date Employed	Date Terminated	NAME OF EMPLOYER

Year 19__ Payroll Period	REG. TIME Hrs.	@	OVERTIME Hrs.	@	EARNINGS Regular Earnings	Overtime	Other Remuneration	Total Earnings	AMOUNT TAXABLE Fed. O. A. Unemp. Ins.	DEDUCTIONS Fed. O. A.	Withholding Tax	Total	NET EARNINGS Amount	Date Paid
Br't. Fw'd.														
TOTAL 3rd Qtr.														
TOTAL 9 MOS.														
TOTAL 4th Qtr.														
YEARLY TOTAL					69 50	10 96		80 46		1 95	7 40			

D-113

Commission Exhibit No. 2237—Continued

FD-302 (Rev. 1-25-60)

FEDERAL BUREAU OF INVESTIGATION

Date 1/29/64

1

On January 28, 1964, Mr. MAURY GOODMAN, sales manager, Berland Shoe Company, 4241 Folsom Avenue, St. Louis, Missouri, was interviewed and at first could not recall ever having known LEE HARVEY OSWALD. Upon mention by the interviewing agent of Mrs. MARGUERITE OSWALD having worked for GOODMAN at the Dolly Shoe Company, in New Orleans, Louisiana, GOODMAN was able to recall LEE HARVEY OSWALD. GOODMAN stated that he could not recall the exact dates of employment for either OSWALD or OSWALD's mother, but felt that it was sometime in 1955. GOODMAN stated that he, GOODMAN, joined the Dolly Shoe Company in February, 1955, as a partner, but left the company in October, 1957. He does not know who would have the books of the company or the original pay records.

GOODMAN recalled that MARGUERITE OSWALD was a cashier and sales clerk at the company, and recalled that she was a very pleasant person and a very good worker. GOODMAN said that at one time, she had asked him to employ her son LEE, so as to "help keep the boy off the street and give him something to do."

GOODMAN said that LEE HARVEY OSWALD worked for him mostly on Saturdays and sometimes a day or two during the week, but that his employment was strictly on a part time basis. He said that basically LEE HARVEY OSWALD was a stock boy, but that they had attempted at one time to train him in sales work, but with no success.

GOODMAN remembered OSWALD as being a "nice, pleasant little boy, but with not much sense." GOODMAN was unable to recall much of OSWALD's character, but stated that to the best of his recollection, he had never heard OSWALD make any threats against the U. S. Government or anyone in it, nor could he recall OSWALD as ever having expressed any interest in any subversive groups or parties.

GOODMAN said that OSWALD's mother, MARGUERITE, **left** the Dolly Shoe Company while, he, GOODMAN, was **still** the manager, but he could not recall what her next **employment** was.

On 1/28/64 at St. Louis, Missouri File # SL 105-3665

by SA JOHN H. CREECH:sam Date dictated 1/29/64

COMMISSION EXHIBIT No. 2238

SL 105-3665
2

Mr. GOODMAN said that he, GOODMAN, now resides at 9774 Lindley Drive, Olivette, Missouri.

COMMISSION EXHIBIT No. 2238—Continued

FD-302 (Rev. 3-3-59) FEDERAL BUREAU OF INVESTIGATION

1

Date December 13, 1963

Mrs. JAMES L. TAYLOR, 4936 Collinswood, stated that she is the managr of the apartment building at that address. She stated that according to her records, she rented the upper west apartment at that address on July 1, 1956 to Mrs. MARGUERITE OSWALD. Mrs. OSWALD was accompanied by her two sons, LEE and ROBERT. Mrs. OSWALD was in the act of moving to Fort Worth from New Orleans, Louisiana. Mrs. OSWALD remained in this apartment until June 1, 1957. At the time she departed from the apartment, she owed Mrs. TAYLOR $6.60 for utility bills. Mrs. OSWALD moved to 1031 West 5th Street in Fort Worth. Mrs. TAYLOR contacted Mrs. OSWALD at that address on two or three occasions, and Mrs. OSWALD refused to pay the utility bills.

Mrs. TAYLOR stated that a few weeks after the OSWALDs moved into the apartment, ROBERT married and moved away from this address. She stated that LEE was 16 years of age and about three months after they moved into the apartment, he became 17 and at that time he quit school and enlisted in the United States Marines. He was attending Arlington Heights High School at the time he quit school. She stated that she never did see LEE OSWALD after he enlisted in the United States Marines. She also stated that she has never seen Mrs. OSWALD or ROBERT since the mother moved out of this apartment on June 1, 1957.

During the time Mrs. OSWALD resided at her apartment, Mrs. OSWALD was engaged in selling ladies' hose in a shoe store in Fort Worth. She stated the store was Paul's Shoe Store. On one occasion, Mrs. OSWALD told her that she had been fired from a job because she refused to do some chore which the manager requested.

[redacted]

Commission Exhibit No. 2239

on 12/12/63 at Fort Worth, Texas File # DL 100-10461

by Special Agent ROBLEY D. MADLAND and B. TOM CARTER/rms Date dictated 12/13/63

This document contains neither recommendations nor conclusions of the FBI. It is the property of the FBI and is loaned to your agency; it and its contents are not to be distributed outside your agency.

COMMISSION EXHIBIT No. 2239

FD-302 (Rev. 3-3-59) FEDERAL BUREAU OF INVESTIGATION

1

Date December 13,1963

Mrs. EDWIN ENOCHS, 4936 Collinswood, stated that she lived in the adjoining apartment to the one occupied by Mrs. OSWALD and her two sons. Mrs. ENOCHS stated that LEE OSWALD was a lone wolf type individual just like his mother, Mrs. MARGUERITE OSWALD. She stated that LEE remained in the apartment practically all the time and was constantly reading books and when he was not reading, he was playing with a bird, a parakeet, which he owned. She stated that ROBERT was only in the apartment for a very short time before getting married and after he was married, he moved away. She stated that Mrs. MARGUERITE OSWALD in her opinion had a persecution complex against society in general.

She explained that Mrs. OSWALD was constantly complaining that everyone was against her and that her employers were not fair to her. Mrs. OSWALD told her that she had been fired from two jobs while she was residing in the apartment. Mrs. ENOCHS stated that as she recalls, LEE never played with any other boys and so far as she recalls, only one boy came by to see him on one occasion. This is the only time she remembers seeing anyone in company with LEE.

on 12/12/63 at Fort Worth, Texas File # DL 100-10461

by Special Agent ROBLEY D. MADLAND and B. TOM CARTER/rms Date dictated 12/13/63

This document contains neither recommendations nor conclusions of the FBI. It is the property of the FBI and is loaned to your agency; it and its contents are not to be distributed outside your agency.

COMMISSION EXHIBIT No. 2239—Continued

FD-204 (Rev. 3-3-59)

UNITED STATES DEPARTMENT OF JUSTICE
FEDERAL BUREAU OF INVESTIGATION

Copy to:

Report of: SA RICHARD L. KESLER   Office: CHARLOTTE
Date: 12/18/63

Field Office File #: 105-1731   Bureau File #:

Title: LEE HARVEY OSWALD

Character: INTERNAL SECURITY - RUSSIA

Synopsis: Records of Socialist Party maintained by Duke University, Durham, N. C., contain handwritten letter dated 10/3/56 from one LEE OSWALD, 4936 Collinwood, Ft. Worth, Texas. Letter advises writer is 16 years of age, a Marxist and has been studying Socialist principles for over 15 months. Letter requested information regarding "Youth League." Records also contain advertisement coupon of "The Socialist Call," New York, which was filled in with name and address of LEE OSWALD as above and requested more information about the Socialist Party. Following handwritten notation appeared at bottom of this coupon: "Sent additional lit. 10/9/56."

\- P -

DETAILS:

AT DURHAM, NORTH CAROLINA

Set forth hereinafter is information concerning correspondence with Socialist Party from one LEE OSWALD, Ft. Worth, Texas, in 1956.

[redacted]

Commission Exhibit No. 2240

COMMISSION EXHIBIT No. 2240

FD-302 (Rev. 1-25-60)

FEDERAL BUREAU OF INVESTIGATION

Date 12/18/63

On December 18, 1963, Dr. BENJAMIN E. POWELL, Librarian, Duke University Library, Durham, North Carolina, advised that during routine processing of inactive files of the Socialist Party of America in possession of the Duke University Library Manuscript Collection, the following items were found:

A. Handwritten letter dated October 3, 1956, which reads as follows:

"Oct. 3, 1956

"Dear Sirs;

"I am sixteen years of age and would like more information about your youth League, I would like to know if there is a branch in my area, how to join, ect., I am a Marxist, and have been studying socialist principles for well over fifteen months_ I am very interested in your Y.P.S.L.

"Sincerely

"/s/ Lee Oswald

"(Addrese over)

"Send To;

"Lee Oswald
4936 Collinwood
Forth Worth,
Tex."

B. Advertisement coupon of "The Socialist Call," 303 4th Avenue, New York 10, New York. This advertisement coupon contained three blocks to be checked as follows:

___ Enclosed please find.........($3.00 for one year's subscription) for a subscription to the Socialist Call.

On 12/18/63 at Durham, N. C. File # Charlotte 105-1731

by SA CHARLES S. MILLER/cjs Date dictated 12/18/63

COMMISSION EXHIBIT No. 2240—Continued

CE 105-1731

_____ I want more information about the Socialist Party.

_____ I want to join the Socialist Party.

The only block which was checked was the second one above and the following name and address was hand printed on the coupon:

"LEE OSWALD
4936 Collinwood
Forth Worth
Texas"

The following handwritten notation appeared on the bottom of the coupon:

"Sent additional lit. 10/9/56."

Photostat copies of these items were made available. The originals are being maintained in the Manuscript Collection of the Library. In the event it is necessary to subpoena them the subpoena should be directed to Dr. MATTIE RUSSELL, Curator of Manuscripts, Duke University Library, Durham, North Carolina.

3

COMMISSION EXHIBIT No. 2240—Continued

FD-302 (Rev. 3-3-59)

FEDERAL BUREAU OF INVESTIGATION

Date January 17, 1964

1

Mr. SANER DAVIS, King Candy Company, 813 E. Ninth, furnished the following information. Records of this company reflect Mrs. MARGUERITE OSWALD was employed by King Candy Company in August of 1958. She terminated her services in June of 1959. During this time, she was employed as a Saleslady in the candy department of Fair Ridglea Department Store. During the latter part of her employment, a jar fell from a shelf and hit her on the nose. She filed a claim against the company and employed an attorney. The injury was slight, but the case was settled for approximately $2750. LEE HARVEY OSWALD was never employed by this company. There was no derogatory information concerning the loyalty of Mrs. OSWALD.

— Commission Exhibit No. 2241 —

on 1/16/64 at Fort Worth, Texas File # DL 100-10461

by Special Agent EARLE HALEY:mja Date dictated 1/16/64

COMMISSION EXHIBIT No. 2241

— Commission Exhibit No. 2242

FD-302 (Rev. 3-3-59)

FEDERAL BUREAU OF INVESTIGATION

1

Date November 29, 1963

Doctor COLEMAN JACOBSON, 6121 Preston Haven Drive, Specialist in Dermatology, advised he has been acquainted with JACK RUBY for about 8 years, during which time he has seen him on a professional basis, perhaps six or eight times. He stated his treatments of RUBY were for minor skin irritations, such as fungus. He stated there was nothing in his medical history insofar as he knew which would reflect upon the recent action of RUBY, namely the assassination of LEE HARVEY OSWALD.

Dr. JACOBSON stated that RUBY told him a number of years ago that he had a "metal plate" in his head but JACOBSON stated he knew none of the details concerning this and was only reminded of this after reading the reports of RUBY's background in the local newspapers.

Dr. JACOBSON stated that a number of years ago he learned RUBY was single, after which he occasionally invited RUBY to his home during holidays to visit. He stated RUBY appeared to be a very pleasant and congenial individual and insofar as he knew, honorable. Dr. JACOBSON stated he never noted anything impulsive about RUBY's personality and considered him very sentimental and sensitive, particularly concerning animals, as RUBY kept a number of dogs, which he seemed to love dearly. Dr. JACOBSON stated RUBY seemed to adore children and enjoyed associating with them very much.

Dr. JACOBSON stated that he knew of nothing "shady" about the endeavors of RUBY. He further stated that he had been in the night club operated by RUBY not more than an average of once a year, and the close acquaintances and associates of RUBY were unknown to Dr. JACOBSON. He heard RUBY say on a number of occasions he carried a gun because of the fact that he frequently maintained the proceeds from his business establishments on his person. He stated he last saw RUBY personally about September, 1963.

Dr. JACOBSON stated at approximately 4:00 or 5:00 p.m. on Friday, November 22, 1963, he received a telephone call

on 11/27/63 at Dallas, Texas File # DL 44-1639

by Special Agent S NORMAN W. PROPST & URAL E. HORTON, JR./csh Date dictated 11/28/63

204

2

DL 44-1639

at his office from RUBY who wanted to know at what time the memorial services for former President KENNEDY were to be held at the synagogue. Dr. JACOBSON recalled RUBY was extremely emotional during their short conversation and stated in view of the President's assassination he was very desirous of going to the synagogue for services. Dr. JACOBSON could recall no other discussion during the short telephonic conversation.

Dr. JACOBSON advised he did not recall hearing JACK RUBY ever relate his political views, and he could not recall RUBY speaking of former President KENNEDY in any manner.

Dr. JACOBSON advised he had seen EVE GRANT, the sister of JACK RUBY, on just a couple of occasions and did not know whether she was married or divorced. He stated the other relatives and the family history of JACK RUBY are unknown to him.

Dr. JACOBSON stated he would review his medical history records of JACK RUBY in an effort to determine additional facts concerning the medical history of JACK RUBY.

(4)

205

FD-302 (Rev. 1-25-60) 'EDERAL BUREAU OF — Commission Exhibit No. 2243 [redacted]

1

Date 11/26/63

ALEXANDER P. GRUBER, 5222 West Olympic Boulevard, Los Angeles, California, on November 25, 1963, advised he has known JACK RUBY for approximately 40 years. He stated they lived in the 20th Ward of Chicago and attended the same grammar school. He advised that when they were approximately 20 years of age, they shared an apartment for about one year which was on the corner of Wilson Avenue and Claredon in Chicago. He stated that he always know RUBY as JAKE RUBENSTEIN.

He advised that after living in the apartment with RUBY that he, GRUBER, moved to New York and had no contact whatsoever with RUBY for many years. He stated about ten years ago, while he was passing through Dallas, Texas, he again met with RUBY, at which time RUBY owned a bar called the Silver Spur. GRUBER recalled on that occasion that he observed RUBY in a fight in the Silver Spur when RUBY ejected two men who he did not want on the premises. He recalled that RUBY told him he always stayed in shape.

GRUBER stated he last saw RUBY about two weeks ago when he was returning from the East and passed through Dallas. He again met with RUBY at his night club. He recalled that RUBY told him that the police liked him because he stays out of trouble and runs a good place. On the occasion of this last visit, RUBY told GRUBER that a number of years ago, a former prize fighter had a "beef" with RUBY and said he was going to get RUBY. RUBY stated he purchased a gun to protect himself and then notified friends on the Dallas Police Department that he had been threatened and that he had purchased a gun. The police officers told him to let them have the gun, that he did not need it because he could take care of himself and it would only get him into trouble. RUBY stated he gave the gun to the officers. Later the prize fighter appeared at RUBY's bar when Dallas police officers were present. RUBY and the fighter started to fight and Dallas police officers told observers to leave them alone and to let them settle it themselves. RUBY told GRUBER that he gave the prize fighter a good beating and after it was all over, Dallas police officers gave RUBY's gun back to him.

GRUBER stated that RUBY told him on the occasion of his last visit that he was having business trouble with his sister, EVE GRANT.

On 11/25/63 at Los Angeles, California File # Los Angeles 44-895

by SA ROBERT K. BURESH and SA VINCENT W. HUGHES/bje Date dictated 11/26/63

273

COMMISSION EXHIBIT No. 2243

2
LA 44-895

GRUBER stated he stayed in Dallas one night and part of the following day and returned directly to Los Angeles. He stated he had no further contact with RUBY until the day the President was shot. He stated that about twenty minutes after the news of the shooting was on television, he received a long distance telephone call from Dallas from JACK RUBY. He stated RUBY was very upset and talked "like a guy who had blown his top." GRUBER stated the conversation was as follows:

RUBY: "Did you hear what happened?"
GRUBER: "You mean the shooting of the President?"
RUBY: "Yes, ain't that a terrible thing. I'm all upset and my sister is hysterical. You don't know this AL, but I started all of my programs with a patriotic number."

GRUBER stated that at that point, RUBY began to cry and he told GRUBER, "I'm crying and I can't talk to you any more" whereupon he hung up the telephone.

GRUBER referred interviewing agents to Mr. AL DUNN as a person who was acquainted with RUBY.

GRUBER stated that at 12:45 a.m. on November 25, 1963, an anonymous telephone call was received at his residence asking for AL GRUBER. When advised that Mr. GRUBER was not home, the anonymous caller stated, "Ask him if he likes livin" then hung up. GRUBER stated he assumed this was an anonymous threat because his name had appeared in the newspapers as an acquaintance of JACK RUBY.

274

COMMISSION EXHIBIT No. 2243—Continued

— Commission Exhibit No. 2244 — —

FD-302 (Rev. 3-3-59)

FEDERAL BUREAU OF INVESTIGATION

Date 11-25-63

1

Lieutenant JAMES R. GILMORE, Platoon Supervisor, Vice Section, Dallas, Texas, states he has known JACK RUBY for approximately 12 years during which time he, GILMORE, has had quite frequent contact with RUBY while on duty. He stated during the nights when he is on duty he usually makes an appearance at the Carousel and Vegas Night Clubs, operated by RUBY, as well as many similar establishment throughout the city of Dallas. He stated his duties were of a supervisory nature as he has subordinates on duty in various areas. He states his contacts with RUBY have never been on a social level and he denied ever having lengthy conversations with RUBY during these contacts.

GILMORE informed he had never been employed by RUBY nor had he accepted any gratuities from RUBY. He further advised he never knew RUBY to carry a gun nor had RUBY ever expressed to him any of his political beliefs.

GILMORE stated he believed RUBY dated some girl steadily approximately three years ago, however, he does not know her identity nor did he know the identity of any present close female associate of RUBY. GILMORE had no information relating to possible homosexuality on the part of RUBY.

GILMORE stated he was in the Dallas Police Department Building on Friday night after the afternoon assassination of President KENNEDY at which time he recalled seeing RUBY in one of the passage ways. He stated he chatted briefly with RUBY, who, he stated did not appear any more upset or disturbed than anyone else over the activities of the day.

RUBY told GILMORE he had distributed some sandwiches to the KLIF Radio Station employees who were in the building. GILMORE recalled seeing RUBY in the basement of the building that same night, however, he stated he did not pay him any attention in view of all the other activities.

GILMORE stated he did not know if RUBY was associated with LEE HARVEY OSWALD and further that he had no idea how RUBY might have gained entrance to the basement of the Police Department Building at the time OSWALD was assassinated.

GILMORE specifically stated, as near as he could recall, that he actually saw RUBY on two occasions, at which time he was associated with no one in particular, on the night of the assassination of President KENNEDY, at the police station.

on 11-25-63 at Dallas, Texas File # DL 44-1639

by Special Agent NORMAN W. PROPST & URAL E. HORTON, JR. - md Date dictated 11-26-63

322

2

DL 44-1639

The first time was approximately midnight in the Police Assembly Room where District Attorney HENRY WADE was holding a press conference.

GILMORE was of the belief that he had also seen him a few minutes later in one of the outside passageways near the Police Department Records Bureau. GILMORE stated RUBY appeared to be just standing and watching the activities on each occasion but he could not be sure.

GILMORE stated that on Sunday, November 24, 1963, at which time he was at home, he observed the shooting of OSWALD by RUBY on television.

323

FD-302 (Rev. 3-3-59)

FEDERAL BUREAU OF [redacted]

1

Date 11/26/63

Mr. BILL ALEXANDER, Assistant District Attorney, Dallas, Texas, telephonically advised at 5:37 p.m. that on November 21, 1963, JACK RUBY came to the District Attorney's Office regarding four bad checks which had been written by one ROBERT E. CRAVEN. He said that three of these checks were in the amount of $100.00 and one was in the amount of $122.59. He said they determined that CRAVEN had been arrested in Los Angeles recently but had made bond. However, CRAVEN's wife had written to them in an effort to make good the checks. He said that the letterhead for CRAVEN's wife was RITA CRAVEN, dba Craven Contracting Company, 407 E. Peco Boulevard, Room 800, Los Angeles, California, telephone 474-5866. He said that CRAVEN had been in Dallas in October, 1963, and had a display at the Texas State Fair entitled "How Hollywood Makes Movies". He advised that their office or members of the Check Squad of the Dallas Police Department, had contacted Los Angeles Police Department and verified that CRAVEN had been arrested in Los Angeles and had made bond. His whereabouts is unknown. He said he felt that RUBY had been in the office merely to make inquiry concerning CRAVEN, who was a friend of his, and that he possibly made the inquiries at the request of CRAVEN.

on 11/26/63 at Dallas, Texas File # DL 44-1639

by Special Agent ROBERT E. BASHAM:jj:cv Date dictated 11/26/63

FD-302 (Rev. 3-3-59)

FEDERAL BUREAU OF INVESTIGATION

1

Date 11/26/63

PHILLIP P. MILLER, 1122 Apartment D, Central Park Place, advised he is the owner of Phil's Delicatessens, located at 3531 Oaklawn, Dallas, Texas, and at 11111 Central Expressway, Dallas, Texas. Mr. MILLER advised he has known JACK RUBY for approximately eleven years, as RUBY has been a good customer during that period of time and has frequented his business establishments. He advised he has never had any social relationships with JACK RUBY, but from all of his observations of Mr. RUBY when RUBY happened to be in one of his places of business, RUBY seemed to be a very fine person. He advised Mr. RUBY was a regular church-goer and a member of the Shearith Israel Synagogue on Douglas Street, Dallas. He advised he has never observed Mr. RUBY in the company of LEE HARVEY OSWALD, and he, MILLER, has never met OSWALD.

Mr. MILLER advised he does not know any of the political beliefs of JACK RUBY and could furnish no information as to background or associates other than the above.

Mr. MILLER advised he was not in his Oak Lawn Store on the night of November 22, 1963, but had been at his Oak Lawn Store on the night of November 21, 1963, at which time JACK RUBY was in the store. He said he did not talk with RUBY and as best he could recall, RUBY was by himself or possibly with his sister, EVA GRANT. He advised he could not say for sure, however, because he was very busy at the time and recalls only the fact that RUBY was in the store for a few moments.

on 11/26/63 at Dallas, Texas File # DL 44-1639

by Special Agents RAYMOND M. LESTER, JR AND JAMES S. WEIR: mam Date dictated 11/26/63

FD-302 (Rev. 3-3-59)

FEDERAL BUREAU OF INVESTIGATION

1

Date 11/25/63

MARGUERITE VEA RIEGLER, in care of Smith Hall, SMU, Dallas, Texas, advised that on Friday night, November 22, 1963, she was at Phil's Delicatessen, 3531 Oak Lawn, Dallas, Texas, in the company of RITA SILVERMAN, a friend, BILL NICHOLS, DENNIS MARTIN and BOB SINDELOR (phonetic), sophomores at SMU. She advised that they went to Phil's Delicatessen at approximately 10:30 p.m. to have a coke and as they were sitting at their table a man walked up to the table and took their newspaper. The man opened the newspaper, began looking at it and very rudely asked if he might look at their paper to which they replied, "Yes". She advised he looked at the amusement section of the newspaper and immediately went to a telephone located approximately 25 to 30 feet from where they were sitting and dialed a number. She advised none of the group paid any attention, and she could not state whether or not he actually talked on the telephone but that approximately ten minutes later he returned to their table and again asked if he might look at the paper. Miss RIEGLER stated permission was again given and he repeated his former action and about ten minutes later again returned to the table this time somewhat embarrassed and pointed out to them in the paper advertisements for the Carousel and Vegas Clubs. He asked them if they knew of these clubs and stated that he was the owner of the clubs. He made conversation concerning some musicians who had played at the clubs and then proceeded to make a third telephone call. She said that after he finished the third telephone call he returned to the table to talk with one of the boys in the group about musicians who had played at the club. As he left the table he turned to the front page of the paper which was covered with news and photographs concerning the shooting of President KENNEDY and made the remark, "Wasn't that a horrible thing". Miss RIEGLER advised that on Sunday when the news concerning the murder of LEE HARVEY OSWALD was broadcast on television she immediately recognized the photograph of JACK RUBY as being the person who had been at Phil's Delicatessen on Friday night and talked with her and her company. She said while he was at the delicatessen RUBY was alone but appeared to be very familiar with the store and with the persons working in the store. She described him as appearing as though he were at home.

Miss RIEGLER advised she could furnish no information concerning the telephone calls or attempted telephone calls made by RUBY.

on 11/25/63 at Dallas, Texas File # DL 44-1603

by Special Agent RAYMOND M. LESTER, JR. cv Date dictated 11/25/63

673

This document contains neither recommendations nor conclusions of the FBI. It is the property of the FBI and is loaned to your agency; it and its contents are not to be distributed outside your agency.

COMMISSION EXHIBIT No. 2247

FD-302 (Rev. 3-3-59)

FEDERAL BUREAU OF INVESTIGATION

Date 11/29/63

1

Detective RICHARD M. SIMS, Homicide & Robbery Bureau, Dallas Police Department, residence, 8483 Sweetwater Drive, Dallas, Texas, was contacted for the purpose of verifying a telephone call JACK RUBY claimed to have been made to Detective SIMS during the evening of November 22, 1963.

Detective SIMS recalled answering the telephone in the Homicide & Robbery Bureau, Dallas Police Department, during the evening of November 22, 1963, on one occasion, when the person calling said, "This is JACK RUBY. I know you are busy. I've got some sandwiches for you." SIMS said he told RUBY the Homicide & Robbery Bureau Officers had already eaten (in relays) and that the sandwiches would not be needed. He recalled he thanked RUBY and that RUBY said, "Alright."

SIMS said he did not recall RUBY mentioning anything about Radio Station KLIF, Dallas, during the conversation, and he (SIMS) did not know what disposition RUBY made of the sandwiches. SIMS advised, however, he gained the definite impression during the course of the telephone conversation that RUBY had already bought the sandwiches and had them with him at the time he made the call to the Homicide & Robbery Bureau. He further related that RUBY gave no information as to his whereabouts at the time he made the above telephone call.

SIMS advised it is his best recollection the above telephone conversation with RUBY occurred sometime between 9:00 PM and 10:30 PM, November 22, 1963. He said it is also his definite recollection this call was made sometime prior to taking LEE HARVEY OSWALD to an assembly room in the Dallas Police Department Headquarters for a "show-up," attended by Dallas County District Attorney HENRY WADE, law enforcement officers, and representatives of the press, radio and television media. SIMS said he helped escort OSWALD to the assembly room where the above "show-up" was held; however, he does not recall seeing RUBY during the time he was escorting OSWALD to the assembly room. He said, in fact, he does not recall seeing RUBY in or about the premises of the Dallas Police Department at any time Friday night, November 22, 1963. SIMS volunteered, however, it would have been quite possible for RUBY to be somewhere around the Dallas Police Department Friday night, November 22, 1963, without his, SIMS, having seen RUBY.

SIMS volunteered he knows RUBY by sight, and has known him

on 11/28/63 at Dallas, Texas File # DL 44-1639

by Special Agent CASTON C. THOMPSON/eah 674 Date dictated 11/28/63

This document contains neither recommendations nor conclusions of the FBI. It is the property of the FBI and is loaned to your agency; it and its contents are not to be distributed outside your agency.

COMMISSION EXHIBIT No. 2248

DL 44-1639
GCT:eah

2

for approximately fifteen years, having been assigned to the South Dallas area approximately fifteen years ago when RUBY operated the "Silver Spur" in that area of Dallas. SIMS said he has never been employed by or worked for RUBY and has never associated with him on a social basis.

675

COMMISSION EXHIBIT No. 2248—Continued

Commission Exhibit No. 2249

December 24, 1963

Mr. J. E. Curry
Chief of Police

Sir:

You will find attached a summary and individual reports of investigations made by the unit you appointed on November 29, 1963, to investigate the shooting of Lee Harvey Oswald in the basement of the City Hall.

These reports are supplemental to the original report already transmitted and concerns investigations not directly connected with the shooting.

Respectfully,

O. A. Jones
O. A. Jones
Captain of Police

OAJ:mw

COMMISSION EXHIBIT No. 2249

December 24, 1963

Mr. J. E. Curry
Chief of Police

Subject: Investigations conducted in connection with the Jack Ruby case that were not Directly Involved with the Events of Sunday, November 24, 1963

Sir:

The investigative team appointed to conduct the investigation of events surrounding the shooting of Lee Harvey Oswald by Jack Ruby in the basement of the City Hall at 11:20 a.m., November 24, 1963, made many contacts that were not directly connected with the assigned work. The attached reports are the result of many such contacts.

The first attachment listed as A-I is a report of the temporary detention of William Frank Goffney, 3132 Morgan Drive, Dallas, Texas. The investigation disclosed Goffney had no connection with the shooting.

The reports listed as I are a series of reports confirming the fact that Jack Ruby was in the basement of the City Hall on November 22, 1963, and in other areas of the City Hall on November 22 and November 23, 1963. Several reports also indicate that Jack Ruby was near the County Jail and the Texas Depository Building on November 23, 1963.

The attached reports #2 are concerning previous arrests of Jack Ruby for carrying prohibited weapons. These incidents occurred on July 26, 1953 and May 1, 1954.

The attachments #3 are negative reports of investigation regarding leads that Lee Harvey Oswald and Jack Ruby were acquainted.

The attachments #4 are negative reports of investigations regarding reports of Dallas Police officers being involved with Jack Ruby.

The Attachment #5 is a report of the investigation regarding a lead from the F.B.I. that Dallas Police Car #207 stopped in front of 1026 N. Beckley at approximately 1:00 p.m. on November 22, 1963, at which time it is believed Lee Harvey Oswald entered his apartment.

Other investigations were made by this unit but reports were forwarded to the Homicide and Robbery Bureau as the information obtained was considered of use only in the criminal prosecution of Jack Ruby.

Respectfully,

O. A. Jones
Captain of Police

OAJ:mw

2.

COMMISSION EXHIBIT No. 2249—Continued

December 17, 1963

Mr. J. E. Curry
Chief of Police

Subject: William Frank Goffney c/m/31
3132 Morgan Drive

Sir:

We received information that the above subject was arrested running from the City Hall after the shooting of Lee Harvey Oswald.

I contacted Sergeant J. F. Everett December 13, 1963. Sergeant Everett stated as follows:

"I was on duty in the Dispatcher's Office and had walked into the hall of the third floor at the time of the shooting. Someone shouted to secure the building and I ran down the steps to the first floor. There I saw the subject William Goffney run towards the Harwood Street exit. Sergeant Putnam, Officer R. T. Davis #1887 and myself apprehended the subject on the steps of the City Hall. He was taken to the Homicide Bureau and interrogated by Detective T. L. Baker. It was determined this subject was apparently sightseeing on the first floor. He was later released.

This person works for Cockrell and Winniford, 2712 Live Oak, Telephone TA4-6741 - Home Phone, CA4-3419."

This investigation of William Goffney has not been carried any farther at this time.

Respectfully submitted,

P. G. McCaghren, Lieutenant
Burglary & Theft Bureau

PGM:mw

3

COMMISSION EXHIBIT No. 2249—Continued

December 23, 1963

Mr. J. E. Curry
Chief of Police

Sir:

The attached reports confirm that Jack Ruby was in the basement of the City Hall on November 22, 1963, on the third floor of the City Hall on November 22, 1963 or November 23, 1963, as well as near the County Jail and the Texas Depository Building on November 23, 1963.

Respectfully submitted,

O. A. Jones
Captain of Police

OAJ:mw

4

COMMISSION EXHIBIT No. 2249—Continued

INTERVIEW WITH WES WISE KRLD-TV NEWSMAN

I interviewed Wes Wise at 7:30 p.m. on November 29, 1963, at 1107 Camp, the KRLD-TV Newsroom.

Wes Wise said that about 3:00 p.m. Saturday, November 23, 1963, he was trying to retrace Lee Oswald's steps of the day before, as far as they could. He had parked his mobile unit on Houston Street across from the Texas Depository Book Building. His unit was parked headed diagonally in a southeasterly direction. Wise stated that he returned to his unit and as he was using his radio to communicate with his office, he saw someone walking to the unit from the direction of the railroad tracks which were located north of him.

Mr. Wise stated he rolled the window up as the figure neared his unit but the person remained outside until he completed his message. Wise said he then rolled the window down and the man stuck his hand in the window and said "I'm Jack Ruby". Wise then recognized him. Jack Ruby then said "All this was a shame and particularly for the President's children". Wise said he then told Ruby about going out to the Trade Mart and taking pictures of the box of saddles that had been a present to be given to the President for his children. He said that upon hearing this, Ruby's eyes misted over. He did not start crying, however.

Mr. Wise said that on Friday night, November 23, 1963, about 11:00 p.m. or later he heard a broadcast over KLIF that gave what the announcer thought was some exclusive lead or material. It concerned Mr. Henry Wade, the District Attorney, and gave Jack Ruby the credit for the lead.

Mr. Wise asked Ruby about this Saturday afternoon and Ruby said "yes, he had given that to them and would have done the same thing for him if he had been there". Wes thought the announcer's name might have been Russ Knight. He was not sure about this and does not know a "Russ Knight".

Mr. Wise also said that the only time he was in the City Hall was from 1½ to 2 hours or more before the shooting, when he drove through the basement of the City Hall and let some cameraman off. He did not see any officers at the Main Street entrance at this time. He did not see Jack Ruby at all and there were very few people in the basement.

Mr. Wise promised to let me know if he remembered anything further.

5

COMMISSION EXHIBIT No. 2249—Continued

December 12, 1963

Mr. J. E. Curry
Chief of Police

Subject: Jack Ruby Case

Sir:

Information was received that Officer Velt O'Dell had driven a car out the Main Street entrance shortly before Lieutenant Pierce emerged from this entrance. O'Dell was interrogated concerning this and he stated that he was not at the City Hall, but was summoned to the City Hall after Oswald was shot, and he drove a Squad Car into the Basement at that time, and when he left the City Hall he exited at the Commerce St. ramp.

Respectfully submitted,

W. R. Westbrook

W. R. Westbrook
Captain of Police
Personnel Bureau

WRW:fb

6

COMMISSION EXHIBIT No. 2249—Continued

December 16, 1963

Mr. J. E. Curry
Chief of Police

Subject: Jack Ruby

Sir:

On Saturday, November 23, 1963, Sergeant D. V. Harkness #471 was working traffic at the corner of Elm and Houston Streets. About 2:30 or 3:00 p.m. that date Sergeant Harkness observed Jack Ruby standing in the street and directed Ruby to get back on the sidewalk. This was on the corner by the Records Building.

Sergeant Harkness stated that he is acquainted with Jack Ruby and knows him on sight.

Respectfully submitted,

H M Hart

H. M. Hart, Detective
Special Service Bureau

HMH:nw

7.

COMMISSION EXHIBIT No. 2249—Continued

December 18, 1963

Mr. J. E. Curry
Chief of Police

Subject: Jack Ruby

Sir:

On Saturday, November 23, 1963, Patrolman P. N. Cooper, #1283 was assigned as point-control at Elm and Houston Streets. About 3:00 p.m. that date subject walked up to Officer Cooper and stated that it was a terrible thing that President Kennedy had been killed. Officer Cooper stated that Ruby had walked from the curb at the corner of the Records Building, crossed the street to Dealey Plaza.

Patrolman Cooper is not personally acquainted with Jack Ruby, however, has seen him on numerous occasions.

Respectfully submitted,

H M Hart

H. M. Hart, Detective
Special Service Bureau

HMH:mw

9.

COMMISSION EXHIBIT No. 2249—Continued

December 18, 1963

Mr. J. E. Curry
Chief of Police

Subject: Jack Ruby

Sir:

On Saturday, November 23, 1963, between 3:00 and 4:00 p.m. Patrolman James M. Chaney #469 was assigned in the Elm, Houston Streets area. Officer Chaney saw Jack Ruby in the park area near the Texas School Book Depository. Officer Chaney stated that Ruby approached him, pointed out 2 men across the street and asked if these men were Chief Curry and Captain Fritz, to which Officer Chaney replied "Yes". Jack Ruby then stated to Officer Chaney "It's a terrible thing that it had to happen in Dallas".

Officer Chaney has known Jack Ruby for several years.

Respectfully submitted,

H M Hart

H. M. Hart, Detective
Special Service Bureau

HMH:mw

9.

COMMISSION EXHIBIT No. 2249—Continued

November 27, 1963

Interview with Mr. Sam Pate, KBOX Radio.

Present Chief Batchelor.

Deputy Chief Stevenson.

Friday night, November 22, Mr. Pate observed Ruby in the Assembly Room, basement of the City Hall. He was about 4 or 5 rows of seats back from the platform on which a desk is located. Ruby was standing on a chair, table or something and was well above the majority of others present. Mr. Pate was sitting on the front edge of the platform facing the back of the room. When Ruby stood up, he saw no press badge on him. Ruby held in his hand a small,(looked like spiral) notebook - or it was about that size. He looked directly toward the platform on which Mr. Wade and others were standing, held up the small notebook which was open. Mr. Pate stated there appeared to be some writing (in pencil) on the notebook.

Mr. Pate stated that he remarked to Jerry Kunkle, also of KBOX, who was with him at the time, "There's Jack Ruby. How did he get in here?" Mr. Pate stated he knew Ruby well. After they left the Assembly Room, but still in the basement, Mr. Pate introduced Jack Ruby to Jerry Kunkle. Ruby had a handful of passes to the Carousel Club. He offered each of them a pass. Kunkle accepted a pass - Mr. Pate did not accept the pass.

Mr. Pate stated that he believes Ruby wrote down Mr. Kunkle's name on the back of one of the Club Passes which he held in his hand.

Mr. Pate stated that he did not see Ruby after this as he was not at the City Hall on Saturday or Sunday.

10.

November 27, 1963.

Subject: Interview with Ron Jenkins, KBOX

At approximately 11 AM, Chief Batchelor and Chief Stevenson interviewed Mr. Ron Jenkins of Radio Station KBOX regarding some information he had given Art Hammett regarding Jack Ruby being in the Police & Courts Building. Art Hammett was also present.

Mr. Jenkins stated he saw Jack Ruby on the Third Floor Friday night. That he was in about 5 or 6 feet of him.

He stated Sunday afternoon he heard a KLIF broadcast of a tape cut in conversation with Ruby's sister. She stated on the broadcast she believed Jack had a press pass or card.

Mr. Jenkins states he observed a man wearing a press badge bearing name of Jim Magnum, Associated Press. The man wearing the badge was not Magnum. He remarked to the man 'Jim Magnum' the man replied, "No, I just found it and put it on." He did know this man, however it was not Jack Ruby. He also states he found a press badge on the floor which belonged to a CBS reporter. He knew the man personally and returned it to him. He had lost it from his jacket.

He stated that Jack Ruby is quite an avid radio fan. That he is always offering members of the Radio Stations and press passes to his night clubs.

Mr. Jenkins stated that he had difficulty gaining admission Sunday morning to the City Hall. He was checked at Commerce Street entrance to the City Hall. He was checked at the top of the stairs leading from the first floor to the basement and was checked at the foot of the stairs in the basement by a plainclothes man.

11.

December 1, 1963

Mr. J. E. Curry
Chief of Police

Re: Jack Ruby

Sir:

On Firday night, November 22, 1963 at around 11:50 pm, I was going off duty in the Burglary and Theft Bureau. I left the third floor and went to the basement of the Police Building with Lt. George Butler who was going to drive me to where my car was parked. He told me that he wanted to listen to a press conference in the Police Assembly Room which was being held for the purpose of the press interviewing District Attorney Henry Wade and giving them an opportunity to photograph Lee Harvey Oswald, suspected assassin of President Kennedy and Officer J. D. Tippitt.

As we entered the police assembly room, it was entirely filled from back to front with press people and police officers and officials. I estimate that there were about 300 people in this room, many of them standing on the desks and chairs. Deputy Chief Charles Batchelor was at the front of the room near Mr. Wade. He saw me at the door of the room and motioned for me to come over to him. He then instructed me to stand in a line of officers at the front of the room to keep the press or anyone from rushing Oswald when he was brought into this room. I was standing at the right end of the line, next to Captain Glenn King who was on my left. This was immediately prior to Oswalds being brought into this room. I did observe Jack Ruby at this time, standing on a desk next to the east wall and about 25 feet from the front of the room. He had a notebook and pen in his hand as if to take notes. At this time someone near the door shouted to him about what he was doing in this room. He shouted back that he had "brought the sandwiches." He then shouted "I'm interpreting for a Jewish newspaper." At this time, Oswald was brought into the room and Ruby was forgotten.

After Oswald was taken from this room, Mr. Wade conducted his interview. He had trouble being heard due to the noise and clamer in this room, so I turned on the loud speaker system for him. Being unable to leave Mr. Wade's platform, I remained at his right side until he finished his interview. I then left the building with Lt. Butler. I have known Jack Ruby since about 1951 and did not know that he had a police record.

Respectfully submitted,

[signature]
T. B. Leonard, Lieutenant
Burglary & Theft Bureau

lh

12.

COMMISSION EXHIBIT NO. 2249—Continued

December 11, 1963

Mr. J. E. Curry
Chief of Police

Re: Interview with Jimmy Darnell,
Cameraman WBAP-TV

Sir:

The subject was interviewed on December 10, 1963.

Darnell was not present in the basement on Sunday, November 24, 1963.

Darnell stated the only time he ever saw Jack Ruby was Friday night, November 22, 1963, or early Saturday morning, November 23, 1963. He said he took about 500 feet of film in the Assembly Room during Mr. Henry Wade's press conference. He said a few minutes later out in the hallway outside of the Records Bureau, Reporter John Rutledge of the Dallas Morning News pointed out a man that Rutledge said was "a very mean man". Darnell told him something about Ruby biting a man's nose off and the man stating that Ruby "fought like a woman". Rutledge said he had talked to the victim but did not remember who he was. Rutledge told Darnell it occurred about eight or ten years ago.

Darnell said he did not recall any other information that might be of value to us.

Respectfully submitted,

[signature]
O. A. Jones
Captain of Police

OAJ:mw

13.

COMMISSION EXHIBIT NO. 2249—Continued

Mr. J. E. Curry
Chief of Police

December 5, 1963

Re: Interview with John Rutledge,
Dallas Morning News

Sir:

I interviewed Mr. Rutledge at 6:00 p.m. on Monday evening, December 2, 1963.

He denied ever seeing Jack Ruby with a press pass and had no information that any officer had told Jack Ruby that he could go up and see Oswald.

He remembers that before 6:00 p.m. on November 22, 1963, that he was standing by the door leading into the Burglary and Theft Bureau and that he saw Jack Ruby standing real close to some newsmen. Captain Fritz was being interviewed by a group of newsmen. Some newsman asked who was being interviewed and Rutledge said Ruby answered thusly: "Will-W I L L, Fritz-F R I T Z. Mr. Rutledge saw about 4 officers speak to Ruby during the time of the interview. He also saw Ruby at another time standing near newsmen just outside the door leading to the Forgery Bureau. He does not remember Ruby talking to anyone at this time.

Rutledge states that almost everytime he saw Ruby, that Ruby was physically crowding himself against newsmen.

Mr. Rutledge says on another ocassion, does not remember if it was Friday, November 22, 1963 or Saturday, November 23, 1963, he was near the elevator on the third floor of the Police and Courts Building. Uniformed guards were checking people entering the third floor. He saw two newsmen walk from the elevators to the hallway leading to the CID Bureau Offices. These two men were newsmen but he does not know who they were. Jack Ruby was pushed up between them with his left arm around the newsman to his left and a piece of folded paper in his other hand. This paper had some writing on it but Rutledge did not know what the writing was. Ruby was talking and waving the paper to the two newsmen as they turned down the hallway toward the Homicide Office. He did not see a press identification or pass on Ruby and the officers apparently allowed the 3 to pass them without checking identification. Rutledge said about midnight of Friday, November 22, 1963, there was a press conference and

14.

Page 2

show-up in the Assembly Room in the basement of the City Hall. He said Oswald was shown. Henry Wade also gave a press conference. Rutledge said that the conference was divided in two parts. The first part was to a roomful of newsmen and upon conclusion of this conference some of the TV newsmen requested that Henry answer some more questions so the TV cameras could get it. Rutledge said he saw another Dallas news reporter, Harry McCormack and asked Harry if he would cover the rest of the conference while he, Rutledge, was phoning in what he had already obtained.

Mr. Rutledge left to phone in his report and when he returned, many of the newsmen had gone. He remembers that he could not find Harry McCormack and while looking for him, he continued looking around the room. Mr. Henry Wade was at the desk and Judge David Johnston was seated across the desk in front of Mr. Wade. Mr. Rutledge saw Jack Ruby standing between the second and third row desk directly in front of Judge Johnston. He saw Ruby lean over toward Judge Johnston as far as he could and hand a business type card that had a red circle on one end of the card in his hand. Judge Johnston leaned toward him as far as he could and took the card.

Mr. Rutledge then left the assembly room through a rear door that led into the Records Bureau. He went to the second desk north of Captain Slaughter's Office in the first row of desks that are west of the row of filing cabinets running north and south through the center of the Records Bureau.

Mr. Rutledge used a phone on this desk and he saw Jack Ruby using a telephone on the first desk south of him. This would be the first desk in the same row as was the desk Rutledge was using, and would be the desk closest to the entrance to the Records Bureau adjacent to Captain Slaughter's Office.

The District Attorney, Mr. Henry Wade, then entered the Records Bureau through the entrance near Captain Slaughter's Office. Jack Ruby was calling and motioning Mr. Wade to come to the telephone and said into the phone, "Mr. Wade is here now, I'll let you talk to him." At the same time a reporter was calling

15.

Mr. Wade to the telephone on the counter on the east side of the Records Bureau and requesting that he come to that phone as they were on the air at that time. Mr. Wade hesitated momentarily and then went to the phone on the counter. Mr. Rutledge left his line open and stood near Mr. Wade while he was talking. Mr. Rutledge stated that upon completion of this call, Mr. Wade went to the desk where Jack Ruby was and engaged in a conversation with the person to whom Ruby had been talking.

Mr. Rutledge said that he engaged in a conversation with Cameraman Jimmy Darnell of BBAP-TV, Channel 5 at one time regarding Jack Ruby, but he does not remember if this was on Friday or Saturday.

Mr. Darnell will be interviewed regarding this.

Mr. Rutledge was not present in the basement of the City Hall on Sunday, November 24, 1963.

Respectfully submitted,

O. A. Jones
Captain of Police

OAJ:nw

16.

COMMISSION EXHIBIT No. 2249—Continued

December 23, 1963

Mr. J. E. Curry
Chief of Police

Sir:

The attached reports are concerning previous arrests of Jack Ruby for carrying prohibited weapons.

The incidents occurred on July 26, 1953 and May 1, 1954.

Respectfully submitted,

O. A. Jones
Captain of Police

OAJ:nw

17.

2

COMMISSION EXHIBIT No. 2249—Continued

City of Dallas
OFFICE MEMORANDUM

To- Mr. N. T. Fisher
Deput Chief of Police
Patrol Division

December 11, 1963

Subject: Arrest of Jack Ruby at the Vegas Club, 3508 Oak Lawn.

Sir:

I arrested Jack Ruby at 12:50 P.M., May 1, 1954, at the Vegas Club, 3508 Oak Lawn Avenue.

I do not remember whether he was inside or outside when arrested.

I do not remember what he was charged with.

Respectfully submitted,

James F. Holcomb
JAMES F. HOLCOMB
SERGEANT OF POLICE

JFH/pf

18

The only reason you and I are here is to assist the people of Dallas

2

COMMISSION EXHIBIT No. 2249—Continued

December 13, 1963

Mr. J. E. Curry
Chief of Police

Subject: Arrest of Jack Ruby, w/m/43
May 1, 1954 for Carrying
Concealed Weapon (Pistol)

Sir:

On May 1, 1954 at 12:50 p.m., while working District #33 with Officer J. F. Holcomb, we received a disturbance call at the Vegas Club, 3508 Oak Lawn. Upon arrival, we found Jack Ruby and another white male named Alkona fighting near the front entrance inside the building. A waitress behind the bar stated "that man (Ruby) has a gun." Jack Ruby had a loaded Smith & Wesson .38 Special pistol in his right coat pocket.

The man named Alkona was employed as Manager of the Vegas Club owned by Jack Ruby. The fight started when Jack Ruby accused Alkona of taking money from the Club.

Respectfully,

C. M. Barnhart

C. M. Barnhart
Patrolman #924
Traffic Division

CMB/kc

2

19.

COMMISSION EXHIBIT NO. 2249—Continued

December 12, 1963

Mr. J. E. Curry
Chief of Police

Sir:

Re: Previous Arrests of Jack Ruby

On July 26, 1953 I was working with W. M. Wall, 859, on squad 56, I believe. That particular night Doctor George Boswell, a resident physician at Parkland Hospital, was with us.

We stopped at the B and B Cafe, 3520 Oak Lawn, about 3:45 a.m. At that time Jack Ruby was sitting at the counter with a small snub nose pistol in his pocket.

We waited until Ruby was through with his meal and contacted him outside the cafe. We then arrested him for carrying a pistol. When questioned about the pistol, Ruby stated that he had just closed his club at 1717 South Ervay, had carried his money home, and had forgotten to take the pistol out of his pocket.

Respectfully submitted,

C. W. Deloney

C. W. Deloney, 751
Detective
Criminal Investigation Division

20.

2

COMMISSION EXHIBIT NO. 2249—Continued

December 12, 1963

Mr. J. E. Curry
Chief of Police

Re: Arrest and release of Jack Ruby charged with Carrying Concealed Weapon

Sir:

On July 26, 1953 at 3:34 A. M. Jack Ruby was arrested at 3520 Oak Lawn. He was arrested by Officers W. M. Wall 859 and C. W. DeLoney 751, and was charged with Carrying Concealed Weapon. He was released by R. L. Patton and P. Dillehay by permission of Captain Westbrook.

Detectives Patton and Dillehay do not remember any other details.

Respectfully submitted,

P. Dillehay

P. Dillehay
Detective
Burglary & Theft Bureau

R. L. Patton

R. L. Patton
Detective
Burglary & Theft Bureau

PD/lh

21.

COMMISSION EXHIBIT No. 2249—Continued

5 Copies to H.P.A.

54-20984 ARREST NO.

IDENT. NO.

POLICE DEPARTMENT
CITY OF DALLAS

ARRESTING OFFICER'S REPORT TO DETECTIVE DIVISION ON SUSPECT

Name of person arrested JACK (N) RUBY Date 5-1-54
Address of suspect 1719½ S. ERVAY Time 12:50 P.M.
Sex M Nationality W Age 43
Occupation NIGHT CLUB OWNER Where arrested 3508 OAK LAWN
Offense suspected INV. C.C.W. (PISTOL)
Date offense committed 5-1-54 Where 3508 OAK LAWN
Name of complainant Phone
Address of complainant

Give complete details as to what you know, what you saw or what you were told about suspect which prompted this arrest:

Suspect was fighting with Jimmy Alkona when officers arrived on a radio call to 3508 Oak Lawn. Suspect is part owner in the club Vegas which Jimmy Alkona operates. Suspect claims Alkona is cheating him out of some money. Suspect had a S&W 38 Special Ser. #11432 in his right front pocket when arrested. Four shells in cylinder. (Pistol in prop. room)

Arresting Officers: John F. Holcomb I.D. No. 708; Charles M. Barnhart I.D. No. 924
Other Officers Present (If any): I.D. No.
Investigation assigned to: By
Results of investigation: Released 5-1-54

22.

COMMISSION EXHIBIT No. 2249—Continued

POLICE DEPARTMENT
CITY OF DALLAS

ARRESTING OFFICER'S REPORT TO DETECTIVE DIVISION ON SUSPECT

65478 ARREST NO.
IDENT. NO.

Name of person arrested JACK RUBY Date 26-JULY
Address of suspect 1717 S. ERVAY Time 3 45 A.M.
Sex M Nationality W Age 42
Occupation NITE CLUB OWNER Where arrested 3520 OAKLAWN
Offense suspected INV. C.C.W.
Date offense committed 26-JULY Where 3520 OAKLAWN.
Name of complainant ARR. OFF. Phone
Address of complainant

Give complete details as to what you know, what you saw or what you were told about suspect which prompted this arrest:

THIS MAN WAS CARRYING A 38 S&W SNUB NOSE REVOLVER SER. NO 44735 IN HIS RIGHT HAND PANTS POCKET. GUN PLACED IN PROPERTY ROOM. (SUS. HAD TEAR GAS PEN ON HIS PERSON) (GUN FULLY LOADED) STATED HE HAD BEEN TO THE BANK

Arresting Officers: W. M. WALL I. D. No. 859; C. W. DELONEY I. D. No. 751
Other Officers Present (If any): I. D. No. / I. D. No.
Investigation assigned to: By
Results of investigation: Released by ... Capt. Westbrook 4 PM - 7-26-53 ...

23

COMMISSION EXHIBIT No. 2249—Continued

December 4, 1963

Mr. J. E. Curry
Chief of Police

Subject: Driver of Car #207

Sir:

Officer J. M. Valentino was operating Car #207, and this car was parked at Houston and Elm, and Valentino was assisting in the search of the School Depository Building.

The keys to Car #207 were given to Sgt. J. A. Putnam along with keys from other cars parked in the immediate vicinity, and released to the Third Platoon Commander at the City Hall at approximately 3:30 P. M.

Respectfully submitted,
W. R. Westbrook
W. R. Westbrook
Captain of Police
Personnel Bureau

WRW:RW

24

COMMISSION EXHIBIT No. 2249—Continued

December 12, 1963

Mr. J. E. Curry
Chief of Police

Subject: Jack Ruby

Sir:

Our files show that on June 1, 1954, Arrest #54-20984 that Jack Ruby was arrested for Carrying a Concealed Weapon (a pistol).

Our files also show that Jack Ruby was released by me on the same date, June 1, 1954.

Due to the length of time that has passed since the offense was committed, I do not remember anything about the case. I do not remember Jack Ruby and would not have known him should I have seen him.

Respectfully,

E. R. Gaddy
Detective 60

ERG:ms

25

COMMISSION EXHIBIT No. 2249—Continued

December 23, 1963

Mr. J. E. Curry
Chief of Police

Sir:

The attached reports concern information regarding possible connections between Lee Harvey Oswald and Jack Ruby.

All reports are negative.

Respectfully submitted,

O. A. Jones
Captain of Police

OAJ:mw

26

2

COMMISSION EXHIBIT No. 2249—Continued

2

December 10, 1963

Mr. J. E. Curry
Chief of Police

Re: Interviews conducted in Ft. Hood, Austin, and Houston, Texas

Sir:

On December 4, 1963, Lieutenant Jack Revill and Lieutenant F. I. Cornwall departed from Dallas enroute to Ft. Hood, Texas. The purpose of this trip was to interview Mr. Robert F. Huffaker, Jr. who is presently serving 2 weeks active duty with the U. S. Army Reserves. Mr. Huffaker resides in Dallas at 4700 East Side Avenue, Apartment 115, and is employed by Radio Station KRLD-TV.

Mr. Huffaker was on duty as a newsman in the basement of the City Hall on November 24, 1963, at the time of the Lee Harvey Oswald shooting.

Mr. Huffaker was interviewed on December 4, 1963, and the results of said interview have been submitted previously.

After the interview with Mr. Huffaker, Lieutenant Jack Revill and Lieutenant F. I. Cornwall traveled to Austin, Texas. While in that city, they interviewed Mr. Frank B. Johnston of 3011 Whitis Avenue, Apartment 205. Mr. Johnston is employed by the UPI and is assigned to the Austin Office. He was on duty as a photographer in the basement of the City Hall on November 24, 1963, at the time of the Lee Harvey Oswald shooting.

The interview of Mr. Johnston was conducted on December 5, 1963, during the early a.m. hours and the results of said interview have been submitted previously.

On December 5, 1963, Lieutenant Jack Revill and Lieutenant F. I. Cornwall departed from Austin, Texas, enroute to Houston, Texas. While in that city they interviewed Mr. Warren Ferguson of 5406 Windswept. Mr. Ferguson is a free lance newsman and was employed by ABC on November 24, 1963, as a soundman in the basement of the City Hall. He was present at the time of the Lee Harvey Oswald shooting.

A report covering this interview has been submitted previously.

On December 6, 1963, Lieutenant Jack Revill and Lieutenant F. I. Cornwall interviewed Miss Helen K. Smith, aka Pixie Lynn.

27

COMMISSION EXHIBIT No. 2249—Continued

Page 2

Miss Smith is an exotic dancer and is a friend of Jack Ruby. A sworn statement was taken from Miss Smith and has been submitted previously.

On December 7, 1963, Lieutenant Jack Revill and Lieutenant F. I. Cornwall returned to Dallas.

Respectfully submitted,

Jack Revill

Jack Revill, Lieutenant
Special Service Bureau

F. I. Cornwall

F. I. Cornwall, Lieutenant
Special Service Bureau

JR:mw

3

28

December 9, 1963

Mr. J. E. Curry
Chief of Police

Re: Interview of Helen K. Smith

Sir:

Attached is the sworn statement of Helen K. Smith, also known as Pixie Lynn. This statement was taken in the office of Mrs. Smith's attorney, W. G. Smith, Houston, Texas.

Information was previously received that Helen K. Smith had made the statement that she had observed Jack Ruby and Lee Harvey Oswald together at a party which was recently held in Dallas, Texas.

The purpose of this interview was to determine if Helen Kay Smith had actual knowledge of any connection between Ruby and Oswald.

The sworn statement received from this individual refutes this information.

Respectfully submitted,

Jack Revill

Jack Revill, Lieutenant
Special Service Bureau

F. I. Cornwall

F. I. Cornwall, Lieutenant
Special Service Bureau

JR:mw

3

29

City of Houston)
County of Harris) SS:
State of Texas)

Statement of Helen Kay Smith:

I have been asked for any knowledge I may have of Jack Rubenstein alias Jack Ruby and Lee Harvey Oswald. This statement is voluntarily made by me in the presence of my attorney, Mr. W. G. Smith, of my own free will and accord.

I am 24 years of age and reside at 4409 Greeley Street, Houston, Texas. My occupation is that of Exotic Dancer, and I usually work in Houston or out of state.

I met Jack Rubenstein, also known as Jack Ruby, in Dallas, Texas, about 1957 at the Club Vegas, which he then operated. I went to the Club Vegas with Juanita Dell Phillips, also known as Candy Bar, to dance. Someone at the table pointed out Jack Ruby to me.

I later saw Ruby at the Club Vegas on two or three occasions over a period of the next year.

The next time I saw Ruby was during the Christmas holidays of 1961 at the Carosel Club in Dallas. On this occasion I went to the Carobel with Torri Shane also known as Evelyn Webster, another dancer. As we entered the club he was standing around near the door and I spoke to him at that time. He later came to our table, sat down and talked to us briefly and asked me where I had been working. Although we were at the club for approximately an hour I talked to Ruby for only a few minutes. I have not seen him since that time. I would also like to add that I have not been in Dallas, Texas since about July of 1963.

I had never heard of Lee Harvey Oswald prior to the assassination of President Kennedy on November 22. I did see pictures of Oswald in the newspapers and on TV and I never, to my knowledge, saw the man in person.

I have been asked if I ever attended a party at which Jack Ruby and Lee Harvey Oswald were present. My answer to that question is absolutely no. I have never attended a party at which they were present or at which either of them were present.

During the two-week period ending November 30, 1963 I was employed at the Tam O'Shanter on Old Spanish Trailj from 2:30 P. M. until 6:00 P. M. I also worked at the Midnight Lounge, 401 Westheimer Street, Houston, from 8:30 PM until 12:00 midnight. During the first week ending November 23 I arrived at the Midnight

3

39.

Page Two of Statement by Helen Kay Smith 12/6/63

Lounge at approximately 7:30 P. M. The latter week ending November 30 I arrived at approximately 8:00 - 8:30 P. M. because my show started at 8:30. I did not appear at the airport on November 21 when the President and Vice President arrived in Houston. I did not attend the dinner at the Coliseum on the evening of November 21.

On the afternoon or evening of November 22 after learning through the news media of the assassination of President Kennedy I did not discuss Jack Rubenstein also known as Jack Ruby.

I have been asked if I know an attorney by the name of Barbara L. Welz, who reportedly has a wooden leg and resides in Dallas, Texas. I do not know this lady and to the best of my knowledge I never heard of her before this date. I did not have a discussion with anyone regarding Barbara L. Welz on the afternoon or evening of November 22, 1963. During the afternoon or evening no one mentioned the names Jack Ruby or Barbara L. Welz in my presence.

I would like to add that my feelings toward President Kennedy were friendly and if there is any way I can help in clearing up any of the aspects of his assassination I would gladly to so.

I was present when this statement was dictated and helped in same and have read and had a chance to read and had a chance to correct this statement before signing and it is the truth to the best of my knowledge and belief.

Helen Kay Smith

Subscribed and sworn to byfore me this sixth day of December, 1963.

Lane Bertram, Special Agent In Charge
U. S. Secret Service

WITNESSES:

W. G. Smith

Lt. Jack Revill

J. D. Rollins

3

31.

COMMISSION EXHIBIT No. 2249—Continued

COMMISSION EXHIBIT No. 2249—Continued

December 2, 1963

Mr. J. E. Curry
Chief of Police

Re: Information regarding Jack Ruby and Lee Oswald

Sir:

This report is in regards to information received from a David Van Meter, 3815 Mt. Washington, FR 1 1325. Van Meter had stated a subject by the name of Julius Hardie, employee Industrial Electric Equipment Company, had quoted another employee of the same firm as saying that Jack Ruby and Lee Oswald had roomed together. Investigaters contacted Hardie by phone and learned that this other employee was Gaston Powell, 3122 Rockford, no phone.

Powell related that this was only idle conversation he had heard from another source and later found out it was not true.

There is no basis for the above information.

Respectfully submitted,

F. G. McCaghren, Lieutenant
Burglary & Theft Bureau

C. C. Wallace, Lieutenant
Juvenile Bureau

lh

32

3

Mr. J. E. Curry
Chief of Police

December 3, 1963

Re: Interview with Wilburn Waldon Litchfield regarding association of Jack Ruby with Lee Harvey Oswald

Sir:

On December 2, 1963, Patrolman Don Green of the Narcotics Section, Special Service Bureau, called the undersigned officers and stated that a Mr. Litchfield had contacted him stating that he had information in regards to seeing Lee Harvey Oswald in company with Jack Ruby.

Approximately at 10:30 a.m. Mr. Litchfield came to the Special Service Bureau and was interviewed regarding this incident. A copy of his affidavit is attached. Upon completion of this interview Mr. Litchfield was given a polygraph examination regarding this incident by Detective R. D. Lewis. It is the opinion of Detective Lewis that Mr. Litchfield was untruthful to the questions asked. A copy of the report submitted by Detective Lewis is attached.

After the polygraph examination, Mr. Litchfield was taken to the office of Captain Fritz where he was interviewed by same along with Agent Jim Bookout of the Federal Bureau of Investigation. A copy of Mr. Litchfield's affidavit was given to Captain Fritz.

Respectfully submitted,

F. I. Cornwall
Lieutenant, Special Service Bureau

Jack Revill
Lieutenant, Special Service Bureau

Enclosures: Report of Detective Lewis
Affidavit

33

3

PAGE 1

AFFIDAVIT IN ANY FACT

THE STATE OF TEXAS
COUNTY OF DALLAS

BEFORE ME, Betty Dunagan

a Notary Public in and for said County, State of Texas, on this day personally appeared Wilburn Waydon Litchfield, aka Robert, 2454 South Zange apartment 120, WH8 9503, Business: Spencer Press, 8428 Kate.

Who, after being by me duly sworn, on oath deposes and says: Sometimes within the first two weeks of November, 1963, either on a Tuesday or Thursday night, (Idon't remember the exact date, but this will help establish the date: It was the night that the strippers had their pictures made for the National Magazine at the Carosel. Three of them signed the release and one didn't. I do not remember the man's name who took the pictures) I went to the Carosel Club. I had an appointment with Jack Ruby between 10:00 and 10:30 pm. I entered and asked for Jack Ruby and was told by the doorman that Mr. Ruby was not in, but I could wait. There were three people already waiting to see him. The doorman was a man in his late 40's or early 50's about 5'7" to 5'9", stocky build, close curly hair, silver colored without a part, and he spoke with a northern or mid western accent. He was wearing a blue suit, dark blue tie with light blue and red in it, and white shirt with collar unbuttoned. He offered me a seat at the first table to the left of the door, and said I could wait until Mr. Ruby arrived. While I was waiting, I had a cup of coffee and watched the show and observed the people in the Carosel.

While I was watching the crowd which consisted of about 28 people, I noticed about 4 tables directly in front of me, a man in a white sweater. The reason I noticed this man was that everyone else in the Carosel was either in a suit, sport coat, or in uniform.

After I had been waiting approximately one hour, the door opened. In came a dash hound, and in came Jack Ruby. Jack greeted me, said just a minute, spoke to the doorman, came back and asked me if I'd mind waiting that he had to see some other people, took his hat off, turned left, and went to the back towards his office. He came back into the club area, and the first person he saw was a fellow in his late 30's or early 40's, black wavey hair, real stocky build, who was sitting at the table directly by the door to the back, next to the wall. I was later informed by the doorman and Jack Ruby

[signature]

SUBSCRIBED AND SWORN TO BEFORE ME THIS 2nd DAY OF December A.D. 1963

BETTY DUNAGAN [signature: Betty Dunagan]
Notary Public, Dallas County, Texas

CPS-GF-413

3 4.

3

COMMISSION EXHIBIT No. 2249—Continued

PAGE 2

AFFIDAVIT IN ANY FACT

THE STATE OF TEXAS
COUNTY OF DALLAS

BEFORE ME, Betty Dunagan

a Notary Public in and for said County, State of Texas, on this day personally appeared

Who, after being by me duly sworn, on oath deposes and says:
that this gentleman was an old friend from California. Jack spoke to this man roughly 15 to 20-minutes.

The next man that Jack saw was a photographer for a national magazine similar to Stag or Male, etc. The reason I know this man was a photographer for a national magazine is that during my discussion with Jack Ruby, this man was introduced to me (although I don't remember his name) as a photographer for the above type national magazine.

The next man that Jack saw was the man mentioned earlier who was sitting 4 tables in front of me wearing a white sweater. Jack came and got this man nd they walked back toward his office. They were gone about 15 to 20 minutes. They both came out and Jack stopped at the table by the wall and spoke to the man from California again. The gentleman in the V neck white sweater and grey slacks walked by me under neath a bright light by the door. He was approximately two feet from where I was sitting.

After Jack got through talking to the man from California, he came over and gotme and carried me back to his office. We discussed a private club. I asked him if he would sell the Vegas. He said no, it had about $40,000 Federal taxes against it, but that he had a good, terrific idea for a private club at a location in Northeast Dallas. I asked him if he had a lease, what the idea was and what the location was. Jack did not say. He said he was afraid someone would steal his idea from him. I left around 1:20 to 1:45 am. After President Kennedy was assasinated, and this fellow Oswald's picture was on televisionand in the paper, I remembered that he was the man that I saw in the white V neck sweater the night that I was at the Carosel Club to see Jack Ruby. I didn't say anything for about a week until Sunday, December 2, 1963, and then I called Don Green, a friend of mine, and told him about it, and asked his advise. He suggested that I come in and talk to the Police.

[signature]

SUBSCRIBED AND SWORN TO BEFORE ME THIS 2nd DAY OF December A.D. 1963

BETTY DUNAGAN [signature: Betty Dunagan]
Notary Public, Dallas County, Texas

CPS-GF-413

3 5.

3

COMMISSION EXHIBIT No. 2249—Continued

3

City of Dallas

OFFICE MEMORANDUM

To- Mr. W. P. Gannaway
Captain of Police

December 2, 1963

Subject: Wilburn Waldon Litchfield W/M/30
Polygraph Examination

Sir:

A polygraph examination was given Mr. Litchfield upon the request of Lt. Jack Revell on this date. The examination was given to determine if Litchfield was being truthful about seeing Lee Harvey Oswald at the Club Carousel which is operated by Jack Ruby. Below is a list of pertinet quiestion asked.

1. Have you told the complete truth about seeing Oswald at the club the night you were there? Answer: Yes

2. Have you made up any of this story about seeing Oswald at the club the night you were there? Answer: No

3. Are you looking for any personal gain or notoriety from making this statement? Answer: No

4. Have you deliberately lied about your thinking this was Oswald? Answer: No

Mr. Litchfield tried for the first half of the examination to control his breathing pattern.

It is the opinion of this Examiner that this person has been untruthful to the above questions.

Respectfully submitted,

R D Lewis

R. D. Lewis
Detective of Police
Identification Bureau

RDL/mel

36 3

The only reason you and I are here is to assist the people of Dallas

December 3, 1963

Mr. J. E. Curry
Chief of Police

Re: Information from Captain Arnett (Police Reserve) that Oswald and Ruby may have been related

Sir:

The information furnished by Captain Arnett was that a Mrs. Conine used to operate a beer joint on Main Street in Dallas several years ago, and at that time she had a waitress working for her, but does not remember the waitress' name. She believes that the waitress is now working at a cafe across from 429 Second Avenue. Also that this waitress knew both Oswald and Ruby and that Oswald was the illigitimate son of Jack Ruby. Mrs. Conine was suppose to have told a Mrs. Laura Sims, aka Stagman, the above information.

We have contacted Mrs. Cleo Conne, who's last name is now Henderson. She works at 429 Second, Parkland Sportswear, TA3 4164. She denied having any knowledge of this information nor has she heard this rumor.

We contacted Mrs. Laura Sims, 2846 Falls Drive, FE7 0038. She is also an employee of Parkland Sportswear and denies having ever heard this rumor. She does not know Jack Ruby nor did she know Oswald.

We also went to the cafe at the corner of Hickory and Second and contacted the manager, Mrs. Mable Dunning of 508 North Winnetka. She denies having ever heard this story nor does she know a waitress that use to work on Main Street some 10 years ago. There was one waitress present at the time of the interview at the cafe, and she also denied ever having known Oswald or Jack Ruby.

Respectfully submitted,

C. C. Wallace

C. C. Wallace, Lieutenant
Juvenile Bureau

P. G. McCaghren

P. G. McCaghren, Lieutenant
Burglary & Theft Bureau

lh

37 3

December 7, 1963

Mr. J. E. Curry
Chief of Police

Re: Interview with Former Landlord of Jack Ruby - Mrs. Cloe Stansell, 4160 Hawthorne LA8-0174

Mrs. Stansell was the manager of the apartment house located at 4156 Hawthorne at the time Jack Ruby was a tenant. Mrs. Stansell stated that Jack Ruby moved into the apartment in early 1957 and moved on January 3, 1959. During the time that Mr. Ruby was a tenant, there were no unusual incidents involving him or any visitors to his apartment.

Mrs. Stansell stated that on 2 or 3 separate occasions, an unknown white male moved into the apartment with Mr. Ruby but each of these men only stayed a few days. She never questioned Jack Ruby about these persons. She considered Ruby to be an excellent tenant.

Mrs. Stansell states that she has not seen nor talked to Jack Ruby since he moved from the apartment. She further stated that she is not acquainted with Mrs. Eva Grant, sister of Jack Ruby.

When questioned about Lee Harvey Oswald, Mrs. Stansell stated that she has never seen this man nor did she ever know him to visit Jack Ruby at the time that Ruby was her tenant.

Respectfully submitted,

H. M. Hart
Detective of Police

HMH:nw

38. 3

COMMISSION EXHIBIT No. 2249—Continued

December 7, 1963

Mr. J. E. Curry
Chief of Police

Re: Interview with Former Landlord of Jack Ruby - Mrs. Rex Goodman 3929 Rawlins - Apartment A LA 6-5714

Mrs. Goodman is the manager of an apartment house at 3929 Rawlins and 3921 Rawlins. Information has been received that Jack Ruby had lived at 3929 Rawlins, Apartment 1 in 1961. Mrs. Goodman stated that Jack Ruby had never lived at that location, however, his sister, Mrs. Eva Grant, is a present tenant in Apartment I and has been since July, 1961.

Mrs. Goodman states that on numerous occasions she has seen Jack Ruby enter the apartment but denies that she has ever seen Lee Harvey Oswald.

Mrs. Goodman further stated that she had been contacted by another person that showed her a photograph of Lee Harvey Oswald requesting information. She stated that this photograph was a mug shot taken by the New Orleans Louisiana Police Department. She declined to identify the person presenting this photograph.

She further stated that she is a close friend of Mrs. Eva Grant and that Mrs. Grant has visited in her apartment on numerous occasions.

Respectfully submitted,

H. M. Hart
Detective

HMH:nw

39. 3

COMMISSION EXHIBIT No. 2249—Continued

December 7, 1963

Mr. J. E. Curry
Chief of Police

Re: Interview with Former Landlord of Jack Ruby - Mrs. Linda Jackson Manager of the Continental House Apartments 4828 Alcott - TA 3-3815

Mrs. Linda Jackson is the present manager of the apartment house where Jack Ruby lived.

Mrs. Jackson presented records indicating that Jack Ruby moved into Apartment 105 at 4727 Homer on January 3, 1959 and moved from this location on July 1, 1961. These records further indicate that Mrs. Eva Grant, sister of Jack Ruby also lived in this apartment. At the time Ruby rented the apartment, he gave personal references as Stanley Kaufman, a local attorney and Alice Nichols of DA1-3687.

Mrs. Jackson states that she does not know Jack Ruby nor has she ever seen him and the tenant records in her office do not reflect any unusual circumstances occurring during the time Ruby was a tenant.

Respectfully submitted,

H M Hart

H. M. Hart
Detective of Police

HMH:mw

40

December 9, 1963

Mr. J. E. Curry
Chief of Police

Re: George Butler, Lieutenant of Police

Sir:

On December 9, 1963, the undersigned officers were approached by Lieutenant Butler and he related that he had information that Lee Harvey Oswald was the illegitimate son of Jack Ruby.

Lieutenant Butler further stated that he had information that Jack Ruby had applied for a visa to Mexico about the same time that Lee Harvey Oswald visited that country. He suggested that we contact the Mexican Consul to confirm this information.

Respectfully submitted,

Jack Revill

Jack Revill, Lieutenant
Special Service Bureau

H. M. Hart, Detective
Special Service Bureau

JR:mw

46.

December 3, 1963

Mr. J. E. Curry
Chief of Police

Re: Information concerning vehicle damage by gun shot

Sir:

This report is in regards to information received that a Mrs. Joe Baily Blackwell, 1210 Holly Glen Drive, FR4 7117, had informed another person that her sister and husband were driving their car in almost the exact spot where the President was shot approximately one week before, when a bullet entered the rear window on the left side of their automobile.

Investigators determined that this report was started by Mrs. Blackwell's sister, Mrs. Luther Howle, 910 Winters, WH1 1429. This report was traced through Mrs. Howle back to a Mrs. Margaret Leath, an employee of Western Union Office, 2000 Main.

Investigators talked to Mrs. Leath and to her supervisor, a Mr. Johnson, who stated approximately five weeks ago Mrs. Leath was in the vicinity of the Continental Street under pass when the left side rear window shattered. There was no hole in the glass. A report was not given to the police. The glass has already been replaced.

Investigators examined the car, a 1957 Rambler, and could find no evidence of a bullet having entered the car.

Respectfully submitted,

B. G. McCaghren, Lieutenant
Burglary & Theft Bureau

C. C. Wallace, Lieutenant
Juvenile Bureau

lh

42. 3

COMMISSION EXHIBIT No. 2249—Continued

AFTER FIVE DAYS RETURN TO

PALMDALE, CALIFORNIA

LANCASTER, DEC 3 7-PM 1963 CALIF.

SUPPORT ... TB ASSOCIATION

Dallas Police
Dallas
Tex

RECEIVED DEC 5 1963

13. 3

COMMISSION EXHIBIT No. 2249—Continued

Oswald Case -:

Check either Howard or Spencer

Perhaps Howard Spencer

Link Ruby—Oswald

14.

COMMISSION EXHIBIT No. 2249—Continued

December 23, 1963

Mr. J. E. Curry
Chief of Police

Sir:

The attached reports concern reports of officers being familiar with Jack Ruby.

The reports indicate that none of the officers were in or near the City Hall on November 24, 1963.

Respectfully submitted,

O. A. Jones
Captain of Police

OAJ:mw

15.

COMMISSION EXHIBIT No. 2249—Continued

4

December 12, 1963

Mr. J. E. Curry
Chief of Police

Subject: Jack Ruby Case

Sir:

A membership card to the Carousel Club, listed in the name of Ray Hawkins, business address City Hall, signed by Ray Hawkins, is attached to this report. This card was discussed with Officer Hawkins and he stated that he had been to the Carousel Club two or three times and on one occasion Jack Ruby told him that he was going to give him a permanent pass, and that he would sign a card, but had not received the pass.

On the day that Lee Oswald was killed, Hawkins was on a day off and was at home, and did not come in or near City Hall.

Respectfully submitted,

W. R. Westbrook
W. R. Westbrook
Captain of Police
Personnel Bureau

WRW:fb
Enclosure

16.

COMMISSION EXHIBIT No. 2249—Continued

December 12, 1963

Mr. J. E. Curry
Chief of Police

Subject: Jack Ruby Case

Sir:

It was revealed to this Investigator by Captain O. A. Jones that two Traffic Officers were on the visiting list of Jack Ruby. This list is on record at the ~~City Hall.~~ County Jail.

This Investigator interviewed Officer T. M. Hanson and he stated that he did not know why his name would have been placed on the list. He stated that he is well acquainted with Ruby, but not any more so than many businessmen in or near Main and Akard Streets.

This Investigator interviewed Officer W. E. Barnett and he also expressed surprise at being on the visiting list. He also was acquainted with Ruby, but no more so than any other businessman in or near Commerce and Akard Streets.

Officer Hanson and Barnett were off duty when Oswald was shot. Neither Officer came in or near the City Hall on that day.

Respectfully submitted,

W. R. Westbrook
W. R. Westbrook
Captain of Police
Personnel Bureau

WRW:fb

47

COMMISSION EXHIBIT No. 2249—Continued

November 30, 1963

Mr. J. E. Curry
Chief of Police

Sir:

I have known Jack Ruby for eight years. I have never associated with him socially and I have never shared an apartment with him.

I have never been to his apartment or residence.

I was not at the City Hall, November 23 or November 24, because I was off duty these two days.

I have not seen Jack Ruby in approximately four or five months.

Respectfully submitted,

James P. Hargis
James P. Hargis

RW

48

COMMISSION EXHIBIT No. 2249—Continued

December 23, 1963

Mr. J. E. Curry
Chief of Police

Sir:

The attached report concerns a lead from the F.B.I. regarding Dallas Police Car 207 stopping in front of 1026 N. Beckley at 1:00 p.m. on November 22, 1963.

Captain Westbrook ascertained that Squad Car 207 was at the City Hall when the officer driving the car, Patrolman J. M. Valentine, heard of the assassination. He went immediately to the scene of the shooting.

The keys to the car were released to Sergeant J. M. Putnam. Sergeant Putnam released the keys to the Third Platoon commander at approximately 3:30 p.m.

Captain Westbrook did not determine what police car was involved in this report.

Respectfully submitted,

O. A. Jones
Captain of Police

OAJ:nw

49.

COMMISSION EXHIBIT No. 2249—Continued

December 2, 1963

STATEMENT OF J. M. VALENTINE:

I was working the 2nd Platoon on November 22, 1963, and was driving Police Car #207.

I was in the Juvenile Bureau when I was informed of the shooting of President Kennedy. I left immediately and went to the building where the President was shot.

I helped search this building for quite a length of time, and turned my keys over to Sergeant J. M. Putnam. I never did drive to Oak Cliff.

50.

COMMISSION EXHIBIT No. 2249—Continued

December 4, 1963

Mr. J. E. Curry
Chief of Police

Subject: Driver of Car #207

Sir:

Officer J. M. Valentine was operating Car #207, and this car was parked at Houston and Elm, and Valentine was assisting in the search of the School Depository Building.

The keys to Car #207 were given to Sgt. J. A. Putnam along with keys from other cars parked in the immediate vicinity, and released to the Third Platoon Commander at the City Hall at approximately 3:30 P. M.

Respectfully submitted,
W. R. Westbrook
W. R. Westbrook
Captain of Police
Personnel Bureau

WRW:RW

5 b.

COMMISSION EXHIBIT No. 2249—Continued

11/29/63

1

Mrs EARLINE ROBERTS, 1026 Beckley, Dallas, Texas advised she could not furnish the exact time that Oswald returned to his room at 1026 Beckley after the assignation of the President but said a rough guess would be 1 pm. Mrs ROBERTS received a telephone callfrom a friend telling her the President had just been shot, and Mrs ROBERTS turned on the television andrecalled the announceb saying President KENNEDY had just been shot and was at Parkland Hospital. Mrs ROBERTS advised after OSWALD returned and entered his room at about 1 pm on November 22, 1963 she looked out the front window and saw Police Car No. 207 with two uniformed uniformed policemen in thecar which slowed up and stopped in front of the residence at 1026 Beckley, and one of the officers blew the horn on the car and then slowly drove on Beckley toward Zangs Boulevard. Mrs ROBERTS said the reason she recalled the number of the car was because she had worked for twopolicemen who drove Car 170, and she looked to see if these officers were the two officers she knew parked in front of the residence.

COMMISSION EXHIBIT No. 2249—Continued

ASSIGNATION OF PRESIDENT JOHN F. KENNEDY
DALLAS, TEXAS 11/22/63

SUGGESTED LEAD

Dallas PD ascertain identity of officers in Squad Car 207 as approximately 1 pm, November 22, 1963 in front of 1026 Beckley, and if possible the reason for their cruising and stopping in front of this residence.

COMMISSION EXHIBIT No. 2249—Continued

FD-302 (Rev. 1-25-60) FEDERAL BUREAU OF INVESTIGA— Commission Exhibit No. 2250

Date November 29, 1963

Mr. CURTIS LA VERNE CRAFARD, also known as Curtis LaVerne Craford, Larry, C.L. and Smoky, was located at the cabin of ROY PARKS in rural Antrim County, Michigan. He was visiting his sister, Mrs. CORABELLE INGERSOLL. This individual volunteered the following information:

He was born at Farwell, Michigan, on March 10, 1941, raised in Michigan and California, until his family moved to Dallas, Oregon, in 1958. The family were fruit harvest people. In September, 1958, he enlisted in the United States Army and served until November, 1959, when he was given a general discharge under honorable conditions. He married WILMA JEAN TEANNEY, June 16, 1962, and she was from Dallas, Texas. He first went to Dallas, Texas, in March, 1963, to attempt a reconciliation with his wife, but finally they separated in June, 1963, as his wife was a lesbian.

During August, 1963, he started to work with a carnival and followed this work, which accounted for his being at the Texas State Fair in Dallas, Texas, on or about October 15, 1963.

He joined a carnival show which was named "How Hollywood Makes Movies." This was run by a BOB CRAVEN, of Hollywood, California, and he performed the duties of a roustabout. He lived in a tent on the fairgrounds and stayed with this show and another show which was a rock and roll outfit until the fair closed on approximately October 30, 1963.

During the time he was employed with the "How Hollywood Makes Movies", he ascertained that JACK RUBY had approximately $150.00 invested and on or about October 21, 1963, at closing time, he was introduced to RUBY by a "DEEK" MILES, another one of the backers. He saw RUBY two or three times during the Texas State Fair, as RUBY would check on the progress of the show. When the fair closed about the end of October, 1963, RUBY hired him to tear down the stage and take it to the Carousel Club in Dallas, Texas. He worked with a man named HOWARD (Last Name Unknown), a Negro, who had been employed by RUBY for approximately 18 years. After completing this job, RUBY asked him to stay at the club and work for room and board. He had the room in front of RUBY's office. This would be approximately November 1, 1963.

On 11/28/63 at Bellaire, Michigan File # Detroit 44-563

by SA THEODORE S. KRAMER / MOS Date dictated 11/29/63

147

COMMISSION EXHIBIT No. 2250

DE 44-563
2

His job at the Carousel Club consisted of being a handyman, clean up man, part-time bartender and also answering the telephone. It was his duty to take down names and addresses of people calling the club for RUBY. RUBY ran almost an ad every day in the local paper for waitresses and performers. He also had an financial interest in a Twist Board Company at Fort Worth, Texas. Telephone calls in a number of twenty to forty would be received daily and these calls were placed in a stenographers notebook, which he kept on RUBY's desk.

The only odd incident concerning telephone calls was that about three or four times a day during the time he was at the club, a call would come in and the man would ask if Mr. RUBY was there. If RUBY was not there, the man refused to leave his name and on every occasion during this period of time, it was the same person who called. He brought this to RUBY's attention on numerous occasions and RUBY told him to forget about it; however, RUBY was not alarmed.

CRAFARD would stay at the club and eat his meals at the Eat Well Cafe and the drugstore across the street from the club. Money for these meals was taken from the cash register. RUBY also purchased his clothes from the Good Will Store and gave him some spending money.

RUBY had an apartment with an individual named GEORGE (Last Name Unknown), who sold Christmas cards and worked part time on the door at the club. He did not know where RUBY's apartment was located, but had the telephone number, WH. 1-1050.

He would see RUBY every day for about one to two hours and this usually occurred between 12:00 PM and 3:00 PM, at the Carousel. Other than that, RUBY would telephonically contact him almost every hour for any calls. He has no knowledge where RUBY spent his time outside of the club. Usually, RUBY would then return to the club at about 10:00 PM each evening and stay until closing time, which was 1:30 AM during week days and 2:00 AM on the weekends.

He stated RUBY trusted him and he would handle anywhere from $300.00 to $400.00 daily; however, ANDY ARMSTRONG or ALEXANDER, the Assistant Manager and bartender, would handle the money until Midnight and, thereafter, he would close up.

148

COMMISSION EXHIBIT No. 2250—Continued

DE 44-563
3

Most of the time at about 5:00 PM, RUBY would call in from his home and, if needed, he told him he would be available there until he came to the club later. He said most of the affairs of the club were handled by ARMSTRONG, who performed paper work, etc., and this individual was with RUBY for approximately nine years.

Continuing, he said that on a few occasions during the daytime, he would accompany RUBY around the Dallas area. He recalls one day, time unknown, that RUBY went to various companies in regards to the purchase of a safe for the club, as RUBY had the habit of carrying all his money in his pocket. On another occasion, approximately three weeks ago, he went with RUBY when RUBY checked about some sound equipment for the club. This was at an electronics company in about the 2200 or 2300 block of Elm Street. They were there ten or fifteen minutes and did not purchase anything. On this occasion he, CRAFARD, was wearing a suit and he feels they were there at about 3:00 PM or 4:00 PM. He said that when they entered the place of business, the electronic equipment, speakers, public address systems, etc., were on the right and left-hand sides in between a counter and a stairway that went to a storeroom on the second floor. He related that most of RUBY's time at the club was spent talking business and he had the habit of always telling the employees who they could talk to. RUBY was somewhat outspoken, had a quick temper and when mad would use loud language in his relations with the employees.

On November 17, 1963, he recalls telling RUBY that he would desire to cease his employment there on the 18th. He said that RUBY then told him he would put him on a salary and persuaded him to stay indefinitely. CRAFARD said he was not too fond of the work and was not busy enough at the club. He also said RUBY had a .38 caliber revolver which he kept in a money sack locked in the trunk of his car. He said that when transporting money, RUBY kept his money in the trunk with the revolver and always kept the revolver with him when moving money.

In regards to RUBY's temper he said they one night, approximately November 14 or 15, 1963, RUBY was having trouble with an M.C., EARL NORMAN at the Carousel and about 1:30 AM he, RUBY, sent CRAFARD out to the car to get the gun. That was the only time he ever handled RUBY's gun and on that occasion did not take it out of the sack. He said that the gun was believed to be the property of HOWARD, the Negro employee.

149

COMMISSION EXHIBIT No. 2250—Continued

DE 44-563
4

On November 20, 1963, he recalls RUBY coming in at approximately 4:00 or 5:00 in the afternoon and requesting CRAFARD to go work at the Club Vegas. RUBY stayed at the Carousel until approximately 6:30 PM. ANDY, the bartender, was there, along with GEORGE, RUBY's roommate. At the latter time, RUBY returned to his home and came back to the club at about 8:00 PM, when he transported CRAFARD to the Club Vegas. That evening, he called three or four times in regards to the crowd and Mrs. EVA GRANT, RUBY's sister, also called in regards to the crowd. At closing time, which was 2:00 AM, RUBY called and said he would be late as the "law was at the place" and LITTLE LYNN, one of the strippers, was sick and he had to take care of her. He waited there until approximately 3:45 AM, at which time RUBY met him and they had breakfast at the Lucas B and B Restaurant, next door to the club. On this date, RUBY was accompanied by a girl named GLORIA, who did not work at the club and who was about 22, white female, 5'6", 125 pounds, blond hair. This girl would be known to MARGIE (Last Name Unknown), waitress at the Carousel. He said that RUBY returned him to the Carousel at approximately 4:30 AM, on November 21, 1963.

On November 21, 1963, RUBY called the club to wake him up at about 11:00 AM, and then came in later in the afternoon, sometime between 12:00 and 3:00. ANDY was at the club at this time and he recalled there was a woman, along with her husband, who desired a job. Thereafter, RUBY left and later in the afternoon called him again to go to the Vegas as the bartender. At about 7:30 PM, RUBY picked him up and took him to the Vegas Club, and he did not see RUBY again until approximately 2:30 AM, after closing, at which time they again had breakfast at the Lucas B and B, returning to the Carousel at about 3:30 or 4:00 AM.

On November 22, 1963, he said he was awakened by ANDY, the bartender, at 11:30 AM, by way of telephone. He then dropped back to sleep and shortly after Noon, ANDY came to the Club, personally woke him up and stated that the President had been shot. He had not heard from RUBY previously that date and at about 1:30 PM, RUBY came into the club and said the club would be closed that night and the entire weekend. He told ANDY to notify the personnel and, thereafter, called the paper and placed an ad to that effect. CRAFARD said that he was much surprised by this action as the club could not financially stand to be closed and it was strictly his opinion that RUBY did this as a gesture to make good will on behalf of the public. After

150

COMMISSION EXHIBIT No. 2250—Continued

DE 44-563
5

that RUBY said that he was going to his sister's home and asked CRAFARD if he desired to accompany him, which offer was refused.

RUBY left the Carousel at about 3:30 PM, being described by CRAFARD as "pretty well shaken up." They knew at that time there was an arrest of a suspect, but he cannot recall the name of any person being mentioned; however, the name of TIBBITS, the policeman, was mentioned and RUBY said he was acquainted with him. Upon leaving, RUBY was what CRAFARD termed being emotionally disturbed. He told CRAFARD to call Mrs. GRANT's home before he went to dinner and upon his return. This was not an ordinary request and CRAFARD had no knowledge of RUBY's reason.

RUBY then came back to the club or called CRAFARD about 7:30 PM that evening. He did not discuss the assassination, he did not mention being at the police department or anything else. He just wanted to check in regards to telephone calls. He did not see RUBY again until the next day.

On Saturday morning, November 23, 1963, at about 5:30 AM, RUBY called him and told him to meet him downstairs with the Polaroid camera and some film. RUBY was very excited and, in a matter of minutes, a telephone call was received from the fellow at the All Wright Parking Lot, telling him that JACK was there and to hurry up. When he got to the car, GEORGE, RUBY's roommate, was also there and they drove out on the Stemmions Freeway, where RUBY showed him a sign "Impeach EARL WARREN." On the end of this sign it said for further information write Post Office Box 1744 or a similar number.

RUBY instructed him to take three pictures of the sign and they then drove to a waffle shop near the Carousel for coffee. RUBY and GEORGE were talking about the sign and the Post Office Box and they had very little conversation concerning the assassination. RUBY then dropped CRAFARD off at the club at 6:20 AM and said that he and GEORGE were going down to the Post Office to look at that Post Office Box. CRAFARD said that he was completely puzzled, as EARL WARREN was unknown to him. This was the last time he saw JACK RUBY. He also recalled that while being at the waffle shop on Commerce Street, RUBY was reading about LEE HARVEY OSWALD in the newspaper. He, at this time, did not express any previous knowledge or acquaintance with this individual and he (CRAFARD) had never, to the best of his knowledge, heard RUBY or anyone else at the club previously

DE 44-563
6

mention this name. He said that it seemed odd to him that RUBY was more excited about the EARL WARREN sign than about the assassination. RUBY, at this time, made no threats or other comments concerning OSWALD.

After being dropped off at the club, CRAFARD called RUBY at approximately 8:00 AM, at RUBY's apartment and told RUBY that they needed food for the three dachshunds that were kept at the club. CRAFARD said that RUBY berated him for waking him up and he then decided to pack up and leave the club as he did not want to take any other verbal abuse. He did not say anything to anyone about leaving and just packed his clothing, left the club at about 12:00 Noon that date and started hitchhiking north. He proceeded north on 77 to Oklahoma City, Oklahoma, and on to Clare, Michigan, where he arrived on Monday, November 25, 1963, at about 9:30 PM, at the home of a cousin, CLIFFORD ROBERTS. His main reason for coming north was to recontact his sister who had not written him for some time. He had no other explanation for his hasty departure, but said that it is just the way he does things.

Returning to RUBY, he said that he can never recall this individual making any statements concerning revenge on OSWALD. He, CRAFARD, saw RUBY's picture in the newspaper the day after his arrest and said that he never saw OSWALD in the Carousel or Vegas Clubs and he definitely knows that he never took this name down from a telephone call. He said that he first found out that OSWALD had been killed on November 24, 1963, at about 8:00 PM, and did not know RUBY was responsible for it until Monday, November 25, 1963.

In regards to RUBY's contacts, CRAFARD said that most of them were recorded in the stenographer's notebook on the desk and that the only other ones would be MICKEY RYAN, who was a bartender in a gun club located in Dallas. He termed RYAN as a very close friend. He cannot recall RUBY ever saying he had any contacts with the underworld, and the only illegal activity that he could recall RUBY speaking about was that each night at the Carousel, as a promotional stunt, they would have drawings and give away champagne to the ladies and Wilkinson swart edge razor blades to the men. RUBY stressed the fact that these razor blades were a blackmarket product and he had no knowledge from where they were obtained.

152

Concerning RUBY's relations with the police, CRAFARD said that on the average, two men in uniform would visit the club nightly at about 11:30 PM and receive free coffee. CRAFARD said that he had no knowledge himself of any Dallas policemen, but RUBY claimed to know the majority of men on the force. He said he was advised that off-duty policemen could come into the club without paying the $2.00 cover charge and that the ordinary price for beer and set ups was 60 cents and the policemen were to be charged 40 cents. He knows of no police contacts on RUBY's behalf, but said RUBY did keep a police card in the cash register at the Carousel with a name, unknown to him, on it.

Another close friend of RUBY's was a BILL WILLIS, who is the drum player at the Carousel.

He said at no time did RUBY ever demonstrate any homosexual tendencies and that he specifically recalls on one occasion an individual, who was a female impersonator, made a request for employment at the club and RUBY became infuriated and stated that type of act was repulsive.

In closing, CRAFARD said that he intended to stay in the Bellaire, Michigan, area until Friday, December 6, 1963, and his address will always be known to Miss GALE EATON of Harrison, Michigan, and he will advise the Traverse City Resident Agency of the Federal Bureau of Investigation by card of any moves.

Several colored photographs were taken of CRAFARD and the following physical description was obtained from interview and observation:

Name	CURTIS LA VERNE CRAFARD
Aliases	Curtis LaVerne Craford, Larry, C.L., Smoky
Race	White
Sex	Male
Age	22
Born	March 10, 1941, Farwell, Michigan
Height	5'8"
Weight	150 pounds
Hair	Brown
Eyes	Brown

153

Complexion	Medium
Scars	1" scar calf of right leg; ½" scar center of upper lip
Tattoos	None
Education	11½ grades
Occupation	Laborer and carnival worker
Social Security Number	511-56-9651
Parents	HUGH and ALICE CRAFORD, 1219 Birch Street, Dallas, Oregon
Sister	CORABELLE INGERSOLL, Bellaire, Michigan
Sister	NORMA NEAL, age 18, Dallas, Oregon
Sister	ALICE CRAFORD, Dallas, Oregon
Brother	EDWARD CRAFORD, U.S. Army, Los Angeles, California.
Military Service	U.S. Army RA 1962841, September 18, 1958, to November 10, 1959; general discharge under honorable conditions, not eligible for re-enlistment; discharged per AR-635-200-STN 264
Arrests	Police Department, Findlay, Ohio, 1961, taking a minor across a State Line, no prosecution; Police Department, Dallas, Oregon, January, 1963, drunk and disorderly, fined $25.00 and three days.
Marital Status	Separated
Wife	WILMA JEAN TEANNEY CRAFARD
Son	ROBERT GERALD CRAFARD, born March 1, 1963, Dallas, Texas

CRAFARD explained that his surname is CRAFARD rather than CRAFORD as is the rest of the family, because when he entered the Army, his name was misspelled CRAFARD and he has considered this his name ever since.

154

FD-302 (Rev. 3-3-59)

FEDERAL BUREAU OF INVES [redacted]

Commission Exhibit No. 2251

Date 11-30-63

1

GRAHAM KOCH, Partner, Akin, Vial, Hamilton and Koch, Law Firm, Mercantile Security Building, Dallas, Texas, advised JACK RUBY consulted him on November 29, 1962, regarding a tax matter. KOCH stated RUBY needed legal advise concerning a problem involving his payment of delinquent Income and Excise Taxes to the Federal Government. KOCH stated he has seen RUBY infrequently since his first contact, the last of which was a telephone call from RUBY on November 21, 1963, concerning the tax situation. He stated he, KOCH, is required by law to obtain the Power of Attorney from RUBY to represent RUBY in such matters. KOCH stated he had intended to obtain this power from RUBY a number of months ago but had not gotten around to it until November 19, 1963, when RUBY came to his office for that purpose.

KOCH stated the attitude of RUBY was no different, on November 19, 1963, then it was during any previous contact and he had no reason to think that RUBY was contemplating any unusual eventuality.

KOCH stated he did not represent RUBY on any other matters but was of the opinion that Attorney SHANNON JONES, Dallas, Texas, had represented RUBY a number of years ago.

on 11-29-63 at Dallas, Texas File # DL 44-1639

by Special Agent NORMAN W. PROPST & URAL D. HORTON, JR. - md Date dictated 11-30-63

This document contains neither recommendations nor conclusions of the FBI. It is the property of the FBI and is loaned to your agency; it and its contents are not to be distributed outside your agency.

220

COMMISSION EXHIBIT No. 2251

FD-302 (Rev. 3-3-59)

FEDERAL BUREAU OF IN [redacted]

Commission Exhibit No. 2252

Date 12/3/63

1

JOHN LEIF FRICKSTAD, employed as counterman at Phil's Delicatessen, 3531 Oaklawn, residence, 8631 Turtle Creek Boulevard, phone EM. 3-1288, furnished the following information:

He has known JACK L. RUBY by sight for about two years. He has had very little conversation with him, but does recognize him readily.

On the night of November 22, 1963, sometime after 8:00 PM and probably about 10:00 PM, RUBY came into Phil's Delicatessen and ordered eight corn beef sandwiches with mustard and ten cold drinks, eight Black Cherries and two Celery Tonics. He also ordered three cups of butter, one-half loaf of bread, and some extra pickles. Potato salad and pickles were provided with each sandwich. RUBY stated he was taking these sandwiches to the disc jockies at Radio Station KLIF, since they were working late. He said he didn't know how he would get in with the sandwiches, since the radio station was locked up, but he stated he was sure he could get in since he was bringing them sandwiches. He mentioned they were working late on "this case," apparently referring to the news coverage of the story of the assassination of President JOHN F. KENNEDY.

During the time that he was waiting for the sandwiches to be made, FRICKSTAD stated that the assassination of the President was a terrible thing and RUBY agreed with him, although he did not discuss it to any extent. Much of the time while waiting for the sandwiches to be prepared, RUBY was on the telephone and, from what he said, FRICKSTAD was of the opinion he was talking to a secretary or business associate, since he mentioned New York and told the party on the phone he was leaving the delicatessen to go to KLIF and if anything should come up he could be called at the radio station.

As he left, FRICKSTAD carried the order out to RUBY's car, which he recalls was a white, four-door automobile, possibly a Chevrolet. As he recalls, the total bill was $9.50, plus tax, and as a tip RUBY gave FRICKSTAD one of his cards on which he wrote a notation, and told FRICKSTAD that this card would admit him free to either of his clubs,

on 11/30/63 at Dallas, Texas File # DL 44-1639

by Special Agent BARDWELL D. ODUM/eah Date dictated 12/2/63

221

This document contains neither recommendations nor conclusions of the FBI. It is the property of the FBI and is loaned to your agency; it and its contents are not to be distributed outside your agency.

COMMISSION EXHIBIT No. 2252

DL 44-1639

2

The Vegas or The Carousel. FRICKSTAD stated he still has this card at home.

FRICKSTAD stated as he recalled RUBY was wearing a felt hat and stated that everytime he has seen RUBY he was wearing this hat or one similar to it.

222

COMMISSION EXHIBIT No. 2252—Continued

FD-302 (Rev. 1-25-60)

FEDERAL BUREAU OF INVESTIGATION

1

Date December 2, 1963

PETE FISHER, photographer for United Press International (UPI), was interviewed at his office in the studios of WWL-TV, 1024 North Rampart Street, and voluntarily furnished the following information:

He was in Dallas covering the visit of President KENNEDY to Dallas and only saw JACK LEON RUBY on one occasion following the assassination of the President. FISHER was in the basement show-up room of the Dallas Police Department late during the evening of Friday, November 22, 1963, or early during the morning hours of Saturday, November 23, 1963, when the Dallas Police Department brought LEE HARVEY OSWALD down to the show-up room.

Approximately five minutes before OSWALD was brought into the show-up room on this occasion, FISHER noted RUBY standing in the show-up room near the entrance to the room which is to the right of the show-up stage as one faces the stage. FISHER did not think this unusual as he had known RUBY for about two years and had previously seen him around Police Department Headquarters.

The Dallas Police brought OSWALD through this entrance and OSWALD passed not more than three feet from RUBY as he was led up on the stage. FISHER pointed out that if RUBY had wanted to shoot OSWALD at that time he could easily have done it because of the fact that he was so close to OSWALD.

On Sunday, November 24, 1963, FISHER was at the Courthouse in Dallas where he planned to take photographs of OSWALD when the latter was brought to the County Jail by Dallas Police Officers. He was not at Police Headquarters when RUBY shot OSWALD in the basement of the Police Headquarters Building. Immediately after he heard that OSWALD had been shot, FISHER rushed to Parkland Hospital where he photographed OSWALD as the latter was brought into the hospital for emergency treatment. At no time during the day of November 24, 1963, was FISHER in or near Police

On 12/2/63 at New Orleans, Louisiana File # NO 44-2064

by SA FURMAN G. BOGGAN and SA MYRYWIN G. ALDERSON :gas Date dictated 12/2/63

407

COMMISSION EXHIBIT No. 2253

2

NO 44-2064
FGB,MGA:gas

Department Headquarters.

With regard to security at Police Headquarters on the evening of November 22, 1963, FISHER said that uniformed Police Officers were checking credentials of newsmen on the first floor of the Police and Courts Building before newsmen were allowed to take the elevator to the third floor. FISHER said that after arrival at the third floor, all newsmen's credentials were checked again by uniformed Police Officers.

With regard to FISHER's knowledge of RUBY, FISHER said he first met RUBY approximately two years ago when he had a photographic assignment at the Carousel Club operated by RUBY. At that time FISHER was working in Dallas for UPI and was attached to the Dallas Times Herald Newspaper. During the following two years FISHER would see RUBY from time to time at police headquarters and on the streets of Dallas. He said RUBY knew many Dallas Police Officers and often brought coffee to Dallas Police Officers in Police Headquarters when these officers would be working on prolonged investigations where they were working considerable overtime.

FISHER said he had no knowledge nor did he see any activities which would indicate to him that any Dallas Police Officers or City Officials conspired with RUBY in the killing of OSWALD or permitted RUBY to kill OSWALD. He said he had no knowledge that OSWALD and RUBY were acquainted with each other prior to the assassination of the President or at any other time. He stated that he had heard rumors that OSWALD and RUBY knew each other citing as an example the "memory expert" who was interviewed by the press and who claimed he recalled having seen OSWALD in the Carousel Club. FISHER said he discounts all of these rumors, believing none of them. He said he did not think OSWALD was the type of person who would

408

COMMISSION EXHIBIT No. 2253—Continued

3

NO 44-2064
FGB;GMA:gas

frequent night clubs, but OSWALD could conceivably have been in the Carousel Club as there are only three night clubs in the whole city of Dallas, Texas,

409

COMMISSION EXHIBIT No. 2253—Continued

FD-302 (Rev. 3-3-59) FEDERAL BUREAU (Commission Exhibit No. 2254

L

Date December 10, 1963

Mr. RONALD L. JENKINS, KBOX Radio Station, 9900 McCree Road, Dallas, Texas, advised as follows:

He has been employed as newsman for KBOX Radio Station for the past two months.

On November 22, 1963, he participated in the coverage of President JOHN F. KENNEDY's tour of Dallas with DAVID KING, UPI, Dallas. He did not witness the assassination of President KENNEDY. He said KING did not witness President KENNEDY's assassination and KING was not in the Dallas Police Department basement when LEE HARVEY OSWALD was shot, November 24, 1963.

On November 24, 1963, he was just entering the basement area of the Dallas Police Department from the upper floor when OSWALD was shot. He did not witness the shooting of OSWALD. He recalls seeing many policemen and press representatives in the basement area at the time of the OSWALD shooting. Identities of the policemen and news representatives were mainly unknown to him.

He does not personally know JACK RUBY and did not know LEE HARVEY OSWALD.

He arrived at the Dallas Police Department approximately 4:00 P.M., November 22, 1963, subsequent to the assassination, and was at the police station until early Saturday, November 23, 1963. He was present when OSWALD was brought before press, radio and television representatives during the evening of November 22, 1963, to be photographed and interviewed. He recalled there were a large number of press representatives present in addition to a large number of police officers.

After OSWALD was shot, November 24, 1963, he had an opportunity to briefly view JACK RUBY in person and also saw photographs of RUBY in the newspapers and on television. After seeing RUBY on November 24, 1963 and the photographs, he recalled that on the evening of November 22, 1963, between approximately 5:30 to 7:30 P.M., he saw a man believed to be RUBY on the third floor of the police station. RUBY was milling around in the crowd of press representatives and was alone. The third floor of the police station was almost

on 12/10/63 at Dallas, Texas File # DL 44-1639

by Special Agents EDMOND C. HARDIN & ROBERT J. WILKISON/jn Date dictated 12/10/63

This document contains neither recommendations nor conclusions of the FBI. It is the property of the FBI and is loaned to your agency; it and its contents are not to be distributed outside your agency.

424

COMMISSION EXHIBIT No. 2254

completely filled and was so crowded he could hardly move around. He did not see anyone who did not appear to be a policeman or press representative. He believes he saw RUBY talking to an unknown man near the third floor elevator shaft. He believes RUBY was wearing a light colored top coat and no hat. He did not recall whether RUBY was carrying anything at the time.

About 11:00 P.M., the same date, when OSWALD was made available to the press representatives, he believed he again saw RUBY in the crowd. He believes RUBY was standing on a table where some cameramen were standing and that RUBY had a pad of writing paper in his hand. RUBY was wearing a sport jacket at that time. On both occasions, he thought RUBY was just another press representative but did not recall if RUBY had a press card or other type of identification.

He did not recall anyone checking identification when he entered the room where OSWALD was made available for press representatives on November 22, 1963. He had not left the Police Department during the evening so he did not know if persons entering the Police Department were being checked for identification.

On November 24, 1963, he did observe policemen, both in uniform and in civilian clothing, checking identification of persons entering the Police Department. His identification was checked on several occasions. There were also police guards at the elevator entrances and at various doors leading into the basement area.

He recalled that when he was in the press room on the third floor of the police station during the evening of November 22, 1963, he observed several press cards laying on a table and he reported same to a police officer, name unknown to him.

He does not know of any unauthorized person permitted to enter the police station basement, November 24, 1963, or the police station during the period of November 22 and November 23, 1963. He does not know of any person permitted to enter the police station without showing identification.

He has no information that anyone conspired with RUBY or that any police officer or other official conspired with RUBY or willfully permitted the killing of OSWALD.

425

COMMISSION EXHIBIT No. 2254—Continued

He did not talk to RUBY on any occasion or see anyone talking to RUBY other than the one man whom he did not know.

He has no knowledge of any relationship or prior acquaintance between RUBY and OSWALD.

He said that ~~ROBERT THOMPSON,~~ James Robert Thornton employee of WFAA television, Channel 8, Dallas, told him he was in the Police Department basement when OSWALD was shot.

JENKINS said that SAM PATE then employed as announcer by KBOX Radio Station, was at the press conference November 22, 1963, when OSWALD was brought before the newsmen to be photographed.

He said that JERRY KUNKLE, announcer KBOX Radio Station, was also at the same previously mentioned press conference. He believes THOMPSON, PATE and KUNKLE have all been interviewed concerning their observations.

Mr. JENKINS said he had no other information concerning this matter.

426

COMMISSION EXHIBIT No. 2254—Continued

FD-302 (Rev. 3-3-59)

FEDERAL BUREAU OF INVESTIGA ON

Date December 5, 1963

(1)

FERDINAND KAUFMAN, Aka FERD KAUFMAN, 608 Downing Drive, Dallas, Texas, advised as follows:

He is employed as a photographer with the Associated Press with office at Room 353, Dallas News Building, Dallas, Texas. In this capacity he was present during the evening of November 22, 1963, at a show-up in the show-up room of the Dallas Police Department when LEE HARVEY OSWALD was brought in, in order that members of the press might photograph him. He does not recall seeing JACK RUBY present in that group. He does recall seeing MIKE SMITH, an Associated Press photographer from Los Angeles, who was present and who was situated on the other side of the room from KAUFMAN.

KAUFMAN advised that he has no information or knowledge that JACK RUBY was present at a press conference during the evening of November 23, 1963, held by the District Attorney, Dallas, but does recall that later he read in a Dallas newspaper, the name of which he has forgotten, an article stating that RUBY was reportedly present at this press conference and had a camera crew there.

KAUFMAN stated that on November 22, 1963, immediately following the assassination of President JOHN F. KENNEDY, he, KAUFMAN, proceeded to the City Hall in Dallas to perform his official duties. He recalls that sometime between 4 and 4:30 p.m. on that date he was in a corridor on the 3rd floor of City Hall, and someone called to him by saying "EDDIE." This individual, who then was unknown to KAUFMAN, walked over to him and stated that he had made a mistake; that he thought KAUFMAN was EDDIE BENEDICT, who KAUFMAN knew to be a Dallas free-lance photographer, residing on Lippit Street, to the best of his knowledge. The man introduced himself as JACK RUBY and stated that he was the owner of the Carousel Club. He gave KAUFMAN a business card bearing this club's name and RUBY's name and told KAUFMAN that this card would entitle him to be a guest of his at the Carousel Club, and he invited KAUFMAN to come visit his club.

RUBY then stated, to the best of KAUFMAN's recollection, "I'll be the only Dallas businessman who will have an ad in the

on 12/4/63 at Dallas, Texas File # DL 44-1639

by Special Agents EDMOND C. HARDIN and ROBERT J. WILKISON:bnm Date dictated 12/5/63

436

COMMISSION EXHIBIT No. 2255

DL 44-1639
(2)

morning paper saying that his places of business will be closed for 3 days in memory of the assassination of the President." KAUFMAN stated that he felt that this was most improbable inasmuch as he knew the deadline for placing an ad in the Dallas morning paper was 5 p.m. He talked to RUBY for about three minutes and left inasmuch as he had pressing matters to attend to.

KAUFMAN advised that he did not see RUBY again prior to the shooting of LEE HARVEY OSWALD and that he was not present at the time OSWALD was shot. He further stated that he was not acquainted with OSWALD and has no information indicating or establishing that there was a personal connection between RUBY and OSWALD, but added that he has personally felt since the shooting of OSWALD that OSWALD and RUBY must have known each other and must have conspired in some manner with each other in the assassination of the President.

KAUFMAN further stated that on December 4, 1963, he was contacted by an English reporter, BRIAN PARK, of the London Daily Express, who is presently staying at the Statler Hotel, Dallas, for a few days longer. He had known and had been associated with PARK for a few days at Dallas. PARK stated to him that he had heard a rumor to the effect that JACK RUBY had a display ad in the Dallas Morning News, a Dallas daily newspaper, concerning RUBY's night clubs and at 5 p.m. or a moment before on November 22, 1963, RUBY allegedly called the Display Advertising Department of that newspaper and cancelled his ad and substituted another ad in its place to read that his clubs would be closed due to the assassination of the President.

BRIAN PARK further told KAUFMAN that he had heard that shortly before the assassination of President JOHN F. KENNEDY, RUBY appeared at the office of the Dallas News Display Advertising Department located on the second floor front of the building. He allegedly went there to conduct business concerning placing an advertisement in the paper and wished to see the advertising man who usually helped him in this regard. The advertising man was not present and when RUBY was told that he would return at 12:45 p.m., RUBY allegedly waited in the office for him. BRIAN also stated that he had heard that RUBY was present in that office when President KENNEDY was assassinated,

437

COMMISSION EXHIBIT No. 2255—Continued

and that the windows from that office afforded a perfect view of the front of the Texas School Book Depository Building located two or three blocks away, from which building OSWALD shot President KENNEDY. BRIAN informed that he desired to get a story concerning this situation and wanted to take pictures from a window of the Dallas News Display Advertising Department office of the Texas School Book Depository Building and surrounding area.

KAUFMAN stated that BRIAN was subsequently refused permission to take such photographs which refusal was made by the manager of the Dallas News Display Advertising Department.

KAUFMAN stated that he felt that BRIAN was of the opinion that RUBY had made it a point to be present in the above described office when President KENNEDY was driven by in order to witness his assassination; that is, to witness the actual shooting on the part of OSWALD. KAUFMAN said he believed BRIAN was also of the opinion that there must have been a personal connection between RUBY and OSWALD and for this reason BRIAN was most anxious to take the photographs described above.

brann

KAUFMAN said he personally feels that there must have been a personal relationship between RUBY and OSWALD but added that he has no concrete evidence other than what he has stated above, and that his feelings are based merely on opinion.

KAUFMAN advised that he does not know the identity of anyone in the advertising room with RUBY at the time he was allegedly there to place an ad in the paper on November 22, 1963. He also stated he knows of no other newsmen who may have talked with RUBY on November 22 or 23, 1963, or to whom RUBY may have given business cards or invited to visit his clubs.

KAUFMAN advised that prior to interview on December 4, 1963, he had just returned from Fort Worth, Texas, where he was present, with other newsmen, at an interview with LEE HARVEY OSWALD's mother. He added that while in Fort Worth he met a Secret Service Agent whose name he believes was PARR, first name unknown. He related to PARR the information which he furnished interviewing FBI Agents.

KAUFMAN advised he cannot recall any other pertinent information concerning this case, but stated that he will immediately advise the Dallas Office in the event any additional information is received by him.

438

COMMISSION EXHIBIT No. 2255—Continued

FD-302 (Rev. 3-3-59)

FEDERAL BUREAU OF INVESTIGATION

1

Date 12/6/63

JERRY LEE KUNKEL, 1818 Stevens Force, telephone WH. 1440, was interviewed at the Dallas FBI Office, at which time he furnished the following information:

KUNKEL is employed as a Radio Announcer for Radio Station KBOX and has been so employed since about May, 1963. KUNKEL was not at the Police Department on Sunday, November 24, 1963, when RUBY shot LEE HARVEY OSWALD and, consequently, could furnish no information concerning the shooting of OSWALD or security measures maintained by the Dallas Police Department.

KUNKEL met JACK RUBY approximately eighteen months ago while visiting in Dallas. This meeting took place at the Carousel Club where KUNKEL had gone to see the show. KUNKEL has had no contact with RUBY since that time. The last time he saw RUBY was on Friday night, November 22, 1963, or early Saturday morning, November 23, 1963, when he saw RUBY standing on a chair at the Dallas Police Department Show-up Room, where OSWALD was appearing before a local Justice of the Peace and being charged with the assassination of President KENNEDY.

He subsequently saw RUBY in the hallway on the third floor of the Police Department and overheard RUBY ask an unknown local newsman for the number of Radio Station KLIF Newsroom. RUBY wanted this number so he could contact the newsroom as he had sandwiches which he wished to give them.

KUNKEL observed RUBY hand out cards advertising the Carousel Club and handed one of these cards to KUNKEL, although KUNKEL is positive RUBY did not remember him from their previous meeting about eighteen months ago.

KUNKEL could furnish no information indicating any association between OSWALD and RUBY.

on 12/4/63 at Dallas, Texas File # DL 44-1639

by Special Agents JOSEPH G. PEGGS & ALVIN ZIMMERMAN Date dictated 12/6/63
eah

444

COMMISSION EXHIBIT No. 2256

FD-302 (Rev. 3-3-59) FEDERAL BUREAU O— Commission Exhibit No. 2257

1

Date December 4, 1963

SAMUEL MACK PATE, news reporter for KBOX Radio Station, Dallas, Texas, was interviewed at his home at 310 Beautycrest, Dallas, Texas, concerning his presence as a newsman at the Police Department, Dallas, at the time of the shooting of LEE HARVEY OSWALD. PATE stated that he was not at the Police Department when LEE HARVEY OSWALD was shot; that he was home at the time and heard about the shooting on the radio. Consequently, he knew nothing of the security precautions taken by the Dallas Police Department in connection with OSWALD's transfer from the Police Department to the County Jail.

PATE advised he has known RUBY for several years, but only as a casual acquaintance. He has never heard RUBY express any political opinions, never discussed anything concerning politics with him and had never seen LEE HARVEY OSWALD prior to his arrest for the assassination of President KENNEDY. He does not know of any possible contact between OSWALD and RUBY. PATE states he did see RUBY at the Assembly Room of the Dallas Police Department about midnight, Friday, November 22, 1963 at a press conference held by HENRY WADE. PATE said RUBY appeared to be only an interested observer at this conference and he heard RUBY make no statements in the Assembly Room. After the conference, PATE and JERRY KUNKEL, who is also a reporter for KBOX Radio Station, talked with RUBY in the hall outside the Assembly Room. The conversation at this time was primarily about RUBY's night club business. PATE recalls nothing specific about the conversation concerning the assassination of President KENNEDY. He recalls that RUBY did not seem particularly disturbed by the event. He also remembers that RUBY asked for the "hot line" of KLIF and was given the number which he wrote on a business card or a piece of paper. He did not say why he wanted the number. During this conversation, which lasted less than five minutes, RUBY was introduced to JERRY KUNKEL by PATE. RUBY then invited KUNKEL to the Carousel Club and gave him a business card. RUBY was still standing in the hall outside the Assembly Room when PATE and KUNKEL left the area.

PATE states he quit his job with KBOX at 6:00 P.M., Saturday, November 23, 1963 due to a budget cut and has no other information concerning this case.

on 11/30/63 at Dallas, Texas File # DL 44-1639

by Special Agents GARY S. WILSON & RICHARD T. RABIDEAU/jn Date dictated 12/4/63

477

COMMISSION EXHIBIT No. 2257

FD-302 (Rev. 1-25-60) FEDERAL BUREAU OF INVESTIGAT

1

Date 12/1/63

DAVID FLINT "MIKE" SMITH, 2321 Chandler Street, advised that he is employed as a Photographer for Associated Press in Los Angeles and that his office is located in the Los Angeles Times Building, 202 West 1st Street, Los Angeles, California. Mr. SMITH advised that approximately one hour after hearing of the President's assassination in Dallas, Texas on November 22, 1963, he and the Photographing Editor, RICHARD STROBEL, left Los Angeles for Dallas, Texas.

He advised that on Sunday morning, November 24, 1963, all of the news media people had congregated in the Dallas Police Department Building. He advised that he picked a place in the basement about one-third of the way from the door from which LEE HARVEY OSWALD would emerge and approximately two-thirds from where the armored truck was parked. He advised that OSWALD was to emerge from a door where the police have a booking office and would have to walk about eight feet to a driveway. Mr. SMITH stated that he could observe and photograph OSWALD from his vantage point as he walked to the armored truck. At the last moment, however, the Dallas Police Department brought two unmarked cars from the parking space below this area and parked them directly behind the armored truck. SMITH got pushed back from where he wanted to be and he advised that as he tried to maneuver around the back of the second car to gain a vantage point he heard someone say, "Here he comes". Mr. SMITH advised that because of the small hallway from which OSWALD emerged, he could not see him. He stated that almost immediately, about three seconds, after hearing the comment, "Here he comes", SMITH stated that he heard a shot. He looked over the heads of people in front of him and saw the top of OSWALD's head as OSWALD was falling backwards between two detectives. Immediately he observed Dallas Police Officers pounce on a man, who he later determined was JACK RUBY.

Mr. SMITH advised that he was present in the Dallas Police Building during Friday evening, November 22, 1963 and at various times on Saturday, November 23, 1963

On 12/1/63 at Burbank, California File # Los Angeles 44-895

by SAA EUGENE I. TUGGEY, JR.;mjg Date dictated 12/1/63

513

COMMISSION EXHIBIT No. 2258

LA 44-895
2

He advised that the third floor hallway at the Police Department on Friday evening was mass confusion caused by the number of news media people present. He believes that the first time his press identification card was checked was on Saturday afternoon when he emerged from the elevator on the third floor of the Dallas Police Department Building. Mr. SMITH advised that on Sunday morning, November 24, 1963, there was an unusual number of uniformed Dallas Police Officers evident around the halls of the Police Department Building.

He stated that just before OSWALD emerged from the small booking office into the garage, the Dallas Police made the press representatives stand along the east side of the building. He advised that at least 15 detectives appeared at this point along with at least one uniformed captain, one uniformed lieutenant and a uniformed sergeant. The police personnel lined up on the west wall opposite from the press for what Mr. SMITH believes was the purpose of observing the press and OSWALD as he walked to the armored car.

SMITH said he has heard rumors that the Dallas Police Department decided to place OSWALD in the second vehicle behind the armored truck and to lay him crosswise on the back seat with two detectives sitting on the back seat in front of him, rather than to place OSWALD in the armored truck. He understood they felt in this way, they would throw anyone off the track who had any ulterior motives as such a person would believe OSWALD was being transported in the armored truck preceeding the two cars.

Mr. SMITH advised that when he entered the Dallas Police Department on Sunday morning, November 24, 1963, prior to the shooting of OSWALD, his press identification card was checked by a Dallas Officer and his photograph compared with his appearance. He advised that

574

COMMISSION EXHIBIT No. 2258—Continued

LA 44-895
3

when he got out of the elevator on the third floor of the building, his identification and photograph were again checked by an officer. He stated that one of the men from the press got off the elevator with him. SMITH did not know his name. The man apparently was without identification. The officer checking the press identification cards immediately referred this man to a Dallas Police Sergeant.

Mr. SMITH determined that the best place for photographing OSWALD would be in the basement of the Dallas Police Department. He left the third floor and went to the basement of the building where his identification and photograph were again checked by a Dallas Police Officer.

He advised that he knows of no unauthorized people who were present in the basement of the Dallas Police Department on Sunday morning, November 24, 1963, or anyone who was in the building without proper identification.

He advised that he possesses no information that anyone conspired with JACK RUBY in the shooting of LEE HARVEY OSWALD. He further advised that he has no information that anyone in an official capacity with the Dallas Police Department or anyone acting under the cover of law conspired with RUBY in connection with the shooting of OSWALD.

He stated that he did not see or talk with JACK RUBY on Sunday morning, November 24, 1963 prior to the shooting of OSWALD. He advised that he does not know JACK RUBY or LEE HARVEY OSWALD and possesses no information concerning any connection between these two men.

Mr. SMITH advised that after the shooting of OSWALD and the identity of JACK RUBY was made available to the news people, he recalled that he had possibly seen JACK RUBY at a news conference in the Show Up Room of the Dallas Police Department Building sometime between 9:00 and 9:30 p.m. on November 23, 1963. He advised that he

575

COMMISSION EXHIBIT No. 2258—Continued

LA 44-895
4

believes this conference was brought about by the pressure brought upon the Dallas Police Department by the late arriving news media people and that OSWALD was brought into the Show Up Room for about three minutes for the purpose of photographs and questions.

He further advised that he heard from one of the newsmen in Dallas, whom he believes was FRED KAUFMAN, Associated Press, Dallas, Texas, that JACK RUBY was present on Saturday evening, November 23, 1963 when District Attorney WADE held a press conference. He recalls that District Attorney WADE made a comment during the Sunday night press conference that RUBY had asked him a question during the conference of Saturday night and was present in the room with the press.

Mr. SMITH further advised that FRED KAUFMAN advised him that he had received a business card from JACK RUBY and that RUBY had invited him to visit his club. Mr. SMITH does not know where KAUFMAN met RUBY. He assumed it was somewhere around Dallas Police Department on Friday or Saturday, November 22 or 23, 1963. He advised that he is also under the impression that other news media people who had had an occasion to talk to JACK R UBY during November 22 or 23, 1963 had also received such invitations from RUBY and his business card.

576

FD-302 (Rev. 3-3-59)

FEDERAL BUREAU OF INVESTIC ION

1

Date December 7, 1963

JOE CAMPISI, 4445 Ashford, Dallas, Texas, owner of the Egyptian Restaurant, 5610 East Mockingbird Lane, furnished the following information:

On Friday, November 29, 1963, he received a telephone call from Captain DECKER, Dallas County Sheriff's Office, in which Captain DECKER told him that JACK RUBY wanted to see him. He said Captain DECKER told him he was one of several people that RUBY had requested permission to see.

CAMPISI advised on Saturday evening, November 30, 1963, he went to the Dallas County Jail where he talked with RUBY for approximately ten minutes. He said RUBY told him he had received a lot of mail and commented: "All the girls love me." He said RUBY asked him if his, RUBY's, friends were mad at him and also asked him about the lawyer he had retained.

CAMPISI said while he was talking to RUBY, he, RUBY, broke down and started crying and said: "Here I am fighting for my life and feeling sorry for myself, when I really feel sorry for Mrs. KENNEDY and the kids."

CAMPISI said RUBY did not give any indication of why he killed OSWALD, however, he said "Somebody had to kill him." He said RUBY gave no indication of ever having known OSWALD previously.

CAMPISI advised he has known RUBY since about 1948, however, has never associated with him and the only contacts he has ever had with RUBY were when he would stop in at the Carousel Club after he closed his place of business, when RUBY would come to his, CAMPISI's place of business, and at various sporting events which were held in the city.

He said his last contact with RUBY was on the Thursday night before Thanksgiving when RUBY came to the Egyptian Restaurant for a steak.

on 12-6-63 at Dallas, Texas File # DL 44-1639

by Special Agent s ROBERT E. BASHAM ~~JAMES J. WARD~~ mvs Date dictated 12-6-63

2

DL 44-1639

CAMPISI advised RUBY was a very impulsive individual and he has seen him hit guests at his club without provocation. He said RUBY was a "crazy S.O.B."

CAMPISI said he never knew of RUBY to carry a gun and never knew of him to carry large sums of money. He said he was surprised when he heard RUBY had $2,000 on his person at the time of his arrest. He said he had always considered RUBY to be very frugal and close-fisted with his money.

CAMPISI said he knows nothing of RUBY's background or associates and doesn't know of anyone who ever lived with him, as he never socialized with him.

CAMPISI advised he was surprised when Captain DECKER called him and told him that RUBY wanted to see him. He said he doesn't know of anyone else who has visited RUBY and the only person present at the time he talked to RUBY was a Deputy Sheriff.

129

COMMISSION EXHIBIT No. 2259—Continued

FD-302 (Rev. 3-3-59) FEDERAL BUREAU OF Commission Exhibit No. 2260

1 Date 12/10/63

JOSEPH A. GLOWACKI, 3442 Knox, Dallas, Texas, furnished the following information:

On November 22, 1963, he was in the downtown area of Dallas with KRYSTIAN BARCZ, a Polish National who was visiting the U. S. on a State Department study grant. During the afternoon of November 22, 1963, they stopped at the Ritz Delicatessen for lunch and while there he observed JACK RUBY walking around in the delicatessen. He introduced him to Mr. BARCZ and invited him to sit at their table. He declined with the comment that he was just walking around. He was still at the delicatessen when they left.

Mr. GLOWACKI advised that at that time JACK RUBY did not appear to him to be any more agitated or upset than the average citizen. In fact, he asked Mr. GLOWACKI, "JOE, what is this going to do to our business? We're going to lose all of the conventions". It appeared to Mr. GLOWACKI that he was more concerned with the result on business than he was by the actual assassination of the President. Mr. GLOWACKI advised that he has probably known Mr. RUBY since about 1957. He considers him a casual acquaintance and not a friend but has seen him quite often at the B & B Cafe, which is near the Vegas Club, or in the Vegas Club or the Carousel Club.

He estimated that he has been in the Carousel Club on five or six occasions and was last there about six to eight months ago. On the occasions he was in the Carousel Club, he noted that RUBY apparently was acquainted with a large number of people and would move from table to table greeting the patrons. He recalls no instances in which photographers were taking pictures of the patrons of the Carousel Club. He recalls having seen no officers of the Dallas Police Department in the Carousel Club but does recall having seen officers in the Vegas Club on numerous occasions.

He advised that in those instances in which he observed officers at the Vegas Club, they usually came into the club during the late hours, stood around for a few minutes and then left. He saw no instances in which they were obviously being treated at no cost by the management of the Vegas Club. Mr. GLOWACKI advised that he is not well enough acquainted with RUBY to have information

on 12/9/63 at Dallas, Texas File # DL 44-1639

by Special Agents RALPH E. RAWLINGS and JAMES F. GLONEK - LAC Date dictated 12/9/63

157

COMMISSION EXHIBIT No. 2260

DL 44-1639
2

concerning his closest associates, his travels, or other activites. On one occasion some three or four years ago, RUBY asked him to go into partnership with him in the operation of one of the night clubs, but he considered this simply a promotion deal and did not enter into a serious discussion with him.

158

COMMISSION EXHIBIT No. 2260—Continued

FD-302 (Rev. 3-3-59) FEDERAL BUREAU O

Commission Exhibit No. 2261

1

Date December 10, 1963

CECIL HAMLIN, 3227 San Paula, Dallas, Texas, furnished the following information:

HAMLIN is presently union representative of Amalgamated Meat Cutters and Butcher Workmen of North America, AFL-CIO, Dallas, Texas.

HAMLIN met JACK RUBY in the latter part of 1948. At that time RUBY was operating the Silver Spur Club on South Ervay Street, Dallas, and HAMLIN was residing at the old Abbott Hotel located nearby. He began frequenting the Silver Spur Club and was on very friendly terms with RUBY until about 1950. Most of his contacts with RUBY were at the Silver Spur Club on South Ervay Street. In 1950, HAMLIN remarried and he visited the club less frequently but has been a good friend of RUBY since. At times while RUBY was operating the Silver Spur Club, HAMLIN would help out at the club. Subsequently, when RUBY operated the Vegas Club, HAMLIN and his wife would assist RUBY at this club on infrequent occasions. HAMLIN and his wife assisted RUBY on the night RUBY opened the Carousel Club on Commerce Street in downtown Dallas.

HAMLIN knew that RUBY was originally from Chicago but RUBY seldom discussed his background except to mention that he had some pretty hard times when he was young in Chicago.

HAMLIN recalled that while RUBY was operating the Silver Spur and Vegas Clubs in Dallas, he discovered a young Negro boy called "Little Daddy" about four years of age who played drums and danced. RUBY used this boy on shows at his clubs and on one occasion, took the boy to Chicago where RUBY obtained bookings at various clubs. HAMLIN does not recall when this was except probably in early 1950's and he was gone several weeks.

HAMLIN and his wife have attended shows and gone out to dinner with RUBY on a number of occasions since they have known him and he has always acted as a gentleman on these occasions and they never knew him to mistreat or be abusive toward anyone.

RUBY was impulsive and quick tempered and on occasion

on 12/9/63 at Dallas, Texas File # DL 44-1639

by Special Agents PAUL L. SCOTT & JAMES S. WEIR/jn Date dictated 12/10/63

163

COMMISSION EXHIBIT No. 2261

2
DL 44-1639

would argue with and berate employees at his clubs, however, he would get over this quickly and would be sorry for his actions. RUBY also acted as his own bouncer and would occasionally have to throw some unruly customer out of his club.

Since about 1950, RUBY has visited in the HAMLIN home a number of times and has called him frequently at his home. He had not seen RUBY for approximately two months prior to the assassination of President KENNEDY. On Friday night, November 22, 1963, RUBY called HAMLIN and mentioned what terrible thing that had happened. He seemed very emotional at the time of the call and said something to the effect "things are all messed up." He said he was closing his clubs until Monday since he thought people would not feel like going to the clubs. He also mentioned how sorry he felt for President KENNEDY's "kids". He was very fond of HAMLIN's small child and inquired about her. HAMLIN received the impression from this phone call that RUBY was considerably "broken up" over the shooting of the President. HAMLIN does not recall that RUBY even mentioned LEE HARVEY OSWALD during this call. He had never previously heard RUBY mention OSWALD and to his knowledge, RUBY did not even know OSWALD. HAMLIN was not acquainted with LEE HARVEY OSWALD and never saw OSWALD or anyone resembling OSWALD at RUBY's club.

HAMLIN and his wife were deeply shocked when they heard of the shooting of OSWALD by RUBY and could not believe it for some time thinking there must have been some mistake.

Subsequently on Monday, November 25, 1963, RUBY called HAMLIN from the Dallas County Jail. He said he was feeling very "low" and seemed to want to know how HAMLIN and his wife felt toward him. He said he guessed he had ruined his life in just a few minutes and that if he had it to do over again, he sure wouldn't do it. He asked HAMLIN to visit him if he could. He mentioned during this call that he had just parked his car before going to the police building prior to shooting OSWALD and had left the dog in the car. HAMLIN gathered from this remark that RUBY had planned to return to the car in a few minutes and that if he had actually planned the shooting of OSWALD, he would not have taken the dog with him.

HAMLIN does not know of any connections RUBY had in Chicago or elsewhere except other members of his family. He does not know of any extensive travel by RUBY except occasional

164

COMMISSION EXHIBIT No. 2261—Continued

3
DL 44-1639

trips to Chicago. He never mentioned any trips out of the United States. In early November, 1963, RUBY talked about going to New York to contact the AGVA about bookings for shows and he later mentioned that he had gone to New York. HAMLIN believes that some years ago, RUBY may have taken a brief trip to Nevada but he is not certain of this.

HAMLIN has never been an employee of RUBY, except to help out occasionally at his club and has never had any financial interest in any of RUBY's business enterprises.

RUBY is widely acquainted in the Dallas area and knows a number of policemen but HAMLIN does not know of any particular policemen RUBY was friendly with. He would occasionally have policemen at his club but these would be from the "dance hall detail". HAMLIN does not know any of the policemen who worked on this detail.

Although RUBY seemed to be well known in Dallas, he had few close associates. HAMLIN recalled RALPH PAUL and BRECK WALL as associates of RUBY. He does not know the nature of their association.

After RUBY was placed in the Dallas County Jail, HAMLIN requested permission to visit him, however, he was denied permission until Saturday, November 29, 1963, when he received a call from Sheriff BILL DECKER who told him RUBY was feeling "low" and that he could visit with him.

HAMLIN stated he expected to be called as a character witness for RUBY when he is brought to trial for the shooting of LEE HARVEY OSWALD.

HAMLIN advised that he visited RUBY again at the County Jail on about November 31, 1963 and at that time RUBY asked him to handle telegrams, messages and funds relating to the defense of RUBY. HAMLIN at first agreed to do this for RUBY but later after talking to his, HAMLIN's supervisor, he decided that he could not handle this matter for RUBY. He then told RUBY and RUBY's attorney, TOM HOWARD, that he could not handle the messages and defense funds for RUBY. HAMLIN said that in view of his employment he does not intend to become further involved in this matter.

HAMLIN advised he could furnish no additional information.

165

COMMISSION EXHIBIT No. 2261—Continued

FD-302 (Rev. 3-3-59)

FEDERAL BUREAU OF IN[redacted] — Commission Exhibit No. 2262

Date 12-11-63

1

CLIFFORD L. WRIGHT, General Foreman of the Composing Room in the "Dallas Morning News", advised that his department received two advertisements on November 22, 1963. These advertisements were for the Vegas Club and the Carousel Club. Mr. WRIGHT stated that his department got the ad set up and they were taken back. He stated that they were received again in his department at 2:41 p.m. from the Service Department. He pointed out that it appears that there was a small change made on one of the advertisements by the Service Department and it may have been made as a result of a call from RUBY. He further stated that at approximately 7:00 p.m., RUBY either called back or came back and changed one of the ads.

Mr. WRIGHT furnished the following additional information:

His record reflects that at 7:00 p.m., RUBY requested that a change be made for both the Vegas and Carousel Club ad to show that both were to be closed Friday, Saturday and Sunday nights.

At 7:00 p.m. RUBY wanted to changed the ad on the Carousel Club so that it would show "closed tonight and Sunday." Mr. WRIGHT pointed out that RUBY was obviously "balled up" because he was trying to leave out the fact that the clubs would be closed Saturday night.

Mr. WRIGHT stated that he is sure RUBY wanted the ad to reflect that the clubs would be closed Saturday night, too. He pointed out further that when RUBY wanted to make a change at 9:00 p.m., he apparently wanted to make the change for the Carousel Club and not for the Vegas Club. This was further indication to Mr. WRIGHT that RUBY was "balled up."

Mr. WRIGHT advised that JOE COUCH is apparently the man that RUBY made the change of the ads with at 7:00 p.m.

on 12-10-63 at Dallas, Texas File # DL 44-1639

by Special Agent JACK B. PEDEN - md Date dictated 12-11-63

513

COMMISSION EXHIBIT No. 2262

2

DL 44-1639

He further said that COUCH is apparently the man whom RUBY tried to make a change with at 9:00 pm. Mr. WRIGHT advised that the attempt to change at 9:00 p.m. was not made because it was too late to make such changes.

Mr. WRIGHT said that he could not state whether or not RUBY came to the office on the changes of the clubs ads or whether he called in. He stated that most likely JACK RUBY called to make the changes on the ad.

514

COMMISSION EXHIBIT No. 2262—Continued

FD-302 (Rev. 3-3-59) FEDERAL BUREAU OF INV[redacted] — Commission Exhibit No. 2263 —

Date 12-11-63

1

JOHN NEWNAM, Advertising Salesman for the "Dallas Morning News" advised that on November 21, 1963, JACK RUBY did not come to the advertising department of the "Dallas Morning News" to his, NEWNAMS, knowledge. He stated that RUBY did call him, NEWNAM, at approximately noon time and reserved the space for two advertisements. These advertisements were to be advertisements of the Vegas Club and the Carousel Club. He said that at approximately 2:30 p.m., RUBY caled and gave him the copy for the ad.

NEWNAM further advised that on November 22, 1963, the day of the President's assassination when JACK RUBY was in the advertising department of the "Dallas Morning News" between 12:00 and 1:00 p.m., RUBY paid for all advertisements up until Saturday, November 23, 1963. RUBY agreed to pay him again on a later date.

on 12-10-63 at Dallas, Texas File # DL 44-1639

by Special Agent JACK B. PEDEN - md Date dictated 12-11-63

521

COMMISSION EXHIBIT NO. 2263

FD-302 (Rev. 3-3-59) FEDERAL BUREAU OF IN[redacted] — Commission Exhibit No. 2264 —

Date December 4, 1963

1

GEORGIA MAYOR, Secretary in the Advertising Division, Dallas "Morning News," home address 115 West 7th Street, Dallas, Texas, advised that on November 22, 1963, she returned from her lunch hour at approximately 12:30 p.m. She said that when she returned JACK RUBY was sitting in a chair directly in front of her desk. She said she is not sure which way he was looking but she had a faint impression that he was looking out at the scene where President KENNEDY was assassinated. She emphasized that she is not sure of this, however. She pointed out that in the particular chair where RUBY was sitting the Texas School Book Depository Building was clearly visible and further that the particular window from which the assassin shot is clearly visible.

Miss MAYOR stated that she had received information as she was returning from her lunch hour that the President had been shot. She stated that HAL COLEY had furnished her this information and she said that after stopping briefly downstairs to cash a check she came directly to the advertising room by the elevator. She said further that DICK SAUNDERS, the employee whose desk is in front of hers, and in whose chair RUBY was sitting, can verify the above information.

Miss MAYOR stated that when she first saw RUBY she did not notice him looking particularly dazed or pale but that at approximately 1:00p.m. she again saw RUBY at JOHN NEWNAM's desk and at that time he seemed very dazed. She advised that he just stared into space when she noticed him at NEWNAM's desk. Miss MAYOR informed that she does not know the significance of RUBY being at that one particular spot where he could observe the assassination scene and admitted that she realized the distance was approximately 600 to 800 yards from the "Morning News" Building to the Texas School Book Depository Building.

on 12/4/63 at Dallas, Texas File # Dallas 44-1639

by Special Agent S JACK B. PEDEN & JAMES E. GARRIS:BL Date dictated 12/4/63

524

COMMISSION EXHIBIT NO. 2264

— Commission Exhibit No. 2265

FD-302 (Rev. 3-3-59)

FEDERAL BUREAU OF IN[redacted]

1

Date 12/5/63

MAX RUDBERG, AAA Bonding Service, 106 North Record, advised that on Thursday, November 21, 1963, about 11:00 AM, JACK RUBY was at his bonding office, 106 North Record.

RUDBERG stated he believes RUBY remarked he had just come from the District Attorney's Office. RUDBERG stated RUBY talked about a peace bond hearing in which he was the defendant and which hearing was held by Judge W. E. RICHBERG sometime previously. RUDBERG stated RUDY indicated that this peace bond had been filed against him by a strip-teaser named "JADA."

RUDBERG advised that RALPH GISMONT, an attorney, was at the bonding office during the time RUDBERG was there and also talked to RUBY. RUDBERG stated RUBY left the bonding office a little after 11:00 AM and said something about going to the Dallas Morning News to see about his advertisement. RUDBERG stated he is positive that the above incident occurred on November 21, 1963.

RUDBERG advised he has known JACK RUBY for the past five years and at no time has there ever been any indication that RUBY was connected with the "Fair Play for Cuba Committee" or was a communist sympathizer. He stated RUBY has never given any indication of having any type political interests.

RUDBERG stated he knew of no possible connection or association between RUBY and LEE HARVEY OSWALD and RUBY had never given any indication that he knew OSWALD.

on 12/5/63 at Dallas, Texas File # DL 44-1639

by Special Agents JAMES W. BOOKHOUT & GEORGE W. H. CARLSON/eah Date dictated 12/5/63

532

This document contains neither recommendations nor conclusions of the FBI. It is the property of the FBI and is loaned to your agency; it and its contents are not to be distributed outside your agency.

COMMISSION EXHIBIT No. 2265

FD-302 (Rev. 3-3-59)

FEDERAL BUREAU OF INV — Commission Exhibit No. 2266 —

[redacted]

1

Date 12/4/63

JEAN AASE, 20 E. Delaware, Apartment 1405, Chicago, Illinois, advised that she is unemployed. She advised that on November 20, 1963, she accompanied a friend, Mr. LAWRENCE V. MEYERS, to Dallas, Texas from Chicago. She described this as a business trip of Mr. MEYERS. She stated that they arrived in Dallas, Texas, via Braniff Airlines at approximately 8:00 PM, November 20, 1963 and checked into the Ramada Motel where they remained that night. On November 21, 1963 they moved to the Cabana Motel.

She stated that on Thursday, November 21, 1963 she and Mr. MEYERS had dinner and then he asked if she would care to meet a friend of his who ran a "strip show". She agreed, and they then went to the Carousel Club which is operated by JACK RUBY. On arriving at the club, MEYERS introduced her to RUBY and the three of them sat at a table near the doorway and chatted. She advised they stayed at the club for approximately one hour at which time they returned to the Cabana Motel. She estimated this to be at approximately 11:00 PM. Shortly thereafter RUBY joined the party at the Cabana Motel where he stayed for "a few minutes" and then departed saying he had to return to his club. During this period she said there was no discussion of the President of the United States and their conversation was limited to small talk and show people and personalities. She stated that they stayed in Dallas until Monday night, November 25, 1963 at which time they returned to Chicago. She advised she did not see RUBY again during this stay.

She stated her contact with RUBY was limited to this one occasion and she is unable to furnish any information regarding him other than that he was introduced to her as the owner of the Carousel Club in Dallas, Texas.

on 12/3/63 at Chicago, Illinois File # DL 44-1639 CG 44-645

by Special Agent SAs GEORGE H. PARFET and RICHARD B. LEE/Jel Date dictated 12/3/63

532

This document contains neither recommendations nor conclusions of the FBI. It is the property of the FBI and is loaned to your agency; it and its contents are not to be distributed outside your agency.

COMMISSION EXHIBIT No. 2266

— Commission Exhibit No. 2267

FD-302 (Rev. 3-3-59)

FEDERAL BUREAU OF INVE[redacted]

1

Date 12/12/63

Mr. LAWRENCE V. MEYERS, Ero Manufacturing Company, 714 West Monroe Street, Chicago, Illinois, advised that he is employed as sales manager of the Sporting Goods Division of this firm and resides at 3950 North Lake Shore Drive, Chicago, Illinois, with his wife and two children.

Mr. MEYERS advised that during the course of his business contacts he has been required to make frequent trips to Dallas, Texas, over the past several years. On one occasion approximately five years ago he met JACK RUBY at RUBY's night club, and since that time he has visited in RUBY's night club on numerous occasions.

He advised that on November 20, 1963, he flew to Dallas, Texas, where on the night of November 20, 1963, he stayed at the Ramada Motel and checked into the Cabana Motel on the morning of November 21, 1963. He stated he pursued his normal business affairs that date and in the evening following dinner he went to JACK RUBY's Carousel Club. Mr. MEYERS stated that on this trip to Dallas he was accompanied by Miss JEAN WEST whom he had known casually as a resident of 20 East Delaware Street, Chicago, Illinois. He described Miss WEST as a "rather dumb, but accommodating broad". He further pointed out that his association with Miss WEST is not known to members of his family or to his business associates. When he and Miss WEST arrived at the Carousel Club he introduced her to the owner, JACK RUBY, and RUBY joined them at their table, buying Miss WEST two champagne cocktails. He stated that during the course of their stay at the club on that evening the conversation revolved primarily around show personalities, the acts currently appearing at the club and other items of topical interest. He advised that he and Miss WEST remained at the Carousel Club for approximately one hour, returning to their motel at about 11:00 PM. Mr. MEYERS stated while at the Carousel Club he had invited RUBY to join him at the Cabana Motel for a drink with him and his brother, EDWARD MEYERS, and EDWARD's wife, who were attending a convention in Dallas. He said that shortly thereafter JACK RUBY came to the motel where he was introduced to his brother and his wife. RUBY remained at the motel for only a few minutes before he left, saying that he had to return to his club.

on 12/3/63 at Chicago, Illinois File # DL 44-1639

by Special Agent s RICHARD B. LEE and GEORGE H. PARFET - gj Date dictated 12/3/63

533

COMMISSION EXHIBIT No. 2267

DL 44-1639
2

Mr. MEYERS stated that his next contact with JACK RUBY was at approximately 10:30 PM, Saturday, November 23, 1963, when RUBY telephoned him at the Cabana Motel. He said that at this time RUBY seemed greatly disturbed over the President's assassination, and that this feeling was compounded by the fact that, according to RUBY, the Colony Club and the Theatre Lounge, which are operated by ABE and BARNEY WEINSTEIN, were remaining open for business in spite of the fact that all other clubs had closed out of respect for the President. MEYERS said that RUBY asked, "what do you think of this awful thing," and "I've got to do something about this.". MEYERS stated although he did not give it any thought at the time he does not now know upon reflection whether RUBY was referring to the WEINSTEIN brother's clubs remaining open or whether he was referring to the assassination of President KENNEDY, at this time. JACK RUBY invited MEYERS to join him for a cup of coffee, but MEYERS declined the invitation and in return invited RUBY to come to the motel to talk, RUBY in turn declined the invitation and at that time it was agreed that they would meet the following evening for dinner. The conversation ended on this note and MEYERS has not been in further contact with JACK RUBY.

Mr. MEYERS stated that on Sunday, November 24, 1963, he drove to Mc Kinney, Texas, where a factory of his firm is located and then continued on to Sherman, Texas, where he intended to play golf. He said that while enroute he had the car radio on and heard the news that RUBY had killed LEE HARVEY OSWALD in the Dallas Police Station. MEYERS stated that his reaction was one of shock and disbelief that RUBY could actually have been involved in such a deed.

MEYERS stated that upon his return to Dallas he debated whether or not to contact the Dallas Police concerning his recent association with RUBY, but decided that in the light of the apparent hectic activities then ensuing at the police station it would be better if he did not do so. MEYERS also stated that he made no effort to contact RUBY.

MEYERS stated that his observations and associations with RUBY over the past five years have culminated in some rather definite ideas as to RUBY's personality. He stated

534

COMMISSION EXHIBIT No. 2267—Continued

that he regards RUBY as a person who is well aware of his lack of formal education and who, by association with individuals who are well educated and/or well respected, tries to inflate his own position. MEYERS explained that on many occasions RUBY would drop names of well known entertainers, managers and agents, or would make a point of being seen in the company of a public official or respected member of the community. He seemingly felt that by engaging in these activities he would himself, gain stature and importance. He stated that RUBY has always impressed him as a gregarious individual who genuinely liked to be with people and in order to promote this need and to encourage business at his club would pass out drink cards free to any group with which he came in contact. He stated that although he, MEYERS, was never introduced to any police officers in Dallas, RUBY on many occasions would identify various individuals in the club as being members of the Dallas Police Department. He stated that through past conversations with RUBY he is of the impression that RUBY was well known to most of the members of the Dallas Police Department.

MEYERS continued that he does not consider RUBY to be an emotionally stable person and that RUBY has always been very emphatic concerning his likes and dislikes. He stated that RUBY seldom, if ever, takes a middle of the road attitude, but would rather have a strong leaning toward one or the other extreme. MEYERS advised that he feels JACK RUBY would usually act on the spur of the moment, being quick to either help or to fight. In this regard, he commented that JACK RUBY had seemed rather perturbed on his last three or four visits and in fact, poured out his troubles to MEYERS regarding other clubs that were in competition to RUBY's. Specifically RUBY mentioned that the actors unions had caused them to quit engaging in amateur nights wherein girls with no experience would try out as strippers in the night clubs.

MEYERS stated that RUBY had stopped this practice but that the clubs operated by the WEINSTEIN brothers had continued to do this and that he had hoped he could get the union managements to change their rule and allow this practice to continue. Regarding RUBY being "quick to fight" he said he meant he did not mean physically, inasmuch as he had never seen JACK RUBY in a physical fight, but was referring to RUBY's quick and firm convictions.

535

He stated that he had never seen RUBY with a gun but on one occasion when RUBY had closed the club, MEYERS accompanied him to his automobile where he placed the night's proceeds in the trunk of the car. Something was said at the time which gave MEYERS the impression that RUBY sometimes maintained a gun in the trunk of his car because of the sums of money that he was required to remove from the club.

Regarding his general association with RUBY he stated that to his knowledge RUBY drank very little, was a "health nut" and had a deep interest in physical fitness. He said in this regard he at one time had obtained a set of barbells for RUBY's personal use. He continued that he did not know of any close friends or associates of RUBY's, but mentioned that he had met GEORGE SENATOR in RUBY's place of business on several occasions. He advised he does not know if SENATOR had any official connection with the club or not. He stated that he can place no credence in the newspaper queries that RUBY had any connection or acquaintance whatsoever with LEE HARVEY OSWALD or any Chicago hoodlums. He stated that regarding the latter he is sure that knowing MEYERS was from Chicago, he would have at some time or another dropped the name of someone engaged in underworld activities in the Chicago area in hopes of enhancing his own level of importance in MEYERS's eyes. MEYERS also said that although he does not know anything about JACK RUBY's political affiliations RUBY has never given him any reason whatsoever to think that he has any communistic tendencies or interests.

He said that he had formed the opinion that RUBY shot LEE HARVEY OSWALD for one of two reasons, "that RUBY sincerely felt he was ridding the world of vermin in shooting OSWALD" or that he "elected himself executioner because of his deep sympathy for the President's family".

536

[redacted]

Date 12/6/63

1.

ASSOCIATES OF RUBY

EDWARD MEYERS who resides at 1779 East 34th Street, Brooklyn, New York, telephone ES 5-2738, and who is the owner and operator of the Queens Beverage Company, a distributor for Pepsi Cola Company, was interviewed at his office, 9701 Avenue D. Brooklyn, New York, on December 5, 1963. He furnished the following information:

He and his wife had planned to attend the convention of the American Bottlers of Carbonated Beverages, Dallas, Texas, the week of November 18, 1963.

He had decided to combine this with a vacation trip to Mexico City and visit his wife's sister.

Prior to leaving on this trip, his brother, LAWRENCE MEYERS, had visited him in New York and said that he would be in Dallas, Texas, during the same week. They made arrangements to contact one another while in Dallas.

EDWARD MEYERS left with his wife on November 8, 1963, and went to Mexico City. He returned from Mexico City to Dallas, Texas, on the 18th of November via San Antonio, Texas, on American Airlines.

LAWRENCE MEYERS called EDWARD MEYERS at the Adolphus Hotel in Dallas, Texas, on the evening of November 21, 1963, to make arrangements to have dinner together. EDWARD MEYERS was unable to have dinner with his brother, but after subsequent telephone contact, he did meet his brother at the Bon Vivant Room of the Cabana Motel about midnight, November 21. EDWARD MEYERS pointed out that his reservation at the Adolphus Hotel had previously been made for him by the Pepsi Cola Company.

On 12/5/63 at New York, New York File # 44-974

by SAS GERALD V. CASWELL and JAMES J. ROGERS/pm Date dictated 12/6/63

COMMISSION EXHIBIT No. 2268

2.

NY 44-974

At the Bon Vivant Room of the Cabana Motel, LAWRENCE MEYERS introduced EDWARD MEYERS to JACK RUBY. He knew it was just about midnight because it was too late for them to order any drinks due to a local ordinance.

EDWARD MEYERS chatted with RUBY about five minutes. He recalled that RUBY was very talkative and tried to get him interested in a "twist board" which MEYERS said was some type of promotional gimmick. MEYERS told RUBY he was not interested. Then RUBY had to leave to go back to his club. Present at the time were EDWARD MEYERS, his wife, his brother, LAWRENCE MEYERS, and a female companion of his brother, name unknown to EDWARD MEYERS.

EDWARD MEYERS returned to New York, New York via air November 22, 1963, leaving Dallas Airport early in the afternoon. He did observe President JOHN F. KENNEDY's arrival at Dallas at the Dallas Airport.

The above was the only contact he had ever had with RUBY. He knows of no connection between RUBY and OSWALD. He had never seen OSWALD at any time. He has never been in the Carousel Club.

COMMISSION EXHIBIT No. 2268—Continued

FD-302 (Rev. 3-3-59)

FEDERAL BUREAU OF IN[redacted] Commission Exhibit No. 2269

1

Date 12/20/63

Mr. C. WILLIAM SELAH, 507 North Rosemont, Dallas, Texas, who received Carousel Club pass card number 202 from JACK RUBY under the name of BILL SELAH advised as follows:

He is employed in the Sales Department of KRLD Television Station and has known JACK RUBY casually for more than the past five years.

He last saw RUBY on the street in Dallas, November 21, 1963, at which time he, RUBY, gave him Carousel Club pass card number 202, made out in the name BILL SELAH. A couple of weeks prior to that time RUBY had been to the KRLD Television Station and told him he would get him a pass card.

He does not believe that on November 21, 1963, he and RUBY discussed the President's trip to Dallas, November 22, 1963, or discussed anything concerning politics.

RUBY also mentioned he was having union trouble at his night club. Further details not furnished.

Mr. SELAH said he had not previously seen RUBY for approximately six months.

He did not know LEE HARVEY OSWALD and had no information indicating there was any relationship between OSWALD and RUBY. He had no information concerning the shooting of OSWALD.

on 12/19/63 at Dallas, Texas File # DL 44-1639

by Special Agent ROBERT J. WILKISON - gj Date dictated 12/20/63

86

COMMISSION EXHIBIT NO. 2269

FD-302 (Rev. 3-3-59)

FEDERAL BUREAU OF [redacted] Commission Exhibit No. 2270

Date December 20, 1963

1

CONNIE TRAMMEL, 5109 Live Oak, was interviewed in connection with her name and address being found on the person of JACK RUBY at the time of his arrest, November 24, 1963. She related the following:

In April, 1963, she and a group of seniors from the University of Texas, School of Journalism, came to Dallas in connection with the promotion of a boat show. They stayed at the Adolphus Hotel across from the Carousel Club and had a party at the Carousel Club. She met JACK RUBY at that time and had a lengthy conversation with him. She graduated from the University of Texas and returned to Dallas from her home, 1420 Rankin, Ashdown, Arkansas, to try and secure employment. This was about the middle of November, 1963. She sought employment for two or three days and then called JACK RUBY to see if he needed an employee. At this time, he tried to get her to go into show business, which she declined to do. She thought perhaps he could employ her temporarily as a hat check girl or in some capacity while she was trying to find a job in her own line of work. About November 20, 1963, she called RUBY and told him she had an appointment with LAMAR HUNT, a prominent oil man in Dallas. She called him inasmuch as she hoped that RUBY might have a personal acquaintance with Mr. HUNT. RUBY came out to her apartment on November 21, 1963, and they again discussed possible leads for her to secure employment and he drove her down to the office of LAMAR HUNT. She was with RUBY from about 11:00 a.m. to 1:00 p.m., and it was on the day before the President was assassinated. On the way downtown, he stopped at the Merchants State Bank on Ross Avenue for a few minutes. She has not seen or heard from RUBY since.

Miss TRAMMEL stated that LEE HARVEY OSWALD was not known to her and she had no knowledge of any association between RUBY and OSWALD. She knew of no friends or associates of RUBY who were members of the Dallas Police Department and had no idea how RUBY got into the basement of the Police Department in order to shoot OSWALD.

on 12/19/63 at Dallas, Texas File # Dallas 44-1639

by Special Agent ALLEN H. SMITH:BL Date dictated 12/19/63

COMMISSION EXHIBIT NO. 2270

FD-302 (Rev. 3-3-59) FEDERAL BUREAU OF Commission Exhibit No. 2271

1

Date 12/13/63

MARGARET MARY ORNDORFF, 1407 Annex, Dallas, Texas, whose name and address appear in RUBY's property, was interviewed at her place of employment, L & H Cafe, 4202 Ross, Dallas, at which time, she furnished the following information:

Approximately three or four weeks ago, exact date she could not recall, she was fired from her job as waitress at the Eatwell Restaurant, Main Street, Dallas. The same day that she was fired from this job, she was talking briefly with a local policeman whom she had never seen before, and during the conversation had mentioned the fact that she was recently unemployed and was at that time looking for a job. She could recall engaging in a brief conversation with the policeman and he had advised her that she might inquire at the Carousel in efforts to obtain a job as a cocktail waitress. Miss ORNDORFF felt that the uniformed policeman had just mentioned it as a suggestion and was quite sure that he was not attempting to direct girls to the Carousel for any particular reason. She stated that he, the policeman, had mentioned that he had visited the Carousel on his days off and knew that the owner was in need of cocktail waitresses.

She went on to say that she thereafter called the Carousel and spoke to an individual who identified himself as Mr. RUBY. After advising him of her situation concerning a job, RUBY told her to come to the Carousel for an interview and that he could possibly arrange some type of a waitress job for her. Again she could not recall the date, but stated that she did talk to RUBY for a brief period and later decided not to accept a job at the Carousel even though RUBY had offered her a job. She said that this was the only contact she had had with either RUBY or the Carousel and has never contacted RUBY again for any reason whatsoever. She was unable to furnish any background information concerning RUBY, and stated that she has no idea as to why RUBY may have shot LEE HARVEY OSWALD.

A photograph of LEE HARVEY OSWALD was shown to Miss ORNDORFF, at which time she advised that she had never seen this individual before and has never heard the name other than in the papers. She was not aware of any connection that RUBY may have had with LEE HARVEY OSWALD.

on 12/13/63 at Dallas, Texas, File # DL 44-1639

by Special Agents ALTON E. BRAMBLETT and LANSING P. LOGAN :lp Date dictated 12/13/63

205

COMMISSION EXHIBIT No. 2271

DL 44-1639

2

Miss ORNDORFF stated that she did not know why her name and address appeared in RUBY's papers, and that he only possible reason would be the fact that she at one time had talked with him concerning a job.

206

COMMISSION EXHIBIT No. 2271—Continued

FD-302 (Rev. 3-3-59) FEDERAL BUREAU O [redacted] Commission Exhibit No. 2272

1

Date 12/11/63

Mr. DAVID L. JOHNSTON, Justice of Peace, Precinct Number 2, Dallas County, 1411 West Belt Line Road, Dallas, Texas, advised as follows:

He does not personally know JACK RUBY. After RUBY shot LEE HARVEY OSWALD November 24, 1963, he realized that RUBY was someone whom he had seen before sometime in the past. He also remembered that he had seen RUBY at a press conference at the Dallas Police Department late November 22, 1963, or early November 23, 1963.

The press conference was arranged for press representatives to photograph and interview OSWALD. The conference was agreed upon by Captain J. W. FRITZ, Chief J. E. CURRY, Dallas Police Department, HENRY WADE, Dallas County District Attorney and WILLIAM ALEXANDER, Assistant Dallas County District Attorney.

He observed RUBY in the group of press representatives at the conference and at that time he (JOHNSTON) was in the company of District Attorney WADE. He thought RUBY was another press representative when he first saw him. Immediately after the conference, RUBY came up to JOHNSTON, introduced himself as JACK RUBY, shook his hand and gave him a business card for the Carousel Club. After RUBY learned that JOHNSTON was Justice of Peace, he shook his hand a second time. This was about 12:15 AM or 12:30 AM, November 23, 1963. He still has the business card given to him by RUBY. He had not observed RUBY talking to District Attorney WADE or anyone else.

He did not see RUBY say anything to OSWALD at the press conference and had no information indicating that RUBY and OSWALD knew each other.

He had no information concerning security measures taken at the Police Department subsequent to OSWALD's arrest until the time OSWALD was shot. He does not know of any unauthorized person permitted to enter the Police Department.

He was not in the Police Department basement when OSWALD was shot November 24, 1963.

on 12/10/63 at Dallas, Texas File # DL 44-1639

by Special Agents EDMOND C. HARDIN and ROBERT J. WILKISON - gj Date dictated 12/11/63

-220-

COMMISSION EXHIBIT No. 2272

DL 44-1639
2

JOHNSTON said that in his official position of Justice of Peace in Dallas County, he arraigned OSWALD on November 22, 1963, for the murder of J. E. TIPPIT; he arraigned OSWALD on November 23, 1963, for the murder of JOHN F. KENNEDY. On November 23, 1963, he issued a warrant charging OSWALD with assault to murder JOHN B. CONNALLY. OSWALD was arraigned on both occasions in Dallas City Municipal Building. During his contacts with OSWALD, OSWALD made no pertinent remarks.

Mr. JOHNSTON said that after RUBY shot OSWALD, he received information from a confidential source whom he declined to identify that RUBY had been co-signer on some loans obtained at Dallas banks by some Dallas Police Department officers. He told this information to Chief of Police CURRY but did not disclose his source to CURRY. He understands that inquiry was subsequently conducted at Republic National Bank of Dallas and the First National Bank in Dallas and it was verified that RUBY had actually been co-signer on some loans obtained by Police officers at those banks. Mr. JOHNSTON said he had no further details concerning this matter.

-221-

COMMISSION EXHIBIT No. 2272—Continued

FD-302 (Rev. 3-3-59) FEDERAL BUREAU OF Commission Exhibit No. 2273

1

Date 12/30/63

DONALD B. SAFRAN, whose name was furnished by RUBY during interview on December 21, 1963, as an individual with whom RUBY spoke by phone during the afternoon of November 22, 1963, advised as follows:

Mr. SAFRAN advised that he is employed as an Amusement columnist by the "Dallas Times Herald". He stated that by virtue of his position, he has known JACK RUBY on a business basis during the past five years and has visited his clubs on a number of occasions. He stated that he last saw RUBY in person about six weeks ago when RUBY appeared at the "Times Herald" office requesting that SAFRAN publish in the "Times Herald" paper a photograph of a comedian then employed at one of RUBY's clubs.

Mr. SAFRAN stated that he last talked with RUBY on November 22, 1963, by phone on three separate occasions between approximately 2:30 PM and 3:15 PM. He stated that he, SAFRAN, first called the Carousel Club and requested to speak with RUBY. The purpose of his call was to inquire of RUBY if he planned to close his clubs in view of the assassination of President KENNEDY. RUBY was not present but the individual answering the phone stated he would get in touch with RUBY and have him call SAFRAN. RUBY called SAFRAN a few minutes later and when he was asked if he was going to close his clubs, RUBY stated he planned to close the Carousel Club. RUBY called back a few minutes later and stated that he had decided to close both the Carousel and Vegas Clubs. About 3:15 PM, RUBY called the third time and requested SAFRAN not to mention to the others, i. e., the operators of other clubs at Dallas, that he, RUBY, was closing his clubs, explaining that he wanted to get a "scoop" on them.

SAFRAN stated that during the three telephonic conversations he had with RUBY on November 22, 1963, RUBY briefly mentioned the assassination of President KENNEDY by explaining that he felt terrible over this and that this was a terrible tragedy. He also stated that he had been crying because of the assassination of President KENNEDY. SAFRAN added that he does not recall that RUBY mentioned OSWALD by name on any occasion.

on 12/27/63 at Dallas, Texas File # DL 44-1639

by Special Agent EDMOND C. HARDIN - gj Date dictated 12/30/63

338

COMMISSION EXHIBIT NO. 2273

DL 44-1639
2

SAFRAN stated that RUBY has, in his opinion, a persecution complex and has often complained to SAFRAN of being given unfair treatment in respect to publicity of his clubs as compared to publicity given other clubs in Dallas.

Mr. SAFRAN advised that he did not know LEE HARVEY OSWALD and has never received any information indicating a connection or association between RUBY and OSWALD. He advised that he has no information concerning the shooting of OSWALD by RUBY or the manner in which RUBY gained access to the basement of the Dallas Police Department prior to this shooting.

- 339 -

COMMISSION EXHIBIT NO. 2273—Continued

Commission Exhibit No. 2274

FD-302 (Rev. 3-3-59)

FEDERAL BUREAU OF INVE[redacted]

1

Date 1/11/64

SAM CAMPISI, co-owner, Egyptian Lounge, 5616 Mockingbird Lane, furnished the following information relative to JACK RUBY's presence at that restaurant on t' evening of November 21, 1963, corroborating information furnished by JACK RUBY upon interview December 21, 1963:

Mr. CAMPISI, who has been previously interviewed, stated that he recalls seeing RUBY and RALPH PAUL at his restaurant during the evening of November 21, 1963. He stated that he recalls this as a very busy evening and consequently cannot be sure of the details surrounding RUBY's visit. He stated that as best as he recalls, RUBY and PAUL arrived at the restaurant between 9:45 and 10:00 PM and had dinner there, staying some 45 minutes. He stated that he does not recall the identity of any individual to whom RUBY and PAUL spoke while there and does not recall any particular conversation he himself may have had with them.

on 1/9/64 at Dallas, Texas File # DL 44-1639

by Special Agent EDMOND C. HARDIN - gj Date dictated 1/10/64

162

COMMISSION EXHIBIT No. 2274

Commission Exhibit No. 2275

FD-302 (Rev. 3-3-59)

FEDERAL BUREAU OF INVES[redacted]

Date 1/23/64

1

ANDREW ARMSTRONG, JR., Assistant Manager, Big D Copa Club, formerly known as the Carousel Club, 1312-1/2 Commerce Street, Dallas, Texas, furnished the following information with regard to the time period from about 11:53 AM until about 4:00 PM or 4:30 PM, November 22, 1963:

He got on the bus near his home at about 11:53 AM and traveled the regular bus route to the bus stop at Main and Akard Street, Downtown Dallas, at about 12:25 PM. At the time he got off the bus he noticed that the Presidential Motorcade, or a large crowd of people watching the Motorcade, were at Main and Lamar Streets, a few blocks west of where he got off the bus. Upon alighting from the bus, he walked to the Carousel Club, which took him approximately four or five minutes. He estimates he arrived at the Carousel Club at about 12:30 PM.

Upon arrival at the club, he went to a room in the rear of the club and took off his jacket and then went to the men's room. While in the men's room, he heard sirens and it sounded to him as though there were many more than just one or two sirens. He became curious about this and consequently left the men's room and went to another room where he keeps his portable radio. He tuned it to Station KLIF, Dallas, and announcements were being made over the radio that someone had fired at the Presidential Motorcade. He then immediately ran to a room in the club, where CURTIS LAVERNE CRAFARD, commonly known as LARRY, was sleeping, and awakened him. He told LARRY that someone had just shot at the President. LARRY, being a very hard sleeper, did not awaken completely at that time and did not get up.

He, ARMSTRONG, then listened to the radio for two or three more minutes and heard several apparently confused announcements on the radio and heard that the car carrying President KENNEDY was on its way to Parkland Hospital. He then returned to the room where CRAFARD was sleeping and awakened him. CRAFARD got up and got dressed. While he was doing this, they both listened to Radio Station KLIF on ARMSTRONG's portable radio.

Approximately five to fifteen minutes after LARRY got up, JACK L. RUBY telephoned him, ARMSTRONG, at the Carousel Club. He

on 1/22/64 at Dallas, Texas File # DL 44-1639

by Special Agent s ALBERT SAYERS and MANNING C. CLEMENTS - LAC Date dictated 1/23/64

136

COMMISSION EXHIBIT No. 2275

believes that RUBY was calling from the Dallas Morning News Building inasmuch as he heard typewriters in the background and also knew that it was RUBY's habit on Friday morning to go to the newspaper building for the purpose of composing his newspaper ads for his clubs for the week-end. RUBY talked to him for three or four minutes, and he surmised that RUBY was calling to tell him that the President had been shot; however, RUBY apparently heard his radio playing in the background and said, "Oh, you have already heard?" and he told RUBY that he had. RUBY at that time told him, "If anything happens, we are going to close the club." RUBY then told him that he would see him after a short while. ARMSTRONG recalls that RUBY forgot to ask him if he had fed the dogs, which he keeps at the club inasmuch as it was RUBY's regular habit almost every time he called ARMSTRONG to ask him if the dogs have been fed.

He, ARMSTRONG, kept the radio tuned to Station KLIF, Dallas, for the remainder of that afternoon. At approximately 1:30 PM, he heard the official announcement when it was first made that President KENNEDY was dead.

Prior to the announcement of President KENNEDY's death, he had heard several announcements on the radio station to the effect that an officer of the Dallas Police Department had been shot. He does not recall hearing the name of the police officer during these announcements and believes, to the best of his recollection, that the officer had not been identified by name at the time these announcements were made.

About fifteen or twenty minutes after hearing the first official announcement of the death of President KENNEDY, JACK L. RUBY arrived at the Carousel Club. He, ARMSTRONG, believes this was at approximately 1:45 or 1:50 PM. RUBY appeared to be distraught and mumbled something about "What a terrible thing." RUBY's first coherent statement after his arrival at the club was that the club was closed and would be closed for the next three days.

RUBY immediately went to a telephone which has telephone number RI 7-2362 and started making telephone calls. He had completed one or two telephone calls within a matter of less than five minutes when they both overheard an announcement on Radio Station KLIF to the effect that Officer TIPPIT of the Dallas Police

137

COMMISSION EXHIBIT No. 2275—Continued

Department had been shot and killed. RUBY mentioned to him, ARMSTRONG, at that time that he knew Officer TIPPIT. ARMSTRONG said he believes that this may have been the first announcement on Station KLIF which identified by name the officer who had been shot. (It has been established through records of the Dallas Police Department that Officer J. D. TIPPIT was shot and killed at approximately 1:18 PM, November 22, 1963.)

JACK L. RUBY remained at the Carousel Club until approximately 4:00 PM. ARMSTRONG said he could not be accurate about that time but this is the best estimate he could give as to when RUBY left the Carousel Club. During the time RUBY was there, he gave ARMSTRONG instructions to contact all of the Carousel Club employees and tell them that the club would be closed Friday night, Saturday night and Sunday night. He, ARMSTRONG, started making these telephone calls at about 2:30 PM. One of the persons he called was "LITTLE LYNN", who resides in Fort Worth, Texas.

RUBY was on the telephone almost all of the time he was in the club and made several long-distance telephone calls, as well as numerous local telephone calls. RUBY was crying nearly all of this time. He, ARMSTRONG, knows, through hearing names mentioned and cities mentioned by RUBY while making these telephone calls, that long-distance calls were made that day to Arlington, Texas, where RUBY talked to RALPH PAUL, and to Detroit, Michigan; Chicago, Illinois, and Los Angeles, California. The only local telephone calls that he, ARMSTRONG, can identify were calls made to EVA L. GRANT and Dr. COLEMAN JACOBSON.

He, ARMSTRONG, has no personal knowledge of any activities, travels or whereabouts of JACK L. RUBY between the time RUBY called him from the Dallas Morning News Building and the time RUBY arrived at the Carousel Club. RUBY did not discuss that time period with him, and he has no way of knowing of RUBY's activities at that time. RUBY has never mentioned to him any intention of going to Parkland Hospital, Dallas, or of having gone there at any time.

ARMSTRONG advised that he recalls that sometime between 2:00 PM and 3:00 PM he answered the telephone at the Carousel Club and a woman asked to speak to Mr. RUBY. He recalls telling this woman that Mr. RUBY was at that time talking on another telephone and the woman asked him to have Mr. RUBY return her call as soon as possible. This woman gave him a telephone number, and he believes he recalls the name ALICE being mentioned by the woman as her name. He knows that this woman was not among his own

138

COMMISSION EXHIBIT No. 2275—Continued

DL 44-1639
4

acquaintances although he has heard of a woman by the name of ALICE NICHOLS who was a former girl friend of JACK L. RUBY.

ARMSTRONG said with regard to the foregoing information that due to the passage of time since the events set out above and the general state of confusion at the time these events were occurring, he could not be certain to the minute with regard to the times of day set out above. He stated, however, that after reflection, and after going over these stated times of day, he believes they are accurate to within a few minutes, to the best of his recollection.

ARMSTRONG related that he does not recall any woman visiting JACK L. RUBY at the Carousel Club during the afternoon of November 22, 1963, and he does not recall RUBY having gone to his office or having been in his office at the club during that afternoon. He said that RUBY usually does most of his paper work at a table near the front door of the club where the telephone is located. He said there is another telephone in the club which is a pay station and which has telephone number RIverside 1-0289. He said he does not recall JACK L. RUBY using the pay station telephone at any time that day.

139

1

DL 44-1639
MCC/ds

On February 17, 1964, U. S. Attorney BAREFOOT SANDERS, Northern District of Texas, advised he had received information from HILDRED C. BARBER, 315 West Orange, Duncanville, Texas, a former employee of a Dallas newspaper, that RUBY was interviewed by PHILIPPE LABRO, representing "France-Soir", on November 23, 1963.

The following information has been furnished by a confidential source abroad:

Mr. PHILIPPE LABRO, a reporter for "France-Soir", a daily French newspaper, Paris, France, was interviewed at the American Embassy, Paris, on March 5, 1964. He advised that he did not conduct an interview with JACK RUBY on November 23, 1963, at Dallas, Texas. He stated that he did encounter RUBY in the corridor on the third floor of Dallas Police headquarters at about 12:00 o'clock noon on November 23, 1963. At that time there were numerous newspaper reporters in the corridor on the third floor and RUBY was circulating among them and making casual remarks. RUBY encountered Mr. LABRO and asked him who he was and what he did for a living. Mr. LABRO advised RUBY that he was a French newspaper reporter. RUBY's response was "ooh la la Folies Bergere", which, according to LABRO, were probably the only French words known to RUBY. RUBY then presented Mr. LABRO with a card advertising his night club "The Carousel" containing the picture of a nude woman and invited him to stop and have a drink with him. RUBY then walked down the corridor toward a small press office which had been set up at the end of the corridor on the third floor. Mr. LABRO also walked down the hall and he noticed RUBY address several uniformed police officers by their first names. RUBY then walked back up the corridor and again encountered Mr. LABRO, at which time he said, "You fellows are having a tough time of it but you are doing a great job -- keep up the good work." No further conversation was had by Mr. LABRO with RUBY. He stated that during his encounter with RUBY it was his impression that RUBY did not display any unusual emotions and appeared to be entirely relaxed and normal.

3

2

DL 44-1639

Mr. LABRO advised that on November 24, 1963, following the murder of OSWALD, he happened to ride up in the elevator in the Dallas Police headquarters with a woman, who apparently had come to visit RUBY who was then on the fourth floor in the Dallas Police Jail. He presumed the woman to be RUBY's sister. The elevator did not stop en route and thus he saw the woman get off the elevator and walk to the cell to visit RUBY. He recognized RUBY at that time as the man whom he had encountered on the previous day, November 23, 1963, on the third floor. He stated, therefore, that there is no question in his mind as to the identity of the person whom he talked with on November 23, 1963, as RUBY.

COMMISSION EXHIBIT No. 2276—Continued

FD-302 (Rev. 3-3-59)

FEDERAL BUREAU OF INVESTIGATION

Date 4/7/64

1

Mr. WILLIAM GEORGE NIKOLIS advised he was born on November 26, 1944, at Vernon, Texas. His permanent address is with his parents, GEORGE and HELEN NIKOLIS, 243-37 72nd Avenue, Douglaston, New York. He is presently a sophomore at Tyler Junior College, Tyler, Texas, and resides at an apartment at 1926 South Belmont, Tyler, Texas, Telephone LYric 2-6763.

In November, 1963, he was a student at Southern Methodist University, Dallas, Texas, and lived at McElvaney Hall on the campus.

About 8:30 to 9:00 PM, November 22, 1963, he was at Phil's Delicatessen located Oak Lawn Avenue, Dallas, Texas, and was having a sandwich with his friends, DENNIS PATRICK MARTIN, BOB SINDELAR, MARGUERITE VEA RIEGLER and RITA SILBERMAN. All of the above were students at Southern Methodist University with the exception of RITA who was a high school student. He had purchased a DALLAS TIMES HERALD and while sitting at the table, he and his friends were scanning the paper. The front page carried a story concerning the assassination of President JOHN FITZGERALD KENNEDY that day.

A man, whom he now believes was JACK RUBY, who was wearing horn-rimmed glasses and sitting at another table a short distance from them, walked up and took a section of the newspaper from his hands and at the same time said something to the effect, "Let me borrow your paper". RUBY then walked away with the paper and he is not sure if RUBY sat down at his own table or not, however, a minute or two later the man brought the paper back.

NIKOLIS is unable to recall if RUBY said anything at the time he returned the paper.

A few minutes later this man walked up again and asked to borrow the paper for the second time. NIKOLIS and the others made remarks such as why didn't they give the man a nickel so he could buy his own paper and other similar remarks. RUBY then told them he owned the Carousel and Vegas Clubs in Dallas, asked if they had ever heard of the clubs and said something about giving them passes. RUBY said something to the effect he was looking for the club advertisement in the paper, however, NIKOLIS stated it was possible RUBY said he was looking for

on 4/6/64 at TYLER, TEXAS 5 File # DL 44-1639

by Special Agent ROBERT J. STEVENS/les Date dictated 4/6/64

COMMISSION EXHIBIT No. 2277

DL 44-1639
2

closing notices concerning the clubs. RUBY then walked to a telephone and talked to someone on the telephone, but NIKOLIS and his party were unable to hear any of the conversation. RUBY then brought the paper back to the table. NIKOLIS asked RUBY what effect he thought the assassination of President KENNEDY would have on the city of Dallas and RUBY replied to the effect it would hurt business and that Dallas would get no more conventions.

DENNIS MARTIN asked RUBY several times about the passes to the Carousel Club, but RUBY commented that they were too young and never did give them any of the passes. To the best of his recollection this ended the conversation with RUBY and although he is not certain, he believes that he and his party left the delicatessen while RUBY was still there. They drove around town for a short time that evening, then went home. NIKOLIS continued that he was watching television and saw JACK RUBY shoot and kill LEE HARVEY OSWALD and from the many photographs he has seen of RUBY since then, he is almost positive in his own mind that the man in the delicatessen was JACK RUBY. The others of his group who were present at the delicatessen that night were of the same opinion and he was told by BOB SINDELAR that RITA SILBERMAN had called the Dallas Police Department after OSWALD was killed and told them of their encounter with JACK RUBY at the delicatessen. To his knowledge, none of their group were ever interviewed by members of the Dallas Police Department. He continued that to his knowledge, none of his group had ever seen JACK RUBY before, did not know him, and further none of them knew or had ever seen LEE HARVEY OSWALD.

NIKOLIS continued that he expects to leave Tyler, Texas at the end of May, 1964, and during the summer months of 1964 can be contacted in care of his uncle, NICK ZELIOUS, Besco Company, Central Expressway, Dallas, Texas.

6

COMMISSION EXHIBIT No. 2277—Continued

FD-302 (Rev. 3-3-59) FEDERAL BUREAU OF INVESTIGATION

Commission Exhibit No. 2278

Date 4/3/64

RITA LESLIE SILBERMAN advised she resides at 13215 Hughes Circle, Dallas, Texas, where her telephone number is AD 9-5480. She said her stepfather, NORMAN SIEGEL, and her mother, LESLIE RODNEY SIEGEL, reside at that address and their telephone number is AD 9-5546. She said she is a student at Hillcrest High School and she is in the twelfth grade.

She said on November 22, 1963, about 8:00 or 8:30 P.M., she, together with MARGUERITE RIEGLER, DENNIS MARTIN, BILL NIKOLIS and BOB SINDELAR, met at Smith Dormitory at Southern Methodist University, Dallas, Texas. Thereafter they drove to Phil's Delicatessen, which is located in Dallas, Texas, near the Love Field Airport on Oaklawn Avenue. She said they ordered food and while waiting for it to be served they observed a man talking to other patrons and also making a phone call. She said they paid no attention to this person's conversation, but after he finished his call he came to the table where he took a newspaper from BOB SINDELAR, asking him for it and taking it before he got permission to read it. She said this person took the paper and remarked, "How horrible it is", referring to the assassination of President JOHN F. KENNEDY.

Then the man made another telephone call and returned to the table, where he took the paper and talked about his night clubs. She said the man turned to a couple of advertisements in the paper and she recalled that they were for the Carousel and Vegas Clubs, and this man said that he owned the clubs and would give passes to the group. Then he looked them over and remarked he could not give them passes because they were too young. One of the boys in the group jokingly said that he was over 21 and thereupon the man, presumably JACK RUBY, said, "Well, come around sometime and perhaps I'll let you in.

She said JACK RUBY seemed to be "upset" and he remarked how horrible the death of the President was and, like everyone else, he talked generally about the assassination and articles which had been published concerning it.

on 4/2/64 at Dallas, Texas 7 File # DL 44-1639

by Special Agent THOMAS J. CARSON and ARTHUR E. CARTER/ds Date dictated 4/3/64

COMMISSION EXHIBIT No. 2278

2

DL 44-1639

She said this man was only in the delicatessen a short time and left about the time that her group received their food order. She said that they learned of the man's identity as JACK RUBY through his telling them of his ownership of the night clubs and, also, through news articles which were published and radio broadcasts which announced that JACK RUBY killed LEE HARVEY OSWALD on November 24, 1963.

She looked at a Dallas Police photograph of JACK RUBY and remarked it appeared to be the same person who was present in the delicatessen on the night of November 22, 1963. She said the person in the restaurant wore a regular business suit and a hat and he did not look exactly like the police photograph because of his dress and the fact that he was wearing a hat.

She said she had never known or observed this person before this incident and she had never known LEE HARVEY OSWALD and knew of no connection between OSWALD and RUBY.

She said she believed that BILL NIKOLIS is currently enrolled in Tyler Junior College. She did not know the whereabouts of DENNIS MARTIN.

8

COMMISSION EXHIBIT No. 2278—Continued

FD-302 (Rev. 3-3-59)

FEDERAL BUREAU OF INVESTIGATION

1

Date 4/3/64

ROBERT LOUIS SINDELAR advised he has a room, number 362, in McElvaney Dormitory, located on the campus of Southern Methodist University in Dallas, Texas. He said he resides in Apartment # 16 at 4630 Palm Gardens Apartments, where he has telephone number LA 6-0780 in Dallas, Texas. He said his home residence is 1821 Cuyler Avenue, Erwyn, Illinois, where he resides with his father, LOUIS SINDELAR.

He said on November 22, 1963, he joined a group of friends and all of them went to Phil's Delicatessen, 3531 Oaklawn Avenue, about 8:00 P.M. He said his friends were BILL NIKOLIS, DENNIS MARTIN, RITA SILBERMAN and MARGUERITE RIEGLER. He said he recalled they bought a newspaper which they were reading and discussing at a table in Phil's Delicatessen while waiting for their food order to be prepared, and suddenly a man pulled the paper from his hand, at the same time asking him if he could borrow the paper. He said the man glanced at the paper, put it down on the table, and walked to a telephone fifteen or twenty feet away, where he proceeded to make a telephone call.

Mr. SINDELAR said he was unable to understand the conversation that this man had on the telephone, but when he completed his call he returned to the table and asked again if he might see the paper, at which time he advised SINDELAR and his companions he was the owner of the Carousel and Vegas Clubs in Dallas. The man remarked he wanted to see if his advertisements appeared that he had ordered for the paper and remarked that his two clubs were the only clubs that were closed because of the President's assassination. He said the man located the advertisements and showed them to the group, and BILL NIKOLIS asked the man if he thought the death of the President would affect Dallas and the man, later identified as JACK RUBY, replied that it would affect the convention business in the City of Dallas. He said BILL NIKOLIS then told JACK RUBY that he knew a former entertainer at the Vegas Club but he did not name the entertainer and RUBY did not discuss it at any length.

on 4/2/64 at Dallas, Texas 9 File # DL44-1639

by Special Agent WILL HAYDEN GRIFFIN and ARTHUR E. CARTER/ds Date dictated 4/3/64

COMMISSION EXHIBIT No. 2279

2

DL 44-1639

He said RUBY then made another telephone call and then returned to the table a third time where he again looked at the front pages of the paper and remarked, "Maybe I'll give you people free passes to my club." Then he jokingly said he could not give free passes to them because they were not old enough to go to the clubs.

Mr. SINDELAR said he was not positive that this man was JACK RUBY. He said after observing a police photograph of RUBY, that the photograph resembled the man who talked to him at Phil's Delicatessen on the night of November 22, 1963; however, he seemed to recall that the man at the Delicatessen wore heavy, dark-rimmed glasses and was dressed in a business suit and wore a hat which he did not take off. He said the man in Phil's Delicatessen apparently knew other people who were there, but these other people were not known to him, SINDELAR.

He said he presumed this man was JACK RUBY because he claimed he was the owner of the Carousel and Vegas Clubs in Dallas, Texas.

He said he knew of no association between JACK RUBY and LEE HARVEY OSWALD and he had never known either of these individuals prior to the assassination of President KENNEDY on November 22, 1963.

He advised that RITA SILBERMAN is a student at the Hillcrest High School in Dallas, Texas, and the other persons were students at Southern Methodist University on November 22, 1963. He did not know the current addresses of DENNIS PATRICK MARTIN or WILLIAM GEORGE NIKOLIS.

FD-302 (Rev. 1-25-60)

FEDERAL BUREAU OF — Commission Exhibit No. 2280 —

1

Date April 17, 1964

Private DENNIS PATRICK MARTIN, Company C, 2nd Battalion, 3rd Brigade, Fort Ord, California, was interviewed by SA MAX H. FISCHER on April 14, 1964. He furnished the following information concerning an incident which took place on the evening of November 22, 1963, at Phil's Delicatessen, 3531 Oak Lawn, Dallas, Texas:

At about 11:00 p.m. on the evening of November 22, 1963, MARTIN, while in the company of MARGUERITE RIEGLER, a Southern Methodist University (SMU) student; ROBERT L. SINDELAR, a SMU student; WILLIAM NICHOLAS, a student at Tyler, Texas, Junior College; and RITA SILVERMAN, a high school student from Richardson, Texas, went to Phil's Delicatessen and sat down in one of the booths to eat. A man whom MARTIN later identified as JACK RUBY, owner of the Carousel Bar in Dallas, Texas, was already in the delicatessen when the group arrived and appeared to be alone.

One of the persons with MARTIN had a copy of the November 23, 1963, edition of the Dallas Morning News which had come out as an extra on the evening of November 22, 1963, and had a large front page writeup on the assassination of President John F. Kennedy.

Shortly after the group sat down in the booth, the man later identified as RUBY approached the booth and politely asked if he could borrow the paper. He appeared to be interested in something in the classified want-ad section of the paper and seemed to use the classified section of the paper to locate a phone number as immediately after looking at the paper, he went to the pay phone located near the cashier's desk and made a phone call or attempted to make a phone call. He returned the paper to the booth where the youths were sitting and made some comment to the effect that "it was a terrible thing about the President being shot." He did not appear to be overly enraged about the assassination of the President although he did appear to be sincere in the comment about it being a terrible thing.

On 4/14/64 at Fort Ord, California File # SF 44-494

by SA MAX H. FISCHER/ab Date dictated 4/14/64

FD-302 (Rev. 3-3-59) FEDERAL BUREAU OF IN Commission Exhibit No. 2281

1

Date 6/3/64

Rabbi HILLEL SILVERMAN, 6146 Lupton Drive, Rabbi of Temple Shearith Israel, advised the service at the synagogue on the night of November 22, 1963, began at 8:30 P.M. and ended at approximately 9:50 P.M. He said he did not see JACK RUBY enter the synagogue. When the service was over, Rabbi SILVERMAN took a position at the door to greet those leaving the synagogue. At that time he saw RUBY. He said at the time he assumed RUBY had entered at the beginning of the service.

RUBY has subsequently told Rabbi SILVERMAN that he came in very late and missed the greater portion of the service. RUBY has told him that he saw JOE GOLMAN (Dallas City Councilman) and a Mrs. LEONA LANE at the synagogue. Rabbi SILVERMAN said he has confirmed through Mr. GOLMAN that GOLMAN did, in fact, see RUBY. He said he had not been in contact with Mrs. LANE in this regard.

Rabbi SILVERMAN said RUBY looked on the night of November 22, 1963, as if he were in a daze. He appeared to be depressed or "in shock". Rabbi SILVERMAN said RUBY did not, surprisingly, say anything to him relative to the assassination of President KENNEDY, but, rather, thanked the Rabbi for having visited RUBY's sister, EVA GRANT, at Gaston Hospital a few days previously. He said he recalls nothing specifically regarding RUBY's manner of dress on this occasion, but "has the feeling" RUBY was dressed in a dark suit, which was his usual dress when observed at the synagogue. He does not know how long RUBY was there.

With regard to the service on November 23, 1963, Rabbi SILVERMAN stated he did not see JACK RUBY on this occasion, and doubts very much he was present. He said he had stated on previous interview that RUBY had attended this service, his statement being based purely on hearsay. He said there was considerable talk by various people after RUBY's arrest on November 24, 1963, that they had seen RUBY at the synagogue. He said he believes it highly probable

on 6/2/64 at Dallas, Texas File # DL 44-1639

by Special Agent MANNING C. CLEMENTS/ds Date dictated 6/2/64

32

COMMISSION EXHIBIT No. 2281

2

DL 44-1639

these persons were confused about when they saw RUBY, and possibly saw him on the night of November 22, 1963, rather than on November 23, 1963. He said he does not at this time recall the identities of any persons who told him they saw RUBY at the synagogue on November 23, 1963.

Rabbi SILVERMAN said RUBY has, himself, told him that he went to bed very late, possibly at about 5:00 A.M. on the morning of November 23, 1963. RUBY related that he received a call from LARRY CRAFARD, employee of the Carousel, at about 8:00 A.M. He said RUBY has never told him that he was at the synagogue on the morning of November 23, 1963, and that it is his impression that RUBY likely went back to sleep after receiving the call from CRAFARD.

33

COMMISSION EXHIBIT No. 2281—Continued

Commission Exhibit No. 2282

FD-302 (Rev. 3-3-59)

FEDERAL BUREAU OF I[redacted]

1

Date 6/4/64

Mrs. LEONA LANE, Van Gogh Studios, 1710 Jackson Street, who resides at 3786 Northview, Dallas, Texas, furnished the following information:

On the evening of November 22, 1963, she attended special services at Shearith Israel Synagogue in Dallas, Texas, accompanied by her mother, Mrs. ESTHER MILLER, and her sons, SEYMOUR LANE, aged 18, and CARY LANE, aged 16. Following the services, coffee was served for those in attendance, at about 11:00 P.M. She had been in the room where refreshments were being served for about five minutes when she noticed JACK RUBY standing by himself, so she, her mother and sons walked over to talk to JACK RUBY. Mrs. LANE introduced her mother and sons to JACK, and reminded him that he had met them about four years ago when they had Passover Dinner together at the home of SAM RUBY, JACK's brother. After the introductions, Mrs. LANE remarked how terrible the assassination of President KENNEDY had been, and JACK RUBY said, "It is worse than that." Mrs. LANE thought that JACK seemed very nervous, upset, and depressed, and they talked about mutual friends for about five minutes, and they left.

She did not see JACK RUBY talking with anyone else, and did not notice him again after they walked away from him.

Mrs. LANE explained that she was originally from Chicago, Illinois, and moved to Dallas about seven years ago. Someone, she does not now recall whom, told her to look up PHYLLIS RUBY, the wife of SAM RUBY, when she got to Dallas, and she did so. Through Mr. and Mrs. SAM RUBY, she met JACK RUBY, and has probably seen JACK only ten or twelve times during the past seven years. This one occasion has been the only time she saw him at the Synagogue.

From her limited contact with JACK RUBY, she has found him to be always extremely happy, or extremely sad, with no in-between status. On the night of November 22, 1963,

on 6/4/64 at Dallas, Texas File # DL 44-1639

by Special Agent C. RAY HALL/ds Date dictated 6/4/64

35

This document contains neither recommendations nor conclusions of the FBI. It is the property of the FBI and is loaned to your agency; it and its contents are not to be distributed outside your agency.

COMMISSION EXHIBIT No. 2282

2

DL 44-1639

at the Synagogue, everyone present seemed to be shocked and depressed over the death of President KENNEDY. JACK RUBY was well dressed in his appearance, but his conversation and demeanor indicated that he was very sad over the death of President KENNEDY.

36

COMMISSION EXHIBIT No. 2282—Continued

Commission Exhibit No. 2283

FD-302 (Rev. 3-3-59) FEDERAL BUREAU OF IN

1

Date 6/4/64

Mrs. ESTHER MILLER, 3786 Northview, Dallas, Texas, related the following information:

On the night of November 22, 1963, following the death of President KENNEDY, she attended special services at Congregation Shearith Israel Synagogue. The services concluded at approximately 11:00 P.M., and she, her daughter, Mrs. LEONA LANE, and grandsons, SEYMOUR and CARY LANE, went to the room where refreshments were being served. They had been there for only a few minutes, when Mrs. LANE noticed JACK RUBY, and they all went over to talk with him.

Mrs. LANE introduced Mrs. MILLER to JACK RUBY, and reminded him they had met previously several years before. Mrs. MILLER said she did not engage in any conversation with JACK, but Mrs. LANE and JACK talked for about five minutes. Something was said about the death of President KENNEDY, but Mrs. MILLER does not remember just what was said. She does recall that JACK RUBY seemed very sad over the assassination, and seemed nervous and upset. She does not recall seeing anyone else talking with JACK RUBY before they spoke to him, and did not see him again after they left him.

Mrs. MILLER said she formerly lived in Chicago, Illinois, and she knew an aunt of Mrs. PHYLLIS RUBY. This aunt suggested that Mrs. MILLER look up PHYLLIS RUBY when Mrs. MILLER arrived in Dallas, and she did so, thereby becoming acquainted with the SAM RUBY family in Dallas, and meeting JACK RUBY.

on 6/4/64 at Dallas, Texas File # DL 44-1639

by Special Agent C. RAY HALL/ds Date dictated 6/4/64

37

COMMISSION EXHIBIT No. 2283

Commission Exhibit No. 2284

UNITED STATES DEPARTMENT OF JUSTICE

FEDERAL BUREAU OF INVESTIGATION

In Reply, Please Refer to File No.

Los Angeles, California
June 11, 1964

INTERVIEW OF ALEXANDER PHILIP GRUBER REQUESTED BY PRESIDENT'S COMMISSION ON THE ASSASSINATION OF PRESIDENT KENNEDY, BY LETTER TO THE DIRECTOR, FBI DATED JUNE 1, 1964

Alexander Philip Gruber was interviewed at his residence, 5222 West Olympic Boulevard, Los Angeles, California, on June 11, 1964.

Gruber furnished the following information:

He is presently employed as a scrap metal dealer in the Los Angeles area.

He knew Jack L. Ruby in the late 1920's in Chicago, and associated with him for approximately four years when both he and Ruby were in their late teens. During this time, they resided together at a boarding house for a little less than a year.

Gruber left Chicago about 1929 or 1930, and went to New York, at which time he lost contact with Ruby. He has never been very interested in politics and did not even bother to vote while living in New York. He was too busy trying to make a living because during this period, a depression was in progress. During his younger days, he was a member of the Boy Scouts.

He was married in New York and came to Los Angeles with his wife about 1942. He is currently registered as a Democrat, and has never been a member of any organization other than the Democratic party or the Boy Scouts of America.

COMMISSION EXHIBIT No. 2284

INTERVIEW OF ALEXANDER PHILIP GRUBER REQUESTED BY PRESIDENT'S COMMISSION ON THE ASSASSINATION OF PRESIDENT KENNEDY, BY LETTER TO THE DIRECTOR, FBI DATED JUNE 1, 1964

He made a trip to Chicago, Illinois, in 1946 or 1947, and stopped in Dallas, Texas, en route to see Ruby. During the course of a conversation with Ruby in the latter's club in Dallas on this particular occasion, three male patrons were observed by Ruby to be bothering a woman in the club, and Ruby engaged all three of these persons in a fight. Ruby was successful in knocking out all three of these individuals. Gruber left Dallas shortly thereafter and had no contact with Ruby until about two weeks prior to the assassination of former President Kennedy.

On this occasion, two weeks prior to the assassination, while en route to Los Angeles from New York, where he had attended a relative's wedding, he stopped at Joplin, Missouri, to get some information on a car wash facility. Since Dallas, Texas was about 100 miles from Joplin, he decided to visit Ruby in Dallas. While in Dallas, he stayed at a hotel just across the street from Ruby's club and visited Ruby for several days. He did not visit Ruby at his home, but saw Ruby at the Club Carousel, from about 6:00 P.M. in the evening until closing time early the following morning. He and Ruby talked of their past experiences shared in Chicago, and Ruby, on a number of occasions, expressed concern about his business being poor. Ruby mentioned that he had been forced by the union to stop having amateur night at his club, and indicated that his competitors had continued having their amateur night programs. Ruby did mention that he always opened and closed his show at the club with something patriotic, but Gruber could not recall the nature of these patriotic acts mentioned by Ruby. They did discuss business during the course of their conversations, including Gruber's interest in the car wash operation. Politics was never discussed.

- 2 -

COMMISSION EXHIBIT No. 2284—Continued

INTERVIEW OF ALEXANDER PHILIP GRUBER REQUESTED BY PRESIDENT'S COMMISSION ON THE ASSASSINATION OF PRESIDENT KENNEDY, BY LETTER TO THE DIRECTOR, FBI DATED JUNE 1, 1964

About 20 minutes after former President Kennedy was assassinated, he received a long distance call in Los Angeles from Ruby in Dallas. Ruby seemed upset and they talked about a number of things including the car wash business. Ruby said that he would send him (Gruber), a dog, and he subsequently did. Ruby asked if he had heard about the President being killed and then started crying, terminating the conversation by saying that he could not talk any more. He does not know exactly why Ruby called him and can only speculate that Ruby wanted to talk to a friend at a time when he was emotionally upset.

He received a letter from Ruby earlier this year postdated February 4, 1964, with the return address of 505 Main Street, Dallas, Texas. In this particular letter, Ruby acknowledged receipt of a prior letter which he (Gruber), had written earlier to Ruby expressing his sorrow over Ruby's predicament. In his letter, Ruby thanked him for his expression of sympathy, mentioned the dog which he had sent to Gruber and said that he was sorry the phone call to Gruber immediately following President Kennedy's death had caused Gruber so much trouble in that Gruber had been contacted by the FBI. Ruby also mentioned receiving numerous letters and wires from people throughout the country during his confinement.

Gruber is not acquainted with Lewis J. Mc Willie, Lawrence Meyers, Ralph Hall, George Senator, Breck Wall and Joe Peterson. He recalled reading the paper several months ago about Ruby and one George Senator rooming together prior to President Kennedy's assassination. He has no knowledge of any interest in or activities on the part of Ruby concerning the sale of jeeps, guns or

- 3 -

INTERVIEW OF ALEXANDER PHILIP GRUBER REQUESTED BY PRESIDENT'S COMMISSION ON THE ASSASSINATION OF PRESIDENT KENNEDY, BY LETTER TO THE DIRECTOR, FBI DATED JUNE 1, 1964

other war materials for use in Cuba, or the smuggling of refugees out of Cuba. He is not aware of and has never heard Ruby mention making any trips to Cuba. He considers Ruby to be a highly emotional person and he feels that the shooting of Oswald was a spur-of-the-moment action on the part of Ruby. Ruby comes from a very fine family, and is in his opinion, a loyal American. Ruby has never, to his knowledge, been involved in anything illegal prior to the shooting of Oswald.

The following description of Alexander Philip Gruber was obtained from observation and interview:

Sex	Male
Race	Caucasian
Date of birth	February 1, 1911
Place of birth	Chicago, Illinois
Height	5' 10½"
Weight	180
Eyes	Grey
Hair	Black, greying
Social Security Number	347-09-0696

\- 4 -

COMMISSION EXHIBIT No. 2284—Continued

LIFE LINE Order typed copies of broadcast by number. Two for 25¢ — cash, stamps or check. Larger quantities 10¢ per copy; 300 or more copies, 3¢ per copy.

RADIO TRANSCRIPT A weekly mailing of seven transcripts (6 weekday radio public affairs, 1 Sunday sermon) 8 weeks, $2.00; 26 weeks, $5.00; 1 year, $10.00. Great clergymen, speakers and writers value and use this material.

LIFE LINES, 3 times-a-week paper—156 issues, 1 year, $5.00. Enclose cash or check or LIFE LINE will bill you upon your request. LIFE LINES, 620 Eleventh St., N.W., Washington 1, D.C.

Those who order transcripts and subscriptions will be sent CATALOG LISTING of governmental documents, freedom books and other patriotic material LIFE LINE offers for sale.

(260-63)

PROGRAM NUMBER 121
9/17/63
SUBJECT: Free Federal Money

54

OPEN: This is LIFE LINE, Gene Scudder from Washington.

The greatest myth in American history is the myth of so-called "free federal money." Because it is so plausible on the surface, and so utterly false in fact and truth, no stone should be left unturned in the constant effort to expose it for what it is. Every idea for exposing it should be tried, however curious or even "wild." This is not a case where there is need for care not to slander persons or offend minority groups. Nobody can possibly be hurt by learning the truth about "free federal money." Nobody can possibly deny that truth, even those who benefit most from the myth. There can be no argument about this kind of exposure. There is only the selfish hope on the part of the statists that the myth will survive because it is not attacked vigorously enough.

Your patronage helps keep LIFE LINE on the air. Subscribe to LIFE LINES, published three times a week, $5 per year. Send cash or check to LIFE LINE, Washington 1, D. C., or LIFE LINE will bill you at your request.

We'll have more to say about "free federal money" following this message from our LIFE LINE sponsor.

(COMMERCIAL.........45 seconds)

A deep yearning to find some way to get something for nothing is a fundamental if not very creditable element in human nature. It explains the popularity of gambling in all ages. It explains the fantastic financial hauls of famous confidence men down through the ages. Carlos Ponzi of Boston collected nine million dollars by the simple plan of promising everyone a fifty per cent profit on their investment every 45 days. He paid off the earlier "investors" with the money flooding in from later ones -- the same sort of success on a grand scale that has been obtained on a small scale by those cryptic ads saying "Last Chance to Send Your Dollar to P. O. Box 1111." Some people will always send a dollar to anybody if informed it is their last chance to do so.

This almost universal weakness, so cleverly exploited by the Carlos Ponzis and the "last chance to send your dollar" boys throughout history, is the reason so many otherwise sensible people can persuade themselves that tax money grants from Washington are a simple gift of "free federal aid" even when rationally they know better. Why look a gift horse in the mouth? is their feeling, to use an old and revealing proverb. Many persons and communities which oppose federal handouts on principle, and complain vigorously against high federal tax rates, still cannot bring themselves to reject a so-called "gift" when offered it.

Consider the choice recently offered to the voters of Duluth, Minnesota. Duluth wants and needs a large new building for holding conventions in the city. It is expected to cost over six million dollars. The Area Redevelopment Administration offered Duluth an outright grant (for that word, read "gift") of three million dollars -- half the total cost -- if the city would approve a loan, spread over a period of no less than forty years, for the other three million. What an opportunity! Three million "free" dollars plus three million more not to be repaid until the majority of those voting on the issue were dead! Why not? What did the voters have to lose -- but their self-respect? They approved the plan.

The hard fact of the matter is that this project was never approved by anyone whose money was being used to pay for it. The taxpayers of the United States who were to furnish three million dollars of the cost were not consulted. The citizens of Duluth now in their childhood, or yet unborn or in other parts of the country, who will have to pay back the other three million forty years from now -- in the year two thousand and three -- were not consulted, because they can't vote yet. This is the kind of blatant intellectual dishonesty, half silly, half tragic, which can come from the great delusion about "free federal money." No money in this world is ever free. It is the product of the labor and the thought and the ingenuity of men and women. Whenever money is spent, someone, somewhere, sooner or later must pay it. And his right to be consulted and to give approval to commitments for such payment is at the very heart of the republican form of government. It was for this that we went to war against Great Britain and won the American Revolution.

There are just two sources from which any so-called "free federal money" can ever come. One is simple and obvious: taxes. Taxes are not just a matter of payments by the taxpayer. They require a vast bureaucracy to collect and administer. As a means of financing any project, they entail an enormous overhead cost. They are probably the most inefficient and costly method of investment ever known. And they are never enough. A government which accepts handouts as a way of life must always fall back upon deficit spending. This is borrowing against the future, obtaining money now from private sources which the government pledges to pay back, with interest, from future taxes which can be expected to be just as inefficient and just as costly as those we now have.

The case of the Duluth Convention Hall is a perfect example of both of these methods in their very worst forms -- a tax-money grant for a strictly local purpose of no value to the nation, and a deficit financing scheme which burdens the children and grandchildren of those who voted for it, for forty years into the future.

COMMISSION EXHIBIT No. 2285

Far from being "free," money obtained in this way is little better than a fastening of chains upon every citizen. Ask any man deeply in debt, or without control over the money he earns, how free he feels; and you may begin to learn how it is that "free" money paves the quickest and easiest road to slavery.

Subscribe now to our patriotic newspaper LIFE LINES, published three times a week, $5 a year. Send cash or check to LIFE LINE, Washington 1, D. C., or LIFE LINE will bill you at your request.

I'll be back in just a moment.

(COMMERCIAL..........45 seconds)

Another great problem in creating public awareness of the truth about so-called "free federal money" is the withholding system for collecting federal taxes. By this system, the employers of most Americans act as tax collectors for the federal government. The employee never sees the money that is taken from him as taxes and finds it easy to forget that he ever earned it. The majority of Americans pay most of their annual tax bill to the federal government in this painless way. They are hardly aware of how much they are losing; therefore it is easy for them to think of whatever benefits they or their community may receive from Washington, as coming out of someone else's pocket and thus "free" as far as they are concerned.

We do not wish to give the impression, by these remarks or any others, that we oppose the fair and just payment of taxes by Americans. Taxes are a necessary part of civilization; as long as there have been civilized societies and governments there have been taxes; and there will be taxes as long as there are still civilized societies and governments. Taxes are the price we pay for law and order, for the essential services that government everywhere must provide. Americans should be willing and even proud to pay taxes for this purpose, and most Americans are. But a responsible attitude toward the payment of taxes is encouraged, not discouraged, by each taxpayer being vividly aware of just how much he is paying and for what purposes. Arrangements such as the withholding tax which so hide tax payments that they can almost be ignored, are a danger to free and responsible government and work against informed public opinion on the issue of government spending. Let it not be forgotten that wage earners pay 80 per cent of all income taxes collected in this country.

There is a simple test which any American can use to judge whether the federal government is following a fiscal policy which he as a voter and taxpayer could approve. This same test, if consistently applied, could be one of the best weapons against the myth of "free federal money." The test is this: would you, if this government money was yours, spend it in this way? Would you collect it in this way? Would you bind yourself and your children to debt in this way? Would you risk your home and your future in this way? If the answer to any of those questions is "no," then you can be sure that the government is playing fast and loose with your money and your future, that any benefits you receive from this kind of expenditure will do you no more good in the long run than the money that was handed out by Carlos Ponzi.

Some persons, pessimistic and discouraged, will say that the American people will never apply this kind of test, that they will never be able to tear themselves away from the lure of "free federal money." According to this argument, Americans simply will not put truth and principle ahead of immediate material gain. We can never accept this argument and we hope that no constructive anywhere will accept it. The American people have proved time and again throughout a proud history that they can and do put truth and principle ahead of material gain, at least when the truth and principle are great and strong enough and freedom is at stake. If the ever-growing dangers of uncontrolled federal spending can be made clear, and the dishonest kind of thinking which is used to justify it can be exposed, the American people will refuse to take more floods of "free federal money" in exchange for the personal freedom to live and earn and enjoy the fruits of productive work which is our most splendid heritage from an heroic past. Americans have often been fooled in the little things of life; but they have never been fooled about the biggest things. They may, like all men, too often seek something for nothing. But no charlatan or demagogue has ever been able to convince Americans for long that nothing is something, that freedom is not freedom, that slavery to an all-powerful state is the royal road to security and happiness. On that independence of spirit we must rely for the final understanding and the final rejection of the poisonous myth of "free federal money."

This is program number 121. Two typewritten copies for 25¢, cash, check or stamps, or 10¢ each in larger quantities. Write LIFE LINE, Washington 1, D. C. Our three-times-a-week patriotic newspaper, LIFE LINES, $5 a year.

To keep freedom programs on the air, those who approve and listen to them should ask their friends to commend sponsors who advertise with patriotic media.

In just a moment, a final thought.

(COMMERCIAL.........45 seconds)

Until we meet again, remember: Without the freedom to earn and to own, all other freedoms become a mockery and will soon perish.

This is LIFE LINE, Gene Scudder from Washington.

CIRCULATION AND AWARENESS OF FREEDOM MATERIAL IS VITAL. PLEASE MAKE THIS COPY AS WIDELY AVAILABLE AS POSSIBLE TO OTHER READERS.

THIS TRANSCRIPT MAY BE REPRODUCED IN ITS ENTIRETY.

COMMISSION EXHIBIT No. 2285—Continued

LIFE LINE Order typed copies of broadcast by number. Two for 25¢ — cash, stamps or check. Larger quantities 10¢ per copy; 300 or more copies, 3¢ per copy.

RADIO TRANSCRIPT A weekly mailing of seven transcripts (6 weekday radio public affairs, 1 Sunday sermon) 8 weeks, $2.00; 26 weeks, $5.00; 1 year, $10.00. Great clergymen, speakers and writers value and use this material.

LIFE LINES, 3 times-a-week paper—156 issues, 1 year, $5.00. Enclose cash or check or LIFE LINE will bill you upon your request. LIFE LINES, 620 Eleventh St., N.W., Washington 1, D.C.

Those who order transcripts and subscriptions will be sent CATALOG LISTING of governmental documents, freedom books and other patriotic material LIFE LINE offers for sale.

(170-63) PROGRAM NUMBER 31
6/19/63
SUBJECT: Heroism

OPEN: This is LIFE LINE, Gene Scudder from Washington.

Personal heroism is a vital part of the American character and the American dream. The building of this nation from a trackless wilderness, its struggles that won freedom, its war for union, its rise to greatness -- all required the leadership and achievement of heroes. Without heroes, the America we know today would not exist. Without heroes, our America will not survive the threatening years ahead.

Yet how often have we heard it said, in scornful scoffing, to someone, usually quite young, who plans a brave and noble act: "What are you trying to do, be a hero?" The question is asked in a way which leaves no doubt that the questioner can think of nothing sillier than wanting to be a hero -- or being one.

Sneering and scoffing at heroism, downgrading it in our thought and forgetting it in our hearts, lead down an old well-trodden road of national decay. No great nation has ever fallen so long as it still prized its heroes. But nearly all nations, when they do fall, have forgotten what heroism is.

We will continue our discussion after a message from our LIFE LINE sponsor.

(COMMERCIAL.........45 seconds)

Heroism is both an ideal and a reality. It is an ideal because it is something we look up to and strive for, but only rarely attain. It is a reality because all down through history men have from time to time attained it -- often men never suspected of heroic qualities until some great crisis.

But the fact that men and women can be heroes does not insure that they will be. If we do not value heroism there will be less and less of it among us, and what there is will accomplish little in the long run. If we do not remember and celebrate the heroism in our heritage, we will have lost the key to a priceless treasure-house of the spirit.

Heroism is not confined to battle and war, although some of its brightest moments have come during the clash of arms. It is not even confined to emergencies. Every man comes to moments in his life when heroism is called for. Whether he answers the call depends on his character, his values, and the strength of his will. In any case, the decision to act heroically is a decision each man must make for himself, in the innermost recesses of his own mind. Heroism may be mass-admired (though all too often it is not, today); but it can never be mass-produced.

The hero, or the man who aspires to heroism, is first and last an individualist. He relies on his own strength and not the support of any group. The highest goal of any group is and must be a colorless "adjustment." The highest goal of the hero is victory -- not over other men (except in self-defense), but over nature, and over the weaknesses all human beings share.

Consider the man who gives up a safe, comfortable job that will assure him a decent living, convenient fringe benefits and enough to get by on in his old age, but which leads nowhere, offers him no chance to create or produce on a high level, does not begin to challenge his real abilities. To give up that safe but meaningless job and strike out in some new and almost unknown field, perhaps in a new and almost unknown part of the country, is a genuine act of heroism -- sometimes of very great heroism. And heroism is shown also by that man's wife when she supports him in his choice and assumes the risk willingly, as he does. My friends, all life is a risk. But only the hero dares to take the risks of life knowingly, making his own opportunities instead of being shaped by the people around him and the familiar ways of doing things.

It is no accident that our times which have seen such great changes in the American way of life, the shift in goals from victory to security, from self-reliance to grasping dependence, from pride to need -- it is no accident that these times have also seen the decline of the hero, for the two trends go together and are closely connected. A nation and a people which truly value their heroes have no use for a paternal government which always claims to know best. Such a nation and a people cannot be coaxed or conned out of their fundamental liberties. But a nation and a people which find heroism funny, or worse still see it as no better than a fraud, will far more readily surrender freedom to authority. When we value ourselves and our freedoms less, we cannot expect our government to value them more.

Notice how carefully our young men are trained today always to give the most credit for any accomplishment of theirs to the group, to "teamwork." Now, teamwork is very desirable and often very important. But there comes a time in any great undertaking when one man must face a dark and uncertain future boldly, and make a personal decision to carry on the torch. That decision has nothing whatever to do with teamwork. It concerns nothing but one man's soul.

Such a moment came for Admiral Rickover in the early days of the atomic submarine. Such a moment came for Admiral Lewis Strauss when he was chairman of the Atomic Energy Commission and alone against the unanimous opposition of a board of scientists swayed by pacifist and mistaken thinking, ordered the building of the hydrogen bomb. Such a moment came for John Glenn when he rode the Mercury capsule through the searing flare of re-entry, expecting at any moment to lose his heat shield and be burned alive.

Men do not survive such moments with honor and victory unless they find in themselves at least a touch of heroism. Every scorning and every scoffing which kills the roots of that heroism in our people, make it less likely that America as a nation will know honor and victory in the years to come.

Subscribe now to our patriotic newspaper LIFE LINES, three times a week, $5 a year. Send cash or check to LIFE LINES, Washington 1, D. C., or LIFE LINE will bill you on your request.

I'll be back in a moment.

COMMISSION EXHIBIT No. 2285—Continued

CIRCULATION AND AWARENESS OF FREEDOM MATERIAL IS VITAL. PLEASE MAKE THIS COPY AS WIDELY AVAILABLE AS POSSIBLE TO OTHER READERS.

THIS TRANSCRIPT MAY BE REPRODUCED IN ITS ENTIRETY.
(COMMERCIAL..........45 seconds)

Heroism in war, though it is not the only kind, is not a heroism we can ever afford to forget. To honor it in no way implies that we enjoy war and do not love peace. Americans have never wanted any war and they have never started one. But when war comes, only American heroism has made victory possible. Through most of our history we remembered that victorious heroism proudly, and sang its praises. Today there is more often only a great and echoing silence.

Did you know that a recent survey found not one textbook in common use in our elementary and high schools which included the immortal battle cry of John Paul Jones: "I have not yet begun to fight"? Fifty years ago, not one textbook on our history left it out.

Think back a moment -- those of you who are old enough to remember -- to a dark autumn 21 years ago, when a war for the world hung in the balance. The mighty armies of freedom-hating tyranny -- ruthless, victorious, unbeaten -- battered like crashing waves at the last lines of defense still standing against them. There were three outstanding points of encounter: in Russia, at Stalingrad; in Egypt, at Alamein; in the Pacific, at Guadalcanal. Defeat at those points would have meant we would have lost the war. But defeat did not come, victories were snatched out of those terrible encounters.

In Russia the anniversary of Stalingrad is celebrated every year, and is used as one of the strongest popular props for a new tyrant enemy. In England Alamein is a name to conjure with, the last decisive victory Britain won and perhaps the last she will ever win.

In America, not so long ago, 35 bright young university students in a history class were asked to identify Guadalcanal. Less than one third of them had ever heard of it.

They had never heard of a band of Marines who landed in a steaming fever-haunted jungle and were cut off the next day by the Japanese navy, yet survived and hung on and fought like fiends through five terrible months until victory was theirs. They had never heard of a colonel named Edson who held a place called Bloody Ridge with a single company of 200 exhausted men and beat off a final decisive attack against odds of 10 to one -- an attack believed certain to succeed. They had never heard of a cruiser called the San Francisco with just one man left alive on her shell-shattered bridge, and how that one man, a young lieutenant named McCandless, held her on course to fire a point-blank broadside into a Japanese battleship, and then to struggle through to survival. They had never heard of a tropic night hideous with the scream of fourteen-inch shells that spelled what seemed surely the end of hope for the Marines who had fought for the island so long, and of the next night after when an admiral named Halsey sent in all he had left, and the last American battleship able to fire a gun in the South Pacific turned back the Japanese fleet singlehanded from the smoking waves round Savo Island.

They had never heard of any of it. Three thousand years of military history tell no story more splendid than the blazing heroism on Guadalcanal, every bit of it American, as truly American as the log cabin frontier and the open range. But nobody hears of it now. United Nations Day each year gets a hundred times the publicity.

We will not find the courage to survive the long years of our still mightier struggle today, by refusing to look upon the heroism in our past. Yet that heroism is there, in the treasure-house of folk memory and the pages of history. All we have to do is remem-- it.

This is program #31, two typewritten copies for 25¢, cash, stamps or check, or 10¢ per copy in larger quantities. Write LIFE LINE, Washington 1, D. C. Our three-times-a-week patriotic newspaper, LIFE LINES, $3 a year.

You may catch LIFE LINE on these stations in the Dallas-Ft.Worth Area:

New Orleans	870-WWL	5:45 a	Terrell	1570-KTER	5:15 p
Denton	1440-KDNT	6:45 a	Dallas	1080-KRLD	6:15 p
Fort Worth	1540-KCUL	7:30 a	Nashville	1510-WLAC	6:15 p
Bonham	1420-KFYN	7:45 a	Shreveport	1130-KWKH	7:00 p
Corpus Christi	1030-KCTA	8:30 a	Greenville	1440-KGVL	7:15 p
Sherman	1500-KTXO	8:30 a	Waco	1460-WACO	8:00 p
Dallas	730-KPCN	11:00 a	New Orleans	870-WWL	9:15 p
Denton	1440-KDNT	11:45 a	Cincinnati	700-WLW	11:05 p
			Tulsa	1170-KVOO	11:45 p
Tyler	600-KTBB	12:45 p	Shreveport	1130-KWKH	12:45 a
Corpus Christi	1030-KCTA	4:45 p	Nashville	1510-WLAC	2:45 a
Tulsa	1170-KVOO	4:45 p	Nashville	650-WSM	4:45 a

Many are preparing and reproducing flyers, of this nature, in quantities for their city, with a commendation of the product advertised by sponsors of LIFE LINE in their city. There is a good slogan promoting Patriotism: "ASK WHERE YOU CAN BUY PRODUCTS ADVERTISED WITH FREEDOM."

SOME OF THE OTHER 311 LIFE LINE STATIONS

Birmingham	1070-WAPI	8:45 p	Louisville	1240-WENN	7:05 p
Montgomery	1440-WHHY	6:15 p	Baltimore	1570-WAQE	7:30 a
Tuscaloosa	1230-WTBC	6:45 a	Jackson	620-WJDX	6:45 p
Phoenix	550-KOY	7:30 p	St. Louis	1010-KXEN	8:30 a
Fayetteville	1250-KFAY	7:15 a	Black Mt.	1010-WFGW	8:15 a
Fort Smith	950-KFSA	6:00 a	Durham	620-WDNC	6:30 p
Little Rock	1909-KAAY	7:00 p	Cincinnati	700-WLW	11:05 p
Los Angeles	640-KFI	10:15 p	Houston	98 fm-KFMK	6:45 a
San Diego	860-XEMO	12:15 p	San Antonio	1200-WOAI	10:45 p
Jacksonville	600-WPDQ	7:05 p	Salt Lake City	1160-KSL	8:10 p
Atlanta	1480-WYZE	7:00 a	Wheeling	1170-WWVA	4:15 a
Waterloo	1540-KXEL	10:15 p	Tampa	1300-WSOL	8:15 a

The principles and goals of LIFE LINE, a religious and patriotic educational program, can be hear on 311 radio stations daily.

COMMISSION EXHIBIT No. 2285—Continued

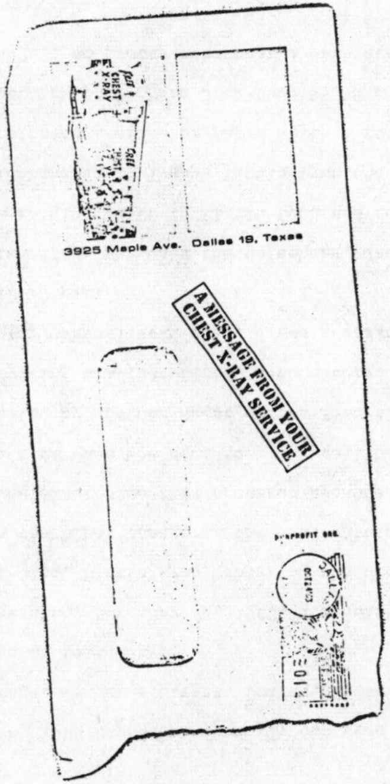

3925 Maple Ave. Dallas 19, Texas
A MESSAGE FROM YOUR CHEST X-RAY SERVICE

COMMISSION EXHIBIT No. 2286

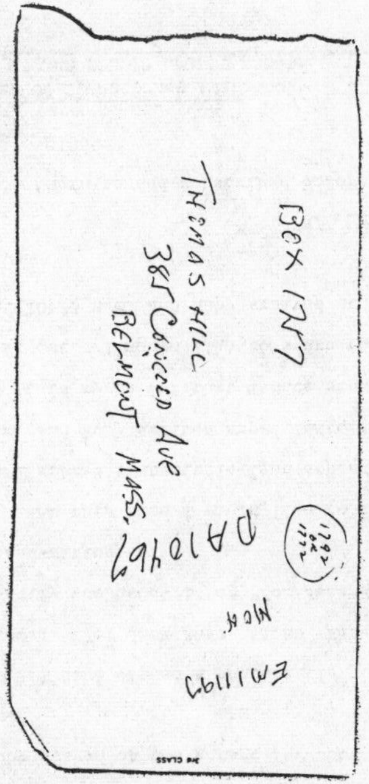

COMMISSION EXHIBIT No. 2286—Continued

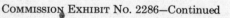

A F F I D A V I T

I, Huey Reeves, 2903 Reynolds, formerly employed as Night Manager for Nichols Garage, Commerce Street, Dallas, Texas, after being duly sworn, depose as follows:

On Saturday evening, November 23, 1963, I recall an employee of Jack Ruby's Carousel Club, Little Lynn, entering the Nichols Garage where I was then the Night Manager. She made a telephone call. I am unable to recall the exact time this occurred because I was not paying attention to the time when she came in. I recall being interviewed on a former occasion by another Agent of the Federal Bureau of Investigation and advising him that Little Lynn entered the garage at approximately 7:30 p.m. When I said this, I was guessing. She could have come in at 10:30 p.m.

A minute or two after she used the telephone, Jack Ruby telephoned and asked me to give $5.00 to Little Lynn and to get a receipt. After the telephone call, I gave Little Lynn the money and wrote the following receipt on a piece of paper which I took off of a Republic Carloading scratch pad: "For Jack Ruby $5.00 received by" and signed "Little Lynn." I am pretty sure that I date stamped

44

this receipt immediately after I wrote it. Little Lynn left the garage after she received the money.

I think Ruby arrived at the garage approximately 20 to 30 minutes later. This would have been about 10:50 p.m. or 11:00 p.m. Jack Ruby stayed at the garage for about 10 or 15 minutes and then he left.

I have viewed a photostatic copy of the receipt described as follows: "For Jack Ruby $5.00 Received by Little Lynn," I can identify the handwriting "For Jack Ruby $5.00 Received by" as my handwriting.

At this time I would like to change my previous statement wherein I stated that Little Lynn appeared at the garage at about 7:30 p.m. and Ruby arrived approximately 30 to 45 minutes later because it is my belief that I date stamped the receipt at the time I made it out. I would like to state that I made this receipt out at about 10:33 p.m. and Ruby arrived at the garage 20 to 30 minutes later.

/s/ HUEY REEVES

Sworn to and subscribed before me this 9th day of June, 1964.

/s/ [illegible] Jr.
Assistant U. S. Attorney (Witness)

/s/ SHIRLEY M. [illegible]
Notary Public

/s/ S/A [illegible] FBI Dallas 6/9/64 (Witness)

45

FD-302 (Rev. 3-3-59) FEDERAL BUREAU OF INVESTIGATION

Date December 16, 1963

(1)

RALPH GISMONT, 1020 Beechview, Dallas, Texas, telephone 7-4373, who is an attorney in Dallas, Texas, was interviewed as to how it could be verified that JACK RUBY was in the office of MAX RUDBERG on November 21, 1963.

Mr. GISMONT advised he was in the office of MAX RUDBERG, AA Bonding Service, on November 21, 1963. He checked receipt number 373 which he had received from the company and which is dated November 21, 1963. Mr. GISMONT said this is the way he is sure it was on November 21, 1963, when he was in RUDBERG's office.

Mr. GISMONT informed that he was introduced to JACK RUBY on that date in RUDBERG's office. He said that the time was between approximately 11 a.m. and 12 noon. GISMONT stated that on that occasion RUBY gave MAX RUDBERG and GISMONT a pass to his Carousel Club and then took the passes back so that he, RUBY, could have the passes laminated.

GISMONT said that this is the only occasion he ever talked with RUBY and he does not know of any connection between RUBY and LEE HARVEY OSWALD.

on 12/14/63 at Dallas, Texas File # DL 44-1639

by Special Agent JACK B. PEDEN:bnm Date dictated 12/16/63

This document contains neither recommendations nor conclusions of the FBI. It is the property of the FBI and is loaned to your agency; it and its contents are not to be distributed outside your agency.

COMMISSION EXHIBIT No. 2288

FD-302 (Rev. 3-3-59) FEDERAL BUREAU OF INVESTIGATION

1

Date 6/19/64

Patrolman H. L. HENLEY, Dallas Police Department, Dallas, Texas, advised that he was assigned to guard the homicide door entrance on the third floor, Dallas Police Department, on the afternoon of November 22, 1963. Officer HENLEY stated that he was relieved at 5:30 P.M. on November 22, 1963. He stated that he knew JACK RUBY and that at no time during the time he was on duty, from approximately 3:00 P.M. until 5:30 P.M. on November 22, 1963, did he see JACK RUBY in the hallway of the third floor of the Dallas Police Department, nor did JACK RUBY attempt to enter the Homicide Bureau office during the period he was stationed there on November 22, 1963.

on 6/17/64 at Dallas, Texas File # DL 44-1639

by Special Agent VINCENT E. DRAIN/ds Date dictated 6/18/64

This document contains neither recommendations nor conclusions of the FBI. It is the property of the FBI and is loaned to your agency; it and its contents are not to be distributed outside your agency.

COMMISSION EXHIBIT No. 2289

FD-302 (Rev. 3-3-59)

FEDERAL BUREAU OF INVESTIGATION

1

Date 6/19/64

ROBERT B. COUNTS, Patrolman, Dallas Police Department, Dallas, Texas, related the following information:

Patrolman COUNTS related that he and CLYDE F. GOODSON relieved Officer H. L. HENLEY at 5:30 P.M. on November 22, 1963, for guard duty on the door of the Homicide Bureau of the Dallas Police Department, Dallas, Texas. He stated this was located on the third floor of the Dallas Police Building. Officer COUNTS related that he knew JACK RUBY when he saw him, and that during the period from 5:30 P.M. until approximately 8:00 P.M. on November 22, 1963, he at no time observed JACK RUBY in the hallway of the third floor of the Police Building or elsewhere. He stated that at no time did RUBY attempt to enter the Homicide Bureau, to his knowledge, while he was doing guard duty with Officer GOODSON.

Patrolman COUNTS stated there is only one entrance to the Homicide Bureau and if JACK RUBY had attempted to get into the Homicide Bureau he would certainly have seen him.

on 6/18/64 at Dallas, Texas File # DL 44-1639

by Special Agent VINCENT E. DRAIN/ds Date dictated 6/18/64

COMMISSION EXHIBIT No. 2289—Continued

UNITED STATES DEPARTMENT OF JUSTICE

FEDERAL BUREAU OF INVESTIGATION

In Reply, Please Refer to File No.

St. Louis, Missouri

June 27, 1964

JACK L. RUBY;
LEE HARVEY OSWALD -
VICTIM
CIVIL RIGHTS

The interview set forth below is predicated upon a request of the President's Commission on the Assassination of President Kennedy, dated June 24, 1964, that Mrs. Wilma Tice, 8406 Lakemont Drive, Dallas, Texas, be interviewed on the basis of information furnished to the Commission by Eileen Kaminsky, sister of Jack L. Ruby, to the effect that Ruby spoke with Mrs. Tice on November 22, 1963, at Parkland Hospital, Dallas, Texas, at which time, according to Mrs. Kaminsky, Mrs. Tice was told by Ruby that he would be willing to donate his kidney to Governor Connally.

Mrs. Wilma Tice, 1919a Park Avenue, St. Louis, Missouri, advised that her home is 8406 Lakemont Drive, Dallas, Texas.

She advised that as near as she can recall the events of November 22, 1963, that after the assassination of the President, she decided to go to Parkland Hospital, where the President and Governor Connally had been taken. She said she had three children in school and that she would have to be home by 3:00 p.m., as they would be home then. As near as she could recall, she either left home or arrived at the hospital at approximately 1:30 p.m. She said she, with a group of bystanders, was near the emergency entrance to Parkland Hospital, which as she recalls is a side entrance just off Harry Hines Street. There is a sloping driveway going into the emergency entrance.

She said a crowd of people had already gathered there. She made her way as near to the front of the crowd as possible and stopped beside a man who was at the time unknown to her, but whom

COMMISSION EXHIBIT No. 2290

she later believed to be Jack Ruby. Her attention was drawn to this man as he had a hat, color or description unknown, in his left hand, hitting it against his leg. She could furnish no description of this man other than to say that she recalls he wore a dark suit, white shirt, and possibly a tie. He was heavily built. She thought by hitting his hat against his leg he would ruin it. He was alone.

She stood about three to four feet from this man when he was approached by another man who stated, "How are you going there, Jack?" Mrs. Tice said that some other individual in the crowd had made the remark that Governor Connally had been shot in the kidney and, when this remark was overheard, the man identified as Ruby stated, "Couldn't someone give him a kidney?" The man who approached Ruby then stated, "Who the hell would give him a kidney?", to which Ruby replied that he would.

Mrs. Tice said that Ruby never called his visitor by name and the visitor never gave Ruby's last name. She said the entire incident during which these two men were together probably did not last more than five minutes.

The man who approached Ruby, Mrs. Tice was unable to describe in any detail other than to say that he was younger and taller than Ruby and was slimmer. She recalls he wore a white shirt and tie and carried a coat over his left arm, but she can not recall the color of his coat, trousers, or tie. She can not recall any facial characteristics of either man. She said the two things which stood out to her during this time was the man identified as Ruby hitting his hat against his leg and his visitor carrying his coat over his left arm.

Mrs. Tice said that shortly after this she had to leave as she had to return to her home by 3:00 p.m., before the children arrived.

Mrs. Tice did not see anyone else in the crowd whom she knew nor did she see or hear Ruby or his visitor speak to anyone else in the crowd.

She said she forgot about this incident until seeing the shooting of Oswald on television, at which time she believed the man hitting his leg with his hat at the Parkland Hospital was the same man who shot Oswald. She then subsequently saw his pictures in the paper and still believed it to be the same individual.

Mrs. Tice said nothing about this to anyone and did not think any more about it at the time. In the meantime she said she felt the remorse that Mrs. Kennedy must be enduring and sent Mrs. Kennedy a sympathy card, to which Mrs. Kennedy replied.

Mrs. Tice advised that on January 23, 1964, she was involved in an automobile accident in Dallas and that she was bedridden until April 21, 1964. During this time in bed, she felt that Eva Grant, Ruby's sister in Dallas, must be undergoing emotional difficulties as a result of the Oswald shooting. She then decided to call Mrs. Grant on the telephone and express her sympathy.

As near as she can now recall, she made the first call either in the latter part of January, 1964, or possibly February, 1964, and believes mid-February would be most likely. She does not recall to whom she spoke when calling the Eva Grant residence, but thinks it was possibly to Eileen Kaminsky, sister of Ruby. She believes the first call was to Eileen, inasmuch as Eileen said on either this call or a subsequent call that Eva Grant would be glad to know there was someone who sympathized with her. It was in this first call that Mrs. Tice told Eileen that she believed she saw Jack Ruby at the Parkland Hospital emergency entrance on November 22, 1963.

Mrs. Tice said it was either in that conversation or her first conversation with Eva Grant, which would have followed in a day or two, that either Eva or Eileen remarked they were glad to have the information that she had seen Ruby at the Parkland Hospital and none of them knew prior to this that he had been there.

Mrs. Tice said that as she recalls, Eva Grant was alone and had just had an operation in a hospital herself. She recalls that Eileen Kaminsky said she lived in Chicago and not in Dallas. She said that Eileen Kaminsky called her possibly three or four times just to talk to her. Mrs. Tice said that Eva Grant would call her frequently, saying she needed someone to talk to, inasmuch as she no longer had any friends after the shooting of Oswald. Eva remarked that people she had considered her friends were now very cool toward her.

Mrs. Tice said that she almost regretted having made her call to Eva Grant because each time Eva Grant would call her, it made her, Mrs. Tice, very nervous. Mrs. Tice explained that she normally did not have a nervous condition, but as a result of her automobile accident, she did.

Mrs. Tice advised that some time shortly after April 21, 1964, when she was no longer confined to bed, she recalls a newspaper man representing station WFAA-TV in Dallas called at her home as a result of the information she had given Eva Grant regarding her having seen Ruby at the Parkland Hospital. This newspaper man wanted pictures of Mrs. Tice and also wanted Mrs. Tice to repeat her story which she had told Eva Grant about having seen Ruby at the hospital. Mrs. Tice told him the same story and he advised her not to talk about this. Mrs. Tice does not know why he gave her such advice, although she refused to permit her picture to be taken by this man or anyone else. She was not contacted by any other newspaper man. She does not know the newspaper man's name.

Mrs. Tice said she could not recall any additional details regarding Ruby's presence at the Parkland Hospital, although she said she desired to make it clear that she had never known or seen, to her knowledge, Jack Ruby or any member of the Ruby family on any occasion prior to November 22, 1963.

- 4 -

COMMISSION EXHIBIT No. 2290—Continued

Commission Exhibit No. 2291

UNITED STATES DEPARTMENT OF JUSTICE

FEDERAL BUREAU OF INVESTIGATION

In Reply, Please Refer to File No.

July 13, 1964
Dallas, Texas

JACK L. RUBY;
LEE HARVEY OSWALD

The investigation reported herein was based on a request in a letter of the President's Commission on the Assassination of President Kennedy for reinterview with Connie Trammel concerning her interview with Lamar Hunt, and information concerning the relationship and office space occupied by Lamar and H. L. Hunt.

Attached are reports of interviews in the above regard.

Attachments

COMMISSION EXHIBIT No. 2291

FD-302 (Rev. 3-3-59)

FEDERAL BUREAU OF INVESTIGATION

1

Date 7/10/64

CONNIE TRAMMEL PENNY, 4607 Monarch, Apartment 114, Dallas, Texas, advised she was recently married and had moved to the new apartment on Monarch on July 8, 1964. Mrs. PENNY is now employed by the General Advertising Agency, Republic National Bank.

Mrs. PENNY advised she was a senior at the University of Texas when she met RUBY, exact date unrecalled. A group of girls from the University were visiting in Dallas and staying at the Adolphus Hotel, which is directly across the street from the Carousel Club that was owned by RUBY at the time. Mrs. PENNY and another girl attended one of the shows at the Carousel Club and Mrs. PENNY had started to the ladies' room when RUBY stopped her and asked Mrs. PENNY if he had not met her before. Mrs. PENNY gave her name, which at that time was CONNIE TRAMMEL, and her telephone number at the University to RUBY.

RUBY made several calls to Mrs. PENNY at the University attempting to get Mrs. PENNY to go to work at the Carousel Club as a stripper. After graduating from the University of Texas, Mrs. PENNY rented an apartment in Dallas and contacted RUBY on several occasions, attempting to obtain employment as a hat check girl or similar employment. RUBY did not have any vacancies but kept insisting that she could work as a stripper.

Mrs. PENNY stated that she had never dated RUBY and had not had too much conversation with RUBY.

On November 21, 1963, RUBY telephonically contacted Mrs. PENNY, asking if she had decided to go to work as a stripper, at which time Mrs. PENNY told RUBY that she had talked with LAMAR HUNT and had made an appointment to see LAMAR HUNT regarding employment. As Mrs. PENNY did not have an automobile, RUBY agreed to meet Mrs. PENNY at her apartment and drive her to the Mercantile National Bank. RUBY told Mrs. PENNY that he had business to transact at the bank and it would be no trouble for him to pick her up. During

on 7/9/64 at Dallas, Texas File # DL 44-1639

by Special Agent WILL HAYDEN GRIFFIN/ds Date dictated 7/10/64

COMMISSION EXHIBIT No. 2291—Continued

2

DL 44-1639

the A.M. of November 21, 1963, exact time she could not recall, RUBY picked up Mrs. PENNY at the apartment and inquired as to how Mrs. PENNY had made the appointment with LAMAR HUNT, at which time RUBY stated that he would like to meet HUNT. Mrs. PENNY explained she had made a personal call to LAMAR HUNT's residence, at which time a maid in the LAMAR HUNT home gave her the telephone number of a straight line into LAMAR HUNT's office. Mrs. PENNY called LAMAR HUNT and made the appointment to talk to LAMAR HUNT in his office in the Mercantile Bank Building. Mrs. PENNY could not recall the suite number where she was interviewed by LAMAR HUNT.

Mrs. PENNY advised she had read in the Dallas newspapers where LAMAR HUNT had owned a bowling alley and was converting the bowling alley into a teen-age club and believed that she could gain employment at the club in public relations as she had obtained a degree from the University of Texas in public relations.

RUBY parked his car in a parking lot near the Mercantile Bank and accompanied Mrs. PENNY to the elevator in the Mercantile Bank, but did not accompany her upstairs. This is the last time that Mrs. PENNY has seen RUBY.

During the trip from Mrs. PENNY's apartment to the bank, RUBY seemed to be impressed with the amount of money that LAMAR HUNT had made, and had mentioned that he knew most of the prominent people in Dallas and could wave at them on the streets of Dallas and be recognized, but that he did not know LAMAR HUNT.

RUBY did not express any views about the political views of LAMAR HUNT or his father, H. L. HUNT, during the trip from Mrs. PENNY's apartment to the bank.

Mrs. PENNY advised she did not obtain the employment with HUNT as he had no plans for any person to work for him in the public relations department for the teen-age club.

COMMISSION EXHIBIT No. 2291—Continued

FD-302 (Rev. 3-3-59)

FEDERAL BUREAU OF INVESTIGATION

1

Date 7/10/64

Mr. H. EDWARD SMITH, Manager of the Mercantile National Bank Building and Mercantile Securities Building, which covers the entire 1800 block of Commerce Street, Dallas, Texas, advised there are numerous entrances from Commerce and Main Streets to both the bank and Securities Building.

SMITH advised LAMAR HUNT is the son of H. L. HUNT and both are interested in numerous business ventures, the principal one being the Hunt Oil Company. The Hunt enterprises have offices on the sixth and seventh floors of both the Securities and Bank Building, and also have offices on the eighth and thirteenth floors of the bank building. The receptionist for all of the offices in both the Securities and Bank Buildings is on the seventh floor of the Mercantile National Bank Building. LAMAR HUNT has his private offices on the seventh floor of the Mercantile Securities Building and H. L. HUNT has his private offices on the seventh floor of the Mercantile National Bank Building.

on 7/10/64 at Dallas, Texas File # DL 44-1639

by Special Agent WILL HAYDEN GRIFFIN/ds Date dictated 7/10/64

Commission Exhibit No. 2292

FD-302 (Rev. 3-3-59)

FEDERAL BUREAU OF INVESTIGATION

Date 7/21/64

1

Mr. JOHN MAZZIOTTA, Chief Photographer, Photographic Department, "The Dallas Times Herald," made available three copies of each of the following described photographs:

Two 8 x 10 inch glossy photographs of the bedroom of JACK RUBY's Marsala Place apartment. According to MAZZIOTTA, these photographs were taken by photographer WILLIAM ALLEN between 4:00 p.m. and 6:00 p.m., November 24, 1963.

One 8 x 10 inch glossy photograph of the front of the Carousel Club. According to MAZZIOTTA, this photograph was taken by photographer WILLIAM BEAL between 7:00 p.m. and 9:00 p.m., November 24, 1963.

MAZZIOTTA advised both photographers, ALLEN and BEAL, are no longer employed by "The Dallas Times Herald." Upon checking his records, MAZZIOTTA stated there were no other photographs taken of either JACK RUBY's apartment or the Carousel Club by "The Dallas Times Herald."

on 7/17/64 at Dallas, Texas File # DL 44-1639

by Special Agent RAYMOND P. YELCHAK:vm Date dictated 7/20/64

FD-302 (Rev. 3-3-59)

FEDERAL BUREAU OF INVESTIGATION

1

Date 7/22/64

Mrs. ELNORA PITTS, 1316 East Jefferson (WHitehall 2-5461), was reinterviewed, at which time she advised she was a cleaning woman for various apartments in Dallas, Texas. She stated JACK RUBY was one of her customers during his residence at the Marsala Place Apartments in Dallas.

Mrs. PITTS indicated that although she had agreed to clean RUBY's apartment between 2:00 and 2:30 PM, on November 24, 1963, she did not go to RUBY's apartment that day. She stated she heard the news of the OSWALD shooting on the radio around noon on that day; therefore, she did not go to RUBY's apartment as agreed.

In view of the above, Mrs. PITTS related she could furnish no information concerning the physical condition of RUBY's apartment on November 24, 1963.

on 7/20/64 at Dallas, Texas File # DL 44-1639

by Special Agent RAYMOND P. YELCHAK/eah Date dictated 7/21/64

COMMISSION EXHIBIT No. 2292—Continued

FD-302 (Rev. 3-3-59)

FEDERAL BUREAU OF INVESTIGATION

1

Date 7/24/64

Mrs. DORIS (CURTIS L.) WARNER (former manager of the Marsala Place Apartments, Dallas, Texas), 914 Joslin, Irving, Texas, was reinterviewed, at which time she furnished the following information:

Mrs. WARNER recalled she heard of the OSWALD slaying sometime before noon on November 24, 1963. She and her husband were almost immediately swamped by newsmen and photographers requesting to see JACK RUBY's apartment. She immediately called the police and let no one in the apartment until three Dallas City Detectives arrived with a search warrant. She estimates the arrival of the detectives at approximately 1:00 PM. She admitted the three detectives and Judge JOE B. BROWN, JR., Justice of the Peace, to the RUBY apartment. She and Judge BROWN remained in the living area while the three detectives searched through the entire apartment.

No photographs were taken by any member of the searching party and Mrs. WARNER stated she at no time permitted any photographers into the apartment. Upon being shown "The Dallas Times Herald" photograph of the interior of RUBY's bedroom taken on November 24, 1963, Mrs. WARNER stated she could furnish no information concerning what items in this room, if any, were disturbed between the time GEORGE SENATOR left the apartment on November 24, 1963, and the photographers arrived, inasmuch as she did not look into the bedroom on that day and she reiterated she did not permit the entry of any photographers.

on 7/21/64 at Irving, Texas File # DL 44-1639

by Special Agent S RAYMOND P. YELCHAK & JAMES W. SWINFORD/eah Date dictated 7/24/64

COMMISSION EXHIBIT No. 2292—Continued

FD-302 (Rev. 3-3-59)

FEDERAL BUREAU OF INVESTIGATION

1

Date 7/24/64

Detective GUY F. ROSE, Homicide & Robbery Squad, Dallas, Texas, Police Department, was interviewed at his residence, 714 Hall Street, Seagoville, Texas. He voluntarily furnished the following information:

ROSE recalled he obtained a search warrant from Judge JOE B. BROWN, JR., Justice of the Peace, at Dallas, on November 24, 1963, to search JACK RUBY's living quarters at the Marsala Place Apartments. ROSE, accompanied by Detectives H. M. MOORE and J. P. ADAMCIK proceeded to RUBY's apartment, where they arrived at approximately 1:00 PM. ROSE stated the owner of the apartment building, name unrecalled, refused to let the detectives enter RUBY's apartment because of an error in the search warrant. He explained RUBY's apartment was No. 207 and the wrong number appeared on the search warrant. He then called Judge BROWN, JR., Justice of the Peace, and Judge BROWN came to the RUBY apartment and corrected the error in the search warrant. A young lady, the resident manager of the apartments, name unrecalled, permitted the three detectives to search the apartment. ROSE estimates they were in the apartment for approximately one hour.

Upon being shown "The Dallas Times Herald" photograph taken of the interior of RUBY's apartment on November 24, 1963, ROSE stated that this is about what the bedroom looked like when he and the other two detectives first entered this room. He said they handled every item in the apartment, but tried to put everything back in exactly the same place they found it. ROSE added neither he nor any of the other detectives took any official police photographs of the apartment and no photographers were permitted to enter the apartment during the search. ROSE stated he and the others left the apartment at about 2:00 PM, at which time the resident manager locked the apartment and the detectives and Judge BROWN departed.

on 7/23/64 at Seagoville, Texas File # DL 44-1639

by Special Agent RAYMOND P. YELCHAK/eah Date dictated 7/24/64

FD-302 (Rev. 3-3-59)

FEDERAL BUREAU OF INVESTIGATION

1

Date 7/20/64

Lieutenant J. C. DAY, Crime Scene Search Section, Identification Bureau, Dallas Police Department, advised that to the best of his knowledge, and after checking records with negative results, no official police photographs were taken of JACK RUBY's living quarters on November 24, 1963. According to DAY, no police photographs were taken of the Carousel Club.

Lieutenant DAY stated he is in charge of the Crime Scene Search Section and if such photographs existed he would be aware of them.

on 7/17/64 at Dallas, Texas File # DL 44-1639

by Special Agent RAYMOND P. YELCHAK/ds Date dictated 7/20/64

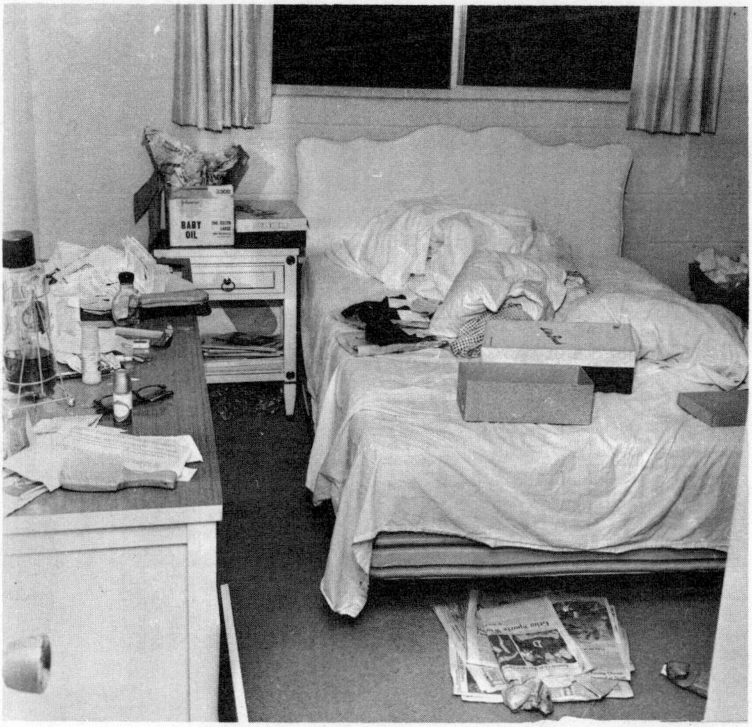

COMMISSION EXHIBIT No. 2292—Continued

COMMISSION EXHIBIT No. 2292—Continued

UNITED STATES DEPARTMENT OF JUSTICE

FEDERAL BUREAU OF INVESTIGATION

In Reply, Please Refer to
File No.

Dallas, Texas
July 23, 1964

JACK L. RUBY;
LEE HARVEY OSWALD

The President's Commission on the Assassination of President Kennedy requested, in a letter dated June 24, 1964, Mrs. Wilma Tice, 8406 Lakemont Drive, Dallas, Texas, be interviewed concerning her allegation she saw Jack L. Ruby at Parkland Hospital on November 22, 1963. The results of interview with Mrs. Tice at St. Louis, Missouri, on June 27, 1964, have been submitted previously.

On July 22, 1964, the Dallas Police Department reported to the Dallas Office of the Federal Bureau of Investigation that Mrs. Tice had, during the preceding night, telephoned concerning a prowler at her residence, had reported an anonymous call of a threatening nature, and had informed she was to give a deposition to the President's Commission on July 24, 1964.

Attached hereto are reports of interviews with Mrs. Tice and her husband, James M. Tice, on July 22, 1964.

The interviewing Agent noted an air of almost open hostility between Mr. and Mrs. Tice. Mrs. Tice gave the appearance of being extremely tense, sat on the edge of her chair nervously wringing her hands throughout the interview, and appeared somewhat reluctant to discuss the matter freely. She gave no indication she has any information that the incidents reported by her have any connection whatsoever with her scheduled appearance before the Commission, or that she has any information as to any phase of the investigation of the assassination and related matters, other than that reported previously.

COMMISSION EXHIBIT No. 2293

FD-302 (Rev. 3-3-59)

FEDERAL BUREAU OF INVESTIGATION

Date 7/22/64

1

Mrs. JAMES M. (WILMA) TICE, 8406 Lakemont Drive, was interviewed in the presence of her husband. She advised they have home telephone No. FL 2-2559.

At the outset of the interview, Mrs. TICE advised that at approximately 10:00 a.m., July 22, 1964, she received a telephone call from a man who identified himself as JIM LEHRER of "The Dallas Times Herald." She stated he inquired of her as to what she was going to testify to before the President's Commission. She said she declined to discuss it with him and he informed her he knew she was to testify before the President's Commission and was to appear at 2:30 p.m., on Friday, July 24, 1964. Mrs. TICE said she declined to discuss this matter with LEHRER and terminated the conversation.

Mrs. TICE advised she does not know how JIM LEHRER obtained the information that she was to testify before the President's Commission in Dallas, Texas. She said that on Sunday, July 20, 1964, she received an airmail special delivery registered letter, return receipt requested, from the President's Commission informing that she was to testify before that Commission in Dallas at 2:30 p.m., on July 24, 1964. She said she did not discuss this letter with anyone, not even her husband.

Mrs. TICE advised that around 1:00 or 1:30 a.m., on July 22, 1964, she was awakened by the ringing of the telephone. She said she picked up the telephone to answer it and the caller hung up. Within a minute or so, Mrs. TICE stated the telephone again rang, she picked it up, and again the caller hung up. By this time, Mrs. TICE advised she was wide awake. She said she lighted a cigarette and sat down in the living room. She advised as she was just about finished smoking the cigarette the doorbell rang. She said she went to window and looked out to see who was at the door but saw no one. At this point, Mrs. TICE stated she awakened her niece, EDITH TICE, age 14, who is visiting at her house. Mrs. TICE stated she was very concerned and both she and EDITH went through the house peering out the windows to see if they could locate any prowlers. Mrs. TICE stated she telephoned her husband who was then at work at

on 7/22/64 at Dallas, Texas File # DL 44-1639

by Special Agent A. RAYMOND SWITZER:vm Date dictated 7/22/64

COMMISSION EXHIBIT No. 2293—Continued

American Airlines, Love Field, Dallas, Texas, to inform him of what had transpired and to seek his advice. She stated her husband came home from work sometime after 2:00 a.m. Mrs. TICE advised she also called the Dallas Police Department and informed she had a prowler around their residence. She said the Dallas Police responded to her call and on inspecting their house discovered a twelve foot two by four homemade ladder wedged against the bottom of the aluminum storm door at the back of the house. She said her husband had made this ladder and it had been stored next to the garage at the rear of the house. She stated the police officers also observed that the spring snap which holds the slatted wooden front screen-storm door secure had been manipulated so that this door could not be opened from the inside without forcing it. She stated police officers also observed that the side gate was open. She stated this gate was closed when she retired for the night.

As set out above, Mrs. TICE advised that on Sunday, July 19, 1964, at about 2:00 p.m., she received the letter from the President's Commission. She said her husband was home at the time and was curious as to why the President's Commission would be corresponding with her. She said she declined to open this letter in the presence of her husband. Mrs. TICE stated her reason for not opening the letter in the presence of her husband was because he "fussed" at her when JACK RUBY's two sisters, EVA GRANT and EILEEN KAMINSKY, visited her on April 30, 1964. Since this time, Mrs. TICE said she has not discussed anything concerning JACK RUBY or the President's Commission with her husband. Mrs. TICE said she had nothing but trouble with her husband after RUBY's two sisters visited her.

Mrs. TICE was questioned as to how she contacted RUBY's sisters or how they knew to contact her. Mrs. TICE declined to answer this question.

Mrs. TICE advised that on Monday afternoon, July 20, 1964, at about 2:00 p.m., she received a telephone call as follows:

COMMISSION EXHIBIT No. 2293—Continued

Mrs. TICE: "Hello"

Unknown Male Caller: "Mrs. Tice?"

Mrs. TICE: "Hello"

Unknown Male Caller: "It would pay you to keep your mouth shut."

Mrs. TICE said the unknown male caller then hung up. She said he had a distinct, mature, well-modulated voice with no detectable accent. She said the voice was not familiar to her and she has no idea who made the call but believes it was a local call.

Mrs. TICE stated she has no information to support her belief but believes there is a connection between the above anonymous call, the incident of a prowler at her residence in the early morning hours of July 22, 1964, and the fact that she is to appear before the President's Commission on Friday, July 24, 1964.

Mrs. TICE related that about one and one half years ago she had received several anonymous telephone calls. She stated at this time many of her husband's fellow employees were having marital difficulties and their families also received anonymous telephone calls. She stated the calls she received then would usually be from a woman inquiring if her husband were home and when she called him to the telephone the caller would have already hung up. She said she considered these calls nuisance, prank-type calls.

Mrs. TICE reiterated that since April 30, 1964, when her husband "fussed" at her because RUBY's two sisters, EVA GRANT and EILEEN KAMINSKY, visited her at her house, she has not discussed anything with him relating to JACK RUBY or the assassination of President KENNEDY. She advised she had no information to offer at this time, but stated that should she receive any information that would be of assistance in this matter she would contact the interviewing Agent.

COMMISSION EXHIBIT No. 2293—Continued

4
DL 44-1639

As interviewing Agent was departing the TICE residence, two men who identified themselves as detectives from Captain FRITZ' office, Homicide and Robbery Bureau, Dallas Police Department, entered the TICE residence and informed they were there at the direction of Captain FRITZ to interview Mr. and Mrs. TICE.

COMMISSION EXHIBIT No. 2293—Continued

FD-302 (Rev. 3-3-59)

FEDERAL BUREAU OF INVESTIGATION

1

Date 7/22/64

JAMES M. TICE, 8406 Lakemont Drive, telephone No. FL 2-2559, was interviewed in the presence of his wife, Mrs. WILMA TICE. Mr. TICE advised he is employed by American Airlines as a Fleet Service Clerk at Love Field, Dallas, Texas.

Mr. TICE advised that sometime after 2:00 a.m., on July 22, 1964, while employed at Love Field he received a telephone call from his wife informing that a prowler had been around their house. Mr. TICE said he returned home. He said when he arrived home he found his wife in an emotional state as she related to him the incident about the prowler or prowlers around their home. He said apparently the prowler or prowlers knew he was at work because "they would not fool around my house, they know better if they know me."

Mr. TICE advised that prior to his arrival home his wife had called the Dallas Police and informed that a prowler had been around their house. He said the police who responded to his wife's call had found a twelve foot homemade two by four ladder wedged against the bottom of the aluminum storm door located at the back of the house. Mr. TICE said he had made the ladder and had previously stored it next to the garage at the rear of the house. Mr. TICE also stated the spring snap which holds the slatted wooden front screen-storm door secure had been manipulated so that the door could not be opened from the inside without forcing it.

Mr. TICE advised that the Dallas Police officers who responded to his wife's call inquired of him if he had any teen-age children. Mr. TICE said he responded negatively to this question. He advised, however, that his niece, EDITH TICE, had been visiting them for about a week. He also stated that he and his wife have three children, ages 7, 8, and 9.

When Mrs. TICE was questioned as to when she was to appear before the President's Commission in Dallas, Texas, she advised she was to appear on Friday, July 24, 1964, at 2:30 p.m., whereupon Mr. TICE stated "That is the first information I have that my wife has to appear before the President's Commission."

on 7/22/64 at Dallas, Texas File # DL 44-1639

by Special Agent A. RAYMOND SWITZER:vm Date dictated 7/22/64

COMMISSION EXHIBIT No. 2293—Continued

2
DL 44-1639

Mr. TICE related that on April 30, 1964, JACK RUBY's two sisters, EVA GRANT and EILEEN KAMINSKY, visited at his house and talked to his wife. He stated he told his wife she had no business talking to those people and that she should not have invited them into their house. He stated he was very annoyed because she had. As a consequence of this, Mr. TICE stated his wife would not discuss with him any information that she might have relating to JACK RUBY or why the President's Commission would want to talk to her. Mr. TICE stated he was at home on Sunday, July 19, 1964, when his wife received the airmail special delivery registered letter, return receipt requested, from the President's Commission. He said his wife would not open it nor would she discuss with him as to what it might contain. He said this annoyed him considerably.

Mr. TICE stated he related the above incident, about his wife receiving a letter from the President's Commission, to his fellow employees at American Airlines.

Mr. TICE advised he is aware his wife received an anonymous telephone call at about 2:00 p.m., on July 20, 1964. He said she informed him that the anonymous male caller had stated to Mrs. TICE that "It would pay you to keep your mouth shut." Mr. TICE stated he has no idea as to who may have made the call or to what the caller was referring but stated it might have something to do with his wife testifying before the President's Commission. He added, however, stating "Hell, nobody tells me anything around here. I guess all I'm supposed to do is chase prowlers and buy groceries." Mr. TICE further stated he is more than a little annoyed with his wife for not discussing the above matters with him.

Mr. TICE stated that about one and one half years ago he received an anonymous telephone call during which the male caller told him not to go to his farm with his little boy because his wife was going to have him killed. He said the caller also said "I will talk to you later at work." Mr. TICE said he did not pay any attention to this call and never learned who made it. He also stated

COMMISSION EXHIBIT No. 2293—Continued

3
DL 44-1639

that a number of his fellow employees had received anonymous telephone calls at about the same time.

Mr. TICE stated he had no information relating to the assassination of President KENNEDY or to the shooting of LEE HARVEY OSWALD by JACK RUBY. He stated, however, that should he receive any information that would be of assistance in this matter he would contact the interviewing Agent.

As interviewing Agent was departing the TICE residence, two men who identified themselves as detectives from Captain FRITZ' office, Homicide and Robbery Bureau, Dallas Police Department, entered the TICE residence and informed they were there at the direction of Captain FRITZ to interview Mr. and Mrs. TICE.

COMMISSION EXHIBIT No. 2293—Continued

KLIF Dallas
KABL San Francisco
WYSL Buffalo
KTSA San Antonio
WYNR Chicago
KILT Houston
XTRA Los Angeles

THE McLendon STATIONS

August 3, 1964

Mr. Bert Griffin
President's Commission
200 Maryland Avenue, N. E.
Washington, D. C.

Dear Mr. Griffin;

In reference to my telephone call with Miss Jane Vida and today's letter from Mr. J. Lee Rankin, I am submitting this letter to the President's Commission of the Assassination of President Kennedy.

I discovered that Jack Ruby's name had, indeed, been mentioned on a KLIF newscast. In listening to a soundscriber tape of the newscast, aired at 2 A. M. on Saturday, November 23, 1963, I found the following:
(portion of newscast, voiced by Glenn Duncan)
following story on the formal charging of Oswald..."Newsman Russ Knight was at the scene when Henry Wade and Police Chief Jesse Curry and Homicide Captain Will Fritz announced the formal charging of Lee Harvey Oswald. Here is his report........"

(voiced by Russ Knight over the telephone in rear of newsroom)
"If I can say it with any believeability, I have just returned from a trip to the Dallas Courthouse on a tip from Jack Ruby, local night club owner......."
(Knight continues with description of his interview with D. A. Wade)

At the time this newscast and report were aired live, Ruby was sitting in the newsroom listening to both. He left shortly afterward, as previously outlined in my testimony at his trial and before Commission Investigator Leon Hubert.

If I can be of any further aid, don't hesitate to call on me for any help or clarification.

Sincerely,
W. Glenn Duncan

W. Glenn Duncan
2921 Dyer
Dallas, Texas

WGD:tr

Commission Exhibit No. 2294

Commission Exhibit No. 2295

UNITED STATES DEPARTMENT OF JUSTICE
FEDERAL BUREAU OF INVESTIGATION
Dallas, Texas
August 6, 1964

In Reply, Please Refer to
File No.

JACK L. RUBY;
LEE HARVEY OSWALD

The President's Commission on the Assassination of President Kennedy requested, in a letter dated July 23, 1964, that Lieutenant James R. Gilmore, Dallas, Texas, Police Department, be re-interviewed concerning his encounters with Jack L. Ruby on Friday, November 22, 1963.

Attached is a report of re-interview with Lieutenant Gilmore.

D-302 (Rev. 3-3-59)

FEDERAL BUREAU OF INVESTIGATION

1

Date 8/6/64

Lieutenant JAMES R. GILMORE, Platoon Supervisor, Vice Section, Dallas Police Department, Dallas, Texas, advised he first saw JACK L. RUBY on Friday night, November 22, 1963, after the assassination of President KENNEDY, inside the Police Department assembly room during the press conference held by District Attorney HENRY WADE at midnight.

GILMORE related that he recalls seeing RUBY at the press conference inasmuch as during this press conference District Attorney WADE was speaking about the organization OSWALD was a member of; however, he was not able to recall the name of this organization, and RUBY "spoke up and remarked, 'the Fair Play for Cuba.'"

GILMORE stated he did not converse with RUBY at this press conference; however, approximately one hour after the press conference he saw RUBY in one of the passageways of the Dallas Police Department, at which time he, GILMORE, asked RUBY what he was doing and RUBY related he was distributing sandwiches to the officers of the Homicide and Robbery Section. GILMORE stated RUBY also commented he was going to "check with KLIF to see if they wanted any sandwiches." Thereafter, he terminated their conversation, departed, and headed for the exit; however, GILMORE did not actually see RUBY leave the building.

on 8/5/64 at Dallas, Texas File # DL 44-1639

by Special Agent JAMES W. SWINFORD/ds Date dictated 8/5/64

Commission Exhibit No. 2295—Continued

Commission Exhibit No. 2296

UNITED STATES DEPARTMENT OF JUSTICE

FEDERAL BUREAU OF INVESTIGATION

In Reply, Please Refer to File No.

Dallas, Texas
July 31, 1964

JACK L. RUBY;
LEE HARVEY OSWALD

By letter dated July 23, 1964, the President's Commission on the Assassination of President Kennedy requested reinterview with Joseph A. Glowacki, Dallas, Texas, and Krystian Barcz, if readily available, relative to their encounter with Jack L. Ruby at Ritz Delicatessen, Dallas, on the afternoon of November 22, 1963, to determine as precisely as possible the time at which they saw Ruby and his conduct at the time.

Available information indicates Mr. Barcz, a Polish National, returned to Warsaw, Poland, in December, 1963. Attached is a report of interview with Mr. Glowacki.

Attachment

Commission Exhibit No. 2296

FD-302 (Rev. 3-3-59) FEDERAL BUREAU OF INVESTIGATION

1

Date 7/31/64

Mr. JOSEPH A. GLOWACKI, 2811 Binkley Avenue, Apartment 210 (EM 3-6794), employed at The Old Warsaw Restaurant, 3914 Cedar Springs, Dallas, Texas, was reinterviewed and furnished the following information:

On November 22, 1963, he was in the downtown area of Dallas with Mr. KRYSTIAN BARCZ, a Polish National, who was visiting the United States on a State Department study grant. They watched the Presidential parade from the corner of Main and Harwood Streets. The parade passed their station shortly after noon at which time they walked to Hoffman's Men's Wear, 1403 Commerce Street, where they learned from Mr. HOFFMAN that the President had been shot.

Mr. GLOWACKI advised he and Mr. BARCZ left Hoffman's shortly after 1:00 p.m. and went to a brokerage house located next to Hoffman's where they watched the news coming in concerning the assassination. They remained at this place for approximately 30 minutes then went back to Hoffman's where they again spoke with Mr. HOFFMAN for a few minutes.

He recalled BARCZ wanted to make a telephone call to his employer, a television station in Warsaw, Poland, to report the news of the assassination. They left Hoffman's and walked to the Southwestern Bell Telephone Company Building, 308 S. Akard, where BARCZ placed his call to Warsaw. GLOWACKI estimated they were in the telephone building for about 30 minutes. From the telephone building they walked to Television Station WFAA, Young and Houston Streets, where BARCZ asked to see the Station Manager, MIKE SHAPIRO. GLOWACKI related parenthetically that BARCZ was a guest of this station. SHAPIRO spoke briefly with them and they left the television station and walked to the Ritz Delicatessen, 205 Browder, for lunch. He estimated their arrival at the delicatessen at approximately 3:30 p.m. or possibly a little later. While at the delicatessen, he observed JACK RUBY standing near the front of the delicatessen listening to the broadcast coming in on the radio. He called RUBY over to his table and introduced him to BARCZ. GLOWACKI invited RUBY to sit at their table, but RUBY declined.

on 7/30/64 at Dallas, Texas File # DL 44-1639

by Special Agent RAYMOND P. YELCHAK:vm Date dictated 7/30/64

2

2
DL 44-1639

GLOWACKI advised that at that time RUBY did not appear to him to be any more agitated or upset than the average citizen. In fact, RUBY asked Mr. GLOWACKI, "Joe, what is this going to do to our business? We're going to lose all of the conventions." It appeared to GLOWACKI that RUBY was more concerned with the result on business than he was by the actual assassination of the President. GLOWACKI now recalls RUBY may have commented, "Do they have that son-of-a-bitch that did it?" and "Joe, whether you think they should do to the bastard -- they should shoot him right away!"

GLOWACKI indicated he and BARCZ continued with their lunch after the brief conversation with RUBY and estimated they left the delicatessen at approximately 4:00 p.m. RUBY was still at the delicatessen when they left.

GLOWACKI further advised his friend BARCZ has since returned to Poland.

3

UNITED STATES DEPARTMENT OF JUSTICE

FEDERAL BUREAU OF INVESTIGATION

In Reply, Please Refer to File No.

Dallas, Texas
August 24, 1964

JACK L. RUBY;
LEE HARVEY OSWALD

By letter dated July 30, 1964, the President's Commission on the Assassination of President Kennedy requested one Mr. Griffin, an employee of "The Dallas Times Herald", be identified and interviewed, it being pointed out that Griffin, according to Roy A. Pryor, saw Jack L. Ruby at about 4:00 a.m., Saturday, November 23, 1963. Attached are reports of interviews with Roy A. Pryor and Kenneth E. Griffith.

It is noted that on August 3, 1964, Paul Pope, Personnel Manager, "The Dallas Times Herald", Dallas, Texas, advised that there is no employee of "The Dallas Times Herald" with the surname of Griffin; however, Mr. Pope noted that one Kenneth E. Griffith is an employee assigned to the Composing Room of this newspaper.

COMMISSION EXHIBIT No. 2297

FD-302 (Rev. 3-3-59)

FEDERAL BUREAU OF INVESTIGATION

Date 8/7/64

1

ROY A. PRYOR, 8544 Foxwood Lane, advised that he is employed as a printer by "The Dallas Times Herald" and that he and a man named GRIFFIN or GRIFFITH, first name unknown, had both worked two hours overtime the morning of November 23, 1963. Both had made up time sheets and were about ready to leave "The Dallas Times Herald" composing room when JACK RUBY came in at approximately 4:10 a.m. PRYOR spoke to RUBY but does not recall if he introduced RUBY to "GRIF." If RUBY and "GRIF" spoke at all, it would have only been to say hello. PRYOR stated that "GRIF" would not have been in RUBY's presence more than five or ten seconds before "GRIF" left. PRYOR stated that "GRIF" is approximately 39 years of age.

on 8/7/64 at Dallas, Texas File # DL 44-1639

by Special Agent JOHN J. O'DONNELL:vm Date dictated 8/7/64

COMMISSION EXHIBIT No. 2297—Continued

FD-302 (Rev. 3-3-59)

FEDERAL BUREAU OF INVESTIGATION

Date August 21, 1964

1

KENNETH E. GRIFFITH, Apartment 1, 3817 Hawthorne, Dallas, Texas, advised that he is employed in the Composing Room at "The Dallas Times Herald" newspaper in Dallas, Texas, and was so employed during the early morning of November 23, 1963.

Mr. GRIFFITH stated that he knows of no employee at the newspaper with the surname of "GRIFFIN", whether it be in the Composing Room or any other department of this newspaper.

Mr. GRIFFITH stated that around 3:00 a.m. on Saturday, November 23, 1963, as he was just getting off work, a person previously unknown to him and whom he thought was another newspaper employee came into the Composing Room with an advertising insert in his hand.

GRIFFITH did not know the name of this man, but heard someone (identity not now recalled) refer to this individual as "JACK".

GRIFFITH stated he was in "JACK's" presence about five or six minutes as he, GRIFFITH, was trying to get out of the building and go home as it had been a hectic night with many of the advertising merchants changing their regular advertisements to ones expressing condolences over the tragic death of President KENNEDY in Dallas on the previous day.

While in "JACK's" presence these few minutes, he recalls that "JACK" appeared to be in a very jovial mood and not at all remorseful, and laughingly had mentioned that he had been hanging around the Dallas City Hall that night although he was not supposed to be there. "JACK" said he

on 8/20/64 at Dallas, Texas File # DL 44-1639

by Special Agent RICHARD J. BURNETT /jtf Date dictated 8/21/64

3

DL 44-1639
2

had done favors in the past for unnamed individuals and had been allowed to enter City Hall that night.

"JACK" also mentioned that "we" (not further identified) are trying to find out who the man really is that placed the ad in "The Dallas Morning News" on November 22, 1963, prior to the President's death making strong accusations against the President . "JACK" by all outward indications acted as if he did not know who this advertiser was (BERNARD WEISSMAN). "JACK" said, "It is probably someone posing as a Jew".

GRIFFITH stated he then continued on his way and never thought anything more of "JACK" or his comments.

GRIFFITH stated that he was home on Sunday, November 24, 1963, watching television when the television showed JACK RUBY shooting OSWALD. Even at this time, GRIFFITH stated he had not connected RUBY with the "JACK" he had seen briefly early Saturday morning, November 23, 1963, in the newspaper building.

GRIFFITH stated that it was not until Thanksgiving morning, November 28, 1963, when someone unrecalled, a fellow newspaper employee, mentioned to him that RUBY was the same "JACK" that he, GRIFFITH, had met in "The Dallas Times Herald" Composing Room early Saturday morning, November 23, 1963, that he, GRIFFITH, realized that "JACK" was the same person who shot OSWALD. Up to this time GRIFFITH had not made the connection of "JACK" being the same person as JACK RUBY.

GRIFFITH added that he had never known RUBY previously and did not recall ever having seen RUBY in person prior to or after November 23, 1963.

4

FD-302 (Rev. 3-3-59) FEDERAL BUREAU

1

Date December 12, 1963

Records of Southwestern Bell Telephone Company show that at 10:19 A.M., November 24, 1963, an individual at Fort Worth, telephone number JEfferson 4-8525, called JACK RUBY at Dallas telephone number WHitehall 1-5601 and this call lasted two minutes and twenty seconds.

Records of the Telephone Company reflect JE 4-8525 is an unlisted number to BRUCE RAY CARLIN, 3809 Meadowbrook Drive. (Investigation has established this is the residence of KAREN BENNETT, also known as KAREN BENNETT KARLIN, "LITTLE LYNN", an entertainer.)

This information is obtainable only through issuance of a subpoena duces tecum to RONALD G. MAPLES, Exchange Supervisor, Southwestern Bell Telephone Company, Fort Worth, Texas.

on 12/10/63 at Fort Worth, Texas File # DL 44-1639

by Special Agent JOSEPH L. SCHOTT/ln Date dictated 12/10/63

509

This document contains neither recommendations nor conclusions of the FBI. It is the property of the FBI and is loaned to your agency; it and its contents are not to be distributed outside your agency.

COMMISSION EXHIBIT No. 2298

FD-302 (Rev. 1-25-60) FEDERAL BUREAU OF

Date 3/13/64

1

The records of the Illinois Bell Telephone Company Chicago, Illinois, reflect that HAROLD KAMINSKY, 6724 North Talman, Chicago, Illinois, is assigned telephone number HO 5-3280. This phone was established prior to August 16, 1957, and has been continuously assigned to this party since that date. No other telephone number at 6724 North Talman is assigned to HAROLD or EILEEN KAMINSKY.

The records of the Illinois Bell Telephone Company reflect the following information concerning toll call charges to number HO 5-3280 during the period September 26, 1963, through November 22, 1963:

72

On 3/12/64 at Chicago, Illinois File # CG 44-645

by SA CHARLES L. BROWN, JR./vmm/phk Date dictated 3/12/64

This document contains neither recommendations nor conclusions of the FBI. It is the property of the FBI and is loaned to your agency; it and its contents are not to be distributed outside your agency.

COMMISSION EXHIBIT No. 2299

2

CG 44-645

Date	Place Called	Number	Charges	Time	Type of Call
9/25/63	Los Angeles, California	WE 6-2287	$ .90	3 minutes	Station 9:03 p.m.
9/28/63	Detroit, Michigan	BR 3-3000	$1.30	3 minutes	Person-to-person - call to EARL RUBY from sister 12:14 p.m.
9/28/63	Los Angeles, California	WE 9-9901	$3.15	12 minutes	Station 9:37 p.m.
10/14/63	Los Angeles, California	AN 9-3438	$5.65	22 minutes	Station 9:13 p.m.
10/16/63	Los Angeles, California	WE 6-2287	$3.15	12 minutes	Station 9:51 p.m.
11/12/63	Dallas, Texas	TA 3-8101	$ .70	1 minute	Station 9:0[illegible] p.m.
11/13/63	Dallas, Texas	LA 6-6258	$5.10	25 minutes	Station 9:48 p.m.
11/22/63	Dallas, Texas	LA 6-6258	$4.10	------------	Station 9:20 p.m.

The above information should not be made public without the issuance of a subpoena duces tecum to an appropriate official of the Illinois Bell Telephone Company.

Date 6/12/64

1

Records of Southwestern Bell Telephone Company, Dallas, disclose no toll charges were incurred to telephone WH 1-5601, unpublished number of JACK RUBY, Apartment 207, 223 South Ewing Street, Dallas, subsequent to November 22, 1963.

Records disclose the following as to toll charges to LA 6-6258, unpublished number in the name of JACK RUBY at 3929 Rawlins, Apartment 1, Dallas, on dates indicated:

DATE	TIME CALL PLACED	DURATION OF CALL	PERSON PLACING CALL	PERSON CALLED	NUMBER & CITY CALLED
11/23/63	10:44 PM	9 min.	Station to Station		CR 5-4891, Arlington, Texas
11/24/63	11:50 AM	1 "	" " "		SH 3-0984, Chicago, Illinois
"	12:07 PM	1 "	" " "		CR 5-4891, Arlington, Texas
"	12:29 PM	1 min. 37 sec.	" " "		SH 3-0984 Chicago, Illinois
"	1:12 PM	4 min.		EARL RUBY	353-2730, Southfield, Michigan
"	3:38 PM	39 sec.	Station to Station		CR 5-4891, Arlington, Texas
"	4:40 PM	13 min.	" " "		CR 5-8113, Arlington, Texas

on 6/8-10/64 at Dallas, Texas File # DL 44-1639

by Special Agent MANNING C. CLEMENTS/eah Date dictated 6/11/64

COMMISSION EXHIBIT No. 2300

2
DL 44-1639

The following toll charge was charged to LA 8-4775, listed to Vegas Club, Dallas, Texas:

DATE	TIME CALL PLACED	DURATION OF CALL	PERSON PLACING CALL	PERSON CALLED	NUMBER & CITY CALLED
11/23/63	12:49 AM	47 min.	EVA GRANT	Station call	765-7625, No. Hollywood, Cal.

Longhand notations among records of the telephone company disclose that on November 29, 1963, information was furnished to a Special Agent of the Federal Bureau of Investigation that a toll charge was made based on a call, to WH 1-5601 at 11:50 AM, November 22, 1963, to SH 3-0984, Chicago, Illinois. Official records disclose no call at 11:50 AM, November 22, 1963, as indicated in the longhand notes, but that a call was made as follows:

DATE	TIME CALL PLACED	DURATION OF CALL	PERSON PLACING CALL	PERSON CALLED	NUMBER & CITY CALLED
11/22/63	9:02 PM	7 min.	Station to Station		SH 3-0984, Chicago, Illinois

Longhand notations among telephone company records show that on November 29, 1963, information was furnished to a Special Agent of the Federal Bureau of Investigation that telephone toll charges were incurred to LA 6-6258 as follows:

11/24/63 Chicago, Illinois, SH 3-0984, 11:50 AM

" Chicago, Illinois, SH 3-0984, 12 noon

" Arlington, Texas, CR 5-4891, 2:30 PM

" Arlington, Texas, CR 5-8113, 4:00 PM

" Smithfield, Michigan, 353-2730 (EARL RUBY)

147

COMMISSION EXHIBIT No. 2300—Continued

3
DL 44-1639

Official records disclose correct information relative to toll charges to LA 6-6258, on November 24, 1963, were as shown previously above.

Subpoena duces tecum for production of the above-described records should be directed to R. A. BURROW, Chief Special Agent, Southwestern Bell Telephone Company.

COMMISSION EXHIBIT No. 2300—Continued

FD-302 (Rev. 1-25-60)

FEDERAL BUREAU

Commission Exhibit No. 2301

Date 6/15/64

The records of the Chesapeake and Potomac Telephone Company, 930 H Street, N.W., Washington, D.C., indicate that the following toll calls charged to Washington, D.C. telephone number DI 7-7750 were made from Dallas, Texas, on November 22, 1963. The above telephone number is listed to Scripps-Howard Newspaper Alliance, 1013 13th Street, N.W., Washington, D.C.

Call From	Call To	Amount	Type	Time	Length of Call
Dallas, Texas Kantor Telephone 743-9711	Washington D.C. DI 7-7750	$1.30	Station Collect	9:51 p.m.	1 minute
Dallas, Texas Kantor - Telephone 351-9072 (pay phone)	Washington DC 347-7750	$2.15	Station Collect	3:23 p.m.	3 minutes 20 seconds
Dallas, Texas Kantor - Telephone 748-9711	Washington DC 347-7750	$ .80	Station Collect	11:43 p.m.	2 minutes 14 seconds
Dallas, Texas Kantor - Telephone 631-5050	Washington DC 347-7750	$1.70	Station Collect	1:52 p.m.	1 minute 51 seconds
Dallas, Texas Kantor - Telephone 748-9711	Washington DC 347-7750	$3.95	Station Collect	5:43 p.m.	8 minutes 7 seconds
Dallas, Texas Kantor Telephone 748-9711	Washington DC 347-7750	$1.30	Station Collect	8:50 p.m.	2 minutes 38 seconds

On 6/15/64 at Washington, D.C. File # WFO 44-520

by SA WILLIAM D. CAMPBELL 220 RWK:kmn Date dictated 6/15/64

COMMISSION EXHIBIT No. 2301

WFO 44-520

Dallas, Texas Cantor - Telephone 748-9711	Washington DC 347-7750	$ .80	Station Collect	11:46 p.m.	26 seconds
Dallas, Texas Cantor - Telephone 631-5050, extension 430	Washington DC 347-7750	$12.05	Station Collect	1:02 p.m.	25 minutes 40 seconds

The above information is confidential and is not to be made public except upon the issuance of a subpoena duces tecum issued to Mr. C. D. SCHULTZ, Manager, Chesapeake and Potomac Telephone Company, 725 13th Street, N.W., Washington, D.C.

221

COMMISSION EXHIBIT No. 2301—Continued

FD-302 (Rev. 1-25-60)

(1)

FEDERAL BUREAU OF INVEST Commission Exhibit No. 2302

Date 3/17/64

1

Records of the Southwestern Bell Telephone Company, 301 South Akard, disclosed that telephone service for Jack Ruby, 223 South Ewing, Apartment 207, Dallas 3, Texas, was established on November 27, 1962, under non-published number WHitehall 1-5601. Pursuant to an order received from Mrs. EVA GRANT, this phone service was disconnected effective December 9, 1963.

The records reveal that during the period September 26, 1963, through November 22, 1963, the following toll charges were made against this number:

WHitehall 1-5601

DATE	TIME CALL PLACED	DURATION OF CALL	PERSON PLACING CALL	PERSON CALLED	NUMBER & CITY CALLED
9/26/63	11:46 AM	2 mins.	Station to Station		CR 5-4891 Arlington, Texas
9/27/63	10:21 PM	15 mins.	" " "		SH 3-0984 Chicago, Illinois
9/27/63	5:57 PM	4 mins.	" " "		CR 5-5352 Arlington, Texas
10/1/63	7:01 PM	3 mins.	Jack Ruby	Adams	ED 5-1266 Ft. Worth, Texas
10/1/63	6:46 PM	2 mins.	Station to Station		TE 4-0847 Ft. Worth, Texas
10/1/63	6:41 PM	3 mins.	" " "		CR 5-5352 Arlington, Texas

9

On 3/12/64 at DALLAS, TEXAS File # DL 44-1639

by SA RAYMOND C. ECKENRODE/les Date dictated 3/14/64

COMMISSION EXHIBIT No. 2302

DL 44-1639
2

DATE	TIME CALL PLACED	DURATION OF CALL	PERSON PLACING CALL	PERSON CALLED	NUMBER & CITY CALLED
10/1/63	6:04 PM	1 min.	Station to	Station	CR 5-4891 Arlington, Texas
10/12/63	6:42 PM	8 min.	" "	"	CR 5-5352 Arlington, Texas
10/13/63	1:30 PM	16 min.	" "	"	CR 5-4891 Arlington, Texas
10/18/63	12:33 PM	11 min.	unknown	Wayne Keller	CE 1-7766 St. Louis, Missouri
10/19/63	7:39 PM	3 min.	Station to	Station	PE 7-5553 Ft. Worth, Texas
10/19/63	3:53 AM	32 mins.	" "	"	OL 2-3849 Beverly Hills, California
10/19/63	12:09 PM	2 mins.	" "	"	PE 7-5553 Ft. Worth, Texas
10/19/63	12:42 PM	7 mins.	Ruby	Mike Raiff	CE 14552 St. Louis, Mo.
10/20/63	1:15 PM	7 mins.	Station to	Station	PE 7-5553 Ft. Worth, Texas
10/20/63	1:05 PM	3 mins.	Unknown	Walker	PE 7-5553 Ft. Worth, Texas

COMMISSION EXHIBIT No. 2302—Continued

DL 44-1639
3

DATE	TIME CALL PLACED	DURATION OF CALL	PERSON PLACING CALL	PERSON CALLED	NUMBER & CITY CALLED
10/21/63	7:46 PM	10 mins.	Station to	Station	CR 5-4891 Arlington, Texas
10/21/63	7:57 PM	3 mins.	" "	"	PE 7-5553 Ft. Worth, Texas
10/25/63	10:09 AM	18 mins.	Ruby	Mike Shore	956-2687 New York, New York
10/27/63	1:23 PM	- -----	Station to	Station	CR 5-4891 Arlington, Texas
10/29/63	10:06 AM	10 mins.	" "	"	"
10/29/63	2:55 AM	3 mins.	" "	"	JE 4-8525 Ft. Worth, Texas
10/30/63	6:24 PM	5 mins.		"	JE 4-8525 Ft. Worth, Texas
10/30/63	6:32 PM	3 mins.	" "	"	PE 2-1519 Ft. Worth, Texas
10/30/63	8:44 AM	15 mins.	" "	"	CR 5-5352 Arlington, Texas
10/30/63	8:34 AM	5 mins.	Jack Ruby	A. L. Davis	PE 8-6469 Ft. Worth, Texas

COMMISSION EXHIBIT No. 2302—Continued

DL 44-1639
4

DATE	TIME CALL PLACED	DURATION OF CALL	PERSON PLACING CALL	PERSON CALLED	NUMBER & CITY CALLED
10/31/63	9:45 AM	12 mins.	Station to Station		CR 5-4891 Arlington, Texas
11/1/63	9:13 AM	6 mins.	" "	"	CR 5-5352 Arlington, Texas
11/2/63	6:42 PM	27 mins.	" "	"	"
11/3/63	3:40 PM	12 mins.	" "	"	CR 5-4891 Arlington, Texas
11/5/63	9:12 AM	3 mins.	" "	"	ED 5-1266 Ft. Worth, Texas
11/5/63	8:58 AM	10 mins.	" "	"	HA 7-3172 Chicago, Illinois
11/9/63	10:50 AM	13 mins.	" "	"	CR 5-4891 Arlington, Texas
11/9/63	1[illegible]:36 AM	2 mins.	" "	"	CR 5-4891 Arlington, Texas
11/11/63	7:03 PM	4 mins.	" "	"	CR 5-5352 Arlington, Texas
11/11/63	9:04 PM	1 min.	" "	"	AT 2-7128 San Francisco, California

12

COMMISSION EXHIBIT No. 2302—Continued

DL 44-1639
5

DATE	TIME CALL PLACED	DURATION OF CALL	PERSON PLACING CALL	PERSON CALLED	NUMBER & CITY CALLED
11/12/63	5:32 PM	3 mins.	Unknown	Herman Flowers	WE 7-3837 Waxahachie, Texas
11/13/63	11:18 AM (3)	4 mins.	Station to Station		CR 5-4891 Arlington, Texas
11/13/63	10:20 AM (2)	5 mins.	" "	"	"
11/13/63	9:25 AM (1)	-----	" "	"	"
11/13/63	11:55 AM (4)	18 mins.	Jack Ruby	Bobby Faye (AGVA)	TN 7-5600 New York, New York
11/14/63	10:48 AM	6 mins.	Station to Station		CR 5-4891 Arlington, Texas
11/15/63	10:07 AM	10 mins.	" "	"	"
11/15/63	12:53 PM	8 mins.	" "	"	"
11/16/63	8:18 PM	10 mins. (5)	Unknown	Miss Smokey Turner	FE 5-3366 Minneapolis, Minn.
11/16/63	11:41 AM	9 mins. (2)	Station to Station		CR 5-4891 Arlington, Texas
11/17/63	6:17 PM	9 mins.	" "	"	"
11/18/63	8:12 PM	5 mins.	" "	"	"
11/19/63	10:37 AM	7 mins.	" "	"	"

13

COMMISSION EXHIBIT No. 2302—Continued

DL 44-1639
6

DATE	TIME CALL PLACED	DURATION OF CALL	PERSON PLACING CALL	PERSON CALLED	NUMBER & CITY CALLED
11/20/63	10:56 AM	8 mins.	Station to	Station	CE 6-5561 Chicago, Illinois
11/20/63	9:32 PM	6 mins.	"	" "	CR 5-4891 Arlington, Texas
11/21/63	6:40 PM	3 mins.	"	" "	CR 5-4891 Arlington, Texas
11/22/63	9:02 PM	7 mins.	"	" "	SH 3-0984 Chicago, Illinois
11/22/63	8:48 PM	3 mins.	"	" "	CR 5-4891 Arlington, Texas

The above information obtained from the records of the Southwestern Bell Telephone Company, Dallas, Texas, is not to be made public except in a usual proceeding following issuance of proper subpoena duces tecum.

Subpoena for these records should be directed to Manager, Southwestern Bell Telephone Company, 301 South Akard Street, Dallas, Texas.

DL 44-1639
RCE:1
1

It has been established through investigation that the following were the subscribers to the indicated telephone numbers as of the dates long distance calls were placed from Dallas Telephone No. WHitehall 1-5601 listed to JACK RUBY, 223 South Ewing, Apartment 207, Dallas, Texas.

CR 5-4891	Bull Pen Drive-In Restaurant, 1936 East Abrams, Arlington, Texas, operated by RALPH PAUL.
SH 3-0984	Hyman Rubinstein, Chicago, Illinois, brother of JACK L. RUBY.
CR 5-5352	Ralph Paul, Copeland Road, Arlington, Texas
ED 5-1266	Plastelite Engineering Company, P. O. Box 412, Fort Worth, Texas
TE 4-0847	Della Jones, 1217 Clarence, Fort Worth, Texas
CE 1-7766	Wayne Keller, Theatrical Agency, 818 Olive Street, St. Louis, Missouri
PE 7-5553	Richard D. Walker, Attorney at Law, 1917-C Hervie Street, Fort Worth, Texas
OL 2-3849	Herbert Eden, 928 Clarke Street, Beverly Hills, California
CE 1-4552	Mike Riaff, Theatrical Bureau, 818 Olive Street, St. Louis, Missouri
956-2687	Curtis Publishing Company, 666 Fifth Avenue, New York, New York
JE 4-8525	Bruce Carlin, 3809 Meadowbrook, Fort Worth, Texas, husband of Karen Bennett Carlin, also known as Little Lynn.

DL 44-1639
RCE:les
2

PE 2-1519	Delbert R. McClinton, 4024 Fairfax, Fort Worth, Texas
PE 8-6469	A. L. DAVIS, 6304 Halifax Road, Fort Worth, Texas
HA 7-3172	Mar-Din Company, 404 South Wells, Chicago, Illinois, Henry Kenter, President-Treasurer
AT 2-7128	Frank Goldstein, 1022 Guerrero, San Francisco, California

It is noted in the investigation conducted previously, it was found that this was in fact a misdirected call intended for a party of similar name, FRANK GOLDSTEIN, 640 Teresita Boulevard, San Francisco, California, Telephone JU 7-7674.

WE 7-3837	Herman Flowers, Jr., 118 Aiken, Waxahachie, Texas
TN 7-5600	American Guild of Variety Artists, 551 Fifth Avenue, New York, New York.
FE 5-3366	Gay 90's Bar and Restaurant, 408 Hennepin, Minneapolis, Minnesota
CE 6-5561	American Guild of Variety Artists, 162 North State Street, Chicago, Illinois.

16

COMMISSION EXHIBIT No. 2302—Continued

FD-302 (Rev. 3-3-59)

FEDERAL BUREAU OF [redacted]

Commission Exhibit No. 2303

Date 3/17/64

1

Records of Southwestern Bell Telephone Company, Dallas, Texas, reflect telephone number RIverside 7-2362, listed to Carousel Club, 1312½ Commerce Street, Dallas, was connected November 10, 1959. Records disclose the following telephone toll charges to this number from September 26, 1963, to November 22, 1963, inclusive:

Date 1963	Time Call Placed	Duration of Call	Person Placing Call	Person Called	Number and City Called
9/27	4:36 p.m.	3 min.	Station to Station		ED 5-1266 Ft. Worth, Texas
10/3	11:53 p.m.	1 min.	" "	"	CR 5-4891 Arlington, Texas
10/3	11:03 p.m.	13 min.	" "	"	ME 1-3753 Shreveport, Louisiana
10/7	10:54 p.m.	4 min.	" "	"	265-7630, Montgomery, Alabama
10/8	12:04 a.m.	6 min.	" "	"	CR 5-4891 Arlington, Texas
10/13	11:00 p.m.	1 min.	" "	"	"
10/15	9:06 p.m.	1 min.	" "	"	CR 5-5352 Arlington, Texas
10/16	11:25 p.m.	13 min.	" "	"	JE 8-4082 Miami, Florida
10/16	1:26 a.m.	3 min.	Unknown	Carme or Paul	CA 2-1900 Houston, Texas
10/17	9:07 p.m.	7 min.	RUBY	Body, c/o San Souci Club	"

19

on 3/12/64 at Dallas, Texas File # DL 44-1639

by Special Agent RA' 'OND C. ECKENRODE:vm Date dictated 3/16/64

COMMISSION EXHIBIT No. 2303

2
DL 44-1639

Date 1963	Time Call Placed	Duration of Call	Person Placing Call	Person Called	Number and City Called
10/17	11:34 p.m.	1 min.	Station to Station		CR 5-4891 Arlington, Texas
10/18	11:58 p.m.	3 min.	Unknown	Marino, c/o Domino Club	JA 4-1069 Atlanta, Georgia
10/18	2:10 a.m.	4 min.	"	Dick Asher, c/o Merry-Go-Round	367-6300 Louisville, Ky.
10/18	7:12 p.m.	6 min.	JACK RUBY	BILL FRAYS (phonetic)	WO 1-8310 Detroit, Michigan
10/19	11:10 p.m.	9 min.	Unknown	SAL VINCENT	CA 5-1781 Houston, Texas
10/19	11:58 p.m.	1 min.	Station to Station		PE 7-5553 Ft. Worth, Texas
10/19	12:10 a.m.	3 min.	Unknown	Showman, Rainbow Room	AL 6-0981 Nashville, Tenn.
10/21	12:33 a.m.	12 min.	HAROLD TANNENBAUM	Collect call from New Orleans, La.	RI 7-2362, Dallas
10/23	11:10 a.m.	3 min.	RUBY	JACK PAGAN	TU 4-4061, Corpus Christi, Texas
10/26	10:17 p.m.	3 min.	Unknown	MIKE SHORE	BR 2-9836, Los Angeles, Calif.
10/26	12:07 p.m.	12 min.	Unknown	WEINER	SH 3-6865 Chicago, Ill.

3
DL 44-1639

Date 1963	Time Call Placed	Duration of Call	Person Placing Call	Person Called	Number and City Called
10/26	10:02 p.m.	2 min.	Station to Station		CR 5-4891 Arlington, Texas
10/27	4:57 p.m.	1 min.	Station to Station		"
10/28	6:36 p.m.	12 min.	" "	"	"
10/29	12:09 p.m.	11 min.	JACK RUBY	MIKE RIAFF	CE 1-4552 St. Louis, Mo.
10/30	9:30 p.m.	4 min.	Station to Station		CR 5-5352, Arlington, Texas
10/30	3:53 p.m.	18 min.	" "	"	JE 4-8525 Ft. Worth, Texas
10/30	9:29 p.m.	1 min.	" "	"	CR 5-4891 Arlington, Texas
10/30	3:12 p.m.	1 min.	" "	"	CR 5-5352 Arlington, Texas
10/30	9:13 p.m.	1 min.	" "	"	CH 2-5431, New Orleans, La.
10/30	10:14 p.m.	21 min.	HAROLD TANNENBAUM	Collect Call – from New Orleans, La.	RI 7-2362, Dallas, Tex.
10/31	9:38 p.m.	4 min.	Station to Station		CR 4-0043, Beverly Hills, Calif.
10/31	9:44 p.m.	2 min.	" "	"	CR 5-5352 Arlington, Texas

4
DL 44-1639

Date 1963	Time Call Placed	Duration of Call	Person Placing Call	Person Called	Number and City Called
10/31	9:43 p.m.	1 min.	Station to Station		CR 5-4891 Arlington, Texas
10/31	4:23 p.m.	19 min.	"	"	UN 3-0400 Detroit, Mich.
10/31	4:57 p.m.	14 min.	Unknown	BUDDY	ED 5-1266 Ft. Worth, Texas
11/1	1:00 p.m.	6 min.	Station to Station		HA 7-3172 Chicago, Ill.
11/1	11:52 a.m.	3 min.	"	"	UN 3-0400 Detroit, Mich.
11/1	4:43 p.m.	1 min.	Station to Station		UN 3-5590 Detroit, Mich.
11/1	1[illegible]:16 p.m.	15 min.	"	"	"
11/1	3:57 p.m.	1 min.	"	"	TE 4-0847 Ft. Worth, Texas
11/1	11:43 p.m.	3 min.	"	"	CR 5-4891 Arlington, Texas
11/1	3:14 p.m.	5 min.	"	"	TE 4-0847 Ft. Worth, Texas
11/3	12:38 a.m.	3 min.	Unknown	JACK PAKIS Southern Club	NA 3-8295, Hot Springs, Arkansas
11/3	7:42 p.m.	20 min.	Station to Station		SH 3-0984 Chicago, Ill.

22

COMMISSION EXHIBIT No. 2303—Continued

5
DL 44-1639

Date 1963	Time Call Placed	Duration of Call	Person Placing Call	Person Called	Number and City Called
11/3	1:08 a.m.	1 min.	Station to Station		CR 5-4891 Arlington, Texas
11/3	1:09 a.m.	3 min.	"	"	CR 5-5352 Arlington, Texas
11/3	10:29 a.m.	7 min.	"	"	CR 5-4891 Arlington, Texas
11/4	10:13 p.m.	9 min.	HAROLD TANNEBAUM, New Orleans, La.	Collect call to RI 7-2362	
11/5	1:13 p.m.	7 min.	Unknown	"Mike Riass"	CE 1-4552 St. Louis, Mo.
11/5	3:47 p.m.	13 min.	"	BILL DeMAR	JA 4-4241 Jackson, Kansas
11/5	3:01 p.m.	5 min.	Station to Station		CR 5-5352 Arlington, Texas
11/5	(?)	6 min.	"	"	JA 4-1069 Atlanta, Ga.
11/5	1:08 a.m.	1 min.	"	"	FA 3-6269 Houston, Texas
11/5	12:06 a.m.	8 min.	"	"	CR 5-4891 Arlington, Texas
11/5	2:16 a.m.	5 min.	TAG POWELL Atlanta, Georgia	Collect Call to RI 7-2362	

23

COMMISSION EXHIBIT No. 2303—Continued

6
DL 44-1639

Date 1963	Time Call Placed	Duration of Call	Person Placing Call	Person Called	Number and City Called
11/6	2:02 a.m.	8 min.	Unknown	DeMAR	JA 4-9269 Jackson, Kansas
11/6	5:01 p.m.	10 min.	"	BUDDY HEARD	KE 3-6827 El Paso, Texas
11/6	10:04 p.m.	9 min.	Station to Station		HO 5-3280 Chicago, Ill.
11/6	10:14 p.m.	18 min.	" " "		SH 3-0984 Chicago, Ill.
11/6	5:18 p.m.	16 min.	" " "		UN 3-5590 Detroit, Mich.
11/6	10:33 p.m.	6 min.	" " "		CR 5-4891 Arlington, Texas
11/6	3:58 p.m.	1 min.	" " "		CR 5-5352 Arlington, Texas
11/7	2:12 p.m.	7 min.	BARNEY BAKER, Chicago, Ill.	Collect Call to RI 7-2362	
11/8	4:47 p.m.	4"	Unknown	Dusty Miller, Eden Rock Hotel	JE 2-2561 Miami, Fla.
11/8	12:02 a.m.	1 min.	Station to Station		CR 5-4891 Arlington, Texas
11/8	6:01 p.m.	5 min.	" " "		"

24

7
DL 44-1639

Date 1963	Time Call Placed	Duration of Call	Person Placing Call	Person Called	Number and City Called
11/8	1:12 p.m.	2 min.	Station to Station		JE 4-8525 Ft. Worth, Texas
11/8	5:22 p.m.	14 min.	" " "		RA 8-4031 Chicago, Ill.
11/9	4:30 p.m.	1 min.	" " "		CR 5-4891 Arlington, Texas
11/9	10:13 p.m.	5 min.	" " "		"
11/9	12:38 a.m.	7 min.	Station to Station		CR 5-5352 Arlington, Texas
11/9	9:56 p.m.	1 min.	" " "		340-0980 Canoga Park, Calif.
11/9	10:04 p.m.	9 min.	" " "		766-1193, North Hollywood, Calif.
11/10	1:30 a.m.	7 min.	Unknown	DEMAR	JA 4-9167 Jackson, Kansas
11/10	5:32 p.m.	6 min.	Station to Station		TE 4-0847 Ft. Worth, Texas
11/10	10:48 p.m.	4 min.	" " "		CR 5-4891 Arlington, Texas
11/11	3:10 p.m.	8 min.	" " "		"
11/11	7:30 p.m.	1 min.	" " "		767-7905 Wichita Falls, Tex.

25

8
DL 44-1639

Date 1963	Time Call Placed	Duration of Call	Person Placing Call	Person Called	Number and City Called
11/12	12:43 p.m.	14 min.	JACK RUBY	JUANITA BLUSHER	OL 7-5257 Edna, Texas
11/12	10:15 p.m.	10 min.	Unknown	FRANKIE GOLDSTEIN	JU 7-7674 San Francisco, Calif.
11/12	9:56 p.m.	9 min.	Station to Station		CR 5-5352 Arlington, Texas
11/13	4:57 p.m.	---	" " "		CR 5-4891 Arlington, Texas
11/13	4:35 p.m.	8 min.	JACK RUBY	BOB FAY (AGVA)	TN 7-5600 New York, N.Y.
11/13	5:09 p.m.	3 min.	JACK RUBY	BOBBY FAY American Guild	"
11/14	1:13 p.m.	1 min.	Station to Station		CR 5-4891 Arlington, Texas
11/15	10:06 p.m.	3 min.	" " "		CR 5-5352 Arlington, Texas
11/15	10:05 p.m.	1 min.	" " "		CR 5-4891 Arlington, Texas
11/15	2:28 p.m.	2 min.	" " "		ED 6-2823 Ft. Worth, Texas
11/16	12:22 a.m.	2 min.	" " "		CR 5-4891 Arlington, Texas

26

COMMISSION EXHIBIT No. 2303—Continued

9
DL 44-1639

Date 1963	Time Call Placed	Duration of Call	Person Placing Call	Person Called	Number and City Called
11/16	11:51 p.m.	3 min.	Station to Station		CR 5-4891 Arlington, Texas
11/16	2:37 p.m.	4 min.	" " "		CR 5-5352 Arlington, Texas
11/16	2:07 p.m.	1 min.	" " "		CR 5-4891 Arlington, Texas
11/19	9:41 p.m.	17 min.	" " "		PA 9-0891 Houston, Texas
11/22	2:37 p.m.	3 min.	" " "		WE 5-1082, Los Angeles, Calif.
11/22	2:05 p.m.	8 min.	" " "		HO 5-3280 Chicago, Ill.
11/22	1:45 p.m.	1 min.	" " "		JE 4-8525 Ft. Worth, Texas
11/22	2:42 p.m.	--	" " "		CR 5-4891 Arlington, Texas
11/22	2:43 p.m.	2 min.	" " "		CR 5-5352 Arlington, Texas
11/22	1:51 p.m.	3 min.	" " "		CR 5-4891 Arlington, Texas

A subpoena duces tecum should be directed to Mr. R. A. BURROW, Chief Special Agent, Southwestern Bell Telephone Company, Dallas, Texas, for production of the above records.

27

COMMISSION EXHIBIT No. 2303—Continued

1
MCC:vm
DL 44-1639

Investigation has established that the persons or entities listed below were subscribers to the telephone numbers indicated as of the dates of telephone calls to such numbers from Riverside 7-2362, Carousel Club, 1312½ Commerce Street, Dallas, Texas:

ED 5-1266, Fort Worth, Texas - Plastelite Engineering Company, Post Office Box 412, Fort Worth, Texas

CR 5-4891, Arlington, Texas - Bullpen Drive-In, 1936 E. Abrams, Arlington, Texas (RALPH PAUL)

ME 1-3753, Shreveport, Louisiana - ELIZABETH ANN MATTHEWS, 7204 S. Lakeshore, Shreveport, Louisiana

265-7630, Montgomery, Alabama - BONNIE KELLOUGH, 39 N. Capitol Parkway, Montgomery, Alabama

CR 5-5352, Arlington, Texas - RALPH PAUL, Copeland Road, Arlington, Texas

JE 8-4082, Miami, Florida - SAMUEL TANNENBAUM, 911 Meridian Avenue, Miami Beach, Florida

CA 2-1900, Houston, Texas - Sans Souci Club, Houston, Texas

JA 4-1069, Atlanta, Georgia - Domino Lounge, 350 Peachtree, Atlanta, Georgia

367-6300, Louisville, Kentucky - Merry-Go-Round Nightclub, Louisville, Kentucky

WO 1-8310, Detroit, Michigan - Royal Palm Hotel, 2305 Park Avenue, Detroit, Michigan

CA 5-1781, Houston, Texas - Continental Houston Hotel, Houston, Texas

PE 7-5553, Fort Worth, Texas - RICHARD D. WALKER, Attorney, 1917-C Hervie Street, Fort Worth, Texas

COMMISSION EXHIBIT No. 2303—Continued

2
DL 44-1639

AL 6-0981, Nashville, Tennessee - Rainbow Club, 4th Avenue, North, Nashville, Tennessee

TU 4-4061, Corpus Christi, Texas - Pagan-Lewis Motors, Inc., 924 N. Water Street, Corpus Christi, Texas

BR 2-9836, Los Angeles, California - MICHAEL SHORE, 109 N. Almont, Los Angeles, California (employed by Reprise Records)

SH 3-6865, Chicago, Illinois - IRWIN S. WEINER, 7345 N. Damen, Chicago, Illinois

CE 1-4552, St. Louis, Missouri - MIKE RIAFF, Theatrical Bureau, 818 Olive Street, St. Louis, Missouri

JE 4-8525, Fort Worth, Texas - BRUCE RAY CARLIN, 3809 Meadowbrook, Fort Worth, Texas

CH 2-5431, New Orleans, Louisiana - Tropical Court, 6027 Chef Menteur Highway, New Orleans, Louisiana (N. J. PECORA)

CR 4-0043, Beverly Hills, California - MICHAEL SHORE, 109 N. Almont, Beverly Hills, California

UN 3-0400, Detroit, Michigan - Cobo Cleaners, 18135 Livernois, Detroit, Michigan (EARL R. RUBY)

HA 7-3172, Chicago, Illinois - Mar-Din Company, 404 S. Wells, Chicago, Illinois (HENRY KENTER, Pres.-Treas.)

UN 3-5590, Detroit, Michigan - Cobo Cleaners, 18135 Livernois, Detroit, Michigan (EARL R. RUBY)

TE 4-0847, Fort Worth, Texas - Mrs. DELLA JONES, 1217 Clarence Street, Fort Worth, Texas (Tami ?)

COMMISSION EXHIBIT No. 2303—Continued

NA 3-8295, Hot Springs, Arkansas - JACK PAKIS, Hot Springs, Arkansas (Southern Club)

SH 3-0984, Chicago, Illinois - NATHAN CARROLL, 1044 W. Loyola Street, Chicago, Illinois (husband of sister of RUBY, MARIAN)

JA 4-4241, Jackson, Kansas - Casa Siesta Motel, 4449 S. Broadway, Wichita, Kansas

FA 3-6269, Houston, Texas - Gaiety Club, 1212 Texas Avenue, Houston, Texas

JA 4-9269, Jackson, Kansas - T-Bone Club, Jackson, Kansas

KE 3-6827, El Paso, Texas - BUDDY HEARD, 100 N. Florence, El Paso, Texas

HO 5-3280, Chicago, Illinois - HAROLD KAMINSKY, 6725 Talman, Chicago, Illinois (husband of RUBY's sister, EILEEN)

JE 2-2561, Miami, Florida - Eden Roc Hotel, Miami, Florida

RA 8-4031, Chicago, Illinois - ROBERT B. BAKER, 5900 Sheridan Road, Chicago, Illinois

340-0980, Canoga Park, California - IRVIN MAZZEI, 22915 Burton, Canoga Park, California

766-1193, North Hollywood, California - IRVIN MAZZEI, 12231 Hesby Street, North Hollywood, California

JA 4-9167, Jackson, Kansas - Pay phone, T-Bone Club, 220 E. 47th Street, South, Wichita, Kansas

767-7905, Wichita Falls, Texas - W. T. KNIGHT, 1800 McGregor, Wichita Falls, Texas

OL 7-5257, Edna, Texas - JUANITA SLUSHER, Edna, Texas (Candy Barr)

JU 7-7674, San Francisco, California - FRANK GOLDSTEIN, 640 Teresita, San Francisco, California

TN 7-5600, New York, New York - American Guild of Variety Artists, 551 5th Avenue, New York, New York

ED 6-2823, Fort Worth, Texas - Casa del Sol Club, Westchester House, 554 S. Summit, Fort Worth, Texas

PA 9-0891, Houston, Texas - BILLY CHESTER CARR, 6027 Ettrick, Houston, Texas

WE 5-1082, Los Angeles, California - ALEXANDER P. GRUBER, 5222 W. Olympic, Los Angeles, California.

FD-302 (Rev. 3-3-59) EDERAL BUREAU OF I— Commission Exhibit No. 2304

Date 3/16/64

1

Records of the Southwestern Bell Telephone Company, 301 South Akard, disclosed telephone service in the form of a non-published number LAkeside 6-6253, was installed in the name of JACK RUBY at 3921 Rawlins, Apartment 1, Dallas. This service was connected on March 15, 1956, and continues as an active number in the name of the indicated subscriber at the present time. It is noted whereas this service for billing purposes is listed in the na of JACK RUBY, it has been ascertained in prior investigation that the address 3929 Rawlins, Apartment 1, Dallas, Texas, is the residence of Mrs. EVA GRANT, sister of JACK L. RUBY.

Records of the telephone company disclosed during the period September 26, 1963, through November 22, 1963, the following long distance telephone calls were placed from this number:

LAkeside 6-6258

	TIME CALL PLACED	DURATION OF CALL	PERSON PLACING CALL	PERSON CALLED	NUMBER & CITY CALLED
10/6/63	4:35 PM	3 min.	Station to Station		CR 5-4891 Arlington, Texas
11/15/63	8:31 PM	5 min.	Station to Station		526-4356 Simi, California

The above information was obtained from the records of the Southwestern Bell Telephone Company, Dallas, Texas, and is not to be made public except in a usual proceeding following issuance of proper subpoena duces tecum.

Subpoena should be issued to Manager, Southwestern Bell Telephone Company, 301 S. Akard, Dallas, Texas.

on 3/11/64 at Dallas, Texas File # DL 44-1639

by Special Agent RAYMOND C. ECKENRODE/atd Date dictated 3/13/64

17

COMMISSION EXHIBIT No. 2304

RCE/atd

DL 44-1639

AT DALLAS, TEXAS

Investigation has determined the subscribers to the telephone numbers called from Dallas telephone number LAkeside 6-6253, listed to JACK RUBY, 3929 Rawlins, Apartment 1, were the following as of the dates such calls were made:

CR 5-4891, Arlington, Texas, is listed to the Bull Pen Drive-In Restaurant, 1936 East Abrams, Arlington, Texas, operated by RALPH PAUL.

526-4356 Simi, California, is listed to RONALD DENNIS MAGID, 1294 Agnew, Simi, California, son of Mrs. EVA GRANT.

18

COMMISSION EXHIBIT No. 2304—Continued

FD-302 (Rev. 3-3-59)

FEDERAL BUREAU OF Commission Exhibit No. 2305

Date 3/16/64

1

Records of the Southwestern Bell Telephone Company, 301 S. Akard, disclosed telephone number LAkeside 8-4775 was connected on March 15, 1956, at 3508 Oak Lawn, Dallas, with listing in the name of the Vegas Club, as well as JACK RUBY, Office. This is a published number and service continues in force at the present time.

Toll charges to the above number during the period September 26, 1963, through November 22, 1963, reflects the following long distance telephone calls were placed from this number during above period:

LAkeside 8-4775

DATE	TIME CALL PLACED	DURATION OF CALL	PERSON PLACING CALL	PERSON CALLED	NUMBER AND CITY CALLED
9/29/63	(toll ticket missing)		Station to Station (night)		Simi, California
10/12/63	6:28 PM	6 min.	Station to Station		526-4356 Simi, California
11/3/63	Unknown	26 min.	Station to Station		765-7625 N. Hollywood, California
11/22/63	Unknown	31 min.	Station to Station (late night)		SH 3-0984 Chicago, Illinois

The above information was obtained from the records of the Southwestern Bell Telephone Company, Dallas, Texas, and is not to be made public except in a usual proceeding following issuance of proper subpoena duces tecum.

Subpoena should be issued to Manager, Southwestern Bell Telephone Company, ,301 S. Akard, Dallas, Texas.

32

on 3/11/64 at Dallas, Texas File # DL 44-1639

by Special Agent RAYMOND C. ECKENRODE/atd Date dictated 3/13/64

COMMISSION EXHIBIT No. 2305

RCE/atd
1

DL 44-1639

The following have been identified as subscribers to telephone numbers as of the dates long distance telephone calls were placed from LAkeside 8-4775, listed to the Vegas Club and JACK RUBY, Office, 3508 Oak Lawn, Dallas, Texas:

526-4356, Simi, California, listed to RONALD DENNIS MAGID, 1294 Agnew, the son of Mrs. EVA GRANT.

765-7625, North Hollywood, California, is listed to CHARLES J. HIRSCH, 12200 Wixon, North Hollywood, California.

SH 3-0984, Chicago, Illinois, listed to HYMAN RUBINSTEIN, Chicago, Illinois.

33

COMMISSION EXHIBIT No. 2305—Continued

SOUTHWESTERN BELL TELEPHONE COMPANY

308 SOUTH AKARD STREET, DALLAS 2, TEXAS

AREA CODE 214

TELEPHONE RIVERSIDE 7-8311

ROY A. EURY
MANAGER

September 18, 1964

President's Commission on the
Assassination of President Kennedy
Mr. J. Lee Rankin, General Counsel
200 Maryland Avenue N.E.
Washington, D.C. 20002

Mr. Rankin:

This is in regard to your letter of August 25, 1964, requesting certain information on the account of Mrs. Eva Grant, LA6-6258.

Per my investigation, Mrs. Grant placed a call from her LA6-6258 number on November 23, 1963 to North Hollywood, California. This call was placed at 11:49 p.m. and lasted for 46 minutes and 30 seconds. Our records also indicate that Mrs. Grant requested the call to be third number billed to LA8-4775.

On November 24, 1963, two calls were placed to Chicago, Illinois to SH3-0984. This first call was placed at 11:50 a.m. and lasted for one minute. The second call was placed at 12:29 p.m. and lasted for one minute and 37 seconds. Our records show a call to Chicago, Illinois on November 22, 1963, but no other information could be obtained.

Sincerely,

Roy A. Eury

Manager, Unit III
Dallas, Texas

COMMISSION EXHIBIT No. 2306

1
MCC:vm
DL 44-1639

Previous investigation has established identities of subscribers to telephones called from WH 1-5601, LA 6-6258, and LA 8-4775, Dallas, during the period November 22-24, 1963, as follows:

CR 5-4891, Arlington, Texas - Bull Pen Drive In,
1936 E. Abrams, Arlington
(RALPH PAUL)

SH 3-0984, Chicago, Illinois - Nathan Norman Carroll,
1044 W. Loyola,
Chicago, Illinois

353-2730, Southfield, Michigan - Earl R. Ruby,
2995 Woodland Drive,
Southfield, Michigan

CR 5-8113, Arlington, Texas - John W. Jackson,
1602 Browning, Arlington
(Manager, Bull Pen Drive In)

765-7625, North Hollywood, California
Charles J. Hirsch,
12200 Wixon,
North Hollywood, California

749

COMMISSION EXHIBIT No. 2306—Continued

FD-302 (Rev. 3-3-59)

FEDERAL BUREAU OF IN[redacted] Commission Exhibit No. 2307

Date 4/23/64

1

Records of the Southwestern Bell Telephone Company, Dallas, Texas, reflect telephone RI 7-2362 was listed to Carousel Club, 1312½ Commerce Street, Dallas, Texas, during the period considered below. Records reflect the following toll charges to this telephone, which was available to JACK L. RUBY, his financial associate, RALPH PAUL, and possibly other persons during the period November 23 - December 1, 1963:

DATE 1963	TIME CALL PLACED	DURATION OF CALL	PERSON PLACING CALL	PERSON CALLED	NUMBER AND CITY CALLED
11/23	23:47 (5)	1 min.	Station-to-Station		CR 5-5352 Arlington, Texas
11/23	23:36 (7)	2 mins.	" "	"	"
11/23	23:18 (6)	3 mins.	" "	"	"
11/23	23:18 (1)	1 min.	" "	"	CR 5-4891 Arlington, Texas
11/23	23:44 (4)	2 mins.	" "	"	SO S-8022 Galveston, Texas
11/25	14:58	1 min.	" "	"	JE 4-8525 Fort Worth, Texas
11/25	19:29	4 mins.	" "	"	CR 5-4891 Arlington, Texas
11/25	16:47	1 min.	" "	"	"
11/25	18:23	1 min.	" "	"	"
11/25	15:58	1 min.	" "	"	CR 5-5353 Arlington, Texas

32

on 4/20-23/64 at Dallas, Texas File # DL 44-1639

by Special Agents C. RAY HALL & MANNING C. CLEMENTS/ash Date dictated 4/23/64

COMMISSION EXHIBIT No. 2307

DL 44-1639

2

DATE 1963	TIME CALL PLACED	DURATION OF CALL	PERSON PLACING CALL	PERSON CALLED	NUMBER AND CITY CALLED
11/25	15:59	2 mins.	Station-to-Station		CR 5-5352 Arlington, Texas
11/25	14:14	1 min.	" "	"	CR 5-4891 Arlington, Texas
11/26	16:59	1 min.	" "	"	"
11/26	17:01	1 min.	" "	"	CR 5-5352 Arlington, Texas
11/27	14:14	1 min.	" "	"	CR 5-4891 Arlington, Texas
11/27	13:08	3 mins.	" "	"	"
11/29	20:27	1 min.	" "	"	"
11/29	14:10	1 min.	" "	"	"
11/30	21:18	1 min.	" "	"	"
11/30	21:19	1 min.	" "	"	CR 5-5352 Arlington, Texas

Subpoena duces tecum for production of these records should be directed to R. A. BURROW, Chief Special Agent, Southwestern Bell Telephone Company, Dallas.

33

COMMISSION EXHIBIT No. 2307—Continued

DL 44-1639
MCC:eah

1

Investigation has established the following were subscribers to indicated telephone numbers as of dates of long-distance telephone calls placed from or charged to RI 7-2362, Carousel Club, 1312½ Commerce Street, Dallas, Texas, which telephone would have been available to JACK L. RUBY and RALPH PAUL, his associate, who took over management of Carousel Club subsequent to RUBY's arrest on November 24, 1963:

CR 5-4891 Arlington, Texas	Bull-Pen Drive-In, 1936 East Abrams, Arlington, operated by RALPH PAUL
CR 5-5352 Arlington, Texas	RALPH PAUL, Copeland Road, Arlington, Texas
SO 3-8022 Galveston, Texas	THOMAS J. MC KENNA, 1527 Broadway, Galveston (call to BILLY RAY WILSON aka Breck Wall)
JE 4-8525 Fort Worth, Texas	BRUCE CARLIN, 3809 Meadowbrook, Fort Worth, Texas

It appears the call on November 25, 1963, to CR 5-5353, Arlington, Texas, at 15:58 was intended for CR 5-5352, identified above.

34

Commission Exhibit No. 2308

FD-302 (Rev. 3-3-59)

FEDERAL BUREAU OF INVESTIGATION

1

Date 11/27/63

The following information was obtained from records of the Southwestern Bell Telephone Company, re telephone WH 15601 (unpublished), of JACK RUBY, 223 South Ewing, Apt. 207:

Date	Minutes	Telephone Number	Place Called
5/7/63	21	AL 5-6160	Nashville, Tennessee
5/7/63	3	523-9468	New Orleans, Louisiana
5/9/63	1	CR 5-4891	Arlington, Texas
5/9/63	3	CA 2-1351	Houston, Texas
5/12/63	8	YU 2-2805	New York, New York
5/12/63	12	476-2438	Drakesbor, Kentucky
5/13/63	1	CR 5-4891	Arlington, Texas
5/15/63	10	CR 5-4891	Arlington, Texas
5/24/63	9	CR 5-5352	Arlington, Texas
6/5/63	28	523-0930	New Orleans, Louisiana
6/10/63	1	PE 8-1951	Fort Worth, Texas
6/11/63	10	PE 8-1951	Fort Worth, Texas
6/12/63	6	CR 5-9365	Arlington, Texas
6/12/63	8	CR 5-4891	Arlington, Texas
6/15/63	4	CR 5-9365	Arlington, Texas
6/16/63	3	CR 5-9665	Arlington, Texas
6/16/63	3	SW 9-2770	Waco, Texas
6/16/63	7	EL 6-0919	Southfield, Michigan
6/19/63	8	523-0930	New Orleans, Louisiana
6/20/63	9	ED 5-1291	Fort Worth, Texas
6/20/63	18	CR 5-5352	Arlington, Texas
6/21/63	11	523-0930	New Orleans, Louisiana
6/23/63	9	CR 5-4891	Arlington, Texas
7/3/63	5	CR 5-4891	Arlington, Texas
7/4/63	11	PE 8-0058	Fort Worth, Texas
7/16/63	3	CR 5-4891	Arlington, Texas
7/18/63	11	ID 5-1536	Biloxi, Mississippi
7/21/63	14	GL 4-3087	Gloversville, New York
7/21/63	21	CR 5-5352	Arlington, Texas
7/21/63	1	CR 5-4891	Arlington, Texas
7/22/63	1	CR 5-4891	Arlington, Texas
7/22/63	2	CR 5-4891	Arlington, Texas
7/24/63	31	CH 2-3401	New Orleans, Louisiana
7/24/63	1	523-0930	New Orleans, Louisiana
7/30/63	16	FL 3-7178	Jackson, Mississippi
7/31/63	4	PE 2-4729	Fort Worth, Texas
8/1/63	6	CR 5-4891	Arlington, Texas
8/2/63	1	HO 6-8211	Los Angeles, California

on 11/27/63 at Dallas, Texas File # DL 44-1639

by Special Agent ROBERT C. LISH /nlf 688 Date dictated 11/27/63

2

DL-44-1639

Date	Minutes	Telephone Number	Place Called
8/2/63	2	HO 4-4785	Los Angeles, California
8/2/63	7	CR 4-0043	Beverly Hills, California
8/2/63	4	TE 1-8877	New York, New York
8/2/63	8	766-1193	North Hollywood, California
8/3/63	10	CR 5-5352	Arlington, Texas
8/4/63	3	CI 7-4915	New York, New York
8/4/63	1	CR 5-5352	Arlington, Texas
8/4/63	5	735-4111	Las Vegas, Nevada
8/7/63	34	NE 1-1489	Chicago, Illinois
8/11/63	24	CR 5-5352	Arlington, Texas
8/15/63	3	JU 2-7700	New York, New York
8/15/63	3	JU 2-7700	New York, New York
8/18/63	8	CR 5-5352	Arlington, Texas
8/18/63	1	CR 5-4891	Arlington, Texas
8/18/63	23	CR 5-4891	Arlington, Texas
8/19/63	1	735-4111	Las Vegas, Nevada
8/20/63	2	735-4111	Las Vegas, Nevada
8/22/63	7	735-4111	Las Vegas, Nevada
8/22/63	7	CR 4-0043	Beverly Hills, California
8/24/63	6	HO 5-3280	Chicago, Illinois
8/25/63	16	CR 5-4891	Arlington, Texas
8/28/63	8	CR 5-5352	Arlington, Texas
8/28/63	1	CR 5-4891	Arlington, Texas
8/28/63	1	CR 5-4891	Arlington, Texas
9/1/63	7	CR 5-4891	Arlington, Texas
9/9/63	11	CR 5-4891	Arlington, Texas
9/19/63	8	HO 5-3280	Chicago, Illinois
9/24/63	1	ED 5-1266	Fort Worth, Texas
9/26/63	2	CR 5-4891	Arlington, Texas
9/27/63	15	SH 3-0984	Chicago, Illinois
9/27/63	4	CR 5-5352	Arlington, Texas
10/1/63	3	ED 5-1266	Fort Worth, Texas
10/1/63	2	TE 4-0847	Fort Worth, Texas
10/1/63	3	CR 5-5352	Arlington, Texas
10/1/63	1	CR 5-4891	Arlington, Texas
10/12/63	8	CR 5-5352	Arlington, Texas
10/13/63	16	CR 5-4891	Arlington, Texas
10/18/63	11	CE 1-7766	St. Louis, Missouri
10/19/63	3	PE 7-5553	Fort Worth, Texas
10/19/63	32	OL 2-3849	Beverly Hills, California
10/19/63	2	PE 7-5553	Fort Worth, Texas
10/20/63	7	PE 7-5553	Fort Worth, Texas
10/20/63	3	PE 7-5553	Fort Worth, Texas

689

COMMISSION EXHIBIT No. 2308—Continued

3

DL-44-1639

RE: Calls Made From Telephone Number RI 7-2362

Date	Minutes	Telephone Number	Place Called
4/10/63	3	885-4323	Sulphur Springs, Texas
4/21/63	1	CR 5-4891	Arlington, Texas
4/23/63	1	CR 5-4891	Arlington, Texas
4/24/63	5	OL 7-4411	Edna, Texas
4/27/63	3	CR 5-4891	Arlington, Texas
5/1/63	6	CR 5-5352	Arlington, Texas
5/5/63	24	CA 2-1351	Houston, Texas
5/7/63	2	OL 7-4554	Edna, Texas
5/12/63	6	735-4111	Las Vegas, Nevada
5/12/63	11	OL 2-9658	Cicero, Illinois
5/12/63	15	SH 3-0984	Chicago, Illinois
5/12/63	2	OL 7-4554	Edna, Texas
5/12/63	9	CR 5-4891	Arlington, Texas
5/19/63	1	OL 7-4554	Edna, Texas
5/19/63	6	CR 5-4891	Arlington, Texas
5/20/63	6	CR 5-4891	Arlington, Texas
5/24/63	3	CR 5-5352	Arlington, Texas
5/26/63	11	CR 5-4891	Arlington, Texas
5/27/63	7	CR 5-5352	Arlington, Texas
5/31/63	3	OL 7-3025	Edna, Texas
5/31/63	2	OL 7-4554	Edna, Texas
6/4/63	12	CR 5-5352	Arlington, Texas
6/9/63	3	CR 5-4891	Arlington, Texas
6/10/63	16	OL 7-3025	Edna, Texas
6/10/63	20	SE 1-2789	San Francisco, California
6/10/63	1	CR 5-4321	Arlington, Texas
6/11/63	3	523-9468	New Orleans, Louisiana
6/13/63	7	CR 5-4321	Arlington, Texas
6/14/63	7	523-0930	New Orleans, Louisiana
6/15/63	12	SH 3-0984	Chicago, Illinois
6/16/63	18	CR 5-4891	Arlington, Texas
6/17/63	3	CR 5-4891	Arlington, Texas
6/19/63	1	CR 5-4891	Arlington, Texas
6/19/63	1	CR 5-4891	Arlington, Texas
6/19/63	4	523-0930	New Orleans, Louisiana
6/23/63	4	FA 3-6269	Houston, Texas
6/23/63	6	CR 5-4891	Arlington, Texas
6/27/63	7	735-4303	Las Vegas, Nevada

690

COMMISSION EXHIBIT No. 2309

4

DL-44-1639

Date	Minutes	Telephone Number	Place Called
6/28/63	7	CR 5-4891	Arlington, Texas
6/29/63	5	CR 5-4891	Arlington, Texas
7/3/63	8	CR 5-5352	Arlington, Texas
7/4/63	8	CR 5-4891	Arlington, Texas
7/6/63	12	523-0930	New Orleans, Louisiana
7/13/63	7	FA 2-7654	Monroe, Louisiana
7/15/63	3	CR 5-4891	Arlington, Texas
7/16/63	8	CR 5-4891	Arlington, Texas
7/21/63	10	PL 2-7365	Waco, Texas
7/23/63	2	CR 5-5352	Arlington, Texas
7/25/63	7	CR 5-4891	Arlington, Texas
7/27/63	3	EX 7-6488	San Francisco, California
7/28/63	9	CR 5-4891	Arlington, Texas
7/28/63	8	SH 3-0984	Chicago, Illinois
7/31/63	7	CR 5-4891	Arlington, Texas
8/2/63	6	735-4303	Las Vegas, Nevada
8/2/63	5	CR 5-4891	Arlington, Texas
8/2/63	3	735-4111	Las Vegas, Nevada
8/2/63	3	TE 1-8877	New York, New York
8/4/63	1	CR 5-5352	Arlington, Texas
8/4/63	4	CR 5-4891	Arlington, Texas
8/4/63	14	CH 2-3401	New Orleans, Louisiana
8/2/63	7	CR 1-9722	Beverly Hills, California
9/5/63	3	CR 5-4891	Arlington, Texas
9/11/63	6	CR 5-4891	Arlington, Texas
9/12/63	25	SH 3-0984	Chicago, Illinois
9/13/63	1	CR 5-4891	Arlington, Texas
9/16/63	4	CR 5-4891	Arlington, Texas
9/16/63	1	CR 5-4849	Arlington, Texas
9/24/63	6	TE 4-9484	Fort Worth, Texas
9/27/63	3	ED 5-1266	Fort Worth, Texas
9/6/63	1	CR 5-4891	Arlington, Texas
9/7/63	6	ED 5-1291	Fort Worth, Texas
9/8/63	2	CR 5-4891	Arlington, Texas
9/8/63	3	ED 6-3265	Fort Worth, Texas
10/3/63	1	CR 5-4891	Arlington, Texas
10/3/63	13	ME 1-3753	Shreveport, Louisiana
10/7/63	4	265-7630	Montgomery, Alabama
10/8/63	6	CR 5-4891	Arlington, Texas
10/13/63	1	CR 5-4891	Arlington, Texas
10/15/63	1	CR 5-5352	Arlington, Texas

691

5

DL-44-1639

Date	Minutes	Telephone Number	Place Called
10/16/63	13	JE 8-4082	Miami, Florida
10/16/63	3	CA 2-1900	Houston, Texas
10/17/63	7	CA 2-1900	Houston, Texas
10/17/63	4	RE 3-0024	Houston, Texas
10/17/63	1	CR 5-4891	Arlington, Texas
10/18/63	3	JA 4-1069	Atlanta, Georgia
10/18/63	4	367-6300	Louisville, Kentucky
10/19/63	9	CA 5-1781	Houston, Texas
10/19/63	1	PE 7-5553	Fort Worth, Texas
10/19/63	3	AL 6-0981	Nashville, Tennessee
10/26/63	3	BR 2-9836	Los Angeles, California
10/26/63	12	SH 3-6865	Chicago, Illinois
10/26/63	2	CR 5-4891	Arlington, Texas
10/27/63	1	CR 5-4891	Arlington, Texas
10/28/63	12	CR 5-4891	Arlington, Texas
10/29/63	11	CE 1-4552	St. Louis, Missouri
10/30/63	4	CR 5-5352	Arlington, Texas
10/30/63	18	JE 4-8525	Ft. Worth, Texas
10/30/63	1	CR 5-4891	Arlington, Texas
10/30/63	1	CR 5-5352	Arlington, Texas
10/30/63	1	CH 2-5431	New Orleans, Louisiana
10/30/63	4	CR 4-0043	Beverly Hills, California
10/31/63	2	CR 5-5352	Arlington, Texas
10/31/63	1	CR 5-4891	Arlington, Texas
10/31/63	12	UN 3-0400	Detroit, Michigan
10/31/63	14	ED 5-1266	Fort Worth, Texas
11/1/63	6	HA 7-3172	Chicago, Illinois
11/1/63	3	UN 3-0400	Detroit, Michigan
11/1/63	1	UN 3-5590	Detroit, Michigan
11/1/63	15	UN 3-5590	Detroit, Michigan
11/1/63	1	TE 4-0847	Fort Worth, Texas
11/1/63	3	CR 5-4891	Arlington, Texas
11/1/63	5	TE 4-0847	Fort Worth, Texas
11/3/63	3	NA 3-8295	Hot Springs, Arkansas
11/3/63	20	SH 3-0984	Chicago, Illinois
11/3/63	1	CR 5-4891	Arlington, Texas
11/3/63	3	CR 5-5352	Arlington, Texas
11/3/63	7	CR 5-4891	Arlington, Texas

692

6

RE: Calls Made From
Telephone No. LA 6-6258

Date	Minutes	Telephone Number	Place Called
6/4/63	3	CR 5-4891	Arlington, Texas
10/6/63	3	CR 5-4891	Arlington, Texas

RE: Calls Made From
Telephone No. LA 8-4775

Date	Minutes	Telephone Number	Place Called
6/12/63	13	HO 5-3280	Chicago, Illinois
7/25/63	38	HO 5-3280	Chicago, Illinois
8/21/63	8	HO 5-3280	Chicago, Illinois
9/2/63	3	526-4356	Simi, California
9/11/63	11	388-1249	Denver, Colorado
10/12/63	6	526-4356	Simi, California

The above information was obtained pertaining to telephone numbers listed to JACK RUBY at the residences shown and at the clubs in which he reportedly has an interest, The Carousel and The Vegas.

The above information is available only upon the issuance of a subpoena duces tecum directed to Mr. R. A. BURROW, Chief Special Agent, Southwestern Bell Telephone Company, Dallas, Texas.

693

COMMISSION EXHIBIT No. 2309—Continued

FD-302 (Rev. 3-3-59) FEDERAL BUREAU OF Commission Exhibit No. 2310

1 Date 6/12/64

Records of Southwestern Bell Telephone Company, Dallas, reflect a pay station at Phil's Delicatessen, 3531 Oak Lawn, Dallas, was assigned number LA 6-9425, as of October 20, 1963. The "agent" for the telephone is shown as Phil's, Inc., same address.

The coin box in connection with this telephone was emptied on November 26, 1963, at which time tabulation was made of the money as follows:

$2.00 in quarters, $53.90 in dimes, and $6.90 in nickels

The toll charge to Arlington, Texas, is 25 cents, no tax.

Toll tickets involving long distance calls from a pay station, such as the one in question, are not maintained with the same precision as in the case of toll tickets made from ordinary telephones where calls are made "on credit." Tickets with regard to this pay station are mixed in with literally hundreds of other toll tickets involving other pay stations.

Four of the quarters taken from the coin box on November 26, 1963, were believed identified with a call to Omaha, Nebraska, not identifiable in any way with JACK L. RUBY or RALPH PAUL. A telephone company representative advised to check all of the toll tickets involved and to say with certainty a particular charge was identifiable with JACK L. RUBY or to say none was identified with him would require an enormous expenditure of man-hours.

Records concerning the above telephone can be obtained through issuance of a subpoena duces tecum directed to R. A. BURROW, Chief Special Agent, Southwestern Bell Telephone Company.

on 6/10/64 at Dallas, Texas File # DL 44-1639

by Special Agent MANNING C. CLEMENTS/eah 959 Date dictated 6/11/64

This document contains neither recommendations nor conclusions of the FBI. It is the property of the FBI and is loaned to your agency; it and its contents are not to be distributed outside your agency.

COMMISSION EXHIBIT No. 2310

Commission Exhibit No. 2311

FD-302 (Rev. 3-_-59) FEDERAL BUREAU OF IN

Date 4/22/64

1

On November 28, 1963, RALPH PAUL, Arlington, Texas, advised SA MANNING C. CLEMENTS the following telephones at Arlington were available to him:

CR 5-4891, which is the Bull Pen Drive-In;

CR 5-5352, listed to RALPH PAUL on Copeland Road, Arlington;

CR 5-8113, which is listed to JOHN W. JACKSON, 1602 Browning.

The records of the Southwestern Bell Telephone Company, Arlington, Texas, were examined for Arlington telephone number CR 5-4891. The records reflected the following telephone calls were made long distance to or from this number from September 26, 1963 to December 1, 1963:

DATE	TIME CALL PLACED	DURATION OF CALL	PERSON PLACING CALL	PERSON CALLED	NUMBER & CITY CALLED
9/26/63	9:39 PM	3 minutes	Colony Club		RI 2-4247, Dallas
9/27/63	2:36 PM	1 minute	Ross Sharp		TU 7-4048, Mabank, state not listed
10/2/63	1:03 PM	1 minute	[illegible]		DA 4-4694, Dallas
10/7/63	6:54 PM	2 minutes	[illegible]		FE 7-2447, Dallas
10/7/63	10:51 PM	1 minute	Carousel		RI 7-2362, Dallas

on 4/21/64 at Arlington, Texas File # DL 44-1639

by Special Agent JOSEPH M. MYERS/eah Date dictated 4/21/64

This document contains neither recommendations nor conclusions of the FBI. It is the property of the FBI and is loaned to your agency; it and its contents are not to be distributed outside your agency.

20

COMMISSION EXHIBIT No. 2311

DL 44-1639
2

DATE	TIME CALL PLACED	DURATION OF CALL	PERSON PLACING CALL	PERSON CALLED	NUMBER & CITY CALLED
10/7/63	10:54 AM	1 minute	[illegible]		WH 2-6003, Dallas
10/8/63	11:26 AM	1 minute	[illegible]		RI 2-5614, Dallas
10/9/63	10:10 PM	10 minutes	Mrs. FLOYD 275-4891, Dallas	RALPH PAUL	CR 5-4891, Arlington
10/12/63	11:13 AM	1 minute	Gerald Weaver		FE 9-9945, Dallas
10/12/63	3:00 PM	2 minutes	Ruby		WH 1-5601, Dallas
10/13/63	Not listed	5 minutes	Lee Berry		CY 5-1623, New York, New York
10/14/63	7:46 PM	2 minutes	Ruby		WH 1-5601, Dallas
10/23/63	12:06 PM	2 minutes	USMC Reserve →		FL 7-8160, Dallas
10/25/63	11:37 AM	1 minute	Coca Cola		FL 7-8146, Dallas
10/27/63	11:43 AM	5 minutes	Ruby		WH 1-5601, Dallas
10/27/63	12:03 PM	7 minutes	Lee Berry		CY 5-1623, New York, New York

21

COMMISSION EXHIBIT No. 2311—Continued

DL 44-1639
3

DATE	TIME CALL PLACED	DURATION OF CALL	PERSON PLACING CALL	PERSON CALLED	NUMBER & CITY CALLED
10/30/63	11:32 AM	3 minutes	Lee Renny		CY 5-1623, New York, New York
11/6/63	12:10 PM	3 minutes	RALPH PAUL 275-4891, Dallas	Bull Pen	CR 5-4891, Arlington
11/6/63	5:49 PM	2 minutes	P.O. Hunt		FR 4-8155, Dallas
11/10/63	1:34 PM	1 minute	Ruby		WH 1-5601, Dallas
11/10/63	12:02 PM	8 minutes	Lee Renny		CY 5-1623, New York, New York
11/13/63	11:34 PM	2 minutes	Carousel		RI 7-2362, Dallas
11/13/63	6:06 PM	11 minutes	Carousel		RI 7-2362, Dallas
11/13/63	5:02 PM	3 minutes	Carousel		RI 7-2362, Dallas
11/15/63	6:10 PM	3 minutes	BETTY HAYS or HARP 275-4891, Dallas	RALPH PAUL	CR 5-4891, Arlington
11/22/63	5:07 PM	Not listed	Weiner		FE 9-9945, Dallas

22

COMMISSION EXHIBIT No. 2311—Continued

DL 44-1639

DATE	TIME CALL PLACED	DURATION OF CALL	PERSON PLACING CALL	PERSON CALLED	NUMBER & CITY CALLED
11/22/63	7:19 PM	3 minutes	Carousel		RI 7-2362, Dallas
11/22/63	Not listed	3 minutes	Minnie Sweat		CA 4-2829, Danieldal (state not listed)
11/24/63	11:56 AM	5 minutes	Lee Renny		CY 5-1623, New York, New York
11/25/63	10:36 AM	10 minutes			EV 1-3965, Dallas
11/25/63	11:23 PM	1 minute			RI 7-2362, Dallas
11/25/63	6:42 PM	6 minutes			WH 2-3268, Dallas
11/25/63	11:07 PM	5 minutes			FL 2-1034, Dallas
11/27/63	11:03 PM	3 minutes			RI 7-2362, Dallas
11/29/63	4:30 PM	3 minutes			RI 7-2362, Dallas
11/30/63	11:42 PM	Not listed			RI 7-2362, Dallas

23

COMMISSION EXHIBIT No. 2311—Continued

...1639

	TIME CALL PLACED	DURATION OF CALL	PERSON PLACING CALL	PERSON CALLED	NUMBER & CITY CALLED
11/30/63	Not listed	4 minutes			Oklahoma City to Arlington, Texas (no toll ticket on file and no way to determine numbers called)
12/1/63	12:02 PM	15 minutes	Lee Berry		CY 5-1623, New York, New York
12/1/63	12:18 PM	3 minutes			LA 6-6258, Dallas

The records for Southwestern Bell Telephone Company were examined for Arlington, Texas, telephone number CR 5-5352 and the toll calls made from September 26, 1963 to December 1, 1963, are as follows:

10/1/63	6:35 PM	3 minutes			FE 7-2447, Dallas
10/6/63	11:45 PM	3 minutes	Mrs. FLOYD 275-5352, Dallas	RALPH PAUL	CR 5-5352, Arlington
10/9/63	3:29 PM	3 minutes	Winnie Floyd		DA 4-4694, Dallas
11/3/63	12:15 AM	1 minute	Carmel		RI 7-2362, Dallas
11/19/63	2:35 PM	4 minutes	Winnie May Floyd		DA 4-4694, Dallas

DL 44-1639
6

DATE	TIME CALL PLACED	DURATION OF CALL	PERSON PLACING CALL	PERSON CALLED	NUMBER & CITY CALLED
11/25/63	3:50 PM	2 minutes			RI 7-2362, Dallas
11/25/63	8:13 PM	18 minutes	Lee Berry		CY 5-1623, New York, New York
11/26/63	5:51 PM	1 minute	Winnie Floyd		DA 4-4694, Dallas
11/26/63	5:49 PM	1 minute	Winnie Floyd		DA 4-4694, Danieldal
11/29/63	2:38 PM	3 minutes			RI 7-2856, Dallas

The records for Southwestern Bell Telephone Company were examined for Arlington, Texas, telephone number CR 5-8113 and the toll calls from September 26, 1963 to December 21, 1963, were as follows:

10/1/63	9:50 PM	29 minutes			CA 7-5274, Blackwood, New Jersey
10/2/63	3:01 PM	4 minutes			CA 7-5274, Blackwood, New Jersey
10/4/63	9:34 PM	53 minutes			CA 7-5274, Blackwood, New Jersey
10/5/63	2:23 PM	34 minutes			CA 7-5274, Blackwood, New Jersey

DL 44-1639
1

DATE	TIME CALL PLACED	DURATION OF CALL	PERSON PLACING CALL	PERSON CALLED	NUMBER & CITY CALLED
10/26/63	12:38 PM	19 minutes			DA 4-6434, Philadelphia, Pennsylvania
10/27/63	11:58 AM	7 minutes	Not listed	ANNA RANIWSKI, Room 300E, St. Joseph Hospital	CE 6-3700, Philadelphia, Pa.
10/30/63	7:50 PM	10 minutes			DA 4-6434, Philadelphia, Pennsylvania
11/22/63	3:08 PM	23 minutes			CA 7-5274, Blackwood, New Jersey
11/24/63	12:15 PM				CA 7-5274, Blackwood, New-Jersey
11/26/63	12:26 AM	5 minutes		Carousel	RI 7-2362, Dallas
11/27/63	6:46 PM	1 minute			DA 4-6434, Philadelphia, Pennsylvania
11/27/63	6:49 PM	11 minutes			CA 7-0014, Blackwood, New Jersey

The above records may be obtained only through issuance of a subpoena duces tecum directed to Mr. ARCHIE MARX, Supervisor, Southwestern Bell Telephone Company, Arlington, Texas.

26

COMMISSION EXHIBIT No. 2311—Continued

1
MCC:vm
DL 44-1639

Investigation has established the following were subscribers to telephones indicated, as of the dates of telephone calls placed from or charged to CR 5-4891, listed to Bull-Pen Drive-In, 1936 East Abrams, Arlington, Texas, owned by RALPH PAUL:

RI 2-4247 Dallas, Texas	Abe's Colony Club 1322½ Commerce, Dallas, Texas
TU 7-4048 Mabank, Texas	ROSS SHARPE, no street address, Mabank, Texas
DA 4-4694 Dallas, Texas	WINNIE FAYE FLOYD, 847 Peavy Road, Dallas, Texas (hostess, Colony Club)
FE 7-2447 Dallas, Texas	BILLY WRIGHT, 2026 Wilbur, Dallas, Texas
RI 7-2362 Dallas, Texas	Carousel Club, 1312½ Commerce, Dallas, Texas
WH 2-6003 Dallas, Texas	Fausett's Lee Auto Service, 833 West 7th, Dallas, Texas
RI 2-5614 Dallas, Texas	Wholesale Meat Company, 905 Fort Worth Avenue, Dallas, Texas
FE 9-9945 Dallas, Texas	GERALD WEAVER, 131 Mt. Hood, Dallas, Texas
WH 1-5601 Dallas, Texas	JACK L. RUBY, 223 S. Ewing, Dallas, Texas
CY 5-1623 New York, New York	LEE BERRY, 2265 Sedgwick, Bronx, New York (billed to MAC BERRY, same address)

27

COMMISSION EXHIBIT No. 2311—Continued

2
DL 44-1639

FL 7-8160 Dallas, Texas	U. S. Army, Marine Reserve Corps, 9638 Harry Hines, Dallas, Texas
FL 7-8146 Dallas, Texas	Coca Cola Company, Fountain Sales Department, Mockingbird and Lemmon Avenue, Dallas, Texas
FR 4-8155 Dallas, Texas	P. O. HUNT, 705 Oak Park, Dallas, Texas
CA 4-2829 Danieldale (Dallas), Texas	MINNIE E. SWEAT, 8833 Beckley, Dallas, Texas
EV 1-3965 Dallas, Texas	Mrs. MATTIE WILLIS, 6922 Forney Road, Dallas, Texas
WH 2-3268 Dallas, Texas	KAY COLEMAN, 325 N. Ewing, Apartment 111, Dallas, Texas
FL 2-1034 Dallas, Texas	PAPPY DOLSEN, Pappy Dolsen's Showland, 3930 Shorecrest, Dallas (billed to CARL DOLSEN)
LA 6-6258 Dallas, Texas	J. RUBY, 3929 Rawlins (EVA GRANT), Dallas, Texas

1
MCC:vm
DL 44-1639

Investigation has established the following were subscribers to telephones indicated as of the dates of telephone calls placed from or charged to CR 5-5352, listed to RALPH PAUL, Copeland Road, Arlington, Texas:

FE 7-2447 Dallas, Texas	BILLY WRIGHT, 2026 Wilbur, Dallas, Texas
DA 4-4694 Dallas, Texas	WINNIE FAYE FLOYD, 847 Peavy Road, Dallas, Texas (hostess, Abe's Colony Club)
RI 7-2362 Dallas, Texas	Carousel Club, 1312½ Commerce, Dallas, Texas
CY 5-1623 New York, New York	LEE BERRY, 2265 Sedgwick, Bronx, New York (billed to MAC BERRY, same address)
RI 7-2856 Dallas, Texas	C. A. DOLSEN, Interurban Building, Dallas, Texas.

DL 44-1639
MCC:eah

1

Investigation has established subscribers to telephone numbers indicated, as of dates of calls placed from or charged to telephone CR 5-8113, Arlington, Texas, listed to JOHN W. JACKSON, 1602 Browning, Arlington (previously identified as Manager of Bull-Pen Drive-In, owned by RALPH PAUL), were as follows:

CA 7-5274 Blackwood, New Jersey	JOHN P. BIEHL, 528 East Church Street, Blackwood
CA 7-0014 Blackwood, New Jersey	Mary's Cold Cut Center, 508 East Church Street, Blackwood (billed to JOHN P. BIEHL, above)
DA 4-6434 Philadelphia, Pennsylvania	MIKOL J. CYBAK, 4420 North 19th Street, Philadelphia
CE 6-3700 Philadelphia, Pennsylvania	St. Joseph's Hospital, 17th Street and Gerard Avenue, Philadelphia
RI 7-2362 Dallas, Texas	Carousel Club, 1312½ Commerce Street, Dallas

20

COMMISSION EXHIBIT No. 2311—Continued

Commission Exhibit No. 2312

FD-302 (Rev. 3-3-59)

FEDERAL BUREAU OF INVES[redacted]

Date 6/22/64

1

RALPH PAUL, Bull-Pen Drive-In, 1936 East Abrams, telephone CR 5-4591, was informed a notation, believed to be a telephone number, "JE 8-7475," was found in the effects of JACK L. RUBY following his arrest on November 24, 1963. He was asked if he could identify such a number.

He promptly stated this is the telephone number of his brother, DAVID PAUL. Referring to a notebook in his possession, Mr. PAUL stated the number is JE 8-7475 and is that of his brother, DAVID PAUL, 1152 College Avenue, Bronx, New York.

PAUL stated he had given the telephone number of DAVID PAUL to RUBY as a number through which he, RALPH PAUL, could be reached should he be absent from his residence and visiting his relatives in the New York City area.

on 6/22/64 at Arlington, Texas 247 File # DL 44-1639

by Special Agents MANNING C. CLEMENTS & J. JAMES WOOD/eah Date dictated 6/22/64

COMMISSION EXHIBIT No. 2312

1

DL 44-1639
MCC/ds

The 1964-65 New York Telephone Directory for Bronx County, New York, lists LEE PAUL, 1152 College Avenue, Bronx, New York, as having telephone JE 8-7475. Investigation has established LEE PAUL is the wife of DAVID PAUL, same address.

248

COMMISSION EXHIBIT No. 2312—Continued

1
DL 44-1639
MCC:eah

Previous investigation has been conducted with negative results to identify telephone "TE 8-7475" which appeared in a "Jot It Down" pad among possessions of RUBY following arrest. Investigation tended to eliminate this as being a Dallas, Texas, number, there being no "TE" prefix, and subscribers to telephones with other prefixes by the same digits having been eliminated.

The notation involving this telephone number followed the notation "RALPH PAUL
CY 5-1623."

PAUL has been previously identified as operator of the Bull Pen Drive-In, Arlington, Texas. It has been established telephone CY 5-1623, New York, New York, has been called from a telephone at Bull Pen Drive-In, and that LEE DERRY, 2265 Sedgwick, Bronx, New York, is the subscriber.

The questioned notation is followed immediately by the following: "American Airlines
Tuesday, October 9 - 985
11 - 11:30 AM"

On June 3, 1964, Miss ELLEN CASTLE, American Airlines, Information & Reservations, advised while American Airlines presently has a flight numbered 985, there was no Flight 985 as of October 9, 1963.

The New York Office has advised TEmpleton 8-7475 is listed to A. SNYMAN, 250 East 65th Street, New York, New York, the name of SNYMAN has not appeared heretofore during this investigation.

On June 3, 1964, W. R. LOVEJOY, Southwestern Bell Telephone Company, Dallas, advised he had made examination of various manuals of the telephone company and finds there are numerous "TE 8" as well as "838" designations which are assigned to exchanges

-4-

COMMISSION EXHIBIT No. 2312—Continued

2
DL 44-1639
MCC:sah

throughout the United States and Canada. Examination of such locations disclosed a "TErminal" exchange, Fort Worth, Texas. There follows an interview with Mrs. CARL M. APPLEWHITE, 2513 Thomas Road, Fort Worth, Texas, who, with her husband, is subscriber to TE 8-7475.

-5-

COMMISSION EXHIBIT No. 2312—Continued

FD-302 (Rev. 3-3-59)

FEDERAL BUREAU OF INVESTIGATION

Date 6/4/64

1

Mrs. CARL M. APPLEWHITE, 2513 Thomas Road, furnished the following information:

She and her husband have had telephone No. TE 8-7475 for approximately ten years. They are not acquainted with JACK RUBY and they have never had any dealings with JACK RUBY. To their knowledge RUBY has never called their home. Mrs. APPLEWHITE stated that CHARLES APPLEWHITE, a well-known singer, entertainer, and night club operator, is a cousin to her husband. She related that CHARLES APPLEWHITE did operate a night club in Dallas and sang at some of the clubs in Dallas. She stated that over a period of three or four years they have received numerous telephone calls from unknown persons trying to locate this CHARLES APPLEWHITE. They have called their number as CHARLES APPLEWHITE formerly lived in Fort Worth and she assumes they believe C. M. APPLEWHITE might be the father of CHARLES APPLEWHITE. Mrs. APPLEWHITE advised that her husband is employed as a welder for the Premier Oil Company of Fort Worth. He has never had any dealings with JACK RUBY.

Mrs. APPLEWHITE believed that whoever had the number TE 8-7475 was possibly trying to get in touch with CHARLES APPLEWHITE.

on 6/4/64 at Dallas, Texas File # DL 44-1639

by Special Agent EARLE HALEY:vm Date dictated 6/4/64

-6-

COMMISSION EXHIBIT No. 2312—Continued

Commission Exhibit No. 2313

FD-302 (Rev. 3-3-59)

FEDERAL BUREAU OF INV[redacted]

1

Date 3/10/64

The records of the Southwestern Bell Telephone Company were examined for Fort Worth telephone number JE 4-8525. The records reflected that this telephone number was listed to BRUCE CARLIN, 3809 Meadowbrook Drive, Fort Worth, Texas, and was a non-published telephone number. This telephone was connected on October 23, 1963, and prior to October 23, 1963, the number was WA 4-0113, listed to BRUCE CARLIN. The telephone number WA 4-0113 was shown to be connected at the residence at 909 East Harvey Street, Fort Worth, Texas, until it was changed on October 23, 1963, to JE 4-8525 at 3809 Meadowbrook Drive, Fort Worth, Texas.

There is still owing on this bill after the phone was disconnected by the telephone company an amount of $82.79 by BRUCE CARLIN.

WITH REFERENCE TO WA 4-0113

Date 1963	Time Call Placed	Duration of Call	Person Placing Call	Person Called	Number and City Called
9/26	8:32 P.M.	3 min.	Not shown	KING	CH 7-5014, Farmers Branch, Texas
9/26	2:21 PM	3 min.	Not shown	C. A. DOLSEN	RI 7-2842, Dallas, Texas
9/26	2:45 PM	3 min.	BRUCE CARLIN	EULESS	282-2162, Hurst, Texas (Billed to WA 4-0113)
9/27	2:45 PM	3 min.	Not shown	CAMERON KING	CH 7-5014, Farmers Branch, Texas

54

on 3/10/64 at Fort Worth, Texas File # DL 44-1639

by Special Agent JOSEPH M. MYERS/ds Date dictated 3/10/64

COMMISSION EXHIBIT No. 2313

2

DL 44-1639

Date 1963	Time Call Placed	Duration of Call	Person Placing Call	Person Called	Number and City Called
9/27	6:51 PM	3 min.	Not shown	TOM PALMER	FE 1-3746, Dallas, Texas
9/27	5:53 PM	3 min.	Not shown	CAMERON KING	CH 7-5014, Farmers Branch, Texas
9/27	2:53 PM	3 min.	LYNN	PAPPY DOLSEN	RI 7-2842, Dallas, Texas
9/29	6:31 PM	2 min.	Not shown	DOROTHY HAMMOND	EM 8-4304, Dallas, Texas
9/29	Not shown	1 min.	Not shown	Not shown	FL 7-5237, Dallas, Texas
10/3	1:49 PM	3 min.	LYNN	DOLSEN	RI 7-2842, Dallas, Texas
10/4	9:05 AM	3 min.	Not shown	Manager, Theater Lounge	RI 2-2677, Dallas, Texas
10/6	6:27 PM	3 min.	Not shown	LARRY BENNETT	OX 1-9575, Miami, Florida
10/8	Not shown	5 min.	Not shown	Not shown	CH 7-5014, Farmers Branch, Texas

55

COMMISSION EXHIBIT No. 2313—Continued

3

DL 44-1639

Date 1963	Time Call Placed	Duration of Call	Person Placing Call	Person Called	Number and City Called
10/9	3:35 PM	7 min.	Not shown	Manager, Connor's Grocery	GR 5-2501, McGregor, Texas
10/10	11:20 PM	7 min.	KAREN CARLIN Dallas, Texas, RI 1-0447 (Collect)	BRUCE CARLIN	JE 4-5901, Fort Worth, Texas
10/13	3:38 PM	5 min.	Not shown	KING	CH 7-5014, Farmers Branch, Texas
10/13	10:34 PM	3 min.	KAREN, Dallas, Texas RI 1-0559	AUTREY	WA 4-1423, Fort Worth, Texas
10/14	1:55 PM	4 min.	LITTLE LYNN	PAPPY DAWSON	RI 7-2842, Dallas, Texas
10/14	2:27 PM	3 min.	BRUCE CARLIN	KEN AZLIN	LY 4-4375, Weatherford, Texas
10/16	10:38 AM	3 min.	BUNKER, Dallas, Texas, DI 8-9956 (Collect)	CARLIN	WA 4-0113, Fort Worth, Texas
10/18	Not shown	5 min.	Not shown	Not shown	CH 7-5014, Farmers Branch, Texas

56

COMMISSION EXHIBIT No. 2313—Continued

4

DL 44-1639

Date 1963	Time Call Placed	Duration of Call	Person Placing Call	Person Called	Number and City Called
10/19	2:31 PM	3 min.	Detective MOTE, Dallas, Texas, RI 8-9711 (Collect)	Mrs. KAREN COLLINS BENNETT	WA 4-0113, Fort Worth, Texas
10/21	8:10 PM	3 min.	Fort Worth, Texas, WA 4-0113	PAPPY DAWSON, Theater Lounge	RI 2-2677, Dallas, Texas
10/21	3:43 PM	3 min.	BRUCE CARLIN Kennedale, Texas, CR 2-6591 (charged to WA 4-0113)	Mrs. MARTIN, Hill & Martin Ice Co.	252-5191, Irving, Texas
10/22	9:10 PM	3 min.	BRUCE CARLIN, Fort Worth, Texas, JE 5-9526 (billed to WA 4-0113)	Theater Lounge	RI 2-2677, Dallas, Texas
			WITH REFERENCE TO JE 4-8525		
10/24	10:27 AM	3 min.	BRUCE CARLIN, Arlington, Texas, CR 5-2886 (charged to JE 4-8525)	JERRY BUNKER	278-9601, Garland, Texas

57

COMMISSION EXHIBIT No. 2313—Continued

5

DL 44-1639

Date 1963	Time Call Placed	Duration of Call	Person Placing Call	Person Called	Number and City Called
10/27	11:45 P.M.	3 min.	KAREN CARLIN Dallas, Texas RI 1-0559 (charged to JE 4-8525)	BRUCE CARLIN	JE 4-5901 Fort Worth, Texas
10/30	1:35 PM	3 min.	KAREN CARLIN Fort Worth, Texas	LIZA SUMMERS	CH 7-5228 Farmers Branch, Texas
10/30	6:35 PM	5 min.	Not shown	CAMERON KING	CH 7-5014, Farmers Branch, Texas
10/30	Not shown	3 min.	Not shown	Not shown	CH 7-5228, Farmers Branch, Texas
10/30	12:09 PM	3 min.	BRUCE CARLIN Fort Worth, Texas WA 6-0331 (charged to JE 4-8525)	JOHNNY AMONS	AN 2-9278 Grand Prairie, Texas
10/31	1:39 PM	9 min.	Not shown	TOM PALMER	RI 2-8292 Dallas, Texas
10/31	6:33 PM	3 min.	Not shown	LIZA SUMMERS	CH 7-5228 Farmers Branch, Texas

58

COMMISSION EXHIBIT No. 2313—Continued

DL 44-1639

Date 1963	Time Call Placed	Duration of Call	Person Placing Call	Person Called	Number and City Called
11/1	5:21 PM	3 min.	Not shown	BARNEY WEIN-STEIN	EM 8-6980 Dallas, Texas
11/3	4:15 PM	3 min.	LITTLE LYNN	C. A. DOLSEN	FL 2-1034 Dallas, Texas
11/4	3:22 PM	3 min.	LITTLE LYNN	JUNE	CH 7-5228 Farmers Branch, Texas
11/4	4:07 PM	3 min.	Not shown	JACK RUBY	RI 7-2362 Dallas, Texas
11/5	9:04 PM	3 min.	Not shown	WEIN-STEIN, Theater Lounge	RI 2-2677 Dallas, Texas
11/5	9:15 PM	3 min.	Not shown	JACK RUBY, Theater Lounge	RI 7-2362 Dallas, Texas
11/6	11:50 AM	8 min.	Not shown	PACHEY NESPICA	OL 1-5000 Cleveland Ohio
11/6	1:30 PM	6 min.	Not shown	JACK RUBY	RI 7-2362 Dallas, Texas

59

COMMISSION EXHIBIT No. 2313—Continued

7

DL 44-1639

Date 1963	Time Call Placed	Duration of Call	Person Placing Call	Person Called	Number and City Called
11/8	Not shown	1 min.	Not shown	Not shown	RI 7-2362 Dallas, Texas
11/13	11:46 PM	3 min.	KAREN CARLIN Dallas, Texas, RI 1-0289 (billed to JE 4-8525)	BRUCE CARLIN	JE 4-5901 Fort Worth, Texas
11/13	8:55 AM	5 min.	CAMERON KING Farmers Branch, Texas CH 7-5014 (Collect)	BRUCE CARLIN	JE 4-8525 Fort Worth, Texas
11/14	12:41 AM	9 min.	KAREN CARLIN Dallas, Texas, RI 1-0289 (Collect)	Not shown	JE 4-8525 Fort Worth, Texas
11/16	3:58 AM	4 min.	KAREN CARLIN Dallas, Texas LA 6-9097 (Collect)	Not Shown	JE 4-8525 Fort Worth, Texas
11/18	9:03 AM	3 min.	Not shown	CAMERON KING	CH 7-5014 Farmers Branch, Texas
11/19	9:32 PM	5 min.	Not shown	CAMERON KING	CH 7-5014 Farmers Branch, Texas

60

COMMISSION EXHIBIT No. 2313—Continued

8

DL 44-1639

Date 1963	Time Call Placed	Duration of Call	Person Placing Call	Person Called	Number and City Called
11/20	9:42 PM	3 min.	JERRY BUNKER Houston, Texas 928-9124 (charged to JE 4-8525)	BRUCE CARLIN, Carousel Club	RI 1-0289 Dallas, Texas
11/20	2:38 AM	18 min.	BRUCE CARLIN Fort Worth, Texas, JE 5-9526	Not shown	RI 1-0638 Dallas, Texas
11/20	3:00 AM	3 min.	Not shown Fort Worth, Texas JE 5-9526 (billed to JE 4-8525)	KAREN CARLIN	RI 1-0638 Dallas, Texas
11/21	4:38 ...	4 min.	Not shown	BRUCE CARLIN and JERRY BUNKER, Vagabond Motel	OX 5-6406 Houston, Texas
11/21	7:34 PM	3 min.	Not shown	JACK RUBY Carousel Club	RI 7-2362 Dallas, Texas (Talked to someone named LARRY)

61

COMMISSION EXHIBIT No. 2313—Continued

9

DL 44-1639

Date 1963	Time Call Placed	Duration of Call	Person Placing Call	Person Calling	Number and City Called
11/21	1:34 AM	3 min.	BRUCE CARLIN Room 120, Houston, Texas, 695-6406	Not shown	RI 7-2362 Dallas, Texas

The above records may be obtained only through issuance of a subpoena duces tecum directed to Mr. JOHN MOORE, Supervisor, Southwestern Bell Telephone Company, Fort Worth, Texas.

1

DL 44-1639

It has been established by investigation that the following were subscribers to indicated telephone numbers as of the dates long-distance calls were placed from Fort Worth, Texas from WA 4-0113 and JE 4-8525 listed to BRUCE CARLIN, reported husband of KAREN BENNETT CARLIN, aka Little Lynn:

Telephone No.	Subscriber
CH 7-5014	CAMERON L. KING, 2952 Hollindale, Farmers Branch, Texas
RI 7-2842	C. A. DOLSEN, Theatrical Agency, 500 Interurban Building, Dallas, Texas
282-2162	Hi-Lo Supermarket, 740 West Pipe Line, Hurst, Texas.
FE 1-3746	T. STEWART PALMER, 2728 West Davis, Apartment 125, Dallas, Texas.
EM 8-4304	DOROTHY HAMMOND, 5945 Fredricks Square, Dallas, Texas.
FL 7-5237	SHIRLEY BERRY, 4557 Shady Hill, Dallas, Texas.
RI 2-2677	Theatre Lounge, 1326 Jackson Street, Dallas, Texas, operated by BARNEY WEINSTEIN.
OX 1-9575	A public pay telephone located at Cy's Wee Wash It, 3390 East 4th Avenue, Hialeah, Florida.
GR 5-2501	Connors Food Store, Highway 84, McGregor, Texas
RI 1-0447	Hickory House Barbecue, 217 South Akard, Dallas, Texas
JE 4-5901	312 Club, 2701 East Lancaster, Fort Worth, Texas.
RI 1-0559	A public telephone located at Theatre Lounge, 1326 Jackson St., Dallas, Texas

2
DL 44-1639

Telephone No.	Subscriber
WA 4-1423	O. L. AUTREY, 2265 Evans Street, Fort Worth, Texas.
LY 4-4375	W. E. AVLIN, West Highway 80, Weatherford, Texas
DI 8-9956	HENRY S. MILLER Company, Inc., Plano Road and Northwest Highway, Dallas, Texas.
RI 8-9711	Dallas City Hall and Police Building, Dallas, Texas.
CR 2-6591	A. L. Davis Food Store, Kennedale, Texas
252-5191	Hill and Martin Ice and Cold Storage Company, 226 West 4th Street, Irving, Texas.
JE 5-9526	Public pay phone at the Fort Worth Terminal of the Fort Worth-Dallas Turnpike.
CR 5-2886	Not presently a working number and records to identify subscriber in October, 1963 are no longer auilable. This is an Arlington, Texas exchange number.
278-9601	This is a Garland, Texas exchange number; however, phone company records indicate it has never been assigned.
CH 7-5228	LILLIE BECK, 3111 Colchester, Farmers Branch, Texas.
WA 6-0331	Kissinger Discount Auto Supply Store 4117 Hemphill Street, Fort Worth, Texas
AN 2-9278	Public pay phone at H & H Petroleum Corporation, 1808 West Main Street, Grand Prairie, Texas.

64

COMMISSION EXHIBIT No. 2313—Continued

3
DL 44-1639

Telephone No.	Subscriber
RI 2-8292	American Guild of Variety Artists, 1500 Jackson Street, Dallas, Texas
EM 8-6980	BARNEY WEINSTEIN, 3815 Northwest Highway, Dallas, Texas
FL 2-1034	PAPPY DOLSEN, 3930 Shorecrest, Dallas, Texas.
RI 7-2362	Carousel Club, 1312½ Commerce Street, Dallas, Texas, operated by JACK L. RUBY.
OL 1-5000	American Greetings Corporation, 1300 West 78th Street, Cleveland, Ohio.
RI 1-0289	Public pay phone listed to the Sovereign Club, 1312½ Commerce Street, Dallas, Texas. It is noted this is the same address as the Carousel Club operated by JACK L. RUBY.
LA 6-9097	Lucas B & B Restaurant, 3520 Oak Lawn, Dallas, Texas.
RI 1-0638	Nichols Brothers Garage, 1320 Commerce Street, Dallas, Texas.
OX 5-6406	Vagabond Motor Hotel, 4805 North Freeway, Houston, Texas.

65

COMMISSION EXHIBIT No. 2313—Continued

FD-302 (Rev. 3-3-59)

1

Date 3/10/64

WELDON L. THOMAS, 3809 Meadowbrook Drive, Fort Worth, Texas, advised that BRUCE CARLIN and his wife, KAREN CARLIN, rented Mr. THOMAS's garage apartment from October 16, 1963, to January 4, 1964, when they moved out. Mr. THOMAS stated that BRUCE CARLIN formerly resided at that garage apartment about four to six weeks in March 1963, but moved out after this time. Mr. THOMAS stated that subsequently BRUCE CARLIN contacted him sometime just prior to October 16, 1963, and asked Mr. THOMAS if he could rent the apartment again for him and his wife, KAREN.

Mr. THOMAS stated that he did not allow BRUCE or KAREN CARLIN to use THOMAS's telephone during this period in Mr. THOMAS's house and, therefore, no long distance calls were made from Mr. THOMAS's house by either BRUCE or KAREN CARLIN.

Mr. THOMAS stated that BRUCE and KA CARLIN now reside at 2937 Meadowbrook Drive, Fort Worth, Texas.

6S

on 3/9/64 at Fort Worth, Texas File # FW 44-1639

by Special Agent JOSEPH M. MYERS/ds Date dictated 3/9/64

Commission Exhibit No. 2314

UNITED STATES DEPARTMENT OF JUSTICE

FEDERAL BUREAU OF INVESTIGATION

In Reply, Please Refer to File No.

Dallas, Texas
September 14, 1964

JACK L. RUBY;
LEE HARVEY OSWALD

The President's Commission on the Assassination of President Kennedy, by letter dated September 4, 1964, requested examination of toll charges to telephone JEfferson 4-8525, Fort Worth, Texas, for the period November 22, 23, 24, 1963. The Commission had previously, by letter dated March 2, 1964, requested examination of such toll charges for the period September 26 - November 22, 1963, and by letter dated April 14, 1964, for the period November 26 - December 1, 1963.

Attached are the results of investigation requested. It has been established previously that Dallas telephone WH 1-5601 was formerly listed to Jack L. Ruby at 223 South Ewing Street, Apartment 207.

ATTACHMENT

FD-302 (Rev. 3-3-59) FEDERAL BUREAU OF INVESTIGATION

1

Date September 14, 1964

The records of the Southwestern Bell Telephone Company were examined for Fort Worth telephone number JE 4-8525, for any long distance telephone calls, from November 22 through 25, 1963.

DATE	TIME CALL PLACED	DURATION OF CALL	PERSON CALLING	PERSON CALLED	NUMBER CALLED AND LOCATION
11/24/63	Not Shown	3 minutes	Not Shown	Not Shown	WH 1-5601 Dallas, Texas
11/25/64	Not Shown	3 minutes	Not Shown	Not Shown	Number not shown, Dallas, Texas

It was determined from CAROL DAVIS that the above calls were not person-to-person calls and the above information is the only information contained in the records of Southwestern Bell Telephone Company.

The above records may be obtained through issuance of a subpoena duces tecum, directed to Mr. CAROL DAVIS, Legal Department, Southwestern Bell Telephone Company, Fort Worth, Texas.

on 9/11/64 at Fort Worth, Texas File # DL 44-1639

by Special Agent JOSEPH M. MYERS/nc Date dictated 9/14/64

COMMISSION EXHIBIT No. 2314—Continued

Commission Exhibit No. 2315

FD-302 (Rev. 1-25-60) FEDERAL BUREAU OF INVE[redacted]

Date 4/21/64

1

The records of Southwestern Bell Telephone Company were examined for Fort Worth telephone No. JE 4-8525 listed to BRUCE CARLIN, 3809 Meadowbrook Drive, Fort Worth, during the period November 26, 1963, through December 1, 1963. The toll calls from this telephone are as follows:

Date	Time Call Placed	Duration of Call	Person Placing Call	Person Called	Number and City Called
11/26/63	Not Listed	3 minutes			Collect Call from Dallas, Texas, to JE 4-8525, Fort Worth. Person and number from Dallas not listed.
11/27/63	Not Listed	3 minutes			Dallas, Texas, RI 7-9349.

The above records may be obtained through issuance of a subpoena duces tecum directed to Mr. WILLIAM SLATE, Supervisor, Southwestern Bell Telephone Company, Fort Worth, Texas.

On 4/21/64 at Fort Worth, Texas 18 File # DL 44-1639

by IC JAMES VON WHITE:vm Date dictated 4/21/64

COMMISSION EXHIBIT No. 2315

1
MCC:vm
DL 44-1639

It has been established by investigation that the following was subscriber to indicated telephone number as of the date of a long-distance call placed from JE 4-8525, listed to BRUCE CARLIN, 3809 Meadowbrook Drive, Fort Worth, Texas:

Telephone Number	Subscriber
RI 7-9349	Good Luck Oil Company, District Office, 2219 Pittman, Dallas, Texas.

19

COMMISSION EXHIBIT No. 2315—Continued

FD-302 (Rev. 3-3-59)

FEDERAL BUREAU OF IN[redacted]

Commission Exhibit No. 2316

Date 6/3/64

1

Mrs. JESSE CALDWELL, Auditor's Office, Adolphus Hotel, advised BRECK WALL and JOE PETERSON were registered at the Adolphus Hotel, Dallas, Texas, from August 31, 1963, to February 17, 1964. WALL and PETERSON produced and starred in "Bottoms Up" which was playing at the Century Room at the Adolphus Hotel.

The following is a list of telephone calls made by WALL and PETERSON and calls made to WALL and PETERSON. If these records should be needed, a subpoena duces tecum should be directed to RAY NEWBURN, Auditor, Adolphus Hotel:

Date 1963	Time Call Placed	Duration of Call	Person Placing Call	Person Called	Number and City Called
* 8/13	--	--	Call placed from San Francisco	WALL	Adolphus Hotel Dallas, Texas
9/30	6:30 p.m.	--	--	TRESSLER	No number, Collect to Fort Worth, Texas
10/1	4:08 p.m.	1 min.	WALL	--	WA 4-9306, Fort Worth, Texas
10/3	5:31 p.m.	1 min.	WALL	--	WA 4-9306, Fort Worth, Texas
10/4	5:21 p.m.	1 min.	WALL	--	WA 4-9306, Fort Worth, Texas
- 10/7	4:39 p.m.	8 min.	JOSEPH PEARSON	--	871-4921, New York

Mrs. CALDWELL advised she believed that the call from San Francisco to Dallas was collect and after WALL and PETERSON checked into the Adolphus Hotel the telephone call was charged to their room.

on 6/2/64 at Dallas, Texas File # DL 44-1639

by Special Agent WILL HAYDEN GRIFFIN:VM Date dictated 6/2/64

7

COMMISSION EXHIBIT No. 2316

Date 1963	Time Call Placed	Duration of Call	Person Placing Call	Person Called	Number and City Called
10/10	12:06 p.m.	1 min.	WALL	--	WA 4-9306, Fort Worth, Texas
10/15	6:38 p.m.	1 min.	WALL	--	CE 5-3048 Oklahoma City, Oklahoma
10/16	1:55 p.m.	5 min.	STUART, called from No. 342-9288, Omaha, Nebraska	PETERSON	Adolphus Hotel, Dallas, Texas
10/17	11:45 a.m.	1 min.	WALL	LEADS	CE 5-3048, Oklahoma City, Oklahoma
10/21	12:49 p.m.	5 min.	JOE PETERSON	JUDELINE	FR 4-8164, Henderson, Nevada
10/26	6:23 p.m.	5 min.	WALL	JOE PETERSON	HU 9-3111, Malakoff, Texas
10/28	8:06 p.m.	2 min.	WALL	--	WA 4-9306, Fort Worth, Texas
10/31	11:09 a.m.	1 min.	WALL	Dr. THOMPSON	536-1329, Fort Worth, Texas
11/3	10:22 p.m.	3 min.	WALL	MARK CHESLEY	359-6528, Pecan Gap, Texas
11/8	7:40 a.m.	--	WALL	--	No number, Collect to Commerce, Texas

8

COMMISSION EXHIBIT No. 2316—Continued

Date 1963	Time Call Placed	Duration of Call	Person Placing Call	Person Called	Number and City Called
11/12	6:24 p.m.	2 min.	JOE PETERSON	Mrs. NESBIT	MO 3-7425, Little Rock, Arkansas
--	8:20 p.m.	6 min.	Collect call from Lompoc, California, no number given	JOE PETERSON	Adolphus Hotel, Dallas, Texas
11/19	1:51 p.m.	1 min.	WALL	--	_24-9306, Fort Worth, Texas
11/22	6:28 p.m.	1 min.	WALL	--	WA 4-9306, Fort Worth, Texas
11/22	6:14 p.m.	2 min.	WALL	--	WA 4-9306, Fort Worth, Texas
11/23	5:27 p.m.	1 min.	WALL	--	SO 3-8022, Galveston, Texas
11/29	6:24 p.m	1 min.	WALL	--	WA 4-9306, Fort Worth, Texas
11/30	10:25 p.m.	1 min.	REYDAN CUDNEY	--	CR 4-2403, Arlington, Texas
12/1	11:21 p.m.	7 min.	WALL	KAY SUTTON	323-5111, Reno, Nevada
12/5	4:07 p.m.	16 min.	JOE PETERSON	--	TR 1-4921, New York

9

COMMISSION EXHIBIT No. 2316—Continued

4
DL 44-1639

Date 1963	Time Call Placed	Duration of Call	Person Placing Call	Person Called	Number and City Called
12/5	6:16 p.m.	1 min.	WALL	--	WA 4-9306, Fort Worth, Texas
12/11	2:29 p.m.	1 min.	WALL	--	WA 4-9306, Fort Worth, Texas
12/11	12:20 a.m.	--	Collect call from Reno, Nevada, no number given	WALL	Adolphus Hotel, Dallas, Texas
12/12	12:25 a.m.	5 min.	PETERSON	LARRY GRAYSON	CA 5-1781, Houston, Texas
12/14	4:55 p.m.	2 min.	PETERSON	TOM McKENNA	763-8022, Galveston, Texas
12/14	4:54 p.m.	10 min.	PETERSON	LARRY GRASON	665-8637, Houston, Texas
12/21	12:50 a.m.		Call from Lompoc, California, no number given	PETERSON	Adolphus Hotel, Dallas, Texas
12/24	2:44 a.m.	9 min.	JOE PETERSON	--	871-4921, Brooklyn, New York
12/25	1:45 p.m.	6 min.	WALL	--	WO 3-8032, Galveston, Texas
12/26	2:15 p.m.	2 min.	JOE PETERSON	FRED MOSK	CA 8-0428, Houston, Texas

10

COMMISSION EXHIBIT No. 2316—Continued

5
DL 44-1639

Date 1963	Time Call Placed	Duration of Call	Person Placing Call	Person Called	Number and City Called
12/28	10:16 p.m.	2 min.	WALL	--	SO 3-8022, Galveston, Texas
11/29	--	9 min.	WALL	HENRY ATCHISON	263-8700, Calgary Alt. Canada
11/29	11:05 a.m.	20 min.	WALL	Mrs. J. E. KOYLEO	932-5660, Coushatta, Louisiana
11/29	12:00 p.m.	11 min.	WALL	ARTHUR B. FOX	435-4861, "LB" (illegible)

11

1
MCC:vm
DL 44-163_

Investigation has established that the persons or entities listed below were subscribers to telephone numbers indicated, associated with toll charges of BRECK WALL (true name BILLY RAY WILSON) and JOE PETERSON, Adolphus Hotel, Dallas, Texas, as of the dates of such calls:

WA 4-9306, Fort Worth, Texas - EDWARD M. PARKER, General Clerk, Fort Worth and Denver Railway, 2709 Mission Street, Fort Worth, Texas

JE 6-1329, Fort Worth, Texas - Dr. RICHARD W. THOMSON, Osteopath and Chiropractor, 3751 E. Lancaster, Fort Worth, Texas

CR 4-2403, Arlington, Texas - GRIFF O'NEIL, 212 S. Cooper, Apartment 111, Arlington, Texas, Student, Texas Christian University

HU 9-3111, Malakoff, Texas - M. T. DODD, Malakoff, Texas

359-6528, Pecan Gap, Texas - R. D. RODERICK, Pecan Gap, Texas

871-4921, New York, New York - ALMA M. JABLONKA, 572 51st Street, Brooklyn, New York

CE 5-3048, Oklahoma City, Oklahoma - Mitchell L. Leeds Theatrical Agency, 317 Municipal Auditorium, Oklahoma City

342-9288, Omaha, Nebraska - Pay Station, Junior Bar, 414 N. 16th Street, Omaha, Nebraska

FR 4-8164, Henderson, Nevada - JOHN D. NICHOLSON, 618 Federal Street, Henderson, Nevada

12

COMMISSION EXHIBIT No. 2316—Continued

2
DL 44-1639

MO 3-7425, Little Rock, Arkansas - ALEXANDER W. NISBET, 2701 N. Grant, Little Rock, Arkansas

SO 3-8022, Galveston, Texas - TOM J. McKENNA, 1527 Broadway, Galveston, Texas

323-5111, Reno, Nevada - Golden Club, 219 N. Center, Reno, billed to W. and J. TOMERLIN, same address

CA 5-1781, Houston, Texas - Continental Houston Motor Hotel, 101 Main, Houston, Texas

665-8637, Houston, Texas - J. O. BERLOWITZ, 7100 Kirby Drive, Apartment D, Houston, Texas

WO 3-8032, Galveston, Texas - See below

CA 8-0428, Houston, Texas - Mosk's Store for Men, 808 Main, Houston, Texas

932-5660, Coushatta, Louisiana - J. E. COLLIER, Route 4, Highway 1, Coushatta

Effort is being made to identify subscriber to telephone 263-8700, Calgary, Alberta, Canada.

The Little Rock Office has advised telephone 435-4861 is not identifiable as a listing in Little Rock, Arkansas.

The Houston Office has advised there is no telephone listing WO 3-8032 in Galveston, Texas. It is to be noted this number is similar to SO 3-8022, Galveston, which number is identified above with THOMAS J. McKENNA who was interviewed at Galveston, Texas, January 2, 1964. McKENNA identified true name of BRECK WALL as BILLY RAY WILSON.

13

COMMISSION EXHIBIT No. 2316—Continued

3
DL 44-1639

Files of the Dallas Office reflect BILLY RAY WILSON, aka Billy Roy Appleton, was declared delinquent by an Austin, Texas, Selective Service Board on June 30, 1958, for failure to keep his local board informed of his current address, failure to report for physical examination, and failure to report for induction. WILSON was interviewed by SAs EUGENE F. WHITMORE and JOSEPH L. SCHOTT at Fort Worth, Texas, on November 12, 1958, concerning his delinquencies. At that time, he furnished the name of TOM McKENNA, 623 N. Rosemount, Dallas, Texas, as a person through whom he could be located. WILSON identified himself as a producer of stage shows and as a homosexual. The file reflects he was subsequently rejected for military service, the delinquencies were removed, and prosecution was declined.

Files of the Dallas Office reflect that on November 13, 1963, GRIFF O'NEIL, Apartment 111, 212 S. Cooper, Arlington, Texas, telephone CR 4-2403, advised SA JOSEPH L. SCHOTT he was a professional baton twirling teacher and contest judge at the time enrolled as a student at Arlington State College. O'NEIL reported at the time, a then unknown person had been using his name and names of other baton twirlers to solicit funds from acquaintances of the persons whose names he was using by long distance telephone. The unknown person was subsequently identified and admitted using the name of O'NEIL and others in connection with fraud by wire violations. This person identified himself as a homosexual and alleged that a number of individuals whose names he had used were also homosexuals. He did not specifically name O'NEIL or any of the other persons whose names he admitted using.

14

FD-302 (Rev. 3-3-59)

FEDERAL BUREAU OF INVESTIGATION

Date 6/11/64

1

Mrs. JESSE CALDWELL, Auditor's Office, Adolphus Hotel, Dallas, Texas, advised JACK RUBY, RALPH PAUL, and GEORGE SENATOR were not registered at the Adolphus Hotel during November, 1963. BRECK WALL and JOE PETERSON were registered in rooms No. 1980 and No. 1981 and made the following calls:

DATE	PERSON PLACING CALL	NUMBER CALLED
November 22, 1963	PETERSON, from room 1980	EMerson 1-4534
November 23, 1963	PETERSON, from room 1980	RIverside 2-6811
November 23, 1963	BRECK WALL, from room 1980	RIverside 8-4361
November 23, 1963	BRECK WALL, from room 1980	RIverside 8-1434

Mrs. CALDWELL advised the hotel does not keep any record of incoming calls and that on all local calls originating from the hotel the time of the call and length of the call are not recorded.

WALL and PETERSON occupied room No. 1703 from December 31, 1962, to February 15, 1963; room No. 1809-10 on February 15, 1963; room No. 1719 on April 17, 1963. They occupied rooms 1980-81 continuously from September 22, 1963, to January 4, 1964.

on 6/10/64 at Dallas, Texas File # DL44-1639

by Special Agent WILL HAYDEN GRIFFIN:vm Date dictated 6/11/64

Commission Exhibit No. 2317

UNITED STATES DEPARTMENT OF JUSTICE

FEDERAL BUREAU OF INVESTIGATION

In Reply, Please Refer to
File No.

Dallas, Texas
August 11, 1964

JACK L. RUBY;
LEE HARVEY OSWALD

By letter dated July 20, 1964, the President's Commission on the Assassination of President Kennedy requested examination of telephone toll charges to Fort Worth and Arlington, Texas, from all telephones, public or official, located in Dallas Police and Courts Building, Dallas, Texas, for the period from 10:00 P.M., Saturday, November 23, 1963, through Sunday, November 24, 1963.

Attached hereto are the results of investigation in the above connection. Investigation has established the subscriber to Fort Worth telephone ED 2-7241 as of November 23, 1963, was the City of Fort Worth, including Fort Worth Police Department. The subscriber to Fort Worth telephone ED 2-0606, as of November 24, 1963, was State Cafe, 1211 Main Street.

COMMISSION EXHIBIT No. 2317

FD-302 (Rev. 3-3-59)

FEDERAL BUREAU OF INVESTIGATION

1

Date 8/11/64

Records of the Southwestern Bell Telephone Company reflect the following information concerning long distance telephone calls placed from public or official telephones, at the Dallas Police and Courts Building insofar as they show calls to Fort Worth and Arlington, Texas, during the period from 10:00 P.M., Saturday, November 23, 1963, through Sunday, November 24, 1963. The following long distance calls were made from RI 8-9711:

Date	Time Call Placed	Duration of Call	Person Placing Call	Person Called	Number and City
11/23/63	--	3 min.	--	Lt. HOPKINS Ext. 488	ED 2-7241 Fort Worth
11/23/63	--	3 min.	--	Missing Persons	ED 2-7241 Fort Worth
11/24/63	--	3 min.	--	JOE Mc___ Attorney	ED 2-0606 Fort Worth

In addition to the above, records of long distance calls were found charged to the following telephone numbers: RI 2-2431; RI 8-2393; and, RI 8-4128. No calls were made to Fort Worth or Arlington, Texas, on the above telephones.

By letter dated August 5, 1964, L. H. CURTWRIGHT, District Manager - Central, Southwestern Bell Telephone Company, advised he enclosed all toll tickets and statements of toll calls charged to the telephone numbers listed above. (This is for the months of November and December 1963.)

The following is a list of all telephones, public and official, located in the Dallas Police and Courts Building, and, with the exception of the numbers listed above, no records were located of any toll calls charged during November 1963:

on 8/6/64 at Dallas, Texas File # DL 44-1639

by Special Agent ROBERT C. LISH/ds Date dictated 8/6/64

COMMISSION EXHIBIT No. 2317—Continued

2

DL 44-1639

RI 7-4317 - Third floor, Radio Room
RI 2-2431 - Third floor, Radio Room
RI 2-2432 - Third floor, Radio Room
RI 2-2433 - Third floor, Radio Room
RI 2-2434 - Third floor, Radio Room
RI 2-2435 - Third floor, Radio Room
RI 2-2436 - Third floor, Radio Room
RI 2-2437 - Third floor, Radio Room
RI 2-2438 - Third floor, Radio Room
RI 2-2439 - Third floor, Radio Room
RI 2-2430 - Third floor, Radio Room

RI 7-7342 - Second floor, North Hall
RI 8-4128 - Second floor, North Hall
RI 8-3054 - Fourth floor, Crime Lab

RI 7-2966 - Third floor, South Hall
RI 8-2393 - Third floor, South Hall
RI 7-7888 - Third floor, South Hall
RI 7-7200 - Third floor, South Hall
RI 7-3905 - Third floor, South Hall
RI 7-1152 - Third floor, South Hall
RI 7-3485 - Third floor, South Hall

RI 8-3243 - Third floor, North Hall
RI 2-6503 - Third floor, North Hall

RI 7-3426 - Second floor, South Hall

RI 1-0139 - First floor, South End Hall
RI 1-0249 - First floor, South End Hall

RI 1-0439 - Basement, South End
RI 1-0379 - Basement, South End
RI 8-6879 - Basement, South End

RI 7-4388 - Third floor, South East
RI 2-5275 - Third floor, South East

COMMISSION EXHIBIT No. 2317—Continued

3.

3

DL 44-1639

RI 7-2745 Second floor, South East

RI 7-3865 - First floor, South East

RI 8-3998 - Fifth floor, South West

RI 7-3954 - Second floor, South West

RI 7-8520 - In front of Tax office, first floor
RI 7-4564 - In front of Tax office, first floor
RI 2-7036 - In front of Tax office, first floor

Old building of City Hall, PBX Trunks

RI 8-M503 ("hot line") - works from third floor Radio Room, Old City Hall
RI 8-9784 - Third floor Radio Room - Old City Hall
RI 8-9785 - Third floor Radio Room - Old City Hall
RI 8-9786 - Third floor Radio Room - Old City Hall
RI 8-9787 - Third floor Radio Room - Old City Hall
RI 8-9773 - Third floor Radio Room - Old City Hall
RI 8-9774 - Third floor Radio Room - Old City Hall
RI 8-9775 - Third floor Radio Room - Old City Hall
RI 8-9776 - Third floor Radio Room - Old City Hall
RI 8-9777 - Third floor Radio Room - Old City Hall
RI 8-9778 - Third floor Radio Room - Old City Hall
RI 8-9779 - Third floor Radio Room - Old City Hall
RI 8-9770 - Third floor Radio Room - Old City Hall
RI 8-9772 - Third floor Radio Room - Old City Hall
RI 8-9755 - Third floor Radio Room - Old City Hall
RI 8-9781 - Third floor Radio Room - Old City Hall
RI 8-9782 - Third floor Radio Room - Old City Hall
RI 8-9751 - Third floor Radio Room - Old City Hall
RI 8-9752 - Third floor Radio Room - Old City Hall
RI 8-9753 - Third floor Radio Room - Old City Hall
RI 8-9756 - Third floor Radio Room - Old City Hall
RI 8-9754 - Third floor Radio Room - Old City Hall
RI 8-9757 - Third floor Radio Room - Old City Hall
RI 8-9758 - Third Floor Radio Room - Old City Hall

COMMISSION EXHIBIT No. 2317—Continued

4.

4

DL 44-1639

Old building of City Hall, PBX Trunks

RI 8-7947 - Third floor Radio Room - Old City Hall
RI 8-7948 - Third floor Radio Room - Old City Hall
RI 8-7949 - Third floor Radio Room - Old City Hall

The above is confidential and is not to be made public except upon the issuance of a subpoena duces tecum, which should be directed to R. A. BURROW, Chief Special Agent, Southwestern Bell Telephone Company, Dallas.

5

COMMISSION EXHIBIT No. 2317—Continued

FD-302 (Rev. 3-3-59) FEDERAL BUREAU OF — Commission Exhibit No. 2318

1

Date 12/16/63

Patrolman HARRY OLSEN, 325 North Ewing Street, Dallas, was interviewed in Room 222, Methodist Hospital, Dallas, where he is recuperating from injuries received in an automobile accident. OLSEN furnished the following information:

He has been employed by the Dallas Police Department during the past five and one-half years. He has known JACK RUBY for two years and has been in RUBY's Carousel Club on several occasions and has talked with RUBY a number of times. He stated that he is a close friend of KAY COLEMAN, former employee of RUBY at this Carousel Club. He advised that he has never liked RUBY, mainly because RUBY has objected to his associating regularly with Miss COLEMAN and for taking up so much of Miss COLEMAN's time.

He last saw RUBY at about 1:30 AM on either November 23 or 24, 1963, when he and Miss COLEMAN were sitting in his automobile on a parking lot at the corner of Jackson and Field Streets, Dallas, when RUBY drove by in his car, recognized them and stopped and talked with them for about ten minutes. RUBY did not state where he came from or where he was going on that occasion. RUBY was traveling west on Jackson Street and was alone at the time. He recalls that they all mentioned the assassination of President KENNEDY but RUBY said nothing to indicate he had ever seen or known OSWALD and did not appear to be any more upset over the tragedy than the average individual.

He has never known RUBY to carry a gun on his person but recalls that several months ago, when a burglar was suspected of being in the Carousel Club, the police were called and he noticed RUBY carrying a gun in his hand inside the club. He suggested to RUBY that he should put his gun away and leave the matter to the police.

OLSEN stated that he has never been employed by RUBY and knows of no other police officer who may have been employed by him. He has never heard RUBY speak about politics or mention any strong like or dislike for President KENNEDY. He considers RUBY to be quick-tempered and unpredictable but would never have considered him to be capable of committing murder.

on 12/12/63 at Dallas, Texas File # DL 44-1639

by Special Agent s RAYMOND C. HARDIN and ROBERT J. WILKISON - LAC Date dictated 12/13/63

138

This document contains neither recommendations nor conclusions of the FBI. It is the property of the FBI and is loaned to your agency; it and its contents are not to be distributed outside your agency.

COMMISSION EXHIBIT No. 2318

DL 44-1639
2

OLSEN stated that he has no information indicating that RUBY had any connection with OSWALD; that RUBY had any assistance in planning the murder of OSWALD or that RUBY was intentionally permitted to enter the basement area prior to shooting OSWALD.

OLSEN stated that to his knowledge GEORGE SENATOR a former roommate of RUBY, was about as close an associate of RUBY as anyone else. He has not talked with SENATOR concerning RUBY and knows of no pertinent information SENATOR may have. He added that a former police officer, namely HUGH GENE SMITH, associated with RUBY several months ago.

139

COMMISSION EXHIBIT No. 2318—Continued

Commission Exhibit No. 2319

FD-302 (Rev. 3-3-59)

FEDERAL BUREAU OF INVESTIGATION

1

Date 12/16/63

KATHLEEN C. ROOT, residence 1911 Moser Street, Telephone Number TA 7-1569, employed by Dr. ISRAEL S. PERLSTEIN, National Bankers Life Building, furnished the following information in connection with "Kathleen, c/o Dr. Perlstein, TA _1569" being in the possession of JACK RUBY:

She and Dr. PERLSTEIN visited the Carousel Club two or three months ago at which time she met JACK RUBY, who was at the club door welcoming patrons.

On November 21, 1963, between 3:00 PM and 3:30 PM, while awaiting a bus on Commerce Street, she again saw JACK RUBY. RUBY told her, "With your looks, you should be in show business." RUBY asked her for a dinner date and she declined. He then asked for her phone number and wrote it down on a piece of newspaper. She had no other contact with RUBY.

She does not know LEE HARVEY OSWALD and does not know of any connection between OSWALD and RUBY.

on 12/14/63 at Dallas, Texas File # DL 44-1639

by Special Agent R. NEIL QUIGLEY :lp Date dictated 12/16/63

144

Commission Exhibit No. 2320

FD-302 (Rev. 3-3-59)

FEDERAL BUREAU [redacted]

1

Date 12/16/63

SAMUEL C. SMITH, 5311 Morningside Street, Dallas, whose name, with his place of employment, Dallas Times-Herald, appeared in a list of items obtained from JACK RUBY's property taken from his automobile following his arrest by the Dallas Police Department, furnished the following information:

SMITH advised he is employed in the Advertising Department of the Dallas Times-Herald, and in this capacity he has known JACK RUBY for two and one-half years inasmuch as RUBY has come to him regularly about once each week for assistance in placing advertisements concerning RUBY's places of business. SMITH added that he has been to the Carousel Club on several occasions but has never had social contacts with RUBY. He last saw and talked with RUBY about 4:00 or 4:30 PM on November 21, 1963, when RUBY was at the Dallas Times-Herald Building in connection with advertisements. He noticed nothing out of the ordinary in RUBY's demeanor or conversation.

SMITH stated that he has never discussed politics with RUBY and has no information concerning RUBY's activities or whereabouts following the assassination of President KENNEDY. He stated he has no information indicating a connection between RUBY and LEE HARVEY OSWALD or concerning the shooting of OSWALD on the part of RUBY. He knows of no conspiracy which may have existed between RUBY and others in connection with the shooting and in connection with RUBY's gaining entrance to the basement area of City Hall prior to the shooting. He has never seen RUBY carrying a gun but several months ago he recalls making a remark to RUBY that he should be afraid to carry so much cash on his person, as was his practice, whereupon RUBY replied that he was not worried about anyone taking this money, which remark made SMITH assume that RUBY did carry a gun for his protection while carrying large sums of money.

SMITH stated that the only close associates of RUBY he knows of are Mr. and Mrs. WALLY WESTON. He stated that WESTON is a comedian and Mrs. WESTON is a dancer using the theatrical name of SHERRY ANGEL. She worked for RUBY as well as her husband until about August 1963.

on 12/13/63 at Dallas, Texas File # DL 44-1639

by Special Agent s EDMOND C. HARDIN and ROBERT J. WILKISON - LAC Date dictated 12/13/63

151

COMMISSION EXHIBIT No. 2320

Commission Exhibit No. 2321

UNITED STATES DEPARTMENT OF JUSTICE

FEDERAL BUREAU OF INVESTIGATION

In Reply, Please Refer to File No.

New Orleans, Louisiana

July 31, 1964

JACK L. RUBY;
LEE HARVEY OSWALD - DECEASED - VICTIM

Reference is made to the President's Commission's letter dated July 23, 1964, which requested a re-interview with Gladys Craddock at Dallas, Texas, to determine where she saw Jack Ruby at "The Dallas Morning News" Building on November 22, 1963, the time at which she saw him, and the conversation and conduct of Ruby.

On July 29, 1964, the Dallas Office of the Federal Bureau of Investigation advised that Gladys Craddock had terminated her employment with "The Dallas Morning News" and it was believed that she was residing at Gloster, Mississippi.

On July 30, 1964, Gladys Beall Ivey, Nee Craddock was located and interviewed by a Special Agent of the Federal Bureau of Investigation at which time she furnished the following information:

She advised that on November 22, 1963, she was employed in a clerical capacity in the Classified Advertising Department of "The Dallas Morning News" newspaper, Dallas, Texas. She advised that the Classified Advertising Department is located on the ground floor on the newspaper building.

Mrs. Ivey stated that to the best of her recollection it was about 11 A.M., on November 22, 1963, when she observed Jack Ruby in the Classified Advertising Department. She stated she affixes the time as approximately 11 A.M., because prior to this time she had temporarily left the building to conduct some personal business in the area and was hurrying to return to the building by 11 A.M., as her supervisor, Mrs. Claire Conlon, had

COMMISSION EXHIBIT No. 2321

JACK L. RUBY;
LEE HARVEY OSWALD-DECEASED-VICTIM

indicated that she wanted to go to lunch on time so that she, Mrs. Conlon, could return to the building to watch the Presidential Motorcade. Mrs. Ivey stated that it was Mrs. Conlon's normal custom to go to lunch at 11 A.M.

Mrs. Ivey stated that upon returning to the newspaper building she walked through the lobby on the ground floor and walked around behind the counter to the area where she normally waits on the customers. As she was walking behind the counter she glanced toward the lobby and observed Jack Ruby walking across the lobby in the direction of the elevator. At approximately the same instant she observed Ruby, Ruby also observed her and at this instant turned towards her and raised his voice and said "Hi, the President is going to be here today." Ruby also during the conversation waved his hand in her direction. She stated that it was necessary for Ruby to raise his voice because he was quite a distance from her and that she then lost sight of Ruby and does not know whether he went to the elevator or left the building.

Mrs. Ivey stated that she had no other conversation with Jack Ruby and in these few moments that she observed Ruby on the morning of November 22, 1963, there was nothing in his conduct or actions which she considered unusual.

Mrs. Ivey stated that in her contacts with Ruby prior to November 22, 1963, it always seemed to her that Ruby was in a hurry to complete whatever he might be doing and that Ruby's contacts with her were always friendly.

- 2 -

COMMISSION EXHIBIT No. 2321—Continued

Commission Exhibit No. 2322

UNITED STATES DEPARTMENT OF JUSTICE

FEDERAL BUREAU OF INVESTIGATION

In Reply, Please Refer to
File No.

Los Angeles, California
July 24, 1964

INTERVIEW WITH ROY WILLIAM PIKE

Reference is made to the letter of the President's Commission on the Assassination of President Kennedy, to the Director, FBI, dated July 20, 1964, requesting that Roy William Pike be re-interviewed.

On July 23, 1964, Roy William Pike, who also uses the name of Mickey Ryan and Mike Pike, was located and interviewed by a Special Agent of the FBI at Stockton Quincy Ford, Inc., 1522 Westwood Boulevard, Los Angeles, California, where he is presently employed as a car salesman under the name of Mike Pike. Pike advised as follows:

He first met Jack Ruby approximately one year prior to November 22, 1963, when he was standing outside Ruby's night club in Dallas, Texas, looking at the poster photographs of the strip-teasers who were then appearing at Ruby's club. He was approached by Ruby, who asked him if he would like to see the show as his guest. He accepted Ruby's invitation and was later that day offered a job as Ruby's bookkeeper. He worked for Ruby for approximately two months until he left Dallas to take a job in Fort Worth, Texas, as a car salesman. During the two months he was employed by Ruby he attended a few parties with Ruby.

He is of the opinion that Ruby was conducting a strictly legitimate business, had no association with the underworld or the Communist Party. He said Ruby liked to give people the impression he was a "tough customer" and liked to surround himself with well-dressed, clean-cut men because it made him feel important.

COMMISSION EXHIBIT No. 2322

After leaving Dallas to work in Fort Worth, he occasionally visited Ruby's club in Dallas, where he had dates with some of the girls working for Ruby. The girls he dated most were his present wife and another stripper, whose name he cannot recall but who is presently living with Cullen Briggs, a retired District Judge in Corpus Christi, Texas.

He was watching television with Ramona Wagner, also known as Tuesday Ryan (his wife from whom he is presently seeking a divorce), on November 22, 1963, when he heard a news flash that President Kennedy had been shot. He does not recall exactly what his activities were on November 23, 1963, but does remember that he was watching television with his wife on November 24, 1963, when Lee Harvey Oswald was shot. He definitely did not see Ruby on November 22, 23, or 24, 1963. He was working as a bartender at the North Park Inn, Dallas, Texas, during this period of time and was always home during the day. He does not recall meeting Ruby at the Carousel Club on November 21, 1963. He believes he last saw Ruby approximately two weeks prior to November 22, 1963. He said he also believes that he last saw George Senator, Ralph Paul, Harry Olsen, "Kathy Kay" Coleman, Karen Bennett Carlin, also known as "Little Lynn," Bruce Carlin, Tammie True, Breck Wall, and Joe Patterson approximately two weeks prior to November 22, 1963. He is positive he did not see these individuals on November 22, 23, or 24, 1963.

His decision to leave Dallas, Texas, on approximately November 30, 1963, was prompted by a fight which he had had with his wife and not by any actions of Ruby or by any connections which he, Pike, had had with Ruby.

He never made any long-distance telephone calls from the Carousel Club and he is positive that Ruby never made any long-distance calls from his, Pike's, phone.

He considered Ruby to be emotionally unstable because he displayed a violent temper on occasions and because of the fact that he liked to surround himself with

- 2 -

COMMISSION EXHIBIT No. 2322—Continued

clean-cut, well-dressed, "Hollywood-type" men to make himself feel important. He never knew Lee Harvey Oswald and believes that Ruby was not acquainted with Oswald.

- 3 -

COMMISSION EXHIBIT No. 2322—Continued

Commission Exhibit No. 2323

FD-302 (Rev. 3-3-59)

FEDERAL BUREAU OF INVESTIGATION

Date 11/26/63

1

ALTON CONRAD SHARPE, 1422 North Sedgewick, advised RUBY telephoned him about one week ago complaining that other clubs in Dallas were giving "amateur shows" which was against the rules of the American Guild Variety Artists (AGVA). RUBY said he was in receipt of a letter from AGVA prohibiting "amateurs" which he was forwarding for SHARPE to read. RUBY stated THOMAS S. PALMER, Branch Manager, AGVA in Dallas, would not give him a fair shake so he was calling SHARPE for his help. SHARPE told RUBY to forward the letter to Chicago and he would see what could be done.

SHARPE said he became acquainted with RUBY in Dallas during the period 1961 to 1962. At this time SHARPE represented AGVA at Dallas. SHARPE said his relationship with RUBY was a business one and he was unacquainted with RUBY's associates other than entertainers at RUBY's club.

SHARPE described RUBY as a person who became excited when a disagreement occurred. He explained that during business discussions RUBY often began to shout and pound the table during disagreements, but he "cooled" down quickly and SHARPE never saw him cause physical violence.

SHARPE said he (SHARPE) was suspended by AGVA on Thursday, November 21, 1963, when a new group took over the guild. On Saturday, November 23, 1963, SHARPE and his wife called the Dallas Office of AGVA to see if PALMER had been suspended. While SHARPE's wife was talking to PALMER's secretary, WILMA HUGHES, SHARPE remembered the letter RUBY was forwarding. SHARPE said he was afraid that if the new AGVA representative in Chicago got RUBY's letter it might cause PALMER to lose his job. With this in mind, SHARPE told his wife to leave a message with HUGHES for RUBY to "Tell JACK not to send the letter today, it would be awkward in Chicago."

SHARPE said he did not know LEE OSWALD and does not know if RUBY knew him. He is not acquainted with any other members of RUBY's family.

SHARPE said for theatrical purposes he legally changed his name from BROWN to SHARPE at Denver, Colorado.

on 11/25/63 at Chicago, Illinois File # CG 44-645 DL 44-1639

by Special Agents GEORGE C. HORNER & JACK C. HAMMACK/eah 419 Date dictated 11/25/63

This document contains neither recommendations nor conclusions of the FBI. It is the property of the FBI and is loaned to your agency; it and its contents are not to be distributed outside your agency.

COMMISSION EXHIBIT No. 2323

FD-302 (Rev. 3-3-59)

FEDERAL BUREAU OF INVESTIGATION

Date 11/28/63

1

JAMES M. CHANEY, 2728 Oats Drive, Dallas, advised he is a motorcycle patrolman on the Dallas, Texas, Police Department.

CHANEY advised he is acquainted with JACK RUBY, the owner and operator of several clubs in the Dallas area. He advised that on the day after the assassination of President KENNEDY, which would have been Saturday, November 23, 1963, he was called to return to duty shortly after noon and dispatched to the area of the assassination scene to assist in controlling the crowd of spectators.

CHANEY stated that, at approximately 3:30 PM, JACK RUBY came by the scene of the assassination on foot and stopped and talked with him. RUBY seemed to be solemn and made comments as to the tragedy of what had happened to the President. He remained about four or five minutes, then walked off in the direction of town. CHANEY advised that a few moments later RUBY pulled up to where he was standing, at which time RUBY was driving his 1960 white Oldsmobile. RUBY asked him if two men who were standing in the area several hundred feet away were not Captain FRITZ and Chief CURRY, of the Dallas Police Department. CHANEY said he looked at the men to which RUBY referred and said they were, to which RUBY replied, "Good, I just told reporters up the street that they were down here." With this RUBY drove off and he did not see RUBY again that day.

on 11/28/63 at Dallas, Texas File # DL 44-1639

by Special Agent RAYMOND M. LESTER, JR./eah 682 Date dictated 11/28/63

This document contains neither recommendations nor conclusions of the FBI. It is the property of the FBI and is loaned to your agency; it and its contents are not to be distributed outside your agency.

COMMISSION EXHIBIT No. 2324

FD-302 (Rev. 3-3-59) FEDERAL BUREAU OF INVESTIGATION

1

Date 11/25/63

THOMAS J. O'GRADY, 939 Bluewood Drive, Dallas, who is employed as a guard at the General Motors Parts Division, 10788 Harry Hines Boulevard, Dallas, furnished the following information:

He formerly worked as a patrolman for the Dallas Police Department from about 1946 to 1950. During this period, while patroling on South Ervay Street, he became acquainted with JACK RUBY, who was at that time, operating the Silver Spur on South Ervay. Mr. O'GRADY left Dallas in 1950 and did not return until about 1955. About 1956, he first ran into RUBY again at the Vegas Club. He began working for RUBY on Saturday nights at the Vegas Club as a bouncer and continued working in this capacity until about 1958 or 1959. Since 1959, he has seen RUBY only on infrequent occasions. He would occasionally go to the Carousel Club with a group of people on a party and he was always welcomed in a friendly manner by RUBY. He recalled that about two years ago, he worked for RUBY on only one night at the Carousel Club, at the time of the Oklahoma - Texas football game. He did not visit RUBY socially and did not call upon him. They had no discussions about political matters and so far as he knew, RUBY was not intently interested in political matters. He did not seem to be more than a normal admirer of President KENNEDY. There was never any indication that he was affiliated with any particular political party or group of persons interested in political activities.

O'GRADY advised he had no knowledge of trips that RUBY may have made away from Dallas, except for two trips to Chicago to visit his ailing father, and to subsequently attend his father's funeral.

O'GRADY advised to his knowledge, he had no affiliation with gambling or booking interests in Dallas or elsewhere.

He had no knowledge of the identities of persons who may have been affiliated with RUBY in the operation of various clubs in Dallas.

O'GRADY advised RUBY's closest friend appeared to be

on 11/25/63 at Dallas, Texas File # DL 44-1639

by Special Agents RALPH E. RAWLINGS & EDMOND C. HARDIN/cah Date dictated 11/25/63

ECH 685

COMMISSION EXHIBIT No. 2325

2
DL 44-1639

RALPH PAUL, who worked with RUBY in the operation of the Vegas Club.

At approximately 8:30 PM, on November 23, 1963, RUBY telephoned O'GRADY and talked to him for approximately five minutes. He did not seem unusually agitated or emotional during these conversations and at no time mentioned the name of OSWALD. He seemed to be particularly interested in two points, first, he told O'GRADY that he was closing the Carousel Club since he did not believe there should be any revelry in the City of Dallas because of the assassination of the President. He complained because some of his competitors were keeping their places of business open, and secondly, he complained about a poster on a building in Dallas, which was critical of Chief Justice WARREN. O'GRADY said that it was unusual for RUBY to call him by telephone and the only reason he believes RUBY called him was that O'GRADY came originally from Boston and is of the Catholic faith, and also, that he has always been able to exert a calming influence on RUBY when the latter became agitated. He advised that RUBY is very hot tempered and would occasionally shout at people when he became angry, however, on the occasion of his telephone call, he did not seem to be agitated and gave absolutely no indication that he intended to do physical harm to OSWALD.

Mr. O'GRADY advised that he had never seen OSWALD in person and had no information indicating a prior connection between RUBY and OSWALD.

686

COMMISSION EXHIBIT No. 2325—Continued

Commission Exhibit No. 2326

FD-302 (Rev. 1-25-60)

FEDERAL BUREAU OF INVESTIGATION

Date December 3, 1963

FRANK BERNARD JOHNSTON, photographer, United Press International, American Statesman Building, Austin, Texas, home address 3011 Whitis, Apartment 205, advised Special Agent H. T. BURK on November 30, 1963, as follows:

JOHNSTON holds press cards issued by the Austin Police Department and the Texas Department of Public Safety, Austin, Texas. He went to Dallas on November 22, 1963, and after covering an assignment to secure photographs at a rooming house where LEE HARVEY OSWALD lived, he was assigned to cover the third floor of the City Hall in Dallas on the night of November 22, 1963, where OSWALD was being questioned. No one asked him for identification and none was shown by him. He remained on this assignment until after midnight and perhaps as late as 2:00 a.m., November 23, 1963.

Those present during this time were: PETE FISCHER, United Press International photographer, New Orleans, Louisiana; FRED KAUFMAN, photographer, Associated Press, Dallas; an unknown TV cameraman and several reporters, but the names of the papers they represented are not known to JOHNSTON.

JOHNSTON does not know whether there was anyone present on the third floor other than the photographers and reporters and police since he has never worked in Dallas before and knows very few people there.

On November 23, 1963, JOHNSTON returned to the third floor of City Hall, Dallas, between 6:00 a.m. and 7:00 a.m. and relieved WILLIAM RAILEY, United Press International, Bureau Manager of Houston, Texas. During this day there were so many people in and out of the third floor it was impossible to formulate any idea of their identity as to whether they were police, reporters, or curious citizens. OSWALD's mother, wife, and brother

On 11/30/63 at Austin, Texas File # SA 44-748

by SA H. T. BURK / njs Date dictated 12/1/63

This document contains neither recommendations nor conclusions of the FBI. It is the property of the FBI and is loaned to your agency; it and its contents are not to be distributed outside your agency.

427

2.

SA 44-748

were all in and out of the third floor this day. On one occasion on November 23, 1963, OSWALD was brought out of the elevator on the third floor into an interrogation room and JOHNSTON made photographs of him as well as the above mentioned relatives. JOHNSTON cannot recall ever having spoken to JACK RUBY at any time and has never met him officially. He recalls having seen RUBY on the third floor of City Hall during the day of November 23, 1963. JOHNSTON went off duty after 11:00 p.m. on November 23, 1963, after spending all day on the third floor. About 4:30 a.m. November 24, 1963, JOHNSTON relieved PETE FISCHER in the basement of City Hall, Dallas. FISCHER had his rented car parked in the basement of City Hall at that time just opposite the hallway where OSWALD was shot. JOHNSTON recalls asking FISCHER how he happened to get his car into that location and FISCHER replied that he just drove it there and parked it.

JOHNSTON showed no identification to get into the City Hall basement but recalls introducing himself to Lieutenant WIGGINS, Booking Desk, Dallas Police Department basement and told him orally that he was a United Press International photographer. JOHNSTON recalls seeing a free-lance photographer, name not known, in the basement of City Hall that morning with a 35 milimeter Nikon-F Camera, described as 24 to 25 years of age, white male, 6' tall, dark hair, 150 to 165 pounds, and slender build. This man said he had been there all night and stood near JOHNSTON waiting for a considerable time.

Others known to have been in the City Hall basement in Dallas on November 24, 1963, are as follows:

1. MIKE SMITH, Associated Press photographer, Los Angeles, California.

2. JACK BIERS, Photographer, Dallas Morning News.

428

3. BOB JACKSON, Photographer, Dallas Times Herald.

4. A man with National Broadcasting Company who had a movie rig, name unknown.

5. Another movie cameraman who had a sound man helping him, names unknown.

6. Unknown United Press International Newsreel Cameraman from Chicago, Illinois.

7. Numerous persons thought to be newspaper reporters.

8. Lieutenant WIGGINS and his staff.

9. JACK RUBY who was not observed in the basement until about the time OSWALD was brought out and RUBY seemed to come up from behind where JOHNSTON was standing, then pushed in front of JOHNSTON as OSWALD approached.

JOHNSTON took three photographs of OSWALD: one when he was about ten feet away; one in which RUBY jumped in front of JOHNSTON and blocked his view of OSWALD; and one was made of Dallas Police Department Detective grappling with RUBY after the shooting of OSWALD.

Prior to OSWALD being brought out of the elevator in the City Hall basement, a large number of police "made a chain" along the route OSWALD would take from the elevator to a waiting car. Captain WILL FRITZ, Dallas Police Department preceded OSWALD out of the elevator with two other detectives on each side of OSWALD. Someone remarked "Here he comes." After JOHNSTON took his first photograph of OSWALD, he recalls seeing RUBY's immage in his view finder of his camera before he snapped the second photograph and he recalls RUBY remarked "You son of a bitch," then JOHNSTON saw a flash from what he supposed was a gun that sounded

427

COMMISSION EXHIBIT No. 2326—Continued

FD-302 (Rev. 3-3-59)

FEDERAL BUREAU OF IN[...] Commission Exhibit No. 2327

(1)

Date December 2, 1963

FRANCOIS PELOU, representative of the France Press News Agency, Washington, D. C., who resides at 128 Bank Street, New York, New York, was interviewed in the Statler-Hilton Hotel, Dallas, Texas. PELOU stated he arrived in Dallas at 8:30 p.m., November 22, 1963, and that same evening he saw LEE HARVEY OSWALD for the first time in the assembly room, Dallas Police Headquarters, where a conference was being held for the press. He did not interview OSWALD on that occasion.

PELOU believes he first saw JACK RUBY on Saturday afternoon, November 23, 1963, at Dallas Police Headquarters where RUBY was passing out sandwiches to members of the press. PELOU said he did not talk to RUBY on that occasion, nor did he see RUBY talk to anyone else.

PELOU related that on Sunday, November 24, 1963, he arrived at Dallas Police Headquarters at approximately 8 a.m. and shortly thereafter he went to the basement of the building to arrange a telephone line to his office in New York City. From approximately 8 a.m. until 10:30 a.m. of the same morning PELOU was either in the basement or on the first floor of the Dallas Police Headquarters. He related that at 10:30 a.m. he went to the basement of the building and remained there until approximately 11:30 a.m. when OSWALD made his appearance with Dallas Police Officers. A man who was identified as JACK RUBY immediately slipped from the crowd in the basement and shot OSWALD. PELOU said RUBY moved forward and fired the shot at OSWALD so quickly that, in his opinion, no one could possibly have prevented the incident.

PELOU advised that when he first entered the Dallas Police Headquarters on the morning of November 24, 1963, he was requested to identify himself as a member of the press and on several occasions from approximately 8 a.m. until 10:30 a.m. on that date, while inside Dallas Police Headquarters, his identification was sought by members of the Dallas Police Department. He said that while in the Dallas Police Headquarters on that date he particularly noticed extremely adequate security measures at each entrance to the building as well as within the building itself. He knew of no unauthorized person who was permitted to enter the basement, and he knew of no one permitted to enter the building, including the basement, without showing proper identification.

on 12/1/63 at Dallas, Texas File # DL 44-1639

by Special Agents JAMES E. GARRIS and R. NEIL QUIGLEY:bnm Date dictated 12/2/63

478

COMMISSION EXHIBIT No. 2327

DL 44-1639
(2)

PELOU further stated he had no knowledge of anyone conspiring with JACK RUBY and he saw no one talking with RUBY at any time. PELOU also advised he had no knowledge of any relationship or prior acquaintance between JACK RUBY and OSWALD. He added that he did not know RUBY or OSWALD and he never had the opportunity to interview either.

PELOU advised that on Monday, November 25, 1963, he and other members of the press interviewed a Mr. HOWARD, RUBY's attorney, who commented that he had just seen RUBY and RUBY had been crying and was brooding when he left him. According to PELOU, HOWARD related that RUBY's comment to the press was that he (RUBY) saw OSWALD for the first time in the assembly room at Dallas Police Headquarters on Friday night, November 22, 1963, which was the same day "he (OSWALD) killed our President."

PELOU estimated the crowd in the basement at the time OSWALD was brought out and subsequently shot by RUBY as easily fifty persons. He advised MILT SOSIN (phonetic), a Miami, Florida newspaperman; IKE PAPPAS (phonetic), a New York City Radio Station representative; and BILL or BOB NEWMAN (phonetic), a Chicago, Illinois, newspaperman, were present in the basement at the time of the shooting. He could not name any of the others present; however, he recalls that representatives of other news media were there. Also, he recalls a short, stocky Reserve Police Captain, name unknown, who was near the ramp entrance where RUBY allegedly entered, approximately 10 minutes prior to the shooting.

FD-302 (Rev. 3-3-59) EDERAL BUREAU (Commission Exhibit No. 2328

1

Date 12/4/63

FRANK GOLDSTEIN, who describes himself as a professional gambler, residing at 640 Teresita Boulevard, San Francisco, California, with his wife, MARY, was interviewed December 4, 1963, at San Francisco by SAs WILLIAM N. KIDWELL, JR., and EDWARD C. SERNETT. GOLDSTEIN stated that he was acquainted with JACK RUBY as JACK RUBENSTEIN or by the nickname SPARKY, having met him in San Francisco in approximately 1933. He stated that he, GOLDSTEIN, was at that time operating a subscription crew for the San Francisco "Call Bulletin," a daily newspaper, and he employed RUBY and his sister, EVA GRANT, in this work from approximately 1933 until 1938 or 1939. He advised that RUBY and EVA both engaged in door-to-door sales of subscriptions to the aforementioned newspaper. EVA may also have done telephone soliciting work for the newspaper. GOLDSTEIN recalled that EVA GRANT and RUBY, together with EVA's son, RONNIE, lived in an apartment located between Eddy and Ellis Streets on Jones Street in San Francisco. He recalled that EVA married FRANK GRANT in San Francisco, whom she later divorced. He stated he believes FRANK GRANT is now somewhere in the Los Angeles, California, area. He has not, however, seen this person for many years. GOLDSTEIN advised that during the period mentioned above he and RUBY were able to make a good living considering the fact that they were so employed during the depression years. He remembers RUBY as a quiet, well-mannered young man. He stated he was honest and completely trustworthy. He was a soft-spoken individual, extremely conscious of his appearance and dress. GOLDSTEIN believes RUBY left San Francisco in late 1939 or early 1940. GOLDSTEIN states he does not know of any other employment RUBY had in San Francisco other than selling newspaper subscriptions.

He was aware that RUBY was in the night club business in Dallas, as EVA GRANT visited with GOLDSTEIN and his wife in San Francisco approximately three years ago. This was a social call, as apparently EVA had not been in San Francisco for many years.

Approximately four weeks ago, during the first part of November, 1963, RUBY telephoned GOLDSTEIN at GOLDSTEIN's unlisted home telephone number JU 7-7674. RUBY could have

on 12/4/63 at San Francisco, California File # SF 44-494 / DL 44-1639
by Special Agent s WILLIAM N. KIDWELL, JR. & EDWARD C. SERNETT:rap/csh Date dictated 12/4/63

SF 44-494
DL 44-1639

obtained this number from EVA GRANT, as she was aware of the number, having visited in the GOLDSTEIN home. GOLDSTEIN stated he had not heard from RUBY for over twenty years until the occasion of this telephone call. He was surprised to hear from him and after a short inconsequential conversation asked GOLDSTEIN if he knew anyone in the "AGVA", which GOLDSTEIN concluded was in reference to the American Guild of Variety Artists. RUBY made some reference to the fact that he was having trouble with this organization in Dallas and he asked GOLDSTEIN if he would get in touch with a man named IRVING MAZZIO or MAZZI, who was reportedly AGVA representative somewhere in Los Angeles. RUBY stated the difficulties he was experiencing involved the Carousel Club in Dallas and he made some reference to a Dallas newspaperman, first name DON, not further described. He furnished GOLDSTEIN with his home telephone number WH 1-5701 and his night club telephone number RI 7-2362. GOLDSTEIN told RUBY that while he knew a lot of people, he doubted that he could help him in connection with this problem. They spoke for a moment or two longer and then ended the call.

GOLDSTEIN advised he has taken no action on this basis of this call because he frankly did not understand what RUBY was requesting of him. He advised that he invited RUBY to visit him should he come to San Francisco.

GOLDSTEIN stated that he recognized RUBY on national television following the murder of LEE HARVEY OSWALD in Dallas. He advised that he cannot understand why RUBY killed OSWALD. He remembers RUBY as a patriotic citizen, who has no radical tendencies. He stated he never has known RUBY to engage in any association with any hoodlum or underworld element. He stated he does not remember RUBY as an individual who would do anything against the best interests of the United States.

269

COMMISSION EXHIBIT No. 2328—Continued

Commission Exhibit No. 2329

FD-302 (Rev. 3-3-59)

FEDERAL BUREAU OF INVESTIGATION

1

Date 12/23/63

ROBERT LARKIN, 500 North Harwood Street, Dallas, Texas, volunteered the following information:

Mr. LARKIN advised he is presently manager of the Mont Martre Club at 206 Browder Street, Dallas, and formerly managed the Colony Club located next door to the Vegas Club, operated by JACK RUBY and his sister, EVA GRANT. He stated that by virtue of his occupation he has known JACK RUBY during the past eight years and has seen him at more or less regular intervals at one of the other of their clubs. Occasionally, he would find himself in the same party with RUBY and, on each occasion, he would usually chat with RUBY for some time.

He stated that about five years ago, possibly four, he managed RUBY's Vegas Club during the three summer months, during which period RUBY vacationed in Cuba.

LARKIN stated he last saw RUBY at about 5:50 PM, on November 23, 1963, when he met him at the corner of Browder and Commerce Streets, where they were both walking in opposite directions. RUBY was going west on Commerce. They stopped and chatted on the street for five or ten minutes and the first part of the conversation concerned the assassination of President KENNEDY in a general way. He does not recall that the name of LEE HARVEY OSWALD was mentioned by either. He recalls that RUBY merely stated he felt the assassination was a terrible tragedy. RUBY said nothing to indicate he was under an unusual mental or nervous stress or that he contemplated doing anything about it. The conversation changed to their personal affairs when RUBY asked him why he did not go into partnership with him in the Carousel Club.

LARKIN stated he does not recall discussing politics with RUBY at any time. He continued he considered RUBY to be a man of extreme emotions and one who was quick to become angry. He stated that if RUBY became angry with

on 12/20/63 at Dallas, Texas File # DL 44-1639

by Special Agent EDMOND C. HARDIN/eah Date dictated 12/20/63

202-

COMMISSION EXHIBIT No. 2329

DL 44-1639

2

a customer for any reason, such as obscene language, he would immediately grab the individual and shove him out of the club and occasionally would strike the individual without first trying to reason with him.

LARKIN stated that by the very nature of his business RUBY made it a point to be friendly with police officers, and a number of officers knew him and dropped by his establishment from time to time. He recalls that one Lieutenant JAMES GILMORE, of the Dallas Police Department Vice Squad, was particularly friendly with RUBY. GILMORE was occasionally accompanied by his partner on his rounds when he would stop by to visit JACK's place and often would view the show. LARKIN added that he has no information which would indicate RUBY ever did any unusual favors for police officers, in order to get them obligated to him and he does not recall ever hearing that RUBY would throw parties for police officers at his place or elsewhere, or ever picked up the tab for any sort of social entertainment for police officers.

LARKIN advised he did not know LEE HARVEY OSWALD and never had any reason to suspect that there ever existed a relationship or acquaintance between OSWALD and RUBY. He added he has no information concerning the shooting of OSWALD by RUBY, or how RUBY may have gained entrance to the basement of the Dallas Police Department prior to the shooting.

COMMISSION EXHIBIT NO. 2329—Continued

Commission Exhibit No. 2330

FD-302 (Rev. 3-3-59)

FEDERAL BUREAU OF [redacted]

1

Date 1/14/64

Mr. DOYLE STOKES, 213 South Ewing, who was reported to have seen RUBY on Sunday morning, November 24, 1963, furnished the following information:

Mr. STOKES advised he is employed by the Veterans Administration Hospital where he is in charge of the Morgue. He works five days a week, Monday through Friday, and weekends when emergencies arise. Mr. STOKES last saw JACK RUBY on Saturday afternoon, November 23, 1963, sometime between 1:00 and 1:30 PM, as RUBY drove his automobile out of the driveway which runs along side of the STOKES' residence. He knows definitely it was Saturday afternoon because he was called back to the hospital to work and after he received his call to go back to work, he telephoned Mrs. STOKES to tell her that he had to work. Mr. STOKES did not see JACK RUBY on Sunday morning November 24, 1963.

Mr. STOKES has known JACK RUBY for three or four months having met him in the neighborhood when RUBY was walking his dogs. Mr. STOKES knows nothing concerning RUBY's personal life or political beliefs. He stated he knows of no connection between RUBY and LEE HARVEY OSWALD.

on 1/11/64 at Dallas, Texas File # DL 44-1639

by Special Agent JOSEPH G. PEGGS - gj Date dictated 1/14/64

168

FD-302 (Rev. 1-25-60) FEDERAL BUREAU OF INVESTIG...ON

Date 1/6/64

1

BARNEY BAKER is a former organizer for the Central States Conference of the International Brotherhood of Teamsters Union and was a reported muscle and bagman for Teamster President JAMES RIDDLE HOFFA.

BARNEY BAKER was interviewed at his residence, 5900 Sheridan Road, Apartment 5E. He advised that he was released from Sandstone Penitentiary June 7, 1963, and is presently employed as field representative for the Chicago Loop Auto Refinishing Company, Incorporated, paint factory, 3216 South Shields Avenue, Chicago.

BAKER advised that on November 11, 1963, his wife CAROLINE called him at his office and told him that he had just received a long distance telephone call from Dallas, Texas, at his home phone of RA 8-4031. His wife stated that it was requested that he return the call and ask for LOU. BAKER advised that he cannot recall the telephone number that he called in Texas, but stated he did return the call the same day from his office telephone which is Chicago number 225-0560. He stated that upon completion of the call to the Dallas number he told the person who answered that he was BARNEY BAKER and that he was returning a call to someone at that number. He stated that the person on the other end of the line said "That's me. My name is (BAKER could not recall the first name) RUBY." This person then told BAKER "You don't know me but we have mutual friends." BAKER said he asked who the mutual friends were but RUBY simply said "We got friends but I don't want to talk over the phone." According to BAKER, RUBY then related that he was in the burlesque and strip show business in Dallas and that competitors were "attempting to knock me out." He advised that he needed a favor and BAKER asked what the favor was. RUBY related that he had several strip shows operating in the Dallas area and said that the American Guild of Variety Artists (AGVA) "are giving me a headache." He told BAKER that competitors through the help of the AGVA were "giving me a fit." BAKER stated that RUBY suggested that "mutual friends" had advised that BAKER was familiar with unions

On 1/3/64 at Chicago, Illinois File # 44-645

by SAs JOHN R. BASSETT & WILLIAM F. HOOD, JR./sbw Date dictated 1/3/64

172

This document contains neither recommendations nor conclusions of the FBI. It is the property of the FBI and is loaned to your agency; it and its contents are not to be distributed outside your agency.

COMMISSION EXHIBIT No. 2331

2
CG 44-645

and handling matters such as this and requested that BAKER contact the AGVA and "straighten them out."

BAKER advised that he had not known JACK RUBY prior to the call but RUBY spoke in a fast and erratic manner making it rather difficult to understand him. BAKER stated that he advised RUBY that he had been released from prison in June, 1963, and that part of the provisions of his five years probation were that he should not engage in any labor management relations activities during the probation period. BAKER recalled that RUBY attempted to persuade him to intercede with the AGVA for him but BAKER concluded the conversation by firmly declining to offer any assistance in the matter.

BAKER advised that as a result of his former capacity as union organizer, he had many friends some of whom were influential politicians and high ranking hoodlums. He stated, however, that he forgot about the conversation with RUBY and did not attempt to determine who the "mutual friends" were who had referred RUBY to him at that time. He stated, however, that after the assassination of President JOHN F. KENNEDY and the subsequent murder of LEE HARVEY OSWALD by JACK RUBY, he made inquiry of numerous persons in an attempt to determine who referred RUBY to him. He stated the results of the inquiry were negative and he still has no idea as to the identity of the individual who suggested that RUBY contact him at Chicago.

173

COMMISSION EXHIBIT No. 2331—Continued

FD-302 (Rev. 1-25-60) FEDERAL BUREAU

Commission Exhibit No. 2332

Date 3/13/64

1

The records of the Illinois Bell Telephone Company show telephone number RA 84031 is listed to ROBERT BAKER, 5900 North Sheridan, Apartment 5-E. This telephone was established on July 12, 1963, and wascontinuously assigned to Mr. BAKER during the period September through november, 1963.

The following are toll charges made to telephone number RA 84031 during the period September 26, 1963, through November 22, 1963:

75

On 3/12/64 at Chicago, Illinois File # CG 44-645

by Special Agent JERRY H. BREIDENFELD/fef/phk Date dictated 3/13/64

COMMISSION EXHIBIT No. 2332

2.

CG 44-645

Date	Place Called	Telephone Number	Charges	Time	Additional Information
9/29	St. Louis, Missouri	PA 13794	$3.50	17"	Station call at 9:58 p.m.
10/3	Harlan, Iowa	SK 51248	1.10	4"	Station call made from number 728-4031 at 6:05 p.m.
10/5	St. Louis, Missouri	PA 13794	3.95	17"	Person call to Stanley Rosen-bloom from Baker made at number 728-4031 at 8:19 p.m.
10/7	Hicksville, New York	WE 13178	5.50	15"	Person call to Pat Mc Gee, 63 Raymond Street, made from number 728-4031 at 6:48 p.m.

76

COMMISSION EXHIBIT No. 2332—Continued

3

CG 44-645

Date	Place Called	Telephone Number	Charges	Time	Additional Information
10/9	Los Angeles, California	OL 57980	$6.06	10"	Person call to Mrs. Rule - Secretary, from Barney Baker, from number 728-4031 at 3:03 p.m.
10/27	Harlan, Iowa	SK 51248	1.85	9"	Station call at 10:13 p.m.
10/29	Brooklyn, New York	ES 78554	4.45	14"	Station at 6:11 p.m.
11/3	Sullivan, Illinois	6224	.55	1"	Station call at 4:54 p.m.
11/13	St. Louis, Missouri	GA 15356	2.10	6"	Person call to Stanley Rosenbloom from Barney Baker made from number 728-4031 at 4:23 p.m.

77

COMMISSION EXHIBIT No. 2332—Continued

4

CG 44-645

Date	Place Called	Telephone Number	Charges	Time	Additional Information
11/17	Harlan, Iowa	SK 51248	$2.35	9"	Station 7:39 p.m.
11/18	Denver, Colorado	333-8193	1.55	1"	Station cal 5:00 p.m.
11/19	Denver, Colorado	333-8193	3.00	9"	Station 7:45 p.m.
11/21	Miami, Florida	JE 83255	2.25	3"	Person call to Dave 6:17 p.m.

78

COMMISSION EXHIBIT No. 2332—Continued

5.

CG 44-645

The above information should not be made public without the issuance of a subpoena duces tecum to an appropriate official of the Illinois Bell Telephone Company, Chicago, Illinois.

79

COMMISSION EXHIBIT No. 2332—Continued

1

DL 44-1639
MCC/cms

Investigation has established subscribers to telephones called on dates indicated from RA 8-4031, listed to ROBERT BAKER, 5900 North Sheridan, Apartment 5E, Chicago, Illinois, were as follows:

Telephone No.	Subscribers
PA 1-3794, St. Louis, Missouri	STANLEY ROSENBLUM, Attorney, 901 Gay, St. Louis
SK 5-1248, Harlan, Iowa	JAKE MORE, 1209 13th Street, Harlan
WE 1-3178, Hicksville, New York	PATRICK E. MC GEE, 63 Raymond Street, Hicksville
OL 5-7980, Los Angeles, Calif.	EARL SCHEIB, Auto Painting, Exec. Office, 8737 Wilshire, Beverly Hills
ES 7-8554, Brooklyn, New York	ROSE BAKER, 1947 Ocean, Apartment A12, Brooklyn
6224, Sullivan, Illinois	IVAN V. SCHRODT, 109 East Blackwood, Sullivan
GA 1-5356, St. Louis, Missouri	STANLEY ROSENBLUM, Attorney, 818 Olive, St. Louis
333-8193, Denver, Colorado	SONNY LISTON, 3395 Monico Parkway, Denver
JE 8-3255, Miami, Florida	DAVID YARAS, 4410 Adams Avenue, Miami Beach, Florida

80

COMMISSION EXHIBIT No. 2332—Continued

FD-302 (Rev. 1-25-60)

FEDERAL BUREAU OF

Date 3/10/64

The records of the Pacific Telephone and Telegraph Company, 74 New Montgomery Street, San Francisco, list telephone number JU 7-7674 to FRANK GOLDSTEIN, 640 Teresita Boulevard, San Francisco. The account record for this number does not list toll charges for a long distance call from Dallas, Texas to San Francisco or from San Francisco to Dallas during the period September 26, 1963 to November 22, 1963.

The following toll charges appear in the company account for telephone number JU 7-7674 during the aforementioned period:

9/27/63	Call to Santa Monica, Calif., EX 9-3980, made from San Francisco MO 1-1184 and charged to JU 7-7674; charges $1.25.
9/28/63	Call to Santa Monica, EX 9-3980; charges $1.05.
10/1/63	Collect call from Santa Monica EX 9-3980 to JU 7-7674; charges $.80.
10/10/63	Collect call from Santa Monica 399-3980; charges $1.40, 4 minutes, station night call.
10/20/63	Collect call from Santa Monica 399-3980; charges $1.05, 3 minutes, station night call.
10/20/63	Call to Santa Monica 399-3980; charges $1.05, 3 minutes, station night call.
10/20/63	Call to Santa Monica 213-EX 9-3980 at 1703.
10/20/63	Call to Santa Monica 213-EX 9-3980; charges $1.05, 3 minutes at 1644.
10/21/63	Call to Santa Monica EX 9-3980; charges $1.25, day call, 3 minutes at 0745.
10/22/63	Collect from Santa Monica 394- for 3 minutes; charges $1.25, station day call.
10/22/63	Collect call from Beverly Hills 657-9248; charges $1.25 for 3 minutes, day station call.
10/22/63	Call to Santa Monica EX 3-0148; charges $2.25, 3 minutes, person day call.
10/22/63	Call to Santa Monica EX 9-3980; charges $1.25, 3 minutes, station day call.
10/24/63	Collect call from Santa Monica 399-3980; charges $1.80, 7 minutes.

140

On 3/10/64 at San Francisco, Calif. File # SF 44-494

by SA WILLIAM N. KIDWELL, JR. :ab/mal Date dictated 3/10/64

COMMISSION EXHIBIT No. 2333

2

SF 44-494
WNK:ab/mal

10/24/63	Call to Santa Monica 213-399-3980; night call, 1 minute, $1.05 at 1929.
11/7/63	Call to Brooklyn, N.Y., BE 2-4731; 4 minutes $1.25, late evening.
11/9/63	Call to Santa Monica, EX 9-3980; 2 minutes $1.05, 7:33 p.m.
11/13/63	Call to Santa Monica EX 9-3980; 1 minute, $.80, late evening.
11/18/63	Call to Los Angeles OL 6-0846; 1 minute, $1.05, 7:49 p.m.
11/19/63	Call to Los Angeles CL 6-0846; 1 minute, $1.25, 9:06 a.m.
11/19/63	Call to Los Angeles OL 6-0846; 1 minute, $1.25, 7:05 a.m.
11/19/63	Call to Santa Monica EX 6-0841; 2 minutes, $1.25, 6:58 a.m.
11/22/63	Call to Salt Lake City EM 4-4062; 13 minutes, $2.65, 9:31 p.m.

Should testimony be desired regarding the above records, a subpoena duces tecum should be directed to DOUGLAS R. HAYDEN, Chief Special Agent, Pacific Telephone and Telegraph Company, 74 New Montgomery Street, Room 300, San Francisco, California.

DL 44-1639
MCC/wvm

Investigation has established that the persons listed below were subscribers to the telephone numbers indicated as of the dates of telephone calls to such numbers from JU 7-7674, FRANK GOLDSTEIN, 640 Teresita Boulevard, San Francisco, California:

EX 9-3980,	Santa Monica, California - MORRIS GOLDSTEIN, 40 Sunset Avenue, Venice, California
657-9248,	Beverly Hills, California - Public telephone, Mount Sinai Hospital, 873 Beverly Boulevard, Beverly Hills, California
EX 3-0148,	Santa Monica, California - CHARLES F. ROW, physician, 1137 Second Street, Santa Monica, California
BE 2-4731,	ANTHONY RODIS, 1866- 58th Street, Brooklyn, New York
OL 6-0846,	Los Angeles, California - THEODORE SCHOENFELD, 1016 North Edinburgh, Apartment 6, Los Angeles, California
EX 6-0841,	LILLY R. LYNCH, 31 Avenue 20 - 6, Venice, California
EM 4-4062,	EVA B. SERGAKIS, 345 S. Second West, Salt Lake City, Utah

Commission Exhibit No. 2334

UNITED STATES DEPARTMENT OF JUSTICE

FEDERAL BUREAU OF INVESTIGATION

In Reply, Please Refer to File No.

Dallas, Texas

June 10, 1964

JACK L. RUBY;
LEE HARVEY OSWALD (Deceased)

The investigation reported herein was based on a request from the President's Commission on the Assassination of President KENNEDY in a letter dated June 4, 1964, that HUBY REEVES, Nichols Garage, Dallas, Texas, be reinterviewed and a receipt executed by Little Lynn on November 23, 1963, for $5.00 advanced to her by REEVES on behalf of JACK L. RUBY be exhibited to him, in order to clarify the time Little Lynn and, in turn, RUBY were in the garage on the night of November 23, 1963.

In interview by a Special Agent of the Federal Bureau of Investigation on December 17, 1963, HUEY REEVES, who identified himself as night manager of Nichols Garage, Commerce Street, Dallas, stated Little Lynn had appeared at the garage at approximately 7:30 PM, November 23, 1963, had made a telephone call, and that shortly thereafter, REEVES received a telephone call from RUBY asking REEVES to advance $5.00 to Little Lynn and get a receipt, that he, RUBY, would be at the garage later that evening to repay the $5.00 loan. REEVES stated RUBY appeared approximately thirty to forty-five minutes later and repaid REEVES.

On June 8, 1964, HERMAN HILL, Property Room, Dallas, Texas, Police Department, furnished reproduced copies of an item taken from the possessions of RUBY following his arrest on November 24, 1963. The item is in the nature of a receipt made in longhand on a piece of paper from a scratch pad of Republic Carloading and reads, "For JACK RUBY $5.00 Received By Little Lynn." A date-stamp impression, "1963 Nov 23 PM 10 33," appears on the receipt.

The results of interview with HUEY REEVES, 2903 Reynolds, Dallas, Texas, on June 8 & 9, 1964, with a copy of an affidavit executed by REEVES in the office of the United States Attorney, Dallas, on June 9, 1964, are attached.

COMMISSION EXHIBIT No. 2334

FD-302 (Rev. 3-3-59)

FEDERAL BUREAU OF INVESTIGATION

Date 6/9/64

Mr. HUEY REEVES, 2903 Reynolds, telephone TA 4-8428, was interviewed at his residence in order to clarify the time that $5.00 was given to LITTLE LYNN by a Nichols Garage employee.

At the outset of the interview, REEVES was asked to recall his meeting with JACK RUBY on the evening of November 23, 1963. REEVES was unable to recall the exact time that LITTLE LYNN entered the Nichols Garage where he was then employed as the Night Manager.

In an effort to pinpoint the time, he refreshed his memory by reading a typed copy of his previous interview by an Agent of the Federal Bureau of Investigation. REEVES, at this point, said LITTLE LYNN could have come into the garage at 7:30 or 10:30 p.m. He was not paying any attention to the clock when she entered the garage on November 23, 1963, and he could not recall the exact time. He said when he told the other Agent of the Federal Bureau of Investigation it was 7:30 p.m., he was just guessing. He further stated after viewing the receipt described as follows: "For Jack Ruby $5.00 Received by Little Lynn" which was date stamped "1963 Nov 23 PM 10 33" that she must have entered the garage at about that time and RUBY arrived at the garage about 20 to 30 minutes later. He advised he made a mistake in the time and wished to change this statement and made the following affidavit on June 9, 1964, in the office of the United States Attorney, Dallas, Texas.

on 6/8/64 and 6/9/64 at Dallas, Texas File # DL 44-1639

by Special Agent EDWARD DENNIS KENNEY:vm Date dictated 6/9/64

2

This document contains neither recommendations nor conclusions of the FBI. It is the property of the FBI and is loaned to your agency; it and its contents are not to be distributed outside your agency.

COMMISSION EXHIBIT No. 2334—Continued

A F F I D A V I T

I, Huey Reeves, 2903 Reynolds, formerly employed as Night Manager for Nichols Garage, Commerce Street, Dallas, Texas, after being duly sworn, depose as follows:

On Saturday evening, November 23, 1963, I recall an employee of Jack Ruby's Carousel Club, Little Lynn, entering the Nichols Garage where I was then the Night Manager. She made a telephone call. I am unable to recall the exact time this occurred because I was not paying attention to the time when she came in. I recall being interviewed on a former occasion by another Agent of the Federal Bureau of Investigation and advising him that Little Lynn entered the garage at approximately 7:30 p.m. When I said this, I was guessing. She could have come in at 10:30 p.m.

A minute or two after she used the telephone, Jack Ruby telephoned and asked me to give $5.00 to Little Lynn and to get a receipt. After the telephone call, I gave Little Lynn the money and wrote the following receipt on a piece of paper which I took off of a Republic Carloading scratch pad: "For Jack Ruby $5.00 received by" and signed "Little Lynn." I am pretty sure that I date stamped

3

this receipt immediately after I wrote it. Little Lynn left the garage after she received the money.

I think Ruby arrived at the garage approximately 20 to 30 minutes later. This would have been about 10:50 p.m. or 11:00 p.m. Jack Ruby stayed at the garage for about 10 or 15 minutes and then he left.

I have viewed a photostatic copy of the receipt described as follows: "For Jack Ruby $5.00 Received by Little Lynn." I can identify the handwriting "For Jack Ruby $5.00 Received by" as my handwriting.

At this time I would like to change my previous statement wherein I stated that Little Lynn appeared at the garage at about 7:30 p.m. and Ruby arrived approximately 30 to 45 minutes later because it is my belief that I date stamped the receipt at the time I made it out. I would like to state that I made this receipt out at about 10:33 p.m. and Ruby arrived at the garage 20 to 30 minutes later.

/s/ HUEY REEVES

Sworn to and subscribed before me this 6th day of June, 1964.

/s/ [illegible]   /s/ [illegible]
Asst. U. S. Attorney (Witness)   Notary Public
/s/ S/A EDWARD [illegible] 6/6/64.

4

FD-204 (Rev. 3-3-59)

UNITED STATES DEPARTMENT OF JUSTICE
FEDERAL BUREAU OF INVESTIGATION

Copy to:

Report of:	SA EDWIN DALRYMPLE	Office:	HOUSTON
Date:	December 4, 1963		
Field Office File #:	Houston file 105-1291	Bureau File #:	62-109060
Title:	LEE HARVEY OSWALD		

Character: INTERNAL SECURITY - R

Synopsis: Subject's address book reported to contain name of HORACE TWIFORD with Houston address and telephone number. Subject reportedly informed his wife on 9/23/63 he might proceed to Houston, Texas from New Orleans. HORACE TWIFORD identified as merchant seaman who left Houston on 10/10/63 for South America and will return approximately 12/14/63. Mrs. ESTELLE TWIFORD and attorney KENYON HOUCHINS interviewed on 12/2/63. They stated Mr. and Mrs. TWIFORD distributed literature for Socialist Labor Party (SLP). Mrs. TWIFORD exhibited envelope apparently used by OSWALD in corresponding with SLP at New York. HORACE TWIFORD reportedly mailed OSWALD literature at Dallas in September, 1963 after this envelope was sent to him by SLP. Mrs. TWIFORD reported she received telephone call from man identifying himself as OSWALD on date she believed to be in late October, 1963. OSWALD informed her he was flying to Mexico and desired to speak to HORACE TWIFORD. Mrs. TWIFORD has never seen OSWALD and feels certain HORACE TWIFORD not acquainted with OSWALD. H. WARNER KLOEPELER, whose name also in possession of OSWALD, not identified in area of Houston, Texas.

-P-1

COMMISSION EXHIBIT No. 2335

HO 105-1291

PREDICATION

On December 2, 1963 the Dallas Office of the FBI reported the following data had been recorded in the address book of LEE HARVEY OSWALD:

HORACE TWIFORD
7018 Schley
MI 9-3500
WA 3-5492.

H. WARNER KLOEPELER
UN 6-3089
UN 6-2741, Extension 276.

The Dallas Office further advised that information had been received that OSWALD's wife and Mrs. RUTH PAINE had last seen OSWALD in New Orleans, Louisiana on 9/23/63 at which time he indicated he had a friend in Houston, Texas and might proceed either to Houston or to Philadelphia, Pennsylvania. When OSWALD next contacted his wife and Mrs. PAINE at Irving, Texas on October 4, 1963 he reportedly claimed he had been in Houston, Texas looking for a job.

RESULTS OF INVESTIGATION

RE: HORACE ELROY TWIFORD

On December 2, 1963 Mrs. DAISY BROWN, Credit Bureau of Greater Houston advised her agency had maintained a record since June, 1956 pertaining to HORACE ELROY TWIFORD. This record was last revised in September, 1962 at which time TWIFORD was reported to be 39 years of age and residing at 7018 Schley, Houston, Texas with his wife ESTELLE TWIFORD. His employment was listed as second mate with Local #20 of the International Organization of Masters, Mates and Pilots. TWIFORD was reported to have been so employed for 10 or 12 years at a salary of approximately $9,000 per year. He had previously resided at 7823 Dixie Drive, Houston, Texas, at several other Houston addresses, and prior to 1956 at Manteo, North Carolina. Mrs. BROWN stated TWIFORD had a good credit record at Houston.

2

COMMISSION EXHIBIT No. 2335—Continued

This file also contained a credit report dated June 27, 1956 from Elizabeth City, North Carolina indicating TWIFORD had recently moved to 4315 West Alabama Street, Apartment 5, Houston, Texas but had previously resided for several years at Manteo, North Carolina. TWIFORD was reported to have been single in 1956, had been a seaman since World War II and he was well regarded at Manteo, North Carolina.

On December 2, 1963 Detective D. D. COLLINS, Intelligence Unit, Houston, Texas Police Department advised he had checked the arrest records of that department on that date and had found no record indicating that HORACE TWIFORD had ever been arrested in Houston, Texas. COLLINS stated HORACE TWIFORD had become known to the Houston, Texas Police Department inasmuch as he had been publicly identified in 1962 as the head of a committee appointed by the American Civil Liberties Union (ACLU) at Houston which was referred to as the "Due Process Committee." COLLINS stated that this committee was reportedly formed to look into allegations of police brutality at Houston and another member of this committee was attorney KENYON HOUCHINS. COLLINS stated this committee actually never functioned beyond writing a few letters in the Houston area. COLLINS stated several people with whom he talked considered TWIFORD to be rather immature inasmuch as he frequently wore a goatee and impressed people as being of college age.

On December 2, 1963 Mrs. ESTELLE TWIFORD, 7018 Schley Street was interviewed by SAS JAMES W. RUSSELL and EDWIN DALRYMPLE. Mrs. TWIFORD stated her husband, HORACE TWIFORD, was the second mate on the "SS Del Monte" operated by the Delta Lines, Inc. She stated this vessel left Houston in late October for a trip to South America and was scheduled to return to Houston on December 14, 1963.

Mrs. TWIFORD first stated that she had never heard of LEE HARVEY OSWALD except for newspaper reports she had read since the assassination of President KENNEDY. She stated she had never seen OSWALD and felt sure her husband was not acquainted with him. Mrs. TWIFORD acknowledged that she and her husband distributed various types of literature including literature of the Socialist Labor Party in which

they were active. She acknowledged that her husband had records of people to whom he had mailed such literature but she initially refused to consult these records or to furnish any information from them.

Mrs. TWIFORD then acknowledged that she did have other information about OSWALD but declined to discuss the matter until she had telephoned attorney KENYON HOUCHINS. HOUCHINS arrived at the TWIFORD residence within a few minutes, stated that he was thoroughly familiar with the matter and instructed Mrs. TWIFORD to cooperate completely.

Mrs. TWIFORD then stated that she and her husband were among the few members of the Socialist Labor Party in Texas and the headquarters of this organization at New York, New York frequently furnished them the names of any persons in the Texas area who made inquiry about the organization. She recalled her husband had received OSWALD's name in this manner and had mailed him literature of the Socialist Labor Party to a post office address in Dallas, Texas.

Mrs. TWIFORD related that at some time which she believed to be in late October or early November she answered a telephone call and the man making this call identified himself as LEE OSWALD. OSWALD asked for her husband and stated he had received a copy of the "Weekly People" and wanted to know how HORACE TWIFORD had obtained his name. Mrs. TWIFORD explained that the "Weekly People" is a newspaper published by the Socialist Labor Party. Mrs. TWIFORD stated her best recollection was that OSWALD stated on that occasion that he was flying to Mexico, had a few hours, and desired to talk with Mr. TWIFORD. She believes OSWALD identified himself as a member of the Fair Play for Cuba Committee but stated neither she nor her husband was a member of that organization and to the best of her knowledge the Fair Play for Cuba Committee had never been active in the Houston area. A characterization of the Fair Play for Cuba Committee is set forth in the appendix of this report.

Mrs. TWIFORD stated she informed OSWALD that her husband was then at sea but if he desired to correspond with Mr. TWIFORD he could direct a letter to 7018 Schley, Houston, Texas.

Mrs. TWIFORD attempted to recall more specifically the date of this telephone call by relating it to some other event and finally stated she still believed it had been received in late October or early November, 1963. She was sure that it came a few days before HORACE TWIFORD left Houston for his current trip to South America. She states her husband had left Houston on the "SS Del Monte" and had proceeded to Louisiana, back to Freeport and Corpus Christi, Texas and back to Houston, Texas where it remained a very short time before leaving Houston for South America. Mrs. TWIFORD recalled that the telephone call from OSWALD was received while her husband was on this coast wise trip because she told her husband of this telephone call during the few hours he had at home before leaving for South America. She said that when she told HORACE TWIFORD that OSWALD had called her husband did not show any particular reaction at all and it appeared to her that the name OSWALD did not mean anything to him. Mrs. TWIFORD stated that she had in fact recalled this incident only since the publicity about the assassination. She stated it should be possible to check records of the Delta Lines, Inc. to determine the approximate date of this telephone call by relating it to the coast wise trip made by this vessel. Mrs. TWIFORD stated OSWALD made no mention of looking for a job in Houston and did not specifically say he was in Houston and she assumed it was a local telephone call because no telephone operator was involved and because of the remark of OSWALD to the effect that he only had a few hours and desired to talk with her husband. She stated she actually had no information concerning OSWALD's exact whereabouts when this call was made.

Mrs. TWIFORD further stated that except for the above incident she had never had any contact whatever with OSWALD, has never seen him, and to the best of her knowledge HORACE TWIFORD has never had any personal contacts with OSWALD at any time. Mrs. TWIFORD also stated that she has never known JACK RUBY and that she could furnish no information whatever concerning the persons involved in the assassination of President KENNEDY, the later murder of OSWALD or the possible motives involved.

Mrs. TWIFORD then obtained from her records a small manilla envelope printed and bearing the address of the New

York Labor News Company, 61 Cliff Street, New York 38, New York, P. O. Box 76. She identified this as the envelope which had been mailed to her husband by the Socialist Labor Party. It was noted the upper left corner of this envelope carried the return address, in hand printing as follows:

"L. H. Oswald
Box 2915
Dallas, Texas.

The above envelope was originally post marked at Dallas, Texas on November 10, 1962 and a rubber stamp impression indicated it was received at New York, New York on November 13, 1962. There was no indication of the date on which this envelope had been mailed to HORACE TWIFORD. A handwritten note across the front of this envelope contained the words "Labor Day issue WP, 9/11/63." Mrs. TWIFORD stated this was the handwriting of her husband and this note indicated to her her husband had mailed to OSWALD on September 11, 1963 the above issue of the "Weekly People". Mrs. TWIFORD stated she would retain this envelope permanently.

Attorney KENYON HOUCHINS, 1207 Welch Street was also interviewed on the above occasion at the residence of Mrs. TWIFORD. HOUCHINS stated he was likewise active in the Socialist Labor Party and noted that there were actually only 5 or 6 members of this organization in the entire State of Texas. HOUCHINS explained it was fairly common when the New York headquarters of this organization received an inquiry from anyone in Texas for that organization to advise HORACE TWIFORD just in case TWIFORD might have an opportunity to make a personal contact. HOUCHINS stated he did not know of the receipt of the above telephone call by Mrs. TWIFORD until a few days after the assassination of President KENNEDY at which time he had discussed the matter thoroughly with Mrs. TWIFORD. HOUCHINS stated he also at that time telephoned DAN RATHER, a member of the NBC news staff to inform RATHER on a confidential basis of the receipt of this telephone call. HOUCHINS stated he had not reported this matter to the FBI or any other law enforcement agency. HOUCHINS stated he had discussed with TWIFORD various individuals in Texas who had shown an interest in the Socialist Labor Party but to the best of his knowledge HORACE TWIFORD had never known LEE HARVEY OSWALD. HOUCHINS volunteered the following comments as being of possible value in this investigation:

HOUCHINS recalled that TWIFORD once told him he had received correspondence from someone in Arlington, Texas requesting information concerning the program of the Socialist Labor Party. TWIFORD informed HOUCHINS he had written that person but no names were mentioned. HOUCHINS stated he mentioned this incident only because he believed he had read that LEE OSWALD had a brother or some relative residing in the area of Arlington, Texas between Dallas and Fort Worth In connection with this incident HOUCHINS located a notation dated May 22, 1963 containing the name JACK E. GRIMMER, 500 South Cooper, Arlington, Texas. HOUCHINS stated he could not recall for sure but GRIMMER may have been the person who requested the above literature.

HOUCHINS further recalled that during the summer of 1963 HORACE TWIFORD had received the name of some man in Fort Worth, Texas who was also interested in the Socialist Labor Party. He stated that HORACE TWIFORD made a trip to Fort Worth and later remarked to him he had seen two or three people in Fort Worth who appeared to be interested in this organization but that one man in particular showed the most interest. HOUCHINS recalled TWIFORD described this man as a young man who indicated he could not discuss the Socialist Labor Party at his residence and when they got together elsewhere this man had very little to say and acted rather strangely. HOUCHINS stated this is a very vague recollection but he volunteered it on the remote chance the man referred to could have been OSWALD.

Both Mrs. TWIFORD and KENYON HOUCHINS stated they were not acquainted with JACK RUBY and that no additional information had come to their attention which might relate in any way to this investigation.

Mrs. TWIFORD stated she felt sure her husband would be glad to cooperate in this investigation but it would be impossible to interview him prior to December 14, 1963 except by radio telephone which would not afford any security.

Mrs. TWIFORD stated she and her husband have had telephone number WA 3-5492 since they moved to 7018 Schley in November, 1962. She pointed out their previous telephone number was MI 9-8500 when they resided at 7823 Dixie Drive.

She stated the old address and telephone number still appear in the current (January, 1963) Houston telephone directory because the directory had already been prepared at the time they changed residences.

On December 2, 1963 N. J. RAITHEL, Assistant Man. Delta Lines, Inc., 1300 Texas Street furnished the following information concerning the recent movements of the "SS Del Monte" operated by his company:

8/31/63	Departed Brazil enroute to Houston
9/16/63	Arrived Houston
9/23/63	Departed Houston for New Orleans, with brief stop at Galveston, Texas on 9/23,24/63
9/26/63	Arrived New Orleans, Louisiana
9/30/63	Departed New Orleans, Louisiana
10/1/63	Arrived Houston, Texas
10/3/63	Departed Houston, Texas
10/4/63	Departed Galveston, Texas for Freeport, Texas
10/5/63	Departed Freeport for Lake Charles, Louisiana
10/6/63	Proceeded from Lake Charles to Corpus Christi, Texas
10/9/63	Corpus Christi, to Houston, Texas

Commission Exhibit No. 2336

UNITED STATES DEPARTMENT OF JUSTICE

FEDERAL BUREAU OF INVESTIGATION

In Reply, Please Refer to
File No.

Dallas, Texas
July 29, 1964

JACK L. RUBY;
LEE HARVEY OSWALD

By letter dated July 17, 1964, the President's Commission on the Assassination of President Kennedy requested re-interviews with John Henry Branch, Harry Lee Jackson and Eva Grant relative to the allegation of Branch that Ruby was in the Empire Room, 1710 Hall Street, Dallas, on the night of November 23, 1963, as opposed to the statement of Harry Lee Jackson that he saw Ruby at the location on November 17, 1963.

Attached are reports of interviews with Branch, Jackson, Grant and Patrolman William M. Starks in the above connection.

COMMISSION EXHIBIT No. 2336

FD-302 (Rev. 3-3-59)

FEDERAL BUREAU OF INVESTIGATION

Date 7/27/64

1

Mr. JOHN HENRY BRANCH, residence, 3722 Greenleaf, business address, 1710 Hall Street, telephone number TA. 4-9062, was interviewed at his place of business and advised as follows:

He last saw JACK RUBY Saturday, November 23, 1963, at about 9:05 PM. He stated the band began playing that evening at approximately 9:00 PM and he saw JACK RUBY just a few minutes after the band began playing. He said he was sure it was Saturday, November 23, 1963, because it was the Saturday between the Presidential assassination and the shooting of LEE HARVEY OSWALD by RUBY.

BRANCH said this was not a prearranged appointment. RUBY just happened to come by the Empire Room to discuss hiring a new piano player on behalf of his sister, EVA GRANT. RUBY told BRANCH his sister was not satisfied with her pianist. She didn't like this pianist because he did not play what she wanted. BRANCH told RUBY he would get a piano player, but he did not advise RUBY whom he would hire. BRANCH said RUBY and he discussed the hiring of a piano player for approximately thirty minutes and then RUBY left for the Carousel Club.

BRANCH said it is possible he saw HARRY LEE JACKSON that evening, but he could not be certain that he actually saw him.

BRANCH said that when he saw RUBY on November 23, 1963, RUBY had on dark blue or black pants, white shirt, string, western-type tie, grey sport coat, and a black Fedora hat. RUBY did not wear this hat at the bar.

When RUBY left BRANCH accompanied him to the door. The Hall Diner is next door to the Empire Club and he last saw RUBY walk from the diner towards Ross Avenue, where he had parked his car.

on 7/23/64 at Dallas, Texas File # DL 44-1639

by Special Agent EDWARD DENNIS KENNEY/eah Date dictated 7/27/64

COMMISSION EXHIBIT No. 2336—Continued

2
DL 44-1639

Since RUBY shot OSWALD on the following day, it would have been futile for BRANCH to hire a piano player on RUBY's behalf. BRANCH never contacted a piano player to honor RUBY's request of November 23, 1963. BRANCH stated he never contacted Mrs. GRANT concerning the hiring of this piano player. BRANCH stated that he had, on several previous occasions, discussed the hiring of Negro musicians with Mrs. GRANT, but he did not discuss the hiring of a piano player with her.

BRANCH was unable to recall anyone who might have seen RUBY talking to him at the Empire Club on November 23, 1963. He stated that Patrolman WILLIAM STARKS, Dallas Police Department, may have been present that evening and might be able to verify RUBY's presence at the club on November 23, 1963.

FD-302 (Rev. 3-3-59)

FEDERAL BUREAU OF INVESTIGATION

Date 7/27/64

1

Mr. HARRY LEE JACKSON, 2536 Romine Street, Dallas, Texas, telephone number HA 1-4594, was interviewed at his residence and advised as follows:

The last time he saw JACK RUBY was Sunday, November 17, 1963, the Sunday before RUBY killed OSWALD. JACKSON walked into the Empire Room, 1710 Hall Street, between 8:30 PM and 9:00 PM. He was unable to recall the specific time.

When JACKSON entered the Empire Room, he immediately saw RUBY standing at the bar. RUBY was engaged in a conversation with JOHN HENRY BRANCH. JACKSON was not aware of the conversation between BRANCH and RUBY. RUBY offered JACKSON a beer, which he declined. RUBY then invited JACKSON to drop in at the Carousel Club whenever JACKSON was in the neighborhood and have a drink. JACKSON stated this was the extent of the conversation between himself and RUBY at that time. Following this, JACKSON walked off to mingle with the patrons in the Empire Room.

JACKSON stated that when he arrived at the Empire Room the band was already playing. On Sundays the band begins playing at about 8:30 PM and JACKSON's habit was to arrive at a dance early in the evening. He stated this was why he estimated that the time was between 8:30 PM and 9:00 PM.

JACKSON recalled that when he saw RUBY on November 17, 1963, RUBY was wearing dark colored slacks, a light colored sport shirt, and a dark colored suit jacket. JACKSON was unable to remember the exact color of RUBY's clothing. He thought the suit jacket matched the pants, but he was not certain. When JACKSON saw RUBY, he was not wearing a hat.

on 7/23/64 at Dallas, Texas File # DL 44-1639

by Special Agent EDWARD DENNIS KENNEY/eah Date dictated 7/27/64

FD-302 (Rev. 3-3-59)

FEDERAL BUREAU OF INVESTIGATION

Date 7/27/64

1

Mrs. EVA GRANT, JACK RUBY's sister, 3929 Rawlins, Dallas, Texas, advised as follows:

JOE JOHNSON, band leader and saxophone player, left her employ on or about November 2, 1963. LEONARD WOODS, who was JOHNSON's pianist, elected to remain as pianist at the Vegas Club. However, a few days later, Mrs. GRANT determined that WOODS was unable to read music and deemed his services as unsatisfactory.

On Thursday or Friday of the week prior to the assassination, she telephonically contacted JOHN HENRY BRANCH, Booking Agent, concerning the hiring of a piano player to replace LEONARD WOODS. She was certain that any discussion she had with her brother, JACK RUBY, concerning the hiring of a piano player transpired prior to the assassination of President JOHN F. KENNEDY.

She does not know her brother spoke to BRANCH at all concerning the piano player, although this is possible. She stated that, if he did speak to BRANCH, it is probable it was at the same time she spoke to BRANCH.

She stated she spoke to her brother, JACK, about midnight, November 23, 1963, and he did not mention he had contacted BRANCH about the piano player. She stated it was probable that if he did speak to BRANCH it occurred on a Sunday, since many Negro musicians gather at the Empire Room on Sunday evenings.

on 7/27/64 at Dallas, Texas File # DL 44-1639

by Special Agents EDWARD DENNIS KENNEY & MANNING C. CLEMENTS/eah Date dictated 7/27/64

5

COMMISSION EXHIBIT No. 2336—Continued

FD-302 (Rev. 3-3-59)

FEDERAL BUREAU OF INVESTIGATION

Date 7/27/64

1

Patrolman WILLIAM M. STARKS, Shield No. 610, Dallas Police Department, 3202 Carpenter Street, was interviewed at his home and advised as follows:

He is acquainted with and has known JOHN HENRY BRANCH, Manager of the Empire Room, for approximately sixteen years.

He never met RUBY or had any contact whatsoever with him. The only time he heard of RUBY was after LEE HARVEY OSWALD was shot. Following this, he remembered seeing RUBY somewhere before, but could not recall the location.

STARKS worked from 3:30 PM to 11:30 PM, Saturday, November 23, 1963, and, therefore, was not at the Empire Room that night, November 23, 1963.

STARKS is certain he was at the Empire Room on Sunday, November 17, 1963, but does not specifically remember seeing BRANCH at the club that evening. STARKS stated he cannot recall ever seeing RUBY at the Empire Room and has never seen RUBY engaged in conversation with JOHN HENRY BRANCH.

on 7/24/64 at Dallas, Texas File # DL 44-1639

by Special Agent EDWARD DENNIS KENNEY/eah Date dictated 7/27/64

This document contains neither recommendations nor conclusions of the FBI. It is the property of the FBI and is loaned to your agency; it and its contents are not to be distributed outside your agency.

6

COMMISSION EXHIBIT No. 2336—Continued

UNITED STATES DEPARTMENT OF JUSTICE

FEDERAL BUREAU OF INVESTIGATION

In Reply, Please Refer to
File No.

Dallas, Texas
July 31, 1964

JACK L. RUBY;
LEE HARVEY OSWALD

By letter dated July 17, 1964, the President's Commission on the Assassination of President Kennedy requested Mrs. Louis (Anice) Byrum be interviewed concerning the presence of Jack L. Ruby at the Pago Club on Saturday night, November 23, 1963.

Attached are reports of interviews with Mrs. Byrum and Mrs. Virginia Thompson Humphries in the above connection.

Attachments.

1

COMMISSION EXHIBIT No. 2337

FD-302 (Rev. 3-3-59) FEDERAL BUREAU OF INVESTIGATION

Date 7/29/64

1

Mrs. VIRGINIA THOMPSON HUMPHRIES, 3600 Gillespie, Apartment No. 5, presently employed as a waitress at the Capri Lounge, 3913 Cedar Springs, Dallas, Texas, advised she is a casual acquaintance of JACK RUBY.

Mrs. HUMPHRIES stated she was formerly employed as a waitress at the Pago Club, 2822 McKinney Avenue, Dallas, Texas.

Mrs. HUMPHRIES recalled that on Saturday night, November 23, 1963, at approximately midnight, JACK RUBY entered the Pago Club alone. She seated RUBY at a table near the middle of the club. RUBY ordered a plain Coke. Upon being served the Coke, RUBY asked, "Why are you open?" According to Mrs. HUMPHRIES, RUBY asked this question as though it were a sacrilege to be open. Mrs. HUMPHRIES stated she said, "Ask my employer," in answer to RUBY's question and she then walked away from RUBY's table, having no further conversation with him.

Mrs. HUMPHRIES related that a few minutes had passed by when she observed BOB NORTON, owner of the Pago Club, sit down and join RUBY at RUBY's table. NORTON called Mrs. HUMPHRIES over to the table and he also ordered a plain Coke. Mrs. HUMPHRIES served NORTON the Coke. She had no further conversation with either of the men and has no knowledge as to the nature of the conversation between them.

Mrs. HUMPHRIES further advised at approximately 1:00 AM, on November 24, 1963, she was getting her "tabs" ready for her customers to pay, as 1:00 AM was the club's closing time. She observed RUBY was not at his table and had apparently left without paying his tab. Mrs. HUMPHRIES did not see RUBY leave the club and does not know how long he remained in the club after she served NORTON at RUBY's table. She looked around the club for RUBY, but could not find him. NORTON was still in the club, but RUBY was not. Mrs. HUMPHRIES stated she then gave RUBY's tab to the Club Manager, Mrs. LAURA BYRUM, stating she was not going to pay for another club owner's tab. The tab amounted to

on 7/28/64 at Dallas, Texas File # DL 44-1639

by Special Agent RAYMOND P. YELCHAK/eah Date dictated 7/28/64

2

COMMISSION EXHIBIT No. 2337—Continued

2
DL 44-1639

either 50¢ or 80¢, exact amount unrecalled.

Mrs. HUMPHRIES stated RUBY never mentioned the name LEE HARVEY OSWALD and she knows of no association between OSWALD and RUBY.

3

COMMISSION EXHIBIT No. 2337—Continued

FD-302 (Rev. 3-3-59)

FEDERAL BUREAU OF INVESTIGATION

1

Date 7/23/64

Mrs. LAURA A. BYRUM, 6039 Singing Hills Drive, employed as the manager of the Pago Club, 2822 McKinney Avenue, Dallas, Texas, advised she is a casual acquaintance of JACK RUBY.

Mrs. BYRUM stated that on Saturday night, November 23, 1963, JACK RUBY entered the Pago Club alone. Mrs. BYRUM stated RUBY was seated at a table near the front of the club by waitress VIRGINIA THOMPSON HUMPHRIES, who is now employed as a waitress at the Capri Lounge, 3913 Cedar Springs, Dallas, Texas. Mrs. BYRUM advised RUBY sat alone at the table and spoke to no one. RUBY ordered a plain Coke and sipped on this Coke for about thirty minutes. At this time, BOB NORTON, owner of the Pago Club, approached RUBY, and Mrs. BYRUM stated RUBY and NORTON exchanged greetings.

Mrs. BYRUM stated that during the time RUBY was seated alone at the table, she (Mrs. BYRUM) passed by RUBY's table and said, "Hi, JACK." RUBY exchanged the greeting and commented that the Pago Club had a "nice crowd."

Mrs. BYRUM stated that RUBY has never mentioned the name LEE HARVEY OSWALD and she knows of no association between OSWALD and RUBY.

on 7/23/64 at Dallas, Texas File # DL 44-1639

by Special Agent ROBERT J. ANDERSON/ds Date dictated 7/23/64

4

COMMISSION EXHIBIT No. 2337—Continued

Commission Exhibit No. 2338

UNITED STATES DEPARTMENT OF JUSTICE

FEDERAL BUREAU OF INVESTIGATION

In Reply, Please Refer to File No.

408 Post Office Building
Baltimore, Maryland 21202

August 19, 1964

JACK LEON RUBY;
LEE HARVEY OSWALD - VICTIM

RE: INTERVIEW OF ROSEMARY HELMICK,
2123 SPARROWS POINT ROAD,
SPARROWS POINT, MARYLAND

By letter dated August 11, 1964, the President's Commission on the Assassination of President Kennedy requested that Rosemary Helmick be interviewed to determine if she had ever received a letter from Wanda Helmick, in which Wanda Helmick told Rosemary Helmick that she had overheard a telephone conversation between Ralph Paul and Jack Ruby, in which Paul had made an exclamation about a gun and Ruby's being "crazy".

On August 18, 1964, Rosemary Helmick, 2123 Sparrows Point Road, Sparrows Point, Maryland, advised that Wanda Helmick, who resides at 2630 Rock Island Road, Irving, Texas, is her sister-in-law. Wanda Helmick is married to Donald, the brother of Rosemary Helmick, and this couple has been married for approximately two years.

Rosemary Helmick informed she has never personally met Wanda Helmick and has never been to the State of Texas. Wanda Helmick has never visited Rosemary Helmick in Baltimore, Maryland and their acquaintanceship has been confined to the exchange of approximately five letters during the period of the past year.

Rosemary Helmick recalled that some time after the assassination of President Kennedy and prior to Christmas 1963, she had received a letter from Wanda Helmick in which Wanda had made mention of Jack Ruby and "something about a gun". Miss Helmick could not specifically recall in what connection Jack Ruby's name

1

was mentioned and she did not remember in what connection a gun was mentioned in this letter. She did not recall the name Ralph Paul being mentioned in this letter and she had no recollection of Ruby being referred to as "crazy", although she stated that it was entirely possible all of these statements could have been made and due to the passage of time, she could not recollect these statements. She does not know and has never met Jack Ruby or Ralph Paul.

Miss Helmick said that she did not recall what she had done with the above-referred-to letter and a search by Miss Helmick of her correspondence and personal effects failed to locate this letter.

Miss Helmick did locate among her correspondence a letter addressed to her from Wanda Helmick, postmarked March 10, 1964 at Irving, Texas. The only mention of Jack Ruby in this letter is as follows:

> "They are sure having a lot of trouble with the Jack Ruby trial these day. 6 prisinor escaped day before yesterday. Two have still not been cought, they were in the same jail as Ruby."

> "I talk to Ralph Ruby partner in the Bull pen he told me Ruby wasn't in his right mind every sence the president had been shot."

2

2638 Rock Island
Irving, Texas

Dear Rosie & Rod

How is every thing there? Don's work is very heavy these days. And we don't have time to do anything anymore. We have been getting up at 5.30 in the morning and getting in bed about 11:00 at night. I have been running the station while he work. the boy I had working for me didn't show up today so I guess he won't be back any more.

We got a Card in the mail yesterday Don said it must have been about the tool you said you would send. There sure must have been a lot of them. (if that what it was he suppost to pick them up today.)

Next day: Well Don never did pick up the pakeage. Sure hope they didn't send it back.

I don't know if Don has told you about this dog we have or not. He really pretty, we he got to me. He house broke himself (thank goodness.) ~~that~~ Other than that he

1

COMMISSION EXHIBIT No. 2339

-2-

is a monster always wanting to play- if you don't want to play he bite you. We have him here a the station and every car that come up he runs under it and I have to get down on my hands and knees and get him out. We have been offered $45.00 for him but Don't would take it.

Its raining here in Irving and every thing is so quite you can't hear yourself think trains coming but every 30 min. Is his being sunday every body in a hurry. Their going by so fast they don't give this place a second thought.

They are sure having a lot of trouble with the Jack Ruby trial these day. 6 prisinor escaped day before yesterday. Two have still not been caught. They were in the same jail as Ruby.

I talk to Ralph Ruby partner in the Bull pen he told me Ruby wasn't in his right mind every sence the president had

2

Commission Exhibit No. 2339—Continued

-3-

been shot.

I work for two more week there. I got a tommer that made it imposable for me to work for a week and Donna was sick for a week (lets say I didn't work it was just on payroll.) but when I went back to work He didn't let me have my job back. That when we were going to Come to see all of you but we had to spend Our saving.

When Dan had to go up there it was impossable for us to make a payment on our house and we were already on the line. When Don did get back to work Mr. Harper would let us make up the payments so we are staying at my mother's until we can find an apartment.

He has be so bussie the last two weeks and yesterday my brother called and had 10,000 more sheets of rock he wanted him to hang.

Dan has plains to go hunting this year in Colo. and Faye wants me to come and stay with her while he gose hunting but I don't think I want too.

3

Commission Exhibit No. 2339—Continued

-6-

It only cost him $65.00 to get up there and back on bus. To be with you. And if thing work out I know it won't be hard for me to talk him into letting me spend a week with you. That would give you a change to see me and the baby, and to if I went to Colo. and took the baby I might deside to go hunting with Don.

Dreams, just watch thing will prebley be ruff and will still have this old station and things allways work out that I have to stay here and work while he takes a vaction.

I told him a day or two ago that I was going to have to see a "brain doctor" if I didn't get away from this place.

Don just came in and we are going to close so I can't finish this now.

— Boy, what a relife to get out of here a little while.

Don, thought it nice for me to come up there, but he did say any thing for sure.

We got the color ~~pictures~~ pitures back. we took on your antinues I'll send the one of the baby and also

1

Commission Exhibit No. 2339—Continued

-5-

of Don as soon a we have them redeleupe.

We I guess you kind of tired of reading. Sure hope it don't take you as long to ~~too~~ read this as it took me to wright it.

I know I just going to love everyone of you. Don love you so I know I will.

Love Always,
Don & Wanda
& Donna

P.S. How do you like my writing paper.

5

COMMISSION EXHIBIT NO. 2339—Continued

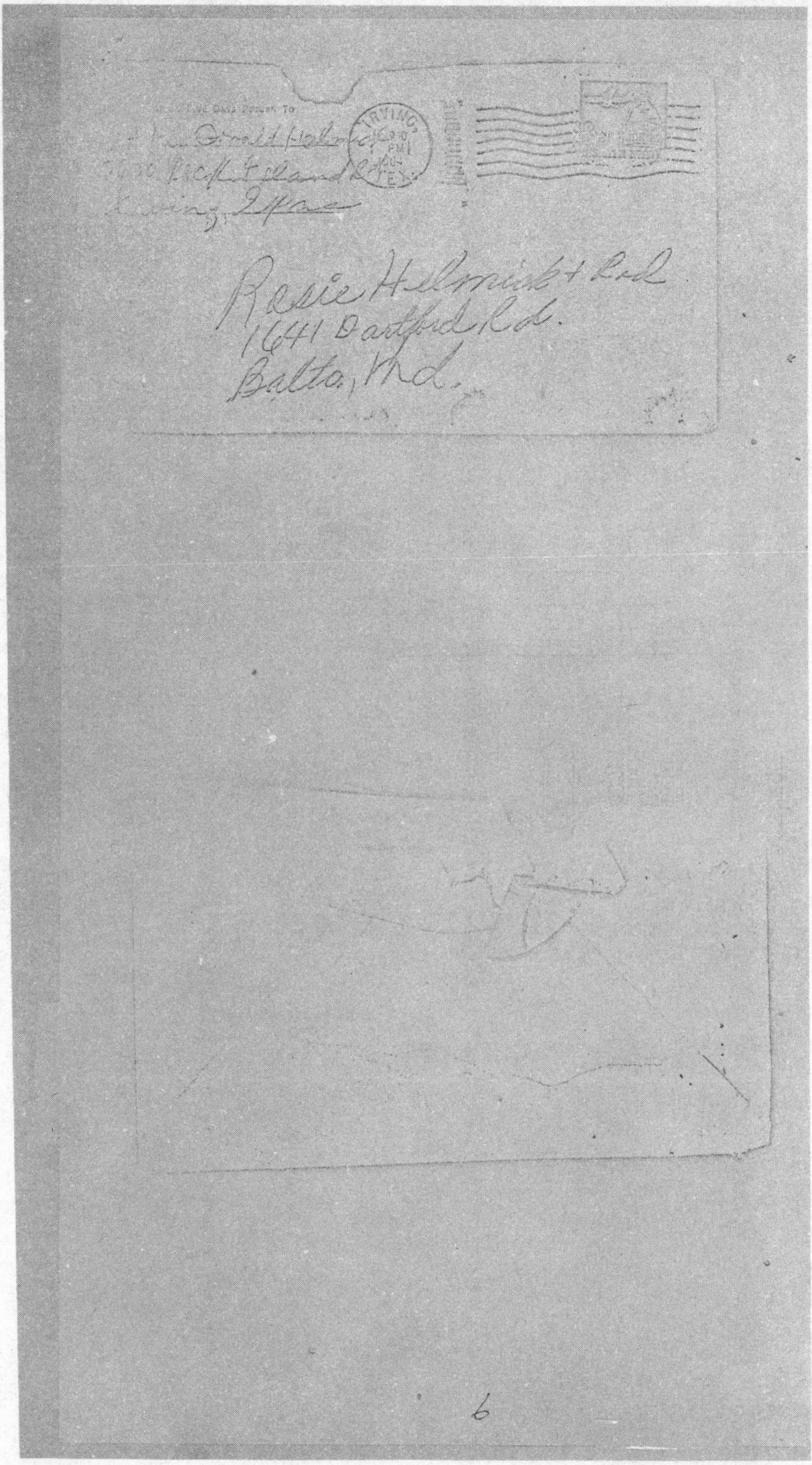

COMMISSION EXHIBIT No. 2339—Continued

 FEDERAL BUREAU OF INVESTIGATION

Date 6/13/64

JEFFERSON D. STOKES, employed as a mortician, Veterans Administration Hospital, 4500 South Lancaster, Dallas, Texas, advised he is the father-in-law of BUDDY MUENSTER, and is a former neighbor of JACK RUBY at the Marsala Place Apartments, 213 South Ewing, Dallas.

STOKES advised he spoke with RUBY strictly on a neighborly basis several times during the one year they were neighbors. He recalled a brief conversation with RUBY on Saturday, November 23, 1963, around noon. RUBY mentioned something about fixing STOKES a hamburger, but STOKES declined as he had to report to work autopsy on that day.

STOKES said he cannot recall seeing RUBY on November 24, 1963, and can recall having no conversation with RUBY on that day.

STOKES advised he was not well acquainted with RUBY, and knows nothing of RUBY's acquaintances or background.

STOKES said he and RUBY never discussed the assassination of President KENNEDY and he, STOKES, knows nothing about LEE HARVEY OSWALD.

on 6/10/64 at Dallas, Texas File # DL 44-1639

by Special Agent ROBERT J. ANDERSON/ds Date dictated 6/10/64

COMMISSION EXHIBIT No. 2340

(EXACT COPY) — Commission Exhibit No. 2341

FEDERAL BUREAU OF INVESTIGATION

Date 11/29/63

1

THOMAS RAYMOND BROWN, an employee of the Allright Parking Company, Dallas, Texas, advised that on Saturday November 23, 1963, he was working at Nichol Brothers Parking Garage, 1320 Commerce Street, Dallas.

BROWN advised that between 1:30 and 2:00 PM, JACK RUBY came into the garage, at which time he did not appear to be upset. He stated RUBY made a local telephone call and he overheard RUBY inform the other party to the conversation as to the whereabouts of Chief of Police CURRY, Dallas Police Department.

BROWN stated that RUBY later called and informed that two men would be by the garage asking for him. He requested that BROWN inform them that he would not be open that night. BROWN stated that one man came by later and asked for RUBY and he told him what RUBY had said. He described this man as a white male, 35 to 40 years of age, short, sandy hair, heavy build, and stated he does not recall ever having seen him before.

BROWN further advised that CLAUDE HALLMARK, General Manager, Nichol Parking Garage, was present at the time RUBY placed the above telephone call to an unknown individual and informed this individual as to the whereabouts of Chief of Police CURRY.

He stated he has known HALLMARK for a number of years and has always found him to be honest and, in his opinion, he would be willing to assist in every manner possible in this investigation.

on 11/28/63 at Dallas, Texas File # DL 44-1639

By Special Agent sARTHUR E. CARTER & JOHN V. eah. Date dictated 11/29/63

680

COMMISSION EXHIBIT No. 2341

OFFICE OF THE DIRECTOR

Commission Exhibit No. 2342

UNITED STATES DEPARTMENT OF JUSTICE

FEDERAL BUREAU OF INVESTIGATION

WASHINGTON, D.C. 20535

September 17, 1964

By Courier Service

Honorable J. Lee Rankin
General Counsel
The President's Commission
200 Maryland Avenue, Northeast
Washington, D. C.

Dear Mr. Rankin:

Reference is made to your letter of September 12, 1964, with which you transmitted a change-of-address card purportedly signed by Lee Harvey Oswald when he opened P. O. Box 2915 in Dallas, Texas. This card has been designated as FBI Exhibit D-253.

It was concluded that the hand printed wording "Fort Worth, Tex." on the face of D-253 and the hand printing and Oswald signature on the back of D-253 were written by Lee Harvey Oswald whose known handwriting and hand printing specimens are designated as FBI Exhibits D-3, D-4, D-5, and D-67.

FBI Exhibit D-253 and two photographic copies of this exhibit are returned to you herewith.

Sincerely yours,

J. Edgar Hoover

Enclosures (3)

COMMISSION EXHIBIT No. 2342

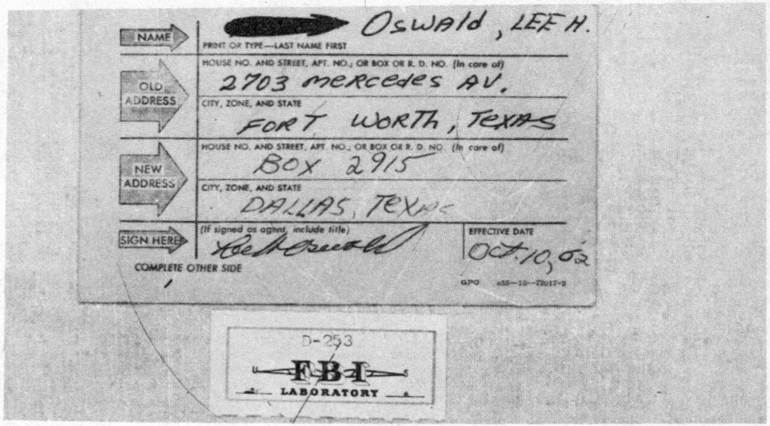

COMMISSION EXHIBIT No. 2342—Continued

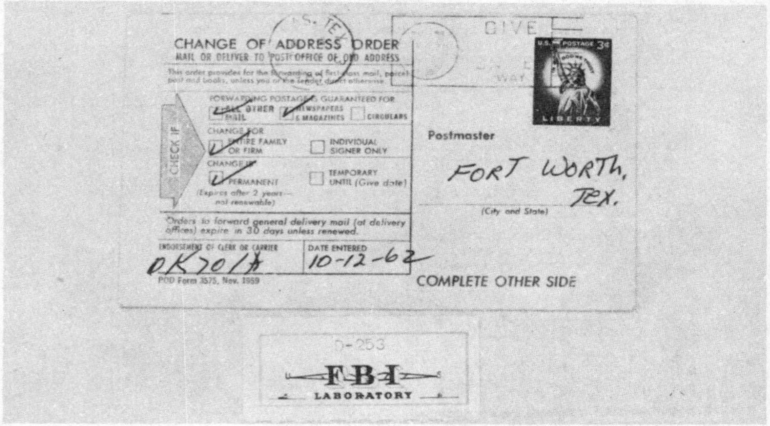

COMMISSION EXHIBIT No. 2342—Continued

FD-302 (Rev. 3-3-59) FEDERAL BUREAU OF IN[redacted]

Date 7/27/64

1

Mrs. EVA GRANT, 3929 Rawlins Street, telephone LA 6-6258, voluntarily advised that on July 24, 1964, Mrs. WILMA TICE telephoned her during the afternoon and asked if she could come to Mrs. GRANT's apartment. She said she invited her to come and Mrs. TICE appeared shortly thereafter.

Mrs. TICE related to Mrs. GRANT that she had given a deposition to the President's Commission on the same date. She said she and her husband had left their children at a theatre and at a time when they went to the theatre to pick the children up she, Mrs. TICE, had run away from her husband, who had threatened her. Mrs. TICE spent approximately four hours in Mrs. GRANT's apartment.

Mrs. GRANT stated she considers Mrs. TICE is "balmy," is "put out" because she was not more closely associated with the events of the assassination, and is seeking publicity. She said she believes the Commission can "discount" anything Mrs. TICE may have told them. She said, however, Mrs. TICE, in claiming she had seen RUBY at Parkland Hospital on November 22, 1963, had rather accurately described the clothing RUBY was wearing. She repeated that she believes Mrs. TICE is "balmy."

on 7/27/64 at Dallas, Texas File # DL 44-1639

by Special Agents MANNING C. CLEMENTS & EDWARD DENNIS KENNEY/esh Date dictated 7/27/64

93

COMMISSION EXHIBIT No. 2343

Commission Exhibit No. 2344

CHRONOLOGY OF RUBY'S ACTIVITIES FROM SEPTEMBER 26 through NOVEMBER 21, 1963.

Date	Place	Activity	Reported
9-28		Ruby saw Deke Miles.	CE 2345
10-1	Dallas	Barbara Hemby saw Ruby.	CE 2346
10-2	Street in front of Baker Hotel	Ruby says he's interested in Carribean cruise.	CE 2347
10-3		Ruby first meets Marv Gardner of Hollywood show.	CE 2348
10-4	Dallas	Ruby took treatments for balding from Bruce McLean.	CE 1494
10-5	Carousel Club	Mrs. Johnnie Hayden saw Ruby	CE 1495
		Ruby took treatment for balding from Bruce McLean.	CE 2349
10-7		Laurence Meyers in Dallas.	CE 2350
10-8		Laurence Meyers in Dallas.	CE 2350
10-9		Ruby noted American Airlines Flight 985, Tuesday, October 9.	13 H 473
10-10		Meyers in Dallas at "How Hollywood makes Movies".	CE 2350
10-12	Dallas	Amos C. Flint saw and talked to Ruby.	CE 2351
	Adolphus Hotel	Michael P. Doyle saw and talked to Ruby.	CE 2352
10-15	Dallas	Ruby visited office of Dr. Coleman Jacobson; was seen by Bonnie H. Bell during day.	CE 2242 CE 2353
		Wanda Minnix saw Ruby at Spa, health club.	CE 2354
	Dallas	"How Hollywood Makes Movies" closes.	CE 2348 Crafard DE 5226

COMMISSION EXHIBIT No. 2344

Date	Place	Activity	Reported
1963			
10/16	Cabana Club Dallas	Jewel Brown saw and talked to Ruby - several occasions during week.	CE 2355
19-18	State Fair	Rock & Roll Show produced by Seay (friend of Groom) closes and Larry Crafard starts to work for Ruby.	CE 2348
10-19		Ruby ran ad for Little Egypt even though not performing at at Carousel. Curtis complains.	CE 2356
10-20	Dallas	Richard H. Sheppard saw and talked to Ruby.	CE 2357
10-21	State Fair		
		At this time inquires of Dallas Police Department re installation of safe.	Standifer DE 1.
		Ruby contacted Swenson re business property.	CE 1509
10-22	Dallas	Ruby took trichology treatment for balding from Bruce McLean.	CE 1494
		Ruby and Robert T. Brown visit project at 2917 Maple Ave. with decorator.	CE 1509
10-24		Jada gets sick and doesn't work.	CE 1561
10-25	Near Adolphus Hotel, Dallas.	J. D. Turner and Robert Franklin aka O'Doud, meet Ruby on street and talk about 2 minutes.	CE 2358
	Mercantile Nat'l Bank	Joe A. Helm saw and talked to Ruby.	CE 2359
		Jada doesn't work.	CE 1561

COMMISSION EXHIBIT No. 2344—Continued

Date	Place	Activity	Reported
10-26	Dallas	Ruby rec'd traffic ticket #734946 in 1500 Block of Commerce Street.	CE 2342
		Last night Jada worked.	CE 1561
10-28	Dallas	Dr. Herman Ulevitch telephoned Ruby re operation for Eva L. Grant.	CE 2360
10-29	Dallas	Dr. Herman Ulevitch saw Ruby; examined Eva L. Grant.	CE 2360
10-30	Dallas News	Ruby placing ad for partner	CE 2252
		Ruby sends letter to Mike Shore outlining AGVA troubles, Special Delivery.	CE 1507
11-1	Carousel	Larry starts work for Jack Ruby.	CE 2361
		Ruby is arrested in connection with Jada dispute.	CE 1561
		Crafard leaves slip of paper with names at Graphic Studios while ordering Twist Board brochures.	CE 1567 CE 2368
11-2	Contract Electronics	Ruby and Larry visit store in 2200-2300 block on Elm Street.	Crafard DE 5226
		Raymond Jones quits as handyman for Vegas club some time in November.	CE 2362
11-3		Joe Johnson's band quit Vegas club about this date.	CE 1560
11-4	Dallas	Ruby's car rec'd parking ticket #738471 in the 2000 block of Main St.	CE 2342
	Graphic Studios	Ruby talked to Bryan Powell and John Lacy re printing job for advertising.	CE 2368 CE 1567
	Carousel Club	Johnny Turner starts as MC at Carousel	CE 1563

COMMISSION EXHIBIT No. 2344—Continued

Date	Place	Activity	Reported
11-5		Called Henry Kenter, Mar-Sen Co. Chicago re twist boards.	CE 2363
11-6		Called Buddy Heard in El Paso re playing Carousel as comedian.	CE 2364
		Approximate date of Eva Grant's operation.	CE 2403
	Vegas	Ruby sees Pauline Hall in evening.	CE 2403
	Dallas	Ruby took trichology treatment for balding from Bruce McLean.	CE 2349
		Visited home of Ed Pullman in early November. (Probably to discuss Twist Board)	**Pullman DE 1**
11-8	Tommy Tucker Plastics Inc.	Tommy T. Tucker saw Ruby re cost of business cards.	CE 2366
	Carousel	Rackley and Craddock see Ruby.	CE 2367 CE 1479
	Carousel	John Lacy sees Ruby	CE 2368
		Ruby picks up hand bills for twist boards.	CE 1567
11-9	Tailor, Dallas	Ruby visited Edw. Fein tailor shop for suit.	CE 2369
	Dallas	Ruby telephone Eva L. Grant from Dr. Ulevitch's office.	CE 2360
	Carousel	Turner quits as MC	CE 1563
11-10	Carousel	Laurence Meyers meets Joyce Lee McDonald. Is in Dallas 2 or 3 days and visits State Fair.	CE 1606
	Carousel	Harvey Lawill Wade saw Ruby at Carousel Club.	CE 2370

COMMISSION EXHIBIT No. 2344—Continued

Date	Place	Activity	Reported
11-10	Carousel Club	Jada paid $125.00 in full.	CE 1322
	Dallas	De Mar arrives in Dallas.	CE 2076
11-11	Ruby's unlisted phone.	Telephone call to Frank R. Goldstein No. AT 2-7128 at San Francisco-wrong number.	CE 2371
		Ruby called Barney Baker, Chicago ex-con and former teamster organizer re "help" in fight with AGVA.	CE 2331
		Alex Gruber visited Ruby.	CE 2243
		Ruby came in to Dr. Ulevitch's office. Dr. Ulevitch saw and talked to Ruby who came in suffer-from a bad cold.	CE 2360
		Ruby MC.	Crafard DE 5226
		De Mar starts work at club.	CE 2076 CE 2372
11-12	Stork Club Dallas	William Edward Howard visited with Ruby.	CE 1477
	Carousel	Paul Roland Jones sees Ruby. Ruby complains competitors had become his enemies.	CE 1300
11-13		Ruby sends letter to Faye re business troubles includes breakdown of receipts.	CE 1322
11-12-13		Ruby in composing room KLIF	15 H 556 Pryor
11-14	Carousel	Linda Zumwalt talked to Ruby about employment	CE 2373
		Ruby telephoned Rose Sandra Renfroe regarding employment.	CE 2374
11-14, 15	Carousel	Curtis LaVerne Crafard saw Ruby at Carousel Club arguing with Earl Norman.	Crafard DE 5226

COMMISSION EXHIBIT No. 2344—Continued

Date	Place	Activity	Reported
11-15			
		B. A. Bates, Jr. saw and talked to Ruby at the Dallas Morning News Building.	CE 1630
	Dallas	Mary Martin saw and talked to Ruby at corner of Ervay & Bryan Streets.	CE 2375
	Merchants State Bank Dallas	Charles Straeght saw Ruby.	CE 2376
	Vegas Club.	George C. Arnett, Lt., Dallas Police Department saw Ruby.	CE 1615
		Ruby receives letter from Bobby Faye.	CE 1322
11-16	Ranch of Buck Sheaver	Rumored hunting party.	CE 2377
		Ruby called Smokey Turner at Minneapolis regarding employment.	CE 2378
11-16,17		Gloria Fillmon talked to Ruby by telephone at Dallas.	CE 2379
11-16	Carousel	Harvey Davis Bostick saw and talked to Ruby.	Ce 2380
	Gay 90s in Mnpls. 8:00-8:30	Ruby called Smokey Turner re hiring as stripper.	CE 2378
11-17		Larry Crafard threatened to quit and Ruby put him on salary.	Crafard DE 5226
	Empire Room 1710 Hall P.M.	H. L. Jackson shook hands with Ruby.	CE 2381
		Probably saw Branch re piano player.	CE 2336 15 H 574, Branch Branch DE 1 15 H 334

COMMISSION EXHIBIT No. 2344—Continued

Date	Place	Activity	Reported
11-17		Norma Jean Bostick telephoned Ruby - talked to him.	CE 2382
		Curtis LaVerne Crafard talked to Ruby re leaving Ruby's employ.	Crafard DE 5226
	Dallas	Vern A. Davis, Oklahoma City saw Ruby at Ed's Bar, 813 Exposition St., Dallas.	CE 2383
11-18	Dallas & Fort Worth	Dallas and Fort Worth newspaper articles re Presidential arrival.	CE 2342
		Telephone conversation with Mrs. Carr re Impellas.	CE 2384
		Telephone conversation with Mr. Carr.	CE 2385
	Carousel	Bertha Cheek visited with Ruby for several hours.	Cheek DE 5354
		Frank J. Boerder present.	CE 2386
		Robert Craven telephone Ruby talked to him regarding lumber purchases in connection with State Fair. (Probably had to do with bad checks.)	CE 1535
		L. F. Dauer observed Ruby going downstairs at Ruby's apartment house with dogs.	CE 2387
	Carousel	Thomas Stewart Palmer saw Ruby at Carousel Club. There to pick up money for performer.	CE 1448
	Carousel	Anne Listak talked to Ruby about employment.	CE 2388
11-19	Office of Graham Koch	Consulted re tax problem - Income and excise taxes.	CE 2389
		Called Mrs. Carr in Houston re Impellas.	CE 2384
	Dallas	Travis Hall saw and talked to Ruby.	CE 1634
	Dallas	Henry D. Akin saw Ruby when Ruby visited law offices of Akin, Vial, Hamilton and Koch.	CE 1614

COMMISSION EXHIBIT No. 2344—Continued

Date	Place	Activity	Reported
11-19	Dallas	Nancy Powell saw Ruby. She quit.	CE 2390
	Holiday Inn, Dallas.	Willard P. DeLacy saw Ruby at 1:00 PM. Operates Prevue of Dallas. Ruby wanted publicity re twist boards.	CE 2501
	Sol's Turf Bar, Dallas.	Robert Y. Black saw Ruby. Later saw Ruby at the Carousel. Bell hop who held Carousel Card #148.	CE 2391
11-19,20	Coffee Shop Cabana Motor Hotel	Milton Joseph saw Ruby 1 a.m.	CE 2392 CE 2252 CE 1453 CE 2393
11-19	Carousel	Karen Green Williams saw and talked with Ruby re employment. Answered ad. Hired for $90.00 per week.	CE 2394 Hall DE 1.
11-20	Tanglewood Apt. 104	Alleged party with JADA, Frederico and Bryant and Tortoriello.	CE 2395 CE 2396 CE 2397
	Carousel	Seen by Herb Kravitz.	Kravitz DE 1.
		10:50 a.m. Ruby calls Alton Sharpe, AGVA, Chicago, complains re strippers.	CE 2323 CE 2302
		Telephone conversation with Mrs. Carr.	CE 2384
		Asks Larry to work at Vegas Club.	Crafard DE 5226
		Joseph P. Rossi saw and talked with Ruby re a new club which Ruby wanted to open.	Rossi DE 1.
11-19,20	KLIF	Ruby in composing room.	15 H 556 Pryor
11-20	Carousel	Crafard saw Ruby between 4 or 5 pm and 6:30 p.m.	Crafard DE 5226
	Carousel	Crafard saw Ruby leave the Club about 6:30 p.m. Ruby went home and returned to Carousel about 8 p.m.	Crafard DE 5226.
	Carousel Club Vegas Club	Ruby took Crafard from Carousel to the Vegas Club, Dallas, about 8 p.m. Ruby called Crafard by telephone 3 or 4 times that night.	Crafard DE 5226

COMMISSION EXHIBIT No. 2344—Continued

Date	Place	Activity	Reported
11-20		Aycox quit at Vegas.	Aycox DE 1.
	Carousel	Elaine Rogers saw Ruby.	CE 1459
		Ruby took trichology treatment from Bruce McLean- 6 to 6:30 p.m.	CE 1494
	Dallas	Connie Trammel telephoned Ruby re employment.	CE 2270
11-20 or 21	Dallas	Patrolman Welcome Eugene Barnett, Dallas Police Department saw Ruby in downtown.	CE 2398
	Vegas Club	James Aycox saw Ruby	Aycox DE 1
11-20,21	Carousel & B & B Restaurant	Gloria Fillmon was with Ruby.	CE 2379
11-21	B & B Restaurant	Ruby picks up Larry at Vegas Club and both have breakfast with Gloria Fillmon at 3:00 a.m.	CE 2379
		Telephone conversation with Mrs. Carr re Impellas.	CE 2384
	Dallas	Allegedly in DA's office.	CE 2265
	Max Rudberg AAA Bonding	Talked about peace bond in previous case re JADA	CE 2265
		Called Dallas News about two ads at noon, brought copy about 2:30 .	Newman DE 2
		Called Dalls attorney re tax problems.	CE 2389
		Rumored to be in Houston as early as 2:30 PM.	CE.2399
		Ruby at Carousel Club in afternoon with Mickey Ryan - made long distance telephone calls.	Crafard DE 5226
	211 W. ERvay	Ruby bought cashiers check and paid $500 rent.	CE 1669 CE 2399

COMMISSION EXHIBIT No. 2344—Continued

Date	Place	Activity	Reported
11-21			
3:00 p.m.		At office of Dallas DA Bill Alexander re bad checks written by Craven.	CE 2245
7:30 p.m.	3531 Oaklwan Carousel	At Phil's Delicatessen	CE 2246
		Took Larry to Vegas Club.	Crafard DE 5226
	Carousel	Meyers and "Ann" meet Joyce McDonald at Carousel. Ruby did not talk.	CE 1606
		With Meyers privately.	
9:45 or 10:00 p.m.	Etyptian Lounge	Ruby with Paul for 45 minutes dinner.	CE 2274
12 midnight	Cabana	Ruby saw Larry and Meyers at Bon Vivant Room.	CE 2266
2:30 a.m.	**Cabana**	**Ruby mad because not notified of earlier call.**	**Crafard DE 5226**
		Picked up Larry and went to B & B for breakfast.	**Crafard DE 5226**
	Carousel	Ruby telephoned Crafard to wake him up.	Crafard DE 5226
	AA Bonding Co.	Ralph Gismont saw Ruby	CE 2288
		Connie Trammel was with Ruby fm. 11 am. til 1:00 p.m. He droveher to office of Lamar Hunt. Stopped by Merchants State Bank.	CE 2270
		Hunt says he didn't see Ruby.	CE 2400
	Dallas	Billy Don Williams saw Ruby.	CE 1527'
	Dallas	Becky Jones saw Ruby	CE 2401
	Carousel	Crafard saw Ruby betw. 12 noon and 3 p.m. Ruby talked to a woman and her husband re a job for the woman.	Crafard DE 5226

COMMISSION EXHIBIT No. 2344—Continued

Date	Place	Activity	Reported
11-21		William Selah saw and talked to Ruby on the street.	CE 2402 CE 2269
		Ruby telephoned Mrs. Carr, Houston, re hiring of band "The Impellas."	CE 2334
	Carousel	Ruby called Crafard wanting Crafard to work that night at the Vegas Club.	Crafard DE 5226
	Carousel	Ruby took Crafard from the Carousel to the Vegas Club.	Crafard DE 5226
	Dallas	Kathleen C. Root saw and spoke to Ruby on Commerce Street.	CE 2319
	Herald Bldg.	Samuel C. Smith saw and talked to Ruby about ads for Ruby's clubs in Dallas.	CE 2320
	Vegas	Pauline Hall saw Ruby	CE 1221
	Carousel	**Charles Miller and Dave Larkin see Ruby eject patron.**	**CE 2434 CE 2435**

COMMISSION EXHIBIT No. 2344—Continued

Commission Exhibit No. 2345

UNITED STATES DEPARTMENT OF JUSTICE

FEDERAL BUREAU OF INVESTIGATION

In Reply, Please Refer to File No.

Los Angeles, California
August 17, 1964

INTERVIEW WITH DEROSTUS MC COLLOUGH MILES

Reference is made to the letter of the President's Commission on the Assassination of President Kennedy to the Director, FBI, dated July 16, 1964, requesting that Mr. Derostus M. Miles be re-interviewed.

Mr. Derostus Mc Collough Miles, 984 South Normandie Avenue, Apartment Number 101, Los Angeles, California, manager of the apartment house at this address, was interviewed on August 14, 1964, by Special Agents of the FBI, at which time he advised as follows:

He met Jack Ruby at the Carousel Club in Dallas, Texas, a week before the fair opened on October 5, 1963, which would make the meeting date with Ruby about September 28, 1963. He subsequently met with Ruby three or four times prior to October 6, 1963, when his show, "How Hollywood Makes Movies" opened at the fair. These visits occurred at the Carousel Club, were usually between 12:00 PM midnight and 2:00 AM in the morning, and would vary in duration from one to two hours. He usually had someone with him when he visited Ruby, and it was always someone affiliated with his show. His show personnel included Bob Craven, Harry Lovejoy, Sam Dougherty, Joe Randulla, and Marvin Gardner, and one or two of these persons would accompany him when he visited Ruby at the Carousel Club.

The topic of conversation during the above-mentioned meetings included show business, dogs, Ruby's bar, and his twist board. Politics were never discussed at these meetings, to the best of his recollection. He took a personal liking to Ruby and enjoyed talking to him.

COMMISSION EXHIBIT NO. 2345

INTERVIEW WITH DEROSTUS MC COLLOUGH MILES

He has no recollection of seeing Ruby at any time, either in Dallas or at the fair grounds prior to the opening of the show on October 6, 1963, other than the above-mentioned contacts. Subsequent to the opening of the show, Ruby visited his show site three to five times. Ruby was alone upon the occasion of these visits which occurred in the morning or the afternoon, and lasted from one to two hours. During the period October 6 through October 19, he and some of his show people visited Ruby at the Carousel Club approximately seven to ten times, usually in the late evening hours. On one occasion, the entire personnel of his show visited the Carousel Club.

Sometime between October 1, 1963, and October 6, 1963, he visited Ruby at the Carousel Club and borrowed several items used as props for his show. One item was a three-foot square mirror taken from Ruby's office and a large cooler unit about three feet square and eighteen inches in depth. Both items were obtained from Ruby at the same time and were brought to his show site by Ruby who was assisted by one of his Negro workers.

He does not recall Ruby obtaining any political radio script called "Life Line" or that Ruby ever commented on any Right Wing literature. Politics were never a topic of conversation at any of the meetings with Ruby, as best he can recall.

An itinerant worker, Larry Crafard, had been working at a show located next to his show at the fair grounds but was fired from his job. He felt sorry for Crafard and hired him since Crafard appeared to need money for living expenses. One night Crafard and another individual also employed at the fair grounds engaged in a fight and Crafard had several teeth knocked out. He does not know what prompted the fight and was not present at the time the fight took place. Crafard appeared to be an illiterate individual and an ordinary itinerant worker. He lost contact with Crafard when the show closed on October 19, 1963.

- 2 -

COMMISSION EXHIBIT NO. 2345—Continued

INTERVIEW WITH DEROSTUS
MC COLLOUGH MILES

During his contacts with Ruby he became aware of the fact that Ruby carried a gun in a shoulder holster. Ruby also carried large amounts of money on his person, believed to be about $1,000 or more. He is of the opinion that Ruby tried to impress people with the idea that he was a successful businessman and night club operator.

COMMISSION EXHIBIT No. 2345—Continued

Commission Exhibit No. 2346

FD-302 (Rev. 3-3-59)

FEDERAL BUREAU OF [redacted]

Date 12-20-63

1

BARBARA (Mrs. CHARLES L.) HEMBY, 7947 Claremont, related the following with regard to her name, Mrs. HEMBY, telephone RI 2-6293. This telephone number is that of her employer, National Life and Accident Insurance Company, First National Bank Building, Dallas. She has known JACK RUBY for about three years. She first went into the Carousel Club about three years ago and been there on two occasions; on both occasions being there with her husband. Her regular employment is as a receptionist in the National Life and Accident Insurance Company, but she occasionally work as a waitress for JACK RUBY on one or two nights a week, this being in the latter part of September, 1963, and continued until sometime about the first of October, 1963. She later saw RUBY on or about that day.

She does not know LEE HARVEY OSWALD and knew nothing about any possible association between RUBY and OSWALD. She knew of no conspiracy on the part of RUBY with anyone to kill OSWALD and did not know how RUBY got into the basement of the Police Department. She knew of no close associates of RUBY who were members of the Dallas Police Department. She said her husband CHARLES L. HEMBY was a former member of the Dallas Police Department and it was through her husband that she originally met RUBY.

on 12-20-63 at Dallas, Texas File # DL 44-1639

by Special Agent ALLEN H. SMITH - md Date dictated 12-20-63

122

COMMISSION EXHIBIT No. 2346

FD-302 (Rev. 3-3-59) FEDERAL BUREAU OF INVESTIGA N

1 Date 12/10/63

NATHAN WYLE, Associate, Travel Inc., 1213-14 Adolphus Towers, Dallas, advised that he has known JACK RUBY since 1948 but only through business contacts. He explained that in 1948, he, WYLE, was employed as a reporter by the "Dallas Morning News" and for several years as such he regularly made the rounds of the various night clubs and lounges in the city. Thus, he had occasion to see and speak to RUBY from time to time but he never associated with RUBY on a social basis.

Mr. WYLE stated that the last time he saw and spoke to RUBY was on about October 2, 1963, on the street in front of the Baker Hotel. At that time, RUBY mentioned that he was interested in taking a Caribbean cruise at a later date, exact date not mentioned, during his anticipated vacation. Consequently, Mr. WYLE mailed some literature concerning such a cruise to RUBY on the following date, but RUBY never followed through and never contacted Mr. WYLE's office concerning this cruise. WYLE stated that to his knowledge, RUBY did not take such a cruise. Mr. WYLE added that he was in the Orient from November 1 to November 24, 1963, and consequently was more or less out of touch with local news and naturally did not see or talk to RUBY during that time. WYLE advised that he always considered RUBY a friendly talkative individual who appeared to be extremely fond of publicity for himself. He stated that he was shocked to learn that RUBY resorted to violence by killing LEE HARVEY OSWALD and in his own mind he felt that RUBY's love for publicity might have influenced him on the spur of the moment to commit such an act.

on 12/9/63 at Dallas, Texas File # DL 44-1639

by Special Agent EDMOND C. HARDIN - gj Date dictated 12/10/63

This document contains neither recommendations nor conclusions of the FBI. It is the property of the FBI and is loaned to your agency; it and its contents are not to be distributed outside your agency.

431

COMMISSION EXHIBIT No. 2347

FD-302 (Rev. 1-25-60) FEDERAL BUREAU OF INVE— Commission Exhibit No. 2348

1 Date November 29, 1963

MARVIN GARDNER, Electronic Technician, 7223 Melrose, telephone WE 1-2070, WE 5-0373 and WE 5-1442, telephoned the FBI Office in Los Angeles on November 27, 1963, and stated that he had seen the interview of AL DAVIDSON on television and DAVIDSON had made it appear that he knew JACK RUBY very well, but this is not true. GARDNER said that he and other individuals were part of a group that put on a show at the Dallas State Fair in October, 1963, called "How Hollywood Makes Movies." DAVIDSON was connected with the group in that he was to handle the publicity, but he did very little work, and met RUBY only casually. GARDNER stated that he talked to RUBY probably more than DAVIDSON did, and GARDNER would be happy to furnish any information he knew, if the FBI was interested.

GARDNER on November 27, 1963, furnished the following information:

GARDNER was employed by ROBERT CRAVEN and DEROSTUS "DEKE" MILES, who produced the show "How Hollywood Makes Movies." A group of eight persons went to Dallas on Sunday, September 29, 1963, and the show opened at the Dallas State Fair on October 5, 1963. It was about October 3 or 4, 1963, that GARDNER first met JACK RUBY, who had met CRAVEN previously.

CRAVEN is a promoter who has lived in Los Angeles about three years but originally was from New England. CRAVEN's wife, RITA CRAVEN, has a clothing business known as Craven Contracting Company, 407 East Pico, Los Angeles.

RUBY was very friendly with this Hollywood group and assisted them by loaning articles needed as props in the show. He was given a pass to the show and invited the members of the group to come to his night club, the Carousel, in downtown Dallas.

On 11/27/63 11/29/63 at Los Angeles, California File # Los Angeles 44-895

by SA WILLIAM W. COLBY:elc Date dictated 11/29/63

This document contains neither recommendations nor conclusions of the FBI. It is the property of the FBI and is loaned to your agency; it and its contents are not to be distributed outside your agency.

74

COMMISSION EXHIBIT No. 2348

GARDNER does not know any background of RUBY, except that RUBY said he came from Chicago several years ago. RUBY was friendly with JOY DALE, a stripper at the Carousel. GARDNER was never at RUBY's house. He does not know any of RUBY's associates. GARDNER described RUBY as having nervous drive but did not think him to be an emotional individual. GARDNER never heard of LEE OSWALD and knows of no connections between OSWALD and RUBY. GARDNER does not know of any police connections of RUBY, but he heard that RUBY knew everyone on the Dallas Police Department.

The Hollywood show closed on October 15, 1963, and those in the group left that city on October 16, 1963, to return to Los Angeles. The show was a financial failure and the members of the cast did not get paid. While they were in Dallas, they stayed the first few days at the Baker Hotel and then moved to a rooming house on Gaston Street, possibly 3900 block. The rooming house was operated by a DOC (last name unknown), a retired auctioneer, and a man named HENRY (last name unknown), who ran a beauty shop in Dallas. DOC and HENRY and the Hollywood group were the only persons staying in the rooming house at the time.

Those persons in the Hollywood show were, in addition to CRAVEN, MILES and GARDNER; HARRY LOVEJOY, a part-time actor, 15325 South Freeman, Lawndale, California; JOE RADULA, an insurance man who was the cameraman in the show, residence 2415 North Gower, Hollywood, California, HOllywood 3-7724; SAM DAUGHERTY, an actor and beautician, 635 30th Street, Manhattan Beach, telephone FR 2-9093, FR 2-5077; JANE SMITH, an actress, address unknown, who has left Hollywood and returned to her home in Connecticut; and CARYN MURPHY, an actress, address unknown, who has left Hollywood and gone to New York.

RADULA knew RUBY slightly. GARDNER did not think DAUGHERTY knew RUBY at all. LOVEJOY became acquainted with RUBY, and the two women met him.

MARVIN GARDNER telephonically informed SA WILLIAM W. COLBY on November 29, 1963, the following:

75

There was an individual by the name of LARRY (last name unknown), age about 20, who worked as a carnival worker around the tent of the show "How Hollywood Makes Movies" in October, 1963, at the Dallas State Fair, Dallas. LARRY told GARDNER that he once used to work in rodeos but was injured so was then doing carnival work. LARRY had a nervous twitch in his eyes. GARDNER believes that LARRY was from the State of Washington. He does not know LARRY's present whereabouts.

After the show closed on Tuesday, October 15, 1963, LARRY continued working in the same tent for the show that followed. The show that followed was a rock and roll show produced by JESSIE SEAY of Dallas. SEAY was in charge of the rides on the midway. GARDNER understood that SEAY was a friend of DEWEY GROOM, owner of the Longhorn Ranch Night Club, Dallas. The rock and roll show lasted only about two nights because of trouble with the musicians. Where LARRY went after that GARDNER does not know, but he heard that JACK RUBY may have given him a job. GARDNER thinks it was CRAVEN who mentioned this.

LARRY knew a lot of the carnival people working at the fair. One person he knew was a man named BULL, white male, American, age in the thirties, husky build, 6 feet. LARRY and BULL had previously worked in some other show, possibly the Memphis Fair. Between Tuesday, October 15, 1963, 12:00 midnight, and 2:00 a.m., October 16, 1963, LARRY and BULL had a fist fight in the tent. the Dallas Police came to the tent to investigate the matter. LARRY told the police he fell over a chair so did not involve BULL.

Another person who knew LARRY at the carnival was a girl named "JOHNNIE." She is a thin-looking blonde who follows the carnivals. Her whereabouts are unknown to GARDNER.

GARDNER does not know of any subversive, hoodlum or gambling connections that RUBY might have.

76

Commission Exhibit No. 2349

FD-302 (Rev. 1-25-60) FEDERAL BUREAU OF INV...

Date 11/23/63

1

Mrs. ISABELLA GREGORY, 414 Emerald Street, New Orleans, Louisiana, and owner of property located 4905-4911 Magazine Street signed a Consent to Search form giving permission to search the premises at 4905 Magazine Street, specifically the apartment and porch formerly occupied by LEE HARVEY OSWALD.

The following described pamphlet was found in the middle row, center shelf of a set of cabinets located on the porch at the rear of 4905 Magazine Street at 10:05 a.m. by SA JOHN B. LEE, JR., on November 23, 1963:

An 8" x 10" cardboard with a paper bearing the words "Hands off Cuba!" "Join the Fair Play for Cuba Committee" "New Orleans Charter Member Branch" "Free Literature, Lectures" "Location: L. H. OSWALD, 4905 Magazine Street, New Orleans, Louisiana" "Everyone welcome! " pasted on this cardboard.

On 11/23/63 at New Orleans, Louisiana File # NO 89-69

by SA JOHN B. LEE, JR. :sab Date dictated 11/23/63

This document contains neither recommendations nor conclusions of the FBI. It is the property of the FBI and is loaned to your agency; it and its contents are not to be distributed outside your agency.

COMMISSION EXHIBIT No. 2349

FD-302 (Rev. 1-25-60) FEDERAL BUREAU OF

1

Date 3/13/64

The records of the Illinois Bell Telephone Company show telephone number ST 2-8920 (782-8920) is listed to Ero Manufacturing Company, 7146 Monroe, Chicago, Illinois. This phone was established prior to November, 1944.

The following toll calls were charged to telephone number ST 2-8920 during the period September 26, 1963, through November 22, 1963:

102

On 3/12/64 at Chicago, Illinois File # CG 44-645

by SAs JERRY H. BREIDENFELD and CHARLES L. BROWN, JR./fef/dmj Date dictated 3/13/64

This document contains neither recommendations nor conclusions of the FBI. It is the property of the FBI and is loaned to your agency; it and its contents are not to be distributed outside your agency.

COMMISSION EXHIBIT No. 2350

2
CG 44-645

Date	Place Called	Telephone Number	Charges	Time	Additional Information
9/28	Memphis, Tennessee	276-0411	$ 1.55	4"	Station Call 10:38 a.m.
10/1	Sterling, Illinois	626-3988	.60	2"	Station Call 4:11 p.m.
10/2	Hazelhurst, Georgia	FR 5-2551	6.25	15"	Station Call 5:42 p.m.
*9/26	NYC, NY	No number	5.05	47"	Person to person charged to credit card, made from Trenton, New Jersey
*9/26	NYC, NY	No number	.80	3"	Person to person day call, credit card used, made from Camden, New Jersey

103

COMMISSION EXHIBIT No. 2350—Continued

3
CG 44-645

Date	Place Called	Telephone Number	Charges	Time	Additional Information
10/3	Olney, Illinois	EX 3-2991	$ 2.20	4"	Person to person day call
*9/28	Newark, New Jersey		.40	3"	Station to station day call, credit card used made from Trenton, New Jersey
*9/28	Newark, New Jersey		.60	5"	Station to station day call made from Trenton, New Jersey, credit card used
10/16	Pagosa Springs, Colorado		.95	1"	Person to person call, credit card used from Santa Fe, New Mexico, to Gibson, Harvey's Motel made 5:34 p.m.

104

COMMISSION EXHIBIT No. 2350—Continued

4

CG 44-645

Date	Place Called	Telephone Number	Charges	Time	Additional Information
10/3	Richmond, Virginia		$ 4.40	14"	Station call at 6:16 p.m. credit card used, made from number 439-1926, at Chicago, Illinois
10/11	Milwaukee, Wisconsin	GR 6-3670	1.10	5"	Person to person call at 4:00 p.m. to Abevar Wisnewski, Milwaukee Board of School Directors, from Anderson at number 782-8921
10/7	McKinney,	LI 2-6574	3.23	27"	Call at 6:40 p.m. to Sherwood Smith, made from number 748-8161, credit card used at Dallas, Texas

105

COMMISSION EXHIBIT No. 2350—Continued

5

CG 44-645

Date	Place Called	Telephone Number	Charges	Time	Additional Information
10/8	Monroe, Louisiana	FA 5-8949	$ 1.45	3"	Person call at 2:04 p.m. to McDonald-Gibson, credit card used at Dallas, Texas
10/7	Philadelphia, Pennsylvania	WA 2-3300	3.40	6"	Person call at 10:24 a.m. to Henry from Farrell, credit card used at Elk Grove, Illinois
10/9	Chicago, Illinois	AM 2-9491	3.25	10"	Station call at 6:40 p.m. from number 748-8161, credit card used at Dallas, Texas
10/9	Chicago, Illinois	WE 5-5348	3.25	10"	Station call at 6:26 p.m. made from number 748-8161, credit card used at Dallas, Texas

106

COMMISSION EXHIBIT No. 2350—Continued

6

CG 44-645

Date	Place Called	Telephone Number	Charges	Time	Additional Information
10/9	Philadelphia, Pennsylvania	WA 2-3300	$ 3.80	7"	Person call at 1:05 p.m. to Weiter Henry from number 921-9882, credit card used at Fond du Lac, Wisconsin
10/9	St. Louis, Missouri	GA 1-5900	2.25	4"	Person call at 4:25 p.m. to Harold Katz, Famous Barr Sporting Goods, credit card used at Dallas, Texas
10/9	Kansas City, Missouri	WE 1-4333	3.30	10"	Station call at 4:30 p.m., credit card used at Dallas, Texas

107

COMMISSION EXHIBIT No. 2350—Continued

6 a

CG 44-645

Date	Place Called	Telephone Number	Charges	Time	Additional Information
10/10	Highland Park, Illinois	ID 2-6639	$ .70	3"	Call at 7:20 p.m. credit card used (Brigin?), Missouri
10/8	McKinney, Texas	LI 2-6574	.83	7"	Call at 6:57 p.m. to Sherwood Smith from number 748-8161, credit card used at Dallas, Texas
10/24	Chicago, Illinois	935-5348	1.65	5"	Station call at 6:23 p.m., credit card used at Huron, South Dakota
10/21	Rockford, Illinois	962-4411	1.75	5"	Person call at 4:17 p.m. to Phillip Sheik Weisses Department Store, from Ferrell, number 782-8921

108

COMMISSION EXHIBIT No. 2350—Continued

7
CG 44-645

Date	Place Called	Telephone Number	Charges	Time	Additional Information
10/15	Rockford, Illinois	962-7747	$ .55	3"	Call at 9:43 a.m. to Be-Mac Transportation, 1860 Seminary Street, phone number 782-8921
10/21	Waukegan, Illinois	MA 3-5070	.35	1"	Station call at 10:16 a.m.
*10/13	Lake Forest, Illinois		10.75	33"	Person night call, credit card used in Easton, Pennsylvania
*10/14	Newark, New Jersey		.45	3"	Station day call, credit card used at Easton, Pennsylvania
10/19	Paducah, Kentucky	443-7533	1.05	1"	Station call at 8:49 a.m.

109

COMMISSION EXHIBIT No. 2350—Continued

7a

CG 44-645

Date	Place Called	Telephone Number	Charges	Time	Additional Information
10/19	Sumter, South Carolina	773-8121	$ 2.25	5"	Station call at 10:26 a.m.
*10/14	Philadelphia, Pennsylvania		1.55	12"	Person day call, credit card used Easton, Pennsylvania
*9/28	Elizabeth, New Jersey		.35	3"	Station day call, credit card used at Trenton, New Jersey
10/28	Roseville, Michigan	PR 2-4244	.85	1"	Station call at 3:55 p.m.
*9/27	New York City, New York		3.45	31"	Person night call, credit card used at Trenton, New Jersey
10/4	Los Angeles, California	MA 8-6324	2.45	4"	Station call at 4:53 p.m.

110

COMMISSION EXHIBIT No. 2350—Continued

8

CG 44-645

Date	Place Called	Telephone Number	Charges	Time	Additional Information
10/5	Maplewood, New Jersey	PO 1-5050	$ 1.45	3"	Station call at 9:08 a.m.
10/7	Muskegan, Michigan	PA 8-2325	.60	2"	Station call at 4:30 p.m.
10/9	Crystal Lake, Illinois	459-1751	.40	3"	Station call at 2:59 p.m.
10/11	Hazelhurst, Georgia	FR 5-2551	2.65	6"	Station call at 10:54 a.m.
10/12	Raleigh, North Carolina	TE 3-3036	1.40	2"	Station call at 11:17 a.m.
10/12	Crystal Lake, Illinois	459-4120	.40	3"	Station call at 12:38 p.m.
10/29	Joliet, Illinois	726-3631	.55	5"	Station call at 2:13 p.m.

J11

COMMISSION EXHIBIT No. 2350—Continued

9

CG 44-645

ate	Place Called	Telephone Number	Charges	Time	Additional Information
*10/25	Lake Forest, Illinois		$ 1.40	6"	Station after 9 PM, credit card used at Miami, Florida
11/1	Crystal Lake, Illinois	459-4120	.40	1"	Station call at 4:47 p.m.
11/4	Waukegan, Illinois	ON 2-4480	.35	1"	Station call at 10:34 a.m. to Ellis Fuqua from Anderson, CH 4-0770
10/25	Chicago, Illinois	225-5533	3.05	6"	Person call at 8:50 a.m. to Miss Elsa Hecker, Room 696, Michael Reese Hospital, from Huron, South Dakota

J12

COMMISSION EXHIBIT No. 2350—Continued

10

CG 44-645

Date	Place Called	Telephone Number	Charges	Time	Additional Information
11/4	Atlanta, Georgia	JA 2-3558	$ 3.05	6"	Person call at 8:23 a.m., M. Wm. Bath, Number 782-8921, from Anderson
10/31	Akron, Ohio	253-1131	.70	3"	Credit card used in Cleveland, Ohio
11/6	Waukegan, Illinois	CH 4-0770	.65	3"	To Ellis Fuqua from Anderson at number 782-8921; call made at 2:57 p.m.
11/1	Port Huron, Michigan	982-0134	.75	2"	Person call, at 2:10 p.m. credit card used at Detroit, Michigan, call to Carol, Carol's Store, from 2635, H.T. Farrel

113

COMMISSION EXHIBIT No. 2350—Continued

11

CG 44-645

Date	Place Called	Telephone Number	Charges	Time	Additional Information
11/1	New York, New York		$ 5.30	10"	Person day call, credit card used at Miami, Florida
11/12	Mundelein, Illinois	LO 6-5700	.35	3"	Station call at 1:24 p.m.
11/7	Chicago, Illinois	935-5348	4.75	15"	Credit card used at Brooklyn, New York, station call at 8:16 p.m.
11/5	Missoula, Montana	549-8201	2.05	9"	Credit card used at New York City, station call at 11:42 p.m.
11/12	Chicago, Illinois	ST 2-8920	2.05	6"	Person call, at 12:40 p.m. collect call from Field at Dayton, Ohio Number 222-4633

114

COMMISSION EXHIBIT No. 2350—Continued

12
CG 44-645

Date	Place Called	Telephone Number	Charges	Time	Additional Information
11/13	Hazelhurst, Georgia	FR 5-2521	$ 2.65	6"	Station call at 2:56 p.m.
11/13	Ottawa, Illinois	HE 4-0947	.85	5"	Call to Lacy and Minor at 12:45 p.m.
11/10	Chicago, Ill.	935-5348	1.80	5"	Station call at 8:35 p.m. credit card used at Jacksonville, Florida
11/9	Hazelhurst, Georgia	375-2551	.95	3"	To Quinn Res. Chester Brezinski call at 4:46 p.m.
11/15	Mundelein, Illinois	LO 6-5700	.35	1"	Station call at 11:31 a.m.
11/15	Mundelein, Illinois	LO 6-5700	.35	1"	Station call at 3:27 p.m.
11/15	Mundelein, Illinois	LO 6-5700	.35	1"	Station call at 1:16 p.m.
11/15	Escanaba, Michigan	ST 6-6544	.90	1"	Station call at 1:01 p.m.

115

COMMISSION EXHIBIT No. 2350—Continued

13
CG 44-645

Date	Place Called	Telephone Number	Charges	Time	Additional Information
11/16	Crystal Lake, Illinois	459-4120	$ .60	5"	Station call at 9:53 a.m.
11/13	Chicago, Illinois	935-5348	1.15	5"	Station call at 9:25 p.m credit card used at New Orleans, Louisiana
11/11	Hazelhurst, Georgia	375-2551	.75	4"	Station call at 2:34 p.m. credit card used at Jacksonville, Florida
11/18	Crystal Lake, Illinois	459-4120	.70	6"	Station call at 2:29 p.m.
11/19	Peoria, Illinois	673-8165	1.30	3"	Person call at 1:08 p.m. to Foster

116

COMMISSION EXHIBIT No. 2350—Continued

14

CG 44-645

Date	Place Called	Telephone Number	Charges	Time	Additional Information
11/19	Springfield, Illinois	522-5622	$ .75	1"	Station call 1:50 p.m.
11/20	Hammond, Indiana	WE 2-2535	.35	6"	Station call at 2:40 p.m.
11/22	Crystal Lake, Illinois	459-4120	.40	2"	Station call at 7:43 a.m.
11/20	Cincinnati, Ohio	381-2100	1.45	2"	Person call at 7:37 a.m. to Lennox from #439-1926, Elk Grove, Ill. credit card used
11/20	Chicago, Illinois	WH 4-4970	1.70	3"	Person call at 9:09 a.m. credit card used, Kansas City, Missouri to Miss A. Asie, Room 1405
11/21	McKinney, Texas	LI 2-3325	1.20	8"	Station call at 1:50 p.m., credit card used at Seagoville, Texas, Ero Manufacturing Company

117

COMMISSION EXHIBIT No. 2350—Continued

15
CG 44-645

Date	Place Called	Telephone Number	Charges	Time	Additional Information
11/21	Chicago, Illinois	ST 2-6944	$ 2.20	3"	Call at 12:20 p.m. credit card used at Dallas, Texas, Miss Hacker from number 748-8161
11/21	Evansville, Indiana	422-3281	1.15	2"	Person call at 5:30 p.m. to Kerswake, from Room 653, telephone number 621-6600, credit card used in Cincinnati, Ohio
11/21	Chicago, Illinois	AM 2-9491	4.75	15"	Station call at 6:33 p.m. credit card used at Dallas, Texas, from number 748-8161

118

COMMISSION EXHIBIT No. 2350—Continued

16

CG 44-645

*The calls marked by an asterisk set forth above were disputed by the subscriber of telephone ST 2-8920, Ero Manufacturing Company, Chicago, Illinois, and the customer is to be rebilled at a later date deleting these calls.

The above information should not be made public without the issuance of a subpoena duces tecum to an appropriate official of the Illinois Bell Telephone Company, Chicago, Illinois.

119

COMMISSION EXHIBIT No. 2350—Continued

FD-302 (Rev. 3-3-59) FEDERAL BUREAU OF Commission Exhibit No. 2351

1 ~~Other Individuals~~ and Organizations Involved or Interviewed Date 12/19/63

AMOS C. FLINT, 5010 Live Oak, Apartment C, employed at Southland Life, advised that he observed an ad in a newspaper advertising membership in the Sovereign Club located on Commerce Street, to which ad he applied. He stated that he became a member of the club and met JACK RUBY, and he believed he gave JACK $20.00 or $25.00 for membership fee. He stated that thereafter he went to the club about ten or twelve times before the club folded up about two or three years ago. He said that he did not see JACK RUBY from that time until the Texas and Oklahoma football game this year, when he was standing on the street after the game and an individual called out his name: FLINT. He said he turned around and recognized JACK RUBY, that he was surprised RUBY recalled his name since the lapse of time.

He said during this brief meeting on the street RUBY was passing out little cards advertising the Carousel Club, one side of which contained a picture of an exotic and the other with the name JACK RUBY. He said he never saw RUBY again and during their association strictly as a member of the Club Sovereign, he never heard RUBY mention LEE HARVEY OSWALD and knew of no association between the two.

He said that he first heard of OSWALD during the Presidential assassination. He advised that RUBY was the type of person who was constantly talking and bragging about his feats but never mentioned or talked about politics. He said that he was a crude salesman, the type that always went around slapping people on the back. He said that he had never observed RUBY swear, push anyone around or fight with them in public, and he was surprised to read about this part of RUBY's nature in the papers.

He said that he met RUBY's sister once and he was impressed by her since she was more sophisticated and suave than JACK RUBY. He said that he had known RUBY owned the Vegas Club in Oak Cliff but had never been in the club. He further advised that he never knew where RUBY lived and never knew any of RUBY's associates. He said that he was surprised when RUBY shot OSWALD. He advised that he joined the Sovereign Club with CHARLES PETTIGREW, who works for the City Planning Commission, City of Dallas, and who lives in an apartment building on North Henderson off the Central Expressway, exact address unknown.

69

on 12/17/63 at Dallas, Texas File # DL 44-1639

by Special Agents JAMES J. WARD and ROBERT E. BASHAM - LAC Date dictated 12/17/63

COMMISSION EXHIBIT No. 2351

FD-302 (Rev 3-3-59) FEDERAL BUREAU OF

Date 12/17/63

1

MICHAEL P. DOYLE, District Manager, Waukesha Sales, 2635 Manana Drive, was found to be identical to a person named MICKEY DOYLE, which name was found in a book which was the property of JACK RUBY.

Mr. DOYLE was contacted at his office, at which time he advised he has known JACK RUBY since about 1955 and became acquainted with him at the Vegas Club. DOYLE stated that, although he was on a first-name basis with RUBY, he knows nothing of a personal nature concerning him and only attended his club when entertaining customers from out of town.

DOYLE stated he never heard of LEE HARVEY OSWALD prior to the assassination of the President and has no knowledge of the murder of OSWALD by RUBY, other than what he has read in the newspapers and has seen on television.

DOYLE stated the last time he saw RUBY was on the evening of October 12, 1963, in the Century Room of the Adolphus Hotel when he talked with RUBY for about an hour between 8:00 PM and 10:00 PM. DOYLE recalls this date as it was the week end of the Texas - Oklahoma Football Game.

on 12/16/63 at Dallas, Texas File # DL 44-1639

by Special Agent EDWARD J. MABEY/eah Date dictated 12/16/63

82

FD-302 (Rev. 3-3-59) FEDERAL BUREAU OF INVESTIGATION

1

Date December 16, 1963

BONNIE H. BELL, whose name appears on a Carousel Club pass card, advised as follows:

Mrs. BELL stated that she has been employed as a nurse for several years by Doctor COLEMAN JACOBSON with office in the Doctors Building, Dallas. She stated that for several years she has seen RUBY from time to time who came to Doctor JACOBSON as a patient. She advised that she went to the Vegas Club four or five times during this period and talked briefly with RUBY two or three times while there as a customer. She went to the Carousel Club several months ago but did not see RUBY at that time. She stated that about October 15, 1963, RUBY, while visiting Doctor JACOBSON, took her name and promised to send her a permanent pass to the Carousel Club which she did not receive.

Mrs. BELL stated that she knew RUBY only through business associations and at times, she visited his clubs as related above and never discussed politics with him and that she feels she did not become well enough acquainted with him to estimate his character, personality or disposition. She added that she is not acquainted with RUBY's associates or background.

Mrs. BELL stated that she did not know LEE HARVEY OSWALD and has no information indicating any relationship which may have existed between OSWALD and RUBY and further that she has no information concerning the shooting of OSWALD by RUBY or of any conspiracy or assistance which may have helped RUBY gain access to the basement area of the Dallas Police Department prior to shooting OSWALD. Mrs. BELL stated she last saw RUBY on about October 15, 1963, when he was at Doctor JACOBSON's office.

on 12/16/63 at Dallas, Texas File # DL 44-1639

by Special Agent EDMOND C. HARDIN/jn Date dictated 12/16/63

41

Commission Exhibit No. 2354

FD-302 (Rev. 3-3-59)

FEDERAL BUREAU [redacted]

Date 12-20-63

1

Mrs. WANDA MINNIX, 4317 Irving, Dallas, Texas, was interviewed concerning the name WANDA MINX, DA 7-5639, which name was found in the personal affects of JACK RUBY at the time of his arrest. She related the following:

She formerly resided at 2420 Greenport Drive, Dallas, telephone DA 7-5639. About one year ago that there was an ad in the paper seeking the services of a hostess. There was a telephone number to call and she called this number and left her name and telephone number. She was requested to come to the Carousel Club for an interview. She did go to the Carousel Club but did not see JACK RUBY. During her visit, however, she saw what type of establishment this was and had no further interest in seeking employment. She has not been in the Carousel Club since and this was the only occasion she has ever been in this place.

Mrs. MINNIX knew RUBY prior to the time she answered the ad, having met him socially while visiting a night club known as the Music Club. She is presently employed as a hostessat the SPA, a health center at 4883 Turtle Creek, Dallas, and has seen RUBY on two or three occasions when the SPA had open house. She explained that the SPA has steam baths, handball courts, badminton, shuffle board, etc., and sells memberships for $100, plus $16 a month dues. She last saw RUBY about October 15, 1963, when the SPA was having an open house.

Mrs. MINNIX did not know LEE HARVEY OSWALD. She knew of no connection between OSWALD and RUBY or why RUBY killed OSWALD.

on 12-19-63 at Dallas, Texas File # DL 44-1639

by Special Agent ALLEN H. SMITH & TOM E. CHAPOTON - md Date dictated 12-20-63

69

This document contains neither recommendations nor conclusions of the FBI. It is the property of the FBI and is loaned to your agency; it and its contents are not to be distributed outside your agency.

COMMISSION EXHIBIT No. 2354

FD-302 (Rev. 1-25-60)

FEDERAL BUREAU O [redacted] Commission Exhibit No. 2355

Date 12/9/63

ASSOCIATES AND EMPLOYEES OF RUBY

JEWEL BROWN was interviewed at the Wellington Hotel, 55th Street and 7th Avenue. She furnished the following information:

JIM DOLAN of the American Guild of Variety Artists, Dallas, Texas, in 1959 contacted her relative to her working in the Club Sovereign, which was owned by JACK RUBY. DOLAN told her RUBY was trying to break the racial barrier, and therefore was interested in employing her as an entertainer at the Club Sovereign.

RUBY contacted her at that time, and arrangements were made between herself and RUBY, whereby she would be the sole performer at the club. She did work for RUBY at the Club Sovereign for about seven months, but quit suddenly as the result of a disagreement with RUBY. She indicated this disagreement resulted from his attempted advances toward her.

At the request of the American Guild of Variety Artists, she returned to the club and worked several more days until her contract expired.

BROWN was then employed by the LOUIS ARMSTRONG band, which went on an overseas tour for the United States State Department. She remained with the band on tour until the band's vacation period August 27 to October 24, 1963.

She worked in the Cabana Club, Dallas, Texas, during the week beginning October 16, 1963.

RUBY was a visitor at the Club Cabana this week on several occasions. This was the first time she had seen or heard from him since she quit working at the Club Sovereign in 1960. Her conversations with him were of a general nature, and at no time did she ever hear him speak of LEE HARVEY OSWALD.

On 12/6/63 at New York, New York File # NY 44-974

by SA EDWARD S. LENEHAN:aam 29 Date dictated 12/9/63

This document contains neither recommendations nor conclusions of the FBI. It is the property of the FBI and is loaned to your agency; it and its contents are not to be distributed outside your agency.

COMMISSION EXHIBIT No. 2355

NY 44-974

She has no knowledge of any prior relationship or acquaintance between RUBY and LEE HARVEY OSWALD. She has no knowledge of RUBY ever being affiliated with any subversive organizations.

2.9.35

COMMISSION EXHIBIT No. 2355—Continued

FD-302 (Rev. 1-25-60)

FEDERAL BUREAU OF I— Commission Exhibit No. 2356

Date 1/20/64

Charles Curtis was interviewed at the New York Office of the Federal Bureau of Investigation (FBI). He resides at 2223 Cortelyou Road, Apartment 3D, Brooklyn, New York, telephone number BU 7-3658. He furnished the following information:

He is the personal manager of Little Lorraine Egypt, who dances professionally as a "belly dancer" under the name Little Egypt.

Little Egypt had been engaged to perform for ten days, beginning October 17, 1963 at a private supper club in Dallas, Texas, known as the "Gay Life." He exhibited a brochure reflecting that Little Egypt was to appear at this club beginning October 17, 1963, and she was billed as "The World's Foremost Egyptian Dancer."

After he had been in Dallas for several days, Curtis noticed an ad in the October 19, 1963 issue of the Dallas Morning News for the Carousel Club. This ad indicated that Jada and several other "strip" dancers were performing at this club. The ad also appeared to indicate that Little Egypt and Ann Corio were also performing at this club. However, Curtis noticed that underneath Little Egypt in small type a statement appeared reflecting that Little Egypt's belly album was given away free and underneath the name Ann Corio in small type was indicated that Corio's stripper album was being given away free.

Curtis determined that legally he could do nothing about this type of advertising. However, he wanted to contact the Manager of Carousel and inform him that he did not appreciate this type of advertising.

Therefore, during the above-mentioned engagement at the "Gay Life" Club, he and Little Egypt went to the Carousel Club about 2 a.m. after Little Egypt had finished her performance at the "Gay Life." They were accompanied by Glen (Last Name Unknown) who was the maitre d' of the "Gay Life" Club, and Glen's wife.

Jack Ruby came over to their table at the Carousel Club and introduced himself. Ruby asked if Little Egypt would

On 1/16/64 at New York File # NY 44-974

by SAS GERALD V. CASWELL & JAMES J. ROGERS/smb Date dictated 1/20/64

This document contains neither recommendations nor conclusions of the FBI. It is the property of the FBI and is loaned to your agency; it and its contents are not to be distributed outside your agency.

32

COMMISSION EXHIBIT No. 2356

2.

NY 44-974

perform at the Carousel Club and Curtis informed him that Little Egypt did not appear in "strip" clubs. Curtis informed Ruby that he would appreciate Ruby taking Little Egypt's name off his advertising. Ruby did not indicate whether he would do so or not.

Curtis had no additional information about Ruby and had never met him on any other occasion. He does not know Lee Harvey Oswald and does not know of any connection between Oswald and Jack Ruby.

33

COMMISSION EXHIBIT No. 2356—Continued

FD-302 (Rev. 1-25-60)

FEDERAL BUREAU [redacted]

Commission Exhibit No. 2357

1

Date 12/21/63

RICHARD H. SHEPPARD, 4518 Marlborough, advised that he was acquainted with RUBY in that about a year ago he transacted business with him in Dallas when he sold him lettering for the Marquee of the Carousel Club.

Since this transaction in the latter part of 1962, SHEPPARD advised he has been in Dallas on numerous occasions and quite frequently visited the Carousel Club, which is located across the street from the Adolphus Hotel, where he stays on his business trips. His last trip to Dallas was approximately the 20th of October, 1963, and he stayed at the Adolphus and talked with RUBY mostly about the advertising business.

SHEPPARD further advised that in his numerous conversations with RUBY the name OSWALD was never mentioned, and he never knew of RUBY belonging to any organization or club.

SHEPPARD concluded by saying that he could produce proof of his trips to Dallas and the specific dates, if it be necessary, in that he has all the records at his business office.

SHEPPARD stated that he was in the neon sign and advertising business.

On 12/21/63 at Houston, Texas File # HO 44-939

by SA DANIEL F. BODINE/lc Date dictated 12/21/63

95

COMMISSION EXHIBIT No. 2357

Commission Exhibit No. 2358

FD-302 (Rev. 3-3-59)

FEDERAL BUREAU OF IN[redacted]

1

Date 11/29/63

ROBERT FRANKLIN, also known as Bobbie O'Dowd, 429 Wrightwood Avenue, advised that he was on a business trip in the State of Texas approximately four weeks ago selling stamp machines. He stated that on approximately October 25, 1963, while in Dallas, he had lunch with a former heavy weight prize fighter known as J. D. TURNER. He advised that as they walked from the Baker Hotel to FRANKLIN's car, TURNER stopped an individual near the Adolphus Hotel in Dallas and introduced FRANKLIN to a person whom he identified as JACK RUBY. FRANKLIN stated they talked for approximately two minutes and it was apparent that TURNER and RUBY were well acquainted. As they departed RUBY's company, TURNER described RUBY as a good guy and the owner of a strip joint located across the street from the Adolphus Hotel.

FRANKLIN stated he has no personal knowledge of RUBY, but advised that TURNER resides on Prairie Street in Dallas, Texas, and is listed in the local telephone directory as J. TURNER, Prairie Street.

on 11/25/63 at Chicago, Illinois File # DL 44-1639 CG 44-645

by Special Agent JOHN R. BASSETT/ss Date dictated 11/25/63

COMMISSION EXHIBIT No. 2358

Commission Exhibit No. 2359

FD-302 (Rev. 3-3-59)

FEDERAL BUREAU [redacted]

1

Date December 20, 1963

Mr. JOE A. HELM, Mercantile National Bank, Dallas, Texas, whose name appeared on a Carousel Club pass card, furnished the following information:

He has known JACK RUBY for about ten years, however, had not had any contact with him for approximately seven years up until three or four weeks prior to the assassination of President KENNEDY.

Mr. HELM advised it was late on a Friday evening approximately four weeks prior to the assassination of President KENNEDY when JACK RUBY came into the bank attempting to get a cashier's check cashed. He said at this time RUBY asked him if he had been to his club. He said he had not and at that time RUBY gave him a pass for four to the Carousel Club. He said he signed the pass and RUBY then took it back saying he was going to have it laminated and would mail it back to him. He said that was the last contact he had with RUBY.

Mr. HELM stated he was formerly in the bookkeeping department of the Mercantile National Bank and while in that department, had frequent contacts with RUBY and knows that he had one or two checking accounts with the bank but does not recall the names in which these accounts were carried.

Mr. HELM advised RUBY always carried a big roll of bills in his pocket, but never put much money in the bank and when asked why, he said he could not as the Government had a lien against him.

Mr. HELM advised he visited the Vegas Club on several occasions and RUBY was always cordial and friendly, however, he always thought of him as a big promoter.

Mr. HELM advised he does not know of any associates, acquaintances or friends of RUBY and his only contacts with him were in connection with the banking business in the aforementioned infrequent visits to the Vegas Club.

Mr. HELM advised he does not recall ever having seen LEE HARVEY OSWALD prior to observing him on television after the assassination of President KENNEDY.

on 12/20/63 at Dallas, Texas File # DL 44-1639

by Special Agents JAMES J. WARD & ROBERT E. BASHAM/jn Date dictated 12/20/63

43

COMMISSION EXHIBIT No. 2359

FD-302 (Rev. 3-3-59)

FEDERAL BUREAU — Commission Exhibit No. 2360 —

Ruby, Jack 2-2

Date 12-13-63

Other Individuals and Organizations

1

Dr. HERMAN ULEVITCH 915 St. Joseph Street, Dallas, Texas, was interviewed regarding his name being listed on property found in RUBY's car, listed as follows:

On October 28, 1963, Dr. ULEVITCH was advised by his answering service about 7:30 p.m. that he had been called by a Mr. RUBY and Mr. RUBY desired him to return the call. Dr. ULEVITCH stated he called one of the numbers left by RUBY which was answered at the Carousel Club and he was advised that RUBY had gone home and for him to call him there. Dr. ULEVITCH said he tried to call RUBY, but was unable to reach him. Later that evening, Dr. ULEVITCH called RUBY at his home and RUBY advised him that his sister, EVA GRANT, had been advised to have an operation and that one of his, RUBY's, friends had suggested that he call Dr. ULEVITCH and arrange to have his sister re-examined. Dr. ULEVITCH continued that he hade an appointment for October 29, 1963, and Mrs. GRANT and JACK RUBY came to his office at 3:00 p.m. RUBY waited while Mrs. GRANT was examined by Dr. ULEVITCH and after the examination, Dr. ULEVITCH talked to both RUBY and Mrs. GRANT and explained the need for the operation.

Dr. ULEVITCH stated he visited the Gaston Hospital on November 6, 1963, and November 9, 1963, while Mrs. GRANT was recovering from the operation. Dr. L. B. ARONOFF, who has offices in the Medical Tower was Mrs. GRANT's doctor.

While Dr. ULEVITCH was talking to Mrs. GRANT on November 9, 1963, she received a telephone call from JACK RUBY inquiring about her condition.

Dr. ULEVITCH continued that he did not see RUBY again until November 11, 1963, when RUBY came to his office suffering a bad cold. Dr. ULEVITCH gave RUBY a prescription and x-rayed RUBY's chest, a routine matter.

on 12-13-63 at Dallas, Texas File # DL 44-1639

by Special Agent TOM E. CHAPOTON & ALLEN H. SMITH - md Date dictated 12-13-63

157

COMMISSION EXHIBIT No. 2360

2

DL 44-1639

Dr. ULEVITCH stated that until October 28, 1963, he had never talked to JACK RUBY in his life and that he has not seen or talked to RUBY since November 11, 1963. Dr. ULEVITCH stated that he is a member of the downtown YMCA and had seen RUBY at the YMCA, but he did not know who RUBY was and had never talked to him there. He further stated that he had no idea who is RUBY's associates or any of RUBY's business dealings he may have had, any connections that RUBY may have had with the Dallas Police Department or whether or not RUBY was associated with LEE HARVEY OSWALD.

158

COMMISSION EXHIBIT No. 2360—Continued

FD-302 (Rev. 3-3-59)

FEDERAL BUREAU OF IN[redacted]

— Commission Exhibit No. 2361

(1)

Date December 4, 1963

RICHARD J. POTTER, 4309 University Avenue, Dallas, Texas, advised that on Sunday, November 24, 1963, at approximately 11:30 a.m. he, in company with three companions, were in Athens, Texas, in connection with the opening of a motel in that city.

POTTER and his group were entering the Old Spanish Trace dining room of this motel when a waitress dressed in a red toreador costume (presumably the hostess) informed his group that OSWALD had just been shot. This girl informed POTTER that she used to work for JACK RUBY, and during the time she was working for RUBY she was living with a Detective of the Dallas Police Department who told her that RUBY was a "shady character." She also volunteered the information that RUBY had at one time told her, "You don't know how many Communists there are in the United States."

POTTER described this person as:

Race	White
Sex	Female
Age	Approximately 35
Build	Slender, tall
Height	Approximately 5'7" or 5'8"
Complexion	Dark
Hair	Dark, upswept

POTTER thought it was unusual that this person would volunteer information of this type, inasmuch as he and his three companions were complete strangers.

on 12/3/63 at Dallas, Texas File # DL 44-1639

by Special Agents JAMES C. KENNEDY and WILL HAYDEN GRIFFIN:bnm Date dictated 12/3/63

This document contains neither recommendations nor conclusions of the FBI. It is the property of the FBI and is loaned to your agency; it and its contents are not to be distributed outside your agency.

107

COMMISSION EXHIBIT No. 2361

FD-302 (Rev. 3-3-59)

FEDERAL BUREAU OF [redacted]

— Commission Exhibit No. 2362

1

Date 1/21/64

RAYMOND JONES (reported to be a former employee of RUBY), 2729 South Boulevard, furnished the following information:

JONES worked for EVA GRANT, RUBY's sister, at the Vegas Club in Dallas as a handy-man for approximately three months during the Fall of 1963. He quit in November, 1963, when he found better employment. JONES knows RUBY on a very casual basis having seen him and talked to him on several occasions when RUBY visited the Vegas Club.

JONES knows nothing concerning RUBY's personal life or political beliefs. He does not know LEE HARVEY OSWALD or does he know of any connection between OSWALD and RUBY.

on 1/20/64 at Dallas, Texas File # DL 44-1639

by Special Agent JOSEPH G. PEGGS - gj Date dictated 1/21/64

79

This document contains neither recommendations nor conclusions of the FBI. It is the property of the FBI and is loaned to your agency; it and its contents are not to be distributed outside your agency.

COMMISSION EXHIBIT No. 2362

FD-302 (Rev. 3-59)

FEDERAL BUREAU OF Commission Exhibit No. 2363

1

Date December 2, 1963

Telephone number HA 7-3172 is listed to Mar-din Company, 404 South Wells Street, Chicago, according to a Public Service Telephone Operator.

On November 29, 1963, HENRY KENTER, President and Treasurer, Mar-Din Company, home address 1428 Madison Street, Evanston, Illinois, was interview and stated that he has headed the firm for the last 25 years and the firm was incorporated in 1956. Mr. SIDNEY KOLLER, 1900 Lake Shore Drive, Chicago, is the Vice President and Secretary. The firm is engaged in the business of selling promotional items, executives/gifts, dealer loading items, safety awards and incentive gifts. Up until about five years ago, his firm did business with Earl Products Company, which was orginally operated by EARL, SAM, and JACK RUBY. A sister was also connected with the firm, but he did not know her name. As he recalled, the first business he had with Earl Products Company was concerning the sale of Aluminum salt and pepper shakers, which was probably about twenty years ago. He recalled meeting JACK RUBY on only one occasion about that time, however, knew nothing concerning his personal life or the personal lives of other members of the RUBY family. As he recalled, JACK RUBY sold his share of the business about 18 years ago and moved to Dallas, Texas, however, he did not know the reason behind his leaving Chicago. He believed that EARL RUBY sold the business about five years ago and he has had no contact with him since that time.

Sometime between November 1, and November 5, 1963, a telephone call was received from JACK RUBY at his place of business, however, he was out to lunch at the time and did not speak with RUBY. On about the fifth of November, he spoke with RUBY over the phone from Dallas, and JACK RUBY advised him that EARL RUBY had told him to call Mar-Din Company as concerns the sale of a twist waist exerciser. RUBY was very enthusiastic about this item and he understood RUBY to be the sales agent for it. When he learned of the price RUBY was asking for the item, he told him that he would not be interested. At a later date, RUBY mailed a twist waist exerciser and promotional material bearing the name Earl Products Company, Post Office Box 5475, Dallas, Texas. Also included was an advertisement from the Sanger Harris Store in Dallas concerning the twist waist exerciser, which was apparently printed in a

on 11/29/63 at Chicago, Illinois File # CH 44-645 DL 44-1639

by Special Agents JOHN E. DALLMAN & JAMES W. GERBLICK/jn Date dictated 12/2/63

41

2
DL 44-1639

local Dallas paper.

He believed that he called RUBY after RUBY had attempted to call him in Chicago, and this therefore, would have been the first conversation he had had with JACK RUBY in the last 17 or 18 years. Nothing other than the twist waist exerciser was discussed and he has not heard from RUBY personally since that time.

He could furnish no information concerning RUBY's personal life or political beliefs.

FD-302 (Rev. 1-25-60)

FEDERAL BUREAU OF INVESTIGATION

Date December 31, 1963

1

WALTER ERVIN (BUDDY) HEARD, Manager HEARD and HEARD Insurance Agency, 100 N. Florence, El Paso, Texas, residence Room 109, Hotel Laughlin, 311 W. Franklin, furnished the following information:

He stated that he has been a singer and comedian, but is presently in partnership with his father in the insurance business.

He stated that he was employed as a singer and comedian by JACK RUBY, at the Carousel Club, Dallas, Texas for approximately four or five weeks in May or June, 1961, the exact dates unrecalled. During this period of employment he resided at a hotel, the exact name and location unrecalled.

While employed by RUBY he was friendly with RUBY, and occasionally took his meals with him. He reported that during this employment and social meetings with RUBY, their conversations dealt primarily with the night-club business and the field of entertainment.

He stated that at no time did RUBY mention the name LEE HARVEY OSWALD. Further, RUBY did not mention or discuss politics, or his feelings toward the late President JOHN F. KENNEDY.

He continued that in approximately September or October, 1962 he was a singer and comedian with the Chuck Cabot Orchestra and during this employment, played an engagement at the Sheridan Hotel, Dallas, Texas for a grocer's, or food convention of some kind.

On one evening, the exact date unrecalled, while in Dallas during this period, he went to the Carousel Club

On 12/31/63 at EL PASO, TEXAS File # EP 44-274

by SA DEAN N. RAY/gc Date dictated 12/31/63

— 174 —

COMMISSION EXHIBIT No. 2364

EP 44-274
2

and saw and spoke to RUBY for approximately five munutes. This conversation involved an exchange of pleasantries only.

Since last seeing RUBY in September or October, 1962, he reported that RUBY has talked to him on two or three occasions by long distance telephone, one time being November 6, 1963.

During this conversation, and those earlier made, RUBY requested him to make a return engagement at the Carousel as a comedian. He stated that other entertainment, and business commitments have always interfered with his accepting RUBY'S offers.

He stated that RUBY kept a gun in his desk at the Carousel, but he never knew or saw RUBY carrying a firearm.

He continued that RUBY, in his opinion, was a temperamental person, but not violent in nature.

He stated that he was very surprised and shocked when he heard that RUBY was formally charged with the murder of LEE HARVEY OSWALD.

COMMISSION EXHIBIT No. 2364—Continued

FD-302 (Rev. 3-3-59) FEDERAL BUREAU Commission Exhibit No. 2365

1 Date 12/18/63

JEAN MASON, care of Mrs. MICHAEL FLORES, 2310 Marvel Drive, telephone number BL 4-7209, Dallas, Texas, furnished the following information:

She advised that her mother, Mrs. MICHAEL FLORES, advised her that she was being sought for interview by the FBI. She stated the only reason she could think of that a piece of paper with her name and address 1502 Ritchie and telephone number BL 4-7209, was found in the possession of JACK RUBY was because she had worked for him for two nights about two years ago. She stated she got the job by going to the Carousel Club and applying for work as a cashier. She worked as a cashier for two nights and met RUBY very briefly during that time. She stated she knew nothing concerning RUBY's background, personal life or political convictions. She stated she has no idea as to why RUBY shot LEE HARVEY OSWALD and knows of no connection between the two men. She had never heard of LEE HARVEY OSWALD prior to the President's assassination.

on 12/18/63 at Dallas, Texas File # DL 44-1639

by Special Agent JOHN E. DALLMAN - gj 223 Date dictated 12/18/63

COMMISSION EXHIBIT No. 2365

FD-302 (Rev. 3-3-59) FEDERAL BUREAU Commission Exhibit No. 2366

1 Other Individuals and Organizations Involved or Interviewed Date December 13, 1963

Mr. TOMMY T. TUCKER, JR., President, Tommy Tucker Plastics, Inc., 3411 Kiest Street, Dallas, Texas, telephone number WH 3-4581, whose name and telephone number appeared on an item secured from JACK RUBY's property in connection with a search of RUBY's car, advised as follows:

There is no one named SAMMY TUCKER at his establishment and he does not know anyone by that name. He believes that the name SAMMY TUCKER, telephone number WH 3-4581, actually refers to himself.

He never personally met JACK RUBY. Approximately two weeks prior to the assassination of President JOHN F. KENNEDY, JACK RUBY came to the Tommy Tucker Plastics, Inc., and made inquiry at the office concerning the cost of business cards. No order was placed by RUBY and RUBY did not recontact his establishment. Mr. TUCKER said that apparently, RUBY was given his name and telephone number at that time.

Mr. TUCKER said he had no information concerning the shooting of LEE HARVEY OSWALD. He has no personal information concerning the past activities of RUBY.

on 12/13/63 at Dallas, Texas File # DL 44-1639

by Special Agent ROBERT J. WILKISON/ln Date dictated 12/13/63

247

COMMISSION EXHIBIT No. 2366

Commission Exhibit No. 2367

FD-302 (Rev. 3-3-59) FEDERAL BUREAU O[redacted]

1

Date 11/25/63

I. T. (TROY) RACKLEY, Emory, Texas, was interviewed, at which time he was advised of the identity of the interviewing agents. RACKLEY then furnished the following information:

On Friday night, November 8, 1963, he was on his way back from Wichita Falls, Texas to Emory, Texas when he stopped in Dallas, Texas with intentions of doing some work on Saturday, November 9, 1963 at the Standard Oil Company of Texas offices. He said he stopped at the Baker Hotel where he planned to register then "see some sights". On the way into the Baker Hotel lobby, he said he met a "man from the Texas Company" whose name is something like "FARRAGUS" and that this man told him the company offices would not be open on Saturday. RACKLEY asked him where he could see some of the sights and this man told him to go to the Carousel Club which is northeast of the Baker Hotel and about two blocks away.

RACKLEY said he walked to this club and entered some time between 9:30 p.m. and 10:00 p.m. RACKLEY stated he had had about two drinks before he went to the club and that when he entered his waitress, who was blonde and wearing a "negligee type dress over very little else" served him bourbon and water. At this time RACKLEY said he noticed two men sitting about 15 feet from him at a table and he asked the waitress who these men were. She said the big guy was her "boss" and she referred to him as "JACK". RACKLEY explained that JACK was the same man known to him from television pictures as JACK RUBY, the Manager of the Carousel Club, and the man who shot "the assassin of President KENNEDY". However, RACKLEY stated the waitress called the other man "BETTIT" or "PE TTIT," he couldn't recall which name she used. He continued by identifying the waitress as the blonde-haired girl who was on television Sunday night, November 24, 1963 from a Dallas television station and the one who said she did not like RUBY and did not get along with him very well. He said that "BETTIT" or "PE TTIT" was the man who was shot by RUBY Sunday morning in Dallas, Texas.

on 11/25/63 at Emory, Texas File # DL 44-1639

by Special Agents DEL D. DRAKE & JOE A. COPELAND/jt Date dictated 11/25/63

7-8-7

This document contains neither recommendations nor conclusions of the FBI. It is the property of the FBI and is loaned to your agency; it and its contents are not to be distributed outside your agency.

COMMISSION EXHIBIT No. 2367

DL 44-1639
2

RACKLEY could not describe the Carousel Club other than there was a bar, many tables, and that when he went in the lights were all bright and later they were dimmed. He stated he had to leave before the show started because the drinks hit him and he recalled having only three bourbon and waters at $1.00 each. RACKLEY also recalled paying an unrecalled cover charge to get in and that there were pictures of girls displayed outside the Carousel Club.

RACKLEY stated after he left he drove his pickup truck to what he believes was the Hillside Tourist Court on old Highway 67 where he spent the night.

RACKLEY further described the Carousel Club as being "near the new telephone building past the Continental Bus Station". He described "JACK", the waitresses "boss" as being a white male, age 40, 5' 10" or 5' 11", but nothing else noted except he was identical with the television picture of JACK RUBY.

RACKLEY could not describe "BETTIT" or "PETTIT", other than being a white male except that he was identical with the "killer of President KENNEDY."

COMMISSION EXHIBIT No. 2367—Continued

FD-302 (Rev. 3-3-59) FEDERAL BUREAU Commission Exhibit No. 2368

1

Date 12/9/63

JOHN LACY, employee Graphic Studios, 1310 Main Street, advised he first met JACK RUBY on about Monday, November 4, 1963, or a day or two later, when RUBY came into the plant to discuss making up printed material for the Carousel Club with Mr. POWELL. His only contact with RUBY at that time was in connection with this work. At the time RUBY was in, he gave POWELL and LACY pass cards to the Carousel Club. He has not used his pass card. The only time he has been in the Carousel Club was on November 8, 1963, when he delivered the printed material to RUBY. RUBY paid him in cash for the order.

LACY advised that his only contact with RUBY was in connection with the above material.

He advised he is not acquainted with LEE HARVEY OSWALD and knows of no association between RUBY and OSWALD.

on 12/6/63 at Dallas, Texas File # DL 44-1639

by Special Agent JAMES F. GLONEK - gj Date dictated 12/9/63

320

COMMISSION EXHIBIT No. 2368

FD-302 (Rev. 3-3-59) FEDERAL BUREAU O. Commission Exhibit No. 2369

Date 12-16-63

1

EDWARD FEIN, tailor, Room 302, 1521 Commerce, Dallas, Texas, was advised that RUBY's records indicated he had been issued Carousel Club pass card no. 143 and he was asked for details concerning his acquaintance with RUBY. Mr. FEIN advised that RUBY brought some trousers to his place of business to be altered about November 9, 1963, to the best of his recollection, and he has never returned for the trousers. Prior to that, he was contacted only on one or two occasions by RUBY, in each instance RUBY came to his place of business for tailer work. RUBY gave him the pass card on one of these occasions.

FEIN has never been to the Carousel Club and has had no opportunity to learn anything concerning Mr. RUBY's background, personal live, activities or associates. He does not know LEE HARVEY OSWALD and has no information to indicate a connection between RUBY and OSWALD.

on 12-16-63 at Dallas, Texas File # DL 44-1639

by Special Agent RALPH E. RAWLINGS & JAMES F. GLONEK - md Date dictated 12-16-63

85

COMMISSION EXHIBIT No. 2369

FD-302 (Rev. 3-3-59) **FEDERAL BUREAU OF INVESTIGATION**

1

Date 11/26/63

HARVEY LAWILL WADE, 818 Donaldson Road, Chattanooga, Tennessee, employed as a building inspector in the City of East Ridge, Tennessee, furnished the following information:

WADE attended Southern Building Congress Convention Dallas, Texas, November 10-14, 1963. He arrived the afternoon of November 10, 1963, and stayed at the Baker Hotel, Dallas. At 11:00 PM, November 10, 1963, WADE visited the Carousel Night Club alone and remained until 1:00 AM. The entertainment consisted of three strippers and emcee BILL DEMERIS (PH). A stripper wearing a platinum wig invited a customer to dance with her on the stage as part of her act at about 12:00 midnight. A Carousel employee, a young white male wearing a white waiter's jacket, took two flash photographs with a Poloroid-type camera. From the angle the photograph was taken, three men seated at the bar connected to the stage on the right side of the night club were between the photographer and the stage and possibly in the photographs. WADE believes one of these three men was LEE HARVEY OSWALD, who was dressed in a coat-length jacket, light colored white dress shirt, open collar, no tie, and dark colored pants.

The person believed OSWALD was accompanied by two unknown men. The number one man is described as a white male, early twenties, 5 feet 8 inches, 140 pounds, long black hair, very fair pale complexion, and slender build. He had no unusual characteristics and wore a dark colored suit. He resembled OSWALD in appearance.

The number two man is described as a white male, 30-32 years old, 200 pounds, 5 feet 10 inches, stocky build, long black hair, dark complexion, oval face, and Mexican or Spanish in appearance. He had numerous bumps on his face and was believed to have a one-inch scar in the eyebrow of his left eye.

The customer on the stage with the stripper was a white male, 5 feet 10 inches, 35 years old, 180 pounds, flat-top dark hair, dress not recalled, and was at the table with one girl and three or four men.

on 11/24/63 at Knoxville, Tennessee File # KX 89-27 DL 44-1639

by Special Agent GEORGE C. WELBORN: mam Date dictated 11/24/63

789

COMMISSION EXHIBIT No. 2370

KX 89-27
DL 44-1639
GCW: mam
2

The waitress who waited on WADE and the three men in the group, including person believed to be OSWALD, is described as a white female, 37 or 38, 5 feet 1 inch, 110 pounds, black-grey hair shoulder length, ruddy complexion, and a very small face.

BILL DEMERIS, emcee, made the statement, following photographing, they were for blackmail purposes. JACK RUBY, manager, walked over to the photographer, talked to him, and yelled that the photographs did not turn out. The emcee had a memory skit. The person believed OSWALD and his two companions took part in the skit. The person believed OSWALD and friends were in the club when WADE arrived and still at the table at WADE's departure. WADE was seated within ten feet of the person believed OSWALD and his group. WADE alone did not see anyone during the visit known to him. He believes he could identify photographs of the men accompanying the person believed OSWALD.

The person believed OSWALD and his friends were not observed talking to anyone outside their group while at the club. He estimated 75 to 80 customers were present when he arrived and 25 or less when he departed. WADE had no further information.

790

COMMISSION EXHIBIT No. 2370—Continued

Commission Exhibit No. 2371

1

DL 44-1639

The following investigation was conducted by SA WILLIAM N. KIDWELL, JR.:

AT SAN FRANCISCO, CALIFORNIA:

Regarding RUBY's long distance telephone call, November 11, 1963, to San Francisco telephone AT 27128:

Telephone AT 2-7128 assigned FRANK GOLDSTEIN, 1022 Guerrero Street, San Francisco, and has been in service since February, 1961.

On December 4, 1963, FRANK RICHARD GOLDSTEIN, 1022 Guerrero, was interviewed by SA WILLIAM N. KIDWELL, JR. GOLDSTEIN stated he is employed as warehouseman, Rox Automobile Imports, 2345 Harrison Street, San Francisco. He was born at San Francisco, March 23, 1925. His wife is BEVERLY FRANCES GOLDSTEIN, Nee Mirabella, also born in San Francisco. He has been employed with aforementioned company since 1955 and served in U.S. Merchant Marine, 1952 to 1954. GOLDSTEIN stated he has never been in Dallas, Texas, and has had no contact of any kind with subject. He explained that during the past two years he and his wife have received a great many "wrong number" telephone calls. He could not recall having received any telephone call from Dallas. In particular he cannot remember such a call occurring on or about November 11, 1963.

Mrs. BEVERLY FRANCES GOLDSTEIN was interviewed on December 4, 1963, by SA KIDWELL. She stated that she has no friends or acquaintances who live in Dallas, Texas. She stated she has never visited that city nor has she been visited by anyone from that city. She was asked if she had received a long distance telephone call from Dallas. She replied that she had not. She explained that she has been the

v63

2

DL 44-1639

recipient of many wrong number telephone calls. She specifically recalled that she received a telephone call from New York City on one occasion, during which the caller asked for FRANK GOLDSTEIN or his wife, MARY GOLDSTEIN. She stated she is not acquainted with the people referred to in this call. She stated that she knew nothing of the subject or LEE HARVEY OSWALD prior to the recent events in Dallas.

No record San Francisco indices, San Francisco Police Department and no unfavorable credit record regarding above individuals.

v64

FD-302 (Rev. 1-25-60) F[?]ERAL BUREAU OF INVI— Commission Exhibit No. 2372

1

Date 1/24/64

JAMES E. JONKER, Manager T-Bone Supper Club, 220 East 47th Street South, advised as follows:

Telephone number JA 4-9269 is a public telephone located in the T-Bone Club, and is available for the use of all patrons of the club. Since this is a public telephone, there is no way of knowing who uses this telephone.

JONKER advised that he has no recollection of JACK L. RUBY ever using a telephone while RUBY was in his club. He stated it was very possible that RUBY, the strippers, MC's or other entertainers may have used this telephone while in the club. He added, however, that if one of these persons had received a call on this telephone the caller would have to know the telephone number as this number is not the one listed for the T-Bone Supper Club.

JONKER made a search of his records and advised that during the period from October 28, 1963 to November 11, 1963, comic BILL DE MAR and stripper FROSTIE CONNERS were appearing at the club. He stated he had booked CONNERS through the Wayne Keller Theatrical Agency, St. Louis, Missouri, and it was his recollection that DE MAR went to RUBY'S Carousel Club in Dallas following his appearance at the T-Bone. JONKER stated that DE MAR was appearing at the Carousel at the time of the death of President KENNEDY. He stated that since DE MAR went to Dallas from Wichita he would be of the personal opinion that someone in Dallas may have contacted DE MAR at the T-Bone on November 6, 1963 regarding his appearance in Dallas at the Carousel Club. JONKER said he could furnish no other information regarding any telephone calls to the T-Bone from Dallas, Texas or specifically from JACK L. RUBY.

On 1/22/64 at Wichita, Kansas File # KC 44-497 DL 44-1639

by SA JAMES F. MILLER:bjc Date dictated 1/23/64

123

COMMISSION EXHIBIT No. 2372

Commission Exhibit No. 2373

DL 44-1639
ECH:gj
1

The following investigation was conducted by SA EDMOND C. HARDIN at Dallas, Texas:

On December 15, 1963, ELNORA PITTS, 1316 East Jefferson Street, Dallas, telephone number WH 2-5461, advised that she is identical to the "ELINOR, WH 2-5461" which name and telephone number was secured from JACK RUBY's property in connection with a search of his person following his arrest on November 24, 1963. Miss PITTS added that she was previously interviewed on November 27, 1963, by SA JACK A. FRENCH and has no additional information to furnish concerning this case.

On December 13, 1963, Mrs. JOE GARCIA, also known as SHERRI LINN, SHERRY LINN, 1938 Las Cruces Street, Dallas, telephone number EX 1-3932, advised that she is identical to the "SHERRY EX 1-3932" whose name and phone number were secured from JACK RUBY's property in connection with a search of his car following his arrest on November 24, 1963. Mrs. GARCIA stated that she was previously interviewed on November 30, 1963, by SA CHARLES BROWN and added that she has no additional information to furnish relative to this case.

On December 13, 1963, LINDA ZUMWALT, 6435 Vanderbilt Street, Dallas, telephone number TA 3-6014, whose name and phone number were obtained from JACK RUBY's property in connection with a search of his car following his arrest on November 24, 1963, advised as follows:

Miss ZUMWALT advised that she is presently a student and is also employed part time as a saleswoman in a downtown gift shop. She stated she noticed an advertisement on November 14, 1963, in a local newspaper by JACK RUBY for employment in the field of dancing. She answered this advertisement by appearing in person at the Carousel Club on the same day and then learned from RUBY the nature of the dancing involved, namely stripping, and since she realized that this was not the type of dancing employment she desired, she declined to accept the employment. She stated that this was the only occasion she ever had to meet JACK RUBY and has no other information concerning him, his activities, travels or associates.

166

COMMISSION EXHIBIT No. 2373

DL 44-1639
2

Miss ZUMWALT stated she did not know LEE HARVEY OSWALD, has no information concerning any possibly relationship between OSWALD and RUBY nor concerning the shooting of OSWALD by RUBY.

On December 15, 1963, EMMA SHIP, Route 6, Box 66, Forest Lane, Dallas, telephone number CH 7-7243, whose name and phone number appeared among items obtained from RUBY's property in connection with a search of his car following his arrest on November 24, 1963, advised as follows:

Miss SHIP advised that on about November 14, 1963, she noticed an advertisement in a local newspaper relative to employment in the field of dancing, which advertisement was placed by RUBY, Carousel Club. She stated she telephoned RUBY on that day inquiring as to the nature of the employment and when RUBY told her it would involve exotic dancing, she told him she was not interested in such employment. She advised that this was her only contact with RUBY and that she has never seen him and has no additional personal information concerning him.

Miss SHIP advised that she did not know LEE HARVEY OSWALD and has no information concerning any possible connection between OSWALD and RUBY or concerning the shooting of OSWALD by RUBY. She added she has received no information concerning how RUBY gained access to the basement of the Dallas Police Department before shooting OSWALD.

The following individuals, all employees of the Merchants State Bank, 5217 Ross Avenue, Dallas, advised that they have known JACK RUBY from one to two years, only as a customer in their bank; that on about November 15, 1963, RUBY took their names and addresses and promised to mail them each a pass card to his Carousel Club, which card was not received. They further stated that they did not know LEE HARVEY OSWALD and have no information concerning any relationship which may have existed between OSWALD and RUBY or concerning the shooting of OSWALD by RUBY:

167

DL 44-1639
3

JACK ETHERIDGE, Assistant Cashier, 10420 Newcombe Drive,
(previously interviewed on November 29, 1963
by SAs RALPH E. RAWLINGS and EDMOND C. HARDIN);

SUE BLAKE, Teller, Garland, Texas;

DONALD WILEY, Teller, 3438 Daniels Avenue, Dallas, Texas;

PAULINE FOSHEE, Teller, 8726 La Panto Street, Dallas, Texas;

MISS TOMMIE HUNTLEY, Teller, 5747 Oram Street, Dallas, Texas.

168

FD-302 (Rev. 3-3-59) FEDERAL BUREAU O[redacted] — Commission Exhibit No. 2374 —

Other Individuals and Organizations
Family of interviewed

Date 12/12/63

1

ROSE SANDRA RENFROE, 2020 Lee Crest, Dallas, Texas, residence phone FR 1-8413, furnished the following information:

She is twenty-one years of age and unemployed. As she recalls, on November 14, 1963, she observed an ad in the Dallas Morning News Newspaper concerning the employment of women at $35.00 a day. The advertisement did not state what type of work was involved and, as she recalled, the number to call had the prefix LA 1. When she called the number, the woman who answered was apparently employed by an answering service, as she told her she would have to take her name, but she did not know who had placed the ad in the paper.

On the same date, she was telephonically contacted by JACK RUBY, who identified himself as owner of the Carousel Club. He advised that he was interested in hiring exotic dancers and, with that, she told him she was not interested and terminated the conversation. She stated RUBY undoubtedly got her number from the answering service and had apparently been the one who placed the ad in the paper.

She recalled meeting JACK RUBY at his Carousel Club during the Winter of 1963, when she visited the club with a girl friend. She stated all she recalled concerning RUBY was that he talked about nothing but his dogs. She knew nothing concerning his background, personal life, or political convictions.

on 12/12/63 at Dallas, Texas File # DL 44-1639

by Special Agent JOHN E. DALLMAN/eah Date dictated 12/12/63

350

COMMISSION EXHIBIT NO. 2374

FD-302 (Rev. 3-3-59) FEDERAL BUREAU [redacted] — Commission Exhibit No. 2375

Date 12-20-63

1

MARY MARTIN, 5015 Bryan, Apartment 201, was interviewed in connection with the name MARY MARLIN, RI 1-5181, being found among JACK RUBY's personal affects. She related the following:

Her office telephone Praetorian Insurance Company is RI 1-5181.

She met JACK RUBY for the first time about four years ago when a date took her to the Vegas Club for an evening of entertainment. She has seen RUBY perhaps four times since first meeting hime. The last time she saw him, which was about November 15, 1963, when she ran into him at Ervay Street and Bryan Street in downtown Dallas. He invited her to visit the Carousel Club. She stated that on one or two occasions RUBY tried to interest her in becoming a show girl, but she always declined.

MARTIN did not know LEE HARVEY OSWALD and knew of no connection or association between RUBY and OSWALD. She had no idea why RUBY shot OSWALD and was not acquainted with any Dallas Police Officers who were friends of RUBY. She said that during her visits to the Vegas Club, she had observed uniformed Police Officers, but did not know who they were.

on 12-20-63 at Dallas, Texas File # DL 44-1639

by Special Agent ALLEN H. SMITH - md Date dictated 12-20-63

64

COMMISSION EXHIBIT NO. 2375

FD-302 (Rev. 3-3-59) FEDERAL BUREAU O

— Commission Exhibit No. 2376 —

1

Date 12/14/63

CHARLES STRAEGHT, 531 Gilpin, employed Ridgewood Barber Shop, 10012 Monroe Drive, furnished the following information:

In 1951, he was employed for seven months as a band leader by JACK RUBY at the Silver Spur. He and RUBY did not get along well during his employment. He has only seen RUBY occasionally on the streets of Dallas, since 1951. The last time he saw RUBY was November 15, 1963, at about 4:00 PM, in the afternoon, at the Merchants State Bank in Dallas. He is definite regarding the above time and place since he, STRAEGHT, was in the bank signing papers regarding the purchase of an automobile.

He stated RUBY always had a short temper and acted on impulse frequently. He was not particularly surprised when he heard RUBY had shot LEE HARVEY OSWALD. He does not know of any political organization or other club or association that RUBY was associated with.

He does not know OSWALD and does not know of any relationship between RUBY and OSWALD.

on 12/12/63 at Dallas, Texas DL File # 44-1639

by Special Agent SA R. NEIL QUIGLEY :lp Date dictated 12/14/63

2/2

COMMISSION EXHIBIT NO. 2376

— Commission Exhibit No. 2377 —

1
DL 44-1639
ECH/jn

On November 30, 1963, Houston adivsed as follows:

On November 30, 1963, ROBERT MILLER, Chief Deputy Sheriff, Jim Wells County, Texas, stated he was informed that JACK RUBY was a member of a hunting party shortly after the opening of the season, November 16, 1963, at the ranch of BUCK SHEARER, well known Texas rancher.

On November 30, 1963, San Antonio advised as follows:

LEE SHEARER, Oak Grove Ranch, Mason County, Texas, advised Special Agent JOSEPH C. WEBB, JR., that JACK LEON RUBY was not known to have been a member of a hunting party at his ranch this year. He stated that the San Saba Ranch, five miles north of Pontotoc, Texas, is owned by SHEARER and leased for hunting to W. H. COOPER, 3017 Valwood, Dallas, Texas,for six members. The members include GORDON OGEE, 1552 Eastus Drive, ROLAND WRIGHT, 2438 Southwood and W. G. WRIGHT, 1731 Timber Grove, all of Dallas. The other two members of the lease were unknown to SHEARER. SHEARER stated that ROLAND WRIGHT had indicated to him that he knew RUBY and considered RUBY to have a poor reputation and to associate with prostitutes in Dallas.

AT DALLAS, TEXAS

On December 6, 1963, W. H. COOPER, 3017 Valwood Parkway, operator of Ship's Lounge, Dallas, advised Special Agents EDMOND C. HARDIN and ROBERT J. WILKISON as follows:

He and the other members of his hunting lease have never hunted with JACK RUBY and JACK RUBY has never hunted on this lease during the current season or at any other time to his knowledge. COOPER identified the other two members of his hunting lease as RICHARD L. KOSTER, Ft. Worth Avenue, Dallas, and JACK H. EASON, street address unknown, Dallas.

COOPER stated that he met RUBY about three months ago at the Carousel Club where he was a customer. RUBY introduced himself and inquired as to whether COOPER was enjoying himself. COOPER added that he did not engage RUBY in any further conversation and has not seen him since.

COMMISSION EXHIBIT NO. 2377

2
DL 44-1639

COOPER advised that he does not know LEE HARVEY OSWALD and has no information concerning any possbile relationship which may have existed between RUBY and OSWALD. He stated that during a recent conversation with LEE SHEARER and others on about November 24, 1963, he mentioned that he had met RUBY and thus may have given the impression that he was familiar with RUBY's background and activities. COOPER stated that he has no additional information concerning this case.

On December 7, 1963, ROLAND O. WRIGHT, 2438 Southwood, who is owner of the Day and Night Automotive Motor Company, 505 West Commerce Street, Dallas, advised Special Agents EDMOND C. HARDIN and ROBERT J. WILKISON as follows:

He has never met JACK RUBY or LEE HARVEY OSWALD and has no personal knowledge of either individual or of any relationship which may have existed between them. He stated that on November 24, 1963, he recalls discussing RUBY and OSWALD with LEE SHEARER and others and did not indicate that he was acquainted with RUBY but may have volunteered the information that W. H. COOPER, also present, had stated to him that he had met RUBY. Mr. WRIGHT stated that he has no information concerning this case.

COMMISSION EXHIBIT No. 2377—Continued

FD-302 (Rev. 1-25-60) FEDERAL BUREAU O— Commission Exhibit No. 2378

Date December 4, 1963

-1-

On December 3, 1963, Miss SMOKEY TURNER advised that she is a dancer presently employed at the Gay 90's Bar and Restaurant, 408 Hennepin, Minneapolis. She said that her non-stage name is GLORIA MERRIFIELD.

She was employed at the Gay 90's on November 16, 1963. Between 8:00 and 8:30 P.M. on that date, she received a long distance telephone call from a man identifying himself as JACK RUBY of Dallas. RUBY told her that JOY DALE, one of his dancers had recommended SMOKEY to him and he wanted to know if she desired to come to Dallas and work in one of his clubs. She said that she was interested and RUBY asked her to send photographs of her and some publicity material. She said that she did send this and the next thing she heard from RUBY was she saw him on television involved in the LEE OSWALD matter.

She said that she had never met RUBY and knows nothing about him. The only discussion on the telephone had to do with an offer to work in one of his night clubs and the condition of the work.

On 12/3/63 at Minneapolis, Minnesota File # MP 44-248

by SA GEORGE C. BURTON and SA RAY W. GANNON / kik Date dictated 12/4/63

369

COMMISSION EXHIBIT No. 2378

FD-302 (Rev. 3-3-59)

FEDERAL BUREAU OF INVESTIGATION

Date December 17, 1963

1

GLORIA FILLMON, also known as Gloria Rettig, 5207 Gaston, Dallas, Texas, furnished the following information:

Mrs. FILLMON was employed as a champagne girl at the Carousel Club for approximately three weeks through the weekend of November 16, 1963. She advised that she got her employment at the Carousel Club by answering an advertisement in a Dallas newspaper citing employment for cocktail waitresses at the Carousel Club. She stated that she appeared at the Carousel Club and was immediately hired under the name of GLORIA RETTIG. She advised that JACK RUBY did not know that she was married and that her married name was Mrs. FRED FILLMON. She stated that while she was in the employ of RUBY, RUBY on a few occasions attempted to date her and he also attempted to recruit her as a stripper. She advised that she repulsed RUBY on both approaches. On the basis of the above, Mrs. FILLMON thought it best that she terminate her employment at the Carousel Club and on approximately November 16 or 17, 1963, she advised RUBY of her decision to terminate her employment. She advised that RUBY appeared to be angry and hung up the phone on her. Mrs. FILLMON advised that due to her short period of employment at the Carousel Club she had no knowledge of any associates of RUBY. She stated that she did not know LEE HARVEY OSWALD and to the best of her knowledge OSWALD had never appeared at the Carousel Club while she was employed there and she has no knowledge of any acquaintanceship or association between OSWALD and RUBY.

on 12/16/63 at Dallas, Texas File # Dallas 44-1639

by Special Agent JAMES E. WEIR:BL Date dictated 12/17/63

904

COMMISSION EXHIBIT No. 2379

FD-302 (Rev. 3-3-59)

FEDERAL BUREAU OF INVESTIGATION

Date December 19, 1963

1

Mrs. GLORIA FILLMON, Nee GLORIA RETTIG, 5207 Gaston Avenue, Dallas, Texas, was contacted to determine if she were identical with one "GLORIA" reported to have been in the company of JACK RUBY at the Lucas B&B Restaurant, Dallas, Texas, during the early morning hours of November 21, 1963.

Mrs. FILLMON advised she terminated her employment as a cigarette girl and "champagne pusher" at the Carousel Club operated by RUBY on a Wednesday night, exact date unrecalled but possibly November 20, 1963. She stated on this date, RUBY offered to take her home after the club closed, which offer she accepted and en route to her residence they stopped at the Vegas Club, also operated by RUBY and located on Oak Lawn Avenue, where they picked up an individual known only to her by the first name LARRY. She stated it was her understanding LARRY was an employee of RUBY but she had not previously met him.

After picking up LARRY, all three of them then went to the Lucas B & B Restaurant, Oak Lawn Avenue, arriving there approximately 3:00 a.m. the following morning (Thursday). FILLMON said she recalled while at the restaurant RUBY talked to several people unknown to her. FILLMON reiterated she was unable to establish the exact date of the above occurrence, but did recall it was a day or two prior to the assassination of President JOHN F. KENNEDY.

on 12/19/63 at Dallas, Texas File # Dallas 44-1639

by Special Agents WILL HAYDEN GRIFFIN & JAMES C. KENNEDY:BL Date dictated 12/19/63

905

COMMISSION EXHIBIT No. 2379—Continued

FD-302 (Rev. 3-3-59)

FEDERAL BUREAU OF [redacted]

Commission Exhibit No. 2380

Date December 15, 1963

1

HARVEY DAVIS BOSTICK, 617 Cheyenne Road, Dallas, Texas, was interviewed as an employee for the S & R, Incorporated, doing business as the Carousel Club during 1961 and 1962. BOSTICK advised that he and his wife, NORMAN JEAN, stage name "MARGO," came to Dallas about May, 1961, looking for employment and they obtained jobs at JACK RUBY's Carousel Club. He worked as a bartender and doorman and his wife worked as cashier and part-time dancer. They worked for RUBY until about December, 1961. BOSTICK and his wife went on the road where his wife danced at other clubs. They returned to Dallas about December, 1962, and again worked for RUBY until March, 1963. On this occasion he worked at the Vegas Club as a doorman and on occasions when needed at the Carousel Club. His wife worked as a part-time dancer. About March, 1963, BOSTICK and his wife again went on the road returning to Dallas during the early part of November, 1963. On November 16, 1963, his wife, "MARGO" went to the Carousel Club to visit with employees working there and while there she talked to RUBY a few minutes. On November 17, 1963, RUBY sent a telegram to her at 617 Cheyenne Road, Dallas, in which he asked her to call him at home. On November 17, 1963, she called RUBY at about 1:30 p.m. and RUBY invited BOSTICK and his wife to come down to the Carousel Club and be his guests, telling them that they were always welcome. RUBY did not offer them work at this time. This is the last time they saw or talked to JACK RUBY.

BOSTICK stated the only close associates of RUBY known to him were GEORGE SENATOR, RUBY's roommate, and RALPH PAUL. He did not have any information concerning RUBY's business dealings or whether or not RUBY had any connections with any police officers. BOSTICK was of the opinion that if RUBY did have any connections with the police department they were very poor because RUBY often complained of having to pay parking tickets. He did not know LEE HARVEY OSWALD and had no idea whether there were any associations or connections between RUBY and OSWALD.

on 12/13/63 at Dallas, Texas File # Dallas 44-1639

by Special Agent S ALLEN H. SMITH & TOM E. CHAPOTON:BL Date dictated 12/14/63

181

This document contains neither recommendations nor conclusions of the FBI. It is the property of the FBI and is loaned to your agency; it and its contents are not to be distributed outside your agency.

COMMISSION EXHIBIT No. 2380

FD-302 (Rev. 3-3-59)

FEDERAL BUREAU O [redacted]

Commission Exhibit No. 2381

Date December 16, 1963

1

HARRY LEE JACKSON, 2536 Romine, Dallas, Texas, residence telephone HA 1-4594, furnished the following information:

He is a professional musician and plays the organ and the piano. During about 1961 he played with bands led by a ROBERT MOSS and a JOE JOHNSON at the Vegas Club in Dallas. He was hired through the band and met JACK RUBY during the course of his work there. He conversed with RUBY occasionally but learned nothing concerning his background, personal life or political convictions.

The last time he saw JACK RUBY, as best he could recall, was on a Sunday night one week prior to November 24, 1963. He was at the Empire Room, 1710 Hall Street, a night club. While sitting at the bar he saw RUBY, shook his hand, and conversed with him briefly. RUBY told him to drop by his Carousel Club if he had the opportunity. RUBY knew many people in Dallas, particularly entertainers and public officials. He could think of no one who was a close personal friend of RUBY.

He has no idea why RUBY shot LEE HARVEY OSWALD and knows of no connection between OSWALD and RUBY. He never heard of OSWALD prior to the President's assassination.

on 12/16/63 at Dallas, Texas File # Dallas 44-1639

by Special Agent JOHN E. DALLMAN:BL Date dictated 12/16/63

112

This document contains neither recommendations nor conclusions of the FBI. It is the property of the FBI and is loaned to your agency; it and its contents are not to be distributed outside your agency.

COMMISSION EXHIBIT No. 2381

FD-302 (Rev. 3-3-59)

FEDERAL BUREAU OF

Commission Exhibit No. 2382

Date December 16, 1963

1

NORMA JEAN BOSTICK, Nee SMITH, stage name "MARGO," 617 Cheyenne Road, Dallas, Texas, was interviewed as a former employee of the Carousel Club. She related that she and her husband, HARVEY BOSTICK, have worked for JACK RUBY at the Carousel Club during the period May - December, 1961 and December 1962 to March, 1963. She worked as a cashier, hostess, stage light operator and part-time dancer. Her husband worked as a bartender-doorman. She stated that they left Dallas about March, 1963 and went on the road. Thereafter they returned to Dallas during the early part of November, 1963. She stated that on November 16, 1963, she went to the Carousel Club to visit with the employees there and talked to JACK RUBY for a few moments. On November 17, 1963, she received a telegram from JACK RUBY at her residence which asked her to call him at home. On November 17, 1963, she called RUBY about 1:00 or 2:00 p.m. and RUBY asked her and her husband, HARVEY, to come down to the Carousel Club to visit and renew acquaintances. This was the last time she talked to JACK RUBY.

She stated that JACK RUBY did not talk too much about his part while she was working there but had mentioned very vaguely that he had worked in Chicago prior to coming to Dallas and while in Chicago had "helped organize unions in Chicago,"but she did not elaborate. The only close associates of RUBY that she knows are RALPH PAUL and GEORGE SENATOR. She has no knowledge of any ofRUBY's business activities or any connections, if any, he might have had with police officers. She related that there was one police officer she knew whom RUBY did not like. This was a red-headed officer on the Vice Squad who was continually chec'ing the club in an effort to file some law violation so that the club could be closed. She continued that she had never heard of LEE HARVEY OSWALD and had no idea as to whether RUBY and OSWALD were acquainted.

on 12/13/63 at Dallas, Texas File # Dallas 44-1639

by Special Agents ALLEN H. SMITH & TOM E. CHAPOTON:BL Date dictated 12/14/63

182

COMMISSION EXHIBIT NO. 2382

Commission Exhibit No. 2383

FD-302 (Rev. 1-25-60)

FEDERAL BUREAU OF INVESTIGATION

Date 11/26/63

1.

VERN A. DAVIS, 6120 S.E. 6th Street, advised that he was born in Oklahoma City, Oklahoma, on May 27, 1917, and was employed as an income tax accountant and salesman, his last occupation being with the Midwest Publishing Company, Midwest City, Oklahoma, in advertisement sales. DAVIS stated that he phoned the managing editor of The Daily Oklahoman concerning the information reported in an article in The Daily Oklahoman on November 25, 1963. He said that he went to Dallas, Texas, on November 17, 1963, his purpose being to join the Lone Star Showman's Club which he described as a club consisting of carnival and concessionnaire people. He said while in Dallas, at about 7 or 7:30 P.M., at what used to be Jack's Bar, now believed to be Ed's Bar at 813 Exposition Street, he was discussing various topics of conversation with some "carnival people." He said while there, an individual joined the group and began making derogatory statements about then Vice President LYNDON JOHNSON and his forthcoming trip to the Trade Mart. He said at no time was President Kennedy's name mentioned by this individual.

He said he believed this individual to be LEE HARVEY OSWALD, whose picture he saw both in the newspaper and television. He said he then left the bar for a short period of time and when he came back he noticed the individual he thought to be OSWALD had left and JACK RUBY was standing at the bar. He said he had met JACK RUBY about ten years ago in Dallas, Texas, and he said JACK RUBY was a gambler who followed the fairs and carnivals throughout the country "hustling" poker games. He said he asked JACK RUBY if he knew anyone at the Lone Star Showman's Club and RUBY told him he knew an individual named COTTON WHEELER. He said COTTON WHEELER later sponsored his application for the Lone Star Showman's Club. He said further he did not know RUBY as a night club operator but only as a gambler going from carnival to carnival.

DAVIS said specifically that in further reflection about the identity of OSWALD, he was not really as sure that OSWALD was in the club as he had been the day before.

On 11/25/63 at Oklahoma City, Oklahoma File # OC 44-430

by SA DAVID S. BYERLY and SA GLENN E. SILVEY:ca 8/2 Date dictated 11/25/63

COMMISSION EXHIBIT NO. 2383

2.
OC 44-430

He said he saw JACK RUBY at the Topeka Fair about two years previous but he did not know anything about his background other than he was a gambler. RUBY's picture was exhibited to DAVIS and he said he believed this was the same JACK RUBY that he had seen in Jack's Bar.

DAVIS said he had served time for burglary in the Oklahoma State Penitentiary at McAlester, the burglary having been committed at Chickasha, Oklahoma, in 1945. He said he also served time at Folsom Penitentiary and at the penitentiary in Tracy, California, for a burglary in Sacramento, California. DAVIS claimed he had only three or four beers the night he saw JACK RUBY in the bar.

COMMISSION EXHIBIT No. 2383—Continued

FD-302 (Rev. 3-3-59)

FEDERAL BUREAU OF I[redacted] Commission Exhibit No. 2384

1

Date November 26, 1963

Mrs. BILLY CHESTER CARR, 6027 Ettrick, telephone PA 9-0891, was interviewed in the presence of her husband. She advised that she and her husband manage a band called the Impellas. She and her husband telephonically contacted JACK RUBY on November 18 and 20, 1963, in an effort to book the band at the Vegas Club, Dallas, Texas, in the near future. RUBY telephonically contacted her on November 19 and 21, 1963, in an effort to agree on a price for the band's appearance. She advised that she and her husband mailed a package containing a recent recording of the Impellas along with photographs of the band to JACK RUBY at an unrecalled address on Oak Lawn Street, Dallas, which will probably be delivered on November 26, 1963. In a telephone conversation, RUBY indicated he had a partner in the Vegas Club, whom he did not name. She stated that her and her husband's only other contact with RUBY was in August, 1958, when they had a one-night appearance at the Vegas Club to promote a recording.

Mrs. CARR stated that her and her husband's contacts with RUBY were entirely of a business nature and that she and her husband are unable to furnish any information regarding RUBY's social, political, romantic or other activities. She stated that LEE HARVEY OSWALD is unknown to her and her husband.

on 11/25/63 at Houston, Texas File # DL 44-1639

by Special Agent PAUL W. HAYMES & JERRY C. DANIEL/csh/bl Date dictated 11/26/63

This document contains neither recommendations nor conclusions of the FBI. It is the property of the FBI and is loaned to your agency; it and its contents are not to be distributed outside your agency.

COMMISSION EXHIBIT No. 2384

FD-302 (Rev. 1-25-60) FEDERAL BUREAU O[redacted] Commission Exhibit No. 2385

1

Date November 25, 1963

Mr. BILLY CHESTER CARR, 6027 Ettrick, telephone PA 9-0891, advised that he telephoned JACK RUBY, owner of the Vegas Club, Dallas, Texas, on November 18, 1963 to book a band called the "Impellas". He said that the operator was unable to reach RUBY at the Vegas Club and subsequently reached him at the Carrousel in Dallas, at which time he described the "Impellas" to RUBY and told him that their services could be obtained for $500.00 a week. CARR stated that the "Impellas" have recently made a fast selling record called the "Continental Whip" and are due to have another record released in the first week of January, which they anticipate being a possible hit. CARR advised that RUBY was interested in the band and stated that he would be in touch with CARR.

CARR advised that the only other contact he had ever had with RUBY was in August, 1958 when he appeared one night at the Vegas Club as a singer under his stage name of BILLY COSTA. He stated that RUBY remembered him from this appearance.

CARR advised that his dealings with RUBY were of a business nature and could furnish no information concerning RUBY's political, social or other business contacts.

CARR advised that LEE HARVEY OSWALD was unknown to him prior to the assassination of President KENNEDY.

On 11-25-63 at Houston, Texas File # HO 44-939

by SAS PAUL W. HAYMES and JERRY C. DANIELS:djw 5 76 Date dictated 11-25-63

COMMISSION EXHIBIT No. 2385

FD-302 (Rev. 3-3-59) FEDERAL BUREAU O[redacted] Commission Exhibit No. 2386

1

Date 12/19/63

Mr. FRANK J. BOERDER, 1211 Mountain Lake Road, Dallas, whose name appeared as "FRANK BORDEN, WH 1-5938" in RUBY's personal property, was interviewed at his place of employment, Boerder Studios, 835 West 7th Street, WH 1-5938, at which time he advised that it would be very logical that his name and business telephone number had appeared in JACK RUBY's personal belongings. He went on to say that he had been associated with JACK RUBY for several years strictly on a business association and explained that RUBY may have spelled his name wrong inasmuch as several people have a hard time spelling his name.

Mr. BOERDER stated that he is self-employed as an architect and because of his occupation, he becomes acquainted with several business owners throughout the Dallas area. He has been decorating night clubs in Dallas for 23 years and could recall meeting JACK RUBY almost fifteen years ago when an individual by the name of JOE SLATIN introduced RUBY to him. He could recall that JOE SLATIN was at that time the owner of the Sovereign Club and knew that it was later owned by JACK RUBY. He could vaguely recall RUBY becoming involved in the night club business throughout the years and after RUBY had obtained the Vegas Club, he, BOERDER, decorated the club for RUBY. Since that time he has worked decorating RUBY's clubs, the Carousel and the Vegas, throughout the years and advised that his association with RUBY was very pleasant. He described him as being "a hell of a nice guy".

BOERDER went on to say that approximately two weeks prior to the assassination of President KENNEDY, exact date he could not recall, RUBY approached him and advised him that he was interested in obtaining a new location for a private club. He could recall RUBY saying that his new proposed club would be at the corner of Mc Kinney and Maple, Dallas, Texas. Although BOERDER was not aware of all the specific details concerning this proposed club, he could recall RUBY mentioning that his plan was to obtain $5,000.00 from a local real estate lady and that he would put in $1,000.00 himself in efforts to start the club. BOERDER's connections with this matter and the reason he knew of the proposed club was the fact that RUBY had approached him concerning the designing of

on 12/13/63 at Dallas, Texas File # DL 44-1639

by Special Agent LANSING P. LOGAN - gj Date dictated 12/18/63

COMMISSION EXHIBIT No. 2386

the club. Although BOERDER could not recall the name of the real estate lady that RUBY approached concerning the $5,000.00, he did recall that RUBY referred to her as "BERTHA" and described her as being 35 to 40 years old, approximately 5 feet 5 inches tall, slender build and very attractive.

Mr. BOERDER further stated that RUBY had mentioned the new proposed club on one or two occasions, but after that had heard absolutely nothing in regard to this new proposed club. He advised that it was his impression that the new club was never built and has never heard anything more concerning this club.

The only other information he could recall concerning the new proposed club was that RUBY had planned to name the club "Club Bistro".

Mr. BOERDER advised that he knew very little concerning RUBY's background and could offer no information regarding his social friends or associates. He had never discussed any type of political views with RUBY and therefore did not know of RUBY's political convictions. However, BOERDER did state that RUBY was a very easy individual to get along with and could recall one specific time at the Carousel Club when RUBY had displayed very good character and tact. He explained this by saying that he, BOERDER, was present when RUBY had fired one of his strippers by the name of JADA and that RUBY was not only very nice to her but was also very considerate in the manner that he approached her. Mr. BOERDER stated that he later learned that JADA had made several allegations against RUBY and that as far as he was concerned they were all false. He explained that he has seen RUBY approach numerous customers and businessmen and could not recall ever seeing any type of friction between RUBY and other individuals.

Although Mr. BOERDER could not be sure, he was under the impression that the name JEANNIE BORDEN which appeared in RUBY's personal property on several occasions was possibly his ex-sister-in-law, whose name is now JEANNIE BAILEY. He stated that he knows of no connection between RUBY and JEANNIE but it would be conceivable that RUBY may have written her name down as JEANNIE BORDEN.

6

Mr. BOERDER was unable to furnish any information concerning LEE HARVEY OSWALD and stated that he knew of no connection whatsoever between OSWALD and RUBY. He knew of no one who conspired with RUBY to shoot LEE HARVEY OSWALD.

Mr. BOERDER could offer no information of value concerning the assassination of the President or the shooting of LEE HARVEY OSWALD other than what he had read in the local newspapers.

7

Commission Exhibit No. 2387

FD-302 (Rev. 3-3-59)

FEDERAL BUREAU OF I[redacted]

Date 11/25/63

1

L. F. DAUER, Apartment 106, Marsala Place Apartments, 223 Ewing Street, Dallas, Texas, who is the Market Manager of Charley's Ranch Market, 6100 Luther Lane, Dallas, furnished the following information:

JACK RUBY moved into the apartment a few weeks after its completion in November, 1962, but outside of casual meetings on the street, he did not know RUBY. They did not discuss RUBY's business or what he did, but he was aware that RUBY managed the Carousel Club in downtown Dallas. RUBY conducted himself like a gentleman around the apartments. He swam in the pool mostly by himself and acted as though he were taking exercise, because he would never stop at the edge of the pool and talk. He also took sun baths on the roof of the apartments alone.

DAUER stated he noted he had been quoted in the newspapers, but wanted to correct this, since he had been misquoted, and what he actually said was that he had never known RUBY to have any parties in his apartment and if he did he never heard them.

He did see RUBY leaving about 5:00 or 6:00 PM to go to work, but did not see him return and did not know what time he actually returned.

The last time he saw RUBY was last Monday when RUBY was coming down the stairs with his dogs. At that time they stopped and talked about the dogs that RUBY kept in his apartment. He has never seen anyone other than RUBY and GEORGE, whose last name he did not know, but who formerly lived in another apartment until about three weeks ago, when he moved in with RUBY, go in this apartment.

DAUER stated he could only recall one female visitor who came during the Summer of 1963. He recalled her because her car was hot and she asked him to look at it. She then saw RUBY, who was sitting at one corner of the pool, and seemed to know him, and they later went upstairs together. He has never seen her again around the apartments.

DAUER stated he has never seen LEE HARVEY OSWALD around the apartments and did not know him.

on 11/25/63 at Dallas, Texas File # DL 44-1639

by Special Agent LOUIS M. KELLEY/eah Date dictated 11/25/63

640

This document contains neither recommendations nor conclusions of the FBI. It is the property of the FBI and is loaned to your agency; it and its contents are not to be distributed outside your agency.

COMMISSION EXHIBIT No. 2387

FD-302 (Rev. 3-3-59)

FEDERAL BUREAU O[redacted]

Commission Exhibit No. 2388

Date December 15, 1963

(1)

Mrs. ANNE LISTAK, previously referred to as HISTAK, was contacted at 321 Washington Street, Dallas, Texas, inasmuch as her name was found in connection with the search of JACK RUBY's car.

Mrs. LISTAK advised that on Monday, November 18, 1963, she contacted JACK RUBY regarding obtaining a job at the Carousel Club. On the night of the 18th she went to the Carousel Club and had an interview with RUBY, but after seeing the club she was not interested in working there. She could furnish no additional information regarding RUBY inasmuch as this was her only contact with him.

She stated that she did not know LEE HARVEY OSWALD and knew of no connection between OSWALD and RUBY.

on 12/13/63 at Dallas, Texas File # DL 44-1639

by Special Agents ALVIN ZIMMERMAN and JOSEPH PEGGS:bnm Date dictated 12/13/63

This document contains neither recommendations nor conclusions of the FBI. It is the property of the FBI and is loaned to your agency; it and its contents are not to be distributed outside your agency.

127

COMMISSION EXHIBIT No. 2388

Commission Exhibit No. 2389

UNITED STATES DEPARTMENT OF JUSTICE

FEDERAL BUREAU OF INVESTIGATION

In Reply, Please Refer to File No.

Oklahoma City, Oklahoma
June 26, 1964

WILLIAM McEWAN DUFF, Also Known As William McEwan McDuff, "Sandy," "Scottie," "Scotty"
INFORMATION CONCERNING ALLEGED ASSOCIATION BETWEEN GENERAL EDWIN A. WALKER AND JACK L. RUBY

Investigation concerning William McEwan Duff and subsequent information which he reported has been predicated on information supplied on December 10, 1963, by Mr. Joe Loria, a Restaurant operator, Dallas, Texas. Mr. Loria advised that some 7 or 8 months previously he had seen an individual known to him only as "Scottie" -- subsequently identified as Duff -- with an individual believed to have been Lee Harvey Oswald. Mr. Loria, who had based his identification on photographs of Oswald which had appeared in Dallas newspapers, advised that he could recall only one time that he thought he had seen Oswald and "Scottie" together.

On January 24, 1964, William McEwan Duff, U. S. Army Serial Number RA 18 678 666, Fort Sill, Oklahoma, identified as "Scottie," was interviewed concerning his reported association with Oswald, an allegation which he denied. On this occasion he reported employment during the period November, 1962, to about April, 1963, in the household of General Edwin A. Walker, Dallas, Texas. Concerning Jack Ruby, Duff stated on January 24, 1964, that he had seen many photographs of Ruby in the newspapers; that he was positive he had never seen Ruby at any place, and had no information about him. He said he had never been in Ruby's night club in Dallas. On May 25, 1964, however, Duff laid claim to an association between Ruby and General Edwin A. Walker, alleging that he had seen Ruby at the Walker residence, according to information supplied by James R. Cantrell, Special Agent, Secret Service, U. S. Treasury Department, at Oklahoma City, Oklahoma, as follows:

COMMISSION EXHIBIT No. 2389

William McEwan Duff

On May 26, 1964, James R. Cantrell, Special Agent, Secret Service, U. S. Treasury Department, Oklahoma City, Oklahoma, advised that in an interview of William McEwan Duff on May 25, 1964, Duff had claimed evidence of an association between Jack Ruby and General Edwin A. Walker, Dallas, Texas; that during the period December, 1962, through March, 1963, while Duff was employed by General Walker and resided in his home, Ruby visited on the basis of about once a month, each time in the company of two unidentified white males, arriving in a Ford car, not further described.

Duff claimed identification of Ruby through photographs, having heard him addressed only as Jack. The others he described as follows:

(1) White male, mid 30's, 5'11" to 6', weighing 145 pounds, dark receding hair; said to be a member of John Birch Society.

(2) White male, in late 40's, heavy build, dark complexion.

Duff advised that the three had always convened with Walker in the living room of the Walker residence. Duff at no time overheard their conversation.

When questioned concerning other witnesses, Duff said it is possible others in the Walker household, whom he could not name, might have identified Ruby, but he considered it doubtful they would assist, out of loyalty to General Walker. He mentioned one Bob Sutton as a possible witness. Sutton, employed by a paper or printing firm in Dallas, was said to have visited at the Walker residence.

Duff had no explanation as to why he had not reported this in previous interviews, both by Agents of the Federal Bureau of Investigation and of the Secret Service, other than to state a fear of General Walker. He said he felt that he knew too much of Walker's operation and of the persons visiting his residence, intimating that Walker was diverting funds collected for the John Birch Society to a personal account at the Highland Park Bank, Dallas, Texas.

- 2 -

COMMISSION EXHIBIT No. 2389—Continued

Duff said he had known nothing of Lee Harvey Oswald.

Agent Cantrell said that his receipt of this information from Duff, predicated on an earlier interview on April 8, 1964, at Fort Sill, Oklahoma, and several subsequent telephone calls, both from Duff and his wife, Peggy Marie Duff, indicate Duff may be using this means to impress his wife and to restore their marital relationship. Duff's wife had threatened divorce on grounds he had misrepresented his background, even claiming to have the rank of Captain in the U. S. Army.

Duff had called Agent Cantrell on long distance telephone from Lawton, Oklahoma, on May 20, 1964, to advise that the man who had offered him $10,000 to kill General Walker had been following him at Lawton; that he, in turn, had followed this man to the Capri Motel, Lawton, Oklahoma, where he established that the man was Cliff Roberts of the Oklahoma Crime Bureau. Roberts had interviewed Mrs. Duff, informing her that warrants were outstanding for Duff. Cantrell said the purpose of Duff's call was to enlist his aid in clearing this matter with Mrs. Duff; to inform her that no warrants were outstanding. In a later call on the same evening, Duff had put Mrs. Duff on the telephone for this purpose, although it had taken three or four minutes to do so, as the two were in an apparent argument. At this time, Mrs. Duff had asked that Cantrell call her on the following day at her office. She is said to have been employed for some 17 years by the Consolidated Supply Company, Lawton, Oklahoma. She railed against Duff, stating he had lied to her.

Cantrell said on the following day he had been unsuccessful in reaching Mrs. Duff. On May 25, 1964, he received a long distance telephone call from Mrs. Duff in which she stated her husband had vital information in the case concerning the assassination of President Kennedy. A meeting was arranged on that evening at the police station in Chickasha, Oklahoma. It was at this time that Duff, in the presence of his wife, related the information concerning the alleged association of Jack Ruby and General Edwin A. Walker.

Agent Cantrell said he had taken Duff aside in an effort to establish the truth, pointing out that if the information were found not to be true, Duff could be subject to prosecution. He invited Duff to change his story, if it were not the truth, while maintaining the fiction to his wife. Duff insisted on its truth and volunteered that he would submit to a polygraph examination if desired. Duff requested that the polygraph examination await his discharge from the Army on June 1, 1964, on grounds of fraudulent enlistment. He claimed to have been in the Air Force from December, 1957, to December, 1960, and had not so indicated when enlisting in the Army.

Agent Cantrell advised he had been informed by Cliff Roberts, Oklahoma Crime Bureau, that Duff had been examined by psychiatrists at Fort Sill, Oklahoma, and had been diagnosed as a pathological liar.

On June 12, 1964, Peggy Marie Duff, 1213 Lawton Street (ELgin 5-8009), Lawton, Oklahoma, a civilian employee of the U. S. Army in the Consolidated Supply Department (ELgin 1-4208), at Fort Sill, Oklahoma, advised of the following in a telephone conversation initiated for the purpose of locating William McEwan Duff for interview.

Mrs. Duff said that she is now divorced from William McEwan Duff, a divorce filed by her attorney, J. Merrill Oakes, on February 14, 1964, in Comanche County, Lawton, Oklahoma, effective June 3, 1964.

Duff, she said, had been discharged from the U. S. Army at Fort Sill, Oklahoma, on June 2, 1964, under Section 606 for fraudulent enlistment and has left the Lawton area.

Although Mrs. Duff said she had not seen Duff since June 3, 1964, he had called her on the telephone on June 12, 1964, from Oklahoma City, Oklahoma. At this time Duff, who would not give his address, perhaps because he is to pay $100 per month alimony in connection with his divorce, advised Mrs. Duff that he had secured employment at Oklahoma City through General Clyde Watts whom he described as an attorney at Oklahoma City and counsel for General Edwin A. Walker, Dallas, Texas. Duff claimed that he was living at the time with an elderly friend of General Watts, a friend who was retired. In order that Mrs. Duff might return a telephone call which he had requested, Duff supplied the telephone number for the residence of this individual with whom he said he was residing; the telephone number being VIctor 3-3075.

Mrs. Duff stated that on the evening of June 12, 1964, she had called the number VI 3-3075 at Oklahoma City to contact Duff. The telephone was answered by an individual who sounded as though he were elderly and who had summoned Duff to the telephone by addressing him as "Bill." Mrs. Duff said that this was a collect telephone call to the number, charges which Duff accepted, and that the call lasted for well over an hour, terminating at about 12:25 a.m., June 13, 1964.

In her conversation with Duff at this time, Mrs. Duff said that she had reminded Duff that he was to contact Agent James R. Cantrell, Special Agent of the Secret Service at Oklahoma City, Oklahoma, for purposes of taking the polygraph examination to which he had agreed following his discharge from the military for fraudulent enlistment. According to Mrs. Duff, Duff responded to this by saying "You notify Cantrell, and I'll be gone." Mrs. Duff stated that she would judge by this statement by Duff that he had no intention of pursuing this matter in which he had alleged that Jack Ruby had visited the residence of General Walker on occasion during Duff's employment in the Walker residence.

Mrs. Duff stated she had no additional information concerning the current allegation by Duff and had no information other than as related concerning his whereabouts. She advised that should Duff contact her at any time in the future, she would notify the Federal Bureau of Investigation immediately.

On June 12, 1964, James D. Andrews, 1st Sergeant, F Battery, 1st Training Battalion, U. S. A. T., Fort Sill, Oklahoma, advised that William McEwan Duff had been discharged under Section 606 -- Fraudulent Enlistment -- on June 2, 1964.

On June 12, 1964, Private First Class William H. Grim, Transfer Point, Fort Sill, Oklahoma, advised that Duff's personnel file had been forwarded to the Department of the Army on June 3, 1964.

On June 16, 1964, William McEwan Duff, 1211 Tedford Way, Oklahoma City, Oklahoma, advised that since the date of his previous interview on January 24, 1964, with a Special Agent of the Federal Bureau of Investigation at Lawton, Oklahoma, he had been discharged from the U. S. Army, divorced from his wife Peggy Marie Duff and had moved to Oklahoma City, Oklahoma, as of June 2, 1964.

With regard to his current status, Mr. Duff said that he had been discharged from the U. S. Army at Fort Sill, Oklahoma, on June 2, 1964, under Section 606, Fraudulent Enlistment, for the reason he had failed to disclose on his enlistment that he previously had served in the Air Force from which he had been discharged for failure to adapt. He said his wife had filed for divorce at Lawton, Oklahoma, in February, 1964, a divorce effective June 2, 1964.

Duff said a week before moving to Oklahoma City he had visited General Clyde Watts, an Oklahoma City attorney, who is counsel for General Edwin A. Walker by whom Duff had been employed in 1962 and 1963 at Dallas, Texas. He said he had met General Watts when the General had visited General Walker in Dallas.

It had been through General Watts that he had obtained temporary living quarters with Marion W. Osborne at 1211 Tedford Way, Oklahoma City, Oklahoma, Osborne being a friend of General Watts. With the same recommendation he had obtained temporary employment at a firm managed by Mr. Osborne at the Paul T. Blakeney Company, 330 Northeast 38th Street, Oklahoma City, Oklahoma, a firm which distributes and repairs lawn mowers of commercial and home type. Mr. Duff said he anticipates General Watts will find employment for him as a heavy equipment operator in road construction at Oklahoma City by reason of his former association with General Walker.

Mr. Duff said that the information that he previously had related and would now relate was based on that gained in connection with his employment by

William McEwan Duff

General Edwin A. Walker from November, 1962, to April, 1963. He said he had been employed by General Walker as his "batman." He defined batman as a British military term for an orderly, valet, or personal aide, stating he previously had had such experience in England. Mr. Duff said he had applied for the job on impulse as one day he had passed the residence of General Walker in Dallas, a house which he had identified by the flags of the United States and Texas flying in front of the house, along with the name of the General. He said he had known nothing of General Walker until he had gone to Dallas; that he had learned of General Walker through newspaper accounts of the activities of the General. He said he had applied for the job in a personal contact with General Walker, who had been summoned by a volunteer aide when Duff had appeared at the door; that he had supplied no references; none were asked.

Mr. Duff said that his duties at the Walker residence largely concerned looking after the personal needs of the General, including cooking and chauffeuring for him. He said his day started each morning with the raising of the two flags in front of the house, and concluded when the house was locked and the General retired. Duff said that he was quartered upstairs, the front room to the left. He received no remuneration, only room, board and other personal requirements. Although he had access to the entire house, General Walker and his volunteer workers would use care that Duff neither saw correspondence nor overheard conversations of a business nature.

Duff said that during this period and in performance of his duties, he observed that Walker had numerous visitors.

When photographs of Jack Ruby appeared in the newspaper in November, 1963, after his shooting of Lee Harvey Oswald, Mr. Duff said he believed him to be one

of two individuals who had visited at the WALKER residence once each month in December, 1962, January and February, 1963. Mr. DUFF said that he is "not sure" of his identification; that there is "doubt in his mind"; that he "would not swear definitely" as to his identification of this individual as JACK RUBY. He said there are a lot of men who look like RUBY, adding "I saw one (of RUBY's likeness) in Oklahoma City the other day."

Mr. DUFF said that what identification he had made was on the basis of personal appearance only, a likeness which he had noted upon seeing the photographs of RUBY in the newspapers; that never had he heard Gen. WALKER or anyone else in WALKER's household mention RUBY in any respect nor had he any other basis which would indicate an association between JACK RUBY and Gen. WALKER.

Mr. DUFF stated that to his knowledge the two individuals in question had visited on these three occasions only, each time in the late afternoon at about 4:30 p.m. In December and January he had not observed their arrival but had only seen their departure, observing them as they stood at the doorway conversing with Gen. WALKER for several minutes after emerging from the sitting room where they had conversed behind the closed French doors. Mr. DUFF stated that he had heard none of the conversation. He said WALKER always conducted his business in this manner, not wishing to be disturbed. On the occasion of the third visit of these individuals in February, 1963, DUFF said he had seen them arrive, parking a 1958 Ford at the corner. Mr. DUFF was not able to provide further description of the Ford vehicle. Mr. DUFF said his view of the man whom he thought to be JACK RUBY was only a profile and view of the man's back only.

Mr. DUFF described the man whom he had considered might be JACK RUBY as follows:

White male American, 40 to 50 years of age, 5'8", 125 pounds, grayish white hair, wearing a business suit. DUFF described this individual as being very thin in appearance.

The second individual DUFF described as a white male American, in his late 40s, 5'11" to 6', 210 pounds, with an evident paunch. This man had very black hair and was believed to have been of Italian or Mexican descent according to DUFF. He was described as wearing a dark business suit. Neither man carried brief cases or dispatch cases of any type.

Mr. DUFF stated that he previously had not informed of this possible association between JACK RUBY and General WALKER based on his personal identification because on the occasion of his interview in January, 1964, he had been interviewed at the hospital at Fort Sill and was more concerned about his personal welfare and physical condition than the matter which he reported.

Mr. DUFF reiterated that while he cannot now be certain that the individual who visited WALKER actually was JACK RUBY, in his view, this possibility alone was sufficient to require his reporting it to the Federal Bureau of Investigation. He volunteered to take a polygraph test concerning the matters which he had reported.

Mr. DUFF was asked whether or not he was acquainted with one ANDRE ANGELES. Mr. DUFF said he was not acquainted with such an individual and knew of none in his acquaintanceship who had traveled to Dallas, Texas on November 22, 1963.

DUFF stated that never had he seen nor had he been in any association with LEE HARVEY OSWALD; that he has never seen anyone of OSWALD's description at the residence of Gen. WALKER.

Mr. DUFF stated that he had left the employment of WALKER because of friction between himself and several women of the office staff. He said he was supposed to have time off from his present duties when the General was away but the women on the staff became very demanding of him instructing that he make coffee, tea and expecting him to do other chores for them. He said he finally had had enough of this and left.

- 9 -

COMMISSION EXHIBIT No. 2389—Continued

William McEwan Duff

Mr. Duff stated that in the event a later interview might be required, he would advise of any change of address in order that he might be located readily.

It is noted that information, as originally obtained from Special Agent James R. Cantrell, U. S. Secret Service, as reported herein, indicated the presence of two men with the individual believed to have been Jack Ruby, on the occasions of the reported visits to the residence of General Walker. Mr. Duff advised there was not a third man, only two, one whom he thought might have been Ruby. He said if three men had been reported, it was in error.

On June 16, 1964, Mr. Marion W. Osborne, 1211 Tedford Way, Oklahoma City, Oklahoma, employed as manager for the Paul T. Blakeney Company, 330 Northeast 38th Street, Oklahoma City, Oklahoma, advised he had given temporary residence and employment to William McEwan Duff upon the recommendation of General Clyde Watts, an attorney for the Blakeney firm, Oklahoma City, Oklahoma.

Mr. Osborne, who advised he had been general manager of the Twentieth Century Fox Films, Inc., at Oklahoma City, Oklahoma, from 1925 until he retired several years ago, said he knew nothing of the background of Mr. Duff or of the basis for Duff's interview sought by the Federal Bureau of Investigation.

On June 16, 1964, Clyde J. Watts, attorney, 219 Couch Drive, Oklahoma City, Oklahoma, contacted the Oklahoma City Office by telephone from Fort Worth, Texas, and furnished the following information:

William Duff contacted Watts in Oklahoma City on approximately June 7, 1964, indicating he had just been discharged from the Army by reason of fraudulent enlistment, and was in need of employment.

Watts had known Duff to be formerly associated with former General Edwin Walker in Dallas, Texas, and believed Duff possibly had information concerning the assassination attempt on General Walker. Watts believed that if he kept Duff around where he could talk with him there would be a

- 10 -

COMMISSION EXHIBIT No. 2389—Continued

chance Duff would reveal his knowledge of the Walker assassination attempt. Watts contacted a friend at the Paul Bl..keney Company, a lawn mower service company in Oklahoma City, obtaining a job for Duff.

Interviewed on a previous occasion, January 8, 1964, Mr. Watts had advised of the following concerning William McEwan Duff, information he had gained as counsel and friend of General Edwin A. Walker:

Mr. Watts advised he is a long-time personal friend of Edwin A. Walker, Dallas, Texas, former General of the United States Army; that he presently is acting as legal counsel for General Walker.

In the Spring of 1963, shortly after someone shot at General Walker in his home in Dallas, Texas, Watts hired two private investigators in Oklahoma City to go to Dallas and attempt to ascertain the identity of the person who had shot at Walker. These investigators were Bill Keester, former member of the Oklahoma City Police Department, and Cliff Roberts, former Oklahoma State Narcotics Bureau Agent.

During the investigation conducted by Keester and Roberts, information was received that one Bill Duff, a Scotsman, who was at one time employed by Walker or Walker's staff, had allegedly remarked he was the person who had shot at Walker. Keester and Roberts made contact with Bill Duff without disclosing their true identity or capacity as private detectives, and offered Duff $5,000 to shoot General Walker. Duff was interested in the proposition and discussed with Keester and Roberts a plan to shoot General Walker. A tape recording was made of the discussion and this recording, along with the results of the investigation by Keester and Roberts, was turned over to the Dallas Police Department. At no time did Duff ever admit to Keester and Roberts that he was the person who had previously attempted to shoot General Walker. At the time Keester and Roberts were in contact with Bill Duff, he resided at 5420 Lewis Street, Dallas, Texas.

On January 16, 1964, Cliff Roberts, Investigator, Oklahoma State Crime Bureau, Oklahoma City, Oklahoma, was interviewed concerning his employment as a private investigator

by Clyde J. Watts, attorney, Oklahoma City, Oklahoma, representing General Edwin A. Walker. He had been retained, he said, with an associate, Bill Keester, for purposes of investigating the attempted shooting of General Walker. In connection with this matter, he had conducted investigation concerning William McEwan Duff, offering Duff $5,000 to shoot Walker, in an effort to establish whether he had information concerning the earlier attempt. During the discussions with Duff relative to this plan, Duff never made any admissions which would indicate he was guilty of the earlier shooting, although he attempted to show some knowledge, in an apparent attempt to impress Roberts and Keester. Roberts said he considered Duff to be a "complete phoney" in every respect, and was convinced he had gone along with Roberts and Keester merely in an attempt to get some money out of them.

Investigation concerning William McEwan Duff has disclosed the following background data concerning him:

William McEwan Duff was born November 4, 1931, at Grangemount, Sterlingshire, Scotland, and on January 24, 1964, was serving in the United States Army at Fort Sill, Oklahoma. He is enlisted under serial number RA 18 678 666 and was connected with Battery D, First Training Battalion, USATC-FA, Fort Sill, Oklahoma.

Duff, when interviewed on January 24, 1964, claimed he had been a member of the British Army, the "Argyles," an infantry unit, from 1949 to 1952. He worked for a number of years for the British National Railroad as an engine driver, and came to Dallas, Texas, in November, 1962. He said at that time the newspapers were full of news of General Edwin A. Walker and he felt he might get a job with the General as his "Batman." Duff, according to his own statement, went to the General's home in Dallas, was hired, and resided at the Walker house as an employee from November, 1962, to April, 1963. He left the employ of General Walker because of friction with a woman on the General's staff.

In August, 1963, he left Dallas and went to Oklahoma City, Oklahoma, where he enlisted in the United States Army and was sent to Fort Polk, Louisiana, for basic training, and on December 10, 1963, left Fort Polk and went to Fort Sill, Oklahoma.

William McEwan Duff

He claimed in July, 1963, he was investigated by the Dallas Police Department in connection with the attempted shooting of General Walker. He said he took a lie detector test and was "completely cleared" as a result. He is reportedly a former chauffeur and handyman for General Walker.

Duff is described as follows:

Race	White
Sex	Male
Date of Birth	November 4, 1931
Place of Birth	Grangemount, Sterlingshire, Scotland
Citizenship Status	Entered the United States in 1957, alien registration number A11330675
Height	5 feet 9 inches
Weight	150 pounds
Eyes	Blue
Hair	Brown and receding
Relatives:	
Father	Deceased
Sister	Margaret Lawson, 715 West Mission, Alhambra, California
Brother	Robert Duff, living near Long Beach, California
Uncle	William McEwan, 7614 Glendon Way South, San Gabriel, California
Relative (possibly ex-wife)	Judie Loraine Duff, Post Office Box 253, Broadus, Montana
Characteristics	Described as "con man," pathological liar and lazy
FBI Number	483264E
Dallas Police Department Number	52495
Los Angeles Police Department Number	B743533
Former Wife	PEGGY MARIE DUFF 1213 Lawton Street Lawton, Oklahoma

COMMISSION EXHIBIT No. 2389—Continued

FD-302 (Rev. 3-3-59)

1

FEDERAL BUREAU OF INVESTIGATION

Date 9/12/64

Mrs. ROBERT D. ROGERS, 3821 Whitehall Road, Dallas, Texas, advised that she has known Miss SYLVIA ODIO for about a year. She stated Miss ODIO's family were acquaintances of friends of her husband's family in Miami, Florida, from pre-BATISTA days.

Mrs. ROGERS stated when Miss ODIO's parents were arrested and put in jail in Cuba by the CASTRO government, Miss ODIO and all of her brothers and sisters were able to get out of Cuba and they all came to the United States. She stated Miss ODIO went to Puerto Rico with her husband and children, but became involved in marital troubles in Puerto Rico and eventually divorced her husband. She understands that the husband actually obtained the divorce from Miss ODIO, but they have some sort of written agreement permitting her to have the children.

She stated that when Miss ODIO arrived in Dallas, Texas, she was quite upset emotionally and has undergone psychiatric treatment at the Southwestern Medical School. For a while she resided with Mrs. ROGERS' brother-in-law, JOHN B. ROGERS, at 4626 Watauga Road in Dallas.

Mrs. ROGERS stated Miss ODIO had stayed a short time with the JOHN B. ROGERS' family due to the family ties that went back beyond the BATISTA days in Cuba. However, when she was able to bring her four children to Dallas from Puerto Rico, she moved into her own apartment.

Mrs. ROGERS described Miss ODIO as a very well educated person who has a typical "Latin" personality, that is, she is very excitable and emotional. However, Mrs. ROGERS stated she is a truthful person, who is not believed to be the type who would make up a story to impress others of her importance. Mrs. ROGERS stated she has never known Miss ODIO to lie to her about anything.

Mrs. ROGERS stated that she has had very little contact with Miss ODIO in recent months and has never heard anything

on 9/11/64 at Dallas, Texas File # DL 100-10461

by Special Agent RICHARD J. BURNETT /rmb [redacted] dictated 9/11/64

Commission Exhibit No. 2390

COMMISSION EXHIBIT No. 2390

2

DL 100-10461

concerning Miss ODIO having seen OSWALD at her apartment prior to the assassination of President JOHN F. KENNEDY.

COMMISSION EXHIBIT No. 2390—Continued

FD-302 (Rev. 3-3-59)

FEDERAL BUREAU OF INVESTIGATION

Date 9/8/64

1

OSWALDO AURELIO PINO PINO, a Cuban national, who presently resides at Dallas at the address 719 North Bishop Street, Dallas, and is employed at the El Chico Restaurant Warehouse, 171 Howell Street in Dallas, was interviewed at his place of employment.

PINO stated he is a member of the anti-CASTRO group known as Second National Front of the Escambray (Operation Alpha 66) (SNFE) but does not belong to any other organizations in Dallas.

PINO stated he does not know SYLVIA ODIO and has never met her to his knowledge. He said he remembers that a general reunion of various Cuban refugees had been held several months ago at a picnic ground near White Rock Lake, and that a woman by the name of ODIO had made a short speech at the reunion.

PINO advised he had never been to the home of SYLVIA ODIO to his knowledge. He said he had not visited the home of any Cuban woman along with two other male persons. He advised he had not known LEE HARVEY OSWALD and had never met or seen OSWALD to his knowledge. He advised he knew nothing concerning the reported visit to the home of SYLVIA ODIO by three persons, one of whom was reported to have the appearance of OSWALD.

on 9/8/64 at Dallas, Texas File # DL 100-10461

by Special Agent WALLACE R. HEITMAN/tll Date dictated 9/8/64

This document contains neither recommendations nor conclusions of the FBI. It is the property of the FBI and is loaned to your agency; it and its contents are not to be distributed outside your agency.

COMMISSION EXHIBIT No. 2390—Continued

FD-302 (Rev. 3-3-59)

FEDERAL BUREAU OF INVESTIGATION

Date 9/8/64

1

FELIX GUILLERMO OTHON PACHO, a Cuban national, who now resides at Dallas, Texas, at 3901 Prescott Street, and is employed by Forrest and Cotton Engineers, Mercantile Continental Building, Dallas, was interviewed at the Dallas Office of the FBI. He said for business purposes he is known as BILL OTHON in Dallas among Americans.

OTHON advised he is a Cuban national and is a refugee living in Dallas. He advised he is the official delegate of an anti-CASTRO Cuban group, Directorio Revolucionario Estudentil (Revolutionary Student Directory) (DRE). He advised there is no formal organized Dallas unit of the DRE nor has there ever been such an organized group in Dallas to his knowledge. He said the official Dallas delegate for the DRE had previously been SARITA CASTILLO, who has now departed Dallas and is residing in New York where she is employed. OTHON said he had been designated as the delegate of the DRE in approximately September or October, 1963, when MANUEL SALVAT, secretary general of the national organization of DRE had come to Dallas from Miami along with two other persons who are members of the DRE, JOAQUIN PINCILLAS and another person, ANITA (last name unknown). SALVAT designated OTHON as the delegate of the DRE in Dallas for the purpose of organizing a unit of the organization in Dallas. OTHON advised he had worked with the DRE in Cuba and was therefore familiar with the organization. OTHON explained that SALVAT had wanted a male delegate in Dallas instead of a female such as SARITA CASTILLO. OTHON said that because of a lack of students among the Cuban refugees in the Dallas area and because he, OTHON, could not spare enough time to devote to organizational efforts of DRE that the Dallas unit had not been formed. OTHON said he worked at a full time job all day and was attending school at night and for that reason had not been able to devote sufficient time to the organization of the DRE in Dallas.

OTHON said that when MANUEL SALVAT came to Dallas, a meeting had been held in a Dallas bank near the White Rock Lake at which meeting approximately thirty or forty persons attended. Persons in attendance were both

on 9/8/64 at Dallas, Texas File # DL 100-10461

by Special Agent WALLACE R. HEITMAN/tll Date dictated 9/8/64

COMMISSION EXHIBIT No. 2390—Continued

DL 100-10461
2

Americans and Cubans. The meeting had been organized by Mr. DEAN PERKINS who was sympathetic with the purposes of the DRE, which purposes OTHON explained were completely anti-CASTRO. OTHON explained that although Americans could not be full members of the DRE, their cooperation was solicited mainly from the standpoint of financial assistance. It was for the purpose of raising money primarily for the organization that the meeting was held at the bank near White Rock Lake.

OTHON said that about two months ago, Mr. DAMASO OLIVO, who is the national secretary of organization for DRE, had come to Dallas from Miami for the purpose of exhibiting a motion picture film entitled, "Cuba de Ayer" (Cuba of Yesterday). This film was exhibited at the Holy Trinity Church in the Oak Lawn section of Dallas for the purpose of raising money for the DRE. Very little money was raised according to OTHON.

OTHON advised that he intended to relinquish his title as delegate of the DRE in Dallas because he cannot spend enough time for the organization and will suggest that another person be designated as delegate. OTHON explained that he does not know SYLVIA ODIO, although he knows of her as he is acquainted with her sister, SARITA ODIO. OTHON further explained that he has never been to the home of SYLVIA ODIO and has never met her to his knowledge. OTHON further explained that he did not know LEE HARVEY OSWALD and never met OSWALD to his knowledge. OTHON said he knows nothing about a reported visit to the home of SYLVIA ODIO by three persons, one of whom was reported by ODIO to have appeared to be OSWALD and the other two of whom are unknown.

COMMISSION EXHIBIT No. 2390—Continued

Commission Exhibit No. 2391

FD-302 (Rev. 3-3-59)

FEDERAL BUREAU

1

Date Dec. 17, 1963

ROBERT Y. BLACK, 1919 Steven Forrest Drive, Apartment 115, bellman, Sheraton-Dallas Hotel, was advised that investigation had determined he had been issued Carousel Club Pass Card #148. BLACK furnished the following information:

He was formerly employed at the Baker Hotel as a bell man and has known RUBY for the pastten years as a local nightclub owner. He has been employed at the Sheraton-Dallas as a bell boy for about four months. He last saw RUBY on November 19, 1963, at Sol's Turf Bar, 1515 Commerce Street, at which time he drank a beer and talked with RUBY who was drinking a 7-Up. He later saw RUBY that night at the Carousel Club at about 10:00 p.m. He does not recall the conversation he had with RUBY but believed he asked RUBY how his business was going.

BLACK stated he did not consider RUBY a personal friend and did not know of any of RUBY's activities other than as operator of several Dallas nightclubs. He had never heard of LEE HARVEY OSWALD before the assassination of the President and had no personal knowledge of the circumstances surrounding the assassination of the President or the murder of OSWALD and knew of no connection between RUBY and OSWALD. He advised he did not know of any close association between RUBY and the Dallas police force or any travels of RUBY in the United States of to any other country.

on 12/16/63 at Dallas, Texas File # DL 44-1639

by Special Agent EDWARD J. MABEY/csh Date dictated 12/17/63

44

COMMISSION EXHIBIT No. 2391

Commission Exhibit No. 2392

FD-302 (Rev. 3-3-59)

FEDERAL BUREAU OF INVESTIGATION

1

Date 11/29/63

GLENN RAYE SNIDER, 4420 Noth 8th Street, Apartment 12, telephone 264-3657, who is employed as an agent at Forrell Talent Agency, 44443 North 24th Street, Phoenix, advised he first met JACK RUBY when SNIDER was entertaining with a vocal trio at Pat Martin's, now known as Montmarte, in Dallas, about two years ago. RUBY visited Martin's frequently, and persuaded the trio to play one night at the Carousel.

SNIDER saw RUBY almost every day during the four weeks stay in Dallas, and sbusequently saw him on other visits to Dallas, but has not seen him for about eight months. RUBY was usually accompanied by GEORGE SENATOR, who appeared to be his only close friend.

SNIDER described RUBY as high strung, and very emotional, but said he never saw RUBY lose temper, and considered him a very nice person. He said RUBY never exhibited any Un-American sentiments, and expressed high regard for late President KENNEDY, and former President ROOSEVELT.

He said he knew of no hoodlum associates of RUBY, and that RUBY appeared to know most members of Dallas Police Department, probably due to fact that RUBY employed different members of Police Department at Carousel Club on Friday's and Saturday's. SNIDER said he recalled having seen RUBY in company of two Dallas Detectives at one time, but has no knowledge of identities of these detectives.

SNIDER said he does not know LEE HARVEY OSWALD, and knows of no association between RUBY and OSWALD. He also knows of no associates, or contacts which RUBY might have in Phoenix area.

He advised he was told by MILTON JOSEPH, a jeweler whose place of business is on Commerce Street, that RUBY was known in Chicago as "Sparky" because of his high temper. SNIDER advised that JOSEPH has extreme dislike for RUBY, which RUBY claimed was based on fact that he barred JOSEPH from Carousel Club because JOSEPH was bothering the girls.

SNIDER was of opinion that RUBY shot OSWALD in fit

on 11/25/63 at Phoenix, Arizona File # DL 44-1639

by Special Agent ROY W. REGER & ORLAND E. FREEMAN/cjr Date dictated 11/25/63

416

COMMISSION EXHIBIT No. 2392

2
DL 44-1639

of anger because of the President's assassination, based on his past knowledge of RUBY.

COMMISSION EXHIBIT No. 2392—Continued

FD-302 (Rev. 3-3-59)

FEDERAL BUREAU OF [redacted] Commission Exhibit No. 2393

1

Date Dec. 20, 1963

MILTON JOSEPH, wholesale jeweler, National Bankers Life Building, associate of JACK RUBY, furnished the following information:

He has known RUBY since the early 1930's when he used to see him in the Randolph Street area of Chicago, Illinois, and although he knew his name, he had never met him and did not know him personally. He did not know of any associates or activities of RUBY at this time in Chicago. The next time he saw RUBY was in Dallas in about 1946 when RUBY arrived in Dallas from Chicago and opened the Silver Spur night club. He did not know where RUBY obtained the money to open this night club but feels it probably came from relatives in Chicago. He states RUBY never liked him and this has often puzzled him, although on one occasion when he visited one of RUBY's clubs in Dallas, name unrecalled, RUBY, with no apparent reason, told him to get out and never come back. He stated this animosity has always existed between them, but he cannot say exactly why or when it started. He does not know of any political affiliations of RUBY or of any connection with the hoodlum element in Dallas or Chicago or any connection with LEE HARVEY OSWALD prior to the murder of OSWALD.

He last saw RUBY two or three days prior to the assassination of the President in the coffee shop of the Cabana Motor Hotel in Dallas at about 1:00 a.m. where they exchanged a short greeting.

on 12/17/63 at Dallas, Texas File # DL 44-1639

by Special Agent EDWARD J. MABEY/csh Date dictated 12/19/63

52

COMMISSION EXHIBIT No. 2393

FD-302 (Rev. 3-3-59) FEDERAL BUREAU OF IN[redacted]

—Commission Exhibit No. 2394 —

1

Date 11/27/63

KAREN GREEN WILLIAMS who resides at 2064 Kirby, Apartment D, was interviewed at the Carousel Club, 1312½ Commerce Street, at which time she furnished the following information:

Mrs. WILLIAMS was born and grew up in Dade City, Florida, and lived in Dade City until June 8, 1963, at which time she came to Dallas and married BILLY DON WILLIAMS. Her husband up until November 15, 1963, was employed by Melnik Construction Company in Dallas and is presently unemployed. On Tuesday evening, November 19, 1963, Mrs. WILLIAMS and her husband went to the Carousel Club in answer to an ad which appeared in a local newspaper and applied for a job as a strip-tease dancer. Mrs. WILLIAMS talked to RUBY on that evening, and he hired her for $90.00 per week.

The last time Mrs. WILLIAMS saw JACK RUBY was at closing time on Thursday night, November 21, 1963, and she has not seen him nor heard from him since that time.

Mrs. WILLIAMS was shown a photograph of LEE HARVEY OSWALD at which time she stated that OSWALD was unknown to her, and she was certain that she had never seen him in the Carousel Club. She stated that it is almost impossible to recognize anyone in the audience due to the brightness of the lights on the stage. Mrs. WILLIAMS knows nothing concerning RUBY's personal life or political beliefs as her brief acquaintanceship with him has been on a strict employer-employee basis. Mrs. WILLIAMS advised that she dances under the name of FELISA PRELL as she did not want it publicly known that she was working as a strip-tease dancer. During her previous stay at the Carousel Club she has not noted any specific police officers or newsmen with whom RUBY was particularly friendly.

on 11/26/63 at Dallas, Texas File # DL 44-1639 DL 89-43

by Special Agents JOSEPH G. PEGGS & ALVIN J. ZIMMERMAN /cv 780 Date dictated 11/27/63

COMMISSION EXHIBIT NO. 2394

— Commission Exhibit No. 2395 —

NBC reel 105
November 21, 1963

POLICE CHIEF JESSE CURRY TV INTERVIEW

Q. Do you anticipate any trouble on the President's arrival?

CURRY. We're hoping that we don't have any trouble at all, but because of what has happened here previously, we would be foolish, I think, not to anticipate some trouble. I, I don't really, I don't anticipate any violence.

Q. By what's happened here previously do you mean the anti-UN picketing involving Mr. Stevenson?

CURRY. That's correct, yes sir.

Q. It did prompt, you say, extra precautions for the President's arrival?

CURRY. I think it has. I believe had it not been for this incident involving Ambassador Stevenson, we probably would have had less security set up for the Presidential visit than we now have.

Q. What preparations have you made for dealing with any unruly crowds?

COMMISSION EXHIBIT NO. 2395

CURRY. The same that we would make in any situation. If the crowd becomes unruly we would take whatever action was necessary to restore peace and order.

Q. Has any order gone out for special surveillance of any persons for tomorrow?

CURRY. We have had one or two persons under surveillance and have interviewed one or two people previous to today and I would say we would probably be aware of the movements of a few people tomorrow.

COMMISSION EXHIBIT No. 2395—Continued

FD-302 (Rev. 3-3-59)

FEDERAL BUREAU Commission Exhibit No. 2396

Date 1/6/64

1

Mrs. HARRIS D. BRYANT aka Mrs. Ann Bryant, 3909 Inwood Drive, Apartment 106, whose name was furnished by E. MACE NAYLOR as having attended a party on November 20, 1963, at Apartment 104, same address, at which party RUBY was allegedly present, furnished the following information:

Mrs. BRYANT stated that about 1:00 or 1:30 AM, on November 20 or 21, 1963, she was in her apartment alone and at that time FRANK T. TORTORIELLO, who resides in Apartment 104, same address, came to her apartment accompanied by a young woman unknown to Mrs. BRYANT. TORTORIELLO explained he had come to her apartment to request some ice, inasmuch as he had run out and needed same for friends he was entertaining in his apartment. He invited Mrs. BRYANT to his apartment for "a couple of drinks," which invitation she accepted. She went to TORTORIELLO's apartment and stayed thirty or forty minutes and had two or three drinks there. Upon arriving, she noticed that all present, except TORTORIELLO, were strangers. There were at that time, in addition to TORTORIELLO, four men and three women. She was introduced all around hurriedly and did not recall the names of any of the individuals but, after the shooting of OSWALD by RUBY, she saw RUBY's photograph in the newspaper, and noticed that this photograph looked familiar to one of the men present at the TORTORIELLO party. This man was apparently there with a young woman who had what Mrs. BRYANT described as a theatrical appearance. She was about twenty-five years of age, tall, brunette, and spoke with a slight accent, which may have been an accent of someone of Germanic origin. She heard someone, name not recalled, state that this woman was the wife of the man who resembled RUBY's photograph. She and this man left together a few minutes before Mrs. BRYANT left. She does not recall anything this man may have said and cannot recall the gist of any conversation she or any other person there may have had with him.

on 1/6/64 at Dallas, Texas File # DL 44-1639

by Special Agent EDMOND C. HARDIN/eah Date dictated 1/6/64

42

COMMISSION EXHIBIT No. 2396

DL 44-1639

2

Mrs. BRYANT stated that the other two women present were attractive young women, in their mid-twenties. One of the women was an attractive blonde, who was tall and slender, and had a less theatrical appearance than the other two women. The other woman was a brunette, slightly taller than average, who had superficial hair and wore heavy make-up, and had a decided theatrical appearance. These women danced with two young men present and appeared to be rather friendly with them. The third man present, according to Mrs. BRYANT, was a man about fifty-five years of age, who had white hair and who conversed most of the time with TORTORIELLO.

Mrs. BRYANT advised that neither Mr. nor Mrs. JOE FEDERICI was present at the above-described party and she does not know whether they are acquainted with RUBY. She added that she does know they are acquainted with TORTORIELLO, but does not know the extent of their relationship with him. She added that "JADA," an exotic dancer who formerly worked for RUBY, was not present at the party, although she was known to Mrs. BRYANT and was allegedly a girlfriend of TORTORIELLO.

Mrs. BRYANT informed that since the above-described party she has not seen the individual resembling RUBY mentioned above, and is not certain in her own mind that this individual was actually RUBY. She stated she has never known LEE HARVEY OSWALD and has no information concerning the assassination of President KENNEDY or the shooting of OSWALD on the party of RUBY.

43

COMMISSION EXHIBIT No. 2396—Continued

FD-302 (Rev. 3-3-59)

FEDERAL BUREA Commission Exhibit No. 2397

[redacted]

Date December 2, 1963

1

Mr. E. MACE NAYLOR, 3909 Inwood, Tanglewood Apartment #5, Dallas, Texas (telephone FL 7-6835), furnished the following information:

NAYLOR received information from JEAN NELSON, Tanglewood Apartments, possibly apartment 212, that a party was held at apartment 104, Tanglewood Apartments, on Wednesday night, November 20, 1963. The following persons were reportedly in attendance at this party:

FRANK T. TORTORIELLO, boy friend of JADA, exotic dancer at the Carrousel Club;

JACK RUBY;

JOE F. FREDERICI, a nephew of VITO GENOVESE;

SANDY, FREDERICI's wife;

Mrs. ANN BRYANT, who resides in apartment 106, Tanglewood Apartments; and

JADA.

It is NAYLOR's understanding that JOE F. FREDERICI and his wife, SANDY, left Dallas Thursday, November 21, 1963, for New Jersey or someplace in the East.

NAYLOR is not personally acquainted with JACK RUBY although he has seen him in the Dallas area. He has no knowledge of RUBY's activities. NAYLOR is not acquainted with and has never seen LEE HARVEY OSWALD.

NAYLOR said he could furnish no additional information.

vvj

on 11/29/63 at Dallas, Texas File # DL 44-1639

by Special Agents PAUL L. SCOTT and JAMES W. SWINFORD/rms Date dictated 12/2/63

This document contains neither recommendations nor conclusions of the FBI. It is the property of the FBI and is loaned to your agency; it and its contents are not to be distributed outside your agency.

FD-302 (Rev. 3-3-59) **FEDERAL BUREAU OF** Commission Exhibit No. 2398

Date December 12, 1963

1

WELCOME EUGENE BARNETT, Patrolman, Traffic Division, Police Department, Dallas, Texas, furnished the following information:

He is more commonly known as GENE BARNETT and resides at 6018 Menger, Dallas, residence phone EV 1-0726. He has been a member of the Dallas Police Department since 1956 and for the first 2½ years was assigned to the Patrol Division. For the last four years he has directed traffic at the intersection of Commerce and Akard Streets in downtown Dallas. He first met JACK RUBY, while assigned to the Patrol Division during his training period, at the Vegas Club in the Oak Lawn section of Dallas. He stated this was during the course of routine police checks of the club. He has never been in the Vegas Club while off duty. He worked for a period of about five months sometime after his training period in the same section and saw RUBY a number of times during that period. He was assigned to his downtown post before RUBY opened the Carousel Club and one month he would work the 7:00 a.m. to 3:00 p.m. shift and the next month the 3:00 p.m. to 11:00 p.m. shift. He checked the Carousel Club while working on the late shift about once a month as he did the Theater Lounge and the Colony Club. He would only stay in these establishments for a period of 5-10 minutes and would attempt to become familiar with the entertainers who appeared there. He did this so that he could answer questions people would ask him about what entertainment there was in the heart of downtown Dallas.

He has been to the Carousel Club while off duty on one occasion and he was with his wife at the time. He recalled that RUBY was in the club that night and did not let him pay for anything. He also recalled that RUBY would occasionally buy him a cup of coffee but he could recall no other favors he had received from him. He did recall that one Christmas a downtown liquor store owner gave him a pint of whiskey stating that one of the downtown club operators had paid for it. He felt that it was probably RUBY who had purchased the whiskey for him.

He never worked for JACK RUBY and knows of no police officer who has ever worked for RUBY. He never knew RUBY to carry a gun but figured that he did as do most of the business people on his beat.

on 12/11/63 at Dallas, Texas File # Dallas 44-1639

by Special Agent JOHN E. DALLMAN:EL Date dictated 12/11/63

5

COMMISSION EXHIBIT No. 2398

DL 44-1639

2

As concerns RUBY's personal life, he did not believe that he had any close friends. He could recall no specific romantic interests in RUBY's life and if RUBY loved anybody or anything it was his dogs. He volunteered the information that he had heard rumors that RUBY was a homosexual. He could recall no one who specifically mentioned this. He did recall, however, that RUBY would often walk with his entertainers past his intersection and introduce them to him. He always seemed to have an active interest in the women he was with and the men he saw RUBY with were always quite manly in appearance. He recalled that a stripper named JADA was the last girl that RUBY introduced him to. He pointed out that all of his contacts with RUBY or his friends that he met were at the intersection of Commerce and Akard with the exception of his above mentioned visits to the club.

As concerns RUBY's emotions, he recalled that he (RUBY) was so mad at JADA as a result of some difficulty he had with her that he said he felt he would have choked her if she was there at the time he was talking about it. RUBY was highly emotional whenever he discussed the articles concerning the club in the newspapers. He stated whenever an article or advertisement would appear in the papers RUBY would usually bring it to his attention when walking by the intersection. He stated RUBY was always trying to outdo the WEINSTEIN brothers who run the Theater Lounge and the Colony Club. He even said to him at one time in reference to that, that "I'm going to show those Jews." He also recalled that RUBY often made lewd comments concerning women.

He knows nothing concerning RUBY's background and he never discussed politics with him. He stated the conversations always seemed to center around RUBY's business. He has no idea of what RUBY's political convictions were or any organizations or groups he might have been affiliated with.

The last time he saw RUBY was on about November 20, 1963 or November 21, 1963, sometime between 9:30 and 10:00 p.m. He seemed to recall RUBY would walk by his intersection almost every day at one time or another for the past four years.

COMMISSION EXHIBIT No. 2398—Continued

DL 44-1639
3

He stated he has not heard from or seen RUBY since that time. He advised that he has no idea as to why his name would be on the visitor's list at the county jail other than that RUBY likes policemen in general and saw the men who work the downtown intersections almost everyday.

He stated a BUCK NEWSOM told him on December 9, 1963, that JACK RUBY had sent him a postcard and told him to say hello to him and "CATFISH." He was referring to "CATFISH" HANSEN who works the intersection of Main and Akard Streets. NEWSOM said that RUBY wanted him to thank them for remembering him. This is apparently in reference to the fact that about a week after RUBY was arrested he saw the former bar tender at the Carousel Club and asked him how JACK was. This bar tender left the Carousel Club about six months ago and he believes he now works at the Vegas Club. He does not know his name. He stated he has no intention of visiting RUBY and stressed the fact that his relationship with him is strictly based on his downtown traffic assignment.

On November 22, 1963, at the time of the President's assassination he was part of the security detail at Elm and Houston Streets. He stated he had already been interviewed by Agents of the FBI concerning this inasmuch as he was at the sight of the assassination. He was not assigned to the security detail at the Central Police Headquarters on November 22, 1963 or November 23, 1963. He worked the downtown intersection of Commerce and Akard Streets on November 23, 1963, from 4:00 p.m. to 12 midnight. On Sunday, November 24, 1963, he did not work and at no time was at the Central Police Headquarters. He had no knowledge of the security precautions taken after the President's assassination.

He never heard of LEE HARVEY OSWALD prior to the assassination and from photographs he has viewed of him did not recall seeing OSWALD in downtown Dallas. He knows of no connection between JACK RUBY and LEE HARVEY OSWALD.

COMMISSION EXHIBIT No. 2398—Continued

Form No. 1588 (Revised)
Memorandum Report
(7-1-60)

UNITED STATES SECRET SERVICE
TREASURY DEPARTMENT

ORIGIN Field | OFFICE Houston, Texas | FILE NO. CO-2-34,030

TYPE OF CASE	STATUS	TITLE OR CAPTION
Assassination	Continued	Lee Harvey Oswald
INVESTIGATION MADE AT: Houston, Texas	PERIOD COVERED: November 25-27,1963	
INVESTIGATION MADE BY: SAIC Lane Bertram		

DETAILS

SYNOPSIS

Numerous witnesses identify Jack Leon Rubenstein ©Jack Ruby, as being in Houston, Texas on November 21, for several hours, one block from the President's entrance route and from the Rice Hotel where he stayed.

DETAILS OF INVESTIGATION

On November 25, 1963, conference was had with the Houston Police Chief, H. Buddy McGill, Assistant Chief George L. Seber and the Intelligence Unit of the Houston Police Department and later with Chief Deputy Sheriff Lloyd Frazier with the view to having those departments screen all information that might appear pertinent to the investigation into the assassination of the President.

On November 26, Chief Deputy Sheriff Lloyd D. Frazier, Houston, called the Houston Office and requested the writer to come to his office and interview several people available there.

At Chief Frazier's Office interview Deputy Sheriff Bill "Red" Williams (colored). He stated that after pictures of Jack Ruby were published in local papers, he recalled seeing a man during the afternoon of November 21 in the 400 block of Milam St., one block from the Rice Hotel whom he feels sure was Jack Ruby. He advised that he saw the man on two or three different occasions and talked to him about 3 p.m. at which time the subject indicated that he was an oil field worker and had just arrived in Houston and was looking for a man named Joe who ran a pool hall in the vicinity of the 400 block of Milam St. Subject indicated he wanted to get money to Joe to cover pool games.

Deputy Williams advised that he was sure the picture of Ruby appearing in the paper was identical with the man he had observed in the 400 block of Milam St. on the afternoon of November 21.

313

DISTRIBUTION	COPIES	REPORT MADE BY / APPROVED	DATE
Chief (AM)	Orig	SPECIAL AGENT	
Dallas (AM)	2-cc		
New Orleans (AM)	1-cc	SPECIAL AGENT IN CHARGE	12/2/63
San Antonio (AM)	1-cc		
Houston	2-cc		
LB/mts			

(CONTINUE ON PLAIN PAPER)

COMMISSION EXHIBIT No. 2399

Deputy Williams advised that several colored people who were in that neighborhood had reported to him that they had seen Ruby during the afternoon of November 21.

Gloria Reece, 409½ Milam St., Houston, advised that about 2:30 p.m. On November 21, she first saw the white man she now believes to be Ruby. She stated that his hands were dirty as if he had been working, but his clothes were reasonable clean. She stated he appeared to have a day and a half or two days beard and quickly explained that he was not a "bum" as he had money and stated that he had a Cadillac parked around the corner.

She advised that she saw him in the block, 400 Milam, and was present when he made inquiry about "Joe" who ran a pool hall. She stated that a Spanish man operates a pool hall which is owned by Chris' Cafe at the corner of Milam and Prairie Sts. She observed the subject believed to be Ruby enter the steps leading up to this pool hall.

She advised that later at about 7 o'clock or a little after, she again met the subject believed to be Ruby on the street at which time the subject asked her if she was going to the "President's dinner". She advised him that she had not been invited and asked him to buy her a beer and attempted to make a date with him. The subject declined, stating that he was in a hurry and departed going in the direction of the Coliseum where the President was to appear at the Albert Thomas Appreciation Dinner.

Gus Haywood, 1416 Matthews St., Houston, advised that he saw the subject believed to be Ruby at about 3:15 in the 400 block of Milam St. at which time Ruby talked about a club on Washington St. operated by a man he referred to as Jack. Ruby also asked if he would be able to buy a beer at the Milam Club, 401 Milam, which is operated by a colored man.

Marshall Bradley, 1411 Pleasantville Drive, Houston, advised that he saw the subject believed to be Ruby at about 3:30 p.m. and later drank a beer at the same table with the subject in the Milam Club. He stated that the subject repeated that he was not a tramp, that he had money in his pocket and exhibited some money. Subject stated he had just come in from working in the oil fields and that he had a Buick automobile parked around the corner and stated that he had been having transmission trouble with the Buick. He also mentioned to Bradley that he wanted to locate a man by the name of Jack who operates a private club on Washington Avenue.

He advised while he was sitting at the table with the subject, drinking beer, the subject pointed out a faint scar on his left cheek running from just under the left ear to within about 1 inch of his mouth. Bradley advised that he had not noticed the scar until attention was called to it by the subject.

Ira Slater, 409 Milam St., (shoeshine parlor) advised that he saw the subject when he was talking to Deputy Sheriff Red Williams and heard part of the conversation as repeated by Williams.

3/5

COMMISSION EXHIBIT No. 2399—Continued

All persons interviewed advised that the subject was a smooth talker, but talked rather rapidly and appeared nervous.

Telephone call was placed to SAIC Sorrels, Dallas, who was not available. The call was taken by Inspector Thomas Kelley, who was requested to furnish photographs of the subject Jack Ruby.

Two police type photographs were received with memorandum from SA Steuart advising that the Dallas Police Department had developed no information indicating that Ruby was out of Dallas on November 21.

The police photographs were shown to all the persons listed above and all agree that in their opinion Jack Rubenstein was in Houston on November 21 from about 2:30 to 7:15 p.m., in close proximity to the President's route to the hotel and the Rice Hotel itself.

Most of these people obtained a front view of the subject when they were talking to him or when another was talking to him. These persons state that the photograph of Ruby showing a front view is identical with the person they talked to. They do not remember too much about the side view.

Marshall Bradley, 1411 Pleasantville Drive, Houston, who sat to the left side of the subject while drinking a beer with him in the Milam Club, stated that he did not clearly recall the front view but is positive that the side view is definitely Ruby. He was questioned more closely about the feint scar on the left side of Ruby's face and states that he is positive that this scar exists and that in the event Ruby has such a scar, that the person observed on Milam St. on the afternoon of November 21 is without any doubt Ruby.

Doris Griffin, 3321 Memel St., waitress at Milam Club, 403 Milam St., advised that she served beer to the subject and to Marshal Bradley on the afternoon of November 21. She was shown the police photograph of Jack Ruby and advised that in her opinion, Ruby was the person that she had served with Bradley, however, she would not make a positive identification.

Benny Sanchez, 1505½ Congress St., who operates the pool hall located over Chris' Cafe at 419½ Milam St., was interviewed on November 26, 1963. He was shown a photograph of Ruby and stated that he did not recall Ruby visiting the pool hall on the afternoon of November 21. He emphatically denied knowing Ruby or Lee Harvey Oswald. Sanchez is considered unreliable by the Houston Police Department and by the Sheriff's Office.

SUSPECT

Composite description - white male, 5-7-5-8, 180-210, brown hair receding, thin on top, brown eyes, dark complexion, wearing a white shirt, open at collar with an Army type jacket, cloth, Army green, thick with knit cuffs, bottom open, described as heavy material possibly making subject appear larger, wearing dark trousers with small stripe and "engineer's boots" about 12 in. high, black, broad toes with strap across instep.

3/3

3

COMMISSION EXHIBIT No. 2399—Continued

CO-2-34,030
Page 4

Subject was further described as having one to three days' beard and one witness states positively that the subject has a very feint cut scar running across left cheek from just under the ear to within about 1 in. of the mouth.

UNDEVELOPED LEADS

Dallas office is requested to interview Jack Ruby regarding his whereabouts on the afternoon of November 21. It is noted that if Rubenstein has a feint scar on the left side of his cheek as described about, there can be no doubt that he was in Houston on November 21. From his actions and the length of time spent in the 400 block of Milam St., which is a colored area, that his visit very probably had some connection with the President's appearance in Houston.

313

4

COMMISSION EXHIBIT No. 2399—Continued

No. 1588 (Revised)
MEMORANDUM REPORT
(7-1-60)

UNITED STATES SECRET SERVICE
TREASURY DEPARTMENT

ORIGIN: Field (Dallas) | OFFICE: Dallas, Texas | FILE NO. CO-2-34030

TYPE OF CASE: Protective Research	STATUS: Continued	TITLE OR CAPTION: Assassination of President Kennedy
INVESTIGATION MADE AT: Dallas, Texas	PERIOD COVERED: 12/3 and 4/63	George Senator Andrew Armstrong Jack Ruby
INVESTIGATION MADE BY: Special Agent Elmer W. Moore		

DETAILS

SYNOPSIS

Investigation discloses that Ruby was in Dallas on November 21, 1963.

DETAILS OF INVESTIGATION

This inquiry is predicated upon information contained in an M/R of SAIC Lane Bertram, Houston, dated 12-2-63.

George Senator, roommate of Jack Ruby at 223 S. Ewing Street, Dallas, Texas, until December 1, 1963, during an interview at the Dallas office on December 3, 1963, stated that to his knowledge Jack Ruby had not been out of Dallas recently.

Andrew Armstrong, young colored man employed at the Carousel Club, 1312½ Commerce Street, Dallas, interviewed December 4, 1963, stated that Ruby was at the club on Thursday, November 21, 1963 during the afternoon. He recalled that he was with a Mickey Ryan, a bartender who wanted to borrow money from Ruby. Armstrong also recalled that Ruby made several phone calls from the club that day and he believed, however was not certain, that Ruby telephoned long distance to some officials of the American Guild of Variety Artists regarding auditions of amateurs.

Armstrong also stated that he did not know of Ruby having made any long trips away from Dallas recently.

Jack Ruby was interviewed at the Dallas County jail on 12-4-63. He was questioned regarding his whereabouts and movements on the day preceeding the visit of the President to Dallas. Ruby at first stated that the only thing he could think of at this time was that he had talked to a bartender named Mickey Ryan and that the conversation took place at his club, probably in the early afternoon hours. Later in the conversation, Ruby recalled that he had been in downtown Dallas when he went to the Merchants State Bank and got a $500 Cashier's check which he gave to Miss Mary Lewandowski, secretary of Leo F. Corrigan, Jr., for rental of one of his

DISTRIBUTION	COPIES		DATE
Chief	Orig.&2cc	REPORT MADE BY: Elmer W. Moore (signature), SPECIAL AGENT Elmer W. Moore	509 12-6-63
Houston	1 cc	APPROVED: Forrest V. Sorrels (signature), SPECIAL AGENT IN CHARGE	12-6-63
Dallas	2 cc		

(CONTINUE ON PLAIN PAPER)

COMMISSION EXHIBIT No. 2399—Continued

clubs. Interview with Ruby was interrupted due to a visit from his attorney, Tom Howard, and his brother Earl Rubenstein.

Miss Mary Lewandowski, secretary of Leo F. Corrigan, Jr., 211 N. Ervay Street, Dallas, was asked on 12-4-63 if and when she received a $500 check from Ruby. She replied that she had received a $500 check for rent from Ruby and that while she could not immediately give the day of the month, she clearly recalls that she received it on Thursday, the day before the assassination of President Kennedy.

Ruby has no noticeable facial scars as reported by SAIC Bertram.

DISPOSITION

Inquiry closed.

ELM:mla

COMMISSION EXHIBIT No. 2399—Continued

The following investigation was conducted by SA LANSING P. LOGAN at Dallas, on December 17, 1963:

Mr. LARMAR HUNT, 2969 Binkley, telephone number EM 8-7708, who is the owner of the Kansas City Chiefs, American League football club and whose name appeared as "LAMAR HUNT" in a book which was the property of JACK RUBY, was contacted at his office located on Orchard Lane with telephone number EM 8-4835. He advised that he has never been acquainted with JACK RUBY and has no information whatsoever concerning RUBY's background, associates, political views or his, RUBY, motive for killing LEE HARVEY OSWALD. The only information he possessed concerning either the assassination of President KENNEDY or the shooting of LEE HARVEY OSWALD is that which he had obtained through the local newspapers and television.

Mr. HUNT advised that he could not think of any reason why his name would appear in JACK RUBY's personal property and stated that he has had no contact whatsoever with RUBY to the best of his knowledge. HUNT is not acquainted with LEE HARVEY OSWALD and has only heard his name mentioned in connection with the assassination of President KENNEDY. He knew of no connection between RUBY and LEE HARVEY OSWALD.

268

COMMISSION EXHIBIT No. 2400

Commission Exhibit No. 2401 [redacted]

FD-302 (Rev. 3-3-59) FEDERAL BUREAU [redacted]

1

Date 11/27/63

BECKY JONES, 115 North Adams Street, was interviewed at the Carousel Club, 1312½ Commerce Street, where she is employed as a cigarette girl.

JONES advised that she has known JACK RUBY for the past four months as he hired her to go to work in his club at that time.

JONES stated that she last saw RUBY on Thursday, November 21, 1963, and therefore had no opportunity to talk with him regarding the death of President KENNEDY. She advised that the Master of Ceremonies at the Carousel Club had made the statement that he had seen LEE HARVEY OSWALD in the Carousel Club strictly for publicity reasons; that no one else in the club has said that they saw OSWALD there. JONES viewed a photograph of LEE HARVEY OSWALD and advised that she had never seen him before.

JONES stated that RUBY was friendly with numerous policemen and that he liked the police. She knew of no specific police officers or newsmen with whom he was particularly familiar or friendly.

on 11/26/63 at Dallas, Texas File # DL 89-43 / DL 44-1639

by Special Agents JOSEPH G. PEGGS & ALVIN J. ZIMMERMAN /cv Date dictated 11/27/63

Commission Exhibit No. 2401

Commission Exhibit No. 2402 [redacted]

DL 44-1639
PLS:cv
1

The following investigation was conducted by SA PAUL L. SCOTT at Dallas, Texas:

On December 18, 1963, DENNIS G. BREWER, 1607 Post Oak, Irving, Texas, whose name appeared in the personal effects of JACK RUBY, advised he first met RUBY at the Silver Spur Club on South Ervay Street in Dallas. He has been a casual acquaintance of RUBY since that time. About three or four years ago when RUBY organized the Sovereign Club on Commerce Street in Dallas, BREWER was a charter member of this club and attended the club approximately once a month. BREWER had also been to the Vegas Club formerly operated by JACK RUBY on several occasions. He has been to the Carousel Club, the most recent club operated by RUBY, on one occasion. During the time he has known RUBY, RUBY impressed him as an individual with definite convictions and one who liked attention. He recalled that RUBY formerly had a close associate by the name of BUDDY TURMAN, however, he does not know any other associates of RUBY. He has no knowledge of RUBY's activities other than operation of the various clubs in Dallas, Texas. BREWER recalled that sometime ago RUBY gave him tickets to a private club located on Lovers Lane, Dallas, however, he did not attend this club and does not recall the name of the club or what connection RUBY had with this particular club.

BREWER did not know LEE HARVEY OSWALD and has no knowledge of any connection between RUBY and OSWALD.

On December 18, 1963, JENNINGS RALPH LYLES, known as Ralph Lyles, residence 1203 South Buckner, Dallas, whose name appeared in the personal effects of JACK RUBY, advised he first met JACK RUBY about four years ago at the Vegas Club on Oaklawn in Dallas. He was single at that time and occasionally frequented the various clubs in Dallas. LYLES does not drink, and after he had been to the Vegas Club on two or three occasions JACK RUBY inquired as to whether or not he was a policeman since he came into the club and did not drink. Subsequently, about three years ago LYLES became a member of the Sovereign Club

Commission Exhibit No. 2402

on Commerce Street operated for a time by JACK RUBY. LYLES went to this club twice during the time it was open. He has not seen JACK RUBY in over three years and has no knowledge of his recent activities or knowledge of any of his associates. He recalled that one time while at the Sovereign Club he, LYLES, had talked to his partner during the show, and RUBY had become violently angry with him. He presumed from this action that RUBY had a violent temper.

LYLES did not know LEE HARVEY OSWALD and has no knowledge of any connection between OSWALD and RUBY.

On December 18, 1963, KENNETH L. TOPLETZ, 4361 San Carlos Drive, Dallas, employed as Vice President, Byer-Rolnick Hat Corporation, Garland, Texas, whose name appeared in the personal effects of JACK RUBY, advised that three or four years ago his company received several membership cards in the mail from the Sovereign Club, Dallas, directed to the attention of TOPLETZ. TOPLETZ did not join the Sovereign Club and never attended this club. He has never met JACK RUBY and has never seen him to his knowledge. He may have attended the same synagogue with RUBY, however, he does not recall seeing RUBY at the synagogue. TOPLETZ has no knowledge of RUBY's activities or associates.

TOPLETZ did not know LEE HARVEY OSWALD and has no knowledge of any connection between RUBY and OSWALD.

On December 18, 1963, REX SANDERS, residence 1752 Mapleton, Dallas, employed as Vice President of the Bank of Services and Trusts, 1115 Commerce, Dallas, whose name appeared in the personal effects of JACK RUBY, advised he first met JACK RUBY in 1959 or 1960. At that time, JOE SLAYTON, who operated a club on Commerce Street, Dallas, had an account at the bank under the name S & R Company. At this time, RUBY took over the club from SLAYTON, and the club was reorganized as the Sovereign Club. When SANDERS first met RUBY he was getting the club ready to open, and he invited SANDERS to attend the opening of the club. SANDERS may have received a membership card for the Sovereign Club, however, he does not recall receiving such a card and never attended the club after it opened. He was there on

one occasion while they were remodeling. He has had occasional contact with RUBY since that time at the bank and on the streets in downtown Dallas. RUBY impressed him as a gregarious individual who was well known in the Dallas area. SANDERS has had no other contact with RUBY and has no knowledge of his associates or activities other than operation of the clubs in Dallas.

SANDERS did not know LEE HARVEY OSWALD and has no knowledge of any connection between JACK RUBY and OSWALD.

On December 18, 1963, A. HENRY SANCHEZ, President, Southern Posters, Inc., 2609 South Ervay, Dallas, residence 2224 Van Cleave Drive, Dallas, whose name as HENRY SANCHEZ appeared in the personal effects of JACK RUBY, advised he joined the Sovereign Club operated by JACK RUBY about three or four years ago. It is his recollection that he joined the club after a visit with the chef, name not recalled, of Anthony's Lounge in Dallas. SANCHEZ never attended the Sovereign Club and is not personally acquainted with RUBY. SANCHEZ recalled that he tried to attend the Vegas Club several years ago and was refused admission to this club. He said his brother, MARIO SANCHEZ, worked for JACK RUBY a short time at the Vegas Club and is acquainted with RUBY. SANCHEZ has no knowledge of recent activities of RUBY or any of his associates. He does not know LEE HARVEY OSWALD and knows of no connection between RUBY and LEE HARVEY OSWALD.

On December 18, 1963, JOHN BROWN, also known as Jim Brown, 1435 Dalview Street, Dallas, whose name as JIM BROWN appeared in the personal effects of JACK RUBY, advised that about two years ago he had been doing some painting for Nichol Brothers on Commerce Street in downtown Dallas. When he finished at Nichol Brothers they sent him to the Carousel Club telling him that this club might need a painter. He contacted a Mr. JACK, a big man at the Carousel Club, and this person sent him to a building located near the intersection of Oaklawn and Lemmon Avenue. At this location, he painted the front of the building and the two restrooms of what appeared to him to be a night club. Mr. JACK's sister, name not recalled, was at this place. He worked two days at this building. He never did know the name of the individual who hired him to do this painting other than Mr. JACK. He has learned since that it was probably JACK RUBY. This was his only contact with JACK RUBY, and he has no knowledge of RUBY's activities or associates. BROWN did not know LEE HARVEY OSWALD and has no knowledge of any connection between OSWALD and RUBY.

On December 18, 1963, DAN TOBIAS, Dan Tobias Advertising Agency, 2114 North Akard, Dallas, whose name appeared on a Carousel Club pass card, advised that about a month and a half ago he was standing on the street in downtown Dallas talking to Mr. CLARENCE SELAH, a representative of KRLD-TV. While talking to Mr. SELAH, JACK RUBY approached and began talking to them. RUBY apparently had previously been acquainted with Mr. SELAH. At this time RUBY gave SELAH a pass card to the Carousel Club and also handed TOBIAS a pass card to the club which he asked TOBIAS to sign. TOBIAS signed the card and returned it to RUBY who stated he would have the card encased in plastic and mailed to TOBIAS. TOBIAS never received the Carousel Club pass card. He had never seen RUBY prior to that time and has not seen him since. TOBIAS has no knowledge of RUBY's activities or associates.

TOBIAS did not know LEE HARVEY OSWALD and has no knowledge of any connection between RUBY and OSWALD.

On December 18, 1963, BETTY JANE TOMPKINS, 3612 Schley Street, Dallas, reportedly a former employee of JACK RUBY, furnished the following information:

On August 12, 1960, TOMPKINS and another girl, name not recalled, were referred by the Texas Employment Office to the Sovereign Club in the 1300 block of Commerce Street, Dallas, for employment. TOMPKINS and the other girl went to the Sovereign Club which was to be a private club and was just preparing to open. They worked two days at this club sending out brochures announcing the opening of the Sovereign Club. They worked under the supervision of an older woman whose name TOMPKINS does not recall. TOMPKINS did not see JACK RUBY during the two days she was employed at the Sovereign Club and has in fact never seen JACK RUBY. She has no knowledge of RUBY's activities

or associates.

TOMPKINS did not know LEE HARVEY OSWALD and has no knowledge of any connection between RUBY and OSWALD.

1

Date November 28, 1963

Mrs. PAULINE HALL, 1606 Pratt, Apartment 6, advised she has been acquainted with JACK RUBY for approximately 6 years. She stated she has worked for JACK RUBY and EVE GRANT, his sister on infrequent occasions over that period of time. Mrs. HALL said she is probably as close a friend as EVE GRANT has. She said her employment with them would have been mostly on weekends when, for reason or another, they needed her to help them.

Mrs. HALL pointed out that work has been quite infrequent and said she had seen very little of JACK RUBY during the past six years. She pointed out, however, that Mrs. GRANT had an operation on approximately November 6, 1963, and that she, Mrs. HALL, took over the operation of the Vegas Club, 3508 Oaklawn, until Mrs. GRANT recovered.

Mrs. HALL said since November 6, 1963, she has seen JACK RUBY more frequently and estimated she has seen him approximately three times a week since, November 6, 1963.

She said RUBY has been coming by the club since November 6, 1963, and would "MC" floor shows on Friday and Saturday nights at the Vegas Club. Mrs. HALL said she last saw JACK RUBY on the Thursday night before the President's assassination on Friday, November 22, 1963. She stated she has not seen him since that time.

Mrs. HALL, who had been present during the interview with Mrs. GRANT at Mrs. GRANT's request, said that she had talked with Mrs. GRANT on Friday and Saturday, November 22 and 23, 1963. She informed that Mrs. GRANT furnished her the same information on Friday and Saturday that she furnished to the interviewing Federal Bureau of Investigation Agents when Mrs. GRANT was interviewed.

Mrs. HALL said she never discussed political matters with JACK RUBY and did not know what his thinking was regarding political matters. She did state she never received any indication he had any foreign or communistic sympathy.

on 11/26/63 at Dallas, Texas File # DL 44-1639

by Special Agent s LELAND D. STEPHENS & JACK B. PEDEN/csh Date dictated 11/27/63

315

2

DL 44-1639

She advised that although she cannot swear that JACK RUBY did not know LEE HARVEY OSWALD, she is positive that he never saw OSWALD before the assassination. She was most emphatic in this statement, although she admitted she could not definitely state he was not associated with OSWALD. She stated JACK RUBY is a highly emotional person and is almost as emotional as EVE GRANT, his sister. Mrs. HALL said that if RUBY hates a person he "really hates him", but "if he likes you, he will give you the shirt off his back." She stated it is a generally accepted fact among his acquaintances that on many occasions RUBY would start out with considerably money to pay bills but would end up being unable to pay them because he would give away about $100.00 a day to persons he felt were needy.

Mrs. HALL advised she never saw JACK RUBY with a gun but that he often carries money.

Mrs. HALL was questioned regarding an individual named "LARRY" who Mrs. GRANT had stated was with RUBY between the time of the President's assassination and the time RUBY allegedly shot OSWALD. She said she had talked with "LARRY" over the telephone on one or two occasions, and had seen him on approximately two occasions for a short period of time.

She said it is her understanding "LARRY' tok $5.00 either from one of the businesses or from RUBY and left. She stated this apparently was Saturday morning, November 23, 1963.

She described him as being approximately 23-24 years, white male, 5'10", 155 pounds, brown hair and with no front teeth. She said he was "creepy" and, in effect, "looked like a bum."

316

Commission Exhibit No. 2404

1
DL 89-43

Under date of November 25, 1963, the following information was furnished to FBI, Dallas, Texas, by the FBI Laboratory:

"Specimens received 11/25/63

"Q17 Fingernail scrapings from right hand of Lee Harvey Oswald
"Q18 Fingernail scrapings from left hand of Lee Harvey Oswald

"K7 Head hair sample from head of Lee Harvey Oswald
"K8 Axillary hair sample from Lee Harvey Oswald
"K9 Chest hair sample from Lee Harvey Oswald
"K10 Limb hair sample from right forearm of Lee Harvey Oswald
"K11 Pubic hair sample from Lee Harvey Oswald
"K12 Limb hair sample from right leg of Lee Harvey Oswald

"Results of examination:

"Several brown limb hairs and brown pubic hairs, all of Caucasian origin, were found in the debris previously removed from the Q12 blanket that matched in microscopic characteristics the K10 limb hairs and K11 pubic hairs of Oswald. Accordingly, these hairs originated either from Oswald or from another Caucasian person whose limb and pubic hairs exhibit the same individual microscopic characteristics.

"No fibers were found in the Q17 and Q18 fingernail scrapings of Oswald that could be associated with the Q12 blanket.

"Specimens Q17, Q18 and K7 through K12 are being retained in the Laboratory for possible future comparison purposes.

"No hairs were found on the 6.5 millimeter Mannlicher-Carcano rifle, K1, or on the paper bag, Q10, previously submitted."

144

COMMISSION EXHIBIT No. 2404

Commission Exhibit No. 2405

(page 15)

DON CAMPBELL,

a witness called by the State, being first duly sworn, testified on his oath as follows:

DIRECT EXAMINATION

BY MR. ALEXANDER:

Q Your name is Don Campbell?
A It is, sir.
Q What age man are you, Mr. Campbell?
A Forty-six.
Q And what is your business or occupation?
A Advertising salesman with the Dallas Morning News.
Q I will ask you where the Dallas Morning News building

COMMISSION EXHIBIT No. 2405

is located where you work?

A It is at the corner of Young and Houston Streets.

Q I will ask you if that is approximately two or three blocks from here?

A Approximately two blocks from here.

Q Yes sir. Directing your attention to Friday, November, 22nd, 1963, I will ask you if you were also employed at the Dallas News in the advertising section?

A I was.

Q What floor of the Dallas News Building is your advertising office located on?

A On the second floor.

Q And I will ask you if that office is one large open space for the most part?

A Yes, for the most part it is.

Q And what time did you come to work that morning, if you recall?

A At 8:30.

Q And I will ask you if you recall whether or not that was the day that President Kennedy participated in a parade in downtown Dallas?

A It was.

Q Do you know the Defendant in this case, Jack Ruby?

A I do.

Q Do you see him in the courtroom here today?

COMMISSION EXHIBIT No. 2405—Continued

A I do.

Q Will you point him out to the Court and Jury.

MR. BELLI: We will stipulate the identification, Your Honor.

THE COURT: All right.

Q On November 22, 1963, did you know the Defendant, Jack Ruby?

A I did.

Q And for what period of time had you known him -- by knowing him, I mean have you been able to recognize him, if you saw him?

A Yes sir.

Q And how long had you known him?

A Oh, approximately four years.

Q I will ask you if in the course of your business with the Dallas News, if you had occasion to discuss the advertising of his business with him?

A Yes sir, quite often.

Q And directing your attention again to November 22, 1963, at around 12:00 o'clock noon, I will ask you if you saw the Defendant, Jack Ruby?

A I did.

Q And where was it that you saw him?

A In the Advertising Department of the Dallas Morning News, second floor.

COMMISSION EXHIBIT No. 2405—Continued

Q I will ask you if you had a conversation with him there that morning?
A I had.
Q And what was that conversation pertaining to?
A To the advertising of his night club, the advertisement inserted in the following morning paper.
Q And do you recall the name of those two night clubs?
A I do.
Q And what were they?
A The Carousel and the Vegas Club.
Q Now, about what time did your conversation with him begin, if you can approximate that for us?
A I can. It was a little after 12:00 o'clock noon.
Q And at what time did you finish your conversation with him?
A About 12:25.
Q All right, did you go anywhere else, after your conversation with him?
A Yes, I left the building.
Q When did you again return?
A It was after, I guess 2:00 in the afternoon.
Q Was the Defendant, Jack Ruby, still there when you returned after 2:00?
A I can't recall.
Q You don't recall whether he was or not. Then I take

COMMISSION EXHIBIT NO. 2405—Continued

it that your conversation occupied the period from approximately 12:00 o'clock noon until 12:25 when you left?
A That's right.
Q Now, do you know the building in downtown Dallas known as the Texas School Book Depository?
A I do.
Q Is it possible to see the Texas School Book Depository from the second floor windows of your office there at the Dallas News?
A It is possible to see the building from about four windows, on our floor, on the second floor.
Q All right sir, I will show you what we will mark as State's Exhibit No. 1. And number 2.

(Thereupon two photographs handed to the Reporter were marked as State's Exhibits Nos. 1 and 2, respectively, for identification.)

MR. BELLI: May we see the pictures before they are offered?

MR. ALEXANDER: Yes sir, I will show them to you before.

MR. BELLI: All right.

Q Let me ask you if you have stood in the windows of your office there and you, yourself, looked at the Texas School Book Depository?
A I have.

COMMISSION EXHIBIT NO. 2405—Continued

Q And I will ask you if at the corner of the second floor office, from which it is possible to see the Texas School Book Depository, a Mr. Jefferys has a small glassed in office there?
A He has.
Q And I will ask you if standing outside Mr. Jefferys' door, looking through that second window from the corner, if it is possible to see the Texas School Book Depository?
A Yes, most of the building.
Q I will show you State's Exhibits Nos. 1 and 2, and please do not display them to the Jury, but look at them yourself.

MR. BELLI: May we see those first before the witness does?

THE COURT: Let him identify them, and then show them to him.

MR. ALEXANDER: I am going to get him to identify them, and then I will show them to you.

Q I will ask you to examine those exhibits and tell me if you can identify the scene they seek to represent?
A Yes sir, I can.
Q I will ask you if those two exhibits truly and accurately portray the scene they seek to represent?
A They do.
Q And what scene is that?
A Looking out the -- on this particular one, one of the

windows on the second floor, approximately Mr. Jefferys' office, looking toward the School Book Depository; --
Q And the other one?
A About the same scene.
Q Yes sir. And I will ask you, sir, if these exhibits truly and accurately portray the scene they represent?
A They do.

MR. ALEXANDER: We offer those into evidence as State's Exhibits Nos. 1 and 2.

MR. BELLI: Objection, as being incompetent, irrelevant and immaterial.

THE COURT: Overrule your objection to them, Counsel.

MR. TONAHILL: Exception.

THE COURT: They are admitted in evidence.

(State's Exhibits Nos. 1 and 2, photographs, were admitted into evidence. Reproductions of same hereto attached)

?

Q Now, as to State's Exhibit No. 1, Mr. Campbell, I will ask you to step down before the Jury and ask you to indicate to the Jury the building known as the Texas School Book Depository.

And let the record reflect that the witness has pointed to a building.

And I will ask you if the building in the right portion

of the picture, is the Dallas-Jefferson Hotel?
A Yes, it is.
MR. BELLI: Here?
A Yes sir.
Q That will be the Dallas-Jefferson Hotel.
And I will ask you if the white building in the left upper portion of the picture is the Terminal Annex?
A Commonly called the Post Office.
Q Now, Mr. Campbell, I will ask you if the building known as the Dallas School Book Depository, which you have pointed out in the picture, is in between the Post Office and the Dallas-Jefferson Hotel?
MR. TONAHILL: Your Honor, we object to leading the witness.
A It is.
MR. BELLI: That's all right.
Q I will show you State's Exhibit No. 2 and ask you if the Texas School Book Depository Building appears in that photograph?
A It does.
Q And I will ask you if it appears between the Post Office Building and the Dallas-Jefferson Hotel.
A It does.
Q I will ask you whether or not the State's Exhibit No. 2 was taken from back inside of the Dallas News Office?

COMMISSION EXHIBIT No. 2405—Continued

3

A It appears to be.
Q And I will ask you if it would appear, from this photograph, that the photograph was taken from right in front of Mr. Jefferys' door?
MR. BELLI: Wait just a minute, the picture speaks for itself, Your Honor. I don't know what the purpose is yet, but it seems that it was taken inside there?
Q Let me ask the witness, does State's Exhibit No. 2 appear to have been taken from inside the building?
A It does.
Q Shooting through the window?
A It does.
Q Now, Mr. Campbell, where was Jack Ruby in the office at the time that you left at 12:25?
A He was sitting at a desk directly behind mine belonging to Mr. John Newnam.
Q And what was he doing at the time you last saw him?
A He was writing some copy for his night club ad.
Q Now, Mr. Campbell, have you dealt with him about his adsover a period of years?
A Yes, off and on. If Mr. Newnam wasn't present when Mr. Ruby came in, someone on the floor would help him out with the copy, and also write out the insertion order.
Q On this day of November 22nd, 1963, did you notice

COMMISSION EXHIBIT No. 2405—Continued

anything peculiar or unusual about his behavior?
A No.
Q Was his behavior similar to that he exhibited on other occasions that you had seen him?
A Yes.
MR. ALEXANDER: Thank you sir. Pass the witness.

CROSS EXAMINATION

BY MR. BELLI:
Q Mr. Campbell, I don't quite understand, where was Jack Ruby with reference to this picture, was he anywhere near this office here, and by this I refer to Exhibit No. 2?
A No, sir, he was not.
Q He was nowhere near this, is that right?
A He was not.
Q Were you in this office, No. 2?
A Not at that time, no.
Q Which floor was he on, on this floor or on another floor?
A On that floor, the second floor of the building.
Q Do you know if he ever was in this office or near this office?
A Not to my knowledge.
Q He wasn't in this office, is that right?
A He wasn't in that office.

COMMISSION EXHIBIT No. 2405—Continued

Q Now, what time here in Dallas was the President assassinated?
A According to the newspaper stories about 12:35.
Q About 12:35. And Jack was with you from 12:00 to 12:25, is that right?
A Yes sir.
Q And then he left you just before the assassination, is that right?
A I left him.
Q You left him. Well, the two of you departed just before the assassination?
A I left the building at 12:25.
Q When you saw him at that time, up until then, there didn't appear to be anything wrong with him, he appeared usual, calm, collected and so forth, is that right?
A He was just Jack Ruby, that I knew.
Q Well, we are going to leave psychiatry to the other man, to the psychiatrist, but to you as a layman he was not upset at that time, was he?
A No.
Q And when you say he was just Jack Ruby, in answer to my question, that was a pretty volatile individual that you knew as Jack Ruby, was it not?
A Yes.
Q And had you seen him the night before, you had seen

COMMISSION EXHIBIT No. 2405—Continued

26

him the night before at the Egyptian Club, and wanted him to go some place, am I right on that, the Egyptian Restaurant?

A I can't recall whether it was the night before I had seen him, I believe during that week before.

Q Were you talking on the night before, there was some problem that someone had taken his band away from him at the place that he was running, and someone had pirated his band; was there some problem that was on Jack's mind with reference to that?

A Possibly it was the band that had been playing at the Vegas Club, that had an engagement at this other club.

Q And one of the problems that he discussed with you in placing the ad the next day, was the financial condition of the economics of the club that he was running, didn't he discuss that with you, that he was sort of scrounging to get customers back to the place, and he was concerned about the ad?

A He was worried because his band that had been with him for years had left him, and he was worried about the business.

Q Did you and he discuss anything about the parade and seeing the President pass by?

A No.

Q You were working at that time, that's the reason you didn't see it; and he was working at that time, and that's the reason he didn't see it. That would be a fair statement,

COMMISSION EXHIBIT No. 2405—Continued

27

wouldn't it?

A Yes, it would.

Q And had you not been working, and had he not been working, I guess both of you would have tried to see the parade go by?

A I think so.

Q Okay. Well, for what it may be worth, the reason he didn't want to go to some restaurant that you were talking about, was that they had taken his band away, is that right? The proprietor of the restaurant?

A Well, I didn't realize the implication at that time, I just wanted Jack to meet this other friend of mine.

MR. BELLI: That is all, thank you very much.

REDIRECT EXAMINATION

BY MR. ALEXANDER:

Q Just a couple more questions, Mr. Campbell. You say Ruby was a very volatile individual in his manner?

A Not wholly, no I wouldn't say that.

Q Did he write his own ads, or did you all write his ads for him, or did you all work together in writing the ads?

A Most of the time he wrote his own ads, and we would help him out once in awhile.

Q And was he fairly competent in writing his own ads, and taking care of his business?

A I think very.

COMMISSION EXHIBIT No. 2405—Continued

WILLIAM E. HOWARD

a witness called by the Defendant, having been first duly sworn, testified on his oath as follows:

DIRECT EXAMINATION

BY MR. BURLESON:

Q Would you state your name to the jury?

A William E. Howard.

Q Where do you live?

MR. WADE: I didn't get the name.

A Howard.

MR. WADE: H-O-W-A-R-D?

A That's right.

Q (By Mr. Burleson) Mr. Howard, where do you live?

A 4029 North Central Expressway.

Q What is your business?

A Well, principally oil. I've been in the oil business for thirty some years here.

Q I'll ask you whether or not you know Jack Ruby, the defendant in this case?

A Yes, I do.

Q Approximately how long have you known him?

A Oh, twelve or thirteen years.

Q What has been your relationship with him? Have you known him socially, in business, or what?

A I've known him socially.

COMMISSION EXHIBIT No. 2406

Q Have you known him as a club operator here in town?

A Yes, sir.

Q Have you ever been in his club?

A Yes, I have.

Q I'll ask you whether or not at anytime during the period of time that you've known him, whether or not you have witnessed any emotional outbursts on behalf of Jack Ruby, or by Jack Ruby?

A Well, I guess you'd call it an emotional outburst. I've seen him in his various clubs getting into fights and brawls and things of that nature.

Q All right. Now, directing your attention, can you recall any specific instances wherein he had an emotional outburst?

A Oh, yes.

Q Could you give us an example or two of that?

A Well, on one particular occasion, there was a young fellow who was straddling a chair in one of his places, the Silver Spur, and Jack commanded him to turn around and face the table and be seated properly, which he did. But when he went by him again, he had straddled the chair again, and they had some words, and the first thing I knew there was a big commotion, and Jack went off the handle and kind of beat this fellow up.

Q All right. Now, would he do this in a sudden manner?

COMMISSION EXHIBIT No. 2406—Continued

4-117

A Yes, sir, quite sudden.

Q All right. Would you say he was quick tempered?

A Oh, yes. Jack is quick tempered.

Q After this emotional outburst, or this blow up, would he then calm down?

A Yes, he would be calm.

Q Would he also calm down very quickly?

A Well, things didn't seem to disturb Jack too much. He would get into an upset, and then it would be all over.

Q Now, how many of these such have you witnessed, do you think, over the last ten or twelve or thirteen years that you have known Jack?

A Oh, any number of them. Maybe eight or ten or twelve, or something like that. And lots more that I've heard about.

Q I'll ask you whether or not at various times you've had conversations with Jack?

A Yes.

Q During these conversations would you describe how his speech was?

A Well, sometimes his speech became disjointed, and it would lack continuity, but not all the time.

Q But on some occasions?

A On some occasions, that's right.

Q Would he be the type of person, in talking and having conversation, would he complete his sentences or would often-

4-118

times he stop in the middle of the sentence?

A Well, sometimes he would ramble and go off on a tangent.

Q Go on a what?

A A tangent. He would divert from the basic subject.

Q Have you seen or talked to Jack about his dogs?

A Oh gosh, yes.

Q Did you ever hear Jack refer to his dogs as anything other than dogs?

A Well, they're his babies.

Q Babies?

A Yes, sir.

Q Did you ever hear him refer to them as children?

A Well, in a sense, yes.

Q Did you ever have any contact with Jack when he was with his dogs?

A Oh, yes. I've been in his apartment, or home, and I have been in his club where he kept his dogs.

Q How would he treat these dogs?

A Just like they were children. He patted them, pampered them, talked with them.

Q Did he have a particular favorite?

A Well, I guess he liked them all.

Q He liked them all. Did he take the dogs with him, or one of them with him?

A He always had them with him.

Q All right. Do you know his sister, Eva Grant?
A Yes, sir, I do.
Q How long have you known her?
A Oh, I don't know. Four or five years, when she come back from California. I believe she was in California, and came back after about, I guess about four or five years ago, whatever it was.
Q Have you known here through her connection with the Club Vegas?
A That's right.
Q Have you visited out there when she's been there?
A Yes, sir, I've been around her.
Q All right. Have you ever seen Jack cry on any of these occasions?
A Well, no, but I've seen him on the verge of breaking up, but I haven't witnessed any tears.
Q Have you noticed any change in the Jack Ruby as you knew him ten or twelve years ago, up until recently?
A Any change?
Q Yes, in his personality, his mental make up, as you viewed it?
A Well, no. However, I think as time when on, and he became more financially involved his attitude was a little different, I suppose. But basically, he was the same, he was very unpredictable.

COMMISSION EXHIBIT No. 2406—Continued

Q Did you form a conclusion as to whether or not Jack was rational at all times?
A Well, I don't know if you would call it rational or not, but lots of times we'd maybe have dinner or something, and he would get up and he would leave for no reason whatsoever, and then the next day when I'd question him, he had some unfinished business he had to take care of, so --
Q He'd just get up and leave?
A Yes.
Q Can you think of any other instances like this straddled chair, that you can relate to the jury at this time?
A Oh, I've seen lots of them. He would ask people out on the dance floor not to do certain things, and they would pay no attention to him.
Q Then he would have one of these emotional outbursts? Or one of these blow ups?
A Whatever it is, yes.
Q You would see him after he did that?
A Yes.
Q And he would appear calm then?
A Oh, yes.
Q Would you say that Jack Ruby was a kind and considerate type person?
A I presume in his way, he is, yes.
Q In his way. Have you seen him do acts of kindness?

COMMISSION EXHIBIT No. 2406—Continued

A Oh, I've seen him loan people money at different times and make contributions to different things, yes.

Q Have you ever made any contributions to anything that he had any connection with, any organization or fund or drive that he had any connection with?

A No, sir.

Q When was the last time that you saw Jack prior to November, 1963?

A Well, it was the early part of November, I believe.

Q The early part of November?

A Yes.

Q Do you recall where that was?

A Yes. I have a supper club here in town. It's the Stork Club. And Jack came by one day and said he had some trouble with one of his strippers. Her name was Jada.

Q All right. Did you talk to him on that occasion?

A Well, he talked to me. He wanted to let his emotions out, I believe, so I sat there and listened to him.

Q Was he upset at that time?

A Well, yes he was. He was disturbed.

Q How was his conversation on that date?

A Well, he told me he had a law suit or something --

Q No, I say how was his conversation, not what was it.

A Oh, he just wanted to get it off his chest, I think; telling me the circumstances, the situation had occurred, and

COMMISSION EXHIBIT No. 2406—Continued

-120

his difficulties with this help of his.

Q Would you describe how he talked?

A Well, of course, Jack talks in a staccato manner all the time anyway, so it didn't vary too much. But he was upset about it, naturally.

Q Have you, based upon what you have seen from Jack, seen of his actions, hearing him talk, knowing Jack as you have known him, have you formed any type of opinion as to Jack's mental status, or mental state?

A Well, with apologies to Jack, I've always considered him --

MR. BOWIE: To which we object, Your Honor.

THE COURT: Sustain the objection.

MR. TONAHILL: He's qualified to give an answer, Judge.

Q (By Mr. Burleson) Have you formed such an opinion?

A Yes, sir, I have.

Q Would you tell us what that opinion is, as to whether or not you feel like --

MR. BOWIE: We object, Your Honor.

Q (By Mr. Burleson) What is the opinion?

A Well, --

THE COURT: Do you object to it?

MR. ALEXANDER: Yes, sir, we object to it.

THE COURT: Sustain the objection.

COMMISSION EXHIBIT No. 2406—Continued

MR. BURLESON: Note our exception.

MR. TONAHILL: Exception. May we complete the Bill now?

THE COURT: No, sir.

MR. TONAHILL: Note our exception.

MR. BURLESON: We'll pass him.

CROSS EXAMINATION

BY MR. WADE:

Q Mr. Howard?

A Yes, sir.

Q I believe you said that you knew the defendant, Jack Ruby, socially as a club operator. Is that right?

A Yes, sir.

Q You're not in business with him in any way?

A No, sir.

Q You hven't financed him or anything, down there?

A No, sir.

Q I believe you said he always had one or more of his dogs with him wherever he went?

A Yes, sir.

Q I believe you said you never had seen him cry, did you?

A No, I don't believe --

Q Did you?

A No, I haven't seen tears roll down his cheeks, in that sense of the word.

Q Was he the type person, Mr. Howard, that always liked to be known, or you might say a name dropper, or that type of person?

A Yes, sir, that's true.

Q He liked to know or call so and so important people as his friends, isn't that right?

A Yes, he's very outgoing.

Q He's very outgoing and was he the type that liked to be well thought of, I guess is one way of putting it?

A This is true.

Q And he, I assume, would tell you who he knew and who was at his place, and one thing and another, that might be some people prominent in some field in Dallas, is that right?

A No, I don't think that he was what you might classify as a social climber, not in that sense.

Q No, I'm talking about one that wanted to be liked, and wanted to know important people. In a sense you might say egotistical, in that sense?

A This is true, yes, sir.

Q In other words, I'm not saying it very well, but he liked to -- he sought the limelight, of a sort?

A This is very true.

Q That's very true. And, for instance, if he was up in the City Hall on Friday night, in the middle of all the cameras and telling them who everybody was, assuming he was, that's the type thing he would like, don't you think? Explaining it to the cameramen who everybody was around the City Hall?

A Well, he liked to be in the middle of things, no matter what it was.

Q No matter what it was, he always liked to be right in the middle of it?

A Yes.

Q Now, I believe you said when he came to talk to you about Jada, and he said that he had some controversy?

A I believe so, yes, sir.

Q Some two or three weeks before that. What kind of controversy was that?

MR. BURLESON: We object to him going into that, as irrelevant and immaterial what the conversation was.

MR. WADE: He's already gone into the conversation, Your Honor.

THE COURT: What was the question?

MR. BELLI: If Your Honor please, even if something is asked that is irrelevant on direct, but not objected to, it can't be broken into on cross. It's irrelevant. We say it's time wasting to go into any controversy he might have had with a strip teaser, or with Jada. Now, if Your Honor thinks it's important, as we haven't anything to hide, let's go into it.

THE COURT: What was the question?

MR. BELLI: The controversy with Jada, a strip teaser.

MR. WADE: I'll withdraw it.

Q (By Mr. Wade) I believe the F.B.I. interviewed you, did they not?

A Yes, they did.

Q I believe you told them that he was quick tempered, a rough and tumble scrapper, didn't you?

A That's right.

Q As a matter of fact, he went to the YMCA to build his body up all the time. You know about that?

A He was quite a health fadist, yes, sir.

Q He was quite a health fadist. And he was an egotist to some extent?

A I would presume so.

Q You would think so. And wherever anything was going on, he liked to be right in the middle of it?

A Well, he was of that nature.

Q And wherover he went he had cards of his club, that he would pass out or give away, according to the situation, would he not?

A This is true.

Q He did that many times in your presence, didn't he?

A Yes, he did.

Q He was trying to promote business for his club?
A That's true.
Q But he always carried them in his pocket and he would spread them out when you were with him?
A Yes, that's true.
Q And he tried to, or did, give the impression that he was tough enough to keep down trouble in his club, is that right?
A I don't know whether he tried to give that impression or not, but when it came to a show-down, he was right there.
Q He was pretty tough, wasn't he?
A Yes, he was.
Q And you've seen him throw people out of his club?
A Yes, I have.
Q Down the steps?
A Well, not exactly. on those particular occasions, but I have seen him in his mix-ups, yes.
Q Did you ever see him carry a gun outside the club?
A Yes, he always had a gun with him.
Q Always had a gun with him?
A Yes, sir.
Q You never did report that to the police or anything?
A No, I didn't report it.
Q You never did?
A No, sir. When I say he had a gun, he always had it in

COMMISSION EXHIBIT No. 2406—Continued

the money bag. I used to see it when he would throw it in the car, if we went someplace. We would have dinner or something like that, and he would throw this bag down, with the gun in the money.
Q Did he carry that into wherever he was eating? The gun?
A No, he would sometimes leave it in the car, I think.
Q Sometimes lock it up in the car?
A That's right.
Q According to where he was at the time, I presume?
A That's right.
Q He had a place to lock it up in his glove compartment?
A I think he put it in the back end of the car, in the trunk.
Q You've seen him do that on occasion?
A Yes, sir.
Q Have you ever been target practicing with him?
A No.
Q You never have seen him shoot the gun?
A No.
Q But usually when he went -- I assume you all ate at nice restaurants when you were with him, as a general rule?
A Oh, yes. Nice places, hotels.
Q He would generally lock his gun up in the car, rather than take it inside with him, into the restaurant?

COMMISSION EXHIBIT No. 2406—Continued

4-129

661

A Well, this wasn't always the occasion. Lots of times he wouldn't have it on his person, or it might be in the car, when he would open the back of the car and fish in the back to get what he wanted, it would be obvious it was there.

Q To be more specific then, many times you said, I believe that he didn't have it with him?

A This is true.

Q And many times when he had it with him in your presence, he would lock it up in the car, accordong to the place you were going into?

A Well, he didn't wait until he went some place to lock it up. It was usually in the back of the car.

Q He usually carried it in the back of the car?

A Yes.

Q You would say that he is quick or high tempered, if you would describe him, would you not?

A Yes, I would.

Q And you would say he was a rough and tumble fighter?

A Yes, sir.

Q That he liked to be in the center of things, whatever is going on? The center of attraction to some extent, in that if anything is going on, he wants to be in the middle of it. Is that right?

A Well, I would say he's been in the middle of a lot of things on a lot of occasions, yes.

COMMISSION EXHIBIT No. 2406—Continued

4-130

662

Q How long have you lived in Dallas, Mr. Howard?

A Thirty-two, three years.

Q Thirty-two or thirty-three years.

MR. WADE: Pass the witness.

REDIRECT EXAMINATION

BY MR. BURLESON:

Q Mr. Howard, you knew that Jack Ruby was in a foster home when he was five years old?

A Yes.

MR. WADE: We object to that. It's leading and suggestive.

THE COURT: Sustain the objection to it.

MR. WADE: When he was five years old? Did he say something -- Have you known Ruby since he was five years old?

A No.

MR. BURLESON: Mr. Wade isn't allowed to ask questions. We have him on direct examination.

MR. WADE: Well, I didn't hear the question.

MR. BURLESON: Then we can ask the court reporter to read it back.

THE COURT: Go ahead, Mr. Burleson.

Q (By Mr. Burlesan) Now, you say in answer to Mr. Wade's question, that Jack liked to be in the center of things, is that right?

COMMISSION EXHIBIT No. 2406—Continued

A I say he's an outgoing person. He's not an introvert. He is a person that's always in the middle of things. When he's out on the street walking around he's talking to people, going to parties, and he makes himself known.

Q Did you know that Jack had arranged an interview for Mr. Wade?

MR. BOWIE: To which we object as leading, Your Honor.

THE COURT: Sustain the objection.

Q (By Mr. Burleson) State the facts with reference to whether or not you knew about the interview that Jack Ruby arranged for Mr. Wade?

THE COURT: I sustained the objection, Mr. Burleson. Get on to something else.

MR. BURLESON: I thought the objection was to leading.

THE COURT: You rephrased the question to ask the same question.

MR. TONAHILL: Note our exception. There wasn't any objection to the next question, Judge.

MR. ALEXANDER: He disobeyed the Court's ruling on it, Your Honor.

Q (By Mr. Burleson) Now, you say Jack handed out cards. Is that correct?

A Yes, sir.

Commission Exhibit No. 2406—Continued

Q That was for his Carousel Club?

A Yes, sir.

Q Now, did he hand those out much like politicians handing them out?

A Well, he would hand them out to anybody that was a prospective customer.

Q Much like a politician would when he was looking for a vote?

A Well, I wouldn't know about that.

Q Now, on these occasions that you saw Jack with a gun, did you always see money with him?

A Yes.

MR. BURLESON: That's all.

RECROSS EXAMINATION

BY MR. WADE:

Q Do you own a club yourself?

A I operate and manage a club, yes, sir.

Q What club is that?

A The Stork Club.

Q Is that --

A It's a private club.

Q It's not a strip club, is it?

A Oh, no. It's a supper club.

Q Where is that located?

A On Oak Lawn, across from the Village. I've had it for

Commission Exhibit No. 2406—Continued

4-133 335

about three years now.

Q It's a private club?

A Yes, sir.

Q But you don't have --

A Oh, no. It's a supper club.

MR. WADE: That's all.

MR. BURLESON: That's all.

THE COURT: The court will be recessed until nine o'clock Monday morning.

COMMISSION EXHIBIT No. 2406—Continued

29

D. V. HARKNESS

a witness called by the State, being first duly sworn, testified on his oath as follows:

DIRECT EXAMINATION

BY MR. ALEXANDER:

Q You're Sgt. D. V. Harkness?

A Yes, sir.

Q What bureau or division of the Dallas Police Department are you assigned to?

A Traffic Division.

Q And were you so employed and assigned back on November 23, 1963?

A Yes, sir.

Q That would have been a Saturday, would it not?

A Yes, sir.

Q Directing your attention to around two-thirty or three o'clock in the afternoon on that Saturday, November 23, 1963, I'll ask you if you were assigned to the vicinity of the entrance of the County jail to assist in traffic and handling people?

A Yes, sir, I was.

Q Now I'll ask you if you were anticipating the transfer of Oswald at around four o'clock?

A Yes, sir, we were.

Q Now, sometime after three o'clock, I'll ask you if a

COMMISSION EXHIBIT No. 2407

crowd began to block the driveway of the entrance to the County jail?
A Yes, sir. A crowd had merged to the entrance and was making it difficult for the Sheriff's department to operate.
Q All right sir. And at that time I'll ask you if you notified the Sheriff's department that they should block that off with either men or ropes?
A Yes, sir, I did.
Q And was that done?
A Yes, sir.
Q Now Sgt. Harkness, I'll ask you if you, yourself, participated in moving the crowd back from the driveway of the County jail entrance there on Houston Street?
MR. TONAHILL: We object to him leading him. Let him testify what he did.
THE COURT: All right. I'll sustain the objection.
Q (By Mr. Alexander) Tell what you did with regard to moving the crowd back?
A I went into the Sheriff's department and contacted Mr. Charlie Player, and he gave me some rope and we took some rope and roped off all the area across the street. And then we moved barricades back on the east side of Houston.
Q That would be on the jail entrance side?
A Yes, sir. The jail entrance to Houston, to move the

COMMISSION EXHIBIT No. 2407—Continued

crowd back away from the entrance to the jail.
Q All right. Do you know the defendant in this case, Jack Ruby?
A Yes, sir.
Q I'll ask you if you saw Jack Ruby in that crowd that you moved back from the jail entrance?
A Yes, sir.
Q And did you see which direction he went after you moved him back?
A No, sir. The last I had seen of him was at Elm and Houston, on the jail side, on the east side of Houston.
Q Now that was on Saturday afternoon, just before four o'clock?
A Yes, sir.
MR. ALEXANDER: Pass the witness.

CROSS EXAMINATION

BY MR. BELLI:
Q Officer, this crowd, was that an ugly crowd, or a murmurming crowd, or a sinister crowd or an ominous crowd? An ugly crowd?
A No, sir. It was an orderly crowd.
Q An orderly crowd. And at that time when you saw Jack Ruby, could you describe him to us? What was his appearance? Do you recall?
A No, sir. I just observed him in the crowd, and the

COMMISSION EXHIBIT No. 2407—Continued

best I recall --

Q And that's the time that Mr. Oswald was to have been moved first, four o'clock on Saturday afternoon, is that right?

A We had no knowledge of the time. We were anticipating him.

Q And then plans were changed and he was held over to be moved at ten o'clock Sunday morning?

A I didn't know about the plans, when they were changed. It was just crowd control.

Q Were there a number of people there that were saying "hi" to the reporters or the t.v. camera back and forth?

A I don't recall any of those.

Q Did you see Mr. Ruby at that time do anything different, or appear any different, than the other score of heart broken citizens who were there?

A No, sir. I just observed him in the crowd.

Q More of a curious crowd than anything else, wasn't it?

A I wouldn't -- sight seers.

MR. BELLI: That's all.

REDIRECT EXAMINATION

BY MR. ALEXANDER:

Q Did you know whether Ruby was armed or not at that time?

A No, sir.

Q Did you have any reason to think that he was armed?

A No, sir.

MR. ALEXANDER: That's all.

RECROSS EXAMINATION

BY MR. BELLI:

Q Did you know that he carried a gun for the last several years, and went out and bought that gun in the company of a policeman?

A No, sir, I did not.

Q And carried large sums of money continuously, and carried the gun to protect himself and his money?

MR. ALEXANDER: We object to that. That's assuming facts not in evidence.

THE COURT: Sustain the objection.

MR. BELLI: That's all. Thank you, Officer.

THE COURT: The court will stand in recess until 1:45.

\- - -

GEORGIA MAYER,

a witness called by the State, being first duly sworn, testified on her oath as follows:

DIRECT EXAMINATION

BY MR. ALEXANDER:

Q Your name is Georgia Mayer?

A Yes.

Q And how are you employed?

COMMISSION EXHIBIT No. 2408

5

A Secretary, Dallas Advertising.

Q What company is that, please?

A The Dallas Morning News.

Q And I will ask you if you work in the same office area with Mr. Campbell and Mr. Newnam?

A Yes, sir.

Q I will ask you if that is an extremely large office that occupies almost the second floor of the Dallas News Building?

A Yes.

Q Do you know the Defendant, in this case, Jack Ruby?

A Yes.

Q How long have you known him there at the Dallas News?

A A year and a half.

Q Directing your attention to November 22, 1963, which was the Friday that President Kennedy was in Dallas, I will ask you if you had occasion to be working on that date?

A Yes.

Q And did you see Jack Ruby on that occasion?

A Yes.

Q About what time of day was it when you saw him?

A 12:30 or 12:35.

Q And what was he doing when you saw him first?

A He was sitting at Dick Saunders' desk.

Q Could you tell what he was doing at Dick Saunders desk?

COMMISSION EXHIBIT No. 2408—Continued

A Nothing.
Q I believe you had just come back from lunch when you saw him there?
A That's right.
Q What did you do after you came back from lunch and you had seen him there at the desk?
A I went to Mr. Jeffery's office and watched television.
Q All right, did you have any conversation with Jack Ruby?
A No.
Q Do you know how long he stayed there at the Dallas News office?
A I saw him around 1:00, or sometime later.
Q And I will ask you if you saw him over at Mr. Jeffery's office watching the television?
A I don't recall.
Q You don't recall that, but you first saw him there between 12:30 and 12:35, and you last saw him sometime after 1:00 or around 1:30?
A That's right.

MR. ALEXANDER: Pass the witness.

CROSS EXAMINATION

BY MR. BELLI:
Q You were all upset, Miss Mayer, at that time -- we all were in this country, weren't you?

A Yes.
Q And Jack was upset too, wasn't he?
A Yes.
Q And did you notice whether he was crying at that time?
A No.
Q Or how upset he was, did you notice anything particular about it?
A Well, later when he was sitting at Don Campbell's desk back from Mr. Newnam's, his eyes were fixed toward the back of the office, toward Mr. Rector's office in back of me.
Q You mean fixed, like a fixed stare?
A Yes, and dazed.
Q And that's something that you recollect, back when you say fixed, that connotes to me someone who was sitting and staring at something, is that what he was doing?
A Yes.
Q What was he doing with this fixed -- was he looking at something or someone?
A Well -- just like I was staring back at the back of the room right now, his eyes were just fixed.
Q How long was he in that fixed stare just looking, staring, that was visible?
A Well, I only looked at him a couple of seconds.
Q You don't know how long before he had been in that condition of a fixed stare, or how long after you had stopped

looking at him he was in it?
A No.
Q But it was something that was remarkable, was it not?
A Yes.
Q Have you seen people in states of epilepsy or otherwise, when they have been in this sort of a fixed stare?
A No.
Q He wasn't moving any parts of his body when he was in this fixed stare, was he?
A No.
Q Did he have his hands down or did you notice how his hands were?
A No.
Q Did you notice whether he was perspiring at the time when he was in the fixed stare?
A No, sir.
Q Did you notice whether he was pallid or whether his color had changed at all?
A No, I just noticed his stare.
Q Had you ever seen him before in this fixed stare?
A No.
Q And he wasn't saying anything at that time?
A No.
Q Did you notice whether he was sitting upright or how he was when he was in this fixed stare?

Commission Exhibit No. 2408—Continued

A He was just sitting in the chair like this, just staring. That is all I can recall.
Q He didn't make any motion, attempt to wipe his eyes or anything when he was in the fixed stare, did he?
A No.
Q Do you see him like that today?
A No sir.
Q Did anyone talk to him and say "Jack -- Jack", and he still was in the fixed stare?
A No sir.
Q Who else was in the room at the time he was in this fixed stare?
A Well, that I couldn't say for sure.
Q But there were other people in and around the room, when Mr. Ruby had that fixed stare, that was unusual enough to attract attention to it?
A Yes.

MR. BELLI: That is all I have. Thank you, ma'am.

REDIRECT EXAMINATION

BY MR. ALEXANDER:
Q Just one other question. That was about the same shape that most everybody was in --

MR. TONAHILL: We object to leading, Your Honor.

Commission Exhibit No. 2408—Continued

Q -- after the assassination, wasn't it?

MR. TONAHILL: We object to leading questions, Your Honor.

THE COURT: Sustain the objection to it.

MR. ALEXANDER: I believe that is all. May this young lady be excused?

MR. BELLI: We stipulate that she may be excused.

THE COURT: All right.

\- - -

COMMISSION EXHIBIT No. 2408—Continued

[redacted]

T. D. McMILLON

a witness called by the State, being first duly sworn, testified on his oath as follows:

DIRECT EXAMINATION

BY MR. WADE:

Q State your name to the jury.

A Thomas Don McMillon.

Q How are you employed, Mr. McMillon?

A As a police officer for the City of Dallas, Texas.

Q How long have you been with the City of Dallas Police?

A Seven and a half years.

Q In what department are you presently in, Mr. McMillon?

A In the Auto Theft Bureau.

Q Auto Theft Bureau. Mr. McMillon, on the 24th of November, last year, were you assigned to any special duty in the City Hall?

A Yes, sir, I was.

Q Tell the jury what that was?

A It was for the purpose of security in the moving of Lee Harvey Oswald from the Dallas City jail to the Dallas County jail.

Q Where were you stationed, or where was your position in the basement of the City Hall?

A I was just outside the jail office door. North side.

Q Step down here and let me show you what has been marked,

COMMISSION EXHIBIT No. 2409

this is what's been marked as State's Exhibit 13, which is a picture of the basement, that being a swinging door in the basement. Where were you standing? Can you get that picture?

A Right along here.

Q You're standing right along there?

A Yes, sir.

Q Right there?

A Yes, sir.

Q Now, Mr. McMillon, did you see Lee Harvey Oswald come out between Officer Levelle and Officer Graves?

A Yes, sir, I did.

Q They passed right in front of you, I presume, didn't they?

A Yes, sir, they did.

Q Headed for a car that Officer Daugherty was in. Did you see the car?

A No, sir.

Q You couldn't see it?

A No, sir.

Q Now, as they approached the entrance to the driveway there that goes down in the City Hall, and out on the other side, what, if anything, happened at that time? Did anything unusual happen?

A Yes, sir, there did.

Q Did you see a person come out of the crowd?

COMMISSION EXHIBIT No. 2409—Continued

MR. TONAHILL: We object to him leading him.

THE COURT: Sustain the objection.

Q (By Mr. Wade) With reference to that, what did you see?

A I saw a man dart from the crowd, with a gun in his hand.

Q Did you see the gun as it was raised, or when did you first see the gun, Mr. McMillon?

A As he was raising it up, as he was coming up with the gun.

Q Tell the jury what position he was in, with reference to standing, or crouched over, or running, or what was he doing?

A This man was kind of in a lunging motion. He was in a crouch, and this all appeared to be one movement; the crouch and the movement and the gun coming up at the same time.

Q Now, did you actually see where he came from in the crowd?

A No, sir, I couldn't tell that.

Q He was out of the crowd when you first saw him?

A He had already come through our line, through our barrier there when I first saw him.

Q About how many steps did you see him take towards Lee Harvey Oswald?

A About two.

COMMISSION EXHIBIT No. 2409—Continued

101

Q Have you later learned who that man was?
A Yes, sir, I have.
Q Is that the defendant, Jack Ruby, in this case?
A Yes, sir, it is.
Q Now, when you first saw him and prior to the shooting -- he did shoot Oswald, didn't he?
A Yes, sir, he did.
Q Prior to the shooting, did you hear him say anything?
A Yes, sir, I did.
Q Tell the jury what you heard the defendant, Jack Ruby, say at that time, Mr. McMillon?
A He said, "You rat son of a bitch, you shot the president." And then a shot rang out.
Q Was that all right the second before the shot went off, or about the same time as the shot went off?
A Yes, sir.
Q And what did you do at that time, Mr. McMillon?
A Well, I broke and tried to get to him.
Q Did you eventually get to him?
A Yes, sir, I did.
Q At that time, was there utter confusion in the basement of the City Hall?
A Yes, sir, there was.
MR. BELLI: Can the answer hold pending the objection? Can he describe what the confusion was?

Q (By Mr. Wade) Well, describe the number of people, the total number of people and what they were doing and saying about that time, by way of whether it was quiet or noisy, or what?
A It was very noisy. There was t.v. cameras, reporters, newsmen around the place. There were a number of officers there in the basement, and then of course, there were a number of officers trying to get to the man besides myself.
Q How many officers do you think were trying to get to the man?
A I don't know, sir. Quite a number.
Q Quite a number. Were you excited yourself to some extent?
A Well, yes, sir.
Q Now, when you got to him, what did you all do with Ruby, or what was done with Ruby?
A Well, a scuffle followed and we hit the floor there for just a little bit, and of course, we were trying to take the gun away from him, trying to get the gun. I had his right arm, and later on several other officers and I took the man inside this door into the jail office and put him on the floor, and we handcuffed him there.
Q From the time after the shooting, as you were carrying him inside to get on the floor, did the defendant, Jack Ruby, say anything at that time?

A Yes, sir, he did.

MR. TONAHILL: We object to anything he said.

THE COURT: Overrule the objection.

Q (By Mr. Wade) What did he say?

MR. TONAHILL: We object to anything he said while under arrest as being in violation of his statutory and Constitutional rights.

THE COURT: Overrule the objection.

MR. TONAHILL: Note our exception.

Q (By Mr. Wade) What did the defendant, Jack Ruby, say at that time?

MR. TONAHILL: Same objection.

MR. BELLI: No foundation.

A He said, "I hope I killed the son of a bitch. I hope I killed the son of a bitch." He said it more than once.

Q (By Mr. Wade) Said it more than once?

A Yes, sir.

Q Did you hear him say anything with reference to who he was?

A Yes, sir, I did.

Q What did he say along that line?

A He kept hollering, "You know me, you know me, I'm Jack Ruby."

MR. TONAHILL: Just a minute. Do we have a full running Bill to anything said under arrest?

COMMISSION EXHIBIT No. 2409—Continued

THE COURT: You can take that as you go along, counsel.

MR. TONAHILL: All right. We object to anything he said while he was under arrest.

THE COURT: Overrule the objection.

Q (By Mr. Wade) Where was he at the time he said that, Mr. McMillon?

MR. TONAHILL: Said what? What's he talking about?

MR. WADE: "I'm Jack Ruby."

A This was during the scuffle and during the time we were taking him in through the jail office there.

Q (By Mr. Wade) Part of that was out in the corridor there where the shooting took place, where you took him in, he was saying that?

A Yes, sir.

Q And what was the other statement he made?

A Well, he kept hollering "I hope I killed the son of a bitch. I hope I killed the son of a bitch."

MR. TONAHILL: Your Honor, we object and ask that it all be stricken.

THE COURT: Overrule the objection. You may have your exception.

MR. TONAHILL: Exception.

Q (By Mr. Wade) Where was he when he said that, the first time you heard him say it?

COMMISSION EXHIBIT No. 2409—Continued

804

A This was during the scuffle and then after we got in the jail office too.

MR. TONAHILL: We have a full Bill on this, Your Honor?

THE COURT: Yes.

Q (By Mr. Wade) He said that also after he got on the floor of the jail? Did he make that statement in there also?

A Yes, sir, he did.

Q Now Mr. McMillon, did you assist in handcuffing him?

A Yes, sir, I handcuffed him.

Q Whose handcuffs did you use?

A Mine.

Q You used yours?

A Yes, sir.

Q And then I believe you and Officer Archer and somebody else --

MR. TONAHILL: Again we object to telling him what he wants him to say, Judge.

Q (By Mr. Wade) Well, what did you do then with him, Mr. McMillon?

A Well, after he was handcuffed, we gave him a very fast preliminary search, and we took him directly to the fifth floor of the men's jail.

Q And proceeded to take all of his clothes off there, I believe?

COMMISSION EXHIBIT No. 2409—Continued

805

A Yes, sir. Almost all of them.

Q Let me ask you, from the time of the shooting until the time you got up to the fifth floor of the jail, can you estimate in minutes how long it probably was?

A Probably no more than three minutes.

Q At that time was -- were you and everybody else still excited over the shooting to some extent?

A Yes, sir, I was.

MR. TONAHILL: We object to that "everybody else."

MR. BELLI: Because we already know that Ruby was calm.

THE COURT: Overrule the objection.

MR. TONAHILL: Exception.

Q (By Mr. Wade) How long did he keep saying the statement, "I hope I killed the son of a bitch"?

MR. TONAHILL: We have a full running Bill of Exception on that? Statements made by Ruby, Judge?

THE COURT: Yes, sir.

Q (By Mr. Wade) Was he still saying that when you got up on the fifth floor?

A No, sir, he didn't say that up there.

Q When you got up to the fifth floor, what did he say? The defendant, Jack Ruby.

MR. BURLESON: Object to anything he said while he was on the fifth floor and under arrest.

COMMISSION EXHIBIT No. 2409—Continued

THE COURT: Overrule the objection.

MR. BURLESON: Note our exception.

Q (By Mr. Wade) This was a matter of less than three minutes, you say, after the shooting?

A Yes, sir.

Q What was said at that time, Mr. McMillon?

MR. TONAHILL: Now, Your Honor --

A Well, he said, "I meant to shoot three times --"

MR. TONAHILL: You've been a witness before. You know you're not supposed to --

THE COURT: Make your objection.

MR. TONAHILL: All right, Judge. Do we understand the Court's ruling to mean that we have a full, running Bill of Exception on any and all statements made by the defendant, any and all times while under arrest?

THE COURT: Yes, sir.

MR. BELLI: Then we don't have to object, Your Honor, and we won't every time.

Q (By Mr. Wade) All right now, Mr. McMillon, what did the defendant, Jack Ruby, say at the time you got him out of the elevator on the fifth floor?

A He said that he meant to shoot the man three times.

MR. BELLI: We'd like to have the exact words, Your Honor. He said that "he meant". We'd like to have the conversation as nearly as he thinks he can

remember it.

THE COURT: All right.

Q (By Mr. Wade) Do you recall more of his exact words, of what he said? As you recall them?

A Well, he made this statement, sir. Detective Archer had told him, "Jack, I believe you killed him." And he said that he meant to kill him, that he meant to shoot the man three times, but that we moved too fast for him and had prevented him from doing so.

Q And he didn't get the three shots off?

A No, sir, he didn't.

Q While you were stripping him down there, did Officer Dean arrive?

A Yes, sir, he did.

Q And then did someone else arrive also?

A Yes, sir, they did.

Q Was that Sorrells of the Secret Service?

A Yes, sir. Mr. Sorrells was there.

Q He was there? And they started talking to him at that time while he was undressed, I believe. Is that right?

A Yes, sir.

Q Did you say how many minutes it was before -- between the time of the shot and the time that Dean arrived there? Estimate it in minutes.

A Seven or eight minutes.

Q Something of that nature?
A Yes, sir.
MR. WADE: I believe that's all.

CROSS EXAMINATION

BY MR. BELLI:
Q You recall -- Did you call him Jack?
A Mr. Ruby, did I refer to him as Jack?
Q Yes.
A Yes, sir, I did.
Q Did you know him before?
A Yes, sir, I did.
Q And was he a peculiar character around town?
A Well, I didn't know him that well, sir. I knew him by sight though.
Q Then not knowing him very well still would you characterize him as peculiar?
A I don't believe I knew him well enough to characterize him.
Q But you had heard of him as being a peculiar character?
MR. WADE: We object to that. He's testified.
MR. BELLI: Character is proved by hearsay only, it can't be proved by specific events, Your Honor.
THE COURT: Go ahead. I'll let him answer.
Q (By Mr. Belli) Did you know of him by hearsay as being a rather unusual man about town?

110

A Well, the things I had heard about him, I knew he had had some trouble with the police before, had been arrested several different times, and that he did run some taverns. And that's about my extent of knowledge. I don't know him real well.
Q Now by being arrested before, he was arrested two times with reference to the license at the club, wasn't it?
A I'm not at all sure what all the arrests was for. I just know that he did have some trouble with the police before and that he had been arrested.
Q There were no arrests for any robbery, burglary, rape, mayhem, kidnapping, child molesting, or sex offenses, or anything that involves moral turpitude, that's correct, isn't it?
A I don't know what the total arrest record consists of.
Q All right. At least being acquainted, if not socially, professionally then, with the Police Department, you did know him in that regard, did you not?
A I knew him through the police department, yes, sir.
Q And the word was around that he was a sort of a queer character, is that right?
MR. BOWIE: We object to that, Your Honor.
MR. BELLI: Foundation, Your Honor.
MR. BOWIE: We object to the terminology used.
MR. BELLI: Withdraw.
Q (By Mr. Belli) You regarded him as being unusual,

didn't you? And the rest of the police?

A I didn't know him that well, sir.

Q Let me ask you by reference to hearsay, you not knowing him, you had heard about him as being unusual, hadn't you?

A No, sir, I didn't hear anything particular about him. I knew that he had those arrests, but I didn't know him very well at all myself.

Q Well, after the event, now I ask you his reputation after the event of the shooting, you heard that he was unusual, didn't you? Not normal?

MR. WADE: We object to that, Your Honor, after the shooting what he had heard.

THE COURT: Sustain the objection.

MR. BELLI: Well, Dr. Guttmacher hadn't met him until after the shooting, and he is going to testify as to whether he's normal or abnormal.

MR. BOWIE: We object to any other witness, and the proper question is available to ask if he wants to ask it, and that is not the proper question.

MR. BELLI: Did Your Honor sustain the objection?

THE COURT: Yes, sir.

MR. TONAHILL: Exception.

Q (By Mr. Belli) Now, that was the prelude to what I come to now. You recall Jack Ruby saying that he meant to shoot Oswald three times, but that you police moved too fast

COMMISSION EXHIBIT No. 2409—Continued

and prevented me from doing so, is that right?

A Yes, sir. He answered that in reply to Don Archer's statement.

Q Who have you gone over this with, this testimony with? The District Attorney?

A I don't understand the question, sir.

Q Well let me put it to you clear. Have you discussed this testimony with Mr. Alexander or Mr. Wade?

A I have discussed this testimony with the District Attorney's office.

Q Well, I asked specifically Mr. Alexander or Mr. Wade.

A I have gone over what facts I could testify to with both Mr. Alexander and Mr. Wade.

Q At different times?

A Yes, sir.

Q How many times?

A I believe that I've discussed the case with them three times with Mr. Alexander, I believe, and once with Mr. Wade.

Q Do you have a pretty good memory?

A I'd say at least average.

Q Who was doing most of the remembering in this conversation, you or the District Attorney?

A I don't understand that.

Q Did you remember that -- did you tell them three times, or was it four times you went over it with them?

COMMISSION EXHIBIT No. 2409—Continued

113

A With who, sir?
Q The District Attorneys, Mr. Wade and Mr. Alexander.
A I discussed it once with Mr. Wade, three times with Mr. Alexander.
Q Four times, and you went over four times this statement -- Will you repeat that statement again that Mr. Ruby said?
A Which statement?
Q The statement that, "I meant to shoot him three times, but you police moved too fast and prevented me from doing so." Is that what he said?
A That's about what it consisted of, yes, sir.
Q Now, would you repeat that into the record, please? Will you repeat what he said into the record, just so we'll have it?
A Don Archer told him, "Jack, I believe you killed him."
Q "Jack, I believe you killed him."
A Right.
Q Yes, and what did Jack say?
A Jack said, "Well, I meant to shoot him three times but you all moved too fast and prevented me from doing so."
Q I thought before you said, "I intended to shoot him three times." He used the words, "I meant to shoot him three times"?
A Well, they mean the same.
Q What did he say? I meant to shoot him three times?

COMMISSION EXHIBIT No. 2409—Continued

A Yes, sir.
Q All right. "I meant to shoot him three times, but you all moved too fast and prevented --" what was the rest?
A From getting off but one shot.
Q From getting off one shot?
A But one shot.
Q But one shot. Now this is the thing that you went over with the District Attorney four times before you took the stand, sort of a rehearsal?
A This is part of the facts that I went over, that I could testify to, with Mr. Alexander and Mr. Wade.
Q All right. Did you go over anything else with the District Attorney, other than this statement, "I meant to shoot him three times, but you all moved too fast and I could only get off one shot"?
A I went over the facts with Mr. Wade and Mr. Alexander that I could testify to, pertaining to this case.
Q All right. And you had given a statement, had you not, to your superior in the police department?
A Yes, sir, I did.
Q Who was your superior in the police department?
A Captain Nichols.
Q And there is a rule in the Civil Service Commission in Dallas that you were not allowed to give a statement to defense counsel, is that true?

COMMISSION EXHIBIT No. 2409—Continued

MR. BOWIE: To which we object, Your Honor.
THE COURT: Sustain the objection.
MR. BELLI: We offer to prove that, Your Honor. May we have an offer of proof and full Bill of Exceptions, Your Honor, on that?
THE COURT: Yes.
MR. TONAHILL: You say we have a full Bill?
THE COURT: Yes.
Q (By Mr. Belli) And how long after this event did you give this statement to the police officer, your superior?
A I started writing on the report around four o'clock, sir.
Q And in that statement you have exactly what you have testified to on the witness stand, is that right?
A What I have testified to on the witness stand is in there, I believe.
Q Are you sure?
A Yes, sir.
Q When did you look at it last?
A I believe that was about two or three days after the shooting.
Q Have you seen it since then?
A No, sir, I haven't.
Q And the statement that you made, you have to make after any unusual occurrence; shooting or robbery or any crime, right?

COMMISSION EXHIBIT No. 2409—Continued

A No, sir, that's not correct.
Q Who asked you to make this statement?
A I was instructed by Captain Nichols to write a special report, covering -- regarding this incident -- covering this incident.
Q You did write that and you did sign it?
A Yes, sir.
Q And was it in duplicate, or was it just the original?
A I wrote it out in longhand, printed it in longhand.
Q All right. And when you looked at it again, everything that you had written on there the first time was still on there, right?
A Yes, sir.
Q Hadn't been changed?
A No, sir.
MR. BELLI: We ask for that statement, for Your Honor's inherent power, for an impeaching document; whether it be oral, whether it be in the ordinary course of business of whether it be a mnemonic or memory aid.
THE COURT: The Court will refuse your request, counsel.
MR. BELLI: We also ask for it for the purpose of impeachment, not for its probative value or substative value in evidence. We offer to impeach this witness by

COMMISSION EXHIBIT No. 2409—Continued

means of that statement, Your Honor.

THE COURT: Same ruling.

MR. ALEXANDER: Let the record reflect that the District Attorney's office does not have a copy of the statement referred to. And we ask that the record show that the witness doesn't have a copy of the statement, under his testimony, his having testified he had not seen it since two or three days after the writing.

MR. TONAHILL: Let the record show that the District Attorney has the complete report from Chief Jesse Curry on this entire matter, and he has failed and refused and denied to give us the report --

THE COURT: Let's not go into all that, Mr. Tonahill.

Q (By Mr. Belli) Let's see. I couldn't get all of this down here. Let me try it once again. He said, "I meant to shoot him three times --" and what?
A "You policemen moved too fast and prevented me from doing it."
Q What?
A "That you policemen moved too fast and I only got off one shot."
Q "I only got off one shot." Okay. Now, if he said that, was he calm at that time? I would presume just a man being shot, he must have been agitated?

A I don't know if he was agitated or not, sir.
Q Well, how did he look to you?
A He looked about like he does now, I guess.
Q Was he talking in a normal tone of voice?
A It appeared normal to me
Q And he didn't raise his voice when he said this, did he?
A No, sir.
Q After he said that, was anything else asked him, or anything else said?
A Well, there was several different things said, but I wasn't present when all of them was said. That's all during the course of my time with him.
Q You just happened to be there when this was said, but not the rest, is that right?
A We were in the process of searching him.
Q All right. Would you say first that there was other conversation?
A During the time that we were with him?
Q No. First, was there other conversation after this was said, "I meant to shoot him three times"?
A What was the question, sir?
Q Was there other conversation with Jack Ruby after this conversation, "I meant to shoot him three times"?
A Yes, sir. During the day there was lots of other conversation.

Q What was the next conversation?
A I don't recall. I may or may not even have been present then.
Q All right. Now let's move to the other end. Was there conversation just prior to this being said, if it was said?
A Yes, sir.
Q And what was the conversation just prior to this being said?
A I didn't hear that. If I did, I don't recall it. I may not have been in a position to hear it.
Q You didn't hear anything said to Jack just before this?
A I was about the jail taking care of some other details with regard to Mr. Ruby.
Q So before Jack said, "I meant to shoot him three times," you didn't hear anybody say anything to him?
A I had just come back, I believe.
Q Let me refresh your memory. You told us earlier today that you had heard one of your brother officers tell him that Oswald was going to die. Don't you recall that now?
A Yes, sir.
Q You do recall that?
A Yes.
Q All right. Let me see if I can refresh your memory a little bit more. When was that said, if that was said, that Oswald was going to die? How long before Mr. Ruby said,

COMMISSION EXHIBIT No. 2409—Continued

"I meant to shoot him three times"?
A Sir, I believe I can clarify the deal there. After we arrived up in the jail, I stepped around the corner there a minute to, like I said, to take care of some other details. And I believe this is going to be one of those times that I came back and Archer was telling him this.
Q You believe it was one of the times that you came back that Archer was telling him this?
A Yes, sir, but I won't swear it.
Q Well, how much else was Mr. Archer telling him?
A Well, I didn't hear that, sir.
Q But he was telling him something else?
A I don't know if he was or not. I wasn't there. I didn't hear it.
Q Well, was everything quiet and all of a sudden, we get these lines, "Oswald is going to die", Ruby answers, "I meant to shoot him three times, but you all moved too fast and I could only get one shot off"?
A No, sir. Everything wasn't just completely quiet. I did hear Archer make that statement, and I did hear Mr. Ruby reply with that answer.
Q Was there sort of a hush up there when Archer said, "Oswald is going to die"?
A No, sir, but I was close enough at that point to hear that.

COMMISSION EXHIBIT No. 2409—Continued

Q You just happened to go over there and hear Archer, and then hear Ruby and then you went away?
A No, sir, I didn't just happen to go over there. I told you I was returning.
Q All right. You just happened to be returning?
A Well, I was returning from taking care of these other details.
Q But you went away afterwards? Right?
A I left at several different times during the period of time that we were with him.
Q Who did you leave with Mr. Archer and Mr. Ruby?
A Detective Clardy, my partner.
Q Now, did you come up in the jail elevator with them?
A Yes, sir.
Q It was a rather quiet ride, wasn't it, up in the elevator?
A No, sir, not especially so. I mean, about like most rides are up and down in an elevator.
Q Well, it doesn't make much noise, the machinery, does it?
A Most of the time it doesn't.
Q Can you hear people talking in the elevator?
A Yes, sir.
Q How many people were in the elevator?
A I don't know the total number, sir.

COMMISSION EXHIBIT No. 2409—Continued

122

Q Well, was it filled to capacity?
A No, sir, I'm sure that it wasn't.
Q Well, you had room enough to turn around?
A Yes, sir.
Q So there was you, Officer Archer and Ruby, and who else?
A Captain King.
Q Captain who?
A Captain King.
Q K-I-N-G?
A Yes, sir. I believe that's right.
Q Anyone else?
A Detective Clardy.
Q C-L-A-R-K?
A No, sir. C-L-A-R-D-Y.
Q Anyone else?
A Yes, sir, but I don't recall who they were.
Q That's one of those elevators that's semi-freight and semi-passenger; carries quite a few and goes slowly, doesn't it? Withdraw. Isn't that a slow moving elevator?
A It moves about like the elevators here in the courthouse.
Q And it makes about as much noise as the one here? Right?
A When it's working properly it doesn't make a whole lot of noise.
Q It was working properly on this day, wasn't it?
A As far as I know it was.

COMMISSION EXHIBIT No. 2409—Continued

Q And then you went from the basement to what floor?
A To the fifth floor.
Q To the fifth floor?
A Yes, sir.
Q Now, from the basement to the fifth floor, was anything said?
A Yes, sir.
Q What was said?
A I believe -- I'll correct that and say --
Q I didn't hear what you were going to correct. First, why don't you tell me that and then go on?
A All right, I will. I started that statement --
Q Are you correcting a story that you've memorized?
A I haven't memorized --

MR. BOWIE: To which we object, Your Honor.

THE COURT: Sustain the objection.

Q (By Mr. Belli) Well, tell me what you were going to correct.
A I started my statement by the words, "I believe."
Q Go ahead.
A Captain King asked the man, somewhere between the basement there, after we had handcuffed him, and the fifth floor, -- and whereabouts in between --
Q Well, this elevator goes up and down, it doesn't run out into the basement?

COMMISSION EXHIBIT No. 2409—Continued

A Well, the point I'm trying to make, sir, I don't know at what point, whether it was on the elevator or whether it was getting on the elevator or not. But somewhere between the time that I handcuffed him and the time we got to the fifth floor, Captain King told the man, "Of all the low life things that's happened and all, this took the cake," and he asked him why that he did it.
Q Captain King told all the low life -- I don't get that.
A He made some statement about "Of all the low life things, and scum and all, why did you do it"?
Q "All the low life things, why did you do it?" Is that right?
A Well, I don't --

MR. WADE: I believe he said "scum" too, didn't he?

A Yes, sir. I don't know exactly how Captain King worded that, but he wound up with why did he do it.
Q (By Mr. Belli) And what did Jack Ruby answer? Anything?
A Well, Mr. Ruby replied that somebody had to do it, somebody had to take care of him, that we couldn't do it.
Q "Someone had to do it, someone had to do it, we can't do it". Right?
A No, he said someone had to do it, that we couldn't do it.
Q Who did he refer to as "we"?

COMMISSION EXHIBIT No. 2409—Continued

A He said "you guys."
Q "You guys"?
A Yes, sir.
Q And you think this might have been said in the elevator?
A Well, I don't know at what point it was said. It was some time between the time we handcuffed him and the time we got to the fourth floor -- the fifth floor.
Q All right. Do you think this might have been said in the elevator?
A I don't know at what point it was said.
Q Could it have been said in the elevator?
A I don't know at what point it was said, sir.
Q Well, I'll ask you, was it said in the elevator?
A I don't know at what point it was said.

MR. WADE: He said he didn't know.

Q (By Mr. Belli) What was said in the elevator? Anything?
A There was some conversation, but I don't recall what it was.
Q You don't recall what it was, but there was conversation in the elevator?
A Yes, sir.
Q Did you put it in your report, the conversation that was in the elevator?
A No, sir.

COMMISSION EXHIBIT No. 2409—Continued

Q It was fresher in your mind at that time, wasn't it?
A Well, I was trying to catch my breath at the time.
Q You were trying to catch your breath when you were going up in the elevator?
A Yes, sir. We had just been in this scuffle.
Q And that's the reason you don't remember what you heard in the elevator?
A I couldn't hear all of it. I wasn't paying any attention to it. I was holding onto the prisoner.
Q Let me see if I can help you. Was something said about s.o.b. to Jack in the elevator? "Jack, you s.o.b."?
A I didn't hear that, sir.
Q Did you hear Jack say anything in the elevator?
A I recall him talking. What statements he made, I don't know.
Q But you did hear Jack talking in the elevator?
A Yes, sir, I'm sure he was.
Q Did you hear him ask what he was doing there?
A I don't recall what the conversation was in the elevator, sir.
Q He could have said, "What am I doing here"?
A I don't recall what was said, sir.
Q But there were some words said that you don't remember?
A At which time, sir?
Q In the elevator.

COMMISSION EXHIBIT No. 2409—Continued

A I couldn't -- I made no point to remember. I don't know what was said there. There was some conversation though, sir.

Q You do remember these other two occasions; number one, "I meant to shoot him three times" and also number two, of Captain King, "All the low life scum things, why did you do it." You can remember that? Right?

A That's not Captain King's exact statement. I said that it was words to that effect. And exactly how he put it, and in what order it came in, I don't know.

Q Well, your statement has this in it, doesn't it?

A No, sir.

Q You don't have this in your statement?

A No, sir.

Q When did you come up with this then, if it was not in that statement that was made right afterwards?

A When did I come up with what, sir?

Q Captain King saying, "All of the low life scum things, why did you do it". You didn't put that in the statement you made right after the shooting?

A No, sir, I did not.

Q When did you recall that, or who helped you to remember this?

A That's one of the things that sticks freshest in my mind, just like the rest of the things. I know there's more

COMMISSION EXHIBIT No. 2409—Continued

that happened, that I should have seen, but I didn't see it all. There's more that's been said. I didn't see it all, and I didn't see it. I just didn't see it, sir.

Q All right. We're not criticizing you for what you see. We'll come to that later. We're asking you now about what you heard. Now, which of the four conversations that you had with the District Attorney, did you finally remember that someone said, "All the low life scum, why did you do it" and Mr. Ruby answered, "Someone had to do it"? Did you tell that to the District Attorney on the first conversation, on the third conversation, or on the second conversation, or did it take to the fourth conversation before you remembered that? The fourth?

A That fact came out the second time that I discussed the case. It was not with the District Attorney, but with Mr. Alexander.

Q The second time you discussed it with Mr. Alexander, that fact came out?

A Yes,sir.

Q Out of whose mind?

A That's what I heard, sir.

Q From Mr. Alexander?

A No, sir.

MR. BELLI: Does Your Honor want to take the recess now? I'll be quite some time.

COMMISSION EXHIBIT No. 2409—Continued

THE COURT: You will be?

MR. BELLI: I think so, Judge.

THE COURT: We'll recess until 1:45 for lunch.

(Whereupon the court was in recess until 1:45 P.M., at which time the following proceedings were had)

Q (By Mr. Belli) Mr. McMillon, were you there later, after all of these events that you have testified to, transpired, when Captain Fritz asked Mr. Ruby, "Why did you do it" and Mr. Ruby answered, "Do what?"

A I wasn't present during Captain Fritz' interrogation at all, sir.

Q Did you see that transpire on the television subsequently, of Captain Fritz talking to Mr. Ruby?

A No, sir. I didn't see Captain Fritz talking to him; either on television or in person.

Q You didn't hear Jack answer to Captain Fritz' "Why did you do it", Jack Ruby answer, "Do what?"

A No, sir, I didn't.

Q Okay. Now, let's take the sequence of events. First let me ask you, did you have occasion to refresh your memory from any instruments or documents during the noon hour?

A No, sir, I didn't.

Q Did you talk with anyone during the noon hour about this case?

A Yes, sir, I did.

Q Who did you talk with?

A Mr. Wade, Mr. Alexander, Mr. Bowie, of the District Attorney's office.

MR. ALEXANDER: Was your question today at noon?

Q (By Mr. Belli) That was today at noon?

A Yes, sir.

Q Your memory certainly can remember back to about half an hour ago. Where did you go to discuss this case at noontime, Mr. Wade, you, Mr. Bowie and Mr. Alexander?

A We were in Mr. Wade's office.

Q And how long did you discuss it?

A Oh, probably some ten minutes.

Q What phase of it did you particularly discuss that you weren't sure of?

A Well, there wasn't any of the facts that I've testified to that I'm not sure of, sir. We went over the facts again that I could testify to.

Q You went over the facts again that you had testified to, is that right?

A No, sir. We went over what facts that I could testify to.

Q That you could testify to?

A Yes, sir.

Q Well, does that mean then there are some things that they have brought out in your memory that you haven't testified to yet?

A No, sir, they didn't bring anything out that I hadn't already told them about. It just hasn't come out in the trial yet.

Q What was this ten minutes that you talked with three District Attorneys that you could testify to? You understand that?

A No, sir.

Q I understood you to say that you talked with Mr. Wade, Mr. Alexander and Mr. Bowie in the District Attorney's office?

A Yes, sir.

Q During the noon hour?

A Yes, sir.

Q For at least ten minutes?

A Yes, sir.

Q About some things you could testify to in the case?

A Yes, sir. Some of them I have already testified to, and some additional things that I could testify to. Some additional facts that I might have.

Q What additional things now do you have for us?

A I don't understand what you mean, sir. You mean --

Q Why did you go over that which you have already testified to?

A We didn't go over that.

Q What did you go over?

COMMISSION EXHIBIT No. 2409—Continued

A The facts that I have testified to and could testify to.

Q Well, just so I understand, "could" means future to me. Does it to you?

A Well, if it were to be admissible in court, yes, sir.

Q I mean if I were to ask you things in certain areas, you were told by Mr. Wade, Mr. Alexander and Mr. Bowie to answer in a certain manner?

A They didn't instruct me how to answer, sir.

Q Well, did they instruct you at all?

A No, sir.

Q What did you go over?

A Facts that I could testify to and some that I had already testified to.

Q Let me ask you, you understand what the word "could" means, don't you?

A Yes, sir.

Q And you say you went over facts that you could testify to? Right?

A Yes, sir.

Q I'll ask you, what are those facts?

A Well sir, they're very numerous.

MR. ALEXANDER: Go ahead and tell the man.

MR. BELLI: I didn't hear what Mr. Alexander said. What are the instructions that Mr. Alexander gave the witness?

COMMISSION EXHIBIT No. 2409—Continued

332

MR. ALEXANDER: Now Your Honor, some of these things at this point are probably not admissible. Now he's asked the question and he realizes what he's asked and what he's doing, then we tell the witness to go ahead.

MR. BOWIE: If he wants to go into all that happened after that, then we have no objection.

MR. BELLI: Let's do this. Let's see what they've tried to bait this man with, so that --

MR. ALEXANDER: We object to that in the presence of the jury.

THE COURT: Sustain the objection.

MR. BELLI: Then we ask to have this out, out of the presence of the jury.

THE COURT: Mr. Belli, let the Court act on the objection before you go on. The Court would sustain the State's objection to the word "bait". Let's don't use it any more.

MR. BELLI: All right.

Q (By Mr. Belli) What did they tell you with reference to answering any questions this afternoon?

A Sir, the only thing that Mr. Wade or Mr. Bowie or Mr. Alexander, or any of them has ever told me, is to tell the truth. They want to know what facts there is that I could testify to. The truth.

COMMISSION EXHIBIT No. 2409—Continued

333

Q Did they also tell you if you were asked to say, "to tell the truth"? That, "I've been told to tell the truth"?

A Sir?

Q Did they also tell you if I asked you about this luncheon conversation, that you were to say, if you had been told anything, to answer, "Yes, I've been told to tell the truth"?

A They instructed me that if I was asked about the luncheon conversation, to tell the truth. They didn't tell me to answer that way. They instructed me to tell the truth.

Q To tell the truth?

A Yes, sir.

Q All three of them told you to tell the truth?

A All three were present. I believe Mr. Wade told me that.

Q All right. Now, this will make the fifth conversation that you had with the District Attorney's office, is that right? We had four this morning, and this is the fifth?

A Those three covered -- didn't cover four times. There were two times with Mr. Alexander, once again with Mr. Alexander and Mr. Wade, and then again this time with Mr. Alexander and Mr. Wade and Mr. Bowie.

Q I count five. Is that right?

A Well, I don't count five, sir. That's four.

Q Let's do it again to be sure. Twice with Mr. Alexander,

COMMISSION EXHIBIT No. 2409—Continued

or three times with Mr. Alexander?

A Twice with Mr. Alexander alone.

Q Yes.

A Once with Mr. Alexander and Mr. Wade. That's together. I'm counting that as the third time. And then this time is the fourth.

Q So you only went over this case with them four times. Is that right?

A As to what facts I could testify to.

Q And coming back to the statement, you say that you didn't have in your statement when you were finishing this morning, about "all the low life scum things, why did you do it"? You didn't have that in the statement?

A No, sir.

Q You told us you told Mr. Wade about that, or Mr. Alexander about that, in the second conversation that you had with him. Right?

A Sir?

Q The second conversation that you had with Mr. Alexander you told him about this occurrence you say happened, that Captain King said, "Of all the low life scum things, why did you do it?"

A I don't recall which conversation it was that we discussed that. It may have been in all four.

Q Well this morning you said it was the second. Do you

recall that?

A I don't recall telling you that this morning. Maybe it was. But I have discussed it with them, sir.

Q All right. Now, suppose you tell us, from the beginning if you will, and we'll have it in sequence for the first time. How close --

MR. WADE: He said it had been a secret so far, and we object to that feature of the statement.

MR. BELLI: Sequence.

MR. WADE: Sequence. Oh, I thought you said secret. Withdraw the objection.

Q (By Mr. Belli) Sequence. One event following another in historical activity. Have you got it? Are you with me?

A Yes, sir.

Q Let's go. Oswald is brought out of the basement. Right?

A Yes, sir.

Q When he is brought out of the basement there's a tremendous hubbub there, isn't there?

A There's a lot of activity, yes, sir.

Q And a lot of talking and a lot of shouting?

A Yes, sir.

Q And did they ask Oswald, "Why did you do it, why did you do it"?

A I heard that question being asked.

Q That question, "Why did you do it, why did you do it?"

A I heard that question, yes, sir.
Q Did you hear him referred to as an s.o.b.?
A No, sir.
Q Did you hear him referred to as a rat, or anything else?
A Yes, sir.
Q And did you see him at that time, give the Communist salute, with one hand like that, when he was in handcuffs?
A No, sir.
Q You didn't see that at that time?
A No, sir.
Q Now, you standing over to the corner. Let's see how we can do this. You were over in this corner here, and that looking at number thirteen, you were over in this corner here against the wall?
A I'm sorry sir, but I can't see what he's pointing to.

MR. WADE: Stand up and show him.

Q (By Mr. Belli) See this corner here? Is that where you made that "M"?
A No, sir. I didn't make that "M".

MR. TONAHILL: Mr. Wade made it for him.

Q (By Mr. Belli) Is there where you were, where that "M" is?
A I was about center ways, or between the door and the edge, right here, sir.
Q Between the door and the edge?

Commission Exhibit No. 2409—Continued

A This opening right here.
Q All right. Would that "M" be about where you were?
A That would be about where I was standing.
Q Now, if we come down here when at the time of the shooting, we should see you in there, shouldn't we?
A Not in this picture, no, sir.
Q Well, that's the time of the shooting.
A I'm right over here.
Q Well, can we see you there?
A No, sir. I'm between this man and this man.
Q Well, is this you here?
A No, sir, that's not me.
Q Then you are in back of here, aren't you?
A I'm behind in here.
Q All right.
A I'll correct that. I believe that's Mr. Graves.
Q All right. So anything that was said at the time of the shooting, the sound would have to come through all of these men in front of you, wouldn't it?
A No, sir.
Q It came over them?
A No, sir.
Q And you heard Mr. Ruby just at the time of the shooting?
A Well, I was looking straight at him.
Q Through these men?

Commission Exhibit No. 2409—Continued

A No, sir.

Q Well, would you step down here and we'll hold this up and see if we can see. Here is a picture with Ruby coming up-- and by "here" I'm referring to -- this is number nine again. Here's Ruby coming up. You don't see yourself in that picture, do you?

A In this picture?

Q Yes.

A Yes, sir.

Q Where are you there?

A Right here.

Q Is this you here?

A Yes, sir. That's me.

Q All right. You're looking the other way, is that right?

A Well, I am according to the picture.

Q Well, according to you. The picture may be wrong.

A I don't know if the picture is wrong or not, but I looked around from this way.

Q This officer was in front of you at that time, wasn't he?

A He came right by the side of me.

Q All right. And this is about at the exact time of the shooting, isn't it?

A No, sir. That's going to be a second before the shooting.

Q All right. Well, this is seconds after the shooting, and these men are in front of you, aren't they?

A I don't know if that was after the shooting or not.

Q Well, here's Officer Levelle, and here's Oswald holding his side where apparently he's been shot. Right?

A I don't know if he's been shot at this point or not.

Q And you say that you heard somewhere at the time that Ruby shot Oswald, what? What did you hear?

A Just after the same moment? The same moment?

Q Right about this moment here.

A No, sir, it wasn't right about this moment. It was after I turned, and he said, "You rat son of a bitch, you shot the president."

Q All right. And where was Ruby at that time?

A He had moved on in closer once the shot was completed.

What point are you talking about?

Q At the time you heard him say, if you did, "You rat son of a bitch, you shot the president."

A He was in a position similar to this one. He was in a crouch, and moving up.

Q Well, if he was moving up he would be in front of this man, wouldn't he, and you would be back here?

A No, sir. I don't know what you mean.

Q Well, I'll make it very clear to you, sir. This picture here is Ruby in action; Ruby moving forward towards Oswald, isn't he?

COMMISSION EXHIBIT No. 2409—Continued

COMMISSION EXHIBIT No. 2409—Continued

A I don't know whether that's Ruby in action or not. That's a still of him. That looks like him.

Q All right. And he kept moving forwards towards Oswald, didn't he?

A All in one motion.

Q All right. He kept moving forward towards Oswald. This would be the next step. He's closer and you're back here where you can't see anything. Right?

A No, sir. That's not right. I don't know whether this would be the next step or not. This is probably a step up, but I don't know if that's the next step or not.

MR. TONAHILL: Your Honor, I'd like to point out under the subpoena duces tecum, Captain Nichols is here and has this man's written statement, and we would like to have Mr. Nichols brought in for examination purposes.

THE COURT: I'm not having him brought in for examination purposes. We've gone through that before and I won't go through it again. You cannot have the statement. Just take your exception.

MR. BELLI: May we have the statement marked for identification, Your Honor?

THE COURT: No, sir.

MR. TONAHILL: May we have a full Bill of Exceptions?

THE COURT: Yes, sir.

COMMISSION EXHIBIT No. 2409—Continued

Q (By Mr. Belli) Now, you heard that prior to this, in just the second it took from the time that Oswald came out of the door, until the time of the shooting, it took matters of seconds, if that long. Is that right?

A I didn't catch all of that.

Q From the time that Oswald came out of the door, until the time he was shot it was a matter of seconds?

A Yes, sir, it was.

Q All right. In those seconds, you heard people say to Oswald, "Why did you do it, why did you do it?" Is that right?

A Yes, sir. Conversation.

Q And then within those seconds you say you also distinctly heard Ruby say, "You rat s.o.b. you shot our president"?

A Yes, sir.

Q Then what is the next thing you heard Ruby say?

A Well during this scuffle, sir, and at the time we were taking him into the jail office, he was hollering, "I hope I killed the s.o.b." and then he was hollering -- he said that several times. And then he said, "Don't you know who I am, don't you know who I am? I'm Jack Ruby. I'm Jack Ruby."

Q Now, which did he say first? "I'm Jack Ruby, I'm Jack Ruby"?

A I believe he said "I hope I killed the son of a bitch" first.

Q He said, "I hope I killed the son of a bitch" first?

COMMISSION EXHIBIT No. 2409—Continued

A This was during the scuffle.

Q Were you still standing back over here when he said that, "I hope I killed the son of a bitch"?

A No. Now when these statements were being made, this is during the struggle and at the time we were going into the jail office.

Q They were struggling back over to this direction, weren't they?

A Well, I can't --

Q To the right of this picture here. And this picture I refer to looks like number eight.

A I don't -- I can't tell from the picture. I can't see it all the way, exactly what you're pointing at, sir.

Q The struggle, the action, was going in this direction here, wasn't it? That way, and Oswald was going that way?

A Oswald was coming out.

Q Now, after Oswald was shot, Oswald went down this way, to the left of this picture, Ruby went to the right. Isn't that right?

A Sir, I don't know which way Oswald went. I had Mr. Ruby's right arm there, and I held on with everything that I had. I don't know what they did with Oswald. Now, what transpired during that time -- I held onto the man's right arm.

Q Who was holding on to Ruby's pistol?

COMMISSION EXHIBIT No. 2409—Continued

A I don't know. I don't know who got the pistol. I have since been told, or learned who got it, but I didn't know at that time, even when we got him in the jail office and had him handcuffed, I still didn't know who had that pistol.

Q Well, when you got hold of Ruby's arm, was there anyone holding onto his pistol?

A I couldn't tell. There was somebody else had hold of his arm besides me.

Q I'm talking about -- were there two people holding his arm, and one person holding his pistol?

A I don't know.

Q Don't you know whether they had a hand on the pistol, and that the pistol was being worked? Didn't you see that?

A I saw the pistol in his hand, and I had my hand on his right arm, and holding on for dear life because the man had a pistol in his hand.

Q When you saw the pistol in his hand, did you see anybody else's hand on that pistol?

A No, sir, I couldn't tell. I saw the pistol --

Q Yes or no?

A Yes or no what? What's the question, sir?

Q MR. WADE: He doesn't have to answer yes or no. He said he didn't see it.

Q (By Mr. Belli) Well, let's see if your answer is the same as Mr. Wade's. When the pistol was being held down at

COMMISSION EXHIBIT No. 2409—Continued

the side, was anyone else's hand on the pistol?

A I couldn't tell that sir. We were in a scuffle and we went to the floor there shortly after the scuffle started. I held onto that right arm. Who wound up with the pistol, or who got it, I didn't know at the time, and didn't learn until later.

Q Is it your answer that you don't know whether anyone else was holding onto the pistol? Is that your answer?

A I didn't see anyone holding on.

Q All right. Did you see the pistol at that time?

A Yes, sir, I did.

Q And you didn't see anyone else holding onto it?

A No, sir.

Q And which way was it pointing?

A When I saw that pistol, it was pointed right about here.

Q And you were over to the right, over in this direction here? Is that right?

A No, sir, that's not right.

Q Well, you didn't move over to the left, did you?

A But I'm -- I'm not where you're pointing, sir.

Q Did you at any time -- would you come down here -- Did you at any time, move to the left side of this picture? Weren't you at all times over at the right side of the picture?

A I came out here, right around here to Mr. Ruby, hanging onto his right arm, right here.

Q All right. And the gun was pointed right at you? Right?

A During part of the scuffle there.

Q And Oswald was over to this side, is that correct?

A Well, I don't know where Oswald was.

Q You didn't see him, is that correct?

A I could see him in the circle, but I was watching the man with the gun.

Q Where was Levelle, do you know?

A I don't know. I wasn't watching Levelle.

Q Will you resume up there please? Now when Jack Ruby was down on the ground -- was he down on the ground at any time?

A Yes, sir. We were both on the ground. I say "ground", I mean concrete, the floor.

Q Well now, what is the answer? Was he down on the ground?

A Well, no, sir. He wasn't on the ground.

Q I didn't hear what you said.

A I said, he wasn't on the ground.

Q He wasn't on the ground at any time? Is that right?

A During the scuffle he wasn't on the ground, no, sir.

Q Well, was he on the ground any time before he was taken into the jail?

A He wasn't on the ground. He was on the floor.

Q Was he on the ground, floor, deck or covering that we walk upon at any time from the time of the shooting until the time that you took him into the jail?
A He was on the concrete floor.
Q On his back?
A We were on our knees where the scuffle took place. As we took him into the jail we laid him face down on the floor.
Q Was he on the floor before you took him inside? Is my question clear to you?
A No, sir, it's not.
Q Floor, deck, covering, ground. Right?
A Right.
Q Was Jack Ruby at any time on the floor, deck, covering or ground before you took him through this door, or this door, inside?
A Yes, sir, he was.
Q And what did he say when he was down?
A During the time that he was down -- now, this is part of the scuffle, and during part of this scuffle there -- I don't know --
Q Do you have the question in mind?
A I think I do. I thought I heard you.
Q Could you answer it?
A I'm trying, sir.
Q Just tell us what he said.

COMMISSION EXHIBIT No. 2409—Continued

A Well, it's a chain of events, sir.
Q Never mind the chain. We'll come to those. Tell me what he said while he was down on the ground.
A All right, sir. As best I can. During this scuffle, at which part of the time we were down on the ground, this is part of the time that Mr. Ruby was hollering, "I hope I killed the son of a bitch."
Q Now, when did he say, "I'm Jack Ruby"?
A I remember him saying, "I'm Jack Ruby" -- now this is as we were taking him into the jail office, and after we had gotten him into the jail office.
Q After you had gotten him into the jail office?
A Yes, sir. On the way, and while we were in the jail office.
Q Well then it was rather redundant, wasn't it, for the other officer, Archer, to say later on, "Jack, I believe you killed him" if Ruby had already said, "I hope I killed the son of a bitch"?
A I don't know what Mr. Archer testified to, sir.
Q Didn't you hear -- What did you hear Archer say to him?
A At what point, sir?
Q At any point.
A After we had reached the fifth floor of the jail, and as I was returning, I heard him say, "Jack, I believe you've killed him."

COMMISSION EXHIBIT No. 2409—Continued

948

Q But Jack had already said that he hoped he had killed him when he was downstairs?

A Yes, sir.

Q All right. And this is in your report, is it? Let me put it to you this way. That's not in your report, is it? Under oath?

A What is not in my report?

Q What you have told us now.

A What is the question, sir?

Q The statements that you've made are not in your report to your official, are they?

A Maybe not --.

Q I beg your pardon?

A Maybe not worded exactly as you have put it, but it is covered in my report.

Q It's covered?

A Yes, sir, it's covered.

Q Are the statements that you have given us here, to the ladies and gentlemen of the jury, "I hope I killed the son of a bitch", are those in your report?

A Yes, sir.

Q All of them?

A Everything I have testified to is covered in my report.

Q And is the statement in there about "you scum, why did you do this" in your report?

COMMISSION EXHIBIT No. 2409—Continued

949

A No, sir, it isn't.

Q That's the only thing of all of these statements that isn't in your report?

A I don't know if that's the only thing or not.

Q Is your statement that you have given us here with reference to shooting him three times, in your report?

A Yes, sir, it's included in the report. Sure is.

Q Did you tell this to the F.B.I.?

A Yes, sir, I did.

Q You wouldn't have any objection to us seeing this report, would you, if it's in there?

MR. BOWIE: To which we object, Your Honor.

THE COURT: Sustain the objection.

MR. TONAHILL: Exception.

Q (By Mr. Belli) And you went over this part that I'm talking to you now, with three District Attorneys during the lunch hour, didn't you?

A Which part is that, sir?

Q The part about shooting him three times?

A I believe that was discussed, yes, sir.

Q You say you believe it was discussed. Do you mean to tell us that you don't know whether you discussed this with the three District Attorneys during the lunch hour?

A Oh, I know we discussed it. I don't know if all three were present. Part of them were there.

COMMISSION EXHIBIT No. 2409—Continued

Q Well, what was the purpose of discussing that? You had just testified, and you knew that you were a witness under oath, going back on the stand, and witnesses are not supposed to be in the courtroom. You know all that, don't you?
A Sir?
Q What was the purpose of going over this with you during the lunch hour, do you know?
A I was instructed not to discuss the case with anybody but counsel, and that's what we did.
Q Discuss it with anybody but the District Attorney, isn't that right?
A I believe that's going to be correct.
Q Is there any doubt about that?
A Not in my mind.
Q Mr. Not in mine [illegible]. Now, in the elevator, we've gotten to the elevator, what was said in the elevator?
A I don't know all the conversation that was said in the elevator, sir.
Q There was some conversation in there?
A Yes, sir.
Q And did someone say, "Jack, why did you shoot him" in the elevator?
A I don't know, sir.
Q Did Jack say anything in the elevator?
A He was making some statements. I don't know what they

COMMISSION EXHIBIT No. 2409—Continued

were. There was conversation in the elevator.
Q And you can't remember or separate those conversations out, but these other conversations that you have given us here, you do separate those out and remember those?
A What I testified to I remember, yes, sir.
Q How long were you in the elevator with the other officers?
A Long enough for it to go from the basement up to the fifth floor.
Q That takes about a minute?
A I don't know how long it takes, sir.
Q And there were how many officers in the elevator?
A I don't know, sir.
Q Was Jack answering in a calm, quiet voice?
A Well, the conversation was pretty -- or seemed average and normal to me.
Q And you can remember a pretty average conversation, the tone of voice and everything else, but you can't remember one word of what was said in that conversation in the elevator, or you won't. Is that right?
A It's not that I won't, sir. I don't remember it, so I can't say that I do.
Q Can you tell us what the subject matter was?
A I'm sure it possibly had something to do with the shooting, or some of the events. I don't recall what it was about.

COMMISSION EXHIBIT No. 2409—Continued

Q You say "probably" had something to do with that?
A Probably did, yes, sir.
Q All right. Jack was handcuffed at that time?
A Yes, sir, he was.
Q And did you have -- were you facing him? Did you have an opportunity to look at him?
A Part of the time.
Q And when you looked at him part of the time, you were out of breath, and you were panting, weren't you?
A I was breathing kind of hard, yes, sir.
Q Was Jack just calm, and not breathing hard?
A He wasn't breathing any harder than I was.
Q Well, was he breathing hard then?
A I don't recall.
Q What was the appearance of his face at that time? Was it flushed, or was it like it appears here?
A Parts of his face -- when I say face, I mean including the forehead -- was red.
Q Parts of the face were red?
A Yes, sir.
Q Well, there's only so many parts to a face, so could you tell us which parts were red?
A Yes, sir. He had an abrasion on one part, I believe. On the forehead. And that part was redder than the rest of the face, sir.

COMMISSION EXHIBIT No. 2409—Continued

Q Do you know how he got the abrasion on the forehead?
A I didn't see it happen. Probably during the scuffle.
Q Was that the time that he was down on the ground, and he was saying, "I'm Jack Ruby, I'm Jack Ruby. Let me up."?
A I don't know, sir. I didn't see him get injured. I say it was probably during that time, but I didn't see anybody get --
Q You didn't see him get injured?
A No, sir.
Q But yet you say that you saw him with the gun, and you saw him down on the ground and you heard him say, what?
A What is the question, sir?
Q What did you hear him say when he was down on the ground, when he was getting injured?
A I don't know at what point he got injured, sir. I don't even know at what point I got injured.
Q Wasn't he injured when he was on the ground?
A I don't know, sir.
Q You saw him all the time he was on the ground?
A I had hold of him all the time he was on the ground.
Q That's not my question. You saw him all the time he was on the ground?
A Possibly glanced away some, trying to get a better hold.
Q Probably what?
A Probably turned away, trying to see the gun or something,

COMMISSION EXHIBIT No. 2409—Continued

if I'm being asked was I staring him face to face all the time, I wasn't, sir.

Q I didn't ask you that. Did he say that which you said he said before you looked away or afterwards?

A I don't know at what point that was, sir.

Q And when you looked away, how long did you look away getting a better hold?

A I don't know that, sir.

Q And you don't know if that's the time someone had their knee on his head?

A No, sir.

Q And you don't know if that was the time that he said, "I'm Jack Ruby, I'm Jack Ruby"?

A At what point are you talking about, sir?

Q At the time he was injured. "Let me up, I'm Jack Ruby."

A I don't know when he was injured, sir.

Q All right. Now, after that you then took him in the jail and laid him face down on the floor, is that right?

A Yes, sir. We put him face down on the floor.

Q What did he say when he was face down on the floor?

A During part of that time, he said again, "I hope I killed the son of a bitch."

Q While he was lying face down on the floor?

A Yes, sir.

Q And how long was he lying face down on the floor?

COMMISSION EXHIBIT No. 2409—Continued

A I don't know how long. Just a very short while.

Q And before he said, "I hope I killed the son of a bitch," you heard a number of people yelling out there, "Oswald is shot, Oswald is shot, Oswald is shot" didn't you?

A I heard someone yell from the outside, yes, sir.

Q The answer to my question is "yes" so there will be no question?

A Yes, sir.

Q And you also heard people yelling, "Jack Ruby did it, Jack Ruby did it" didn't you?

A No, sir.

Q Didn't you hear someone say, "Jack, you scum, why did you do it"?

A During part of the time he was in my custody I heard him referred to as that.

Q No, no, I didn't ask you that. Didn't you say that you heard someone say to Jack, "Jack, you scum --" Let me get your exact words here. And I think it was Captain King, "All the low life scum things, why did you do it". Didn't you hear Captain King say that?

A I heard Captain King use those words in talking to him.

Q Where? In the elevator?

A Sir, I have already told you, I don't know at what point I heard Captain King ask him that.

Q Did you hear Captain King say that, put that question

COMMISSION EXHIBIT No. 2409—Continued

to him before Jack said, "I hope the s.o.b. dies"?
A I didn't get that.
Q What's the sequence of events, the sequence, the happening of the events? When was it that Captain King said that, "All the low life scum things, why did you do it"? When he was on the ground?
A No, sir. He didn't ask him that while he was on the ground.
Q Then he must have asked him while he was in the elevator, is that right?
A I don't know whether he asked him that in the elevator, on the way up in the elevator, or as we were putting him on the elevator, or not sir. I don't know at what point Captain King asked him that.
Q That could have happened while he was on the elevator?
A I don't know when it happened, sir.
Q What did Jack answer to that? "Why did you do it"?
A "You guys couldn't do it. Somebody had to do it."
Q And that was in the elevator. Right?
A Sir, I don't know at what point Captain King asked him that.
Q Well it certainly didn't happen when he was lying on the ground outside, did it?
A No, sir.
Q And it certainly didn't happen when he was lying on his

face on the deck inside the jail, did it?
A I don't know at what point from there, after we got him in the jail, I don't know at what point it happened, sir.
Q You don't know when that happened, and you don't know when that happened in the sequence of events of people yelling out there, "Oswald is shot, Oswald is shot"? Is that right?
A What was the question, sir?
Q You don't know at what time this happened? Captain King -- this is the one thing that isn't just memorized by you, isn't it, sir?

MR. WADE: We object to that, Your Honor.

THE COURT: Sustain the objection.

Q (By Mr. Belli) It's the one thing, you say, that's not in your report, is that right?
A Sir, I don't know at what point Captain King asked him that.
Q Do you understand my question?
A No, sir, I don't believe I do.
Q * This is the one thing you say is not in your report, is that right?
A It wasn't in the report.
Q This is in your report?
A No, sir. It's not in the report.
Q Do you know why you meticulously put in this language of these other sayings in your report, and left this out?

A I don't understand the question, sir.

Q Do you know why you left this out of your report, if it happened, "All the low life scum things, why did you do it"? Answer: "Someone has to do it, and I knew you guys couldn't do it." Why did you leave that out of your report, if it happened?

A It's one of the things that I didn't recall. There's some more things that I didn't recall too, so I'm sure they must have happened, but I didn't see them or didn't hear them or didn't know about them.

Q And this you say you recalled on your second visit to Mr. Alexander, is that right?

A I don't know what visit it was. It might have been the second one, but on one visit.

Q All right. Now, you've told us the time that the other things occurred. Could you try and remember when Captain King said this to Mr. Ruby?

MR. ALEXANDER: That's repetitious, Your Honor.

MR. BELLI: We haven't had an answer yet.

MR. ALEXANDER: He's asked it at least five times and the man told him he couldn't tell him at what point.

MR. BELLI: We can't get an answer then?

MR. ALEXANDER: Get on to something else.

MR. BELLI: I'll take my orders from Your Honor as to getting on to something else.

COMMISSION EXHIBIT No. 2409—Continued

THE COURT: I'll sustain the objection. I think it's repetitious.

MR. BELLI: So we have it then in the record, Your Honor, that he can't tell us when that happened, if it did happen in the jail elevator. Is that right?

MR. TONAHILL: Exception.

MR. BOWIE: He's already answered the question, Your Honor. It's repetitious.

Q (By Mr. Belli) Now you left the room that Jack was in upstairs about what time? Do you recall?

A Which time, sir?

Q Well after you heard Jack say -- let me get you correctly here so I won't misquote you -- "I meant to shoot him three times, but you all moved too fast and prevented me from getting the other two shots off." And after that you walked away, is that right?

MR. ALEXANDER: Now, Your Honor, we object to that. That is not the statement in evidence. Counsel is misquoting.

MR. BELLI: Withdraw.

Q (By Mr. Belli) Will you tell us what you said, or what he told to you?

A At a point after we arrived on the fifth floor, sir, I returned from handling some other details regarding the case. As I returned, I heard Archer ask him --

COMMISSION EXHIBIT No. 2409—Continued

Q Go ahead.
A Asked him there --
Q Well, tell us what Archer said and what he said, so I'll have it right.
A Well, I heard Archer tell him, "Jack, I believe you've killed him."
Q And Jack said?
A He said he meant to shoot the man three times.
Q Go ahead.
A But that we moved a little too fast for him, that he only got off one shot.
Q Then what did you do after that?
A I was still standing by, still guarding the man, still keeping him under surveillance, going about handling some of the other details.
Q Did you see Jack at all after that?
A Well yes, sir.
Q That evening?
A Yes, sir.
Q And did he appear about the same that evening when you saw him later?
A The last time I saw him he appeared about the same as when I first saw him that day, and kind of like, maybe like now.
Q Was the red mark still on his face?

Commission Exhibit No. 2409—Continued

A From the injury?
Q Well, I don't know what it was from. You said it was from the injury.
A Yes, sir. This abrasion was still showing.
Q Now, we have all this period of time, from the time that you first saw Ruby until the last time you saw him that evening, that he appeared to be cool, calm, collected, not agitated or excited, or emotional. That's correct, isn't it?
MR. ALEXANDER: That's a multifarious question.
THE COURT: Break it down, counsel.
Q (By Mr. Belli) All right. The last time you saw him he was calm, not agitated, not emotional. Right?
A I don't know if he was agitated, or what he was. He appeared about --
Q The same as before?
A Yes, sir.
Q And about the same as when he was lying on the floor covering outside of the door and about the same as when he was lying on the ground inside the door. Right?
A No, sir, he didn't appear --
Q. It may be funny to you, Officer. It's not as funny to me.
A It's not funny to me at all.
Q It's difficult for me to cross examine you, I assure you. If I had your statement I could do a much better job.

Commission Exhibit No. 2409—Continued

If you want to smile, that's your privilege. Do you have the question?

MR. WADE: We object to him referring to the statement.

THE COURT: Let's leave the statement alone, because it's not in evidence.

MR. BELLI: I know it isn't, Your Honor.

Q (By Mr. Belli) Now, did he seem to be the same as far as his facial expression went, from the time that he was lying on the floor outside of the door, to the time he was lying on the floor inside the door, and you seeing him in the elevator? No change?

A I can't answer that with a yes or no, sir.

Q Well, tell us. Answer it any way. Just give us the truth.

A During the time he was lying face down in the jail office floor, and during the time -- during all the time we were in this scuffle, I couldn't see what his facial expressions were all the time, so I don't know if they were the same as when we -- as when I last saw him or not, sir.

Q But you could hear him very plainly, couldn't you? Above all of the din and all of the tumult and all of the noise, you could hear him very plainly enunciate these words that you've told us, couldn't you?

A What I testified here I did hear, yes, sir.

COMMISSION EXHIBIT No. 2409—Continued

Q And that was a normal tone of voice, wasn't it?

A I don't know if it was normal or not, sir.

Q Well, was he shouting?

A It was loud enough to hear.

Q Was he shouting when he said this upstairs, "I meant to shoot him three times"?

A No, sir, he wasn't shouting them. Just conversation.

Q Was that the same conversational tone he used downstairs when he said, "You rat s.o.b."?

A No, sir, it wasn't.

Q Then he did shout when he said that, is that right?

A Well, by tone I thought you meant volume. It was a little louder downstairs there than it was upstairs.

Q Now, did you face him in the elevator, or did you have your back to him?

A I don't recall what position I had. I saw him some.

Q Did you see him in the elevator?

A Yes, sir.

Q All right. Tell the ladies and gentlemen of the jury whether he seemed to be agitated in the elevator?

A I don't know if he was agitated or not, sir.

Q Did you see his face in the elevator?

A I saw him some.

Q Was there perspiration on his face?

A I don't recall if there was or not, sir.

COMMISSION EXHIBIT No. 2409—Continued

Q Did you notice whether he was breathing hard?
A I don't recall that. I believe that he was, but I'm not sure. I think that he was. I knew that I was.
Q Were the other officers breathing hard, panting too?
A I don't know, sir.
Q Wouldn't you say when you saw him in the elevator, that Ruby was the calmest of the lot there, that he was not perspiring, his face was not flushed, he was not breathing hard, and he was standing very quiet?
A No, sir. I couldn't answer that by saying yes to all of that question.
Q You couldn't answer it by saying no?
A Not to all that question. Parts of it's true, parts of it's not true.
Q What part is untrue?
A Well, you just asked me -- I would say he was about as calm as any of the rest of us. His face, part of it's going to be red, it's got this abrasion on it. Things like that.
Q Did he make any effort to get away, or cause you any trouble as you went in there?
A At what point, sir?
Q At any point?
A No, sir. Just scuffling there. I didn't know whether he was trying to get away there or what.
Q Was he trying to get away there?

COMMISSION EXHIBIT No. 2409—Continued

A Well, I don't know, sir.
Q All right. Did he say anything about the dog in the car?
A Later on in the day that came out.
Q All right. Tell us what he said? That he had left his dog in the car across the street?
A Yes, sir.
Q What did he say with reference to that?
A Well, I don't recall all that conversation, sir, but he did tell us that he had a dog parked over in the parking lot somewhere, in the car. The dog and the car was parked over across the street.
Q How did he refer to the dog?
A I believe he called that dog by name, but I don't recall the name.
Q Sheba?
A I don't recall the name, sir.
Q Well, whatever the dog's name, he said that he had left the dog in the car, to go over and send the wire, didn't he?
A I can't recall all that conversation. He told us he had the dog in there, and there was some conversation about the wire. Now word for word, the exact conversation, I don't recall all that, sir.
Q You don't recall it exactly like you do the other conversation, is that right?

COMMISSION EXHIBIT No. 2409—Continued

A I don't recall all this conversation here that you're talking about.

Q What did he say in general about the wire?

A Part of the details on that, I believe he said that he had sent the wire to someone in Ft. Worth.

Q Someone that needed it for the rent, one of the girls that worked for him?

A They needed it for something, I believe.

Q And did he also tell you that she had called him about five minutes after ten that morning and asked him to send that money, come downtown and send it to her?

A At some point. Now, the exact time that he mentioned I don't know. He did mention sending this wire. Now, the exact conversation, word for word, I don't know it, sir.

Q Indeed, he told you that she phoned him at the exact time that you had announced over the radio the night before, that Oswald was to have been moved, at ten o'clock. Is that right?

A I don't know. I don't remember the time, sir.

Q Just this one area then we'll try to run through this as fast as we can. No one from the press went up in the elevator with you, did they?

A Not that I know of, sir.

Q Well, there's no doubt in your mind about that, is there just so we can nail that down?

COMMISSION EXHIBIT No. 2409—Continued

A I didn't see any when we got off and I don't recall any being on there.

Q Now, if Ruby had said "You guys couldn't do it, someone had to do it" what was the answer to that?

A I don't know. I don't recall what answer there was. I didn't know exactly how he had worded the thing. Like I told you a while ago.

Q May I suggest to you that if that did happen, you left that out of your report because you thought it would embarrass the police department?

A Sir?

Q You didn't leave that out of your report, if it did happen, because it would embarrass the police department, did you?

A I left it out of the report because I didn't recall it.

Q And you wrote this report how long after the event?

A I started writing this one report, probably around four or four-thirty that afternoon.

Q And the other report, when?

A That is the only one that I wrote. I gave a statement a time or two after that.

Q A time or two?

A Yes, sir.

Q To whom did you give those statements?

A One was departmental investigation of the incident, and

COMMISSION EXHIBIT No. 2409—Continued

then I talked to one team, and that would be two F.B.I. agents. And then later on I talked to another team. That would be two more F.B.I. agents.

Q And there was a departmental secretary taking down what you were saying? Right?

A No, sir.

Q And even though you had made one report, talked to two departmental investigations and the F.B.I., it wasn't until the second talk with Mr. Alexander that you remembered this conversation that you say, "All the low life scum things, why did you do it", and Ruby answering, "Someone had to do it, you guys couldn't"? Fair enough?

A I still don't understand the question.

Q I'll make it clear to you. You tell us that wasn't in your original report, this statement, "All the low life scum things, why did you do it" and Ruby answered, "Somebody had to do it, you guys couldn't do it." That wasn't in your original report, right?

A That's correct.

Q Now after that you had two departmental investigations, right?

A Yes, sir.

Q And you went through all this alleged statement, is that correct?

A No, sir. We had one departmental investigation that I

attended.

Q One that you attended?

A Yes, sir.

Q But you made two other statements, didn't you, that you told us?

A I talked to the F.B.I. on the deal, twice.

Q And you talked with the F.B.I. twice, right?

A Yes, sir.

Q All right. In none of these, until you come to the second conversation with Mr. Alexander, did you mention the subject of all the low life scum. Fair enough?

A No, sir, that's not the way it happened.

Q Tell us the way it happened.

A At the departmental investigation that point was included on the report.

Q Oh, that was on the report then before you talked to Mr. Alexander, right?

A At the departmental investigation, sir.

Q So it wasn't true that you told us this morning that the first time you mentioned that was on the second conversation with Mr. Alexander, right?

A I didn't testify to that this morning, sir. If I did I misunderstood you.

Q All right. Is that what you discussed during the ten minutes during the noon hour with the District Attorney?

171

A We discussed that point some.
Q You discussed that point some? Is that what you said?
A Yes, sir.
Q And, what did you say about it?
A I don't recall how the conversation went, sir.
Q Well, would you try and recollect back now about an hour and a half, and see if you can't give us the substance of that conversation? Three District Attorneys and you. Were you in the room with the three of them with the door closed?
A Parts of the time.
Q Part of the time? Well, let's take the part of the time that you were in the room with them first, with the door closed. What did you discuss some about this statement, "All the low life scum," "someone had to do it". What did you discuss about that?
A It was just mentioned. It wasn't any big issue. It was just mentioned.
Q By whom?
A I don't recall which one of the three of them mentioned it.
Q Did you say then that you didn't remember it until the second time you had the conversation with Mr. Alexander?
A Did I say what, sir?
Q Do you tell us now that in your departmental investigation you did mention this?

192

A That he had stated that he meant to shoot the man three times?
Q No. No. That wasn't said at the same time that you say that Captain King said, "All the low life scum things, why did you do it", to which Ruby answered, "Someone had to do it, you people couldn't". Now, did you mention that in the departmental investigation?
A Sir, I don't understand.
Q What is the answer, yes or no?
A Well, I don't understand the question. There's been about four or five different deals here. I've discussed the case with them --
Q Well, I don't have any deals with the District Attorney, so I wouldn't know.
A I don't understand what you mean sir, at which point you mean, sir.
Q I'll make it perfectly clear. Do you understand that you testified this morning, that Captain King had told Mr. Ruby, or put the question to him, "All the low life scum things, why did you do it" and Mr. Ruby answered, "I know that you fellows couldn't do it, some guy had to do it for you." Now you say that that was said on that morning, or that day, is that right?
A On what day, sir?
Q The day of the shooting.

A Captain King made the statement, or asked Ruby that the day of the shooting.
Q And you don't know when he asked him that?
A At what point I don't recall.
Q You don't recall whether it was upstairs, downstairs, at any time, is that right?
A I don't recall at what point. I don't know where we were when Captain King made the statement, where we were at the time, whether we were on the elevator or what.
Q Now I asked you if that was in your original report, and you said "no". So far we're together, right?
A Yes, sir. That's not in the original report.
Q Then you had a departmental investigation in which you gave a statement, is that right?
A Yes, sir.
Q And was that given to the departmental investigators?
A It was covered in that, sir.
Q Was it given to him in these words?
A Wait a minute, sir. I don't understand what you mean.
Q I'll withdraw and make it clear. In the departmental investigation did you say what you have told us here, that Captain King said to Ruby, and what Ruby said back to him? Did you tell that to the departmental investigation?
A No, sir.
Q When was the first time you told anybody that this

happened, or that you heard this? Is that clear to you?
A No, sir.
Q All right. You told us that Captain King said something to Ruby this morning, and Ruby answered, with reference to scum and if you people couldn't do it he had to do it. Have you got the subject of the conversation?
A Yes, sir.
Q All right. Now, when was the first time that you told anybody about that, that you had heard that, allegedly, or had heard it? The first time that you ever told anybody was the second conversation with Mr. Alexander?
A No, sir. That's not the first time.
Q When was the first time?
A I don't know when the first time was. I discussed the case some with the officers that were in the jail with me that day.
Q I didn't get the last.
MR. BELLI: Would you read his answer, please?
(Whereupon the last answer is read back by the court reporter)
Q (By Mr. Belli) All right. Did you discuss that with them in jail that day?
A I don't recall if I did or not. I discussed --
Q Were you getting together on any story in jail at that time?

A No, sir.
Q Well, if you had this testimony in your memory, could you tell us why this four or five conversations with the District Attorney's office? What were you doing? Were you telling them the same thing repeatedly?
A Sir, there was preparation for the bond hearing, and preparation for the trial. As to what facts I could testify to.
Q But it was the same thing every time, is that right?
A I went over the same facts I could testify to, what I saw and heard.
Q Did you have any notes that you have made at any time, other than the statement?
A No, sir.
Q Do you keep a notebook for notes on criminal activities that you reduce to report later on?
A No, sir.
Q Did you, right after that event, make some rough notes, like a rough log, to later on reduce them to a smooth log?
A No, sir. I wrote that statement.
Q Were the other officers with you at the time that you wrote the statement?
A Some of them were.
Q Were you all writing out about the same statement?
A I assume they were writing what they had seen and heard.

COMMISSION EXHIBIT No. 2409—Continued

Captain Nichols instructed us to write a report of what everybody had seen and what they knew about the incident, and he instructed us not to talk to each other about the deal.
Q But you had been talking to each other, hadn't you, right then about these events?
A I had discussed it with Clardy, Archer, some of the jail personnel probably that was on duty at the time.
Q Did you discuss this silent elevator ride?
A Sir?
Q Did you discuss the silent elevator ride?
A Well sir, the elevator ride wasn't silent.
Q I don't think it was either. Tell us what was said during the elevator ride?
A Sir?
MR. WADE: Your Honor, we object to that. It's repetitious. He's been over that a dozen times.
THE COURT: Sustain the objection.
Q (By Mr. Belli) Just one further subject of inquiry. Who did Jack say, "You guys couldn't do it and someone had to do it for you"? To whom did he say that?
A I'm assuming that he was answering Captain King's question.
Q And Captain King didn't answer, and no one else answered Right?
A There was some conversation on the elevator, but what

COMMISSION EXHIBIT No. 2409—Continued

answer or other conversation there was, I don't know, sir.
Q In the departmental investigation, in the daily press and the F.B.I., they all wanted to know if there was any connection between Ruby and the Police Department, didn't they?
A Yes, sir.
Q And if that is true, didn't you think that this was important, if it did happen, that Ruby said, "You guys couldn't do it, I did it for you." Didn't you think that would be sort of a solution to that when they asked you that question, particularly the F.B.I.?
A Regarding the what, sir?
Q The subject of inquiry was by the F.B.I. and by the police investigation, as to whether there was any collusion allowing Jack to get into the jail so he could shoot Oswald, is that right?
A I don't understand the question, sir.
Q Withdraw. We'll take it again. There was considerable discussion in the newspaper and considerable discussion in the department, that perhaps this shooting was the result of the police making it easy for someone to get in there and shoot Oswald. Do you recall that discussion?
A Yes, sir.
Q All right. And that was put to you as a question, wasn't it, if you knew anything about that?
A Had I seen him around down in there?

Q No. Wasn't the question put to you, do you know anything about whether it was made easy for Ruby or anyone else to get in there?
A Well sir, there was an investigation conducted, and that question wasn't asked to me during this investigation word for word like you've asked it.
Q Not word for word, but generally that question was put to you, wasn't it?
A During the investigation I assume that they tried to determine if I had knowledge of how he had gotten down in there.
Q And as to whether the police had been lax?
A I assume that was part of it too.
Q If you assumed all of that, then if you really knew, and Ruby had said that, wouldn't you have thought that it would have been extremely important to say that he said, "If you guys couldn't do it, someone had to do it for you"?
A I didn't remember it at the time.

MR. BELLI: That's all.

MR. WADE: We want to introduce these two statements into evidence for the State at this time. This is State's Exhibit 14. The statement is dated November 30, 1963, Lt. Wallace and McAghran. One dated the 24th of November, 1963, addressed to Chief of Police J. E. Curry. State's Exhibit 15. We introduce them in evidence.

MR. BELLI: We ask for a new trial at this time, Your Honor. And very sincerely and very urgently, we would like to argue this motion for a mistrial, and particularly on the grounds we were refused the privilege and the right to examine this man and the other man on any statements. We offer to Your Honor that there is a Civil Service rule that defense counsel cannot get a statement from a policeman. We have not seen this statement, I don't know what is in it, I'm not bound by the statement because it will be self serving.

Now, if I were to stand up and say, after asking to see the statement, that I don't want it into evidence the jury, being unlettered in the law, might think that I am not sincere. But we know as lawyers, Your Honor, that I don't have to offer this into evidence, because I have this for the purpose of impeaching this witness. I want to see the statement and have this marked for identification, and on the basis I have urged, we ask for a mistrial.

THE COURT: All right. I overrule your motion.

MR. WADE: We offer it in evidence, Your Honor.

MR. BELLI: May I see it, Your Honor? And then may it be marked for identification? May we call now

COMMISSION EXHIBIT No. 2409—Continued

too, Your Honor, for the other statement that we have subpoenaed?

THE COURT: No, sir.

MR. BELLI: Well, Judge, do I understand when they feel that they have something here that is self serving, after a luncheon conference we're handed something that they can introduce, and we cannot see the other statement?

THE COURT: They want to introduce it in evidence. Do you object to it?

MR. BELLI: I haven't read it. I haven't seen it. We're not entitled to see these things until we call for them in court. I would like to read it now, and we ask likewise that we have the other statement to compare with it, because the other officer was there with him at the time and he said they talked them over together.

THE COURT: The Court's not going to let you have it, Mr. Belli. I wouldn't let you have this one, except the State tendered it.

MR. BELLI: So that I'll have the record clear, let me ask this.

Q (By Mr. Belli) There was a statement made by you on, what date was it? Was it Sunday the 24th?

A Yes, sir. I wrote one of those reports on the 24th.

Q I beg your pardon?

COMMISSION EXHIBIT No. 2409—Continued

A I wrote one of them on Sunday, following the shooting.

THE COURT: We'll take a fifteen minute recess.

(Whereupon the court was in recess until 3:15 P.M., at which time the following proceedings were had.)

MR. BELLI: I understand this instrument, consisting of --

MR. WADE: I haven't examined him. I think you passed him back.

MR. BELLI: Let me get this into the record. This instrument, consisting of seven pages, has been admitted into evidence?

THE COURT: No, sir, it hasn't. It's only been tendered, as I understand it.

MR. WADE: We offer it into evidence.

THE COURT: All right.

MR. BELLI: We object to it being offered into evidence, but we do want to examine this officer on it, Your Honor, first.

THE COURT: The Court will sustain the objection. You may return it to the State.

MR. BELLI: I want to use it, Your Honor.

THE COURT: You can't use it unless you put it in evidence.

MR. WADE: We have no objection to him using it, Your Honor. We're not through examining the witness

yet. I have another matter here. Here is a statement of D. R. Archer. We have obtained copies of them now, Your Honor.

(Whereupon the exhibit is marked State's Exhibit 15 by the court reporter)

MR. WADE: We offer it in evidence, Your Honor.

MR. BELLI: We haven't seen this, and we cite that as misconduct and ask for a mistrial, in the presence of the jury offering the statement in evidence, or calling for a stipulation that we may want to object to for legal grounds. And I wish Your Honor would instruct the jury now that we do have the right to make legal objections, to object to the offering of any evidence, and that should not prejudice in anywise, may it please Your Honor.

THE COURT: Yes. I think the jury understands that, counsel, that you have a right to make objections.

MR. BELLI: In this context, I understand here has been an instrument that was offered after the recess into evidence. We have not seen it, we do not know what is in this statement here. I'm going to object to this presently. I may read it, I may feel that it is self serving, and I may feel that at that time I may object to it, and if I object to it in the presence of the jury, the jury then may feel that I am holding probative

382

evidence out. So that's the reason that I say that is misconduct for the District Attorney to do that, may it please Your Honor. Now, the jury can't separate legal objections from substance. It's difficult enough to even have lawyers do that.

MR. WADE: Judge, he can argue the case later, if he wants to argue it.

MR. BELLI: I just want to be sure, and I hope we don't have to argue it later in any other court. That's the reason I'm so careful here. All right. This has been offered, Your Honor. We had a recess, we have not had the opportunity to look at this, and I would like to --

THE COURT: All right. You keep it, Mr. Belli, and at the proper time --

MR. TONAHILL: Your Honor, this is the same statement that Mr. Alexander took from Mr. Nichols and refused to permit us to see this morning, and that we ordered here by subpoena duces tecum.

MR. BOWIE: There were no such statements made, and the record won't reflect any. This is a misstatement. This was the statement that was given --

MR. TONAHILL: Well, Mr. Nichols can come here and make this statement Mr just made, a pure, one hundred percent falsehood, Judge.

COMMISSION EXHIBIT No. 2409—Continued

383

MR. BOWIE: He did not make a written statement to Mr. Alexander. The record so reflects.

MR. TONAHILL: Mr. Alexander took the statement away from Mr. Nichols that we ordered here by subpoena duces tecum, and wouldn't permit us to see it, and now we want to know if this is one and the same statement, Your Honor.

MR. WADE: I think that's a copy of it.

MR. TONAHILL: This is the one you all wouldn't permit us to see.

MR. WADE: No, that isn't the one. We discussed those.

MR. TONAHILL: We want the one you wouldn't let us see this morning.

MR. WADE: There's a copy of it, right there.

THE COURT: All right, Mr. Tonahill, take your seat.

REDIRECT EXAMINATION

BY MR. WADE:

Q You are Officer McMillon, is that right?

MR. BELLI: I haven't finished my cross examination.

THE COURT: You've already passed him back.

MR. BELLI: No I haven't, Your Honor.

THE COURT: What does the record show, Mrs.

COMMISSION EXHIBIT No. 2409—Continued

Stinebaugh?

MR. BELLI: If the record does show that, I have no knowledge of making any statement that I'm finished with the cross examination.

MR. WADE: He asked a question, Your Honor, when I offered the statement, but I have some questions I want to ask him, then they'll have a chance to question him.

THE COURT: All right.

MR. BELLI: I would like to continue the cross examination. Now I'm offered the statements --

THE COURT: Well, the State has him.

MR. ALEXANDER: Let's see what the record shows.

THE COURT: All right. What was the last question?

(Whereupon the last question and answer were read back by the reporter)

MR. WADE: That was voir dire. Go back further than that, just before I introduced the statements.

MR. BELLI: To be sure, Your Honor, so we'll have our record here, the statement was then proferred into evidence, and I was not permitted to cross examine on the statement during the examination. Now I ask leave to cross examine on the statement for inconsistencies.

THE COURT: You'll have a chance, but you have passed him.

MR. BELLI: I'm still cross examining him.

THE COURT: No, you passed the witness back to the State.

MR. BELLI: Well, it's probably my unfamiliarity with Texas law.

THE COURT: You'll not be deprived of an opportunity, Mr. Belli.

MR. BELLI: I'd like to do it in sequence, Your Honor.

Q (By Mr. Wade) Mr. McMillon --

MR. BELLI: Excuse me just a minute. For the record, could we have the original of these instruments rather than photostats? These are photostats, and I object to the use of photostats. We ask for the best evidence. We say this is hearsay, there's been no foundation and we would like to see the originals, Your Honor. And there's a statement here 24 November, and then there's something attached to it of November 30th that I haven't heard of before, and I would like to see the originals.

THE COURT: You can ask him when you get him on recross examination, Mr. Belli.

MR. BELLI: Well, I've been handed these to look at, Judge. If those are proffered as the statements I object to them. I want the originals. Can we have them?

THE COURT: No, sir.

MR. BELLI: These are hearsay and secondary evidence, and there's been no foundation. We don't know if they have been done on the Cash and Carry Printing Press, the D.A.'s printing press, or whose. We're certainly entitled to see the originals, are we not?

THE COURT: Mr. Belli, they're worth exactly what they are, whatever they're worth to you, sir.

MR. ALEXANDER: May it please the Court, the State of Texas is not in possession of the originals of these. We phoned the Police Department and they were kind enough to make a Zerox copy for us, and this is the best we can do.

MR. BELLI: We produced the originals, and the originals were here and sent back.

THE COURT: I have released the originals, and will do so again, Mr. Belli. Now the State has proffered you those. You take them for whatever they're worth.

MR. BELLI: Judge, these may be as valid as a Chinese laundry ticket, as far as I know. I have no way of knowing whether these are authentic. There's interlineations here. I can cross examine to show that these were put in later on.

MR. BOWIE: Then do it.

COMMISSION EXHIBIT No. 2409—Continued

MR. BELLI: Why should I have to? Are we back in the Middle Ages, Judge, that we can't see the original of a document?

THE COURT: Yes, sir.

Q (By Mr. Wade) Mr. McMillon, directing your attention back to the lunch hour and that ten minute conversation, what are the facts with reference to whether or not we asked you about the conversation that followed after you got on the fifth floor?

MR. BELLI: That's leading and suggestive.

MR. TONAHILL: Hearsay.

THE COURT: Overrule your objection.

MR. TONAHILL: Exception.

Q (By Mr. Wade) What are the facts with reference to whether we asked you if you heard the conversation between Officer Dean and Ruby?

MR. TONAHILL: Leading and hearsay.

THE COURT: Overrule your objection.

MR. TONAHILL: Exception.

Q (By Mr. Wade) You did recall part of that conversation, didn't you?

A Yes, sir, I did.

MR. BELLI: Leading and suggestive.

THE COURT: Overrule the objection.

A Yes, sir.

COMMISSION EXHIBIT No. 2409—Continued

Q (By Mr. Wade) Now let me ask you a second question. On cross examination by Mr. Belli, he's asked you about if Ruby told you he had a dog in the car, I believe. Is that right?
A Yes, sir.
Q He also asked you if Ruby told you about going to Western Union and sending a telegram. Was that conversation even following the Dean conversation up in the jail?
A Yes, sir, it occurred later on, up in the jail on the fifth floor.
MR. TONAHILL: We object to anything with reference to any conversation with Dean up on the fifth floor. The defendant was under arrest.
MR. WADE: That's the conversation they went into.
THE COURT: Overrule the objection.
MR. TONAHILL: Exception.
Q (By Mr. Wade) Now, as a matter of fact, did you and other officers stay with Ruby until you took him to Homicide later that afternoon?
A There was some detective with him at all times. I was not present with Mr. Ruby at all times. I was in and out.
Q You were up there on the fifth floor though?
A Yes, sir, I was.
Q Until about what time that afternoon?

Commission Exhibit No. 2409—Continued

A I believe it was after three. Three or three-thirty, something like that.
Q What did you do with Ruby at that time?
A We assisted some Homicide detectives in taking the man to Captain Fritz' office.
Q Now, after the conversation that defense counsel asked about the Western Union, going to the Western Union, did the defendant, Jack Ruby, at that time, tell you how he got into the basement of the City Jail?
MR. TONAHILL: We object to that, Your Honor, as being a statement made while the defendant was under arrest.
MR. WADE: That's the same conversation.
MR. TONAHILL: It's in violation of the statutory and Constitutional rights, and violation of Article 727 of the Code of Criminal Procedure.
THE COURT: Overrule your objection.
MR. TONAHILL: Exception.
Q (By Mr. Wade) Let me ask you again, following the --
MR. TONAHILL: Same objection. Same ruling?
THE COURT: Yes, sir.
Q (By Mr. Wade) In the same conversation that the defendant, Jack Ruby, told you about sending a telegram, did he also -- in the conversation inquired about by defense counsel Belli, did he tell you how he got into the basement of the

Commission Exhibit No. 2409—Continued

City Jail?

MR. BELLI: Leading and suggestive.

THE COURT: Overrule the objection.

Q (By Mr. Wade) On the day of the killing of Lee Harvey Oswald?

A Yes, sir, he did.

Q Tell the jury how he told you he got in?

MR. BELLI: Same objection, same exception. After custody, after arrest, after jail, after held in confinement.

MR. TONAHILL: Prejudicial as well.

THE COURT: Overrule your exception.

MR. TONAHILL: Exception to the Court's ruling.

Q (By Mr. Wade) Go ahead and tell us.

A I was present when Mr. Ruby stated how he had gotten into the basement.

MR. BELLI: I can't hear you.

A I was present when Mr. Ruby made a statement about how he got into the basement of the City Hall. He stated that as Lt. Rio Sam Pierce was pulling out of the basement in the squad car, or in a car, --

Q (By Mr. Wade) On what street?

A Main Street side, sir. That he just walked right by this officer that was there, between the wall and the car.

Q Did he say an officer called him?

A He said someone hollered at him, but --

Q Did he say he kept on walking?

A Yes, sir.

Q On down into the -- Did he mention that the officer on guard there was assisting Rio Pierce in getting out into traffic, or out onto Main Street?

A If he did I don't recall that, sir.

Q Now, is that an entrance rather than an exit on Main Street?

A Yes, sir. It's an entrance.

Q This was a car going the wrong way coming out of the basement?

A Yes, sir, that's right.

Q It was a police car?

A Yes, sir, it was.

Q He said some officer or someone called to him and he just kept on walking fast?

A Yes, sir.

Q Do you remember anything else in that conversation dealing with why he killed Lee Harvey Oswald?

MR. BELLI: Same objection, same exception.

THE COURT: All right.

MR. TONAHILL: Under arrest and prejudicial.

THE COURT: Overruled.

MR. TONAHILL: Note our exception.

A Yes, sir, there was quite a bit of conversation as to why he had — why he had killed him, later on during the day.

Q (By Mr. Wade) Did he mention seeing him Friday night there in the assembly room?

MR. BELLI: May the answer go out pending the objection? No proper foundation, persons present, time and place. We are entitled to that, Your Honor.

THE COURT: All right. Sustain the objection.

Q (By Mr. Wade) Is this the same conversation in which he told you about the Western Union telegram, and also the information about the dog that defense counsel asked you about?

MR. BELLI: Leading and suggestive.

Q (By Mr. Wade) What are the facts with reference to whether or not this took place in the same conversation that defense counsel asked you about concerning the dog and the Western Union telegram?

MR. TONAHILL: We object to that, Your Honor. He's trying to get him to change his answer. He's already said it took place later on in the day. It's an entirely different conversation.

THE COURT: Go ahead and answer the question.

A I don't recall what point of the day all this conversation took place. He did tell us about being down there Friday night. And at what point of the day this was while he was in

our custody, I don't recall.

MR. BELLI: I just want to protect our record. We object and ask that the answer go out. It could not be part of the res gestae, Your Honor.

THE COURT: Overrule your objection.

MR. WADE: Pass the witness.

RECROSS EXAMINATION

BY MR. BELLI:

Q At some time later in the day, Ruby told you when you had told him that he had shot Mr. Oswald,"you all won't believe this, but I didn't have this planned. I couldn't have planned it so perfect." He said he had just got there and Oswald happened to be coming out and it was a coincidence. Did he say that?

A I believe that's not my statement, sir.

Q What?

A I don't think that's my statement.

Q I'm not asking whether this is your statement. We're going to come to that.

A What was your question?

Q Didn't he say that?

MR. WADE: Judge, we think counsel can sit at the table to question the witness.

MR. BOWIE: He's cross examining him off of another witness's statement.

THE COURT: Come on over here, Mr. Belli. Let's take one thing at a time.

MR. BELLI: All right.

Q (By Mr. Belli) Let's take this very slowly now, sir, so we can understand. On 24 November, 1963, you wrote out a statement. Is that right?

A Yes, sir. I wrote a statement on that day.

Q And the subject of that statement was "assignment for security of Lee Harvey Oswald." Right?

A Yes, sir.

Q All right. Now, you told us this morning and this afternoon, that we would find in that statement where someone called him rat scum and he said that he had to do it because someone else did it. That's right?

A What was that, sir?

Q Do you recall what Captain King said?

MR. ALEXANDER: I didn't understand what he said. Did or did not?

Q (By Mr. Belli) Well, do you recall that you said that Captain King told him that you are a rat scum or something like that? Why did you do it? And he said, that he had to do it because you people couldn't do it?

A I told you this morning sir, that I didn't recall exactly how Captain King worded it. But he did ask him why he did it.

COMMISSION EXHIBIT No. 2409—Continued

Q You also told us you wouldn't find that in this statement, didn't you?

A If I did I don't recall it, sir.

Q Is that in this statement?

A No, sir. Not that I recall.

Q It's not in that statement?

A Not that I know of.

Q Well you know it's not in there, don't you?

A I don't recall it being in there, sir.

Q Let me interrogate you on the other thing now, sir. You recall telling us this morning and this afternoon --

THE COURT: Take your seat, Mr. Belli.

MR. BELLI: Do I have to?

THE COURT: Yes, sir.

Q (By Mr. Belli) Do you recall telling us this morning or this afternoon, probably one of the most damaging things that you've said about Ruby, if he said this, and that is, to-wit; "I shot him three times, and I tried to get off another bullet. I tried to shoot him three times, but you fellows were too fast and I couldn't get off the other bullet." Right?

A I don't --

Q Let me get it exactly for you, sir. "I meant to shoot him three times, but you all moved too fast and prevented me from doing so. I could only get off one shot." Right?

A Yes, sir. I told you that.

COMMISSION EXHIBIT No. 2409—Continued

Q And you told the ladies and gentlemen of the jury this morning under oath, and this afternoon, that also was in this statement, didn't you?
A I said that I had that in a statement, yes, sir.
Q And it's not in there, is it?
A It's in a statement, sir.
Q It is in there?
MR. WADE: Look down at the bottom on the other statement.
MR. BELLI: The other statement?
MR. TONAHILL: Is Mr. Wade going to testify now, Judge?
MR. WADE: He wants to know -- Let him look at it.
MR. TONAHILL: Let him get up in the witness chair with the witness if he's going to do some testifying, Judge.
THE COURT: Take your seat, Mr. Tonahill.
Q (By Mr. Belli) Did you not tell us this morning that that was in the written statement that you made?
A Which time, sir?
Q Are you in doubt now what I'm asking you about?
A I'm asking you which statement, sir.
Q Did you make more than one written statement?
A I wrote one myself. I gave a statement on the departmental investigation.

COMMISSION EXHIBIT No. 2409—Continued

Q Do you know what the word "written statement" means?
A Yes, sir, I do.
Q How many written statements did you make?
A Several.
Q You made several written statements? That you signed?
A Yes, sir.
Q You told us this morning that you only made one written statement, didn't you?
A No, sir. I told you that I wrote one myself, and that is my writing on my copy of the statement.
Q All right. I'll show you here what purports to be a photostat, 24 November, 1963, and at the end of it it has, "Respectfully submitted, T. D. McMillon." Is that your signature there?
A Yes, sir. That's my signature.
Q All right. That is a written statement by you, is that right?
A That's right.
Q Will you tell the ladies and gentlemen of the jury if you made another written statement?
A I gave a statement to Lt. Wallace and Lt. McAghren, I believe was conducting that investigation.
Q Would you answer my question now?
MR. ALEXANDER: I think he did answer it, Your Honor.

COMMISSION EXHIBIT No. 2409—Continued

Q (By Mr. Belli) You gave another written statement to them?

A Yes, sir.

MR. BELLI: May we have that other written statement?

Q (By Mr. Belli) Where is the other written statement?

A I don't know, sir. I thought you had it.

MR. WADE: That's one you've got right there.

Q (By Mr. Belli) You tell us now, sir, that you made more than one written statement, is that right?

A I told you that before. I did, sir.

Q You did tell us that before?

A Yes, sir.

Q All right. We'll check the record. How many written statements did you make? I know this is facetious to you, but it isn't to me.

MR. WADE: We object to that statement, Your Honor.

THE COURT: All right. Let's get on with this.

Q (By Mr. Belli) Trying to get back and forth on the question now, if you'll direct your attention to this we'll be through and go on to something else. How many written, W-R-I-T-T-E-N statements did you make?

A Sir, I wrote this statement myself. On the Saturday, I gave this statement right here to Lt. Wallace and Lt.

COMMISSION EXHIBIT No. 2409—Continued

McAghran. These are two separate statements. You have both of the statements that I'm talking about right here, sir.

Q One was oral, was it not?

A I signed one. The one that I wrote, the original, the first one here.

Q The first one that you signed was November the 24th, is that right?

A I wrote that myself, yes, sir.

Q All right. After that then you gave an oral statement to Lt. Wallace. Right?

A Yes, sir. I gave a statement.

Q And that is not in your handwriting, it is typewritten. Is that correct?

A Yes, sir.

Q And that is not signed by you, but it is signed by Wallace and McAghran. Right?

A Yes, sir.

Q So the only written statement which you've ever made which you signed, was 24 November, 1963. Is that right?

A I wrote that one myself, yes, sir.

Q All right. And after you wrote that statement, you read it, did you not?

A Yes, sir.

Q And you went back and added some corrections, did you not?

COMMISSION EXHIBIT No. 2409—Continued

A Yes, sir.

Q And you were very careful that everything in there reported everything that happened that you could remember on that afternoon, is that right?

A That report that I wrote at that time, sir, is the truth as best that I remembered it then.

Q All right. And in that report, you don't say anything about what Captain King is supposed to have said to Ruby, do you?

A I don't believe I do in the original report, sir.

Q Well, you know you don't. Is that right?

A Yes, sir.

Q All right. But secondly, you don't say anything that happened upstairs about Ruby saying that he intended to shoot him three times either, do you?

A I didn't remember that when I wrote my first one.

Q And if you told us this morning that would be in the written report, written report, if we could get it, you overspoke yourself. Is that right?

MR. ALEXANDER: We object to that, Your Honor. Both of them are written there. One typed and one in the officer's own hand.

THE COURT: Sustain the objection.

Q (By Mr. Belli) Now, on the front of this, what you call your report, is something dated November 30, 1963, J. E.

Curry, Chief of Police, re shooting of Lee Harvey Oswald, signed by Lt. of Juvenile and Lt. of Burglary." Right?

A I believe Lt. Wallace and Lt. Mc[illegible]ghran are --

Q Did you see this after they wrote it?

A Yes, sir.

Q When did you see this?

A Four or five days later, I believe, sir.

Q Did you initial it?

A I don't recall if I did or not, sir.

THE COURT: Take your seat, counsel.

Q (By Mr. Belli) Now, in that report, that's the one in which you say, or which Lt. Wallace says, reporting about you, that you had said, that Ruby had said -- you're following me, aren't you?

A No, sir.

Q Well it's difficult for me too, but this is the way I have to do it.

A All right.

Q Here is a report that is supposed to be submitted by two other policemen, without your signature on it, without your identification on it, to the Chief of Police. It's attached to this report of the 24th and this is dated the 30th, in which you say that Ruby had told you that he had come from the Western Union office, where he wired the girl in Ft. Worth some money. Right?

A I believe that report shows there that I heard him say that he had been to Western Union.
Q All right. And did he tell you that he saw Rio Pierce standing out in the basement?
A I heard him make that statement.
Q And did he say he walked past the policeman standing there?
A The last question you just asked, he didn't tell me he saw him standing out there. He told me he passed him. He was guiding the car.
Q Well, did you notice this error on this when you read it over as you've told us?
A What error, sir? I don't understand what error you're talking about.
Q Ruby said that he walked past the policeman standing there.
A Did I notice the error when? That error in the way you asked me that question a while ago?
Q Which question do you want me to put to you, sir?
A You said that Mr. Ruby saw Mr. Pierce standing in the basement.
Q Here's a report by Wallace to the Chief of Police, saying that he had talked to you over and above your report, and he says that you told him, "He, Ruby, walked past the policeman standing there." Is that right or wrong?

A I heard Mr. Ruby make a statement that he walked down the ramp past Lt. Rio Sam Pierce.
Q Who was standing there?
A No, sir. He was driving out in the car.
Q Well then, this statement is wrong. Did you say it was wrong, if you ever really and honestly read it before. Did you read it before?
A Well certainly I read it before.
Q Well didn't you notice that it said he walked past the policeman standing there?
A That's not Lt. Pierce you're talking about standing there, sir.
Q What?
A That's not Lt. Pierce he's talking about standing there.
Q He said he saw a policeman who hollered at him. Is that right?
A He said he saw a policeman standing there.
Q And he said he saw a policeman and hollered at him. Is that right? Is that what Ruby told you?
A No, sir. He said he saw a policeman standing there and someone yelled or hollered at him. He didn't know if it was a policeman or who it was, but as he was going down the ramp somebody yelled or hollered at him.
Q You say he didn't know if it was a policeman or who it was?

A No, sir.

Q I put it to you that this report says that you said that Ruby said, he Ruby, said a policeman hollered at him, but he ducked his head and kept going. Is that right or wrong?

A He said someone hollered at him, he didn't know if it was a policeman or not.

Q Then this is an error here where he said it was a policeman. Right? Do you follow me?

A No, sir, I don't.

Q Well, I'm having a little trouble today. This report says, that was written by Wallace to the Chief November 30th, that you told him, Wallace, Ruby told you that when he went down the ramp he saw a policeman and hollered at him. Wrong or right? That's a simple question.

A What is the question, sir? I don't understand what the question is.

Q Is this a correct statement of what Ruby told you? That he, Ruby, told you that as he went down the ramp a policeman hollered at him?

A Mr. Ruby told me that as he went down the ramp someone hollered at him. He didn't know if it was a policeman or not, but he just kept on going.

Q All right. So if this says that Ruby told you that a policeman hollered at him, that's in error. Right?

A Yes, sir.

Q All right. And he ducked his head and kept going. Is that correct?

A Mr. Ruby told me he just ducked his head and kept going.

Q And he said he knew he could always act like a reporter?

A Yes, sir.

Q All right. Then he said "Yall --" Y-A-L-L "Yall won't believe this, but I didn't have this planned." Is that right?

A Yes, sir.

Q "I couldn't have planned it so perfect." Right?

A Right.

Q And by that he meant that he was over at Western Union at eleven-seventeen, and the shooting happened about eleven -- what? Twenty-one at the very latest, wasn't it?

A I'm not sure at all of the time on that.

Q All right. He said he just got there and Oswald happened to be coming out at the time, isn't that correct?

A Yes, sir.

Q That's what he told you? Right?

A I heard him make those statements.

Q He also told you he had no premeditation to kill Oswald or anything else, didn't he?

A No, sir. He didn't tell me that.

Q He didn't tell you that?

A No, sir, he sure didn't.

Q What did he mean when he said he just got there and

Oswald was coming out?

A I don't know what he meant. I guess he meant they were getting ready to transfer him from City to County.

Q He also told you that he always carried a gun in the car because he always had some money. Right?

A Yes, he said he usually had large sums of money on him.

Q All right. And you overheard, you overheard Ruby say that after coming out of the Western Union office, he saw the armored car there and came out to see what was going on?

A Would you repeat that, sir?

Q Yes, sir, I sure will. Will you listen?

A I'm trying sir.

Q Here is a statement written by Lt. Wallace to the Chief of Police. And in that statement he is supposed to be quoting you. Some of these things you say are right, some of them you say are wrong. He says that you told him, "I overheard Ruby say that after coming out of the Western Union office, I saw the armored car there and came to see what was going on."

A I don't recall that part of the conversation at all.

Q Well, where did Wallace get that from? Do you know?

A If it's in that report, I'm sure that I told him that. I don't recall that at this time though, sir.

Q Then the next sentence is the first time that anything is ever mentioned. "Ruby said he figured he could get off at least three shots before he would be caught." Now, you don't

COMMISSION EXHIBIT No. 2409—Continued

say anything about that in this original, detailed report, do you? In your own handwriting, which you read over, which your chief told you to give in full and in detail, right? And which you corrected.

A I don't understand what the question is.

Q For the first time that you say anything about Ruby saying he could get off at least three shots before he would get caught, appears as hearsay in this report from Wallace purporting to talk to you orally. That is not in your original, detailed, written and signed report in your handwriting, which you read before you signed, and which you corrected, and which you dated, pursuant to the request of your superior to put anything down that happened according to this event. Right?

A I don't know if it's in that report or not, sir.

Q I can assure you it isn't, and can you explain to me why it isn't, if it happened?

A I can't remember every little detail on one report, sir.

Q It's not a little detail. That's the most damning thing that you've said to date.

MR. ALEXANDER: That was labeled "Investigation of Breach of Security" and counsel well knows that that report was made for a different purpose, investigating a security breach.

MR. TONAHILL: Counsel doesn't know anything of the kind, Your Honor.

COMMISSION EXHIBIT No. 2409—Continued

MR. BOWIE: It's in the record, Your Honor. It's the title of the report, and was put in this record.

MR. TONAHILL: It has eighteen corrections in it.

Q (By Mr. Belli) These are both on security breach, aren't they?

A I would assume that second one you have, the top page that you have, probably is, but it's departmental investigation.

Q They're both departmental investigation, aren't they?

A The first one is what we call a special report that's written on major incidents involving police personnel. I wrote it because I was instructed to do so. What it might be used for, I didn't ask. They told me to write, I wrote it.

Q You checked this out and you made some eighteen corrections in it, didn't you, according to this Zerox?

A Before it was typed.

Q It was typed up then after that, and submitted?

A I assume that it was. I intended for it to be typed when I turned it in.

Q And you intended this to be your official report on everything that transpired then, didn't you?

A That was to be the one that was to be typed from.

Q Which did you think was the most important, to say that Jack was searched, and Jack was clad in his B.V.D.'s, or if it happened, that he said that he wanted to get away three shots

before he was caught, but you fellows are too fast for me? Did you think the latter was just a detail, if it happened? It slipped your mind?

A Well, of course, I wasn't thinking about which was important and which wasn't, when I wrote that report. I wrote a report that covered everything I could remember, the best I could remember, at the time it happened.

Q But you left out the two main things that you tell us about today; one, "all the low life scum things, why did you do it?" "I did it because you guys couldn't." And the other one, "I tried to get away three shots and I couldn't. You guys were too fast for me." Those minor details you left out of your original report, that you did for your supervisor. Subject: Assignment for the Security of Lee Harvey Oswald. Right?

- MR. WADE: Judge, that's all repetitious. He's been through that five or six times.

Q (By Mr. Belli) Let me go into something now that we haven't gone into. In your report you say that before he got upstairs, you took him to property, didn't you?

A Took him where?

Q Do you know what property means? I'm using the jargon as I thought the police department did. Don't you call it property? Don't you call it property department in your police department?

A No, sir. We have a property room.

Q Oh, property room. I said department. It should be property room. Did you take him to the property room?

A No, sir.

Q You didn't. When did he go to the property room, if ever?

A I don't know that he ever went.

Q All right. He would have to go there before he was clad in his B.V.D.'s, wouldn't he?

A No, sir.

Q I know it's funny.

A No, sir, it's not funny.

Q Well, you didn't tell us about him being searched. You put your handcuffs on this man, "and Detective Clardy, Archer, Capt King and I took the man directly to the fifth floor, men's jail, after a preliminary search." So, when was the preliminary search done, and where?

A I believe I testified this morning that the record will reflect it, that I stated before we placed him on the elevator, he was given a preliminary search.

Q When?

A Just as we had taken him up, lifted him up from the floor and stood him on his feet, right there in the jail office. We gave him a real brief one for other weapons, and so on.

COMMISSION EXHIBIT No. 2409—Continued

Q For other weapons. Did you find some eighteen hundred dollars on him at that time?

A I didn't. He had some money on him. I don't know how much.

Q In that preliminary search, did you take that money from him?

A No, sir.

Q Who took that money from him?

A It wasn't done in the preliminary search, sir.

Q What?

A It wasn't done during this preliminary search.

Q Who took the money from him on booking?

A I don't know.

Q "Booking", is that word strange to you?

A Yes, sir. Part of it. The procedure there.

Q All right. You preliminary searched him, is that right?

A Yes, sir.

Q Then you took him upstairs? Right?

A Yes, sir.

Q And the searching wasn't done in that jail office, was it?

A No, sir.

Q But you say in your statement you did a preliminary search in the jail office. Now which is correct?

A Are you talking about the searching, the actual searching

COMMISSION EXHIBIT No. 2409—Continued

A I'm talking about the --

MR. WADE: We object to that. He's answered every question.

MR. BELLI: May I approach the witness, Your Honor?

THE COURT: If you want to use the statement, yes, sir.

Q (By Mr. Belli) You state here, "I took the man to, directly to the fifth floor man's jail, after a preliminary search in the jail office." Now, where is the jail office?

A Right on the floor where he was laying, where we handcuffed him.

Q Well, isn't that inside that foyer? This isn't the jail office here, is it? Let me put it up here so you can see it. This isn't the jail office here, is it? Out here, is this the jail office?

A I can't tell from that picture there whether that's the jail office or not.

Q You can't tell by these pictures. You've got your "M" over here. You don't know where you were standing?

A There's more to that.

Q Where is the elevator here? Could you tell us where the elevator is?

A As you go in through --

Q On this one, so we won't have to extrapolate. I mean

so we won't have to orient ourselves on something else.

A If this is the jail office, the elevator door would be at an angle back over here where the bars are.

Q All right. The jail office is a different room from the elevator, isn't it, of course?

A Yes, sir.

Q And the jail office is an office that's off to the side of this door here in this picture, isn't that correct? If you look through here?

A That's similar to it.

Q When you say here, that you did a preliminary search in the jail office, that wasn't inside of the elevator, was it?

A It possibly could have been, sir. They're in the same -- the jail office has an entrance to the elevator on it.

Q Is the jail office seperate from the entrance to the elevator? Is there a door and partition between the jail office and the hallway to the elevator?

A Sir, in the jail office there's a section that's partitioned off.

Q Partitioned off. Right?

A Stands up, say, about this high.

Q And it was behind those partitions that there was a preliminary search made? Right?

A No, sir, there was not.

Q Then when you said here, "After a preliminary search in

the jail office" that's not correct. Right?

A It is correct, sir.

Q Then on the fifth floor, was Ruby searched and stripped?

A With the exception of his shorts.

Q Now, will you tell the ladies and gentlemen of the jury if this was before he said, "I wanted to shoot him three times," or did he say that while they were taking his pants off?

A I don't recall at what point that was. It was when I was returning.

Q Try and see if you can help us a little bit on that, would you?

A I tried this morning, Mr. Belli. I don't know at what point it was that I came back. It was at the point that I was coming back that I heard him tell Detective Archer this.

Q Well let's see if we can go a little slower on that. He comes up to the fifth floor, and as soon as he got up on the fifth floor, you instructed the jailers to search this man and strip him. Now, did you have a conversation with him before that was done?

A There was probably some words spoken. I don't recall them.

Q When were these words spoken, if they were spoken, about the shooting three times, but you fellows were too fast for me?

A As I was returning from taking care of some other

details.

Q So you do remember now that it was after he had his pants off, is that right, sir?

A No, sir, I don't know whether he had his pants off or on, or what.

Q Well, you would know certainly, if the man was clad just in his shorts, wouldn't you, when he said this, that you don't have in your report?

A As I was returning from taking care of these other details, like I told you, sir, he was telling Detective Archer that. Detective Archer had asked him that, and this conversation was going on.

Q You think that it was after he was stripped and searched, right?

A I don't know, sir.

Q All right. Let's get the sequence of events. As soon as you got to the fifth floor you instructed the jailers to search this man and strip him, leaving him clad only in his shorts, right?

A Yes.

Q And you also instructed the jail doctor to come and examine him, right?

A No, sir, I didn't personally instruct the jail doctor to examine him.

Q Someone has added this into the statement then, if you

218 416

didn't do that. Do you want to look at this part?

A It's in there. We instructed them to go for the --

Q When did you look at this last, that you remembered it was in there? At noon time?

A No, sir.

Q When did you last look at that?

A A while ago when you handed it to me.

Q Well, I didn't show you that page.

A I don't know whether you did or didn't, sir.

Q Well I do. What I showed you was the other page.

A Could have been. That's the last time I saw the report was when you handed it to me a while ago, sir.

Q Let's go on. You told the jail doctor to come and examine him immediately, right?

A I didn't personally tell the jail doctor.

Q Well, someone told him while you were there, is that right?

A We left instructions for the jail personnel to send up the doctor, to examine the man.

Q How long was it before the jail doctor got there?

A It was later on in the afternoon, sir.

Q About what time?

A Well, I don't know, sir.

Q And then you said, "I stayed with this prisoner from eleven-twenty-five A.M. until relieved by Homicide detectives

COMMISSION EXHIBIT No. 2409—Continued

219 417

at three-twenty-five in the afternoon."

MR. WADE: Judge, I believe you instructed counsel to sit down. He can ask all these questions from over there.

MR. BELLI: It's hard to break a habit of some thirty years, Judge, but I'll try.

THE COURT: I'll help you, Mr. Belli.

MR. BELLI: I know Your Honor will, and that's the reason I did it before Your Honor helped me.

Q (By Mr. Belli) Now, you stayed with him from eleven-twenty-five A.M., you didn't -- when you changed the front of the statement at approximately eleven-twenty-five A.M. where did you get that information that the shooting was eleven twenty-five A.M., rather than eleven twenty-one?

A I'm just -- at that time, I was just trying to think back how long I had been down there. I knew about what time I got to the basement. I was trying to figure about how long I had been there before it happened.

Q When did you say you had fixed it at eleven twenty-five? You know now it's eleven twenty, twenty-one, don't you?

A I don't know what time it was, sir.

Q All right. But you changed it back over here on the first page of the statement, or the second page. Right?

A Well, I don't know. If it's changed -- let's see if it's my writing.

COMMISSION EXHIBIT No. 2409—Continued

Q I'd be interested in that too.
A What part are you talking about?
Q Right here. "Approximately eleven twenty-five."
A No, sir, I didn't change that. That's just the beginning of the sentence that I added onto it.
Q It's something that you added onto it?
A Yes, sir. That's the way I wanted to start the sentence.
Q You put eleven twenty-five in the body over here on page -- let's see what this is here -- page five, and then you come back and interlineate on the second page. Had you been discussing this with any of your brother officers at that time?
A Captain Nichols -- No, sir, I hadn't. Captain Nichols told us to write the thing, and there was several officers in the room there, that had some part in the security detail, and everybody was writing their own. He instructed us to do it that way.
Q You were all in one room writing your report, is that right?
A I say we were all there. I don't know if all the officers out of our Auto Theft Bureau were in this one room. Part of them may have been in the Lieutenent's office, or the Captain's office, but a bunch of us was in this one room.
Q Let me ask you the direct question. Who was in the one room writing reports?

COMMISSION EXHIBIT No. 2409—Continued

221

A Myself and several other detectives.
Q Who? Who?
A Detective Clardy was there, Detective Archer, Detective Dawson was there, and I don't know who else.
Q Did you discuss your reports with the other officers?
A No, sir. Captain Nichols told us to write them ourselves.
Q Did you discuss the report with the other officers before you wrote them?
A Did I -- Sir?
Q Did you talk about the reports you were going to write before you started writing them?
A We didn't know we were going to have to write them.
Q Did you discuss the events with the other officers before you were told to write a report?
A Yes, sir.
Q About what time was that?
A Oh, I don't know at what point. It was during this four hours that we were in and out of the jail up there.
Q Did you tell us what time the doctor showed up?
A I told you sir, that I didn't know what time the doctor showed up. It was later in the day.
Q When did you take your handcuffs off of Ruby?
A After we had arrived on the fifth floor.
Q And when you took your handcuffs off of him, he was

COMMISSION EXHIBIT No. 2409—Continued

clothed in his civilian clothes, right?
A Yes, sir, he was.
Q And the next thing that was done was that he was searched and stripped, is that right?
A I don't know exactly -- if that was exactly the next detail or not, but shortly thereafter he was searched and stripped.
Q And that's your regular procedure? You take him upstairs and search and strip him immediately, isn't it?
A No, sir, it is not.
Q But your recollection in this case, is that what you did?
A Yes, sir, we did take him upstairs.
Q And who was the man into whose custody you gave him to search and strip him?
A I don't recall for sure what jailer or jail guard that was, sir. One of the men that was on duty that day, sir.
Q Was Archer standing there next to you then?
A Archer and Clardy and I were there during this. I was in and out some.
Q And where did they search and strip him, in that room or in another room?
A Next to the telephone booth that the prisoners use in the jail.
Q All right. But you didn't go into the room where they

Commission Exhibit No. 2409—Continued

were searching and stripping him?
A It wasn't a room. It was more or less the hallway, sir.
Q All right. Well, was he within your sight all that time?
A No, sir.
Q So what he said during that time, or what was said to him, you don't know?
A No, sir.
Q And you didn't see him again then for how long, about ten or fifteen minutes?
A No, sir. I wasn't gone that long. I was maybe around to check on if his hat was sent up, to check on that, to see if it was his or if it was mine, and around on some other details like that, sir.
Q Mr. Sorrels from the secret service came up to see him, and Mr. Hukl of the F.B.I. What time did they get there?
A Mr. Sorrels came in with Sgt. Dean. Sgt. Dean brought him up there. And that was about -- after we had been on the fifth floor -- that was about five minutes after we had gotten there.
Q After you submitted this report, how long did you say it took you to write this report of November 24?
A Probably forty-five minutes on that, sir.
Q And after you submitted that report, then you next heard from Lt. Wallace, didn't you?

Commission Exhibit No. 2409—Continued

A Well, we were advised to be at this departmental investigation, and learned that Lt. Wallace and Lt. McAghran were doing part of the investigation, sir.

Q Then at that time, had you thought about your report in the meantime?

A Yes, I suppose I had, not especially though, sir.

Q What?

A I suppose that I had.

Q Now, Did Wallace interrogate you, or did you make voluntary statements to Wallace in this report that he sent on to Chief Curry?

A It was sort of a question and answer interview.

Q Did he make suggestions, or did you furnish all the information?

A He asked me some questions. I answered them the best I could. I told the man the truth.

Q You told him that you had been interviewed by the Federal Bureau of Investigation?

A Yes, sir, I did.

Q And when did you tell him that the Federal Bureau of Investigation had interviewed you?

A I don't know if I told him that or not, sir.

Q I want you to listen carefully, if you will, to these next few questions. We have on the 24th of November, the report of six pages that you signed, right?

COMMISSION EXHIBIT No. 2409—Continued

A I don't know how many pages is in it. I wrote a report on the 24th.

Q I have what purports to be a Zerox copy of something here. There was something that was attached to this too. Do you know what was attached to this? It shows the clips on there, but there is nothing attached to this now.

A Probably where they unstapled it when they typed it.

Q There's no staples over here. You don't know what was attached to it?

A No.

Q All right. That's on 24 November, then on 30 November --

MR. ALEXANDER: I believe you pulled that up, because I stapled that myself in full view of the Court a while ago.

MR. BELLI: I'm referring to these staples over here, on the side.

MR. BOWIE: It's not in evidence.

MR. TONAHILL: Everything there is in evidence.

MR. WADE: Tonahill says it's all in evidence, so let's let it --

MR. BELLI: Mr. Belli doesn't say that though.

MR. BOWIE: We have no objection.

MR. BELLI: I know you don't, but I'm not putting in a self serving statement by a man that I can't cross

COMMISSION EXHIBIT No. 2409—Continued

225

examine; to-wit, Wallace and McAghran.

Q (By Mr. Belli) Now, between the 24th of November and the 30th of November, did you tell the F.B.I. these two things; one, what King is reported to have said to Ruby, and two, what Ruby is reported by you to have said upstairs about trying to fire three times? You didn't tell that to the F.B.I., did you? If it were true.

A Well, it is true, sir. And I did tell them about him going to fire three times, and I don't remember if I told them about this other, or not. But I don't believe I did.

Q You don't believe you told them that? Are you positive you told about Ruby saying that he wanted to get three bullets off?

A Yes, sir.

Q When did you remember that then, after 24 November?

A When did I remember what, sir?

Q Well, you don't have it in this report. You don't have either of those things in this detailed report. You now say between 24 November and November 30th you remembered one of them. You told one to the F.B.I.?

A I guess I remembered it all the time. I just failed to put it in the report. I didn't remember it then. I probably knew it.

Q Is it your best recollection that you told that to the F.B.I.?

227

A I told the F.B.I. everything that I could recall about the case, as best I could at the time.

Q What is the answer to my question? Did you tell the F.B.I. these two subjects; one, the King statement, "You rat why did you shoot him? I had to because you wouldn't." And two, the statement in the jail, if it happened, "I tried to get off three shots, but you were too fast and I couldn't." What did you tell the F.B.I.?

MR. ALEXANDER: Judge, we object to it. The question has been asked and a definite answer has been had. It's repetitious.

THE COURT: Sustain the objection. Let's move on.

MR. BELLI: We had one this morning, and it's at variance with this one.

MR. TONAHILL: I haven't heard any definite answer out of this man yet, Judge. I've seen a lot of evading.

MR. BOWIE: We object, Your Honor. This is no call for such a statement.

MR. TONAHILL: There shouldn't be any call for it.

Q (By Mr. Belli) Now, where was Jack interviewed by the F.B.I.? In which room?

A Part of this interview took place in one of the halls, back near the jail cells.

Q Where is it?

A In a little hallway, in one of the cell blocks, near

the jail cells.

Q Was anyone present from the Dallas Police when the F.B.I. interviewed him?

A I was present part of the time. Clardy was present some of the time, Archer was present some of the time.

Q Did the F.B.I. take notes of what was said?

A The man was making some notes. I'm assuming that's what he was taking.

Q All right. And did not Jack Ruby tell the F.B.I. that he didn't know about shooting Oswald? What did he tell the F.B.I. about whether he had shot Oswald or not?

A I didn't hear that part, sir.

Q You mean to say the F.B.I. was talking to him there about Oswald being dead, and you were there and you didn't hear Ruby say anything about whether he intended to shoot Oswald or did shoot Oswald?

A I wasn't present all the time. I didn't hear them ask him that statement, and I didn't hear Mr. Ruby answer that statement to the F.B.I. agent.

Q You didn't hear that statement asked by the F.B.I.?

A No, sir. There was quite a bit of conversation as I recall. I didn't hear that question asked by the F.B.I.

Q There was a quite a bit of conversation about what subject? The shooting of Oswald?

A One thing that I remember that this F.B.I. agent

seemed to be getting into, he was trying to get a lot of background history on Mr. Ruby. Exactly how that conversation went, word for word, I don't remember, but that seemed to be the point or the purpose.

Q Didn't you tell the F.B.I. "Ruby just told us he wanted to shoot him three times"?

A Yes, but that's not what you asked me.

Q Well, I ask you now, did you tell that to the F.B.I. at that time?

A I don't know at what point I told it to him.

Q Did you tell the F.B.I. at that time, that afternoon, when Ruby was talking with the F.B.I., "Why, Ruby told us he wanted to shoot Oswald three times"?

A I told the F.B.I. that in my statement. I didn't interfere with the man while he was talking to Mr. Ruby.

Q You didn't do what?

A I didn't interfere with the F.B.I. agent while he was talking to him.

Q And all the time the F.B.I. and Ruby were talking, at no time did he say anything about intending to shoot Oswald, or shooting Oswald, or anything else in that line, did he?

A I didn't hear that question asked to him, or I didn't hear an answer, not to this agent.

Q Not to the agent. How long was that agent there?

A I don't know, sir. He was there quite a while.

Q About an hour and a half?
A Probably so.
MR. BELLI: That's all I have.

REDIRECT EXAMINATION

BY MR. WADE:
Q Now, let me see this statement here, Mr. McMillon. With reference to this statement Archer made to Ruby on the fifth floor of the Dallas County Jail, is it your testimony that between the 24th of November and the 30th, you related that to the F.B.I.?
MR. BELLI: Wait a minute. There's nothing in that report whatsoever of any statement Archer made in the jail, in either the so-called original report, or the report by Wallace.
MR. TONAHILL: It would be hearsay to the defendant.
THE COURT: Read that question back, will you Mrs. Stinebaugh?
(Whereupon the last question was read by the court reporter)
MR. BELLI: Now, are you referring to a statement made in here, or --
MR. WADE: I'm referring to the statement made by Jack Ruby on the fifth floor, where he said in substance, "I thought I could get off three shots before

I was stopped." Roughly to that effect.
Q (By Mr. Wade) Did you relate that to the F.B.I. between the 24th of November and the 30th of November?
A Yes, sir, I did.
Q Now, I'll direct your attention to the 30th of November, when you were interviewed by Lt. Wallace and P. C. McAghran, did you inform them at that time that the defendant, Jack Ruby, on the fifth floor of the jail, as you have testified, said he meant to shoot three times, but he was stopped before he could?
A Yes, sir.
MR. WADE: That's all.
MR. BELLI: I have no further questions. May we have the statement for identification?
MR. WADE: We'll leave it with the court reporter here, for the record. It's marked for identification.
THE COURT: We'll stand in recess until 9:00 o'clock tomorrow morning.

AFTERNOON SESSION

MARCH 4, 1964

(Following the noon recess period proceedings were resumed before the Jury, as follows:)

JOHN RUTLEDGE,

a witness called by the State, being first duly sworn, testified on his oath as follows:

DIRECT EXAMINATION

BY MR. WADE:

Q Your name is John Rutledge?

A Yes.

Q And how are you employed sir?

A I am a newspaper reporter, Dallas Morning News.

Q How long have you been with the Dallas News, Mr. Rutledge?

A About twelve years.

Q Do you have any certain beat you are covering or were covering on the 24th of November, last year?

A Yes, I am the night police reporter.

Q For the Dallas News, at the City Hall?

A Yes sir.

Q Directing your attention back to the afternoon and evening of the 22nd of November, the day of the assassination of the President, where were you at that time?

COMMISSION EXHIBIT No. 2410

A At the time the shot was fired?

Q Later on in the afternoon?

A Well, I am night police reporter, I come to work about 5:00 o'clock in the afternoon, but I came in early, I reported directly at the police station on the third floor, and was covering the activities inside Captain Fritz's office.

Q Now, you are familiar with the layout on the third floor of the police department, are you not?

A Yes.

Q Will you tell the Jury generally how it is laid out, what offices, and where with reference to the Homicide Office?

A Well, directly across the hall from the Homicide Office is the Burglary and Theft Bureau; at one extreme end of the hall is the Press Room. And the opposite direction from the Press Room, past Captain Fritz's office, is where Homicide is located. And there is a door that enters into the elevator used as the jail elevator to take prisoners either up to the jail or downstairs to the jail desk.

Q Now, that is a long corridor down that way; and there's one down the other way also?

A Yes sir, on the other end of the corridor or the office of the Police Chiefs.

Q The elevator corridor comes in from the side, is that right?

A Yes, that's right.

COMMISSION EXHIBIT No. 2410—Continued

Q That is the main elevator.
A Yes.
Q On that occasion, did you see the Defendant, Jack Ruby, there on the third floor of the Dallas Police Department?
A Yes. I saw him right outside of Captain Fritz's office, in the hall.
Q Now, directing your attention back to the elevator first, did you at any time -- you recognize the Defendant sitting in the courtroom over here, do you not, as Jack Ruby?
MR. BELLI: We will stipulate the identification if he knows him.
A Yes sir.
Q Did you see how he gained entrance from the elevator into the third floor?
A That's a public elevator.
Q A public elevator?
A Yes sir. At one time I saw him come from the elevator door, past the police guards who were keeping everybody except members of the Press out of that hallway, in front of the Homicide Office.
MR. ALEXANDER: Could you talk a little bit louder, please sir.
Q About what time of night was this, do you know?
A Oh, it was sometime probably between 6:00 o'clock and 8:00 o'clock.

Q Go ahead and tell how you saw him get by the guard -- before I ask you that, describe to the Jury what was in all the corridors on the third floor of that building, by way of television cameras, or the Press present from other parts of the country?
A Well, at the entrance to the corridor that leads to Captain Fritz's office, in which I often sit, there was a tangle of cables, and there were three tripods; and on each one of those tripods, there were a lot of bright lights that were shining down the hall, blinding if you looked at them, and a couple of live television cameras were there; and the rest of the hall was a packed mass of newspaper and television reporters and camera men, jammed in like sardines in a can on this floor.
Q Now, let's go back, were there police guards at the elevator, as you came in, to check all who were coming in?
A Yes.
Q Now, go ahead and tell us, how you saw, if you did see Jack Ruby, the Defendant, get by the guards there?
A Well, I saw Jack and two out-of-State reporters, whom I did not know, leave the elevator door and proceed toward those television cameras, to go around the corner where Captain Fritz's office was. Jack walked between them. These two out-of-State reporters had big Press cards pinned on their coats, great big red ones, I think they said, "President

Kennedy's visit to Dallas -- Press", or something like that.

And Jack didn't have one, but the man on either side of him did. And they walked pretty rapidly from the elevator area past the policeman, and Jack was bent over like this -- writing on a piece of paper, and talking to one of the Reporters, and pointing to something on the piece of paper, he was kind of hunched over.

Q And did that put him in the corridor on the third floor of the Police City Hall up there?

A That's right. The three of them just walked past the policeman, around the corner, past those cameras and lights, and on down the hall.

Q Now, directing your attention to Captain Fritz's and the Homicide office, that opens into the corridor there, did you see while you were there, Lee Harvey Oswald being brought in or out of the Homicide, more than once, or once, or any time?

A Yes sir, several times they brought him out from Homicide.

Q Is that where they were interrogating him, in Homicide, as far as you know?

A Yes sir, that's where he was being interrogated.

Q Now, did you ever see the Defendant, Jack Ruby -- let's get the time again, approximately what time on Friday night was this -- did you see him outside of the Homicide Bureau?

COMMISSION EXHIBIT No. 2410—Continued

A The first I saw him was, he was standing right outside the Homicide Bureau door. It must have been around 6:00 or 7:00 o'clock.

Q 6:00 or 7:00 o'clock?

A I am not real sure of the time.

Q It was early in the evening though, you hadn't been there too long, I presume?

A No sir. I think I had been there a couple of hours at least before that.

Q Now, during that time, tell the Jury what, if anything, he did with reference to -- was he saying or doing anything there outside the Homicide Department, where they were interrogating Oswald?

A Sure was.

Q Tell the Jury what you remember.

A He was explaining to members of the out-of-State Press, who everybody was that came in and out of that door; occasionally, for instance, if Captain Fritz stepped out the door and addressed the Press and told them the progress of the investigation, all these reporters were making notes of everything that was said, and then Captain Fritz would go back in the office. And then all the reporters, being strangers in town, would start asking each other who that was -- "Was that Sheriff Decker?"

I heard Jack say, "No, that was not Sheriff Decker.

COMMISSION EXHIBIT No. 2410—Continued

That was Captain Fritz."

Someone would ask, "Who is Captain Fritz?"

"How do you spell it?"

There would be a thousand questions shot at him at once, and Jack would straighten them all out and tell them -- "You spell it W-i-l-l F-r-i-t-z, he is the Homicide Captain."

And then they would say, "Who is the Sheriff, we thought he was the Sheriff?"

And then he would spell out Sheriff Decker's name.

One time the District Attorney, Mr. Wade came out and then went back in, and they asked who that was, if that was Captain Fritz, and Jack explained to all of them and told them that it wasn't Captain Fritz, that it was Henry Wade, that he was the District Attorney.

Q He was just generally furnishing all the out-of-State Press, who everybody was that was there?

A Yes sir. He was very good making identification to the strangers.

Q Now, let me ask you, did any officer or somebody from over toward across the hall, ask Jack Ruby anything with reference to what he was doing there?

A Yes sir. I heard two, possibly three detectives speak to him. One of them I remember was standing near the Burglary and Theft Bureau door.

MR. BELLI: I didn't hear you, I am sorry.

A I was standing near the Burglary and Theft Bureau door, which is directly across the hall and offset to it, maybe two or three feet from Captain Fritz's door.

Q How wide is that corridor, could you judge it, say between you and the rail here at the Jury box, from one wall to the other?

A I suppose it's as far as from myself to the first Juror over there.

Q That is the width of the one corridor?

A The width of the hall, yes sir.

Q Was he asked any questions by anyone that you heard?

A One of these detectives knew him and yelled -- he had to yell almost at the top of his voice in the hallway to be heard, in fact all this I have testified to previously about the things Jack told the visiting reporters, that was shouted at the top of his lungs, everybody had to shout to be heard by the man right next to him, and they were all crammed together pretty tight.

This detective hollered over in the crowd and said words something like, "Hey Jack, what are you doing here?"

Q What did Jack Ruby say, if anything?

A He raised -- he got his arm out of that mass of people and waved his hand at this detective and said, "Hello there" -- and he called him by his first name and he said, "I am helping all these fellows." And he turned around and he pointed.

Q He said he was helping out, indicating the members of the Press that were jammed in that corridor?
A Yes sir. And he was helping them.
Q Now, that was 6:00 or 7:00 o'clock in the evening. And now, later on that night did you see him anywhere?
A Later on that night I saw him, it was after that I saw him come past the police guard, from the public elevator down in the corridor.
And then I saw him again about midnight, in the basement, in the assembly room.
Q Was that on Friday night the 22nd of November?
A Yes sir.
Q 1963?
A Yes, it was.
Q Was that the conference where they brought Oswald in there in front of the Press?
A Yes sir, it was.
Q Where was Ruby, the best of your recollection at that time?
A At the time that Oswald was interviewed by the Press?
Q Yes.
A Well, I didn't see him while Oswald was there. My attention was focussed on Oswald. And Oswald was all I could see.
Q Well, Oswald was there a couple of minutes, or three

minutes probably?
A Yes.
Q And after he was gone, the Press then started asking me some questions. I was there, was I not?
A Yes, you were there.
Q Did you see at that time Jack Ruby in the audience anywhere?
A Yes sir. He was just about directly in front of you, about as far from you as you and I are now, I believe. There were two little tables in this assembly room, and you were on the platform, and he was behind the second table.
Q During that conference there, was the question asked something about some Cuban movement, with reference to Oswald; did someone ask me about that?
A Some reporter asked you if Oswald was linked with being a member of the Cuban movement in this country.
Q I believe I answered something about the free Cuba movement, or something to that effect, didn't I?
A Yes, you did.
Q Now, at that time did the Defendant, Jack Ruby, say anything from out in the audience; did he volunteer any information?
A That's the time he answered the question, before you could answer it.
Q And he gave the name of the "Fair Play for Cuba

8

Committee," I believe?

A He gave the accurate name.

Q I had called it the organization --

A You had it a little bit wrong, and he knew it, and he straightened you out on it.

Q He said it's the Fair Play for Cuba, is that about right, or something to that effect?

A Yes sir, that's right.

Q And this went on until say 12:30 or 1:00 o'clock in the morning, on Saturday morning the 23rd?

A Yes sir, it was at least that late, 1:00 or 1:30.

MR. WADE: Pass the witness.

CROSS EXAMINATION

BY MR. BELLI:

Q Did he speak that very bitterly, in answer to Mr. Wade, that Mr. Oswald was a member of the Fair Play for Cuba Committe, I mean as though he were angry, an angry shout from the crowd?

A No sir. That was not my impression. It was more that it was shouted because nearly everything was shouted.

Q You had to shout.

A You had to shout as loud in the assembly room as you did up in the hall. It was more of an explanatory statement.

Q That is the subversive group, isn't it? At least, we are led to believe, the Fair Play for Cuba?

COMMISSION EXHIBIT No. 2410—Continued

4-32 [redacted]

WILLIAM G. SERUR

a witness called by the Defendant, having first been duly sworn, testified on his oath as follows:

DIRECT EXAMINATION

BY MR. TONAHILL:

Q Please state your name, your age, your occupation, and place of residence to the Court and jury?

A My name is William G. Serur. I live at 1248 Stevens Ridge Drive. I'm self employed. I'm a salesman for myself. I sell out of my car, and I travel Dallas and Ft. Worth.

Q How do you spell your last name?

A S-E-R-U-R.

Q How old are you?

A Fifty-one.

Q You live here in Dallas?

A Yes, sir.

Q You're fifty-one?

A Yes, sir.

Q How long have you lived here?

A About twenty-seven or twenty-eight years.

Q And you are a salesman?

A Yes, sir.

Q What do you sell?

A Drug sundries and novelties.

Q Did you ever engage in the upholstery business?

COMMISSION EXHIBIT No. 2411

A Yes, sir.
Q Do you know Jack Ruby, the defendant here?
A Yes, sir. I know him very well.
Q How long have you known Jack?
A I would say in the neighborhood of around eleven or twelve years.
Q Have you had occasion to visit him in his place of business, or elsewhere?
A Yes, sir.
Q Do you know Jack Ruby's personality and his mental make-up, his behavior pattern and so forth?
A Well, sir, I met Jack about -- are you asking me what did I think about him when I met him?
Q I said do you know his behavior pattern, his personality, his temperment and disposition?
A Yes, sir. I found him to be a very emotional man.
Q That's what I want to know. You say you found him to be a very emotional man?
A Yes, sir.
Q Just what do you have in mind?
A Well, he -- in my opinion he wasn't like most of the men that I've met, the people I've met. He was high strung and he was -- well, he was just the type man that he would never stay in one place long enough to really talk with him. He was on the go all the time. And I tried to make him out

COMMISSION EXHIBIT No. 2411—Continued

from the beginning, but it was awful hard for me to figure him out.
Q You consider him then to be highly emotional, and a very unstable person?
A I would say that's right.
Q Have you had occasion to witness quick and instantaneous outbursts of rage by Jack Ruby while you were present?
A Well, the -- I have noticed that at his Vegas Club, yes, sir.
Q Did you ever have occasion to visit one of his competitors and find that they were overflowing with business, and then go to see Jack when his business wasn't so good, and tell him about it?
A Yes, sir, I have.
Q Tell us about it. What happened? What was Jack's reaction?
A Well, Jack always didn't like me coming up and telling him about any of his competitors. He said, "I don't want to hear anything about my competitors."
Q Just start at the beginning now, and tell us what you saw and what you went over and told Jack about? What happened?
A This was the last Saturday in October, or I would say it was the first Saturday in November. I cannot recollect that -- which date it was. That night about ten o'clock, I took my wife home, and I told her I was going downtown. I had

COMMISSION EXHIBIT No. 2411—Continued

heard someone tell me that Abe's Colony Club had a terrific show, and I found great relaxation in going to shows, so I decided I'd go there. I got up there about ten-thirty that night, on a Saturday night, and when I got up to the top of the steps, the smoke was pouring out of there, and people were standing there waiting to go in, and there was no seating there available at that particular time, so I had to stand at the wall. And the M.C. was terrific and the girls they had was real good, and I was enjoying it even though I didn't have a seat. So, I guess I stayed there until about eleven-thirty. And the show was over, and I enjoyed it much, and I said, I guess I'll take a little run and go over and see Jack. When I got to where the Carousel Club entrance is, I walked up the stairs, and when I got to the top of the stairs, I looked to the right there and left, and I couldn't see anything except -- his club was real dark, and I guess there was about five or six people in there. I looked over to my left, to the post that I always found Jack at, where he turns the lights on the stage. Jack had his hands to his back and pacing back and forth, looking at the floor. And I stood there for a minute, and I said, I'm really surprised at the kind of crowd that Jack has here. So I said, I guess I'll just walk over to where he is. I walked about ten steps and turned to my left, and Jack was still pacing back and forth. I walked up to Jack and he looked at me, and he didn't say a word for a second. And the

lights was shining right on Jack's face, the light was showing right on him, and I said, say Jack, I just got in -- came in from Abe's Colony Club and he had a tremendous crowd, one of the largest crowds that I have ever seen. I can't figure this out. Jack kind of tilted his head over to one side, I could see the intent in his eyes. What the intent was, I didn't know, but Jack started in on me and he said, what do you mean coming up here telling me about this competitor of mine. I'm not interested in my competitors. I feel bad enough as it is. Do you see the crowd I have? Don't you do this to me any more. I froze and was petrified. I couldn't even move for a second, and I didn't -- I just dared not say a word. I just didn't say another word.

Q Mr. Serur, describe again what he did. He turned his head, twisted sideways?

A Jack, when he gets mad, he doesn't walk to you straight and look at you. He kind of tilts a little bit, and he explodes without warning, and that's the way he did me. And I just stood there.

Q What kind of a look did he have in his eyes?

A I kept looking at those eyes, and I got scared. And I knew I said too much. He kept raving like a mad man, and he said, "Don't you ever do this to me again. If you want to come to my club I don't want to hear this kind of stuff any more. I'm telling you now and you'd better be careful."

Q All right. Did he have a wild look in his eyes?
A he looked wild enough to me, he had me scared.
Q Why were you scared?
A Because I wasn't used to Jack getting into that type of outburst.
Q Well, did he get over it suddenly, or what?
A I kept my back to him when he walked away, and I walked about two or three feet and I saw a little table and a chair, and I decided I'd better get right there, but first I decided I'd better leave. And I said, "No, Jack will get mad." So I looked towards the bar, the bar is over to the left, and he walked to the bar and the man gave him a glass of water, the bartender. And then Jack disappeared into the right corner. And I was sitting there and didn't know what to do, and I was pretty scared. I would say about seven or eight minutes later, then I said, "This is it" and Jack started walking toward me and I said, "Now, what's he going to say", and he walked up to me. When he walked up to me he was a different person altogether and he walked right straight to me and he laid his shoulder on my hand, and said, "Kid, you want a cup of coffee?" He said, "Get me one too, black coffee, no sugar and no milk."
Q You just said he laid his shoulder on your hand.
A I mean laid his hand on my shoulder.
Q What did he say about the coffee?
A He said, "Why don't you get yourself a cup of coffee,

COMMISSION EXHIBIT NO. 2411—Continued

and fix me one, black, no cream and no sugar." I think that's what he wanted. He said, "You'll find the coffee behind that little wall, right behind that little wall."
Q Was he calm?
A He was just as cool and calm as I ever saw him.
Q Did he apologize for what he'd just said to you?
A I never found Jack to be an apologetic type person.
Q Did he appear to you as though he realized he had just bawled you out in a fit of emotional rage?
A He acted as if nothing had happened, or as if he had said nothing.
Q How long did you stay there and talk?
A He stood up drinking this coffee and said, "I don't want you to leave. I've got this girl, Jada, and I want you to see her and tell me what you think about her."
Q Have you see Jack in these outbursts on numerous occasions?
A Yes, I have.
Q Does he cool off rather quickly, and not mention them as though nothing ever happened?
A I will say this with true respect for Jack, that when he explodes and gets mad, he does it quicker than any person I ever seen, but he can cool off quicker than any person I ever saw.
Q Have you always been astounded and terrified by those

COMMISSION EXHIBIT NO. 2411—Continued

88-381 O—64—vol. XXV——33

instantaneous violent tempers of his?

A Yes, sir. I saw a lot of that at the Vegas Club on Oak Lawn.

Q Did you ever see Jack with his dogs, or talk to him about his dogs?

A Yes, sir.

Q What did he refer to the dogs as?

A He called them my children and my kids.

Q How did he feel about those dogs?

A Well, in order to tell you about that, I would have to tell you about the telephone call I received from Jack.

Q Go right ahead.

A I received a telephone call from Jack one day, and he said he wanted me to put seat covers on his automobile. I said, "What's wrong with your seat covers, Jack?" And he said, "Well, I'll let you look at them and then you can tell me what I'll need." So I said, "Jack, I won't be able to see you today, but tomorrow evening at three o'clock I'll drive down there and see you." And he said, "Look Bill, I'll be parked on the Field Street side, or my car might be in the garage" but he said, "I'll meet you then." I said, "Fine, I'll be there at three o'clock." So at three o'clock the next morning -- I mean the next day, I drove to Field Street and noticed an Oldsmobile parked, but I didn't look into it because I wanted to get around there quick to where Jack was.

When I made the corner to go where the Carousel Club was, I looked to the left and Jack was stooping down opening up dog food. There was a little ledge inside of the garage, the parking station, and I would say there was three or four dogs -- and Jack used to always tell me, "I don't want you to refer to them as dogs." He said, "Those are my children." He said, "Don't you have children?" He said, "Don't you respect them?" He said, "I respect my kids." He said, "They go wherever I go and I want you to not call them dogs any more." So he had names for them, but I couldn't recall what the names was. So as he was opening up the dog food, his left hand was bleeding profusely. It wasn't scratches, it was deep gashes.

Q He cut it on the can?

A As he was opening up -- he had that type that you go up and down, but he was cutting his hand. And I said, "Jack, how come your hand's all cut up?" And he said, "It'll be all right." And about that time, blood was all over his hand, and the largest of the dogs was licking the blood off of his hand. I said, "Jack, I wouldn't let those dogs lick that blood. I'd be afraid of them." And he said, "I told you not to call these children of mine dogs any more." And he stood up and looked at me right straight in the face, and I didn't say no more. And I said, "That's all right, Jack. I'm sorry." He said, "These are my children, and I respect them just like you respect your kids." He said, "You tell me you've got three kids."

Q Did he have that twist in his neck and head, and that look in his eye?

A Well, I didn't notice too much the twist that particular time, but he said, "Would you help me get these dogs upstairs?" He said, "Then we'll go look at the car." And we got upstairs, and he's got a big white towel that you dry dishes with, and he wrapped it around his left hand.

Q Did you help him get his children upstairs?

A I helped him get the dogs upstairs, and when he opened the door I had to turn because I couldn't stand the odor coming from the room where he kept his dogs.

Q Well, did you ever do anything for him about the upholstery on his car?

A Yes, sir. We went back down to his car. He opened the door, and when he did, I burst out laughing. And he looked at me, and he said, "What are you laughing about?" He kind of tilted his head that time. I said, "I want to know what did this. I've never seen seat covers like this."

Q Did what?

A Did this to his seat covers. They were all eat out. All the upholstery was all over the back floor board, and all over the front floor board. The only thing left of the seat covers was the outer shred of the seat covers. They were nylon material that Oldsmobile usually puts, but they ate out the pockets. I called it pockets. The only thing they left

was the outer edges. If I could describe it to you. They left the outer edges, but they ate out the whole thing and you could see the springs protruding. I said, "Jack, what did this?" He said, "My children." He said, "Anything wrong with that?" He kind of tilted his head, and I said, "I can't figure this out. You mean the dogs?" And he said, "What did I tell you about my dogs?" He said, "My children did it." He said, "What do you want to do, cause an argument out here?" He said, "I asked you to come down here and give me a price on these seat covers, and now you want to criticize my children." I said, "Wait just a minute, Jack. Will you give me a little time to see what you're going to need here?" I said, "What type of seat covers do you want?" He said, "I want something that my children can't eat up too quick." I said, "Well, the only thing I would suggest would be naugahyde." And he wanted to know if that was the same material that they use on cafe booths, and I said, "Jack, that is the only thing that you could put to keep them from getting to it too quick." I said, "I don't guarantee you that they won't chew it all up." He said, "That's all right. What are you going to charge me?" And I said, "Now, Jack let me tell you something. If you went to any seat cover place in Dallas, Texas, they would charge you anywhere from a hundred to two hundred dollars to fix this car." And when I said that, he tilted his head and said, "I didn't ask you to give me any reference to other seat cover

COMMISSION EXHIBIT No. 2411—Continued

companies. I called you because you are my friend." And he said, "I don't appreciate you telling me anything about anybody else. I called you because I wanted you to fix this car for me. I wanted to help you out."

Q Did you consider it unusual that he referred to those dogs of his as his children?

A Yes, I couldn't figure that out.

Q But he was insistant that you call them his children, wasn't he?

A He demanded I call them.

Q Well, did you ever have any trouble with him about the -- some furniture, or something in the living room of his apartment, that his dogs chewed up that you went to fix there?

A No, sir, I didn't have any trouble --

Q About some wall paper, or something?

A He asked me to come to his apartment, which was off of Fitzhugh. This apartment was behind the Holiday Central, or whatever you call that big, nice apartment motel that's up there on Central Expressway. And I visited him one Sunday morning, and when I went into his apartment that Sunday morning, the first thing I noticed, the baseboard was all eat out, and the couch was all eat up, part of it. And I said, "Jack, what in the world happened?" And he said, "My children." He said, "Anything wrong in that?" He said, "My children eat it up." He said, --

Q In other words, whenever you acted as though his children had been bad children, he didn't like that? He would get mad and get in an uproar?

A Well, he just wanted to take up for his kids, I guess. I don't know. That's what --

Q Have you seen him have any of these episodes or violent outbursts over trivial things?

A Yes, sir, I have.

Q On many occasions?

A Yes, sir.

Q You consider him then to be a highly emotional and unstable person, don't you?

A I would say that from the time that I first met Jack, I didn't think that, but right here in the last few years I thought that he might have been suffering from some form of disturbance, mental disturbance, by the way he acted.

Q There's no doubt in your mind about that now, is there?

A Sir?

Q There's no doubt in your mind about that now, but that Jack has a mental disturbance?

A I would almost say that I was sure of it.

Q You're positive now, aren't you?

A I'm positive that it can hit him most any time. That's the way I've got it figured.

Q Have you ever seen him cry?

A Never have.
Q Emotionally?
A No, sir.
Q Where do you live now?
A 1248 Stevens Ridge Drive.
MR. TONAHILL: That's all.

CROSS EXAMINATION

BY MR. WADE:
Q You never have seen him cry?
A I never have.
Q How long have you known him?
A About twelve years.
Q You've known him twelve years? How often have you seen him during that time?
A Well, the first time I recollect meeting Jack Ruby was at the Silver Spur.
Q Out on South Ervay. When he got mad he scared you to death, didn't he?
A Well, I just don't like to be around people that hollers at me.
Q You kept on going back to see him though, didn't you?
A Well, I --
Q For twelve long years?
A Well, now --
Q You didn't have to go out there, did you?

COMMISSION EXHIBIT No. 2411—Continued

MR. BELLI: Wait a minute. I suggest if you want an answer, let him answer first.
Q (By Mr. Wade) Did anybody make you go out there?
A Jack didn't --
MR. BELLI: Now we've got three questions.
A Jack didn't get into any outbursts when I first met him.
MR. TONAHILL: Your Honor, it's argumentative anyhow.
Q (By Mr. Wade) Have you ever seen him throw anybody out of his club up there?
A I've seen him walk them out of his club, yes, sir.
Q What for?
A Well, I can tell you of a lot of instances that -- he knew them all. The minute they entered his club, he said, "I don't want you in here, and I told you don't come out here any more."
Q How about carrying a pistol? Did he throw them out of there for carrying a pistol, or did everybody in the club carry a pistol?
MR. TONAHILL: We object to it and ask him to break it down. That's three questions.
THE COURT: All right. Break it down.
Q (By Mr. Wade) Did everybody up there carry a pistol?
A No, sir.
Q Did you carry one?

COMMISSION EXHIBIT No. 2411—Continued

A No, sir.

Q Do you carry one all around town while you're traveling?

MR. TONAHILL: That's not material.

MR. WADE: I think it's important.

THE COURT: Sustain the objection.

A No, sir.

Q (By Mr. Wade) You're a traveling salesman, aren't you?

A That's right, but I don't fool with pistols.

Q You don't fool with them?

A No, sir.

Q I thought everybody in Dallas carried them?

A I've never owned one in my life.

MR. TONAHILL: Your Honor, we'll stipulate if the District Attorney thinks everybody in Dallas carries a pistol.

MR. WADE: That's according to the defense lawyers. They said everybody carried a pistol, Your Honor.

MR. TONAHILL: Mr. Wade said, "I thought everybody in Dallas carried a pistol" and if he want's to say that and think it --

MR. WADE: That's all you've been --

A Mr. Wade, you don't insinuate I carried a pistol?

Q (By Mr. Wade) Do you carry a pistol?

A No, sir. Never.

THE COURT: Talk one at a time, gentlemen.

Q (By Mr. Wade) Did you --

MR. BELLI: Judge, we can't get a record, in fairness to the reporter here --

Q (By Mr. Wade) In all of this time, you say he took the dogs with him nearly everywhere he went, didn't you? In his car, didn't he?

A He told me he carried them wherever he went.

Q No matter where he went, he had the dogs with him?

A That's right.

Q Did he have them up in the club?

A Yes, sir.

Q Where were they up there during the strip acts?

A He had them in a room to the left of the kitchen.

Q I imagine after this incident that you told about when you were so scared you didn't know what to do, that you reported that to the police, didn't you?

A No, sir.

Q Did you report any instance you ever saw with the defendant, to the police?

A No, sir.

Q Never reported anything?

A No, sir. Had no occasion to.

Q Well, you were scared, you said almost to death when he was threatening you.

A I get scared every day of some people, but I can get over it pretty quick myself.

Q Did you keep going back to him the next day?

A I don't -- sometimes when I get in a little wrangle with Jack, I may stay away from his place two or three weeks, but I always go back.

Q Always go back, because you like him?

A I like him very much.

Q You like that atmosphere up there, don't you?

A Well, yes, sir, I found great relaxation there.

Q Great relaxation --

MR. BELLI: Judge, we just can't get a record --

MR. WADE: She's not complaining.

MR. BELLI: Well I am. And I want a record, and I want a good record here, with every word.

MR. TONAHILL: That's something the District Attorney doesn't want, is a record.

MR. BELLI: That's exactly it. The District Attorney doesn't want a record here, Your Honor, but we do.

MR. WADE: Judge, we object to all that, and ask the jury not to consider what he's saying there about our not wanting a record.

MR. TONAHILL: Ask the jury not to consider Mr. Wade's questions too, Judge.

COMMISSION EXHIBIT No. 2411—Continued

Q (By Mr. Wade) I guess when he came over there and you were complaining about his business being not as good as next door, that did make him mad, because he liked to make money, didn't he?

A I think he did, yes, sir.

Q He liked to be in the lime light, didn't he? He liked to be known by people?

A Jack was well known, in my opinion.

Q He liked -- he was always looking for a plug here and there, wherever he could get it?

A I don't know about the plugs, but I knew that he knew a lot of people.

Q Did he like to have good looking girls with him?

A I don't know. I never have seen Jack on any of his dates, or anything after leaving the club, no, sir.

Q I'm talking about, you've never seen him in a public place with any girl?

A Not that I know of, no, sir.

Q In twelve years?

A No.

Q Never have seen him with any girl in twelve years?

A No, sir.

Q You've seen him once or twice a week, I guess, haven't you?

MR. BELLI: Judge, I hardly know what grade of

COMMISSION EXHIBIT No. 2411—Continued

4-101 633

character that would prove or disprove, someone who didn't want to be seen someplace with a good looking girl, and I say that with my wife in the audience.

MR. ALEXANDER: Now, Your Honor, this witness doesn't need any coaching from Mr. Belli. We object to his comments.

Q (By Mr. Wade) And you never have seen him cry in all your life?

A Never.

Q I assume after that last time when he got so mad with you, and threatened you, that you were afraid to even leave, is that right?

A For a little minute, yes, sir, I thought I better not leave because Jack might get mad at me.

Q You didn't want to make him mad at you?

A No, sir.

Q You wanted to keep his friendship?

A Yes, I learned the way to get around Jack, and I understood Jack better than a lot of people.

Q You understood him a lot better, so understanding his problem I assume you took him to a psychiatrist, or a doctor, to treat him, didn't you?

A No, sir, I didn't.

Q Didn't you ever take him to a doctor with all that outburst that he was giving you?

COMMISSION EXHIBIT No. 2411—Continued

4-102 634

A No, sir.

Q You didn't? And you kept going back to see him, and see his show there?

A Yes, sir. Every time he had a good headliner there, I made up my mind to go there. I was a free paid patron. I never paid a dime to go in Jack Ruby's place.

Q You never paid a dime?

A No, sir.

Q Who was your favorite stripper there?

MR. BELLI: That's objected to. It's incompetent, irrelevant and immaterial.

THE COURT: Sustain the objection to it.

A I didn't show no favoritism to any stripper.

Q You never --

MR. BELLI: Don't get in an insulting match with the District Attorney, because he can out insult anyone in the room.

THE COURT: Let's keep the sidebar remarks out. The Court's going to sustain the objection to the last question. Go ahead.

Q (By Mr. Wade) You kept on coming back? You were in there the night before -- a day or two before the assassination, weren't you?

A No, sir, I wasn't.

Q You weren't?

COMMISSION EXHIBIT No. 2411—Continued

A No, sir.

Q Were you off on the road?

A No, sir. I was in town, but I -- after Jack -- a few little things go on sometimes, I just don't go up there to see him. I just stay away sometimes, but he always wants to know why I haven't been around.

Q Why you haven't been around. But you liked him quite a bit, and was a good friend of his?

A Yes, sir.

Q You'd do nearly anything to help him, wouldn't you?

A Well, he -- I thought I was helping him a lot of times, but he helped me a great deal.

Q He's helped you a lot and you'd be glad to help him, you'd do anything you could for him?

MR. TONAHILL: Let him be specific, Your Honor.

A Well, I don't know what you mean, Mr. Wade by --

Q (By Mr. Wade) You'd testify for him, wouldn't you?

A Well, I would just say that Jack was fine up until about -- until he took over the Carousel Club, and then he begun to do so many crazy things, that I started forming my opinion that Jack was becoming to be a sick man of some type.

Q Did you ever carry him to a doctor of any kind?

A No, sir. He didn't ask me to.

Q He didn't ask you to?

A He didn't tell me that he was ailing with any troubles.

COMMISSION EXHIBIT No. 2411—Continued

Q You were his friend, weren't you?

A Yes, sir, but he didn't disclose his personal feelings or his health to me.

Q He was running a business there that took in hundreds of dollars every night, didn't it?

MR. TONAHILL: What's that got to do with this law suit? It's irrelevant and immaterial.

MR. WADE: It has a lot to do with it.

THE COURT: Sustain the objection.

Q (By Mr. Wade) He was running a business and handling money, and making money out of it, wasn't he?

MR. TONAHILL: Same objection heretofore imposed.

MR. WADE: Judge, that's important on the mental state, whether a man could run a business out here for twelve years. That's the first time he knew him.

Q (By Mr. Wade) He's been in business for twelve years, since you've known him, hasn't he?

A Yes, sir.

Q Where all has he been in business, what clubs that you can recall that you've been in?

A Well, the first club that I recall meeting Jack, it was so far back there, was the Silver Spur.

Q Where was that located?

A On South Ervay Street.

Q What type of place was that?

COMMISSION EXHIBIT No. 2411—Continued

A Well, after going down there a few times I decided that that wasn't the part of town that I wanted to be, so I didn't go down there too much.
Q All right. Where is the next club you saw him running?
A Then came the Studio Lounge. This was out on Oak Lawn, and Jack Ruby took that over and called it the Vegas Club. I would say that's about nine or ten years ago.
Q Nine or ten years ago. You went out there often, didn't you?
A Sir, I was out there practically every other night, or every night.
Q Every night. Are you a married man?
A Yes, sir.
MR. BELLI: That's insulting, if Your Honor please. "Is he a married man." And I say this man is a master at insult as any District Attorney I've ever heard, and I've tried them all in this country and abroad. I think he can insult with the best of them. Now, to ask him if he's a married man, what has that got to do with the --
MR. WADE: I think it's important.
MR. BELLI: He can outshout me too, but what has that got to do with this man on trial for murder, asking him if he's a married man. I submit, Your Honor, that that's incompetent, irrelevant and immaterial.

Dirty, salacious, meretricious and insulting.
MR. BOWIE: Your Honor, he's already testified that he's a married man.
MR. BELLI: Then why does he ask him repeatedly again? To put in a little more prejudice in the case that he's got so full of prejudice here, Judge?
MR. WADE: Judge, he's just making a speech, he's not making an objection.
MR. BELLI: That's right, whenever it's necessary --
THE COURT: All right. Sit down, Mr. Belli. Go ahead, Mr. Wade.
MR. TONAHILL: Did I understand you to sustain the objection?
THE COURT: I did.
MR. TONAHILL: Exception.
Q (By Mr. Wade) Now, you were there -- what was the last question -- you were there every night at the Vegas Club?
A I wouldn't say every night, Mr. Wade, but I was there practically every night.
Q Practically every night?
A Towards the weekend, every night.
Q On the weekend nearly every night?
A Friday, Saturday and --
Q Well, when did you move from there to the Carousel Club?

A Well, Eva Grant took over the Vegas Club, and about the summer of '60, I think, Jack took over the Carousel Club which was called the Sovereign Club. He took it over from Joe Slayton. That was the man that I was dealing with up there at that particular time.

Q Joe Slayton?

A That's right.

Q And he operated the Vegas Club for how long?

A Jack Ruby?

Q Yes.

A I would say that he took the club over out there which used to be called the Studio Lounge, I would say that was in the early fifties, probably '51, '52, '53, somewhere in there. I can't recall the exact date. About nine or ten years, I'd say.

Q And how long has he been running the Carousel Club?

A I would say that he's been at the Carousel Club a little over three years, there about, somewhere. I don't know exactly the exact time.

Q Have you ever seen him throw anybody out of there for carrying a gun?

A Not at the Carousel, no, sir.

Q How about the Vegas?

A Yes, sir.

Q What would he do? Would he throw them out and keep the

COMMISSION EXHIBIT No. 2411—Continued

gun?

A No, sir. One night I was at the Vegas Club, and some man came running up to Jack, and he says, "That man standing back there at that booth has a pistol on him." And Jack left us so quick that I couldn't even tell what happened to Jack, and here come Jack marching him out of the club. Jack had his hands back of his belt, and had the gun in his other hand, and he didn't have it pointed at the man, he was just kind of holding it. He took it off the man. And he said, "You leave my club and don't you ever come back in here any more." And Jack Ruby called the police and they came. I was still there when they came.

Q Did they come and get him for carrying a gun?

A Came and got who?

Q The other man I guess.

A No, sir. The other man got away.

Q He got away?

A Jack Ruby shoved him out the front door.

Q Why did he need the police? Did he tell the police to go after him?

A The police did go after him.

Q Did they get him?

A They followed the car that he got into. Jack knew it was an old model car and I did too, because I ran out there to see the car when he sped away down Lemon Avenue.

COMMISSION EXHIBIT No. 2411—Continued

Q What happened to the gun?

A Jack had it right there at the club when the police came.

Q He kept the gun?

A I don't know what happened to the gun. I never did see it any more.

Q You never have, in all your friendship and close relationship with him, you never have taken him to a doctor at any time to be treated?

MR. BELLI: That's been asked many times.

THE COURT: Sustain the objection.

Q (By Mr. Wade) You haven't even suggested it, have you? Not in all your life?

MR. BELLI: Did you sustain the objection, Your Honor.

THE COURT: Yes, sir.

MR. BELLI: I thought so too.

Q (By Mr. Wade) And you're not trying to tell this jury that Jack Ruby didn't know what he was doing when he was running those clubs?

A Jack Ruby knew what he was doing when everything was going swell, but Jack was easy -- he was always upset with the cold drink man and the people who brought him -- he was fussing with them all the time.

Q He was fussing with them and he was high tempered too,

wasn't he?

A Definitely high tempered, high strung, emotionally upset a lot of times, I found him to be that way.

Q When he was high tempered he was also mean, wasn't he?

A I wouldn't say he was mean, no, sir.

Q Well, you were afraid of him, weren't you?

A No, sir, it just frightens me sometimes when a man hollers at me.

Q It frightens you?

A It kind of gets me --

Q That was a good --

MR. BELLI: Let him answer.

A Say that again?

Q (By Mr. Wade) Your counsel -- I think you answered the question.

MR. BELLI: That's a typical modus operandi that we see of the District Attorney on television, but I think Your Honor runs a more dignified court.

THE COURT: Make your objection to it, Mr. Belli.

MR. BELLI: Object to him cutting off the witness before he has a chance to answer.

Q (By Mr. Wade) Go ahead and answer the question.

A What was that question, sir.

Q I don't know. We can let the reporter read it back, but he said you were still talking and I thought you were through with it.

MR. BELLI: He was asking what the question was, Mr. Wade. Can't you remember?

MR. ALEXANDER: May it please the Court, counsel over here on the left is not cross examining Mr. Wade, and we object.

MR. BELLI: I'd love to though.

THE COURT: One more statement like that, counsel, and I'm going to hold you in contempt. I'm not going to put up with this. We've had enough of it. About fifteen minutes of it is all I can take. I'm not going to take any more of it.

MR. BELLI: I apologize to the Court.

Q (By Mr. Wade) Do you know why he wanted you to look at Jada?

MR. TONAHILL: Now what's that got to do with it?

MR. WADE: He testified that he did, and I was wondering if he helped him select his girls.

MR. BELLI: I think that was in answer to the District Attorney's question that I was going to object to at the time as incompetent, irrelevant and immaterial, and I object now.

THE COURT: Sustain the objection.

Q (By Mr. Wade) Did you go with him to New Orleans at one time to look at some strippers?

COMMISSION EXHIBIT No. 2411—Continued

A No, sir.

MR. BELLI: That's objected to, and cited as misconduct. It's only meant to confuse irrelevancies.

Q (By Mr. Wade) Have you been down there with him?

MR. BELLI: May we have a ruling?

THE COURT: Overrule your objection.

MR. BELLI: It's also incompetent, irrelevant and immaterial and ask that it go out.

THE COURT: Overrule your objection.

MR. TONAHILL: Exception.

Q (By Mr. Wade) Did you go to Cuba with him, back in '59?

A No, sir. I didn't even know he went to Cuba until I read it in the paper.

Q You didn't know it until you read it in the paper?

A That's right.

Q At that time he was gone two or three weeks. Didn't you miss him?

MR. TONAHILL: There's no evidence here to support that, Judge.

THE COURT: Sustain the objection to it.

MR. WADE: All right. We pass him back.

REDIRECT EXAMINATION

BY MR. TONAHILL:

Q Now, with reference to Jack being mean, was Jack a kind, charitable individual?

COMMISSION EXHIBIT No. 2411—Continued

A If Jack liked you there wasn't anything in the world he wouldn't do for you, but if he didn't like you he'd try to avoid you.

Q You knew when Officer Mullinax died he took up a collection for his widow and gave a hundred and fifty dollars --

MR. WADE: We object to that.

THE COURT: Sustain the objection.

A I had heard something about --

THE COURT: Don't answer the question. Sustain the objection.

Q (By Mr. Tonahill) What had you heard about Officer Mullinax --

MR. BOWIE: We object, Your Honor. That's a leading question.

THE COURT: The Court sustained the objection to it. Go on to something else.

Q (By Mr. Tonahill) Now, you know Officer Blankenship?

A No, sir.

Q Did you ever hear of the time that Jack Ruby --

MR. BOWIE: To which we object. It's a leading question.

THE COURT: Get on to something else, counsel.

MR. WADE: We ask you to instruct counsel not to ask either of those questions of this or any other witness.

THE COURT: Sustain the objection.

MR. WADE: So instruct him.

THE COURT: Not this witness or any other witness.

Q (By Mr. Tonahill) Mr. Serur, you say Jack was a kind and generous individual, and not mean?

MR. WADE: Judge, that's leading. Just telling the witness what to say.

A I would say that he was very unusually --

THE COURT: Don't be so anxious to answer the question. Sustain the objection.

MR. TONAHILL: That's all.

MR. WADE: That's all.

RALPH TEMPLIN

a witness called by the Defendant, having first been duly sworn, testified on his oath as follows:

DIRECT EXAMINATION

BY MR. TONAHILL:

Q Would you state your name, your age, your occupation, and place of residence to the Court and Jury?

A I'm Ralph Templin, I'm forty-two years old. I work for the Southwestern Bell Telephone Company, District Manager, Ft. Worth, Texas.

Q Ft. Worth, Texas. How long have you been with Southwestern Bell?

A About eighteen years.

Q And, as District Manager for Southwestern Bell in Ft. Worth, do you have the telephone and telephone exchanges under your jurisdiction?

A Yes, sir, I have. I have them under my general supervision.

Q Back on November 24, 1963, was this telephone number JE 48525 then under your jurisdiction in Ft. Worth?

A Yes, sir, it was.

Q In whose name was that telephone listed, and where was it located, the address?

A The service was located at 3809 Meadow Brook Drive, and it's a non-published number, but we billed it to Bruce Ray

COMMISSION EXHIBIT No. 2412

Carlin. C-A-R-L-I-N.

Q And in response to a subpoena duces tecum, did you bring with you, the official records of your company with reference to that particular telephone number, and a long distance call having been made the morning of November 24, 1963, from that number to an individual in Dallas named Jack Ruby?

A Yes, I did.

Q Would you please get those records out, so that we can have them identified?

(The witness produces the records)

MR. TONAHILL: Would you mark this please?

(Whereupon the record is marked D-3 by the court reporter)

Q (By Mr. Tonahill) I hand you this card here, which you have just handed to the court reporter. It appears to be one of those IBM cards, I believe, and I would ask you to please explain what that is.

A This card is a record of a call that an operator prepared on November 24th, where a call was placed from the number you described, Jefferson 48521, to Dallas, Texas, and the number dialed in Dallas was Whitehall 15601. It was a person to person call to one Jack Ruby. And the call --

Q Was that record made in the usual and customary course of business, and constitute a business record of your firm?

A Yes, it is.

COMMISSION EXHIBIT No. 2412—Continued

Q It's 428 -- what is the number on it? Jefferson 48525?
A Jefferson 48525. Yes.
MR. TONAHILL: we offer it into evidence.
MR. WADE: We have no objection to anything this gentleman says is their records.
Q (By Mr. Tonahill) What time does it show that the telephone call was made from the Ft. Worth number, Jefferson 48525, to Jack Ruby in Dallas on November 24, 1963?
A Ten eighteen A.M.
Q Ten eighteen in the morning, is that right?
A Yes.
Q It was made to Jack Ruby at Whitehall 15601, in Dallas?
A Yes, sir, that's correct.
MR. TONAHILL: I believe that's all.

CROSS EXAMINATION

BY MR. WADE:
Q Do you know, Mr. Templin, how long the conversation was? Is it on that card?
A It's on the card. I believe it's two minutes and nineteen seconds, roughly.
Q Roughly like that?
A That's correct.
MR. WADE: That's all. Thank you, sir, for coming down.

COMMISSION EXHIBIT No. 2412—Continued

WESLEY A. WISE

a witness called by the State, being first duly sworn, testified on his oath as follows:

DIRECT EXAMINATION

BY MR. ALEXANDER:
Q Your name is Wes Wise?
A Wesley A. Wise is the full name.
Q And how are you employed, please sir?
A Newsman at KRLD.
Q I believe that station is the one affiliated with the Dallas Times Herald?
A Right.
Q Directing your attention back to Saturday, November 23, 1963, were you working in your capacity as a newsman for KRLD?
A I was.
Q And directing your attention to about three o'clock that afternoon, did you have occasion to be across the street from the School Book Depository, down here on Houston Street?
A I did.
Q And what, if anything, were you doing there?
A I was on assignment to retrace as close as possible, the steps of Lee Harvey Oswald, after he allegedly shot the president.
Q All right. At that time did you know the defendant in this case, Jack Ruby?

COMMISSION EXHIBIT No. 2413

A I did.
Q And did you see Jack Ruby there that afternoon?
A I did.
Q And where was he when you first saw him?
A I tried to gain entrance to the building and failed to do so, so went back to my unit, called in to the station there, and I didn't particularly want anybody to hear the transmission. I had rolled up the window on the drivers side, and after I -- or right near the end of the transmission, somebody, as I recall, knocked on the window and I put it down and it was Jack. And he re-introduced himself to me.
Q Did you have a conversation with him then?
A I did.
Q And what was the nature of your conversation?
A Well, it's hard to recall the details, but we discussed the killing of the president, general conversation about how terrible it was. I mentioned that I had been at the Trade Mart the day before when he was due -- when the president was due to arrive. And we discussed the reactions of -- the terrible reaction there to the president's killing.
Q Now, would you tell the layout of the streets at this intersection that your car was parked close to? Let me help you a little bit with it. Elm Street runs nearly east and west, passes the Records Building, crosses Houston Street,

COMMISSION EXHIBIT No. 2413—Continued

and then as it goes in front of the School Book Depository, makes a turn before going under the triple underpass, doesn't it?
A Right.
Q Then the School Book Depository would be on the northwest corner and the Records Building; that is, this building, would be on the southeast corner, and across the street west, across Houston Street, would be Dealy Plaza where the fountains and the statues are?
A Yes.
Q Now where, in relation to the intersection of Houston Street and Elm Street, was your mobile unit parked?
A I was close to the northeast corner, parked cata-cornered across the street from the Texas School Book Depository Building.
Q I take it then that your car would have been facing north, or towards the railroad tracks?
A No, my car would be facing northeast actually, because I was cata-cornered, you see.
Q Did you see what direction Jack Ruby came from?
A He came from in the general direction of the railroad tracks, which is north, I believe.
Q That would be north of the School Book Depository?
A Yes.
Q Let me ask you if he mentioned that Captain Fritz and

COMMISSION EXHIBIT No. 2413—Continued

18

Chief Curry were in the near vicinity at that time?

A As I recall it, we held a conversation, oh, maybe eight, nine, ten minutes there, then I believe I got ready to leave, and he came back -- as I remember it, he came back to the car and said, "Did you know that Will Fritz and Jesse Curry were here?" And I said, "No, where are they?" And he said, "Well, they're over there looking at the flowers which had been placed there by people in Dallas." And I think hinted that I might want to take pictures, which I did.

Q Was there anything unusual about your conversation with him?

A The only thing I noticed was that when I mentioned that at the Trade Mart I had gone into the room where President Kennedy's rocking chair and straight line to Washington were located, and saw the two large presents meant for Caroline and John, and they were western saddles that were going to be given to Kennedy to give to his children, and I mentioned to him that I had taken pictures of them, and I noticed tears in his eyes.

Q Did he appear excited at that time?

A I wouldn't say excited. I would say touched.

Q And where did he go when you last saw him?

A He walked back in a northerly direction, back toward the railroad tracks.

Q This was in the vicinity of three o'clock on Saturday afternoon?

19

A Right. I'd say probably by the time he left, it would probably be around three-twenty, because we held a conversation and I went and took pictures of Mr. Fritz and Mr. Curry, and then he spoke -- I thanked him on the way back to my unit. I turned to him and said, "I sure thank you. I would have missed that if you hadn't told me they were here." And he smiled and left.

Q At that time had the crowd begun to assemble around the County jail, anticipating the transfer of Oswald at four o'clock?

A I don't believe, as far as I remember, that there was a crowd around the County jail at that time. There was quite a crowd around -- down at the slant, where the flowers were being placed, and I noticed as I left that Jack took pictures of a lot of people walking along the street, taking flowers to the slant.

Q Well now, let me ask you this. At the time you had your conversation, they had not roped off the area around the driveway entrance to the jail and the rest of the block towards Elm?

A I don't believe. I don't believe. In fact, I can't remember now whether we knew at that time that Oswald would probably be moved the next day or not. I don't remember whether -- what I'm getting at, I didn't know there was a discussion that he might be moved at four o'clock.

Q But at that time the crowd hadn't gathered around the driveway entrance to the County jail?

A No, I don't believe so.

MR. ALEXANDER: I believe that's all.

CROSS EXAMINATION

BY MR. TONAHILL:

Q Mr. Wise, when you discussed the saddles for the little Kennedy children on that occasion with Jack, the fact that you had been out there and seen them and photographed them, did Jack break down and cry?

A I wouldn't describe it as breaking down and crying. I'd say that tears definitely came to his eyes. He was touched.

Q He was touched very deeply, was he not?

A I would say so, yes.

Q And you have known Jack for a long time, have you not?

A I'd say about five or six years.

Q Over the period of time you've known him, you've come to appreciate the fact that he is a highly emotional man and sometimes irrational, due to a violent state of mind?

A Frankly I didn't know that of my own personal experience, Mr. Tonahill. I had heard that.

Q Did you ever work as a sportscaster?

A Yes.

Q Attend some prize fights here?

A Oh, yes.

Q Did you see Jack at any of those fights?

A Yes. All of them.

Q Did Jack ever react violently at any of the prize fights as a result of disagreeing with some of the decisions of the judges?

A Yes, I'd say -- I don't know whether you'd use the term "violently" or not. He would take exception to some of the decisions more than most, yes.

Q Describe how he would do that, if you would?

A He would -- in the first place, he would always have a ringside seat, I believe. And he would always -- as I remember this now -- he would see someone that he knew, either at the press table, or at ringside, and go over there and say, "Did you hear that? Don't you think that so and so --" You know, that type thing. That kind of excitement.

Q He would take exception to the decisions in pretty strong --

A I'd say so, yes. More than most.

Q Did he ever tell you how he had witnessed the Barney Ross fight, and he bet against Barney and Barney had won the fight, and Barney's a good friend of his, and he passed out and had a blackout seizure after Barney won?

MR. ALEXANDER: That we object to, Your Honor.

THE COURT: Sustain the objection.
Q (By Mr. Tonahill) Did he ever discuss his friend, Barney Ross, with you?
A I knew that he knew Barney Ross.
Q Did he ever discuss seeing Barney win a fight that upset him?
A Well, I can't remember whether Jack himself told me that, or whether I had heard that from someone else.
Q You had heard that?
A Yes.
Q When Jack left you that afternoon, did you later see him in his car and he tooted his horn at you and kind of waved and acknowledged he had done you a favor in pointing out that Captain Fritz and Chief Curry were there so you could interview them and photograph them at the scene?
A Well, I don't remember his calling from his car. I remember his speaking to me about it, and I remember my thanking him. My recollection was that he was on foot and going back to his car. He may have been in his car and turned and waved at me and said that. I don't really remember the details. But I do remember my acknowledging and thanking him and his -- you know, returning the thanks.
Q Wes, you have seen Jack react rather violently to various episodes in his night clubs, the Carousel and the Vegas Club, have you not, over some disputes with people?

A I have observed that once, yes. I don't know whether I'd use the term "violently." I just don't know whether I would use that term or not. Excitable, yes.
Q He's a highly excitable individual?
A Yes.
Q And have you seen him there in his night club where he would reprimand his employees in a highly emotional, excitable state?
A I don't believe I ever saw him reprimand an employee, but I haven't been in his night clubs too often.
Q Have you seen him reprimand customers for interfering in an act?
A Yes.
Q He gets pretty excited about that, when customers interfered with the act?
A Yes.
Q Now, you know Jack to be more or less a character around town, do you not Wes, sort of a Damon Runyon character?
A Yes.
Q When he walked up to you that afternoon, did he not say, "I'm Jack Ruby of the Carousel Club, do you remember me?" Or words to that effect?
A Yes.
Q And you remembered him right away?
A Yes.

Q Was Jack concerned about the effect of the tragic loss of the president upon his widow, Mrs. Kennedy, and the children?

A Yes.

Q You all discussed that?

A Yes.

Q Did Jack impress you as being a patriotic citizen?

A I never knew that until I read it. We never discussed that.

Q You are impressed with that fact?

A Now?

Q Yes.

A Yes, from what I've read, yes. That's just hearsay though. I would gather that he was. Are you relating that to the Kennedy assassination?

Q Yes.

A If you're relating it to the Kennedy assassination, he was disturbed from what I gather, from seeing him at the School Book Depository Building, about the president having been shot.

Q Did you ever see him when Buddy Turman fought?

A Yes.

Q Did he get upset about any of his fights or any of the decisions?

A I just can't place it specifically to Buddy Turman's

COMMISSION EXHIBIT No. 2413—Continued

fights, but I have seen him excited at fights.

Q He was pleased, was he not, with the fact that he called your attention to the fact that Chief Curry and Captain Fritz were down there looking at the flowers, and pleased because he had told you about it so you could go down and interview them?

A Yes. I got the impression -- I had kidded him about the fact that he had given KLIF a scoop the night before, which I had heard on the radio on the way home.

Q Was that the scoop where he got Mr. Wade on the telephone so that he could tell the KLIF people about the fact that the Oswald case was broken and he wants the death sentence?

A I only -- yes, I believe that was. I remember it related to Wade, but I don't remember specifically what it was. If I may say this, I didn't really consider it a real, big beat, but I was listening to the competition in order to see what they were doing.

Q You were just pulling his leg, like a good reporter --

A Yes. I got the impression he could have taken it a little more seriously, and was trying to -- you know --

Q Jack likes to get along with you men of the press because he asks you to give him plugs every now and then and he appreciates that type thing, doesn't he?

A I don't think he ever requested me to give him a plug.

COMMISSION EXHIBIT No. 2413—Continued

I think he knows I probably wouldn't.

Q Now when you and Jack were talking there, shortly before Chief Curry and Captain Fritz came up, and discussing the loss of the president, the tragedy, did he at any time joke or appear to be joking to you?

A The only time I saw any sign of that was when I said something to him about the KLIF scoop.

Q And when you were talking about the loss of the president, the great tragedy, and the saddles to the children, tears welled up in his eyes at that time? He was touched very deeply?

A Yes.

Q Now, do you recall when the news broke that Oswald was to be moved at ten o'clock on Sunday, November 24th?

A No. I heard that Mr. Curry had said to the newsmen, I suggest that you be alert, or aware, or something like that, at ten o'clock the next morning.

Q Ten o'clock. Then word did get out to you folks that Oswald was to be transferred from the City jail to the County jail at ten o'clock Sunday morning?

A Sometime after ten o'clock.

Q Where were you at the time of the shooting of Oswald?

A I was at the -- I was on the street out there at the County courthouse. I was awaiting the arrival of Oswald at the County jail.

Q There were a number of people here at the County Building awaiting the arrival of Oswald, isn't that right?

A Yes, there was.

Q About how many?

A My guess would be around three, four hundred. Something like that.

Q And when the news was released there to the crowd that Oswald was shot, what reaction did it have on that crowd?

MR. BOWIE: To which we object.

THE COURT: Sustain the objection to it.

MR. BELLI: It's offered for the state of mind of Mr. Ruby, both before and after, Your Honor.

THE COURT: Sustain the objection.

Q (By Mr. Tonahill) Where were you standing when it was announced to the crowd that Oswald had been shot?

A I was standing in the street, which had been roped off, or else the police were holding the traffic off. I was standing in the street with a microphone.

Q Didn't loud cheers go up?

MR. BOWIE: To which we object, Your Honor.

THE COURT: Sustain the objection.

MR. TONAHILL: Exception.

That's all.

REDIRECT EXAMINATION

BY MR. ALEXANDER:

Q Just a couple more questions. At the time that Ruby walked up to your mobile unit there on Saturday afternoon, did he give you the impression that he wanted to be interviewed?

A No.

Q Did he impress you as a person that seeks publicity and wants to be included in everything?

A He was -- he liked to be friends with the newsman and that sort of thing, but I don't believe he really -- he knew that I -- in other words, if I had been Tony Zoppi or the amusements editor, then he might have expected that. He knew that there was nothing I could do for him in the way of a plug.

MR. ALEXANDER: Thank you. That's all.

Call Officer Harkness.

COMMISSION EXHIBIT No. 2413—Continued

— Commission Exhibit No. 2414 —

FD-302 (Rev. 3-3-59)

FEDERAL BUREAU OF INVESTIGATION

1

Date ~~11/25/63~~ 11-30-63

BILLY JOE WILLIS, 6922 Forney Road, furnished the following information:

WILLIS advised he has been employed as a drummer at the Club Carousel for approximately two years. During this period he has become well acquainted with JACK RUBY. RUBY's closest friends appear to be GEORGE SENATOR and RALPH PAUL. He believes PAUL may have a financial interest in the Club Carousel.

WILLIS is personally interested in history and has tried unsuccessfully to draw RUBY into conversations of history and politics. RUBY seemed to be uninterested in current events and politics. At one time he did become emotionally disturbed and was practically in tears over a discussion of the persecution of the Jews in Germany. WILLIS has heard RUBY speak of CASTRO in such a derogatory manner that it was obvious he did not like him and was not in sympathy with the CASTRO government in Cuba.

WILLIS advised that it has become common in the entertainment world to put on harmless skits making fun of the KENNEDY family and often after the presentation of such skits, RUBY would off-stage, openly express great admiration for President KENNEDY.

WILLIS talked by telephone to RUBY on the afternoon of November 22, 1963, and at that time, RUBY informed him the Club Carousel would be temporarily closed because of the President's assassination. RUBY said that the assassination was the most horrible thing that had ever happened and expressed great personal distress over the incident. He said,"Can you imagine what a miserable critter that OSWALD is". He was half sobbing during the conversation and WILLIS was amazed at the manner in which RUBY was affected by the tragedy. Nothing further was said about OSWALD and he did not see RUBY or talk to him again.

WILLIS stated that RUBY is a highly emotional person who has no control over his emotions. He was prone to argue with his employees and acquaintances over trivial matters and to fire his employees with the slightest provocation. He reacted violently when aroused and was often involved in brawls.

506

on 11/26/63 at Dallas, Texas File # DL 44-1639 89-43

by Special Agents RALPH E. RAWLINGS & ERR EDMOND C. HARDIN/cah ECH Date dictated 11/26/63

This document contains neither recommendations nor conclusions of the FBI. It is the property of the FBI and is loaned to your agency; it and its contents are not to be distributed outside your agency.

COMMISSION EXHIBIT No. 2414

2

DL 44-1639
89-43

As an example of his highly explosive nature, about one year ago, he became angry with a patron who had ignored his request to pay his admission to the Club Carousel or leave and beat him severely and threw him down the stairs. This was done so quickly that Vice Squad officers on duty at the club, were not even aware of the incident.

WILLIS stated that he knows from personal recollection that RUBY was at the Club Carousel every night for approximately two weeks prior to November 22, 1963, inasmuch as RUBY participated in the shows on these nights. He would arrive at the club no later than 10:30 PM each night. He knew that RUBY had a .38 caliber revolver which he carried with him when handling proceeds from the operation of the club. He did not know whether RUBY carried the gun on other occasions.

WILLIS advised that he was aware of the statements made by BILL DeMAR, master of ceremonies at the Club Carousel to the effect that a patron, similar in appearance to OSWALD, had participated in the show recently at the club. WILLIS had talked to DeMAR and tried to pin him down as to the particular night the particular patron he had reference to, and had found DeMAR very vague and non-specific. WILLIS advised that he thought also that the photographs of OSWALD resembled a patron who had participated in the show a few nights ago. He recalled that this man was alone at a table near the front and was wearing a blue denim jacket and a white T-shirt. He came early and stayed late. At no time did he talk to JACK RUBY within WILLIS' presence. WILLIS stated he is not sure he has the same man in mind that DeMAR has referred to. He believes it is only remotely possible this man is identical to OSWALD, and is personally convinced there was only a superficial resemblance.

507

COMMISSION EXHIBIT No. 2414—Continued

— Commission Exhibit No. 2415

FD-302 (Rev. 3-3-59)

FEDERAL BUREAU OF INVESTIGATION [redacted]

1

Date 6/26/64

SA MANNING C. CLEMENTS, with HERMAN HILL, Property Room Supervisor, Dallas, Texas, Police Department, examined inventory records in Mr. HILL's office relative to property taken from JACK L. RUBY following his arrest on November 24, 1963. The records do not indicate an overcoat or topcoat.

SA CLEMENTS, with First Assistant District Attorney A. D. JIM BOWIE, Dallas County District Attorney's office, examined clothing of RUBY which had been turned over to the District Attorney's office by Dallas Police Department. No overcoat or topcoat was among such clothing. A dark brown suit, coat and trousers, bearing a Neiman-Marcus Store label, was observed. It was noted this suit appears almost black from a distance of a few feet.

SA CLEMENTS reviewed newspaper and television photographs of the shooting of LEE HARVEY OSWALD on November 24, 1963, and noted RUBY did not have an overcoat or topcoat on at the time, and that the suit he was wearing appears similar in color to that observed in the District Attorney's office.

on 6/25/64 at Dallas, Texas File # DL 44-1639

68

by Special Agent MANNING C. CLEMENTS/ds Date dictated 6/26/64

COMMISSION EXHIBIT No. 2415

FD-302 (Rev. 3-3-59)

FEDERAL BUREAU OF INVESTIGATION

1

Date 6/25/64

EDDIE BARKER, News Director, KRLD-TV, advised records of his office reflect as follows concerning official temperature and humidity (U. S. Weather Bureau, Dallas Love Field) on November 24, 1963:

Time	Temperature	Humidity
6 A.M.	34	75
7 A.M.	33	82
8 A.M.	32	92
9 A.M.	36	85
10 A.M.	43	57
11 A.M.	48	46
12 N.	50	43

on 6/25/64 at Dallas, Texas File # DL 44-1639

by Special Agent MANNING C. CLEMENTS/ds Date dictated 6/25/64

This document contains neither recommendations nor conclusions of the FBI. It is the property of the FBI and is loaned to your agency; it and its contents are not to be distributed outside your agency.

COMMISSION EXHIBIT No. 2415—Continued

FD-302 (Rev. 3-3-59)

FEDERAL BUREAU OF INVESTIGATION

Date 6/26/64

1

SAM RUBY, 11616 Jamestown Road, telephone EM 8-5083, advised he has no recollection of seeing his brother, JACK L. RUBY, wearing a topcoat in Dallas.

Mr. RUBY said he has no information as to the type and color of a topcoat, if any, owned or worn by GEORGE SENATOR.

on 6/25/64 at Dallas, Texas File # DL 44-1639

by Special Agent MANNING C. CLEMENTS/eah Date dictated 6/26/64

This document contains neither recommendations nor conclusions of the FBI. It is the property of the FBI and is loaned to your agency; it and its contents are not to be distributed outside your agency.

COMMISSION EXHIBIT No. 2415—Continued

FD-302 (Rev. 3-3-59)

FEDERAL BUREAU OF INVESTIGATION

Date 6/26/64

1

EVA GRANT, 3929 Rawlins, Apt. 1, telephone LA 6-6258, advised she knows JACK L. RUBY, her brother, owned and wore a topcoat while living in Chicago prior to coming to Dallas, Texas. She said, however, she does not recall ever seeing RUBY wear a topcoat in Dallas and does not believe he possessed and wore a topcoat. She said she had seen RUBY regularly during the last four years and lived with him during a part of this period. He occasionally wore sweaters under his suit coats during cold weather.

Mrs. GRANT said she believes GEORGE SENATOR wore a Navy-blue raincoat on occasions but does not recall ever seeing him with a topcoat on and does not believe he owned one.

on 6/26/64 at Dallas, Texas File # DL 44-1639

by Special Agent MANNING C. CLEMENTS/eah Date dictated 6/26/64

This document contains neither recommendations nor conclusions of the FBI. It is the property of the FBI and is loaned to your agency; it and its contents are not to be distributed outside your agency.

FD-302 (Rev. 3-3-59)

FEDERAL BUREAU OF INVESTIGATION

Date 6/26/64

1

Mrs. LINDEN (JEANNE) LAUVE, 6011 Gaston, telephone TA 7-7002, advised GEORGE SENATOR has been known to her and her husband for some time and lived with them following the shooting of LEE HARVEY OSWALD by JACK L. RUBY until some three weeks after completion of RUBY's trial in March, 1964. She received a call from SENATOR sometime thereafter, at which time he said he was living with his sister, Mrs. A. J. WEISBERG, 2255 Grand Concourse, Bronx, New York, telephone SE 3-1671.

Mrs. LAUVE stated someone gave SENATOR a topcoat about one year ago, and this was the only topcoat she knew him to have as of November, 1963. She described the coat as "loud, dark tan or brown checked and gaudy." She remembered commenting to SENATOR when she first saw the coat on the apparent taste of the donor for gaudy clothing.

Mrs. LAUVE recalled further SENATOR made a trip to see his family in the New York City area between RUBY's bond hearing and murder trial. On his return to Dallas, he told her his brother-in-law had noted the topcoat described above had a hole in it and had given SENATOR another one.

on 6/26/64 at Dallas, Texas File # DL 44-1639

by Special Agent MANNING C. CLEMENTS/eah Date dictated 6/26/64

This document contains neither recommendations nor conclusions of the FBI. It is the property of the FBI and is loaned to your agency; it and its contents are not to be distributed outside your agency.

FD-302 (Rev. 3-3-59)

FEDERAL BUREAU OF INVESTIGATION

1

Date 6/26/64

CHARLES R. GAMBULOS, 3104 Amherst, was interviewed at his place of employment, Eatwell Restaurant, 1404 Main Street.

GAMBULOS said he does not have any specific recollection of ever having seen JACK RUBY in a top or overcoat. He said GEORGE SENATOR had a brownish-tweed overcoat of heavy-looking wool type and this is the only coat of other than suit-coat type he recalls having ever seen SENATOR wear. He said, as he remembers, this coat looked quite worn. GAMBULOS does not know whether SENATOR had any grayish top or overcoats, but, if he did, he does not have any recollection of having seen him wearing them.

on 6/26/64 at Dallas, Texas File # DL 44-1639

by Special Agent KENNETH C. HOWE/ds Date dictated 6/26/64

This document contains neither recommendations nor conclusions of the FBI. It is the property of the FBI and is loaned to your agency; it and its contents are not to be distributed outside your agency.

COMMISSION EXHIBIT No. 2415—Continued

FD-302 (Rev. 3-3-59)

FEDERAL BUREAU OF INVESTIGATION

1

Date 6/26/64

MILDRED POLLARD, 5319 Ash Lane, was interviewed at her place of employment, Eatwell Restaurant, 1404 Main Street.

Mrs. POLLARD said she has no recollection of what color or type of top or overcoat GEORGE SENATOR owned, and does not remember having ever seen him in one, although she presumes he did have and occasionally did wear an overcoat of some type. To her best recollection, when she saw SENATOR in the Eatwell on the morning LEE HARVEY OSWALD was shot, he was wearing only a suit-coat and did not have a top or overcoat of any kind with him.

Mrs. POLLARD never knew JACK RUBY, and had no knowledge who RUBY was until after the Sunday on which OSWALD was shot.

on 6/26/64 at Dallas, Texas File # DL 44-1639

by Special Agent KENNETH C. HOWE/ds Date dictated 6/26/64

This document contains neither recommendations nor conclusions of the FBI. It is the property of the FBI and is loaned to your agency; it and its contents are not to be distributed outside your agency.

COMMISSION EXHIBIT No. 2415—Continued

FD-302 (Rev. 3-3-59)

FEDERAL BUREAU OF INVESTIGATION

1

Date 6/26/64

WILFORD JAMES (JIM) MARTIN, attorney, 706 Main Street, said that on most occasions when he had seen JACK RUBY in the past it was indoors and he would not, of course, have been wearing any type of outer garment other than a suit coat. He cannot remember whether he ever saw him in a top coat.

As to GEORGE SENATOR, MARTIN said he was much closer to him, and certainly believes he must have, at one time or another, seen SENATOR in a top or overcoat of some type, but he could not specifically bring to mind any such occasion, and was unable to give any description of any such type garment SENATOR might have had. MARTIN said he admittedly is very unobservant in connection with matters of this kind, and could not even state whether SENATOR was wearing any type of outer garment on the occasion when he came to his home following the shooting of LEE HARVEY OSWALD.

on 6/26/64 at Dallas, Texas File # DL 44-1639

by Special Agent KENNETH C. HOWE/ds Date dictated 6/26/64

COMMISSION EXHIBIT No. 2415—Continued

FD-302 (Rev. 1-25-60)

FEDERAL BUREAU OF INVESTIGATION

Date 7/1/64

1

GEORGE SENATOR was interviewed at the New York Office of the Federal Bureau of Investigation (FBI). He furnished the following information:

He presently resides at the Chesterfield Hotel, 130 West 49th Street, New York, New York and he is not employed. His present residence is not permanent, but he can always be located through his sister, Mrs. A. J. WEISBERG, 2255 Grand Concourse, Bronx, New York.

He was living with JACK RUBY in Dallas, Texas on November 24, 1963. He reaalled that he arose about 8:00 a.m. that day and RUBY was asleep at the time. He did not know what time RUBY had gotten home during the night.

RUBY did not leave the apartment with anyone on the morning of November 24, 1963 until approximately 10:30 a.m. This was shortly after RUBY had received a telephone call from "LITTLE LYNN" a striptease performer. SENATOR believed RUBY might have had something to eat, washed up after the telephone call and then left the apartment with his dog.

SENATOR recalled that RUBY was wearing a blue suit and had when he left the apartment. He did not wear a topcoat and to SENATOR's knowledge RUBY did not own a topcoat.

SENATOR did not own a "greyish topcoat" at that time. SENATOR does own a brown plaid English tweed topcoat, but he did not wear it on November 24, 1963.

SENATOR left the apartment about one hour after RUBY and was having coffee in a restaurant at the time that LEE HARVEY OSWALD was shot.

On 6/30/64 at New York, New York File # NY 44-974

by SAS EUGENE W. O'NEILL and JAMES J. ROGERS:rea Date dictated 7/1/64

COMMISSION EXHIBIT No. 2415—Continued

Commission Exhibit No. 2416

UNITED STATES DEPARTMENT OF JUSTICE

FEDERAL BUREAU OF INVESTIGATION

In Reply, Please Refer to File No.

Dallas, Texas
August 19, 1964

JACK L. RUBY;
LEE HARVEY OSWALD

By letter dated June 4, 1964, the President's Commission on the Assassination of President Kennedy requested the Federal Bureau of Investigation to determine the existence of phonographic records and papers, which former Dallas County Sheriff Steve Guthrie claimed were made in connection with the Dallas Crime Investigation, 1946-1948; and if they do exist, how they are now maintained; how extensive they are, and whether or not they are indexed to show any mention of Jack L. Ruby.

Attached hereto are results of additional investigation and review of the recordings, located in the possession of Lieutenant George E. Butler, Police Department, Dallas, Texas.

COMMISSION EXHIBIT NO. 2416

FD-302 (Rev. 3-3-59)

FEDERAL BUREAU OF INVESTIGATION

1

Date 8/10/64

CARL F. HANSSON, 1230 Ridgeway Drive, interviewed at his residence, advised he was formerly Chief of Police, Dallas, Texas, until early January 1960. He was the Chief of Police at Dallas during the pertinent periods of 1947 and 1950.

HANSSON stated that during the time he was Chief of Police he was well informed on the investigation regarding PAUL ROWLAND JONES. He also stated that he is well acquainted with the part former Dallas County Sheriff STEVE GUTHRIE and Police Lieutenant GEORGE BUTLER took in the JONES investigation.

HANSSON stated he does not know the present whereabouts of transcriptions of the phonograph records taken of the various interviews between JONES, GUTHRIE and BUTLER. However, he did note that during the course of the JONES investigation, he had on several occasions read these transcripts and does not recall the name of JACK RUBY ever being mentioned. HANSSON stated he positively does not think that the name of JACK RUBY ever came up in the recorded interviews of JONES by GUTHRIE and BUTLER.

HANSSON noted he does not have a good opinion at all of STEVE GUTHRIE and would not place any confidence in any statement by GUTHRIE to the effect that JONES had mentioned the name of JACK RUBY during the interviews.

Regarding the reported return of the transcriptions of the phonograph records to the Dallas Police Department on December 2, 1950, from the Clerk of the Court of Criminal Appeals, State of Texas, Austin, Texas, HANSSON advised this would have been a routine matter and he would surmise the transcriptions were indeed returned at that time to the Dallas Police Department, but he nevertheless does not recall the specific incident.

on 8/5/64 at Richardson, Texas File # DL 44-1639

by Special Agent RICHARD J. BURNETT/ds Date dictated 8/6/64

COMMISSION EXHIBIT NO. 2416—Continued

FD-302 (Rev. 1-25-60)

FEDERAL BUREAU OF INVESTIGATION

Date August 13, 1964

1

Assistant Chief of Police GEORGE L. LUMPKIN, Administrative Division, Dallas Police Department, was interviewed in his office regarding the possible location of a transcript of the original recordings taken by the Dallas Police Department in connection with other local law enforcement agencies during the period 1946-1948 in their joint investigation concerning PAUL ROWLAND JONES.

LUMPKIN advised that inasmuch as the investigation was many years ago and the matter regarding JONES has been handled in the courts, he would assume that any such old records have been long since destroyed.

However, LUMPKIN stated on August 6, 1964, that he would have his Records Bureau conduct a thorough search to try and locate the pertinent phonograph records and/or their transcriptions.

LUMPKIN subsequently advised on August 10, 1964, that a search by his Records Bureau regarding instant matter was unproductive.

On 8/6/64 and 8/10/64 at Dallas, Texas File # DL 44-1639

by Special Agent RICHARD J. BURNETT/jtf Date dictated 8/11/64

COMMISSION EXHIBIT No. 2416—Continued

FD-302 (Rev. 3-3-59)

FEDERAL BUREAU OF INVESTIGATION

Date August 13, 1964

1

Lieutenant GEORGE E. BUTLER was interviewed in his office located in the Juvenile Bureau at the Police Department, Dallas Texas.

Lieutenant BUTLER advised on August 6, 1963, in regard to the present whereabouts of phonograph records and/or transcriptions of recordings made by former Dallas County Sheriff STEVE GUTHRIE and himself in connection with their departments' joint investigation of PAUL ROWLAND JONES around 1946 - 1948, he did not believe either the recordings or their written transcriptions were still in existence.

Lieutenant BUTLER stated that when he picked up the recordings from the Clerk of the Court of Criminal Appeals, State of Texas, Austin, Texas, reportedly in December, 1950, in behalf of former Dallas Chief of Police CARL F. HANSSON, he believes it was to deliver the recordings to the Kefauver Committee then holding sessions in Chicago, Illinois.

Lieutenant BUTLER stated he took the recordings to the Kefauver Hearings in Chicago, Illinois.

He noted he would make a search of his "personal" records at his home (6447 Velasco Avenue, Dallas, Texas) to see if he could locate any copy of the transcript of these recordings.

On August 11, 1964, Lieutenant BUTLER advised he had located the original recordings, consisting of twenty-two (22) discs, at his home, but could find no written transcriptions of same or an index.

He stated that when he located the recordings at his home, he noted that they were still packaged in the original, unopened container by which they were returned to him in 1960 from the McClellan Committee.

on 8/6/64 and 8/11/64 at Dallas, Texas File # DL 44-1639

by Special Agent RICHARD J. BURNETT /jtf Date dictated 8/11/64

COMMISSION EXHIBIT No. 2416—Continued

BUTLER stated that he now remembers that he had loaned the recordings to the McClellan Committee for their use sometime in late 1959 or early 1960.

It was noted that the package by which these twenty-two records were returned to Lieutenant BUTLER had never been opened and had been sent by "Registered Mail - Return Receipt Requested" on March 17, 1960, from the office of Senator McClellan to Lieutenant GEORGE BUTLER, Dallas Police Department, Dallas, Texas. The Post Office stamp on the outside of the package indicated that the package had arrived in Dallas, Texas, on March 21, 1960. The package bore Registry Number 220346.

Upon opening the package in the interviewing Agent's presence, it was noted to contain twenty-two records, which Lieutenant BUTLER described as the recordings taken by former Dallas County Sheriff STEVE GUTHRIE and himself in their joint investigation in regard to the joint intelligence investigation of PAUL ROWLAND JONES around 1946 - 1948, the exact dates of which he does not now recall.

Lieutenant BUTLER stated he has retained these twenty-two recordings in his "personal" possession and intends to continue to do so in order to be sure of their whereabouts at all times.

He advised that if the President's Commission desires to personally review the recordings, the Commission should contact him "personally" and not through anyone else at the Dallas Police Department.

BUTLER stated that he had no objection whatsoever to the Federal Bureau of Investigation or the President's Commission taping these twenty-two records or making written transcriptions of them for official use.

Lieutenant BUTLER stated he has not listened to these records for years and cannot positively state whether or not the name of JACK L. RUBY is mentioned in any of the records. However, he stated to the best of his recollection, he does not believe that the name of JACK L. RUBY is mentioned in any of the recordings.

Regarding previous written transcripts and/or an index of names mentioned in any of the records, Lieutenant BUTLER stated that while transcripts had been made years ago, he does not know of their present location or even if they still exist. Concerning any index, Lieutenant BUTLER stated he believes the discs may have been indexed years ago, but he does not know of the present whereabouts or even of the present existence of such an index.

BUTLER added it is entirely possible that the McClellan Committee may have transcribed the contents of these twenty-two recordings for their records.

FD-302 (Rev. 3-3-59)

FEDERAL BUREAU OF INVESTIGATION

Date August 19, 1964

1

The twenty-two recordings made available for review by the Federal Bureau of Investigation, with the permission of Lieutenant GEORGE E. BUTLER, Juvenile Division, Police Department, Dallas, Texas, were monitored on August 14, 1964, in the Dallas Office of the Federal Bureau of Investigation by Special Agent RICHARD J. BURNETT.

It is noted that at no time on any of the twenty-two recordings was the name of "JACK L. RUBY" or "RUBY" mentioned. The records furnished by Lieutenant BUTLER were twenty-two in number. They are marked and identified as follows:

1. Recordings #1 through #19, inclusive, were recorded on Nov mber 1-2, 1946, between the hours of 8:00 p.m. and 2 a.m. The conversations recorded thereon were between STEVE GUTHRIE, GEORGE BUTLER and PAUL ROWLAND JONES. They are described as the "first meeting".

It is noted that recordings #8 and #17 which would be on the same record, but opposite sides, are missing.

2. Recordings #20 through #28, recorded between 3:10 p.m. and 6:00 p.m. on November 6, 1964, were recordings of conversations between STEVE GUTHRIE, GEORGE BUTLER, PAUL ROWLAND JONES, and a fourth individual named as "KNAPP". These records pertain to the second meeting of GUTHRIE, BUTLER and JONES.

3. Recordings #29 through #37 were recorded between 8:40 a.m. and 11:40 a.m., on November 7, 1946. The persons involved in these recordings are STEVE GUTHRIE, GEORGE BUTLER, PAUL ROWLAND JONES, "KNAPP", and a fifth individual called "MANNING". These records are referred to as the "third meeting".

on 8/14/64 at Dallas, Texas File # DL 44-1639

by Special Agent RICHARD J. BURNETT /jtf Date dictated 8/19/64

DL 44-1639
2

4. Recordings #38 through #42 were recorded on December 13, 1946 (time not indicated), between STEVE GUTHRIE, GEORGE BUTLER and PAUL ROWLAND JONES. These recordings are described as the "fourth meeting".

While the names of JACK L. RUBY or RUBY were not noted to have been mentioned in these recordings, of particular significance might be comments made on recordings #9 and #18 made at the "first meeting" between GUTHRIE, BUTLER and JONES on November 1-2, 1946.

During the conversation between JONES, GUTHRIE and BUTLER regarding the setting up of a gambling joint in the Dallas area by an outside group, JONES mentioned to GUTHRIE, who was then a Sheriff-elect and not as of that time officially in office, that he wanted GUTHRIE to choose his own man to operate the proposed gambling joint in Dallas and JONES stated "You pick the man," and JONES continued, "I'm going to train the man you pick." GUTHRIE stated that he would send in only one man from the outside to be connected with this gambling venture, and this would be a "crap shooter". JONES emphasized that "It's got to be local." JONES in describing the individual (the crap shooter), who he would bring in from the outside, stated that he looks like a preacher, "not a Dago, not a Jew".

FD-302 (Rev. 3-3-59)

FEDERAL BUREAU OF INVESTIGATION

Date August 19, 1964

1

On August 17, 1964, the twenty-two recordings pertaining to the transcriptions made of the four meetings between former Dallas County Sheriff STEVE GUTHRIE, GEORGE E. BUTLER and PAUL ROWLAND JONES during November and December, 1946, were returned personally to Lieutenant GEORGE E. BUTLER, Juvenile Division, Dallas Police Department. Lieutenant BUTLER stated that he does not know where or what might have happened to recordings # 8 and # 17 of the "first meeting" between JONES, GUTHRIE and himself on November 1, 1946. BUTLER stated these twenty-two recordings, which he had furnished to the FBI on August 11, 1964, were all of the recordings which had been returned to him by the Mc Clellan Committee in 1960. BUTLER stated that he does not recall any questions in the past regarding the absence of any specific records pertaining to the interviews between GUTHRIE, JONES and himself in 1946. He stated that he does not know at this time whether the "missing record" might possibly be an error in transcribing numbers some years ago or whether such a record actually existed at one time.

Lieutenant BUTLER noted that all of these twenty-two recordings were made during four separate meetings in November and December, 1946, between JONES, GUTHRIE and himself in the home of former Dallas County Sheriff STEVE GUTHRIE. He stated that these records are the original recordings of these transcribed accounts of the four meetings.

on 8/17/64 at Dallas, Texas File # DL 44-1639

by Special Agent RICHARD J. BURNETT /jtf Date dictated 8/19/64

This document contains neither recommendations nor conclusions of the FBI. It is the property of the FBI and is loaned to your agency; it and its contents are not to be distributed outside your agency.

COMMISSION EXHIBIT NO. 2416—Continued

Commission Exhibit No. 2417

UNITED STATES DEPAR[redacted]

FEDERAL BUREAU OF INVESTIGATION

In Reply, Please Refer to
File No.

Dallas, Texas
August 27, 1964

JACK L. RUBY;
LEE HARVEY OSWALD

The President's Commission on the Assassination of President Kennedy by letter dated July 23, 1964, in Item Six, requested certain property receipts, included in a Dallas Police Department Report, be initialed by one or both of the officers who executed the documents and that one or more of the individuals be interviewed with respect to certain questions.

Attached are reports of interviews with Willie Mills Dickey, Charles Batchelor and B. W. Reuben, Dallas Police Department, and Billie Joe Smith, former Dallas Police officer.

The four property receipts supplied by the Commission have been initialed. In addition the Dallas Police Department has supplied a copy of property receipt number 14580G, which has been initialed by Mr. Smith.

Attachments (4)

COMMISSION EXHIBIT NO. 2417

FD-302 (Rev. 3-3-59)

FEDERAL BUREAU OF INVESTIGATION

1

Date 8/4/64

WILLIE MILLS DICKEY, 4807 Skillman, advised he was employed as a property clerk for the Dallas Police Department, Dallas, Texas, on November 25, 1963, in the property bureau of the Dallas Police Department, Dallas, Texas. Mr. DICKEY stated he was a retired captain in the regular United States Navy. Mr. DICKEY observed Dallas Police Department Property Clerk's Invoice No. 11105G which was an invoice reflecting property received by Mr. DICKEY and B. J. SMITH, a property clerk, on November 25, 1963. Mr. DICKEY related that this property was property received from Lieutenant RICHARD SWAIN and Lieutenant VERNON SMART of the Dallas Police Department. Mr. DICKEY advised that he checked this property and filled out Invoice No. 11105G and placed it in the property room of the Dallas Police Department. Mr. DICKEY affixed his initials on a copy of this invoice. This property was received from Lieutenant SWAIN and Lieutenant SMART, according to Mr. DICKEY, and tagged with the date of November 24, 1963.

Mr. DICKEY viewed a photostat of Dallas Police Department Property Invoice No. 11107G which contained a listing of property taken from JACK RUBY on November 24, 1963. Mr. DICKEY stated this property was taken from JACK RUBY by Lieutenant VERNON SMART and Lieutenant RICHARD SWAIN on November 24, 1963, tagged, and brought to the property room of the Dallas Police Department on November 25, 1963, where this invoice was made up by him and property clerk B. J. SMITH, and, thereafter, this property was placed in the files of the property department of the Dallas Police Department on November 25, 1963. Mr. DICKEY initialed this photostat reflecting receipt of property contained on Dallas Police Department Invoice No. 11107G.

Mr. DICKEY observed Dallas Police Department Invoice No. 11109G which contained the property of JACK RUBY. This invoice reflected that this property had been received from the jail on November 25, 1963. Mr. DICKEY stated that it was the policy of the Dallas Police Department that when property was removed from prisoners it was to be tagged and placed inside a vault similar to a night safety depository of a bank. Mr. DICKEY related that the property contained on Invoice No. 11109G of the Dallas Police Department was taken from JACK RUBY on November 24, 1963, by Patrolman KENNETH H. HAAKE of the Dallas Police Department, tagged, and placed

on 7/31/64 at Dallas, Texas File # DL 44-1639

by Special Agent VINCENT E. DRAIN:vm Date dictated 8/3/64

2

2
DL 44-1639

in the jail safe. Mr. DICKEY related that no persons have a key to this safe except authorized property clerks and that once dropped into the slot in the top of this safe this property cannot be tampered with until removed by authorized clerks of the Dallas Police Department. Mr. DICKEY placed his initials on the photostat of Dallas Police Department Invoice No. 11109G reflecting that the property contained on this invoice was received by him on November 25, 1963, and thereafter placed in the vault in the property room of the Dallas Police Department.

Mr. DICKEY stated that he was not aware of any property not listed in these invoices that was taken from RUBY at the time of his arrest and, as far as he knew, all such property normally would be listed in a property invoice. He stated he was not aware of any other property invoices that were completed upon RUBY's arrest which had not been exhibited to him. Mr. DICKEY also stated that he was not aware of any loose press cards or badges having been found lying in the basement after RUBY's apprehension on November 24, 1963.

3

FD-302 (Rev. 3-3-59)

FEDERAL BUREAU OF INVESTIGATION

Date 8/5/64

1

Assistant Chief of Police CHARLES BATCHELOR, Dallas Police Department, Dallas, Texas, advised that the only additional invoice of property of the Dallas Police Department that he could find in the property room reflecting property of JACK RUBY taken from him at the time he was arrested was Dallas Police Department Invoice No. 14580G which was property reflecting a .38 caliber revolver, five live rounds of .38 caliber Special ammunition, one .38 caliber cartridge case, and one .38 caliber slug. Assistant Chief BATCHELOR stated this property was used in the trial of JACK RUBY. This invoice reflected that this property was received by property clerk B. J. SMITH from Captain WILL FRITZ, Detectives L. C. GRAVES, M. JOHNSON, and L. D. MONTGOMERY. Assistant Chief BATCHELOR stated that B. J. SMITH was no longer with the Dallas Police Department and was presently working for the Texas Instrument Company at Metairie, Louisiana, which is a suburb of New Orleans, Louisiana. He stated that Mr. SMITH's full name was BILLIE JOE SMITH and that his headquarters was in the Ingram Building, 2848 Veterans Highway, New Orleans, Louisiana.

on 8/1/64 at Dallas, Texas File # DL 44-1639

by Special Agent VINCENT E. DRAIN:vm Date dictated 8/4/64

This document contains neither recommendations nor conclusions of the FBI. It is the property of the FBI and is loaned to your agency; it and its contents are not to be distributed outside your agency.

COMMISSION EXHIBIT No. 2417—Continued

FD-302 (Rev. 3-3-59)

FEDERAL BUREAU OF INVESTIGATION

Date 8/11/64

1

B. W. REUBEN, Property Clerk, Dallas Police Department, advised that Dallas Police Department Property Invoice No. 11474G was made out by him and witnessed by B. J. SMITH. He stated that the money listed on this invoice was previously furnished to the property room of the Dallas Police Department by Lieutenant RICHARD SWAIN and Lieutenant VERNON SMART of the Dallas Police Department. Mr. REUBEN stated this was a supplement to invoice No. 11105G. Mr. REUBEN placed his initials on this invoice certifying that it was a copy of the original invoice of the property room of the Dallas Police Department and was prepared by him.

on 8/10/64 at Dallas, Texas File # DL 44-1639

by Special Agent VINCENT E. DRAIN and ROBERT J. BURNETT:vm Date dictated 8/10/64

This document contains neither recommendations nor conclusions of the FBI. It is the property of the FBI and is loaned to your agency; it and its contents are not to be distributed outside your agency.

COMMISSION EXHIBIT No. 2417—Continued

FD-302 (Rev. 1-25-60)

FEDERAL BUREAU OF INVESTIGATION

1

Date 8/14/64

BILLIE JOE SMITH, 2848 Veterans Highway, Metairie, Louisiana, advised that he was employed by the Dallas Police Department on February 18, 1964, and prepared Invoice No. 14580G. Mr. SMITH stated he was a property clerk, and to the best of his knowledge received the items on invoice from Dallas Police Officers GROVES, JOHNSON, and MONTGOMERY. The items listed on this invoice were listed by him and are the only property he recalls seeing that belonged to RUBY; however, he believes an unknown amount of money was accepted by Mr. HILL, the property room supervisor.

On 8/12/64 at Metairie, Louisiana File # DL 44-1639 NO 44-2064

by SA ALEXANDER JAMIESON: mam Date dictated 8/14/64

This document contains neither recommendations nor conclusions of the FBI. It is the property of the FBI and is loaned to your agency; it and its contents are not to be distributed outside your agency.

COMMISSION EXHIBIT No. 2417—Continued

Form CPS—PC—447

POLICE DEPARTMENT

CITY OF DALLAS

PROPERTY CLERK'S INVOICE OR RECEIPT

25 Nov. 1963 19

Received of Lt. Swain & Lt Smart the following described articles,

§ recovered stolen property:

Evidence in Offense No. Arrest No. Charge inv. murder

QUANTITY	ARTICLE	BIN NO.	DISPOSITION
	Rep. Nat'l Bank money bag with		
$124.87	one hundred twenty four dollars & eighty seven cents	Sf-dr-9	
	(50 ones, 602 dimes, 242 nickels, 257 pennies)		
	Envelope containing		
$131.41	one hundred thirty one dollars & forty one cents		
	(2 tens, 38 ones, 1 silver dollar, 47 halves, 154 quarters, 58 dimes, 86 nickels, 31 pennies)		
	First Nat'l money bag containing		
$795.50	seven hundred ninety-five & fifty cents		
	(80 fives, 320 ones, 47 halves, 82 quarters, 269 dimes, and 92 nickels)		
	(Total - $1051.78)		
1	blue canvas money bag		
1	khaki canvas money bag with leather trimmed top and fitted for locking seal missing the latch		
	tag dated 11-24		
	ARR: RUBY, Jack w/m/52 3929 Rawlins		

№ 11105 G

W M DICKEY & B J SMITH
Property Clerk

If neither evidence nor recovered stolen property, write on face of this form in detail reason for police possession.

260

COMMISSION EXHIBIT No. 2417—Continued

Form CPS—PC—447

POLICE DEPARTMENT

CITY OF DALLAS

PROPERTY CLERK'S INVOICE OR RECEIPT

25 Nov 1963 19

Received of Lt. Smart & Lt Swain the following described articles,

§ recovered stolen property:

Evidence in Offense No. Arrest No. Charge inv. murder

QUANTITY	ARTICLE	BIN NO.	DISPOSITION
1	paper sack containing blk. plastic briefcase with business	77-30	
	correspondence	N-18	
3	Newspapers dtd. 23 Nov. 1963, 2 The Dallas Morning News, & 1 The Dallas Times Herald		
1	envelope containing 2 Polaroid pictures, 3 negatives		
	misc. receipts		
1	envelope containing		
	1 small notebook		
	1 tan plastic billfold with		
	1 Tex oper's license in name of Jack Leon Ruby, 3929 Rawlins		
	1 passenger car lic. receipt, same name		
	misc. papers, cards		
1	envelope containing 1 newspaper page		
	from The Dallas Morning News, 22 Nov. 1963		
	1 pc. of paper with the word "Closed"		
1	small cardboard box with Carousel Club passes & business papers		
	1 small btl. of brn. liquid		
1	envelope containing 2 razor blade dispensers, 2 advertisement pictures		
1	carton of 18 razor blade dispensers		
1	book of 25 stamps (8¢)		
1	book of 20 stamps (5¢)		
2	pr. metal "Knuks"		
12	brn. lea. holster		
1	Wynnewood State Bank money bag		
1	Empire State Bank money bag with misc. papers		
1	stack of envelopes		
1	Merchants State Bank money bag		
1	Rep. Nat'l Bank money bag w/ misc. papers		
1	lea. keycase with 4 keys		

tag dated 11-24 · ARR: RUBY, Jack Leon w/m/52
3929 Rawlins

B J SMITH & W M DICKEY
Property Clerk

Nº 11107 G

If neither evidence nor recovered stolen property, write on face of this form in detail reason for police possession.

8

251

COMMISSION EXHIBIT No. 2417—Continued

Form CPS—PC—447

POLICE DEPARTMENT

CITY OF DALLAS

PROPERTY CLERK'S INVOICE OR RECEIPT

25 Nov 1963 19

Received of jail the following described articles,

§ recovered stolen property:

Evidence in Offense No. Arrest No. Charge inv. murder

QUANTITY	ARTICLE	BIN NO.	DISPOSITION
$2015.33	two thousand fifteen dollars & thirty three cents	Safe Dr 9	
1	man's "Le Coultre wrist watch w/clear stones on face		A-13823
3	Amer. Exp. Company travelers checks, #DA49 990 257, DA49 990 258, DA49 990 259 all three in amt. of $20.00 - in name of Samuel Baker		
1	Gents w/g ring with 3 clear stones	Safe dr 9	A-13823
1	envelope containing	G-25	
	1 pr. eyeglasses, blk. plastic frames		
3	ball pt. pens		
1	small "Trim-Trio" knife		
4	Polaroid pictures, "Impeach Earl Warren" signs		
1	blk. lea. belt		
1	key		
1	blk. lea. belt		
1	necktie		
2	address book		
1	pr. blk. lea. shoes	W-30	
1	white dress shirt	N-18	
1	cot underwear		
1	brn. suit		
1	gray felt hat		
	tag dated 11-24		
	ARR: RUBY, Jack Leon w/m/52 3929 Rawlins		

B J SMITH & W M DICKEY
Property Clerk

Nº 11109 G

If neither evidence nor recovered stolen property, write on face of this form in detail reason for police possession.

9

261A

COMMISSION EXHIBIT No. 2417—Continued

Form CPS—PO—447

POLICE DEPARTMENT

CITY OF DALLAS

PROPERTY CLERK'S INVOICE OR RECEIPT

3 Dec 1963 19

Received of Lt Smith & Lt. Smart the following described articles,

§ recovered stolen property:

Evidence in Offense No. Arrest No. Charge inv. murder

QUANTITY	ARTICLE	BIN NO.	DISPOSITION
$42.00	forty two dollars	Sf dr 9	
	(all one dollar bills)		
12-4-63 Held Continue			
	tag dated 11-24-63		
	ARR: RUBY, Jack w/m/52		
	3929 Rawlins		
	money on invoice 111050 was recounted after F.B.I. agents recorded serial numbers on 12-2-63, and found to exceed the indicated total by the amount of $42.00. This $42.00 is shown on this invoice as a supplement to invoice 111050		

DWR

B J SMITH & D W REUBEN
Property Clerk

№ 11474 G

If neither evidence nor recovered stolen property, write on face of this form in detail reason for police possession.

~~EN-394 URD~~

COMMISSION EXHIBIT No. 2417—Continued

Dead - hold - Do not rel. - Murder filed more Johnson & Gentile 2/20/64

Form CPS-PO—447

POLICE DEPARTMENT

CITY OF DALLAS

PROPERTY CLERK'S INVOICE OR RECEIPT

18 Feb 1964 19

Received of Capt Fritz, L C Graves, M Johnson, L D Montgomery the following described articles,

§ recovered stolen property:

Evidence in Offense No. Arrest No. Charge inv. murder

QUANTITY	ARTICLE	BIN NO.	DISPOSITION
X 1	revolver, 38 cal. Colt 'Cobra', 2" bbl.,	A-215	
	shielded hammer, blue steel with		
	brown plastic grips (left grip chipped)		
	Ser#2744-LW		
X 5	live rounds 38 SPL ammo		
X 1	38 cal. cartridge case		
X 1	38 cal. slug		
	CSS#7992		
	tag date 11-24-63		
	ARR: RUBY, Jack		
	DECEASED: Lee Harvey Oswald		

RECEIVED OF D W Reuben
OF THE PROPERTY ROOM ON FEB 28 1964
ARTICLES AS CHECKED (X) ON INVOICE # NUMBER 14580 G. TAKEN OUT FOR REASON OF Judge Brown's Court
SIGNED: M Johnson 879
RETURNED: DATE:

B J SMITH B J S
Property Clerk

№ 14580 G

44-2064-387

If neither evidence nor recovered stolen property, write on face of this form in detail reason for police possession.

COMMISSION EXHIBIT No. 2417—Continued

4 Commission Exhibit No. 2418

UNITED STATES DEPARTMENT OF JUSTICE

FEDERAL BUREAU OF INVESTIGATION

In Reply, Please Refer to
File No.

Dallas, Texas
September 1, 1964

JACK L. RUBY;
LEE HARVEY OSWALD

By letter dated August 25, 1964, the President's Commission on the Assassination of President Kennedy requested that one "Johnnie" (Last Name Unknown), an employee in November, 1963, of a parking garage near the corner of Jackson and Field Streets, in Dallas, Texas, be located and interviewed regarding a conversation on Saturday morning, November 23, 1963, between Harry Olsen, his wife, and Jack Ruby.

Attached are the results of the interview of John J. Simpson, Jr., Hurst, Texas, who is known as "Johnny", and who on Saturday morning, November 23, 1963, was employed at Simon's Garage, 1300 Jackson, corner of Field Street, Dallas, Texas.

Attachment

COMMISSION EXHIBIT No. 2418

FD-302 (Rev. 3-3-59)

FEDERAL BUREAU OF INVESTIGATION

Date September 1, 1964

1

JOHN J. SIMPSON, JR., advised he resides with his sister, Mrs. GRADY AILES, at 731 Norwood Drive, Hurst, Texas, and is currently employed as a service station attendant at the Gulf Service Station located at the corner of Pipe Line Road and Harrison Lane, Hurst, Texas.

SIMPSON advised that he is commonly known by the nickname of "JOHNNY". He stated that from late Friday night, November 22, 1963, until 6:00 a.m., Saturday morning, November 23, 1963, he was employed as the night parking attendant at Simon's Garage, 1300 Jackson, Dallas, Texas.

He recalls that around 1:00 a.m., Saturday morning, November 23, 1963, a Dallas police officer named OLSEN (whom SIMPSON believes is no longer employed as a Dallas police officer) came to Simon's Garage and got his car. OLSEN then pulled up to the garage exit to wait for his girl friend, name unknown, who was working as a dancer at JACK RUBY's night club, located just one block away on Commerce Street. When the girl friend came and got into OLSEN's car, they started to drive off, but the girl apparently saw JACK RUBY walking down the street and she yelled a greeting to him. RUBY called back, and OLSEN stopped his car when RUBY came up to the car to talk to OLSEN and the girl.

SIMPSON stated that RUBY, the girl, and OLSEN must have conversed at least an hour and possibly longer at this time by the garage.

SIMPSON stated he did not take part in any of the conversation and does not know what the three talked about. He does recall having overheard RUBY remark that he had been to police headquarters that same night and had taken coffee and eats to the police officers. SIMPSON stated he knows JACK RUBY

on 8/29/64 at Hurst, Texas File # DL 44-1639

by Special Agent RICHARD J. BURNETT /jtf Date dictated 8/31/64

This document contains neither recommendations nor conclusions of the FBI. It is the property of the FBI and is loaned to your agency; it and its contents are not to be distributed outside your agency.

COMMISSION EXHIBIT No. 2418—Continued

DL 44-1639
2

by sight but is not a personal friend of RUBY's. He knew OLSEN as a member of the Dallas Police Department, and he recognized the girl with OLSEN as one of the dancers at RUBY's night club, but SIMPSON stated he was not a close friend of any of the three individuals. He would have had no reason to listen to or to partake in their private conversations.

COMMISSION EXHIBIT No. 2418—Continued

FD-302 (Rev. 1-25-60)

FEDERAL BUREAU OF IN — Commission Exhibit No. 2419 —

[redacted]

Date 8/28/64

GEORGE SENATOR advised that he presently resides at the Bristol Hotel, Room 1211, 129 West 48th Street, New York, New York. He also advised that he is employed as a cashier at the Mr. Kiska Delicatessen, 150 West 49th Street, New York, New York.

SENATOR gave the following account of his activities during the morning of November 24, 1963:

I arose around 8:00 a.m. and made myself a cup of coffee. RUBY got up later and made himself two eggs and coffee, however, I did not eat.

RUBY left the apartment around 10:30 a.m. alone. RUBY, while in the apartment, was mumbling to himself, and when I asked him what he was saying he replied nothing. RUBY never mentioned anything about killing OSWALD.

I did not make a phone call to WILLIAM DOWNEY on this day and I never recall ever offering to make breakfast for DOWNEY or his wife at their apartment. DOWNEY is a traveling salesman and a very heavy drinker, and when drinking he does a lot of talking and exaggerates a great deal.

When I left Dallas, Texas, DOWNEY and I were not on speaking terms.

On the morning of November 24, 1963, I left the apartment around 11:00 or 11:30 a.m. and went to the "Eat Well Restaurant" on Main Street for breakfast. While I was in the restaurant one of the waitresses told me that she had just heard on the radio that OSWALD had been shot by an unknown man. I immediately called my friend JIM MARTIN, who is an attorney, to tell him the news. JIM's daughter answered the phone and told me he was at church and would be home soon.

Shortly thereafter the radio announced that RUBY had shot OSWALD. I immediately went to JIM MARTIN's home, and when I arrived there he told me he had just seen the shooting on television. At this time both MARTIN and myself went to the court house where I remained all day.

On 8/27/64 at 1215 Third Avenue, New York, New York File # NY 44-974

by SA EUGENE W. O'NEILL/lac Date dictated 8/28/64

COMMISSION EXHIBIT No. 2419

WU 6278 (R 9-54)

RECEIPT

MF DALLAS, TEXAS — Nov 24 1963

OFFICE — DATE

RECEIVED FROM Jack Ruby

ADDRESS 1312½ Commerce

Twenty Five Dollars $ 25.00

☐ Account for the month of ______ 19__

☐ Telegraphic Money Order

☐ Telegram or Cable

☐ Deposit on Collect Telegram Returnable after 24 hours

☐ Account No. For Remittance

TO Karen Bennett

Address WU

Place Ft Worth Texas

MONEY	Chgs	$ .55
ORDER	Tolls	$ 1.20
CHARGES	Tax	$ .12
PAID	TOTAL	$ 1.87

THE WESTERN UNION TELEGRAPH COMPANY

BY [illegible signature]

Commission Exhibit No. 2420

1963 NOV 24 AM 11 16

...S TEXAS

Commission Exhibit No. 2421

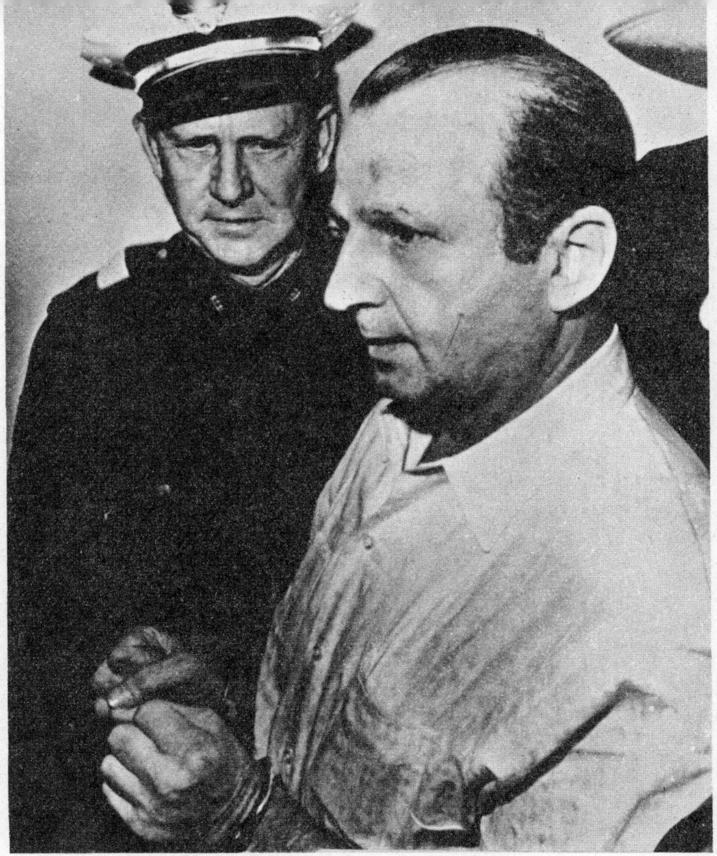

Commission Exhibit No. 2422

Commission Exhibit No. 2423

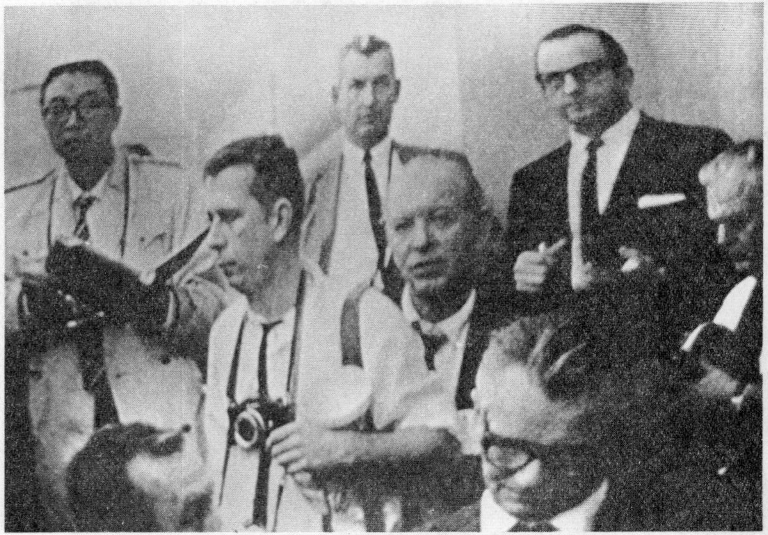

Commission Exhibit No. 2424

COMMISSION EXHIBIT No. 2425

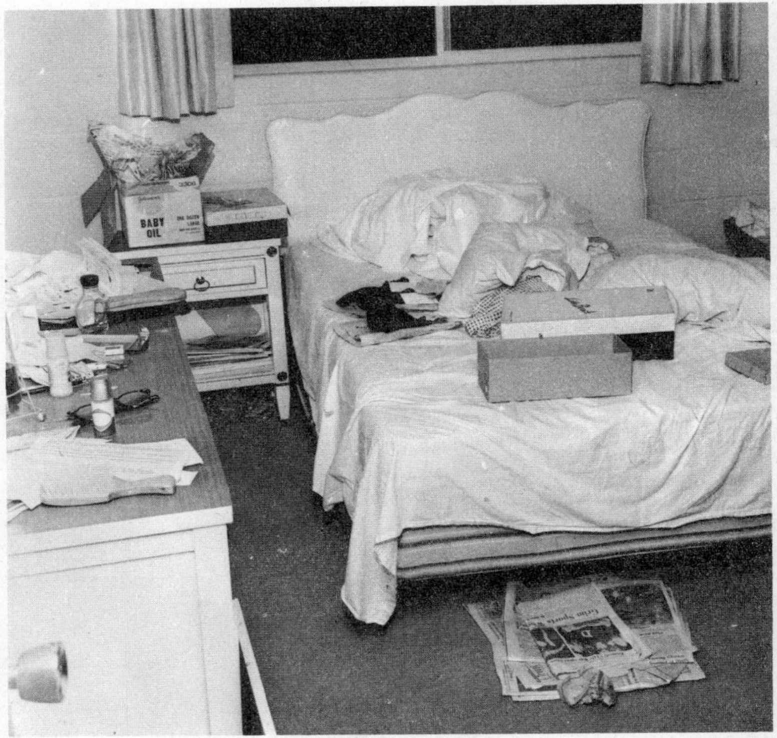

COMMISSION EXHIBIT No. 2426

COMMISSION EXHIBIT No. 2427

Commission Exhibit No. 2428

PRESIDENT'S COMMISSION
ON THE
ASSASSINATION OF PRESIDENT KENNEDY
200 Maryland Ave. N.E.
Washington, D.C. 20002
Telephone 543-1400

September 14, 1964

M E M O R A N D U M

TO: J. Lee Rankin
General Counsel

FROM: Burt W. Griffin

Pursuant to your request, the Federal Bureau of Investigation has provided for examination all reports in its files pertaining to the activities in the Dallas-Fort Worth area during the year 1963 of all persons associated with the anti-Castro Cuban groups known as ALFA 66, JURE and Directorio Revolutionario Estudiantil (DRE).

I have examined those reports and have found no names or activities mentioned which are recognizable by me in any way as being connected with Jack Ruby, with any of Jack Ruby's known associates or any activities in which Jack Ruby participated.

Burt W. Griffin

COMMISSION EXHIBIT No. 2428

FD-302 (Rev. 1-25-60)

FEDERAL BUREAU OF INVESTIGATION

Date June 8, 1964

1

Mrs. GALE ANN CASCADDAN, nee Eaton, 202 West Birch Street, Harrison, Michigan, furnished the following information:

CURTIS LAVERNE CRAFARD, also known as "Larry", is Mrs. CASCADDAN's first cousin. Her mother and CRAFARD's father are sister and brother. Mrs. CASCADDAN has known CRAFARD for the past twelve years, however, personal contact with him during that period has been quite limited and intermittent. During the early part of September, 1963, CRAFARD visited Mrs. CASCADDAN's parents (EDWARD and ESTHER EATON) at the latter's residence, 202 West Birch Street, Harrison. Mrs. CASCADDAN saw him on that occasion. CRAFARD departed from Harrison the following day, stating that he was going to join a carnival (name unknown) at Allegan, Michigan. This carnival was destined for Memphis, Tennessee, to play at the Mid-South Fair in that city during the latter part of September. CRAFARD apparently obtained a job with this carnival through his brother-in-law, CHAUNCEY INGERSOLL, who was employed by it. The latter is married to CORA BELLE INGERSOLL, CRAFARD's sister, who now resides in Clare, Michigan. Presently, CHAUNCEY INGERSOLL is incarcerated in the State Prison of Southern Michigan, Jackson, Michigan, serving a term for burglary which involved the theft of firearms.

When CRAFARD was in Harrison during the early part of September, 1963, he made no mention of going to Texas and gave no indication whatsoever that he had met or knew JACK RUBY. Subsequent to his departure from Harrison on that occasion, his whereabouts and activities remained unknown until Mrs. CASCADDAN received an air mail letter from him which was postmarked at Dallas, Texas, on October 29, 1963. This letter revealed that he was living at "1312½ Commerce", Dallas, and was employed by the Carousel Club there as "...a combination janitor and bookkeeper".

Mrs. CASCADDAN was next contacted by CRAFARD on November 26, 1963, when he appeared at her parents' home in Harrison. CRAFARD remained over night and then left

On 6/5/64 at Harrison, Michigan File # Detroit 44-563
Dallas 44-1639

by SA (A) DOUGLAS C. CANNELL:sal Date dictated 6/5/64

93

COMMISSION EXHIBIT No. 2429

DE 44-563
2

the next day to hitchhike to Kalkaska, Michigan, and visit his sister, CORA BELLE INGERSOLL. While in Harrison on that occasion, CRAFARD said he had been employed by JACK RUBY at the Carousel Club in Dallas, Texas. In addition to being a bookkeeper and janitor for RUBY, he "worked the lights" during the floor shows and "...got tired of watching naked women". CRAFARD claimed that he also served as JACK RUBY's "personal secretary"; he had coffee with RUBY in the latter's office; and he and RUBY occasionally sat at the end of the bar near the rear door of the Carousel Club and talked. According to Mrs. CASCADDAN, these statements by CRAFARD were apparently designed to demonstrate that CRAFARD was not only an employee, but also a "buddy" of RUBY. Too, CRAFARD gave the impression that his employment by RUBY was a "big deal" and it had been an honor to work for him.

CRAFARD talked of only one occasion when he and RUBY were together away from the Carousel Club. This occurred while CRAFARD was employed by RUBY and involved photographing signs advertising the Carousel Club. Mrs. CASCADDAN stated that her mother (ESTHER EATON) learned through a conversation with CRAFARD on February 29, 1964, that the latter had had dinner on at least one occasion with RUBY at the home of EVA GRANT, RUBY's sister, in Dallas. This ostensibly took place while CRAFARD was working for RUBY.

CRAFARD said that he first learned of the assassination of President KENNEDY on the same day that event occurred. He was sleeping in his room, apparently at the Carousel Club, when a "buddy" (not further identified) awakened him and told him about it. CRAFARD did not mention what he did following the receipt of this information. Specifically, he made no mention of discussing it with JACK RUBY or even being in contact with RUBY after that. However, Mrs. CASCADDAN stated that her mother (ESTHER EATON) informed her that CRAFARD said RUBY was upset when he received the news of President KENNEDY's death and RUBY "walked around". CRAFARD made no mention of being at the Carousel Club on the night of November 22, 1963, or engaging in a telephone conversation with anyone. Additionally, he did not talk about RUBY's emotional reaction to the news of the President's assassination. In fact, CRAFARD did not discuss in Mrs. CASCADDAN's presence what he, CRAFARD, did between the time he first learned of President KENNEDY's death and his (CRAFARD's) departure from Dallas on the following day (November 23, 1963).

94

COMMISSION EXHIBIT No. 2429—Continued

DE 44-563
3

In Mrs. CASCADDAN's opinion, CRAFARD exhibited an indifferent attitude toward the assassination of the President. While CRAFARD was visiting Mrs. CASCADDAN's parents in Harrison on November 26-27, 1963, a considerable amount of time was being devoted by the television networks to the assassination and its aftermath involving RUBY's murder of LEE HARVEY OSWALD. Mrs. CASCADDAN, her parents, and her brothers spent most of their time watching programs on television pertaining to the assassination. CRAFARD seemed mildly interested in these programs, and spent some time upstairs reading comic books. This seemed strange to Mrs. CASCADDAN. She thought that CRAFARD should have had an avid, continuing interest in this matter because he was a "buddy" and former employee of RUBY. In Mrs. CASCADDAN's vernacular, CRAFARD seemed about as disturbed over the President's assassination as he would be "over killing a cat".

Mrs. CASCADDAN advised that neither she nor her parents could understand why CRAFARD departed from Dallas to hitchhike back to Michigan on the day following the assassination. Specifically, she asked CRAFARD why he left Dallas at that time and he never answered her question. As she recalls, he merely shifted the conversation to another topic. Too, her parents had been unable to secure an answer to this question from CRAFARD. Why CRAFARD would not furnish a reason or reasons for this action is unknown to Mrs. CASCADDAN.

In respect to his departure from Dallas on November 23, 1963, CRAFARD stated that he did not contact JACK RUBY and tell RUBY he was leaving. At the time, RUBY owed him wages and CRAFARD did not attempt to collect them. CRAFARD explained that he did not mention the departure to RUBY, because he and RUBY were "buddies" and RUBY would not want him to leave.

CRAFARD did not discuss, even in a general way, activities which took place while he was hitchhiking from Texas to Michigan during November, 1963. However, he did mention that en route he learned that RUBY had shot and killed LEE HARVEY OSWALD. No doubt, CRAFARD was fortunate in securing rides during this trip for he reached Clare, Michigan, in two days and spent the night at the home of his cousin, CLIFFORD ROBERTS, 307 East 7th Street, Clare. At that time, CRAFARD's sister, CORA BELLE INGERSOLL, was also residing at that address. On the following day (November 26, 1963), CRAFARD visited Mrs. CASCADDAN and her parents in Harrison.

95

COMMISSION EXHIBIT No. 2429—Continued

FD-302 (Rev. 1-25-60)

FEDERAL BUREAU OF INVESTIGATION

1

Date 6/8/64

Mrs. EDWARD (ESTHER) EATON, 202 West Birch Street, Harrison, Michigan, was present during part of the interview of her daughter, Mrs. GALE ANN CASCADDAN, on June 5, 1964.

Mrs. EATON confirmed Mrs. CASCADDAN's assertion that CURTIS LAVERNE CRAFARD never explained to her (Mrs. EATON) or other members of the EATON family why he (CRAFARD) left Dallas, Texas, the day following President KENNEDY's assassination. Mrs. EATON observed that CRAFARD expressed relative unconcern over the assassination, and his only mention of its effects on JACK RUBY was the statement that RUBY was "upset" and "walked around a great deal". Mrs. EATON cannot recall any further information furnished by CRAFARD which related to RUBY's emotional state or activities at that time. Also, she noted that CRAFARD was not specifically asked by her nor did he discuss in her presence his activities from the time that he first learned of President KENNEDY's death until he departed from Dallas on the following day.

On 6/5/64 at Harrison, Michigan File # Detroit 44-563
Dallas 44-1639

by SA(A) DOUGLAS C. CANNELL:sal (?) Date dictated 6/5/64

COMMISSION EXHIBIT No. 2429—Continued

OFFICE OF THE DIRECTOR

UNITED STATES DEPARTMENT OF JUSTICE

FEDERAL BUREAU OF INVESTIGATION

WASHINGTON, D.C. 20535

September 4, 1964

BY COURIER SERVICE

Honorable J. Lee Rankin
General Counsel
The President's Commission
200 Maryland Avenue, Northeast
Washington, D. C.

Dear Mr. Rankin:

Reference is made to my letter dated August 27, 1964, concerning the display of photographs of Officer J. D. Tippit and Mr. Bernard Weissman to six individuals having a connection with the Carousel Club.

Enclosed are two copies each of two communications from our Portland Office dated August 21, 1964, and August 31, 1964. In the enclosed communications you will note Mr. Crafard states Mr. Jack Ruby told him that he knew Officer Tippit and that he, Crafard, had seen Mr. Weissman at the Carousel Club on a number of occasions.

For your information, my letter dated August 27, 1964, enclosed a communication from our Dallas Office dated August 21, 1964. On page two of the Dallas communication Mr. Andrew Armstrong, Jr., during an interview on August 20, 1964, stated after viewing photographs of Officer Tippit and Mr. Weissman that he had never seen either individual before. Mr. Armstrong also stated that Mr. Ruby had told him that the "Tippit" who was shot was not the one he knew. Further, beginning on page three of the Dallas communication Detective Gayle M. Tippit, during interview on December 16, 1963, acknowledged that he was very well acquainted with Mr. Ruby.

COMMISSION EXHIBIT No. 2430

Honorable J. Lee Rankin

When the results of our efforts to verify Mr. Weissman's employment in Dallas on November 14, 1963, as requested in your letter dated August 31, 1964, are received, you will be promptly advised concluding our inquiries into this particular matter.

Sincerely yours,

J. Edgar Hoover

Enclosures (4)

-2-

COMMISSION EXHIBIT No. 2430—Continued

UNITED STATES DEPARTMENT OF JUSTICE

FEDERAL BUREAU OF INVESTIGATION

In Reply, Please Refer to
File No.

Portland, Oregon
August 21, 1964

ASSASSINATION OF PRESIDENT
JOHN FITZGERALD KENNEDY,
NOVEMBER 22, 1963, DALLAS, TEXAS
MISCELLANEOUS - INFORMATION CONCERNING

Curtis La Verne Crafard, 1219 Birch Street, Dallas, Oregon, advised Special Agent Vern F. Davis that he had been employed by Jack Ruby at Ruby's Carousel Club and also at his Vegas Club in Dallas, Texas, principally as lights operator for the stage acts but also occasionally as bartender and doorman, and this employment covered the period around November 14, 1963. Interview was conducted on August 21, 1964.

Relative to Officer J. D. Tippit, the photographs of Tippit were shown to Crafard at his above address in Dallas, Oregon. He said that he does not recognize the photographs of Tippit as anyone he had seen in either of the above clubs. He does recall the name "Tippit" and recalls that he was in the presence of Ruby at the time the news came over the air concerning the assassination of President Kennedy and the death of Officer Tippit, and at that time Crafard recalls hearing Ruby refer to Tippit by name in a manner indicating to Crafard that Ruby knew Tippit. Crafard was unable to recall specifically what Ruby said.

Concerning Bernard Weissman, Crafard was shown the photographs of Weissman. He recalled the photographs as being of a man he recognizes as having been at the Carousel Club, belonging to Ruby in Dallas, Texas, on a number of occasions. He has heard Ruby refer to Weissman by the name of "Weissman," and on several occasions has served Weissman drinks at the Carousel Club.

Crafard stated he was employed by Ruby on November 14, 1963, but he is quite certain he was at the Vegas Club on that date. Crafard has no recollection of Ruby, Weissman and Tippit meeting at the Carousel Club or elsewhere on November 14, 1963, or on any other date.

COMMISSION EXHIBIT No. 2430—Continued

UNITED STATES DEPARTMENT OF JUSTICE

FEDERAL BUREAU OF INVESTIGATION

In Reply, Please Refer to
File No.

Portland, Oregon
August 31, 1964

ASSASSINATION OF PRESIDENT
JOHN FITZGERALD KENNEDY
NOVEMBER 22, 1963, DALLAS, TEXAS
MISCELLANEOUS - INFORMATION CONCERNING

Curtis La Verne Crafard, 1219 Birch Street, Dallas, Oregon, furnished the following information to Special Agents Vern F. Davis and Harold G. Brack on August 27, 1964:

It is Crafard's definite recollection that he was in the presence of Jack Ruby when the news came over the air concerning the assassination of President Kennedy and the death of Officer J. D. Tippit on November 22, 1963. At that time, Ruby referred to Officer Tippit by his first name or a nickname, neither of which Crafard can recall, and said he knew him quite well. He definitely was referring to the Dallas, Texas, Police Department officer, Tippit, who was shot the day of the assassination.

Concerning an individual named Weissman, Crafard has a very vague recollection of having heard either Ruby or the man in charge of the Carousel Club in Ruby's absence, whose name is either Andy Alexander or Andy Armstrong, mention the name Weissman. He does not remember in what connection the name was mentioned, unless possibly it was simply an order to serve Mr. Weissman. Crafard believes he served such a "fellow" two or three times at the bar at the Carousel Club in the late evening and that he was a detective from the Dallas, Texas, Police Department. He does not recall Weissman's first name but is inclined to think it may have been Johnny. He does not recall anyone else who knew Weissman, and the only description Crafard can furnish of Weissman is as follows:

Race	White
Sex	Male
Nationality	American
Age	38 to 43 years

COMMISSION EXHIBIT No. 2430—Continued

ASSASSINATION OF PRESIDENT
JOHN FITZGERALD KENNEDY
NOVEMBER 22, 1963, DALLAS, TEXAS
MISCELLANEOUS - INFORMATION CONCERNING

Height	Six feet
Weight	180 to 185 pounds
Hair	Dark

Crafard does not recall whether Weissman may have been at the Carousel Club early in the period he, Crafard, worked there or at a later date. Actually, Crafard said, he has "practically forgotten all that happened when I was in Dallas and I could have my recollection of a Mr. Weissman mixed up with someone else."

Crafard stated that if previous to August 21, 1964, he had not furnished information as to his recollection of an acquaintanceship between Ruby and Officer J. D. Tippit and also his recollection of a possible acquaintanceship between Ruby and a Mr. Weissman, it is because these points had not been specifically covered with him previously. He said he knows of no other information that he has which would be pertinent to this matter.

COMMISSION EXHIBIT No. 2430—Continued

Commission Exhibit No. 2431

UNITED STATES DEPARTM [redacted]

FEDERAL BUREAU OF INVESTIGATION

In Reply, Please Refer to
File No.

Dallas, Texas
September 2, 1964

JACK L. RUBY;
LEE HARVEY OSWALD

The President's Commission on the Assassination of President Kennedy by letter dated August 21, 1964, advised that Mrs. Wanda Yvonne Helmick in her deposition before a Commission staff member stated that on Saturday night, November 23, 1963, at about 9:00 p.m. or later, she had overheard a telephone call at the Bull Pen Drive-In between Ralph Paul and Jack Ruby in which Paul made a remark about Ruby's possessing a gun and was heard to exclaim "Are you crazy!"

The President's Commission desired that certain employees of the Bull Pen Drive-In be identified and interviewed regarding this specific telephone call.

Attached are the results of the interviews of these employees.

It is noted that upon the original contact on August 27, 1964, at the Bull Pen Drive-In, Arlington, Texas, Mr. Ralph Paul presented himself and volunteered to assist in identifying and locating present and former employees of his drive-in and offered to be of any assistance possible to this investigation.

Attachments

COMMISSION EXHIBIT No. 2431

FD-302 (Rev. 3-3-59)

FEDERAL BUREAU OF INVESTIGATION

Date September 1, 1964

1

RALPH PAUL, Copeland Road, Arlington, Texas, was interviewed at his restaurant, the Bull Pen Drive-In, East Abrams, Arlington, Texas.

Mr. PAUL advised that on Monday, August 24, 1964, he had been interviewed at Fort Worth, Texas, by a representative of the President's Commission regarding information of value he might have concerning his association with JACK L. RUBY. Mr. PAUL stated that he was questioned regarding the telephone call he reportedly had received on the night of Saturday night, November 23, 1963, at the restaurant from JACK RUBY, in which he had apparently made the remark, "Are you crazy?" over the phone to RUBY.

Mr. PAUL stated this remark was probably true, but pertained to the fact that RUBY had mentioned to him that he was going to close his night club for three days, which he, PAUL, thought was ridiculous.

PAUL stated at no time during any of the telephone conversation he had with RUBY on November 23, 1963, had RUBY mentioned to him anything about having a revolver.

Mr. PAUL stated he has positively not told anyone that RUBY had called him that Saturday night stating he had a gun. He had not told anyone this as it is untrue.

Regarding the identities of former and present employees of the Bull Pen Restaurant, whose nicknames are "ROSE", "TOYO", "BONNIE", "CURLY" and "JOE," Mr. PAUL furnished the following information:

"ROSE" is actually ROSE JACKSON, wife of JOHN W. JACKSON, manager of this drive-in, and ROSE is employed as a cashier.

on 8/27/64 at Arlington, Texas File # DL 44-1639

by Special Agent RICHARD J. BURNETT /jtf Date dictated 8/31/64

This document contains neither recommendations nor conclusions of the FBI. It is the property of the FBI and is loaned to your agency; it and its contents are not to be distributed outside your agency.

2

DL 44-1639
2

"TOYO" is a Japanese girl, whose last name is unknown to Mr. PAUL, but who is currently working at the Bull Pen Drive-In.

"BONNIE" is VERNA LOU CORNETT, a former waitress, who is currently living at an unknown address in Arlington, Texas.

"CURLY" is unknown by nickname to Mr. PAUL, who advised that he does not recall ever having any employee at the Bull Pen Drive-In by this nickname.

"JOE" is identical to JOYCE ANGELL, who resides at 1017 Craven Road, Arlington, Texas, and who in November, 1963, would have been working as a curb waitress during the daylight hours.

3

FEDERAL BUREAU OF INVESTIGATION

Date September 1, 1964

1

JOHN W. JACKSON, 1602 Browning, Arlington, Texas, advised he is the manager of the Bull Pen Drive-In, and held such position on November 23, 1963.

Mr. JACKSON advised he does not recall ever having heard RALPH PAUL, the owner of the Bull Pen Drive-In, mention that RUBY had told him he had a gun, or that PAUL thought RUBY was crazy and was going to shoot OSWALD.

JACKSON stated the only person at this restaurant who is known by the nickname of "JOHNNIE" is himself. He stated RALPH PAUL has never, to his knowledge, been referred to by such a nickname.

JACKSON stated he does not recall any telephone call received by RALPH PAUL at the Bull Pen Drive-In on Saturday night, November 23, 1963, from JACK RUBY.

JACKSON stated that BRUCE CARLIN and "LITTLE LYNN" are unknown to him; however, he stated that TAMMI TRUE is a frequent customer at this drive-in restaurant and he believes, but he is not positive, that she might have visited this restaurant on Saturday, November 23, 1963, or Sunday, November 24, 1963.

JACKSON stated that by the time he saw RALPH PAUL on Sunday, November 24, 1963, PAUL had already heard of JACK RUBY's having shot OSWALD. He stated PAUL appeared to be generally upset over this event.

JACKSON advised he is sometimes referred to by a few customers by the nickname of "CURLY; however, this restaurant has not, to his knowledge, in recent years, had any employee, male or female, who used the nickname of "CURLY" commonly.

on 8/27/64 at Arlington, Texas File # DL 44-1639

by Special Agent RICHARD J. BURNETT /jtf Date dictated 8/31/64

4

COMMISSION EXHIBIT No. 2431—Continued

Date September 1, 1964

1

ROSE JACKSON, 1602 Browning, Arlington, Texas, advised she is the wife of JOHN W. JACKSON, the manager of the Bull Pen Drive-In, Arlington, Texas. She stated she is also employed at this restaurant as the cashier and was so employed as of Saturday, November 23, 1963.

Mrs. JACKSON stated she does not recall RALPH PAUL receiving a telephone call from JACK RUBY on the night of November 23, 1963, at the Bull Pen Drive-In. As she now recalls, PAUL had not been feeling well that night, and she and her husband had sent him home earlier in the evening prior to closing time.

Mrs. JACKSON stated she positively did not overhear any telephone conversation between RALPH PAUL and JACK RUBY on Saturday, November 23, 1963, and has never heard RALPH PAUL make any statement indicating that RUBY had called him that night and had told him he had a gun.

Mrs. JACKSON stated RALPH PAUL has never been known to her to have been referred to by one of the employees by the nickname "JOHNNIE". She stated the only such individual, who has this nickname and who is employed at this restaurant, is her husband.

Mrs. JACKSON stated that BRUCE CARLIN and "LITTLE LYNN" are unknown to her; however, TAMMI TRUE is a frequent customer at this restaurant, but she is not in a position to say whether or not TAMMI TRUE was at this drive-in on either Saturday night, November 23, 1963, or the following day.

She stated that on Sunday, November 24, 1963, when she first saw RALPH PAUL that day, he had already heard of RUBY's shooting OSWALD, and he, PAUL, seemed to be visibly upset.

on 8/27/64 at Arlington, Texas File # DL 44-1639

by Special Agent RICHARD J. BURNETT /jtf Date dictated 8/31/64

This document contains neither recommendations nor conclusions of the FBI. It is the property of the FBI and is loaned to your agency; it and its contents are not to be distributed outside your agency.

5

COMMISSION EXHIBIT No. 2431—Continued

DL 44-1639
2

Mrs. JACKSON said that she knows of no former employee at the Bull Pen Drive-In by the nickname of "CURLY".

FD-302 (Rev. 3-3-59)

FEDERAL BUREAU OF INVESTIGATION

Date September 2, 1964

1

GERALDONE TOYO, 415 Northwest 19th Street, Grand Prairie, Texas, advised she is commonly known by her nickname "TOYO".

TOYO advised that she speaks very little English and finds it difficult to understand English spoken to her unless it is spoken quietly and slowly. Accordingly, she stated it is impossible for her to overhear a telephone conversation in all the noise that accompanies the Saturday night business at the Bull Pen Drive-In, and she does not recall Mr. PAUL having spoken to JACK RUBY on Saturday night, November 23, 1963.

TOYO advised that on the busy nights, of which Saturday nights are the busiest, she works outside the drive-in as a curb waitress, and she would have no reason to have been inside near the telephone.

TOYO stated that the only person known to her by the nickname of "JOHNNIE" at this restaurant is JOHN JACKSON, the manager. She has never heard RALPH PAUL referred to by this nickname.

She stated she does not know BRUCE CARLIN, "LITTLE LYNN" or TAMMI TRUE by name.

She stated that by the time she saw RALPH PAUL on Sunday, November 24, 1963, PAUL had already heard of RUBY's shooting OSWALD, and PAUL appeared to be visibly shaken over the news.

on 8/27/64 at Arlington, Texas File # DL 44-1639

by Special Agent RICHARD J. BURNETT /jtf Date dictated 8/31/64

7'

FD-302 (Rev. 3-3-59) FEDERAL BUREAU OF INVESTIGATION

Date September 2, 1964

1

JOYCE ANGELL, 1017 Craven Road, Arlington, Texas, advised she is commonly known by the nickname "JOE".

Mrs. ANGELL advised she is employed as a curb waitress by the Bull Pen Drive-In, Arlington, Texas, and was so employed on Saturday night, November 23, 1963. Mrs. ANGELL advised she does not recall overhearing any telephone conversation on the night of November 23, 1963, between RALPH PAUL and JACK RUBY. She stated neither does she recall ever having heard PAUL mention that RUBY had called him and had said he had a gun. Mrs. ANGELL stated that RALPH PAUL has never been known to her to use the nickname of "JOHNNIE". She noted that the only individual employed by this restaurant, who has such a nickname, is the manager, JOHN JACKSON. She stated that BRUCE CARLIN and "LITTLE LYNN" are unknown to her, but she does know TAMMI TRUE who is a regular customer at this restaurant.

However, Mrs. ANGELL stated she cannot say whether or not TAMMI TRUE had visited this drive-in on Saturday night, November 23, 1963, or the following day.

Mrs. ANGELL added that she was not around the drive-in when RALPH PAUL first heard the news concerning RUBY's shooting OSWALD and she does not know his reaction.

on 8/27/64 at Arlington, Texas File # DL 44-1639

by Special Agent RICHARD J. BURNETT /jtf Date dictated 8/31/64

8

COMMISSION EXHIBIT No. 2431—Continued

Commission Exhibit No. 2432

UNITED STATES DEPARTMENT OF JUSTICE

FEDERAL BUREAU OF INVESTIGATION

In Reply, Please Refer to File No.

Knoxville, Tennessee
September 1, 1964

JACK L. RUBY;
LEE HARVEY OSWALD - VICTIM
CIVIL RIGHTS

On September 1, 1964, Mr. HARVEY LAWILL WADE, 818 Donaldson Road, Chattanooga, Tennessee, advised an Agent of the FBI that he telephoned the FBI Office, Knoxville, Tennessee, on the afternoon of November 24, 1963, to report he had information of possible value regarding assassination of JOHN FITZGERALD KENNEDY. He was interviewed by Agents of the FBI on the night of November 24, 1963, from 9:18 p.m. to 10:16 p.m. Mr. WADE advised he had not received any information prior to his contacting the FBI regarding possibility LEE HARVEY OSWALD had visited in the Carousel Club, Dallas, Texas. He stated he was not aware anyone had reported similar information at the time he reported this matter to the FBI on November 24, 1963.

On September 1, 1964, the five photographs furnished the FBI by Mr. J. LEE RANKIN, General Counsel for the President's Commission on the Assassination of President Kennedy by letter dated August 25, 1964, were exhibited to Mr. WADE. Mr. WADE advised none of the persons included in any of the above five photographs resembled the individual whom he believed and previously reported resembled LEE HARVEY OSWALD. He reported he did not recall seeing the individual identified in the photographs as HARRY CRAFARD at the Carousel Club or the individual indicated by an arrow in two of the above photographs who appeared to be wearing a long-sleeved sport shirt with both sleeves turned up two or three rolls partway exposing the forearms of this individual. Mr. WADE stated he definitely recalled the unidentified patron in white shirt with pants legs rolled up who appeared in the photographs dancing with one of the strippers. He also recalled the unidentified patron assisting one of the strippers with a zipper as shown in one of the

1.

COMMISSION EXHIBIT No. 2432

JACK L. RUBY

photographs. He stated that when the above two photographs were taken the three men previously described by him were seated at the extreme end of the bar on the right side facing the stage. He did not see any of the three men described by him previously in any of the five photographs exhibited to him.

He again repeated the description of the individual he believed resembled LEE HARVEY OSWALD. He stated this man was white male, early 20's, 5'8", 140 lbs., long black hair, very fair pale complexion, slender build. He had no unusual characteristics and wore a dark-colored suit. He resembled OSWALD in appearance.

This document contains neither recommendations nor conclusions of the FBI. It is the property of the FBI and is loaned to your agency; it and its contents are not to be distributed outside your agency.

-2-

COMMISSION EXHIBIT No. 2432—Continued

Commission Exhibit No. 2433

UNITED STATES DEPARTMENT OF JUSTICE

FEDERAL BUREAU OF INVESTIGATION

In Reply, Please Refer to File No.

Dallas, Texas
August 11, 1964

JACK L. RUBY;
LEE HARVEY OSWALD

The President's Commission on the Assassination of President Kennedy requested, in a letter dated July 23, 1964, that examination be made of all existing long distance telephone calls made from telephones listed to Mr. Harry Olsen and Mrs. Harry Olsen (Kathie Kay Coleman), formerly of 325 North Ewing Street, Dallas, Texas.

Attached are the results of such examination of toll charge records now available in Dallas, Texas.

Records of Southwestern Bell Telephone Company, Oklahoma City, Oklahoma, disclose the subscriber to telephone GA 7-6531, as of December 26, 1963, and at present, is Oklahoma Tire and Supply Company, retail store at 1612 N.E. 23rd Street, Oklahoma City.

In a letter dated July 20, 1964, the Commission made a request for similar toll charge information for the period from 10:00 P.M., Saturday, November 23, 1963, through Sunday, November 24, 1963. It is observed this period was covered in the examination.

COMMISSION EXHIBIT No. 2433

FD-302 (Rev. 3-3-59)

FEDERAL BUREAU OF INVESTIGATION

1

Date 7/31/64

Records of Southwestern Bell Telephone Company reflect no telephone service has ever been listed in the name of Mr. HARRY OLSEN or to a Mrs. HARRY OLSEN.

There was found a listing to a KAY COLEMAN, residence 325 N. Ewing Street, Apartment 111. This service was installed on December 14, 1962, and disconnected on February 1, 1964.

KAY COLEMAN had a deposit of $30 with the telephone company and a refund check of $21.48 wasmailed upon the discontinuance of the service to a Mrs. HALL, Apartment 115, 325 N. Ewing Street, Dallas, on February 5, 1964. This check was returned unclaimed and has never been claimed to date having been sent to the Southwestern Bell Telephone Company headquarters, St. Louis, Missouri.

The above information is confidential and is not to be made public except upon the issuance of a subpoena duces tecum which should be directed to R. A. BURROW, Chief Special Agent, Southwestern Bell Telephone Company, Dallas, Texas.

2

on 7/29/64 at Dallas, Texas File # DL 44-1639

by Special Agent ROBERT C. LISH:vm Date dictated 7/30/64

This document contains neither recommendations nor conclusions of the FBI. It is the property of the FBI and is loaned to your agency; it and its contents are not to be distributed outside your agency.

COMMISSION EXHIBIT No. 2433—Continued

FD-302 (Rev. 3-3-59)

1

FEDERAL BUREAU OF INVESTIGATION

Date 7/31/64

Records of the Southwestern Bell Telephone Company reflect the following information concerning subscriber KAY COLEMAN, residence 325 North Ewing, Apartment 111, telephone number WH 2-3268:

DATE	TIME CALL PLACED	DURATION OF CALL	PERSON PLACING CALL	PERSON CALLED	NUMBER AND CITY
11/14/63		9 min.		Mrs. TAMMY TRUE	TE 4-0847, Fort Worth (State not shown)
11/27/63		7 min.		TAMMY TRUE, Room 6, Siesta Motel	GA 4-4646, Oklahoma City, Okla.
12/1/63		3 min.		"	"
12/1/63		6 min.	KAY COLEMAN (Collect call)		WH 2-3268, Dallas (State not shown)
12/22/63		6 min.		HARRY D. OLSON	538-4682, Henrietta (State not shown)
12/26/63	1:33 p.m.	2 min.			GA 7-6531, Oklahoma City, Okla.

The above are the only long distance calls available on bills rendered KAY COLEMAN and no long distance calls appeared on the final bill, which was rendered February 5, 1964.

The records of the Southwestern Bell Telephone Company reflect telephone number 538-4682 is listed to HARRY L. OLSEN, residence 415 West Ikard, Henrietta, Texas. This person is part owner of the Olsen

3

on 7/30/64 at Dallas, Texas File # DL 44-1639

by Special Agent ROBERT C. LISH/eah/pm Date dictated 7/30/64

This document contains neither recommendations nor conclusions of the FBI. It is the property of the FBI and is loaned to your agency; it and its contents are not to be distributed outside your agency.

COMMISSION EXHIBIT No. 2433—Continued

DL 44-1639
2

Stelzer Boot Company.

The above is confidential and is not to be made public except upon the issuance of a subpoena duces tecum, which should be directed to R. A. BURROW, Chief Special Agent, Southwestern Bell Telephone Company, Dallas.

4.

COMMISSION EXHIBIT No. 2433—Continued

FD-302 (Rev. 3-3-59)

FEDERAL BUREAU OF INVESTIGATION

1

Date August 27, 1964

Sergeant H. H. STRINGER, Personnel Office, Dallas Police Department, said the records of that office reflect HARRY NEAL OLSEN, former patrolman, discharged December 29, 1963, was born February 16, 1934, at Wichita Falls, Texas.

The file further showed HARRY LEE OLSEN to be the father of HARRY NEAL OLSEN.

HARRY LEE OLSEN, part owner of Olsen Stelzer Boot Company, Henrietta, Texas, is shown only as having an address of Post Office Box 45, Henrietta, Texas.

5.

on 8/26/64 at Dallas, Texas File # DL 44-1639

by Special Agent ROBERT C. LISH/pm Date dictated 8/26/64

COMMISSION EXHIBIT No. 2433—Continued

UNITED STATES DEPARTMENT OF JUSTICE

FEDERAL BUREAU OF INVESTIGATION

In Reply, Please Refer to
File No.

Los Angeles, California
August 13, 1964

REPORT OF LONG DISTANCE TELEPHONE CALLS MADE FROM TELEPHONES LISTED TO MR. AND MRS. HARRY OLSEN, LONG BEACH, CALIFORNIA

The President's Commission on the assassination of President KENNEDY, by letter to the Director, FBI, dated July 23, 1964, requested a report of all existing long distance telephone calls made from telephones listed to Mr. HARRY OLSEN and Mrs. HARRY OLSEN (KATHIE K.COLEMAN) formerly of 325 North Ewing Street, Dallas, Texas, who presently resides at 315 Obispo Avenue, Apartment 12, Long Beach, California. Mr. and Mrs. OLSEN now conduct a Doctor's Business Bureau, Room 1006 Hartwell Building, 19 Pine Avenue, Long Beach, California.

Investigation by a Special Agent of the FBI disclosed the following:

HARRY W. OLSEN, 315 Obispo, Apartment 12, Long Beach 14, California has a non-published telephone number 433-6289, which was installed April 30, 1964. There were no toll calls from this telephone subsequent to installation, except the following:

June 25, 1964, to Riverside, California, telephone number 688-0291; duration 14 minutes; cost $3.00.

July 17, 1964, to Las Vegas, Nevada, telephone number 735-9111; duration 3 minutes; cost 85 cents.

The Doctor's Business Bureau, Hartwell Building, 19 Pine Avenue, Room 1006, Long Beach, California, has telephone number HE 5-6315. The following toll calls were made from this telephone during the period December 1963 through July 13, 1964:

COMMISSION EXHIBIT No. 2433—Continued

REPORT OF LONG DISTANCE TELEPHONE CALLS

DATE	PLACE CALLED	NUMBER CALLED	MINUTES	CHARGE
12/12	Newport Beach	646-7443	1	.25
12/12	Anaheim	828-8394	3	.25
12/20	Anaheim	774-1450	4	.30
1/3	Anaheim	827-0290	5	.35
1/7	Garden Grove	534-4545	2	.20
1/8	Buena Park	521-3169	1	.20
1/9	Westminster	TW3-4521	9	.45
1/13	Santa Ana	547-4898	1	.25
12/12	Los Angeles	MA7-1252	4	.30
1/10	Alhambra	AT2-9121	3	.30
12/12	Anaheim	776-7111	2	.25
12/16	Buena Park	521-5405	1	.20
12/18	Santa Ana	549-1448	2	.25
12/20	Santa Ana	549-1448	1	.25
12/27	Green Camp, Ohio	LA8-7445	1	2.10
12/30	Buena Park	521-7040	2	.20
12/30	Anaheim	772-8111	2	.25
1/3	Anaheim	533-4585	2	.25
1/6	Garden Grove	534-6040	4	.25
1/7	Anaheim	828-6974	1	.25
1/7	Buena Park	522-2935	1	.20
1/7	Orange	633-2087	1	.25
1/9	Anaheim	527-8844	1	.25
1/9	Huntington Beach	VI7-6031	2	.20
1/13	Newport Beach	646-7443	2	.25
12/12	Anaheim	828-8394	1	.25
12/13	Garden Grove	534-3681	4	.25
12/18	Anaheim	828-7383	2	.25
12/20	Anaheim	774-3818	5	.35
12/27	Buena Park	521-7040	1	.20
12/27	Anaheim	828-1559	3	.25
1/4	Santa Ana	545-5057	1	.25
1/8	Anaheim	527-8849	3	.25

2

COMMISSION EXHIBIT No. 2433—Continued

REPORT OF LONG DISTANCE
TELEPHONE CALLS

DATE	PLACE CALLED	NUMBER CALLED	MINUTES	CHARGE
1/9	Anaheim	527-8844	1	.25
1/9	Buena Park	521-5405	1	.20
1/10	Brea	529-3016	1	.25
12/16	Fullerton	871-1078	1	.25
12/18	Anaheim	722-7130	1	.25
12/19	Buena Park	521-9795	1	.20
12/20	Santa Ana	544-6333	1	.25
12/20	Westminster	TW7-4817	2	.15
12/20	Garden Grove	534-3681	5	.30
12/26	Garden Grove	534-3681	2	.20
12/26	Garden Grove	534-3681	4	.25
12/27	Garden Grove	534-3681	2	.20
12/30	Buena Park	521-7742	2	.20
12/30	Buena Park	521-7742	1	.20
12/31	Garden Grove	537-8420	2	.20
12/31	Garden Grove	534-3681	4	.25
1/2	Anaheim	828-7797	2	.25
1/2	Anaheim	828-7797	2	.25
1/2	Anaheim	828-7797	3	.25
1/3	Buena Park	521-7742	1	.20
1/3	Buena Park	522-1988	3	.20
1/6	Garden Grove	534-3681	1	.20
1/6	Placenta	528-6661	1	.30
1/6	Garden Grove	534-3681	5	.30
1/7	Santa Ana	542-3809	1	.25
1/7	Garden Grove	534-3681	2	.20
1/8	Garden Grove	537-5160	1	.20
1/8	Fullerton	525-7043	1	.25
1/8	Santa Ana	545-0416	2	.25
1/9	Anaheim	527-8844	1	.25
1/9	Westminster	TW7-6963 MY	1	.15
1/13	Anaheim	828-8307	1	.25
1/13	Garden Grove	534-3681	1	.20
1/8	Anaheim (collect from)	527-8849	8	.70

COMMISSION EXHIBIT No. 2433—Continued

REPORT OF LONG DISTANCE
TELEPHONE CALLS

DATE	PLACE CALLED	NUMBER CALLED	MINUTES	CHARGE
1/7	Gardena (Collect From)	534-(?)	3	.30
1/7	Gardena (Collect From)	534-3681	3	.30
1/9	Gardena (Collect From)	534-3681	3	.30
1/9	Gardena (Collect From)	534-3681	5	.50
1/20	Westminster	TW7-6580	3	.15
1/21	Newport Beach	646-3246	1	.25
1/21	Orange	633-2087	1	.25
1/21	Buena Park	522-8471	6	.35
1/22	Fullerton	525-1153	1	.25
1/28	Westminster	TW3-3633	2	.15
1/29	Newport Beach	548-3471	1	.25
1/29	Anaheim	772-8111	2	.25
1/30	Morongo Valley	342-2831	1	.75
1/30	Santa Ana	542-0681	1	.25
1/30	Santa Ana	545-8151	1	.25
1/30	Santa Ana	547-5526	1	.25
2/4	Santa Ana	547-3333	2	.25
2/6	Santa Ana	542-4705	1	.25
2/7	Newport Beach	646-2431	2	.25
2/11	Santa Ana	531-5700	1	.25
2/12	Buena Park	522-1131	1	.20
1/16	Santa Ana	545-4900	1	.25
1/20	Santa Ana	547-7251	5	.35
1/20	Anaheim	722-8111	5	.35
1/21	Anaheim	772-2267	7	.45
1/23	Santa Ana	549-1167	2	.25
1/23	Anaheim	527-4600	3	.25
1/28	Santa Ana	545-5180	1	.25
1/28	Santa Ana	541-3663	2	.25
1/29	Santa Ana	543-0518	1	.25
1/29	Newport Beach	548-3471	1	.25
1/29	Newport Beach	548-3471	1	.25
1/29	Huntington Beach	VI7-6287	3	.20
1/30	Newport Beach	548-3471	1	.25
1/30	Newport Beach	548-3471	6	.40
1/31	Buena Park	522-3114	1	.20

COMMISSION EXHIBIT No. 2433—Continued

REPORT OF LONG DISTANCE
TELEPHONE CALLS

DATE	PLACE CALLED	NUMBER CALLED	MINUTES	CHARGE
2/4	Huntington Beach	VI7-1090	1	.20
2/5	Newport Beach	548-3471	2	.25
2/5	Anaheim	772-8111	4	.30
2/5	Garden Grove	539-1425	6	.35
2/11	Westminster	TW3-7931	1	.15
2/11	Redlands	PY7-4406	3	.55
1/15	Garden Grove	534-3681	5	.30
1/28	Anaheim	527-9370	4	.30
1/30	Santa Ana	531-9487	2	.25
1/31	Garden Grove	534-3681	5	.30
2/7	Santa Ana	546-0683	1	.25
2/7	Garden Grove	537-8269	1	.20
2/7	Garden Grove	537-3379	1	.20
2/7	Anaheim	533-4376	1	.25
2/10	Anaheim	774-6845	3	.25
2/12	Westminster	TW7-7991	1	.15
2/12	Westminster	TW3-1101	3	.15
1/13	Gardena (Collect from)	534-3681	3	.30
1/23	Gardena (Collect from)	534-3681	3	.30
1/30	Gardena (Collect From)	534-3681	3	.30
2/3	Gardena (Collect From)	534-3681	12	.90
1/29	Los Angeles (Collect From)	624-8054	3	.30
1/14	Anaheim	774-1450	3	.25
1/17	Anaheim	527-6517	1	.25
1/17	Placenta	528-6240	1	.30
1/21	Anaheim	772-4410	2	.25
1/21	Garden Grove	534-6040	2	.20
1/28	Santa Ana	544-6068	4	.30
1/30	Santa Ana	542-2381	3	.25
1/31	Buena Park	521-2000	1	.20
1/31	Buena Park	522-3114	2	.20
2/7	Garden Grove	537-3141	1	.20
2/10	Buena Park	521-0253	4	.25
2/11	Newport Beach	548-3471	1	.25
1/14	Los Angeles	MA7-1252	6	.40
1/17	Los Angeles	MA7-1252	13	.75

5

COMMISSION EXHIBIT No. 2433—Continued

REPORT OF LONG DISTANCE
TELEPHONE CALLS

DATE	PLACE CALLED	NUMBER CALLED	MINUTES	CHARGE
1/28	Los Angeles	MA7-1252	6	.40
1/14	Orange	633-2087	1	.25
1/14	Buena Park	522-3114	1	.20
1/14	Huntington Beach	VI7-2327	9	.50
1/14	Garden Grove	530-4950	4	.25
1/15	Anaheim	772-9643	1	.25
2/22	Thousand Oaks	495-4979	2	.50
2/24	Garden Grove	534-6454	1	.20
2/24	Santa Ana	546-0683	2	.25
2/24	Newport Beach	646-9347	3	.25
2/25	Fullerton	879-8444	1	.25
2/25	Santa Ana	549-1167	1	.25
2/25	Buena Park	522-5142	1	.20
2/26	Garden Grove	534-3681	1	.20
2/28	Anaheim	535-2826	9	.55
3/4	Garden Grove	534-3681	3	.20
3/4	Garden Grove	534-3681	4	.25
3/5	Garden Grove	534-3681	2	.20
3/6	Anaheim	535-2826	2	.25
3/6	Anaheim	535-2826	3	.25
3/6	Garden Grove	534-3681	3	.20
2/18	Gardena (Collect From)	534-3681	3	.30
3/3	Gardena (Collect From)	534-3681	3	.30
2/14	Buena Park	522-5142	3	.20
2/17	Newport Beach	646-3246	1	.25
2/19	Buena Park	522-6138	3	.20
2/21	Laguna Beach	HY4-9057	3	.35
2/21	Newport Beach	548-3700	7	.45
2/25	Santa Ana	549-1167	1	.25
2/27	Anaheim	772-5151	2	.25
2/28	Anaheim	527-4600	3	.25
2/28	Santa Ana	547-8251	5	.35
2/24	Alhambra	AT2-9121	3	.30
2/28	Los Angeles	MA7-1252	5	.35
3/11	Los Angeles	MA7-1252	2	.25
2/17	Buena Park	521-3512	1	.20
2/20	Westminster	TW7-2833	1	.15

6

COMMISSION EXHIBIT No. 2433—Continued

REPORT OF LONG DISTANCE
TELEPHONE CALLS

DATE	PLACE CALLED	NUMBER CALLED	MINUTES	CHARGE
2/20	Santa Ana	531-8214	3	.25
2/21	Santa Ana	542-4642	2	.25
2/21	Westminster	TW7-4234	2	.15
2/24	Fullerton	525-7714	9	.55
2/25	Anaheim	827-5515	6	.40
2/27	Newport Beach	548-3471	1	.25
2/27	Brea	529-3049	3	.25
2/28	Buena Park	521-4045	1	.20
2/28	Garden Grove	534-3681	2	.20
2/28	Anaheim	527-4600	6	.40
3/2	Anaheim	527-4600	1	.25
3/2	Huntington Beach	VI7-8209	1	.20
3/3	Santa Ana	544-6068	1	.25
3/4	Santa Ana	546-3090	1	.25
2/13	Westminster	TW3-3616	1	.15
2/13	Westminster	892-2819	1	.15
2/20	Santa Ana	531-6853	1	.25
2/21	Buena Park	522-6908	2	.20
2/25	Huntington Beach	VI7-8817	5	.30
2/27	Anaheim	527-4900	1	.25
2/28	Rialto	875-3030	1	.55
2/28	Santa Ana	531-8214	2	.25
3/2	Buena Park	521-4688	2	.20
3/3	Santa Ana	544-6068	1	.25
3/6	Garden Grove	534-3681	5	.30
2/13	Westminster	TW3-1423	1	.15
2/14	Anaheim	827-3733	2	.25
2/17	Anaheim	828-2408	2	.25
2/17	Garden Grove	534-3681	4	.25
2/18	Huntington Beach	LE6-9872	1	.20
2/18	Garden Grove	537-6414	2	.20
2/18	Garden Grove	530-1000	4	.25
2/20	Orange	538-6024	2	.25
2/22	Anaheim	527-8003	2	.25
2/22	Westminster	TW3-3633	2	.15

7

COMMISSION EXHIBIT No. 2433—Continued

REPORT OF LONG DISTANCE
TELEPHONE CALLS

DATE	PLACE CALLED	NUMBER CALLED	MINUTES	CHARGE
3/12	Anaheim	535-1143	3	.25
3/16	Anaheim	776-0110	2	.25
3/16	Anaheim	533-4585	2	.25
3/17	Santa Ana	547-5526	1	.25
3/17	Anaheim	533-4585	1	.25
3/17	Buena Park	521-9991	1	.20
3/18	Huntington Beach	VI7-4590	1	.20
3/18	Anaheim	533-4585	2	.25
3/18	Buena Park	521-1033	7	.40
3/19	Garden Grove	534-3681	4	.25
3/20	Anaheim	772-8111	3	.25
3/23	Santa Ana	547-5526	1	.25
3/25	Huntington Beach	VI7-3488	3	.20
3/26	Huntington Beach	VI7-8817	3	.20
4/2	Garden Grove	537-6895	2	.20
4/3	Anaheim	772-0584	4	.30
4/9	Huntington Beach	VI7-8817	1	.20
3/18	Los Angeles	FA1-0786	3	.20
3/27	Los Angeles	MA7-1252	9	.55
4/2	Los Angeles	MA2-8748	7	.45
3/9	Buena Park	522-2935	1	.20
3/12	Buena Park	522-2935	1	.20
3/13	Anaheim	827-4267	1	.25
3/16	Santa Ana	531-8214	1	.25
3/16	Santa Ana	549-1167	3	.25
3/17	Anaheim	828-1096	5	.35
3/18	Brea	529-2505	1	.25
3/20	Anaheim	772-8111	2	.25
3/23	Orange	633-3521	2	.25
3/24	Anaheim	827-2130	1	.25
3/24	Orange	633-3407	4	.30
3/24	Buena Park	522-2807	5	.30
3/25	Fullerton	526-3465	1	.25
3/26	Buena Park	522-2935	1	.20
3/26	Fullerton	525-0237	1	.25
4/8	Westminster	TW7-1948	2	.15
3/9	Buena Park	522-3114	1	.20

8

COMMISSION EXHIBIT No. 2433—Continued

REPORT OF LONG DISTANCE
TELEPHONE CALLS

DATE	PLACE CALLED	NUMBER CALLED	MINUTES	CHARGE
3/9	Orange	633-6406	3	.25
3/10	Anaheim	828-9257	1	.25
3/10	Santa Ana	545-9815	2	.25
3/11	Anaheim	527-8003	2	.25
3/17	Orange	633-2087	1	.25
3/18	Santa Ana	545-6711	1	.25
3/19	Orange	633-3407	11	.65
3/20	Buena Park	521-9991	1	.20
3/23	Santa Ana	549-1167	3	.25
3/24	Orange	633-4300	3	.25
3/24	Orange	633-4300	4	.30
4/8	Anaheim	827-4447	1	.25
4/9	Garden Grove	539-1425	4	.24
3/9	Anaheim	535-2826	1	.25
3/9	Santa Ana	547-5526	2	.25
3/10	Anaheim	772-0584	2	.25
3/11	Santa Ana	531-8214	2	.25
3/11	Garden Grove	534-3681	3	.20
3/16	Anaheim	535-2826	2	.25
3/17	Santa Ana	547-5526	1	.25
3/17	Brea	529-2505	1	.25
3/17	Garden Grove	534-3681	1	.20
3/18	Garden Grove	534-3681	3	.20
3/20	Anaheim	774-5683	6	.40
3/24	Orange	532-2511	1	.25
3/24	Anaheim	535-2826	4	.30
3/24	Garden Grove	534-3681	5	.30
3/24	Orange	633-4300	5	.35
3/26	Santa Ana	541-3303	1	.25
3/26	Buena Park	522-7706	2	.20
3/26	Santa Ana	541-3303	6	.40
3/27	Santa Ana	547-3333	9	.55
3/30	Placenta	528-6661	1	.30
3/31	Garden Grove	534-3681	6	.35
4/2	Garden Grove	534-3681	4	.25
4/3	Anaheim	772-0584	1	.25
4/3	Anaheim	828-7770	3	.25

9

COMMISSION EXHIBIT No. 2433—Continued

REPORT OF LONG DISTANCE
TELEPHONE CALLS

DATE	PLACE CALLED	NUMBER CALLED	MINUTES	CHARGE
4/6	Garden Grove	534-3681	3	.20
4/7	Placenta	528-6661	1	.30
4/8	Anaheim	527-7707	1	.25
4/9	Garden Grove	534-2131	2	.20
3/20	Fullerton (Collect From)	526-2488	5	.50
3/18	Fullerton (Collect From)	526-3465	1	.30
3/18	Fullerton (Collect From)	526-3465	6	.60
3/23	Fullerton (Collect From)	526-3465	4	.40
3/19	Fullerton (Collect From)	871-0998	1	.30
4/27	Placenta	528-6661	1	.30
4/27	Placenta	528-6661	3	.30
5/1	Garden Grove	534-3681	3	.20
5/7	Garden Grove	534-3681	2	.20
5/7	Anaheim	535-8532	2	.25
5/7	Newport Beach	646-4886	2	.25
5/7	Anaheim	828-3320	12	.70
5/12	Santa Ana	541-3325	1	.25
5/13	Garden Grove	534-3681	8	.45
5/5	Gardena	HE5-6318	3	.30
4/16	Anaheim	772-9222	6	.40
4/17	Newport Beach	548-5533	2	.25
4/28	Santa Ana	547-6184	3	.25
4/28	Santa Ana	547-8251	5	.35
5/1	Anaheim	772-5151	3	.25
5/8	Garden Grove	534-1150	4	.25
4/29	Los Angeles	MA7-1252	4	.30
5/5	Alhambra	AT2-9121	3	.30
5/6	Los Angeles	MA7-1252	6	.40
5/7	Los Angeles	MA7-1252	6	.40
4/10	Anaheim	828-1096	1	.25
4/10	Anaheim	772-8111	2	.25
4/13	Santa Ana	547-6256	1	.25
4/15	Fullerton	525-5241	1	.25
4/16	Garden Grove	537-3253	1	.20
4/22	Santa Ana	549-1167	1	.25
4/22	Buena Park	521-3512	1	.20
4/23	Santa Ana	547-3333	4	.30

10

COMMISSION EXHIBIT No. 2433—Continued

REPORT OF LONG DISTANCE
TELEPHONE CALLS

DATE	PLACE CALLED	NUMBER CALLED	MINUTES	CHARGE
4/28	Westminster	TW3-7121	1	.15
5/1	Santa Ana	531-5162	1	.25
5/1	Garden Grove	534-3681	3	.20
5/1	Santa Ana	542-1101	9	.55
5/4	Huntington Beach	VI7-6018	1	.20
5/11	Fullerton	526-5581	3	.25
4/10	Garden Grove	539-0926	2	.20
4/13	Santa Ana	542-1101	6	.40
4/13	Huntington Beach	VI7-7689	9	.50
4/13	Fullerton	525-1079	2	.25
4/14	Garden Grove	539-1425	1	.20
4/14	Anaheim	527-2584	1	.25
4/14	Santa Ana	545-1171	2	.25
4/14	Garden Grove	539-1425	3	.20
4/15	Fullerton	525-8241	7	.45
4/17	Anaheim	533-4376	1	.25
4/17	Fullerton	525-8473	1	.25
4/24	Anaheim	828-5425	1	.25
4/24	Placenta	528-5677	5	.50
4/29	Garden Grove	539-1822	1	.20
4/30	Anaheim	527-2233	1	.25
5/1	Buena Park	522-5142	1	.20
5/9	North Hollywood	765-6325	14	1.45
5/12	Placenta	528-6661	1	.30
4/13	Huntington Beach	VI7-6018	4	.25
4/14	Garden Grove	539-1425	4	.25
4/20	Placenta	528-6661	1	.30
4/20	Anaheim	828-3977	2	.25
4/22	Garden Grove	534-3681	6	.35
5/28	Buena Park	521-2264	1	.20
5/29	Garden Grove	534-3681	4	.25
6/1	Garden Grove	534-3681	4	.25
6/9	Thousand Oaks	495-5741	2	.50
6/9	Thousand Oaks	495-5741	4	.65
5/15	Gardena	HE5-6315	3	.30
6/5	Gardena	HE5-6315	3	.30
5/19	Fullerton	525-8714	3	25

11

COMMISSION EXHIBIT No. 2433—Continued

REPORT OF LONG DISTANCE
TELEPHONE CALLS

DATE	PLACE CALLED	NUMBER CALLED	MINUTES	CHARGE
5/19	Anaheim	533-4376	3	.25
5/19	Anaheim	533-4376	3	.25
5/20	Anaheim	828-8098	1	.25
5/21	Garden Grove	539-2724	3	.20
5/21	Oxnard	486-2641	4	1.45
5/21	Buena Park	521-1235	2	.20
5/22	Anaheim	722-8111	1	.25
5/22	Anaheim	772-8111	4	.30
6/1	Huntington	VI7-6524	1	.20
6/1	Westminster	TW7-6963	7	.35
6/5	Anaheim	828-2694	1	.25
6/5	Anaheim	527-2314	2	.25
6/8	Anaheim	535-2891	5	.35
6/10	Anaheim	827-5806	1	.25
5/25	Beverly Hills	CR6-2403	4	.40
5/27	Pomona	NA2-2937	3	.40
5/27	Lomita	DA6-2533	3	.15
6/12	Los Angeles	MA7-1252	6	.40
5/15	Fullerton	525-8473	1	.25
5/19	Buena Park	521-8121	4	.25
5/19	Fullerton	871-1441	1	.25
5/19	Garden Grove	534-3681	3	.20
5/21	Anaheim	533-4376	1	.25
5/22	Garden Grove	537-3158	3	.20
5/25	Huntington Beach	VI7-6524	1	.20
5/27	Santa Ana	531-8580	3	.25
5/28	Anaheim	776-7780	3	.25
5/28	Anaheim	535-2891	4	.30
5/28	Anaheim	774-4192	5	.35
6/5	Newport Beach	548-5882	2	.25
6/5	Huntington Beach	LE6-8891	4	.25
6/10	Anaheim	776-5485	1	.25
5/18	Garden Grove	530-5750	8	.45
5/19	Newport Beach	548-2266	6	.40
5/27	Santa Ana	546-0683	7	.45
5/28	Anaheim	535-2891	1	.25

12

COMMISSION EXHIBIT No. 2433—Continued

REPORT OF LONG DISTANCE TELEPHONE CALLS

DATE	PLACE CALLED	NUMBER CALLED	MINUTES	CHARGE
6/5	Anaheim	772-8111	3	.25
6/9	Garden Grove	534-3681	2	.20
6/9	Thousand Oaks	495-5741	4	.65
6/11	Anaheim	828-8080	3	.25
5/14	Garden Grove	534-2331	1	.20
5/18	Newport Beach	548-2266	2	.25
5/21	Garden Grove	534-3681	6	.35
6/18	Garden Grove	534-3681	3	.20
6/18	Garden Grove	534-3681	7	.40
6/19	Newport Beach	646-6492	1	.25
6/22	Newport Beach	646-5492	1	.25
6/22	Westminster	TW3-2468	3	.15
6/22	Newport Beach	646-6492	10	.60
6/23	Garden Grove	534-3681	4	.25
6/23	Newport Beach	646-2491	14	.80
6/24	Garden Grove	534-3681	5	.30
6/25	Anaheim	828-7383	2	.25
6/29	Orange	538-6089	7	.45
7/1	Placenta	528-6661	2	.30
7/1	Garden Grove	534-3681	3	.20
7/1	Huntington Beach	VI7-1093	3	.20
7/2	Orange	538-6089	8	.50
7/6	Garden Grove	534-3681	3	.20
7/6	Orange	538-6089	5	.35
7/7	Orange	538-9528	5	.35
7/8	Orange	538-8892	12	.70
7/13	Buena Park	521-1266	1	.20
7/13	Huntington Beach	VI7-1093	1	.20
7/13	Garden Grove	534-3681	3	.20
6/9	Los Angeles	HO4-1890	14	1.50
6/29	Gardena	HE5-6315	3	.30
6/30	Gardena	HE5-6315	3	.30
7/3	Westminster	HE5-6315	3	.30
6/10	Garden Grove	534-3681	2	.20
6/15	Pomona	NA9-4171	3	.40
6/16	Anaheim	828-1096	1	.25

13

COMMISSION EXHIBIT No. 2433—Continued

REPORT OF LONG DISTANCE TELEPHONE CALLS

DATE	PLACE CALLED	NUMBER CALLED	MINUTES	CHARGE
6/18	Fullerton	871-9132	1	.25
6/19	Newport Beach	646-6492	2	.25
6/19	Garden Grove	534-3681	3	.15
6/22	Garden Grove	534-6712	29	1.50
7/6	Westminster	TW3-3536	1	.15
7/8	Anaheim	828-5425	3	.25
6/11	Santa Ana	545-5581	1	.25
6/16	Santa Ana	547-2511	1	.25
6/16	Laguna Beach	HY4-1131	1	.35
6/17	Santa Ana	547-6184	2	.25
6/18	Santa Ana	545-3298	20	1.10
6/19	Newport Beach	646-6492	4	.30
6/19	Newport Beach	646-6492	4	.30
6/22	Anaheim	776-8080	3	.25
6/22	Anaheim	828-7726	4	.30
6/23	Newport Beach	646-8986	1	.25
6/24	Anaheim	776-2430	7	.45
6/24	Westminster	TW7-3058	2	.15
6/24	Garden Grove	534-3681	5	.30
6/29	Huntington Beach	VI7-1211	1	.20
7/1	Anaheim	776-7780	1	.25
7/1	Buena Park	521-0517	1	.20
7/1	Anaheim	527-1493	1	.25
7/2	Anaheim	828-1096	1	.25
7/6	Anaheim	776-1361	1	.25
7/7	Anaheim	774-0330	6	.40
7/10	Anaheim	772-8111	4	.30
7/13	Newport Beach	646-2672	2	.25
6/12	Riverside	685-4315	1	.50
6/16	Huntington Beach	VI7-2196	4	.25
6/19	Anaheim	828-5425	1	.25
6/23	Westminster	TW3-7576	4	.20
6/24	Huntington Beach	VI7-0184	2	.20
6/25	Westminster	TW7-7641	1	.15
6/25	Buena Park	522-3161	6	.35
6/29	Anaheim	827-1531	1	.25
6/29	Buena Park	522-5344	1	.20

14

COMMISSION EXHIBIT No. 2433—Continued

REPORT OF LONG DISTANCE
TELEPHONE CALLS

DATE	PLACE CALLED	NUMBER CALLED	MINUTES	CHARGE
7/1	Huntington Beach	VI7-1093	1	.20
7/1	Westminster	TW3-5086	4	.20
7/2	Anaheim	776-2430	4	.30
7/6	Anaheim	776-7652	3	.25
7/9	Orange	538-8892	7	.45
6/11	Garden Grove	534-3681	6	.35
6/15	Garden Grove	534-3681	3	.20
6/16	Riverside	685-4315	1	.50
6/16	Garden Grove	534-3681	5	.30
6/17	Garden Grove	534-3681		.20

15

COMMISSION EXHIBIT No. 2433—Continued

REPORT OF LONG DISTANCE
TELEPHONE CALLS

Page number one of this memorandum shows that on June 25, 1964, a call was made from telephone number 433-6289 listed to Harry W. Olsen, 315 Obispo, Apartment 12, Long Beach, California, to Riverside, California, telephone number 688-0291. This telephone number, 688-0291, is listed to Walter A. Belk, 6585 Rexford Drive, Riverside, California.

Pages two through fifteen of this memorandum show calls made from the Doctor's Business Bureau, Hartwell Building, 19 Pine Avenue, Room 1006, Long Beach, California, telephone number HE 5-6315. The subscribers to these telephone numbers are set forth hereafter, showing the date or dates on which the number was called.

Investigation has disclosed that telephone number LA 8-7445 in Green Camp, Ohio, which was recorded as having been called from telephone number HE 5-6315 on December 27, 1963, is a non-existent number.

-16-

COMMISSION EXHIBIT No. 2433—Continued

REPORT OF LONG DISTANCE
TELEPHONE CALLS

Telephone Number	Subscriber	Dates Called
541-3663	Honda Santa Ana 1320 South Main, Santa Ana, California	1/28/64
542-4642 associated with 542-4713	American Pipe and Construction Company 2501 West 5th Street, Santa Ana, California	2/21/64
546-3090 disconnected 8/26/64	L.M. BACKUS 1141 Mohawk Drive, Santa Ana, California	3/4/64
544-6068 non-published	BOB FORD 12552 Del Rey Drive, Santa Ana, California	1/28/64 3/3/64 (2 times)
545-5057	Laurentide Corporation 1859 Harbor, Costa Mesa, California	1/4/64
545-4900	MARGARET NEWLON 2131 Orange Avenue, Santa Ana, California	1/16/64
547-4898	RICHARD E. GAWRYCHOWSKI 306 South Sullivan, Space 66, Santa Ana, California	1/13/64
531-6853	EDWARD J. ROWE 9410 Madison Avenue, Westminster, California	2/20/64
545-9815 Public telephone	3801 South Harbor Boulevard, Agent Voit Rubber Company, Santa Ana, California	3/10/64

-17-

COMMISSION EXHIBIT No. 2433—Continued

REPORT OF LONG DISTANCE TELEPHONE CALLS

Telephone Number	Subscriber	Dates Called
542-3809	STANLEY WOOD 1726 West Hall Avenue, Santa Ana, California	1/7/64
545-6711	Household Finance Company, 909 East Warner Avenue, Santa Ana, California	3/18/64
542-4705	Wright Transfer and Storage Company, 1101 East 6th, Santa Ana, California	2/6/64
521-4688	Jerry's Barbecue 6050 Manchester, Boulevard, Buena Park, California	3/2/64
521-4045	PAUL A. STROHMAN 15026 Campellos Road, La Mirada, California	2/28/64
521-7040	A & J Manufacturing Co. 6461 Roland Avenue, Buena Park, California	12/27/63 12/30/63
521-1033	GORDON P. SMITH, M.D. 5781 Beach Boulevard, Buena Park, California	3/18/64
521-2000	Cal-Russ Construction Corporation 555 South Harbor, La Habra, California	1/31/64
521-9991	Ayers Secreterial Service 4301 West Commonwealth Avenue, Suite D 4, Fullerton, California	3/17/64 3/20/64

COMMISSION EXHIBIT No. 2433—Continued

REPORT OF LONG DISTANCE TELEPHONE CALLS

Telephone Number	Subscriber	Dates Called
522-1988	PAUL A. STROHMAN 15026 Campellos Road, La Mirada, California	1/3/64
522-2935 disconnected 3/23/64	U.S. Eagle Fertilizer Company, 5582 Orangethorpe Avenue, Buena Park, California	3/26/64
522-2934	Commander DAVID W. BERGER 6327 Morgan Way, Buena Park, California	1/7/64 3/9/64 3/12/64
522-6908 non-published	WILLIAM TRASK 7604 9th Street, Apartment B, Buena Park, California	2/21/64
522-2807	Beach Architectural Products 6880 A Oran Circle, Buena Park, California	3/24/64
521-9795	Tolo Patterns, Inc. 4250 Artesia Avenue, Fullerton, California	12/19/63
530-1000	Metropolitan Life Insurance Company 13163 Brookhurst, Garden Grove, California	2/18/64
530-4950	Family Finance Company 12111 Brookhurst, Garden Grove, California	1/14/64
539-0926	W.T. KING 9571 Vons Drive, Garden Grove, California	4/10/64
537-6895	JAMES D. PORTER 12551 Twintree Lane, Garden Grove, California	4/2/64

COMMISSION EXHIBIT No. 2433—Continued

REPORT OF LONG DISTANCE
TELEPHONE CALLS

Telephone Number	Subscriber	Dates Called
539-1822 non-published	MERLE R. NEWLAND 10132 Malinda Lane, Garden Grove, California	4/29/64
539-2724	Wells and Sons Wholesale Provisions, 11162 Wasco Road, Garden Grove, California	5/21/64
530-5750	Laurentide Finance Corporation, 12190 Brookhurst, Garden Grove, California	5/18/64
534-6712 non-published	CLARENCE HARRISON 12132 Bluebell Avenue, Garden Grove, California	6/22/64
534-4545	Grove Rambler Sales, Inc. 12222 Garden Grove Boulevard, Garden Grove, California	1/7/64
534-6454	Kerko Cabinet Company 7592 Acacia, Garden Grove, California	2/24/64
539-1425	ALFRED B. DRAIS 12201 Sheridan Lane, Garden Grove, California	2/5/64 4/9/64 4/14/64 (3 times)
537-8420	TOUFIGH, RIAZ 4036 El Rancho Avenue, Apartment B, Orange, California	12/31/63
646-2672	Hyatt Drapery 1670 Superior Avenue Costa Mesa, California	7/13/64

COMMISSION EXHIBIT No. 2433—Continued

REPORT OF LONG DISTANCE
TELEPHONE CALLS

Telephone Number	Subscriber	Dates Called
646-8986 disconnected 7/15/64	Cadillac Gage Company 1796 Monrovia Avenue, Costa Mesa, California	6/23/64
646-4886	HOWARD D. STERN 508 Redlands Avenue, Newport Beach, California	5/7/64
548-5882	A.W. HOWE 315 East 18th, Apartment A, Costa Mesa, California	6/5/64
548-3700	WILLIAM E. GOLDEN 2345 Elden Avenue, Costa Mesa, California	2/21/64
548-5533	Rosan, Inc. 2901 West Coast Highway, Newport Beach, California	4/17/64
646-6492	ROLAND J. BOUCHARD 796 Joan, Costa Mesa, California	6/19/64 (4 times) 6/22/64 (2 times)
646-2491	Cadillac Gage Company 1866 Whittier Avenue, Costa Mesa, California	6/23/64
548-3471	Theo Robins Ford 3100 West Coast Highway, Newport Beach, California	1/29/64(3 times) 1/30/64(2 times) 2/5/64 2/11/64 2/27/64
646-7443	B & H Office Supply and Equipment Company 541 Center, Costa Mesa, California	12/12/63 1/13/64

COMMISSION EXHIBIT No. 2433—Continued

REPORT OF LONG DISTANCE TELEPHONE CALLS

Telephone Number	Subscriber	Dates Called
646-2431	United California Bank Newport Beach Mariners Office, 2712 West Coast Highway, Newport Beach, California	2/7/64
646-9347	Not a working number no records	2/24/64
548-2266	RALPH FRANKLIN, M.D. 2011 Westcliff Drive, Suite 1, Newport Beach, California	5/18/64 5/19/64
646-3246 disconnected April, 1964	Bay Motors, 2054 Harbor Boulevard, Costa Mesa, California	1/21/64 2/17/64
527-2584	CLARENCE HARBIN 10732 Knott Avenue, Stanton, California	4/14/64
533-4585	Coast Data Processing, Inc., 2021 West Lincoln Avenue, Suite A 5, Anaheim, California	1/3/64 3/16/64 3/17/64 3/18/64
527-7707	JOSEPH TSEN, M.D. 3321 West Lincoln Avenue, Anaheim, California	4/8/64
828-7726 non-published	ERNIE MARKLEY 9744 Holder, Buena Park, California	6/22/64
827-3733	CHARLES L. STEVENS 6261 San Lorenzo Drive, Buena Park, California	2/14/64

-22-

COMMISSION EXHIBIT No. 2433—Continued

REPORT OF LONG DISTANCE TELEPHONE CALLS

Telephone Number	Subscriber	Dates Called
828-7770	Arrowhead Products of Division of Federal - Mogul - Dower Ball-bearings, Inc., 4411 Katella Avenue, Los Alamitos, California	4/3/64
776-7780	Schaefer's Discount 2138 East Lincoln Avenue, Anaheim, California	5/28/64 7/1/64
827-5806	WILBUR M. PRICE 7406 Glenoaks Drive, Stanton, California	6/10/64
828-7797	LEON KRAUS, M.D. 3414 West Ball Road, Suite F, Anaheim, California	1/2/64 (3 times)
774-3818 non-published disconnected 3/16/64	DANIEL COPAFIAN 1807 W. Glen Avenue, Anaheim, California	12/20/63
535-2826	ROBERT L. MARTIN, Ins. 433 West Lincoln Avenue, Suite 1, Anaheim, California	2/28/64 3/6/64 (2 times) 3/9/64 3/16/64 3/24/64
527-8844	Thriftymart, 8228 La Palma Avenue, Buena Park, California	1/9/64 (3 times)
774-6845	JOHN M. BERTELO 1873 West Elm Place, Anaheim, California	2/10/64
527-8849	WARREN F. DAILEY, Dr. 8810 Knott Avenue, Buena Park, California	1/8/64 (2 times)

-23-

COMMISSION EXHIBIT No. 2433—Continued

REPORT OF LONG DISTANCE
TELEPHONE CALLS

Telephone Number	Subscriber	Dates Called
535-2891	Bank of America, NT&SA, 150 East Lincoln Avenue, Anaheim, California	5/28/64(2 times) 6/8/64
527-4900	JOHN CARL KNOTEK, SR. 8607 Harrison Way, Buena Park, California	2/27/64
828-6974	HENRY NANCE 10305 Diane Avenue, Buena Park, California	1/7/64
828-3977 non-published	GUNDA MC GRATH 128 South Bella Vista, Apartment 12, Anaheim, California	4/20/64
527-8003	HENRY RICHMOND 8601 Lola Avenue, Stanton, California	2/22/64 3/11/64
776-8080	Orange County of Anaheim-Fullerton Judicial District, 1170 North Anaheim Boulevard, Anaheim, California	6/22/64
828-8080	Bank of America, Stanton Branch, 10518 Beach Boulevard, Stanton, California	6/11/64
828-1096	Stanton Nurseries, Inc. 3730 West Ball Road , Anaheim, California	3/17/64 4/10/64 6/16/64 7/2/64
828-8098	YNOCENTE RIOS 6501 Christine Circle , Buena Park, California	5/20/64

COMMISSION EXHIBIT No. 2433—Continued

REPORT OF LONG DISTANCE
TELEPHONE CALLS

Telephone Number	Subscriber	Dates Called
527-4600	Security Construction Company, 9741 Graham, Cypress, California	1/23/64 2/28/64(2 times) 3/2/64
774-5683	Luskey Brothers and Company, Main Office, 608 East Broadway, Anaheim, California	3/20/64
776-7652	Dell's Real Estate 413 South Brookhurst, Anaheim, California	7/6/64
772-9643 non-published	JAMES DURON REECE 10651 Hedlund Drive, Anaheim, California	1/15/64
828-2694	LUTHER LINDSEY 10582 Asbury Avenue, Stanton, California	6/5/64
528-5677 non-published	JIM BENAUIDEZ 17251 Regulus Drive, Yorba Linda, California	4/24/64
528-6661	Western Hills Golf and Country Club, Carbon Canyon Road, Chino, California	1/6/64 3/30/64 4/7/64 4/20/64 4/27/64(2 times) 5/12/64 7/1/64
528-6240 disconnected 7/30/64	DAVID C. ANDERSON 4672 Plumbosa, Yorba Linda, California	1/17/64
529-3049	Esco Rubber Products 130 North Brea Boulevard, Brea, California	2/27/64

COMMISSION EXHIBIT No. 2433—Continued

REPORT OF LONG DISTANCE
TELEPHONE CALLS

Telephone Number	Subscriber	Dates Called
529-3016	OLIVER A. TAYLOR 1442 Evergreen, Fullerton, California	1/10/64
529-2505	Brea Frozen Foods and Lockers 241 North Brea Boulevard, Brea, California	3/17/64 3/18/64
534-3681	K.C. DANFORD 1916 Robert Lane, Anaheim, California	12/13/63 12/20/63 12/26/63 (2 times) 12/27/63 12/31/63 1/6/64 (2 times) 1/7/64 (3 times) 1/9/64 (2 times) 1/13/64 (2 times) 1/15/64 1/23/64 1/30/64 1/31/64 2/3/64 2/17/64 2/18/64 2/26/64 2/28/64 3/3/64 3/4/64 (2 times) 3/5/64 3/6/64 (2 times) 3/11/64 3/17/64 3/18/64 3/19/64 3/24/64 3/31/64 4/2/64 4/16/64 4/22/64

COMMISSION EXHIBIT No. 2433—Continued

REPORT OF LONG DISTANCE
TELEPHONE CALLS

Telephone Number	Subscriber	Dates Called
534-3681 (continued)	K.C. DANFORD	5/1/64 (2 times 5/7/64 5/13/64 5/19/64 5/21/64 5/29/64 6/1/64 6/9/64 6/10/64 6/11/64 6/15/64 6/16/64 6/17/64 6/18/64 (2 times) 6/19/64 6/23/64 6/24/64 (2 times) 7/1/64 7/6/64 7/13/64
534-6040	Pacific Finance Corporation 13183 Harbor Boulevard, Garden Grove, California	1/6/64 1/21/64
537-6414	Star Construction Company 12796 Brookhurst, Garden Grove, California	2/18/64
537-3379	VIRGIL VAN SKYOCK 12502 Twinleaf Lane, Garden Grove, California	2/7/64
534-2331	Swan Pools, Inc. 1269 Harbor Boulevard, Garden Grove, California	5/14/64
537-8269	JAMES O. KRUEGER 12502 Volkwood, Garden Grove, California	2/7/64

COMMISSION EXHIBIT No. 2433—Continued

REPORT OF LONG DISTANCE
TELEPHONE CALLS

Telephone Number	Subscriber	Dates Called
537-3253	Belisle's Restaurant 12001 Harbor Boulevard, Garden Grove, California	4/16/64
537-3158	Beneficial Finance Company of Garden Grove, 9654 Garden Grove Boulevard, Garden Grove, California	5/22/64
537-5160	Palm Harbor General Hospital, 12860 Palm, Garden Grove, California	1/8/64
534-1150	Randolph Rubber Company 10631 Stanford Avenue, Garden Grove, California	5/8/64
537-3141	U.S. Grovernment Post Office Department, 10642 Garden Grove Boulevard, Garden Grove, California	2/7/64
534-2131	First Western Bank and Trust Company 12976 South Euclid, Garden Grove, California	4/9/64
546-0683	HENRY A. ROY 3142 Gibralter Avenue, Costa Mesa, California	2/7/64 2/24/64 5/27/64
542-0681	JOHN K. HERNANDEZ 1637 West Wisteria Place, Santa Ana, California	1/30/64
521-7742 non-published	EVERETT ARCHER 4200 West Franklin, Fullerton, California	12/30/63(2 times) 1/3/64

-28-

COMMISSION EXHIBIT No. 2433—Continued

REPORT OF LONG DISTANCE
TELEPHONE CALLS

Telephone Number	Subscriber	Dates Called
522-7706	CHARLES H. FOSTER 8344 Philodendron Way, Buena Park, California	3/26/64
521-0517 working with 521-2010	La Mirada Bowling Lanes, 15011 Adelfa Drive, La Mirada, California	7/1/64
521-3512	Stanley Chevrolet, Inc. 11980 East Firestone Boulevard, Norwalk, California	2/17/64 4/22/64
522-8471	Pacific Finance 8431 La Palma, Buena Park, California	1/21/64
521-5405	DON BAXTER 14746 Rayfield Drive, La Mirada, California	12/16/63 1/9/64
522-5344	ROBERT BURNS 7925 La Costa Circle, Buena Park, California	6/29/64
521-1266	B & G Electric 7612 Commonwealth Avenue, Buena Park, California	7/13/64
521-2264	Hartshorn Plumbing, Inc. 7010 Dale Avenue, Buena Park, California	5/28/64
521-0253	Ross-Loos Medical Group 7811 Commonwealth, Buena Park, California	2/10/64
521-1235	H.J. PRZYBYLOWSKI 5943 Western Avenue, Buena Park, California	5/21/64

-29-

COMMISSION EXHIBIT No. 2433—Continued

REPORT OF LONG DISTANCE
TELEPHONE CALLS

Telephone Number	Subscriber	Dates Called
521-3169 non-published	LYLE H. CAMERON 15346 San Bruno Drive, La Mirada, California	1/8/64
522-3161	VALENTINE BORBON 7975 Lamona Circle, Buena Park, California	6/25/64
522-5142 disconnected 6/12/64	CELESTINO MARTINEZ 7641 Knott, Buena Park, California	2/14/64 2/25/64 5/1/64
522-6138	Ward Concrete Products Company, 5270 East Houston, Buena Park, California	2/19/64
522-1131	Knotts Berry Farm Grand, Buena Park, California	2/12/64
521-8121	JOE FERRIERA 5529 Burlingame Avenue, Buena Park, California	5/19/64
522-3114	Paul Crouch Fence Company, 7122 Orangethorpe, Buena Park, California	1/14/64 1/31/64(2 times) 3/9/64
871-9132 non-published to 871-5290 non-published	BETTY J. MC CALL 519 South Highland Avenue, Apartment A, Fullerton, California	6/18/64
525-1153	DAVID B. KERR, Atty., 1305 West Valencia Drive, Fullerton, California	1/22/64
525-0237	ROGER C. HOPE, Atty., 246 West Commonwealth, Fullerton	3/26/64

-30-

COMMISSION EXHIBIT No. 2433—Continued

REPORT OF LONG DISTANCE
TELEPHONE CALLS

Telephone Number	Subscriber	Dates Called
525-5241	ALICE D. MC CARTHY 333 West Whiting Avenue, Fullerton, California	4/15/64(2 times)
871-1441	Autonetics Division of North American Aviation, Inc., 392 West Walnut, Fullerton, California	5/19/64
879-8444 disconnected 7/30/64	Harvey Concrete, 2500 West Orangethorpe, Fullerton, California	2/25/64
531-5700	GILBERT MILLER 10632 Hazard, Garden Grove, California	2/11/64
545-5581	Borg Warner Controls Division of Borg Warner Corporation 3300 Newport Avenue, Santa Ana, California	6/11/64
531-8580	MAROLYN STAFFIERI 14392 Warren, Westminster, California	5/27/64
547-5526	Liberty Mutual Insurance Company, 116 B South Broadway, Santa Ana, California	1/30/64 3/9/64 3/17/64(2 times) 3/23/64
543-0518	JEROME MOORE 1202 Linwood Avenue, Santa Ana, California	1/29/64
547-2511	General Motors Acceptance Corporation, 1077 West 17th, Santa Ana, California	6/16/64

-31-

COMMISSION EXHIBIT No. 2433—Continued

REPORT OF LONG DISTANCE
TELEPHONE CALLS

Telephone Number	Subscriber	Dates Called
531-9487	Reverend G.B. CUNNINGHAM 329 South Harbor Boulevard, Space 92, Santa Ana, California	1/30/64
549-1448	Pink Garter, 1400 West McFadden, Unit 9, Santa Ana, California	12/18/63 12/20/63
545-0416	Medical-Dental-Hospital Bureau of Orange County, Inc., 1914 Newport Boulevard, Costa Mesa, California	1/8/64
542-2381 disconnected 8/5/64	Great Western Leasing Company, 123 East 11th, Santa Ana, California	1/30/64
544-6333	GRAHAM H. BELL 1311 Lucinda Way, Tustin, California	12/20/63
547-3333	Title Insurance and Trust Company, 800 North Main, Santa Ana, California	2/4/64 3/27/64 4/23/64
526-3465 disconnected 6/11/64	Parkersburg Sales and Service, 4301 West Commonwealth, Fullerton, California	3/18/64(2 times) 3/23/64 3/25/64
525-8473	McGuire's Sheet Metal Office, 1213 South State College Boulevard, Fullerton, California	4/17/64 5/15/64

-32-

COMMISSION EXHIBIT No. 2433—Continued

REPORT OF LONG DISTANCE
TELEPHONE CALLS

Telephone Number	Subscriber	Dates Called
526-2488	Instrumental and Mechanical Service 413 West Amerige, Fullerton, California	3/20/64
526-5581	Astro Electronics 1160 East Ash, Fullerton, California	5/11/64
525-7714	J. PIERCE CONATY, M.D. 1431 North Harbor, Fullerton, California	2/24/64
525-8714	Maan Oil Company 2045 West Commonwealth Avenue, Fullerton, California	5/19/64
871-0998	HOWARD C. KAYLOR 1523 North Highland Avenue, Fullerton, California	3/19/64
525-7043	HELEN L. SMITH 235 South Pacific Drive, Fullerton, California	1/8/64
871-1078 non-published	DANNY J. SILVA 424 West Avenue, Apartment C, Fullerton, California	12/16/63
525-1079 disconnected 6/11/64	Shermans Automatic Transmission 236 South Brookhurst, Fullerton, California	4/13/64
633-6406	CHARLES PALEN 4034 Del Valle Avenue, Orange, California	3/9/64
633-4300	Farmers Insurance Group, 2401 West Chapman, Santa Ana, California	3/24/64(3 times)

-33-

COMMISSION EXHIBIT No. 2433—Continued

REPORT OF LONG DISTANCE TELEPHONE CALLS

Telephone Number	Subscriber	Dates Called
772-8111	Autonetics Division of North American Aviation 3311 East La Palma, Anaheim, California	12/30/63 1/20/64 1/29/64 2/5/64 3/20/64 (2 times) 4/10/64 5/22/64 (2 times) 6/5/64 7/10/64
776-7111	City of Anaheim Police Department 425 South Harbor Boulevard, Anaheim, California	12/12/63
776-0110	City of Anaheim City Hall 204 East Lincoln Avenue, Anaheim, California	3/16/64
772-7130 disconnected 3/25/64	Murray Manar Liquors 911 North Brookhurst, Anaheim, California	12/18/63
535-1143	Cone Brothers Chevrolet 215 North Anaheim; (used car lot) 1044 North Los Angeles Anaheim, California	3/12/64
827-2130	Walker & Lee Inc. 8031 Stanton Avenue, Cypress, California (Real Estate)	3/24/64
772-5151	Laura Scudders 1525 North East Street, Anaheim, California	2/27/64 5/1/64

COMMISSION EXHIBIT No. 2433—Continued

REPORT OF LONG DISTANCE TELEPHONE CALLS

Telephone Number	Subscriber	Dates Called
774-4192	Security First National Bank, 347 West Lincoln Avenue, Anaheim, California	5/28/64
772-9222	Autonetics Division of North American Aviation 1001 East Ball Road, Anaheim, California	4/16/64
527-2233	Delco-Remy Division General Motors Corp. 1201 North Magnolia Avenue, Anaheim, California	4/30/64
828-9257	MARY VIDRINE SARGIS 6881 San Alto Way, Buena Park, California	3/10/64
827-4267	JOSEPH G. SMALLEY 6584 Lassen Drive, Buena Park, California	3/13/64
772-2267 non-published	DELWIN LARKIN 10162 Gilbert, Anaheim, California	1/21/64
765-6325	FRANK PAPPALARDO 7633 Whitsett, North Hollywood, California	5/9/64
HO 4-1890	GEORGE W. ELDER 2630 Creston Drive, Los Angeles, California	6/9/64
CR 6-2403	DENIS FABIAN, M.D., 442 South Rexford Apt. 306, Beverly Hills, California	5/25/64

COMMISSION EXHIBIT No. 2433—Continued

REPORT OF LONG DISTANCE TELEPHONE CALLS

Telephone Number	Subscriber	Dates Called
FA 1-0786	Craven Tool and Dye Company 1736 West 130th Street, Gardena, California	3/18/64
MA 2-8748 non-published	Doctor's Business Bureau 617 South Olive 4th Floor, Los Angeles, California	4/2/64
MA 7-1252	Doctor's Business Bureau of Southern California 617 South Olive Street 4th Floor, Los Angeles, Calif- ornia	12/12/63 1/14/64 1/17/64 1/28/64 2/28/64 3/11/64 3/27/64 4/29/64 5/6/64 5/7/64 6/12/64
624-8054	Security Consulors 257 South Spring Street, Los Angeles, California	1/29/64
AT 2-9121	General Business Forms 539 West Main Street, Alhambra, California	1/10/64 2/24/64 5/5/64
DA 6-2533	E. E. Meyer Contractor 23204 Walnut, Torrance, California	5/27/64
HE 5-6318	Doctor's Business Bureau 10 Pine - Room 1210 Hartwell Building, Long Beach, California	5/15/64 6/5/64 6/29/64 6/30/64
HE 5-6315	The Doctor's Business Bureau, Room 1210, Hartwell Building, Long Beach, California	5/15/64 6/5/64 6/29/64 6/30/64

-36-

COMMISSION EXHIBIT No. 2433—Continued

REPORT OF LONG DISTANCE TELEPHONE CALLS

Telephone Number	Subscriber	Dates Called
875-3030	JOSEPH PARROS 110 East Morgan Avenue, Rialto, California	2/28/64
685-4315	JOHN SHEFFIELD 7418 Font, Riverside, California	6/12/64 6/16/64
342-2831	PATRICK L. BENSON 19526 Hartland, Reseda, California	1/30/64
827-0290	Dr. CHRISTOPHER J. SMITH 129 A. South Topango Drive, Anaheim, California	1/3/64
828-8307 disconnected 7/23/64	DANIEL CHAMBERS 10571 Court Avenue, Stanton, California	1/13/64
527-2314 non-published	NICKIE DELLACIOPPA 10588 Asberry Avenue, Stanton, California	6/5/64
828-3320	WALTER J. SCHOEPPNER 10201 Beaver Circle, Cypress, California	5/7/64
774-0330	Jewell Tea Company, Inc. 1000 East Ball Road, Anaheim, California	7/7/64
776-1361	First Republic Finance Company 305 South State College Boulevard, Anaheim, California	7/6/64
527-9370	Public Telephone 3450 West Ball Road, Anaheim, California	1/28/64

-37-

COMMISSION EXHIBIT No. 2433—Continued

REPORT OF LONG DISTANCE
TELEPHONE CALLS

Telephone Number	Subscriber	Dates Called
533-4376	D & L Drive-All 548C Central Park Avenue, Anaheim, California	2/7/64 4/17/64 5/19/64 (2 times) 5/21/64
828-7383	Mobile Holdings Corp. 4656 Lincoln Avenue, Cypress, California	12/18/63 6/25/64
828-8394	C. HERBERT EACHUS 8612 Stanton Avenue, Anaheim, California	12/12/63 (2 times)
828-2408 non-published	R. D. WALKER 10021 Blanchi Circle, Buena Park, California	2/17/64
772-4410	Pacific Finance Branch Office Anaheim 532 West Lincoln Avenue, Anaheim, California	1/21/64
828-5425	MIKE MC GONIGAL 630 South Knott Avenue, Apt. D, Anaheim, California	4/24/64 6/19/64 7/8/64
776-2430	Weaver, Radzik and Elias - Attorneys 1695 West Crescent, Anaheim, California	6/24/64 7/2/64
827-4447	PAUL F. BONELLA 2673 West Trojan Place, Anaheim, California	4/8/64
774-1450	Anaheim Memorial Hospital 1111 West La Palma Avenue, Anaheim, California	12/20/63 1/14/64
776-5485 non-published	HERMON B. NIELSEN 116 West Stueckle Avenue, Anaheim, California	6/10/64

COMMISSION EXHIBIT No. 2433—Continued

REPORT OF LONG DISTANCE
TELEPHONE CALLS

Telephone Number	Subscriber	Dates Called
527-1493 disconnected 8/21/64, moving	MILTON E. RAMEY 10271 Sentry Drive, Stanton, California	7/1/64
827-5515	CECIL D. BELLAMY 3518 Mungall Drive, Apt.4, Anaheim, California	2/25/64
527-6517	J. L. KELLUM 6215 San Ricardo Way, Buena Park, California	1/17/64
827-1531	WINTON A. BURNETT 8532 Tamarock Way, Buena Park, California	6/29/64
535-8532	Macres Florist 701 West Lincoln Avenue, Anaheim, California	5/7/64
828-1559 disconnected 8/8/64	JACK VAN HEEL 6363 San Revaldo Circle, Buena Park, California	12/27/63
772-0584	WALTER C. RALSTON, M.D. 1701 Euclid Avenue, Anaheim, California	3/10/64 4/3/64 (2 times)
541-3325	Damian's Cleopatra Beauty Salon 1525 East 17th Street, Santa Ana, California	5/12/64
541-3303	First Fidelity Mortgage Company 2114 North Broadway, Santa Ana, California	3/26/64 (2 times)
545-3298	R. J. RICHARDSON, SR. 2885 Ballow Lane, Costa Mesa, California	6/18/64

COMMISSION EXHIBIT No. 2433—Continued

REPORT OF LONG DISTANCE
TELEPHONE CALLS

Telephone Number	Subscriber	Dates Called
547-6256	Prudential Acceptance Corp. 221 East 17th, Santa Ana, California	4/13/64
547-8251	Universal C.I.T. Corp. Suite E, 1104 East 17th Street, Santa Ana, California	2/28/64 4/28/64
547-7251	Security Title Insurance Company 825 North Broadway, Santa Ana, California	1/20/64
531-8214	DOUGLAS KENT NIXON 9391 Madison Avenue, Westminster, California	2/20/64 2/28/64 3/11/64 3/16/64
547-6184	Katnik-Katnik Cuvard, Attorneys 1205 North Broadway, Santa Ana, California	4/28/64 6/17/64
545-5180 disconnected 5/11/64	Jackson Auto Building 2525 South Birch , Santa Ana, California	1/28/64
545-1171	Seaboard Finance Company 2300 Harbor Boulevard , Costa Mesa, California	4/14/64
549-1167	Allied Asphalt Paving Company 1409 East Warner , Santa Ana, California	1/23/64 2/25/64 (2 times) 3/16/64 3/23/64 4/22/64
531-5162	MARSHALL R. KING 5428 Highland , Santa Ana, California	5/1/64

-40-

REPORT OF LONG DISTANCE
TELEPHONE CALLS

Telephone Number	Subscriber	Dates Called
545-8151	Glass-Laminates 849 West 18th, Costa Mesa, California	1/30/64
542-1101	Telephone Company Business Office, 1015 North Main Street, Santa Ana, California	4/13/64 5/1/64
538-6089	W. E. MEYER 11502 East Santiago Boulevard, Orange, California	6/29/64 7/2/64 7/6/64
633-2087	ROBERT I. BUCHBINDER 16872 Albian Lane , Orange, California	1/7/64 1/14/64 1/21/64 3/17/64
538-6024	JAMES K. SEIRUP 1801 East Witson Avenue , Apt. 3 E , Orange, California	2/20/64
538-8892	Orange Credit Service 550 A East Chapman Avenue , Orange, California	7/8/64 7/9/64
538-9528	Orange Credit Service 550 A East Chapman Avenue , Orange, California	7/7/64
633-3521	Silman Chevrolet Co. 402 West Chapman Avenue, Orange, California	3/23/64
532-2511	Farmers Insurance Group 1137 West Chapman Avenue, Orange, California	3/24/64
633-3407	ART FISHER 334 East Chestnut Avenue, Orange, California	3/19/64 3/24/64

-41-

REPORT OF LONG DISTANCE TELEPHONE CALLS

Telephone Number	Subscriber	Dates Called
495-5741	N. J. DURANT 706 Combs Road Thousand Oaks, California	6/9/64 (3 times)
495-4979	OSCAR RICHEY 2445 Calle Narciso Thousand Oaks, California	2/22/64
486-2641	Ventura County 242 West 2nd Street Oxnard, California	5/21/64
NA 2-2937	M & M Printing & Plastic Product 432 West Monterey Pomona, California	5/27/64
NA 9-4171	Los Angeles County of Agriculture Commission 350 West 5th Street Pomona, California	6/15/64
TW 3-1432 non-published	JACK L. RISLEY 13652 Monroe Westminster, California	2/13/64
TW 7-4234	KENNETH R. PIETTY 6942 Sowell Avenue Westminster, California	2/21/64
TW 3-1101	JOHN E. MC PHERSON 6002 Calvin Circle Huntington Beach, California	2/12/64
TW 3-7121	RICK LESHER 15841 Topaz Circle Westminster, California	4/28/64

COMMISSION EXHIBIT No. 2433—Continued

REPORT OF LONG DISTANCE TELEPHONE CALLS

Telephone Number	Subscriber	Dates Called
HE 5-6315	Dr Business Bureau #10 Pine Heartwell Building Room 1210 Long Beach, California	7/3/64
TW 3-4521	Bank of America 6951 Westminster Westminster, California	1/9/64
TW 3-7576	Riley Realtor 14341 Beach Westminster, California	6/23/64
TW 3-3536	Michael C. Inc. 8501 East Bolsa Avenue, Midway, California	7/6/64
TW 7-6580 non-published	BETTY ANN ERNA 7322 21st Street, Apt. 24 Westminster, California	1/20/64
TW 7-4817	D. SPRANKLE 6642 Halifax Huntington Beach, California	12/20/63
VI 7-3488	WILLIAM H. RIALE 16132 Warren Huntington Beach, California	3/25/64
VI 7-6524	EDWARD WING 16251 Honolulu Huntington Beach, California	5/25/64 6/1/64

COMMISSION EXHIBIT No. 2433—Continued

REPORT OF LONG DISTANCE
TELEPHONE CALLS

Telephone Number	Subscriber	Dates Called
LE 6-9872	HERSHEL ENGLISH 9581 Albacore Drive Huntington Beach, California	2/18/64
VI 7-8817	RONALD CORRIGAN 16251 Fairway Huntington Beach, California	2/25/64 3/26/64 4/9/64
VI 7-4590	RICHARD G. BEGIN 17108 Edgewater Huntington Beach, California	3/18/64
VI 7-1211	La Rue Realty Company 17081 Beach Boulevard Huntington Beach, California	6/29/64
VI 7-2327	W. F. CARDINAL 18662 Florida Avenue Huntington Beach, California	1/14/64
LE 6-8891	Marshal of Orange County 520 Magnolia Huntington Beach, California	6/5/64
VI 7-6018	Altadena Escrow Corp. 17847 Beach Boulevard Huntington Beach, California	4/13/64 5/4/64
VI 7-6031	Fantastic Fair 16672 Beach Boulevard Huntington Beach, California	1/9/64
VI 7-1090	CLYDE A. DAWSON 6911 Clara Huntington Beach, California	2/4/64

-44-

COMMISSION EXHIBIT No. 2433—Continued

REPORT OF LONG DISTANCE
TELEPHONE CALLS

Telephone Number	Subscriber	Dates Called
VI 7-1093	C. E. WAYMIRE 16231 Fairway Lane Huntington Beach, California	7/1/64 (2 times) 7/13/64
892-2819	D. M. CARTERING 11550 Western Avenue Stanton, California	2/13/64
TW 7-2833	ROBERT W. OWENS 12851 Taylor Garden Grove, California	2/20/64
TW 3-2468	La Rue Realty Corp. 15541 Beach Westminster, California	6/22/64
TW 3-7931	MARTIN QUIJAS 7702 Yorkshire Avenue Stanton, California	2/11/64
TW 7-1948 non-published	WILLIAM L. ROSE 7972 Lampson Avenue, Apt. 11 Garden Grove, California	4/8/64
TW 7-6963	JOHN ROSS 9172 Glenridge Avenue Westminster, California	1/9/64 6/1/64
TW 7-3058	J. L. SLOAN 7692 Yorkshire Avenue Stanton, California	6/24/64
TW 7-7991	J. C. KALEBAUGH 7201 21st Street Westminster, California	2/12/64

-45-

COMMISSION EXHIBIT No. 2433—Continued

REPORT OF LONG DISTANCE
TELEPHONE CALLS

Telephone Number	Subscriber	Dates Called
TW 3-5086	Household Finance Corp. 14015 Beach Westminster, California	7/1/64
TW 3-3616	B. M. SIMMONS 13841 Linnert Garden Grove, California	2/13/64
TW 3-3633	Mitchells Retreading Service 12943 South Sycamore Garden Grove, California	1/28/64 2/22/64
TW 7-7641	JAMES A. BLAISDELL 5882 Andy Avenue Garden Grove, California	6/25/64
VI 7-8209	SUDA BROWN 16557 Graham Place Huntington Beach, California	3/2/64
VI 7-2196	P. E. POSKIMS 8572 Glasgow Circle Huntington Beach, California	6/16/64
VI 7-6287	BURYLE C. HEMERICK 17472 Zeider Huntington Beach, California	1/29/64
VI 7-0184	H. W. COTTRELL 17530 Santa Domingo Fountain Valley, California	6/24/64

COMMISSION EXHIBIT No. 2433—Continued

REPORT OF LONG DISTANCE
TELEPHONE CALLS

Telephone Number	Subscriber	Dates Called
VI 7-7689	Unable to locate; appears to be an off group	4/13/64
HY 4-9057 (Paystation)	Laguna Canyon Club 21162 Laguna Road Laguna Beach, California	2/21/64
HY 4-1131	Tommy Ayres Chevrolet 350 Broadway Laguna Beach, California	6/16/64
PY 7-4406	PAUL A. HARDING 190 East Pine Altadena, California	2/11/64

COMMISSION EXHIBIT No. 2433—Continued

UNITED STATES DEPARTMENT OF JUSTICE

FEDERAL BUREAU OF INVESTIGATION
Las Vegas, Nevada
August 22, 1964

In Reply, Please Refer to
File No.

JACK L. RUBY, also known as;
LEE HARVEY OSWALD, also
known as - Victim

The July, 1964, telephone directory of the Central Telephone Company, Southern Nevada Division, Las Vegas, Nevada, reflects that telephone number 735-9111 is listed to the Sands Hotel, 3317 Las Vegas Boulevard South, Las Vegas, Nevada.

COMMISSION EXHIBIT No. 2433—Continued

FD-302 (Rev. 3-3-59)

FEDERAL BUREAU OF INVESTIGATION

Date 12-21-63

1

ROBERT G. LANDERS, Service Representative, "Dallas Morning News" newspaper, advised he had only been acquainted with JACK RUBY as a customer placing ads in the newspaper since early November, 1963. He was not well enough acquainted with RUBY to be familiar with his habits or associates.

About six weeks ago, RUBY issued him a permanent Carousel Club pass card number 190. On Thursday night, November 21, 1963, he went to the Carousel Club with another employee, CHARLES MILLER. They saw RUBY there but did not talk to him. During an intermission, RUBY was on the stage giving away prizes. There was a man who appeared to be drunk creating a disturbance in the crowd, in that he was using foul language, telling RUBY to get off the stage and to bring on the girls.

RUBY had a verbal argument with the man after which the man left the Carousel Club. RUBY did not have to use any force to get the man to leave. He apologized to the audience for the disturbance after the man left.

Sometime on Friday morning, November 22, 1963, he saw RUBY at the "Dallas Morning News" but did not talk with him other than to just say hello.

LANDERS was not acquainted with LEE HARVEY OSWALD, knew of no association between RUBY and OSWALD and knew of no association by other individuals with these two men in connection with the shootings.

on 12-21-63 at Dallas, Texas File # DL 44-1639

by Special Agent JAMES F. GLONEK - md Date dictated 12-21-63

COMMISSION EXHIBIT No. 2434

FD-302 (Rev. 3-3-59)

FEDERAL BUREAU OF IN[redacted]

Commission Exhibit No. 2435

Date 12-21-63

1

CHARLES MILLER, Clerk and Messenger, "Dallas Morning News", advised he has been casually acquainted with JACK RUBY for about the past year in connection with RUBY coming to the paper to place ads. He has never developed a personal acquaintanceship with RUBY and is not aware of his friends, associates, or habits.

MILLER stated he has been in the Carousel Club about three times during the past year. On several of the occasions, RUBY would write him an informal pass to attend the club while RUBY was at the paper to place an ad.

About six weeks or so ago, the last time that he saw RUBY at the newspaper, RUBY issued him a Carousel Club pass card number 138 sealed in plastic.

On the night of Thursday, November 21, 1963, he and ROBERT LANDERS, another employee, went to the Carousel Club with their passes. They did not talk with RUBY at the club, but saw him there. During an intermission, RUBY was at the microphone on the stage giving away prizes. There was a man in the audience who appeared to be intoxicated, who was creating a disturbance by using dirty language, telling RUBY to get the prizes over with and to bring on the girls. RUBY told the man to behave, which the man refused to do. RUBY made a statement something to the effect that he wanted to "flip a coin with the man to pay for the furniture that would be busted if the man did not leave the place." The man then left the club at RUBY's insistence peacefully and RUBY did not have to use any force to eject him. RUBY then apologized to the audience for the disturbance and the show continued.

MILLER was not acquainted with LEE HARVEY OSWALD, knew of no association between OSWALD and RUBY and knew of no association by other individuals with these two men in connection with the shootings.

on 12-21-63 at Dallas, Texas File # DL 44-1639

by Special Agent JAMES F. GLONEK JFG - md Date dictated 12-21-63

260

This document contains neither recommendations nor conclusions of the FBI. It is the property of the FBI and is loaned to your agency; it and its contents are not to be distributed outside your agency.

COMMISSION EXHIBIT No. 2435

FD-302 (Rev. 3-3-59)

FEDERAL BUREAU OF [redacted]

Commission Exhibit No. 2436

Date December 4, 1963

1

DON J. CAMPBELL, Advertising Salesman, Dallas "Morning News," home address 5514 Swiss, telephone number TA 1-0792, furnished the following information:

JACK RUBY has in the past for a number of years been a regular advertising customer with the Dallas "Morning News." It is the usual thing for him to be in the Dallas News Building with his advertisements on a Friday morning.

On Friday, November 22, 1963, at approximately 12:00 noon, CAMPBELL returned to the Advertising Office and JACK RUBY was in the office at that time. CAMPBELL heard from some unrecalled source that RUBY ate breakfast at the cafeteria of that building on that particular day. CAMPBELL, who has handled RUBY's accounts for the past few years, and RUBY discussed business and at the conclusion of that business, RUBY talked to CAMPBELL about his, RUBY's, business.

On this particular day, RUBY mentioned what a "lousy" business he was in and talked about some of the problems of running a night club. He spent some time talking about some of the physical fights he had been in in connection with his night club and informed CAMPBELL that he, RUBY, was a very capable fighter. At that time he made a statement to CAMPBELL that any time he felt like he was fixing to have trouble with someone, he would always get a gun and have it on his person.

RUBY did not at this time or at any other time to CAMPBELL's recollection, mention anything about President KENNEDY, the parade which was going on at that time, or discuss any kind of politics.

CAMPBELL had another customer he had to see and left the building at approximately 12:25 p.m. CAMPBELL advised he did not return to his office before RUBY's departure. He further advised that while he was in the office RUBY was not near the desk of Miss GEORGIA MAYOR to his (CAMPBELL's) knowledge.

on 12/4/63 at Dallas, Texas File # Dallas 44-1639

by Special Agents JACK B. PEDEN and JAMES E. GARRIS:BL Date dictated 12/4/63

523

This document contains neither recommendations nor conclusions of the FBI. It is the property of the FBI and is loaned to your agency; it and its contents are not to be distributed outside your agency.

COMMISSION EXHIBIT No. 2436

FD-302 (Rev. 3-3-59)

Commission Exhibit No. 2437

FEDERAL BUREAU OF [redacted]

Date 7/22/64

1

JAMES M. TICE, 8406 Lakemont Drive, telephone No. FL 2-2559, was interviewed in the presence of his wife, Mrs. WILMA TICE. Mr. TICE advised he is employed by American Airlines as a Fleet Service Clerk at Love Field, Dallas, Texas.

Mr. TICE advised that sometime after 2:00 a.m., on July 22, 1964, while employed at Love Field he received a telephone call from his wife informing that a prowler had been around their house. Mr. TICE said he returned home. He said when he arrived home he found his wife in an emotional state as she related to him the incident about the prowler or prowlers around their home. He said apparently the prowler or prowlers knew he was at work because "they would not fool around my house, they know better if they know me."

Mr. TICE advised that prior to his arrival home his wife had called the Dallas Police and informed that a prowler had been around their house. He said the police who responded to his wife's call had found a twelve foot homemade two by four ladder wedged against the bottom of the aluminum storm door located at the back of the house. Mr. TICE said he had made the ladder and had previously stored it next to the garage at the rear of the house. Mr. TICE also stated the spring snap which holds the slatted wooden front screen-storm door secure had been manipulated so that the door could not be opened from the inside without forcing it.

Mr. TICE advised that the Dallas Police officers who responded to his wife's call inquired of him if he had any teen-age children. Mr. TICE said he responded negatively to this question. He advised, however, that his niece, EDITH TICE, had been visiting them for about a week. He also stated that he and his wife have three children, ages 7, 8, and 9.

When Mrs. TICE was questioned as to when she was to appear before the President's Commission in Dallas, Texas, she advised she was to appear on Friday, July 24, 1964, at 2:30 p.m., whereupon Mr. TICE stated "That is the first information I have that my wife has to appear before the President's Commission."

on 7/22/64 at Dallas, Texas File # DL 44-1639

by Special Agent A. RAYMOND SWITZER:vm Date dictated 7/22/64

COMMISSION EXHIBIT No. 2437

2
DL 44-1639

Mr. TICE related that on April 30, 1964, JACK RUBY's two sisters, EVA GRANT and EILEEN KAMINSKY, visited at his house and talked to his wife. He stated he told his wife she had no business talking to those people and that she should not have invited them into their house. He stated he was very annoyed because she had. As a consequence of this, Mr. TICE stated his wife would not discuss with him any information that she might have relating to JACK RUBY or why the President's Commission would want to talk to her. Mr. TICE stated he was at home on Sunday, July 19, 1964, when his wife received the airmail special delivery registered letter, return receipt requested, from the President's Commission. He said his wife would not open it nor would she discuss with him as to what it might contain. He said this annoyed him considerably.

Mr. TICE stated he related the above incident, about his wife receiving a letter from the President's Commission, to his fellow employees at American Airlines.

Mr. TICE advised he is aware his wife received an anonymous telephone call at about 2:00 p.m., on July 20, 1964. He said she informed him that the anonymous male caller had stated to Mrs. TICE that "It would pay you to keep your mouth shut." Mr. TICE stated he has no idea as to who may have made the call or to what the caller was referring but stated it might have something to do with his wife testifying before the President's Commission. He added, however, stating "Hell, nobody tells me anything around here. I guess all I'm supposed to do is chase prowlers and buy groceries." Mr. TICE further stated he is more than a little annoyed with his wife for not discussing the above matters with him.

Mr. TICE stated that about one and one half years ago he received an anonymous telephone call during which the male caller told him not to go to his farm with his little boy because his wife was going to have him killed. He said the caller also said "I will talk to you later at work." Mr. TICE said he did not pay any attention to this call and never learned who made it. He also stated

COMMISSION EXHIBIT No. 2437—Continued

3
DL 44-1639

that a number of his fellow employees had received anonymous telephone calls at about the same time.

Mr. TICE stated he had no information relating to the assassination of President KENNEDY or to the shooting of LEE HARVEY OSWALD by JACK RUBY. He stated, however, that should he receive any information that would be of assistance in this matter he would contact the interviewing Agent.

As interviewing Agent was departing the TICE residence, two men who identified themselves as detectives from Captain FRITZ' office, Homicide and Robbery Bureau, Dallas Police Department, entered the TICE residence and informed they were there at the direction of Captain FRITZ to interview Mr. and Mrs. TICE.

COMMISSION EXHIBIT No. 2437—Continued

1
DL 44-1639
MCC:eah

On July 13, 1964, JARRETT BOREN, 3815 East Beverly, Dallas, Texas, telephone LA 8-7400, advised telephonically he had been in the King Tailor Shop, Elm Street, Dallas, about ten days previously and had observed a photograph on the wall. The photograph included the car of President KENNEDY on the parade route on November 22, 1963. BOREN stated Mr. KING had pointed out an individual in the photograph as being RUBY.

On July 14, 1964, GORDON KING, King the Tailor, 2020 Elm Street, Dallas, Texas, exhibited to SA MANNING C. CLEMENTS the photograph in question. He said he purchased the picture shortly after November 22, 1963, from some Negro boys, who had said a man in a dark hat in the picture was JACK RUBY.

SA CLEMENTS recognized the photograph as one which has been brought to his attention on at least two different occasions previously by other persons. On the basis of having interviewed RUBY on December 21, 1963, over a period of three to four hours and having seen RUBY daily during his murder trial, SA CLEMENTS concluded the individual in question is definitely not RUBY.

COMMISSION EXHIBIT No. 2438

— Commission Exhibit No. 2439 —

FD-302 (Rev. 3-3-59)

FEDERAL BUREAU OF INVES[redacted]

1

Date September 7, 1964

ANDREW ARMSTRONG, JR., Apartment C, 3821 Dixon, Dallas, Texas, was interviewed at one of his places of employment, the Connecticut Village Apartments, Connecticut Lane, Dallas, Texas. Mr. ARMSTRONG reviewed all six photographs and stated as follows:

Photograph No. 1 - ARMSTRONG identified JACK L. RUBY as the person wearing glasses appearing in the upper right side of the photograph.

Photograph No. 2 - ARMSTRONG identified JACK L. RUBY as the individual wearing glasses in the upper right corner of the photograph.

Photograph No. 3 - ARMSTRONG pointed out RUBY as the individual whose back portion of the head appears in the center of the picture.

Photograph No. 4 - ARMSTRONG stated that RUBY is the bald man in the foreground with his right hand in his pocket and his back to the camera.

Photograph No. 5 - ARMSTRONG stated that JACK L. RUBY is the individual standing in the foreground in about the center of the photograph.

Photograph No. 6 - ARMSTRONG stated that JACK L. RUBY is identical to the individual standing in the foreground in about the center of the photograph

There was no doubt whatsoever in ARMSTRONG's mind that JACK RUBY is identical to the person appearing in the aforementioned photographs.

on 9/5/64 at Dallas, Texas File # DL 44-1639

by Special Agent RICHARD J. BURNETT/pm Date dictated 9/7/64

COMMISSION EXHIBIT NO. 2439

FD-302 (Rev. 3-3-59)

FEDERAL BUREAU OF INVESTIGATION

1

Date September 7, 1964

BRUCE W. McLEAN, owner, McLean Hair Experts, Room 1423, Dallas Athletic Club, 1805 Elm Street, Dallas, Texas, who resides at 7306 Mimosa Lane, Dallas, was interviewed in his office.

Mr. McLEAN stated that JACK L. RUBY is the person who is depicted in the upper right side of photographs 1 and 2. In these photographs RUBY is wearing dark glasses and is attired in a business suit.

In regard to photographs 3 through 6, McLEAN stated that while the individual is believed by him to be RUBY, he does not feel that he can make a positive identification of RUBY being pictured in any of these photographs. He stated that he is just not positive of this identification of RUBY, and would not want to make the positive statement that RUBY is depicted in any of these photographs.

2

on 9/5/64 at Dallas, Texas File # DL 44-1639

by Special Agent RICHARD J. BURNETT/pm Date dictated 9/7/64

COMMISSION EXHIBIT NO. 2439—Continued

FD-302 (Rev. 3-3-59) **FEDERAL BUREAU OF INVESTIGATION**

1

Date September 7, 1964

CLYDE F. GOODSON, Police Officer, Dallas Police Department, was interviewed at his residence, 6529 Oleta Drive, Dallas, Texas.

Mr. GOODSON viewed the six photographs furnished by the President's Commission and commented that he does not feel that he knew RUBY well enough to make an unqualified identification of RUBY in any of these six photographs.

Officer GOODSON stated that RUBY appears to him to be identical with the individual in the upper right corner of photographs 1 and 2 In regard to photographs 3 through 6, GOODSON stated that he cannot say one way or the other whether the individual believed to be JACK L. RUBY in these photographs is positively RUBY.

3

on 9/5/64 at Dallas, Texas File # DL 44-1639

by Special Agent RICHARD J. BURNETT/pm Date dictated 9/7/64

This document contains neither recommendations nor conclusions of the FBI. It is the property of the FBI and is loaned to your agency; it and its contents are not to be distributed outside your agency.

COMMISSION EXHIBIT No. 2439—Continued

FD-302 (Rev. 3-3-59) **FEDERAL BUREAU OF INVESTIGATION**

1

Date September 7, 1964

VICTOR F. ROBERTSON, JR., employee, Dallas radio station WFAA, was interviewed at his residence, 414 South Willomet, Dallas, Texas.

Mr. ROBERTSON identified, without any qualifications, the individual appearing in the upper right corner of photographs 1 and 2, attired in a business suit and wearing glasses, as JACK L. RUBY.

ROBERTSON stated that the individual believed to be RUBY in photograph No. 3 is "possibly" RUBY; however, he cannot make a positive statement to this effect.

In regard to photographs 4, 5 and 6, ROBERTSON stated he, himself, appears in these photographs, but he does not recall having seen RUBY behind him at the time these photographs were taken. He noted that the individual believed to be RUBY in these photographs is thinner than what he remembers JACK RUBY to be. He added that he personally does not feel that RUBY is the individual depicted in photographs 4, 5 and 6, as the bald-headed man standing in the foreground of these three pictures.

4

on 9/5/64 at Dallas, Texas File # DL 44-1639

by Special Agent RICHARD J. BURNETT/pm Date dictated 9/7/64

This document contains neither recommendations nor conclusions of the FBI. It is the property of the FBI and is loaned to your agency; it and its contents are not to be distributed outside your agency.

COMMISSION EXHIBIT No. 2439—Continued

FD-302 (Rev. 3-3-59) FEDERAL BUREAU OF INVESTIGATION

1

Date September 7, 1964

GABRIEL D. MACIAS, Badge No. 1374, Dallas Police Department, a resident of 3005 Klondike, Dallas, Texas, was interviewed at the Dallas Police Department.

MACIAS viewed photograph No. 6 and identified himself as the police officer who appears on the right-hand side of the photograph who is moving in the direction of the man believed to be JACK RUBY.

MACIAS stated he was on duty for only a few minutes on the third floor of the Police Department on the night of November 22, 1963, and his assignment was to keep the reporters and cameramen in the hallway moving in order to keep the aisle cleared. MACIAS stated that he only vaguely knows JACK L. RUBY, and he does not recall having seen RUBY on the third floor of the Police Department during the very short time he was on duty at that assignment.

Officer MACIAS viewed photograph No. 6, in which he is shown, and stated that he cannot identify RUBY as being an individual shown in that photograph as he does not feel that he knew RUBY well enough to make an identification from this photograph.

5

on 9/5/64 at Dallas, Texas File # DL 44-1639

by Special Agent RICHARD J. BURNETT/pm Date dictated 9/7/64

This document contains neither recommendations nor conclusions of the FBI. It is the property of the FBI and is loaned to your agency; it and its contents are not to be distributed outside your agency.

COMMISSION EXHIBIT No. 2439—Continued

FD-302 (Rev. 1-25-60) FEDERAL BUREAU OF INVESTIGATION

Date 9/9/64

GEORGE SENATOR who resides at the Bristol Hotel, 129 West 48th Street, room 1211 and is employed as a cashier at the Mr. Kishka Restaurant, 150 West 49th Street, Manhattan, New York, was interviewed on September 8, 1964.

The six photographs furnished by the President's Commission on the Assassination of President KENNEDY were exhibited to GEORGE SENATOR.

He identified JACK RUBY in photographs one and two as the man standing in the last row, right hand side, dressed in a dark suit, wearing a tie and carrying a hankerchief in his breast pocket.

On observing photographs three and four, SENATOR said he believed RUBY in photograph three was the slightly bald man in the center of the picture shown walking out of the door and in photograph four he believed that RUBY was the slightly bald man in the foreground with his right hand in his pocket and his back to the camera. SENATOR believed that JACK RUBY was the man shown in photograph five and six who is depicted standing in the foreground in about the center of the photographs.

SENATOR was unable to identify the police officer who appears on the right hand side of photograph six.

6

On 9/8/64 at New York, New York File # NY 44-974

by SA JAMES J. ROGERS/dmb Date dictated 9/9/64

This document contains neither recommendations nor conclusions of the FBI. It is the property of the FBI and is loaned to your agency; it and its contents are not to be distributed outside your agency.

COMMISSION EXHIBIT No. 2439—Continued

Commission Exhibit No. 2440

FD-302 (Rev. 3-3-59) EDERAL BUREAU OF INV[redacted]

1

Date 6/10/64

Mr. MIKE WHITAKER, United Press International, Dallas, Texas, advised that he was at the Dallas Police Department on the afternoon of November 22, 1963, and was on the third floor practically all the time near the Homicide Bureau and that he does not recall seeing JACK RUBY at any time on the third floor of that building.

Mr. WHITAKER could furnish no information relative to JACK RUBY's activities, of his own personal knowledge, on November 22, 23 or 24, 1963.

on 6/10/64 at Dallas, Texas File # DL 44-1639

by Special Agent VINCENT E. DRAIN/ds Date dictated 6/10/64

COMMISSION EXHIBIT No. 2440

COMMISSION EXHIBIT No. 2441

COMMISSION EXHIBIT No. 2442

FD-204 (Rev. 3-3-59)

UNITED STATES DEPARTMENT OF JUSTICE
FEDERAL BUREAU OF INVESTIGATION

Copy to: 1-Legat, Mexico City

Report of: SA ERVIN B. BRUNINGA   Office: Birmingham
Date: 2/11/64

Field Office File #: BH 105-908   Bureau File #: 105-82555

Title: LEE HARVEY OSWALD

Character: INTERNAL SECURITY - R

Synopsis: JOHN HOWARD BOWEN states he rode on bus from Nuevo Laredo, Mexico, to Mexico City, Mexico, 9/26-27/63, and sat next to unidentified young man whom he was unable to identify as subject OSWALD. BOWEN claims to be itinerant Baptist preacher for past 50 years, traveling extensively in the United States, and for past 20 years in Mexico. He claims he has never been to any other foreign countries, other that Bermuda. BOWEN acquainted with ALBERT OSBORNE, from Canada, who is about his same size and age, and who is also itinerant Baptist preacher or missionary who has traveled in Mexico, and who was reportedly in that country in December, 1963, and January, 1964.

- RUC -

DETAILS:

This document contains neither recommendations nor conclusions of the FBI. It is the property of the FBI and is loaned to your agency; it and its contents are not to be distributed outside your agency.

COMMISSION EXHIBIT No. 2443

FD-302 (Rev. 1-25-60)

FEDERAL BUREAU OF INVESTIGATION

Date 2/11/64

JOHN HOWARD BOWEN was interviewed February 8, 1964, and he furnished the following information:

BOWEN advised that he has been in the Russellville, Alabama, area, speaking at various rural Baptist churches, and has been residing at the residence of WYLIE UPTAIN, Rural Route, Russellville, Alabama. He stated he intended leaving the Russellville, Alabama, area February 11, 1964, en route back to Laredo, Texas, by way of New Orleans, Louisiana.

BOWEN stated to the best of his knowledge, he was born at Chester, Pennsylvania, on January 12, 1885, and his father's name was JAMES A. BOWEN, and his mother was EMILY BOWEN. He did not know his parents, but he was reared in an orphanage in Philadelphia, Pennsylvania. His grandmother, SARAH HALL, participated to a limited extent in giving him guidance and shelter during the early years of his life. His grandmother and relatives are all deceased, and he has no known relatives of any kind.

BOWEN attended elementary school intermittently in the Philadelphia, Pennsylvania, area, but took correspondence courses and has completed the equivalent of about two years of college. He also took a correspondence course in theology, which he completed in about 1914. About fifty years ago, he was ordained as a minister by the Plymouth Brethren Church, in Trenton, New Jersey, and about forty-five years ago, he was ordained as a minister by the Northern Baptist Convention at Binghamton, New York. He also is recognized as an ordained minister by the Missionary Baptist Convention and he currently considers himself associated with that church body.

BOWEN stated he considers himself an itinerant gardener and preacher. He was formerly a member of the First Baptist Church at Knoxville, Tennessee, and more recently was a member of the First Baptist Church at Laredo, Texas. He has visited and worshiped at the latter church intermittently for the past twenty years.

On 2/8/64 at Florence, Alabama File # BH 105-908

by SA ERVIN B. BRUNINGA:ela Date dictated 2/10/64

This document contains neither recommendations nor conclusions of the FBI. It is the property of the FBI and is loaned to your agency; it and its contents are not to be distributed outside your agency.

COMMISSION EXHIBIT No. 2443—Continued

About thirty years ago, BOWEN applied for a job as a juvenile counselor, with the Tennessee Valley Authority at Knoxville, Tennessee, and recalled that he was fingerprinted on that occasion. From about 1929 to about 1934, BOWEN worked with juvenile delinquents for the City of Knoxville, Tennessee. While doing this work, he became well acquainted with Dr. A. D. MUELLER, who is now associated with the Veterans Hospital in Memphis, Tennessee, and lives at 4035 Tutwiler Road, Memphis, Tennessee. He also became well acquainted with Miss MARY ELLIOTT, who is a prominent social worker in the Knoxville, Tennessee, area.

BOWEN states since becoming ordained about fifty years ago, he has traveled extensively in the United States, particularly in the Stanton, Virginia, area, and in the Southern part of the United States, as an itinerant Baptist minister. During the past twenty years, he has also made numerous trips as an itinerant Baptist minister throughout Mexico. He stated he has never been to Canada or England or any other foreign country, except in about 1939, he once visited Bermuda. On these itinerant preaching tours, he resides in the homes of the host pastor, and he moves from place to place frequently. He considers his home to be the St. Anthony Hotel, Laredo, Texas, and he is well known there by the manager OSCAR FERRINA. He has been residing at that hotel intermittently for the past twenty years, and has made trips to Mexico for the past twenty years as an itinerant preacher.

BOWEN stated he has no passport, but carries for identification purposes, the following items:

Social Security Card in the name of JOHN HOWARD BOWEN, Social Security Number 449-36-9745.

Texaco Company Credit Card #T-11372, in the name of J. H. BOWEN, P. O. Box 3042, Knoxville, Tennessee.

Gold Star Insurance Company Card, Policy Number N3176.

Card from Laredo National Bank, in the name of JOHN HOWARD BOWEN, 920 Salinas Avenue, Box 308, Laredo, Texas, Account Number 10-7400-1.

BOWEN stated that in 1956, he contacted an unrecalled attorney in Philadelphia to apply for Social Security. This attorney experienced great difficulty in obtaining a date of birth for him. The attorney was not able to completely verify his birth, but furnished him with a card reflecting the following data:

Name:	JOHN HOWARD BOWEN
Born:	January 14, 1880
Father:	JAMES A. BOWEN
Mother:	EDITH MONTGOMERY
Place of Birth:	Chester, Pennsylvania
File Number:	D-869-1880
Filed:	March 6, 1956

The above card bore the signature of a person which appeared to be DERWIN F. WATKINS, as the person who executed the birth data form. BOWEN stated he doubted if the above was exactly correct, but it was the best birth data which the attorney could obtain through unknown sources. He could not recall the name of this attorney, and was not certain if WATKINS was his name or not. BOWEN stated he had been unable to obtain Social Security benefits because of his inability to obtain correct birth data.

BOWEN states that in about 1958, he was residing at the Reece Hotel, Oaxaco, Mexico, and also residing in that same hotel was ALBERT OSBORNE, who was a retired itinerant Baptist minister from Canada. OSBORNE was about 70 years of age, 5'8" tall, 190 pounds, hair gray and balding, and had an English or Scottish accent. BOWEN acknowledged that OSBORNE was about his same size and age.

A census of some type was then being taken by Mexican authorities, and BOWEN was unable to locate his identification papers. He therefore borrowed the identification papers of OSBORNE on that occasion, and exhibited them to the Mexican authorities. He thereafter returned these papers to OSBORNE. He later found his own identification papers, and states he has never before or since claimed to be anyone other than JOHN HOWARD BOWEN.

BOWEN stated he next saw OSBORNE in about the Spring of 1961 or 1962, at the Railway Express Company Office in Mexico City, Mexico. He pointed out he corresponds occasionally with OSBORNE, but has not seen him since the above occasion. He recalled having heard through friends in Mexico that OSBORNE was traveling in Mexico as an itinerant Baptist preacher in December, 1963, and January, 1964, but he was planning on returning to Canada, and possibly taking upon residence in the vicinity of Vancouver, Canada.

BOWEN observed a photograph of a man standing in front of a castle-like building, holding what appeared to be a camera, and he identified that person as being ALBERT OSBORNE. BOWEN explained that he has a copy of that same photograph, which was sent to him by OSBORNE, and it apparently was taken during a trip to England or Scotland.

BOWEN also observed a photograph of a man in a zippered jacket and a helmet, and identified that as being a photograph of himself, which had been taken about twenty years ago at Veracruz, Mexico. BOWEN stated that ALBERT OSBORNE has traveled in the same areas in Mexico as an itinerant Baptist preacher, and OSBORNE has stayed at the two independent churches in Texmelucan, Mexico, where the churches maintain a home for ministers. Those churches also distribute food for children from destitute families. He explained that it was entirely possible persons might confuse him with OSBORNE, because they are both itinerant Baptist preachers, are about the same size and age, and both travel extensively in Mexico.

BOWEN stated he was not interviewed in Mexico at Texmelucan or anywhere else by the FBI, regarding OSBORNE or subject OSWALD. He pointed out when he came to Laredo, Texas, recently, he learned that the FBI had been making inquiries there regarding his recent trip to Mexico. He stated that he thereafter looked through his papers and files at Laredo, and learned that he had made a trip by bus from Nuevo Laredo, Mexico, to Mexico City, on September 26-27, 1963.

BOWEN explained that at the bus station in Nuevo Laredo, Mexico, at about 3:30 P.M., September 26, 1963, he boarded a bus en route to Mexico City, and signed his own name, JOHN HOWARD BOWEN, to the roster of passengers. He sat in the third seat from the front on the right side. A young man who apparently boarded the bus at the same time sat in the seat adjacent to him. He described this person as follows:

Sex:	Male
Race:	White
Age:	29
Height:	5'8"
Weight:	150 pounds
Hair:	Blond and thin
Complexion:	Dark

He explained this passenger had a small zipper bag which he placed in the rack above his feet. He did not talk to this person or hear him speak to anyone else on the bus. He presumed this person was Mexican or Puerto Rican, because he was dark complected and did not appear to be an American. He recalled that directly in front of him was a man and a woman who were about sixty years of age. The man was retired from the Bermuda Police Department, and he apparently had been traveling extensively since his retirement. BOWEN recalled that two Mexican women and a small child occupied the seat directly behind him. He could not recall who the other passengers might have been on the bus. He did recall that the bus was fully occupied when it left Nuevo Laredo.

BOWEN stated the young man sitting next to him went to sleep shortly after getting on the bus, and did not converse with him or anyone else. At about 4:30 or 5:00 P.M. on September 26, 1964, the bus stopped for a lunch stop at Sabinas Hidalgo, Mexico. This young man went to the restroom and ate a lunch at the bus station. When he returned to the bus, he went to the rear of the bus where he reclined on a rear seat and went to sleep.

BOWEN stated he did not recall seeing the above person again during the trip to Mexico City, and has not seen him before or since that time. He did not know where the above person got off the bus. BOWEN stated he does not recall having specifically seen a particular photograph of subject LEE HARVEY OSWALD, but is rather certain he had seen some newspaper photographs of him. He stated he does not feel that the above person was identical to LEE HARVEY OSWALD, because the above person was quite dark complected and appeared to be a Mexican or Puerto Rican.

BOWEN stated he arrived in Mexico City on the above bus about 9:30 AM., September 27, 1963. He thereafter boarded another bus in Mexico City, and went to Puebla, Mexico, where he resided at the St. Augestine Hotel. The next day, he boarded a night train at Puebla and traveled to the Railroad Hotel in Jesus Carranga, which is north of Juchitan, Mexico. He remained in this area for about one week, contacting various native ministers, and delivering Bibles to them. He preached some in Juchitan, and Tehuantepec, area. He then returned to the area of Puebla, Mexico, where he resided with various persons connected with Baptist churches in that vicinity. He then traveled back to Laredo, Texas, in about the middle of November, 1963. While in Mexico City, he usually resides at the Canada Hotel Annex, which is on Cinco De Mayo Street. BOWEN stated at no time on this trip did he again see the above mentioned person who had been on the bus with him from Neuvo Laredo.

BOWEN stated he intends to travel from the Russellville, Alabama, area, to Laredo, Texas, by way of New Orleans, and expects to be at the St. Anthony Hotel, Laredo, Texas, about February 15-17, 1964, where he will remain indefinitely. He stated that at Laredo, he could locate the bus ticket which would verify the date of the above mentioned trip into Mexico in September, 1963. He stated he may also have there correspondence from ALBERT OSBORNE.

BOWEN stated he has never taught school, has never been to any foreign countries, other than Mexico and Bermuda. He stated he has never written a book, knew nothing about the Lisban earthquake of 1775. He could not recall seeing any American girls on instant bus, and knew of no one on the bus who might have talked to the young man sitting in the seat adjacent to him.

BOWEN stated he definitely is not identical to ALBERT OSBORNE, and with the one exception, he has never posed as ALBERT OSBORNE. BOWEN stated he would cooperate fully in this matter. He volunteered to have his photograph and fingerprints taken on this occasion.

BOWEN furnished the following descriptive data regarding himself:

Name:	JOHN HOWARD BOWEN
Sex:	Male
Race:	White
Date of Birth:	January 12, 1885
Place of Birth:	Chester, Pennsylvania
Height:	5'8"
Weight:	190 pounds
Hair:	Gray and thin
Eyes:	Blue
Build:	Heavy
Complexion:	Medium
Scars and Marks:	Small round sore or scar on right temple.

BH 105-908

Characteristics:	Wears heavy, dark rimmed glasses for reading
Occupation:	Itinerant Baptist preacher.

9*

COMMISSION EXHIBIT No. 2443—Continued

DL 100-10461
RPG:eah

A. FBI Laboratory Examinations

COMMISSION EXHIBIT No. 2444

1

DL 100-10461
RPG:mja

Under date of December 20, 1963, the FBI Laboratory furnished the following information concerning a photographic examination requested by the Dallas Office, December 5, 1963:

Specimens received 12/6/63

K51 One Bell and Howell Zoomatic 8mm motion picture camera SN AS13486, obtained from Mr. Abraham Zapruder

Result of examination:

The K51 8mm motion picture camera has been tested to determine the running speed of this camera, and it has been determined that this camera when operated at normal "RUN" speed operates at 18 1/3 frames per second.

While it is not possible to establish accurately from the film the moment of impact of the first two shots, applying the above camera speed to the film previously submitted which was exposed by Abraham Zapruder and which recorded the assassination, it has been determined that the best estimate of the elapsed time between the first and third shots lies between approximately five and six seconds. It is noted that the President's car moves behind a signboard at about the time of the first shot, and the President's movements during this period are not observable. However, he begins to fall forward immediately upon emerging from behind the sign.

1
DL 100-10461
RPG:gmf

Under date of December 27, 1963, the FBI Laboratory furnished the following information concerning a document examination requested by the Dallas Office on December 13, 1963:

"Specimens received 12/20/63

K52 A replica sack made at the Texas School Book Depository Building from paper and tape available in the shipping room of the Texas School Book Depository

Result of examination:

It was determined that the paper and tape used for specimen K52 is different from the paper and tape used for the Q10 paper bag that was previously submitted in this case."

1
DL 100-10461
RPG:mvs

Under date of December 20, 1963, the FBI Laboratory furnished the following information concerning an examination requested by the Dallas Office on November 27, 1963:

Specimens received November 27, 1963

Q228 Pamphlets entitled "The Crime Against Cuba" by Corliss Lamont (Dallas Item #303)

Q229 Booklet entitled "The Socialist Workers Party" by Joseph Hansen (Dallas Item #305)

Q230 Russian book dated 1962 at Sofia (Dallas Item #324)

Result of examination:

In these specimens certain letters, words and entire phrases have been excised.

No cryptographic significance could be attached to this material.

44

COMMISSION EXHIBIT No. 2444—Continued

DL 100-10461
RPG:cv
1

Under date of December 18, 1963, the FBI Laboratory furnished the following information concerning a firearms examination requested by the Dallas Office on December 10, 1963:

Specimens received December 12, 1963

Q258 - Q261 Four 6.5 mm cartridge cases obtained from Mrs. VIRGINIA GOODWIN

Results of examination:

The four cartridge cases, Q258 through Q261, were compared with OSWALD's rifle, K1. As a result of this comparison, it was determined that Q258 through Q261 could not have been fired in this rifle.

40

COMMISSION EXHIBIT No. 2444—Continued

DL 100-10461
RPG:cv
1

Under date of December 16, 1963, the FBI Laboratory furnished the following information concerning a document examination requested by the Dallas Office on December 13, 1963:

Specimens received December 14, 1963

Q265 Brown paper envelope bearing handwritten address "Lee Oswald 601 West Nassaus St Dallas Texas," postmarked "IRVING, TEX. 5-30 AM 1963 (date illegible)

Q266 Accompanying portion of long, narrow paper bag and strip of brown corrugated paper

Result of examination

The papers of specimens Q265 and Q266 were found to differ in observable physical characteristics from the paper of specimen Q10, a wrapping paper in the shape of a large bag which was previously submitted and believed to have contained the assassination rifle.

50

COMMISSION EXHIBIT No. 2444—Continued

1

DL 100-10461
RPG:mja

Under date of December 23, 1963, the FBI Laboratory advised as follows concerning a firearms examination requested by the Dallas Office, on December 11, 1963:

Specimens received 12/16/63

Q267 - Q331 Sixty-five cartridge cases

Results of examination:

The 65 cartridge cases, Q267 through Q331, were examined and two of them were found to be the same caliber as Oswald's rifle, K1. It was determined, however, that these two cartridge cases could not have been fired in Oswald's rifle.

51

COMMISSION EXHIBIT No. 2444—Continued

1

DL 100-10461
RPG:mja

Under date of December 17, 1963, the FBI Laboratory furnished the following information concerning a document examination requested by Confidential Informant Dallas T-3 on December 13, 1963:

Specimens received 12/16/63 from Confidential Informant, Dallas T-3

Q332 Transportes Frontera bus company passenger list covering a trip made by bus No. 340 from Mexico City to Laredo, Texas, 10-2-3-63, bearing the name "Oswald" in the space for seat No. 4

Result of examination:

It was concluded that the name of the passenger and the destination on Line 4 of Q332 were not written by LEE HARVEY OSWALD, whose known writing appears on K4 and K5 in this case.

Due to the limited amount of comparable writing, no conclusion was reached whether the name and destination on Line 4 of Q332 were written by the writer of other entries on this specimen.

52

COMMISSION EXHIBIT No. 2444—Continued

1

DL 100-10461
RPG:mja

Under date of December 18, 1963, the FBI Laboratory furnished the following information concerning a document examination requested by Confidential Informant, Dallas T-3 on December 11, 1963:

Specimens received 12/17/63 from Confidential Informant Dallas T-3

Qc333 Photocopy of page of registry book of Hotel Del Comercio, Calle Sahagun 19, Mexico City, with signatures of guests registering on September 27, 1963, Line 18 bearing signature "Lee Harvey Oswald"

Result of examination:

It was concluded that the Lee Harvey Oswald signature on Line 18 of Qc333 was written by LEE HARVEY OSWALD, whose known writing appears on K4 and K5 in this case.

53

COMMISSION EXHIBIT No. 2444—Continued

1

DL 100-10461
RPG:mja

Under date of December 23, 1963, the FBI Laboratory furnished the following information concerning a document examination requested by the Dallas Office, on December 5, 1963:

Specimens received 12/9/63

Q334 Torn portion of a sheet of paper bearing handwritten message beginning "Father on Sept. 26th I was ....." and ending ".....of a True Catholic. Thank you" and signed "Fabian McElroy"

Result of examination:

Q334 was searched in the Anonymous Letter File without effecting an identification. Copies have been added to this file for future reference.

No fingerprint cards have been located for persons using the names or aliases Fabian McElroy and Fabion McElroy.

It was concluded that LEE HARVEY OSWALD, K4 and K5, did not prepare the questioned handwriting on Q334.

54

COMMISSION EXHIBIT No. 2444—Continued

1

DL 100-10461
RPG:mja

Under date of December 20, 1963, the FBI Laboratory advised as follows concerning a document examination requested by the New Orleans Office, on December 16, 1963:

Specimens received 12/18/63

Q335 Hand printed employment agency application #500188, obtained from the Commercial Employment Agency, 1001 National Bank of Commerce Building, New Orleans, La., dated 5/7/63

Q336 Agency Agreement dated 5/7/63, bearing signature "Lee H. Oswald"

Result of examination:

It was concluded that the questioned hand printing on specimen Q335 (exclusive of the handwriting and other notations in red on the front and back of this specimen) and the signature "Lee H. Oswald" on specimen Q336 were written by LEE HARVEY OSWALD whose known handwriting is designated as specimens K4 and K5, et cetera, in this case.

55

COMMISSION EXHIBIT No. 2444—Continued

1
DL 100-10461
RPG:mvs

Under date of December 20, 1963, the FBI Laboratory furnished the following information concerning a document examination requested by the Dallas Office on December 13, 1963:

Specimens received December 20, 1963

Q337 Four-page handwritten and hand printed interview record form of the Devilbiss Company, Toledo, Ohio, bearing signature "Lee H. Oswald"

Q344 White envelope bearing writing "New Orleans Public Libery, New Orleans, La."

Q345 Accompanying letter beginning "Dear Sirs: Through a clearical errow of yours..." and ending "... handleing the returned books, yours Truly"

ALSO SUBMITTED: New Orleans Public Library gift acknowledgment card

Result of examination:

It was concluded that the OSWALD signature and other writing on Q337, except the hand printing under item 13 of Q337, were written by LEE HARVEY OSWALD, whose known writing appears on K4 and K5 in this case.

No conclusion was reached whether the hand printing under item 13 of Q337 was prepared by OSWALD because of variations which were not accounted for based on the available writings.

It was also concluded that the handwriting on Q344 and Q345 was written by LEE HARVEY OSWALD, K4 and K5.

56

COMMISSION EXHIBIT No. 2444—Continued

1

DL 100-10461
RPG:mja

Under date of December 20, 1963, the FBI Laboratory furnished the following information concerning a document examination requested by the Dallas Office, December 14, 1963:

Specimens received 12/20/63

Q338 One sample of gummed paper tape from the home of Mrs. RUTH PAINE, Irving, Texas

Q339 One sample of gummed paper tape from the home of Mrs. RUTH PAINE, Irving, Texas

Result of examination:

The tapes Q338 and Q339 were found to be nonidentical to the gummed tape on the wrapping in the shape of a sack believed to have contained the assassination rifle.

COMMISSION EXHIBIT No. 2444—Continued

1

DL 100-10461
RPG:mja

Under date of December 23, 1963, the FBI Laboratory furnished the following information concerning a docume[illegible] examination requested by the Dallas Office, on December [illegible], 1963:

Specimens received 12/20/63

Q340 Hand printed "COTTON PICKIN' APPLICATION", dated October 4, 1963, bearing the signature "Lee H. Oswald"

Result of examination:

It was concluded that the signature "Lee H. Oswald," on the reverse side of specimen Q340 was prepared by LEE HARVEY OSWALD, whose known specimens are designated as K4, K5, et cetera.

58

COMMISSION EXHIBIT No. 2444—Continued

1
DL 100-10461
RPG:mvs

Under date of December 20, 1963, the FBI Laboratory furnished the following information concerning a document examination requested by the Dallas Office on December 13, 1963:

Specimens received December 20, 1963

Q341 White correspondence-type envelope obtained from property of LEE and MARINA OSWALD at the home of Mrs. Ruth Paine, 2515 West 5th Street, Irving, Texas

Q342 White airmail-type envelope obtained from property of LEE and MARINA OSWALD at the home of Mrs. Ruth Paine, 2515 West 5th Street, Irving, Texas

Result of examination:

The envelopes, Q341 and Q342, were examined for development of indented writing. No intelligible indentations were developed.

53

COMMISSION EXHIBIT No. 2444—Continued

1
DL 100-10461
RPG:gmf

Under date of December 26, 1963, the FBI Laboratory furnished the following information concerning a document examination requested by the Dallas Office on December 14, 1963:

"Specimens received 12/24/63

Qc343 Photocopy of a United States Marine Corps Certificate of Service identification card in the name 'Alek James Hidell'

Result of examination:

An examination of Qc343 discloses that this item is a photograph of a fraudulent and counterfeit card made directly or indirectly from the retouched negatives of a United States Marine Corps Certificate of Service identification card in the name of LEE HARVEY OSWALD, 1653230. These negatives are a part of Qc65a submitted previously."

COMMISSION EXHIBIT No. 2444—Continued

1
DL 100-10461
RPG:gmf

Under date of December 26, 1963, the FBI Laboratory advised as follows concerning a document examination requested by the Charlotte Office under date of December 18, 1963:

"Specimens received 12/24/63

Qc346 Photocopy of two-page letter dated Oct. 3, 1956, first page handwritten, beginning 'I am sixteen years of age...' and signed 'Lee Oswald,' second page bearing hand printed notation 'SEND TO: LEE Oswald 4936 Collinwood Fort Worth, TEX.'

Qc347 Photocopy of advertisement coupon of 'The Socialist Call 303 Fourth Ave. New York 10, N.Y.' bearing the hand printed name and address 'LEE Oswald 4936 Collinwood Fort Worth TEXAS'

Result of examination:

It was concluded that the questioned handwriting and hand printing on Qc346 and the questioned hand printing on Qc347 were prepared by LEE HARVEY OSWALD, whose known writing appears on K4, K5, and K13 in this case."

61

COMMISSION EXHIBIT No. 2444—Continued

DEPARTMENT OF STATE
WASHINGTON

June 15, 1964

Dear Mr. Rankin:

Enclosed is a copy of a note from the Cuban Ministry of Foreign Affairs to the Swiss Ambassador in Cuba, together with a copy of a translation of the note by the Department's Division of Language Services. A copy of the covering note from the Swiss Embassy in Washington to the Department is also enclosed.

Sincerely yours,

Leonard C. Meeker

Leonard C. Meeker
Acting Legal Adviser

Enclosures:

As stated.

The Honorable
J. Lee Rankin,
General Counsel,
President's Commission on the
Assassination of President Kennedy,
200 Maryland Avenue, N.E.,
Washington, D.C.

COMMISSION EXHIBIT No. 2445

AMBASSADE DE SUISSE

The Embassy of Switzerland presents its compliments to the Department of State and has the honor to enclose herewith the original of a note of the Cuban Government, dated June 9, 1964, which because of its urgency the Embassy of Switzerland in Havana transmitted directly to this Embassy.

The Embassy of Switzerland avails itself of this opportunity to renew to the Department of State the assurance of its highest consideration.

Washington, D.C.,
June 12, 1964.

Encl.

COMMISSION EXHIBIT No. 2445—Continued

REPUBLICA DE CUBA
MINISTERIO DE RELACIONES EXTERIORES

La Habana, 9 de junio de 1964

Señor Embajador:

Tengo el honor de referirme a la Nota número 103 que, en vuestro carácter de representante de los intereses de Estados Unidos de América,- se sirvió enviar el día 28 de mayo del presente año.

El Gobierno Revolucionario de Cuba accede a remitirle al Señor Magistrado Earl Warren, en respuesta al pedimento que hiciera, por conducto del Departamento de Estado del Gobierno norteamericano, los informes que - posee en torno a la visita que efectuara al Consulado de Cuba en México, D.F., el señor Lee Harvey Oswald, presunto asesino del Presidente John F. Kennedy.- Parece pertinente dejar expresa constancia, ante todo, que desde el instantemismo en que tuvo conocimiento de ese hecho, nuestro Gobierno ordenó realizar la más escrupulosa investigación al respecto.

Según los datos que obran en poder del Gobierno Revolucionario, el señor Lee Harvey Oswald se personó, el día 27 de septiembre de 1963,- en el Consulado de Cuba en México, D.F., formulando una solicitud de visado -

/para

Excelentísimo Señor Emil Anton Stadelhofer,
Embajador Extraordinario y Plenipotenciario de Suiza,
La Habana.

COMMISSION EXHIBIT No. 2445—Continued

para viajar a Cuba, en tránsito hacia la Unión de Repúblicas Socialistas Soviéticas, a cuyo efecto llenó el formulario correspondiente. De este aparece que el prenombrado dijo haber nacido el 18 de octubre de 1939, en Nueva Orleans, Estados Unidos de América, y, residir permanentemente en 4907 Magazine St., Nueva Orleans; de ocupación fotógrafo comercial y portador del pasaporte norteamericano número D-092526. Propuso como fecha para viajar a Cuba el 30 de septiembre de 1963, para una estancia de dos semanas, y, si fuera posible, por más tiempo, con objeto de continuar viaje hacia la Unión de Repúblicas Socialistas Soviéticas.

En su citada visita al Consulado de Cuba en México, D.F., el señor Lee Harvey Oswald fue atendido por la empleada Silvia Durán, de nacionalidad mexicana, quien le hizo saber que su solicitud, de acuerdo con los procedimientos usuales, debía ser trasmitida al Ministerio de Relaciones Exteriores, en La Habana, con objeto de que decidiera sobre el otorgamiento o denegación de la visa interesada, señalándole, a la vez, que dicho trámite podía demorar alrededor de dos semanas. Ante esta circunstancia, el señor Oswald expresó, en forma airada y descompuesta, su contrariedad, dando lugar a que el Cónsul cubano, señor Eusebio Azcue, saliera de su despacho para atenderle y le reiterara las explicaciones de la señora Durán. Después de hacer impertinentes recriminaciones e insistir en su incorrecta actitud, el señor Oswald abandonó el Consulado de Cuba, con visibles muestras de disgusto y violencia.

Durante la conversación entre el señor Oswald y la señora Du-

/rán,

COMMISSION EXHIBIT NO. 2445—Continued

rán, ésta hubo de escribir una nota, a mano, al primero, con el número de teléfono del Consulado, a fin de que pudiera inquirir telefónicamente por el resultado de su solicitud de visa.

Recibida en el Ministerio de Relaciones Exteriores de Cuba la solicitud de visa de tránsito en cuestión, el día 7 de octubre, y examinada con arreglo a las normas establecidas, se instruyó al Consulado en México, D.F., el día 15 del mismo mes, en el sentido de que el visado debía ser denegado, en virtud de que el interesado carecía de la visa de entrada en el país de destino, en este caso la Unión de Repúblicas Socialistas Soviéticas.

Con posterioridad al hecho relatado, ni el Ministerio ni el Consulado en México, D.F., tuvieron más noticias sobre el señor Oswald.

Finalmente, el señor Lee Harvey Oswald no ha viajado a Cuba en momento alguno y el Gobierno Revolucionario carece, por ende, de informaciones adicionales sobre su persona y actividades.

Aprovecho la oportunidad para reiterar a Vuestra Excelencia el testimonio de mi más alta consideración.

Raúl Roa

COMMISSION EXHIBIT NO. 2445—Continued

DEPARTMENT OF STATE
DIVISION OF LANGUAGE SERVICES

(TRANSLATION)

LS NO. 16093
T-52/R-XX
Spanish

REPUBLIC OF CUBA
MINISTRY OF FOREIGN AFFAIRS

Habana, June 9, 1964

Mr. Ambassador:

I have the honor to refer to note No. 103 which, in your capacity as representative of the interests of the United States of America, you sent on May 28 last.

In response to the request that was made through the Department of State of the United States Government, the Revolutionary Government of Cuba agrees to send to Chief Justice Earl Warren, whatever information it has concerning the visit to the Cuban Consulate at Mexico City of Lee Harvey Oswald, alleged assassin of President John F. Kennedy. It appears appropriate to state first of all that as soon as our government learned of that event, it ordered that a most careful investigation be made.

According to the information in the possession of the Revolutionary Government, Lee Harvey Oswald appeared on September 27, 1963 at the Cuban Consulate in Mexico City

His Excellency
Emil Anton Stadelhofer,
Ambassador Extraordinary and Plenipotentiary of Switzerland, Habana.

COMMISSION EXHIBIT No. 2445—Continued

-2-

and requested a visa to go to Cuba in transit for the Union of Soviet Socialist Republics, for which purpose he filled out the proper form. That form shows that Mr. Oswald stated that he was born October 18, 1939, in New Orleans, United States; that his permanent address was 4907 Magazine Street, New Orleans; that he was a commercial photographer; and that he was the bearer of United States passport No. D-092526. He fixed September 30, 1963 as the date to go to Cuba, where he planned to remain two weeks, and if possible longer, before continuing his trip to the Union of Soviet Socialist Republics.

On his visit to the Cuban Consulate at Mexico City, Lee Harvey Oswald was attended by Mrs. Silvia Durán, a Mexican citizen, who informed him that, in accordance with the customary procedure, his application had to be sent to the Ministry of Foreign Affairs in Habana for its decision on granting or refusing the visa in question. He was also told that that procedure might take about two weeks. Hearing that, Mr. Oswald, angry and upset, expressed his dissatisfaction, which caused Mr. Eusebio Azcue, Cuban Consul, to come out of his office to talk to him, and he repeated what Mrs. Durán had told him. Expressing bitter recriminations and giving additional indications of an improper attitude, Mr. Oswald left the Cuban Consulate with visible signs of anger and violence.

In the conversation between Mr. Oswald and Mrs. Durán, the latter wrote down her name and the telephone number of the Consulate for Mr. Oswald so that he could inquire about the decision on his visa application.

COMMISSION EXHIBIT No. 2445—Continued

-3-

The transit visa application in question was received in the Ministry of Foreign Affairs of Cuba on October 7, and after it was examined in accordance with the regulations, the Consulate at Mexico City was instructed on October 15 that the visa application should not be granted, because Mr. Oswald did not have an entry visa for the country of destination, in this case, the Union of Soviet Socialist Republics.

After this incident, neither the Ministry nor the Consulate at Mexico City heard any more about Mr. Oswald.

Finally, Lee Harvey Oswald did not go to Cuba at any time, and so the Revolutionary Government has no other information about him or his activities.

I avail myself of the opportunity to renew to Your Excellency the assurances of my highest consideration.

[s] Raúl Roa

COMMISSION EXHIBIT No. 2445—Continued

FD-302 (Rev. 3-3-59)

FEDERAL BUREAU OF INVESTIGATION

Date December 7, 1963

1

Mrs. OPAL ROBERTSON was interviewed at 104 Woodland Drive, Irving, Texas, where she and her husband, WADDELL ROBERTSON, are employed by Mr. ELLIS DUNN as servants.

OPAL ROBERTSON stated she was with her husband during the latter part of August or early part of September, 1963 when they observed a white man in his 20's fire a rifle in the Trinity River Bottom located behind 104 Woodland Drive, Irving, Texas. Mrs. ROBERTSON said they observed this man around 5:00 or 5:30 one afternoon. Mrs. ROBERTSON said after she had seen pictures of LEE HARVEY OSWALD in newspapers and on television, she believed the man they saw firing the rifle in the river bottom looked like OSWALD. Mrs. ROBERTSON said the man was accompanied by a woman in her 20's, 5' 6", 130 lbs. with dark hair, and a small boy about four years old. A dark-colored car of an old model was parked nearby.

On that particular afternoon, the man was firing a rifle at a homemade bullseye target which he had placed on the levee in the river bottom.

Four or five days later, Mrs. ROBERTSON and her husband were at the river bottom fishing, and the same man came up and spoke to them and carried on a friendly conversation with them for five or ten minutes. She recalled the man saying he was from Irving, Texas, after he had asked them where they were from.

on 12-7-63 at Irving, Texas File # DL 100-10461

by Special Agent ROBERT P. BUTLER / CHARLES T. BROWN Date dictated 12-7-63

MVS

This document contains neither recommendations nor conclusions of the FBI. It is the property of the FBI and is loaned to your agency; it and its contents are not to be distributed outside your agency. — Commission Exhibit No. 2446

COMMISSION EXHIBIT No. 2446

FD-302 (Rev. 3-3-59)

FEDERAL BUREAU OF INVESTIGATION

1

Date December 14, 1963

Mr. WILLIAM RAY FULLER advised he resides at 410 Staffordshire, Dallas, Texas, and that he is known as "BILL," and owns a business known as "Bill's Decorating," which is located at 209 Martha at Euless, Texas.

Mr. FULLER said he observed two persons sighting in a rifle on a makeshift range located on Highway 183 at Belt Line near Irving, Texas, a day or two before the President was assassinated, and he said after President KENNEDY's assassination he telephoned LEON POWERS, Assistant Chief of Police, at Irving, Texas, on Saturday, November 23, 1963, to give him the information because he believed this makeshift range would be a good place to check to determine if LEE HARVEY OSWALD might have used the range to practice shooting. He said that he did not get close enough to these two individuals to get a good description of them but he recalled one of the individuals wore a tan cloth jacket and was bare headed, and after seeing OSWALD's photograph on TV and in the newspapers he felt there might be some slight resemblance. He said the other person appeared to be a young boy in his late teens but he paid no particular attention to either of these men. He did not observe whether they had a car and did not stop to look at them so he was unable to furnish any more definite information concerning these people.

Mr. FULLER said he had never known LEE HARVEY OSWALD or JACK RUBY at any time and had never actually seen either of them until the TV and news media produced photographs of them.

on 12/14/63 at Euless, Texas File # DL 100-10461

by Special Agent ARTHUR E. CARTER /gmf Date dictated 12/14/63

This document contains neither recommendations nor conclusions of t[redacted] your agency; it and its contents are not to be distributed outside your

Commission Exhibit No. 2447

COMMISSION EXHIBIT No. 2447

FD-302 (Rev. 3-3-59)

FEDERAL BUREAU OF INVESTIGATION

1

Date December 5, 1963

On December 4, 1963, Mrs. LOVELL T. PENN, Belt Line Road, Cedar Hill, Texas, advised that she had located one spent shell which had been fired in her pasture on October 6, 1963, by the man she thought might have been OSWALD. Mrs. PENN made this shell available.

on 12/4/63 at Cedar Hill, Texas File # DL 89-43

by Special Agent DAVID H. BARRY/gmf Date dictated 12/5/63

This document contains neither recommendations nor conclusions of [redacted] your agency; it and its contents are not to be distributed outside yo[redacted]

Commission Exhibit No. 2448

COMMISSION EXHIBIT No. 2448

UNITED STATES DEPARTMENT OF JUSTICE
FEDERAL BUREAU OF INVESTIGATION

In Reply, Please Refer to
File No.

WASHINGTON 25, D. C.

June 10, 1964

LEE HARVEY OSWALD

BASIS FOR INQUIRY

The President's Commission has advised that it has evidence that on Friday or Saturday, September 27 or 28, 1963, LEE HARVEY OSWALD had his photograph taken for use on a visa application at the Cuban Embassy in Mexico City.

RESULTS OF INVESTIGATION CONDUCTED AT PHOTOGRAPHIC STUDIOS IN VICINITY OF HOTEL DEL COMERCIO, MEXICO CITY, CUBAN AND SOVIET EMBASSIES, MEXICO CITY, AND TRAVEL AGENCY, MEXICO CITY, AT WHICH OSWALD IS BELIEVED TO HAVE PURCHASED A BUS TICKET AS H. O. LEE

A confidential source, who has furnished reliable information in the past, furnished the following information on June 6, 1964:

A street-to-street canvass in the vicinity of the Hotel Del Comercio, Bernardino de Sahagun No. 19, Mexico City, failed to disclose the existence of any photographic studios in the area. The source pointed out that the area surrounding the Hotel Del Comercio is one in which many bus terminals and small business establishments are located and does not appear to be an area which would be conducive to the operation of a photographic studio.

A second confidential source, who has furnished reliable information in the past, furnished the following information on June 8, 1964:

The personnel at the photographic studios located in the vicinities of the Cuban and Soviet Embassies in Mexico City were interviewed concerning the possibility that a

COMMISSION EXHIBIT No. 2449

photograph of OSWALD had been taken. The source also reviewed the negatives retained by these studios for photographs taken on September 27 and 28, 1963, but no negative was located which appeared to be the negative of a photograph of OSWALD. The studios contacted are listed below:

The photographic studio of Mrs. MARIA LUISA MALDONADO DE GUTIERREZ, located at Salamanca No. 21, Mexico City, and the branch office of this photographic studio located at the corner of Pachuca and Juan Escutia Streets, Mexico City.

The photographic studio, "Aviles," owned by Mr. JACINTO AVILES, located at Tamaulipas No. 202, Local 16, Mexico City.

The photographic studio at Tamaulipas No. 224-B, Mexico City, owned by Mrs. CELIA C. DE GOODMAN.

The photographic studio, "Alori," owned by Mrs. ANA MURILLO, located at Campeche No. 249, Mexico City.

The photographic studio, "Fatima," located at Campeche No. 382, Mexico City, owned by Mr. KHAN RASAK BEK KHADJIEFF.

The photographic studio, "Rosales," Calzada de Tacubaya No. 165-3, Mexico City, owned by Mrs. YOLANDA MENDOZA DE ROSALES.

The photographic studio, "Cameras," located at Benjamin Franklin No. 22, Mexico City, owned by Mr. OSMAR CAMERAS.

A confidential source abroad furnished the following information on June 8, 1964:

The personnel were interviewed and the negatives of photographs taken on September 27 and 28, 1963, were reviewed on June 8, 1964, at the following photographic studios which are located seven or eight blocks from the Hotel Del Comercio, mentioned above, and are also in the

- 2 -

COMMISSION EXHIBIT No. 2449—Continued

immediate vicinity of the Agencia de Viajes, Transportes Chihuahuenses, S. A. de C. V. (Chihuahuenses Transportation Travel agency, Inc.), with offices at Paseo de la Reforma No. 52, Room 5, where LEE HARVEY OSWALD, as H. O. LEE, is believed to have purchased a bus ticket for his return trip from Mexico City to the United States:

"Arte Fotografica," Lafragua No. 4, Mexico City.

"Danubio Studio," Avenida Reforma No. 12, Mexico City.

The photographic studio located at Calle Antonio Caso No. 31, Mexico City.

It is noted that investigation disclosed that the negatives are retained by these photographic studios by date only and the names of the persons photographed are not recorded.

COMMISSION EXHIBIT No. 2449—Continued

1

SA 105-2909

The following investigation conducted by Special Agent HAROLD H. CROSSETT was done to attempt to locate FRANCISCO MORALES and ERNESTO LIMA JUAREZ, both of whom were reportedly at the Hotel Del Comercio in Mexico City during or about the same time LEE HARVEY OSWALD was reportedly there.

AT REYNOSA, TAMAULIPAS, MEXICO:

On June 15, 1964, SA T-1, a confidential source abroad, advised he had determined that ERNESTO LIMA JUAREZ is a masonry contractor who, until recently, was on a job in Rio Bravo, Tamaulipas, Mexico, but had returned to Reynosa, Tamaulipas, Mexico.

On June 16, 1964, SA T-1 advised that ERNESTO LIMA JUAREZ furnished the following information:

He was in Mexico City during the last few days of September, 1963, and possibly the first day or two of October, 1963. He stayed at the Hotel Del Comercio in Room Number 8 with FRANCISCO MORALES whom he was attempting to aid in obtaining employment.

While there he noticed an American whom he later recognized from news media photographs as LEE HARVEY OSWALD. He did not associate with OSWALD, and as far as he knows, MORALES did not associate with OSWALD. He pointed out that at that time he had no reason to pay any particular attention to OSWALD, assuming that OSWALD was merely an American tourist.

During the time he was staying at the Hotel Del Comercio he also noticed four Cubans, one of whom he heard, probably from MORALES, was from the State of Florida, U. S. A. He described this individual as a white male, 55 to 56 years of age, 5 ft. 8 in. in height, slender build, fair complexion, and grey hair. He did not associate with the Cubans and did not learn their names or addresses. However, MORALES had some drinks with them on one or two occasions and might possibly have their names or other information pertaining to them.

COMMISSION EXHIBIT No. 2450

SA 105-2909

He saw OSWALD with the Cubans at the hotel on one or two occasions, but these meetings appeared to be social in nature.

LIMA further stated that GABRIEL CONTRERAS V., a retired railroad man who resides at Primera de Mayo Number 1, Ciudad Camargo, Chihuahua, Mexico, was also staying at the Hotel Del Comercio and may have some information pertaining to the Cubans. CONTRERAS probably saw OSWALD at the hotel.

SA T-1 also advised he had located a sister of FRANCISCO MORALES in Reynosa who stated her brother left Mexico City and traveled to Victoria, Tamaulipas, Mexico, seeking employment. He was unsuccessful and recently went to Monterrey, Nuevo Leon, Mexico, where he is currently located; however, she does not have an address for him at the present time. She stated she expects to hear from him in the near future and will obtain an address.

COMMISSION EXHIBIT No. 2450—Continued

SA 105-2909

As has been previously reported, OSWALD was registered from September 27, 1963, through October 1, 1963, in Room Number 18 of the Hotel del Comercio located at Calle Bernardino de Sahagun Number 19, Mexico, D. F., Mexico.

The records of the hotel reflect that ERNESTO LIMA JUAREZ, Reynosa, Tamaulipas, Mexico, was registered in Room Number 8 on September 26, 1963, and FRANCISCO MORALES, also of Reynosa, was registered in Room Number 8 from September 27, 1963, through October 1, 1963.

COMMISSION EXHIBIT No. 2450—Continued

SA 105-2909

The following investigation was conducted by Special Agent JAMES R. WILSON:

AT REYNOSA, TAMAULIPAS, MEXICO

On July 10, 1964, SA T-1, a confidential source abroad, advised that on June 28, 1964, the Source had located and interviewed FRANCISCO MORALES of Reynosa, Tamaulipas, Mexico, in Ciudad Victoria, Tamaulipas, Mexico. MORALES advised the Source as follows:

MORALES was in Ciudad Victoria seeking employment, and he might leave in the near future to travel to Guadalajara, Jalisco, Mexico, for the same purpose.

MORALES was registered with ERNESTO LIMA in the Hotel del Comercio in Mexico City in September and October, 1963, exact dates unrecalled, while seeking employment with the federal government. He does not recall having seen LEE HARVEY OSWALD during his stay there. The only other hotel guests at that time whose names he recalls were GABRIEL CONTRERAS of Chihuahua, Mexico, and one ARTURO CHAVEZ MARTINEZ, a Mexican Federal employee who is supposed to reside at Zaragoza Number 58, Ciudad de Maiz, San Luis Potosi, Mexico, and who was supposed to be assigned to work at Bahia de Todos Santos, Baja California, Mexico. CHAVEZ attempted to sell MORALES an illegal Customs receipt for use in bringing an automobile into Mexico without paying import duties. On two occasions MORALES had drinks with two Cubans who stayed at the hotel, one of whom was going to Florida and was arranging immigration papers. Both Cubans were in their late forties or fifties, were about five feet eight inches in height, and the one going to Florida wore dark glasses most of the time. The names of these Cubans and other hotel guests should be known to a Hotel del Comercio employee named SEBASTIAN.

The Source advised MORALES was reluctant to discuss the above matters, and Source believes MORALES did not divulge all information in his possession.

COMMISSION EXHIBIT No. 2450—Continued

FD-302 (Rev. 1-25-60) FEDERAL BUREAU OF INVESTIGATION

1

Date July 13, 1964

ERNESTO LIMA JUAREZ, advised as follows:

He is a masonry contractor by trade and is presently out of work. He resides several miles outside of Reynosa on the Monterrey Highway, and is usually in downtown Reynosa during the daytime. His surname is LIMA, JUAREZ being his mother's maiden name.

LIMA, and FRANCISCO MORALES, a close friend, went to Mexico City and registered at the Hotel del Comercio on about September 18, 1963. The purpose of the trip was to attempt to obtain employment for MORALES in the Comision Federal de Electricidad (Federal Electric Power Commission) in Mexico City. They were contacting officials and persons necessary for such purpose during the major portion of each day. When they returned to the hotel, LIMA, age 58, usually went up to the room and MORALES, a younger man, would stay in the hotel lobby. They were not acquainted with any hotel guests prior to registering at the hotel. MORALES became acquainted casually through friendly overtures with several of the hotel guests whom MORALES later introduced to LIMA. They thusly became acquainted with one GABRIEL CONTRERAS of Chihuahua, Mexico, whom LIMA believes to be a retired railroad man. They also became acquainted casually soon after their arrival with three Cubans who were residing at the hotel on the second floor, room numbers unknown. They had drinks with the Cubans, names unrecalled, several times. LIMA believes the three Cubans they met at first were in the hotel when LIMA and MORALES registered. Two of the Cubans were Negro males whom he recalled only as young, tall and slender, and one of them resided with and was supported by a Cuban Negro woman in the hotel. The third Cuban was a white male, age 44-46, 5' 10" to 5' 11", dark hair and eyes, dark complexion. These three Cubans had no apparent occupation.

On about September 23, 1963, these three Cubans went to the airport at Mexico City and met a fourth Cuban who arrived by plane from Cuba. He was described as white, male, age 54-58 years, 5' 7" to 5' 8", brown greying hair,

On 7/10/64 at Reynosa, Tamps., Mexico File # SA 105-2909

by SA JAMES R. WILSON/mjb Date dictated 7/10/64

2

SA 105-2909

grey mustache, who claimed to have owned a large ranch near Havana, Cuba, which ranch was confiscated by CASTRO. The four Cubans were anti-CASTRO and denounced CASTRO for his actions, policies, and political philosophy. The latter Cuban departed Mexico City via plane enroute to Miami, Florida, to join his wife, having received money by check from Florida. His departure was on about October 8, 1963. Sometime before this Cuban departed, a street photographer took a picture of LIMA, MORALES, CONTRERAS, and the two older Cuban men. Each person signed his name on the reverse of his respective likeness in the photograph, and this photograph was retained by CONTRERAS.

On two occasions in about the latter part of September, 1963, LIMA saw a young American male talk briefly in English to the two Cuban Negroes at the entrance of the hotel. LIMA believes these were merely exchanges of friendly greetings, but he is not certain due to his being able to understand only a few English words. This young man and MORALES never met to LIMA's knowledge, nor did LIMA meet this young man. MORALES does not speak or understand English. This young man is described only as about twenty-six years of age, having receding hair at each side of his forehead forming a widow's peak. LIMA believes but is not positive that this young man may be identical with OSWALD. He saw no other individual who resembles OSWALD in any way.

In October, 1963, funds used by LIMA and MORALES were becoming depleted, and the hotel bill could not be paid. LIMA then requested MORALES return to Reynosa, Mexico, to seek funds with which to pay the hotel bill. MORALES then checked out about October 12, 1963, and LIMA remained at the hotel. MORALES never returned with and never sent any money to LIMA, and on about November 18, 1963, LIMA arranged with the hotel to pay the bill at a later date and check out. He returned to Reynosa, Mexico. He later sent the money to the hotel from Reynosa.

When there was later publicity about OSWALD, LIMA saw the photographs of OSWALD in local news media. Those news media photographs, however, were not clear and LIMA at that time was not sure the young man referred to above was OSWALD. Due to the lapse of time, LIMA cannot state, after looking at a good and clear photograph of OSWALD, whether or not this young man at the hotel referred to is identical with OSWALD.

The following investigation was conducted by Special Agent ROBERT L. CHAPMAN at Laredo, Texas, to locate MARTIN SUMAYA, the person who reportedly occupied Room Number 5 at the Hotel del Comercio, Mexico City, on September 27, 1963.

SA T-2 advised on July 10, 1964, that he had located MARTIN SUMAYA residing at Dr. Mier Number 2119, Nuevo Laredo, Mexico, and interviewed SUMAYA relative to his stay at the Hotel del Comercio on September 27, 1963.

SUMAYA advised that he is an employee of the Mexican Petroleum Industry and makes frequent trips to Mexico City and other parts of Mexico. SUMAYA stated that he has known the owner of the Hotel del Comercio for the past twenty years and frequently stays at that hotel when in Mexico City. SUMAYA stated that he recalls nothing concerning his stay in Room Number 5 on September 27, 1963, and definitely does not recall seeing LEE HARVEY OSWALD around the Hotel del Comercio. SUMAYA advised that he did not recall the exact dates he was at the Hotel del Comercio in September, 1963, nor did he recall the exact mode of transportation he was using, but stated that it must have been Transportes Frontera since he always travels by bus and almost always uses Transportes Frontera Bus Lines. SUMAYA further stated that he believes that on this particular trip in September, 1963, that he returned to Nuevo Laredo, Mexico, via Tampico, Mexico.

SUMAYA was shown a photograph of LEE HARVEY OSWALD and stated he still did not recall having seen OSWALD or having heard anything concerning him while in Mexico City in September, 1963.

The following interview with SA T-2 was conducted in an effort to locate one A. MARTINEZ and one HILDA QUEZADA who reportedly traveled on Transportes del Norte bus from Mexico City to Nuevo Laredo, Mexico, on October 2-3, 1963.

The following investigation was conducted by SA ROBERT L. CHAPMAN:

AT LAREDO, TEXAS:

On August 10, 1964, SA T-2 advised that he had conducted continuous investigation in Nuevo Laredo, Mexico, through civil records and other sources of information to locate A. MARTINEZ and HILDA QUEZADA, with negative results. SA T-2 advised that in addition he has checked public records and has checked at leading downtown hotels in an effort to locate these two individuals, all with negative results.

UNITED STATES DEPARTMENT OF JUSTICE
FEDERAL BUREAU OF INVESTIGATION

In Reply, Please Refer to
File No.

WASHINGTON 25, D. C.

June 23, 1964

LEE HARVEY OSWALD

BASIS FOR INQUIRY

As has been previously reported, on September 27, 1963, OSWALD registered at the Hotel del Comercio, Calle (Street) Bernardino de Sahagun No. 19, Mexico City, under the name of LEE, HARVEY OSWALD. His name was continued in the guest records of the hotel through October 1, 1963. He occupied room No. 18.

According to the guest records of the hotel, MARIO RESENDIZ, Saltillo, Coahuila, Mexico, occupied room No. 21 from September 26 through October 1, 1963, and GABRIEL CONTRERAS, Ciudad Juarez, Chihuahua, Mexico, was a resident of room No. 14 from September 26 through October 1, 1963.

INTERVIEW OF MARIO RESENDIZ VILLANUEVA

On June 18, 1964, MARIO RESENDIZ VILLANUEVA was located and interviewed at the Hotel del Comercio by a confidential source abroad, at which time he furnished the following information:

He formerly resided with his sister in Saltillo, Coahuila, Mexico, but now resides at Progreso No. 103, Villa Frontera, Coahuila, Mexico, telephone number 103. He is self-employed, selling religious artifacts, jewelry, and curios which he buys in Tapachula, Chiapas, Mexico, and sells throughout the Republic of Mexico.

He comes to Mexico City at irregular intervals and

usually stays at the Hotel del Comercio. He did not specifically recall staying at the hotel during the September-October, 1963, period mentioned above, but was certain he was there if the hotel record so indicated.

RESENDIZ was shown a number of photographs of LEE HARVEY OSWALD. He said this person was unknown to him by name, photograph, or description and went on to state that he had never noted the presence of an American at the Hotel del Comercio.

INTERVIEW OF GABRIEL CONTRERAS UVINA

The following information was supplied by a confidential source who has furnished reliable information in the past:

On May 23, 1964, the source located and interviewed GABRIEL CONTRERAS UVINA, who operates an electrical appliance shop at the corner of Gonzalez Ortega and Primero de Mayo streets in Ciudad Camargo, Chihuahua, Mexico. The following information was supplied to the source by CONTRERAS:

CONTRERAS was in Mexico City from September 26, 1963, to October 2, 1963, and resided at the Hotel del Comercio during that period. He always stays at this hotel when he visits Mexico City, which is approximately once every month.

Following the assassination of President KENNEDY on November 22, 1963, CONTRERAS observed photographs of OSWALD in the press. He then recalled that on one occasion at lunch time while eating at the small restaurant next door to the Hotel del Comercio he sat down at a table with an unknown American. It was necessary for him to occupy a table with this unknown American due to the crowded condition of the restaurant at the time. After observing the press photographs of OSWALD which appeared in connection with the publicity concerning the assassination, CONTRERAS reached the definite conclusion that OSWALD was identical with the unknown American with whom he had occupied a table in the restaurant. CONTRERAS advised the source that he did not exchange a single word with OSWALD since it appeared that the latter spoke no Spanish and CONTRERAS does not understand English.

CONTRERAS told source that during his stay at the Hotel del Comercio from September 26 through October 1, 1963, this was the only time he observed OSWALD, and he could furnish no other information concerning OSWALD.

-3-

COMMISSION EXHIBIT No. 2450—Continued

UNITED STATES DEPARTMENT OF JUSTICE

FEDERAL BUREAU OF INVESTIGATION

In Reply, Please Refer to
File No.

Washington, D. C.

July 10, 1964

LEE HARVEY OSWALD

BASIS FOR INQUIRY

As has been previously reported, OSWALD was registered from September 27, 1963, through October 1, 1963, in Room No. 18 of the Hotel del Comercio, located at Calle Bernardino de Sahagun No. 19, Mexico, D. F., Mexico.

The records of the hotel reflect that ERNESTO LIMA JUAREZ, Reynosa, Tamaulipas, Mexico, was registered in Room No. 8 on September 26, 1963, and FRANCISCO MORALES, also of Reynosa, was registered in Room No. 8 from September 27, 1963, through October 1, 1963.

On interview in Reynosa on June 16, 1964, ERNESTO LIMA JUAREZ, a masonry contractor, advised he was in Mexico, D. F., Mexico, where he stayed in Room No. 8, Hotel del Comercio, for a few days in the latter part of September, 1963, and possibly the first day or two in October, 1963. He was in Mexico, D. F., on business and was accompanied by FRANCISCO MORALES, whom he was attempting to aid in securing employment.

While at the hotel, LIMA JUAREZ noticed an American, whom he later recognized from news media photographs as LEE HARVEY OSWALD. He did not associate with OSWALD, and as far as he knows, MORALES did not associate with OSWALD. He pointed out that at that time he had no reason to pay any particular attention to OSWALD.

COMMISSION EXHIBIT No. 2451

LIMA JUAREZ also saw four Cubans at the hotel and saw OSWALD associating with these Cubans on one or two occasions, but these meetings appeared to be social in nature. He did not associate with the Cubans and did not learn their names or addresses; however, MORALES had some drinks with them on one or two occasions and might possibly have their names or other information pertaining to them. LIMA JUAREZ heard, probably from MORALES, that one of the Cubans was from the State of Florida, U. S. A. He described this individual as a white male, 55 to 56 years of age, 5 feet 8 inches in height, slender build, fair complexion, and grey hair.

INQUIRIES AT HOTEL DEL COMERCIO
CONCERNING ALLEGATIONS OF
ERNESTO LIMA JUAREZ

On July 6, 1964, a confidential source abroad obtained the following information:

GUILLERMO GARCIA LUNA, owner and manager of the Hotel del Comercio, pointed out that a previous examination of the hotel register, which lists the nationality of each guest, showed that OSWALD was the only guest who did not list his nationality as Mexican during the entire period that OSWALD was at the hotel. GARCIA LUNA recalled that there were several Cubans who resided at the hotel some time prior to the arrival of OSWALD there. These Cubans were awaiting the issuance of United States visas from the American Embassy in Mexico, D. F., in order to proceed to the United States. He recalled very definitely that all of the Cubans departed the hotel before the arrival of OSWALD and emphasized that there were no Cubans at the hotel during the period of OSWALD's residence there.

GARCIA LUNA said that the records of the hotel show that ERNESTO LIMA JUAREZ of Reynosa, Tamaulipas, Mexico, was a guest at the hotel from September 15, 1963, through October 1, 1963, occupying Room No. 8 during this period. LIMA JUAREZ occupied this room with FRANCISCO MORALES, also of Reynosa. GARCIA LUNA pointed out that the procedure of the hotel is to list in the hotel register on a daily basis the name of the guest

- 2 -

COMMISSION EXHIBIT No. 2451—Continued

for each room that is occupied. Where a room is occupied by two or more guests, the name of only one of them is listed for the room. He explained that this was the reason why the name of LIMA JUAREZ appeared as occupying Room No. 8 on September 26, 1963, and the name of FRANCISCO MORALES was shown as occupying the same room from September 27, 1963, through October 1, 1963. He was not well acquainted personally with these two persons but recalled that when they departed, they owed some money to the hotel and left a suitcase as security. Later, a girl, perhaps a daughter of LIMA JUAREZ, came by and paid the debt and picked up the suitcase.

GARCIA LUNA could recall no group of four Cubans who stayed at the hotel during the period when LIMA JUAREZ and MORALES were there; however, he did recall that two Cuban families with children and an older Cuban man had been guests at the hotel during at least part of this period. He knew of no mutual connection among these Cuban people. Inasmuch as the hotel register for the period was not available, he could not locate the names of these people, but he did recall that the older Cuban man was named JULIAN HUERTA and that he was the last of the Cubans to depart the hotel.

GARCIA LUNA checked other records of the hotel and determined that JULIAN HUERTA checked out of the hotel on September 22, 1963. He recalled HUERTA as a white male, about 55 to 60 years of age, about 5 feet 8 inches in height, medium build, grey hair, and fair complexion. GARCIA LUNA very definitely recalled that HUERTA was the last of the Cubans to leave the hotel and concluded that OSWALD could not have associated with any of these Cubans since HUERTA checked out of the hotel on September 22, 1963, five days before OSWALD registered at the hotel.

SEBASTIAN PEREZ HERNANDEZ, desk clerk at the Hotel del Comercio, corroborated the information furnished by GARCIA LUNA. PEREZ HERNANDEZ added that he recalled that FRANCISCO MORALES was a young man about 21 years of age and that ERNESTO LIMA JUAREZ, an older man, was trying to help MORALES find employment.

- 3 -

COMMISSION EXHIBIT No. 2451—Continued

Both GARCIA LUNA and PEREZ HERNANDEZ advised that there is no restaurant or bar in the Hotel del Comercio and no liquor is sold there. Neither is there any establishment in the vicinity of the hotel which sells liquor, although beer is served in some of the restaurants in the vicinity of the hotel.

The following information was obtained by the confidential source abroad on July 6, 1964, from the records of the Visa Section of the American Embassy in Mexico, D. F.:

An application for a United States immigration visa was made on August 20, 1963, by JULIAN FRANCISCO HUERTA-OLIVA, a Cuban citizen, born January 28, 1902, in Marinao, Havana, Cuba. The local address at the time the visa application was made was given as the Hotel del Comercio, Sahagun No. 19. He was the bearer of Cuban Passport No. 99428. An O-1 United States immigration visa was issued to him on September 20, 1963. At that time he indicated that he planned to join his wife, ROSELIA ESCALONA, 221 Alton Road, Apartment 21, Miami Beach, Florida. His visa file contained a letter from ROSA QUARANTO, owner of the New Richmond, Miami Beach, Florida, which letter guaranteed employment for HUERTA-OLIVA upon arrival in Miami Beach.

- 4 -

COMMISSION EXHIBIT No. 2451—Continued

[redacted]

OFFICE OF THE DIRECTOR

Commission Exhibit No. 2452

UNITED STATES DEPARTMENT OF JUSTICE

FEDERAL BUREAU OF INVESTIGATION

WASHINGTON 25, D.C.

April 14, 1964

BY COURIER SERVICE

Honorable J. Lee Rankin
General Counsel
The President's Commission
200 Maryland Avenue, N. E.
Washington, D. C.

Dear Mr. Rankin:

We have acquired through a confidential source abroad a block of passenger lists of the Transportes Frontera Company which was used in connection with the operations of that Company in Mexico City during most of the month of October, 1963. These forms, which are bound together at the top in pad form by a gum-type substance, have been designated Specimen K74. We have also acquired the original of Specimen Q332 which is the passenger list of the Transportes Frontera Company covering the trip by bus 340 from Mexico City to Nuevo Laredo on October 2 and 3, 1963. The name "Oswld" appears in handwriting on line four of Specimen Q332. On examination of aforementioned specimens, it was determined that the handwriting, format, and appearance of the block of passenger lists, Specimen K74, agree with the handwriting, format, and appearance of Specimen Q332. In addition, indented writings and extraneous marks were noted on Q332 which indicate that this sheet was originally on top of the present top sheet in K74.

No indentations were found on the present top sheet in K74 which correspond to the writing in black ink on the top two lines of Q332, the black ink writing on line 40 and immediately below this line, or the handwritten notation in red at the top of Q332 in the wording "Transportes Frontera."

With respect to the handwritten entries on Q332, fragmentary portions of these entries were found to be indented on the present top sheet of K74 except no indented

COMMISSION EXHIBIT No. 2452

Honorable J. Lee Rankin

handwriting was found to correspond to the "Oswld" entry on line four of Q332, and the handwritten entries on lines eight and thirteen of Q332 did not produce any corresponding identifiable indented impressions on the top sheet of K74.

For the present, we intend to retain the original documents comprising Q332 and K74. As the indented writings on the present top sheet of K74 are difficult to photograph, you may desire a member of your staff to personally examine the original documents in question.

Sincerely yours,

J. Edgar Hoover

- 2 -

COMMISSION EXHIBIT No. 2452—Continued

UNITED STATES DEPARTMENT OF JUSTICE
FEDERAL BUREAU OF INVESTIGATION

In Reply, Please Refer to
File No.

WASHINGTON 25, D. C.

April 8, 1964

LEE HARVEY OSWALD

A confidential source abroad advised as follows:

On March 31, 1964, GILBERTO LOZANO GUIZAR, Manager of the Mexico City terminal of the Transportes Frontera Lus Company, Buenavista Street No. 7, Mexico, D. F., Mexico, emphatically advised that the original passenger list or manifest relating to departure No. 2, bus No. 340, on October 2, 1963, of the Transportes Frontera Bus Company, is an authentic record of data pertaining to that particular trip. It is noted that further details concerning the above-described passenger list or manifest were contained in a memorandum dated March 12, 1964.

LOZANO pointed out that a passenger list is compiled at the Mexico City terminal of the company for trips originating in Mexico City and that, after the departure of the bus, information relating to this trip, that is, the number of passengers destined to particular points, is radioed ahead to one of their main offices located along the point of travel. In the case of the above-described trip, the information, according to LOZANO, was reported by radio to their Monterrey, Mexico, office. LOZANO advised that, once the information is relayed ahead and the trip is completed, for all practical purposes they have no further need of conserving the passenger lists as a permanent record.

He advised that the passenger lists for all their trips originating in Mexico City are recorded chronologically on a gummed block of forms maintained on a clip board at the ticket sales counter of the terminal in Mexico City. He stated the above-described manifest dated October 2, 1963, was handled in such a manner. He advised that, when the block of forms covering trips over a period of a month's time has been completely recorded, the block of forms will be replaced on the clip board by a new block of forms for

COMMISSION EXHIBIT No. 2453

the succeeding month and the old forms which contained the passenger lists for the preceding month will be set aside for discarding. He stated that there are times when the recorded block of forms containing the passenger lists is immediately discarded, and on other occasions there may be an accumulation of forms covering trips over a period of months prior to their being discarded. He stated that the company maintains no fixed policy with relation to the destruction of the forms.

He advised that officers of the Presidential Staff appeared at the bus terminal shortly after the assassination of President KENNEDY, seeking to review passenger lists of the bus company for early October, 1963, and it was found at that time that the completed block of forms for most of the month of October, 1963, which included the above-described passenger list, was still in the baggage room at the terminal prior to being discarded. He stated he had torn the October 2, 1963, manifest from the block of forms and furnished it to one of the officers. LOZANO advised that one Lieutenant ARTURO BOSCH, an officer with the Presidential Staff, reviewed the above-described manifest.

LOZANO advised that, upon further reflection, it is his opinion that ARTURO BOSCH had filled in the blanks in ink at the top of the form as to the time, destination, trip number, bus number, and date, including the crossing out of the date "November 1" and replacing it with the notation "October 2" which appeared on the above-described manifest. LOZANO stated BOSCH did so on the basis of information he and FRANCISCO ALVARADO, the ticket salesman at the Transportes Frontera bus terminal, had furnished BOSCH and as an aid to his investigation of the matter.

LOZANO also stated that the hand printed notation appearing at the bottom of the manifest, "Driver, DIONISIO REYNA, FCO. SAUCEDO," was also filled in by BOSCH.

LOZANO, commenting on the manifest in question, advised that there was definitely only one section of bus No. 340 which departed Mexico City at 1:00 p.m. on October 2, 1963, en route Monterrey, Mexico, and Nuevo Laredo, Mexico. He explained that the notation

- 2 -

COMMISSION EXHIBIT No. 2453—Continued

"Departure No. 2" appearing on the top of the manifest and which he believed BOSCH had filled out merely indicates the second departure of a Transportes Frontera bus on that particular day, October 2, 1963. The first departure of one of their buses on that day from the Mexico City terminal occurred at 9:00 a.m., with the terminal point being Monterrey, Mexico. He stated that the second departure of a Transportes Frontera bus from the Mexico City terminal on October 2, 1963, was the departure at 1:00 p.m., with the terminal point being Nuevo Laredo, Mexico, and the passengers on this bus were reported on the above-mentioned manifest of October 2, 1963. He stated that there were three other departures on that day from their Mexico City terminal, the third departure having occurred at 2:30 p.m., with the terminal point being Matamoros, Tamaulipas, Mexico; the fourth departure having occurred at 9:00 p.m., with terminal point at Nuevo Laredo; and the fifth departure at 10:00 p.m., with terminal point being Ciudad Juarez, Chihuahua, Mexico. LOZANO advised that the only bus operating on their line which would have arrived at Nuevo Laredo between the hours of 12:00 a.m. and 8:00 a.m. on October 3, 1963, is bus No. 340, which departed from their Mexico City terminal at 1:00 p.m. on October 2, 1963.

LOZANO reiterated that he is of the firm opinion that the person designated as "OSWLD" on the October 2, 1963, passenger manifest did not purchase a ticket and did not travel on that trip. He stated that it is his opinion that a reservation was made, but it was never used, and that their bus company has no further information which would shed any light on the matter.

A second confidential source abroad advised as follows:

On March 25, 1964, FRANCISCO ALVARADO, ticket salesman and dispatcher for the Transportes Frontera Bus Line at Mexico City, advised that the above-described manifest is an authentic document. He stated, as he had in the past, that he had prepared most of the handwriting which appears on the manifest. ALVARADO related that with

- 3 -

COMMISSION EXHIBIT No. 2453—Continued

regard to the notations appearing at the top of the manifest as to the time, destination, trip number, bus number, and date, it is his opinion that those notations were filled in by one of the Presidential Staff investigators who had reviewed the manifest at the bus terminal shortly after President KENNEDY's assassination. He advised that the hand printed notation appearing at the bottom of the page of the manifest, "Driver, DIONISIO REYNA, FCO. SAUCEDO," was also in his opinion made by one of the Presidential Staff investigators, and he believed this person was Lieutenant ARTURO BOSCH. ALVARADO believed he had furnished this information to BOSCH.

On March 25, 1964, ALVARADO made available one block of forms of the Transportes Frontera Bus Line which contained passenger lists during most of the month of October, 1963. However, the passenger list for October 1, 1963, was not included in this block of forms. ALVARADO advised that he had made efforts to locate the manifest for October 1, 1963; however, he had been unsuccessful. He stated he would continue efforts to locate that manifest.

It is noted that the ticket numbers on the above-mentioned manifest of October 2, 1963, appear to be in sequence with manifests for subsequent trips which were located for the month of October, 1963.

On March 25, 1964, FRANCISCO SAUCEDO, bus driver for the Transportes Frontera Bus Company, advised in Mexico City that he had been one of the bus drivers who had driven the Transportes Frontera bus No. 340 on October 2, 1963, which departed Mexico City at 1:00 p.m. on that day en route to Monterrey and Nuevo Laredo. He stated that seats No. 1 and No. 3 on that bus had been reserved by him under tickets No. 39633 and No. 39634. However, he advised that he does not recall for whom he had made the reservations. He said that on occasion he reserves seats in advance for only friends or relatives and never does so for anyone with whom he is not acquainted. However, he could not recall which of his friends or relatives had utilized those seats on that particular day. He stated he was certain that seats No. 1 and No. 3 were not used by OSWALD or ANGEL PEREZ, whom SAUCEDO advised he does not know.

On March 25, 1964, DIONISIO REYNA, who was co-driver with SAUCEDO on Transportes Frontera bus No. 340 of October 2, 1963, advised at Mexico City that he could furnish no information regarding the individuals who had utilized seats No. 1 and No. 3 on that trip. He added that he was quite certain that neither OSWALD nor ANGEL PEREZ did so. REYNA again stated that he was quite certain that OSWALD did not travel on that particular bus.

Information was received on March 24, 1964, that one J. M. DE CUBA and his wife, both of whom, according to Mexican Immigration records, departed Mexico at Nuevo Laredo, Tamaulipas, on October 3, 1963, and were checked out at Nuevo Laredo by the same Mexican Immigration Inspector who handled OSWALD's exit, stated they believed they had traveled to Nuevo Laredo on that occasion on a Transportes Frontera bus. Mr. DE CUBA, while disclaiming any knowledge of OSWALD, recalled that there was a young man he presumed to be an American who rode to Nuevo Laredo on the bus on which he and his wife had traveled. He advised that he could not identify the American passenger but recalled the individual had trouble making himself intelligible to the Mexican border officials.

On March 25, 1964, FRANCISCO SAUCEDO advised that he does not know the DE CUBAs and also was quite certain they had not utilized seats No. 1 and No. 3 on the above-mentioned trip.

A third confidential source abroad advised as follows:

On March 30, 1964, the records of the Transportes del Norte Bus Company, Avenida Insurgentes Sur No. 137, Mexico, D. F., were reviewed and a passenger manifest was located at that bus company listing two seats for J. M. DE CUBA and showing that J. M. DE CUBA had been a passenger on bus No. 332 of that company which departed Mexico City at 8:30 a.m. on October 2, 1963, and which had as its final destination Laredo. The above records located at the Transportes del Norte bus line indicated that J. M. DE CUBA and his wife actually traveled on a Transportes del Norte bus rather than on a Transportes Frontera bus.

Commission Exhibit 2454

UNITED STATES DEPARTMENT OF JUSTICE

FEDERAL BUREAU OF INVESTIGATION

In Reply, Please Refer to
File No.

Dallas, Texas
August 21, 1964

LEE HARVEY OSWALD

By letter dated August 6, 1964, the President's Commission requested additional investigation be conducted concerning the possibility that Lee Harvey Oswald had a telescopic sight mounted on a rifle and sighted at the Irving Sport Shop, 221 East Irving Boulevard, Irving, Texas. The President's Commission noted previous testimony regarding this matter has raised questions concerning which they desired additional investigation.

It was desired the following persons be interviewed: Mrs. Gertrude Hunter; Roy Truly; Charles Woodrow Greener; friends of Mrs. Hunter whose names were furnished as Mr. and Mrs. "Dominick," as well as determine the date of the Irving - Richland Hills High School football game, which occurred in November, 1963.

On August 11, 1964, Mrs. Gertrude Hunter, 141 South Hastings, Irving, Texas, furnished the following information regarding the proposed trip of her relatives, "James and Doris Dommney" of Houston, Texas.

Mrs. Hunter stated that the "Dommneys" had not directly told her that they planned to visit her in November, 1963, but that her sister-in-law and mother of "Doris Dommney," one Mrs. Patterson, had written her that the "Dommneys" were planning a visit to the Dallas area in November, 1963, and would probably visit her in Irving, Texas.

Mrs. Hunter stated that Mrs. Patterson died on or about June 13, 1964.

COMMISSION EXHIBIT No. 2454

LEE HARVEY OSWALD

Mrs. Hunter does not have the letter in which Mrs. Patterson mentioned that the "Dommneys" planned to visit the Dallas area in November, 1963.

Mrs. Hunter stated that the "Dommneys" did not visit her in Irving, Texas, in November, 1963.

Mrs. Hunter furnished the address of "James and Doris Dommney" as 8133 Locksley, Houston, Texas.

She does not know if the Dommneys still have their old station wagon, but might now have a newer Chrysler automobile.

On August 11, 1964, Rex Andrews, Police Officer, Irving, Texas, advised that the football game between Irving High School and Richland Hills High School was played on Friday, November 8, 1963, at Richland Hills, Texas (a suburb of Fort Worth, Texas).

On August 13, 1964, Roy S. Truly, Superintendent, Texas School Book Depository, 411 Elm Street, Dallas, Texas, advised his company does not utilize a "time clock" system for its employees to check in and out of work. A notation is merely made that a particular employee is at work in the morning and is still at work at the end of the same day, at which time the individual is credited with eight hours work.

Warehouse employees are given forty-five minutes for lunch, and although it is possible for employees to take a few minutes longer, any excess absences would be noted and the employee would have wages deducted from his pay. Truly does not recall Oswald's being away from his employment at any time on an extended lunch period.

-2-

COMMISSION EXHIBIT No. 2454—Continued

LEE HARVEY OSWALD

Mr. Truly advised he believed Oswald rode to work from Irving, Texas, with a fellow employee, Wesley Frazier, in Frazier's automobile. To his knowledge, Oswald was not known to have an automobile of his own and arrived at work either by bus or riding with Frazier.

Truly stated Mr. H. S. Aiken, a leadman in the warehouse, keeps the daily employment records of each employee.

Truly stated that while a warehouse employee such as Oswald would have noted on a bill of lading that he was the particular employee filling the book order, the particular bills of lading would not indicate the time of the day the work was started or finished nor would they indicate the amount of time utilized in filling a particular order. Mr. Truly noted small book orders can be filled in a few minutes while large orders may take hours to fill.

Mr. Truly stated further that the orders and bills of lading are filed by towns and cities and that to locate a particular order filled by Oswald on November 6 or 7, 1963, would be an enormous task. In addition, in the event such bills of lading were located, they would not contain a notation as to the time of the day the order was filled by Oswald or the amount of time taken to fill the particular order. Consequently, Mr. Truly stated such a review would not determine how much time Oswald was off on his lunch period on the dates in question. Mr. Truly concluded that his company did not have any record which would indicate an employee was gone for a longer period of time than forty-five minutes on his lunch period.

On August 13, 1964, Mr. H. S. Aiken, Leadman, Texas School Book Depository, 411 Elm Street, Dallas, Texas, advised he keeps the daily employment records of warehouse employees.

COMMISSION EXHIBIT No. 2454—Continued

LEE HARVEY OSWALD

He stated the employees do not use a time clock to record their time of arrival, departure or time taken for lunch. He stated that he is advised in the morning as to who is at work and at the end of the workday who is still at work. The normal workday consists of eight working hours.

Aiken stated that no notation of any sort is made of the time an employee takes his forty-five minute lunch period, that is, the employee's time of departure for lunch and the time of his return.

Aiken noted his time record for Lee Harvey Oswald indicates that during the week of November 4 through November 8, 1963, Oswald was credited with having worked eight hours each day from Monday, November 4, 1963, through Friday, November 8, 1963.

Aiken stated that if an employee was gone for a period of time much longer than the employee's forty-five minute lunch period, he would have reported this information, and the time would have been deducted from the employee's pay for the day. In Oswald's particular case, there had been no notation that Oswald was gone for lunch on either November 6 or November 7, 1963, for any extended period of time in excess of his normal forty-five minute lunch period, and AIKEN would surmise that Oswald had not overstayed his lunch period on those days.

Aiken added that he knows of no company records which would indicate how much work a particular employee did in the morning or in the afternoon.

On August 13, 1964, Wesley Frazier, 1413 West Shady Grove, Apartment 27, Irving, Texas, who is employed in the warehouse of the Texas School Book Depository, advised

COMMISSION EXHIBIT No. 2454—Continued

Lee Harvey Oswald used to ride to work with him from Irving, Texas, in his (Frazier's) 1954 Chevrolet, four-door sedan, black in color. Frazier further described this vehicle as rather "beatup" looking with most of its chrome missing. The car has power-glide transmission as well as "loud pipes."

Frazier stated that Oswald has never driven this car and at no time did he ever loan the car to Oswald, including any short period of time such as a lunch period.

Frazier further advised that he has never heard of any of the other Texas School Book Depository employees loaning their car to Oswald at any time.

Frazier noted that his car had previously been photographed by a representative of the President's Commission investigating the assassination of President Kennedy.

On August 18, 1964, Charles Woodrow Greener, owner, Irving Sport Shop, 221 East Irving Boulevard, Irving, Texas, advised his memory regarding past events and dates has always been very poor and he was not positive that the information he was about to furnish regarding his whereabouts between Friday, November 22, 1963, and Thanksgiving Day, Thursday, November 28, 1963, would be absolutely correct, but that his information was based on the best of his present recollection.

Greener stated that between November 22, 1963, and November 28, 1963, he had been in Irving, Texas, at either his place of business or his home. If he had left Irving at any time during this period, it would have been for only a few hours and not overnight.

COMMISSION EXHIBIT No. 2454—Continued

Greener stated that during this week's period he naturally had conversed on numerous occasions with his employee, Dial D. Ryder, at work, but he did not recall Ryder ever mentioning to him that the Irving Sport Shop had worked on a gun for Oswald. At no time, according to Greener, did Ryder advise him between November 22, 1963, and November 28, 1963, that he, Ryder, had located a work ticket bearing Oswald's name.

Greener stated that the first he knew about any work slip in the name of Oswald was when he read about it in "The Dallas Times Herald" newspaper on Thanksgiving Day, November 28, 1963, and the news article was a complete shock to him. Greener stated he was at home on Thanksgiving Day when he read this newspaper article. He then, on the same day, went down to his store and saw the work ticket for a person named "Oswald".

COMMISSION EXHIBIT No. 2454—Continued

OFFICE OF THE DIRECTOR

UNITED STATES DEPARTMENT OF JUSTICE

FEDERAL BUREAU OF INVESTIGATION

WASHINGTON 25, D.C.

March 10, 1964

By Courier Service

Honorable J. Lee Rankin
General Counsel
The President's Commission
200 Maryland Avenue, Northeast
Washington, D. C. 20002

Dear Mr. Rankin:

Reference is made to my letter dated January 10, 1964, advising that arrangements were made with the Atomic Energy Commission to process by nuclear analytical techniques items relating to the assassination of President Kennedy.

The paraffin casts from Lee Harvey Oswald were examined by neutron activation analyses at the Oak Ridge National Laboratories, Research Reactor Site, Oak Ridge, Tennessee.

These analyses were made to determine if the paraffin casts from Oswald which were made, chemically treated and washed by the Dallas law enforcement authorities, bear any primer deposits from the rifle cartridge cases found in the Texas School Book Depository Building following the President's assassination.

As a result of these examinations, the deposits found on the paraffin casts from the hands and cheek of Oswald could not be specifically associated with the rifle cartridges. Elements (barium and antimony) were found on the casts; however, these same elements were found in residues both from the above rifle cartridge cases and

COMMISSION EXHIBIT No. 2455

Honorable J. Lee Rankin

from the revolver cartridge cases which were fired from Oswald's revolver reportedly between the time of the assassination and the time of apprehension.

No characteristic elements were found by neutron activation analyses which could be used to distinguish the rifle from the revolver cartridges.

In view of the fact that the paraffin casts were not made until after the reported firing and handling of the revolver, no significance could be attached to the residues found on the casts other than the conclusion that barium and antimony in these residues are present in amounts greater than would be expected to be found on the hands of an individual who has not recently fired a weapon or handled a fired weapon.

Sincerely yours,

J. Edgar Hoover

2

COMMISSION EXHIBIT No. 2455—Continued

UNITED STATES DEPARTMENT OF JUSTICE
FEDERAL BUREAU OF INVESTIGATION

Copy to:

Report of: HARRY H. WHIDBEE
Office: Los Angeles, California
Date: 6/11/64

Field Office File #: 105-15823
Bureau File #: 105-82555

Title: LEE HARVEY OSWALD

Character: INTERNAL SECURITY - RUSSIA - CUBA

Synopsis: EULALIO RODRIGUEZ-CHAVEZ, a Mexican citizen, located and interviewed at Los Angeles. RODRIGUEZ positively identified a photograph of LEE HARVEY OSWALD as passenger on Transportes del Norte bus which traveled from Mexico City, Mexico, to Laredo, Texas, 10/2/63 and then by Greyhound bus from Laredo, Texas, during early morning hours of 10/3/63. RODRIGUEZ recalled OSWALD was one of two men passengers taken off this bus for further questioning regarding his documents by examining immigration officers at Mexican Immigration check station, located a few miles from the Mexican-United States border. RODRIGUEZ had no personal contacts or conversations with OSWALD.

- P -

DETAILS:

COMMISSION EXHIBIT No. 2456

1

Date 6/11/64

EULALIO RODRIGUEZ CHAVEZ, a Mexican citizen, 62 years of age, presently unemployed and residing at 3418½ East Michigan Avenue, Los Angeles, California, advised the following in the Spanish language:

He recalled having made three trips to the United States by bus from Mexico City, Mexico, during the year of 1963. He refreshed his recollection from some personal letters and some documents, and determined that on October 2, 1963, he departed aboard a Transportes del Norte bus at Mexico City about 8:00 a.m. en route to Houston, Texas, via Monterrey, State of Nuevo Leon, Mexico, and Laredo and San Antonio, Texas. He had made reservations at the Transportes del Norte bus station located on Calle (street) Insurgentes in Mexico City about two days previous to his departure and remembered that he then received his bus ticket and was assigned a seat number. He could not recall the exact number of the latter. He departed from Mexico City en route to Houston, Texas, to engage in a dump truck business.

Previously, he had traveled to Dallas, Texas, because of the death of a friend, and subsequent to the above trip to Houston, Texas, he again traveled to Houston with his wife and daughter from Mexico City in the latter part of November, 1963.

He recalled that on the bus trip from Mexico City to Laredo, Texas, on October 2, 1963, he was assigned either seat number five or eight aboard the bus and he was certain that he sat about three rows back of the bus driver in an aisle seat. He was very certain about the latter because he does not like to ride in a bus sitting by a window. He kept the same seat on the bus during the trip from Mexico City to Laredo, Texas. He recalled that when he boarded the bus at Mexico City on the morning of October 2, 1963, he was late in arriving and had difficulty obtaining assistance in getting his large suitcase placed in the trunk carrier of the bus. He remembered that when he boarded the bus, most of the other passengers already were seated.

He remembered clearly that he sat next to a young woman who sat on his left next to the window and he could not recall

On 6/11/64 at Los Angeles, California File # Los Angeles 105-15823

by SA HARRY H. WHIDBEE and SA FREDERICK E. RODERICK:dmr Date dictated 6/11/64

COMMISSION EXHIBIT No. 2456—Continued

whether a man or a woman sat next to him across the aisle. He spoke to the young woman, who was seated in the bus when he boarded, and he described her as being of Mexican descent, about eighteen or nineteen years of age, thin build, good looking, and spoke Spanish fluently. The young woman advised him that she had been vacationing in Mexico City, that she was married and was returning to her residence in Houston, Texas. He did not learn the young woman's name but she was supposed to have been met at the Greyhound bus station in Houston, Texas, by her husband.

After being processed by United States Immigration, Public Health, and Customs at Laredo, Texas, he boarded a Greyhound bus and proceeded to San Antonio, Texas, where he boarded another bus for Houston, Texas.

He recalled that the bus stopped at Monterrey and all passengers alighted, but he did not recall if it was the same or a different bus which they boarded when they departed from Monterrey. He remembered that there were several rest stops while en route to Laredo, Texas, from Mexico City, which allowed the passengers to drink a soda or eat a sandwich but these stops were short.

The bus was full and he did not have any conversation with anyone else except the young woman who sat next to him. He could not recall specifically if any additional passengers boarded the bus at Monterrey but he was certain that he kept his same seat all the way from Mexico City to Laredo, Texas. He remembered that the arrival at Monterrey was at about 9:00 or 10:00 p.m. and that it was then dark.

A few miles before reaching the border at Nuevo Laredo, State of Tamaulipas, Mexico, the bus stopped and the lights in the bus were turned on to allow a Mexican Immigration official to examine the travel documents of all the passengers aboard the bus. He remembered that at this Mexican Immigration check station there were two men taken from the bus for questioning, apparently about their travel documents. He saw these two men who left the bus and considered that they were not Mexicans because there was some sort of problem with regard to their travel documents. He remembered that one of these men had sat across the aisle from him either to the rear or just ahead, and that the other man was sitting to the rear of him on his side of the bus.

He could recall that only one Mexican Immigration official boarded the bus, but when the men were taken off the bus they were taken to talk with another Mexican Immigration official whom he assumed was higher in rank with the Mexican Immigration Service and whom he stated probably was "a Sergeant".

The two men were allowed to return to the bus and the stop at this check station delayed the bus about fifteen to twenty minutes. He believed that this stop was made at about 1:00 or 1:30 a.m. on the morning of October 3, 1963.

He described one of the men who was taken off the bus and who sat someplace across the aisle as "a foreigner to Mexico", about fifty some odd years old, black hair, graying, heavy set, and fair complexion. He could not recall the type of clothing this man wore.

He described the second man who sat behind him as "a foreigner to Mexico", a young man, shorter than the above described man, fair complexion, wore a jacket "coffee-colored tan" which was a gabardine type, and he tried to speak some Spanish to the Mexican Immigration official when approached at the check station for his travel documents but he was unable to communicate his Spanish properly. This man did not get off at the rest stops with the other passengers and once he was observed eating a banana which he had taken from a paper bag he carried. This individual was observed once talking with a middle aged woman, a passenger whose description he could not recall, and their conversation and the language used could not be recalled as well as exactly when this took place aboard the bus.

He recalled that after departure from the Mexican Immigration check station, the bus proceeded to Nuevo Laredo where again a Mexican Immigration official boarded the bus to hurriedly check the travel documents of the passengers. Then the bus traveled on the bridge across the Rio Grande River to Laredo, Texas, where all passengers alighted from the bus and were processed first by the United States Immigration Service, then by the United States Department of Public Health for a small pox vaccination, and then their luggage was examined by United States Customs. Following this, RODRIGUEZ CHAVEZ boarded a Greyhound bus at about 2:00 or 2:30 a.m. on October 3, 1963, for San Antonio, Texas. Here he boarded another Greyhound bus for Houston, Texas, where he arrived at about 6:00 or 7:00 a.m. on the same day.

At this point he could not recall anything specific about any of the other passengers with regard to their identities, their descriptions and their purpose for travel because he did not engage in conversation with any of them except the young woman who sat next to him and who traveled to Houston, Texas.

A photograph of LEE HARVEY OSWALD taken on August 9, 1963, at New Orleans, Louisiana, which consists of a side and front view and a full length front view of him standing, was exhibited for identification and RODRIGUEZ CHAVEZ immediately recognized OSWALD as the second man described above, who sat to his rear, who tried to speak to the Mexican Immigration official in Spanish, and who was taken off the bus at the Mexican Immigration check station before arrival at the Mexican-United States border. He was positive about this because he explained that this photograph was that of the man who kept an overhead reading light on, in the bus, after about 10:00 p.m. on October 2, 1963, which disturbed RODRIGUEZ CHAVEZ from sleeping on the bus. He remembered that the man in the photograph shown him was reading either a book, a magazine, or a newspaper and this bothered him because the man was no inconsiderate to leave the light on when he as well as others were trying to sleep. He remembered that the man was reading because RODRIGUEZ CHAVEZ turned to look at him.

He could not be certain as to the exact seat the man in the photograph sat but he was certain that the man sat to his rear and to his left.

He was asked if he knew the man in the photograph shown him and he stated that he did not. He was told that the photograph was that of LEE HARVEY OSWALD and he stated that OSWALD was a "desgraciado" (disgraceful person). He then expressed a deep emotional feeling for President JOHN F. KENNEDY, losing his composure and crying at length. After composing himself, he advised the following additional information:

He remembered that OSWALD not only did not turn off the reading light when others were trying to sleep, but he was "a loner" because he did not get off the bus with the other passengers at various rest stops en route and always appeared to be "alone", not associating with other passengers.

He recalled having seen OSWALD last when the passengers alighted from the Greyhound bus at San Antonio, Texas, and he did not recall that OSWALD boarded the Greyhound bus with him en route from San Antonio, Texas, to Houston, Texas.

He did see the young woman who sat next to him on the bus, at the Greyhound bus station in Houston, Texas, when her husband failed to appear and she stated that she was taking a taxi to her residence in Houston.

He could not recall having seen OSWALD at the bus station in Mexico City or having been aware of his presence on the bus at the time it departed from Mexico City. The was crowded and during the first hour or two of the trip, he got accustomed to his seat and conversed with the unknown young woman sitting next to him. He said he was not aware of OSWALD until possibly the second rest stop when he observed that OSWALD did not get off the bus with the others but remained in his seat.

He was asked to furnish any other specific knowledge he might have regarding OSWALD. He said that he did not recall observing any activities of OSWALD at the time the bus stopped at Monterrey, Mexico. He definitely recalled that OSWALD was on the bus when it crossed the border into the United States and stopped for processing. He said, however, that he was most concerned with his own papers and the United States Customs check of his belongings, and he was not alert to the activities of the other passengers. He did not remember observing OSWALD being processed by the United States authorities. He did recall seeing OSWALD board the same Greyhound bus with him at Laredo, Texas, when the bus proceeded to San Antonio, Texas. He could not recall where OSWALD sat on this bus. He stated that during the entire trip he had no personal contact or conversation with OSWALD.

He was asked specifically whether he could recall any information regarding other passengers on the busses. He stated that except for the young woman who sat next to him, who was returning to her residence in Houston, Texas, he remembered only one other who was a student. The citizenship and origin of this student were unknown to him, but he did remember that this young man had a "long string of tickets" and he was traveling from Mexico City to San Antonio, Texas, en route to Chicago, Illinois, and then some other "far away place." He did not sit next to or across from any male passenger whom he could recall, and he

6
LA 105-15823

could not remember where the student sat on the busses. He could not recall a description of the student.

He was asked specifically if he had realized, prior to this interview, that OSWALD, who allegedly assassinated President JOHN F. KENNEDY, was identical with the passenger whom he had seen on the bus during the trip. He stated that he had not. He advised that he cannot read or speak English; that he does not own a television set; and had not seen OSWALD on television or in magazines. He said that he saw OSWALD's photograph once in a newspaper. He admitted that he had not recognized the photograph in the newspaper of OSWALD as that of the passenger on the bus. He said that apparently it was not a good likeness. On the other hand, when shown the photograph of OSWALD reflecting three poses, he immediately recognized the photograph as identical with the passenger on the bus because he stated the photograph was "so lifelike".

He could not think of any other information regarding the activities of OSWALD while a passenger on the busses between Mexico City and San Antonio, Texas. He stated that he had never met OSWALD previously and had no contacts with or knowledge of OSWALD after the trip on October 2 - 3, 1963.

- 7*-

COMMISSION EXHIBIT No. 2456—Continued

UNITED STATES DEPARTMENT OF JUSTICE

FEDERAL BUREAU OF INVESTIGATION
Los Angeles, California
May 7, 1964

In Reply, Please Refer to
File No.

LEE HARVEY OSWALD

Lee Harvey Oswald, traveling as H. O. Lee, is believed to have departed from Mexico City at 8:30 AM, October 2, 1963, on bus number 332 of the Transportes del Norte line, which arrived at Monterrey, Mexico, at 9:15 PM on the same date. At Monterrey, Oswald and passengers for Laredo transferred to bus number 373.

Manifest of bus number 332 shows the passenger in seat number 4, second window seat on the driver's side, was occupied by one Margaret A. Wolff, whose destination was listed as Laredo.

Records of the Passport Office, U. S. Department of State, Washington, D. C., reflect a passport application dated May 6, 1963, for a Margaret Wolff. She was born December 22, 1899, at Berlin, Germany, and resided at 1176 3/4 South Norton Avenue, Los Angeles 19, California. Her approximate date of departure was May, 1963. She intended to visit Germany to see her mother. Passport number D113012 was issued on May 10, 1963. She was a widow.

On May 7, 1964, Mrs. Margaret Clara Wolff, who resides at 1176 3/4 South Norton Avenue, Los Angeles, advised that she was born December 22, 1899, at Berlin, Germany. She and her husband, Frederick Wolff, who is now deceased, entered the United States for permanent residence in 1945. In May, 1963, she applied for and was issued U. S. Passport D113012 for travel to Germany. She departed the United States in the latter part of May, 1963, and traveled by air transportation to Berlin, Germany, where she visited her mother. She returned to the United States by Pan American Airlines during the last week in October, 1963. She stated that she flew direct from Germany to London, England, and then non stop to Los Angeles. She stated that she has never been in Mexico and specifically stated that she was not a passenger on a bus traveling through Mexico in October, 1963.

COMMISSION EXHIBIT No. 2457

DEPARTMENT OF STATE
WASHINGTON

June 24, 1964

Dear Mr. Rankin:

Enclosed are copies of a telegram and Security Report in which you may be interested. Also attached, at Mr. Coleman's request, are two copies of Passport Notice 2300 of April 8, 1964 which amends the Passport Office Lookout File Information Code.

Sincerely,

Leonard C. Meeker
Acting Legal Adviser

Enclosures:

1. Copy of telegram No. 1590, June 9, 1964, from Caracas.
2. Security Report dated June 9, 1964, from Caracas.
3. 2 copies of Passport Notice 2300.

The Honorable
J. Lee Rankin,
General Counsel,
President's Commission on the
Assassination of President Kennedy,
200 Maryland Avenue, N.E.,
Washington, D.C.

LIMITED OFFICIAL USE

COMMISSION EXHIBIT No. 2458

INCOMING TELEGRAM *Department of State*

Action
SY

Info
RMR

Control:
Rec'd:

FROM: CARACAS

ACTION: SECSTATE 159Ø, PRIORITY

DATE:

SY CHANNEL

SUBJECT: LEE HARVEY OSWALD.

AFTER REPEATED EFFORTS CARACAS TO LOCATE MARIA CRISTINA MURACCIOLE (DAVILA) DE PIEDRA AND MATILDE MURACCIOLE (DAVILA) RESULTED IN LOCATING BROTHER WHO INFORMS SISTERS NOW RESIDING AT HOTEL ROOSEVELT, AVENUE INSURGENTES 287, MEXICO CITY.

ADVISE WHETHER THIS OFFICE OR HEADQUARTERS WILL SEND LEAD TO MEXICO.

REPORT WITH AVAILABLE INFORMATION TO DATE BEING POUCHED TODAY.

RSO NOW VISITING KINGSTON AND WILL HANDLE PENDING PORTION THERE.

STEWART

OFFICE OF SECURITY

JRB/22

COMMISSION EXHIBIT No. 2458—Continued

FORM DS-838
4-26-56

DEPARTMENT OF STATE
OFFICE OF SECURITY

TITLE			CASE CLASSIFICATION
OSWALD, Lee Harvey			IA-25.03(1)
FIELD OFFICE	DATE REPORTED	DATES INVESTIGATED	REPORTING AGENT
Caracas	6/9/64	3/30/64 - 6/9/64	M. B. Lustgarten

SYNOPSIS

Translation of interview of Mr. and Mrs. DE CUBA by the Netherlands Antilles Police Forces set out. Attempts to locate Matilde MURACCIOLE (Davila) and Maria Cristina Muracciole (Davila) de PIEDRA in Caracas revealed women now residing in Mexico City. Pending at Kingston.

- PENDING -

REFERENCE: O:SY/I memoranda 1/27/64, 3/27/64, 4/3/64
RSO Caracas report 3/6/64

DETAILS:

INVESTIGATION IN CURACAO, N.A.

By investigative report dated May 29, 1964, the Post Security Officer at American Consulate General, Curacao forwarded a report from the Netherlands Antilles Police Force which stated the following:

"On the 22nd of May 1964, Mr. Cornelis BRINKENBERG, Sub-Inspector of the Netherlands Antilles Police Forces interrogated in Aruba Juan Matheo DE CUBA, born in Aruba February 8, 1935, customs-officer, residence - Savaneta No. 237A, Aruba, and his wife, Ada Francisca BISLIP, born in Aruba, January 6, 1935, same address.

APPROVED

MBL
Michael B. Lustgarten
Regional Security Officer
(Special Agent in Charge)

DO NOT WRITE IN THIS SPACE

DATE RECEIVED

COPIES REFERRED
3 - O:SY/I
1 - File

REVIEWED BY AGENT SUPERVISOR

(Date) (Initials)

1584

COMMISSION EXHIBIT No. 2458—Continued

OSWALD, Lee Harvey

"A verbal report of this interrogation in the Dutch language was written by Mr. BRINKENBERG, duly signed under his oath of office on the 25th of May 1964.

"After having brought back to their memory the journey in Mexico, Mr. BRINKENBERG started to interrogate Mrs. Ada DE CUBA - BISLIP.

Q: Can you remember with which transportation company you travelled to Nuevo Laredo?

A: Yes, it was the Transportes del Norte line.

Q: Where did you board the bus and where did you cross the border between Mexico and the U.S.A.?

A: My husband and I boarded the bus in Mexico City. I cannot remember the name of the town where we reached the border, but it was in the vicinity of Nuevo Laredo, where the bus went after the border check.

Q: Can you remember something about the procedure of the immigration officers at the Mexican border?

A: I cannot recall this exactly. I think that I remained in the bus.

Q: Can you remember a young man sitting in the bus, who got in trouble with the immigration authorities at the Mexican border?

A: Yes, I remember a young man, who was ordered by the immigration to leave the bus. I suppose that he was an American; apparently he did not speak Spanish. I did not hear what he said or what was said to him.

Q: Do you know the reason why he was ordered to leave the bus or what kind of trouble he had?

A: No, I don't know, but I got the impression that he had trouble about his papers, that his passport was not good or something the like. But I am not sure of this, it is just an impression.

-2-

COMMISSION EXHIBIT No. 2458—Continued

OSWALD, Lee Harvey

Q: Can you give a description of this young man. Do you know where he boarded the bus and where he went?

A: I estimate this man to be not older than 30 years. He was slim and as tall as you are (reporter measures bare feet 5 feet, 10 inches). He did not wear a hat nor a coat. He was dressed in a sport shirt. I don't know where this man went. After the border check we went to Nuevo Laredo and there we changed into a Greyhound bus. I don't know if this man also changed busses. I cannot remember having seem him again afterwards. I suppose that this man entered the bus in Mexico City, but I am not sure of this. I would not recognize this young man and I did not recognize him from the picture you showed me.

Q. On what date and hour did you leave Mexico City and did you arrive in Nuevo Laredo?

A: We left Mexico City on the 2nd of October 1963 about 8:30 a.m. and arrived at the border in the night. About one hour later we arrived in Nuevo Laredo. This was on the 3rd of October 1963, about 2:00 a.m.

Q: How many people were there in the bus and where was your seat?

A: I don't know how many people there were in the bus. I presume that we were sitting in the middle of the bus.

Q: Where did you buy tickets for the bus?

A: My husband took care of it. I think that he bought them in Mexico City.

"Thereupon Mr. Juan M. DE CUBA was interrogated.

Q: Can you remember with which transportation company you travelled to Nuevo Laredo?

A: Yes, with a bus of the Transportes del Norte.

-3-

OSWALD, Lee Harvey

Q: Where did you enter the bus and where did you cross the border between Mexico and the U.S.A.?

A: My wife and I entered the bus in Mexico City. At the border, I cannot recall the name of the town, we had first the Mexican immigration and immediately thereupon the U.S.A. immigration.

Q: Can you remember the procedure of the immigration at the Mexican border?

A: We were checked twice, first by the Mexican immigration and afterwards by the American immigration. I think my wife remained in the bus, but I am not sure of this. It is possible that I had to show my papers in the bus but it is also possible that all the passengers had to leave the bus. However, I had no difficulties at the border. But I cannot recall the details.

Q: Can you remember a young man, sitting in the bus, who had trouble with the immigration authorities?

A: Yes, I remember a young man who was ordered by the Mexican authorities to leave the bus. I presume that he was an American, for he could not speak Spanish. Otherwise I did not hear what he said or what was said to him.

Q: Do you know why he had to leave the bus or what was wrong with him?

A: No, I don't know. I thought that there was something wrong with his passport or papers. I just got this impression.

Q: Can you describe this young man. Do you know where he boarded the bus and where he went?

A: I estimate the age of this man between 20 and 30 years, anyhow not older than 30 years. He wore ^no^ hat nor coat. He wore a sport shirt. He was slim and shorter than you are. I don't know where this man went. I believe that he did not enter the bus in Mexico City but at one of the bustops between Mexico City and the border. After the border check he went, as far as I know, with the bus to Nuevo Laredo. There my wife and I changed into a Greyhound bus and I have not seen the man anymore. It is not impossible that he also got

OSWALD, Lee Harvey

into the Greyhound bus, but I can impossible say so, for I have not seen this man anymore. I would not recognize this man, neither do I recognize him from the picture you showed me.

Q: On what day and hour did you leave Mexico City and when did you arrive in Nuevo Laredo?

A: We left Mexico City in the morning of the 2nd of October 1963 about 8:30 and arrived at the border station close after midnight. Approximately one hour later we arrived in Nuevo Laredo, this was on the 3rd of October 1963 about two o' clock in the night.

Q: How many people were there in the bus and where were you seated?

A: I don't know how many people there were in the bus. The bus was not full. I was sitting about the middle of the bus and I think that the young man was sitting diagonally behind me.

Q: Where did you buy the bus tickets?

A: I bought the tickets already at the beginning of my journey. Thus I had them already. However before the beginning of our bus trip I went in Mexico City to the office of the Greyhound in order to make reservations.

"Mr. DE CUBA added that he was not in Dallas during this trip. They passed by Dallas, but did not leave the bus there. He does not know if anybody left the bus in or near Dallas.

"This translation into the English language was duly done by me, Hendrik J. VISSER, Sub-Inspector 1st class of the Netherlands-Antilles Police Force, attached to the Staff of the Chief-Commissioner of Police, Willemstad, Curacao, and signed under my oath of office on this 20th of May 1964.

/s/ H. J. Visser

"Visé by the Chief-Commissioner Netherlands-Antilles Police Force:

/s/ J. F. van der Staur, L.L.B."

-5-

OSWALD, Lee Harvey

INVESTIGATION IN CARACAS, VENEZUELA

Matilde MURACCIOLE (Davila), born March 14, 1917 at Tovar, Merida, Venezuela and Maria Cristina Muracciole (note variance in spelling - Caracciola) (Davila) de PIEDRA, born September 10, 1917 at Merida, Venezuela could not be located. However, information from their brother, Jose Ramon MURACCIOLE, revealed that his sisters are now residing in Mexico City, Mexico at Hotel Roosevelt, Av. Insurgentes 287.

Record checks with the following agencies in the name of the sisters MURACCIOLE were non derogatory:

Venezuelan Bureau of Identification, Caracas
Judicial Technical Police, Caracas
Direccion General of Police, Caracas

NOTE: Final report will be submitted upon receipt of portion now pending at Kingston, Jamaica.

-4-

OFFICE OF THE DIRECTOR

UNITED STATES DEPARTMENT OF JUSTICE

FEDERAL BUREAU OF INVESTIGATION

WASHINGTON, D.C. 20535

June 29, 1964

BY COURIER SERVICE

Honorable J. Lee Rankin
General Counsel
The President's Commission
200 Maryland Avenue, N. E.
Washington, D. C.

Dear Mr. Rankin:

There are enclosed two copies of a Department of State, Office of Security, report in the Lee Harvey Oswald case dated June 9, 1964, at Caracas, Venezuela, dealing in part with reinterview of Mr. and Mrs. Juan M. De Cuba. The De Cubas were fellow passengers of Oswald on the buses of the Transportes del Norte line from Mexico City, Mexico, to Laredo, Texas, on October 2 and 3, 1963. The De Cubas were reinterviewed at our request.

The enclosed report also makes reference to the Muracciole sisters, formerly of Caracas, Venezuela, who are said to presently reside in Mexico City, Mexico.

In light of recent developments which have established that Oswald departed from Nuevo Laredo, Mexico, on October 3, 1963, by Transportes del Norte bus and as the Muracciole sisters departed from Nuevo Laredo, Mexico, on October 3, 1963, by air en route to Caracas, Venezuela, we do not intend to conduct further inquiry to locate and interview them.

Sincerely yours,

J. Edgar Hoover

Enclosures (2)

COMMISSION EXHIBIT No. 2459

FORM DS-836
4-26-54

DEPARTMENT OF STATE
OFFICE OF SECURITY

TITLE			CASE CLASSIFICATION
OSWALD, Lee Harvey			IA-26.00(4)
FIELD OFFICE	DATE REPORTED	DATES INVESTIGATED	REPORTING AGENT
Caracas	6/9/64	3/30/64 - 6/9/64	M. B. Lustgarten

SYNOPSIS

Translation of interview of Mr. and Mrs. DE CUBA by the Netherlands Antilles Police Forces set out. Attempts to locate Matilde MURACCIOLE (Davila) and Maria Cristina Muracciole (Davila) de PIEDRA in Caracas revealed women now residing in Mexico City. Pending at Kingston.

- PENDING -

REFERENCE: O:SY/I memoranda 1/27/64, 3/27/64, 4/3/64
RSO Caracas report 3/6/64

DETAILS:

INVESTIGATION IN CURACAO, N. A.

By investigative report dated May 29, 1964, the Post Security Officer at American Consulate General, Curacao forwarded a report from the Netherlands Antilles Police Force which stated the following:

"On the 22nd of May 1964, Mr. Cornelis BRINKENBERG, Sub-Inspector of the Netherlands Antilles Police Forces interrogated in Aruba Juan Matheo DE CUBA, born in Aruba February 8, 1935, customs-officer, residence - Savaneta No. 237A, Aruba, and his wife, Ada Francisca BISLIP, born in Aruba, January 6, 1935, same address.

APPROVED

MBL
Michael B. Lustgarten
Regional Security Officer
(Special Agent in Charge)

DO NOT WRITE IN THIS SPACE

DATE RECEIVED

COPIES REFERRED
3 - O:SY/I
1 - File

REVIEWED BY AGENT SUPERVISOR

(Date) (Initials)

THIS REPORT IS THE PROPERTY OF THE DEPARTMENT OF STATE AND ITS CONTENTS MUST NOT BE DISCLOSED TO UNAUTHORIZED PERSONS.

GPO 831584

ENCLOSURE

COMMISSION EXHIBIT No. 2459—Continued

"A verbal report of this interrogation in the Dutch language was written by Mr. BRINKENBERG, duly signed under his oath of office on the 25th of May 1964.

"After having brought back to their memory the journey in Mexico, Mr. BRINKENBERG started to interrogate Mrs. Ada DE CUBA - BESLIP.

Q: Can you remember with which transportation company you travelled to Nuevo Laredo?

A: Yes, it was the Transportes del Norte line.

Q: Where did you board the bus and where did you cross the border between Mexico and the U.S.A.?

A: My husband and I boarded the bus in Mexico City. I cannot remember the name of the town where we reached the border, but it was in the vicinity of Nuevo Laredo, where the bus went after the border check.

Q: Can you remember something about the procedure of the immigration officers at the Mexican border?

A: I cannot recall this exactly. I think that I remained in the bus.

Q: Can you remember a young man sitting in the bus, who got in trouble with the immigration authorities at the Mexican border?

A: Yes, I remember a young man, who was ordered by the immigration to leave the bus. I suppose that he was an American; apparently he did not speak Spanish. I did not hear what he said or what was said to him.

Q: Do you know the reason why he was ordered to leave the bus or what kind of trouble he had?

A: No, I don't know, but I got the impression that he had trouble about his papers, that his passport was not good or something the like. But I am not sure of this, it is just an impression.

-2-

COMMISSION EXHIBIT No. 2459—Continued

Q: Can you give a description of this young man. Do you know where he boarded the bus and where he went?

A: I estimate this man to be not older than 30 years. He was slim and as tall as you are (reporter measures bare feet 5 feet, 10 inches). He did not wear a hat nor a coat. He was dressed in a sport shirt. I don't know where this man went. After the border check we went to Nuevo Laredo and there we changed into a Greyhound bus. I don't know if this man also changed busses. I cannot remember having seem him again afterwards. I suppose that this man entered the bus in Mexico City, but I am not sure of this. I would not recognize this young man and I did not recognize him from the picture you showed me.

Q, On what date and hour did you leave Mexico City and did you arrive in Nuevo Laredo?

A: We left Mexico City on the 2nd of October 1963 about 8:30 a.m. and arrived at the border in the night. About one hour later we arrived in Nouvo Laredo. This was on the 3rd of October 1963, about 2:00 a.m.

Q: How many people were there in the bus and where was your seat?

A: I don't know how many people there were in the bus. I presume that we were sitting in the middle of the bus.

Q: Where did you buy tickets for the bus?

A: My husband took care of it. I think that he bought them in Mexico City.

"Thereupon Mr. Juan M. DE CUBA was interrogated.

Q: Can you remember with which transportation company you travelled to Nuevo Laredo?

A: Yes, with a bus of the Transportes del Norte.

-3-

COMMISSION EXHIBIT No. 2459—Continued

Q: Where did you enter the bus and where did you cross the border between Mexico and the U.S.A.?

A: My wife and I entered the bus in Mexico City. At the border, I cannot recall the name of the town, we had first the Mexican immigration and immediately thereupon the U.S.A. Immigration.

Q: Can you remember the procedure of the Immigration at the Mexican border?

A: We were checked twice, first by the Mexican immigration and afterwards by the American immigration. I think my wife remained in the bus, but I am not sure of this. It is possible that I had to show my papers in the bus but it is also possible that all the passengers had to leave the bus. However, I had no difficulties at the border. But I cannot recall the details.

Q: Can you remember a young man, sitting in the bus, who had trouble with the immigration authorities?

A: Yes, I remember a young man who was ordered by the Mexican authorities to leave the bus. I presume that he was an American, for he could not speak Spanish. Otherwise I did not hear what he said or what was said to him.

Q: Do you know why he had to leave the bus or what was wrong with him?

A: No, I don't know. I thought that there was something wrong with his passport or papers. I just got this impression.

Q: Can you describe this young man. Do you know where he boarded the bus and where he went?

A: I estimate the age of this man between 20 and 30 years, anyhow not older than 30 years. He wore no hat nor coat. He wore a sport shirt. He was slim and shorter than you are. I don't know where this man went. I believe that he did not enter the bus in Mexico City but at one of the busstops between Mexico City and the border. After the border check he went, as far as I know, with the bus to Nuevo Laredo. There my wife and I changed into a Greyhound bus and I have not seen the man anymore. It is not impossible that he also got

-4-

into the Greyhound bus, but I can impossible say so, for I have not seen this man anymore. I would not recognize this man, neither do I recognize him from the picture you showed me.

Q: On what day and hour did you leave Mexico City and when did you arrive in Nuevo Laredo?

A: We left Mexico City in the morning of the 2nd of October 1963 about 8:30 and arrived at the border station close after midnight. Approximately one hour later we arrived in Nuevo Laredo, this was on the 3rd of October 1963 about two o' clock in the night.

Q: How many people were there in the bus and where were you seated?

A: I don't know how many people there were in the bus. The bus was not full. I was sitting about the middle of the bus and I think that the young man was sitting diagonally behind me.

Q: Where did you buy the bus tickets?

A: I bought the tickets already at the beginning of my journey. Thus I had them already. However before the beginning of our bus trip I went in Mexico City to the office of the Greyhound in order to make reservations.

"Mr. DE CUBA added that he was not in Dallas during this trip. They passed by Dallas, but did not leave the bus there. He does not know if anybody left the bus in or near Dallas.

"This translation into the English language was duly done by me, Hendrik J. VISSER, Sub-Inspector 1st class of the Netherlands-Antilles Police Force, attached to the Staff of the Chief-Commissioner of Police, Willemstad, Curacao, and signed under my oath of office on this 20th of May 1964.

/s/ H. J. Visser

"Visé by the Chief-Commissioner
Netherlands-Antilles Police Forces

/s/ J. P. van der Stour, L.L.B."

-5-

OSWALD, Lee Harvey

INVESTIGATION IN CARACAS, VENEZUELA

Matilde MURACCIOLE (Davila), born March 14, 1897 at Tovar, Merida, Venezuela and Maria Cristina Muracciole (note variance in spelling - Caracciole) (Davila) de PIEDRA, born September 10, 1917 at Merida, Venezuela could not be located. However, information from their brother, Jose Ramon MURACCIOLE, revealed that his sisters are now residing in Mexico City, Mexico at Hotel Roosevelt, Av. Insurgentes 287.

Record checks with the following agencies in the name of the sisters MURACCIO LE were non derogatory:

Venezuelan Bureau of Identification, Caraças
Judicial Technical Police, Caracas
Direction General of Police, Caracas

NOTE: Final report will be submitted upon receipt of portion now pending at Kingston, Jamaica.

-6-

COMMISSION EXHIBIT No. 2459—Continued

UNITED STATES DEPARTMENT OF JUSTICE
FEDERAL BUREAU OF INVESTIGATION

In Reply, Please Refer to
File No.

WASHINGTON, D.C. 20535

March 31, 1964

LEE HARVEY OSWALD

BASIS FOR INQUIRY

The information set out below was made available by a confidential source abroad.

According to the records of the Department of Immigration, Mexican Ministry of "Gobernacion" (Interior or Government), Mexico, D. F., Mexico, among tourist cards surrendered by "aliens" departing from Mexico at Nuevo Laredo, State of Tamaulipas, as tourists on October 3, 1963, was the tourist card of Herbert Robert VOORHEES. This card was an FM-5 permit bearing No. 4325846. It was valid for 180 days' stay in Mexico. This tourist card was issued by the Mexican Immigration Service in Nuevo Laredo on June 5, 1963, and the following data was recorded thereon:

VOORHEES entered Mexico at Nuevo Laredo on June 5, 1963, by train with final destination designated as Mexico, D. F. He was described on the tourist card as a male, American citizen; 73 years of age; a widower; retired; born in Beloit, Wisconsin; residence, Overland Park, Kansas. He presented a birth certificate as proof of citizenship. This tourist card carries the typewritten Spanish word "tren" (meaning train), and the Mexican Immigration form FM-11 which constitutes a recapitulation of departures of tourists at Nuevo Laredo on October 3, 1963, records that VOORHEES departed from Mexico by railroad with the final destination of "Overland, P. K." The departure of VOORHEES from Mexico was handled by Mexican Immigration Service employee ALBERTO ARZAMENDI CHAPA.

COMMISSION EXHIBIT No. 2460

Since VOORHEES departed from Mexico during ALBERTO ARZAMENDI CHAPA's tour of duty between 12:00 midnight and 8:00 AM, October 3, 1963, he was located to determine whether or not he had observed LEE HARVEY OSWALD during his travel.

According to Mexican Immigration records, OSWALD had surrendered his tourist card at Nuevo Laredo to ARZAMENDI CHAPA between 12:00 midnight and 8:00 AM on the same date.

INTERVIEW OF HERBERT ROBERT VOORHEES

A confidential source abroad stated that on March 26, 1964, HERBERT ROBERT VOORHEES was residing at Calle Masones No. 19, Apartment 10, San Miguel de Allende, State of Guanajuato, Mexico, and, upon being located next door to his residence, VOORHEES advised as follows:

His true name is HERBERT FRANCIS VOORHEES, but for unknown reasons his name was listed incorrectly as HERBERT ROBERT VOORHEES on his birth certificate. He uses his true name as a commercial cartoonist.

Until six years ago, he had lived the greater part of his life in Chicago, Illinois, where for twelve years he had resided at the Lake Lane Apartments, 6214 Winthrop Street. He is a widower and for the last six years has traveled, primarily by train, to Mexico, where he has met several friendly Americans and artists in San Miguel de Allende.

He obtains a Mexican tourist card, valid for 180 days' stay in Mexico, which causes him to return to the United States every six months to have his status in Mexico as a tourist re-established for another 180-day period.

He explained that the train from Nuevo Laredo, State of Tamaulipas, Mexico, does not pass through San Miguel de Allende, and he leaves the train at San Luis Potosi, State of San Luis Potosi, Mexico, and travels to San Miguel de Allende by bus.

Initially, he stated he was 74 years of age, hard of hearing, and would have to stop to refresh his recollection

- 2 -

COMMISSION EXHIBIT No. 2460—Continued

before he could be positive about anything which took place in the past, since he has difficulty remembering the exact details of his travels. He was positive that his last departure from Mexico was by bus and not by train.

He affirmed initially that he last departed Mexico by "Greyhound bus" in the early part of October, 1963. He explained that it was a "Greyhound bus" in his mind because the bus on which he traveled in Mexico had "Greyhound dogs" painted on the sides, the ticket he purchased was a "Greyhound bus ticket," and his journey in the United States was continued on the Greyhound Bus Lines, but in Mexico the name of the bus company he used was Transportes del Norte. He entered Mexico by train some months prior to October 6, 1963, since by this date he had to leave Mexico to renew his tourist card.

At first he could not recall any information concerning the trip he repeatedly referred to as the one taken by him on the "Greyhound bus." He could not recall the exact date he entered Mexico at Nuevo Laredo by train from San Antonio, Texas, to which he proceeded from Kansas City, Kansas, via the "Katy Railroad Line," but he was certain that it was several months prior to October 6, 1963, when his Mexican tourist card would have expired.

By writing down the dates of trips made during 1963, he was able to recall that on or about October 2, 1963, he left San Miguel de Allende at 7:30 AM by "a second-class, yellow bus" for San Luis Potosi, where he arrived just before noon the same day.

At the Transportes del Norte bus station at San Luis Potosi he purchased a ticket straight through to San Antonio, Texas, because Transportes del Norte is affiliated with the Greyhound Bus Lines in the United States. He purchased a Greyhound bus ticket to San Antonio, Texas, which included transportation aboard a Transportes del Norte bus in Mexico. His travel to Nuevo Laredo was aboard a Transportes del Norte bus and from Laredo to San Antonio aboard a Greyhound bus.

After purchasing his ticket, he ate lunch and left San Luis Potosi on a Transportes del Norte bus at about 2:40 PM on October 2, 1963.

- 3 -

COMMISSION EXHIBIT No. 2460—Continued

He did not know his ticket number, could not recall if his name was registered on a passenger list, and did not know whether or not the bus he boarded had proceeded from Mexico, D. F., to San Luis Potosi. He saw the bus arrive at the bus station at San Luis Potosi but did not remember whether or not passengers were aboard.

He and other passengers boarded the bus at the Transportes del Norte bus station in San Luis Potosi. He assumed the bus he boarded was made up at this city because "it smelled clean." He stated he did not count them, but there were at least four passengers on the bus and probably several more. He did not notice any other Americans aboard the bus.

The bus arrived at Laredo, Texas, at approximately 2:00 AM, October 3, 1963. While aboard the bus at Nuevo Laredo, State of Tamaulipas, Mexico, he had inquired if it would be possible with his type of bus ticket to leave the bus at Laredo, Texas, and later proceed to San Antonio, Texas. He was told that he could take a Greyhound bus at any time later with the "Greyhound bus ticket" which he had purchased. He was emphatic that after he went through U. S. Customs and U. S. Immigration at Laredo, Texas, he reboarded the bus and, at his request, was allowed to disembark from the bus alone on one of the streets in Laredo in order that he could proceed to the Southland Hotel. He could not recall exactly where U. S. Customs and U. S. Immigration are located in Laredo. After resting at the Southland Hotel, he went to the Greyhound bus depot in Laredo that same day and boarded a Greyhound bus, using his through ticket to San Antonio, Texas.

He was very certain that the bus stopped in Mexico at about 1:00 AM on October 3, 1963, at the "Mexican Immigration check station about twelve miles from the Mexican-American border," the lights in the bus were turned on, and a Mexican Immigration official boarded the bus to check each passenger's identification and travel documents.

VOORHEES First Notices American

At this point the Mexican Immigration official ushered a young American man off the bus. This was the first

time VOORHEES realized an American was on the bus. He described the American as about 20 years of age, five feet nine inches tall, not heavy, of medium build, clean-shaven, bareheaded, coatless, and cleanly attired in shirt, slacks, and shoes. VOORHEES recalled that he had considered the American lightly clad, since he did not wear a coat during the cool night. VOORHEES repeatedly stated "he was not a beatnik." The American was carrying one small bag, either a zipper bag or a small duffel bag. VOORHEES was unable to describe the exact type of bag but was certain the American did not have a suitcase.

VOORHEES was certain he sat on the right side of the bus because he habitually sits on the right side, looking forward. He remembered that he did not sit toward the front or back but somewhere in the middle of the bus.

During the trip VOORHEES talked with a "Mexican-American" man who sat across the aisle from him. The Mexican-American, whom he remembered as a middle-aged, thin-faced man who spoke both English and Spanish well, said he was going to the United States, but VOORHEES could recall neither his destination nor his name. The Mexican-American was traveling on the bus with his wife and VOORHEES believed he was returning to "his business" in the United States. He gave the impression of being very nervous, smoking one cigarette after another. VOORHEES did not know whether the Mexican-American is a Mexican or a United States citizen. During the trip VOORHEES discussed with the Mexican-American the fact that he, VOORHEES, is a commercial artist.

When the American was taken off the bus, he was taken from the back of the bus to the front, and the Mexican-American remarked to VOORHEES that the American was having trouble over his papers. VOORHEES remembered clearly that when the young American was taken off the bus most of the passengers on the bus were sleeping, and he also recalled that at the beginning of the trip at San Luis Potosi there was some sort of discussion between a Mexican woman and the driver of the bus with regard to a seat number. He could describe neither the Mexican woman nor the bus driver. He was certain that he was not acquainted with anyone aboard the bus.

He recalled that, when the American returned to the bus and walked to the back of it, he mumbled in good English, in a grumbling manner, something like, "My papers were in order before and I don't know why they bother me now - they took my pass before." This was the first time VOORHEES had noticed the American, and he could not state when the latter first boarded the bus. He had the impression the American could not speak Spanish and presumed the American was taken off the bus to the "check station office" where someone must have spoken to him in English.

He clearly recalled seeing the American at the U. S. Customs checking station in Laredo, Texas, at about 1:30 AM, October 3, 1963, when a Mexican woman's luggage was being examined and the young American was standing by. The American was trying to dispose of a banana by eating it hurriedly, "gulping it down," and he was told by a Customs officer that he could carry the banana into the United States and did not have to gulp it down so fast.

When asked if he had talked with or been near the American, VOORHEES stated he was not near the young American at any time during the bus trip or while checking through U. S. Customs at Laredo.

VOORHEES did not recall seeing the American again after he saw him at the U. S. Customs checking station in Laredo and could only presume that the American returned to the bus when all passengers left the checking station and reboarded the bus. VOORHEES left the bus at Laredo by himself when the bus driver let him off on an unknown street with an unscheduled stop at about 2:00 AM, October 3, 1963. He believed that all other passengers remained on the bus until it reached its scheduled destination, which he presumed to be the Greyhound bus depot in Laredo.

After refreshing his recollection about the bus trip from San Luis Potosi to Nuevo Laredo, he was certain the bus arrived at Monterrey, State of Nuevo Leon, Mexico, at about 11:00 PM on October 2, 1963, and all passengers had to change to a smaller bus of the same bus line, Transportes del Norte, to proceed to Nuevo Laredo. He did not see the American

- 6 -

COMMISSION EXHIBIT No. 2460—Continued

during this change of buses and did not recall seeing him prior to the "check station stop at the 26 kilometer point before arrival at Nuevo Laredo." He believed that some passengers other than those who traveled from San Luis Potosi had boarded the bus at Monterrey, but was not certain of this.

When shown a photograph of OSWALD among other photographs, he immediately recognized the photograph and exclaimed that this was a photograph of OSWALD. When asked how he knew this to be so, he stated he has been a commercial artist all his life, is a member of the Academy of Fine Arts in Chicago, Illinois, and can recognize a face.

He repeated that he was unable to conclude definitely that the young American aboard the bus was OSWALD, stating he could not be positive, but he affirmed strongly that the American was "the same general type" as OSWALD. VOORHEES then said, "How do you like _that_, if _that_ was OSWALD on _that_ bus and I didn't know it."

When shown a full-length, front-view photograph of OSWALD, he immediately exclaimed that the young American was "about the same size, the same type, and it seems to be _him_," but VOORHEES would not state positively that the young American was OSWALD, pointing out that he could not make a definite identification of someone he saw only momentarily several months earlier. He was emphatic that there was every similarity between the photographs shown to him and his recollection of the young American aboard the bus but he would not be more definite in connection therewith. He expressed the wish that he had been more observant of the young American on the bus.

He attempted to recall other details about the trip to assist in determining whether or not the young American was identical with OSWALD, but he was unable to do so. He stated that, if he were able to recall any other possible details with regard to the above, he would contact the source.

He could not recall any further details of his trip and the young American and was apologetic for not being able to do so. He stated that, if the incident regarding the

- 7 -

COMMISSION EXHIBIT No. 2460—Continued

young American at the "Mexican Immigration check station" had happened during the day, he would have sketched the young American's face, as he generally does when there is an incident, and, had he done so, others could have decided whether or not the young American was identical with OSWALD.

Addresses For VOORHEES

VOORHEES explained that on this occasion he took the bus to make desirable train connections to Kansas City, Kansas, traveling by train from San Antonio, Texas, to Kansas City and from there to the home of his daughter, Mrs. NANCY M. TOUHY, 886 West Army Trail Road, Addison, Illinois, 60101. Upon his return to the United States, he visits his daughter and can be located through her at any time.

He advised that when he is at San Miguel de Allende he can be reached by telephone during the day through RODOLFO PEREZ R., owner of the Auto Mercado Super Market, telephone number 33, which is located next door to Calle Masones No. 19, San Miguel de Allende, State of Guanajuato, Mexico, and he utilizes Post Office Box No. 200, San Miguel de Allende, for receipt of mail.

Efforts to Identity Other Passengers

VOORHEES could not identify photographs of JOHN BOWEN, also known as ALBERT OSBORNE. (JOHN BOWEN was a passenger aboard a bus operated by "Servicios Unidos Autobuses Blancos, Flecha Roja, S. A. de C. V." (The Unified Services of White Autobuses Red Arrow, Incorporated) on which OSWALD traveled from Laredo, Texas, to Mexico, D. F., on September 26-27, 1963.)

VOORHEES also was unable to identify the photographs of JUAN MATEO DE CUBA and ADA FRANCISCA BISLIP DE DE CUBA. (JUAN MATEO DE CUBA and his wife, ADA FRANCISCA BISLIP DE DE CUBA, were among the "aliens" who surrendered their tourist cards to Mexican Immigration upon their departure from Mexico at Nuevo Laredo on October 3, 1963, between 12:00 midnight and 8:00 AM.)

According to VOORHEES, the Mexican-American he talked with aboard the bus en route to Nuevo Laredo had a thinner face than that of JUAN MATEO DE CUBA.

The names of the following individuals on the passenger list of Bus No. 340 of the "Transportes Frontera, S. A. de C. V.," bus line for October 2, 1963, were exhibited to VOORHEES and he was unable to recognize any of these names as persons he might know:

FCO. SAUCEDO
OSWLD (OSWALD)
Sra. LANDEROS
ANDRIAN HERNANDEZ
JUANA
ANGEL GALLEGOS
Sra. MORALES
NICOLAS GONZALEZ
RAFAEL FLORES
GAUTIER ? (GANSTINE)
ANGEL PEREZ
ANTONIO CAZAREZ
Sra. AGUILAR
Sra. FRANCO
CONSTANTINO GARCIA
ELIASAR GONZALEZ
CONSTANTINO GARCIA
YNIGNES (INIQUEZ)

As noted above, the FM-5 No. 4325846 Mexican tourist card issued to VOORHEES has the word "tren" (train) typed toward the top, which must have been typed on this form when VOORHEES entered Mexico by train with this card, as he states he did.

The foregoing information from VOORHEES fully clarifies that he departed from Mexico on October 3, 1963, via a Transportes del Norte bus, and the FM-11 data to the effect that his exit from Mexico was by train is in error. This is further verified by the fact that Mexican Immigration employee ALBERTO ARZAMENDI CHAPA, who handled VOORHEES' departure, was at the Kilometer 26 highway checking station during his tour of duty from 12:00 midnight to 8:00 AM on October 3, 1963, and not at a railroad station.

An examination of the March, 1964, issue of the Mexican "Guia de Transportes Aereo y Autotransportes de Mexico" (Guide for Air Travel and Automobile Transportation in Mexico), which is described as the "official publication in Spanish of airline and automobile bus schedules in Mexico," reflects on page nineteen that Transportes del Norte, which connects with Greyhound Lines, Union Bus Lines, Missouri Pacific Lines, and Winter Garden Bus Lines, between Canada and the United States and Mexico, has bus terminals located at Insurgentes No. 137 Sur, Mexico, D. F., and Juan Mendez No. 1355, Monterrey, Nuevo Leon, Mexico. This guide further reflects bus schedule No. 18 for "Mexico-Guadalajara-San Luis Potosi-Monterrey-Torreon, via Central (highway)," with daily departures of Transportes del Norte buses from Mexico, D. F. From a review thereof, it appears that VOORHEES must have traveled aboard the bus which follows the schedule recorded on page nineteen of the above guide and is copied hereinunder:

Leave Mexico, D. F., 8:30 AM

Arrive San Juan del Rio, Mexico, 10:45 AM
Leave San Juan del Rio, Mexico, 10:45 AM

Arrive Queretaro, Mexico, 11:25 AM
Leave Queretaro, Mexico, 11:25 AM

Arrive San Luis Potosi, Mexico, 2:00 PM
Leave San Luis Potosi, Mexico, 2:20 PM

Arrive Matehuala, Mexico, 4:45 PM
Leave Matehuala, Mexico, 4:45 PM

Arrive Saltillo, Mexico, 7:55 PM
Leave Saltillo, Mexico, 8:00 PM

Arrive Monterrey, Mexico, 9:30 PM
Leave Monterrey, Mexico, 10:00 PM

Arrive Nuevo Laredo, Mexico, 1:30 AM

The foregoing passenger list of Bus No. 340 of the "Transportes Frontera, S. A. de C. V.," bus line for October 2, 1963, was exhibited to VOORHEES for the purpose of establishing that he was correct in his statement that he traveled via Transportes del Norte bus line and that he was not confused with travel on a Transportes Frontera bus line. JUAN MATEO DE CUBA and ADA FRANCISCA BISLIP DE DE CUBA had been interviewed previously and recalled a "young American" who traveled with them on the bus and who had experienced some trouble making himself intelligible to a Mexican border official. They had stated that they believed their travel was by a Transportes Frontera bus, although subsequent inquiry established that they had traveled on the same Transportes del Norte bus as VOORHEES.

The confidential source abroad advised that on March 30, 1964, VOORHEES furnished the following additional data by telephone from San Miguel de Allende:

He was unable to recognize the following names of tourists who departed from Mexico at Nuevo Laredo on October 3, 1963, as being identical with the Mexican-American and wife who were aboard the bus with him:

AGAPITO DEL RIO
MANUEL CAPIZ
GUADALUPE CAPIZ
LAWRENCE LOPEZ
MARIA LUISA CRUZ DE LOPEZ
SALVADOR SEGOBIANO
MARIA SEGOBIANO
ROBERTO BALDAZO
DOLORES BALDAZO ROMERO
ROBERT L. TARIN
ELISABETH TARIN

He stated he had tried to recall the Mexican-American's name and had been unable to do so. He described him as being in his late fifties, tall, slender, and very well-dressed and his wife as also being very well-dressed.

OFFICE OF THE DIRECTOR

UNITED STATES DEPARTMENT OF JUSTICE
FEDERAL BUREAU OF INVESTIGATION
WASHINGTON, D.C.

July 1, 1964

BY COURIER SERVICE

Honorable J. Lee Rankin
General Counsel
The President's Commission
200 Maryland Avenue, N. E.
Washington, D. C.

Dear Mr. Rankin:

There are enclosed two copies each of two memoranda dated June 23, 1964, concerning Mexican aspects of the Lee Harvey Oswald investigation.

Upon detachment from the enclosures, this letter may be regarded as unclassified.

Sincerely yours,

J. Edgar Hoover

Enclosures (4)

COMMISSION EXHIBIT No. 2461

UNITED STATES DEPARTMENT OF JUSTICE
FEDERAL BUREAU OF INVESTIGATION

In Reply, Please Refer to
File No.

WASHINGTON 25, D. C.

June 23, 1964

LEE HARVEY OSWALD

BASIS FOR INQUIRY

As has been previously reported, OSWALD, using the name of H. O. LEE, is believed to have departed Mexico City at 8:30 AM on October 2, 1963, on bus No. 332 of a bus line called "Autobuses Transportes del Norte" (hereinafter referred to as Transportes del Norte). In Monterrey, Nuevo Leon, Mexico, passengers on bus No. 332 who were continuing on to Nuevo Laredo, Tamaulipas, Mexico, and Laredo, Texas, transferred to Transportes del Norte bus No. 373, which was driven by ALVARO IBARRA.

Notations on the trip envelope for bus No. 373 showed that twelve passengers had boarded the bus in Monterrey with a final destination of either Nuevo Laredo or Laredo and that one passenger boarded the bus in Nuevo Laredo for Laredo. When the trip envelope was located at the Transportes del Norte headquarters in Monterrey, Nuevo Leon, Mexico, it was found to contain a total of twenty tickets, ten covering travel from Monterrey to Laredo, nine for travel from Monterrey to Nuevo Laredo, and one for travel from Nuevo Laredo to Laredo.

When interviewed in Nuevo Laredo concerning the discrepancy between the notations appearing on the trip envelope and the actual number of tickets contained in the envelope, ALVARO IBARRA stated that the only explanation he could offer was that tickets from some other trip were intermingled with tickets of bus No. 373 for the trip from Monterrey to Laredo on October 2-3, 1963. He explained that, if the date stamps on the back of the tickets which were in the envelope correspond with the date stamps on the front of the trip envelope, then he, IBARRA, made an error in recording the number of tickets inside the trip envelope. He alleged that all tickets in the trip envelope should bear on the backs of the tickets a stamp similar to the one appearing on the trip envelope itself. The purpose of this inquiry was to establish whether this latter statement of IBARRA is correct.

COMMISSION EXHIBIT No. 2461—Continued

INTERVIEW OF RAMON TREVINO QUEZADA,
VICE PRESIDENT AND GENERAL MANAGER
OF TRANSPORTES DEL NORTE,
MONTERREY, NUEVO LEON, MEXICO

When interviewed by a confidential source abroad on June 16, 1964, RAMON TREVINO QUEZADA, Vice President and General Manager of Transportes del Norte, Monterrey, Nuevo Leon, Mexico, advised that each Transportes del Norte bus ticket is date stamped on the reverse side by the ticket agent to reflect the date on which the ticket was actually sold. He said the date stamp on the ticket may or may not reflect the date on which the ticket was utilized. He pointed out that often tickets are purchased several days before travel is performed in order to insure that the passengers will have seats on the particular date on which they desire to travel.

According to TREVINO, the trip envelope in which the bus driver places the tickets collected by him is also date stamped. He explained that the date stamp on the trip envelope ordinarily reflects the actual date of travel and that the date stamps appearing on the tickets themselves quite often will be different from the date stamp on the trip envelope in which they are placed.

COMMISSION EXHIBIT No. 2461—Continued

UNITED STATES DEPARTMENT OF JUSTICE
FEDERAL BUREAU OF INVESTIGATION

In Reply, Please Refer to
File No.

WASHINGTON 25, D. C.

June 23, 1964

LEE HARVEY OSWALD

BASIS FOR INQUIRY

As has been previously reported, investigation disclosed that one H. O. LEE, believed to be identical with OSWALD, departed Mexico City at 8:30 AM on October 2, 1963, on bus No. 332 of a bus line called "Autobuses Transportes del Norte" (hereinafter referred to as Transportes del Norte). A total of sixteen passengers, including LEE, boarded the bus in Mexico City with destinations of Monterrey, Nuevo Leon, Mexico; Nuevo Laredo, Tamaulipas, Mexico; Laredo, Texas; and points beyond. Ten additional passengers boarded the same bus in San Luis Potosi, State of San Luis Potosi, Mexico.

Among the passengers who boarded the bus at San Luis Potosi were MAXIMINO ESQUIVEL, CECILIO CARDENAZ, PEDRO GONZALEZ, and JOSE CRUZ.

INTERVIEW OF MAXIMINO ESQUIVEL LIMON

On June 14, 1964, MAXIMINO ESQUIVEL LIMON, Amado Nervo No. 2454 Norte, Colonia Bella Vista, Monterrey, Nuevo Leon, Mexico, furnished the following information to a confidential source abroad:

He is a welder. In late September, 1963, he and three friends, CECILIO CARDENAS, PEDRO GONZALEZ, and JOSE CRUZ, all welders from Monterrey, went to Uruapan, Michoacan, Mexico, to seek employment. They were unsuccessful in obtaining work there and started back to Monterrey via Guadalajara, Jalisco, Mexico.

COMMISSION EXHIBIT No. 2461—Continued

On approximately October 2, 1963, ESQUIVEL and his three friends left Guadalajara on a bus of a company called "Camiones Azules" (Blue Buses) bound for San Luis Potosi. Upon arrival in the latter place they transferred to a Transportes del Norte bus which stopped there en route to Monterrey from Mexico City. It was his recollection that the bus left San Luis Potosi at approximately 11:00 AM.

ESQUIVEL observed only two Americans on the Transportes del Norte bus. One was an elderly lady and the other was a young man, about twenty-five years of age, thin build, and having dark hair. The two Americans did not appear to be traveling together, but ESQUIVEL observed that they conversed in English from time to time. The young man appeared to have been assigned a seat in front of the one assigned to the woman. (From investigation previously conducted it would appear that the elderly American woman is possibly identical with MARGARET A. WOLFF, a passenger on the Transportes del Norte bus from Mexico City to Monterrey on October 2, 1963.)

ESQUIVEL did not know the identity of either of the Americans. He stated the young American man resembled the person appearing in photographs of LEE HARVEY OSWALD which were displayed to him, but he could not state definitely that the two were identical.

INTERVIEW OF CECILIO CARDENAS MENDEZ

On June 15, 1964, the confidential source abroad interviewed CECILIO CARDENAS MENDEZ, Porfirio Diaz No. 716 Sur, Monterrey, Nuevo Leon, Mexico, who furnished the following information:

Late in September, 1963, CARDENAS and three friends from Monterrey traveled to Uruapan, Michoacan, Mexico, to seek employment as welders. His three friends were identified as MAXIMINO ESQUIVEL LIMON, PEDRO GONZALEZ YERENA, and JOSE CRUZ CUELLAR. Unsuccessful in their efforts to obtain employment, they decided to return to Monterrey, stopping at Guadalajara en route.

About October 2, 1963, the four departed Guadalajara for San Luis Potosi on a bus of the company called "Camiones

Azules." Arriving in San Luis Potosi, they transferred to a Transportes del Norte bus which was en route to Monterrey from Mexico City. It was his recollection that this bus left San Luis Potosi at about 11:00 AM.

CARDENAS noticed there were two Americans on the Transportes del Norte bus, an elderly lady and a young man. The lady appeared to be about sixty years of age, and the young man was about five feet ten inches in height, had brown hair, wore dark glasses, and appeared to be about twenty-eight years of age.

The lady appeared to be restless and walked up and down the aisle of the bus, occasionally occupying a seat at the rear of the bus where there was more room. She was observed conversing from time to time in English with the young man, who occupied a seat in front of the one designated for the lady. CARDENAS and his friends had boarded the bus with a bottle of tequila, and he recalled that one of his companions offered the lady a drink. She refused the drink, but appeared to be very amused at their antics.

At Matehuala, San Luis Potosi, Mexico, the bus made a stop. Both the lady and the young man were observed by CARDENAS to leave the bus and enter the bus station. In addition to his dark glasses, which he did not remove at any time, the young man wore on his head a dark, narrow-brimmed, felt hat as he left the bus. He was observed going into and coming out of the men's rest room in the bus station. The young man and the lady reboarded the bus before it left Matehuala for Monterrey.

CARDENAS and his companions terminated their trip at Monterrey, and he did not again observe either the young man or the lady.

According to CARDENAS, photographs of LEE HARVEY OSWALD displayed to him resembled the young man he observed on the bus, but he could not positively identify the young man as OSWALD.

CARDENAS stated PEDRO GONZALEZ YERENA is presently employed with "Petroleos Mexicanos" (Mexican Petroleum Company)

at Coatzacoalcos, Veracruz, Mexico, under a foreman named CARLOS GARZA. He believes that JOSE CRUZ CUELLAR is presently employed with "Celulosa de Chihuahua" (Chihuahua Celulose Company) in Chihuahua, State of Chihuahua, Mexico, where the company is constructing a thermoelectric plant.

-4-

COMMISSION EXHIBIT No. 2461—Continued

1

DL 89-43
RPG/rms

Under date of December 2, 1963, the FBI Laboratory advised as follows:

Specimens received 12/1/63 from FBI, San Antonio

Qc68 Eleven photocopies of Texas State Comptroller warrants issued to Lee H. Oswald further identified as follows:

WARRANT NUMBER	WARRANT DATE
F 819610	8/21/63
G 231213	8/7/63
G 246347	8/9/63
G 281852	8/16/63
G 323653	8/26/63
G 353037	9/3/63
G 386726	9/6/63
G 421381	9/13/63
G 459698	9/23/63
G 493187	10/1/63
G 532220	10/8/63

Qc69 Seventeen photocopies of Texas Employment Commission folder forms further identified as follows:

FORM	DATE
TEC B-3 (163)	4/12/63
LA 1B-1	4/29/63
LA 1B-14	4/29/63 (at bottom)

COMMISSION EXHIBIT No. 2462

2
DL 89-43
RFG/rms

FORM	DATE
LA 1B-2	5/7/63
LA 1B-10	4/26/63
LA 1B-2	5/15/63
LA 1B-1	7/22/63
LA 1B-2	7/30/63
LA 1B-10	7/21/__
LA 1B-2	8/6/63
LA 1B-2	8/13/63
LA 1B-2	8/20/63
LA 1B-2	8/27/63
LA 1B-2	9/3/63
LA 1B-2	9/10/63
LA 1B-2	9/17/63
LA 1B-2	9/24/63

Qc70 Photocopies of two Texas Claim cards Form B-4, one dated 10/3/63 and the other dated 10/10/63

Result of examination:

It was concluded that LEE HARVEY OSWALD, K4 and K5 in this case, wrote the signatures and endorsements on Qc68 through Qc70 except no conclusion was reached with respect to the warrants in Qc68 dated 8/9/63, 8/26/63, 9/3/63, 9/13/63, 9/23/63, 10/1/63 and on the LA Forms 1B-2 in Qc69 dated 8/27/63 and 9/3/63 which are too indistinct for an adequate handwriting comparison.

1

DL 89-43

Under date of December 2, 1963, the FBI Laboratory advised as follows:

"Specimens received 12/2/63 from New Orleans

"Qc71 Two Xerox copies of an Application for Tourist Card to Visit Mexico, number 987, in the name Lee Harvey Oswald, dated September 17, 1963

"ALSO SUBMITTED: Film pack containing six exposures of Qc71

"Result of examination:

It was concluded that Qc71 (excluding the numerals in the upper right corner '987' and '24085') was written by Lee Harvey Oswald, K4 and K5 in this case."

FD-302 (Rev. 1-25-60)

FEDERAL BUREAU OF INVESTIGATION

Date December 13, 1963

Records of Flecha Roja (Red Arrow) Bus Line, Nuevo Laredo, Mexico, contain a baggage guide list or baggage manifest (Guia De Equipajes) dated September 26, 1963, Nuevo Laredo, Mexico, for Red Arrow Bus Line No. 516, reflecting this bus departed Nuevo Laredo, Mexico, at 2:15 p.m. en route to Monterrey, Mexico, and Mexico City. The driver of the bus was listed as ROBERTO MORALES. This manifest disclosed that 18 passengers boarded this bus at Nuevo Laredo, Mexico, on September 26, 1963, and that 6 of the 18 passengers were en route to Monterrey, Mexico, and 12 were en route to Mexico City. This list is set out as follows:

Seat No.-Person-Destination	Baggage Claim Check	Type of Baggage	Customs Check
1 PABLO VASQUEZ Mexico City	#257512	Veliz	Marked
2 Line drawn through space indicating either wife or other person traveling with VASQUEZ.-Mexico City	#257513	"	"
3 S. MORAN Mexico City	#257580	"	"
4 ALFREDO BRESENO Mexico City	257577	"	"
5 ROIG SORQUIS Mexico City	#257578	"	"
6 T. GONZALEZ Mexico City	#257579	"	7318060
7 ANDRES MORALES Monterrey	#257575	"	Marked
8 Line drawn through space indicating either wife or other person traveling with MORALES-Monterrey	#257574	Caja (box)	"

10

On 12/6/63 at Nuevo Laredo, Mexico File # SA 105-2909

by SA ROBERT L. CHAPMAN / njs Date dictated 12/13/63

This document contains neither recommendations nor conclusions of the FBI. It is the property of the FBI and is loaned to your agency; it and its contents are not to be distributed outside your agency.

COMMISSION EXHIBIT No. 2463

2.

SA 105-2909

9 APE. MARTINEZ-Monterrey	#257576	Veliz	Marked
10 (FNU) BOWEN-Mexico City	#320438	Maletin (small handbag)	"
11 HARRY J. MITCHELL-Monterrey	#320200	"	"
12 Line drawn through space indicating wife or other person travelling with MITCHELL.-Monterrey	#320202	Veliz	"
13 Line drawn through space indicating wife or other person travelling with MITCHELL-Monterrey	#320201	"	"
14 LEE H. OSWALT-Mexico City	#320435	"	"
15 (FNU) BOWEN-Mexico City	#320441	"	"
16 Line drawn through space indicating wife or other person travelling with BOWEN-Mexico City	#320440	"	"
17 JOHN MC FARLAND-Mexico City	7317276	"	"
18 Line drawn through space indicating wife or person travelling with MC FARLAND-Mexico City	#7317277	"	"

Mexican Customs Inspector of baggage into Mexico indicated on bus manifest as "marked" when luggage or veliz contained clothing and articles of small value. Whenever

11

COMMISSION EXHIBIT No. 2463—Continued

3.

luggage contained clothing or other articles of great value, it was given a customs inspection number for entry into Mexico, thus accounting for the customs inspection numbers as opposed to customs mark of luggage.

12

COMMISSION EXHIBIT No. 2463—Continued

FD-302 (Rev. 1-25-60)

FEDERAL BUREAU OF INVESTIGATION

1.

Date December 13, 1963

GILBERTO CAZARES GARZA, Chief of Mexican Immigration, advised that his records reflect the cancellation of a tourist permit numberFM 8625156, on October 3, 1963, issued to HOMER VAUHAN.

Inasmuch as VAUHAN did not enter Mexico by auto, GARZA stated that his records do not show where or when VAUHAN entered Mexico, and therefore, does not have information reflecting where VAUHAN obtained his tourist card in the United States.

He stated that this information; however, could be obtained from Gobernacion, in Mexico City.

13

On 12/10/63 at Nuevo Laredo, Mexico File # SA 105-2909

by SA LEOPOLDO E. ARMIJO/jmb Date dictated 12/11/63

COMMISSION EXHIBIT No. 2463—Continued

FD-302 (Rev. 1-25-60)

FE[illegible]RAL BUREAU OF INVESTIGATION

1.

Date December 13, 1963

VERNON KLEIN was interviewed at Aaronson Bros. Store, Laredo, Texas, and stated that he resides at 1734 Carthage Street, Brownsville, Texas.

He is District Supervisor for Aaronson Bros. He stated that he went to Monterrey, Mexico, on September 26, 1963, by automobile and entered Mexico, by way of Laredo, Texas, and Nuevo Laredo, Mexico.

He crossed the border into Mexico at Laredo, Texas, about 5:00 p.m. on September 26, 1963.

Upon viewing a photograph of LEE HARVEY OSWALD, he stated that he has never seen this individual in Mexico or any other place.

14

On 12/11/63 at Laredo, Texas File # SA 105-2909

by SA LEOPOLDO E. ARMIJO/jmb Date dictated 12/11/63

This document contains neither recommendations nor conclusions of the FBI. It is the property of the FBI and is loaned to your agency; it and its contents are not to be distributed outside your agency.

COMMISSION EXHIBIT No. 2463—Continued

FD-302 (Rev. 1-25-60)

FEDERAL BUREAU OF INVESTIGATION

Date 12/12/63

1

JOSEPH HARRISON BIRD, residence Box 289, Devine, Texas, was located at his place of employment, S. X. Callahan Company, San Antonio, Texas. Mr. BIRD stated he went through Nuevo Laredo, Mexico, on September 26, 1963, alone, by automobile, en route to Mexico, D. F. He stated that on this trip he saw no one who reminded him of LEE HARVEY OSWALD and prior to having seen photographs of OSWALD on television, following the assassination of the President, he could not recall ever having seen him before.

15

On 12/6/63 at San Antonio, Texas File # SA 105-2909

by SA JOHN RUSSELL GRAHAM eks Date dictated 12/11/63

This document contains neither recommendations nor conclusions of the FBI. It is the property of the FBI and is loaned to your agency; it and its contents are not to be distributed outside your agency.

COMMISSION EXHIBIT No. 2463—Continued

1

SA 105-2909

The following investigation was conducted by Special Agent TOM E. NEAL:

AT SAN ANTONIO, TEXAS:

On December 4, 1963, the following employees of Braniff Airways, Inc., International Airport, San Antonio, were shown a photograph of LEE HARVEY OSWALD. They were unable to identify OSWALD as ever having been a customer or ever having approached the ticket counter of Braniff Airways:

GLENN M. HEDRICK, agent in charge, ticket counter, who worked from 6:30 a.m. to 3:00 p.m., October 2 and 3, 1963;
Mrs. ILEANA ESPARZA, ticket counter, who worked from 10:00 a.m. to 6:30 p.m., October 2, 1963;
JOHN WILLIAMS, agent in charge, ticket counter, normally off duty October 2 and 3, 1963, but could have been at the counter;
R. L. STREET, ticket counter, who worked from 10:00 a.m. to 6:30 p.m., October 3, 1963;
LOU ARMSTRONG, ticket counter, who worked from 6:00 a.m. to 2:30 p.m., October 2 and 3, 1963;
JAMES CARROLL, who worked from 5:00 a.m. to 1:30 p.m., October 3, 1963;
ALLAN STAHLE, ticket counter, who worked from 5:00 a.m. to 1:30 p.m., October 2, 1963;
WAYNE FRAZIER, ticket counter, who worked midnight, October 1, 1963, to 8:30 a.m., October 2, 1963;
DAVID STEWART, ticket counter, who worked 3:00 a.m., to 11:30 p.m., October 2 and 3, 1963;
RICHARD CHAPMAN, ticket counter, who worked midnight to 8:30 a.m., October 2 and 3, 1963;
ROBERT BLOHM, ticket counter, who worked from 6:30 a.m. to 3:00 p.m., October 2 and 3, 1963;
GENE M. DAVIS, agent in charge, who worked from 2:30 p.m. to 4:00 p.m., October 2 and 3, 1963;
BUELL WELBORN, ticket counter, who worked from 4:00 p.m. to 12:30 a.m., October 2 and 3, 1963;
ROBERT D. HOPKINS, ticket counter, who worked from 2:30 p.m. to 11:00 p.m., October 2 and 3, 1963;
ROBERT KERN, ticket counter, who worked 3:00 p.m. to 11:30 p.m., October 2 and 3, 1963.

16

COMMISSION EXHIBIT No. 2463—Continued

2

SA 105-2909

Mr. GLENN M. HEDRICK, agent in charge of the ticket counter, advised that JAMES BRAYMEN who works at the counter from 6:30 a.m. to 3:00 p.m. was on leave and would return to duty December 8, 1963. He furnished his telephone number as OL 5-1794. He stated further that ROBERT ROESLER formerly worked at the ticket counter and was employed there on October 2 and 3, 1963, but had been transferred to JAMTO at Fort Sam Houston, telephone TA 6-5369. He further advised that WILLIAM LINDERMAN who is employed at the ticket counter whose hours are from 10:30 a.m. to 7:00 p.m. was on leave and would return to duty December 9, 1963. He stated that he believed LINDERMAN may be in Minneapolis and that R. L. STREET, one of the ticket counter men, would probably be able to furnish information where LINDERMAN, who is a single man, might be located.

R. L. STREET advised that LINDERMAN's parents have the same name and reside at Dysart, Iowa, and that LINDERMAN was going to visit his parents and go pheasant hunting and from there he was going to Minneapolis. Mr. STREET stated he felt sure that if LINDERMAN could not be located at his parents' home that he could be located through a close friend nicknamed "WHITEY" who is employed by Braniff Airways at Minneapolis, Minnesota.

Mr. W. S. CLARK, Manager, American Airlines, San Antonio International Airport, on December 4, 1963, was shown a photograph of LEE HARVEY OSWALD, and he stated it was not identifiable with anyone he had ever seen at the American Airlines ticket counter. Mr. CLARK stated that R. J. DISHMAN who works at the ticket counter, and W. D. UNGER, a supervisor who also works at the ticket counter at times, were on a deer hunt in west Texas and would not return to work until December 9, 1963. He stated that Mr. DISHMAN's wife would probably know where they could be located. He stated that all other employees were available.

On December 5, 1963, Mrs. JAMES BRAYMEN was contacted at telephone OL 5-1794, and she stated that her husband, who is a ticket agent for Braniff Airways, was in Dallas and she did not know how to locate him but he would return to San Antonio on December 5, 1963, and would report for duty at Braniff on Sunday, December 8, 1963.

17

COMMISSION EXHIBIT No. 2463—Continued

Mr. JOHN H. McLEAN, Station Manager, Trans-Texas Airways, International Airport, San Antonio, advised on December 5, 1963, that he was on duty October 2 and 3, 1963, and occasionally works the ticket counter. He was shown a photograph of LEE HARVEY OSWALD and stated it was not identifiable with any person whom he had ever seen at the airport.

Mr. McLEAN stated that they keep a record of the names of persons who make reservations for flights on their airlines, which includes nearly all of their customers; however, he stated that at times a customer will purchase a ticket shortly before plane departure time and, in such instances, a card is not made on this person, and in such cases, the original copy of the ticket which is known as "auditor's coupon" is mailed directly to their General Accounting Office at Houston, Texas. This ticket will show the passenger's last name.

Mr. McLEAN stated that their office is open from 5:00 a.m. to about 1:00 a.m. The following employees of Trans-Texas Airways who work the ticket counter were shown a photograph of LEE HARVEY OSWALD on December 5, 1963, and they stated that he was not identifiable with any person whom they had ever seen:

OTIS PATTILLO, who worked 7:30 a.m. to 4:30 p.m., October 2, and 3, 1963;
BILLIE BUSCH, who worked 7:30 a.m. to 4:30 p.m., October 2 and 3, 1963;
WILLIAM B. KORNRUM, also operations agent, who worked from 2:15 p.m. to 11:15 p.m., October 2 and 3, 1963;
MICKEY AMACKER (did not work October 2 and 3, 1963);
A. F. SHADROCK, Chief Ticket Agent, day shift;
GIL BROSCH, who worked October 2 and 3, 1963.

On December 5, 1963, Mr. A. E. NOVAK, Station Manager, Braniff Airways, Inc., advised that their flight manifests are destroyed after sixty days. The October manifests will be destroyed December 31, 1963, and the November manifests will be destroyed January 31, 1964. Mr. NOVAK was requested to retain the flight

manifests to be turned over to the San Antonio Federal Bureau of Investigation, and he advised that he would do so.

Mr. TOM QUINLAN, Reservations Manager, Braniff Airways, Inc., on December 5, 1963, made available the flight manifests for October 2, 1963, of flights leaving San Antonio on that day for Dallas, Texas. These manifests were searched for the names LEE HARVEY OSWALD, also known as ALEK JAMES HIDELL, and L. H. LEE, and MARINA OSWALD. These names did not appear on manifests for the following flights on October 2, 1963:

Flight No.	Leaves San Antonio	Arrives Dallas
542	11:40 p.m.	12:27 a.m. (October 3, 1963)
40	5:00 p.m.	5:47 p.m.
50	6:35 p.m.	7:23 p.m.
110	1:15 p.m.	2:45 p.m.
564	9:00 p.m.	10:30 p.m.
154	4:00 p.m.	4:56 p.m.
232	10:10 p.m.	11:55 p.m.
8	7:00 a.m.	7:45 a.m.
392	8:30 a.m.	10:39 a.m.
50	6:35 p.m.	7:23 p.m.

Mr. W. S. CLARK, Manager, American Airlines, San Antonio International Airport, advised they have one flight to Dallas which leaves San Antonio at 11:05 a.m. and arrives Dallas, Texas, 11:52 a.m.

The following American Airlines ticket counter employees were shown a photograph of LEE HARVEY OSWALD

5

SA 105-2909

and they stated that he was not identifiable with any person who had ever been at their counter:

L. R. McBROOM, worked 7:30 a.m. to 4:15 p.m., October 2, 1963;
F. J. KAUPERT, worked 3:10 p.m., to 11:30 p.m., October 2 and 3, 1963;
BILL SETTLE, worked 7:30 a.m. to 4:15 p.m., October 3, 1963;
RAUL HORCASITAS, worked 2:15 p.m. to 11:00 p.m., October 2 and 3, 1963;
C. R. VILLAR, worked from 6:30 a.m. to 3:15 p.m., October 2 and 3, 1963.

On December 9, 1963, Mr. A. F. SHADROCK, Chief Agent, Trans-Texas Airways, International Airport, made available flight manifests of passengers leaving San Antonio for Dallas on October 2, 1963. A search of these records failed to identify OSWALD under his true name or aliases, or MARINA OSWALD.

R. A. ROESLER, Post Transportation, Fort Sam Houston, Building 370, Room 11, advised that he is on loan to the Army. He was on duty with Braniff Airways at the ticket counter, International Airport, on October 3, 1963. He was unable to identify the photograph of LEE HARVEY OSWALD as having contacted Braniff Airways.

Mr. JOHN LIVINGSTON, who is employed at the ticket counter, American Airlines, International Airport, advised that he worked the ticket counter from 2:15 p.m. to 11:00 p.m. on October 3, 1963. He was shown a photograph of LEE HARVEY OSWALD and was unable to identify him as having contacted the airlines.

On December 9, 1963, JAMES BRAYMEN, Braniff Airways, employed at the ticket counter, advised he was on duty from 6:00 a.m. to 2:30 p.m. on October 2 and 3, 1963. He was unable to identify OSWALD's photograph as having contacted the airlines office.

20

COMMISSION EXHIBIT No. 2463—Continued

On December 16, 1963, Mr. MAJOR GREEN, Manager, Continental Trailways Bus Lines, 1314 Tulane Avenue, New Orleans, furnished the following information to SAA JAMES E. SCHMIDT, JR.:

There are four separate buses leaving New Orleans for Houston, Texas. These buses can be identified from the schedule now in effect, which was also in effect during September, 1963. He advised the cost of a one-way ticket from New Orleans is $9.70 and a round-trip ticket costs $17.50.

The daily bus schedules in effect in September, 1963, from New Orleans to Houston, Texas, are as follows:

LEAVING NEW ORLEANS	ARRIVING HOUSTON
8:15 PM	7:00 AM (Next day)
4:40 PM	2:15 AM (Next day)
12:20 PM	10:50 PM (Same day)
6:00 AM	4:30 PM (Same day)

All bus operators leaving New Orleans can be identified through Mr. MAJOR GREEN, if necessary by his contacting the Trailways Alexandria Office.

12

COMMISSION EXHIBIT No. 2464

T-12 advised as follows:

On April 16, 1964, JULIO CASTRO, employee of the accounting department in the offices of the Flecha Roja bus line, Mexico, D. F., made available the ledger of arrivals at Mexico, D. F., for the Flecha Roja buses. The ledger records separate entries for each day, with the exact time of arrival of each bus in Mexico, D. F., at the terminal.

This ledger disclosed that bus No. 516 of the Flecha Roja bus line, which made the trip from Nuevo Laredo, to Mexico, D. F., on September 26-27, 1963, arrived at the Flecha Roja bus terminal, Heroes Ferrocarrileros No. 45, Mexico, D. F., at 10:00 a.m. on September 27, 1963.

106

COMMISSION EXHIBIT No. 2464—Continued

On November 26, 1963, T-14, a confidential source who has furnished reliable information in the past, advised that, following a check of the registration records of numerous middle and lower class hotels in the downtown area of Mexico City, he had ascertained that on September 27, 1963, LEE HARVEY OSWALD had registered at the Hotel del Comercio, located at Calle (Street) Bernardino de Sahagun No. 19 and approximately eight blocks from the commercial heart of the Mexican capital. The records disclosed that OSWALD was registered as the occupant of room No. 18 until October 1, 1963, and was deleted from the hotel guest list on October 2, 1963.

- 46 -

COMMISSION EXHIBIT No. 2464—Continued

According to source, there were only three employees at the hotel, and some of them were able to recognize OSWALD's photograph as having been a guest at that establishment but could recall virtually no information concerning the circumstances relating thereto.

1. OSWALD's Registration at Hotel

T-1 made available photocopies of the registration records of the Hotel del Comercio, Calle Bernardino de Sahagun No. 19, Mexico, D. F., which reflect that on September 27, 1963, OSWALD registered at that hotel as "LEE, HARVEY OSWALD, USA, Texas, PHOTO, US citizen" and was assigned room No. 18.

The owner and manager of the hotel, GUILLERMO GARCIA LUNA, explained on March 3, 1964, that upon arrival, a guest is required to register in his own handwriting; however, as long as he remains at the hotel thereafter, the name is transferred to the registration list for subsequent days by the manager or his assistant.

2. Examination of Handwriting on Hotel Register by FBI Laboratory

On December 11, 1963, a photocopy of the above-described page of the Hotel del Comercio registration book was submitted to the FBI Laboratory for examination of the "LEE, HARVEY OSWALD" signature appearing thereon.

In a laboratory report dated December 18, 1963, the FBI Laboratory stated that examination of "Qc333, photocopy of page of registry book of Hotel del Comercio, Calle Sahagun 19, Mexico City, with signatures of guests registering on September 27, 1963, Line 18, bearing signature 'Lee Harvey Oswald'" had been made with the following result:

"It was concluded that the LEE HARVEY OSWALD signature on Line 18 of Qc333 was written by LEE HARVEY OSWALD, whose known writing appears as K4 and K5 in this case."

The information recorded hereinunder was furnished by T-13.

A signed statement which had been made by SILVIA DURAN to the Federal Security Police on November 23, 1963, as translates from Spanish is recorded hereinunder:

"At the City of Mexico, Federal District, at 6:00 p.m. of November 23, 1963, the undersigned, Captain FERNANDO GUTIERREZ BARRIOS, Assistant Director of the Federal Security (Police), proceeding legally with witnesses present, makes record: that with the presentation in this office of Mrs. SILVIA TIRADO DE DURAN for the purpose of being interrogated concerning the matters which are herein set forth, this document was prepared:

"Promptly upon the presentation of the person who under normal conditions is called SILVIA TIRADO DE DURAN, having been warned to tell the truth and advised of the penalties which are incurred by those who furnish false testimony, described herself as follows: that her name is as recorded, 25 years of age, married, without religious preference, an employee, literate, a native and resident of this city, with domicile at Constituyentes #143, Apartment #3, with respect to the matters under investigation declares: that she has been legally married to Mr. HORACIO DURAN NAVARRO since November 5, 1958, and is the mother of a child named PATRICIA, who, at the present time, is three and one-half years of age; that in the month of July or August of 1961 the deponent was invited to join the Mexican-Cuban Institute of Cultural Relations, which at that time, was directed by Attorney AGUSTIN CUE CANOVAS, as a Coordinator, and, although she does not recall specifically who it was that recommended her, she can clarify that for some time previously she was friendly and visited with frequency the employees of the Cuban Embassy, being a personal friend of Ambassador PORTUONDO, as well as the Cultural Attaches, TERESA PROENZA and LUIS ALVERU, as well as with the female employees, but principally with the secretary of Consul EUSEBIO ASCUE, Miss MARICARMEN OLAVARRI, of Spanish nationality but a relative of ASCUE; that at the Institute the activities were exclusively of a cultural nature and were attended on occasions by the afore-mentioned Cultural Attaches and some Cubans, but in a greater number by Mexicans, always artists and intellectuals, without any political discussions, although she recalls that at the time of the October Cuban crisis in connection with the threatened invasion of Cuba and the subsequent blockade of the island by the North American Government, they listened by shortwave radio to the news from the 'Prensa Latina' (Latin Press), on the basis of which they made up a bulletin which was read of the news that they had listened to directly from Havana, agreeing also to the effect that Cubans and Mexicans attending said meetings discussed the political problem of Cuba on a private basis without doing so in any official character; that the declarant was receiving a salary of 500 pesos ($40 U.S.) monthly in her capacity as Coordinator at the Institute, with her work schedule being from 4:00 to 8:00 p.m. daily, and the money for the maintenance of the Institute itself coming from a monthly subsidy from the Cuban Embassy, the amount of which she is not aware, but also with each one of the members paying a quota, and also contributions were received from persons whose names she does not recall because usually they were made anonymously,

COMMISSION EXHIBIT NO. 2464—Continued

being unable to fix the monthly receipts, although she was the person who personally received all of the funds received at the Institute; that in addition to the speaker, only Mr. FELIPE ROJAS, who worked as a secretary at the Institute during the mornings, received any monthly salary in the same amount of 500 pesos ($40 U.S.), with the remainder of the money which was received being used for the payment of rent and other expenses connected with its operation. That in the month of December of 1961, the declarant and her husband made a trip by air to Havana, Cuba, paying for their own transportation, but all of their expenses of their visit to that city and the greater number of the cities of the island being paid by the Cuban Institute of Friendship with the People and the House of Culture, so-called, 'of the Americas,' the trip having lasted fifteen days without their having any contact or connection during this trip with officials of the Cuban Government. That as the speaker has already stated, she has been a sympathizer of socialism and Marxist doctrine for several years, having studied philosophy and existentialism, and particularly she has sympathized since its inception and sympathizes with the Cuban Revolution. That approximately three months ago she began to occupy the position of Secretary to the Cuban Consul in this city, Mr. EUSEBIO ASCUE, who ceased to function in that capacity some five days ago on Monday, the 18th of this month, having been substituted by Mr. ALFREDO MIRAVAL Y DIAZ, clarifying at this time that from the beginning she began to work in that capacity as a temporary measure as a result of the death in a traffic accident of her friend, MARICARMEN OLAVARRI, who had been occupying that position, until some person should arrive from Cuba who would assume the same, having had under her responsibility the administrative operation and preparing the visas which are issued, as well as handling the applications for such visas which invariably are sent to the

COMMISSION EXHIBIT NO. 2464—Continued

Ministry of Foreign Relations, Government of Cuba, for its approval, having obtained this position directly from former Consul ASCUE, with whom she is very friendly, and for whom the speaker even organized a farewell party in her home, which was attended by almost all of the officials and employees of the Embassy and the Consulate, except the Ambassador. That the speaker does not belong to any political party and never has attended manifestations or meetings, nor has she given lectures or speeches, which her husband has done, since he has written several articles for the newspaper 'El Dia' (The Day) (pro-Communist Spanish language newspaper published in Mexico City); that she has never been arrested for any reason, nor even on the occasion of the visit to Mexico of Mr. JOHN F. KENNEDY, which caused her a great deal of personal satisfaction because of the benefits which it would represent to the country. That yesterday while she was working at the Cuban Consulate, where she is employed from 10:00 to 2:00 and from 4:00 to 6:00 p.m. daily and where she receives a salary of 1,500 pesos ($120 U.S.) monthly, just before their time of departure at noon, a friend commented to her that she had been listening to the radio and heard a news item to the effect that President KENNEDY had suffered an attack in which they had fired three shots at him, as a result of which she called her husband on the telephone and they discussed this news, and he advised her that he already knew about it and referred to said attack as 'monstrous,' and they agreed that upon meeting at their home they would discuss the matter, which they did during their dinner hour, but in a very brief manner since they did not know all the circumstances of the attack and the name and description of the presumed author of the same, its having been only that night that they read in the extra (edition) the news relating thereto, and subsequently on the radio at her residence she heard the name of LEE HARVEY OSWALD, which caused her to remember that this name refers to a North

American who in the last days of September or the first days of the month of October of the present year appeared at the Cuban Consulate and applied for a visa to Cuba in transit to Russia and based his application on his presentation of his passport in which it was recorded that he had been living in the latter country for a period of three years, his work permit from that same country written in the Russian language and letters in the same language, as well as proof of his being married to a woman of Russian nationality and being the apparent Director in the city of New Orleans of the organization called 'Fair Play for Cuba' with the desire that he should be accepted as a 'friend' of the Cuban Revolution, as a result of which the speaker, in compliance with her duties, received all of his data and filled out the appropriate application, and he left to return in the afternoon, this time with his photographs, and the speaker, recognizing that she exceeded her duties, semi-officially called the Russian Consulate by telephone because of her interest in facilitating the handling of the Russian visa for LEE HARVEY OSWALD, but from there they answered her that the operation would require approximately four months, which annoyed the applicant, since as he affirmed he was in a great hurry to obtain the visas which would permit him to travel to Russia, insisting that he was entitled to them because of his background and his partisanship and personal activities in favor of the Cuban movement, the declarant's not being able to specify because she does not remember whether or not he said that he was a member of the Communist Party, but that his wife, of Russian nationality, was at that time in the city of New York from where she would follow him, although his place of origin was the afore-mentioned city of New Orleans; that as soon as OSWALD understood that it was not possible to give him a Cuban visa without his previously obtaining a Russian one, because the former was for transit, he became highly agitated and angry, as a result of which the speaker called Consul ASCUE, who, at that time, was in his private office in company of his ultimate replacement, MIRAVAL, but came out and began to argue in English with OSWALD in a very angry manner and ASCUE concluded by saying to him that, 'As far as he was concerned, he would not give him a visa,' and that 'A person like him, in place of aiding the Cuban Revolution, was doing it harm,' its being noted that in their discussion they had been referring to the Russian socialist revolution and not the Cuban, its being stated by OSWALD that he had two reasons to request the visa with urgency, which were, one, that his permit to be in Mexico was expiring and the other that he had urgent necessity of reaching Russia; that in spite of the argument the speaker handed to OSWALD a piece of paper similar to that which she writes at this time in which she recorded her name, 'SILVIA DURAN,' and the telephone number of the Consulate, which is '11-28-47,' and, at any rate, she initiated the handling of his visa application by sending it to the Cuban Ministry of (Foreign) Affairs, from which a reply was received in the normal manner some fifteen to thirty days later approving the issuance of a visa, but conditioning it on his previously obtaining the Russian (one), although she does not recall whether OSWALD subsequently called her or not on the telephone for the Consulate which she had given him; that all of the conversation which the speaker had with OSWALD, as well as that of Consul ASCUE with him, was in the English language since he did not speak any Spanish, and that upon seeing his photograph which appears in today's newspapers, specifically in the newspaper 'El Dia,' she immediately recognized and identified it as being the same person that she has been referring to as LEE HARVEY OSWALD. That on only one occasion the declarant attended a reception ceremony at the Russian Embassy which was given on the occasion of the visit of the astronauts, GAGARIN and TERESHKOVA, on the personal invitation which the

speaker received from the Russian Consul YACKSOV when the latter visited ASCUE and MIRAVAL and delivered to them their respective invitations at the Cuban Consulate. That with respect to her in-laws, LIDIA and RUBEN DURAN NAVARRO, the former on various occasions attended with the declarant the meetings which were being held at the Institute, whereas the latter only did so on one or two occasions in connection with exhibits of paintings and with respect to BETY SERRATO AZUCAR, the wife of RUBEN, she has always remained aloof from these activities, although all of them are of leftist ideology but do not actively participate in any activities; that BARBARA ANN BLITS TRESMOND ESQUIVEL and AGATA ROSENO GARCIA are friends of BETY and the speaker has known them very little and superficially, as a result of which she knows nothing about their activities and ideologies, and in connection with the gentleman who she now knows is named BENTLEY, she had never seen him before and supposes that he is a friend of BARBARA, since she noticed that he was talking to BARBARA when they were dining at the home of the deponent, being present her husband, AGATA and LIDIA, whereas the others were at the home of her brother-in-law, RUBEN. That she has nothing further to declare and after reading the above, she ratifies and signs the margins in evidence thereof. The above document is closed authorized and witnessed.

Signed, Assistant Director of Federal Security,
Captain FERNANDO GUTIERREZ BARRIOS.
Witnesses: Lic. (Atty.) FERNANDO ORTIZ DE LA PENA;
Lic. CARLOS DURAN LANZ."

House No. 4, Apt. 24
Ul. Kalinina

Kuznetsova, Rosa
Inter. (Intourist ?) Hotel "Minsk"
92-463

House 20, Apt. 8
Ul. Kola Miskneva (?)
Nel Norodovskvim (?)
112 In(stitute) of Foreign Languages

Page 46
English

Ruth Kloefer
306 Pine St.
New Orleans 18, La.

H. Warner Kloepfer
UN 6-0389
UN 6-2741, Ex. 276

Russian Translation

Communist Party U. S. A.
23 West 26th St.
New York

Page 47

Spanish Translation

Mexico City
Consulate of Cuba
Zamora and F. Marquez
11-28-47
Sylvia Duran

Embassy of the Union of Soviet Socialist Republic
15-61 55 (15-60 55)
Department of Consular Matters

Cubano Airlines
Paseo de la Reforma 56
35-79-00

U. S. Embassy
Lafragua 18
46 94 00
Bills 1-5-10-20
12.5 Pesos = $1.00
1 Peso = .08¢ Coins 1-5 pesos.

Page 51

Russian Translation

Medical Institute
LUCIA 31890
Ul. Kalinina 14.

Page 52

Russian Translation

smola (?) 14
stova (?)

Page 53

Russian Translation

Merezhkinsky (man's surname)
Prospect Stalina 12, Apt. 26
veogde (?) 7-14-53

FD-302 (Rev. 3-3-59) FEDERAL BUREAU OF INVESTIGATION

Date 3/16/64

1

ROBERT OSWALD, 1009 Sierra, furnished the following information:

On December 8, 1963, he obtained property of LEE HARVEY and MARINA OSWALD which was in the home of RUTH PAINE, Irving, Texas. Included in this property was a box which contained a two volume history, some Russian books, and a small American-made camera. He stated he had never made this camera available to authorities before February 24, 1964, because he had never been asked for it previously, and because he could see no evidentiary value to anyone interested in the assassination of President JOHN F. KENNEDY, of this cheap camera which belonged to LEE HARVEY OSWALD. He stated it had never occurred to him that anyone would be interested in the camera.

He advised he has no letters in his possession that LEE HARVEY OSWALD had written, and that the only letters he did have have been turned over by him to the President's Commission.

ROBERT OSWALD made available the box which contained this camera, and the items it still contains, all of which were the property of either LEE HARVEY OSWALD or MARINA OSWALD. The first thirteen items are books:

1. V. I. LENIN - MARX - ENGELS - MARXISM
2. "Baby and Child Care" - Dr. BENJAMIN SPOCK
3. "The Iliad" - HOMER
4. "Perfect Lovers Guide and other stories" - STEPHEN LEACOCK
5. "Squibb Product Reference"
6. "Short Russian Reference Grammar"
7. "Russian - Elementary Course I"

8-13. Six books in Russian language. In one book designated as #8, a note is written in the front:

"Dear Lee
Great Congratulations,
"Let all your dreams come true!
18. x 1959
Moscow
Rimma" (October 18 is LEE HARVEY OSWALD's birthday).

468

on 3/15/64 at Denton, Texas File # DL 100-10461

by Special Agent BARDWELL D. ODUM and R. NEIL QUIGLEY:vm Date dictated 3/16/64

COMMISSION EXHIBIT No. 2466

2
DL 100-10461

14. Cellophane tape, one roll
15. One small fuse
16. One pair dice
17. 29 dominoes and one box - "Made in Japan"
18. One pencil sharpener
19. One carriage bolt
20. One clothespin
21. One sheet white bond paper located in book designated as Item #13.

ROBERT OSWALD made available all other property of LEE HARVEY OSWALD still in his possession, which he obtained from the home of RUTH PAINE on December 8, 1963:

1. Val-pak type suitcase
2. One Texas flag - small
3. One Master lock padlock
4. One shower spray attachment
5. One treated cloth in paper container
6. One Marine Corps belt and buckle
7. One pencil
8. One sea bag
9. One carton for "Vegian Chewables"
10. One set long underwear
11. Three ties
12. One pair men's black gloves
13. One brown and grey leather cap
14. Two mufflers
15. One summer khaki overseas hat
16. One chess set - board and 27 pieces and 15 dominoes
17. One extension cord
18. One pair shoe trees
19. One can black shoe polish
20. One pencil sharpener

469

COMMISSION EXHIBIT No. 2466—Continued

3
DL 100-10461

21. One sea shell
22. One green eraser
23. One shoe brush
24. One coloring pencil
25. One shaving brush
26. One Schick box for electric shaver
27. One manicure set
28. One miniature silver spoon - broken
29. One knit shopping bag
30. One green winter overseas hat (USMC).

COMMISSION EXHIBIT No. 2466—Continued

FD-302 (Rev. 1-25-60) 'DERAL BUREAU OF INVESTIGATIC

Date 4/8/64

1

On April 8, 1964, SA J. HALE McMENAMIN purchased a silver-colored identification bracelet from the jewelry counter of the H. L. Green Company, 1623 Main Street, Dallas, Texas. This bracelet was sold as a "girls' hand-engraved expansion ident" bracelet for the retail price of $1.00 and was contained in a gold-colored cardboard box bearing a price tag with the following information:

"McCrory's"
O 12311
1.00
D21

The bracelet and box were marked for identification by SA McMENAMIN.

152

On 4/8/64 at Dallas, Texas File # DL 100-10461

by SA J. HALE McMENAMIN:vm Date dictated 4/8/64

COMMISSION EXHIBIT No. 2467

FD-302 (Rev. 1-25-60) FEDERAL BUREAU OF INVESTIGATION

Date 4/8/64

1

Mr. CHARLES R. PEZET, 5738 Collad Street, Dallas, Texas, advised he operates the H. L. Green Watch Repair Company located in the main floor of the H. L. Green Company Department Store, 1623 Main Street, Dallas, Texas. Mr. PEZET advised that prior to November, 1962, his watch concession was located in the basement of this store; that he moved his operation to the third floor of this same building just prior to Thanksgiving day, 1962, and has been in his present location on the main floor of the H. L. Green Company since March, 1964.

Mr. PEZET was shown photographs of the expansion identification bracelets belonging to LEE HARVEY OSWALD and MARINA OSWALD and he stated he at one time stocked cheap bracelets similar to the ones in the photographs but does not have this type of bracelet in stock at present. He said he was unable to recall whether the bracelets he previously stocked were identical with those in the photographs and would be unable to resolve this since his records would not show the type of bracelet he previously handled. Mr. PEZET advised that bracelets of this type have the decorative border machine engraved on the name plate when they are received and that the only additional engraving would be the name desired by the customer. He examined the engraved name "Marina" on Mrs. OSWALD's bracelet and advised this work was very similar to work done by him. He said it appeared to have been done by an electric Burgess Vibro-graver type machine and that although he does not use one at present he has employed this type of engraver in his work in the past. Mr. PEZET said that in order to be positive he would like to engrave the name "Marina" on some test plates to compare with the name shown in the photograph. He then engraved the name MARINA on two test plates and compared these engravings with the name appearing on Mrs. OSWALD's bracelet. After a careful comparison, Mr. PEZET advised it was his belief he had engraved this name on the bracelet. He observed that due to the vibration of the engraving tool, no two name engravings are exactly identical but that since the formation of the letters in the name MARINA was the same as his writing, it is his belief that he engraved this name.

Mr. PEZET was shown a photograph of LEE HARVEY OSWALD and

153

On 4/8/64 at Dallas, Texas File # DL 100-10461

by SAs J. HALE McMENAMIN and RAYMOND J. FOX:vm Date dictated 4/8/64

2
DL 100-10461

he advised he was unable to recall OSWALD as a customer of his watch shop at any location in the H. L. Green Store.

He added however that it was quite possible OSWALD may have purchased articles in his shop and he would not recall him since he waits on numerous persons during the course of his business day. He stated he could not recall OSWALD as a watch repair customer at his shop. He advised that until one month ago he did not keep a name file on customers and accordingly was unable to determine whether OSWALD might have been a customer of his at any time.

He was shown photographs of the bracelet of LEE HARVEY OSWALD and stated that while the bracelet appeared similar to those sold by him at one time he is positive the name "Lee" engraved thereon was not done by him.

Mr. PEZET was shown a girl's silver-type metal expansion identification bracelet bearing the stamped mark "Japan" which had been purchased by SA J. HALE McMENAMIN on April 8, 1964, at the jewelry counter of the H. L. Green Company. After examining the bracelet construction and machined decorative border engraving on the bracelet, he advised it was his opinion the bracelet was identical to Mrs. OSWALD's bracelet before the name "Marina" was added.

Mr. PEZET recalled that in October, 1963, the electric engraving tool being used by the girls working at the jewelry counter of the H. L. Green Company broke down and he was asked whether they could use his Burgess Vibro-graver. He said since he was using a larger engraving machine at this time he readily agreed.

He advised he did not normally do engraving work for the purchases made by customers at the H. L. Green jewelry counter but does recall that in the first week in October, 1963, he believed on a Thursday evening, he received a call at his shop on the third floor from one of the H. L. Green Company's managers on duty that night who asked him whether he might be able to engrave a purchase for a customer. The manager, who he believed was either KEN WOMACK or BOB WEBER, informed him that the girl who normally did do the

154

3
DL 100-10461

engraving was away from the counter and he desired PEZET to expedite the sale. He said he proceeded to the jewelry counter of the H. L. Green Company on the main floor where he engraved an item purchased by the customer. He was unable to recall whether this was a bracelet or some other item. He said neither could he recall the nature of the engraving nor could definitely say whether he had engraved the name MARINA at this time. Mr. PEZET pointed out that since the article was not purchased from him he paid very little attention to the customer and the article and could not now recall specific details concerning either. He said the jewelry counter was using his engraving machine at this time but had also repaired their own machine and he could not state which machine he used to make this engraving. Mr. PEZET, who is 6' tall, stated that while engraving this purchase he had the impression of a shorter person who was the customer standing near by awaiting the finished article. He added he did not observe this person closely at any time and was unable to say whether it was a man or a woman.

FD-302 (Rev. 1-25-60)

FEDERAL BUREAU OF INVESTIGATION

Date 4/8/64

1

Miss JUANITA DAVALOS, Merchandise Buyer, Jewelry and Cosmetics Department, H. L. Green Company, 1623 Main Street, Dallas, Texas, viewed photographs of a silver-colored expansion identification bracelet bearing the engraved name "Marina" and advised it was similar in design to a bracelet sold by the H. L. Green Company. She then viewed a bracelet presented to her by SA J. HALE McMENAMIN which was purchased from the jewelry counter of this store after which she stated she thought it definitely to be the same design as the bracelet appearing in the photographs. Miss DAVALOS continued that the border design on the name plate of the bracelet is done by the manufacturer and purchased with the border design already etched; however, any names engraved into the name plate are done by employees of the H. L. Green Company.

Similarly, Miss DAVALOS viewed photographs of an expansion bracelet bearing the engraved name "Lee" on the name plate of the bracelet and identified this bracelet also as being handled by the H. L. Green Company. She stated that on occasion she waits on customers at the jewelry counter and when engraving is required is capable of this type of skill but that the names MARINA and LEE as they appear on the above bracelets were not engraved by her.

Miss DAVALOS advised that the H. L. Green Company is one of the stores owned by the McCrory, McLellan, Green Stores Corporation and in the Dallas - Fort Worth area there are four other stores in this chain which handle these bracelets both of which are purchased from Originalities of New York Corporation, 890 Broadway, New York City. She stated the bracelet purchased by SA J. HALE McMENAMIN is purchased as a girl's hand-engraved expansion identification bracelet, order No. 1231, while the bracelet bearing the engraved name "Lee" is believed by her to be identical with order No. 1220 and purchased from Originalities of New York as a men's expansion identification bracelet.

Miss DAVALOS stated she is not aware that any other stores in Dallas carry this bracelet other than the H. L. Green Company at

156

On 4/8/64 at Dallas, Texas File # DL 100-10461

by SAs J. HALE McMENAMIN and RAYMOND J. FOX:vm Date dictated 4/8/64

1623 Main Street, Dallas; McCrory's, 383 W. Jefferson, Dallas; the H. L. Green Company, 901 Houston Street, Fort Worth, Texas; the McCrory's Store, 401 Houston Street, Fort Worth, Texas, and the McCrory's Store, 6305 Camp Bowie Blvd., Fort Worth, Texas.

UNITED STATES DEPARTMENT OF JUSTICE

FEDERAL BUREAU OF INVESTIGATION

In Reply, Please Refer to
File No.

WASHINGTON 25, D. C.

July 23, 1964

LEE HARVEY OSWALD

BASIS FOR INQUIRY

As has been previously reported, investigation disclosed that one H. O. LEE, believed to be identical with OSWALD, departed Mexico City at 8:30 A.M. on October 2, 1963, on bus No. 332 of a bus line called "Autobuses Transportes del Norte" (hereinafter referred to as Transportes del Norte). A total of sixteen passengers, including LEE, boarded the bus in Mexico City with destinations of Monterrey, Nuevo Leon, Mexico; Nuevo Laredo, Tamaulipas, Mexico; Laredo, Texas; and points beyond. Ten additional passengers boarded the same bus in San Luis Potosi, State of San Luis Potosi, Mexico.

INTERVIEW OF JOSE CRUZ CUELLAR

On July 3, 1964, JOSE CRUZ CUELLAR, who was located at the home of his sister, MARIA CRUZ CUELLAR, Calle Naranjo 1318 Norte, Colonia Moderna, Monterrey, Nuevo Leon, Mexico, furnished the following information to a confidential source:

CRUZ CUELLAR stated that he had been employed as a welder at Infiernillo, Michoacan, Mexico, in September, 1963. Late in September, he and nine other welders left their jobs and went to Guadalajara, Jalisco, Mexico. From Guadalajara, he and three other welders, CECILIO CARDENAS MENDEZ, MAXIMINO ESQUIVEL LIMON, and PEDRO GONZALEZ YERENA, proceeded to San Luis Potosi, San Luis Potosi, Mexico, where they were to board a Transportes del Norte bus bound for Monterrey, Nuevo Leon, Mexico.

At San Luis Potosi, CRUZ CUELLAR and his friends purchased three liters of tequila and consumed a large portion of it before they boarded the bus for Monterrey. He

COMMISSION EXHIBIT No. 2468

said that he was very drunk during the trip from San Luis Potosi to Monterrey, but he did notice that there were two persons on the bus who appeared to be Americans. One was an elderly lady approximately sixty years of age and the other was a young man.

CRUZ CUELLAR could not recall the appearance of the young man well enough to describe him, and he was unable to identify the young man as LEE HARVEY OSWALD. He was not able to state that the young man resembled a photograph of OSWALD that was displayed to him.

The confidential source mentioned above has furnished reliable information in the past.

COMMISSION EXHIBIT No. 2468—Continued

OFFICE OF THE DIRECTOR

UNITED STATES DEPARTMENT OF JUSTICE

FEDERAL BUREAU OF INVESTIGATION

WASHINGTON, D.C. 20535

July 16, 1964

BY COURIER SERVICE

Honorable J. Lee Rankin
General Counsel
The President's Commission
200 Maryland Avenue, N. E.
Washington, D. C.

Dear Mr. Rankin:

There are enclosed two copies of a memorandum dated July 9, 1964, dealing with procedures involved in the issuance of tickets at Laredo, Texas, and Nuevo Laredo, Mexico, of the Transportes del Norte bus line.

Upon detachment of the classified enclosures, this letter may be regarded as unclassified.

Sincerely yours,

Enclosures (2)

COMMISSION EXHIBIT No. 2469

UNITED STATES DEPARTMENT OF JUSTICE

FEDERAL BUREAU OF INVESTIGATION

In Reply, Please Refer to
File No.

WASHINGTON 25, D. C.

JUL 9 1964

LEE HARVEY OSWALD

BASIS FOR INQUIRY

As has been previously reported, OSWALD, using the name of H. O. LEE, is believed to have departed Mexico City at 8:30 a.m. on October 2, 1963, on bus No. 332 of a bus line called "Autobuses Transportes del Norte" (Hereinafter referred to as Transportes del Norte). In Monterrey, Nuevo Leon, Mexico, passengers on bus No. 332 who were continuing on to Nuevo Laredo, Tamaulipas, and Laredo, Texas, transferred to Transportes del Norte bus No. 373.

It has also been previously reported that according to Transportes del Norte records, one of the passengers on bus No. 332 on October 2, 1963, was PAULA RUSIONI, holder of ticket No. 9511, which had been issued in exchange for ticket No. 39532.

Extensive investigation has been conducted in an unsuccessful effort to date to locate and interview PAULA RUSIONI. In connection with this investigation, it was deemed desirable to ascertain the procedures involved in the issuance of the RUSIONI ticket.

INTERVIEW OF RAMON TREVINO QUEZADA,
GENERAL MANAGER, TRANSPORTES DEL
NORTE BUS LINE, MONTERREY, NUEVO LEON, MEXICO

On June 1, 1964, RAMON TREVINO QUEZADA, General Manager, Transportes del Norte bus line, Heroes Poniente No. 271, Monterrey, advised a confidential source abroad as follows:

COMMISSION EXHIBIT No. 2469—Continued

The name PAULA RUSIONI does not appear on any of the passenger lists maintained by that bus line at Monterrey. He was not acquainted with any person so named.

The Greyhound Bus Lines office at Laredo, Texas, regularly issues Transportes del Norte bus tickets to persons purchasing tickets in Laredo for travel to Mexico. It does not issue Greyhound tickets for such travel. Through an agreement between the two companies, Greyhound Bus Lines receives a ten per cent commission on each Transportes del Norte ticket sold by it.

Ordinarily, the Greyhound office at Laredo, Texas, is the only one authorized to issue Transportes del Norte tickets, whether a Greyhound ticket was previously involved or not. However, on special occasions the G eyhound office at San Antonio, Texas, may issue Transportes del Norte tickets to members of an excursion group proceeding from that city to Mexico. Special arrangements must be made with Transportes del Norte in such instances.

When arrangements for travel to Mexico are made at Greyhound Bus Lines offices in other parts of the United States, that company issues its own (Greyhound) ticket. When the passenger arrives in Nuevo Laredo, Tamaulipas, Mexico, the pertinent portion of his ticket is exchanged for a Transportes del Norte ticket authorizing travel on that bus line in Mexico. Subsequently, Transportes del Norte notifies Greyhound of the exchange and it is remunerated by Greyhound to the extent that the passenger traveled on that bus line in Mexico.

The same procedure is followed at Transportes del Norte offices in Mexico when it issues its own tickets to purchasers there for travel in the United States. The pertinent portion of the Transportes del Norte ticket is exchanged at the United States border for a Greyhound ticket, and Transportes del Norte later reimburses Greyhound to the extent the passenger traveled on that bus line in the United States.

Ticket No. 39532, believed to have been purchased by PAULA RUSIONI, was a Transportes del Norte ticket sold

COMMISSION EXHIBIT No. 2469—Continued

at the Greyhound Bus Lines office at Laredo, Texas, on September 10, 1963. According to PEDRO MOLINA P., Manager, Transportes del Norte office at Nuevo Laredo, Tamaulipas, Mexico, that ticket was a two-portion ticket authorizing travel from Laredo, Texas, to Mexico, D. F., and from Mexico, D. F., to Laredo, Texas. The proper ticket for such travel should have been a four-portion ticket authorizing travel from Laredo, Texas, to Monterrey, Nuevo Leon, Mexico; Monterrey, Nuevo Leon, to Mexico, D. F.; Mexico, D. F., to Monterrey, Nuevo Leon; Monterrey, Nuevo Leon, to Laredo, Texas. When the ticket agent at the Transportes del Norte office in Nuevo Laredo, Tamaulipas, noticed ticket No. 39532 had been issued in only two portions, he took it from the passenger and exchanged it for Transportes del Norte ticket No. 9511, which was of the proper four-portion type, on September 11, 1963.

- 3 -

COMMISSION EXHIBIT No. 2469—Continued

UNITED STATES DEPARTMENT OF JUSTICE

FEDERAL BUREAU OF INVESTIGATION

In Reply, Please Refer to File No.

Dallas, Texas

February 15, 1964

LEE HARVEY OSWALD

Exhibit D - 106 is a three-page manifest of Transportes Frontera Bus Company covering trip number 2 for bus number 340, departing from Mexico City for Laredo, Texas, on October 2, 1963. The results of the FBI Laboratory examination of this manifest are reflected on page 52 of the report of SA ROBERT P. GEMBERLING dated January 7, 1964.

With respect to the above described manifest, it should be noted that seats one and three are listed in the name "FCO. Saucedo" together with their corresponding ticket numbers and a destination of Monterrey. This individual is identical with Francisco Saucedo Velez, driver of the bus on this particular trip. Saucedo was interviewed at considerable length on December 7, 1963, at which time he explained that frequently he makes reservations for friends of his in his own name simply as a favor to these friends. Although he had no independent recollection concerning this particular trip, he presumed he had made the reservations for two friends who subsequently purchased their tickets and utilized the seats reserved by him.

It should also be noted that seat four is listed under the name of "Oswld" with a destination of "Lared" and that no ticket number is listed. Extensive investigation at the offices of the Transportes Frontera Bus Company in Monterrey on December 10, 1963, resulted in the location there of all tickets whose numbers are listed on the bus passenger list. It was pointed out by them that the ticket numbers prefixed with the number 39 were tickets from Mexico City to Monterrey and those prefixed with the number 10 were tickets covering passage from Mexico City to Nuevo Laredo. Officials of the company were unable to locate

COMMISSION EXHIBIT No. 2470

a ticket covering Oswald's passage. They also pointed out that the figures below the passenger's names, "9 Laredo, 7 Monterrey", indicated the number of passengers for each destination. It will be noted that without taking Oswald into account, there are nine ticket numbers listed with the prefix 10, and seven ticket numbers bearing the prefix 39, indicating passage from Mexico City to Monterrey. Including Oswald, there are actually ten passengers listed with a destination of Laredo.

On January 21, 1964, Gilberto Cazares Garza, Chief of Mexican Immigration, Nuevo Laredo, Mexico, advised that he could find no cancellation of tourist permits for October 3, 1963, on the following persons:

Sra. Landeros
Juana (last name unknown)
Sra. Morlaes
Rafael Flores
Ganstiere
Angel Perez
Sra. Aguilar
Luz Tricarco
Constantino Garcia

The above names appeared on the passenger list of the Transportes Frontera Bus Line, bus number 340, which left Mexico City on October 2, 1963, and the name Oswald appears on the manifest.

Cazares stated that his records did reflect, however, that one Juana Maria Alaniz, married, age 47, American, who had entered Mexico on October 1, 1963, and whose destination in Mexico was Monterrey, tourist card number 626392, had departed Mexico at Nuevo Laredo, Mexico, on October 3, 1963, and her destination in the United States was San Antonio, Texas. Cazares stated that Alaniz was traveling by bus. It was subsequently determined by interview of Alaniz that she was on a different bus line, the Transportes Del Norte, and that she knew nothing about Oswald and after viewing a photograph of him, could not remember ever seeing him.

2

COMMISSION EXHIBIT No. 2470—Continued

UNITED STATES DEPARTMENT OF JUSTICE

FEDERAL BUREAU OF INVESTIGATION

In Reply, Please Refer to
File No.

WASHINGTON 25, D.C.

February 20, 1964

RE: LEE HARVEY OSWALD

As has been previously reported, a confidential source abroad on November 28, 1963, made available a copy of the bus manifest of a company called Transportes Frontera. This manifest covered the trip of the bus of this company which departed Mexico City on October 2, 1963, for Nuevo Laredo. The bus had a scheduled departure time of 1:00 p.m. from Mexico City on October 2, 1963, and a scheduled arrival time at Nuevo Laredo of 6:00 a.m. on October 3, 1963. The passenger listed as occupying seat 4 on this manifest was "OSWLD," no first name given. The destination of this individual was given as "Lared."

No ticket number was listed by the name "OSWLD" although ticket numbers appeared beside the names of the remaining passengers. It is to be noted that this passenger manifest was rather poorly prepared in longhand with the names of some of the passengers being incomplete and in some cases almost illegible. Toward the bottom of the manifest is a notation, "9 Laredo, 7 Monterrey"; however, including the name "OSWLD," 10 passengers appear on the list with a destination of Laredo.

FRANCISCO ALVARADO, ticket salesman and dispatcher at the Transportes Frontera terminal in Mexico City, was interviewed several times by two reliable sources, the last of these interviews being on December 17, 1963. ALVARADO had no personal recollection of OSWALD and could offer no explanation as to why no ticket number appeared beside the name "OSWLD" or as to the reason for the discrepancy in the number of passengers listed for Laredo.

ALVARADO advised that no information concerning the identities of the passengers other than that appearing on the bus manifest is maintained by the bus company.

As has been previously reported, FRANCISCO SAUCEDO VELEZ and DIONISIO REYNA PAZ, chauffours on the trip on which the name "OSWLD" appeared as a passenger, were exhaustively interviewed on two different occasions. They had no personal recollection of OSWALD nor could they offer any explanation concerning the discrepancy in the number of passengers and the fact that no ticket number appeared beside the "OSWLD" entry.

In the course of the second interview SAUCEDO explained that tickets bearing a profix of 39 covered travel from Mexico City to Monterrey and those with a prefix of 10 covered the travel from Mexico City to Nuevo Laredo. SAUCEDO also pointed out that tickets collected from the passengers on a given trip are forwarded to the offices of the bus company in Monterrey.

On 12/9/63 TELESFORO QUIROGA, ticket agent at the Transportes Frontera Office, Calle Zimapan 104, Monterrey, was interviewed. All tickets listed by number on the passenger manifest for the October 2-3, 1963, trip from Mexico City to Nuevo Laredo were located. QUIROGA could offer no explanation as to why no ticket number was listed for "OSWLD," and it was impossible for him to locate a ticket which might have been used by OSWALD.

It has been previously reported that OSWALD stayed at the Hotel Del Comercio, Calle Sahagun 19, Mexico City. On January 20, 1964, GUILLERMO GARCIA LUNA, manager of this hotel, advised as follows:

The hotel does not use a system of registration cards for guests arriving at the hotel, but rather uses a registry book. On the first day a guest arrives he, himself, makes the initial entry in the book, this including the name of the guest, the place from which he is arriving, his occupation, and his nationality. Thereafter on each day the guest continues at the hotel the same information is entered in the book on the page designated for that day, but the entry is made by a hotel employee. No exact home address is obtained from the guest since he is required to pay in advance. As has been previously reported, OSWALD registered at the hotel on September 27, 1963, with the point from which he was arriving being shown as "USA (Texas)," his occupation was shown as "photo," and under the column for nationality was listed "U. S. citizen." The handwriting on this entry in the registry book has been identified with the known handwriting of OSWALD by the FBI Laboratory.

OSWALD was listed as staying in room 18 of the hotel during his entire stay there from September 27 through the night of October 1, 1963. Mr. GARCIA LUNA pointed out that rooms 18 through 23 occupy one floor of the hotel. He examined the registry book for the period OSWALD was at the hotel and was able to furnish information on three of the guests who occupied rooms on the same floor as OSWALD during a part or all of the time that OSWALD was at the hotel. He said he recalled these guests because they frequently stop at the hotel when in Mexico City. The guests he recalled were the following:

Mr. PEREZ PLIEGO, who registered from San Luis Potosi, is a railroad employee who visits the Hotel Del Comercio frequently. He occupied room 19 on September 26, 27, and 28, 1963. A Captain ESQUIVEL of Veracruz occupied room 19 on September 30, 1963. Mr. GARCIA LUNA described him as a Mexican Army Captain whom he believes to be well-known in Veracruz.

MARIO RESENDIZ, a merchant who registered from Saltillo, Coahuila, occupied room 21 from September 26, 1963, to October 3, 1963. This individual reportedly has a merchandising business involving the sale of flowers and miscellaneous items in Monclova, Coahuila. GARCIA LUNA claimed that he is well-known in Monclova.

Mr. GARCIA LUNA could furnish no information on other guests occupying rooms on the same floor as OSWALD which would assist in their location.

On January 21, 1964, ALFONSO PEREZ PLIEGO, home address Espana 304, Guadalajara, Jalisco, Mexico, office address Bolivar 8-401, Mexico City, was interviewed in

-3-

COMMISSION EXHIBIT No. 2471—Continued

Mexico City. He advised that he frequently stops at the Hotel Del Comercio and confirmed that he had resided at the hotel during the period September 26-28, 1963, in room 19. He said that unfortunately he had not noticed OSWALD's presence in the hotel during that time and could furnish no information concerning OSWALD's activities while in Mexico City.

The following investigation was conducted in Veracruz on January 23-24, 1964:

ERNEST HOLM, Vice Consul, American Consulate, contacted logical sources of his office. None of these sources was able to identify Captain ESQUIVEL.

Lt. Commander CHARLES EDSON, assigned to the Mexican Naval Academy as an instructor by the U. S. Navy, was unable to locate any information identifiable with Captain ESQUIVEL.

Inspector ALBERTO MORALES, Veracruz Police Department, contacted sources at the military establishments in the Veracruz area and was unable to obtain any information concerning Captain ESQUIVEL.

Investigation to locate ESQUIVEL is continuing.

Intensive investigation is continuing to locate and interview MARIO RESENDIZ of Monclova who has not been located to date.

-4-

COMMISSION EXHIBIT No. 2471—Continued

UNITED STATES DEPARTMENT OF JUSTICE
FEDERAL BUREAU OF INVESTIGATION

In Reply, Please Refer to
File No.

WASHINGTON 25, D. C.

May 25, 1964

LEE HARVEY OSWALD

BASIS FOR INQUIRY

LEE HARVEY OSWALD is believed to have traveled under the name of H. O. LEE from Mexico City to Laredo, Texas, via buses of the "Autobuses Transportes del Norte" bus line (hereinafter referred to as Transportes del Norte). According to available records, H. O. LEE departed from Mexico City at 8:30 AM, October 2, 1963, on Transportes del Norte bus No. 332 and transferred at Monterrey, Nuevo Leon, Mexico, to Transportes del Norte bus No. 373, which arrived at Laredo, Texas, at approximately 2:00 AM on October 3, 1963. He was assigned seat No. 12 on bus No. 332, a window seat located four rows from the front on the driver's side. Having purchased bus transportation to Dallas, it is believed he departed from Laredo at 3:00 AM, October 3, 1963, on a Greyhound bus en route to Dallas, Texas, via San Antonio, Texas.

INFORMATION REGARDING OTHER TRANSPORTES DEL NORTE BUS PASSENGERS OF OCTOBER 2-3, 1963

As has been reported, the following is the passenger manifest and seat reservations for those passengers on Transportes del Norte bus No. 332, which departed Mexico City at 8:30 AM, October 2, 1963. Those passengers who have been located and interviewed are indicated below. (Further details regarding this passenger manifest are contained in a memorandum dated April 7, 1964.)

COMMISSION EXHIBIT No. 2472

Seat (No.)	Name of Passenger	Destination
2	Miss COSIO	San Antonio
3	Mr. A. MARTINEZ	Nuevo Laredo
4	MARGARET A. WOLFF (Review of tickets reflected WOLFF possibly traveled only as far as Monterrey, Nuevo Leon.)	Laredo
5	ROBERTO P. GONZALEZ	Monterrey
6	M. H. VILLANUEVA (This person did not travel.)	
7	PAULA RUSIONI	Laredo
8	J. M. DE CUBA (Located and interviewed.)	Laredo
9	J. M. DE CUBA (Apparently ADA FRANCISCA BISLIP DE DE CUBA, wife of J. M. DE CUBA, utilized this seat.) (Located and interviewed.)	Laredo
10	Operator (Identified and interviewed.)	
11	AUGUSTO AGUILAR (Located and interviewed.)	Houston
12	Chihuahuenses (Chihuahuenses Transports Travel Agency) (This seat was reserved for H. O. LEE, believed identical with OSWALD.)	Laredo, Tex.
14	Mr. EULALIO RODRIGUEZ	Houston
15	A Viajes (This seat was reserved for ANASTASIO RUIZ MEZA.) (Located and interviewed.)	Laredo
16	PH. VAN DER VORM (PHILIPPE PITER E. VAN DER VORM) (Located and interviewed.)	Laredo, Tex.

-2-

COMMISSION EXHIBIT No. 2472—Continued

Seat (No.)	Name of Passenger	Destination
17	JORGE DAVILA	Monterrey
18	JOSE BARRIGA (Located and interviewed.)	Dallas
19	and wife (Located and Interviewed.)	Dallas
21	AGAPITO DEL RIO (Located and interviewed.)	San Antonio

Of the above-listed 16 passengers who boarded bus No. 332, the following 8 people have been located and interviewed:

Mr. and Mrs. J. M. DE CUBA
AUGUSTO AGUILAR
ANASTASIO RUIZ MEZA
PHILIPPE PITER E. VAN DER VORM
AGAPITO DEL RIO
Mr. and Mrs. JOSE BARRIGA

Upon interview on April 6, 1964, PHILIPPE PITER E. VAN DER VORM recalled that on the bus was a German woman whom he described as about 50 years of age who has been a school teacher in the United States for the past fifteen or twenty years and who had been in Yucatan, Mexico, on vacation. It is believed that the person referred to by VAN DER VORM may be MARGARET A. WOLFF.

In addition to the above passengers it has been determined that ten additional passengers boarded bus No. 332 at San Luis Potosi, State of San Luis Potosi, Mexico, in the early afternoon of October 2, 1963, eight of these passengers having arrived in San Luis Potosi on a feeder bus of the "Linea Azul" (Blue Line), which had departed from Guadalajara, Jalisco, Mexico, at 8:00 AM, October 2, 1963, to make connection with bus No. 332 in San Luis Potosi. The eight who boarded at Guadalajara and the seat numbers assigned them on bus No. 332 are as follows. (Further details regarding this passenger list are contained in a memorandum dated April 7, 1964.)

-3-

COMMISSION EXHIBIT No. 2472—Continued

Seat (No.)	Name of Passenger	Destination
22	HILDA QUEZADA	Nuevo Laredo
23	HILDA QUEZADA	Nuevo Laredo
24	HILDA QUEZADA (This seat was designated for QUEZADA as a half-fare ticket.)	Nuevo Laredo
25	CECILIO CARDENAZ	Monterrey
26	PEDRO GLEZ. (probably GONZALEZ)	Monterrey
24	Illegible (probably JOSE CRUZ) (Seat No. 24 was listed for this person; however, since that seat was also designated for another person, it is believed that perhaps this seat was intended to be No. 29.)	Monterrey
28	MAXIMINO ESQUIVEL	Monterrey
27	Unidentified	Monterrey

The two passengers who boarded Transportes del Norte bus No. 332 at San Luis Potosi are unidentified; however, it appears that one of the passengers was HERBERT ROBERT VOORHEES, who was located and interviewed on March 26, 1964, at San Miguel de Allende, Guanajuato, Mexico. (Detailed information regarding the interview of VOORHEES is contained in a memorandum dated March 31, 1964.)

Two other passengers, who were not listed by name and remain unidentified, boarded the bus at Monterrey (passengers on bus No. 332, who were continuing the trip north, changed to Transportes del Norte bus No. 373 at Monterrey for the trip to the United States-Mexico border) with their destination being Nuevo Laredo, Tamaulipas, Mexico. Another unidentified passenger, who was not listed by name, boarded the bus at Nuevo Laredo for the trip to Laredo, Texas.

-4-

COMMISSION EXHIBIT No. 2472—Continued

EFFORTS TO IDENTIFY BUS PASSENGERS ON TRANSPORTES DEL NORTE BUSES NO. 332 AND NO. 373 FOR TRIP OF OCTOBER 2-3, 1963

At Mexico, D. F., Mexico

On April 2, 1964, a check of the visa files, United States Embassy, was made for the following persons, and no record identifiable with them could be located:

PAULA RUSIONI
MARGARET A. WOLFF
Miss COSIO
EULALIO RODRIGUEZ

It was determined on April 15, 1964, through a check at the Central Office, Immigration and Naturalization Service (INS), Washington, D. C., that the master index of that agency contained a reference to one HILDA QUEZADA QUIROZ. These records disclosed that HILDA QUEZADA QUIROZ was born September 4, 1944, at Mexico, D. F., Mexico (D. F. refers to "Distrito Federal" - Federal District or the Mexican Federal Capital), and admitted to the United States at Laredo, Texas, on May 24, 1963, on a Class B-2 visa valid to June 15, 1963. She was the bearer of Mexican Passport No. 31067, and the visa was issued at Mexico City on May 15, 1963. Her permanent address was given as J. M. Correa No. 196, Mexico, D. F., Mexico, and her address in the United States was recorded as "San Antonio and Houston, Texas." The departure record reflects she departed from the United States at Laredo on May 30, 1963.

T-1, a confidential source abroad, advised on April 30, 1964, that he had located HILDA QUEZADA QUIROZ at Calle Jose Maria Correa No. 196, Colonia Vista Alegre, Mexico, D. F., and QUEZADA stated she did travel on a Transportes del Norte bus from San Luis Potosi, State of San Luis Potosi, State of San Luis Potosi, Mexico, to Nuevo Laredo in May, 1963. QUEZADA affirmed that she did not travel in October, 1963.

T-2, a confidential source abroad, advised that on April 29, 1964, a review of Mexican Government Immigration forms FM-11 listing all persons of record who departed from Mexico at Nuevo Laredo on October 3, 1963, failed to disclose any information identifiable with the following persons who were listed as passengers on the buses in question:

Miss COSIO
A. MARTINEZ
MARGARET A. WOLFF
ROBERTO P. GONZALEZ
PAULA RUSIONI
EULALIO RODRIGUEZ
JORGE DAVILA
HILDA QUEZADA
CECILIO CARDENAZ
PEDRO GONZALEZ
JOSE CRUZ
MAXIMINO ESQUIVEL

On March 23, 1964, MACLOVIO HERRERA, Chief of the Travel Control Files of the Mexican Immigration Department, Mexico, D. F., advised that in a circular instruction dated March 20, 1962, the Chief of the Immigration Department described the Immigration form FM-11 as a "statistical record to be prepared every two weeks on nationals and aliens entering and leaving the country." HERRERA explained that separate FM-11 forms are submitted semimonthly by all Mexican Immigration stations for entries and departures from Mexico, and separate lists are prepared in connection with the various types of travel documents presented and submitted in duplicate (original and one carbon copy) to the Travel Control Files for checking and comparison with the tourist cards or other travel documents on which they are based. HERRERA advised, however, that numerous Mexican nationals traverse the Mexico-United States border on a daily basis without any records being made of their travel.

On May 20, 1964, the following additional review was made of visa records, United States Embassy, Mexico, D. F., for the names of bus passengers as indicated below:

MAXIMINO ESQUIVEL - No record identifiable with this person could be located.

CECILIO CARDENAZ - Visa files contain one card for CECILIO CARDENAS CISNEROS, born June 28, 1933, at El Zapote, Aguililla, Michoacan, a resident at Calle Allende No. 11, Aguililla, Michoacan, who on January 28, 1963, applied for admission to the United States as a nonquota immigrant. No visa had been granted as of May 20, 1964.

JORGE DAVILA - Visa files contain the following references to persons with the name JORGE DAVILA:

JORGE DAVILA MUNOZ, born in October, 1933, occupation travel agent, residing at Bahia de Santa Barbara No. 20, Apartment No. 210, Colonia Veronica Anzures, Mexico, D. F., presented Mexican Passport No. 32084/58 and was issued a visa which expired March 26, 1963.

JORGE DAVILA TELLO, born at Mexico, D. F., (no date given) residing at 5 de Febrero No. 132, Room No. 5, Mexico 8, D. F., Mexican Passport No. 040446/62, received a visa which expired June 9, 1960.

JORGE IGNACIO DAVILA GALVEZ, born August 1, 1946, at Tehuacan, Puebla, residing at Niza No. 81, Apartment No. 12, Colonia Juarez, Mexico, D. F., Mexican Passport No. 31324/63, obtained a one-entry visa which expired on August 16, 1963.

EULALIO RODRIGUEZ - No record identifiable with this person could be located.

ROBERTO P. GONZALEZ - There are several hundred cards on file and in the absence of descriptive data it was not possible to identify this person.

Miss COSIO - There are numerous cards on file for persons who might be known as Miss COSIO and a large number of cards for persons who might be known as Mrs. COSIO. The following are names of persons who might be known as "Miss COSIO" (also commonly spelled "COSSIO") who held United States visas as of October 2, 1963:

-7-

COMMISSION EXHIBIT No. 2472—Continued

CELIA PATRICIA COSSIO RODRIGUEZ, age 10 in 1963, residing at Calle Alvaro Obregon No. 230-10, Mexico, D. F., held a visa issued September 13, 1963, valid to December 13, 1963, for one entry to the United States on a pleasure trip. The visa card was signed by this person's mother, CELIA DE COSSIO.

GUADALUPE COSIO HINOJOSA, holder of Mexican Passport No. 29856/63, a resident of Calle Cuernavaca No. 9, Colonia Condesa, Mexico, D. F., born March 9, 1903, at Mexico, D. F., held a visa issued May 14, 1963, which was to expire on November 14, 1963. Her occupation was listed as housewife-real estate owner. Her visa was secured for a trip to San Antonio, Texas.

JOSEFA COSSIO COSIO, holder of Mexican Passport No. 10026/58, residing at Calle Carmen No. 78, Mexico 1, D. F., held a visa issued August 5, 1963, which was valid to November 5, 1963, for one-week pleasure trip to the United States.

PAULA RUSIONI - No record was located for this person.

T-3, a confidential source abroad, advised on May 21, 1964, that a review of the National Alien Registry of the Ministry of the Interior, Mexico, D. F., failed to reveal any information identifiable with PAULA RUSIONI, which would indicate that, if this person is residing in Mexico, she is not in an alien status.

T-4, a confidential source abroad, advised as follows:

On May 13, 1964, Dr. ARRIGO LOPEZ CELLY of the Italian Embassy, Mexico, D. F., related that no record could be located for PAULA RUSIONI in the files at that Embassy.

On May 20, 1964, T-3 advised he had conducted a review of the Passport records at the Mexican Foreign Ministry, Mexico, D. F., and was unable to identify any of the following persons through a review of those

- 8 -

COMMISSION EXHIBIT No. 2472—Continued

records. Source related that the paucity of information concerning these persons and the fact that the Passport records at the Mexican Foreign Ministry are set up in an alphabetical index according to the year of the issuance of the passports make it exceedingly difficult to locate identifiable data with only partial names.

Miss COSIO
A. MARTINEZ
PAULA RUSIONI
JORGE DAVILA
MAXIMINO ESQUIVEL
CECILIO CARDENAZ
HILDA QUEZADA
EULALIO RODRIGUEZ
PEDRO GONZALEZ
JOSE CRUZ

Regarding bus passenger ROBERTO P. GONZALEZ, source related that he located a record for one ROBERTO PALACIOS GONZALEZ, holder of Mexican Passport No. 26838/62.

Source advised on May 21, 1964, that records of the Passport Office, Mexican Foreign Ministry, disclose that ROBERTO PALACIOS GONZALEZ, holder of Mexican Passport No. 26838/62, resided in 1962 at Calle Oriente No. 300, Colonia Villa de Cortes, Mexico, D. F. His birth date is recorded as March 28, 1941, and his parents were named as EDUARDO PALACIOS and SOLEDAD GONZALEZ. In 1962 he secured a Mexican passport for the purpose of traveling to the United States with New York City listed as his final destination. His Mexican Military Service Card number is registered as No. 4461985. He was described as being single, 5'3" in height, of dark complexion, black hair, brown eyes, occupation "artist." He formerly held Mexican Passport No. 73-5:1519, which had been issued by the Mexican Consulate at Brownsville, Texas.

MARGARITA MUNGUIA, Visa Section, United States Embassy, Mexico, D. F., advised on May 22, 1964, that visa records disclose that one ROBERTO PALACIOS GONZALEZ, born March 28,

-9-

COMMISSION EXHIBIT No. 2472—Continued

1941, and residing in 1962 at Calle Oriente 65 No. 3000, Colonia Villa de Cortes, Mexico, D. F., secured a visa on December 20, 1962, for the prupose of an eight-day pleasure visit to the State of Texas. This person's visa card lists his occupation as "movie actor." (It is noted that records of the Passport Office, Mexican Foreign Ministry, list his residence address in 1962 as Calle Oriente No. 300, Colonia Villa de Cortes, Mexico, D. F.)

At Merida, Yucatan, Mexico

Consul Paul S. Dwyer, United States Consulate, advised he could locate no record in the files of the Consulate for the name MARGARET A. WOLFF.

T-5, a confidential source abroad, advised that FELIX SALAZAR, caretaker in charge of the registry at the Mayan ruins of Chichen-Itza, Yucatan, made available the visitors' signature register. This register was reviewed for the period of August 1, 1963, to October 6, 1963, and no record could be located for the name MARGARET A. WOLFF.

T-2 advised that on May 20, 1964, ERNESTO ABREU GOMEZ, Identification Section, State Judicial Police, Merida, advised that the following persons reviewed the indicated records for the period from August 1, 1963, to October 6, 1963, without locating any record for the name MARGARET A. WOLFF:

Attorney MANUEL CASTANEDA RAMIREZ, Superintendent of the Anthropology Institute, Merida, Yucatan, who reviewed the visitors' signature register at the Mayan ruins of Uxmal, Yucatan.

Attorney HUMBERTO ROSADO ESPINOLA, Barbachano Travel Agency, who reviewed the hotel registers for the Hotel Uxmal located near the site of the Uxmal ruins and for the Mayanland Hotel located near the site of the ruins of Chichen-Itza, Yucatan.

-10-

COMMISSION EXHIBIT No. 2472—Continued

At Monterrey, Nuevo Leon, Mexico

T-6, a confidential source abroad, advised as follows:

On May 19, 1964, it was determined that one MARGARET A. WOLFF registered at the Ambassador Hotel in Monterrey at about 9:55 PM, October 2, 1963, and checked out of the hotel the following morning at 9:07 AM. Inquiry revealed that WOLFF was described as being of German descent and a teacher of languages. Hotel records reflect that WOLFF's residence address is listed as 2 Delaware (probably street or avenue), Dummont (possibly Dumont), New Jersey. It was determined on May 20, 1964, that WOLFF may have made travel arrangements for her trip to Mexico through a travel agency known as the Utell International Travel Agency of New Jersey with addresses listed at 2 Essex House, New York, New York, and what appeared to be 32-A Norwalk, Berjensild (probably Bergenfield), New Jersey.

According to the bus manifest, of the sixteen passengers who boarded Transportes del Norte bus No. 332 at Mexico City on October 2, 1963, Monterrey was listed as the final destination for ROBERTO P. GONZALEZ and JORGE DAVILA.

The following individuals who were named on the manifest of the feeder bus which left Guadalajara on the morning of October 2, 1963, to make connection with Transportes del Norte bus No. 332 at San Luis Potosi listed Monterrey as their final destination:

CECILIO CARDENAZ
PEDRO GONZALEZ
JOSE CRUZ
MAXIMINO ESQUIVEL

In an effort to locate the above-named persons for whom Monterrey was listed as their final destination, T-7, a confidential source abroad, advised on May 8, 1964, that he had located the following persons at Monterrey through a check of the telephone directory, voting records, and public utility

-11-

COMMISSION EXHIBIT No. 2472—Continued

records at Monterrey, and all advised that they had not been passengers on Transportes del Norte bus No. 332 which had departed Mexico City the morning of October 2, 1963:

ROBERTO GONZALEZ, JR., residing at Calle Republica Dominicana No. 103
ROBERTO GONZALEZ, residing at Padre Mier Oriente No. 814
ROBERTO GONZALEZ, residing at Padre Mier Oriente No. 817
ROBERTO A. GONZALEZ, residing at Rio Amazonas Oriente No. 422
ROBERTO L. GONZALEZ, residing at Calle Republica Dominicana No. 219
ROBERTO M. GONZALEZ, residing at Calle Republica Dominicana No. 111
PEDRO A. GONZALEZ, residing at Calle Miguel Nieto Oriente No. 352
PEDRO G. GONZALEZ, residing at Calle Manuel del Llano Oriente No. 334
PEDRO L. GONZALEZ, residing at Serafin Pena Norte No. 714
PEDRO G. GONZALEZ, residing at General Trevino Poniente No. 1221

This source advised that he was continuing efforts to locate and identify JORGE DAVILA, CECILIO CARDENAZ, JOSE CRUZ, and MAXIMINO ESQUIVEL.

It was determined on April 15, 1964, through a check of the Central Office, Immigration and Naturalization Service (INS), Washington, D. C., that the master index contained records of three border crossing cards for persons who could possibly be identical with the Transportes del Norte bus passenger, EULALIO RODRIGUEZ. The information appearing on these border crossing cards is as follows:

Border Crossing Card No. 507572 was issued at Laredo, Texas, November 26, 1958, to EULALIO RODRIGUEZ PERALES, born

-12-

COMMISSION EXHIBIT No. 2472—Continued

May 12, 1934, at Linares, Nuevo Leon, Mexico, residence 23 de Abril Norte No. 1814, Monterrey, Nuevo Leon, Mexico.

Border Crossing Card No. 263316 was issued at Laredo, Texas, April 9, 1957, to EULALIO RODRIGUEZ CARRILLO, born February 12, 1934, at San Luis Potosi, State of San Luis Potosi, Mexico, residence Lago de Pascuaro Poniente No. 101, Monterrey, Nuevo Leon, Mexico.

Border Crossing Card No. 1339074 was issued July 9, 1963, at Laredo, Mexico, to EULALIO RODRIGUEZ GALVAN, born April 16, 1923, at Rio Verde, San Luis Potosi, Mexico, employed as a body mechanic, residence Ruperto Martinez Oriente No. 956, Monterrey, Nuevo Leon, Mexico.

T-2 advised as follows:

On April 30, 1964, EULALIO RODRIGUEZ GALVAN, who resides at Washington Oriente No. 1220, Monterrey, Nuevo Leon, advised that he formerly resided at Ruperto Martinez Oriente No. 956 in Monterrey. He stated he is 40 years of age and an unemployed solderer. He said he had not visited the United States since September, 1963, when he traveled to Brownsville, Texas. He related that he also visited McAllen and Mission, Texas, at that time and was arrested by United States Immigration officers and deported to Mexico. He said he had been required to surrender his border crossing card at that time. He affirmed that he had not returned to the United States since that time and had not been a passenger on the aforementioned Transportes del Norte bus.

On May 1, 1964, JOSE RODRIGUEZ PERALES, who resides at 23 de Abril Norte No. 1814, Colonia Venustiano Carranza, Monterrey, advised that he has a brother named EULALIO RODRIGUEZ PERALES, who for some time has been residing at Alamo, Texas, and is employed at the Jones Office Supply, 1065 Broadway, McAllen, Texas. He did not know EULALIO's street address but stated his mailing address is Post Office Box 175, Alamo.

Efforts are being made to locate and interview EULALIO RODRIGUEZ PERALES at McAllen and Alamo, Texas.

Source reported on May 6, 1964, that he had been unable to locate EULALIO RODRIGUEZ CARRILLO who is registered as residing at Lago de Pascuaro Poniente No. 101, Monterrey, but was continuing efforts to locate this person.

At Guadalajara, Jalisco, Mexico

On April 3, 1964, Vice Consul OTTO WAGNER, United States Consulate General, Guadalajara, reported that no record of a United States visa issued during August, September, and October, 1963, could be located for the following:

HILDA QUEZADA
JOSE CRUZ
CECILIO CARDENAZ
MAXIMINO ESQUIVEL
PEDRO GONZALEZ

T-8, a confidential source abroad, advised on April 19, 22, and 28, 1964, that he had conducted the following investigation at Guadalajara:

A check of the local telephone directory, files of the power and light company, and the Guadalajara Census Bureau failed to locate any information which would aid in identifying the passengers listed below. Source advised that the names are common in the area and that he had interviewed numerous persons with the same surnames without locating anyone who was acquainted with the passengers.

HILDA QUEZADA
JOSE CRUZ
MAXIMINO ESQUIVEL
CECILIO CARDENAZ
PEDRO GONZALEZ

MEMORANDUM REPORT (7-1-50)

UNITED STATES SECRET SERVICE
TREASURY DEPARTMENT

ORIGIN Field (Dallas)	OFFICE Dallas, Texas		FILE NO. CO-2-34030
TYPE OF CASE Protective Research	STATUS Continued	TITLE OR CAPTION Assassination of President Kennedy	
INVESTIGATION MADE AT Dallas, Texas	PERIOD COVERED 11/30 - 12/5/63	Robert H. Klause	
INVESTIGATION MADE BY Special Agents William H. Patterson and Unum Brady		[redacted]	

\- Commission Exhibit No. 2473 —

DETAILS

SYNOPSIS

Photo of late President on derogatory leaflet circulated in Dallas was made for unknown customer by Robert H. Klause. He could probably identify. Actual film shot at Monk Brothers, 2027 Young Street, Dallas, Texas.

DETAILS OF INVESTIGATION

Reference is made to handbills, derogatory in nature, bearing face and profile shots of President Kennedy, captioned: "Wanted for Treason", which were circulated in Dallas during the week of the assassination.

Other Investigation

On November 30, 1963, SA's Brady and Patterson interviewed Mr. J. T. Monk, proprietor of Monk Brothers, photo-engravers, at 2027 Young Street, Dallas, Texas, together with his assistant, Clifford Spencer. After viewing the front and profile of President Kennedy's photo on the inflammatory handbill, Spencer recalled that about a month ago he made these shots on film from newspaper or magazine clipping approximately 3½" high. Spencer made the negative and his customer picked up both the negative and copy. Spencer identified his customer as Bob Klause of 2615 Oaklawn and said there is no question as to the person's identity as he is well acquainted with Klause. This identity was also verified by J. T. Monk, Jr., son of the proprietor.

On November 30, 1963, SA's Brady and Patterson interviewed Mrs. Dorothy Mercer, owner of the Letter Craft Printers, 2615 Oaklawn, who said she could find no record covering this transaction. Mrs. Mercer stated that Klause is her son. He has been employed at the printing company since October 1962, and resides at 1126 S. Waverly. Mrs. Mercer did not disclose the family

DISTRIBUTION Chief Dallas	COPIES Orig.&2cc 2 cc	REPORT MADE BY SPECIAL AGENT	DATE 12-6-63
		APPROVED 482 SPECIAL AGENT IN CHARGE	DATE 12-6-63

(CONTINUE ON PLAIN PAPER) U. S. GOVERNMENT PRINTING OFFICE 16—61508-1

COMMISSION EXHIBIT No. 2473

CO-2-34030
12-6-63

connection between her and Mr. Klause until inquiry developed the information.

On December 1, 1963, Klause was interviewed by SA's Patterson and Brady. He is Robert G. Klause, age 32, and readily acknowledged making the film negative for the questioned shots. Klause said his customer, whose name he does not know, but whom he thought might be another printer, and who was white, male, about 5' 7", short curly hair, maybe in his early 30's, came into the shop between 11:30 A.M. and 12:00 noon one day. Subject was wearing slacks and a sport shirt. Klause said his customer's copy appeared to have been taken from a slick type magazine. The pictures were ragged in appearance, and the customer asked him to make two shots, 4 x 6 or 4 x 5, and arranged so that he could get a border on them together. Klause told his customer that he could make the film, and that he would have same ready during the early afternoon. After one or more unsuccessful attempts, Klause saw that he would be unable to copy the pictures successfully and that the reproduction might involve re-screening. Klause said he took the job to Monk's and obtained the film negative; that he made delivery to his unknown customer on that same day at about 4:00 or 4:30 P.M. He charged the customer $4.00 for the job, which was paid in cash. Klause did not write up this sale, as he said he saw a chance to make a few dollars on the side. Hence no record is available for this transaction. Klause said no other employees were at the shop, as they had gone home for the day. He thought the customer might have been a printer because of the appearance of ink about his nails and on his hands. He conceded this may not be ink and might have been grease or other stain. Klause felt sure that he would know this party if he sees him again. He said he would call us if he did.

Agents agree that the description of the customer by Klause may be different from that of Oswald, but on the other hand a check of the printed text in the subject shows errors of syntax and spelling similar to that contained in known Oswald writings. "He has consistantly appointed Anti-Christians---" "previous marraige and divorce" "insp- ired" instead of in-spired for proper hyphenation. Also, the text states in part "----wanted for treasonous activities" but more accurate usage would have been "----wanted for treasonable acts". These errors are consistent with the type of errors found in Oswald's written expressions. The text is somewhat soft on Cuba, but hard on Russia and Communism. It is recalled that Oswald was disenchanted with the Soviet and avowed he was not a Communist, but a Marxist. The text tends to extreme right, but we feel it is not significant of the unpredictable Oswald in his search of derogatory material for his subject, President Kennedy. This handbill was constructed within weeks of the President's visit.

482

482

COMMISSION EXHIBIT No. 2473—Continued

CO-2-34030
12-6-63

On December 5, 1963 in Dallas, Texas, SA Brady interviewed Mr. Robert G. Klause at 2615 Oaklawn Avenue, and displayed to him two good photos of Lee Harvey Oswald and one of Jack Ruby. After examining the pictures, Mr. Klause said he is able to state that, in his opinion, neither Oswald nor Ruby is the person for whom he obtained the photo film showing face and profile of President Kennedy.

He said that, in his opinion, the purchaser of this film had the general appearance of Oswald and closely resembles him, except that the customer, he recalls, had heavier brown hair in front, which appeared to be somewhat curly, whereas Oswald's hairline appears to be receding. The customer's figure and physical build, otherwise closely parallels that of Oswald. He was in casual dress - sport shirt and slacks.

Mr. Klause said he would promptly report any re-appearance of this customer

DISPOSITION

Continued.

WHP:mla

482

Commission Exhibit No. 2473—Continued

Form No. 1580 (Revised) Memorandum Report (7-1-56)

UNITED STATES SECRET SERVICE
TREASURY DEPARTMENT

ORIGIN Field	OFFICE Dallas, Texas	FILE NO. CO-2-34,030
TYPE OF CASE: Protective Research	STATUS: Continued	TITLE OR CAPTION: Assassination of President Kennedy
INVESTIGATION MADE AT: Dallas, Texas	PERIOD COVERED: 4-29/5-11/64	Robert H. Klause
INVESTIGATION MADE BY: SA John Joe Howlett		[redacted]

Commission Exhibit No. 2474

DETAILS

SYNOPSIS

Investigation has not yet positively identified printer of "Wanted for Treason" leaflets. Investigation continued.

DETAILS OF INVESTIGATION

Reference is made to my M/R dated 4-30-64.

Other Investigations

On 4-29-64 I interviewed Mr. Dean Campbell of the Dallas Times Herald. Mr. Campbell said that their route man, Mr. W. R. Wynn, 14537 Dennis Lane, Farmers Branch, Texas, saw some of the "Wanted for Treason" leaflets.

I interviewed Mr. Wynn and he stated that he found some leaflets around the Magnolia Building, 106 S. Akard, Dallas; United Fidelity Building, 1025 Elm, Dallas; and the Texas Bank Building, 810 Main, Dallas. Mr. Wynn said that these leaflets appeared two or three days prior to the parade and I showed him a copy of the printed "Wanted for Treason" leaflets and they were not the same leaflets. Mr. Wynn described the leaflets that he saw as being on white paper, approximately 8" x 11" or 9" x 12". The writing appeared to be in a red marking pencil and was handwritten and handprinted. He said he threw all of the leaflets away and did not have a sample, but from the best of his memory, they had printed on them, "Wanted for Treason," "J. F. Fink," and "Go Home J. F. Fink." Mr. Wynn said this was the first time he had seen the printed "Wanted for Treason" leaflet and that the ones found in the Dallas Times Herald circulation dispensers were not the same type of leaflet.

Mr. Campbell said that to the best of his knowledge, the leaflets appeared only on the route carried by Mr. Wynn. Mr. Campbell also said that the number of

DISTRIBUTION	COPIES	REPORT MADE BY	DATE
Chief ✓	Orig & 2 cc	[signature] SPECIAL AGENT	5-12-64
Dallas	2 cc	APPROVED: [signature] SPECIAL AGENT IN CHARGE	5-12-64

(CONTINUE ON PLAIN PAPER)

U. S. GOVERNMENT PRINTING OFFICE 16—61506-1

Commission Exhibit No. 2474

2.
CO-2-34,030

leaflets in their street dispensers did not amount to the number indicated in some of the newspaper and magazine articles about the incident. Mr. Campbell said that he did not believe there was over a half dozen or maybe a dozen or so.

On 4-29-64 I telephoned FBI Agent Robert Gemberling and asked how many of the leaflets they had on hand. Mr. Gemberling checked his files and phoned back later to say that his reports do not indicate the number of leaflets that they received, only that they kept a few samples and turned some over to the Secret Service, Dallas. Agent Gemberling said that he was not positive as to the exact number, but guessed that they only had a few samples.

On 4-30-64, I interviewed Sheriff Bill Decker, Dallas County Sheriff, who produced twenty-two leaflets. Sheriff Decker said that his records have no information as to the total number of leaflets distributed and no attempt had been made to determine an estimate.

On 5-5-64 I interviewed Mr. J. T. Monk, of Monk Brothers, 2027 Young Street, Dallas. Mr. Monk said that he was uncertain as to the price of reproducing the pictures, therefore, was unable to determine the exact date that they made the negatives. The reason for this is because to the best of their memory, the pictures were line shots and did not require half-toning, as the pictures would have already been half-toned, but their price indicates that it was a half-tone job. Mr. Monk said that it was possible that in making the charge, that they looked at the picture and saw that it was half-toned and made the charge for this amount even though they simply made a line shot.

Mr. Monk said that he went on a vacation November 15, 1963, and returned to Dallas on November 22, 1963. To the best of his knowledge and that of his wife, Rita Monk, it was just a few days, or possibly the day before, they left on vacation. The tickets for Lettercraft during the month of November 1963 were searched completely and it is believed that the negative was made on either November 13 or November 14, 1963. On 11-13-63 a ticket shows one 5x8, charge $2.90 and one 5x6, charge $2.15, total bill $5.05. Mr. Monk said that he does not believe they would have shot two different size negatives in reproducing the pictures. On November 14, 1963, ticket indicates one 5x8, charge $2.90. Mr. Monk says that he believes this is the ticket for the transaction, however, the charge, $2.90, indicates half-tone pictures. For this reason, Mr. Monk said that he believes a mistake was made in billing the transaction.

Mrs. Rita Monk said that she noticed the negative as it was drying and looked at it. She said that she is fairly sure that there was only one negative, with both front and profile view, and that it was 5x8 inches in size.

Therefore, as best it can be determined, it appears that the negative was made and delivered on November 14, 1963.

COMMISSION EXHIBIT No. 2474—Continued

3.
CO-2-34,030

Mr. Monk stated that they had lost the Lettercraft business since this incident. However, he replied that if they are going to be that way about it, he doesn't care if he ever gets their business again. Mr. Monk produced his records showing that Lettercraft made 10 purchases in September, 12 purchases in October, 16 purchases in November, and 1 purchase in December, 1963. In 1964, they made no purchases in January, 6 purchases in February, 6 purchases in March, and 1 purchase in April. Lettercraft failed to pay their bill, and Mr. Monk said that he contacted them and asked that they pay their bill and asked why they had not been receiving their business. They replied that they had not been doing any work which required the assistance of Monk Brothers. Lettercraft then paid its bill in February which dated back to November and covered the particular transaction under investigation.

Mr. Monk said that they never had received much line work for Lettercraft and that they mostly did half-tone and fine line work.

Mr. Monk said that he had known Robert Klause for several years, but did not know of any organizations or political activities that Klause had engaged in. Mr. Monk said from his experience, Robert Klause is poor to average in his work, and really does not know too much about the printing business.

Mr. Monk examined the circular (leaflet) and said that in his opinion, it was run on a small 1250 type press, running head first, top of the leaflet. Mr. Monk said that there were slurs in the ink running from top to bottom of the printed leaflet, which gave him this impression. Mr. Monk also called attention to the letters - E, A, and O - which gave him this impression. Mr. Monk also called attention to the letters - E, A, and O - which were closing up in places. Mr. Monk said that in his opinion, this indicated to him that the copy stand was not working properly. He said that it could either be insufficient vacuum or a sponge rubber type copy stand.

Mr. Monk said that he could not think of anything or see anything on the leaflet that would be traceable with any degree of certainty.

Mr. Monk also called attention to the fact that a smaller size type could have been used, then an enlarging line photograph taken, to increase the size of the type. Mr. Monk said that in view of the closed Es, As, and Os, and the general appearance of the leaflet, he thought this may be the case. Mr. Monk was asked how it came to his attention that he made the negatives for this leaflet. Mr. Monk said his wife's mother went out into her yard to work on Monday after the assassination and found one of the leaflets in the shrubery and flowers. She kept the leaflet and later showed it to Mrs. Rita Monk, who recognized the photographs to be similar to the negatives she had observed in their shop.

The leaflet was shown to Mr. Clifford Spencer, who actually did the photography, and he said that he believes they are the same. Mr. Clifford Spencer was interviewed and he said that he is not sure if it was a half-tone or line shot,

COMMISSION EXHIBIT No. 2474—Continued

4.
CO-2-34,030

but to the best of his memory, he believes that it was a line shot. Mr. Spencer also said that to the best of his knowledge, there was only one negative made and that the pictures on the "Wanted for Treason" leaflets appear to be the same as the negative that he made.

On 5-5-64 I interviewed Mr. Joseph B. Harman, Office Manager, American Type Founders Company, Incorporated, 2276 Vantage, Dallas. Mr. Harman said that in his opinion, the type would not be traceable because of its common nature. Mr. Harman exhibited samples of all of the type manufactured by American Type Founders and there appeared to be two or three different types that were similar to those used on the leaflet. There was also several different sizes of the similar types. Mr. Harman also called attention to the fact that there are several other different companies that manufacture and sell type in this area.

In view of the common style of type used, the several different companies manufacturing type, and the various sizes within each style of type, it is believed that it is impossible to attempt to trace the type.

On 5-5-64 I reinterviewed Mr. James S. Wagnon, Vice-President, Olmsted-Kirk Paper Company. Mr. Wagnon furnished copies of all the orders for Lettercraft during 1964. All orders, other than the assorted dodger paper, like that used to print the "Wanted for Treason" leaflets, were disregarded. On 1-29-64 10,000 assorted dodgers were purchased. A shipping note said, "Today" and was signed by Billy Eason. On 3-20-64, 15,000 assorted dodgers were purchased. The shipping notice read, "Early Mon. A.M." and was signed by Klause. This was the total assorted dodger purchases for Lettercraft from Olmsted-Kirk Paper Company during 1964.

Mr. C. A. Kirby, Senior Foreman, Sanitation Department, City of Dallas, and Mr. M. O. Satterfield, Foreman, Sanitation Department, City of Dallas, were interviewed. They both stated that they had never seen any of the "Wanted for Treason" leaflets and that none of the Sanitation men had called them to their attention. It was determined that Mr. Ted Brashear, 2407 Community, Dallas, was the driver of the Sanitation Department truck which picked up trash from Lettercraft Printing Company, 2615 Oak Lawn. His assistants were Mr. C. O. Barnes, 4431 Helen, Dallas and Tommy Waters, Jr., 3403 Whateley Place, Dallas. Tommy Waters was interviewed and stated that he had never seen the leaflets before. It was also noted that Mr. Waters can barely read and write. Mr. C. O. Barnes was interviewed and said that he had never seen the leaflets before. It was also noted that he could barely read and write.

Mr. Ted Brashear was interviewed and stated that he had never seen the leaflet before, however, he had picked up three garbage cans full of leaflets containing President Kennedy's picture. He said these were picked up about a week or two before the assassination and while he could not give me the exact address, he could take me to the location. Mr. Brashear said that most of their work is in the alleys and he does not know the street number where these were picked up. Mr. Brashear directed me to the alley behind

5.
CO-2-34,030

Lettercraft Printing Company and pointed out the garbage cans directly in the rear of Lettercraft Printing Company, as the location where these leaflets were picked up.

Mr. Brashear described these leaflets as being on white paper, approximately 12" x 14" and containing a large full face photograph of President Kennedy. To the best of his knowledge, there was no writing under the picture, other than President Kennedy's name. Mr. Brashear said that he remembers this because he was new on the route and had another man driving it while he was learning the route. At this time, Mr. Brashear was working the top of the truck and was the individual that emptied the garbage cans into the truck. He stated that he noticed the picture of President Kennedy and thought that it was a good picture so he got a handful that had not been bent up and soiled. He stated that he put these into the cab of his truck. To the best of his knowledge, he said there three garbage cans full and estimated that there must have been several thousand of them, as they had just been stuffed down in the gargabe cans.

Mr. Brashear stated that he had left these leaflets in the cab of his truck for a couple of weeks, then selected two or three of them and took them home. Mr. Brashear and I proceeded to his home and were informed by Mr. Brashear's wife that she had thrown the leaflets away. Since the time of the assassination, Mr. and Mrs. Brashear have moved twice and Mrs. Brashear said it was during one of these moves that she destroyed the leaflets.

From Mr. Brashear's description, the background of the picture was white instead of black, like the full face photograph on the "Wanted for Treason" leaflets. However, Mr. Brashear said that it was a full face photograph similar to the one on the "Wanted for Treason" leaflet.

On 5-6-64, SA Gene Wofford and I interviewed Robert Klause at Lettercraft Printing Company. Mr. Klause said that to the best of his memory, there were two negatives shot on the front and side profile of President Kennedy. He stated that he had no idea who the person was for whom he had the negatives made. He stated that an individual came to the print shop and asked that he, Klause, make the negatives for him. Robert Klause said that he thought he would be able to make the negatives himself so he took the job. However, he said that he later found out he could not copy the pictures. He said that he was having difficulty getting his screen to line up with the screen already on the picture he was trying to copy. From the way Klause talked, it appeared that he was attempting to half-tone a picture which had already been half-toned. He said that he was coming up with large black specks on his negative.

Robert Klause said that he was willing to cooperate in any way possible to help us identify the printer and/or financier of the leaflets. Klause was asked if he would be willing to take a lie detector test and he stated that he would be.

An attempt was made to run Klause on the polygraph and it was found to be busy. Klause agreed that when we set up the appointment we could contact him and that he would take the test. Later in the day, an appointment was obtained for 1 P.M. and unsuccessful efforts were made to locate Klause. During the afternoon, Klause phoned the Secret Service Office and talked with SA Patterson and informed SA Patterson that he, Klause, had talked with his attorney and his attorney said that he did not have to take the test and that he, Klause, had decided not to take the test. After obtaining this message from SA Patterson, SA Wofford and I attempted to relocate Klause, but without success.

Mr. Billy Easom, printer for Lettercraft Printing Company, was interviewed. Mr. Easom said that he had no idea who had printed the "Wanted for Treason" leaflet and that he had not observed any cuttings, plates, or blanket impressions around the printing shop. Billy Easom was asked if he would be willing to take a polygraph test and he replied that he would. However, he stated that he was going to have to work late to complete a job that had to be delivered the next day and asked that we delay the polygraph test. Billy Easom was informed that we would contact him later about the polygraph test.

On 5-6-64 Mr. and Mrs. Mercer, owners, Lettercraft Printing Company, were interviewed. Robert Klause is the son of Mrs. Mercer. Mrs. Mercer said that she felt sure the "Wanted for Treason" leaflets were not printed in her shop because she has not seen any evidence, spoilage, etc., resembling the "Wanted for Treason" leaflet. Mrs. Mercer also said that they have not done any political printing.

On 5-11-64, Robert Klause was reinterviewed at Lettercraft Printing Company. Robert Klause complained that we were taking him from his work and that he had a wife and three children to feed. He stated that he works strictly on a commission and that he is not making any money while talking with us. Extensive efforts were made to get Robert Klause to go on the polygraph, but he refused to do so. When asked why he agreed to go on it and changed his mind, he stated that he did not know his rights, but after consulting his attorney, he was informed that he did not have to take the test. In response to our questions, Klause admitted that we did not tell him he had to go on the test, but continued saying that he was unsure as to his position at that time, but after consulting an attorney, he does not want to take the test. Extensive efforts were also made to have Robert Klause name the individual for whom he had the negatives made, or printed the leaflets, but he continued to say that he did not know the individual.

Robert Klause said that his attorney was Don C. Alexander, Dallas Federal Savings Building, Phone RIverside 7-0374. In response to my question, Robert Klause said that he did not have an attorney as such, but that he had approached this attorney about the pending incident. Klause said that he had called Mr. Alexander and talked with him over the phone and received advice as to his rights. In response to my questioning, Klause said that he had not used this attorney before,

but that he had simply phoned him and talked with him over the phone. I asked Klause if the attorney would have remembered the incident and Klause replied that he doubted it, as he only talked with him for a few moments. I called Klause's attention to the fact that an attorney's product was his advice and that it seemed peculiar to me that an attorney would talk with a stranger over the phone, furnish advice, and not submit a bill. Klause replied that he didn't know about that. Two or three different attempts were made at questioning Klause along the lines of his attorney, and he continued to say that he didn't know if the attorney would remember it or not, but I was unable to get Klause to change his story.

Mrs. Mercer, owner of Lettercraft Printing Company, became quite upset during our visit. She stated that we were bothering her employees, getting them so excited and nervous, that they were unable to do their work. Mrs. Mercer was visibly disturbed and upset during our interview with her and she mentioned two or three different times why we wanted to run her printer, Billy Easom, on the lie detector. Mrs. Mercer said that she had contacted her attorney and found out that her son, Robert Klause, and her printer, Billy Easom, did not have to take a polygraph test unless they wanted to. Extensive efforts were made through Mrs. Mercer to get her to influence Robert Klause to take a polygraph examination, and get the matter settled. Mrs. Mercer indicated several times that she thought we were picking on her son because he had a prior criminal record and she attempted to name several other printing companies which she thought might run this type of work. It was pointed out to Mrs. Mercer that the leaflet was printed using the negative which her son had made. Since her son had had the negative in his possession, he was unable or would not identify the person to whom he gave it. Since this was the case, she was informed that our investigation would continue at her printing company until we exhausted all possible leads, or were able to trace it to another individual.

Mr. Mercer became quite upset during our visit and stated that we were hurting his business and keeping his employees from working. He also complained about our wanting to run their printer, Billy Easom, on the polygraph and said that he could not understand why Billy Easom should be dragged into this. Mr. Mercer indicated that they were quite busy and asked that we complete this investigation as soon as possible. Mr. Mercer was informed that it was our desire to complete this investigation as soon as we could, and that we felt sure that with the cooperation of Robert Klause we could finish the investigation in considerably less time.

An effort was made to get Robert Klause to accompany us to the office and he became quite upset and asked if we were charging him with anything. He was informed that he was not under arrest and was not being charged with anything, that we simply wanted to go downtown, contact his lawyer, and talk about the matter. Robert Klause asked to leave the room and he departed for a few minutes. Mr. and Mrs. Mercer returned shortly, wanting to know why we were taking Robert Klause downtown and wanted to know if he was being charged with anything. Mr. and Mrs. Mercer were informed that he was not being charged with anything; that we simply asked that he come downtown with us. Mr. Mercer asked if Robert Klause had to go downtown with us and he was informed that we asked Robert Klause to go downtown with us. To this, Mr. Mercer replied, I suggest that he refuse to go downtown with you and stated that they just had too much work to do for Robert Klause to be going downtown with us. Mrs. Mercer was also quite disturbed and asked if Robert Klause was being charged with anything. She also was informed that he was not under arrest and was not being charged with anything; that we simply wanted to go downtown to contact his lawyer and talk about the matter.

Robert Klause stated that he had too much work to do to come downtown with us. He was asked to contact his lawyer and to make arrangements where we could all meet and talk about the matter. Robert Klause advised that he would contact this agent by 4:30 P.M., 5-11-64, or early morning 5-12-64.

During the two visits to Lettercraft Printing Company, the following information was obtained from the company records. On 11-5-63, Lettercraft received an order for 3,000 circulars, using the dodger paper like that used for the "Wanted for Treason" leaflets. The circulars were promised for delivery on 11-10-63. On 11-12-63, Lettercraft received an order for 15,000 circulars using the dodger paper. This was all of the dodger paper used for printing circulars during the months of October, November, and December, 1963. Mr. and Mrs. Mercer, Robert Klause, and Billy Easom, all stated that they used this dodger paper for printing scratch pads. They print 9" x 12" sheets with a Lettercraft Printing Company heading and cut the 9" x 12" sheet into 4 scratch pads which are glued at the top end. While going through the orders for October, November, and December 1963, I noticed several sheets from these scratch pads upon which notes had been made and placed in the files for the various orders. Therefore, it appears that a good deal of this dodger paper is used for the printing of these scratch pads. Billy Easom and Robert Klause both stated that they print about 10,000 sheets of this dodger paper at a time which would cut out to about 40,000 scratch pads. Billy Easom and Robert Klause both said that these scratch pads do not last long, as the salesmen give them away and they usually include some when they deliver orders. Billy Easom said that they usually run these scratch pads about once a month, however, they haven't run any for the last couple of months or so.

The withholding tax records reviewed for the last quarter of 1963 and in addition to Mr. and Mrs. Mercer, Billy Easom, and Robert Klause, they show the following employees: Homer Dwight Hatcher, Social Security Number 452-52-6749, earnings $80; Jasper R. Hawkins, Social Security Number 451-01-2728, earnings $116; Henry Davila, Social Security Number 456-52-3254, earnings $682.66; Margo Frances Brown, Social Security Number 061-38-4061, earnings, $76.80.

During our visit on 5-11-64 Robert Klause was asked to write the words, "consistently" and "marriage." He correctly spelled "marriage" but incorrectly spelled "consistently" however, it was not the same misspelling as that in the "Wanted for Treason" leaflet.

UNDEVELOPED LEADS

Investigation continued.

JJH:wd

Commission Exhibit No. 2475–A

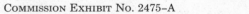

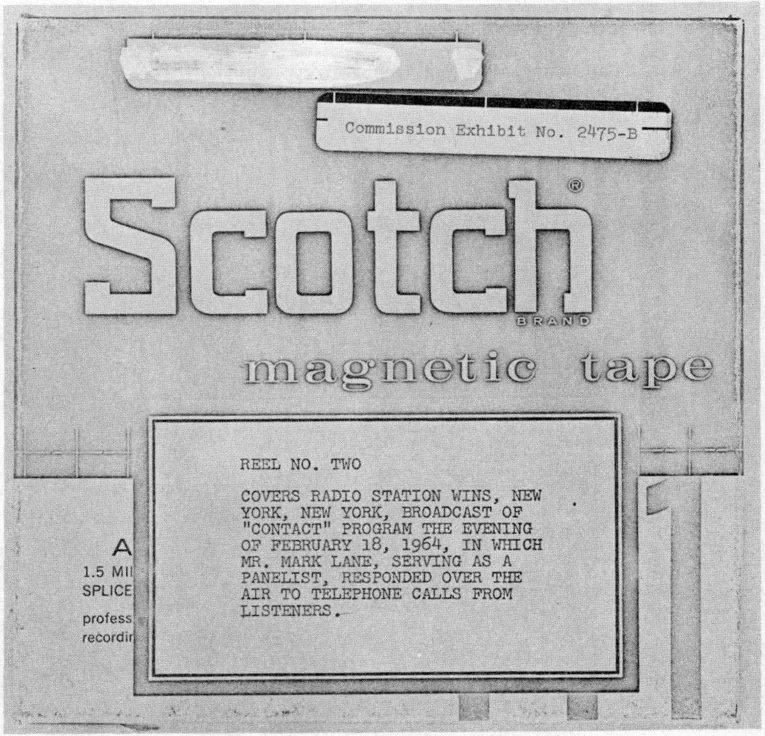

Commission Exhibit No. 2475–B

EXCERPT FROM THE TWO REELS OF TAPE COVERING THE "CONTACT" PROGRAM OF FEBRUARY 18, 1964, OVER RADIO STATION WINS, NEW YORK, NEW YORK, BEING THE CONTENTS OF THE TELEPHONE CONVERSATION BETWEEN MURRAY BURNETT, MARK LANE, AND BERNARD WEISSMAN.

COMMISSION EXHIBIT NO. 2475-C

Mr. Burnett: Good evening here on "Contact".

The Caller: Oh. Hello.

Mr. Burnett: Yes.

The Caller: I'd like to ask Mr. Lane if he doesn't think it's strange that, since the Ruby trial -- since the case was so well covered -- since the Kennedy case was so well covered that no pictures of Officer Tippit appear, even a high school picture. I mean, I got about three newspapers and I didn't see any pictures in the papers.

Mr. Lane: That was an interesting point. I will tell you this. There was a conference which took place just a week before the assassination. Present at that conference was Bernard Weissman, the gentleman who placed the full page ad in the Dallas Morning News that practically accused the President of treason. Also present at that conference was Officer Tippit, and there was a third person whose name I will not mention although I have his name now, but there are reasons for which I cannot reveal it now.

Mr. Burnett: Fascinating.

Mr. Lane: And this conference took place in a strip joint called the Carousel, in Dallas, Texas.

Mr. Burnett: A strip joint called the Carousel?

Mr. Lane: Yes.

* * * * * *

COMMISSION EXHIBIT NO. 2475-C—Continued

And I'm Murray Burnett on "Contact" WINS. Tonight we're talking to Mark Lane, who's the attorney for the mother of Lee Harvey Oswald, the accused assassin of President Kennedy, and also to William M. Kuntzler, whose written a fantastic book called "The Minister and the Choir Singer" which is the story of the Hall Mills murder case and which, at the start of the program is not only a fascinating book but is also going to be turned into a fantastic motion picture, but also has some astonishing similarities at least in press coverage and in confusion to the assassination of the late President Kennedy. And now we'll get back to our phones here at JUdson 2-7000.

Mr. Burnett: Good evening here at "Contact".

Mr. Weissman: Hello, is Mr. Lane present? This is Bernie Weissman.

Mr. Burnett: Yes. Bernard Weissman of Dallas?

Mr. Weissman: Yes. That's right.

Mr. Lane: Yes. Hello.

Mr. Weissman: Mr. Lane?

Mr. Lane: Yes. I saw your ad down there. Very impressed by it.

Mr. Weissman: Yeah, so I understand. You know that there has been several statements you've made this evening, as a matter of fact the newspapers have been bothering me somewhat also about them.

Mr. Lane: Yes.

COMMISSION EXHIBIT No. 2475-C—Continued

Mr. Weissman: That in your capacity in representing the assassin Oswald and his mother Marguerite --

Mr. Lane: Yes.

Mr. Weissman: -- and you're saying that you have evidence that I knew this Patrolman Tippit and that I was in the Carousel bar and so on and so forth.

Mr. Lane: Yes.

Mr. Weissman: Yes, you're being very mysterious. You know I ---

Mr. Lane: Well, did you know Patrolman Tippit?

Mr. Weissman: No, frankly.

Mr. Lane: Never saw him?

Mr. Weissman: I don't have the faintest idea of what he even looks like.

Mr. Lane: Were you ever in the Carousel?

Mr. Weissman: I was never in the Carousel bar, and I don't know Oswald ---

Mr. Lane: Never? In your life?

Mr. Weissman: And I don't know Oswald, or Ruby, or anybody else involved in this thing.

Mr. Lane: I see.

Mr. Weissman: And, this leads me to believe, you know, that it seems to me --

Mr. Lane: Yes.

Mr. Weissman: -- that you're grabbing at straws somehow. That you're looking to throw the case.

COMMISSION EXHIBIT No. 2475-C—Continued

Mr. Lane: Well, let me tell you this, Mr. Weissman. Some very, very respectable citizen in Dallas --

Mr. Weissman: Uh-huh.

Mr. Lane: -- who gave me this information, says you were there. I'd like to see you confront him, and I'd like to see you two discuss this together. Do you think we can arrange that?

Mr. Weissman: Well, I'll tell you something Mr. Lane --

Mr. Lane: Can we arrange that?

Mr. Weissman: This is something I'd like to get straight with you first, you know, because obviously you're hearing one side of the story here, and it's very erroneous.

Mr. Lane: I'd like very much to meet with you, I assure you, Mr. Weissman.

Mr. Weissman: Well, all right. Now, I'm sure you know my address.

Mr. Lane: I don't know your address. But perhaps you can give it to me now.

Mr. Burnett: You can give your address/on the telephone, sir, it's all right.

Mr. Weissman: Can I?

Mr. Burnett: He can. Yes.

Mr. Lane: What is your address, sir?

Mr. Weissman: (chuckle-chuckle) I'm sure you know where to find me.

Mr. Lane: I don't know where to find you. I just read your ad. That's all I know about you.

COMMISSION EXHIBIT No. 2475-C—Continued

Mr. Weissman: The fact is, if you're going to make statements like this --

Mr. Lane: Yes.

Mr. Weissman: --and more or less - not libel me - but to give a very very poor impression, and wrong impression, I would certainly wish that when you do something like this, where a man's entire future is at stake, that you contact them first and try to find out the facts --

Mr. Lane: I told you, I'd like very much to talk with you, I think ----

Mr. Burnett: Wait a minute. I may have a suggestion here. Mr. Weissman, if you - if this program -- I'm not cutting you off, but this program runs until one a.m., and if you would care to call back privately, after one a.m. --- Mr. Lane, would you want to talk with him?

Mr. Lane: Yes. I'd like to get your address, and I'd like to meet with you, and I would like --

Mr. Weissman: That's up to you, sir?

Mr. Lane: Can we arrange that, Mr. Weissman?

Mr. Weissman: Yes. In fact, let's see. I'll call you back at 1:05, how's that?

Mr. Lane: Excellent. I'll be here waiting for your call, very anxiously I assure you.

Mr. Burnett: Mr. Weissman, I'll give you a private number to call. Yes, - - I'll - - I'll give you a number to call. Judson 2-7015.

Mr. Weissman: 2 - 7 - 0 - 1 - 5.

Mr. Burnett: Yes.

Mr. Weissman: All right, fine.

Mr. Burnett: Do you have anything else that you want to say on the air?

COMMISSION EXHIBIT No. 2475-C—Continued

- 5 -

Mr. Weissman: Frankly, no. That's all.

Mr. Burnett: Thank you for calling. Good-bye now.

This is Murray Burnett on "Contact" WINS, the show that puts you in touch and on the air with the most interesting people in the world. And I would like to also to remind you that this is a group W station, Westinghouse Broadcasting in New York. WINS, 1010 on your dial. And I see that I have made a mistake by giving out a telephone number. And I wish people would forget it. All right, let's go and take our next call. Judson 2-7000.

COMMISSION EXHIBIT No. 2475-C—Continued

FD-302 (Rev. 1-25-60)

FEDERAL BUREAU OF INVESTIGATION

Date 7/8/64

LINDA PRIESTLY, Secretary to MURRAY BURNETT, who conducts radio interview program "Contact" broadcast over Radio Station WINS was contacted at WINS studio, 7 Central Park West, New York, New York.

She advised that according to her records MARK LANE appeared as a guest on the "Contact" program February 18, 1964. WILLIAM M. KUNTZLER, Author of the book entitled "The Minister and the Choir Singer" which is about the HALL MILLS murder case that occurred in 1922, was also a guest on the program.

She furnished a copy of a tape of this program, consisting of two reels. She believed that the conversation between Mr. BERNARD WEISSMAN and Mr. MARK LANE was on the first reel.

On 7/6/64 at New York, New York File # 44-974

by SA JAMES J. ROGERS/hjb Date dictated 7/8/64

This document contains neither recommendations nor conclusions of the FBI. It is the property of the FBI and is loaned to your agency; it and its contents are not to be distributed outside your agency.

COMMISSION EXHIBIT No. 2475-D

FD-302 (Rev. 1-25-60)

FEDERAL BUREAU OF INVESTIGATION

Date 7/8/64

MURRAY BURNETT who resides at 2711 Henry Hudson Parkway, Riverdale, Bronx, New York, telephone number KI 9-3723 and who conducts radio interview program "Contact" broadcast over Radio Station WINS, New York, New York, furnished the following information:

MARK LANE had appeared as a guest on the program "Contact" broadcast over WINS on or about February 18, 1964. During this program BERNARD WEISSMAN telephoned the radio station and a conversation between WEISSMAN and LANE was broadcast over the program.

BURNETT said he could furnish no additional information other than that which is on the tape recording of the program.

BURNETT recalled that WEISSMAN did call the radio station WINS about 1:05 a.m. and spoke to MARK LANE. BURNETT believed that WEISSMAN and LANE arranged a meeting between themselves but he did not know whether that meeting actually occurred. This latter conversation was not recorded.

On 7/7/64 at New York, New York File # 44-974

by SA JAMES J. ROGERS/hjb Date dictated 7/8/64

FD-302 (Rev. 1-25-60)

FEDERAL BUREAU OF INVESTIGATION

Date 7/8/64

A copy of a tape of the radio interview program "Contact" conducted by MURRAY BURNETT and broadcast February 18, 1964, over Radio Station WINS, New York, New York, was monitored on July 7, 1964, at the New York Office of the Federal Bureau of Investigation (FBI). During this program a telephone conversation took place between Mr. BERNARD WEISSMAN and Mr. MARK LANE.

The following is a succinct summary of this program:

Mr. MARK LANE said that he had on that day spoken to a Dallas schoolteacher who was a witness to the assassination of President JOHN F. KENNEDY. She had indicated that she was in Dallas, Texas, across the street from the book depository building and that she had heard four to six shots which came from the overpass in front of the Presidential limousine and which did not come from the book depository building. He also indicated that MARY WOODWARD (phonetic), a reporter for the "Dallas Morning News," had written a story in that newspaper that she and three other witnesses also heard shots coming from the direction of the overpass.

LANE indicated his belief that LEE HARVEY OSWALD was not the assassin of President KENNEDY.

A listener telephoned in a question about the lack of photographs appearing in the public press of Dallas Police Officer J. D. TIPPITT. In response to this question LANE stated that a week before the assassination a conference took place in a Dallas strip joint, known as The Carousel. LANE said present at this conference were BERNARD WEISSMAN, Officer J. D. TIPPITT and another person whom LANE said he would not mention at this time. LANE pointed out that Mr. WEISSMAN was the person who placed an ad in the "Dallas Morning News" on November 22, 1963, which practically accused President KENNEDY of treason.

On 7/7/64 at New York, New York File # 44-974

by SA JAMES J. ROGERS/hjb Date dictated 7/8/64

NY 44-974

BERNARD WEISSMAN telephoned the program shortly after the above statement was made and questioned LANE about the alleged conference that LANE had said occurred a week before the assassination.

LANE indicated he had received the information about this conference from a very, very responsible Dallas citizen. LANE wanted WEISSMAN to meet this person and also said that he wanted to meet WEISSMAN himself. WEISSMAN said that he would also like to meet LANE.

MURRAY BURNETT then gave WEISSMAN a telephone number where WEISSMAN could reach MARK LANE at the conclusion of the program. WEISSMAN agreed to call this number at 1:05 a.m., on that morning.

In the second reel of the tape recording, LANE answers several questions about the assassination and reiterates his belief that the Federal Bureau of Investigation (FBI) version of the assassination is not correct.

101

COMMISSION EXHIBIT No. 2475-D—Continued

For Post Office Use Only ENTERED IN DIRECTORY	INITIALS OF CLERK	INITIALS OF CARRIER	BOX NO.
	RJ		30061

THE FOLLOWING MUST BE COMPLETED AND SIGNED BEFORE P.O. BOX IS ASSIGNED

DELIVER MAIL IN ACCORDANCE WITH INSTRUCTIONS CHECKED BELOW

☒ ALL EXCEPT SPECIAL DELIVERY IN BOX ☐ ALL INCLUDING SPECIAL DELIVERY IN BOX ☐ ONLY MAIL ADDRESSED TO BOX IS TO BE PLACED IN IT, ALL OTHER MAIL TO BE DELIVERED AS ADDRESSED.

☐ OTHER INSTRUCTIONS (Explain)

SPECIAL DELIVERY MAIL ONLY (Deliver as checked below)

☐ DELIVER TO LOCAL RESIDENCE AT (No., street, and zone) ☐ DELIVER TO LOCAL BUSINESS ADDRESS AT 657 French (No., street, and zone)

NAMES OF PERSONS ENTITLED TO RECEIVE MAIL THROUGH BOX (If box is rented to a firm, include the full name of each of its members whose mail is to be placed in box.)

A.J. Hidell
Marina Oswald

☐ HAVE READ ITEMS 1 THROUGH 5, ABOVE AND WILL COMPLY WITH THEM.

X L.H. Oswald (Signature of applicant)

POD FORM 1093 JULY 1960 — APPLICATION FOR POST OFFICE BOX

U.S. GOVERNMENT PRINTING OFFICE 16—47410-

COMMISSION EXHIBIT No. 2476

FOR POST OFFICE USE ONLY	POSTMASTER	DATE BOX OPENED	DATE BOX CLOSED	BOX NO.
		6-3-63	9-26-63	30061

APPLICANT PLEASE NOTE: Completion of this application signifies your willingness to comply with all postal rules relative to the renting and use of Post Office boxes.

NAME OF APPLICANT (Print or type): L.H. Oswald

NAME OF FIRM OR CORPORATION (If box is rented for use of either)

KIND OF BUSINESS

BUSINESS ADDRESS (No., street, and zone)

HOME ADDRESS (No., street, and zone): 657 French St. New Orleans

SIGNATURE OF APPLICANT: X L.H. Oswald — DATE OF APPLICATION: June 3

COMMISSION EXHIBIT No. 2476—Continued

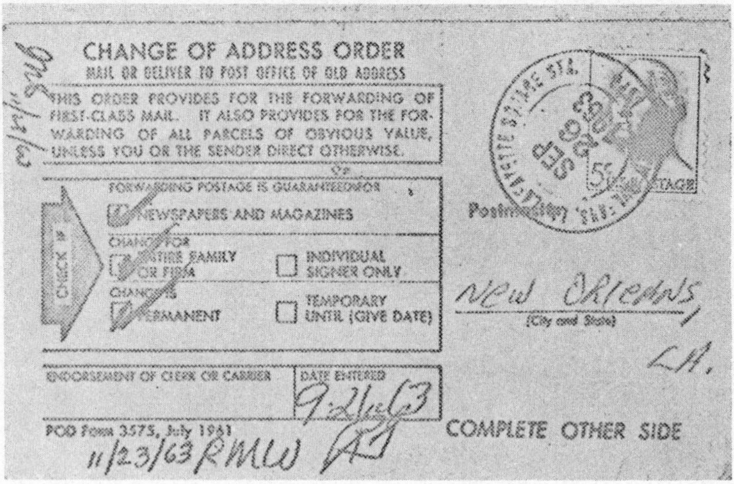
CHANGE OF ADDRESS ORDER
MAIL OR DELIVER TO POST OFFICE OF OLD ADDRESS

THIS ORDER PROVIDES FOR THE FORWARDING OF FIRST-CLASS MAIL. IT ALSO PROVIDES FOR THE FORWARDING OF ALL PARCELS OF OBVIOUS VALUE, UNLESS YOU OR THE SENDER DIRECT OTHERWISE.

CHECK

FORWARDING POSTAGE IS GUARANTEED FOR
NEWSPAPERS AND MAGAZINES

CHANGE FOR
ENTIRE FAMILY OR FIRM
INDIVIDUAL SIGNER ONLY

CHANGE IS
PERMANENT
TEMPORARY UNTIL (GIVE DATE)

ENDORSEMENT OF CLERK OR CARRIER

DATE ENTERED 9-26-63

POD Form 3575, July 1961

11/23/63 RMW

SEP 26 1963

5¢ POSTAGE

Postmaster

NEW ORLEANS, LA.
(City and State)

COMPLETE OTHER SIDE

Commission Exhibit No. 2476—Continued

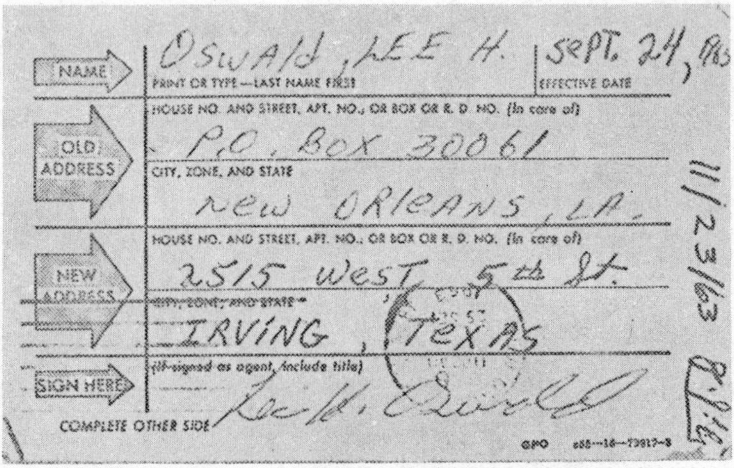
NAME: OSWALD, LEE H.
PRINT OR TYPE—LAST NAME FIRST

EFFECTIVE DATE: SEPT. 24, 1963

OLD ADDRESS
HOUSE NO. AND STREET, APT. NO., OR BOX OR R. D. NO. (In care of)
P.O. BOX 30061
CITY, ZONE, AND STATE
NEW ORLEANS, LA.

NEW ADDRESS
HOUSE NO. AND STREET, APT. NO., OR BOX OR R. D. NO. (In care of)
2515 WEST 5th St.
CITY, ZONE, AND STATE
IRVING, TEXAS

SIGN HERE
(If signed as agent, include title)
Lee H. Oswald

COMPLETE OTHER SIDE

11/23/63

GPO

Commission Exhibit No. 2476—Continued

FD-302 (Rev. 1-25-60) **FEDERAL BUREAU OF INVESTIGATION**

1

Date May 13, 1964

Post Russian Period 2

Other Individuals and Organizations Involved or Interviewed

EVARISTO GILBERTO RODRIGUEZ, whose name as used in Cuba and ~~other Latin American~~ countries would include his mother's maiden name of ORTEGA, i.e., EVARISTO GILBERTO RODRIGUEZ-ORTEGO, in response to a request made to him on May 11, 1964, voluntarily appeared at the New Orleans Office on May 12, 1964, and furnished the following information:

RODRIGUEZ related that approximately in September, 1963, LEE HARVEY OSWALD was observed by him in the Habana Bar, 117 Decatur Street. He explained this statement as follows:

As best he could recall it was in September, 1963, at approximately 3:30 a.m. or 4:00 a.m., day of the week not recalled, that two white males entered the Habana Bar and sat at a table opposite the center of the bar, both facing the entrance to the bar on Decatur Street.

According to RODRIGUEZ based on photographs he had seen of LEE HARVEY OSWALD after the assassination of President JOHN F. KENNEDY he was able to state that one of these two men he has described above was in his opinion LEE HARVEY OSWALD. He related that the person he believes to be OSWALD who entered the bar as stated above was accompanied by a white male, age about 32, a little taller than OSWALD and perhaps a little heavier than OSWALD. He described this man as being about 5'7", medium build with muscular biceps. He explained that this man was wearing a sleeveless slipon vest-like sweater, blue in color and was wearing a white, long sleeve business shirt with a tie, the color of which he does not recall. He was wearing a light sport coat which appeared to have a base color of grey interspersed with dull red lines, checkered in appearance. This man was wearing white pants, was light complexioned, wore no hat and no glasses. RODRIGUEZ was unable to recall the color of this man's hair; however, he did recall that he was able to speak Spanish very well. RODRIGUEZ was not able to state whether this man was Mexican, Cuban, Argentine or a national of any other Spanish speaking country. He related that the

— Commission Exhibit No. 2477 —

On 5/12/64 at New Orleans, Louisiana File # NO 100-16601

by SA WARREN C. DEBRUEYS and SA RICHARD E. LOGAN :gas Date dictated 5/13/64

9

COMMISSION EXHIBIT No. 2477

2

NO 100-16601
WCD:REL:gas

person he believed to be OSWALD wore a short sleeve white sport shirt with an open collar, dark pants. He wore no glasses and no hat and apparently spoke no Spanish.

RODRIGUEZ then related that when these two persons entered the Habana Bar the party he believes was identical with LEE HARVEY OSWALD gave the appearance of being drunk and was assisted to the above mentioned table opposite the bar by the man that accompanied him. RODRIGUEZ related that the man who accompanied the person he believes was OSWALD was seated on the side of the table closer to the bar and the party he shall refer to herinafter as OSWALD was seated closer to the wall opposite the bar. At that time the owner of the bar, ORESTES PENA, was seated at the far end of the bar also facing the entrance on Decatur Street and from this position PENA could observe the backs of the party believed to be OSWALD and his friend.

RODRIGUEZ related that the man with "OSWALD" ordered a tequila in Spanish. RODRIGUEZ carried the tequila to the table where "OSWALD" and his companion were seated and gave the tequila to "OSWALD's" companion and told him "That will be 50 cents." "OSWALD's" companion who spoke Spanish asked RODRIGUEZ in Spanish who the owner was. RODRIGUEZ replied "He is a Cuban but an American citizen." RODRIGUEZ claims that "OSWALD's" companion then stated that "He is an imperialist or a capitalist." RODRIGUEZ claims he advised this man that he is an American who lives off of his business.

According to RODRIGUEZ all the conversation was in Spanish with "OSWALD's" companion. While he was having the described discussion with "OSWALD's" companion, "OSWALD" had begun to drink the tequila which was ordered by his companion and "OSWALD" had commenced to vomit after drinking a half portion of the tequila. "OSWALD's" companion attempted to assist "OSWALD" and ordered a lemonade. RODRIGUEZ claims he walked to the far end of the bar and spoke to ORESTES PENA advising "these two men" wanted a lemonade, and RODRIGUEZ

10

COMMISSION EXHIBIT No. 2477—Continued

NO 100-16601
WCD;REL:gas

mentioned to ORESTES PENA "we don't make lemonades here." RODRIGUEZ then said ORESTES told him to go ahead and make the lemonade with some lemons, sugar and water. RODRIGUEZ claims he went immediately behind the bar and made the lemonade and as he was carrying the lemonade back to the table, stopped at the end of the bar and asked ORESTES how much should he charge for the lemonade and ORESTES advised him "25 cents." RODRIGUEZ claims he carried the lemonade to the table where "OSWALD" and his companion were seated and gave the lemonade to "OSWALD's" companion and speaking to him in Spanish told him that the lemonade was 25 cents and the latter gave him 25 cents. Immediately thereafter "OSWALD" and his companion stood up at the table and "OSWALD" assisted by his companion left the Habana Bar and while leaving "OSWALD's" companion said in Spanish that "the bar will be closed tomorrow." About three or four days later in the afternoon when EVARISTO RODRIGUEZ was returning from a call to see a doctor with ORESTES PENA they drove to Canal Street apparently on Carondelet Street and had turned right on Canal Street and headed towards the Mississippi River. It was at that time that RODRIGUEZ and PENA observed a congregation of people located in front of a theater on Canal Street between St. Charles and the next street closer to the river from St. Charles. In this group of people RODRIGUEZ observed CARLOS BRINGUIER talking to two policemen. He also observed two police cars and a white male entering one of the two police cars. Also on the sidewalk were scattered some yellow handbills. RODRIGUEZ stated that ORESTES PENA was driving his 1959 Mercury yellow four-door sedan and proceeded without stopping to observe the congregation any further. He stated that this is all he recalls about this incident on Canal Street.

On the following day about 12:30 p.m., CARLOS BRINGUIER came into the Habana Bar and advised RUPERTO PENA and ARMANDA JARVIS, the barmaid, that he, CARLOS BRINGUIER, had been in some difficulty with a pro-CASTRO individual who

NO 100-16601
WCD,REL:gas

was distributing handbills on Canal Street. RODRIGUEZ mentioned, however, that at that time he did not know the man with whom BRINGUIER had difficulty on Canal Street was LEE HARVEY OSWALD. He stated that he now assumes that the white male getting in the police car at the time of the incident on Canal Street was LEE HARVEY OSWALD.

RODRIGUEZ explained that after President KENNEDY was assassinated the picture of LEE HARVEY OSWALD appeared on television and in the local newspapers. He believes that this occurred on the day after President KENNEDY was assassinated and that on the afternoon of that same day after seeing the picture of LEE HARVEY OSWALD he told CARLOS BRINGUIER that "OSWALD" had been in the bar previously and told him the story about "OSWALD" being in the bar with an unknown male that spoke Spanish and about "OSWALD" vomiting in the bar as he, RODRIGUEZ, has outlined the story during this interview.

RODRIGUEZ specifically stated that he never told BRINGUIER or anyone that the man who was in the Habana Bar with a person he believed identical with LEE HARVEY OSWALD was being sought by the FBI. He states he knows that he could not have made such a statement because he had no information at any time that the man he described above as being with "OSWALD" at the Habana Bar was wanted by the FBI. In fact he, RODRIGUEZ, had not been talked to by any FBI Agent prior to the date of the assassination of President JOHN F. KENNEDY.

RODRIGUEZ was unable to recall what persons were in the Habana Bar on the morning that he allegedly saw "OSWALD" and a companion of "OSWALD's" in the Habana Bar other than ORESTES PENA. He reiterated that the person he believed to be identical with OSWALD was definitely drunk. This was the only occasion he had seen the man he believed to be OSWALD and the man that accompanied the latter except possibly on the occasion of the incident on Canal Street when he saw a man entering the police car who could have been LEE HARVEY OSWALD.

5

NO 100-16601
WCD,REL:gas

RODRIGUEZ was shown three photographs depicting LEE HARVEY OSWALD distributing handbills in front of the International Trade Mart, New Orleans, which photographs also included numerous other persons. The only person that RODRIGUEZ was able to identify in these photographs as someone he has seen previously was LEE HARVEY OSWALD. He claimed that he did not know the identity of any of the other persons in the photographs nor had he seen any of them previously.

RODRIGUEZ furnished the following background information regarding himself:

Name	EVARISTO GILBERTO RODRIGUEZ, or EVARISTO GILBERTO RODRIGUEZ-ORTEGA
Alien Registration No.	A 15 391 115
Sex	Male
Race	White
Date of Birth	7/26/41
Place of Birth	Gibara, Oriente, Cuba
Height	5'7"
Weight	153 pounds
Hair	Black
Eyes	Brown
Complexion	Olive
Marital Status	Married
Wife	MARIA IRENE ORDAS CANTRERA, aka. MARIA RODAS de RODRIGUEZ, age 27
Residence	1239 Chartres Street, upstairs.
Nationality of Wife	Guatemalan
Date of Arrival in United States	1959 as seaman
Date of Arrival in United States as Resident Alien	January, 1963
Selective Service No.	10-133-41-325, Local Board No. 133.

13

COMMISSION EXHIBIT No. 2477—Continued

6

NO 100-16601
WCD,REL:gas

RODRIGUEZ claimed to have been a seaman aboard the S.S. BARCELONA which sunk in the Gulf of Mexico, January 3, 1963; was picked up by a vessel named San Jose and taken to Costa Rica and subsequently returned to the United States by the firm which owned the S.S. BARCELONA.

RODRIGUEZ claimed he was never a member of the CASTRO government or the militia in Cuba; he claimed to be anti-CASTRO.

14

COMMISSION EXHIBIT No. 2477—Continued

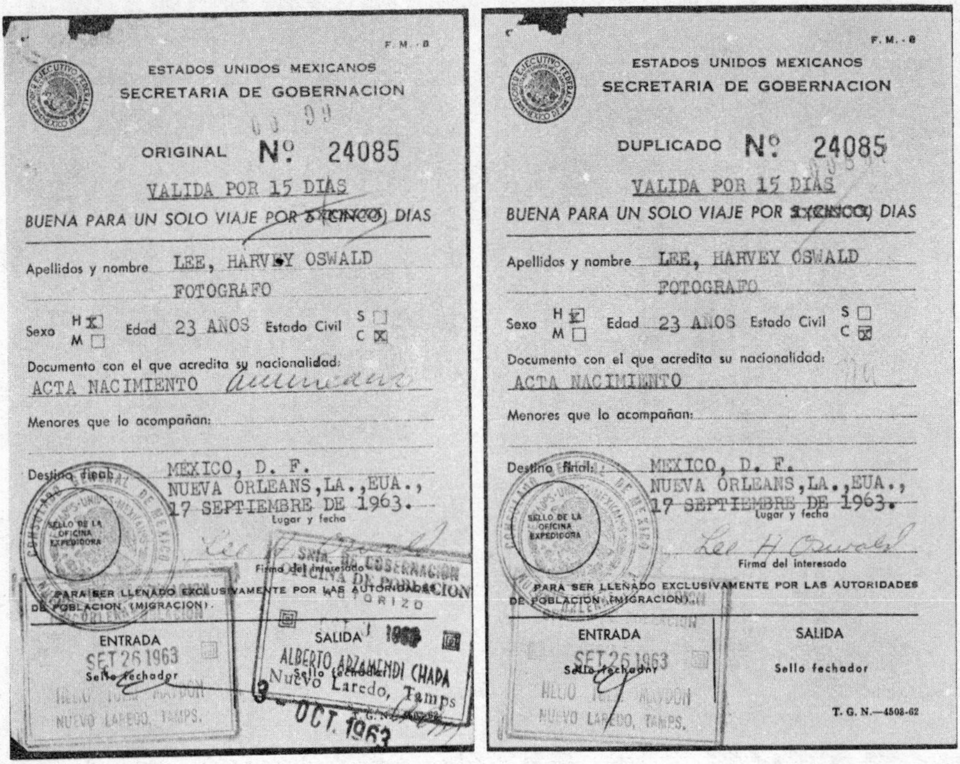

F.M.-8

ESTADOS UNIDOS MEXICANOS
SECRETARIA DE GOBERNACION

ORIGINAL Nº 24085

VALIDA POR 15 DIAS
BUENA PARA UN SOLO VIAJE POR ~~5 (CINCO)~~ DIAS

Apellidos y nombre LEE, HARVEY OSWALD
FOTOGRAFO

Sexo H [X] M [ ] Edad 23 AÑOS Estado Civil S [ ] C [X]

Documento con el que acredita su nacionalidad:
ACTA NACIMIENTO American

Menores que lo acompañan:

Destino final: MEXICO, D. F.
NUEVA ORLEANS, LA., EUA.,
17 SEPTIEMBRE DE 1963.
Lugar y fecha

SELLO DE LA OFICINA EXPEDIDORA

Lee H Oswald
Firma del interesado

PARA SER LLENADO EXCLUSIVAMENTE POR LAS AUTORIDADES DE POBLACION (MIGRACION).

ENTRADA
SET 26 1963
Sello fechador
NUEVO LAREDO, TAMPS.

SALIDA
AUTORIZO
ALBERTO ARZAMENDI CHAPA
Nuevo Laredo, Tamps
3 OCT. 1963
Sello fechador

F.M.-8

ESTADOS UNIDOS MEXICANOS
SECRETARIA DE GOBERNACION

DUPLICADO Nº 24085

VALIDA POR 15 DIAS
BUENA PARA UN SOLO VIAJE POR ~~5 (CINCO)~~ DIAS

Apellidos y nombre LEE, HARVEY OSWALD
FOTOGRAFO

Sexo H [X] M [ ] Edad 23 AÑOS Estado Civil S [ ] C [X]

Documento con el que acredita su nacionalidad:
ACTA NACIMIENTO

Menores que lo acompañan:

Destino final: MEXICO, D. F.
NUEVA ORLEANS, LA., EUA.,
17 SEPTIEMBRE DE 1963.
Lugar y fecha

SELLO DE LA OFICINA EXPEDIDORA

Lee H Oswald
Firma del interesado

PARA SER LLENADO EXCLUSIVAMENTE POR LAS AUTORIDADES DE POBLACION (MIGRACION).

ENTRADA
SET 26 1963
Sello fechador
NUEVO LAREDO, TAMPS.

SALIDA
Sello fechador

T. G. N.—4508-62

COMMISSION EXHIBIT No. 2478

ADVERTENCIAS

1. EL IMPUESTO QUE CAUSA ESTE DOCUMENTO ES DE $ 6.25.
2. Autoriza al titular a permanecer en México 5 (cinco) días improrrogables, a partir de la fecha de su entrada al país.
3. No podrá desarrollar actividades distintas a las de recreo.
4. Si el titular se internó con menores, deberá salir acompañado de ellos.
5. Este documento deberá ser entregado a las Autoridades de Migración del lugar por donde efectúe su salida del país.

ATTENTION

1. TAX APPLICABLE TO THIS DOCUMENT: $ 6.25 MEXICAN CURRENCY (DLS. 0.50).
2. The legal holder of this permit is authorized to remain in Mexico for a period not to exceed 5 (five) days (not renewable) starting from the date of his entry into the country.
3. Issued only for pleasure trips.
4. If bearer enters the country accompanied by minors, upon departure he must leave with them.
5. This document must be surrendered to the Migration Authorities at the time and place of departure from the country.

OBSERVATION IMPORTANTE

1. CE DOCUMENT EST SOUMIS A UN IMPOT DE $ 6.25 PESOS MEXICAINS (U.S. $ 0.50).
2. Le titulaire de ce document est autorisé à séjourner au Mexique pendant une période qui ne pourra, en aucun cas, dépasser 5 (cinq) jours à partir de la date de son entrée dans le pays.
3. Il ne pourra exercer aucune activité autre que celle de touriste.
4. Si le titulaire est entré au Mexique accompagné de mineurs, ceux-ci devront obligatoirement quitter le pays en même temps que lui.
5. Ce document devra être remis aux Autorités Mexicaines du port de sortie au moment du départ du pays.

ADVERTENCIAS

1. EL IMPUESTO QUE CAUSA ESTE DOCUMENTO ES DE $ 6.25.
2. Autoriza al titular a permanecer en México 5 (cinco) días improrrogables, a partir de la fecha de su entrada al país.
3. No podrá desarrollar actividades distintas a las de recreo.
4. Si el titular se internó con menores, deberá salir acompañado de ellos.
5. Este documento deberá ser entregado a las Autoridades de Migración del lugar por donde efectúe su salida del país.

ATTENTION

1. TAX APPLICABLE TO THIS DOCUMENT: $ 6.25 MEXICAN CURRENCY (DLS. 0.50).
2. The legal holder of this permit is authorized to remain in Mexico for a period not to exceed 5 (five) days (not renewable) starting from the date of his entry into the country.
3. Issued only for pleasure trips.
4. If bearer enters the country accompanied by minors, upon departure he must leave with them.
5. This document must be surrendered to the Migration Authorities at the time and place of departure from the country.

OBSERVATION IMPORTANTE

1. CE DOCUMENT EST SOUMIS A UN IMPOT DE $ 6.25 PESOS MEXICAINS (U.S. $ 0.50).
2. Le titulaire de ce document est autorisé à séjourner au Mexique pendant une période qui ne pourra, en aucun cas, dépasser 5 (cinq) jours à partir de la date de son entrée dans le pays.
3. Il ne pourra exercer aucune activité autre que celle de touriste.
4. Si le titulaire est entré au Mexique accompagné de mineurs, ceux-ci devront obligatoirement quitter le pays en même temps que lui.
5. Ce document devra être remis aux Autorités Mexicaines du port de sortie au moment du départ du pays.

COMMISSION EXHIBIT No. 2478—Continued

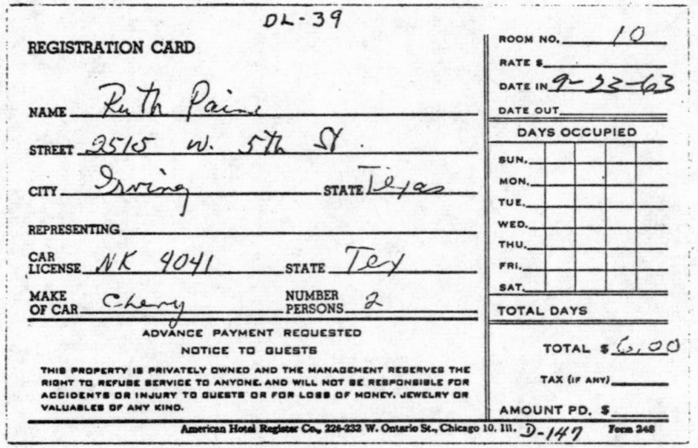

DL-39

REGISTRATION CARD

NAME Ruth Paine	ROOM NO. 10
STREET 2515 W. 5th St.	RATE $
CITY Irving STATE Texas	DATE IN 9-23-63
REPRESENTING	DATE OUT
CAR LICENSE NK 4041 STATE Tex	DAYS OCCUPIED: SUN. MON. TUE. WED. THU. FRI. SAT.
MAKE OF CAR Chevy NUMBER PERSONS 2	TOTAL DAYS
	TOTAL $ 6.00
	TAX (IF ANY)
	AMOUNT PD. $

ADVANCE PAYMENT REQUESTED

NOTICE TO GUESTS

THIS PROPERTY IS PRIVATELY OWNED AND THE MANAGEMENT RESERVES THE RIGHT TO REFUSE SERVICE TO ANYONE, AND WILL NOT BE RESPONSIBLE FOR ACCIDENTS OR INJURY TO GUESTS OR FOR LOSS OF MONEY, JEWELRY OR VALUABLES OF ANY KIND.

American Hotel Register Co., 226-232 W. Ontario St., Chicago 10, Ill. D-147 Form 248

COMMISSION EXHIBIT No. 2479

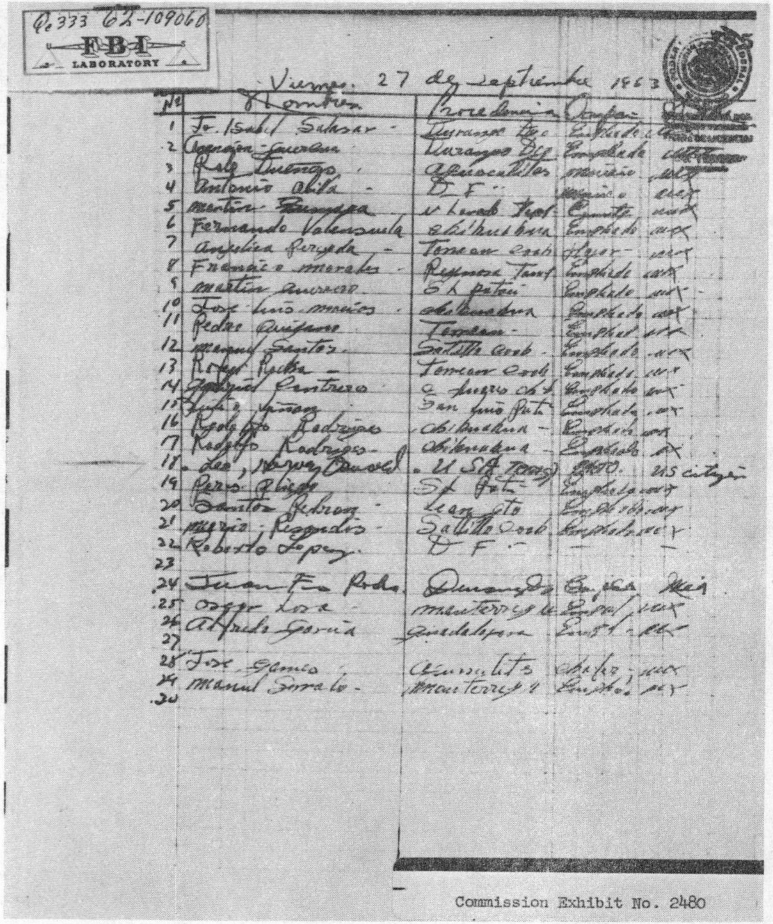

Qe333 62-109060

FBI LABORATORY

Viernes 27 de septiembre 1963

No	Nombre	Procedencia	Ocupación	
1	Jo. Isabel Salasar	Durango Dgo	Empleado	[illegible]
2	[illegible]	Durango Dgo	Empleado	[illegible]
3	[illegible]	Aguascalientes	[illegible]	[illegible]
4	Antonio Avila	D. F.	[illegible]	[illegible]
5	Martin [illegible]	[illegible]	[illegible]	[illegible]
6	Fernando Valenzuela	Chihuahua	Empleado	mex
7	Angelica [illegible]	Torreon Coah	[illegible]	mex
8	Francisco Morales	Reynosa Tamps	Empleado	mex
9	Martin [illegible]	S L Potosi	Empleado	mex
10	Jose Luis [illegible]	Chihuahua	Empleado	mex
11	Pedro [illegible]	Torreon	Empleado	mex
12	Manuel Santos	Saltillo Coah	Empleado	mex
13	[illegible]	Torreon Coah	Empleado	mex
14	[illegible]	[illegible]	Empleado	mex
15	[illegible]	San Luis Pot	Empleado	mex
16	Rodolfo Rodriguez	Chihuahua	Empleado	mex
17	Rodolfo Rodriguez	Chihuahua	Empleado	mex
18	Lee, Harvey Oswald	U S A Texas	Photo	U.S. citizen
19	[illegible]	S L Pot	Empleado	mex
20	Santos [illegible]	Leon Gto	Empleado	mex
21	[illegible]	Saltillo Coah	Empleado	mex
22	Roberto Lopez	D F		
23				
24	Juan [illegible]	Durango Dgo	[illegible]	[illegible]
25	[illegible]	Monterrey	[illegible]	mex
26	Alfredo Garcia	Guadalajara	[illegible]	mex
27				
28	Jose [illegible]	Aguascalientes	[illegible]	mex
29	Manuel [illegible]	Monterrey	Empleado	mex
30				

Commission Exhibit No. 2480

COMMISSION EXHIBIT No. 2480

D-436848 Qc71 AX

FBI LABORATORY

MEXICAN CONSULATE
534 WHITNEY BLDG.,
NEW ORLEANS, LA.

APPLICATION FOR TOURIST CARD TO VISIT MEXICO NO. 987

CONSULAR FEE: $3.00 U. S. Cy. SERIE: 24085

NAME: LEE Harvey Oswald
(Print full name, no initials) (Married women should give maiden given name together with husband's surname)

SEX MALE AGE 23 MARITAL STATUS: married
(State whether single, married, widow or divorced)

PROFESSION OR OCCUPATION: PHOTOGRAPHER

BUSINESS ADDRESS: 640 RAMPART
(Name and address of firm with whom employed)

PLACE OF BIRTH: NEW ORLEANS LA. ORLEANS
(City or Town) (State) (Country)

NATIONALITY BY BIRTH: AMERICAN NATIONALITY AT PRESENT: AMERICAN
(Naturalized American citizens must present their citizenship certificates as such).

HOME ADDRESS: 4907 MAGAZINE NEW ORLEANS LA.
(Number and Street) (City) (State and Country)

PHONE: — RELIGION: CATHOLIC

DESTINATION IN MEXICO: TRANSIT TOURIST

OBJECT OF TRIP: TOURIST DURATION OF TRIP: 15 DAYS

MEANS OF TRANSPORTATION: AUTO ( ) PLANE ( ) TRAIN ( ) BUS (✓) SHIP ( )

APPROXIMATE AMOUNT OF MONEY BEING TAKEN FOR TRIP $ 300. (STATISTICAL PURPOSES)

DOCUMENTS SUBMITTED TO PROVE NATIONALITY: BIRTH CERTIFICATE

(Birth Certificates, Affidavit of Birth, Voter's Registration Card or Poll Tax Receipt, Army, Navy or Air Force Discharge Papers, Passports, etc.).

I hereby declare that the above statements are true and correct; that I shall not engage in business or remunerative work during my sojourn in Mexico, and also take cognizance of the fact that the Mexican Immigration Law establishes penalties for any person convicted of making false statements concerning the nature of trip to Mexico.

Sept. 17, 1963
(Date of Application)

Commission Exhibit No. 2481

COMMISSION EXHIBIT NO. 2481

(Print full name, no initials) (Married women should give maiden given name together with husband's surname)

SEX MALE AGE 23 MARITAL STATUS: married
(State whether single, married, widow or divorced)

PROFESSION OR OCCUPATION: PHOTOGRAPHER

BUSINESS ADDRESS: 640 RAMPART
(Name and address of firm with whom employed)

PLACE OF BIRTH: NEW ORLEANS (City or Town) LA. (State) ORLEANS (Country)

NATIONALITY BY BIRTH: AMERICAN NATIONALITY AT PRESENT: AMERICAN
(Naturalized American citizens must present their citizenship certificates as such).

HOME ADDRESS: 4907 MAGAZINE (Number and Street) NEW ORLEANS (City) LA. (State and Country)

PHONE: — RELIGION: CATHOLIC

DESTINATION IN MEXICO: TRANSIT TOURIST

OBJECT OF TRIP: TOURIST DURATION OF TRIP: 14 DAYS

MEANS OF TRANSPORTATION: AUTO ( ) PLANE ( ) TRAIN ( ) BUS (X) SHIP ( )

APPROXIMATE AMOUNT OF MONEY BEING TAKEN FOR TRIP $ 300. (STATISTICAL PURPOSES)

DOCUMENTS SUBMITTED TO PROVE NATIONALITY: BIRTH CERTIFICATE

(Birth Certificates, Affidavit of Birth, Voter's Registration Card or Poll Tax Receipt, Army, Navy or Air Force Discharge Papers, Passports, etc.).

I hereby declare that the above statements are true and correct; that I shall not engage in business or remunerative work during my sojourn in Mexico, and also take cognizance of the fact that the Mexican Immigration Law establishes penalties for any person convicted of making false statements concerning the nature of trip to Mexico.

Sept. 17, 1963
(Date of Application)

Lee H. Oswald
(Applicant's Signature)

****

NOTICE:

TOURIST CARD must be used within 90 days from date of issuance and is valid for a period of six months stay in Mexico from date of entry.

NO REFUNDS MADE.
NO PERSONAL CHECKS ACCEPTED.

****

SEP 17 1963

COMMISSION EXHIBIT No. 2481—Continued

Servicios Unidos **AUTOBUSES BLANCOS** Flecha Roja, S. A. de C. V.

Correspondiente al Art. 64 de la Ley.

GUIA DE EQUIPAJES

Nuevo Laredo, Tamps. 26 de Sept. 63 de ______ Autobús No. 516

[illegible]VO LAREDO A Mexico D.F. HORA DE SALIDA 1400 hs OPERADOR Roberto Morales

	NOMBRE DEL PASAJERO Y DESTINO		ETIQUETAS DE EQUIPAJE Y MARBETES REVISION ADUANAL				
1	Pablo Vasquez = (Mex)	Etiquetas Equipaje / Marbetes Revisión	257	512	(Velix)		Marcado
2	—— —— (")	Etiquetas Equipaje / Marbetes Revisión	257	513	(")		Marcado
3	S. [illegible] (")	Etiquetas Equipaje / Marbetes Revisión	257	580	(")		Marcado
4	Alfredo Briseño (")	Etiquetas Equipaje / Marbetes Revisión	257	577	(")		Marcado
5	Rosa [illegible] (")	Etiquetas Equipaje / Marbetes Revisión	257	578	(")		7318061
6	T. Gonzalez (")	Etiquetas Equipaje / Marbetes Revisión	257	579	(")		7318060
7	Andres Morales (Mont)	Etiquetas Equipaje / Marbetes Revisión	257	575	(")		Marcado
8	—— —— (")	Etiquetas Equipaje / Marbetes Revisión	257	574	(M[illegible])		Marcado
9	Cope Martinez (")	Etiquetas Equipaje / Marbetes Revisión	257	576	(Velix)		Marcado
10	Rowen (Mex)	Etiquetas Equipaje / Marbetes Revisión	320	438	(Maleta)		Marcado
11	Harry Mitchell (Mont)	Etiquetas Equipaje / Marbetes Revisión	320	200	(")		Marcado
12	—— —— (")	Etiquetas Equipaje / Marbetes Revisión	320	202	(Velix)		Marcado
13	—— —— (")	Etiquetas Equipaje / Marbetes Revisión	320	201	(")		Marcado
14	Lee H Oswald (Mex)	Etiquetas Equipaje / Marbetes Revisión	320	433	([illegible])		Marcado
15	Rowen (")	Etiquetas Equipaje / Marbetes Revisión	320	[illegible]	(")		Marcado
16	—— —— (")	Etiquetas Equipaje / Marbetes Revisión	320	440	(")		Marcado
17	John McFarland (")	Etiquetas Equipaje / Marbetes Revisión	320	437	(")		7317276
18	—— (")	Etiquetas Equipaje / Marbetes Revisión	320	436	(")		7317277
19	(18)	Etiquetas Equipaje / Marbetes Revisión					(18)
20		Etiquetas Equipaje / Marbetes Revisión	[illegible]				
21		Etiquetas Equipaje / Marbetes Revisión					
22	El Vista[illegible]	Etiquetas Equipaje					

D-10[illegible]

COMMISSION EXHIBIT No. 2482

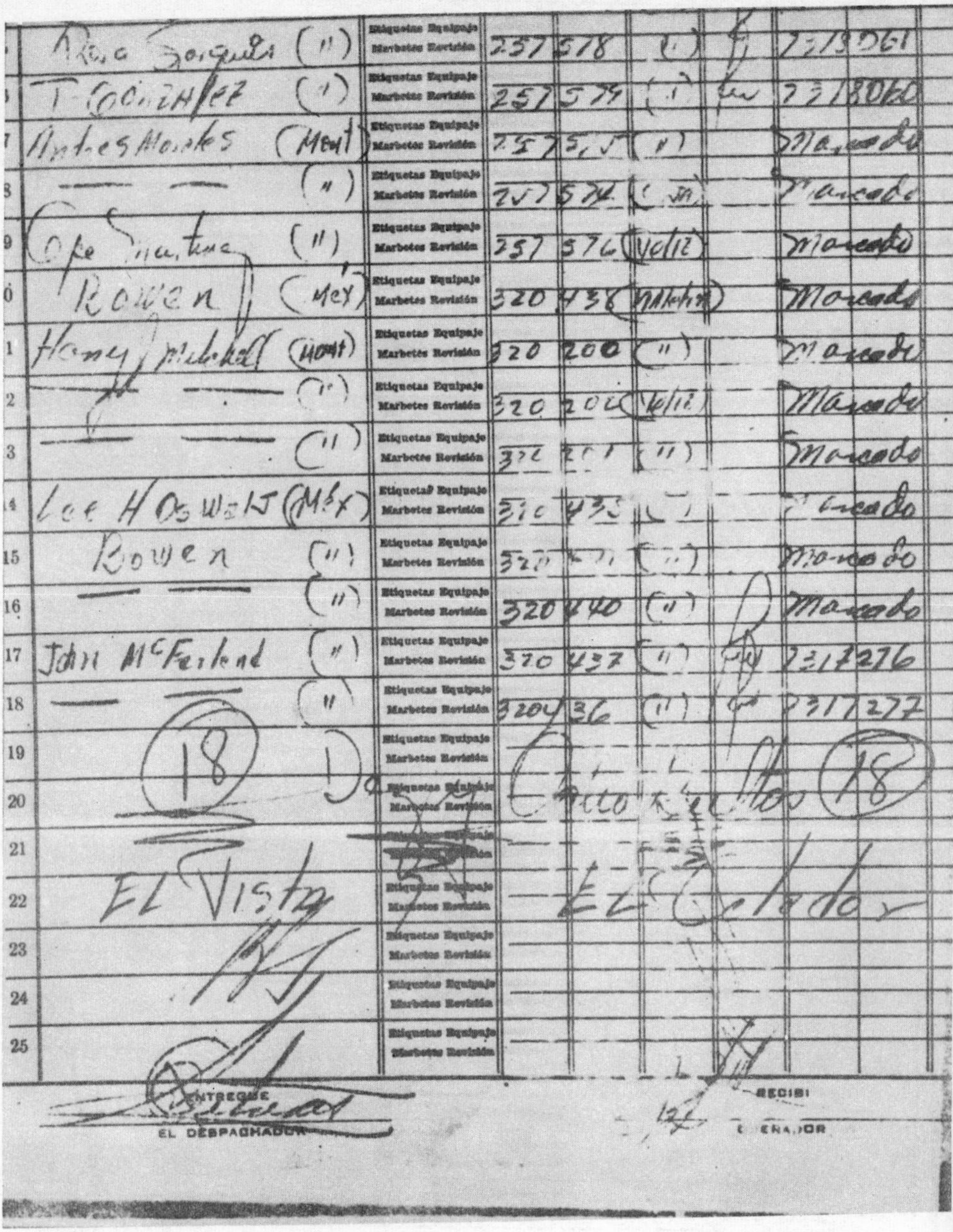

5	Rosa Gonzalez	(")	Etiquetas Equipaje / Marbetes Revisión	257	578	2213061
6	T. Gonzalez	(")	Etiquetas Equipaje / Marbetes Revisión	257	579	2218060
7	Andres Morales	(Mont)	Etiquetas Equipaje / Marbetes Revisión	257	5[illegible]	Marcado
8	—— ——	(")	Etiquetas Equipaje / Marbetes Revisión	257	574	Marcado
9	Ope Martinez	(")	Etiquetas Equipaje / Marbetes Revisión	257	576	Marcado
10	Bowen	(Mex)	Etiquetas Equipaje / Marbetes Revisión	320	438	Marcado
11	Harry Mitchell	(Mont)	Etiquetas Equipaje / Marbetes Revisión	320	200	Marcado
12	—— ——	(")	Etiquetas Equipaje / Marbetes Revisión	320	202	Marcado
13	—— ——	(")	Etiquetas Equipaje / Marbetes Revisión	320	201	Marcado
14	Lee H Oswald	(Mex)	Etiquetas Equipaje / Marbetes Revisión	320	433	Marcado
15	Bowen	(")	Etiquetas Equipaje / Marbetes Revisión	320	[illegible]	Marcado
16	—— ——	(")	Etiquetas Equipaje / Marbetes Revisión	320	440	Marcado
17	John McFarland	(")	Etiquetas Equipaje / Marbetes Revisión	320	437	2317276
18	—— ——	(")	Etiquetas Equipaje / Marbetes Revisión	3204	36	2317277
19	(18)		Etiquetas Equipaje / Marbetes Revisión			
20			Etiquetas Equipaje / Marbetes Revisión	Cotejado (18)		
21			Etiquetas Equipaje / Marbetes Revisión			
22	El Vista		Etiquetas Equipaje / Marbetes Revisión	El Cotejador		
23			Etiquetas Equipaje / Marbetes Revisión			
24			Etiquetas Equipaje / Marbetes Revisión			
25			Etiquetas Equipaje / Marbetes Revisión			

ENTREGUE — EL DESPACHADOR   RECIBI — [illegible]

COMMISSION EXHIBIT No. 2482—Continued

4

DL 89-43

Card of "Fair Play for Cuba Committee, 799 Broadway, New York 3, New York, telephone ORegon 4-8295", issued to LEE H. OSWALD, May 28, 1963, filed by V. T. LEE as Executive Secretary

Card of "Fair Play for Cuba, New Orleans Chapter", issued to L. H. OSWALD, June 15, 1963, filed by A. T.(?) HIDELL, Chapter President (note name HIDELL on fictitious Selective Service card)

Selective Service notice of classification card to LEE HARVEY OSWALD, Selective Service No. 41-114-39-532, IV-A, dated February 2, 1960, from Local Board 114, Fort Worth, Texas

$13.00 in currency, consisting of one $5.00 bill and eight $1.00 bills

Residence 2515 West 5th Street, Irving, Texas, phone BL 3-1628 (residence of wife for past five weeks)

Room in rooming house, 1026 North Beckley, for about five weeks. Phone number unknown.

Previous Residences 4706 Magazine Street, New Orleans, Louisiana, no phone (about three months)

602 Elsbeth, no phone (about seven months), Dallas, Texas

Unrecalled street in Fort Worth, Texas, (a few months), with brother in Fort Worth, Texas, for a few months.

Previously in Soviet Union, until July, 1962

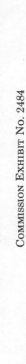

95

COMMISSION EXHIBIT No. 2483

COMMISSION EXHIBIT No. 2484

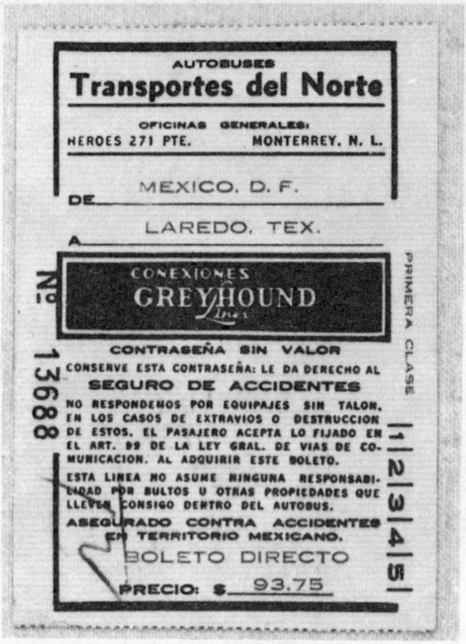

Commission Exhibit No. 2485

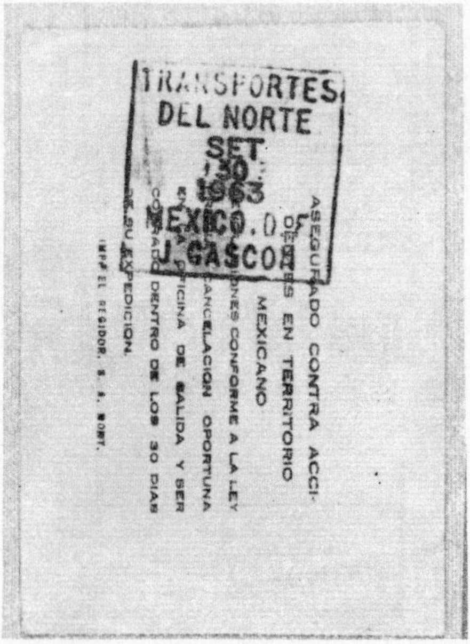

Commission Exhibit No. 2485—Continued

WHAT TO DO, WHAT TO SEE, WHERE AND HOW — QUE VER, QUE HACER, DONDE Y COMO

THIS WEEK - ESTA SEMANA

SEPTEMBER 28-OCTOBER 4, 1963 — SEPTIEMBRE 28-OCTUBRE 4, 1963

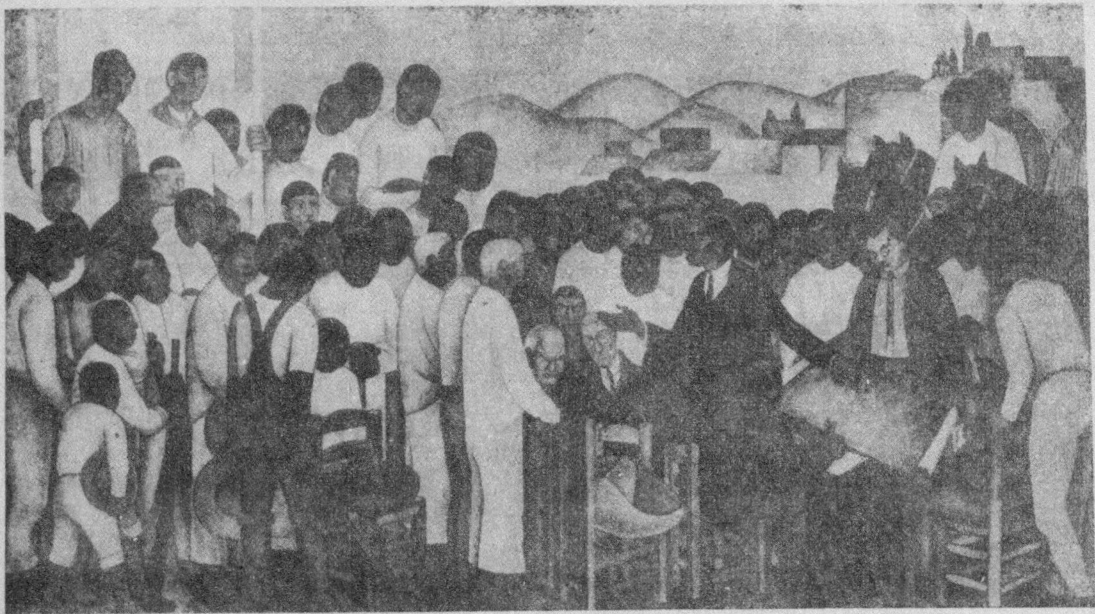

See page 32 — Véase pág. 32

COMMISSION EXHIBIT No. 2486

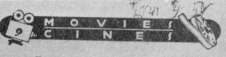

ERS
ROS

[A]LARCON. — Liverpool y Versalles (H-8). A las 7.30 y 9.45 p. m. "Desnúdese Señora", Celia D'Alarcón, Oscar Pulido, Varelita. Reservaciones Tel.: 35-93-20.

[A]RLEQUIN. — Villalongín 24. A las 7.30 y 9.50 p. m. "Niña", con Nadia Haro Oliva, Miguel Manzano, A. Ciangherotti. Reservaciones Tels.: 46-86-73 y 46-16-51.

[CH]OPIN. — Av. Insurgentes y Puebla (G-10). A las 8.30 p. m. "Una vez al año", con Marilú Elízaga, Tito Junco, Raúl Farel, Miguel Suárez. Reservaciones: 11-38-17.

[M]ILAN.—Lucerna y Milán (H-7). A las 8.30 P. M. "La Gobernadora", con Magda Guzmán, Miguel Maciá. Reservaciones: 46-21-46.

[M]USICO.—Vallarta 6 (cerca del Monumento a la Revolución). A las 8.30 p. m. "Aurelia y sus Hombres", con Lucy Gallardo, Enrique Rambal. Reservaciones: Tels. 46-81-50 y 46-07-29.

[P]ALACIO DE BELLAS ARTES.—Cerca del Parque Alameda. Todos los miércoles a las 9.00 p. m. y todos los domingos a las 9.30 a. m. y 5.00 p. m. Ballet "Folklórico de México". Exhibición de la Cortina de Cristal "Tifanny". Reservaciones: 46-79-36.

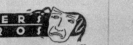

MOVIES
CINES

Shows are at approximately 4, 7 and 9 p. m.
Prices are in Mexican Currency

Las películas pasarán aproximadamente a las 4, 7 y 9 p. m.

ARCADIA.—Balderas & Juárez Av. (K-5). Sept. 28 - Oct. 4. "Amor en Roma", Mylene Demongeot, Peter Baldwin, Elas Martinelli. Spoken in Italian. Sub-tiles in Spanish. $4.00.

ARIEL.—Av. Ejército Nacional 826 (A-7). Sept. 28-Oct. 4. "Mi Novia es del Otro Mundo", Tom Tryon, Brian Keith, Dany Saval. Spoken in English, sub-titles in Spanish. $4.00.

CHAPULTEPEC.—Reforma 505 (near entrance to Chapultepec Park). Sept. 28-Oct. 4. "Las Pícaras Doncellas", Mylene Demongeot, Michael Craig, Anne Heywood. Spoken in English, Sub-titles in Spanish. $4.00.

DIANA.—Av. Reforma & Mississippi (C-5). Sept. 28-Oct. 4. "West **Side Story (Amor sin Barreras). Natalie Wood, Richard Beymer, Rita Moreno. Spoken in English, sub-titles in Spanish. $8.00.**

METROPOLITAN.—Av. Balderas & Independencia (K-5). Sept. 28-Oct. 4. "José Vendido en Egipto". Geoffrey Horne, Belinda Lee. Spoken in English, su-titles in Spanish. $4.00.

MEXICO.—Av. Cuauhtémoc y Alvaro Obregón (I-11). Sept. 28-Oct. 4. "México de mis Recuerdos". Fernando Soler, Joaquín Cordero, Fernando Soto. Spoken in Spanish. No sub-titles. $4.00.

PASEO.—Reforma 35 (I-5). Sept. 28-Oct. 4. "Therese Desqueyroux", Emmanuelle Riva, Edith Scob-Philippe. Spoken in French, subtitles in Spanish. $4.00.

ROBLE.—Reforma 133 (H-7). Sept. 28-Oct. 4. "El Hombre de Papel", Luis Aguilar, Columba Domínguez, Rita Macedo. Spoken in Spanish, sub-titles in English. $4.00.

VARIEDADES.—Av. Juárez (K-5). Sept. 28-Oct. 4. "The Parent **Trap" (Operación Cupido), Maureen O'Hara, Brian Keith, Hayley Mills. Spoken in English, sub-titles in Spanish. $4.00.**

31

BEAUTY SHOPS
SALONES DE BELLEZA

BEAUTY SALON FLORENCIA.—Florencia 69 cor. Liverpool. Tel.: 11-30-30. Specialized personnel. Moderate prices. Personal especializado. Precios moderados. E-10

TRIM LINE STUDIOS of Insurgentes Sur 1339, Phone: 24-08-88, offers the most modern methods in use in Europe and the U. S. A. for the aesthetic culture of the woman. Excellent baths, elegant beauty shops. CLUB HAMBURGO, S. A., of Hamburgo 20, Tel. 46-12-04 offers spacious and modern gymnasiums and service exclusively for men.

TRIM LINE STUDIOS de Insurgentes Sur 1339, Teléfono: 24-08-88, ofrece los métodos más modernos de Europa y los Estados Unidos de América para la cultura estética de la mujer. Excelentes baños, elegantes salones de belleza. CLUB HAMBURGO, S. A., de Hamburgo 20, Tel.: 46-12-04, ofrece espaciosos y modernos gimnasios y servicio exclusivamente para los hombres.

CLUB HAMBURGO, S.A.
·HAMBURGO 20 · TEL. 46-12-04·

STUDIOS TRIM LINES
INSURGENTES SUR 1339

INDISPENSABLE

"THIS WEEK - ESTA SEMANA"
Tiene la información que usted desea para
VIAJES Y DIVERSIONES
en
MEXICO

EN Acapulco... RENTAMOS CASAS AMUEBLADAS!
POR DIAS O MES · 3, 4 o 5 RECAMARAS CON BAÑOS PRIVADOS AGUA CALIENTE · SERVICIO DE LIMPIEZA Y COCINERA · ALBERCA DE AGUA PURIFICADA · EXCELENTE VISTA Y SITUACION · MUY FRESCAS!
RESERVACIONES EN MEXICO D.F. CALLE RAMON ALCAZAR No. 8 · Tels. 46-18-88 35-29-29

Commission Exhibit No. 2486—Continued

38

LEE OSWA

DIPLOMATS IN MEXICO, D.F. / DIPLOMATICOS EN MEXICO, D.F.

15-60 55-

ARGENTINA. — (Embassy-Embajada).—Av. Independencia 59.	Tel. 10-47-16
(Consulate-Consulado).—Independencia 59.	" 13-35-06
BELGICA.—(Chancelry-Cancillería). Melchor Ocampo 463.	" 28-80-53
BRASIL.—(Embassy-Embajada).—Reforma 455.	" 35-96-15
CANADA.—(Embassy-Embajada).—Melchor Ocampo 463.	" 25-15-60
CHILE.—(Embassy-Embajada).—Vallarta 1.	" 35-06-30
CHINA.—(Embassy-Embajada).—Campos Elíseos 69.	" 45-54-46
COSTA RICA.—(Embassy-Embajada).—Temístocles 313.	" 45-12-16
(Consulate-Consulado).—Dublín 5.	25-32-34
CUBA.—(Embassy-Embajada).—F. Márquez 160.	" 14-92-14
(Consulate-Consulado).—Zamora & F. Márquez.	" 11-23-47
CZECOSLOVAKIA (CHECOESLOVAQUIA). — Legation-Legación).—Av. Cedros 213.	" 45-61-80
DENMARK (DINAMARCA).—Embassy-Embajada). — Melchor Ocampo 487.	" 14-46-16
EL SALVADOR. — (Embassy-Embajada). — Independencia 59.	" 13-70-79
(Consulate-Consulado).—Independencia 59.	" 10-90-04
FRANCE (FRANCIA).—(Embassy-Embajada).—Hamburgo 103.	" 11-13-28
(Consulate-Consulado).—Londres 75.	" 14-50-97
GREAT BRITAIN (GRAN BRETAÑA). (Embassy-Embajada).—Lerma 71.	" 11-48-80
GUATEMALA.—(Embassay-Embajada).—Vallarta 1.	" 46-48-76
(Consulate-Consulado).—Vallarta 1.	" 46-89-63
GERMANY (ALEMANIA). — (Embassy-Embajada). — L. Byron 737.	" 45-66-55
HAITI.—(Embassy-Embajada).—Mariano Escobedo 479.	" 45-52-29
HOLLAND (HOLANDA). — Embassy-Embajada). — Londres 40.	" 11-86-21
HONDURAS.—(Embassy-Embajada).—Av. Juárez 64.	Tel. 13-38-59
INDIA.—(Embassy-Embajada).—Av. Juárez 97.	" 12-41-11
INDONESIA.—(Embassy-Embajada).—Hamburgo 187.	" 25-24-91
ITALY (ITALIA).—(Embassy-Embajada).—Varsovia 22.	" 25-48-36
JAPAN (JAPON). — (Embassy-Embajada).—José María Marroquí 1.	" 12-65-79
NICARAGUA.—(Embassy-Embajada).—Explanada 825.	" 20-47-06
(Consulate-Consulado).—Acueducto 29-C.	" 20-47-06
NORWAY (NORUEGA).—Embassy-Embajada).—Virreyes 1460.	" 26-97-74
PERU.—(Embassy-Embajada).—Bahía de Ballenas No. 58, 1er. piso, Esq. Ejército Nacional.	" 45-84-50
PANAMA.—(Embassy-Embajada).—Insurgentes 453.	" 11-78-84
(Consulate-Consulado).—Insurgentes Sur 222.	" 28-86-32
POLAND (POLONIA). — Legation-Legación).—Salamanca 11.	" 14-96-45
PORTUGAL.—(Embassy-Embajada).—Prado Norte 615.	" 20-75-67
SPAIN (ESPAÑA).—Embassy-Embajada).—Londres 7.	" 46-66-14
SWEDEN (SUECIA). — (Embassy-Embajada).—Buenavista 3.	" 46-96-20
(Consulate-Consulado).—Parque Vía 198.	" 46-70-72
SWITZERLAND (SUIZA).—(Embassy-Embajada).—Hamburgo 66.	" 25-46-28
TURKEY (TURQUIA). — Embassy-Embajada).—Av. Luis G. Urbina 128.	" 20-23-44
UNITED STATES OF AMERICA (ESTADOS UNIDOS.—(Embassy-Embajada).—Lafragua 18.	" 46-94-00
URUGUAY.—(Embassy-Embajada).—Av. M. Avila Camacho 137.	" 20-18-04
(Consulate-Consulado).—Lerma 345-101.	" 11-41-57
U. S. S. R. (REPUBLICAS SOVIETICAS).—(Embassy-Embajada).—Calzada de Tacubaya 204.	" 15-69-87
VENEZUELA.—(Embassy-Embajada). — Londres 75, 5o. piso.	" 28-69-71
YUGOSLAVIA.—(Embassy-Embajada). — Av. Prado Sur 225	" 20-69-23

MEMORABLE DATES OF THIS WEEK — 2 — FECHAS MEMORABLES DE ESTA SEMANA

SEPTEMBER / SEPTIEMBRE

Conference in Munich between Hitler, Mussolini, Chamberlain and Daladier, 1938.	29	Conferencia en Munich entre Hitler, Mussolini, Chamberlain y Daladier, 1938.
José María Morelos y Pavón, hero of Mexican Independence born 1765.	30	Nace José María Morelos y Pavón, héroe de la Independencia de México, 1765.

OCTOBER / OCTUBRE

Francisco I. Madero, ex-President of México born 1873.	4	Nace Francisco I. Madero, ex Presidente de México, 1873.
Francisco (Pancho) Villa born 1877.	4	Nace Francisco (Pancho) Villa, 1877.
First airplane flight by the Wright Bros. in 1905.	5	Primer vuelo en avión por los Hermanos Wright, 1905.
John Erskine, American poet born 1879.	5	Nace John Erskine, poeta americano, 1879.

Here in Mexic / Opera, who wi / the 30th Sept / Institution and / pears with a / established by / at the Gallery / at

Aquí en la Ciu / el Tenor de la / tiembre dará / México, D. F. / de Francia. A / de la cría qu / obtuvo en la / calle R

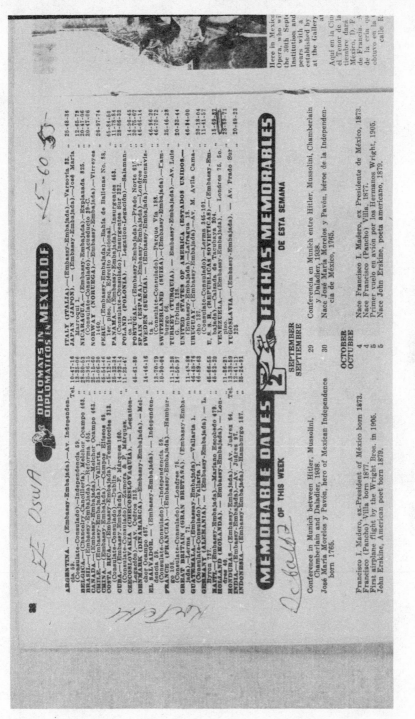

Commission Exhibit No. 2486—Continued

NINA POTAPOVA

LEARNING RUSSIAN

FOREIGN LANGUAGES PUBLISHING HOUSE
Moscow

COMMISSION EXHIBIT No. 2487

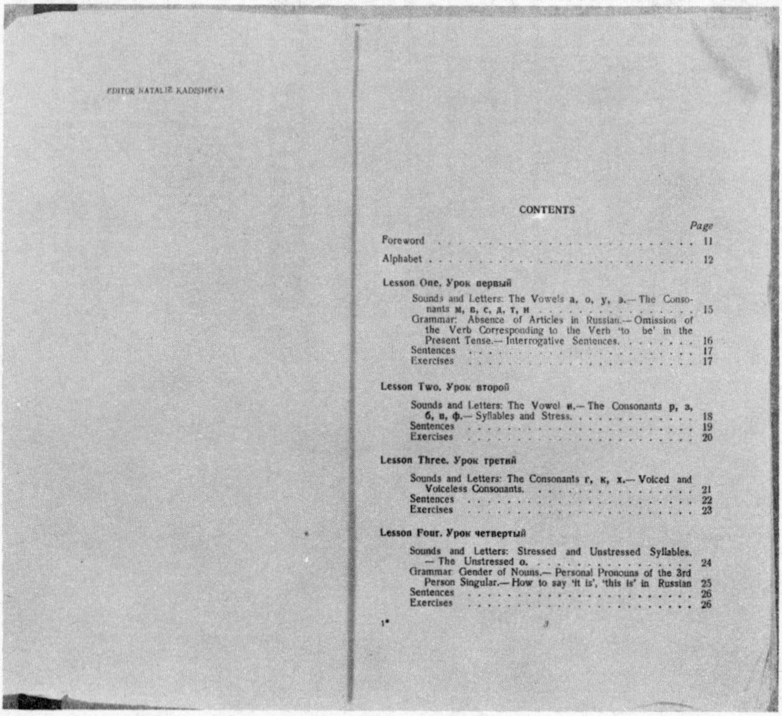

EDITOR NATALIE KADISHEVA

CONTENTS

1* 3

COMMISSION EXHIBIT No. 2487—Continued

Commission Exhibit No. 2487—Continued

Commission Exhibit No. 2487—Continued

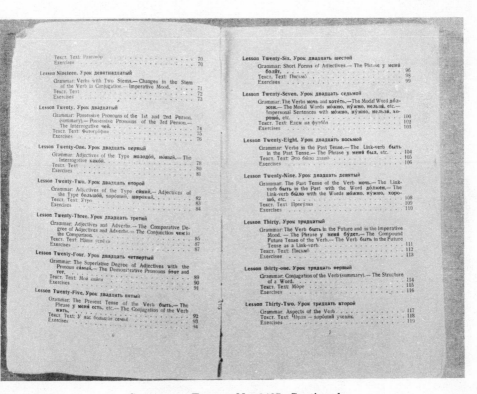

COMMISSION EXHIBIT No. 2487—Continued

FOREWORD

This is the first grade of *Learning Russian*,
differs from *Russian* (Books I and II) by the sa
in which the material is presented, the structure
texts. One of its principal features is the conci
Learning Russian may be used by all begin
though not by very young children. For adults
required to complete the course, for schools a
The aim of the book is to teach the student
sian, to understand easy texts and to carry on
Phonetics is dealt with mainly in the first l
which give a comparison of the characteristic
those of English, pronunciation, reading and s
principles of Russian handwriting.
In grammar, which is expounded concentrica
the gradual mastering of the spoken language
with mainly from the point of view of synta
The vocabulary of the first grade contains
taining to everyday life and therefore indisp
or useful to tourists or for reading easy newsp
The texts deal with everyday subjects reflect
Soviet life and culture.
The key to the exercises supplied at the end
student the opportunity to correct his own mist
help in studying a language, and permits the
without a teacher. A general Russian-English v
the end of the course.
The author will be grateful for any remarks
by students or teachers. Letters may be addres
Textbook Department, Foreign Languages
Zubovsky Boulevard, Moscow, USSR.*

* Москва, Зубовский бульвар 21, Издате
иностранных языках, Редакция учебников.

д, т, н.
ussian.
Corresponding to
e Present Tense.

ussian vowels are
ls are either long
pronounced:
with lips rounded
, though not so
rounded lips;
У у, Э э coin-
—The consonants

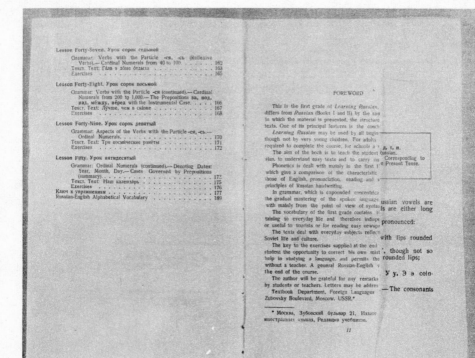

COMMISSION EXHIBIT No. 2487—Continued

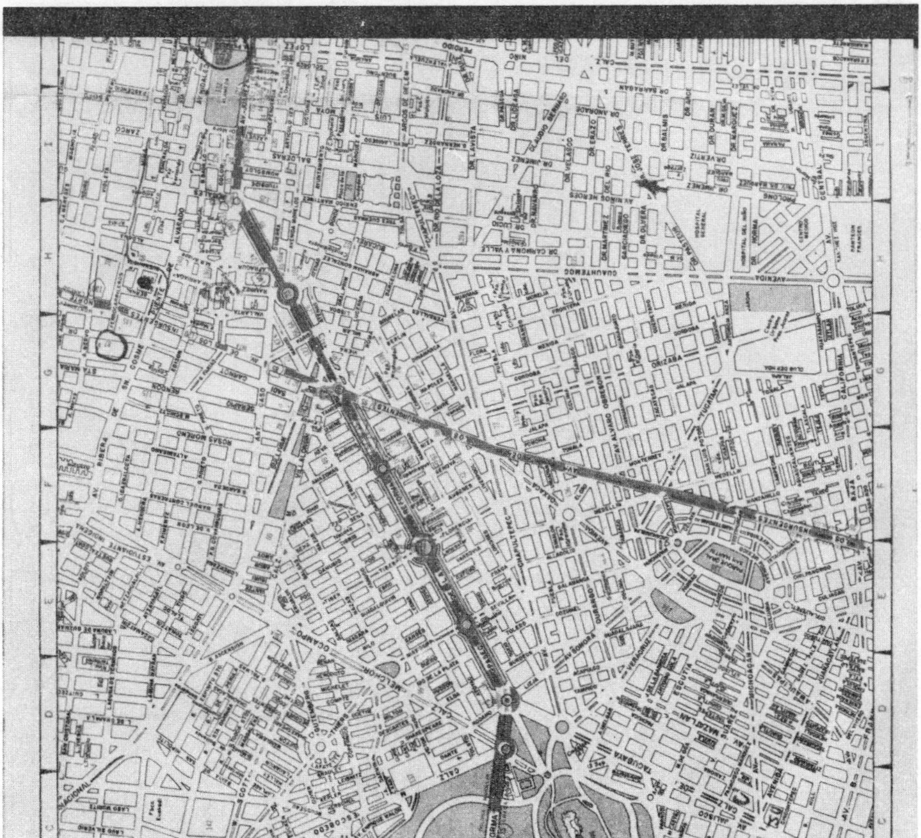

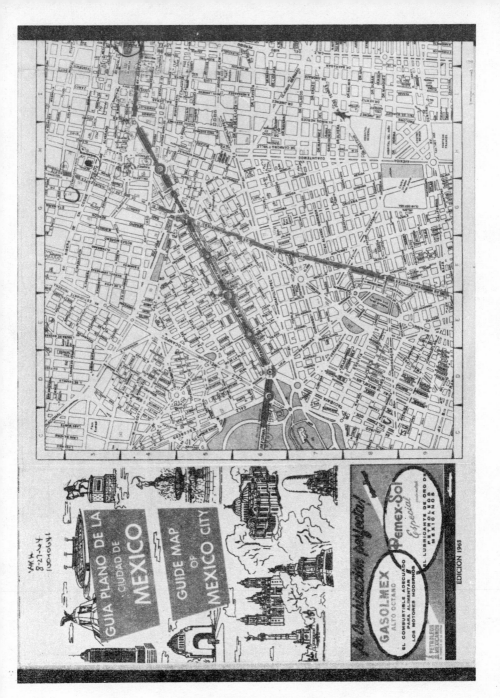

COMMISSION EXHIBIT No. 2488

INDICE / INDEX

PUNTOS DE INTERES / POINTS OF INTEREST

EDIFICIOS DE GOBIERNO
GOVERNMENT BUILDINGS.

1—Palacio Nacional. National Palace L-4
2—Depto. Central. City Hall K-4
3—Suprema Corte de Justicia. Supreme Court of Justice .. L-4
4—Secretaría de Economía. Dep. of Commerce L-4
5—Secretaría de Educación P Dep. of Public Education ... L-3
6—Secretaría de Recursos Hid Dep. Hydraulic Resources ... H-4
7—Secretaría de Marina. Navy Dep. I-4
8—Secretaría de Agricultura. Agriculture Dep. J-4
9—Secretaría del Trabajo. Labor Department .... I 6
10—Secretaría de Relaciones Foreign Relations I-4
11—Dirección de Pensiones. Pensions Building H-4
12—Secretaría de Gobernación. Dep. of the Interior H-5
13—Cámara de Diputados. Chamber of Representatives . K-3
14—Cámara de Senadores. Senate J-3
15—Jefatura de Policía Police Dept. K-6
16—Correo Mayor. Main Post Office J-4
17—Telégrafos Nacionales. National Telegraph Office ... J-3
18—Nacional Monte de Piedad. National Pawn Shop K-4
19—Palacio de Bellas Artes. Palace Fine Arts J-4
20—Estatua de Carlos IV. Charles 4th. Statue H-4
21—Hemiciclo a Juárez. Hemicycle I-4
22—Monumento a la Revolución. Monument to Revolution H-4
23—Estatua a Colón. Columbus Statue H-4
24—Estatua a Morelos I-5
25—Fuente del Salto del Agua. Colonial Fountain J-5
26—Estatua de Washington. G-5
27—Monumento a la Madre. Mother's Monument G-4
28—Castillo de Chapultepec. Castle C-7
29—Monumento a Cuauhtémoc. Cuauhtemoc Statue G-5
30—Monumento de la Indep Independence Monument F-5
31—Monumento a los Niños H Child Heroes Monument .. D-7
32—Estatua a Bolívar. Bolivar Statue D-6
33—Central de Bomberos Fire Dept. M-6

HOTELES

34—Aller I-5
35—El Presidente F-6
36—Bamer I-4
37—Paseo F-5
38—Continental Hilton G-5
39—De Cortés I-3
40—Del Prado I-4
41—Emporio G-5
42—Geneve F-6
43—Hotel María Isabel F-5
44—San Francisco, I-4
45—Francis H-4
45-A—Hunter F-4
46—Alameda, Av. Juárez 50 ... J-4
47—Luma G-6
47-A—Madrid Once G-4
48—Majestic K-4
49—María Cristina F-5
50—Meurice G-6
51—Monte Cassino F-6
52—Montejo F-5
53—Ontario K-5
54—Plaza G-4
55—Prince I-4
56—Reforma G-4
57—Regis I-4
58—Ritz K-4
59—Roosevelt F-8
60—Shirley Courts F-4
60-A—Saxon G-4
61—St. Moritz G-4
62—Virreyes J-5

TRANSPORTACION
TRANSPORTATION

64-A—Royal Dutch Air G-4
145—Omnibus de México G-3
63—Aeronaves I-4
64—Aerovías Guest G-4
65—American Airlines H-4
66—Autos Pullman A.D.O. H-3
67—Eastern Airlines H-4
68—Cía. Mexicana de Aviación. . I-4
73 Pan American H-4
68-A—Cubana de Aviación H-4
68-B—Estrella de Oro .... K 6
69—Ferrocarriles NN. de M Mexican Railways .. J-4
70—Ferrocarriles, Estación. Railroad Depot H-3
70-A—Taca International I-4
71—Transportes del Norte, Bus Terminal (North) G-4
72—Transportes "Galgo" Acapulco Limousines K-6

INFORMACION TURISTICA
TURIST INFORMATION

73—Depto. Nac. Turismo H-4
74—Pemex Travel Club I-4
75—Wagons Lits Cook .. I-4
76—Wells Fargo J-4
77—AMA. (Mex. Auto. Ass.) F-6
78—ANA. (Nat. Auto. Ass.). F-4

MUSEOS BIBLIOTECAS.
LIBRARIES, MUSEUMS

79—Academia de San Carlos. Fine Arts School L-4
80—Biblioteca B. Franklin F-6
81—Biblioteca Nacional. National Library K-5
82—Colegio Americano. Mexico City College G-8
83—Museo Arte Religioso K-4
84—Museo Nacional de Historia. National History Museum . C-7
85—Museo Antropología Anthropology Museum L-4
86—Museo Artes e Inds. Popls. Museum of Popular Arts.... I-4
87—Museo de Historia Natural . G-3

TIENDAS DE ROPA
DEPARTAMENT STORES

89—Centro Mercantil K-4
90—Palacio de Hierro K-4
90-A—Nvo. Palacio de Hierro . E-7
91—El Puerto de Liverpool .. L-4
92—Salinas y Rocha I-4
93—Sears Roebuck F-8
93-A—Woolworth G-4

RESTAURANTES
MAIN RESTAURANTS

94—Centro Vasco, Madero 6 ... J-4
95—Ambassadeurs H-4
96—Angelo's F-6
97—Bellinghausen F-6
98—Bottoms Up Bar P-6
99—Cadillac. Bar D-5
100—Café "Tacuba" K-4
57—Capri (en Hotel Regis) I-4
102—Chalet Suizo F-5
103—Czardas. Danzant D-6
104—El Parador F-5
105—Muralto, Torre Latino J-4
106—Mauna Loa, Hamburgo 127 . E-6
107—Normandie, Reforma y Niza F-5
108—Jena. Bar H-4
109—Focolare F-5
110—1-2-3, Liverpool 123 .... F-6
111—Quid G-6
112—Sanborn's No. 1 .... J-4
41—Sanborn's No. 2 .. I-4
112-A—Sanborn's Reforma H-4
83—Villa Fontana, F-5

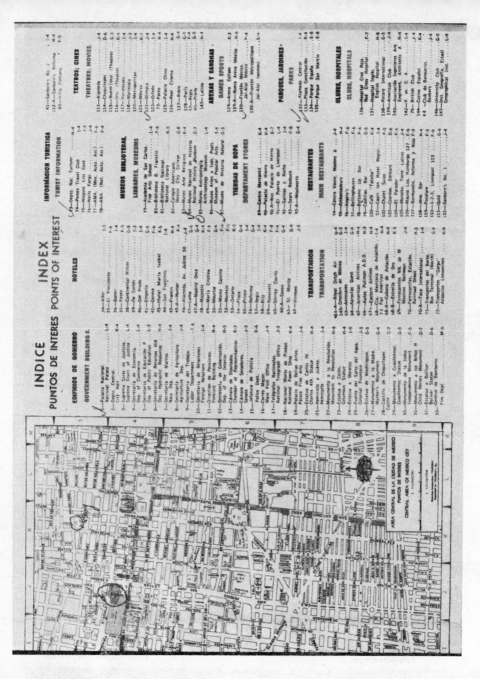

TEATROS; CINES
THEATRES; MOVIES.

113—Alameda J-4
114—Chapultepec D-6
115—Nuevo Ideal (Theatre) .. G-3
116—Iris (Theatre) K-4
117—Variedades I-4
118—Mariscala J-3
120—Metropolitan I-4
121—México H-7
122—Olimpia J-4
123—Orfeón I-4
73—Paseo H-4
125—Palacio Chino I-4
126—Real Cinema H-4
127—Roble G-4
128—París G-5
57—Regis F-4
40—Prado G-5
143—Latino H-4

ARENAS Y CANCHAS .
GAMES SPORTS

129—Arena Coliseo K-3
129-A—Nueva Arena México .. H-6
130—Frontón México. Jai-Alai México H-4
130-A—Frontón Metropolitano Jai-Alai (women) L-4

PARQUES, JARDINES·
PARKS

132—Alameda Central I-4
133—Plaza Constitución K-4
134—Parque España E-8
135—Parque San Martín E-8

CLUBES, HOSPITALES
CLUBS, HOSPITALS

136—Hospital Cruz Roja. Red Cross Hospital F-7
137—Hospital Inglés. English Hospital H-8
138—Rotary International G-5
139—American Club J-4
140—Asociación Ingenieros Arq Engineers, Architects A . H-4
142—Y. M. C. A. I-4
76—British Club J-4
144—Casino Español K-4
44 —Club de Banqueros. Bankers J-4
146—University Club G-5
147—Inst. Geografía, Estadi Geographical Inst. L-4

Commission Exhibit No. 2488—Continued

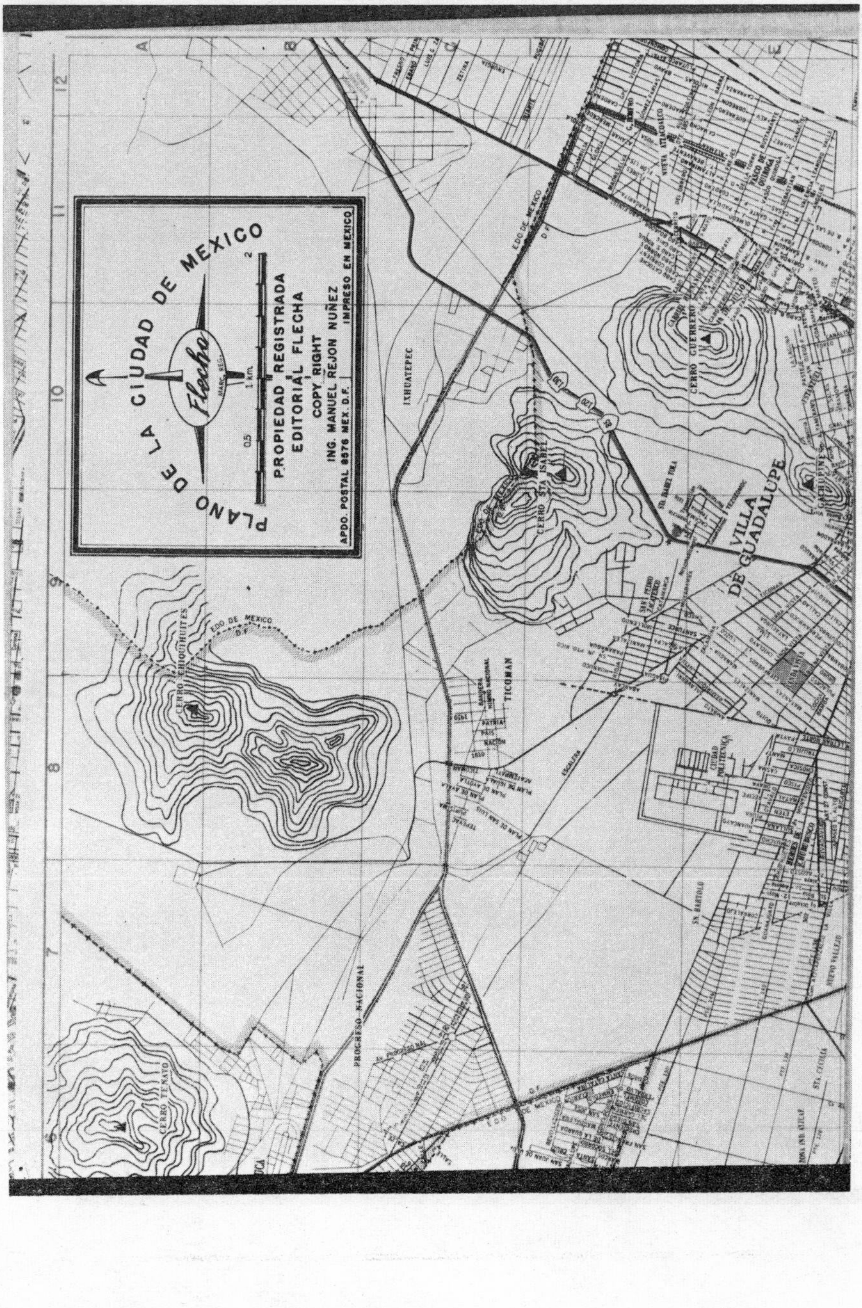

Commission Exhibit No. 2488—Continued

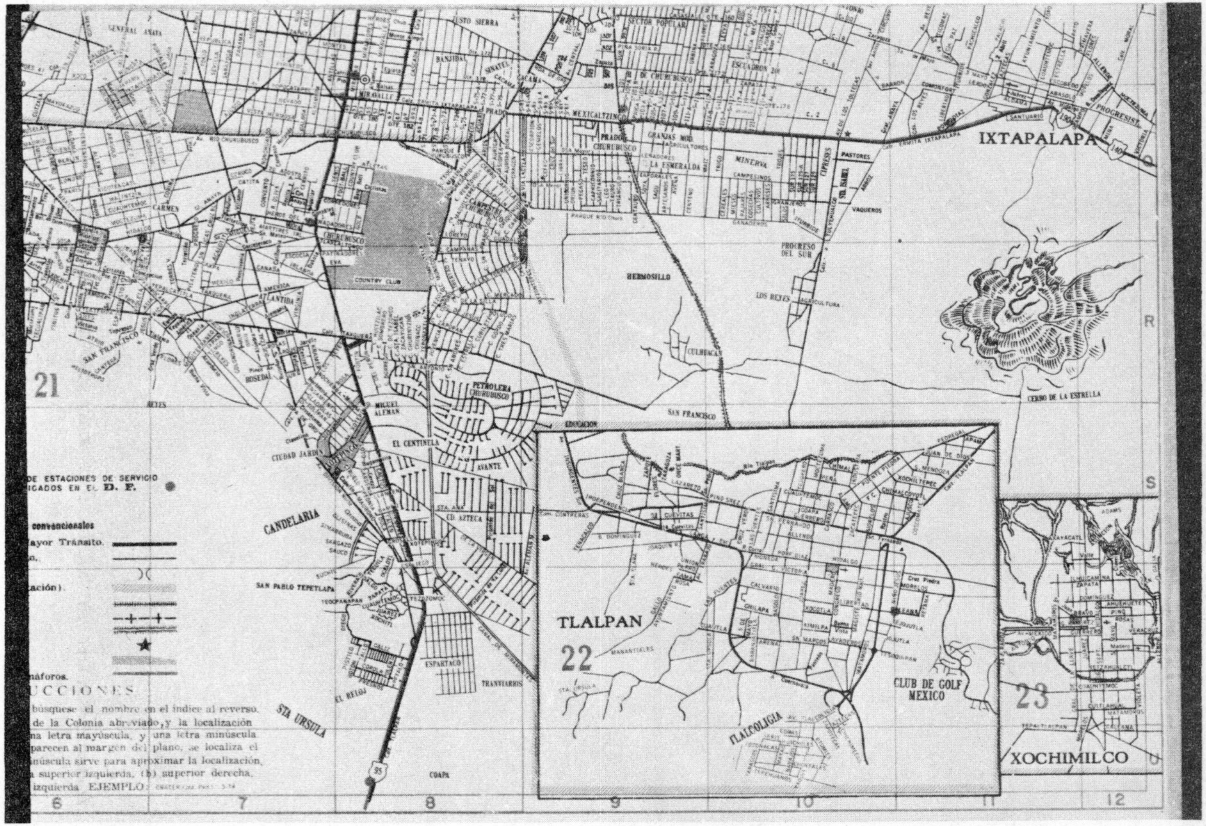

COMMISSION EXHIBIT No. 2488—Continued

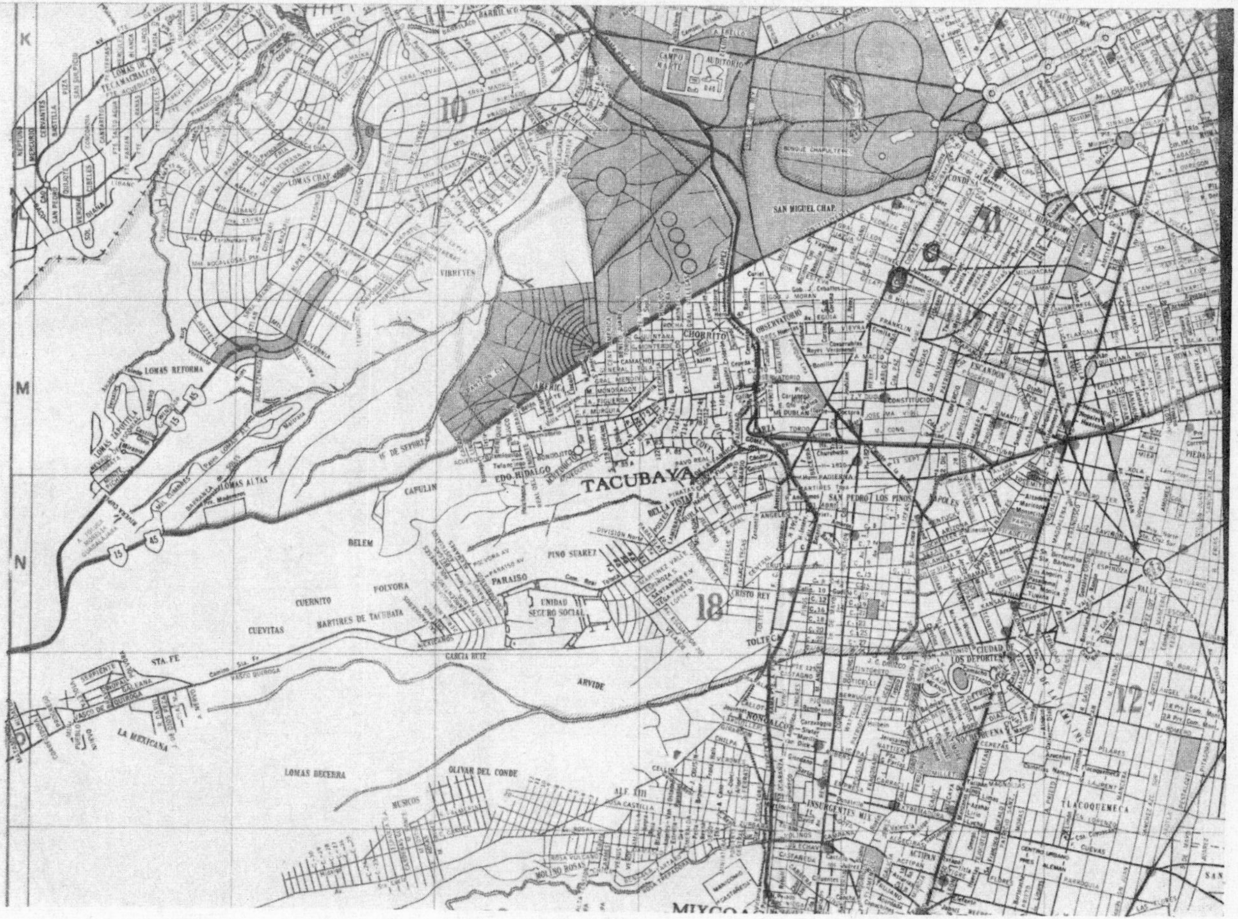

Commission Exhibit No. 2488—Continued

Commission Exhibit No. 2488—Continued

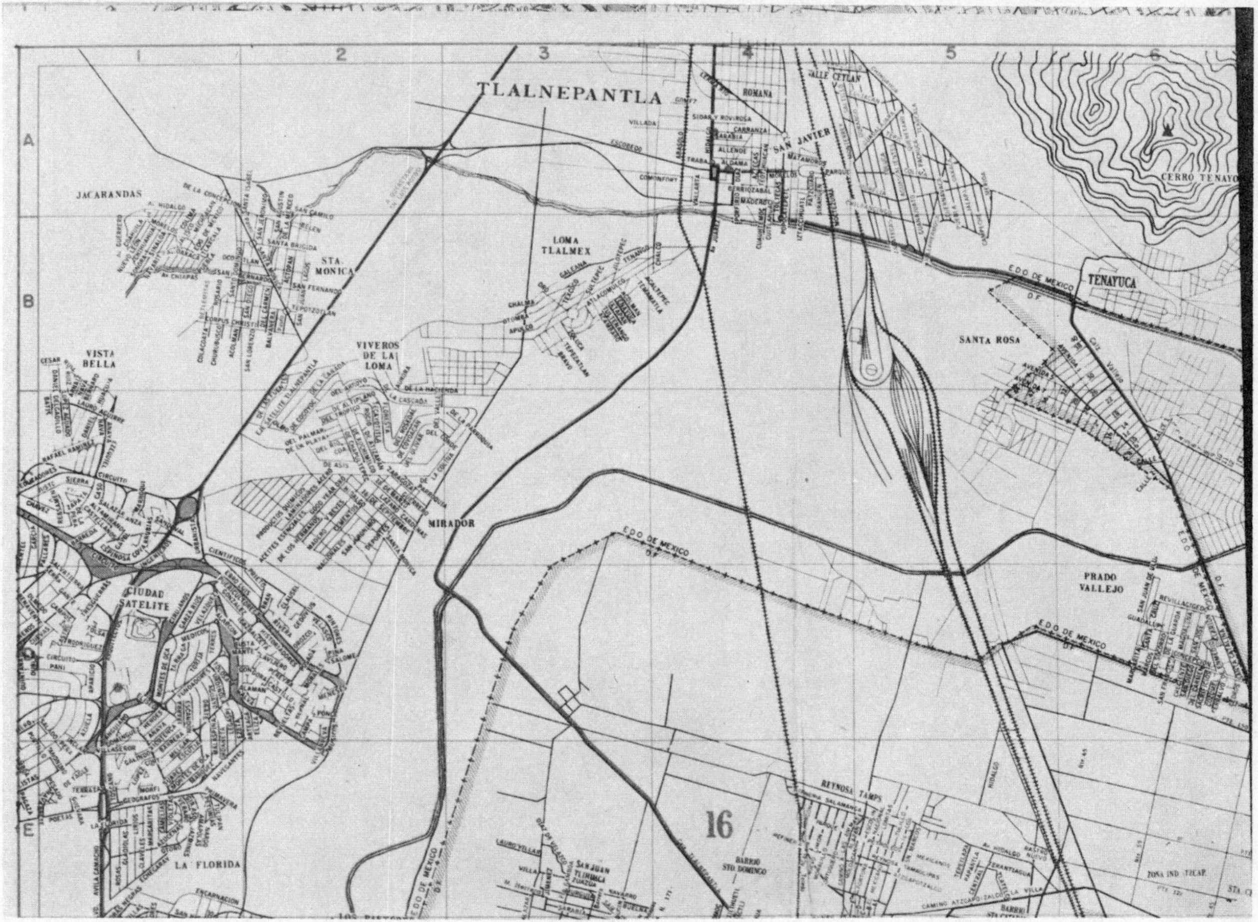

COMMISSION EXHIBIT No. 2488—Continued

Commission Exhibit No. 2488—Continued

Commission Exhibit No. 2488—Continued

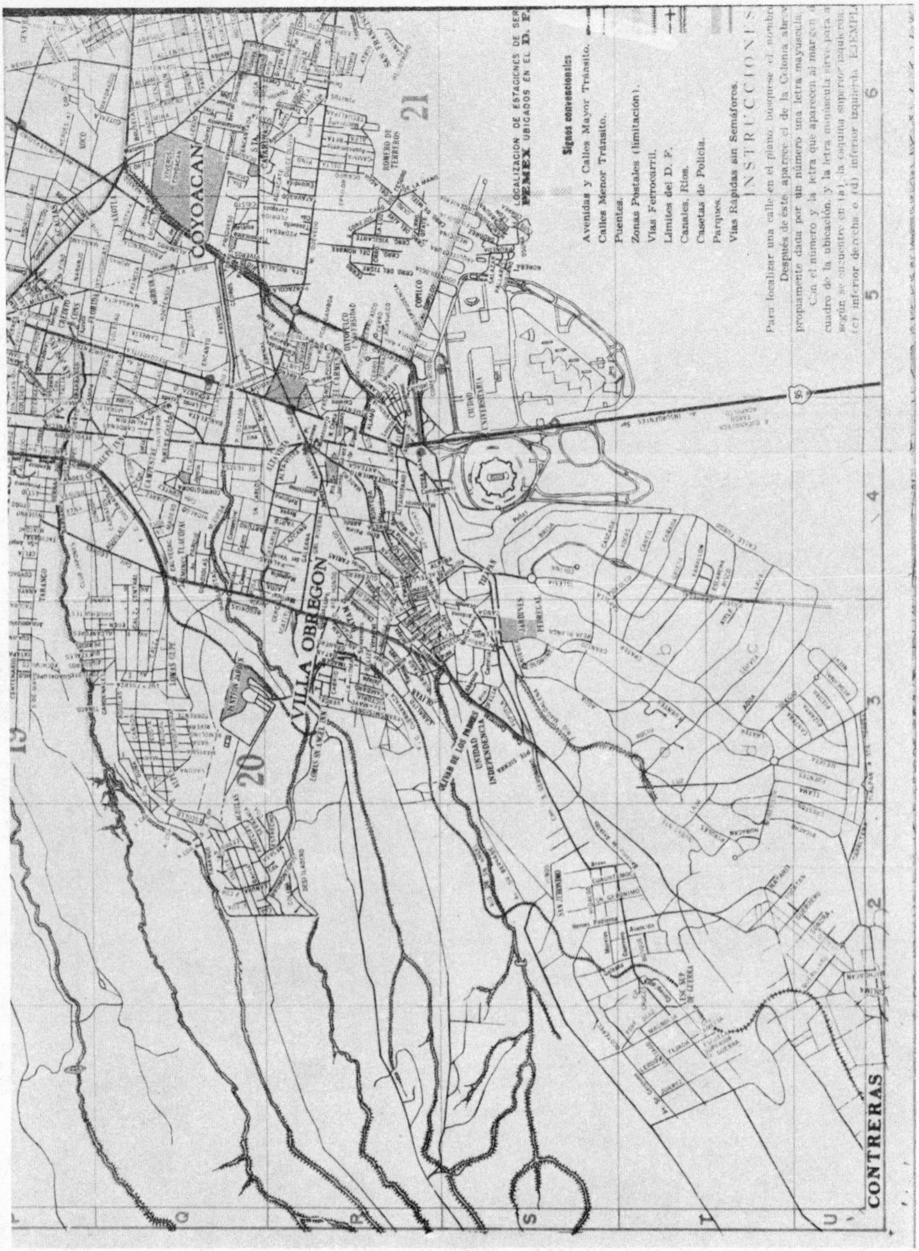

COMMISSION EXHIBIT No. 2488—Continued

INDICE DE

A

B

E

J

N

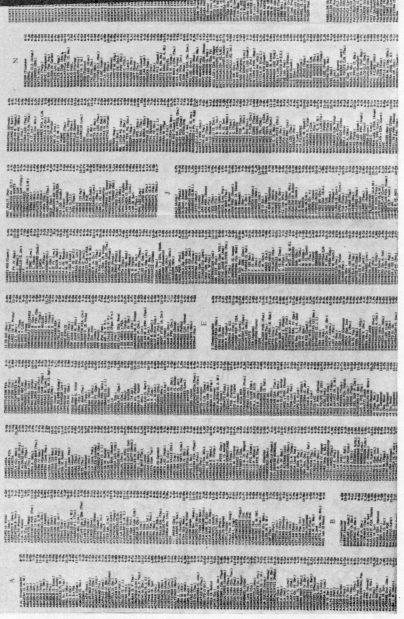

COMMISSION EXHIBIT No. 2488—Continued

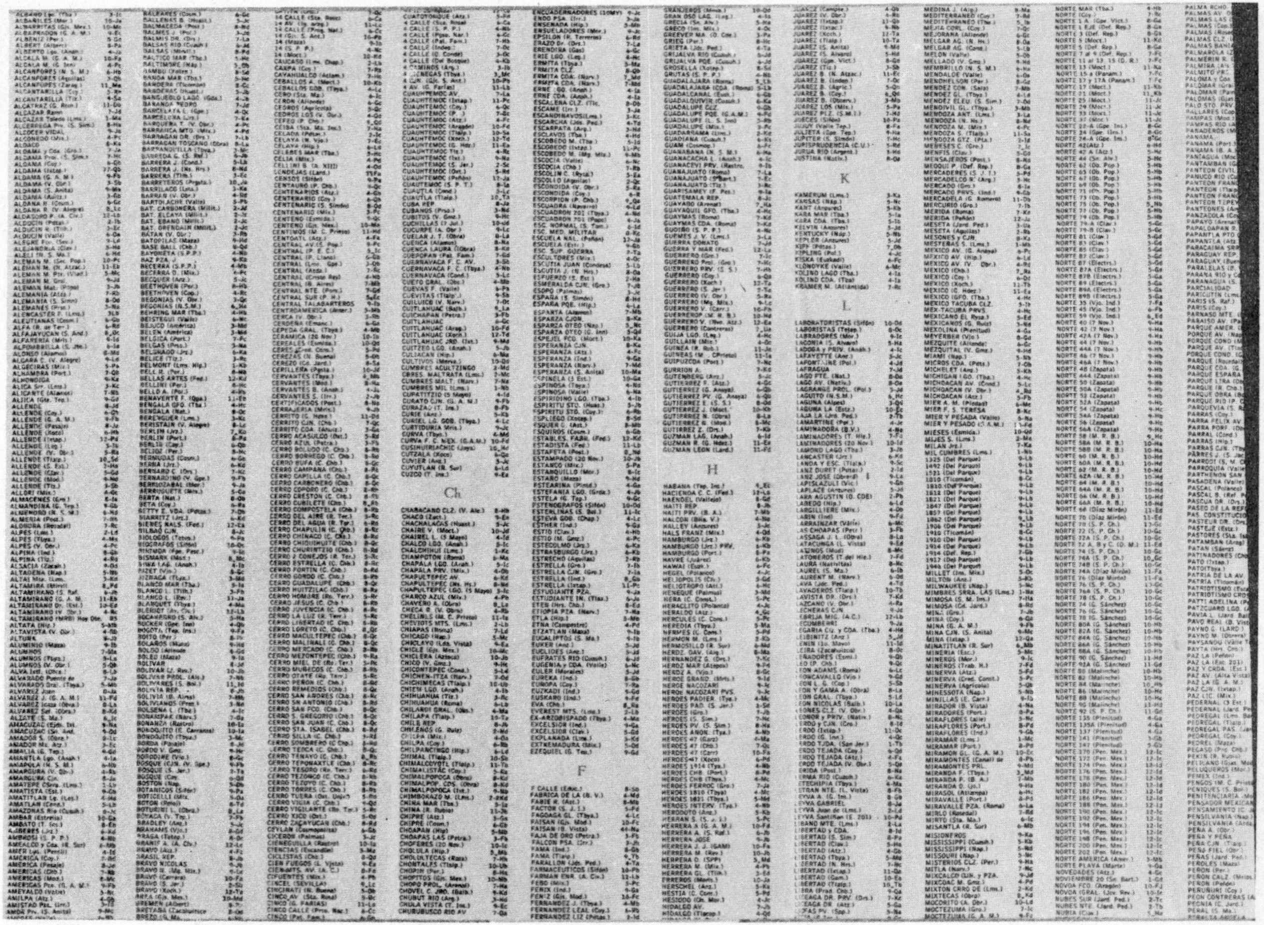

COMMISSION EXHIBIT No. 2488—Continued

COMMISSION EXHIBIT No. 2488—Continued

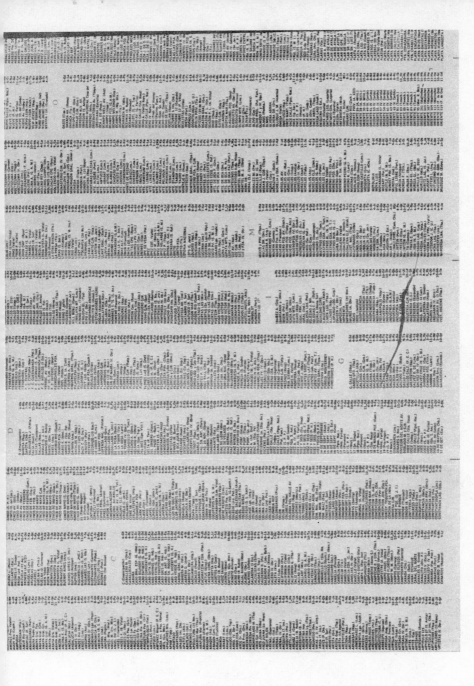

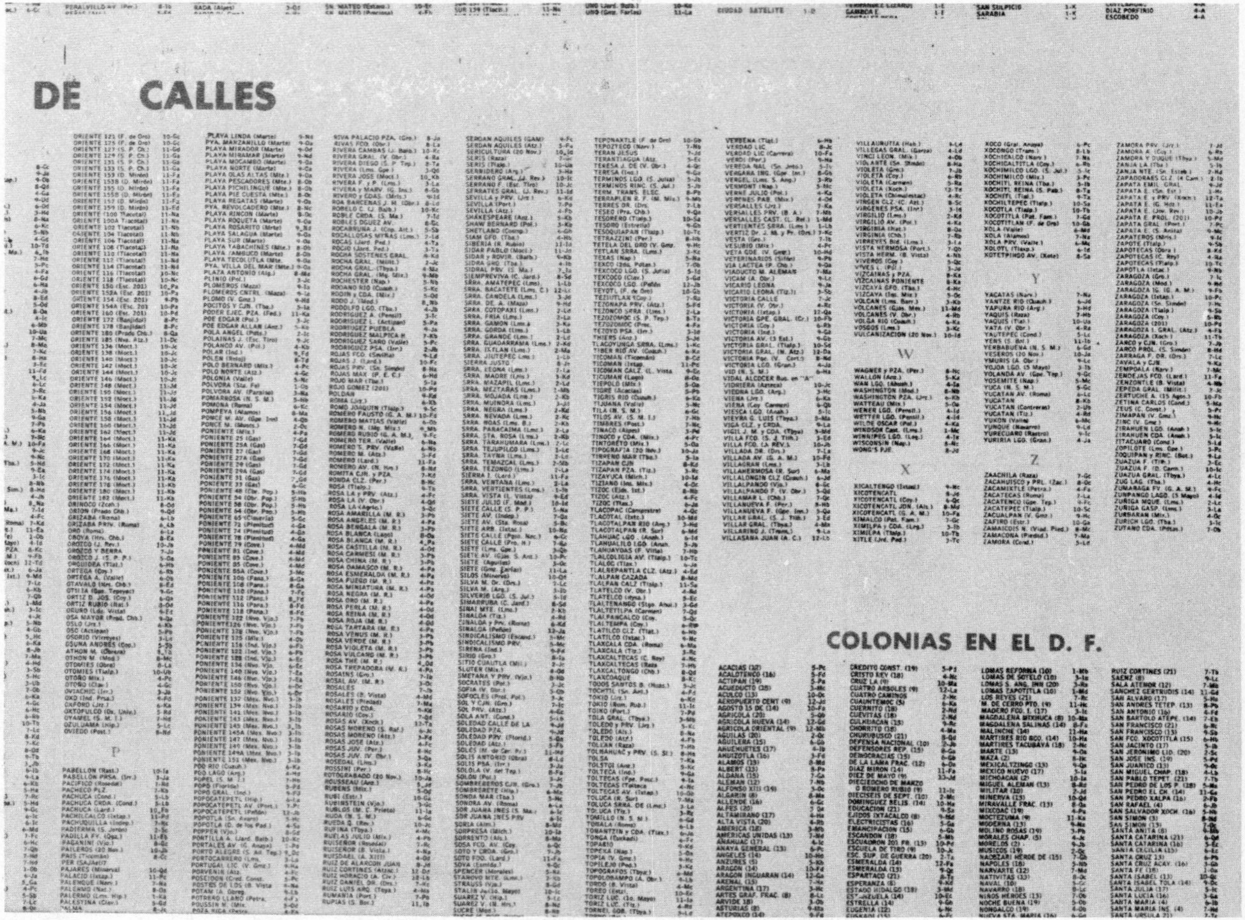

COMMISSION EXHIBIT No. 2488—Continued

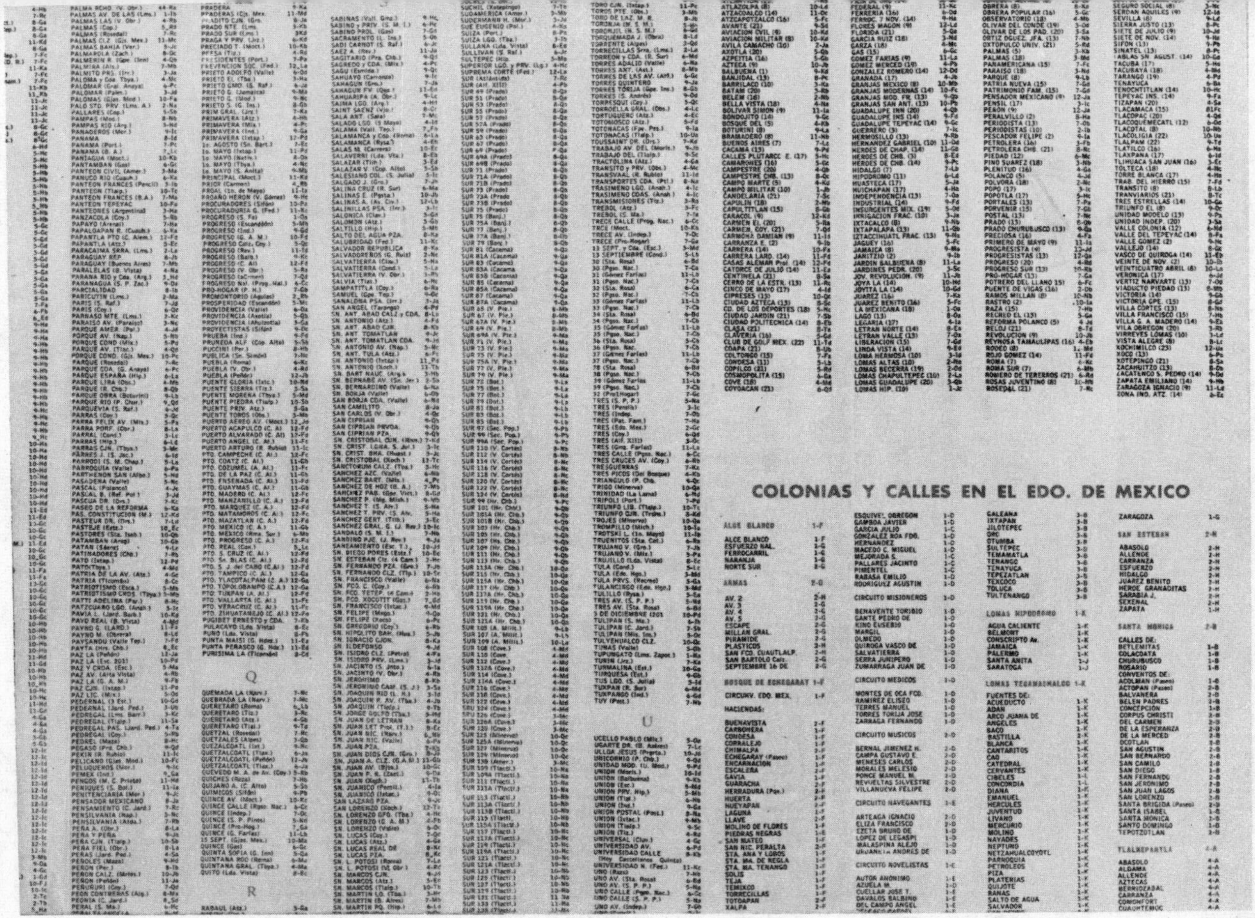

Commission Exhibit No. 2488—Continued

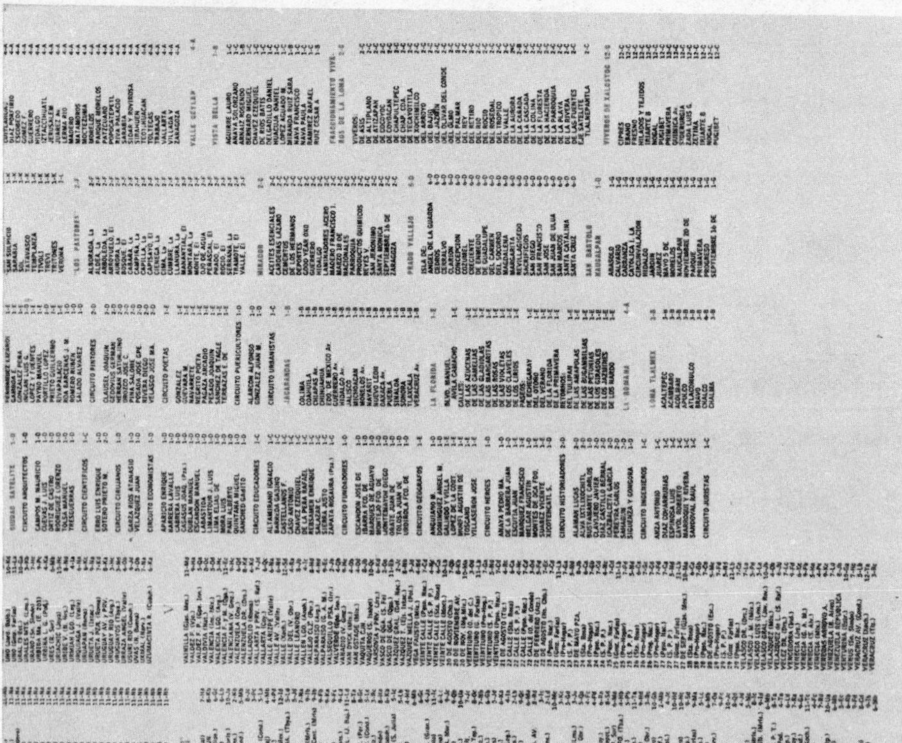

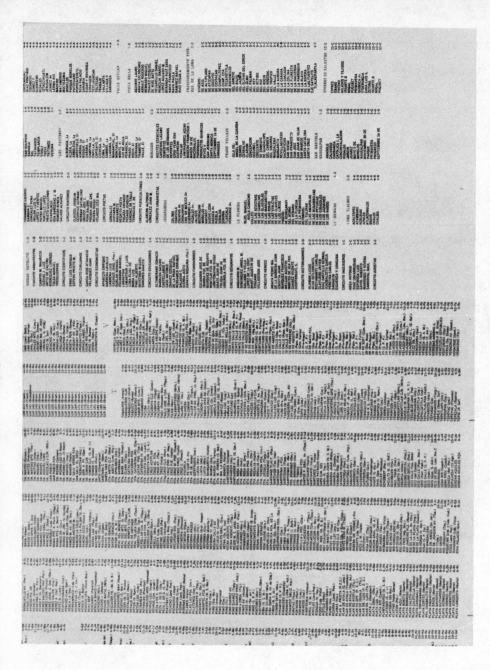

Commission Exhibit No. 2488—Continued

breed was improved with a stud from Pablo Bajumea, and later three more studs from Murube.

ATLANGA. Founded in 1890 with local stock from Atlamaxac and studs from Zotoluca, Piedras Negras, La Laguna, Coaxamalucan, Zacatepec, San Mateo and Rancho Seco.

ZOTOLUCA. Founded in 1908 with Tepeyahualco cows, and studs from Anastasio Martin, Concha and Sierra, Marquis of Saltillo, Duque de Veragua and Miura.

LA LAGUNA. Founded in 1908, with blood from Tepeyahualco mixed with Saltillo.

COAXAMALUCAN. Founded in 1918 with blood from Piedras Negras and Tepeyahualco. Later mixed with studs from Ibarra and Murube.

ZACATEPEC. Founded in 1925 with cows and studs from Piedras Negras and also San Mateo. Back in 1938 this hacienda acquired studs (five) from Carmen de Federico (Murube).

RANCHO SECO. Founded in 1925, with stud bulls from Zotoluca and local bred cows as well as Piedras Negras Stock. Some cows from the Marquis of Saltillo were later brought in to breed with the studs from Carmen de Federico (Murube), and still later on, the blood was improved with studs from Antonio Urquijo and one more from the Count of La Corte.

SAN MIGUEL MIMIAHUAPAN. Founded in 1923 with a section of Ajuluapan, belonging to don Jesus Zamora. Later the same hacienda bought the stock from Torreon de Cañas belonging to don Rafael Gurza.

LA TRASQUILA. Blood from Atlanga, Piedras Negras, Zacatepec and Coaxamalucan. Blooded studs from Arribas Brothers.

LAS HUERTAS. Pure Pasteje blood.

CAROLINA GONZALEZ. A section of Coaxamalucan.

OLIVARES. A section of Zacatepec.

ZACATECAS

SAN MATEO. Founded with local selected breeds but all the stock was rejected in 1908 when the former owner, father of the present proprietor, imported 40 cows and eight stud bulls from the Marquis of Saltillo in the Mother country. One year later, Don Antonio the elder, imported again stock from the Marquis. The Llaguno family, owners of this old hacienda, have managed to put the San Mateo brand in the very first row of the brave bulls breeding haciendas. The elder Don Antonio Llaguno devoted his entire time to his ranch, and took every pain to make of it the great success that it is to the present day.

TORRECILLAS. Founded back in 1932, when the stock from San Mateo was divided between the Llaguno brothers, Don Julian and Don Antonio, the younger. There are cows as well as stud bulls from the Marquis of Saltillo. Several specimens from this Ganaderia have made history in the Mexican bull rings.

Manuel Rodriguez (Manolete) on his first appearance in the old time Toreo in Mexico City, had a brilliant performance with Torrecillas bulls.

CHUCHO CABRERA. Founded back in 1935 by the well known Mexican Torero Lorenzo Garza, who later sold to don Jesus Cabrera the present owner. This ranch was started with 225 cows and five stud bulls from San Mateo and Torrecillas, pure Marquis of Saltillo blood. Several specimens from this hacienda have also made history in the Mexico City arenas.

There are, of course a number of lesser establishments that have managed to stand the competition of the greater names in brave bull breeding. Some of the local stocks are exceptionally good and are remembered with gratitude by the native aficionados who seem never to forget a good Tarde de Toros.

PRINTED IN MEXICO EDITION

100-10461
8-27-64
WRH

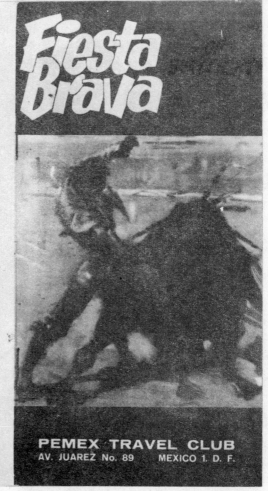

Fiesta Brava

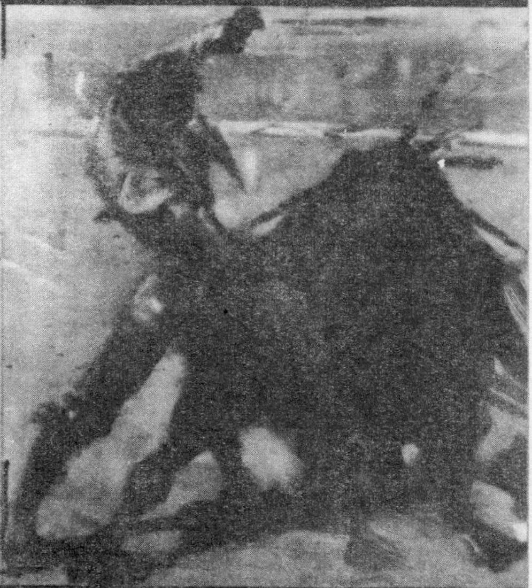

PEMEX TRAVEL CLUB
AV. JUAREZ No. 89 MEXICO 1. D. F.

COMMISSION EXHIBIT No. 2489

На 1962 год

БІЛЕТ № 16031/9132

Прозвішча ______________________

Імя Освальд

Імя па бацьку Ли Харей

Месца працы або вучобы ______________________

Рэгістратар:

Зак. 9546. Тыр. 3500.

Вытрымка з правілаў бібліятэкі

1. Білет абавязкова паказваецца кожны раз пры ўваходзе ў бібліятэку і чытальню.
2. № білета, прозвішча і месца працы або вучобы ўпісваецца ў кантрольны лісток, які разам з білетам прад'яўляецца пры атрыманні кніг.
3. Перадача білета другім асобам забараняецца.
4. При згубе білета дублікат выдаецца праз месяц пасля заявы аб гэтым. Пры згубе дубліката паўторна дублікат не выдаецца.
5. Выносіць кнігі з чытальні ў другія пакоі забараняецца.
6. Чытачы бібліятэкі нясуць матэрыяльную адказнасць за атрыманыя кнігі.
7. Уваход у чытальні са сваімі кнігамі забараняецца.

Commission Exhibit No. 2490

ДЗЯРЖАЎНАЯ БІБЛІЯТЭКА БССР
імя У. І. ЛЕНІНА

Без права перадачы

Commission Exhibit No. 2490—Continued

Commission Exhibit No. 2491

FD-302 (Rev. 3-3-59)

FEDERAL BUREAU OF IN[redacted]

1

Date 11/25/63

JAKE RIFKIN, 869 Faxon, Memphis, Tennessee, a professional gambler, telephonically advised that he, RIFKIN, formerly lived in Dallas, Texas, for a period of twenty years, ending in 1961. In approximately ten years he became casually acquainted with JACK RUBY and subsequently became friendly with him. Seven or eight years ago, RIFKIN underwent an operation at Lisbon Veterans Administration Hospital at Dallas, and at the time of his discharge he was without any money with which to maintain himself. In view of this, JACK RUBY took him in to live with him at RUBY's apartment, the address of which RIFKIN could not recall. He said he remained at this apartment for approximately two months.

According to RIFKIN, he has not seen RUBY since 1961 and had only seen him once or twice during a two or three year period before 1961. He last saw RUBY when RUBY opened a night club known as the Sovereign Club in Dallas.

He said he knew nothing concerning RUBY's parents, relatives or previous life except that RUBY was from Chicago, Illinois.

RIFKIN said he knew nothing of any subversive connections of RUBY. Specifically he knew nothing concerning any activity of RUBY in connection with the Fair Play for Cuba Committee.

Mr. RIFKIN stated he did not know OSWALD and knew of no connection between RUBY and OSWALD. He likewise stated he was not aware of any racial or extremist views or activities of RUBY.

RIFKIN described RUBY as a kindly, gentlemanly, generous man because of RUBY's generosity to him.

on 11/25/63 at Memphis, Tennessee File # DL 44-1639 MH 44-1165

by Special Agent NORMAN L. CASEY: mam Date dictated 11/25/63

COMMISSION EXHIBIT NO. 2491

Commission Exhibit No. 2492

FD-302 (Rev. 3-3-59)

FEDERAL BUREAU OF IN[redacted]

1

Date November 28, 1963

DON TABON, 8546 Forest Hills, Dallas, Texas, furnished the following information.

In early February, 1963, one night, about 8:00 P.M., TABON was at the Burgandy Room at the Adolphus Hotel. He was sitting at a table with two friends, salesmen from out of town.

TABON knows JACK RUBY by sight having seen him on several occasions at various hotels in Dallas passing out cards advertising the Carousel Club. On this particular night, a short time earlier, TABON had seen JACK RUBY in the Adolphus Hotel accompanied by an "exotic blond". While in the Burgandy Room, JACK RUBY passed the table where TABON was seated and as he passed, TABON made a remark to the effect "what became of that crazy blond you had". JACK RUBY turned around and began beating TABON savagely about the head. After RUBY had beaten TABON to the floor, he immediately left the Burgandy Room. TABON was taken to the hotel office for first aid and while there, a police officer came in and TABON made out a complaint against RUBY. TABON was able to walk out of the hotel, however, the next day he found after going to a doctor that he had received serious injuries from the beating, necessitating his going to a neuro surgeon and eye surgeon.

Subsequently, this matter was brought into Corporation Court in Dallas and after TABON testified, JACK RUBY was found not guilty.

TABON recalled that on the night he was attacked by RUBY at the Burgandy Room about midnight, he received a telephone call at his home from a Detective whose first name he believed was TOMMY and this Detective suggested that he drop the complaint against RUBY since if he were found guilty on a charge of assault, he would probably be fined only about $15.00.

TABON said he had considered a civil suit against RUBY in connection with the assault on him, however, his attorney had determined that RUBY did not have a bank account or other property and even if a judgment were obtained against him, it would not be possible to collect the judgment.

on 11/28/63 at Dallas, Texas File # DL 44-1639

by Special Agents PAUL L. SCOTT, & JAMES W. SWINFORD/jn Date dictated 11/28/63

COMMISSION EXHIBIT NO. 2492

Commission Exhibit No. 2493

FD-302 (Rev. 3-3-59)

FEDERAL BUREAU OF I[redacted]

Date 11-27-63

1

Mr. MARION T. STEENSON, 717 N. Hill, Richardson, Texas, furnished the following information:

In early February, possibly about February 15, 1963, STEENSON was in the Burgundy Room at the Adolphus Hotel, this was sometime early in the night. As he was sitting at the bar, he heard a disturbance at his back and turned around and saw two men fighting between tables adjacent to the bar. STEENSON was not acquainted with either of the men who were fighting, however, he recalled that one of the men was a short heavy set man, and this man was doing most of the "slugging" while the other individual appeared to be trying to get away. The fight lasted two or three minutes and sometime later the police contacted STEENSON and asked him for information concerning the fight. He told them at that time he was not acquainted with either of the men and did not know the cause of the fight or any other pertinent information. The man who was being beaten by the short, heavy, fat man, appeared to have been badly beaten and was taken to the Adolphus Hotel Office. There were a number of other persons in the Burgundy Room at this time, however, during the discussion following the fight, no one seem to know the reason for the fight.

STEENSON was told after he went to the hotel office that the short heavy man involved in the fight was JACK RUBY from the Carousel Club in Dallas. The police had indicated to STEENSON that he would be called later as a witness, however, he was never called and he assumed ther[illegible]d been no trial in connection with this altercation at the hotel.

STEENSON said he is not acquainted with JACK RUBY and does not recall ever having seen him except at the time the fight occurred.

on 11-26-63 at Richardson, Texas File # DL 44-11639

by Special Agent PAUL L. SCOTT - md Date dictated 11-27-63

This document contains neither recommendations nor conclusions of the FBI. It is the property of the FBI and is loaned to your agency; it and its contents are not to be distributed outside your agency.

COMMISSION EXHIBIT No. 2493

Commission Exhibit No. 2494

FD-302 (Rev. 3-3-59)

FEDERAL BUREAU OF IN[redacted]

Date December 3, 1963

1

JOE GARCIA, 1938 Las Cruces, Dallas, Texas, advised he has known JACK RUBY for about 7-8 years, having met him in the Silver Spur Club in Dallas. He said RUBY is a hot headed individual who believes in dominating other persons by the use of his fists. He further advised RUBY is the type of person who would perform a favor for an individual and then alienate that person's friendship because of his hot temper. GARCIA has never known RUBY to take any interest in politics and he is not known to harbor any interest in political or civic matters. GARIS has never discussed politics with RUBY and stated RUBY has never shown any hostility toward the President of the United States or any political figures. He said RUBY is mainly interested in making money and in operating his night clubs.

GARCIA recalled incidents when RUBY would appear at the Artists of Dallas Club at which time RUBY would bring the day's receipts from his club with him. On these occasions RUBY would be carrying a gun and he would leave the receipts and the gun with the Artists of Dallas Club operator. GARCIA said this club closed in Dallas about 2 years ago and he knew RUBY was carrying a gun for quite some time prior to the time the club closed. GARCIA advised he recently talked with the band leader at the Carousel Club in Dallas which club is owned by RUBY, at which time they wondered how the entertainer BILL DEMAR could have remembered seeing OSWALD in the Carousel Club. GARCIA said he and the Carousel Band leader were perplexed by this information because DEMAR went through his act so fast in the audience it would be almost impossible for him to remember a particular individual he contacted in the audience in connection with an act. GARCIA said he has worked for JACK RUBY at times in the past providing music for RUBY's night clubs. GARCIA recalled RUBY as being a very unusual person in that RUBY would physically beat someone and then apoligize later to the individual he had beaten. GARCIA said this could only be explained by RUBY's inability to control his hot temper. GARCIA said at the present time RUBY is receiving hair treatments at the McLean's Hair Treatment Parlor located in the Dallas Athletic Club building. GARCIA said persons at the McLean Hair Treatment Parlor would possibly be acquainted with RUBY on a daily basis. GARCIA concluded by advising he knows very little concerning RUBY's background except that RUBY came from Chicago to Dallas.

on 11/30/63 at Dallas, Texas File # Dallas 44-1639

by Special Agent S CHARLES T. BROWN, JR. & ALFRED C. ELLINGTON:BL Date dictated 12/3/63

This document contains neither recommendations nor conclusions of the FBI. It is the property of the FBI and is loaned to your agency; it and its contents are not to be distributed outside your agency.

COMMISSION EXHIBIT No. 2494

DL 44-1639
2

He recalled RUBY has been friendly with numerous Dallas police officers and detectives over a long period of time and RUBY has invited those officers to his clubs for entertainment.

157

COMMISSION EXHIBIT No. 2494—Continued

Commission Exhibit No. 2495.

[redacted]

FD-302 (Rev. 3-3-59)

FEDERAL BUREAU OF INVESTIGATION

Date December 3, 1963

1

Mrs. JOE GARCIA, also known as SHERRI LINN, 1938 Las Cruces, Dallas, Texas, advised she has known JACK RUBY for approximately 15 years. Mrs. GARCIA is an exotic dancer and uses the stage name SHERRI LINN. She said she first became acquainted with RUBY when he was frequenting the old Sky Club in Dallas, which was later known as the Sky View Club. She said this club was formerly operated by a Dallas character by the name of JOE BONDS. She pointed out another Dallas police character by the name of CECIL GREEN, whom she described as a Dallas-Fort Worth gambler, who was killed on the front steps of the Sky Club by other hoodlums. She stated JACK RUBY, JOE BONDS and CECIL GREEN were good friends at that time. She believed BONDS is presently serving a sentence in the Texas State Penitentiary at Huntsville, Texas, on a sodomy charge involving a 15-year old girl. He is also serving time on two other violations at the same time.

Mrs. GARCIA described RUBY as being a person who liked to use his fists to gain his way. She stated he is hot tempered and would fight for no reason at all. She recalled on one occasion RUBY jumped on her brother and was about to kill her brother before someone stopped the fight. She said RUBY hit her brother with a blow from behind with his hand which knocked her brother to the ground after which RUBY kicked him in the face. She continued in her opinion GEORGE SENATOR and RALPH PAUL are perhaps RUBY's closest associates at the present time. She said RUBY is an individual who would like to know a lot of people and for that reason he does on occasions do nice things for people after which he will make a complete change and do something mean to them because of his hot temper. As a result of this temper, RUBY has alienated all of his so called friends.

Mrs. GARCIA advised she has never known RUBY to show any interest in politics or political figures. At first she had the opinion that RUBY shot LEE HARVEY OSWALD for publicity purposes; however, based on information she has obtained through radio and newspapers she now believes RUBY may possibly be involved in the assassination of President KENNEDY along with OSWALD. Mrs. GARCIA stated she was basing the latter opinion strictly on what she had heard on the radio and seen in the newspapers regarding the assassination. She

153

on 11/30/63 at Dallas, Texas File # Dallas 44-1639

by Special Agents CHARLES T. BROWN, JR. & ALFRED C. ELLINGTON:BL Date dictated 12/3/63

COMMISSION EXHIBIT No. 2495

DL 44-1639
2

said a dollar means everything to JACK RUBY and he is the type of person who would do anything for money. Mrs. GARCIA said she worked for RUBY at times during the past 15 years and she had also worked for JOE BONDS when he was operating a night club in Dallas. She stated she knew RUBY was in possession of and was carrying a gun when she first met him several years ago. She did not know the particular reason why he carried the weapon but presumed that he carried same for his own personal protection or because he carried considerable money in his pockets at times from his night club receipts. She said RUBY has never shown any intense hatred for a particular individual over a long period of time and he has never exhibited a dislike for President KENNEDY or any of President KENNEDY's policies. She stated RUBY has never married and the only thing he can talk about is money and his night clubs. She advised he is a real publicity "hound" and he would do anything for publicity. He has never expressed any particular interest in religious matters and she has never engaged him in discussion of politics. She said to the best of her knowledge he has no apparent interest in anything except his night clubs.

With regard to his background prior to coming to Dallas, she advised she knew he came from Chicago and there is nothing more she knows regarding his background. She stated she did know RUBY was friendly with quite a few Dallas police detectives and policemen and he continually invited these persons to visit his night clubs. She recalled RUBY formerly dated an exotic dancer by the name of "JADA", one KATHY KAY and one MILLIE PERELL (phonetic). She said KAY and PERELL are both exotic dancers.

154

COMMISSION EXHIBIT No. 2495—Continued

FD-302 (Rev. 3-3-59) FEDERAL BUREAU OF INVESTIGATION

Commission Exhibit No. 2496

1

Date December 12, 1963

Dr. M.L. GLICKFELD, 1001 Montgomery, Office 103, advised he has residence phone number ED 6-3265.

Dr. GLICKFELD stated that he had been to Dallas, Texas on a number of occasions in the past and had about three months ago gone to the Carousel Club operated by JACK RUBY. Dr. GLICKFELD stated that he was with a friend of his, BERT NELSON, owner of Chez Femme Wig Salon, 4328 Lovers Lane, Dallas, and this friend introduced Dr. GLICKFELD to one of the entertainers who was performing at the Carousel. This girl's name is JADA, one of the strippers that worked at the Carousel. Dr. GLICKFELD stated that he had several dates with JADA and that she had his home telephone number.

Dr. GLICKFELD said that JACK RUBY never did call him at his residence and that he believed that JADA made all of the telephone calls to him from the Carousel. Dr. GLICKFELD stated that he only met JACK RUBY once at the Carousel and believed that this was on an occasion when JADA was sitting at his table with him and NELSON and RUBY came up and was introduced to him. He stated that RUBY did not sit down and he did not carry on any conversation with him. Dr. GLICKFELD said that he got the impression from JADA that RUBY was trying to date her and he did not like the idea.

Dr. GLICKFELD stated further that on nearly every occasion that he was at the Carousel Club, RUBY was always screaming at someone and nearly every time RUBY threw someone out of the club. Dr. GLICKFELD added that JADA told him that RUBY cut the lights off on her act on at least one occasion.

Dr. GLICKFELD also stated that he had never seen LEE HARVEY OSWALD in the Carousel and never did see RUBY talking with anyone even resembling OSWALD.

156

on 12/10/63 at Fort Worth, Texas File # DL 44-1639

by Special Agent JOSEPH M. MYERS/jn Date dictated 12/11/63

COMMISSION EXHIBIT No. 2496

FD-302 (Rev. 3-3-59) **FEDERAL BUREAU O** Commission Exhibit No. 2497

Date 12-8-63

1

IRENE ZASCODA WARD, of 145 Skyline Apartments, Grand Prairie, Texas, was advised of the identity of the interviewing Agents. She was advised that she did not have to make any statement, and that any statement she made could be used against her in a court of law and that she had the right to consult an attorney. She furnished the following information:

WARD stated she arrived in Grand Prairie approximately four months ago from Waco, Texas, where she resided at 1916 Barnard with telephone number PL 2-7365. She stated that she was formerly employed as a hostess and waitress at the Falcon Club, Waco, and the House of Mole, Waco.

She met JACK RUBY in Dallas, Texas, in a cafe - coffee shop and was introduced to him by a TOM RIES, who plays in the band of CLYDE McCOY, "the Sugar Blues Man." This meeting took place in July, 1963. RUBY asked her what she was doing in Waco and WARD advised him what she was doing and also that she was thinking of going to Dallas to seek employment. RUBY offered WARD help in finding employment and gave her his telephone number, both at home and at his club. In July, exact date unknown, WARD called RUBY, telling him that she and a friend named HELEN (LNU), were going to Dallas and RUBY agreed to meet them and helpthem find a job. They met at Kips, believed to be located on Route 77 and went to RUBY's club downtown. RUBY furnished WARD and HELEN (LNU) with lists of names to call and allowed them to use his office to make these calls.

WARD could not find employment from any of the names on the list and returned to Waco and believed that she later called RUBY at his home, advising him that she was going back to Dallas. WARD could not recall RUBY calling her at home or at the Falcon Club. She believes that the last time she saw RUBY was sometime in the middle of July, 1963

on 12-8-63 at Grand Prairie, Texas File # DL 44-1639

by Special Agent EDWARD J. MABEY & KENNETH P. HUGHES - md Date dictated 12-8-63

188

COMMISSION EXHIBIT NO. 2497

FD-302 (Rev. 3-3-59) **FEDERAL BUREAU O** Commission Exhibit No. 2498

1

Date Dec. 10, 1963

JAMES H. RHODES, 719 Exinker Street, advised he is the subscriber of telephone 885-4323 in Sulphur Springs, Texas, and he remembered a telephone call placed to his residence from JACK RUBY about two months ago. RHODES explained that RUBY has called him numerous times on business since RHODES is a photographer and RUBY occasionally asks him to make photographs of new acts at the Carousel Club.

RHODES stated he was employed by RUBY about two years ago when RUBY first opened the Carousel Club. He advised he worked as a bartender, photographer and booking agent for RUBY and once RUBY got the Carousel Club established, RHODES quit and began working as an independent photographer.

RHODES said RUBY was not liked by his employees due to his "high temper" and sudden outbursts of criticism to employees. RHODES said RUBY has always been a "publicity hound" and would stop at nothing to advertise his business.

RHODES further stated that he had never seen or heard of LEE HARVEY OSWALD until he saw his picture on television and had never observed OSWALD in the Carousel Club. RHODES added RUBY has never expressed his political views or governmental affairs to him.

on 12/10/63 at Sulphur Springs, Texas File # DL 44-1639

by Special Agent JOE A. COPELAND/csh Date dictated 12/10/63

351

COMMISSION EXHIBIT NO. 2498

FD-302 (Rev. 3-3-59)

FEDERAL BUREAU OF I [redacted]

Commission Exhibit No. 2499

1

Date December 8, 1963

DANIEL EARL ROWE, 2769 Ann Arbor Street, Dallas, Texas, was contacted at his place of employment, Earl's Barber Shop, 811 Vermont Street, Dallas. He furnished the following information:

He stated he is commonly known as EARL ROWE. During 1950 or 1951, he was a member of the Rowe Brothers Band and was hired to play at the Silver Spur, 1717 Ervay Street, Dallas, by JACK RUBY. His brother, JACK ROWE, was the band leader, and conducted the business arrangements with RUBY at that time. The band played at the Silver Spur for only about two months. Later they had a program on Radio Station KSKY in Dallas which was sponsored by JACK RUBY.

The last time he saw JACK RUBY was five years ago. At that time he was in the Oak Lawn Section of Dallas at a night club run by RUBY, the name of which he cannot recall. While in the club with a group of friends, RUBY recognized him, chatted for a few minutes, and saw to it that the admission fee that he and his friends had paid was returned to them.

He considered RUBY during the short period of time that he was in frequent contact with him, to be a helpful sort of individual and he recalled RUBY had lent him $50 during the time he played at the Silver Spur. He thought he was the type of man who, if he did not like someone, would certainly let them know it but if he did like an individual, he would do almost anything for them.

He knows nothing concerning RUBY's background, personal life, or political convictions. He never heard of LEE HARVEY OSWALD prior to the President' assassination and knows of no connection between JACK RUBY and OSWALD.

on 12/7/63 at Dallas, Texas File # Dallas 44-1639

by Special Agent JOHN E. DALLMAN:BL Date dictated 12/8/63

353

COMMISSION EXHIBIT No. 2499

FD-302 (Rev. 3-3-59)

FEDERAL BUREAU OF

1

Date 12/10/63

LUTHER ROWE, 3017 DuPres, Irving, Texas, residence phone BL-5-6178, furnished the following information:

He operates Rowe's Barber Shop, 116 Irving North Shopping Center at Irving. During the time he was a member of the Rowe Brothers Band, he played with the band at the Silver Spur Club which was operated by JACK RUBY for a brief period of time during 1950 or 1951. He also recalled that RUBY sponsored some of the band's radio programs for a period of about a year during that time. He was not a personal friend of RUBY but merely became acquainted with him during the course of his employment.

The last time he saw JACK RUBY was three or four years ago at a club operated by RUBY on Oaklawn Street in Dallas, the name of the club he could not recall. He was there on a social visit and chatted with RUBY very briefly at that time.

He knows of no close friends of RUBY but felt that probably every musician in the Dallas area would be slightly acquainted with him. He recalled RUBY was very good to him at the time he worked for him and would loan him a few dollars on occasion. He knows nothing concerning RUBY's background other than that he came from Chicago, Illinois. He knows nothing concerning RUBY's personal life, temperament or political convictions.

He had not heard of LEE HARVEY OSWALD prior to the President's assassination and knows of no connection between OSWALD and JACK RUBY. He stated he could furnish no additional information at this time.

on 12/9/63 at Irving, Texas File # DL 44-1639

by Special Agent JOHN E. DALLMAN - gj Date dictated 12/10/63

355

COMMISSION EXHIBIT No. 2500

FD-302 (Rev. 3-3-59) FEDERAL BUREAU C

Date 12/14/63

1

WILLARD P. DeLACY, 5010 Cedar Springs, Dallas, Texas, furnished the following information:

Mr. DeLACY owns and publishes the magazine, "Prevue of Dallas,"a visitors' guide, setting forth the activities in Dallas. He has operated this magazine for approximately four years. Prior to that he was associated with a similar magazine known as, "This Month in Dallas," with which he was associated from approximately 1949 to 1956. DeLACY, while operating the magazine, "This Month in Dallas," met JACK RUBY in the early 1950's when RUBY was operating the Silver Spur Lounge. Periodically RUBY would request DeLACY to carry gossip items pertaining to his club which in turn would encourage business at the Silver Spur Lounge. DeLACY described RUBY as a person who liked publicity and liked to play the roll of a "big shot" and was a typical "huckster."

DeLACY stated that he last saw RUBY on November 19, 1963, at approximately 1:00 p.m., at the Holiday Inn Motel. On that afternoon, DeLACY was at a luncheon and he received a call from RUBY. RUBY wanted to see him in connection with a publicity angle on a twist board that RUBY wanted to produce. DeLACY asked RUBY to come out to the Holiday Inn Motel to see him which RUBY did. At that time, RUBY brought with him a $50 cashier's check for payment for an ad which was run in the November issue of the "Prevue of Dallas" magazine describing the New Carousel Club. DeLACY stated that they discussed the promotion of the twist board and he, DeLACY, advised RUBY that he wanted no part of the operation as the twist is dead and the twist board could not possibly be a good promotional artical at this time.

At the time of the shooting of OSWALD in the basement of the Dallas Police Department, DeLACY was at home and did see the shooting on television. When he learned that RUBY had shot OSWALD, he immediately went down to his photo lab to look through his pictures as he knew there would probably be great demand for any photographs of RUBY. DeLACY found a photograph he had taken of RUBY in a group at the opening of the University Club, Dallas, Texas, in late September. DeLACY recalled that on the evening of the opening of the University Club he and his wife attended the affair. During the evening,

on 12/14/63 at Dallas, Texas File # Dallas 44-1639

by Special Agent JAMES S. WEIR:BL Date dictated 12/14/63

74

COMMISSION EXHIBIT No. 2501

DL 44-1639
2

JACK RUBY and one of his entertainers whose stage name is JADA, appeared at the University Club, between shows at the Carousel Club. Since most of the tables were filled at the University Club, DeLACY suggested to RUBY when he saw him, that RUBY join DeLACY and his wife at their table and at that time DeLACY met JADA for the first time. Later that evening, a group of people were standing together, including JACK RUBY and JADA, and somebody mentioned, "Take a picture of us." DeLACY did take the picture.

On the late afternoon of November 24, 1963, the day of the shooting of OSWALD, DeLACY found the photograph and was immediately made offers on the photograph by representatives of "Life," "Saturday Evening Post," and a French magazine company. Representatives of these firms got into bidding for the photograph and DeLACY sold the photograph to LAWRENCE SCHILLER, 1055 Alskog Street, Sun Valley, California, a photographer for the "Saturday Evening Post."

DeLACY stated that on November 24, 1963, while at the Kincaid Photo Studios in Dallas, which is a gathering place for photographers who want expeditious and outstanding photography work done in the development of film, he and many other photographers and pressmen were discussing the whereabouts of JIMMY RHODES. Representatives of "Time," "Life," "Saturday Evening Post," and other pictorial magazines all were in agreement that if RHODES could be located he would be a source for many photographs pertaining to JACK RUBY and the Carousel Club as RHODES for many years had been in the employ and had been the photographer for RUBY and often took pictures of new acts and the entertainers at the Carousel Club.

On November 27, 1963, while at the Press Club, Dallas, DeLACY heard that "Life" magazine had located RHODES and probably had bought all of RHODES' pictures. On approximately December 4, 1963, RHODES met SHELL HERSHORN of the "Life." magazine Bureau, Dallas, Texas. At that time HERSHORN told DeLACY that "Life" magazine had paid RHODES $5,000 for his entire album of photographs pertaining to JACK RUBY and the Carousel Club. According to HERSHORN, very few of the pictures are the type that can be used by "Life" magazine as most of them border on obscenity and could be classified as lewd. According to DeLACY, who advises he has not himself seen

75

COMMISSION EXHIBIT No. 2501—Continued

DL 44-1639
3

the photographs, some of them are risque shots of RUBY with some of his entertainers.

DeLACY did not know LEE HARVEY OSWALD and knew nothing about any acquaintance between RUBY and OSWALD.

76

COMMISSION EXHIBIT No. 2501—Continued

FD-302 (Rev. 3-3-59) FEDERAL BUREAU OF I— [redacted] Commission Exhibit No. 2502

Date December 17, 1963

1

DONNA FULTON AGEE, 1125 Ridgeview Drive, Mesquite, Texas, furnished the following information:

Mrs. AGEE in 1960 worked for JACK RUBY at the Carousel Club assisting in maintaining his books and receipts. She stated at that time RUBY had a luncheon club and it was her job to assist the cashier in maintaining the day-to-day receipts taken from the operation of the luncheon club. She recalled that she first met JACK RUBY a short time prior to the time that she took employment with him, when she was frequenting the Vegas Club. She stated at the time her name was DONNA FULTON. Mrs. AGEE stated that at that time she was divorced and maintaining a family of two children and that JACK RUBY was aware of the situation and offered her a job. She stated that it was her feeling that RUBY did not need her as an employee; however, he felt sorry for her situation and employed her out of the goodness of his heart. She stated that he was a good man to work for and he was good to his employees. She further advised that RUBY was "a soft touch" and often went out of his way to help people in need. She advised that to the best of her recollection she has not seen RUBY since 1960 when she left his employ at the time of her current marriage. She stated that she did not know LEE HARVEY OSWALD and she has no knowledge of any association or acquaintance between OSWALD and RUBY.

on 12/16/63 at Dallas, Texas File # Dallas 44-1639

by Special Agent JAMES S. WEIR:BL Date dictated 12/17/63

174

COMMISSION EXHIBIT No. 2502

FD-302 (Rev. 3-3-59) FEDERAL BUREAU [redacted] Commission Exhibit No. 2503

1 Date December 15, 1963

Officer J. B. TONEY, Detective, Forgery Bureau, Dallas, Texas, Police Department, was immediately advised of the identity of the interviewing Agents; of the fact that he did not have to make any statement; that any statement he made could be used against him in a court of law; and that he had the right to consult an attorney. He then furnished the following information:

On November 23 and 24, 1963, he was off duty and out of town both Saturday and Sunday.

In 1952, he worked in the police district that covered South Ervay where JACK RUBY had his club. He knew RUBY from visits to the club and in fact, arrested RUBY after he became involved in a fight in the Burgundy Room of the Hotel Adolphus, in February, 1963. He did not work for RUBY nor did he know any other officers who did. He did not see RUBY any time between the November 22-24, 1963, period and he knew of no relationship that existed between RUBY and OSWALD.

With regard to the complaint filed by DON TABON against RUBY in connection with a fist fight in the Hotel Adolphus Burgundy Room, TONEY stated that he did call TABON at home and advised TABON that all he could do against RUBY was to file simple assault charges against him inasmuch as the only weapons RUBY used were his fists. TABON still wished to press the charges and TONEY filed these charges for TABON as TABON's agent. TONEY then called RUBY by telephone and told him he would have to come down and explained to him the charges that were being filed against him. He stated that RUBY did come down and TONEY believes he posted bond. TONEY has been in the Carousel Club both on business and for pleasure. He was investigating an individual by the name of PHYLLIS SHEA who used the stage name, "SUGAR," and who was filed on as a check writer. He was in the club socially in December, 1959 with relatives but could not recall being in the club with one HAROLD TENANT. He explained that he formerly worked with TENANT as a machinist during his off hours from the police department. He could not recall ever taking TENANT to RUBY's clubs or introducing TENANT to RUBY. He reiterated that he did call TABON, but he did not try to get TABON to drop the charges against RUBY. He merely explained to him the simple assault charge and law.

on 12/12/63 at Dallas, Texas File # Dallas 44-1639

by Special Agent S KENNETH P. HUGHES & EDWARD J. MABEY:BL Date dictated 12/13/63

273

This document contains neither recommendations nor conclusions of the FBI. It is the property of the FBI and is loaned to your agency; it and its contents are not to be distributed outside your agency.

COMMISSION EXHIBIT No. 2503

FD-302 (Rev. 3-3-59) FEDERAL BUREAU OF INV [redacted] Commission Exhibit No. 2504

1 Date 12/17/63

ED E. MC LEMORE, 4211 Lakeside Drive, Owner of the Sportatorium, Industrial Boulevard and Cadiz, advised he has known JACK RUBY since RUBY first opened the Silver Spur Night Club on South Ervay Street. He said he used to provide entertainers to RUBY, since he used to handle western acts and RUBY's club primarily dealt with western and hillbilly-type individuals. He said this was in the late 1940's and early 1950's and his association with RUBY was strictly business. He said that RUBY's dealings were very good and that RUBY had attempted to give him membership cards in his private club, The Sovereign, when it first opened in Dallas. He said this was the same club which is now known as The Carousel.

He said he has never been to either The Sovereign or The Carousel and the last time he saw RUBY was over six months ago, when they happened to meet on the street. He said they chatted briefly and departed.

He said he never knew JACK RUBY to carry a gun and he knew of no connection between RUBY and LEE HARVEY OSWALD. In fact, he stated, he did not know OSWALD until the President's assassination.

MC LEMORE advised RUBY used to come to the Sportatorium in the late 1940's and early 1950's when he, MC LEMORE, sponsored wrestling matches. He said RUBY would bring his friends and, naturally, expected to get into the wrestling match free, which he always did. He said RUBY was high-strung, emotional and was hard to get along with, both with his help and his customers. He classified RUBY as a glory seeker, but stated he was surprised to learn RUBY had shot LEE HARVEY OSWALD, because he did not believe RUBY would go so far to seek publicity.

118

on 12/17/63 at Dallas, Texas File # DL 44-1639

by Special Agents ROBERT E. BASHAM & JAMES J. WARD:ch Date dictated 12/17/63

This document contains neither recommendations nor conclusions of the FBI. It is the property of the FBI and is loaned to your agency; it and its contents are not to be distributed outside your agency.

COMMISSION EXHIBIT No. 2504

FD-302 (Rev. 3-3-59)

FEDERAL BUREAU OF IN [redacted] Commission Exhibit No. 2505

1

Date December 20, 1963

Mrs. J. M. (DOLORES F.) BANKSTON, nee MERIDITH, 3542 Rosedale, Highland Park, Texas, whose name appeared on a note pad secured from JACK RUBY, furnished the following information:

Approximately four or five years ago, she met JACK RUBY, through friends of hers, BOB and KATHRYN HEISER, at the Jaz Limited Club in Dallas.

She said she subsequently accompanied the HEISER's and RUBY to various private clubs, the only one which she now recalls is the 3520 Club.

She advised she has not seen RUBY since the aforementioned night, however, about two years ago, she received a phone call from him which he advised her he had learned she had recently been hospitalized and inquired as to her health. She said RUBY asked her if she needed any money and when she replied that she did not, he said he thought she might have been strapped for funds due to her illness and was offering her the money without any strings attached.

Mrs. BANKSTON advised HEISER was formerly associated with the National Cash Register Company and sold their products to various clubs. She said she presumes it was while he was with the National Cash Register Company that HEISER met RUBY.

Mrs. BANKSTON further advised HEISER used to joke with her about RUBY and said that he thought "JACK liked boys".

Mrs. BANKSTON advised she could furnish no further information concerning RUBY. She said she does not recall ever having seen LEE HARVEY OSWALD or of having heard of him prior to the assassination of President KENNEDY.

on 12/19/63 at Highland Park, Texas File # DL 44-1639

by Special Agents JAMES J. WARD & ROBERT E. BASHAM/jn Date dictated 12/19/63

COMMISSION EXHIBIT No. 2505

FD-302 (Rev. 1-25-60)

FEDERAL BUREAU OF INV [redacted] Commission Exhibit No. 2506

Date December 20, 1963

1

TED (NO MIDDLE NAME) MARKS, Apartment Number 2, Fireside Motel, advised he was employed by the American Guild of Variety Artists (AGVA), Chicago, Illinois, in 1958, and in January, 1959, was transferred by the AGVA to Dallas, Texas, to reorganize the AGVA office. He said that as a representative of AGVA he contacted the night clubs in Dallas and through these contacts met JACK RUBY in the Spring of 1959 at RUBY's Vegas Night Club in Dallas.

MARKS stated RUBY also owned the Soverign Night Club located on Commerce Street in Dallas (now the Carosel Club) and that he (MARKS) stayed to work for RUBY some time in September or October, 1960, selling memberships for the Soverign.

MARKS said he found it hard to sell memberships to the Soverign Club primarily because of the number of other clubs in Dallas who were doing the same thing, so after about two months stopped working for RUBY. MARKS said he later obtained employment at the Jazz Limited Night Club and that RUBY often visited this club to review the acts MARKS had working for him in this club.

MARKS said he was never close to RUBY as a friend and had no social contacts with RUBY. He said he did not know if RUBY was married and believed RUBY lived at the Soverign Club. He said he once heard RUBY say that he had once lived in Chicago.

MARKS advised he never discussed politics with RUBY and did not know RUBY's business contacts. He said he heard RUBY on several occasions refer to BARNEY and ABE WEINSTEIN, owners of two successful night clubs in Dallas, and say that he was going to get entertainers for his club in spite of the WEINSTEINs. He said he never heard the WEINSTEINs mention RUBY.

MARKS described RUBY as a "rough character", good, but one who could get mad easily and if he got mad at a customer;for example,would physically throw the person he was mad at out of the club.

On 12/19/63 at Mill Valley, California File # SF 44-494

by SAs RALPH M. LINDSEY and DALE F. NORTON:mep Date dictated 12/20/63

COMMISSION EXHIBIT No. 2506

2
SF 44-494
DFN:mep

MARKS said he had no information as to any close contacts RUBY might have had at the Dallas Police Department and was surprised when he read in the newpapers that RUBY was a "hanger on" at the police department. MARKS said RUBY was a "name dropper" and recalled that when he had coffee on occasions at the Eatwell Restaurant, a restaurant which stayed open after midnight in Dallas, that he often heard RUBY talk with policeman who came in for coffee and call them by their first names.

MARKS advised he did not know LEE HARVEY OSWALD and did not know if RUBY was acquainted with OSWALD.

MARKS stated he left Dallas in August, 1962, for Californ' and has had no contact with RUBY since.

127

COMMISSION EXHIBIT No. 2506—Continued

COMMISSION EXHIBIT No. 2507

FD-302 (Rev. 3-3-59)

FEDERAL BUREAU OF I[redacted] Commission Exhibit No. 2508

1

Date December 21, 1963

Mr. EMMETT JOSEPH HUDSON, 107 South Bishop Street, was recontacted to determine if he has any knowledge as to the acquaintanceship and/or association between LEE HARVEY OSWALD and JACK RUBY. It is noted that Mr. HUDSON had previously been contacted and pointed out that he was in one of the pictures appearing in a local newspaper concerning the assassination of President KENNEDY.

Mr. HUDSON said that he has no knowledge of OSWALD and no knowledge of JACK RUBY. He said that he did not know either of these men and knew of no relationship between them.

on 12/21/63 at Dallas, Texas File # DL 44-1639

by Special Agent JACK B. PEDEN/JB Date dictated 12/21/63

235

This document contains neither recommendations nor conclusions of the FBI. It is the property of the FBI and is loaned to your agency; it and its contents are not to be distributed outside your agency.

COMMISSION EXHIBIT No. 2508

FD-302 (Rev. 3-3-59)

FEDERAL BUREAU OF I[redacted] Commission Exhibit No. 2509

1

Date 1/6/64

JERRY ANTHONY BOLAND, also known as TONY, 2515 Hillburn Drive, Apartment C, whose name appeared in a list of JACK RUBY indicating former employment at one of RUBY's clubs, furnished the following information:

BOLAND stated that he has known RUBY since 1961, at which time he met him due to beginning employment with RUBY's sister, EVA GRANT, about October 1961 at the Vegas Club where he worked as bouncer and emcee and assisted Mrs. GRANT generally in running the club. It was his understanding that RUBY and his sister both owned the club, but it was in Mrs. GRANT's name. At the same time, RUBY owned the Carousel Club, which was a union club, and he understood that RUBY could not register a non-union club such as the Vegas Club in his name. He regularly saw RUBY at the Vegas Club on Friday nights and since that time he has maintained a regular and continous acquaintance, both business and social, with RUBY. His employment at the Vegas Club on this occasion lasted until about April 1962.

In about November 1961 he began working for RUBY, in addition to his employment at the Vegas Club, at RUBY's Carousel Club as bouncer, doorman and overseeing the waitresses. This employment lasted until February 1962. During the fall of 1962 he resumed his employment at the Vegas Club and continued there until January 1963. About August 1963 he resumed his employment by RUBY at the Carousel Club and continued as such until about September 1963.

BOLAND stated that during the latter part of 1961 and January 1962, he stayed with RUBY at the Carousel Club, that is, he was furnished a rollaway bed by RUBY in the hall of this club and, at the same time, RUBY was residing in the back part of the club in a separate room. BOLAND stated that he had numerous occasions to converse with RUBY and feels that he became fairly well acquainted with RUBY's character, personality and disposition. He stated that he considers RUBY to be a friendly, helpful person in the event he likes someone, but he is also impetuous, high-strung and quick-tempered. BOLAND added that RUBY was also quick to return to normal and forget his differences with anyone with whom he became angry.

on 1/4/64 at Dallas, Texas File # DL 44-1639

by Special Agent EDMOND C. HARDIN - LAC Date dictated 1/4/64

75

This document contains neither recommendations nor conclusions of the FBI. It is the property of the FBI and is loaned to your agency; it and its contents are not to be distributed outside your agency.

COMMISSION EXHIBIT No. 2509

DL 44-1639
2

BOLAND stated that he did not know RUBY to carry a pistol regularly although RUBY did always carry his pistol when he brought cash to the club for the evening's operation but after arriving at the club he would usually lock up the gun. Whenever RUBY traveled in his car he would usually put his pistol in the trunk of the car.

BOLAND stated that he rarely discussed politics with RUBY but gained the definite impression that RUBY was more interested in the character and ability of the man running for office than the party itself.

BOLAND stated that RUBY was friendly with and knew many police officers and newsmen and felt a real friendship for them generally. RUBY was the type of person, according to BOLAND, who liked to "keep his nose clean", and although he may have known people in the various rackets, he is sure that RUBY did not work with or conspire with any such individuals. He does not recall RUBY mentioning Officer TIPPIT's name and does not know to what extent RUBY was acquainted with this individual.

BOLAND stated he last saw RUBY in August 1963 and has no information concerning the shooting of OSWALD by RUBY or as to how RUBY entered the basement of the Police Department prior to the shooting. He added that he himself never knew OSWALD and never had reason to believe that RUBY knew or associated with OSWALD at any time. He added that he feels personally quite sure that RUBY did not know OSWALD, explaining that had RUBY known OSWALD, BOLAND would have become aware of same at one time or another.

BOLAND stated that he recalls that on one occasion a year or so ago RUBY carried his pistol on his person for one week inasmuch as he had heard that someone who had just been released from prison was "looking for him". BOLAND stated he does not know the identity of this individual and has no additional information about the incident.

76

COMMISSION EXHIBIT No. 2509—Continued

MARK LANE
ATTORNEY

SUSQUEHANNA 7-6797

164 WEST 79TH STREET
NEW YORK, N. Y. 10024

March 27, 1964

J. Lee Rankin
General Counsel
President's Commission on the Assassination
of President Kennedy
200 Maryland Avenue N.E.
Washington, D.C. 20002

Dear Mr. Rankin:

I'm sorry not to have answered your letter of 3/18/64 sooner, but have been out of New York on matters pertaining to the Oswald case, and have just been advised of the contents of your letter.

I am still working on this matter, and will contact the Commission when I have permission from my source of information to reveal his name.

Sincerely yours,

Mark Lane

Mark Lane

ML:dg

COMMISSION EXHIBIT No. 2510

PRESIDENT'S COMMISSION
ON THE
ASSASSINATION OF PRESIDENT KENNEDY
200 Maryland Ave. N.E.
Washington, D.C. 20002
Telephone 543-1400

April 16, 1964

Mr. Mark Lane
164 West 79th Street
Apartment 14-A
New York, New York

Dear Mr. Lane:

You will recall that during the course of your testimony before the Commission on March 4, 1964, you stated that you had information concerning an alleged meeting involving Bernard Weissman, Jack Ruby and Officer Tippit. You advised the Commission that you would request permission of your informant to reveal his name to the Commission. On March 18, 1964, we asked whether you were in a position to furnish this information and on March 27 you advised us that you would contact the Commission when you had received permission from your source to reveal his name.

In view of the importance of this matter to the work of the Commission, we ask that you reveal promptly the identity of your informant. If you feel that you are unable to furnish this name on a voluntary basis, the Commission will consider invoking the power of subpoena given to the Commission by Congress.

We also call your attention to page 76 of your public testimony in which you were asked whether you possessed any documentary evidence other than that which you submitted to the Commission. Your reply was "Not beyond what I have submitted or made reference to." The Commission has been advised that you have publicly stated that you have a tape recording of a statement by a witness to the Tippit slaying in which this witness states that the man who shot Officer Tippit was short and had bushy hair. I assume that the witness is Miss Helen Markham who, according to your testimony before the Commission, has provided you with information of this nature. In view of the importance of Miss Markham's testimony, we would appreciate receiving from you the tape which you are purported to have claimed to have in your possession. We will return the tape to you after we have had the opportunity to listen to it.

Sincerely,

J. Lee Rankin
General Counsel

COMMISSION EXHIBIT No. 2511

Commission Exhibit No. 2512

MARK LANE
ATTORNEY

164 WEST 79TH STREET
NEW YORK, N. Y. 10024

SUSQUEHANNA 7-6797

April 29, 1964

J. Lee Rankin
General Counsel
President's Commission on the Assassination
of President Kennedy
200 Maryland Avenue N.E.
Washington, D.C. 20002

Dear Mr. Rankin:

I apologize for the delay in answering your letter of April 16, 1964. I have just returned to the United States from abroad.

I will seek permission from my source to reveal his name to your Commission as I previously stated. Absent that permission I will be unable to reveal his name. I hope that the Commission will not seek to reverse what I understood to be its previous position by now seeking to force me, by invoking its power of supoena, to violate a moral commitment.

For the best information regarding statements made by Miss Helen Markham and other eye witnesses I would suggest that you contact, if you have not already done so, those witnesses directly. I am mildly surprised that you seek to secure the working documents of an attorney who had been retained to represent a client and who developed such documents in that capacity.

I was willing to testify before the Commission although your request that I do so coupled with your refusal to permit me to act as counsel for my client was somewhat unusual. I will continue to cooperate with the Commission in all matters that do not require me to violate the attorney client relationship.

This very morning as I left my home I was accosted by two special agents of the Federal Bureau of Investigation who demanded to know if I had any documents from the Federal Bureau of Investigation files in my possession. They sought to secure such documents from my person on that occasion as we stood in the rain. They informed me that they had "confidential information" that I had illegally secured such documents. I informed them that I had given to your Commission information regarding all the documents in my possession. I suggested that they contact you.

I have now secured information proving that the story widely circulated throughout the United States on February 10 that there was

COMMISSION EXHIBIT No. 2512

an eyewitness, a Negro janitor, who actually saw Oswald pull the trigger, was deliberately planted by an agent of the Secret Service. I would suggest that your Commission should show less concern with the sources of my information and more concern with the harassment of an American citizen by the Federal Bureau of Investigation. May I also suggest that you might seek to determine why an agent of the U.S. Secret Service deliberately planted a false story with the media. Should you be interested in conducting such an investigation, I will make known to you all the details, including the names and numbers of the F.B.I. agents and the names of those persons involved in the transmission of the false news story.

One additional matter: in your letter to me of April 16, you sought to imply that I made a false answer to the Commission in calling my attention to my testimony on page 76. In your letter you state, "We also call your attention to page 76 of your public testimony in which you were asked whether you possessed any documentary evidence other than that which you submitted to the Commission. Your reply was 'Not beyond what I have submitted or made reference to.'" You have incorrectly paraphrased your question above. Permit me to call your attention to page 76 and the question which you put to me. "Mr. Rankin. 'Now, is there any documentary evidence beyond which you have submitted that you would like to submit to the Commission?'" In any event, I indicated that I did not wish to make available information beyond that which I had submitted or made reference to. May I now call your attention to page 75 of my public testimony, indicating those statements that I had made reference to. "Mr. Rankin. 'Do you have anything beyond that that you care to submit?' Mr. Lane. 'I have the various statements which I have made reference to from Mrs. Hill and Mrs. Markham, Mr. Klein, Mr. Ryder. But I have given you the essence of those statements. If you are interested in pursuing that, I think it might be best to call them.'"

I am certain that upon rereading the paragraphs that I have called to your attention, a letter of apology from your office will be forthcoming.

Sincerely,

Mark Lane

Mark Lane
per Deirdre Griswold

ML:dg
Dictated but not read.

COMMISSION EXHIBIT No. 2512—Continued

PRESIDENT'S COMMISSION
ON THE
ASSASSINATION OF PRESIDENT KENNEDY
200 Maryland Ave. N.E.
Washington, D.C. 20002
Telephone 543-1400

April 30, 1964

Mr. Mark Lane
164 West 79th Street
Apartment 14-A
New York, New York

Dear Mr. Lane:

This is in reply to your letter of April 29, 1964.

With reference to the story concerning the janitor who allegedly saw Oswald pull the trigger, you state in your letter that you have information that this story was deliberately planted by an agent of the Secret Service. We would appreciate receiving all information in your possession concerning this incident including the names of the agents involved, the persons to whom the information was given, and any further relevant details.

We would also like to receive from you the details of the encounter with two special agents of the Federal Bureau of Investigation to which you refer in the fifth paragraph of your letter.

Concerning the statements which you claim Mrs. Markham made to you, the Commission has heard the testimony of Mrs. Markham and she has denied both the substance of the alleged conversation with you and the fact that such a conversation ever took place. We would appreciate receiving from you any documentary records you have in your possession which would substantiate that you had the conversation with Mrs. Markham referred to in your testimony as well as any evidence in your possession to support your statement that Mrs. Markham described the killer of Officer Tippit as a person who was short and had bushy hair.

The Commission is still most anxious to obtain the name of your source of information concerning the alleged meeting between Jack Ruby, Officer Tippit and Bernard Weissman. Your letter indicates that you are attempting once again to obtain permission from your source to reveal his name. We hope that you will be in a position promptly to advise the Commission on this matter.

Sincerely,

J. Lee Rankin
General Counsel

COMMISSION EXHIBIT NO. 2513

Commission Exhibit No. 2514

MARK LANE
ATTORNEY

164 West 79th Street
New York, N. Y. 10024

Susquehanna 7-6797

May 6, 1964

J. Lee Rankin, Esq.
General Counsel
President's Commission on the
Assassination of President Kennedy
200 Maryland Avenue N.E.
Washington, D.C. 20002

Dear Mr. Rankin:

I have your letter of April 30, in which you requested further information relative to a false story deliberately planted by an agent of the Secret Service and to the details of my encounter with two Special Agents of the Federal Bureau of Investigation. I am gratified that you are interested in a false statement deliberately planted by an agent of the Secret Service, inasmuch as we have been led to believe that the Commission is relying upon the accuracy of the statements made by investigatory agencies including the Secret Service. Under such circumstances, it seems to me that a thorough investigation of the false statement made by the agent of the Secret Service is required.

I am not clear as to whether you would like me to appear before the Commission and present such information while I am under oath. If that is your preference, I will be happy to fly to Washington to testify before the Commission. If you prefer, instead, merely a statement in a letter from me detailing the incidents referred to above, I shall be happy to comply with that request.

I am continuing in my efforts to secure permission to release to you the name of the person who gave me information regarding the meeting which took place prior to the assassination and which was attended by Officer Tippit, Bernard Weissman, and a third person whose name I gave to the Commission while in executive session.

I am, of course, surprised to hear that Mrs. Markham denies that she gave to me the information which I have indicated publicly that she gave to me and am surprised even more to discover that she denies ever having had a conversation with me. Unless there is some gross error

Commission Exhibit No. 2514

J. Lee Rankin, Esq. - 2 - May 6, 1964

involved on either Mrs. Markham's part or on mine, one of us seems to have committed perjury. Perhaps under the circumstances it would be appropriate, therefore, to refer this matter to the appropriate federal authorities in order that criminal action might be instituted against the person who may be guilty of making false statements under oath.

Sincerely yours,

Mark Lane

ML:dg

Commission Exhibit No. 2514—Continued

PRESIDENT'S COMMISSION
ON THE
ASSASSINATION OF PRESIDENT KENNEDY

200 Maryland Ave. N.E.
Washington, D.C. 20002
Telephone 543-1400

MAY 12, 1964

Mr. Mark Lane
164 West 79th Street
Apartment 14-A
New York, New York

Dear Mr. Lane:

This is in reply to your letter of May 6, 1964.

It will be satisfactory for you to prepare a statement, in the form of a letter, dealing with your allegation that a false story concerning an eyewitness to the assassination was disseminated deliberately by an agent of the Secret Service. You may also include in this letter the details of your encounter with the agents of the Federal Bureau of Investigation mentioned in your letter of April 29, 1964.

Concerning the conflict between your testimony and that of Miss Markham, the Commission would like to know whether you have in your possession any documentary evidence in any form whatsoever, including tape recordings, which substantiates your testimony concerning the conversation between you and Miss Markham. If you have such evidence, we would like you to forward it to the Commission. If you do not have such evidence, we would like a definite statement from you to that effect.

The Commission would also like a definite answer from you at this time as to whether you are in a position to reveal the name of your source for the information concerning the alleged meeting between Officer Tippit, Barnard Weissman, and the third person mentioned in your testimony.

We would appreciate your prompt reply.

Sincerely,

J. Lee Rankin
General Counsel

COMMISSION EXHIBIT No. 2515

Commission Exhibit No. 2516

MARK LANE
ATTORNEY

164 West 79th Street
New York, N. Y. 10024

Susquehanna 7-6797

May 18, 1964

J. Lee Rankin, Esq.
General Counsel
President's Commission on the
Assassination of President Kennedy
200 Maryland Avenue N.E.
Washington, D.C. 20002

Dear Mr. Rankin:

As per your request in your letter to me, dated May 12, 1964, I submit a statement relating to the false story planted by an agent of the United States Secret Service with the press.

A Secret Service Agent by the name of Mike Howard, while in the presence of his brother Pat Howard, a Deputy Sheriff of Tarrant County, falsely gave information to Thayer Waldo, a reporter for the Fort Worth Star Telegram. The statement made by Mike Howard consisted of, among other comments, the following:

> "Wait 'till that old black boy gets up in front of the Warren Commission and tells his story. That will settle everything. Yes, sir. He was right there on the same floor, looking out the next window; and, after the first shot, he looked and saw Oswald, and then he ran. I saw him in the Dallas police station. He was still the scaredest nigger I ever seen. I heard him tell the officer, 'Man, you don't know how fast fast is, because you didn't see me run that day.' He said he ran and hid behind the boxes because he was afraid that Oswald would shoot him."

Mike Howard then explained that the Negro witness had been arrested in the past by the Special Services office of the Dallas Police for gambling; and, since he was familiar with that branch of the Dallas Police, he immediately gave himself up to that branch. Mr. Howard alleged that he had visited the Negro witness while he was in the custody of the Special Services in the Dallas jail. Mr. Howard then said that the witness had been moved to another place, but that he, Howard, did not know where the witness had been moved. After Waldo had the

COMMISSION EXHIBIT No. 2516

story published in the Fort Worth Star Telegram, Pat Howard called Waldo and said, "You didn't quote Mike, did you, you didn't mention his name?" When Waldo indicated that he had protected his source, Pat Howard stated, "Well, good boy, good boy. This ought to pick up some excitement."

In addition to the fact that it hardly seems correct that an agent of the United States Secret Service would use such epithets in describing a citizen who pays his salary, one must be concerned that an agency upon which your Commission is relying for accuracy in reporting seems to have planted a false story with the press.

In relation to my encounter with the agents of the Federal Bureau of Investigation, I submit the following statement:

At 10:07 a.m, Wednesday, April 29, as I was leaving my house, two men approached me as I crossed the street from my house diagonally in a northerly and westerly direction. It was raining slightly, and these two men approached me from the rear and then stood in front of me, preventing my forward progress. The first gentleman to speak told me that he wanted to know if I had in my possession files which I held illegally and which I had illegally secured from the office of the F.B.I. I asked him who he was, and he said he was a special agent of the Federal Bureau of Investigation. I asked to see his credentials, which he flashed. But, when I then requested an opportunity to see them more fully, he held them out in his right hand, and there were two cards in a leather-type case hinged horizontally across the middle. The cards purported to identify the gentleman as a Special Agent of the Federal Bureau of Investigation and indicated that his name is William E. Folkner and that his Serial Number is 5954. I repeated the same procedure with the other gentleman. His name was John P. Di Marchi and his Serial Number was 4256.

Mr. Folkner then repeated his request in reference to whether I had information which I illegally secured from the files of the Federal Bureau of Investigation. I asked Mr. Folkner what led him to such a conclusion. He said, "We have confidential information that you have illegally obtained F.B.I. reports." I told Mr. Folkner and Mr. DiMarchi that I had made reference in my testimony before the President's Commission on the Assassination of President Kennedy to all of the documents in my possession and that, since that was a Commission established by the United States Government and since the F.B.I. was an agency of the United States Government, I would direct the F.B.I. to the President's Commission to determine what information was in my possession. I further stated that I did not like to be accosted in the rain in front of my house by agents of the Federal Police Force and that, since I was an attorney and had an office in New York City, the Federal Bureau of Investigation, if it sought any information of me, might do so by writing a letter to me, which is the same system employed by other agencies of the government when they wish to communicate with me. Mr. Folkner then replied that they had nothing to do with the Warren Commission and that

COMMISSION EXHIBIT No. 2516—Continued

they wanted the documents from me directly. He said that my answer seemed to him to be an admission that I did have documents illegally obtained from the files of the Federal Bureau of Investigation in my possession; and, in a loud and firm voice, he stepped closer to me and said, "I now demand that you give to me all of the documents in your possession which you have illegally obtained from the files of the F.B.I."

I left them after excusing myself and hailed a taxi cab driven by Alvin Weinstein, whose cab license is No. 70372.

(End of Statement)

I am not now in a position to reveal the name of my source for the information regarding the meeting between Officer Tippit, Bernard Weissman, and the third person whose name I submitted to the Commission in executive session.

As per your previous request, I enclose the exhibits. I understand that you will copy the exhibits and then return the originals to me.

Sincerely,

Mark Lane

ML:dg

Enclosure

COMMISSION EXHIBIT No. 2516—Continued

PRESIDENT'S COMMISSION
ON THE
ASSASSINATION OF PRESIDENT KENNEDY

200 Maryland Ave. N.E.
Washington, D.C. 20002
Telephone 543-1400

J. LEE RANKIN,
General Counsel

JUN 19 1964

Mr. Mark Lane
Citizens' Committee of Inquiry
Room 422, 156 Fifth Avenue
New York, New York 10010

Dear Mr. Lane:

I am writing this letter pursuant to a telephone conversation yesterday between Mr. Willens of my staff and Miss Deirdre Griswald, Executive Director of the Citizens' Committee of Inquiry.

As you undoubtedly know, this Commission is in the final stages of its investigation and is anxious to make public its report as soon as possible. Prior to ending our investigation, however, the Commission desires to obtain further testimony from you regarding certain matters which have been the subject of correspondence between us since your appearance on March 4, 1964.

The Commission would like you to appear any time at your convenience prior to Wednesday, July 1, 1964. I understand from Miss Griswald that you are currently in Europe and not expected to return until sometime in the middle of July. The Commission regrets the necessity of asking you to interrupt your travels in Europe, but I am sure you share with the Commission its desire to complete this important assignment in the very near future. In view of our request, of course, we are prepared to compensate you for the additional expenses which you are required to incur.

When you appear before the Commission in Washington, D. C. we would like you to bring with you all your records, papers, notes and other documents pertaining to the assassination of President John F. Kennedy, the killing of Dallas Police Officer J. D. Tippit, and the killing of Lee Harvey Oswald, including, but not limited to, those records, papers, notes and other documents pertaining to (1) conversations between you and Miss Helen Markham and (2) an alleged meeting at the Carousel Club concerning which you testified before this Commission on March 4, 1964.

I would appreciate an early response to this letter.

Sincerely,

J. Lee Rankin
General Counsel

COMMISSION EXHIBIT NO. 2517

PRESIDENT'S COMMISSION
ON THE
ASSASSINATION OF PRESIDENT KENNEDY
200 Maryland Ave. N.E.
Washington, D.C. 20002
Telephone 543-1400

J. LEE RANKIN, General Counsel

MAR 18, 1964

Mr. Mark Lane
164 West 79th Street
Apartment 14-A
New York, New York

Dear Mr. Lane:

During the course of your testimony before this Commission you discussed an alleged meeting which was supposed to have taken place in the Carousel Club approximately one week before the assassination of President Kennedy. You advised that present at this meeting were Bernard Weissman, Officer Tippit and Jack Ruby. In executive session, you advised the Commission that you would attempt to obtain permission from your source of information to reveal his name to the Commission.

In view of the possible importance of this information, we would like to know whether you are in a position to reveal your source of information at this time.

Sincerely,

J. Lee Rankin
General Counsel

COMMISSION EXHIBIT NO. 2518

DL 44-1639
LLR:lp

1

On December 12, 1963, LEO L. ROBERTSON, SA, conducted the following investigation:

J. H. KITCHING, Identification Officer in the Identification Division of the Dallas County Sheriff's Office, advised that they had no record of any kind for GEORGE SENATOR.

PAT SIWEC of the Dallas Police Department Records Bureau, checked their file and found that GEORGE SENATOR had arrest # 61-88755. This record reflected that he was a white male, born September 4, 1913, and gave his residence address as 4917 Live Oak Street, Dallas, Texas. He was arresed in the 4800 Block of Bryan Street by Patrolmen N. T. CHRISTOPHER, Badge #670 (now deceased), and R. B. BROOKS, Badge # 1511. This arrest occurred at 10:50 PM, September 12, 1961. He was charged with drunk and disorderly. The records also reflected that he had deposited a cash bond of $10 and then forfeited the bond.

Lieutenant W. F. DYSON, of the Special Service Bureau, was unable to find any record in their files. He also checked the Intelligence files of that bureau, where they keep rumors and things of that nature concerning homosexuals and other abnormal people, and was unable to find any record of SENATOR there.

Lieutenant K. P. KNIGHT of the Identification Bureau of the Dallas Police Department, advised that they had no record of SENATOR.

211

COMMISSION EXHIBIT NO. 2519

Date November 30, 1963

1

Captain JAMES ARNOLD, Commander, First District Station, New Orleans Police Department, advised that on August 9, 1963, he was aware of the fact that Lieutenant WILLIAM GILLIOT, Patrolmen FRANK HAYWARD and FRANK WILSON, had arrested LEE HARVEY OSWALD on Canal Street because he became involved in a disturbance with three Cubans while he, OSWALD, was distributing Fair Play for Cuba Committee literature. Shortly after OSWALD was booked at the district, he stated that Sergeant HORACE J. AUSTIN and Patrolman WARREN ROBERTS of the Intelligence Unit of the New Orleans Police Department came to the district and interviewed OSWALD as well as the other three Cubans who were arrested with OSWALD.

At the outset of this interview with OSWALD, Captain ARNOLD advised he was present and since he was merely there as an observer, he made no notations and did not submit any report or results of the interview since this was the responsibility of AUSTIN and ROBERTS.

As best he can remember, Captain ARNOLD said that the beginning of the interview dealt with general background of OSWALD, such as place of birth, where he lived, who his family was, his employment, etc.

Captain ARNOLD remembered that he asked OSWALD if he knew CARLOS LAMONT, who, according to information he, ARNOLD, possessed was considered to be a Communist. OSWALD responded by saying that CARLOS LAMONT was not a he but was a she and that he had read some of the material written by this female and he did not consider LAMONT to be a Communist. He further commented that he, himself, OSWALD, was not a Communist.

Captain ARNOLD said that he remembered from past knowledge that the name of Professor LEONARD REISSMAN of the New Orleans Council for Peaceful Alternatives, who resided at 1121 Pine Street, New Orleans, had been mentioned as being possibly affiliated with the Fair Play for Cuba Committee, although he did not have any first hand information to the effect that REISSMAN was so connected and when he, OSWALD, mentioned during the interview that some of the meetings of the Fair Play for Cuba Committee had been held on Pine Street,

On 11/29/63 at New Orleans, Louisiana File # NO 89-69

by SA JOHN L. QUIGLEY /cjo Date dictated 11/30/63

NO 89-69 /cjo
2

he immediately recalled the name of REISSMAN. He said that he asked OSWALD if REISSMAN was a member of the Fair Play for Cuba Committee. OSWALD did not give a verbal answer to this question, but Captain ARNOLD said he gathered from the expressions appearing on OSWALD's face and from words he uttered at that time, which he could not recall at this time, that OSWALD knew or was acquainted with REISSMAN. He said that he attempted to pursue this further, but OSWALD refused to admit any knowledge of REISSMAN or ever having been at REISSMAN's home. Captain ARNOLD said previous to this OSWALD had admitted to him that he was a member of the local chapter of the Fair Play forCuba Committee and he was trying to tie OSWALD and REISSMAN together, but was unsuccessful.

At no time during the period when he was present during the interrogation of OSWALD, did OSWALD mention being paid any amount of money for the distribution of Fair Play for Cuba Committee literature.

Captain ARNOLD said that he could not remember any additional details with respect to questioning of OSWALD.

Commission Exhibit No. 2521

Form No. 1588 (Revised)
Memorandum Report
(7-1-60)

UNITED STATES SECRET SERVICE
TREASURY DEPARTMENT

FILE NO. CO-2-34,030

ORIGIN Field	OFFICE Dallas	TITLE OR CAPTION
TYPE OF CASE: Protective Research	STATUS: Continued	Assassination of President Kennedy, Dallas, Texas
INVESTIGATION MADE AT: Dallas, Texas	PERIOD COVERED: December 10, 1963	
INVESTIGATION MADE BY: ATSAIC Leon I. Gopadze		

DETAILS

SYNOPSIS

Additional information received from Marina Oswald regarding attempted assassination of former General Walker. Also concerning whereabouts of Lee Oswald during the month of October 1962.

DETAILS OF INVESTIGATION

Reference is made to memorandum report of ATSAIC Gopadze dated December 10, 1963.

On December 10, 1963, the reporting agent accompanied by SA Kunkel proceeded to the Martin's residence where Marina Oswald was questioned for additional information she may have relative to the attempted assassination of former General Walker by her husband Lee Harvey Oswald. She stated that Lee Oswald also told her that once before prior to taking shot at General Walker on April 10, 1963, he went to the Walker residence for the same purpose but that he changed his mind as the place did not look just right for him, that three days prior to April 10 he took his rifle out of the house and buried it in a field near the Walker's house. According to Marina Oswald, upon her husband's return to the house after he tried to kill General Walker and telling her about it, three days later she saw him taking his military green rain coat for the purpose of wrapping the rifle and bringing it home. However, stated that when he returned home she did not see the rifle but several days later she saw the rifle on a shelf in the apartment where he always kept it. Marina Oswald also stated that the evening her husband shot at Walker, he told her that the church which is located near the Walker's house had some gathering, that there was plenty of noise and that after shooting at Walker he buried the rifle in the same place. Lee Oswald also told her, after reading in newspapers

DISTRIBUTION	COPIES	REPORT MADE BY	DATE
Chief	Orig. & 2	[signature] SPECIAL AGENT	12-11-63
Dallas	2	APPROVED Forrest V. Sorrels [signature] SPECIAL AGENT IN CHARGE	12-11-63

632

(CONTINUE ON PLAIN PAPER)

CO-2-34,030
Page 2

that some young man saw an automobile containing three men pulling away from the scene of shooting, that the Americans always think they should have a car to get away from the scene of the crime and that he would rather use his feet to do so than to have a car. He also told her that he took buses to go to the Walker residence and that he took a different bus to return home after the shooting.

In connection with Lee Oswald's places of residence after he moved from the YMCA on October 19, 1962, she stated that at that time she was staying with Elena Hall, that Lee had some apartment in Dallas but that she did not know where and that when she was moved from the Hall's home to 602 Elsbeth Street in the early part of November, Lee and his friend Gary Taylor moved her there. Regarding Gary Taylor, she stated that Gary was the son-in-law of George De Mohrenschildt and his wife, being married to the daughter of George's wife from the previous marriage by the name of Alexie; that Gary was a taxi driver and that after his divorce from Alexie he moved to live with his parents in Dallas but she did not know where. Marina Oswald was asked if she ever saw her husband doing any dry practice with the rifle either in their apartments or any place else, and she replied in the negative. She also was asked how she was able to explain to her mother-in-law, Marguerite Oswald, concerning the attempted assassination of General Walker by her husband, and she replied that she did to the best of her knowledge of English language and that no one else knew about the shooting except her and her mother-in-law.

Concerning Lee Oswald's being in Mexico City and his visits to the Cuban and Russian Embassies, Marina Oswald stated that she had no prior knowledge of him going to Mexico City, but that due to their family difficulties she on several occasions expressed her desire to return to Russia on which he agreed and that he also expressed a desire to return to Russia to save their marriage and on account of their children. She also stated that in order to return to Russia she wrote to the Russian Embassy in Washington, D. C.

Marina Oswald was asked why her husband used the name of "Aleck" and she stated that the name of "Aleck" was given to him by his co-workers in Russia because they did not like the name of Lee as it usually is connected with Chinese persons. She was also asked if to her knowledge her husband used the name of Aleck Hidell, and she replied in the negative. During the interview with Marina Oswald, she advised the reporting agent that she signed contracts the previous evening with Attorney John M. Thorne to handle her business on 10% commission basis for a period of ten years; that she also signed a contract with Jim Martin to receive 15% as her business manager; and that Robert Oswald also would receive 10% as her adviser. Marina Oswald stated that Robert Oswald examined and approved the contents of the contracts.

UNDEVELOPED LEADS

Possible additional interview with Marina Oswald.

LIG:amr

632

FD-302 (Rev. 1-25-60) FEDERAL BUREAU OF INVESTIGATION

Date 3/12/64

1

Mr. PETER O'DONNELL, with offices at 211 North Ervay Street, Dallas, Texas, was contacted this date, March 10, 1964. Mr. O'DONNELL is Chairman of the Republican Party of Texas. According to Mr. O'DONNELL, former Vice President RICHARD NIXON was in Texas only once in 1963, that being November 21, 1963. Mr. O'DONNELL knows of no invitation or publicity concerning Mr. NIXON in 1963, other than the time when he was here in November, 1963.

Mr. O'DONNELL stated he believed he would know if Mr. NIXON had been in Dallas in the Spring or Summer, 1963, and he was of the opinion Mr. NIXON was neither invited to come to Dallas during this period, nor did he receive any publicity during that period.

He stated their files in the Republican Headquarters do not reflect any publicity concerning Mr. NIXON in 1963.

On 3/10/64 at Dallas, Texas File # 100-10461

by SA VINCENT E. DRAIN/eah Date dictated 3/10/64

221

COMMISSION EXHIBIT No. 2522

FD-302 (Rev. 3-3-59) FEDERAL BUREAU OF INVESTIGATION

1

Date 1/22/64

WARREN REYNOLDS, part owner, Johnny Reynolds Used Car Lot, 500 Jefferson Street, Dallas, advised on the afternoon of November 22, 1963, while sitting in his office, he had observed an individual running south on Patton Avenue toward Jefferson Street and then walking at a fast rate of speed west on Jefferson. As the individual was running down Patton Avenue, he had a pistol or an automatic in his possession and was apparently attempting to conceal same in his belt while he was running. REYNOLDS advised he had previously heard shots coming from the area of Tenth and Patton Streets and, thinking that possibly a marital argument had occurred and a shooting had taken place, he attempted to follow the individual in order that he could inform the Dallas Police Department of the individual's location.

He advised he stayed at a safe distance behind the individual and last observed the individual to turn north by the Ballew Texaco Service Station, and from this point he did not again observe the individual. He advised he made inquiry at Ballew's Texaco Service Station, and they informed him the individual had gone through the parking lot.

REYNOLDS advised approximately five or ten minutes later he was informed by an unknown source that the individual whom he had been "tailing" had shot and apparently killed a uniform officer of the Dallas Police Department.

REYNOLDS was shown a photograph of LEE HARVEY OSWALD, at which time he advised he is of the opinion OSWALD is the person he had followed on the afternoon of November 22, 1963; however, he would hesitate to definitely identify OSWALD as the individual.

On 1/21/64 at Dallas, Texas File # DL 100-10461

by Special Agents JOHN T. KESLER and VERNON MITCHEM - LAC Date dictated 1/22/64

COMMISSION EXHIBIT No. 2523

OFFICE OF THE DIRECTOR

UNITED STATES DEPARTMENT OF JUSTICE

FEDERAL BUREAU OF INVESTIGATION

WASHINGTON 25, D.C.

January 17, 1964

Honorable J. Lee Rankin
General Counsel
The President's Commission
200 Maryland Avenue, N. E.
Washington, D. C.

Dear Mr. Rankin:

For your information, on January 4, 1964, I received a telegram from Attorney Clyde J. Watts of 219 Couch Drive, Oklahoma City, Oklahoma, in which Mr. Watts stated as attorney for retired General Edwin A. Walker, he was requesting the FBI to officially confirm or deny news reports that Lee Harvey Oswald confessed to his wife that he attempted to murder Walker on April 10, 1963. He also desired the FBI to furnish a transcript of all evidence and information pertinent to the alleged attempt by Oswald so that appropriate action could be taken to protect the general.

Mr. Watts and Attorney A. V. Grant of St. Jo, Texas, initially contacted our Dallas Office on December 7, 1963, and indicated they were representing General Walker. Watts stated that aside from being Walker's legal representative he was also a very close personal friend. Watts was of the opinion that there had been an official leak somewhere concerning the disclosure that Marina Oswald had stated her husband was responsible for the attempt on General Walker's life. At this time, the attorneys were advised the FBI had made no such disclosure.

Watts stated he was not asking for information but asked that any information developed relating to Walker's safety be furnished to Walker or the Dallas Police Department. Watts was, of course, advised any such information received would be handled in the same manner as a threat against any individual in that the FBI would promptly advise not only the individual but appropriate local authorities.

COMMISSION EXHIBIT No. 2524

Honorable J. Lee Rankin

Watts concluded by stating he was considering an interview with Marina Oswald as it might aid him in his efforts to protect Walker. He was told whatever decision he made in this matter was entirely up to him and we would not suggest or recommend any course of action.

Of possible interest, immediately following the attempted murder of Walker in April, 1963, our Dallas Office discussed the case with the Dallas Police Department and volunteered to forward the bullet recovered from Walker's home to the FBI Laboratory for examination; however, no such request was ever made. During the course of our current investigation into the assassination of President Kennedy and prior to the interview of Mrs. Oswald on December 3, 1963, wherein she indicated her husband may have been responsible for the shooting at Walker, the possibility that Oswald may have fired at Walker was considered. Our Dallas Office, therefore, on the weekend of November 30, 1963, requested the Dallas Police Department to make available the recovered bullet for examination by the Laboratory. On December 2, 1963, the bullet was forwarded to our Laboratory where it was examined. This examination revealed that the distorted and mutilated bullet had the same general characteristics of bullets from the rifle used by Oswald in the assassination of President Kennedy. However, it was not possible to definitely establish whether or not the recovered bullet was fired from Oswald's gun.

The files of the Dallas Police Department relating to the investigation of the Walker shooting disclose that General Walker reported that at approximately 9:00 p.m., on April 10, 1963, while sitting at his desk in his Dallas residence, a shot was fired above his head into his home. The only suspect developed by the Dallas Police Department in this matter was one William MacEwan Duff who had been employed in some capacity by General Walker or his staff. He was selected primarily because he was considered to be a "con man." After a polygraph examination was given to him by the Dallas Police Department and after they conducted other investigation, Duff was absolved by the Dallas Police Department of involvement in this crime.

- 2 -

COMMISSION EXHIBIT No. 2524—Continued

Immigration and Naturalization Service records disclose that Duff was born on November 4, 1931, in Scotland and entered the United States in 1957. He has been characterized as a "con man" and "nc good." So far in our investigation of the assassination, only one individual, a Dallas lunchroom proprietor, has linked Oswald with Duff in approximately April or May, 1963, as having frequented this lunchroom on one occasion. It should be pointed out that six other individuals who had intimate knowledge of Duff were unable to connect Oswald with Duff. Further, our investigation discloses that during the above period Oswald is known to have been in Dallas, Texas, until April, 1963; however, from late April, 1963, to September, 1963, he was in New Orleans, Louisiana.

On January 8, 1964, Attorney Watts was personally contacted by an Agent from our Oklahoma City Office at which time his January 4, 1964, telegram to me was acknowledged. He was told the results of the FBI investigation into Oswald's activities have been furnished to the President's Commission and we are not in a position to divulge such information to him. It was again reiterated that should any information be received relative to the safety of General Walker it would be promptly furnished to the General and to appropriate law enforcement authorities.

Watts at this time indicated he might possibly communicate with the President's Commission in an effort to obtain the information requested from the FBI.

In addition, Watts advised that shortly after the attempt on General Walker's life he hired two private investigators to look into the incident and they developed one Bill Duff of Dallas as a suspect. Duff, according to Watts, had been employed in some capacity by Walker or his staff. The private investigators were unable to develop any information linking Duff with the Walker shooting and turned over the results of their investigation to the Dallas Police Department. Watts stated he was furnishing this information as a possible link between Duff and Oswald.

We have been endeavoring to locate William MacEwan Duff, the suspect absolved by the Dallas Police Department, for interview. Information developed to date on this individual indicates he remained in Dallas, Texas, until October, 1963, when he was last reported to be en route to Oklahoma City, Oklahoma, by bus.

We will continue our efforts to locate Duff, an alien, for interview, and when this is accomplished you will be advised.

Sincerely yours,

J. Edgar Hoover

Commission Exhibit No. 2525

Form No. 1584 (Revised)
MEMORANDUM REPORT
(7-1-50)

UNITED STATES SECRET SERVICE
TREASURY DEPARTMENT

ORIGIN Field	OFFICE Dallas	FILE NO. CO-2-34,030
TYPE OF CASE: Protective Research	STATUS: Pending	TITLE OR CAPTION: ASSASSINATION OF PRESIDENT KENNEDY, DALLAS, TEXAS
INVESTIGATION MADE AT: Dallas, Texas	PERIOD COVERED: December 2, 1963	
INVESTIGATION MADE BY: Inspector Thomas J. Kelley, ATSAIC Leon I. Gopadze, and SA Max D. Phillips		

DETAILS

SYNOPSIS

Russian note found in Mrs. Marina Oswald's home economic book. This Russian note was translated by ATSAIC Gopadze and gives instructions to Mrs. Marina Oswald in the event that Lee Harvey Oswald is arrested.

DETAILS OF INVESTIGATION

Reference is made to previous reports.

Other Investigations

On December 2, 1963, the Arlington Police Department, Arlington, Texas, hand delivered to the Secret Service Office, Dallas, miscellaneous personal effects belonging to Mrs. Marina Oswald. The Arlington Police had received these miscellaneous personal effects from Mrs. Ruth Paine.

On instruction of Inspector Thomas J. Kelley, the reporting Special Agent examined the miscellaneous personal effects for any documents which were written in Russian for the purpose of having ATSAIC Gopadze translate the Russian documents.

Among the miscellaneous personal effects were two books which were written in Russian:

Book No. 1: Title of book, according to ATSAIC Gopadze, is Book of Helpful Instructions. This book is basically a cookbook and other general home economic subjects. Its color is light green with a light blue back binding.

DISTRIBUTION	COPIES	REPORT MADE BY	DATE
Chief Dallas	Orig.&2 2	SPECIAL AGENT Max D. Phillips	12-3-63
		APPROVED 707 SPECIAL AGENT IN CHARGE	12-3-63

(CONTINUE ON PLAIN PAPER)

COMMISSION EXHIBIT No. 2525

CO-2-34,030
Page 2

Book No. 2: Title of book, according to ATSAIC Gopadze, is Our Child. This book is basically a book on motherhood and infant care. Its color is white with a picture of an infant on the cover.

Upon examination of the book titled, Book of Helpful Instruction, the reporting Special Agent found a folded paper with Russian written on it. See Inspector Thomas J. Kelley's and ATSAIC Leon Gopadze's memorandum reports for specifics concerning translation of Russian note and further investigation.

UNDEVELOPED LEADS

Investigation continued.

MDP: ew

707

COMMISSION EXHIBIT No. 2525—Continued

PROPOSED MANIFEST - AF #1
FORT WORTH TO DALLAS

1. THE PRESIDENT
2. MRS. JOHN F. KENNEDY
3. MR. KENNETH O'DONNELL
4. MR. LAWRENCE O'BRIEN
5. MR. DAVID POWERS
6. BRIG. GEN. GODFREY T. MCHUGH
7. MISS PAMELA TURNURE
8. MISS EVELYN LINCOLN
9. MR. MALCOLM KILDUFF
10. MRS. MARY GALLAGHER
11. DR. GEORGE BURKLEY
12. MISS CHRIS CAMP
13. GOVERNOR CONNALLY
14. MRS. CONNALLY
15. SENATOR R. YARBOROUGH
16. MR. ROY H. KELLERMAN - SS
17. MR. CLINT HILL - SS
18. JOHN J. O'LEARY - SS
19. MR. EMORY ROBERTS - SS
20. MR. JOHN READY - SS
21. MR. DONALD LAWTON - SS
22. MR. WILLIAM T. MCINTYRE - SS
23. MR. HENRY RYBKA - SS
24. MR. WILLIAM GREER - SS
25. CONG. R. ROBERTS
26. CONG. J. BECKWORTH
27. CONG. O. TEAGUE
28. MSGT JOSEPH GIORDANO - USA
29. CWO IRA GEARHART - USA
30. CONG. J. WRIGHT
31. MR. MERRIMAN SMITH - PRESS
32. MR. F. CORMIER - PRESS
33. MR. B. BASKIN - PRESS
34. MR. B. CLARK - PRESS
35. MR. GEORGE THOMAS
36. HMCM ELLIS H. HENDRIX - USN

COMMISSION EXHIBIT No. 2526

Transportes Frontera

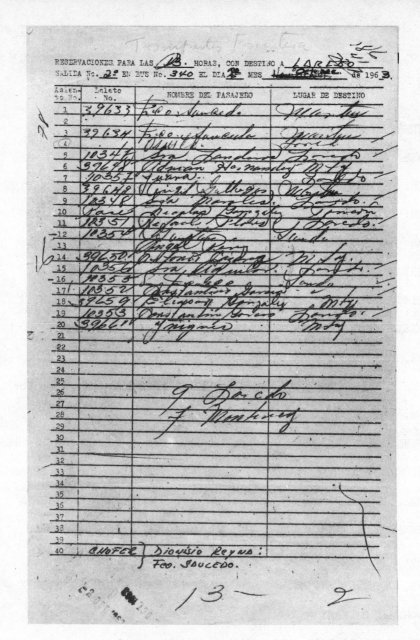

RESERVACIONES PARA LAS 13. HORAS, CON DESTINO A LAREDO
SALIDA No. 2º EN BUS No. 340 EL DIA 2 MES Octubre de 1963.

Asiento No.	Boleto No.	NOMBRE DEL PASAJERO	LUGAR DE DESTINO
1	39633	Fco. Saucedo.	Monterrey
2			
3	39634	Fco. Saucedo	Monterrey
4		Oswald	Laredo
5	10347	Sra. Sandoval	Laredo
6	39648	Adrian Hernandez	Mty.
7	10357	[illegible]	Laredo
8	39649	Miguel Gallegos	Monterrey
9	10348	Sra. Morales.	Laredo.
10	Pase	Nicolas Gonzalez	Tenerm
11	10351	Rafael Flores	Laredo.
12	10354	[illegible]	[illegible]
13		Angel Perez	
14	39650	Antonio Gazorra	Mty.
15	10356	Sra. Aguilar.	Laredo.
16	10355	[illegible]	Laredo
17	10352	Constantino Garza	
18	39659	Eliazar Gonzalez	Mty.
19	10353	Constantino Garza	Laredo.
20	39660	Yñiguez	Mty.
21			
22			
23			
24			
25			
26			
27			
28			
29			
30			
31			
32			
33			
34			
35			
36			
37			
38			
39			
40	CHOFER	Dionisio Reyna: / Fco. Saucedo.	

9 Laredo
F. Monterrey

13 — 2

Commission Exhibit No. 2527

146.30
108.80
255.10

Commission Exhibit No. 2527—Continued

RESERVACIONES PARA LAS________HORAS, CON DESTINO A___________________

SALIDA No.____ EN BUS No.______ EL DIA____ MES__________________ de 196_

Asiento No.	Boleto No.	NOMBRE DEL PASAJERO	LUGAR DE DESTINO
1			
2			
3			
4			
5	2514	Sra de Ponce	Victoria.
6			
7			
8	2513	Nicolas Flores.	Victoria.
9	1154		
10			
11	3693		
12	810		
13			
14			
15			
16			
17			
18			
19			
20			
21			
22			
23			
24			
25			
26			
27			
28			
29			
30			
31			
32			
33			
34			
35			
36			
37			
38			
39			
40			

1430

COMMISSION EXHIBIT No. 2528

MIERCOLES

TRANSPORTES DEL NORTE

MIERCOLES

De MEXICO A LAREDO

Bus. No. 332 Fecha Octubre 2 1963 Hora 8.30

Operadores R. Cuevas - R. Gonzalez

ASIENTO	NOMBRE DEL PASAJERO	DESTINO	No. DE BOLETO
2	Sta. Cosio	S. A.	13920
3	J. A. Martinez	N. Ldo	12619
4	Margaret & Wolff	Mty	61840 Cargo
5	Roberto P. Gonzalez	Mty	7915
5	A. H. Villa	Mty	99232 X
6			
7	Paula Rascone	Ldo.	9511
8	J.M. DE GUBA	Ldo.	8940
9	—	—	41
9			
10	Operador		
11	Augusto Alquelos	Houston	13742
12	Chihuahuenses	San Antonio	13688
13			
14	Sr. Eulalio Rodriguez	Houston	13921
15	A. Veloz	Ldo.	13619
16	Sh van der VORM	Laredo Tex	13407
17	Jorge Davila	Mty	716
18	Jose Barriga	Dallas	13740
19	y Sra.	—	741
20			
21	Sr. Agapito del Rio	S. A.	13928
22	Guadalajara	Jerez	
23	—	—	
24	—	—	
25	—	—	
26	—	—	
27	—	—	
28	—	—	
29	—	—	
30			
31			
32			
33			
34			
35			
36			
37			
38			
39			
40			
41			
42			

(16)

COMMISSION EXHIBIT No. 2529

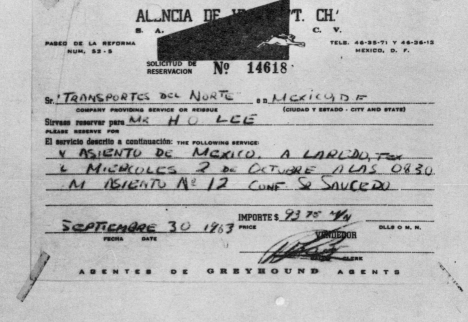

AL_NCIA DE [redacted]T. CH.'

S. A. [redacted] C. V.

PASEO DE LA REFORMA
NUM. 52-5

TELS. 46-35-71 Y 46-36-12
MEXICO, D. F.

SOLICITUD DE RESERVACION Nº 14618

Sr. TRANSPORTES DEL NORTE en MEXICO D.F.
COMPANY PROVIDING SERVICE OR REISSUE (CIUDAD Y ESTADO - CITY AND STATE)

Sirvase reservar para MR H O LEE
PLEASE RESERVE FOR

El servicio descrito a continuación: THE FOLLOWING SERVICE:

1 ASIENTO DE MEXICO A LAREDO, TEX
L MIERCOLES 2 DE OCTUBRE A LAS 0830
M ASIENTO Nº 12 CONF SR SAUCEDO

SEPTIEMBRE 30 1963
FECHA DATE

IMPORTE $ 93 75 M/N
PRICE DLLS O M. N.

VENDEDOR
SALES CLERK

AGENTES DE GREYHOUND AGENTS

Reproduced above is a "Solicitud de Reservacion" (Reservation Request), also described as a "Ticket Purchase Order" of the "Agencia de Viajes Transportes Chihuahuenses" (Transportes Chihuahuenses Travel Agency), Mexico City, issued to Mr. H. O. LEE for "one seat from Mexico to Laredo, Tex. for Wednesday, October 2 at 08:30 for seat No. 12 confirmed Mr. SAUCEDO" in the amount of 93.75 pesos ($7.50 U. S.) and dated September 30, 1963.

COMMISSION EXHIBIT NO. 2530

Commission Exhibit No. 2531

FORM 121
(PRINTED IN U.S.A.)

WESTERN GREYHOUND LINES
(DIVISION OF THE GREYHOUND CORPORATION)
371 MARKET STREET
SAN FRANCISCO, CALIFORNIA

INTERNATIONAL SALES REPORT

PERIOD FROM October 1st. 1963 TO October 31th. 1963

FORM A-10 NUMBER (1)	PASSENGER'S NAME	NO. OF PAS-SEN-GERS	ROUTING IN NORTH AMERICA ORIGIN	DESTINATION	AMOUNT OF ORDER	AMOUNT OF TAX
43598	Mr. Rolando Hernández B.	1	Vancouver	Vancouver	7.30	
43599	Mr. H. O. Lee	1	Laredo, Tex.	Dallas, Tex.	12.80	
43600	CANCELLED					
48251	Mr. Cesar C. Alcocer	3	Laredo, Tex.	Elgin, Ill.	93.50	
48252		2	El Paso, Tex.	Laredo, Tex.	124.12	
48253	Mr. Abraham León K.	1	Miami, Flda.	Miami, Flda.	68.70	
48254	Mr. & Mrs. Adolfo Lara	2	Laredo, Tex.	New York, N.Y.	110.10	
48255	Miss Harlouchet	2	San Ysidro, Calif.	Los Angeles, Calif.	8.30	
48256	Mr. & Mrs. A. Villanueva	2	Laredo, Tex.	Laredo, Tex.	72.90	
48257	Mr. C. Bell	1	Laredo. Tex.	San Antonio, Tex.	4.60	
48258	Mr. Alfredo Barbel & Sra.	2	Laredo, Tex.	Laredo, Tex.	72.90	
48259	Miss Marylin Goodwin	3	Laredo, Tex.	Los Angeles, Calif.	129.45	
48260	Mr. Francisco Fl res	1	Laredo, Tex.	Chicago, Ill.	35.80	
48261	Mr. Arnold Montperous	1	Laredo, Tex.	New York, N.Y.	55.05	
15425	REFUND				(95.70)	
				TOTALS	699.82	

NAME OF AGENCY	AGENCIA DE VIAJES T.CH., S.A. DE C.V.	1	TOTAL OF ORDERS	699.82
STREET ADDRESS	Reforma # 52-5	2	TOTAL TAX	
CITY	Mexico, City	3	MISCELLANEOUS	25.56
COUNTRY	MEXICO	4	TOTAL (LINES 1, 2 AND 3)	725.38
SIGNATURE OF AGENT	[signature]	5	COMMISSION ON LINE 1	69.98
(1) ATTACH AUDITOR'S COPIES OF ORDERS TO ORIGINAL REPORT		6	MISCELLANEOUS	
(2) A CHECK IN U. S. DOLLARS ON A U. S. BANK FOR THIS AMOUNT MUST ACCOMPANY REPORT		7	NET REMITTANCE (LINE 4 LESS LINES 5 AND 6)	655.40

COMMISSION EXHIBIT No. 2531

UNITED STATES DEPARTMENT OF JUSTICE

FEDERAL BUREAU OF INVESTIGATION

In Reply, Please Refer to
File No.

WASHINGTON 25, D. C.

May 11, 1964

LEE HARVEY OSWALD

BASIS FOR INQUIRY

The following information was made available by a confidential source abroad:

The records of the Chihuahuense Travel Agency and the Transportes del Norte bus line terminal at Mexico, D. F. ("D. F." refers to the Federal District of Mexico or the Federal Capital, also known as Mexico City), reflect that one H. O. LEE occupied seat No. 12 on the Transportes del Norte bus No. 332 which departed from Mexico City on October 2, 1963, with Monterrey and Nuevo Laredo, Mexico, as its destination. According to the source, ANASTASIO RUIZ MEZA, a resident of Mexico City, advised that he was a passenger on the above-mentioned bus and identified photographs of LEE HARVEY OSWALD as having been a passenger thereon.

It also had been ascertained that OSWALD traveled from Nuevo Laredo, Tamaulipas, to Mexico City on a bus of the Flecha Roja bus line on September 26-27, 1963, and during the trip had recommended to passengers on that bus that they seek hotel accommodations at the Hotel Cuba in Mexico City.

With respect to OSWALD's luggage, color photographs had been provided of an olive-colored "Bee-4" bag and a blue, canvas, zippered handbag which had been identified as the property of OSWALD.

TRANSPORTES DEL NORTE PASSENGERS ORIGINATING IN GUADALAJARA

On April 3, 1964, a second confidential source abroad advised that the "Linea Azul" (Blue Line) bus company affords

COMMISSION EXHIBIT NO. 2532

service from Guadalajara, Jalisco, Mexico, to San Luis Potosi, State of San Luis Potosi, to make connections with Transportes del Norte for possible further travel to Monterrey and Nuevo Laredo, Mexico. According to this source, a reservations list for the October 2, 1963, 8:00 AM departure of the Blue Line bus from Guadalajara with San Luis Potosi as its destination reflects the following information as best the names and other data thereon could be deciphered:

Name of Passenger	Destination	Ticket No.
HILDA QUEZADA	N. Laredo	77898
--------------	---------	99
(Lines indicate a second passenger or seat reserved in that name.)		
JOSE CRUZ	Monterrey	00751
HILDA QUEZADA	N. Laredo	77900 1/2
(It was explained the "1/2" indicates half fare paid.)		
CECILIO CARDENAZ	Monterrey	00749
JOSE MAZO	San Luis	14128
VICTORIA MAGALLANES	(Apparently did not travel.)	
MAXIMINO ESQUIVEL	Monterrey	00752
PEDRO GLEZ. (GONZALEZ)	Monterrey	00753
AURELIO HDEZ. (HERNANDEZ)	San Luis	1362

Source advised that comprehensive investigation, including a check of the files of the United States Consulate visa records, checks of telephone directories, and numerous interviews of persons listed in the telephone directory with similar names, had been conducted at Guadalajara for the above names of persons traveling beyond San Luis Potosi without identifying anyone who had been a passenger of Transportes del Norte on October 2, 1963.

TRANSPORTES DEL NORTE BUS LINE OPERATIONS, MONTERREY

The following information was furnished by a third confidential source abroad:

COMMISSION EXHIBIT NO. 2532—Continued

On April 19, 1964, RAMON TREVINO QUEZADA, vice president and manager of the Monterrey, Nuevo Leon, Mexico, terminal of the bus line, Transportes del Norte, advised that tickets are taken up by the driver from passengers at the time they board the bus, and he deposits them in a manila envelope, which is provided for that purpose in connection with each trip. He stated the driver makes a notation on the outside of the envelope as to the number of passengers traveling over a determined section of the route, and the tickets inside the envolope should coincide or balance with the notation by the driver on the envelope.

With respect to the records of the company for the trip of its bus No 373 on October 2, 1963, from Monterrey to Nuevo Laredo, Tamaulipas, and Laredo, Texas, TREVINO advised that he was unable to explain the fact that the envelope carries the figure of "12" passengers from Monterrey to Nuevo Laredo and Laredo and "1" passenger from Nuevo Laredo to Laredo, although a total of "20" ticket sections were in the envelope for that particular trip. He stated, however, that the notation by the driver is a clerical function which he handles during the trip, often at night and under considerable stress and pressure, and he can only conclude that the driver made an error in writing "12" rather than "19" upon completing his collection of tickets and delivering the envelope at the conclusion of his run.

It was mentioned to Mr. TREVINO that the baggage manifest for the bus which arrived at Nuevo Laredo in the early morning of October 3, 1963, had listed the number of that bus as No. 396, and he advised that this notation could only be a clerical error by the baggage handler. He displayed a copy of a document referred to as a "Traffic Report" for Transportes del Norte at its Nuevo Laredo terminal for October 3, 1963, which recorded that bus No 373had arrived at that terminal at 1:35 AM with A. IBARRA as the driver. The "Traffic Report" for October 2, 1963, registered the arrival of bus No 396 at Nuevo Laredo as having taken place at 1530 (3:30 PM) on that date, and its departure from Nuevo Laredo for Monterrey was recorded on the report for the following day as having occurred at 2:30 AM. He pointed out that, on the basis of the foregoing records, bus No. 396 would still have been at the Nuevo Laredo

terminal at the time of arrival on October 3, 1963, of bus No. 373, and he assumed that the baggage handler had become confused between them when he made the erroneous notation on the baggage manifest.

EFFORTS TO IDENTIFY BUS
PASSENGER HILDA QUEZADA

It was pointed out to Mr. TREVINO that a HILDA QUEZADA and two accompanying persons, an adult and a child, were recorded as having traveled from Guadalajara, Jalisco, to San Luis Potosi, State of San Luis Potosi, in order to continue their travel on the October 2, 1963, Transportes del Norte bus to Nuevo Laredo. He stated that the name of HILDA QUEZADA is totally unknown to him.

It was determined on April 15, 1964, through a check at the Central Office, Immigration and Naturalization Service (INS), Washington, D. C., that the master index contained a reference to one HILDA QUEZADA QUIROZ. These records disclosed that HILDA QUEZADA QUIROZ was born September 4, 1944, at Mexico, D. F., Mexico, and that she was admitted to the United States at Laredo on May 24, 1963, on a Class B-2 visa valid to June 15, 1963. She was the bearer of Mexican Passport No. 31067, and the visa was issued at Mexico City on May 15, 1963. Her permanent address was given as J. M. Correa No. 196, Mexico, D. F., Mexico, and her address in the United States was recorded as "San Antonio and Houston, Texas." The departure record reflects she departed from the United States at Laredo on May 30, 1963.

A confidential source who has furnished reliable information in the past advised on April 30, 1964, that he had located HILDA QUEZADA QUIROZ at Calle Jose Maria Correa No. 196, Colonia Vista Alegre, Mexico, D. F., and QUEZADA advised that she did travel on a Transportes del Norte bus from San Luis Potosi, State of San Luis Potosi, Mexico, to Nuevo Laredo but in May, 1963. QUEZADA advised that she did not travel in October, 1963.

TICKETING PROCEDURES BY
TRANSPORTES DEL NORTE BUS LINE

The following information was furnished by a fourth confidential source abroad:

On April 20, 1964, RAMON MEDINA BELTRAN, manager of the Mexico City terminal of the Transportes del Norte bus line, advised that this company is affiliated with the Greyhound Lines in the United States and is authorized and is in a position to sell transportation to any point in the United States. He stated that until approximately one year ago the sale of bus transportation in the United States in behalf of Greyhound Lines had been effected through a system of exchange or purchase orders; however, in the interests of simplifying the sales and accounting procedures, Transportes del Norte ticket counters are now stocked with Greyhound Lines tickets and make direct sales in behalf of Greyhound, as well as its own facilities. He stated very definitely that the only record as to the identity of any person purchasing Greyhound transportation through a Transportes del Norte ticket counter would be the recording of the seat reservation on a passenger list at the point of origin or purchase of the ticket.

TRANSPORTES DEL NORTE PREPARES NO PASSENGER
LISTS AT SAN LUIS POTOSI AND MONTERREY

On April 9, 1964, RAMON MEDINA BELTRAN, manager of the Mexico City terminal of the Transportes del Norte bus line, advised that he had contacted the San Luis Potosi, State of San Luis Potosi, terminal of that company in an effort to obtain a list of passengers who had embarked on bus No. 332 of that company on the morning of October 2, 1963, with Monterrey and Nuevo Laredo as their destinations. He stated that he had been advised that no passenger reservations lists or manifests are prepared at that terminal because of the small number of persons who embark at that point.

On April 3, 1964, RAMON TREVINO QUEZADA, vice president of Transportes del Norte, Monterrey, advised the third source abroad that because of the fact that the company operates numerous schedules daily between Monterrey and Laredo,

Texas, no effort is made to prepare reservations or passenger lists in connection therewith.

INTERVIEW OF AUGUSTO AGUILAR,
PASSENGER ON TRANSPORTES DEL
NORTE BUS NO. 332, OCTOBER 2, 1963

According to the first confidential source abroad, the passenger and reservations list for the Transportes del Norte bus No. 332, which departed from Mexico City for Nuevo Laredo on October 2, 1963, recorded that seat No. 11 had been utilized by AUGUSTO AGUILAR, whose final destination was listed as Houston (Texas). In this connection, passenger ANASTASIO RUIZ MÉZA had recalled that seated in front of him on the bus was a person whom he believed to be Mexican and either a missionary or minister, as he was reading a Bible during parts of the trip. RUIZ MEZA believed that the destination of the above-described person was Houston, Texas.

The following information was provided by a fifth confidential source abroad:

Inquiry among various Protestant missionary and religious organizations at Mexico City developed data that the Bible Society of Mexico might have records relating to many of the Protestant missionaries and ministers in Mexico.

On April 29, 1964, JOSE HERNANDEZ J., an officer in the Methodist Church and affiliated with the Bible Society of Mexico, Mexico, D. F., reported that the records of that Society include the name of one AUGUSTO AGUILAR, Calle Juan Alvarez No. 44, Villahermosa, Tabasco. Through the cooperation of the Office of the Military Attache, United States Embassy, Mexico, D. F., which was in communication with members of its staff who were traveling in Villahermosa, it was ascertained on May 4, 1964, that AUGUSTO AGUILAR of Villahermosa had traveled to the United States by bus in early October, 1963.

The information recorded hereinunder was provided by a sixth confidential source abroad:

On May 6, 1964, Mrs. AUGUSTO AGUILAR, Calle 2 de

Abril No. 37 (April 2 Street No. 37), Villahermosa, State of Tabasco, Mexico, advised that her husband, AUGUSTO AGUILAR, who is an Evangelical minister, made a bus trip from Mexico City to the United States the latter part of 1963. She stated her husband was out of the city visiting his sister, Mrs. RITA MARIA AGUILAR DE FONZ, who lives at Calle 35 No. 76 (35th Street No. 76), Ciudad del Carmen, State of Campeche, Mexico, telephone No. 4-37.

She related that her husband is the minister of a church known as the "Templo Bethel, Iglesia Cristiana de las Asambleas de Dios" (Bethel Temple, Christian Church of the Assemblies of God) which is located at Juan Alvarez Street No. 44, in Villahermosa.

Mrs. AGUILAR made available her husband's Mexican Passport No. 21630, issued to JOSE AUGUSTO AGUILAR PINTO, and recorded therein was a United States nonimmigrant visa No. 115356, issued to AGUILAR on October 1, 1963, at the United States Embassy, Mexico, D. F.

A stamped notation of the United States Immigration and Naturalization Service in this passport indicates AGUILAR was admitted to the United States at Laredo, Texas, on October 3, 1963.

On May 6, 1964, JOSE AUGUSTO AGUILAR PINTO was located at the residence of his sister at Calle 35 No. 76, Ciudad del Carmen, State of Campeche, Mexico, and advised that although JOSE AUGUSTO AGUILAR PINTO is his complete name, he is more commonly known as AUGUSTO AGUILAR. He furnished the following information:

He was a passenger on a Transportes del Norte bus which departed Mexico City at 8:30 AM on October 2, 1963, knowing the date to be October 2, 1963, inasmuch as his Mexican passport contains a date stamp that he was admitted to the United States at Laredo, Texas, on October 3, 1963, and he recalls that he boarded the bus in Mexico City on the previous day.

He was not certain of his seat number on the bus but occupied the seat which had been assigned to him. He said his

- 7 -

COMMISSION EXHIBIT No. 2532—Continued

seat was a window seat located on the right side of the bus and several rows from the front. (The passenger manifest for Transportes del Norte bus No. 332, which departed Mexico City at 8:30 AM, October 2, 1963, discloses space was assigned in seat No. 11 for AUGUSTO AGUILAR whose final destination is listed as Houston. Seat No. 11 is a window seat on the right side of the bus opposite the driver's side and two rows from the front.)

He believed there were perhaps ten or twelve other passengers who boarded the bus at Mexico City; however, he cannot recall the identities of these fellow passengers or any details which would aid in identifying them. He did not recall any Americans having boarded the bus.

He related that he had made a bus trip on a Transportes del Norte bus from Mexico City to Mazatlan, State of Sinaloa, Mexico, to attend a religious conclave in Mazatlan, a short time prior to the trip of October 2, 1963, and it is difficult for him to distinguish clearly in his mind the trip to Mazatlan from the trip of October 2, 1963.

When he boarded the Transportes del Norte bus at Mexico City on October 2, 1963, his final destination was Houston, Texas, and after arriving in Houston, he continued to the home of Reverend BILLY SANDERS of Humble, Texas, on whose invitation he had made the trip. While in the United States, he delivered several sermons in the Humble, Texas, area and at Houston and San Antonio, Texas. He was in the United States until about November 20, 1963, at which time he returned to Mexico. He was able to fix his departure from the United States for return to Mexico as November 20, 1963, by the fact that President KENNEDY had been assassinated on November 22, 1963, and he was in Veracruz, Mexico, when he first learned of the assassination, having left the United States about two days previously.

He does not recall exactly where the bus stopped before reaching Monterrey, Nuevo Leon, Mexico, although he assumed the bus stopped at San Luis Potosi as one of the principal cities on the route.

- 8 -

COMMISSION EXHIBIT No. 2532—Continued

He was not certain whether or not there was anyone seated by him on the bus nor could he furnish specific information concerning the passengers who had been seated in his immediate vicinity. He said the bus arrived in Monterrey around 11:00 PM, October 2, 1963, but considered this was only an estimate on his part, remembering it was late at night. He could not remember any details of a stop at Monterrey, changes of bus units, or other data related to that phase of his travel.

He remembered that just prior to arrival at Nuevo Laredo, Tamaulipas, Mexico, the bus stopped and travel and identification documents of the passengers were inspected by Mexican Immigration officials. The interior lights of the bus were turned on and one or two Mexican Immigration officials boarded the bus at this stopping point. It was his impression that one of the officials was a stout individual, but he could remember no further descriptive data concerning this person.

At this Immigration check point, an American youth left the bus with the Mexican Immigration official or officials, and he believed that some question had arisen concerning the youth's documents. He said he considered this person to be an American from his general appearance. He estimated that this person was away from the bus for about ten minutes. He did not recall this person's making any remarks after reboarding the bus, or that other passengers left the bus at this point.

Upon viewing a chart of the seating arrangment of the Transportes del Norte bus No. 332, which departed Mexico City on October 2, 1963, it was AGUILAR's opinion that the American youth was seated in either seat No. 8 or 9 or seat No. 12 or 13. AGUILAR stated he vaguely recalls this person was seated to his left and slightly to his rear.

AGUILAR vaguely recalled that the American youth reboarded the bus at the Immigration check point and took a seat in the area of the seats numbered 8, 9, 12 or 13. He described this person, whose facial features he cannot clearly remember, as follows:

Age:	Under 30 years
Height:	5' 7" to 5' 8"

- 9 -

COMMISSION EXHIBIT No. 2532—Continued

Weight:	121 to 132 pounds
Build:	Slender, thin
Hair:	Light brown
Complexion:	Light

He expressed his general impression that the American was dressed neatly in dark-colored clothing and believed he was wearing a dark suit coat. He did not recall further details regarding the youth's clothing or his luggage.

AGUILAR viewed several photographs of LEE HARVEY OSWALD and could not recognize the photographs as being identical with any of the passengers on the bus or the American youth. He agreed that the American youth could be identical with OSWALD, but affirmed that he could not be certain.

AGUILAR viewed the photograph of JUAN MATEO DE CUBA as it appears on Mexican Government tourist form FM-5 No. 3625296, and of his wife, ADA FRANCISCA BISLIP DE DE CUBA, as it appears on Mexican Government tourist form FM-5 No. 3625295. He also was shown a photograph of PHILLIPE PITER E. VAN DER VORM as it appears on Mexican Government tourist form FM-8 No. 624820. AGUILAR could not recognize the photographs of Mr. and Mrs. DE CUBA and VAN DER VORM as being identical with any of the passengers on the bus.

He could not recall whether the bus from Monterrey to Laredo stopped in Nuevo Laredo but does remember arriving at the offices of the United States Immigration and Naturalization Service and United States Customs near the International Bridge in Laredo.

He recalled that upon arriving in Laredo, the passengers disembarked, obtained their luggage, and walked up a ramp into a large office containing a large counter, where the luggage of the passengers was then examined by United States officials whom he assumed to be United States Customs agents. He recalled going into another large office where the passengers' travel documents were checked by United States authorities.

He does not recall details of contact between the

- 10 -

COMMISSION EXHIBIT No. 2532—Continued

various passengers and United States officials but believed that the American youth who left the bus earlier during the Mexican Immigration check had some discussion with a United States Immigration official during the examination of travel documents; however, he could not furnish further details concerning the discussion.

AGUILAR advised he was not vaccinated upon arrival in Laredo. He estimated that United States Immigration and Customs check lasted about forty minutes and when it was completed, the passengers again boarded the bus.

He could not remember whether he boarded another bus at the bus terminal in Laredo or San Antonio, Texas. He stated that either at Laredo or San Antonio he boarded an "American" bus but could not recall the bus company or any details regarding the number or other passengers on the bus. From San Antonio, he continued his journey to Houston.

The following is a physical description of AGUILAR as obtained from data appearing on his Mexican passport and through observation:

Name:	JOSE AUGUSTO AGUILAR PINTO, also known as AUGUSTO AGUILAR.
Date of Birth:	June 17, 1922
Place of Birth:	Ciudad del Carmen, State of Campeche, Mexico.
Height:	5' 8" to 5' 9"
Weight:	Approximately 185 pounds.
Build:	Stocky
Hair:	Black on the sides; top portion of head completely bald.
Eyes:	Brown
Complexion:	Medium
Occupation:	Evangelical minister
Residence:	Calle 2 de Abril No. 37, Villahermosa, State of Tabasco, Mexico.
Marital Status:	Married

OSWALD'S LUGGAGE

The following information was furnished by the fourth source abroad:

On April 4, 1964, JUAN PEREZ GONZALEZ advised that he is the chief of the baggage department at the terminal of the Flecha Roja bus line, Calle Heroes Ferrocarrileros No. 45, Mexico, D. F. PEREZ viewed photographs of an olive-colored, "B-4" bag with yellow chalk or crayon markings on one side which appeared to be "9/26" and possibly an initial, of fragments of stickers and tags thereon, and of a blue, zippered handbag and affirmed that he has no recollection of those pieces of luggage and did not recognize any of the markings, stickers or tags as being in any way connected with the Flecha Roja operations. He stated, however, that he recently entered Mexico at Nuevo Laredo with a small, zippered handbag of canvas material; and when he went through Mexican Customs, the Inspector placed a green chalk or crayon marking on the bag to indicate it had been inspected.

PEREZ displayed the various photographs to the baggage handlers on duty at the terminal, and they stated they were unable to recall the luggage in question or make any explanation of the tags, stickers and inscriptions on them.

On May 8, 1964, the manager of the Mexico City terminal of the Transportes del Norte bus line, Insurgentes Sur No. 137, viewed the photographs mentioned above and advised that he did not have any recollection with respect to the two pieces of luggage described above nor did he believe that any of the fragments of stickers and tags thereon were connected in any way with the Transportes del Norte baggage handling procedures. He expressed the belief that the yellow chalk markings on the olive-colored bag were typical of the method used by Mexican Customs Inspectors at Nuevo Laredo to mark luggage upon completing examination thereof in lieu of a sticker which they sometimes use.

The manager, RICARDO MEDINA BELTRAN, displayed the photographs to the baggage handlers on duty and they affirmed that they were unable to recognize either piece of luggage in connection with any passenger but stated unanimously that they recognized the crayon or chalk markings on the olive bag as typical of the inspection procedure of Mexican Customs at Nuevo Laredo. MEDINA also displayed the photographs to several Transportes del Norte drivers, and they were of the opinion that the yellow inscriptions on the olive bag had been placed there by the Mexican Customs Inspector at Nuevo Laredo.

On May 4, 1964, SEBASTIAN PEREZ HERNANDEZ, assistant desk clerk at the Hotel del Comercio, Calle Bernardino de Sahagun No. 19, Mexico City, advised that he could not recognize the photographs of either the olive or the blue-colored luggage as having been in the possession of a guest at that hotel.

On May 8, 1964, GUILLERMO GARCIA LUNA, owner of the Hotel del Comercio, affirmed that he was unable to recognize the photographs of the two bags as having any connection with OSWALD or any other guest at the Hotel del Comercio.

MATILDE GARNICA, maid at the Hotel del Comercio, who claimed to remember OSWALD as a guest at the hotel in room No. 18, examined photographs of the luggage on May 8, 1964, and stated she recognized the small, blue, zippered handbag as the luggage which OSWALD had in his room at the hotel. She pointed out that she had been impressed by the fact that he had very few personal effects, had noticed he did some laundry each day and left the wet articles hanging in the bathroom, and she was quite certain she had not seen the larger, olive-colored bag.

On May 9, 1964, PEDRO RODRIGUEZ LEDESMA, night watchman at the Hotel del Comercio, examined the photographs referred to above and stated he was quite certain OSWALD had been carrying the blue handbag on the morning of his departure from the hotel. He claimed to be unable to definitely affirm that OSWALD had been carrying the olive bag, as he could not remember several of its characteristics, but he expressed the firm conviction that OSWALD had been carrying two pieces of luggage. He related that on the morning of his departure OSWALD carried his own luggage down the two flights of stairs and waited in the reception area while RODRIGUEZ went in search of a taxi.

When RODRIGUEZ returned with the taxi, he carried the luggage from the reception area to the taxicab, and still has the strong impression that he had a bag in each hand. RODRIGUEZ admitted that his recollection of the type and color of the luggage is very hazy, and he does not wish to state definitely that he recognizes the photograph of either piece of luggage in connection with OSWALD.

INQUIRIES AT HOTEL CUBA

PATRICIA WINSTON and PAMELA MUMFORD, who were passengers on the same bus with OSWALD from Monterrey, Nuevo Leon, Mexico, to Mexico, D. F., September 26-27, 1963, when interviewed December 17, 1963, related that during the bus trip OSWALD recommended that they stay at the Hotel Cuba in Mexico City. They related that OSWALD claimed he had stayed at that hotel several times before and pointed out that the hotel was inexpensive, mentioning, however, that he was not staying at the Hotel Cuba during his current trip.

Inquiry was conducted to establish whether OSWALD had, in fact, stayed at the Hotel Cuba during a period following his return to the United States from Russia in June, 1962, to November, 1963.

On December 27, 1963, a second confidential source who has furnished reliable information in the past advised that an exhaustive search of the records of the Hotel Cuba located at Calle Republica de Cuba No. 69, Mexico City, for the period June, 1962, to October, 1963, failed to disclose any registration for OSWALD under his name or known aliases.

A seventh confidential source abroad advised as follows:

On March 11, 1964, ANGEL CELORIO, manager, Hotel Cuba, made available records of the hotel, which were rechecked for the period June 9, 1962, to November 22, 1963, and no record could be located for the name of LEE HARVEY OSWALD or his known aliases, O. H. LEE and ALEK JAMES HIDELL. The records did contain a registration for one ROBERTO LEE, who registered

1 NO 100-16601/jas

On December 16, 1963, Mr. MAJOR GREEN, Manager, Continental Trailways Bus Lines, 1314 Tulane Avenue, New Orleans, furnished the following information to SAA JAMES E. SCHMIDT, JR.:

There are four separate buses leaving New Orleans for Houston, Texas. These buses can be identified from the schedule now in effect, which was also in effect during September, 1963. He advised the cost of a one-way ticket from New Orleans is $9.70 and a round-trip ticket costs $17.50.

The daily bus schedules in effect in September, 1963, from New Orleans to Houston, Texas, are as follows:

LEAVING NEW ORLEANS	ARRIVING HOUSTON
8:15 PM	7:00 AM (Next day)
4:40 PM	2:15 AM (Next day)
12:20 PM	10:50 PM (Same day)
6:00 AM	4:30 PM (Same day)

All bus operators leaving New Orleans can be identified through Mr. MAJOR GREEN, if necessary by his contacting the Trailways Alexandria Office.

12

COMMISSION EXHIBIT No. 2533

Form No. 1588 (Revised)
MEMORANDUM REPORT
(7-1-60)

UNITED STATES SECRE[redacted]
TREASURY DEPART_

Commission Exhibit No. 2534

ORIGIN Chief's Office	OFFICE Dallas, Texas	FILE NO. CO-2-34,030
TYPE OF CASE: Protective Research	STATUS: Continued	TITLE OR CAPTION: Assassination of President Kennedy
INVESTIGATION MADE AT: Dallas, Texas	PERIOD COVERED: 8-28-64	
INVESTIGATION MADE BY: SA Roger C. Warner		

DETAILS

SYNOPSIS

Schedule of buses travelling from Dallas and Houston to Laredo, Texas.

DETAILS OF INVESTIGATION:

Reference is made to a telephone call from Inspector Thomas Kelley to SAIC Forrest V. Sorrels on 8-27-64, requesting Continental Trailways Bus schedules effective 9-25-63 for Dallas to Laredo and Houston to Laredo.

Other Investigations

On 8-28-64 at the General Offices, Continental Trailways Bus Lines, Dallas, Texas, I examined Continental bus schedules effective 9-25-63. Examination of these schedules revealed the following:

A Continental Trailways Bus departs Dallas, Texas at 11 P.M. This bus travels through San Antonio, Texas, to Alice, Texas, and arrives at Alice at 10:25 A.M. At this point, persons travelling to Laredo, Texas, change buses and board bus no. 304 which departs Alice, Texas, at 10:35 A.M., arriving Laredo, Texas, at 1:20 P.M. (See Attachment 2)

Persons departing Continental Trailways Bus, Houston, Texas, at 2:35 A.M, arrive at Corpus Christi, Texas, at 8:15 P.M. At that point, they change buses, boarding bus no. 304, and departing Corpus Christi at 8:50 A.M. This bus then travels to Alice, Texas, arriving at 10:05 A.M., and connects with Continental Trailways Bus arriving from Dallas and San Antonio. Bus no. 304 then departs Alice, Texas, at 10:35 A.M., arriving at Laredo at 1:20 P.M.

Persons travelling on to Mexico City then must transport themselves between the Continental Trailways Terminal at Laredo and the Greyhound Bus Terminal

DISTRIBUTION	COPIES	REPORT MADE BY	DATE
Chief	Orig & 2 w/atts	Roger C. Warner, SPECIAL AGENT	8-28-64
Dallas	2 cc	APPROVED Forrest V. Sorrels, SPECIAL AGENT IN CHARGE	8-28-64

(CONTINUE ON PLAIN PAPER)

COMMISSION EXHIBIT No. 2534

2.
CO-2-34,030

at Laredo, a distance of approximately 5 blocks. At that point, they may board a Mexican national bus line, Autobuses Blancos Flecha Roja Bus Line. This line departs Laredo, Texas, at 1:45 P.M., arriving in Mexico City at 9:45 A.M., the next day. (Schedule Houston to Laredo, Texas, via Corpus Christi and Alice - Attachment No. 3)

Attached is a schematic sketch locating routes between Dallas and Houston which meet at Alice, Texas, at approximately 10:35 A.M. (Attachment No. 1)

DISPOSITION

This phase of the investigation is closed.

ATTACHMENTS - Chief

Attachment No. 1 - Routes between Dallas and Houston, meeting at Alice, Texas.
Attachment No. 2 - Schedule Dallas to Laredo, Texas, via San Antonio and Alice.
Attachment No. 3 - Schedule Houston to Laredo, Texas, via Corpus Christi and Alice.

RCW:wd

COMMISSION EXHIBIT No. 2534—Continued

CO-2-34,030

Attachment No. 1

SCHEMATIC OF PERSONS TRAVELING TO MEXICO AND MEETING
AT ALICE, TEXAS
(September 25, 1963)

Party A (September 25, 1963

Depart Dallas - 11:00 P.M.

Arrive Alice, Texas - 10:25 A.M.

(Change to Continental Bus
Run No. 304 to Laredo, Texas)

Party B (September 26, 1963)

Depart Houston - 2:35 A.M.

Arrive Corpus Christi - 8:15 A.M.

(Change to Continental Bus Run
No. 304 to Laredo, Texas)

Depart Corpus Christi - 8:50 A.M.

Arrive Alice, Texas - 10:05 A.M.

Party A & B

Depart Alice, Texas - 10:35 A.M.

Arrive Laredo, Texas - 1:20 P.M. (September 26, 1963)
(Continental Trailways Terminal)

COMMISSION EXHIBIT No. 2534—Continued

Dallas - San Antonio - Alice - Freer
Laredo - Monterrey - Mexico City

READ DOWN ✱			Effective 9-11-61 8303	READ UP		
DAILY AM	DAILY AM	DAILY PM		DAILY PM	DAILY AM	DAILY AM
7 00	2 00	11 00	Lv•DALLAS,TEX..........8252.CTS.Ar	10 05	12 50	5 30
3 35	10 15	6 30	Ar•SAN ANTONIO,TEX.....8252.CTS.Lv	1 45	5 00	10 00
109	107	103	RUN NUMBERS	102	104	108
4 05	1 15	7 45	Lv•SAN ANTONIO,TEX..........CTS.Ar	1 10	4 15	9 30
F	F	F	Lv Leming..........Lv	F	F	F
4 55	2 05	8 33	Lv•Pleasanton..........Lv	12 20	3 25	F
5 20	2 30	8 57	Lv•Campbellton..........Lv	11 52	2 57	F
5 30	2 40	F	Lv Whitsett..........Lv	11 42	2 47	F
F	F	F	Lv Sunniland..........Lv	F	F	F
5 50	3 00	9 25	Ar•Three Rivers.......LB.......Lv	11 26	2 31	7 48
5 52	3 02	9 25	Lv•Three Rivers.......LB.......Ar	11 26	2 31	7 47
6 05	3 15	9 37	Ar•George West.......LB.......Lv	11 11	2 16	7 35
6 05	3 15	9 37	Lv•George West.......LB.......Ar	11 10	2 15	7 35
R6 55	R4 05	10 25	Ar•ALICE..........Lv	10 20	1 25	6 45
326	302	304	RUN NUMBERS	321	303	305
7 10	4 15	10 35	Lv•ALICE..........Ar	10 15	R1 15	R6 30
7 26	4 30	10 50	Lv•San Diego..........Lv	9 59	12 59	6 15
↓	5 05	↓	Ar•FREER..........Lv	↑	12 25	↑
↓	5 05	↓	Lv•FREER..........Ar	↑	12 20	↑
7 51	5 35	11 15	Lv•Benavides..........Lv	9 34	↑	5 50
8 07	F	11 31	Lv•Realitos..........Lv	9 18	↑	5 30
R8 27	R6 05	R11 51	Ar•HEBBRONVILLE..........Lv	8 58	↑	5 15
8 37	6 15	12 01	Lv•HEBBRONVILLE..........Ar	R8 48	↑	R5 05
8 55	6 33	12 18	Lv•Bruni..........Lv	8 30	↑	4 47
9 06	6 44	12 29	Lv•Oilton..........Lv	8 19	↑	4 36
Δ	6 51	12 36	Lv•Mirando City..........Lv	8 12	↑	4 29
9 19	F	F	Lv Aguilares..........Lv	8 03	↑	F
9 55	7 35	1 20	Ar•LAREDO,TEX..........CTS.Lv	7 25	11 00	3 45
	8 00	1 45	Lv LAREDO,TEX.......2042..AB.Ar		10 00	2 00
	8 30	2 15	Ar NUEVO LAREDO,TAMPS.,MEX......Lv		9 45	1 30
	8 30	3 15	Lv NUEVO LAREDO,TAMPS..........Ar		9 30	1 45
	12 30	7 15	Ar MONTERREY,N.L..........Lv		5 45	10 00
	1 00	7 30	Lv MONTERREY,N.L..........Ar		5 30	9 50
	10 30	5 30	Ar TAMPICO,TAMPS..........Lv		6 15	↑
		↓	Lv C.VALLES,S.L.P..........Ar		↑	↑
		9 45	Ar MEXICO CITY,D.F.,MEX.2042.AB.Lv		3 15	7 30

AB- Autobuses Blancos. CTS- Continental Trailways. Δ- Operates to Mirando City road only, except for passengers holding tickets from other points. LB- ''Lock Box'' or other provisions for leaving inbound express during hours when station is closed.

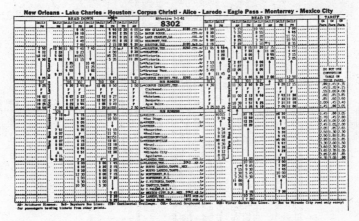

Dallas to Laredo via San Antonio and Alice, Texas. (Red asterisk denotes schedule of Party B)

COMMISSION EXHIBIT No. 2534—Continued

CONTINENTAL TRAILWAYS

Corpus Christi - Laredo & Old Mexico

New Orleans - Lake Charles - Houston - Corpus Christi - Alice - Laredo - Eagle Pass - Monterrey - Mexico City

READ DOWN						✱			Effective 3-1-61 8302	READ UP								TARIFF		
DAILY PM	DAILY PM	DAILY AM	DAILY PM	DAILY AM	DAILY PM	DAILY PM	DAILY PM	DAILY AM		DAILY PM	DAILY PM	DAILY AM	DAILY PM	DAILY AM	DAILY AM	DAILY PM	DAILY PM	OW Fare	OW Fare	OW Fare
			8 15			5 40	12 20	6 00	Lv NEW ORLEANS,LA.......8180.CTS.Ar	11 30		5 15		10 55			7 00			
			10 10			6 55	2 35	8 15	Lv BATON ROUGE..........CTS.Ar	9 30		3 20		8 55			6 45			
			4 00			9 35	9 35	2 15	Lv LAKE CHARLES,LA..........CGL.Ar	4 10		9 05		4 20			11 55			
			4 40			12 05	8 15	2 10	Lv BEAUMONT,TEX..........CTS.Ar	4 00		9 25		3 30			10 55			
			7 00			2 15	10 50	4 30	Ar HOUSTON,TEX.......8180.B&B.Lv	1 15		7 20		1 10	←		8 35			
2 50	12 30	11 30	7 40	7 40		2 35	←	8 05	Lv•HOUSTON,TEX.......8260.CTS.Ar	11 05	4 55	4 55	9 15	11 20	12 35		6 15			
4 32	2 23	↓	9 23	↓		4 00		9 38	Lv•WHARTON..........Ar	↑	2 53	↑	7 33	↑	11 10		4 44			
L8 10	4 00	↓	R10 55	↓		R5 25		R11 10	Ar•Victoria..........Lv	↑	1 20	↑	6 00	↑	9 45		3 15			
6 30	4 20	↓	11 15	↓		5 35		11 20	Lv•Victoria..........Ar	↑	1 00	↑	12 42	↑	9 25		3 05			
↓	↓	2 35	↓	10 46		↓		↓	Lv•Palacios..........Ar	7 53	↑	2 07	↑	8 08	↑		↑			
↓	↓	3 17	↓	11 25		↓		↓	Lv•Port Lavaca..........Ar	7 12	↑	1 27	↑	7 27	↑		↑			
↓	↓	4 00	↓	1 02		↓		↓	Lv•Aransas Pass..........Ar	5 49	↑	12 04	↑	6 04	↑		↑	DO NOT USE CONVERSION TABLE ON THESE FARES		
↓	8 37	↓	↓	↓		↓		↓	Lv•Beeville..........Ar	↑	11 45	↑	↑	↑	↑		↑			
9 05	↓	4 25	1 35	1 35		8 15		1 40	Ar•CORPUS CHRISTI,TEX...8260.....Lv	5 15	↑	11 35	3 00	5 30	7 00		12 50			
314		316	302		310	304		312	RUN NUMBERS	313		311	303	317		305	315			
9 25	↓	6 30	2 45	←	12 05	8 50		1 50	Lv•CORPUS CHRISTI,TEX..........Ar	4 30	↑	11 30	2 50	5 25	↑	8 20	12 15	.00	1.45	4.35
F	↓	F	F		F	F		F	Clarkwood..........	F	↑	F	F	F		F	F	.45	1.70	4.15
F	↓	F	F		F	F		F	Violet..........	F	↑	F	F	F		F	F	.55	1.00	4.00
10 02	↓	6 07	3 22		12 42	9 27		F	•Robstown..........	F	↑	11 00	2 13	4 46		7 43	11 38	.60	.85	3.85
10 12	↓	6 17	3 32		12 52	9 37		F	Banquete..........	F	↑	F	2 03	F		7 33	11 28	.85	.60	3.60
10 24	↓	6 29	3 44		1 04	9 49		F	Agua Dulce..........	F	↑	10 39	1 51	4 25		7 21	11 18	1.00	.45	3.40
10 40	7 00	6 44	R6 00		1 20	R10 05		2 50	Ar•ALICE..........Lv	3 25	10 25	10 25	1 35	4 10		7 05	11 00	1.45	.00	3.05
	326								RUN NUMBERS		321									
	7 10	←	4 15			10 35			Lv•ALICE..........Ar		R10 15	↑	R1 15			R6 30		1.45	.00	3.05
	7 26		4 30			10 50			•San Diego..........		9 59		12 59			6 15		1.70	.45	2.80
	↓		5 05			↓			Ar•FREER..........Lv		↑		12 25			↑		2.45	1.05	2.00
	↓		5 05			↓			Lv•FREER..........Ar		↑		12 20			↑		2.45	1.05	2.00
	7 51		5 35			11 15			•Benavides..........		9 34		↑			5 50		2.05	.85	2.65
	8 07		F			11 31			•Realitos..........		9 18		↑			5 30		2.50	1.30	2.30
	R8 27		R6 05			R11 51			Ar•HEBBRONVILLE..........Lv		8 58		↑			5 15		2.90	1.65	1.85
	8 37		6 15			12 01			Lv•HEBBRONVILLE..........Ar		R8 48		↑			R5 05		2.90	1.65	1.85
	8 55		6 33			12 18			•Bruni..........		8 30		↑			4 47		3.30	2.00	1.50
	9 06		6 44			12 29			•Oilton..........		8 19		↑			4 36		3.60	2.30	1.20
	Δ		6 51			12 36			•Mirando City..........		8 12		↑			4 29		3.65	2.35	1.05
	9 19		F			F			Aguilares..........		8 03		↑			F		3.85	2.65	.85
	9 55		7 35		←	1 20			Ar•LAREDO,TEX..........CTS.Lv		7 25		11 00			3 45		4.35	3.05	.00
			8 00		3 00	1 45			Lv•LAREDO,TEX.......2042..AB.Ar				10 00			2 00				
			8 30		3 30	2 15			Ar NUEVO LAREDO,TAMPS.,MEX......Lv			→	9 45			1 30				
			8 30		4 00	3 15			Lv NUEVO LAREDO,TAMPS..........Ar			7 15	9 30			1 45				
			12 30		8 00	7 15			Ar MONTERREY,N.L..........Lv			3 30	5 45			10 00				
			1 00		8 30	7 30			Lv MONTERREY,N.L..........Ar			3 25	5 30			9 50				
			5 30		1 00	↓			Ar C.VICTORIA,TAMPS..........Lv			11 00	↑			↑				
			10 30		5 30	↓			Ar TAMPICO,TAMPS..........Lv			6 15	↑			↑				
						↓			Ar C.VALLES,S.L.P..........Lv				↑			↑				
						9 45			Ar MEXICO CITY,D.F.,MEX..2042.AB.Lv				3 15			7 30				
						2 20			Lv LAREDO,TEX..........1872.WGB.Ar				10 25							
						5 20			Ar EAGLE PASS,TEX.......1872.WGB.Lv				7 20							

Thru Bus Houston—Alice—Laredo No Change

Thru Bus Laredo—Alice—Houston No Change

AB- Autobuses Blancos. B&B- Bayshore Bus Lines. CTS- Continental Trailways. CGL- Central Greyhound Lines. WGB- Winter Garden Bus Lines. Δ- Bus to Mirando City road only except for passengers holding tickets from other points.

Houston Laredo via Corpus Christi and Alice, Texas. (Red asterisk denotes schedule of Party A)

COMMISSION EXHIBIT No. 2534—Continued

UNITED STATES DEPARTMENT OF JUSTICE
FEDERAL BUREAU OF INVESTIGATION

In Reply, Please Refer to
File No.

WASHINGTON, D.C. 20535

April 7, 1964

LEE HARVEY OSWALD

BASIS FOR INQUIRY

The information recorded below was made available by a confidential source abroad.

The files of the Department of Immigration, Mexican Ministry of "Gobernacion" (Interior or Government), revealed that Lee Harvey Oswald departed from Mexico on October 3, 1963, at Nuevo Laredo, Tamaulipas. The files of the Department of Immigration showed further that on October 3, 1963, from 12:00 midnight until 8:00 AM, immigration official ALBERTO ARZAMENDI CHAPA was in charge of the "Kilometer 26" highway checking station, where tourist cards are picked up from aliens leaving Mexico by highway travel through Nuevo Laredo. The name and date stamp of ARZAMENDI CHAPA on the original tourist card surrendered by OSWALD upon his departure from Mexico on that date was evidence of the fact that his exit from Mexico occurred during those hours.

Source reported that considerable investigation had been conducted by several different agencies of the Mexican Government for the purpose of ascertaining subject's method of travel on departure and that, in view of the fact that the name "OSWLD" had been located on a passenger list for the 1:00 PM trip of the "Transportes Frontera" bus line from Mexico City to Nuevo

COMMISSION EXHIBIT No. 2535

Laredo, Tamaulipas, on October 2, 1963, it was considered that OSWALD had traveled thereon.

Considerable investigation with respect to the passenger list mentioned above, including a check of the ticket stubs at the Monterrey, Nuevo Leon, headquarters of the company, interview of bus drivers and passengers, and numerous interviews of employees of the Mexico City terminal of the bus line, failed to confirm that OSWALD, in fact, had been a passenger on the "Transportes Frontera" bus in question.

CHECKS OF RECORDS OF OTHER BUS LINES

A second confidential source abroad provided the following information:

On March 30, 1964, officials of the "Autobuses Blancos Flecha Roja, S. A.," bus line made available passenger lists for the four scheduled trips of that company from Mexico City to Nuevo Laredo of October 2, 1963, and no information identifiable with OSWALD by any of the names he was known to have used was located on those lists. It was determined, however, that, if the time schedules of that company are maintained, none of its trips to Nuevo Laredo would arrive at the "Kilometer 26" highway checking station between midnight and 8:00 AM.

On the basis of several contacts with Mr. RICARDO MEDINA BELTRAN, Manager of the Mexico City terminal of the "Autobuses Transportes del Norte" bus line (hereinafter referred to as Transportes del Norte), information was received from him to the effect that "Secret Service agents, Presidential investigators, Federal Security agents, and others" had reviewed the passenger lists maintained by his company for its service between Mexico City and Laredo, Texas, and that he had assisted in those checks, which failed to disclose any information identifiable with OSWALD.

MEDINA explained that the passenger list actually is a card form on which reservations and ticket sales are recorded and that after the particular trip for which it was prepared has left the terminal it is cancelled to avoid further

COMMISSION EXHIBIT No. 2535—Continued

confusion, as the reverse side of the form is utilized for a similar record at a later date. He stated that the cancelled lists are not a permanent record and are maintained only for a short period of time following their use. He stated that he had set aside the lists for early October, 1963, in the event there should be further need for them; nevertheless, he was unable to locate them. He pointed out that apparently they had been placed inadvertently in a storeroom where tires, spare parts, boxes of obsolete files and records, and other materials are maintained and that only a thorough review of all material in the storeroom would reveal whether or not the list for October 2, 1963, was still in existence. He related that his company has two direct trips daily to Nuevo Laredo, Tamaulipas, and Laredo, Texas, and that the bus which departs from Mexico City at 8:30 AM is scheduled to arrive in Nuevo Laredo at 2:00 AM the following morning and would arrive at the "Kilometer 26" checking station at approximately 1:00 AM.

TRANSPORTES DEL NORTE PASSENGER LIST FOR OCTOBER 2, 1963

On March 30, 1964, Mr. MEDINA advised that he had located the passenger-reservations list for the 8:30 AM bus of October 2, 1963, and, on the basis of consultation with him and with several reservations and ticket clerks who recognized their handwriting thereon, the following data was obtained therefrom as translated from Spanish:

Wednesday TRANSPORTES DEL NORTE Wednesday

MEXICO TO LAREDO

Bus No. 332 October 2, 1963 8:30

Drivers R. (ROGELIO) CUEVAS - R. (RAMON) GONZALEZ

Seat (No.)	Name of Passenger	Destination	Ticket No.
2	Miss COSIO	S.A.	13920
3	Mr. A. MARTINEZ	N. Ldo.	12619
4	MARGARET A. WOLFF	Ldo.	61840 exchange
5	ROBERTO P. GONZALEZ	Mty.	7915
6	M. H. VILLANUEVA	Mty.	99232
7	PAULA RUSIONI	Ldo.	9511
8	J. M. DE CUBA	Ldo.	8940
9	" "	"	41
10	Operator		
11	AUGUSTO AGUILAR	Houston	13742
12	Chihuahuenses	Laredo, Tex.	13688
13			
14	Mr. EULALIO RODRIGUEZ	Houston	13921
15	A Viajes	Ldo.	13619
16	PH. VAN DER VORM	Laredo, Tex.	13927
17	JORGE DAVILA	Mty.	716
18	JOSE BARRIGA	Dallas	13740
19	and wife	"	741
20			
21	Mr. or Miss AGAPITO DEL RIO	S.A.	13928
22	Guadalajara	Laredo	
23	"		
24	"		
25	"		
26	"		
27	"		
28	"		
29	"		

MEDINA explained that seats No. 12 and No. 15 had been reserved for another bus line or travel agencies and that the company would have no record with respect to the identities of the occupants of those seats.

On March 31, 1964, Miss ROSA MARIA OROZCO, Auditor of the "Auto Viajes Internacionales, S. A.," travel agency (International Auto Travels, Inc.), Lafragua No. 4, Mexico, D. F., advised that she had located a record of the sale by that firm of a ticket for travel on seat No. 15 of the 8:30 AM, October 2, 1963, bus of Transportes del Norte to Laredo to ANASTACIO RUIZ MEZA. She stated that the company had sold this transportation to RUIZ MEZA for travel via the Transportes del Norte bus line to Laredo and from Laredo to Chicago, Illinois, by Greyhound Line.

RECORD OF LOCATION OF
TRANSPORTATION SOLD TO H. O. LEE

A third confidential source abroad provided the information recorded hereinunder:

On April 1, 1964, MACLOVIO PORTILLO G., Superintendent of the Mexico City terminal of the bus line, "Transportes Chihuahuenses, S. A. de C. V.," (Chihuahuenses Transportation, Incorporated with Variable Capital) Bernal Diaz No. 5, Mexico, D. F., and his clerk, MARIA TERESA CASARES, caused the records of that bus line to be searched for all tickets issued for travel on October 2, 1963, in an effort to locate the names LEE HARVEY OSWALD, O. H. LEE, ALEK JAMES HIDELL, and V. L. LEE with particular attention to ticket No. 13688.

PORTILLO advised that no information had been located which could be identified with the foregoing, explaining that tickets sold by his company during that period were in the eighty and ninety thousand series, eliminating the possibility that ticket No. 13688 might have been sold at that office.

PORTILLO suggested that the transportation concerning which inquiry was being made might have been sold at the "Agencia de Viajes, Transportes Chihuahuenses, S. A. de C. V.," (Chihuahuenses Transportation Travel Agency, Inc.) with offices at Paseo de la Reforma No. 52, Room 5. He telephoned

to that agency and was advised by a clerk, ALEJANDRINA M. DE BUTCHER, that the reservation order under No. 13688 was available at that office.

On April 1, 1963, Miss TERESA SCHAEFFER BEQUERISSE, Manager of the above-mentioned travel agency, located the reservation and purchase order No. 13688, and it was determined to be in blank, never having been utilized. She reviewed the Transportes del Norte passenger list for bus No. 332 for October 2, 1963, considering that the order number might be 12688, and this order No. 12688 was located and also found to be blank. She insisted that her office had not handled the reservation noted on the Transportes del Norte passenger list shown her for October 2, 1963. She was requested to review all reservation and purchase orders issued for October, 1963, by her office.

A review of the carbon copies of these reservation and purchase orders was made by the confidential source abroad in the presence of Miss SCHAEFFER, which revealed that reservation and purchase order No. 14618 was issued to Transportes del Norte in Mexico City for Mr. H. O. LEE for seat No. 12 from Mexico City to Laredo, Texas, on Wednesday, October 2, 1963, at 8:30 AM. This information was printed in Spanish, and the reservation was confirmed by a Mr. SAUCEDO. At the bottom of this printed order the date was indicated to be September 30, 1963, and the cost was listed as 93.75 "moneda nacional" (national money or Mexican pesos comparable to $7.50 U.S.). Also at the bottom of this printed order was the printed notice that the "Agencia de Viajes, Transportes Chihuahuenses" is an agent for the Greyhound Bus Line.

Miss SCHAEFFER advised that former employee ROLANDO BARRIOS had signed the reservation and purchase order and apparently made the sale to Mr. H. O. LEE. She stated the original of this form was given to the purchaser in order that he could then obtain his ticket at Transportes del Norte, explaining that an original and two copies of the reservation and purchase order are made and the original is given to the purchaser, one copy is kept at her office, and the third copy is forwarded to the main office of the travel agency which is "Transportes Chihuahuenses, S. A. de C. V.," Avenida 16 de Septiembre No. 274, Ciudad Juarez, Chihuahua, Mexico. She made available the carbon copy of the above-mentioned purchase order and stated she would search her files for any other pertinent records.

Subsequently she advised on the same date by telephone that she had located Greyhound International Exchange Order No. 43599 for presentation to the Greyhound agent at Laredo, Texas, and issued to Mr. H. O. LEE. This order was issued against the Western Greyhound Lines, 371 Market Street, San Francisco 5, California, for travel from Laredo, Texas, to Dallas, Texas, via San Antonio, Texas.

A fourth confidential source abroad advised that on April 1, 1964, Miss SCHAEFFER made available a copy of the Greyhound International Exchange Order mentioned above, which noted that Mr. H. O. LEE was traveling to the port of exit via Transportes del Norte. The order reflected it was issued on October 1, 1963, for $12.80 U.S. by the "Agencia de Viajes, T. Ch. S. A. de C. V.," Reforma 52-5, Mexico City. According to Miss SCHAEFFER, the signature of the issuing agent on this order form was that of ROLANDO BARRIOS.

Miss SCHAEFFER's bookkeeper, Miss NORMA ROMAN, made available the agency's cash receipt and disbursement ledger which Miss SCHAEFFER described as a record of cash receipts and disbursements of the business on a daily basis. These records disclosed that on October 1, 1963, an entry was made in the ledger reflecting receipt of 253.75 pesos ($20.30 U.S.) from Mr. H. O. LEE which was paid to cover the cost of a bus trip from Mexico City to Dallas via Laredo. Miss SCHAEFFER explained that the entry reflecting receipt of cash is made in the cash receipt and disbursement ledger on the day following the actual transaction. She added that of the total 253.75 peso amount, 93.75 pesos ($7.50 U.S.) applied to the portion of the trip from Mexico City to Laredo and 160.00 pesos ($12.80 U.S.) applied to the travel from Laredo to Dallas.

The above record reflected that the total amount of 253.75 pesos was paid on "Agencias de Viaje T. Ch." reservation and purchase order No. 14618 and that H. O. LEE was also issued

- 7 -

COMMISSION EXHIBIT No. 2535—Continued

Greyhound International Exchange Order No. 43599 to cover the trip from Laredo to Dallas.

The above-mentioned cash ledger reflected that the letter "B" appeared beside the name of H. O. LEE, and Miss SCHAEFFER explained that the letter "B" represents the surname initial of ROLANDO BARRIOS, the former employee of the firm who handled the transaction with H. O. LEE.

The cash ledger also revealed that under the figure of 253.75 pesos, the amount of the cash transaction, were illegible handwritten initials, and Miss SCHAEFFER stated that those are the initials of ELSA MAYNEZ, another former employee of the firm, acknowledging receipt of the 253.75 pesos by MAYNEZ from BARRIOS for entry in the cash ledger book.

Miss SCHAEFFER advised that ROLANDO BARRIOS was involved in a financial problem with her agency for which she discontinued his services. She furnished his home address as Bahia de Santa Barbara No. 20-209, Mexico, D. F., and stated he was last known to be employed at the Mauna Loa Restaurant in Mexico City.

On April 1, 1964, Miss SCHAEFFER made available a copy of a form captioned: "Western Greyhound Lines (Division of the Greyhound Corporation), 371 Market Street, San Francisco, California, International Sales Report." This sales report covers the period from October 1, 1963, to October 31, 1963, and Miss SCHAEFFER advised that recorded on this form is a recapitulation of travel sales during the month of October, 1963, made by the agency as agents for the Western Greyhound Lines in connection with which Greyhound International Exchange Orders were issued to the travelers. There were twelve such sales recorded on the above-mentioned sales report, which reflects that the second entry or sale made involved the issuance of Greyhound International Exchange Order No. 43599 to one passenger, Mr. H. O. LEE, for travel from Laredo, Texas, to Dallas, Texas, total fare for that portion of the trip being recorded as $12.80 U.S.

Miss SCHAEFFER advised that the foregoing must be

- 8 -

COMMISSION EXHIBIT No. 2535—Continued

maintained as a matter of permanent record in her office because of Mexican Government regulations.

On April 2, 1964, the third confidential source abroad was advised by Miss SCHAEFFER that MARGARITA LABASTIBA, who also worked in the front office while BARRIOS was present, had informed her that she remembered an American who purchased a travel order but could not recall the date, nor could she state it was OSWALD. Upon interview Miss LABASTIBA could only recall that the American was tall, wore disheveled clothing, and had a great deal of hair. She could not be more specific about the date or the description of the American.

Photographs of LEE HARVEY OSWALD were exhibited to TERESA SCHAEFFER BEQUERISSE, ALEJANDRINA M. DE BUTCHER, NORMA ROMAN, and MARGARITA LABASTIBA at the "Agencia de Viajes, Transportes Chihuahuenses, S. A. de C. V.," offices and these persons were unable to identify OSWALD.

INTERVIEW OF ROLANDO BARRIOS RAMIREZ

On April 2, 1964, the following information was furnished to the second confidential source abroad:

ROLANDO BARRIOS RAMIREZ, Bahia de Santa Barbara No. 20, Apartment 209, Mexico, D. F., advised that formerly he was employed at the Chihuahuenses Travel Agency and now is employed as a cashier at the Mauna Loa Restaurant in Mexico City. BARRIOS reviewed the copy of the reservation and purchase order No. 14618 of the travel agency reflecting the sale on September 30, 1963, of seat No. 12 on the 8:30 AM trip of Transportes del Norte from Mexico City to Laredo, Texas, on October 2, 1963, and definitely identified the handprinting and signature thereon as his own. He also viewed a copy of International Exchange Order No. 43599 dated October 1, 1963, recording the sale to Mr. H. O. LEE of transportation by Greyhound Lines from Laredo, Texas, to Dallas, Texas. He stated that the handprinting and signature on this document were his and that undoubtedly he had handled the transactions represented by the two documents.

BARRIOS viewed photographs of LEE HARVEY OSWALD and

advised that he was unable to affirm positively that he recalled OSWALD in connection with the travel agency. He related that at the time OSWALD's photographs were being published widely in newspapers and magazines he was impressed by the feeling that he had known or met OSWALD at some time, but had been unable to associate the feeling with any particular incident or time.

INTERVIEW OF PERSONNEL AT TRANSPORTES DEL NORTE TERMINAL, MEXICO CITY

On April 3, 1964, the Mexico City Terminal Manager for Transportes del Norte, RICARDO MEDINA BELTRAN, reiterated that he had no recollection whatsoever with respect to OSWALD and explained that he has no contact with passengers except under unusual circumstances since his office is removed from the passenger area of the terminal.

On the same date bus drivers ROGELIO CUEVAS and RAMON GONZALEZ were contacted upon their arrival at the Mexico City terminal and advised that they reside in Monterrey, Nuevo Leon, Mexico, at Magna Vista No. 232 and at Juan Mendez No. 1407 Altos, respectively. Although they had no independent recollection in connection therewith, they were aware of the fact that the company's records reflect that they were the drivers of bus No. 332 between Mexico City and Monterrey on October 2, 1963. They stated that they usually leave the bus at Monterrey, and it was their understanding that on October 2, 1963, all passengers from bus No. 332 were transferred to another unit which transported them to Nuevo Laredo with a relief driver. They viewed all available photographs of LEE HARVEY OSWALD and stated they were unable to recall his having been a passenger. They pointed out that they rarely notice the passengers and would not remember one of them unless an incident or special circumstance created a special reason for noticing and recalling them.

On April 2, 1964, ANGEL CURIEL informed that he is a ticket salesman at the Mexico City terminal of Transportes del Norte and that he recognized his handwriting on the October 2, 1963, passenger list for bus No. 332 in connection with the items listed under "destination" and "ticket number."

He explained that he undoubtedly exchanged ticket No. 13633 for the travel agency purchase order and recorded the number of the ticket before delivering it to the passenger. CURIEL viewed available photographs of OSWALD and stated he could not recall him in connection with his duties at the bus line.

On the same date salesman MIGUEL SAUCEDO advised that the handwriting on the passenger list under "name of passenger" of the word "Chihuahuenses" opposite seat No. 12 indicated that he received the telephonic reservation of the space by the travel agency. SAUCEDO did not recall the matter and was unable to identify photographs of OSWALD in connection therewith.

Ticket salesmen CANUTO S. ROJAS and JUAN GASCON advised that they recognized their handwriting on the October 2, 1963, manifest in connection with some of the reservations and ticket sales, but upon viewing photographs of OSWALD could not recall having seen him at the Mexico City terminal of Transportes del Norte.

MEDINA and the four ticket salesmen mentioned above explained that the diversity of serial numbers for tickets sold on the passenger list in question is occasioned by the fact that they each sell from different blocks of tickets for the various destinations involved.

Commission Exhibit No. 2536

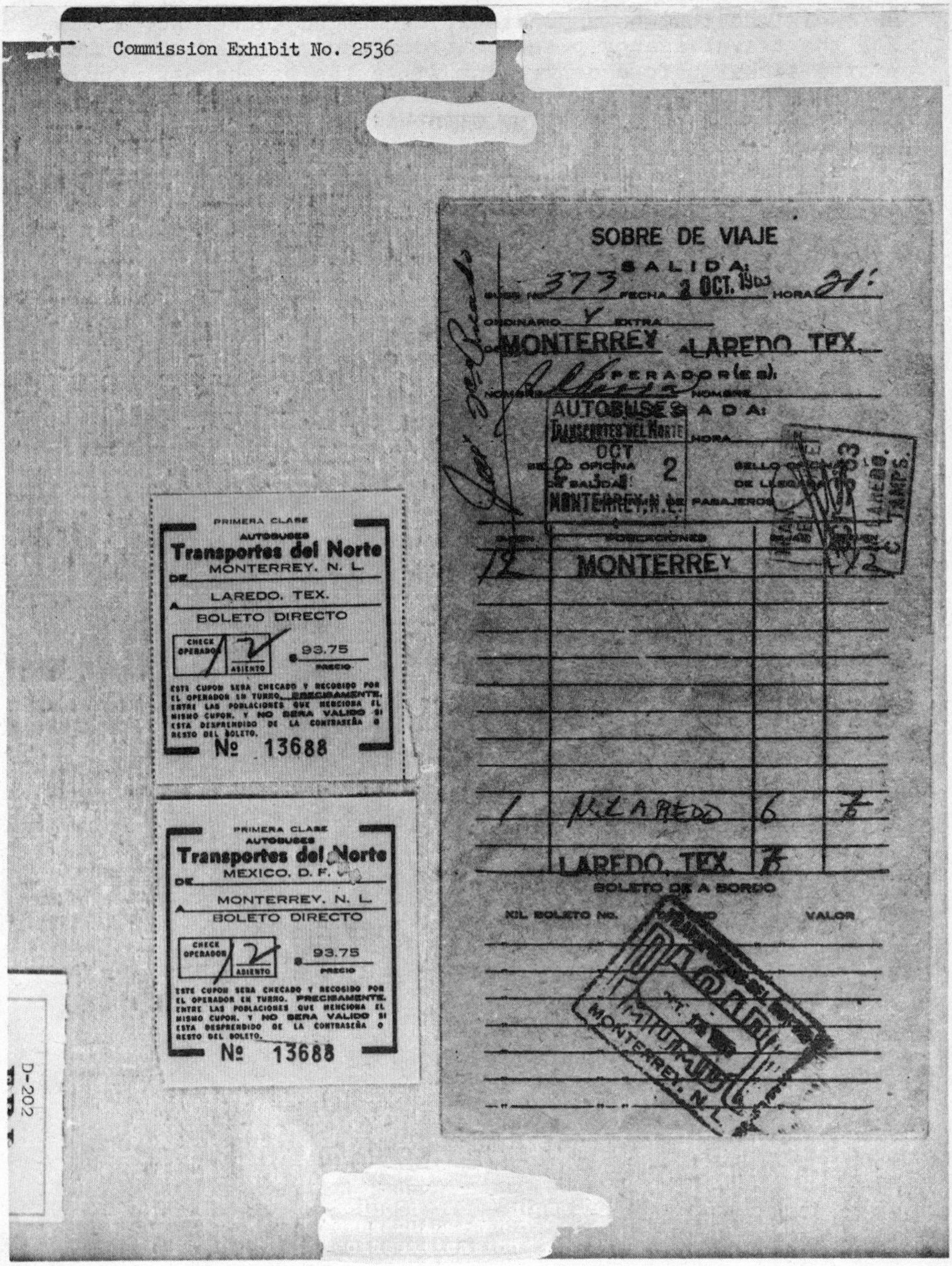

PRIMERA CLASE
AUTOBUSES
Transportes del Norte
DE MONTERREY, N. L.
A LAREDO, TEX.
BOLETO DIRECTO
CHECK OPERADOR 1 | 12 ASIENTO | $ 93.75 PRECIO
ESTE CUPON SERA CHECADO Y RECOGIDO POR EL OPERADOR EN TURNO, PRECISAMENTE, ENTRE LAS POBLACIONES QUE MENCIONA EL MISMO CUPON, Y NO SERA VALIDO SI ESTA DESPRENDIDO DE LA CONTRASEÑA O RESTO DEL BOLETO.
Nº 13688

PRIMERA CLASE
AUTOBUSES
Transportes del Norte
DE MEXICO, D. F.
A MONTERREY, N. L.
BOLETO DIRECTO
CHECK OPERADOR 1 | 12 ASIENTO | $ 93.75 PRECIO
ESTE CUPON SERA CHECADO Y RECOGIDO POR EL OPERADOR EN TURNO, PRECISAMENTE, ENTRE LAS POBLACIONES QUE MENCIONA EL MISMO CUPON, Y NO SERA VALIDO SI ESTA DESPRENDIDO DE LA CONTRASEÑA O RESTO DEL BOLETO.
Nº 13688

SOBRE DE VIAJE
SALIDA:
BUS No. 373 FECHA 2 OCT. 1963 HORA 21:
ORDINARIO ✓ EXTRA
DE MONTERREY A LAREDO, TEX.
OPERADOR(ES):
NOMBRE NOMBRE
AUTOBUSES TRANSPORTES DEL NORTE OCT 2 MONTERREY, N.L.
LLEGADA:
HORA
SELLO OFICINA DE SALIDA
SELLO OFICINA DE LLEGADA
No. DE PASAJEROS

ORDEN	POBLACIONES		
12	MONTERREY		
1	N. LAREDO	6	7
	LAREDO, TEX.	7	

BOLETO DE A BORDO

XIL BOLETO No.		VALOR

D-202

COMMISSION EXHIBIT No. 2536

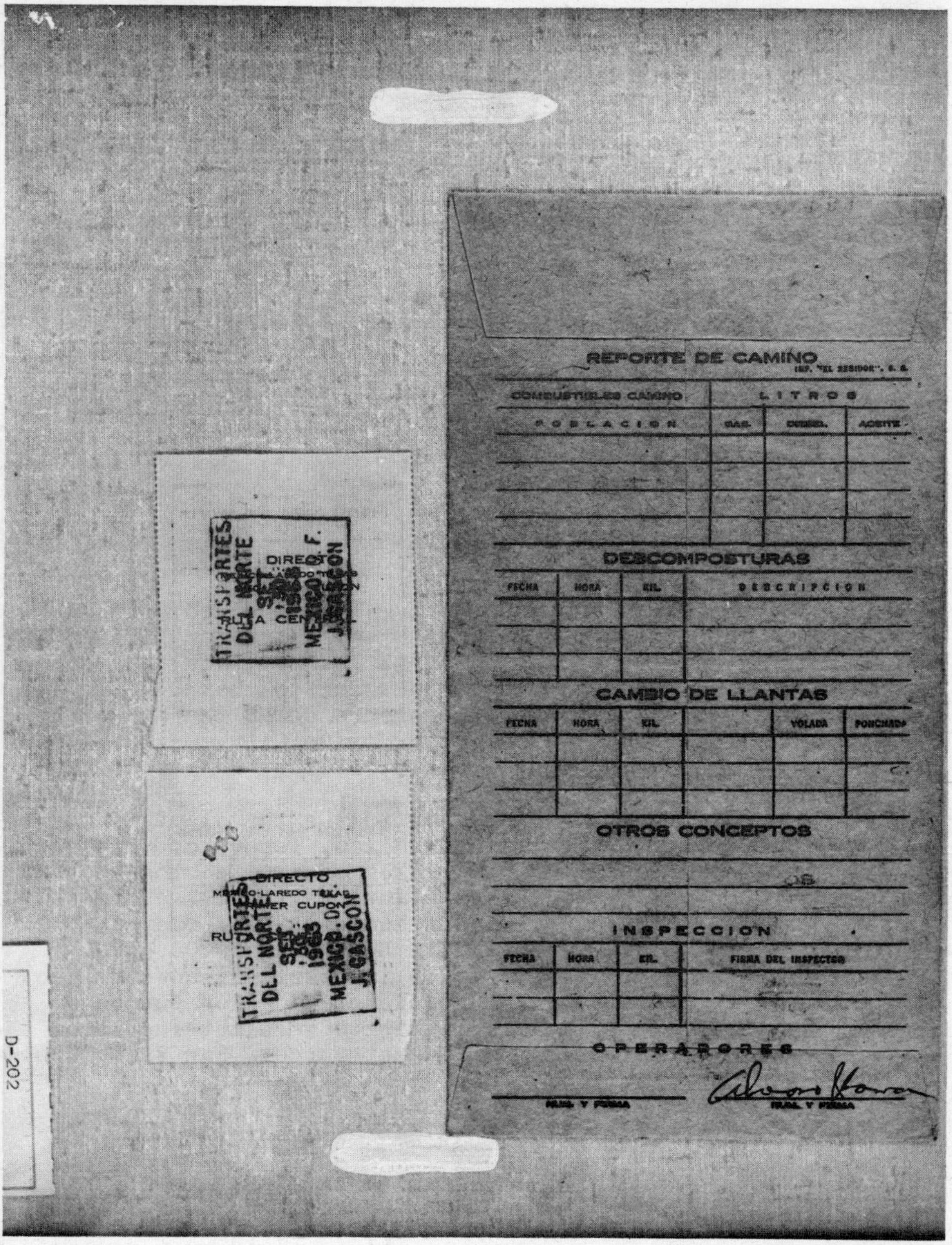

Commission Exhibit No. 2536—Continued

OFFICE OF THE DIRECTOR

UNITED STATES DEPARTMENT OF JUSTICE

FEDERAL BUREAU OF INVESTIGATION

WASHINGTON, D.C. 20535

April 16, 1964

BY COURIER SERVICE

Honorable J. Lee Rankin
General Counsel
The President's Commission
200 Maryland Avenue, N. E.
Washington, D. C.

Dear Mr. Rankin:

Reference is made to our letter dated April 13, 1964, which enclosed two copies of a memorandum in the Lee Harvey Oswald case dated April 7, 1964, and two copies of seven photographs designated Exhibit Number D-202. The enclosures to our letter of reference dealt in part with the travel of one H. O. Lee from Mexico City, Mexico, to Dallas, Texas, on October 2 and 3, 1963.

With further reference to the travel of H. O. Lee between Laredo, Texas, and Dallas, Texas, on October 3, 1963, there are enclosed two copies each of photographs of Exhibit Number D-199, Greyhound International Exchange Order Number 43599, and Exhibit Number D-200, Greyhound Ticket Number 8256009. Exhibits D-199 and D-200 have been processed for latent finger impressions; however, no latent impressions of value for identification purposes were developed on them. The exhibits were obtained from the Western Greyhound Lines, 369 Market Street, San Francisco, California, on April 3, 1964.

Sincerely yours,

J. Edgar Hoover

Enclosures - 8

COMMISSION EXHIBIT NO. 2537

FORM A-10
printed in U.S.A.

(TO PASSENGER)

GREYHOUND

INTERNATIONAL EXCHANGE ORDER

ISSUED BY

WESTERN GREYHOUND LINES

(Division of THE GREYHOUND CORPORATION)

371 MARKET STREET, SAN FRANCISCO 5, CALIF.

PASSENGER NOTE — This order is NOT valid for transportation or other services. It must be exchanged for tickets at point of reissue, as shown below.

REFUND can be secured ONLY in the currency originally paid upon presentation of unused order or tickets to the originating agency.

ON PRESENTATION OF THIS ORDER

43599

GREYHOUND LINES AGENT

AT LAREDO, TEXAS U.S.A (POINT OF REISSUE) WILL ISSUE TO

MR H. O. LEE (NAME OF PASSENGER)

TICKETS AS SHOWN BELOW, VALID FOR MOTOR COACH TRANSPORTATION, AND HOTELS, SIGHT-SEEING OR OTHER FEATURES.

FROM LAREDO, Tex. (ORIGIN) TO DALLAS, Tex. (DESTINATION)

VIA SAN ANTONIO, TEXAS

DIRECT ROUTE ONLY, UNLESS OTHERWISE SPECIFIED ABOVE

PASSENGER TRAVELING TO PORT OF ENTRY VIA T. DEL NORTE (CARRIER)

NAME OF S. S. OR FLIGHT No.

CLASS ____ TICKET No. ____

FROM ____ (POINT OF ORIGIN)

DEPARTURE DATE ____ (FROM POINT OF ORIGIN)

ARRIVAL DATE ____ (AT PORT OF ENTRY)

NO. OF TICKETS	TYPE OF TICKETS	@	AMOUNT
1	O.W. Full Fare	12.80	12.80
	O. W. ½		
	R.T. Full Fare		
	R. T. ½		
	HOTELS — TOUR FEATURES		
	TOTAL COLLECTED		12.80
	NUMBER OF TARIFF OR RATE GUIDE USED	A-20-C	

Entire payment was received by the agency for transportation between points within the United States issued with connecting transportation.

ISSUING OFFICE AGENCIA DE VIAJES T. CH. SA de CV (NAME OF AGENCY)

AT REFORMA 52-5 (STREET ADDRESS) MEXICO CITY (CITY) (COUNTRY)

DATE OF SALE OCTOBER 1st 1963 (SIGNATURE OF AGENT)

COMMISSION EXHIBIT No. 2537—Continued

This order is subject to the regulations of the individual transportation lines over which passenger is to travel. In issuing tickets over routes of other carriers Greyhound Lines acts only as selling agent.

FOR USE OF AGENT AT POINT OF REISSUE

THE FOLLOWING TICKETS ISSUED ON THIS ORDER

COMPANY	FORM NO.	TICKET NOS.	TICKETS OW	TICKETS RT	AMOUNT	
C.G.L.	I	8256009	✓		12	80

OCT 3 - 1963
DATE

R. Figuerina
AGENT

LAREDO, TEXAS
CITY AND STATE

HONORING AGENT
STAMP HERE

AGENCIA DE VIAJES
"T. CH."
OCT 1 1963
REFORMA NUM. 52-5
MEXICO, D. F.

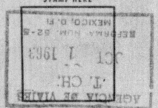

COMMISSION EXHIBIT No. 2537—Continued

GOOD FOR ONE TRIP AS SHOWN BELOW.

PLACE OF ISSUE: CENTRAL GREYHOUND LAREDO TEXAS 06

DATE OF ISSUE: 10 -3 63

BGGE. ☆ ☆ ☆ PUNCH

PASSENGER TICKET

GREYHOUND®

ISSUING CARRIER WILL BE RESPONSIBLE ONLY FOR TRANSPORTATION ON ITS OWN LINES, in accordance with tariff regulations and limitations, AND ASSUMES NO RESPONSIBILITY FOR ANY ACTS OR OMISSIONS OF OTHERS OCCURRING WITHIN OR OUTSIDE THE UNITED STATES except as imposed by law with respect to baggage. Seating aboard vehicles operated in interstate or foreign commerce is without regard to race, color, creed, or national origin. ONE WAY FARES LIMITED TO 2 MONTHS. ROUND TRIP FARES LIMITED TO 1 YEAR. SPECIAL FARES LIMITED AS ENDORSED.

FROM LAREDO TEX REISSU OW

TO Dallas Tex. REISSU O6L

REISSU

REISSU

REISSU

ENDORSEMENTS

F.E.O. 43599

Org. MEXico

PRINTED IN U.S.A.

VOID IF DETACHED

8 7 6 5 4 3 2 1

FARE 12.80

FORM 1

TICKET NUMBER 8256009

COMMISSION EXHIBIT No. 2537—Continued

COMMISSION EXHIBIT No. 2537—Continued

FD-204 (Rev. 3-3-59)

Commission Exhibit No. 2538

UNITED STATES DEPARTMENT OF JUSTICE
FEDERAL BUREAU OF INVESTIGATION

Copy to:

Report of: JOHN P. MC HUGH | Office: SAN FRANCISCO
Date: 4-6-64
Field Office File #: 89-58 | Bureau File #: 105-82555

Title: LEE HARVEY OSWALD

Character: INTERNAL SECURITY - R - CUBA

Synopsis:

Records, Western Greyhound Lines, 369 Market Street, San Francisco, contained an International Exchange Order number 43599 issued in Mexico City on 10-1-63 to one Mr. H. O. LEE for travel from Laredo, Texas to Dallas, Texas via San Antonio. Instant order honored at Laredo, Texas on 10-3-63. Records of the Greyhound Lines, San Francisco, also contained Greyhound ticket number 8256009 issued at Laredo, Texas 10-3-63 for travel from Laredo, Texas to Dallas, Texas, one-way.

\- P -

DETAILS:

COMMISSION EXHIBIT No. 2538

FD-302 (Rev. 1-25-60)

EDERAL BUREAU OF INVESTIGA

1

Date 4-6-64

On April 3, 1964, Mr. JOHN C. CAIN, Auditor of Revenues, Western Greyhound Lines, 369 Market Street, San Francisco, California, furnished the material described below:

Passenger's copy of International Exchange Order number 43599 which reflected that this order was issued by the Agencia de Viajes T. Ch SA de CV, Reforma 52-5, Mexico City, on October 1, 1963.

This International Exchange Order was issued to one Mr. H. O. LEE for travel from Laredo, Texas to Dallas, Texas via San Antonio. The order indicated that travel to the port of entry in the United States would be via T. Del Norte.

The reverse side of the above-mentioned order indicated that the ticket in the amount of $12.80 was for a one-way fare from Laredo, Texas to Dallas, Texas, and, in addition, reflected that the International Exchange Order was honored on October 3, 1963 by agent R. TIJERINA (?) at Laredo, Texas, who issued one-way ticket number 8256009 for the above-mentioned travel.

Mr. CAIN advised that the International Exchange Order referred to above would have been in the passenger's possession from the time it was issued in Mexico City until it was honored at Laredo, Texas, namely from October 1, 1963 to October 3, 1963.

Continuing, Mr. CAIN advised that ticket number 8256009 would have probably been in the passenger's possession from Laredo, Texas to San Antonio, Texas, where the passenger had to change buses to proceed on to Dallas. He indicated that in all probability instant ticket was surrendered by the passenger to the driver of the bus which proceeded from San Antonio, Texas to Dallas, Texas.

In addition to the above, Mr. CAIN made available the above-mentioned Greyhound ticket, number 8256009. This ticket reflected that it had been issued

On 4-3-64 at San Francisco, California File # SF 89-58

by SA JOHN P. MC HUGH:cj Date dictated 4-6-64

COMMISSION EXHIBIT No. 2538—Continued

2

JPM:cj
SF 89-58

on October 3, 1963 by Central Greyhound Lines, Laredo, Texas for travel from Laredo, Texas to Dallas, Texas, one-way. Under the word "Endorsements" was placed a notation in ink, namely "I.E.O. (International Exchange Order) 43599 Org Mexico (origin Mexico)". This ticket reflected that it was issued at Central Greyhound, Laredo, Texas by agent number 06.

Greyhound ticket 8256009 bore no indication as to the name of the passenger using this ticket.

- 3* -

COMMISSION EXHIBIT No. 2538—Continued

UNITED STATES DEPARTMENT OF JUSTICE
FEDERAL BUREAU OF INVESTIGATION

In Reply, Please Refer to
File No.

WASHINGTON, D.C. 20535

September 4, 1964

LEE HARVEY OSWALD

The following was received from a confidential source abroad:

Mr. Roland Barrios, former employee of the Chihuahuenses Travel Agency, Mexico, D.F., Mexico, when shown Photostats of the exchange order (Exhibit D-202) issued in connection with the travel of H. O. Lee from Mexico, D.F., Mexico, to Laredo, Texas, via the Transportes del Norte bus line on October 2-3, 1963, stated that the handprinting and signature on this document were his and that undoubtedly he handled the transaction represented by the document. A photograph of the tourist card (Exhibit J-3) of Lee Harvey Oswald was also displayed to Mr. Barrios. He stated that he would interpret the comma following the name "Lee" on the tourist card to indicate surname of the traveler to be "Lee" and, in order to avoid unnecessary writing on the exchange order, he would have used the initials of the first and middle names appearing on the tourist card which he considered to be "Harvey Oswald."

Mr. Barrios stated he could not recall Lee Harvey Oswald or his dealings with him. On viewing the above-described documents, he affirmed that he would have written the name of the traveler as "H. O. Lee" had he copied this name from Oswald's tourist card.

Mr. Barrios stated that he would attempt to reconstruct the events following issuance of the exchange order in question. However, he subsequently advised that he was unable to recall his contact with the traveler for whom he issued the exchange order in the name "H. O. Lee."

COMMISSION EXHIBIT No. 2539

Name and Residence	Room No.	Dates of Occupancy
ARMANDO RODRIGUEZ San Luis, Guanajuato (San Luis de la Paz)	26	September 30, 1963
GREGORIO PEREZ Puebla, Puebla	28	September 30 through October 1, 1963
RAMIREZ Monterrey, Nuevo Leon	1	October 1, 1963
Cap. DOMINGUEZ Guadalajara, Jalisco	5	October 1, 1963
ROSAS RAMIREZ Celaya, Guanajuato	16	October 1, 1963
Sr. MONTOYA Puebla, Puebla	23	October 1, 1963
FRANCISCO GUTIERREZ Puebla, Puebla (Chauffeur)	25	October 1, 1963
FELIPE ESCOBEDO	26	October 1, 1963
ALFONSO GARCIA Monterrey, Nuevo Leon	27	October 1, 1963

4. Interview of Manager and Other Personnel at Hotel

GUILLERMO GARCIA LUNA advised on March 3, 1964, that he is the owner and manager of the Hotel del Comercio, which is located approximately five blocks north of the main east-west thoroughfare of Mexico City, Paseo de la Reforma, and two blocks east of the principal north-south artery, Avenida Insurgentes. He explained that his hotel caters to commercial travelers, most of whom are Mexican citizens; that it has a total of thirty rooms, most of which are equipped with a private bath; that for a single room the minimum rate, without bath, is 13.00 pesos ($1.04 U.S.) and the maximum, with bath,

- 53 -

COMMISSION EXHIBIT No. 2540

is 20.00 pesos ($1.60 U.S.). He added that the hotel is in the heart of the area of many of the bus terminals in Mexico City and also is only a few blocks from the passenger railroad station.

GARCIA LUNA furnished the following observations concerning the stay of LEE HARVEY OSWALD at the Hotel del Comercio. He received OSWALD and caused him to sign the hotel registration book, which is utilized in place of registration cards. He believed OSWALD's arrival had occurred between 10:00 and 11:00 a.m. The guest makes the initial entry in the registration book with data which includes his name, place of origin, occupation, and nationality; thereafter, so long as the guest remains at the hotel, his name and identifying data are transferred to the registration book page for the current date, after he has made payment in advance for his room for the ensuing night. Inasmuch as payment is made in advance, no effort is made to obtain an exact home address for the registrant.

The hotel has four floors, and OSWALD was assigned room No. 18 (with bath) on the third floor at a daily rate of 16.00 pesos ($1.28 U.S.) The rooms on the latter floor are numbered from 18 through 23. The hotel registration book reflects that OSWALD paid for his room on October 1, 1963, which, according to GARCIA LUNA, indicates he was entitled to and probably slept at the hotel the night of October 1-2, 1963, and departed therefrom during the day of October 2, 1963. GARCIA LUNA stated he could not recall the circumstances of OSWALD's departure nor the hour thereof, but merely was judging normal procedure on the basis of information in his record.

GARCIA LUNA advised that he speaks a few words of English and received the impression that OSWALD neither spoke nor understood any Spanish. He had not observed OSWALD in the hotel during the day nor had he ever seen him accompanied by any individual or individuals. He recalled that OSWALD had been carrying a medium-size, brown handbag, which he believed had a zipper and was either of Naugahyde or canvas material. He did not remember that OSWALD had ever worn a coat and believed he usually appeared in a short-sleeved shirt of a knit variety.

- 54 -

COMMISSION EXHIBIT No. 2540—Continued

Inquiry was made of GARCIA LUNA as to other personnel at the hotel who might recall OSWALD on the basis of having any reason to notice or contact him, and he stated that those persons would be his assistant, SEBASTIAN PEREZ, and the maid who cleans the rooms on the upper two floors, MATILDE GARNICA.

GARCIA LUNA stated that he was acquainted with a few of the guests who were at the hotel during the same period as OSWALD but did not have home addresses for any of them. He mentioned that several of the guests of that period are commercial travelers and return to the hotel from time to time.

MATILDE GARNICA, maid at the Hotel del Comercio, advised on March 3, 1964, that she recognized the photographs of OSWALD as being of the young American who had occupied room No. 18 for almost a week during the latter part of last year. She explained that she handles the daily housekeeping duties for the third and fourth floors of the hotel, comprising rooms numbered 18 through 30, and ordinarily arrives at work between 9:00 a.m. and 10:00 a.m., leaving at 9:00 p.m., upon completion of her working day.

Mrs. GARNICA related that she clearly recalls OSWALD, as few Americans stay at the hotel, and was somewhat intrigued by his presence there. He had very few personal effects, which he carried in what she described as a "small, brown, zippered handbag," which was either of canvas or imitation leather material. She did not believe she had seen OSWALD in the hotel on more than two occasions, the day of his arrival and the following Saturday as he was still in his room when she checked to determine which rooms were available for cleaning. She remembered that when she saw him in the room on the Saturday morning in question, he said "good morning" to her in English, and a short time later left the hotel.

She never saw him with any other person and had no conversation with him, having received the impression that he neither spoke nor understood Spanish.

SEBASTIAN PEREZ HERNANDEZ, desk clerk and assistant to the owner of the Hotel del Comercio, advised on March 10, 1964, that he had not conversed with OSWALD but remembered him clearly inasmuch as very few Americans have stayed at

the hotel. To the best of his recollection, OSWALD left the hotel each morning and did not return until evening; possibly after PEREZ HERNANDEZ had completed his working day and left the hotel. He stated OSWALD was alone whenever he noticed him at the hotel and usually wore a knit, short-sleeved sport shirt and no coat or jacket.

PEREZ HERNANDEZ advised that since OSWALD paid his rent in advance for the night of October 1, 1963, there would have been little reason for contact with him on the presumed date of his departure, October 2, 1963, and he was unable to remember any details in this connection.

On April 18, 1964, PEDRO RODRIGUEZ LEDESMA advised that he resides at Santa Clara, State of Mexico, and for many years has been the night watchman at the Hotel del Comercio, his working hours being from 9:00 p.m. to 9:00 a.m. He explained, however, that he often is able to leave the hotel by 8:00 a.m. or earlier if the owner and manager, GUILLERMO GARCIA LUNA, has arrived to relieve him and handle reception duties. With respect to LEE HARVEY OSWALD's stay at the hotel, he furnished the following information.

He clearly recalls the young American whom he later identified in his mind as OSWALD and remembers that on the date of the latter's departure from the hotel and on the basis of sign language and the word "taxi," which he interpreted to indicate that OSWALD wanted a taxicab, RODRIGUEZ walked around the corner from the Hotel del Comercio to Orozco y Berra and Bernal Diaz Streets where he obtained a taxicab which had just left a passenger at the "Estrella Blanca" (White Star) bus terminal. He stated definitely that he did not know the taxi driver and had not known or discussed with the driver or OSWALD the latter's intended destination. He said OSWALD carried his own luggage downstairs and waited in front of the hotel with the luggage until RODRIGUEZ returned with the taxicab.

He believed OSWALD left the hotel between 6:30 and 7:00 a.m., since it was getting light when he went in search of the taxicab. He could not be more precise concerning the time. He believed that OSWALD gave him a small tip of one or two pesos ($.08 or $.16 U.S.) for his assistance in calling a taxi. RODRIGUEZ commented that while he had little difficulty obtaining a taxi at the early hour, it becomes very difficult to secure taxi transportation between 7:30 and 8:30 a.m. because of the heavy traffic at that time.

RODRIGUEZ related that to the best of his recollection OSWALD always arrived at the hotel late at night, "midnight or thereafter," but he never noticed any indication that OSWALD had been drinking. He never observed OSWALD in the company of any person and did not recall his ever using the only telephone at the hotel, which is located at the reception desk.

-57-

COMMISSION EXHIBIT No. 2540—Continued

4

DL 89-43

Unemployment Claims

Mr. MILLER made available a claim record card which had been forwarded from the New Orleans office of the Louisiana Employment Commission. This reflects that an initial claim for unemployment compensation was made on April 29, 1963 by L. H. OSWALD, 757 France Street, New Orleans, Louisiana, Social Security Number 433-54-3937.

The original address is typed in but penciled notations indicate changes as follows:

French Street instead of France Street; P. O. Box 30061, no city listed; 2515 West 5th, Irving, Texas. The dates of these changes are not shown.

Mr. MILLER advised that this claim card indicates that L. H. OSWALD filed a claim for unemployment compensation at New Orleans based upon employment in Texas and that in addition to April 29, 1963, LEE OSWALD, according to the notations on the card, appeared at the New Orleans office of the Louisiana Employment Commission on the following dates:

May 7, 1963	August 20, 1963
May 15, 1963	August 27, 1963
July 22, 1963	September 3, 1963
July 30, 1963	September 10, 1963
August 6, 1963	September 17, 1963
August 13, 1963	September 24, 1963

During this period no earnings were shown for OSWALD except on July 22, 1963 he reported $58.00.

Mr. MILLER advised this card further reflects that LEE OSWALD appeared at the Dallas office of TEC on October 3, 1963 and October 10, 1963 and noted that on October 10, 1963 OSWALD signed his name on this card when he appeared. He advised that on ~~these dates~~ Oct 3, 1963 OSWALD appeared at the TEC office at 2210 Main Street, Dallas,

212

COMMISSION EXHIBIT No. 2541

Texas, where he was interviewed by HARRY SANDERSON. He appeared at this same address October 10, 1963 where he was interviewed by MC CLUSKEY. Mr. MILLER made this identification of the persons whom OSWALD contacted through initials appearing opposite the contact date on the claim record card.

Mr. MILLER further advised that the unemployment benefits of OSWALD were terminated with the claim which he submitted on October 3, 1963 and that no further benefits were payable or were paid to him.

MILLER advised that he has no record of the exact amount of the check paid on each claim period to OSWALD, and that this record could be located only in Austin, Texas, at the state headquarters of TEC.

213

COMMISSION EXHIBIT No. 2541—Continued

FD-302 (Rev. 1-25-60)

FEDERAL BUREAU OF INVESTIGATION

1

Date 12/3/63

DOUGLAS JONES, Jones Printing Company, 422 Girod, advised after viewing the photograph of LEE OSWALD, that although he could not positively be sure, he said he did not believe the person ordering the printing of the handbills relating to Cuba last May 29th was OSWALD. He said to the best of his recollection the man ordering the handbills was a husky type person, on the order of a laborer. He said he remembered the person ordering the handbills did not have a Cuban accent and did not look like a Cuban to him and he therefore wondered why this person would be involved with the Cubans. He again stated that he could not positively say the person ordering the handbills was not OSWALD but he did not think it was. JONES said he could not furnish any other identifying data concerning the person ordering the handbills.

On 12/3/63 at New Orleans, Louisiana File # NO 89-69

by SA DONALD C. STEINMEYER/bap Date dictated 12/3/63

COMMISSION EXHIBIT No. 2542

FD-302 (Rev. 1-25-60)

FEDERAL BUREAU OF INVESTIGATION

1

Date 12/4/63

ARTHUR B. NUESSLY, Printer, Jones Printing Company, New Orleans, Louisiana, was interviewed at his place of business, and advised that he recalls printing an order for 1,000 copies of a handbill, commencing with the words "Hands Off Cuba" and ending with the words "Everyone Welcome."

He stated that he recalls the order came in several months ago, exact date not recalled, and was completed within a few days. He stated that the printing used on the handbill could be described as Wood Gothic, Chilton Hand Extended, Chilton Hand Bold, Parson's Italic, and Gothic Bold. He advised that he had no contact at all with the person who placed the order. At this point NUESSLY, was shown a photograph of LEE HARVEY OSWALD which he failed to recognize.

On 12/3/63 at New Orleans, Louisiana File # NO 89-69

by SA JOHN M. MCCARTHY /mh Date dictated 12/4/63

This document contains neither recommendations nor conclusions of th [redacted] your agency; it and its contents are not to be distributed outside your [redacted]

Commission Exhibit No. 2543

COMMISSION EXHIBIT NO. 2543

FD-302 (Rev. 1-25-60)

FEDERAL BUREAU OF INVESTIGATION

1

Date December 3, 1963

GLYNN A. YOUNG, President, Direct Mail Enterprises, Inc., 424 Gravier Street, was shown a photograph of LEE H. OSWALD taken by the New Orleans Police Department, on August 9, 1963, and he identified OSWALD as an individual who came alone to his shop and asked for an estimate on the price of printing 1,000 copies of a 4" x 9" form.

YOUNG said he gave OSWALD a price of approximately $9.00 and OSWALD said the price was too high and he wanted something cheaper. Mr. YOUNG said he referred OSWALD to a competitor, the Mailers Service Company, at 225 Magazine Street, and told OSWALD they could possibly print it at a cheaper rate.

YOUNG said JOHN I. ANDERSON, Mailers Service Company, brought the layout of the form to his shop to be typed. YOUNG said ANDERSON's mother and father were on vacation at the time, and there was no one to type it up at Mailers Service. YOUNG said he gave the layout to his typist, VALERIE PICOU, to be typed.

YOUNG said he recalls when OSWALD asked for the estimate he had a handwritten copy on a piece of paper. YOUNG said all he can recall of the contents on the paper was that it had something to do with "donations for Cuba."

YOUNG said he does not know what happened to the handwritten layout given to him by ANDERSON other than that he gave it to Miss PICOU.

On 12/3/63 at New Orleans, Louisiana File # NO 89-69

by SA W. J. DANIELSON, JR. and SA DONALD J. STEINMEYER /dmm Date dictated 12/3/63

This document contains neither recommendations nor conclusions of the FBI. It is the property of the FBI and is loaned to your agency; it and its contents are not to be distributed outside your agency.

COMMISSION EXHIBIT NO. 2544

FD-302 (Rev. 1-25-60)

FEDERAL BUREAU OF INVESTIGATION

Date 12/3/63

1 Mr. JOSEPH J. JOHNSON, employed by James W. Trout Printing, 417 Natchez, advised he currently resides at 4855 Feliciana Drive, New Orleans.

He said that LEE HARVEY OSWALD came into the shop in the late part of July, 1963, and requested 3,000 copies of a handbill at a special price. Mr. JOHNSON said they did not discuss price after OSWALD showed him a hand-written sample of the handbill he desired. Mr. JOHNSON continued that the sample furnished was written in pencil on cheap paper, which appeared to be brown wrapping paper. He said he recalls that a portion read, "Hands Off Cuba." He said OSWALD wanted delivery of the order on the following day. Mr. JOHNSON said he informed OSWALD at that point that he did not desire to do the job, whereupon OSWALD asked JOHNSON to recommend a shop. Mr. JOHNSON said he refused to make such a recommendation, and that OSWALD became annoyed and left. Mr. JOHNSON said he did not know where OSWALD went or even in what direction he traveled after leaving the shop.

He continued that OSWALD had not identified himself, but that he (JOHNSON) recalled OSWALD as the man with whom he spoke following the appearance of the photographs of OSWALD in the newspapers after the assassination of President KENNEDY. Mr. JOHNSON concluded by stating that he recalled OSWALD to have been dressed in a dirty brown khaki jacket and trousers. He said from all appearance, OSWALD was traveling on foot.

On 12/3/63 at New Orleans, Louisiana File # NO 89-69

by SA ROBERT M. WHOMSLEY :jas Date dictated 12/3/63

401

This document contains neither recommendations nor conclusions of the FBI. It is the property of the FBI and is loaned to your agency; it and its contents are not to be distributed outside your agency.

COMMISSION EXHIBIT No. 2545

FD-302 (Rev. 1-25-60)

FEDERAL BUREAU OF INVESTIGATION

1

Date November 25, 1963

CHARLES HALL STEELE, JR. appeared at the New Orleans Office November 24, 1963, in the company of his father. He stated he is 20 years of age, having been born November 5, 1943, and is a student at Delgado Trades School, and works part-time at Muller's Shell Service Station, Paris Avenue and Robert E. Lee Boulevard, New Orleans.

STEELE stated that on Friday, August 16, 1963, he took his girl friend, CHARLENE STOUFF, 2056 Brutus Street, New Orleans, to the Louisiana State Employment Service, for the purpose of her taking a typing test in connection with her application for employment by the Orleans Parish School Board. He stated he can fix this date specifically because his father was on active duty at Fort Polk, Louisiana, returning August 10, 1963, and he, CHARLES JR., left New Orleans August 21, 1963, for a visit to Gatlinburg, Tennessee. He stated he knows that the date he went to the Louisiana State Employment Service was the Friday between August 10, and August 21, 1963.

STEELE related that while his girl friend was taking the typing test, he sat in the reception room waiting for her. He noted an individual talking to various people in the waiting room and overheard him asking an unidentified individual sitting next to STEELE if this person would be interested in making about $2 by distributing some literature. The unidentified man told this person the job would require a few minutes at noon and the person sitting next to STEELE replied he had to be someplace at noon.

STEELE stated that this man who he believed gave his name as OSWALD, then approached him, STEELE, and asked if he would be interested in making $2 for about 15 to 20 minutes work distributing leaflets. STEELE stated he agreed and arranged to meet this person at noon in front of the International Trade Mart building located at Camp and Gravier Streets. STEELE stated that he, STEELE, arrived first and OSWALD walked up with the leaflets in his hand and carrying a briefcase. STEELE stated OSWALD was accompanied by another person whom he described as a white male, 19 - 20 years of age, about 6 feet, slender build, dark hair, olive complexion. He could recall no further

On 11/24/63 at New Orleans, Louisiana File # NO 89-69

by SAs PAUL R. ALKER & STEPHEN M. CALLENDER /sw Date dictated 11/25/63

267

This document contains neither recommendations nor conclusions of the FBI. It is the property of the FBI and is loaned to your agency; it and its contents are not to be distributed outside your agency.

COMMISSION EXHIBIT No. 2546

[redacted]

Commission Exhibit No. 2547

DL 100-10461
KBJ:cv
1

On November 29, 1963, Mr. E. P. BASS, 2019 Ferndale, Dallas, Texas, telephonically advised SA MILTON L. NEWSOM that he is a member of the Lancaster Gun Club and practices firing his rifle at the club range frequently. He said that approximately two weeks before the President's assassination he observed an individual at the Lancaster Gun Club Range that was possibly identical to LEE HARVEY OSWALD. BASS said he is not certain of this identification; however, he recalled that the man was very rude, rough in appearance and appeared to be an excellent shot with the rifle he was using. He said the rifle had a scope and that the magazine protruded in front of the trigger guard exactly like the one pictured in the newspapers that was used in the President's assassination. He said as nearly as he could recall this man's description fit that of OSWALD. BASS advised the President of the Lancaster Gun Club is HUNTER B. BAKER and that Mr. BAKER has been staying at the club during the time practice sessions with rifles have been allowed.

On December 3, 1963, Mr. HUNTER B. BAKER, 717 Winston, Dallas, Texas, advised SA KENNETH B. JACKSON that he is the president of the Lancaster Gun Club and that he spends a great deal of time at the range, usually about four or five days a week. He said some weeks he is there everyday in the week and stated that he had never observed anyone at the range who resembled LEE HARVEY OSWALD and that if a rifle such as OSWALD allegedly used in the assassination of President KENNEDY had appeared on the range in the possession of any member or guest he would have likely remembered it. He referred to this type of rifle as "junky". He said that OSWALD was not a member of this gun club, and he was unable to furnish any information to indicate that anyone resembling OSWALD may have visited the range at any time. He pointed out that there is a gate at the entrance to the range which is normally kept locked and that only members are permitted to have keys to the gate for entry on the premises.

On December 3, 1963, Mr. E. P. BASS was recontacted regarding this matter, and he advised that he was unable to furnish any additional information to identify the individual that he had observed on the range of the Lancaster Gun Club approximately two weeks before the President's assassination. He said that as best he could recall the individual whom he

DL 100-10461
KBJ:cv
2

recalled as possibly resembling OSWALD kept bothering him which he himself did not appreciate because he goes to the range to shoot and does not like interruptions. He said the gun in the possession of the individual whom he thought resembled OSWALD was an ordinary-looking gun and had a telescopic sight. He said it had a mahogany stock which was not an oil-soaked stock. He said that as best he could recall there may have been no others present at the range other than himself and his son and the individual whom he thought resembled OSWALD. BASS said that he did not know this individual as a member of the gun club and had no way of knowing who the person might have been. He said, however, that he probably would have presumed at the time that the man was a member of the gun club since the gun club range is restricted to the use of members and their guests. Mr. BASS said that his son, JAN BASS, age 15, is quite alert and has a better recollection probably of this individual then he himself.

On December 3, 1963, JAN BASS, age 15, 2019 Ferndale, Dallas, Texas, advised that he accompanied his father E. P. BASS to the Lancaster Gun Club Range approximately three weeks previously on an occasion when there were no other persons at the range with the exception of a man who came there with what he described as a gun that looked like a "typical mail order gun". He said that he did not pay much attention to this man, but he feels that the man may have been an inch or two taller than his father who is 5'7½". He stated the man was driving a 1961 blue Falcon sedan, and he was quite certain the man wore glasses. He said he has no recollection of how the man was dressed. He said that after observing photographs of LEE HARVEY OSWALD that he does not have any reason to believe that this individual was OSWALD based upon his recollection of the man.

SA KENNETH B. JACKSON conducted the interviews of E. P. BASS and JAN BASS on December 3, 1963, at Dallas, Texas.

FAIR PLAY FOR CUBA
(FPCC)
NEW ORLEANS

No record was found in New Orleans of the issuance of a parade permit to LEE HARVEY OSWALD during April, 1962.

New Orleans Police Department records indicate he was arrested August 5, 1963, for disturbance of the peace for which he was fined $10.00 on August 12, 1963.

Under the name OSBORNE, OSWALD ordered 1,000 copies printed of "Hands Off Cuba" FPCC handbills from Jones Printing Company, 422 Girod Street, New Orleans, May 29, 1963, which he probably received on June 4, 1963. As LEE OSBORNE he ordered 500 copies printed of an FPCC membership application from the Mailers Service Company, 225 Magazine Street, New Orleans, on June 3, 1963, receiving same on June 5, 1963. Shortly thereafter he ordered 300 copies printed of an FPCC membership card by the same firm.

OSWALD was arrested by the New Orleans Police Department on August 9, 1963, in the 700 block of Canal Street and charged with disturbance of the peace by creating a scene following an altercation with CARLOS JOSE BRINGUIER, CELSO MACARIO HERNANDEZ, and MIGUEL MARIANO CRUZ (members of the anti-Castro Cuba Students Directorate (Directorio Revolucionario Estudiantil)(D.R.E.) while he was distributing FPCC handbills. At the time of arrest, he was in possession of a National FPCC membership card issued May 28, 1963, signed by V. T. LEE, Executive Secretary; New Orleans Chapter FPCC membership card issued June 6, 1963, signed by A. HIDELL, President; and a cardboard sign reading "Viva, Viva FIDEL." During police interrogation, OSWALD stated he had first become interested in the FPCC while a Marine at Los Angeles, California, in 1958; that the New Orleans Chapter of FPCC consisted of 35 persons, five of whom regularly attended monthly meetings on Pine Street; denied being a Communist but stated he was a socialist and embraced the teachings of KARL MARX in "Das Kapital"; and that he would not allow members of his family to learn English as he hated America and did not want them to become Americanized; and that there

COMMISSION EXHIBIT NO. 2548

were "fat stinking politicians in Russia just like over here."

DRE members indicated OSWALD had offered that organization his services as a trainer of guerrilla fighters on August 5, 1963, which offer was refused.

No connection was established between OSWALD and the New Orleans Council for Peaceful Alternatives or the Southern Conference Educational Fund. Copies of the FPCC handbill were found on the campus of Tulane University during the summer of 1963.

OSWALD distributed FPCC handbills in front of the International Trade Mart, Camp and Commerce Streets, New Orleans, on August 16, 1963. A portion of this distribution was televised locally.

OSWALD was interviewed by WILLIAM K. STUCKEY on August 17, 1963, and a portion of the interview was utilized by STUCKEY in his "Latin Listening Post" radio program on Station WDSU, New Orleans, on that date. He also appeared on STUCKEY's "Carte Blanche" radio program on the same station on August 21, 1963, with representatives of DRE and the Information Council of the Americas. During this broadcast, he stated that the FPCC was not a Communist controlled organization and that he was a Marxist.

COMMISSION EXHIBIT NO. 2548—Continued

During this period the only police protection given the District of Columbia was done by several country Constables appointed by Prince George and Montgomery Counties in Maryland, and a small night watch in Alexandria.

President John Adams was the first President to officially live in Washington. He arrived in the city on June 3, 1800, and was met by a large body of citizens on horseback, and escorted to Georgetown where he lived until moving into the partially-completed White House a short time later. Every President from that time on has officially used the White House as his principal residence and Executive Office.

John Adams received the usual annoying and threatening letters. An example of one is cited below:

> President Adams -
>
> Myself and my family are ruined by the French. If you do not procure satisfaction for my losses, when a treaty is made with them, I am undone forever and you must be a villain to your country!!! Assassination shall be your lot, if restitution is lost to America through your means, or if ever you agree to a peace without it. The subsistence of thousands, who have lost their all, depends upon it.
>
> A ruined merchant
> Alas! With ten children!!!
> Made beggars by the French

Threats against the early Presidents were not given serious consideration, and practically no provisions were made to protect the Chief Executives or the White House. It is reported that even on Jefferson's inauguration day, he walked to the Capitol to take his Oath of Office, without being accompanied by a guard of any kind.

With the new Government established in Washington, it became apparent that additional police protection was needed, and accordingly in 1802 the Mayor of Washington was given general police authority. He made no immediate use of this power, however, and it was not until three years later that he appointed a high constable and forty Deputy constables, to police the capitol city.

In 1814, the British Army invaded Washington and burned many of the Government buildings. Very little effort was made to protect the city or the Government. Apparently L'Enfant's defense circles were forgotten about in the haste to evacuate

the city before the British arrived. President Madison was forced to flee for safety and the White House was looted and set on fire. Almost the entire interior of the building was gutted, and cost the Government over $300,000.00 to repair the damage.

It is reported that frequently President John Quincy Adams was faced with dangerous cranks, and threatening letters were received daily. On one occasion a court-martialed Army Sergeant walked into the White House and demanded that Adams have him reinstated. He was told to offer proof that the court had erred, but he could not do so, and his request was turned down. A few days later he again came to the President and informed him that he could have his choice of either being assassinated or ordering the reinstatement. The President paid no attention to the threat and continued to walk about unguarded, both during the daytime and at night. The would-be assassin hung around in the vicinity of the White House, and finally one day he came up to Adams and stated that his threat had been a joke, and he requested that the President give him enough money to pay his way home. The President gave him the money.

The Administration of President Jackson was particularly outstanding in its threats and dangers to the life of the Chief Executive. Jackson was continually receiving threats of assassination.

During the first part of 1833 Jackson made a trip to Fredericksburg, Virginia, to lay a corner stone of a monument to Washington's Mother. While the steamboat was at the dock at Alexandria, a young Naval Lieutenant named Robert B. Randolph came up to the President and hit him in the face so violently with his fist that it caused Jackson to kick over a nearby table. Bystanders stepped in immediately and overpowered the attacker.

On January 30, 1835, Jackson attended the funeral services of a member of the House of Representatives at the Capitol After the sermon, the President filed past the casket with the cabinet members and started to leave. When he entered the rotunda of the Capitol, a man stepped forward from the crowd and pointed a small bright pistol at the Chief Executive's breast. He pulled the trigger and the cap exploded, but the charge failed to fire. Before anyone realized what was happening, the attacker produced another pistol and fired a second time. Again the cap exploded but the charge failed to fire. The President lunged for the attacker and was aided by friends in capturing him.

The two guns were later examined by an expert on small arms, and were found to have been loaded properly in every respect.

of the United States. Believing the President to be the source of all his difficulties, he was still fixed in his purpose to kill him, and if his successor followed the same course, he would put him out of the way. He declared that no power in this country could punish him, because it would be resented by the powers of Europe as well as of this country. The assassin appeared tranquil and unconcerned as to the final result and to anticipate no punishment for his deed."

The physicians examining him found him to be insane. He was tried and found not guilty, and was then committed to an insane asylum. It is a point of considerable interest that among Jackson's many threatening letters was one signed in the name of the father of the assassin who was to take Lincoln's life three decades later, as follows:

Brower's Hotel, Philadelphia
July 4, 1835

"You dam'd old scoundrel if you don't sign the pardon of your fellow men, now under sentence of death, De Ruiz (?) and De Soto, I will cut your throat whilst you are sleeping. I wrote to you repeated cautions; so look out or damn you I'll have you burnt at the stake in the city of Washington."

Your master
Junius Brutus Booth

"You know me! Look Out!"

In spite of these dangers which constantly confronted the President, there is no evidence of any steps being taken to provide protection for the Chief Executive.

In 1842, during John Tyler's administration, the President' political opponents would march past the White House and hoot; and some even went so far as to disfigure the front of the House. One Sunday morning while the President was taking a walk in the grounds south of the White House, an intoxicated painter threw rocks at him.

As a result, on August 23, 1842, Congress passed an act "to establish an auxiliary watch for the protection of the public and private property in the City of Washington." The force was to consist of a Captain and fifteen men. This action was also considered necessary because of the fear of incendiaries.

COMMISSION EXHIBIT No. 2549—Continued

* * * * * *

On November 1, 1950, at about 2:20 P. M., Private Leslie Coffelt, White House Police, proved that a dying man can make words come alive. A succinct paragraph of the Secret Service Manual reads, in part, "Members of the Secret Service must be ready and willing to sacrifice their own lives if necessary in protecting the life of the President..." and it was into those words that Private Coffelt put the breath of life as his final conscious act. The brave words had been written long before the day on which Griselio Torresola and Oscar Collazo attempted to kill President Harry S. Truman but such bold words must be tempered in blood before they ring true. Private Coffelt so tempered them, in his own blood and that of his assassin, and he did it calmly and deliberately as though underlining the key-words in the Manual's command: ready, willing, to sacrifice, if necessary.

Equally ready and willing to sacrifice their lives were the other men on duty with Private Coffelt that fateful day -- Privates Donald T. Birdzell, Joseph O. Davidson, Private Technician Joseph H. Downs, and Special Agent Floyd M. Boring of the White House Detail. But Private Coffelt was the only one whose name on the roll of honor would be marked, "Killed in the performance of his duty."

Private Coffelt was a cheerful and friendly man. He liked his job and he was grateful for having it. Assigned to the Blair House, then the temporary residence of the President of the United States, his post placed him but an arm's length from the stream of pedestrians, many of them sightseers, who strolled along Pennsylvania Avenue in passing the Blair House. Hundreds of the passers-by stopped to ask him a question or two, and each was rewarded with a courteous reply delivered with an engaging smile. But Griselio Torresola was no sightseer, nor did he have any questions to ask. He approached Private Coffelt's guard booth casually. He whipped out a Luger automatic pistol and began shooting -- shooting with deadly accuracy and shooting to kill. Private Coffelt slumped in his chair as three 9mm slugs tore into his vital organs in as rapid succession as the deadly Luger automatic pistol could deliver them. Torresola, sure of his kill, turreted and fired three quick shots at Private Technician Joseph H. Downs,

COMMISSION EXHIBIT No. 2549—Continued

scored a leg wound. But Torresola's orgy of marksmanship--seven shots with seven hits--was over. Private Coffelt had Torresola in his sights. Private Coffelt squeezed the shot off with his rapidly waning strength, the revolver bucked in his hand, and Torresola's head jerked in the unmistakable sign that a brain shot had been scored. Torresola was dead before his gun had cooled.

Collazo, his clip expended, crouched down on the steps of the Blair House to re-load. He was partially screened from the view of Special Agent Boring and Private Davidson by an iron picket fence. The two officers assumed that Collazo had been hit and that the battle with a lone gunman was over. At that time, neither knew that a second assassin had been in action. Private Davidson glanced across the meager front lawn of the Blair House toward Private Coffelt's guard booth and he saw a strange sight. A deadly grim Private Coffelt was leveling his revolver on the crouched form of Collazo.

Private Davidson had seen blood on Collazo's chest. He figured the fight was over.

"Hold it, Coffelt!" Davidson shouted.

Private Coffelt slumped and Death began to take over.

Boring and Davidson had been joined by Special Agent Vincent P. Mroz, and all had fired at Collazo. But, while he was wounded, Collazo was not ready to quit. He came up firing--and then collapsed at the base of the steps which he had chosen so illogically as the road to glory.

Only seconds had elapsed from first shot to last. Private Davidson grabbed the White House Police phone. "Send everything--ambulance!" he shouted.

Special Agent Stewart G. Stout, Jr., holding his post at the foot of the main stairway inside Blair House, re-set the safety on his sub-machine gun.

Chief U. E. Baughman, Assistant Chief Carl Dickson, and all available Inspectors, Special Agents in Charge, and Special Agents proceeded to Blair House at the first word of the shooting. Chief Baughman took personal charge of the investigation as to the attempt to assassinate the President and Metropolitan Police officers began their investigation as to the homicide phases of the case.

The President, in his room on the second floor of the Blair House, continued his preparations to proceed to Arlington National Cemetery where he was scheduled to speak at the

dedication of a monument and, in a few minutes and on schedule, he did depart to keep this appointment. His automobile and the accompanying Secret Service car had to leave by a rear driveway, however, as Private Davidson's cryptic "Send everything!" had accomplished just that. Pennsylvania Avenue, in front of the Blair House, swarmed with people, ambulances, police cars, police motorcycles, and traffic-stalled motor vehicles of almost every description.

Chief Baughman began a systematic gathering of facts and, though starting from scratch, he was, in about an hour, able to hold a press conference at which he disclosed the basis for the attack.

Although the basis for the attempted assassination was quickly established, a still continuing investigation, almost two years later, was day by day bringing to light additional side lights and facets as to the activities of the Nationalist Party of Puerto Rico, the organization responsible for the attempted assassination.

Though no rational man could be expected to understand the violent machinations of the Nationalist Party of Puerto Rico, it was once described as "the lengthened shadow of one man" and that man was, of course, Pedro Albizu Campos, once affectionately known to his few but fanatic followers as "Don Pedro." The angry flame which projected his shadow and inflamed his followers was sustained by his burning hatred for the United States. But, until November 1, 1950, no trained evaluator in the investigating agencies of the Government believed that this little man's hatred was sufficiently intense to ignite a political powder keg which, for a few seconds, projected his shadow all the way from Puerto Rico to the steps of the Blair House, where it fleetingly appeared as a pall of death. President Harry S. Truman, the object of the mad attack by Campos' henchmen, was unscathed and unruffled but Campos, who at the time of the attack on the President, was being besieged by Insular Police in his headquarters at San Juan, was on the road to complete madness, a condition which has since caused some of his followers to dub him "Don Quixote."

To understand the many acts of violence perpetrated by the Nationalist Party of Puerto Rico, it is necessary to know something as to the background of Pedro Albizu Campos, from whom all this violence stemmed. It has been said that Campos hates the United States and that, of course, he has adequately proven by his acts of violence against it. In an objective appraisal of these acts of violence on the part of the Nationalist Party of Puerto Rico, it becomes apparent that the rank and file members of the Nationalist Party of Puerto Rico have been exploited by Campos, in the name of liberty, to act as instruments of his personal hatred.

(10) In Public Law 92 these protective authorities contained from year to year in Secret Service appropriation acts were changed to permanent legislation.

2. Personnel Protection Measures

a. In March, 1894, information was being received of a plot to assassinate President Cleveland by a group of gamblers in Lyons, Colorado. The Chief of the Secret Service was requested to investigate the matter and accordingly ordered Operative Walker, who was stationed in the vicinity, to discontinue his other duties and investigate the reports. Walker hired an informer named Glen and sent him to Lyons. Glen reported that danger did exist from this group. Thereupon, the Chief ordered Walker and his informer to report to Washington, where they were both commissioned as special policemen and assigned to the White House. They were instructed to stay in the vicinity of the White House during the daytime and watch for suspicious persons who might be Western gamblers, Anarchists, or cranks; and in the evenings they were to attend meetings of Coxey's Army, which was then in town. This Detail continued until early summer when the Cleveland family departed Washington for their summer home at Buzzards Bay, Massachusetts.

b. A new Detail of three men went with the family for the summer. Each summer thereafter, a Detail guarded President Cleveland at his summer home, and special Details were provided for the President at Washington, for trips, or social functions at the White House. During the Spanish-American War a Detail was kept continually at the White House.

c. A Special Detail was provided for McKinley on his trips to Buffalo. Three agents were present at the time of the assassination but they merely acted as guards and were not allowed control of the crowd in such a manner that the attack could have been prevented.

COMMISSION EXHIBIT No. 2550

d. After McKinley's death, a regular Presidential Detail was provided for President Roosevelt and it has continued to fully guard the safety of every President since.

3. The White House Police Force

a. Prior to 1864 the protection for the White House and grounds was included as part of the general responsibility of the District of Columbia police in protecting private and public property and persons within the city of Washington. There were no police assigned to the White House or grounds for this purpose.

b. In 1864 a Detail of four Metropolitan policemen was assigned to the White House, both for protection of the President and the White House property.

c. After the Civil War the number of officers was reduced to three and assigned entirely to protection at the White House.

d. During President Cleveland's second administration, he began receiving so many threatening letters that Mrs. Cleveland became alarmed and persuaded the President to increase the number of White House Policemen from three to twenty-seven.

e. Over the years the number of officers assigned to White House protection continued to increase until 1922 the force totaled 54 men.

f. On September 14, 1922, Congress enacted legislation creating the White House Police Force as a separate organization.

(1) Supervision of the Force was delegated to the President of the United States.

(2) The President placed control of the Force under his military aide.

g. On May 14, 1930, Congress placed supervision of the White House Police Force under the Chief of the United States Secret Service.

COMMISSION EXHIBIT No. 2550—Continued

JOHN EDGAR HOOVER
DIRECTOR

Federal Bureau of Investigation
United States Department of Justice
Washington, D. C.

July 2, 1964

Honorable J. Lee Rankin
General Counsel
The President's Commission
200 Maryland Avenue, Northeast
Washington, D. C.

Dear Mr. Rankin:

I received your letter of June 29th requesting copies of documents dealing with the origin and establishment of the Federal Bureau of Investigation.

Enclosed is a copy of an Order dated July 26, 1908, signed by Attorney General Charles J. Bonaparte creating an investigative agency within his Department. Also enclosed is a copy of an Order dated March 16, 1909, signed by Attorney General George W. Wickersham relating to the establishment of the Bureau of Investigation of the Department of Justice. The name of the Bureau of Investigation was changed by Executive Order to Division of Investigation on June 10, 1933, which was approved by Congress. The title, Division of Investigation, was changed to Federal Bureau of Investigation in the FBI's appropriation bill for fiscal year 1936 which was passed on March 22, 1935, by Congress and this title became effective July 1, 1935.

For the purpose of providing additional background, I am enclosing pertinent pages from the Annual Report of the Attorney General for the year 1909 dealing with the establishment of the Bureau of Investigation.

I trust the above will be of help to you and if there are any additional questions on this subject, you may be assured of our desire to be of all possible assistance to you.

Sincerely yours,
J. Edgar Hoover

Enclosures (3)

COMMISSION EXHIBIT No. 2551

Office of the Attorney General,
Washington, D.C.

July 26, 1908.

ORDER

All matters relating to investigations under the Department, except those to be made by bank examiners, and in connection with the naturalization service, will be referred to the Chief Examiner for a memorandum as to whether any member of the force of special agents under his direction is available for the work to be performed. No authorization of expenditure for special examinations shall be made by any officer of the Department, without first ascertaining whether one of the regular force is available for the service desired, and, in case the service cannot be performed by the regular force of special agents of the Department, the matter will be specially called to the attention of the Attorney General, or Acting Attorney General, together with a statement from the Chief Examiner as to the reasons why a regular employee cannot be assigned to the work, before authorization shall be made for the expenditure of any money for this purpose.

CHARLES J. BONAPARTE,
Attorney General.

COMMISSION EXHIBIT No. 2551—Continued

Office of the Attorney General.
Washington, D.C.

March 16, 1909.

ORDER ESTABLISHING BUREAU OF INVESTIGATION OF THE DEPARTMENT OF JUSTICE.

For the purpose of facilitating the investigation work under this Department, the office of the Chief Examiner shall hereafter be called the Bureau of Investigation, and the Chief Examiner is hereby authorized and designated to act as the Chief of the said Bureau, and as such shall have supervision over the work of all persons whose compensation or expenses are paid from the appropriation "Miscellaneous Expenses, United States Courts", or the appropriation "Detection and Prosecution of Crimes", and who are employed for the purpose of collecting evidence or of making investigations or examinations of any kind for this Department or the officers thereof.

Geo. W. Wickersham

Attorney General.

COMMISSION EXHIBIT No. 2551—Continued

307

U.S. Dept. of justice

ANNUAL REPORT

OF

THE ATTORNEY-GENERAL OF THE UNITED STATES

FOR THE YEAR

1909

WASHINGTON
GOVERNMENT PRINTING OFFICE
1909

For the Year 1909

The pros-
Railroad C

EMPLOYERS' LIABILITY CASES.

During the current year the department has adopted the policy of intervening in a number of cases arising in both state and federal courts throughout the country in which the constitutionality of the employers' liability act of 1908 (35 Stat., 65) has been questioned. The United States Circuit Court, Eastern District of Arkansas, in the case of *Watson* v. *St. Louis, Iron Mountain & Southern Railway Company*, upheld the constitutionality of the act. On the other hand, the Supreme Court of Connecticut, in the case of *Mondou* v. *New York, New Haven & Hartford Railroad Company*, decided it to be unconstitutional. The matter will be presented to the Supreme Court at an early date.

HOURS OF SERVICE ACT.

There is pending in the Supreme Court, in the case of *Baltimore & Ohio Railroad Company* v. *Interstate Commerce Commission*, the question of the validity of an order of the commission directing the making of monthly reports to the commission by railroad companies of violations of this law.

THE BUREAU OF INVESTIGATION. ✓

A few days before July 1, 1908, under the direction of my predecessor, the first active steps were taken toward the organization in this department of a comprehensive investigation service, for the purpose of collecting evidence for the use of the Government in cases pending or about to be commenced in the Federal courts, and also for the purpose of making such other examinations and investigations as the business of the department might require.

Prior to that time the department was employing and paying a large number of persons for investigation work of various kinds, which force consisted substantially of the following:

(*a*) From 10 to 20 persons, who were borrowed from the office of the Comptroller of the Currency from time to time, as occasion required, for the purpose of collecting evidence in cases involving violations of the national banking laws, and who were paid from $15 to $25 per day and actual expenses of travel and subsistence.

(*b*) From 2 to 20 or more persons, who were borrowed from time to time from the Secret Service division of the Treasury Department for the purpose of collecting evidence for use in various cases pending or about to be commenced in the Federal courts, who were paid from $3 to $6 per day and a per diem of $4 in lieu of subsistence, together with actual expenses of travel, etc.

(*c*) About 50 persons, who were employed by this department for the purpose of making investigations of various kinds in naturaliza-

For the Year 1909

tion cases, and who were paid from $900 to $2,500 per annum and expenses.

(*d*) Six men, who were permanently employed by the department for the purpose of collecting evidence in matters involving violations of the peonage laws, and who received $4 per day and $3 in lieu of subsistence, together with actual expenses of travel, etc.

(*e*) Seven men, who were permanently employed by the department in investigations in connection with land-fraud cases in the West, and who received from $3 to $5 per day and $3 per day in lieu of subsistence, and also actual expenses of travel, etc.

(*f*) Twelve examiners holding statutory positions at salaries of from $1,800 to $2,500 per annum, and receiving actual expenses of travel and subsistence, and who were charged with the duty of investigating the official acts, records, accounts, etc., of United States attorneys, United States marshals, clerks of United States courts, and United States commissioners.

While all of the persons above mentioned were employed and paid by this department, there was, prior to July 1, 1908, no general organization or systematic cooperation between the different forces. Moreover, there was, with a single exception (the examiners' force, to which reference will be made hereafter), an absence of any permanent, convenient record at the department showing the nature, extent, or cost of the work performed by these persons. Furthermore, the force of departmental examiners which was in charge of the chief examiner was at that time the only investigation force of the department having a definite organization, an officer in charge at Washington, and complete records showing the nature and extent of the work performed by it.

I am advised that about two years prior to July 1, 1908, the question of organizing an investigation service along the lines of the present bureau of investigation was seriously considered by this department, but it appears that no active measures were taken to this end until after the passage of the sundry civil act of May 27, 1908, which prohibited the continuation of the above-mentioned practice of borrowing secret-service operatives from the Treasury Department.

On or about July 1, 1908, under the direction of my predecessor, and by reason of the provision of law above mentioned, and also, as it appears, for the purpose of systematizing the investigation work of the department, 9 men, who had prior to that time been connected with the Secret Service Division of the Treasury Department were appointed as special agents of this department; and these men, together with the thirteen above mentioned (who had for some time previously been employed by this department for the purpose of collecting evidence in matters involving violations of the peonage and land-fraud statutes) and the 12 statutory examiners of this

For the Year 1909

department, were organized into a general investigation service under the designation of "Bureau of Investigation," and the chief examiner was placed in immediate charge of their work.

Of the 35 men above mentioned, all are still connected with the department (with the exception of 5 of the 9 men who were originally secured from the Secret Service). By reason of certain very important cases which required the work of a number of special agents, and on account of the large number of cases throughout the entire country in which it was found that special agents could be used to great advantage in collecting evidence for the Government, and also by reason of the fact that it was found necessary to make some systematic effort to locate and apprehend fugitives from justice who previously had been able to escape arrest in a large number of cases by simply leaving the district in which they were being prosecuted and proceeding to some other part of the United States, a number of additional agents have been secured from time to time, as occasion required.

Upon consideration of the advantages accruing from the organization of the investigation service, as above set forth, and in view of the statements contained in my predecessor's report for the fiscal year ended June 30, 1908, to the effect that, unless such action were prohibited by Congress the department would seriously consider the proposition of organizing its own force of bank accountants for the purpose of collecting and preparing evidence in cases involving criminal violations of the national banking laws, which work was previously done by bank examiners borrowed from the office of the Comptroller of the Currency, as above set forth, a small force of bank accountants has been organized as a part of the bureau of investigation, with compensations of from $1,800 to $2,200, and in one instance of $2,700, per annum, besides actual expenses, or a small, fixed per diem allowance in lieu of subsistence.

As a result of the changes above set forth, all of the investigation work of the department, which was formerly performed by the various forces of men above mentioned (with the exception of the naturalization work, which is now under the Department of Commerce and Labor, and of a few cases in which it is still necessary to employ bank examiners for brief periods, owing to the fact that the force of bank accountants is not as yet entirely complete) is now performed by persons connected with the bureau of investigation, and the department has secured the services of a thoroughly organized and generally efficient force of investigators at a minimum cost, and has available for reference at all times convenient, complete, and permanent records, showing the nature, extent, and result or status, and the cost of all such investigations.

OFFICE OF THE DIRECTOR

UNITED STATES DEPARTMENT OF JUSTICE

FEDERAL BUREAU OF INVESTIGATION

WASHINGTON, D.C. 20535

May 27, 1964

BY COURIER SERVICE

Honorable J. Lee Rankin
General Counsel
The President's Commission
200 Maryland Avenue, N. E.
Washington, D. C.

Dear Mr. Rankin:

Reference is made to my letter of May 14, 1964, relating to appropriation language dealing with the protection of the President and H. R. 4158 introduced on February 25, 1963, by Congressman Emanuel Celler which will codify the laws relating to the organization of the U. S. Government and its employees.

The portion of this bill dealing with the Federal Bureau of Investigation includes a provision concerning the protection of the President,and the Treasury Department, in their analysis of this bill, objected to this item being included in that portion dealing with this Bureau and recommended that it be stricken from the bill.

As you were orally advised by Mr. Malley on May 26, 1964, this language in the appropriation was a safety valve to enable the Federal Bureau of Investigation to render assistance to the Secret Service as we have done since the assassination. If the language is removed it will preclude assistance to the Secret Service on the part of the FBI in the protection of the President and we would not be able to give manpower or assistance to protect the President.

By letter dated May 21, 1964, Deputy Attorney General Nicholas de B. Katzenbach advised that the Department of Justice will advise the Budget Bureau that the Department of Justice would prefer to have the language carried in the appropriation as it is now or amended to read, "to assist in protecting the person of the President."

In view of your interest in this matter and your conversation with Mr. Malley on May 26, 1964, I thought you should be advised of the foregoing.

Sincerely yours,

J. Edgar Hoover

COMMISSION EXHIBIT NO. 2552

TREASURY DEPARTMENT

UNITED STATES SECRET SERVICE

WASHINGTON, D.C. 20220

OFFICE OF THE CHIEF

June 8, 1964

Mr. J. Lee Rankin
General Counsel
President's Commission on the
Assassination of President Kennedy
200 Maryland Avenue, N. E.
Washington, D. C. 20002

Dear Mr. Rankin:

In response to your letter of June 1, we find that many of the old records which might have revealed reliable information about the complement of agents in the past years have been destroyed in accordance with the Retirement and Disposition of Records Program of the Federal Government.

Based on recollections of older members of the Secret Service, we estimate that the first White House Detail, protecting President Theodore Roosevelt, consisted of two or three agents. Apparently they did not work on regularly scheduled shifts, but remained close to the President until he retired for the night. When the President traveled, the number of agents was increased to five or six.

The number of agents of the Detail increased to about ten during World War I.

It cannot be definitely determined when regularly scheduled shifts were established for the Detail, but they were in effect during the administration of President Calvin Coolidge. At that time there were twelve agents on the Detail, one of whom was assigned to Mrs. Coolidge and another to one of the President's sons.

The Detail gradually grew in size through the administrations of President Hoover and President Franklin D. Roosevelt. In 1939, for example, there were sixteen agents and two supervisors, working seven days a week with no days off. In 1940 arrangements were made to provide days off, and the Detail was increased to about twenty-two.

COMMISSION EXHIBIT NO. 2553

When the United States entered World War II it was considered advisable to assign extra men to the protection of the President, and the Detail operated with ten men on each of three shifts, with three supervisors and four drivers, for a total of 37 men.

In October of 1950, thirty-three special agents were assigned to the White House Detail, plus two drivers (Special Employees).

The force level of the White House Detail since 1950 is classified information which we will supply in a separate communication.

There is listed below the legislation which brought about the growth of the White House Police from thirty-three men at the time of its inception in 1922 to a present ceiling of 250 authorized positions.

Public Law	Congress	Date Approved	Authorized Ceilings
300	67th	9-14-22	33
292	68th	12-5-24	39
221	71st	5-14-30	48
80	74th	5-28-35	60
476	76th	4-22-40	80
463	77th	2-21-42	140
90	80th	6-9-47	110
693	81st	8-15-50	133
418	82nd	6-28-52	170
481	87th	6-8-62	250

The number of positions established by the authorized ceilings imposed by the Congress does not necessarily reflect the number of positions for which Congress grants appropriations each year. For instance, the present authorized ceiling for the White House Police is 250 men. The increase in the ceiling provided by Public Law 481 was requested and authorized by Congress to extend protection to the Executive Office Building and permit protection for future buildings as such need is required. The Congress appropriated funds for 213 officers for fiscal year 1964.

There follows a list of the number of positions for which appropriations were granted from the year 1940 through 1964 (prior to 1940 appropriations generally were granted for the authorized ceilings).

COMMISSION EXHIBIT No. 2553—Continued

Year	No. of Positions in Appropriations
1940	60
1941	80
1942	101
1943	94
1944	93
1945	99
1946	102
1947	105
1948	99
1949	102
1950	104
1951	106
2-1-51 (Result of Blair House Shooting)	170
1952	170
1953	166

Year	No. of Positions in Appropriations
1954	163
1954	145
1955	142
1955 *	138
1955 *	156
1955 *	151
1956	156
1957	155
1958	154
1959	153
1959 *	164
1960	164
1960 *	163
1961	162
1962	162
1963	213

(* Represents adjustments made during year due to changes in law.)

Public Law 221, passed in May 1930, placed the White House Police under the direct supervision of the Chief of the Secret Service.

Public Law 87-481, passed in June 1962, placed the White House Police under the control and supervision of the Secretary of the Treasury. The Secretary of the Treasury then delegated the authority for the control and supervision of the White House Police to the Chief of the Secret Service.

Sincerely yours,

James J. Rowley

James J. Rowley

COMMISSION EXHIBIT No. 2553—Continued

OPTIONAL FORM NO. 10
5010-104

UNITED STATES GOVERNMENT

Memorandum

TO : Chief James J. Rowley DATE: November 30, 1963

FROM : SA Lawton, 1-16 - White House Detail

SUBJECT: Activities of this Special Agent in Dallas, Texas on Friday, November 22, 1963

On Friday, November 22, 1963 I was a member of the 8:00AM - 4:00PM shift. I arrived in Dallas, Texas, Love Field at 11:40AM aboard USAF 26000. I was assigned to the Press Area upon arrival and my instructions were to remain at the airport to effect security for the President's departure.

I received information President Kennedy had been shot and that he was being brought back to USAF 26000. I immediately contacted the Police Official in charge of the police detail at the airport and advised him of the situation and requested that strice security be placed in the vicinity of USAF 26000, the terminal, and surrounding area. I advised the Police Offical to caution his men to be on the lookout for people taking pictures, that there was to be no picture taking by anyone.

A short time later I received information that President Kennedy had died and that his body was being brought to Dallas Love Field and placed aboard USAF 26000, for return to Washington, D.C. After a short time the President's body arrived at the airport and I assisted in placing the coffin aboard USAF 26000.

Donald J. Lawton
Donald J. Lawton
Special Agent
1-16, White House Detail

APPROVED:

Gerald A. Behn
Gerald A. Behn
Special Agent in Charge
1-16, White House Detail

COMMISSION EXHIBIT NO. 2554

2

CO-2-34030

FIELD OFFICE - Dallas, Texas
AGENT - Roger C. Warner
DATE - November 22, 1963

On November 22, 1963, I was assigned, in connection with the Presidential Visit to Dallas, to Love Field Airport to provide help for advance preparations for the President's arrival, security of the Air Force I and II during the President's visit to Dallas, and as help in advance for departure of President from Dallas.

I arrived at the airport at approximately 10;30 A.M. in company with Special Agent Jerry Kivet, Vice Presidential Detail. At that time, I undertook duties to aid SA Lawson, Presidential Detail in lining up cars for the motorcade, passing out numbers for the automobiles, and other general duties.

At about 12 Noon the President arrived in Air Force I, and upon his departure from the plane he began shaking hands with citizens gathered along the fence, approximately 75 yards from the ramp on which the President deplaned. During the time the President was shaking hands with these citizens, I provided security and passage for the President to move around the fence meeting the people. The President then moved to his automobile and the motorcade left the airport.

As soon as the motorcade left Love Field I introduced myself to Special Agents Rybka and Lawton and aided them in securing Air Force I and II with armed Air Force sentries. Plans were also made at this time to secure the area for the President's return. Agents Rybka and Lawton, and I then went to the airport to have lunch.

About 12:30, plane crews of Air Force I and II and of the Press plane were alerted by public address system of the airport to return to their planes immediately. Agents Rybka, Lawton, and I immediately returned to the planes at which time we were informed by Special Agent Patterson, who was standing near the boarding area of Air Force I that the President had been shot.

No further information was received at that time relative to the condition of the President. Agents Patterson, Rybka, Lawton, and the undersigned immediately secured the boarding area of Air Force I and II, all buildings, and warehouses adjacent thereto. This was accomplished by directing police officers and airport personnel to clear the areas of both private citizens and airport personnel working in the immediate vicinity. In this manner, the lower end of Love Field adjacent to the terminal was completely secured along with warehouses and various outbuildings of the terminal itself. Also, parking lots were secured with no persons being allowed to sit in cars parked near the fence.

COMMISSION EXHIBIT NO. 2554—Continued

CO-2-34,030
-2-

During the time we were waiting for the President to return to the plane, we were getting reports from various individuals who were listening to the radio, both pocket transistor radios and radios aboard the nearby airplanes, and were therefore able to gather information about the progress of the President to Parkland Hospital.

In a short period of time, I observed two automobiles pull up to the airplane and persons boarding Air Force I. I then subsequently observed Special Agent Rufus Youngblood closing the door on Air Force I and knew the new President Johnson had boarded the airplane.

Approximately ten minutes later, word was received that the coffin containing the body of President Kennedy was returning to the airfield; that Mrs. Kennedy had requested no photographs or persons be allowed near the area where she would board Air Force I. It was also suggested at this time by unknown persons that Air Force I and II be moved to the far side of Love Field. This suggestion was not complied with for the reason that security had been established in the original landing area and it would involve a number of movements to return the planes to the other side of the field and again provide substantial security.

About ten minutes later, a Motorcade containing the body of the President in a bronze colored casket and Mrs. Kennedy appeared and were loaded aboard ship. At this time no photographs were taken with the exception of one photographer who had climbed to the roof of a warehouse approximately 200 yards from the airplane. This photographer was restrained from taking further photographs.

After Mrs. Kennedy and the body of the President were loaded aboard Air Force I, security was maintained until I met with Special Agent James H. Howard who had driven from Fort Worth to the Love Field area in company with Special Agent William Duncan. Special Agent Howard stated that a suspect had been captured by Fort Worth Police and that he wished me to accompany him to Fort Worth to question this suspect. I informed Special Agent Patterson and other Secret Service agents who had accompanied the deceased President Kennedy to the airport that I was about to depart with Agent Howard to question this suspect and they concurred and gave permission to depart. I then left with Agent Howard and traveled to Fort Worth Police Station where we questioned Donald Wayne House, 404 Lula, Ranger, Texas. At the time SA Howard and I left for Fort Worth to question the suspect, the Air Force I had not departed Love Field.

Roger C. Warner
Roger C. Warner

Orig. 7 2 Chief
Dallas 2 cc

COMMISSION EXHIBIT No. 2554—Continued

Duty Assignment Upon Arrival At Dallas, Texas On November 22, 1963.

Upon arrival at Love Field, Dallas, Texas aboard Air Force ONE (26000) at 11:35 am, I proced to the follow-up car 679-X and stationed myself at the right front fender of 679-X and the rear of 100-X. There I stopped everyone from going in between the cars. Once the motor-cade began to move I moved along with it, until the motor-cade picked up speed. From this point I returned to the immediate area of Air Force ONE.

Once the motor cade left the Airport, approximately fifteen minutes later I procedded to the Airport restaurant for a sandwich and coffee. Upon completion of my meal, I saw the crew from the Pan-American chartered plane leaving in a hurry. One of the crew members stated they received word to return to their craft immediately at which time I also left the restaurant and went to the area of Air Force ONE.

After receiving information of what has happened, I assisted other Agents in enforcing security at the Airport. When word was received that the body was to be brought back on the plane I took the post at the rear ramp of the plane, and remained there until departure time. At this time I boarded Air Force ONE and departed at 2:45 pm.

Henry J. Rybka
Henry J. Rybka
SA 1-16

COMMISSION EXHIBIT No. 2554—Continued

4

CO-2-34,030

FIELD OFFICE - Dallas, Texas
AGENT - William H. Patterson
DATE - November 22, 1963

On November 22, 1963, I was assigned to drive the Vice President's car in Fort Worth, Texas, and was therefore not assigned a post during the Dallas visit.

Upon completion of my assigned duties in Fort Worth, Texas, which occurred sooner than anticipated, I departed Carswell Air Force Base in Secret Service car 720-S, and proceeded to Dallas Love Field to assist in the general security in that area. I arrived at Dallas Love Field at approximately 12:20 P. M., and assisted the local police and Special Agents Warner and Lawton in the security of Air Force I and II.

At approximately 12:30 P. M. the crew of Air Force I was alerted to stand by for immediate departure and this was the dirst indication I received that some trouble had occurred with the Presidential visit. Succeeding information was obtained at various intervals from the plane crew and over a pocket radio carried by one of the local police officers. It was by this means that I learned the President had been assassinated.

Upon learning of the President's death, I assisted SA Lawton and SA Warner in direction of local police officers in applying strict security to Air Force I and II and the general landing area and buildings in this vicinity.

I remained in close proximity of Air Force I during the arrival of Vice President and Mrs. Johnson, the President's coffin, and Mrs. Kennedy. I stayed in the vicinity of Air Force I until it departed, at which time I returned to the Dallas Field Office.

William H. Patterson

COMMISSION EXHIBIT No. 2554—Continued

5

THE ASSASSINATION OF PRESIDENT JOHN F. KENNEDY
ON NOVEMBER 22, 1963, AT DALLAS, TEXAS

Statement of Special Agent John J. O'Leary, United States Secret Service, concerning his activities and official duties on November 22, 1963, in Dallas, Texas.

On the morning of November 22, 1963, I departed Fort Worth, Texas, with the Presidential Party aboard Air Force One (U. S. Air Force Plane No. 26000). Departure time from the Fort Worth Airport was at 11:25 a.m. Air Force One arrived at Love Field, Dallas, Texas, at 11:40 a.m. My official duties as a Secret Service agent in connection with this trip of the President was to supervise the handling and security of all luggage aboard Air Force One. This would include all the personal effects of the President, such as his suitcases, loose clothes, hanging bags, bed mattress, Presidential Seal, etc. Baggage for Mrs. Kennedy, who was along on this trip to Texas, was also handled by me.

When we arrived at the Dallas airport I remained aboard the Presidential airplane or in close proximity of the plane during the time the welcoming ceremonies were in progress for the President and First Lady, and after the Presidential motorcade departed for downtown Dallas. None of the President's luggage was to be unloaded in Dallas as this was not to be an overnight stop. My instructions were to remain at the airport until the President's motorcade returned for departure for Austin, Texas. SA Don Lawton remained at Love Field with me.

My first knowledge that the President had been shot was when Colonel Swindle, Presidential pilot, asked me if I had heard that the President and Governor Connally had been shot. I had seen the pilot of the Pan-American chartered Press plane running into the terminal building just before Colonel Swindle told me of the shooting, so I felt that something was wrong. At this point, after learning of the incident, I boarded Air Force One and watched the television coverage of the events following the tragedy. I stayed on the plane until it departed Dallas at 2:47 p.m. Dallas time and arrived at Andrews Air Force Base, Washington, D. C., at 5:58 p.m. that night (Washington time). Before departure from Love Field I was told that we were waiting for the President's body to be put on the plane.

Sometime before departure from Love Field, Dallas, I was asked to witness the swearing in ceremony of Lyndon Johnson as the 36th President of the United States. This was done aboard Air Force One at 2:38 p.m., and all passengers aboard Air Force One were invited to witness the swearing in.

Upon disembarking from Air Force One at Andrews Air Force Base, I entered a White House car and followed the ambulance carrying the President's body to the Bethesda Naval Hospital, Bethesda, Maryland. Departure from Andrews Air Force Base was at 6:10 p.m. and we arrived at the hospital at 6:55 p.m. At the hospital I was present at the autopsy and the official picture taking of the President's body. I eventually departed the hospital about midnight and returned to the White House.. This is a true statement of facts to the best of my knowledge and belief.

Above statement made on Nov. 30, 1963.

John J. O'Leary
Special Agent
U. S. Secret Service

COMMISSION EXHIBIT No. 2554—Continued

TREASURY DEPARTMENT
FISCAL SERVICE
WASHINGTON 25

OFFICE OF
TREASURER OF THE UNITED STATES
IN REPLYING PLEASE QUOTE EQD-454-AC

December 12, 1963

To: Chief, U. S. Secret Service
Attention: Mr. Robert I. Bouck, P.R.S.

From: Office of Examiner of Questioned Documents

Re: Lee H. Oswald
alias Alek J. Hidell

Reference is made to the report from this office dated December 11, 1963. There are transmitted herewith several photographs of the photographic selective service card and of the photographic certificate of service which were the subjects of that report. Three different techniques were used in making these photographs: (1) To show the subjects about as they appear to the eye but by use of a red filter with panchromatic film to improve the contrast of the green and blue inks against the background; (2) The same as 1 but with a very low angle of light to show indentations made by typewriter and by ball point pen; (3) With the same lighting as 2 but on infrared film in an effort to achieve higher contrast of the marks of identation by typewriter and pens. Please note that on the photograph of the selective service card a capital letter "O" is shown about two spaces to the left of the typewritten name "ALEK".

The photograph of the reverse of the photographic certificate of service shows some slight evidence of indentations on the line below signature of individual. Just below the printed word "OF" there is a suggestion of a handwritten capital "H" and other indented vertical lines following could be parts of d's.

The photographs are enlarged about 1.84 diameters of the size of the subjects.

Alwyn Cole
ALWYN COLE,
Examiner of Questioned Documents.

580

COMMISSION EXHIBIT No. 2555

TREASURY DEPARTMENT
FISCAL SERVICE
WASHINGTON, D.C. 20220

OFFICE OF
TREASURER OF THE UNITED STATES
IN REPLYING PLEASE QUOTE EQD-454 -AC

DEC 11 1963

From: Office of Examiner of Questioned Documents

To: Chief, U. S. Secret Service,
Attention: Mr. Robert I. Bouck, P.R.S.

The material described below has been submitted for examination and report. The enclosures transmitted with your reference are returned herewith. Photographs have not been made. If this matter requires further attention, return all documents promptly.
Your reference: Form 1600, 12-6-63, CO-2-34030.

Questioned: (1) A card, 3.7" X 2.4", purporting to be a "Selective Service System Notice of Classification, GPO: 1956--0-381688," issued to one Alek James Hidell, No. 42 224 39 5321, Class IV, Feb. 5 62, bearing an illegible signature over the line for member or clerk of local board, which may be "Good Hoffer", and bearing the signature "Alek J. Hidell" in green ink over the registrant line. On the reverse of this card, the following information (not that in parentheses) has been inserted by faint typewriting or indentations by typewriter: (Color of Eyes) GREY; (Color of Hair) BROWN;(Complexion) FAIR; (Height) 5 (Ft.) 9 (In); Weight I55, and in the frame for local board stamp "TEXAS LOCAL BOARD I, SELECTIVE SERVICE, RN 2226 400 W. VICKERY ST., FORT WORTH, TEX." The face of the card bears a photograph approximately 3/4" square which corresponds to those recently published in newspapers and magazines as being of Lee H. Oswald.

(2) A card 3.15" X 2.05" purporting to be a Certificate of Service, Armed Forces of the United States, United States Marine Corps, DD Form 217MC 1 Jan 51, issued to Alek James Hidell (typewritten insertion), bearing the following information on the reverse by faint typewriting under the heading "Period of Active Duty": (From) Oct. 13, 1958 (To) Oct. 12, 1961, bearing the signature A. G. Ayers, Jr., Lt. USMCR, over a rubber stamp showing that name and title.

REPORT: 580

These cards are not original documents with respect to the printed

COMMISSION EXHIBIT No. 2556

form but each is made up of photographs of the face and reverse of some original card, which photographs are now glued together to simulate an original card. In my opinion the original card bore a name and other information, which insertions were selectively removed or prevented from showing in the photographs either by retouching or by masking, which operations would be performed either on the photographic negative or on the print therefrom or on both negative and print in order to achieve a final print which simulated an original blank form. This form was then further processed by insertion of the information which now appears thereon.

On the photographic Selective Service card the inserted information by typewriter or by indents from a typewriter are as follows, here shown in the approximate relative positions occupied on the card:

ALEK JAMES HIDELL

42 224 39 3321

x (Local Board)

FEB 5 62 Good Hoffer (Illegible signature by ball point pen, blue ink)

Photograph (Corresponding to published photographs of Lee H. Oswald)--and at the left end the signature "Alek J. Hidell" in green ink.--on the reverse:

GREY BROWN

FAIR

5 9 155

TEXAS LOCAL BOARD I
SELECTIVE SERVICE
RN 2226 400 W VICKERY ST.
FORT WORTH, TEX.

On the photographic certificate of service the inserted information on the face is "ALEK JAMES HIDELL" by typewriter, and on the reverse: (From) Oct. 13 1958 (To) OCT. 12, 1961. On this card the signature of the certifying officer is a photographic reproduction along with the remainder of the card.

580

The probable reason for the faintness of the added typewriting on these glossy photographs is that the surface did not readily accept ink, and, in fact, there is, in addition to the typewriting that can be read with fair to poor legibility, evidence of other typewriting of two classes: (1) with a lighter ribbon, and (2) showing an indent only as though the machine lacked a ribbon or was set on stencil. In most instances the other fainter typewriting and the indents repeat the same information as that which has the moderate to poor legibility but there are differences of position and some differences of content. For example on the photographic certificate of service the "From" date is shown by indent "24 OCTOBER 1957" and the "To" date is shown by indent as "23 OCTOBER 1959". While not all of the indentations can be read with complete certainty it appears that none of the others give any information appreciably different from the typewriting that can be read with moderate to poor legibility.

The signature in the name of the member or clerk of local board on the purported Selective Service card was made with a ball point pen and it is recorded partly by a scanty deposit of ink and partly by a sharp indent in the photographic paper. The depth of the indentation from the pen may be the result of an effort to persuade it to deliver ink. It is also possible that some of the extra pressure might be the result of tracing from some other signature; however, the speed of writing is somewhat greater than would be expected in an ordinary tracing. On this card the signature in the name of Alek J. Hidell was made with a fountain pen delivering a green fluid ink and the flow of ink was considerably more than would be obtained from most ball-point pens.

A method for photographing an original document and the subsequent selective removal of information appearing on such original for the purpose of simulating a blank printed form is as follows: Information in certain colors can be prevented from recording on panchromatic photographic film by the use of colored filters over the taking lens, but if the information is in black the photographic negative may be retouched with opaque material (finely divided carbon in a liquid medium which will dry to a thin hard film). The technique is a familiar one in printing and photoengraving shops for the purpose of dropping out unwanted text and for spotting of pinholes in negatives.

580

Where information on the original document crosses a part of the printed form such as a ruled ine, rule. box, or lettering, the opaquing operation will often result in the removal of a section of a line or letters or parts of letters. A method for restoring such lines is to make a photographic print of the opaqued negative (often this print will be enlarged more than actual size in preparation for the next operation to be described). On this print the lines or letters or sections of letters damaged by the opaque and showing impairment in the print are corrected thereon by hand work with pen and ink. The corrected print is then re-photographed and if the print was enlarged it may now be reduced to actual size on the negative. A print from this second negative will now simulate a blank form. A matte finish photographic paper will accept ink fairly well. A glossy paper such as that used for these documents takes ink poorly.

Evidence that the above described operation was performed on some original document is shown on these photographic prints as follows: On the Selective Service card the lower lines of the four boxes for "No." show evidence of hand retouching. The right side of the first box shows the same effect. Other small boxes for "Local Board, Appeal Board, and President" show a similar effect. The center and right of the dotted line following "Class" has been repaired. The right of the ruled line above"(Member or clerk of local board)" shows some evidence of retouching and the word "local" in the legend just given shows serious impairment as does the word "violation" below. This would indicate that some original writing extended through the word "local" and into the word "violation" but not lower than the latter word. On the reverse of this card short sections of the dotted lines after "Eyes, Hair, and Weight" show evidence of retouching.

The face of the photographic certificate of service does not show evidence of retouching. If the original card contained a line of typewriting properly centered this could have been blocked out by opaque without touching any printing of the form proper. On the reverse of this photograph there is evidence of repair or retouching in the letters "U" and to a smaller extend in the "E" of the word "SIGNATURE" and on the ruled line below at the center and to the left of center there is further evidence of retouching. The impairment of the F's of "OFFICER" may also be due to retouching.

The absence of retouching on the line for signature of registrant on the Selective Service card means that there was no original signature cutting through this line or that if one was present it was in a colored ink that could be removed by filters.

There is no evidence of erasure on these photographic cards, although it appears that the original typewriting might have been worn away to some extent as it would not dry as well on this glossy paper as on paper intended to receive typewriting.

580

The photograph of Lee H. Oswald at the lower left of the Selective Service card is of a good photographic quality. It was separately mounted on the photographic card and is not a part of the original copying of the card. This photograph is readily identifiable as being of the same person shown in newspapers and magazines from November 22, 1963, to the present under the name of Lee H. Oswald.

Photographs of the photographic Selective Service and Certificate of Service cards have been made and they will be transmitted by a separate memorandum when completed.

Alwyn Cole

ALWYN COLE,
Examiner of Questioned Documents.

580

UNITED STATES DEPARTMENT OF JUSTICE
FEDERAL BUREAU OF INVESTIGATION

In Reply, Please Refer to
File No.

Dallas, Texas
March 26, 1964

LEE HARVEY OSWALD

The following investigation was conducted in connection with the Imperial Reflex camera identified as Federal Bureau of Investigation Laboratory D-146.

On February 16, 1964, ROBERT LEE OSWALD, 1009 Sierra Drive, Denton, Texas, viewed photographs of a Stereo Realist Camera and a Cuera-2 camera and advised that he did not recognize either of the cameras as having been the property of LEE HARVEY OSWALD, but also stated he was not familiar enough with the cameras owned by LEE HARVEY OSWALD to either state that the cameras in question did or did not belong to LEE HARVEY OSWALD.

On February 17, 1964, a photograph of the "Smena-2" camera (referred to above as the Cuera-2 camera), which is Inventory Item 378, and bears Serial No. 627250, was exhibited to MARINA OSWALD and she identified this camera as identical with the Russian camera owned by LEE HARVEY OSWALD. She was also shown the photograph of the Stereo-Realist camera which is Inventory Item No. 378 and which bears Serial No. A60979, but she could not identify this camera and stated it was not the property of LEE HARVEY OSWALD, as far as she knew.

On February 18, 1964, MARINA OSWALD described the camera with which she took the photograph of LEE HARVEY OSWALD holding a rifle in his hands. She stated she believed she took this photograph with an American camera owned by OSWALD. She stated it was an American-made camera which had a grayish color, somewhat like aluminum and stated it was a box-type camera. She stated she was not completely sure, however, as to whether

COMMISSION EXHIBIT NO. 2557

Re: LEE HARVEY OSWALD

the camera had an extending bellows. She stated she could recall that she sighted the camera by looking down into a viewer at the top of the camera. She stated she did not know the whereabouts of this camera at the present time, but could identify it if she saw it again.

On February 19, 1964, Detective JOHN A. MC CABE, Irving Police Department, Irving, Texas, advised that he was present at the residence of Mrs. RUTH PAINE on November 23, 1963, when the Dallas Police Officers executed a search warrant of Mrs. PAINE's residence.

Detective MC CABE advised that he assisted the Dallas Police Officers in this search and is certain that he saw a light gray box camera in a box in Mrs. PAINE's garage. MC CABE stated that this camera was in a box which contained books and photographs belonging to LEE HARVEY OSWALD. MC CABE stated he searched this box and did not take the camera since he did not consider it to be of evidentiary value.

On March 23, 1964, Detective MC CABE advised that during the search of the garage at the PAINE residence, where most of LEE HARVEY OSWALD's belongings were located, he was going through a box containing some books, some pictures, and a camera. He took the camera out of the box, put it on a dresser and searched the box in detail, and then put the camera back in the box. He described the camera as of a square, reflex type which appeared in such poor condition that he believed it was not capable of taking pictures.

Detective MC CABE was shown Federal Bureau of Investigation Laboratory Photograph D-146 of an Imperial Reflex camera which had been obtained from ROBERT OSWALD on February 24, 1964, and he stated the camera in this photograph appeared identical with the one he described above.

Detective MC CABE stated that in his opinion the Dallas Police Officers, who were also participating in the search, did not see this camera and did not search this particular box. He stated he had already searched the box and told them so. He did not point out the camera to them.

COMMISSION EXHIBIT NO. 2557—Continued

Re: LEE HARVEY OSWALD

On February 19, 1964, Mrs. RUTH PAINE, 2515 West Fifth Street, Irving, Texas, advised that approximately three weeks after the assassination of President KENNEDY, ROBERT OSWALD, accompanied by two individuals whom she later determined were JAMES MARTIN and JOHN THORNE, came to her residence and requested that they take all the remaining property belonging to LEE HARVEY OSWALD and MARINA OSWALD. Mrs. PAINE advised that she pointed out to them the boxes and other materials in her garage belonging to the OSWALDS and they removed this property.

On February 24, 1964, ROBERT LEE OSWALD made available a Duo-Lens Imperial Reflex camera made in the United States of America. It is aluminum colored and has a matching gray plastic carrying strap. The film size is indicated as 2¼ X 2¼ and it uses Roll Film No. 620. ROBERT LEE OSWALD advised that in about 1957, LEE HARVEY OSWALD purchased a camera at about the time he first went into the U. S. Marine Corps. About 1959 when LEE HARVEY OSWALD went to Russia, he left this camera with ROBERT at Fort Worth, Texas. In about August 1962, after returning from Russia, LEE HARVEY OSWALD regained possession of this camera from ROBERT and, to ROBERT's knowledge, retained possession of it until his death on November 24, 1963.

In December 1963 ROBERT stated he obtained this camera, along with other effects of LEE HARVEY OSWALD, from the home of Mrs. RUTH PAINE, Irving, Texas. The above-described Duo-Lens Imperial Reflex camera was the camera described above by ROBERT LEE OSWALD and the camera which he made available on February 24, 1964. To the best of ROBERT's knowledge, the camera did not have film in it at the time he obtained it from Mrs. PAINE's residence and he has no undeveloped film or pictures made with this camera.

On February 25, 1964, the above-described Imperial Reflex camera obtained from ROBERT LEE OSWALD on February 24, 1964, was exhibited to MARINA OSWALD, at which time she identified it as the camera belonging to LEE HARVEY OSWALD with which she had taken the picture of OSWALD holding the rifle and newspaper and wearing the pistol.

Re: LEE HARVEY OSWALD

On March 14, 1964, Detectives JOHN P. ADAMCIK, RICHARD S. STOVALL, GUY F. ROSE, and HENRY M. MOORE of the Dallas Police Department advised that they participated in a search of the PAINE residence, 2515 West Fifth Street, Irving, Texas, on November 22 and 23, 1963.

All four of these individuals were exhibited a Federal Bureau of Investigation Laboratory Photograph No. D-146 of the Imperial Reflex camera obtained from ROBERT LEE OSWALD on February 24, 1964. None of these officers could recall ever having seen this camera and did not recall seeing it during a search of the garage at the PAINE residence. They all stated that if it had been discovered during the search, they would have brought it in.

On March 23, 1964, Detectives STOVALL, ROSE and MOORE all advised that during the search of the PAINE residence they recalled that there were several boxes in the garage at the PAINE residence and that all boxes were searched by one of the officers participating in the search. Each of them stated they could not specifically state which boxes they searched, but all stated they definitely did not see the Imperial Reflex camera pictured in Federal Bureau of Investigation Laboratory Photograph No. D-146, or any other camera in the PAINE garage.

On March 24, 1964, Detective ADAMCIK also stated that there were several boxes in the garage at the PAINE residence and that all boxes were searched by either himself or one of the other officers. He could not specifically state which boxes he searched, but stated he definitely did not see the Imperial Reflex camera pictured in Federal Bureau of Investigation Laboratory Photograph No. D-146, or any other camera in the garage.

On March 15, 1964, ROBERT OSWALD, 1009 Sierra, Denton, Texas, advised that on December 8, 1963, he obtained property of LEE HARVEY OSWALD and MARINA OSWALD which was at the home of RUTH PAINE in Irving, Texas. Included in this property was a box which contained a two-volume history, some Russian books, and a small American-made camera. He stated he had never made this camera available to authorities before February 24, 1964, because he had never been asked for it previously and because he could see no evidentiary value to anyone interested in the assassination of President JOHN FITZGERALD KENNEDY of this cheap camera which belonged to LEE HARVEY OSWALD. He stated that it had never occurred to him that anyone would be interested in the camera.

ROBERT advised he has no letters in his possession that LEE HARVEY OSWALD had written and that the only letters he did have were those turned over by him to the President's Commission.

ROBERT OSWALD made available the box which contained this camera, and the items it still contains, all of which were the property of either LEE HARVEY OSWALD or MARINA OSWALD. The first thirteen items are books:

1. V. I. LENIN - MARX - ENGELS - MARXISM

2. "Baby and Child Care" - Dr. BENJAMIN SPOCK

3. "The Iliad" - HOMER

4. "Perfect Lovers Guide and other stories" - STEPHEN LEACOCK

5. "Squibb Product Reference"

6. "Short Russian Reference Grammar"

7. "Russian - Elementary Course I"

8-
13. Six books in Russian language. In one book designated as No. 8, a note is written in the front:

"Dear Lee

"Great Congratulations,
Let all your dreams come true!
18. x 1959
Moscow
Rimma"

(October 18 is LEE HARVEY OSWALD's birthday.)

14. Cellophane tape, one roll

15. One small fuse

16. One pair dice

17. 29 dominoes and one box - "Made in Japan"

18. One pencil sharpener

19. One carriage bolt

20. One clothespin

21. One sheet white bond paper located in book designated as Item No. 13

ROBERT OSWALD made available all other property of LEE HARVEY OSWALD still in his possession, which he obtained from the home of RUTH PAINE on December 8, 1963:

1. Val-pak type suitcase

2. One Texas flag - small

3. One Master Lock Padlock

4. One shower spray attachment

5. One treated cloth in paper container

6. One Marine Corps belt and buckle

Re; LEE HARVEY OSWALD

7. One pencil
8. One sea bag
9. One carton for "Vegian Chewables"
10. One set long underwear
11. Three ties
12. One pair men's black gloves
13. One brown and gray leather cap
14. Two mufflers
15. One summer khaki overseas hat
16. One chess set - board and 27 pieces and 15 dominoes
17. One extension cord
18. One pair shoe trees
19. One can black shoe polish
20. One pencil sharpener
21. One sea shell
22. One green eraser
23. One shoe brush
24. One coloring pencil
25. One shaving brush
26. One Schick box for electric shaver

- 7 -

COMMISSION EXHIBIT No. 2557—Continued

Re: LEE HARVEY OSWALD

27. One manicure set
28. One miniature silver spoon - broken
29. One knit shopping bag
30. One green winter overseas hat (USMC)

- 8 -

COMMISSION EXHIBIT No. 2557—Continued

OFFICE OF THE DIRECTOR

UNITED STATES DEPARTMENT OF JUSTICE

FEDERAL BUREAU OF INVESTIGATION

WASHINGTON 25, D.C.

February 28, 1964

BY COURIER SERVICE

Honorable J. Lee Rankin
General Counsel
The President's Commission
200 Maryland Avenue, N. E.
Washington, D. C.

Dear Mr. Rankin:

Reference is made to my letter dated February 19, 1964, which reported that Marina Oswald had expressed the belief that she took the photograph of Lee Harvey Oswald with the rifle and pistol using her husband's American camera. She described the camera as grayish in color, something like aluminum.

On February 24, 1964, Mr. Robert Lee Oswald, brother of Lee, furnished to a Special Agent of the Dallas Office of this Bureau a Duo-lens Imperial reflex camera which he stated was the property of Lee. This camera is aluminum colored, uses roll film, number 620, has a matching gray plastic carrying strap and is equipped for use with a flash attachment. Robert advised that he obtained this camera from the residence of Mrs. Ruth Paine, Irving, Texas, in December, 1963. At that time it did not contain film. He advised that this camera was purchased by Lee in about 1957 and Lee subsequently left it with Robert in about 1959 when Lee went to Russia. After Lee returned from Russia, he regained possession of this camera and, as far as Robert is aware, retained possession of it until his death. Robert stated that, although this camera is equipped for use with a flash attachment, he had no knowledge that Lee had such an attachment.

On February 25, 1964, this camera was displayed to Marina Oswald and she immediately identified it as the American camera which belonged to her husband and the one which she used to take the photograph of him with the rifle and the pistol.

COMMISSION EXHIBIT No. 2558

Honorable J. Lee Rankin

On February 24, 1964, Robert also made available to a Special Agent of this Bureau an Eastman Baby Brownie box camera which is currently in an inoperable condition. According to Robert, this camera also belonged to Lee and Robert first saw it in about 1953 in New York City when Robert visited his mother at her home in New York City. Robert last saw this camera in about 1958 when Lee gave it to Robert's daughter Cathy. To the best of Robert's knowledge, Lee did not have this latter camera in his possession subsequent to 1958.

Both of the above-mentioned cameras will be retained by this Bureau along with the other items of evidence in this case.

Sincerely yours,

J. Edgar Hoover

- 2 -

COMMISSION EXHIBIT No. 2558—Continued

OFFICE OF THE DIRECTOR

UNITED STATES DEPARTMENT OF JUSTICE

FEDERAL BUREAU OF INVESTIGATION

WASHINGTON 25, D.C.

March 26, 1964

BY COURIER SERVICE

Honorable J. Lee Rankin
General Counsel
The President's Commission
200 Maryland Avenue, Northeast
Washington, D. C.

Dear Mr. Rankin:

Reference is made to your letter of February 28, 1964, concerning the C14 rifle, a 6.5 millimeter Italian Service Rifle, Serial Number C2766.

Enclosed are two copies of a "Secret" memorandum, nine photographs prepared by the Federal Bureau of Investigation Laboratory and a copy of one page of the shipping manifest, number 3376 relating to the C14 rifle.

This completes your request and upon removal of the classified enclosure this communication becomes unclassified.

Sincerely yours,

J. Edgar Hoover

Enclosures (12)

COMMISSION EXHIBIT No. 2559

UNITED STATES DEPARTMENT OF JUSTICE

FEDERAL BUREAU OF INVESTIGATION

In Reply, Please Refer to
File No.

WASHINGTON 25, D. C.

March 17, 1964

LEE HARVEY OSWALD

The following information was furnished by a confidential source abroad on March 16, 1964:

1. Rifle C14 was manufactured by the Fabbrica Armi Esercito Terni - di Terni (the Army Arms Plant of Terni, Italy).

2. The number C2766 which appears on the barrel of the C14 rifle is the serial number of the rifle.

3. The C14 rifle is the only one of its type which bears serial number C2766.

4. It was not possible to definitely establish how many of this type of rifle were sold. It was established, however, that the Carlo Riva Machine Shop of Brescia, Italy, shipped rifles of the same type to Adam Consolidated Industries, Inc., 404 Fifth Avenue, New York 18, N. Y., telephone number WIsconsin 4-4490. Rifle C14 was one of the rifles in a lot of 5200 so shipped. This shipment, numbered 3376, was shipped from the Port of Genoa, Italy, on the ship "Elettra Fassio" on September 28, 1960.

Concerning the shipment of these rifles to Adam Consolidated Industries, Inc., there is presently a legal proceeding by the Carlo Riva Machine Shop to collect payment for the shipment of the rifles which Adam Consolidated Industries, Inc., claims were defective.

COMMISSION EXHIBIT No. 2559—Continued

The owner of the Carlo Riva Machine Shop, during a visit made to the United States in December of 1960, verified that about 7,000 of the rifles shipped to Adam Consolidated Industries, Inc., were in the possession of a company owned by Louis Feldsott of Yonkers, New York.

There follows a detailed description of the markings and numbers which appear in the photographs of the C14 rifle, serial number C2766.

Photograph 1. Depicts one of the weapons 91/38 modified by the Carlo Riva Machine Shop and sold to the Adam Consolidated Industries, Inc., of New York.

Photograph 2. The number C2766 is definitely the serial number of the rifle. The letters "SD" mean the inspector of the rifle.

Photograph 3. 1940 is the year of manufacture. The inscription "MADE ITALY" was placed on the rifle by Carlo Riva Machine Shop at the request of Adam Consolidated Industries, Inc. The crown emblem means the rifle was tested by the Army Arms Company.

Photograph 4. 1940 is the year of manufacture. "MADE ITALY" is the inscription Adam Consolidated Industries, Inc., wanted inscribed on the weapon prior to shipment. The crown R. E. Terni means the rifle was manufactured and tested by the Army Arms plant of Terni, Italy. "CAL.6.5" indicates the caliber of the rifle.

Photograph 5. The crown and TNI means the barrel of the rifle was inspected by an official of the Army Arms plant of Terni, Italy.

Photograph 6. It was not possible to establish what the letters "AG-47-2" mean; most probably they indicate the quality of steel used to manufacture the rifle and the letters remained after the rifle was completed.

Photograph 7. "Rocca" indicates the name of the designer or artisan of the rifle who manufactured and furnished the bolt cocking piece. Rocca, in fact, is named Giuseppe Rocca, who owned a machine shop in Lumezzane, Brescia, Italy. The shop is no longer in existence.

Photograph 8. P.G indicate the initials of the designer who during the period of manufacture of the rifle furnished the bolt handle.

Photograph 9. The number 40 indicates the year of manufacture while the mark on the extreme right of the photograph is the inscription made by the person who inspected the breech.

UNITED STATES DEPARTMENT OF JUSTICE

FEDERAL BUREAU OF INVESTIGATION

In Reply, Please Refer to
File No.

WASHINGTON 25, D. C.
June 16, 1964

LEE HARVEY OSWALD

On June 16, 1964, the confidential source abroad which had furnished information classified Secret on March 16, 1964, concerning the C-14 rifle, Serial No. C-2766, which information was incorporated into a memorandum dated March 17, 1964, captioned as above, gave permission to declassify all of the information it had provided on March 16, 1964, concerning the C-14 rifle.

COMMISSION EXHIBIT No. 2559—Continued

Memo for the Record

Mr. Eisenberg

Telephone message received from Mr. Meade Werner of the BRL of the Aberdeen Proving Ground on April 6, 1964:

"There were three pieces in the scope examined by the BRL gunsmith. Two pieces were .015 inches thick so placed as to elevate the scope with respect to the gun. One piece was .020 inches thick so placed as to point the scope leftward with respect to the gun. The gunsmith observed that the scope as we received it was installed as if for a left-handed man."

COMMISSION EXHIBIT No. 2560

OFFICE OF THE DIRECTOR

UNITED STATES DEPARTMENT OF JUSTICE

FEDERAL BUREAU OF INVESTIGATION

WASHINGTON 25, D.C.

April 2, 1964

By Courier Service

Honorable J. Lee Rankin
General Counsel
The President's Commission
200 Maryland Avenue, Northeast
Washington, D. C.

Dear Mr. Rankin:

In accordance with the request on March 30, 1964, of Mr. Melvin Eisenberg, paraffin tests were conducted with the assassination rifle, C14, by the FBI Laboratory.

The paraffin test consists of pouring warm paraffin over the hand or cheek, peeling the paraffin cast off and testing the inner surface of the paraffin for the presence of any gunpowder residues. The reagents used in this test, however, are not specific for only gunpowder residues and will react positively with most oxidizing agents. Oxidizing agents that will react are also present in such common substances as fertilizer, urine, tobacco and others, as well as gunpowder residues. In prior experiments conducted by the FBI Laboratory, it has been found that the paraffin test is unreliable as to whether a person recently fired a weapon, since in some instances, positive reactions were obtained on casts from the hands of persons who had not fired weapons and no reactions were obtained on casts from the hands of persons who had fired weapons.

Before conducting the tests with the assassination rifle, control paraffin tests of the right check and both hands were conducted on a Laboratory examiner who had thoroughly washed his face and hands and who had not recently fired a weapon. The paraffin casts were then treated with diphenylbenzidine, a sensitive reagent for the detection of most oxidizing agents. Numerous positive reactions were noted on the casts of both hands

COMMISSION EXHIBIT No. 2561

Honorable J. Lee Rankin

and no reactions were noted on the cheek cast. It is pointed out that warm paraffin can remove the foreign matter that is present on the skin or in the pores.

The assassination rifle was then rapid-fired three times by the same man on which the control tests were made. Paraffin casts of the examiner's right cheek and both hands were then prepared. These paraffin casts were also treated with diphenylbenzidine and there were no reactions.

Sincerely yours,

J. Edgar Hoover

2

COMMISSION EXHIBIT No. 2561—Continued

OFFICE OF THE DIRECTOR

UNITED STATES DEPARTMENT OF JUSTICE

FEDERAL BUREAU OF INVESTIGATION

WASHINGTON 25, D.C.

April 30, 1964

BY COURIER SERVICE

Honorable J. Lee Rankin
General Counsel
The President's Commission
200 Maryland Avenue, Northeast
Washington, D. C.

Dear Mr. Rankin:

Reference is made to your letter dated February 21, 1964, and my letter dated March 27, 1964, relating to the 6.5 millimeter Mannlicher-Carcano Italian military rifle, serial number C2766, and to your request for this Bureau to obtain the originals or photographic copies of all documents relating to this rifle as well as an Italian carbine rifle, serial number 2766.

Enclosed for your assistance are two copies of a twenty-page self-explanatory communication from our Dallas, Texas, Office dated April 22, 1964. This communication describes in a systematic manner the documents obtained by this Bureau in accordance with your request. The documents relating to the rifle bearing the serial number C2766 are described first followed by data on the rifle bearing serial number 2766.

In addition, there are enclosed two photographic copies each of thirty-six documents relating to the above rifles arranged in the same sequence as described in the enclosed Dallas communication.

For your information, copies of exhibits D 17, D 18, D 19, D 77 and J 1 have been previously furnished to you and were consequently not duplicated for this particular request. The originals or copies of the

COMMISSION EXHIBIT No. 2562

Honorable J. Lee Rankin

enclosed documents obtained by this Bureau are being retained in our Laboratory under the indicated exhibit identification numbers.

This concludes inquiries by this Bureau pursuant to the requests set forth in your letter dated February 21, 1964.

Sincerely yours,

J. Edgar Hoover

Enclosures (74)

- 2 -

COMMISSION EXHIBIT No. 2562—Continued

UNITED STATES DEPARTMENT OF JUSTICE

FEDERAL BUREAU OF INVESTIGATION

In Reply, Please Refer to
File No.

Dallas, Texas
April 22, 1964

LEE HARVEY OSWALD

The following is submitted pursuant to a request of the President's Commission to obtain the originals or photographic copies of all documents relating to K 1 (C 10) as well as a 6.5 Italian carbine rifle bearing Serial Number 2766 which was included in a shipment of 6.5 Italian carbine rifles made on July 5, 1962, from Century Arms, Incorporated, of St. Albans, Vermont, to Aldens of Chicago, Illinois:

RE: 6.5 M/M Mannlicher-Carcano
Italian Military Rifle,
Model 91/38, Serial Number C2766
(Exhibit C 10, also identified as K 1)

Mr. Louis Feldsott, President, Crescent Firearms, Incorporated, 2 West 37th Street, New York, New York, advised his company was organized to handle importation of foreign surplus rifles, especially those of an Italian origin, and the purchases of these rifles were made by him personally in Italy from the Italian Ministry of Defense.

The guns purchased were packed by a Crescent company agent in Italy in the presence of Italian authorities and at that time the serial number for each rifle was checked. The rifles were packed in cartons of ten each and a Crescent company shipping slip bearing the serial number for each rifle was attached to the outside of each rifle carton. Other copies of the shipping slip bearing the rifle serial numbers were forwarded to the Crescent company in New York City. Adam Consolidated Industries, 404 Fifth Avenue, New York, New York, was the importer of the rifles and stored them in a bonded warehouse upon their arrival in the United States. The rifles were subsequently cleared by Freedman and Slater Company, New York, New York, who are customs brokers.

COMMISSION EXHIBIT No. 2562—Continued

LEE HARVEY OSWALD

Since the rifles were used and in need of repair, they were subsequently trucked by Mr. Fred Rupp under Crescent company instructions to Perkasie, Pennsylvania, where Rupp serviced the rifles and shipped them to purchasers as directed by the Crescent company.

Office Copy of Ten Shipping Slips Reflecting Carton Numbers (Exhibit D 173)

Office copy, Crescent Firearms, Incorporated, shipping slip No. 3620 pertaining to carton No. 3376, lists a rifle having Serial Number C2766 as the third gun in the carton. This list was prepared at the time the rifles were packed in Italy.

Bill of Lading Number 18 for Motor Ship Elettra Fassio (Exhibit D 174)

This Bill of Lading, dated September 29, 1960, pertains to a shipment of 520 cartons of obsolete rifles to Adam Consolidated Industries, Incorporated, 404 Fifth Avenue, New York 18, New York, by S.N.T. Fratelli Gondrand. The rifles are further described as "No. 1700 Mod. 38 Cal. 6.5" and "No. 3500 Mod. 91 Cal. 6.5." The port of loading is indicated as Genoa and the port of discharge is New York. This Bill of Lading contains cartons "3305/3436" among the cartons listed.

Copy of Inventory List Reflecting Carton Numbers Attached to Above Bill of Lading Number 18 (Exhibit D 175)

This inventory list indicates carton No. 3376 contains ten serial numbers including "C2766."

LEE HARVEY OSWALD

Copy of Notice Dated October 10, 1960, with Estimated Date of Arrival of Shipment from Genoa to Adam Consolidated Industries, Incorporated (Exhibit D 177)

This notice is on the letterhead of Norton, Lilly and Company, Incorporated, 26 Beaver Street, New York 4, New York, and advised a shipment of 520 cartons of obsolete rifles shipped on Bill of Lading Genoa No. 18 via Elettra Fassio was due about "10-15."

Copy of Warehouse Entry Form from Freedman and Slater, Incorporated, No. 52737, dated October 24, 1960 (Exhibit D 176)

This exhibit on Customs Form 7502 Treasury Department pertains to a shipment of 520 cartons of rifles exported from Italy September 29, 1960, at Genoa on Bill of Lading No. 18 via Elettra Fassio. The importer of record is Adam Consolidated Industries, Incorporated, 404 Fifth Avenue, New York, N.Y., and the warehouse is "Harborside Terminal Warehouse." Included are cartons numbered "3305/3436" with the date imported given as "10-17-60."

Copy of a Bill of Lading Dated October 25, 1960, from Adam Consolidated Industries, Incorporated (Exhibit D 178)

This memorandum pertains to 520 cartons of rifles consigned to Harborside Terminal Company, Incorporated, 34 Exchange Place, Jersey City, New Jersey, via Waterfront Transfer Company, Custom House License No. 290, "in bond cargo." The cartons listed include "3305/3436" and the memorandum makes reference to Bill of Lading No. 18 Genoa dated September 29, 1960.

Exhibits D 173 through D 178 were made available by Louis Feldsott, President, Crescent Firearms, Incorporated, 2 West 37th Street, New York City, on March 13, 1964.

<u>Warehouse Receipt Dated November 9, 1960, of Harborside Terminal Company (Exhibit D 189)</u>

The billing copy of this receipt referring to Lot No. 91594 pertains to 520 cartons of rifles "38 E 91 I 6.5 Calibre" with charges for storage to Adams Consolidated from October 26, 1960. Also shown on this instrument are five deliveries to "Rupp" with dates and delivery order numbers. The warehouse receipt indicates a balance of 86 cartons remained as of May, 1963.

<u>Five Delivery Orders Numbered 89138, 14473, 03408, A01640, and A00642 (Exhibit D 190)</u>

The above delivery orders of Harborside Terminal Company, Incorporated, Jersey City, New Jersey, show Fred Rupp signed for deliveries against the account of Adams Consolidated, 404 Fifth Avenue, New York, New York, on August 29, 1962; October 4, 1962; October 16, 1962; October 24, 1962; and October 31, 1962. Only delivery order No. 89138 listed specific cartons of rifles obtained by Rupp.

Exhibits D 189 and D 190 were furnished by Frederick Peterson, President, Harborside Terminal Company, Incorporated, Exchange Place, Jersey City, New Jersey, on March 9, 1964.

<u>Copy of Sales Invoice No. 03408 from Adams Consolidated, 404 Fifth Avenue, Dated October 16, 1962 (Exhibit D 179)</u>

This invoice appears to be identical with delivery order No. 03408 listed under Exhibit D 190 other than it does not bear the notation "70 10-16-62 J. M. Krasnolutsky" and the initial "L" in the upper right corner. This instrument reflects the sale of 70 cartons of rifles "38 E 91 I 6.5 Calibre" to Fred Rupp "Via: Rupp." The signature "Fred Rupp" appears at the bottom as the person receiving the merchandise.

Exhibit D 179 was furnished by Louis Feldsott, President, Crescent Firearms, Incorporated, New York City, on March 13, 1964.

<u>Klein's Purchase Order for One Hundred Rifles Effective January 15, 1962 (Exhibit D 163)</u>

On April 15, 1964, William J. Waldman, Vice President, Klein's Sporting Goods, Incorporated, 4540 West Madison Street, Chicago, Illinois, furnished the following information regarding the above purchase order which was directed to Crescent Firearms, 2 West 37th Street, New York, New York: This purchase order is the bottom page of a multipage document containing data from various purchases, and in this case, all relating to Italian Mannlicher Carcano rifles. The center of the page contains a series of vertical columns each bearing the designation "A/R." Mr. WALDMAN noted that on an unused purchase order blank, in addition to a bottom page similar to this exhibit, there would be other pages with their leading edges extending to the vertical lines of each of the "A/R" columns. Each subsequent page in the purchase order blank would be narrower in width than the succeeding page and as a result would make reference only to one specific vertical column and the data contained thereon.

Mr. Waldman advised the "Effective 1/15/62" appearing on the above exhibit is correct and the date is utilized for administrative purposes only by his firm and indicates when the purchase order was first initiated. This date does not indicate in any way the date the order was placed, shipped, billed, or invoiced.

748-381 O—64—vol. XXV——53

LEE HARVEY OSWALD

This particular purchase order is only concerned with the column headed by Order No. 1243 dated January 24, 1963, and the vertical line drawn through the column makes reference only to a shipment of 100 of the described rifles which he commented is the shipment containing rifle bearing Serial Number C2766. The figures "200 and 400" in adjoining columns have no reference to the shipment of 100 rifles which contained the rifle having Serial Number C2766. Mr. Waldman advised this purchase order as shown makes reference only to an order and subsequent shipment of 100 Italian Mannlicher-Carcano rifles, Klein's Catalog No. C20-T749. The bottom of the purchase order indicates the shipment of 100 rifles consisting of ten packages was received February 21, 1963, via Lifschultz Freight under Bill of Lading No. 3041342 which weighed 750 pounds. He also noted this form under the columns "Accounting Department" and "Extension" bears Klein's Extension No. 85000 which indicates the receipt of the one hundred rifles was recorded for accounting purposes on February 22, 1963.

Exhibit D 163 was furnished by Mr. Waldman on March 12, 1964.

<u>Original Sales Order, Crescent Firearms, Incorporated, No. 3178, Dated February 7, 1963 (Exhibit D 172)</u>

This instrument shows a sale to Klein's Sporting Goods, Incorporated, 4540 West Madison Street, Chicago, Illinois, on Customer's No. 1243 consisting of "100 ea. T-38 6.5 It. Rifles" at $8.50 each. This sales order shows ten cases were shipped February 12, 1963, via Lifschultz and that one of the cases bore number "3376."

Exhibit D 172 was furnished by Louis Feldsott, President, Crescent Firearms, Incorporated, New York City, on March 13, 1964.

COMMISSION EXHIBIT No. 2562—Continued

LEE HARVEY OSWALD

<u>Page from Record Book of Mr. Fred W. Rupp Indicating Shipment on February 12, 1963 (Exhibit D 151)</u>

Fred W. Rupp, Rural Free Delivery Two, Mink Road, Perkasie, Pennsylvania, advised he has a subcontract with Crescent Firearms, Incorporated, New York City, to clean various types of Italian-made rifles and he periodically obtained these guns from Harborside Warehouse Terminal, Jersey City, New Jersey. He said his records do not show the serial number of any individual gun handled by him. The only record he has is the carton number record of the cartons he ships from his place of business to various customers designated by Crescent Firearms, Incorporated, New York City. His shipping book reveals that on February 12, 1963, on Crescent Firearms, Incorporated, Order No. 3178, he turned over carton No. 3376 to North Penn Transfer Company, Lansdale, Pennsylvania, for shipment, however, his records do not reflect to whom the shipment was made because the Bill of Lading furnished to him by North Penn Transfer Company was sent to Crescent Firearms, Incorporated, New York City.

Exhibit D 151 was furnished by Mr. Fred W. Rupp, Perkasie, Pennsylvania.

<u>Bill of Lading No. 3178, Crescent Firearms, Incorporated (Exhibit D 171)</u>

The memorandum copy signed by I. Moore as agent shows ten cartons or cases of guns or rifles weighing 750 pounds were consigned collect to Klein's Sporting Goods, 4540 West Madison Street, Chicago, Illinois. The name of the carrier is shown as "NPT" of Lansdale, Pennsylvania, and the route is indicated as Lifschultz Freight.

This exhibit was furnished by Louis Feldsott, President, Crescent Firearms, Incorporated, New York City, March 13, 1964.

COMMISSION EXHIBIT No. 2562—Continued

<u>Photostat of Undated Bill
of Lading No. 3178
(Exhibit D 152)</u>

This exhibit is the shipping order copy containing the same information as Exhibit D 171 with the exception that it indicates the shipment concerned was received at Ottsville, Pennsylvania, and has the stamped number 394857 in the upper middle of the page.

This exhibit was furnished by Arthur N. Anders, President and General Manager, North Penn Transfer, Incorporated, Route 63 at 202, Lansdale, Pennsylvania.

<u>North Penn Transfer, Incorporated,
Delivery Receipt for Shipping Order
No. 3178
(Exhibit D 153)</u>

The above instrument bearing North Penn Transfer, Incorporated, 'Pro. No. A394857', pertaining to ten cartons or cases of guns or rifles, weighing 750 pounds, shows the shipper as Crescent Firearms, Incorporated, Ottsville, Pennsylvania, Shippers No. 3178, and the consignee as <u>Kelins</u> Sporting Goods, 4540 West Madison Street, Chicago, Illinois, with the connecting carrier indicated as "LIFS FF." A receiving stamp indicates this shipment was received by Lifschultz Fast Freight, February 13, 1963.

This exhibit was obtained from Arthur N. Anders, President and General Manager, North Penn Transfer, Incorporated, Route 63 at 202, Lansdale, Pennsylvania.

<u>Consignee's Memo 'Pro No.
A394857" Dated February 12, 1963
(Exhibit D 168)</u>

This instrument was issued by North Penn Transfer, Incorporated, Lansdale, Pennsylvania, and indicates receipt by Lifschultz Fast Freight, Philadelphia, Pennsylvania, February 13, 1963. This item also bears the stamped number "41342."

<u>Delivery Receipt No. 3-041342
Dated February 13,
(Exhibit D 169)</u>

This instrument was issued by Lifschultz Fast Freight, 28 North Franklin Street, Chicago, Illinois, for a shipment of ten cartons or cases of guns or rifles weighing 750 pounds. The shipper is Crescent Firearms, Pottsville, Pennsylvania, and the consignee is Klein's Sporting Goods, 4540 West Madison, no city shown. This receipt bears the perforated number 48969 and was received at Klein's Sporting Goods, Incorporated, on February 21, 1963.

<u>Cashier's Copy, Chicago
Run Sheet, No. 48969, Dated
February 21, 1963
(Exhibit D 170)</u>

The above run sheet of Lifschultz Fast Freight, driver Jones, No. 293, trailer No. 43, shows a delivery was made to Klein's Sporting Goods consisting of ten pieces weighing 750 pounds on Bill No. 041342.

Exhibits D 168 through D 170 were furnished by Merrill Brown, Lifschultz Fast Freight, Chicago, Illinois, November 25, 1963.

<u>Invoice No. 3178,
Crescent Firearms, Incorporated,
Dated February 7, 1963
(Exhibit D 165)</u>

This invoice shows 100 "T38 6.5 It. rifles" were sold to Klein's Sporting Goods, Incorporated, Chicago, Illinois, on the basis of Order No. 1243 via North Penn Transfer - Lifschultz. The invoice bears the stamped date of "Feb 20 1963" and a vouchering stamp indicating the invoice was paid March 4, 1963.

Five Pages of "Customers Invoice" of Crescent Firearms, Incorporated (Exhibit D 164)

The above accompanied the shipment of rifles to Klein's Sporting Goods, Chicago, Illinois, on invoice No. 3178. There is one "Customers Invoice" for each carton shipped and on it is listed the serial number of each of the ten rifles contained in the carton. "Customers Invoice" No. 3620 which pertains to carton No. 3376 reveals rifle No. C2766 is listed as No. 3.

Exhibits D 164 and D 165 were furnished by William J. Waldman, Vice President, Klein's Sporting Goods, Incorporated, Chicago, Illinois, on March 12, 1964.

Photostat of List Prepared by Mitchell Scibor, Klein's Sporting Goods (Exhibit D 167)

This list is described as a copy of a record made by Scibor upon opening the gun cases on February 22, 1963. The notation "RR 1243" indicates the receiving report number which detailed the method of travel of the guns. The date "2-22-63" indicates when the gun cartons were opened. The bold-face numbers are control numbers assigned to each rifle with the serial number of each listed thereafter as it is taken from the carton and checked for accuracy. Control No. "836" shows a weapon having Serial Number C2766.

Exhibit D 167 was furnished by Mitchell Scibor, Klein's Sporting Goods, Chicago, Illinois, on November 23, 1963.

One Check and Attached Klein's Voucher No. 28966 (Exhibit D 166)

Check No. 28966 of Klein's Sporting Goods, Incorporated, 4540 West Madison Street, Chicago, Illinois, dated March 1, 1963, in the amount of $850 is payable to Crescent Firearms, Incorporated, 2 West 37th Street, New York, New York, and it is drawn on the First National Bank of Chicago, Illinois. The voucher bearing No. 28966 bears the date "2-7" and refers to payment of invoice No. 3178 in the amount of $850.

Exhibit D 166 was furnished by William J. Waldman, Vice President, Klein's Sporting Goods, Incorporated, Chicago, Illinois, on March 12, 1964.

Photograph of Roll of Microfilm from Klein's Sporting Goods, Incorporated, Chicago, Illinois, Which Contains Photograph of Envelope, Order Form, and Order Blank for Italian Carbine, Serial Number C2766 (Exhibit D 77)

This roll of microfilm is further described as Filmfill No. 83, 269688-270596, General Files, and contains photographs of various business documents.

Exhibit D 77 was made available by William J. Waldman, Vice President, Klein's Sporting Goods, Incorporated, Chicago, Illinois, on November 23, 1963.

Photographs Made from Microfilm (Exhibit D 77) of Envelope, Order Form, and Order Blank from Klein's Pertaining to Italian Rifle, Serial Number C2766 (Exhibit J 1)

The envelope postmarked Dallas, Texas, March 12, 1963, is addressed to Klein's and bears the return address of A. Hidell, Post Office Box 2915, Dallas, Texas. The order form which accompanied the envelope is a small advertisement of Klein's. This item is an order for item No. "C20-T750" and indicates the sum of $19.95 is the purchase price. This order form was signed A. Hidell with the address of Post Office Box 2915, Dallas, Texas. Klein's Sporting Goods "Order Blank" bearing the machine date of March 13, 1963, on transaction No. 270502 reflects the purchase of one Italian carbine 6.5 W/4X Scope, Control Number VC 836, Serial Number C2766, at a cost of $19.95. The item number is shown as C20-T750 which was shipped "PP" on March 20, 1963, to the purchaser who was listed as A. Hidell, Post Office Box 2915, Dallas, Texas. The total amount enclosed is shown as "21.45" "MO" which included $1.50 for postage or handling charge.

According to William J. Waldman, Vice President, Klein's Sporting Goods, Incorporated, the money order received in payment of the above rifle was deposited at the First National Bank of Chicago on March 15, 1963, in company account No. 50-91144.

Exhibit J 1 was made available by Mr. Waldman on November 23, 1963.

United States Postal Money Order Payable to Klein's (Exhibit D 19)

Money Order No. 2202130462, in the amount of $21.45, issued at Dallas, Texas, March 12, 1963, is payable to Klein's Sporting Goods and the purchaser is shown as A. Hidell, Post Office Box 2915, Dallas, Texas. This money order is endorsed in favor of The First National Bank of Chicago, Illinois, by Klein's Sporting Goods, Incorporated, Account No. 50-91144.

Exhibit D 19 was made available by Special Agent John H. Grimes, United States Secret Service, Washington, D. C., November 24, 1963.

Application for Post Office Boxes Signed by Oswald (Exhibit D 17)

The application dated October 9, 1962, signed Lee H. Oswald, directed to Postmaster W. B. Hudson, reveals box No. 2915 was opened October 9, 1962, and was closed on May 14, 1963. This item is also identified as Q 34.

Change of Address Order by Oswald (Exhibit D 18)

POD Form 3575 addressed to Postmaster, Dallas, Texas, signed Lee H. Oswald with the effective date of May 12, 1963, changed the address of Oswald from Post Office Box 2915, Dallas, Texas, to 4907 Magazine Street, New Orleans, Louisiana. This form bears the date stamp of "5-14-63." This exhibit is also further identified as K 18.

RE: 6.5 Italian Carbine Rifle, Serial Number 2766, Shipped From Century Arms, Incorporated, St. Albans, Vermont, to Aldens of Chicago, July 5, 1962

Empire Wholesale Sporting Goods, Limited, Invoice No. 1078 (Exhibit 156)

The invoice of Empire Wholesale Sporting Goods, Limited, 360 Craig Street, West, Montreal, Quebec, dated June 29, 1962, reflects the sale of 700 used Italian rifles made in Italy to Century Arms, Incorporated, 54 Lake Street, St. Albans, Vermont. Also included in this invoice were 600 rifles of a different make.

Exhibit D 156 was furnished by James L. Ouimet, owner, Century Arms, Incorporated, St. Albans, Vermont, March 11, 1964.

Original List of Serial Numbers of 700 Carcano Italian Carbines Received by Century Arms, Incorporated, from Empire Wholesale Sporting Goods Limited Montreal, Quebec, Canada. Serial Number 2766 Appears on Last Page of Numbers (Exhibit D 103)

The above list accompanied Empire Wholesale Sporting Goods, Limited, invoice No. 1078. The top of the first page bears notations "Carcano," "Case #'s," and "Italian Carbines." It is noted on pages one through six there are 25 serial numbers listed to each case. On page seven there are listed 50 serial numbers to each case. In addition, the top of the last page bears a notation "Italian Carbine 46"."

Exhibit D 103 was obtained from James L. Ouimet, owner, Century Arms, Incorporated, St. Albans, Vermont, November 23, 1963.

<u>Photostat of Canadian</u>
<u>National Railways Straight</u>
<u>Bill of Lading Dated June 29, 1962</u>
<u>(Exhibit D 180)</u>

This document pertains to a shipment from Empire Wholesale Sporting Goods, Limited, Montreal Quebec, consigned to Century Arms, Incorporated, 54 Lake Street, St. Albans, Vermont. The shipment is described as 41 cases of used guns (1300) and "No further use except for ornamental purposes CLASSIFICATION No.: 73080."

Exhibit D 180 was furnished by William Sucher, owner, International Firearms Company, Limited, 1011 Bleury Street, Montreal, Canada.

In connection with efforts to obtain documentary exhibits from Empire Wholesale Sporting Goods, Limited, Montreal, Canada, it was learned the concern is not active. It is operated by a Mr. Itkovitch, a brother-in-law of William Sucher, owner of International Firearms Company, Limited, Montreal, and is reported as probably fully owned by the latter company.

William Sucher on March 12, 1964, advised he has bought hundreds of thousands of rifles overseas as Italian Government surplus and he does not maintain the serial numbers of these rifles. Many were collected from battlefields and places of improper storage and they were in very poor condition. They were usually bought by the

pound rather than units. Upon arrival in Canada, defective parts were removed and salable rifles were sometimes composed of parts of three or more weapons. Sucher advised the Mannlicher-Carcano rifle was manufactured in Italy from 1891 until 1941 however in the 1930's Mussolini ordered all arms factories to manufacture the Mannlicher-Carcano rifle. Since many concerns were manufacturing the same weapon, the same serial number appears on weapons manufactured by more than one concern. Some bear a letter prefix and some do not. Sucher stated at times he has prepared a listing of serial numbers of rifles in a given shipment for customs purposes and that listing was thereafter transmitted with the shipment. International Firearms Company, Limited, did not maintain a copy of the serial numbers of the rifles and no such listing is required by law.

Sucher located a record of documents listed as Exhibit D 156 which invoice was paid by Century Arms, Incorporated, on August 6, 1962, and Exhibit D 180. He advised there are no additional records of this shipment in the possession of his company and he is sure the serial numbers of the individual weapons involved were not recorded at the point of shipment as he is certain his purchase was on a per pound basis.

<u>Photostat of Consumption</u>
<u>Entry No. 77, Bureau of Customs</u>
<u>(Exhibit D 158)</u>

The above Treasury Department form dated July 6, 1962, shows the port of entry as St. Albans, Vermont, and the "Term Bond No." as "3." The importer of record is indicated as A. N. Deringer, Incorporated, St. Albans, Vermont, for account of Century Arms, Incorporated, St. Albans. The country of importation is Canada with the importing vessel or carrier shown as Central Vermont Railway, Incorporated. The date of "exportation" and "importation" is given as July 1, 1962. The shipment pertains to 700 used Italian rifles and 600 used English rifles.

Photostat of Examination
and Appraisal of Entry No. 77
(Exhibit D 159)

The above document dated July 6, 1962, which is to be attached to the invoice, reflects the merchandise was examined and released under immediate delivery permit No. 3 on July 3, 1962.

Exhibits D 158 and D 159 were furnished by Mark K. Gardner, United States Customs Agent in Charge, St. Albans, Vermont, March 11, 1964.

Century Arms, Incorporated,
Order No. 8934, Dated June 29,
1962, Reflecting Sale of 700 6.5
Caliber Italian Carbines to
Aldens, 5000 West Roosevelt Road,
Chicago, Illinois
(Exhibit D 102)

The above order refers to Aldens Order No. 82803 and bears a handwritten notation that it was shipped July 5, 1962.

Exhibit D 102 was furnished by James L. Ouimet, owner, Century Arms, Incorporated, St. Albans, Vermont, November 23, 1963.

Memorandum for Bill of
Lading from H. P. Welch Company,
Dated June 29, 1962
(Exhibit D 157)

The above memorandum of H. P. Welch Company home office, 400 Somerville Avenue, Somerville, Massachusetts, relates to a shipment from Century Arms, Incorporated, St. Albans, Vermont, to Aldens, 5000 West Roosevelt Road, Department G 33, Chicago, Illinois, consisting of 25 cases containing 700 rifles. It also refers to Order No. 82803, Catalog No. 33-3541M.

Exhibit D 157 was furnished by James L. Ouimet, Century Arms, Incorporated, St. Albans, Vermont, March 11, 1964.

Photostat of H. P. Welch Company
Shipping Order Dated June 29, 1962
(Exhibit D 181)

This Shipping Order pertains to a shipment of 25 cases containing 700 rifles from Century Arms, Incorporated, St. Albans, Vermont, consigned to Aldens, Chicago, Illinois. It bears the stamped impression "E. Ward Truck No. 499 Jul 5 1962." Elmer Ward is the company driver who picked up this shipment at St. Albans on July 5, 1962, and took it to the company terminal at Burlington, Vermont. This order also bears the stamped number "3686."

Exhibit D 181 was made available by Albert C. Penney, Office Manager, H. P. Welch Company, 400 Somerville Avenue, Somerville, Massachusetts, March 17, 1964.

Duplicate of H. P. Welch
Company Waybill No. B-3686
Dated July 6, 1962
(Exhibit D 160)

This waybill indicates a collect shipment from Century Arms, Incorporated, St. Albans, Vermont, to Aldens of Chicago, Illinois, consisting of 25 cases containing 700 rifles and refers to Order No. 82803.

Exhibit D 160 was furnished by Abe Shindel, Manager, H. P. Welch Company, Burlington, Vermont, March 11, 1964.

Yellow Duplicate Copy of
H. P. Welch Company Waybill
No. B-3686
(Exhibit D 182)

This copy bearing No. "7" in upper right corner dated July 6, 1962, pertains to a shipment from Century Arms, Incorporated, St. Albans, Vermont, to Aldens, Chicago, Illinois, consisting of 25 cases containing 700 rifles under Order No. 82803.

The stamped notation "T-MCLEAN 7526" indicates the shipment was loaded on a McLean trailer and transported to Somerville, Massachusetts, the same date by a Welch Company driver where it laid over until Monday, July 9, 1962. On July 9, 1962, the shipment was unloaded from truck No. 7526 at the Somerville terminal of the Welch Company and reloaded on company truck No. 344739 operated by driver J. Dillon as noted by a stamped impression in the upper left corner of the waybill. The shipment was then transferred by Dillon on July 9, 1962, to Eastern Express Company terminal at 260 Western Avenue, Allston, Massachusetts, where it was again unloaded as the Eastern Express Company was to transport the shipment to the consignee at Chicago, Illinois. The signature "Conway" in the lower left corner indicates receipt of the shipment by Eastern Express Company.

Exhibit D 182 was obtained from Albert C. Penney, Office Manager, H. P. Welch Company, 400 Somerville Avenue, Somerville, Massachusetts, on March 17, 1964, who also furnished explanations for the entries.

Photostat of Customer's Copy
of H. P. Welch Company Waybill
No. B-3686
(Exhibit D 183)

This copy of the waybill dated July 6, 1962, bears a penciled notation "191947."

James Mooney, Office Manager, Boston Terminal, Eastern Express Company, 260 Western Avenue, Allston, Massachusetts, on March 17, 1964, advised the number "191947" is the waybill number assigned by his company to this shipment. His company's manifest has been destroyed and he has no records to show the date of receipt by

his company or the date shipped to the consignee in Chicago. The shipment was signed for by Charles Conway, Dock Supervisor, when received by his company.

Exhibit D 183 was furnished by Mr. James Mooney on March 17, 1964.

Delivery Receipt from
Eastern Express, Incorporated
(Exhibit D 201)

This receipt, dated July 9, 1962, bearing "Pro. No." 191947, pertains to a shipment from Century Arms, Incorporated, St. Albans, Vermont, to Aldens, 5000 West Roosevelt Road, Department G 33, Chicago, Illinois, consisting of 25 cases containing 700 rifles on Order No. 82803. It also refers to "Welch B 3686 7/6." The receipt also bears a receiving stamp of Aldens, Incorporated, dated July 12, 1962.

Exhibit D 201 was furnished by James Damron, Assistant Terminal Manager, Eastern Express, Incorporated, 7526 State Road, Bedford Park, Illinois.

Invoice No. 8934,
Century Arms, Incorporated
(Exhibit D 161)

This invoice dated June 29, 1962, pertains to a shipment made to Aldens, 5000 West Roosevelt Road, Department G 33, Chicago Illinois, their Order No. 82803, consisting of 700 6.5 Italian carbines. The invoice bears a block stamp showing the date received as July 9, 1962. Additional stamps indicate the invoice was received in the "Invoice Unit" and the "Accounting Dept." on July 13, 1962. The invoice also bears the handwritten numerals in the upper right corner of "14535."

LEE HARVEY OSWALD

Aldens Checking Slip
No. 293779
(Exhibit D 162)

This document dated July 12, 1962, refers to a shipment having waybill No. 191947 received from Century Arms, Incorporated, via Eastern Express consisting of 25 packages. The catalog number is given as 33 B 3541 and the total received is "700." The bottom of the slip near items "received by" and "checked by" bears the date of July 12, 1962.

Exhibits D 161 and D 162 were furnished by Albert Lesko, Manager, Accounting Department, Aldens, Chicago, Illinois, March 5, 1964, who advised these two items are the only records still available at his company and the serial numbers of the rifles received are not available.

- 20 -

COMMISSION EXHIBIT No. 2562—Continued

[redacted]

Commission Exhibit No. 2563

UNITED STATES DEPARTMENT OF JUSTICE
FEDERAL BUREAU OF INVESTIGATION

In Reply, Please Refer to
File No.

WASHINGTON 25, D. C.
April 20, 1964

LEE HARVEY OSWALD

BASIS FOR INQUIRY

The following information was furnished by a confidential source abroad on March 17, 1964:

The travel document with which LEE HARVEY OSWALD entered Mexico on September 26, 1963, is described as a Mexican Ministry of "Gobernacion" (Interior) FM-8 and is commonly referred to as a tourist card, which consists of two sections, an original and a carbon copy duplicate. At the time of OSWALD's travel to Mexico, the FM-8 was valid for a single entry to the interior of Mexico and residence therein for no longer than fifteen days. The original tourist card utilized by OSWALD, which is reproduced on the following page, records the following data:

FM-8 No.:	24085, valid for 15 days.
Full Name:	LEE, HARVEY OSWALD
	Photographer
Sex:	Male
Marital Status:	Married
Document with Which Nationality Was Established:	Birth Certificate
Final Destination:	Mexico, D. F.
Date and Place (of issuance):	New Orleans, La., USA, September 17, 1963.
Signature of Bearer:	LEE H. OSWALD

It bears the stamp of the Consulate General of Mexico at New Orleans, Louisiana, indicating issuance by that agency, and the date stamp of Mexican Immigration official HELIO TUEXI MAYDON, reflecting entry into Mexico at Nuevo Laredo, Tamaulipas, September 26, 1963. The stamp for departure is that of Immigration official ALBERTO ARZAMENDI CHAPA and the date shown is October 3, 1963. Under normal procedures, the means of travel of the bearer upon entry to Mexico is recorded on both sections of the tourist card at the top thereof with a stamped, typed or handwritten notation; however, this record does not appear on the FM-8 for OSWALD.

COMMISSION EXHIBIT No. 2563

F.M.-8

ESTADOS UNIDOS MEXICANOS

SECRETARIA DE GOBERNACION

ORIGINAL Nº 24085

VALIDA POR 15 DIAS

BUENA PARA UN SOLO VIAJE POR 5 (CINCO) DIAS

Apellidos y nombre LEE, HARVEY OSWALD

FOTOGRAFO

Sexo H [X] M [ ] Edad 23 AÑOS Estado Civil S [ ] C [X]

Documento con el que acredita su nacionalidad: ACTA NACIMIENTO

Menores que lo acompañan:

Destino MEXICO, D. F.

NUEVA ORLEANS, LA., EUA.,

17 SEPTIEMBRE DE 1963.

Lugar y fecha

ENTRADA SET 26 1963

NUEVO LAREDO, TAMPS.

SALIDA

ALBERTO ARZAMENDI CHAPA

Nuevo Laredo, Tamps

OCT. 1963

Copied above is the original portion of the Mexican FM-8 with which LEE HARVEY OSWALD entered Mexico on September 26, 1963, and departed therefrom on October 3, 1963. Although he is known to have traveled by bus from Nuevo Laredo to Mexico City, his mode of travel is not recorded on the FM-8, which was retrieved and cancelled by ALBERTO ARZAMENDI CHAPA at the time of his departure. No space is provided on the card for recording means of travel upon departure, and no such information appears on the above card. The back of the FM-8 contains no information other than printed instructions and warnings to the traveler in Spanish, English and French.

A review of the original tourist cards (FM-5, FM-8, and one FM-17, latter explained below) in the possession of the Immigration Department of the Mexican Ministry of "Gobernacion" revealed that 79 persons documented with those forms had departed from Mexico at Nuevo Laredo, Tamaulipas, on October 3, 1963, among them LEE HARVEY OSWALD.

On March 23, 1964, Mr. MACLOVIO HERRERA, Chief of the Travel Control Files of the Mexican Immigration Department, advised that in a circular instruction dated March 20, 1962, the Chief of the Immigration Department described the Immigration form "FM-11" as a "statistical record to be prepared every two weeks on nationals and aliens entering and leaving the country." Mr. HERRERA explained that separate FM-11 forms are submitted semimonthly by all Mexican Immigration stations for entries and departures from Mexico. He explained that separate lists are prepared in connection with the various types of travel documents presented and are submitted in duplicate (an original and one carbon copy) to the Travel Control Files for checking and comparison with the tourist cards or other travel documents on which they are based.

Under current procedures, twenty names are placed on each page of the FM-11 in alphabetical order by date, and prior to final filing these are reviewed by a clerk who may make corrections and report possible discrepancies which might require investigation in order to make certain that the Immigration Laws of Mexico are not being violated. The items of information which are recorded on the FM-11 in horizontal columns are: chronological number (chronological listing number during fifteen-day period), identification document number, complete name, sex, age, marital status, nationality, occupation, place and country of origin, final destination, date of entry or departure, type of vehicle in which traveling, date of entry, date of departure (latter columns to determine period of residence), and remarks.

A review of the original tourist cards for persons traveling as tourists who departed from Mexico at Nuevo Laredo on October 3, 1963, disclosed that in no instance did any notation appear on the travel documents to indicate manner of travel of the bearer or destination in the United States upon departure from Mexico. Because of an unusual circumstance, however, it was noted that in a single instance a tourist, one JOHN H. BENNETT, had reported to Immigration authorities that he had lost his tourist card, and after being fined he was provided with a special document which would permit his departure from Mexico, an FM-17.

It was observed that on the FM-11 forms, the "destination" of the traveler at the time of departure was completed invariably with the same information as appeared on the tourist card as to place of residence, the place of issuance thereof, or a notation that the information was not available.

REVIEW OF TOURIST CARDS AND FM-11 RECORDS

A review of the FM-11 form listing persons who exited from Mexico on October 3, 1963, at Nuevo Laredo, Tamaulipas, with alien tourist cards revealed that for the 79 persons who were recorded as having departed their means of travel could be defined as follows:

Travel By	Number of Persons
Automobile	25
Bus	17
Railroad	18
Airline	7
Data unavailable	12
Total	79

A review of the original portions of the tourist cards of these travelers disclosed that none contained any information concerning means of transportation utilized by these people on departure from Mexico with the exception of JOHN H. BENNETT, who had lost the original portion of his tourist card.

- 4 -

COMMISSION EXHIBIT No. 2563—Continued

Dear Mr. Rankin:

I am forwarding two documents with translations, concerning the visa application of Lee Harvey Oswald, which were given by the Government of Cuba to Ambassador Stadelhofer on August 26, 1964, and were given by Ambassador Stadelhofer to the Department in New York on August 28, 1964.

The Department is not keeping copies of the original documents and would appreciate copies of them when they are reproduced.

You will note that the translators found certain words illegible. We would be happy to attempt again to translate these words if the Commission is able to have the original documents enlarged or clarified.

Sincerely yours,

Leonard C. Meeker
Acting Legal Adviser

Enclosures:
Visa application of Lee Harvey Oswald, with translation.

The Honorable
J. Lee Rankin,
General Counsel,
President's Commission on the Assassination of President Kennedy,
200 Maryland Avenue, N.E.,
Washington, D.C.

L:L/SCA:RAFrank:pat 8/31/64

COMMISSION EXHIBIT No. 2564

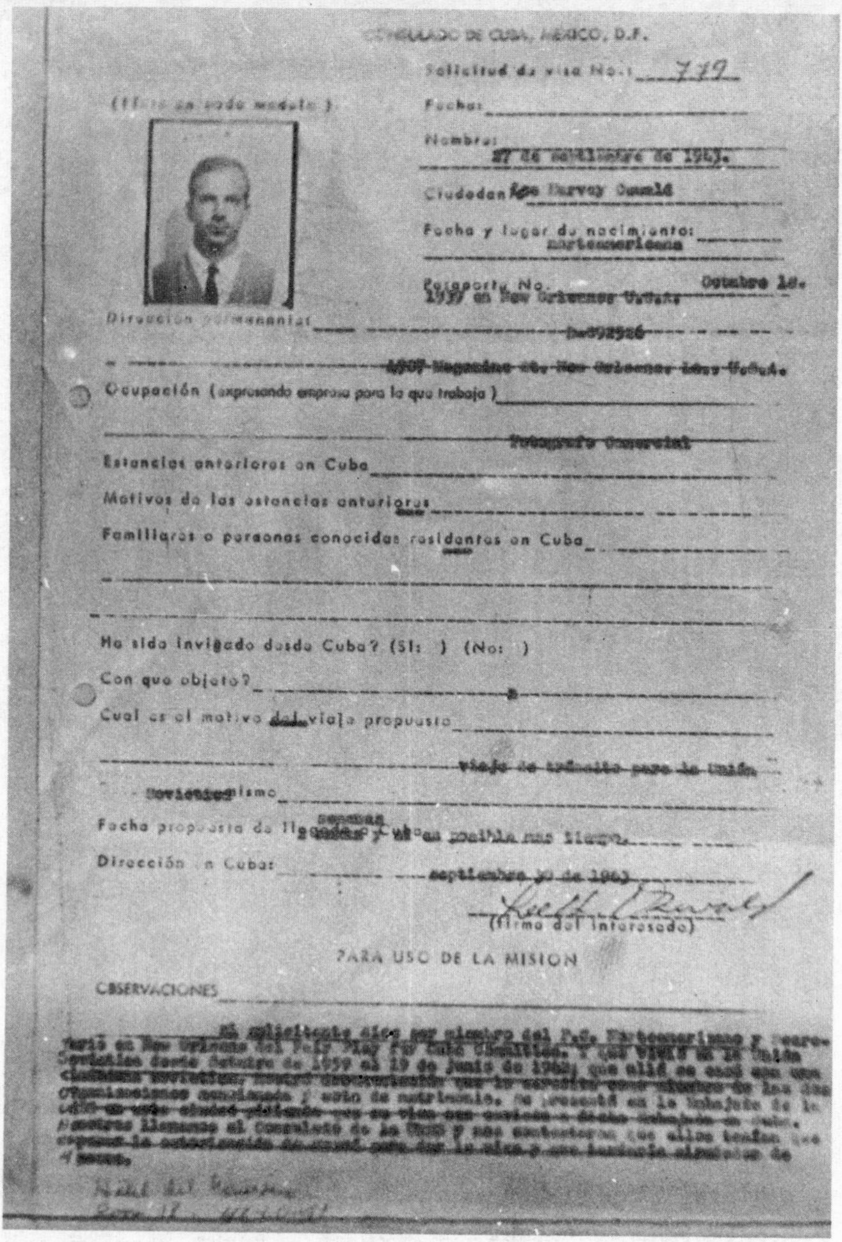

CONSULADO DE CUBA, MEXICO, D.F.

Solicitud de visa No.: 779

(Foto en todo modulo) Fecha:

Nombre:
27 de septiembre de 1963.

Ciudadan Lee Harvey Oswald

Fecha y lugar de nacimiento:
norteamericana

Pasaporte No. Octubre 18.
1939 en New Orleans U.S.A.

Direccion permanente: D-092526

4907 Magazine St. New Orleans [illegible] U.S.A.

Ocupación (expresando empresa para la que trabaja) Fotografo Comercial

Estancias anteriores en Cuba

Motivos de las estancias anteriores

Familiares o personas conocidas residentes en Cuba

Ha sido invitado desde Cuba? (Si:) (No:)

Con que objeto?

Cual es el motivo del viaje propuesto

viaje de tránsito para la Unión Soviética

[illegible]ismo

Fecha propuesta de llegada a Cuba: semanas [illegible] posible mas luego.

Dirección en Cuba: septiembre 30 de 1963

Lee H. Oswald

(firma del interesado)

PARA USO DE LA MISION

OBSERVACIONES

El solicitante dice ser miembro del P.C. Norteamericano y Secretario en New Orleans del Fair Play for Cuba Committee. Y que vivió en la Unión Soviética desde Octubre de 1959 al 1[illegible] de Junio de 1962, que allí se casó con una ciudadana soviética, [illegible] documentación que lo acredita como miembro de las dos Organizaciones [illegible] y acta de matrimonio. Se presentó en la Embajada de la [illegible] en esta ciudad pidiendo que su visa sea enviada a dicha Embajada en Cuba. Nosotros llamamos al Consulado de la URSS y nos contestaron que ellos tenían que esperar la autorización de [illegible] para dar la visa y que tardaría alrededor de 4 meses.

[illegible]

COMMISSION EXHIBIT No. 2564—Continued

DEPARTMENT OF STATE
Division of Language Services

(Translation)

Ls No. 18282
T-39 / R-XX
Spanish

Consulate of Cuba

Mexico, D.F.

(one photo on each form) Visa application No. : 779

Date: September 27, 1963

Name: Lee Harvey Oswald

Citizenship: American

Date and place of birth: October 18, 1939, in New Orleans, U.S.A.

Passport No.: D-092526

Permanent Address: 4907 Magazine Street, New Orleans, La., U.S.A.

Occupation (specifying concern for which you work):Commercial Photographer

Previous visits to Cuba: --

Reasons for previous visits: --

Members of family or acquaintances residing in Cuba: --

Were you invited by persons in Cuba? (Yes:) (No: X)

For what purpose? --

What is the purpose of the proposed trip? In transit on the way to the Soviet Union.

[Two or more words illegible] 2 weeks and longer if possible

Planned date of arrival in Cuba: September 30, 1963

Address in Cuba: --

[Signed] Lee H. Oswald
(Signature of applicant)

TRUE COPY OF TRANSLATION WITH
CORRECTION AS STATED IN LETTER
ATTACHED.

COMMISSION EXHIBIT No. 2564—Continued

FOR USE OF THE MISSION

COMMENTS: The applicant states that he is a member of the American Communist Party and Secretary in New Orleans of the Fair Play for Cuba Committee, and that he lived in the Soviet Union from October 1959 to June 19, 1962, and that he married a Soviet citizen there. He displayed documents in proof of his membership in the two aforementioned organizations and a marriage certificate. He appeared at the Embassy of the U.S.S.R. in this city and requested that his visa be sent to the Soviet Embassy in Cuba. We called the Consulate of the U.S.S.R. and were told that they had to await authorization from Moscow in order to give the visa and that it would take about four months.

[handwritten notation reading: Hotel del Comercio
Room 18 46-50-61]

COMMISSION EXHIBIT No. 2564—Continued

MINISTERIO DE RELACIONES EXTERIORES

SALIDA No. 14857

OCT 17

La Habana, 15 de octubre de 1963

"AÑO DE LA ORGANIZACION"

Estimado compañero:

Cúmpleme notificar a usted, en relación con la solicitud de visa de tránsito del ciudadano norteamericano LEE HARVEY OSWALD, que para acceder a su solicitud debe comunicarnos por cable con respuesta pagada cuando tenga la visa de la Embajada de la URSS autorizada.

Con saludos revolucionarios de "PATRIA O MUERTE", me reitero de usted,

Fraternalmente,

Juan Nilo Otero
Director

Al comp. Alfredo Mirabal Díaz
Cónsul de Cuba en México, D.F.

COMMISSION EXHIBIT No. 2564—Continued

Republic of Cuba

Ministry of Foreign Affairs

SECRETARIAT

(VISA SECTION)

/Stamp/

Ministry of Foreign Affairs

/Several words illegible/

* October 17 /year illegible/

Outgoing correspondence No. 14697

Habana, October 15, 1963

YEAR OF ORGANIZATION

Esteemed comrade:

With regard to the application for a transit visa submitted by LEE HARVEY OSWALD, an American citizen, I respectfully inform you that in order for us to comply with his request, he must inform us by cable, with prepaid reply, when he has the authorized visa of the Embassy of the U.S.S.R.

With revolutionary greetings of FATHERLAND or DEATH, I remain,

Yours fraternally,

By order: /Signed/ Mercy Martínez

Juan Milo Otero

Director

/Stamp of the Ministry of Foreign Affairs/

To Comrade Alfredo Mirabel Diaz

Consul of Cuba, Mexico, D.F.

COMMISSION EXHIBIT No. 2564—Continued

OFFICE OF THE DIRECTOR

UNITED STATES DEPARTMENT OF JUSTICE

FEDERAL BUREAU OF INVESTIGATION

WASHINGTON, D.C. 20535

May 4, 1964

BY COURIER SERVICE

Honorable J. Lee Rankin
General Counsel
The President's Commission
200 Maryland Avenue, N. E.
Washington, D. C.

Dear Mr. Rankin:

There are enclosed two copies each of memoranda dated April 21, April 22 and April 23, 1964, concerning the travel of Lee Harvey Oswald to Mexico.

In connection with Oswald's possible expenditures during the period September 25, 1963, through October 3, 1963, we have determined that the cost of one-way bus transportation via both the Continental Trailways and the Greyhound bus lines on September 25, 1963, from New Orleans, Louisiana, to Houston, Texas, was $9.70 and from New Orleans, Louisiana, to Laredo, Texas, was $20.25. While Oswald's mode of transportation between New Orleans and Houston on September 25, 1963, is unknown, it has been established that he boarded a Continental Trailways bus at Houston on the morning of September 26, 1963, on which he traveled to Laredo, Texas. As set forth in the report in the Oswald case of Special Agent Edwin Dalrymple dated February 20, 1964, at Houston, Texas, one one-way ticket for transportation from Houston, Texas, to Laredo, Texas, was sold by the ticket agent on duty at the Continental Trailways bus terminal in Houston, Texas, between 10:30 p.m. on September 25, 1963, and 6:30 a.m. on September 26, 1963. The price of this ticket was $10.60.

Our investigation of Lee Harvey Oswald's activity between September 25, 1963, and October 3, 1963, is continuing and results will be furnished to you as received.

COMMISSION EXHIBIT No. 2565

Honorable J. Lee Rankin

Upon detachment of the classified enclosures, this letter may be regarded as unclassified.

Sincerely yours,

J. Edgar Hoover

Enclosures (6)

COMMISSION EXHIBIT No. 2565—Continued

UNITED STATES DEPARTMENT OF JUSTICE

FEDERAL BUREAU OF INVESTIGATION

In Reply, Please Refer to File No.

WASHINGTON 25, D. C.

May 4, 1964

LEE HARVEY OSWALD

BASIS FOR INQUIRY

A confidential source abroad has advised that the baggage manifest of bus No. 516 of the "Servicios Unidos Autobuses Blancos Flecha Roja, S. A. de C. V.," (The Unified Services of White Autobuses Red Arrow, Incorporated) commonly referred to as the Flecha Roja bus line, which departed from Nuevo Laredo, State of Tamaulipas, Mexico, on September 26, 1963, and arrived in Mexico, D. F., (D. F. refers to "Distrito Federal" - Federal District or the Mexican Federal Capital) the following day included as a passenger thereon the name of "LEE HARVEY OSWALJ."

According to source, several persons who traveled on that bus as passengers have definitely identified photographs of LEE HARVEY OSWALD as being of a young American who was a passenger thereon.

TIME OF ARRIVAL OF FLECHA ROJA BUS NO. 516 AT MEXICO, D. F., ON SEPTEMBER 27, 1963

A second confidential source abroad advised as follows:

On April 16, 1964, JULIO CASTRO, employee of the accounting department in the offices of the Flecha Roja bus line located at Heroes Ferrocarrileros No. 45, Mexico, D. F., made available the ledger of arrivals at Mexico, D. F., for the Flecha Roja bus line. This ledger contains separate entries for each day, recording the exact time of arrival of each bus in Mexico, D. F., at the terminal.

COMMISSION EXHIBIT No. 2566

These records disclosed that bus No. 516 of the Flecha Roja bus line, on which LEE HARVEY OSWALD reportedly traveled from Nuevo Laredo to Mexico, D. F., on September 26-27, 1963, arrived in Mexico, D. F., at the Flecha Roja bus terminal, Heroes Ferrocarrileros No. 45, at 10:00 AM on September 27, 1963.

JULIO CASTRO advised that Flecha Roja bus No. 516, which departed from Nuevo Laredo, State of Tamaulipas, Mexico, at 2:00 PM, September 26, 1963, had a scheduled arrival in Mexico, D. F., of 9:45 AM, September 27, 1963, but, according to the entry in the ledger book, this bus was late in arriving at Mexico, D. F. He mentioned that the buses from Nuevo Laredo often arrive well in advance of their official schedules.

CASTRO made available another record contained in the office files of the Flecha Roja bus line which is captioned "Control de Llegada" (Arrival Control) and which registers the mechanical condition of a bus upon arrival in Mexico, D. F. This record revealed that upon arrival in Mexico, D. F., on September 27, 1963, one of the operators of bus No. 516 in the portion of the form captioned "condition of the bus" had made the notation "arreglar suspension" (repair suspension). A blank space on this form for time of arrival had not been filled out. CASTRO stated that the notation made by one of the bus operators at the completion of the trip to Mexico, D. F., possibly would explain the reason that bus No. 516 was behind schedule.

CROSSING OF INTERNATIONAL BRIDGE AT NUEVO LAREDO, STATE OF TAMAULIPAS, MEXICO, BY FLECHA ROJA BUS LINE

On April 16, 1964, JULIO CASTRO furnished information concerning the crossing of the International Bridge between Nuevo Laredo, State of Tamaulipas, Mexico, and Laredo, Texas, by the Flecha Roja equipment as follows:

There are two trips daily by the Flecha Roja bus line which leave Mexico, D. F., for Nuevo Laredo, but with a final terminal point of Laredo, Texas. This schedule was in effect in September, 1963. On both of these trips the Flecha Roja

-2-

COMMISSION EXHIBIT No. 2566—Continued

buses cross the International Bridge over the "Rio Bravo del Norte" (Rio Grande River) between Nuevo Laredo, Mexico, and Laredo, Texas, with the buses stopping in Laredo where they discharge passengers and also pick up new passengers in Laredo for the return trip into Mexico with Mexico, D. F., as the final terminal point.

CASTRO advised that on the return trip to Mexico, D. F., Flecha Roja bus No. 516 had a scheduled departure from Laredo, Texas, on September 26, 1963, of 1:30 PM, arriving in Nuevo Laredo a few minutes later, with departure from Nuevo Laredo for the trip to Mexico, D. F., scheduled for 2:00 PM.

-3-

COMMISSION EXHIBIT No. 2566—Continued

T-16, who is in a position to be well-informed with respect to the day-to-day operations of the Mexico City ticket offices of the "Compania Cubana de Aviacion" (Cuban Aviation Company - commonly referred to as "Cubana Airlines"), furnished the following information on April 18, 1964:

Most of the office employees at the Cubana Airlines ticket office, Paseo de la Reforma 56, Mexico City, are Mexican citizens. Source would have an excellent possibility of being informed of any visits or inquiries made at the Cubana Airlines offices by an American, and is thoroughly convinced that LEE HARVEY OSWALD did not appear at those offices during late September and early October, 1963, within the regular working hours. Source viewed various photographs of OSWALD and also consulted with associates at the Cubana Airlines office and reiterated the conviction that

- 113 -

OSWALD had not been at those offices at any time.

This source confirmed that the published and most used telephone number for the Cubana Airlines office is 35-79-00.

- 114 -

COMMISSION EXHIBIT No. 2567

CENTRAL INTELLIGENCE AGENCY
WASHINGTON 25, D.C.

[illegible]

MEMORANDUM FOR: Mr. J. Lee Rankin
General Counsel
President's Commission on the
Assassination of President Kennedy

SUBJECT: Hours of Work at Cuban and Soviet Consulates; Procedures and Regulations for Issuance of Cuban Visas; Mexican Control of U.S. Citizens' Travel to and from Cuba

1. I refer to your earlier memorandum in which you request information on hours of work at Cuban and Soviet diplomatic installations in Mexico City, details of regulations governing the issuance of Cuban travel documents and Mexican control of U.S. citizens travelling to and from Cuba through Mexico.

2. The Soviet Embassy and Consulate are not open to the public; offices in the Soviet compound may be visited by appointment only. A twenty-four-hour guard is mounted at the entrance to the compound in which these Soviet installations are located. Visitors ring the bell at this entrance at all hours. Russian-speaking visitors are permitted to enter at any time, but others are usually turned away by the guard after normal hours of work. Normal work hours during September 1963, when Lee Harvey OSWALD visited the Soviet installation, were 0900 to 1800. However, the hours for Mondays and Fridays have been changed to 0900 to 1400 hours. Sixteen Soviet families live in the compound.

3. The Cuban Embassy and Consulate are located in their own compound, but these installations have separate entrances. Visitors may enter the Cuban Consulate from 1000 to 1400 hours, Monday through Friday. Embassy working hours are 0900 to 1700 on the same days. Visitors to the Embassy, however, usually appear before 1400 hours. These work hours were also in effect during September 1963.

COMMISSION EXHIBIT No. 2568

4. Prior authorization from the Ministry of the Exterior in Havana is required before Cuban visas may be issued. On occasion, requests for permission to issue visas and the resulting decisions are handled by cable. The applicant fills out a visa application form at the Cuban consulate. Cuban visas are normally valid for three months from date of issuance. The Soviets are not known to issue travel permits to Cuba.

5. The Government of Mexico recognizes the passport as an identification document only. Mexican immigration officials do not recognize passport entries prohibiting the bearer's travel to Cuba, if the bearer holds a visa valid for travel to that country. Non-Cubans, including U.S. citizens, entering Mexico from Cuba must have Mexican visas or tourist cards. Depending on their outgoing flight times, non-Cubans transitting Mexico do not always need a transit visa. The passports of all persons travelling between Mexico and Cuba are stamped in Spanish with the phrases "Departed for Cuba" or "Entered from Cuba", as appropriate.

6. We hope that the information given above meets your need for data on travel between Mexico and Cuba.

Richard Helms
Deputy Director for Plans

-2-

COMMISSION EXHIBIT No. 2568—Continued

FD-204 (Rev. 3-3-59)

UNITED STATES DEPARTMENT OF JUSTICE
FEDERAL BUREAU OF INVESTIGATION

Copy to:

Report of: JAMES J. O'CONNOR   Office: MIAMI, FLORIDA
Date: JUL 16 1964

Field Office File #: 105-8342   Bureau File #: 105-82555

Title: LEE HARVEY OSWALD

Character: INTERNAL SECURITY - RUSSIA - CUBA.

Synopsis:

JULIAN FRANCISCO HUERTA OLIVA, Cuban exile residing at Miami, Fla., stated he lived at Hotel Del Comercio, Mexico City, Mexico, from 8/19 to 9/23/63, departing for Miami on the latter date. He saw no other Cubans at the hotel during his stay, and did not see OSWALD.

\- P -

DETAILS:

This investigation is related to information which was developed from ERNESTO LIMA JUAREZ of Reynosa, Mexico, who had stayed at the Hotel Del Comercio in Mexico City, Mexico, from September 15 to October 1, 1963. He said he noticed an American at the hotel whom he later recognized from news photographs as LEE HARVEY OSWALD. He said he also saw four Cubans at the hotel, with whom OSWALD associated on one or two occasions in an apparently social manner.

MM 105-8342

LIMA also advised that a retired railroad man named GABRIEL CONTRERAS, from Ciudad Camargo, Mexico, had also been staying at the Hotel Del Comercio, and might possess information concerning the Cubans, and might also have seen OSWALD at the hotel.

Information was also received through employees of the Hotel Del Comercio that while several Cubans had stayed at the hotel during part of the time that ERNESTO LIMA was there, all the Cubans had departed before the arrival of OSWALD at the hotel. These Cubans were reportedly seeking immigrant visas to the United States, and the last of them to depart was identified as JULIAN FRANCISCO HUERTA OLIVA, who reportedly left the hotel as of September 22, 1963, en route to Miami, Florida.

On July 9, 1964, JULIAN FRANCISCO HUERTA OLIVA, residing at 221 Alton Road, Miami Beach, Florida, displayed his immigrant registration card, #A13 332 144, reflecting his arrival in the United States at Miami, Florida, on September 23, 1963. The card reflected HUERTA's date of birth as January 28, 1902.

Mr. HUERTA related that he had arrived in Mexico from Cuba on August 19, 1963, on which date he took a room at the Hotel Del Comercio in Mexico City while awaiting the issuance of an immigrant visa by the U. S.Embassy in Mexico City. He stated he remained at the HotelDel Comercio for the entire period of his stay in Mexico City, having departed from Mexico City by plane for Miami, Florida, on September 23, 1963. He said that during this entire period, he observed no other Cubans at the Hotel Del Comercio, and did not see anyone resembling LEE HARVEY OSWALD, whose photographs he saw in the newspapers subsequent to the assassination of President JOHN F. KENNEDY.

Mr. HUERTA stated that the Hotel Del Comercio has about thirty rooms, and to his knowledge, there were no Cubans staying at the hotel during the time he was there. He stated he befriended a retired Mexican railroad man named GABRIEL CONTRERAS who is from Ciudad Camargo, Mexico, and was in Mexico City for an eye operation. He stated that CONTRERAS was still as the hotel as of the date HUERTA departed from Mexico City and may have returned to the hotel following his operation. He said he believes CONTRERAS travels frequently from Ciudad Camargo to Mexico City because he possesses a railroad pass.

COMMISSION EXHIBIT No. 2569—Continued

UNITED STATES DEPARTMENT OF JUSTICE

FEDERAL BUREAU OF INVESTIGATION

In Reply, Please Refer to File No.

WASHINGTON 25, D. C.

July 21, 1964

LEE HARVEY OSWALD

BASIS FOR INQUIRY

As has been previously reported, OSWALD was registered from September 27, 1963, through October 1, 1963, in Room No. 13 of the Hotel del Comercio, located at Calle Bernardino de Sahagun No. 19, Mexico, D.F., Mexico.

The records of the hotel reflect that ERNESTO LIMA JUAREZ, Reynosa, Tamaulipas, Mexico, was registered in Room No. 8 on September 26, 1963, and FRANCISCO MORALES, also of Reynosa, was registered in Room No. 8 from September 27, 1963, through October 1, 1963.

On interview in Reynosa on June 16, 1964, ERNESTO LIMA JUAREZ, a masonry contractor, advised he was in Mexico, D.F., Mexico, where he stayed in Room No. 8, Hotel del Comercio, for a few days in the latter part of September, 1963, and possibly the first day or two in October, 1963. He was in Mexico, D.F., on business and was accompanied by FRANCISCO MORALES, whom he was attempting to aid in securing employment.

While at the hotel, LIMA JUAREZ noticed an American, whom he later recognized from news media photographs as LEE HARVEY OSWALD. He did not associate with OSWALD, and as far as he knows, MORALES did not associate with OSWALD. He pointed out that at that time he had no reason to pay any particular attention to OSWALD.

LIMA JUAREZ also saw four Cubans at the hotel and saw OSWALD associating with these Cubans on one or two occasions, but these meetings appeared to be social in nature. He did not associate with the Cubans and did not learn their names or addresses; however, MORALES had some

COMMISSION EXHIBIT No. 2570

drinks with them on one or two occasions and might possibly have their names or other information pertaining to them.

INQUIRIES AT HOTEL DEL COMERCIO
CONCERNING ALLEGATIONS OF
ERNESTO LIMA JUAREZ

A confidential source abroad obtained the following information on July 15, 1964:

GUILLERMO GARCIA LUNA, Owner and Manager, Hotel del Comercio, Sahagun No. 19, Mexico City, Mexico, and SEBASTIAN PEREZ HERNANDEZ, the desk clerk at this hotel, advised on July 15, 1964, that the records of this hotel disclosed that ERNESTO LIMA JUAREZ and FRANCISCO MORALES occupied Room No. 8 at the Hotel del Comercio from September 15 to October 1, 1963. Mr. GARCIA advised that neither name appears on the payment book after that date and the records disclose that they checked out on October 1, 1963, still owing the sum of 106 pesos ($8.48 U.S.), which was later paid by LIMA's daughter.

Mr. GARCIA advised that the only Cuban in residence at that time was JULIAN HUERTA, who had checked out of the hotel on September 23, 1963.

Mr. GARCIA stated that Mr. HUERTA, during his period of residence in the hotel, spent a lot of time in the lobby where he became friendly with GABRIEL CONTRERAS, ERNESTO LIMA, MANUEL SANTOS and FERNANDO VALENZUELA, who were also guests at the hotel. Mr. GARCIA was of the opinion that HUERTA joined some of these individuals for coffee and they possibly may have taken him sightseeing.

Mr. GARCIA and Mr. PEREZ identified a photograph of JULIAN FRANCISCO HUERTA OLIVA, born January 28, 1902, in Havana, Cuba, as the JULIAN HUERTA who was a guest at the Hotel del Comercio.

Neither Mr. GARCIA nor Mr. PEREZ could recall any Negro guests of any nationality during this period with the

exception of ANTONIO OLIVA, described as a tall, slender, male Negro about twenty-nine years old. Mr. GARCIA said that OLIVA has the dark skin and kinky hair of a Negro and for this reason was sometimes referred to as a Cuban; however, OLIVA claimed to be a Mexican from Veracruz, Mexico, according to Mr. GARCIA.

Mr. GARCIA stated that OLIVA claimed employment as a musician, but neither Mr. GARCIA nor Mr. PEREZ noted any music or musical instruments in his possession and believed that OLIVA worked as a waiter in some night club or cafe. Mr. GARCIA said that OLIVA worked nights and lived with a woman about his age who also had a dark complexion but who appeared to be a Mexican.

Mr. GARCIA advised that OLIVA and his companion occupied Room No. 4 on the top floor of the hotel. Other rooms on this floor are numbered 24 through 30. He explained that the space formerly occupied by Room No. 4 on the ground floor had been converted into an office with no room number. Thereafter, an additional room was constructed on the top floor and the number 4 was arbitrarily assigned this room, replacing the Room No. 4 on the ground floor which was converted into an office. This new Room No. 4 on the top floor is one floor above the floor where Room No. 18, occupied by OSWALD, is located.

Mr. GARCIA noted that HUERTA and LIMA were on the top floor and GABRIEL CONTRERAS was on the second floor in Room No. 14 during the pertinent period. Mr. GARCIA and Mr. PEREZ were not certain of the identities of all of the persons on the second floor for this period, but were certain that none of them were Negroes or Cubans.

Mr. GARCIA advised that OLIVA and his companion had no one else staying with them and occupied no other rooms at the hotel.

Mr. GARCIA and Mr. PEREZ checked the hotel records, recalling that two Cuban families had stayed at that hotel for some time in the past while awaiting visas from the United States Embassy to go to the United States; however, a check of the records by Mr. GARCIA disclosed that these individuals had all departed from the Hotel del Comercio prior to the end of August, 1963.

Mr. GARCIA pointed out that OLIVA departed owing the hotel approximately 200 pesos ($16 U.S.), and Mr. GARCIA has not seen or heard anything concerning him since his departure. Mr. GARCIA and Mr. PEREZ believed that his "wife" was working as a waitress, but they had no information concerning the place of her employment.

MATILDE GARNICA, maid, Hotel del Comercio, Mexico City, Mexico, furnished the following information to the above-mentioned confidential source abroad on July 15, 1964:

Miss GARNICA could not recall that any Cubans had resided at that hotel during the pertinent period except Mr. HUERTA, an older man who lived in Room No. 28, and ANTONIO OLIVA. She could not recall that any Negroes had resided at the hotel during the pertinent period except OLIVA. She stated that OLIVA claimed to be a Mexican, but his "wife," IRMA, a Mexican of Indian appearance from Oaxaca, Mexico, told her that actually OLIVA is a Cuban.

IRMA stated that she had an aunt on Sadi Carnot Street in Mexico City, Mexico.

After OLIVA and his companion left the hotel, Miss GARNICA later saw them together on two occasions, once on Chopo Street near the Hotel Museo, and on another occasion at the Metropolitano Movie Theater. On both occasions they appeared to be avoiding her, presumably because of their outstanding bill at the hotel.

On one occasion Miss GARNICA noted that OLIVA had a letter which had been directed to him at Calle Sullivan 23, Mexico City, Mexico.

- 4 -

COMMISSION EXHIBIT No. 2570—Continued

Miss GARNICA did not recall that anyone had stayed with OLIVA and his companion, but recalled that OLIVA has a close friend who may be described as being a dark, slender young Negro who is taller than OLIVA. She believed that this individual was called "TONY."

- 5 -

COMMISSION EXHIBIT No. 2570—Continued

UNITED STATES DEPARTMENT OF JUSTICE
FEDERAL BUREAU OF INVESTIGATION

Copy to:

Report of: SA ROBERT E. SHORTELLE Office: NEW HAVEN
Date: July 28, 1964

Field Office File No.: 100-18158 Bureau File No.: 105-82555

Title: LEE HARVEY OSWALD

Character: INTERNAL SECURITY - R - CUBA

Synopsis:

HUERTA OLIVA, 3 Ely Avenue, South Norwalk, Connecticut, furnished a photograph of himself and four other individuals whom he identified taken on September 20th, 1963, at Mexico City. OLIVA stated all individuals were Mexican and he had met them while he was staying at the Del Comercio Hotel, Mexico City, Mexico, during the period 8/19 - 9/23/63. OLIVA stated that he knew of no Cubans staying at this hotel during this period, with the exception of one negro, who OLIVA was told was Cuban, but because of speech did not believe this individual to be Cuban.

R U C

DETAILS:

Mr. HUERTA OLIVA, 3 Ely Avenue, South Norwalk, Connecticut, was contacted on July 21, 1964, and furnished a photograph which was taken in Mexico City on September 20, 1963. This photograph showed OLIVA seated at a table with four other individuals whom OLIVA advised were staying at the Hotel Del Comercio during the period he resided there from August 19, 1963, to September 23, 1963. OLIVA stated that these individuals were still at the hotel when he departed on September 23, 1963. OLIVA identified

COMMISSION EXHIBIT No. 2571

NH 100-18158

these individuals seated from right to left in the photograph as FRANCISCO MORALES, GRABREIL CONTRERAS, MANUEL SANTOS and ERNESTO L. JUAREZ. In the photograph OLIVA is seated in the middle with MORALES and CONTRERAS to his right and SANTOS and JUAREZ to his left. This photograph is stapled to a white folder, and on the inside of the folder to the left of the photograph appears writing in the Spanish language, which was translated by OLIVA to read: My friend Julian. This is a souvenir of your time in the Mexican Capital from your friends, GRABREIL CONTRERAS, MANUEL SANTOS, PANCHO MORALES (according to OLIVA, another name for FRANCISCO MORALES), ERNESTO L. JUAREZ, and dated September 20, 1963.

On the front of the folder are signatures which OLIVA stated are the signatures of FRANCISCO MORALES, ERNESTO L. JUAREZ (with printed name of JUAREZ below), MANUEL SANTOS and GRABRIEL CONTRERAS.

OLIVA stated that the note below these signatures refers to a FERNANDO VALERZUELA, who was called MARTIN PORRA as a joke, and could not be there at the time the photograph was taken. OLIVA stated the VALERZUELA was another individual staying at the hotel who he had become acquainted with. According to OLIVA, this photograph was taken by a vendor.

In regard to the above-mentioned individuals, OLIVA stated that they were all Mexicans and he was the only Cuban. He advised that to his knowledge there were no other Cubans staying at the hotel during the period of time he stayed there, nor were there any Americans. OLIVA had several conversations with the owner of the hotel whose name he did not know, but called him "MEMO" and he is sure had there been other Cubans staying at the hotel he would have known of this.

There was a negro, according to OLIVA, staying with a woman at the hotel, and OLIVA was told, by whom he did not

2.

COMMISSION EXHIBIT No. 2571—Continued

NH 100-18158

recall, that this person was a Cuban, but although OLIVA did not speak with him he heard his speech and from it did not believe that this person was Cuban but Puerto Rican. OLIVA stated that CONTRERAS had advised him that this person was an artist.

OLIVA stated that when he arrived in Mexico he was met at the airport by a NESTOR CARBONELL, a friend from Cuba who was in the newspaper business, that this was on August 19, 1963, and that he remained at the Hotel Del Comercio until he departed Mexico for Florida on September 23, 1963.

3.*

COMMISSION EXHIBIT No. 2571—Continued

UNITED STATES DEPARTMENT OF JUSTICE
FEDERAL BUREAU OF INVESTIGATION

In Reply, Please Refer to
File No.

WASHINGTON 25, D. C.

August 3, 1964

LEE HARVEY OSWALD

Exhibit D-231 is comprised of a copy of a photograph of Mr. Huerta Oliva and four other individuals and the folder in which the photograph was contained. These items are referred to in report in the Lee Harvey Oswald case of Special Agent Robert E. Shertelle dated July 28, 1964, at New Haven, Connecticut.

COMMISSION EXHIBIT No. 2571—Continued

COMMISSION EXHIBIT No. 2571—Continued

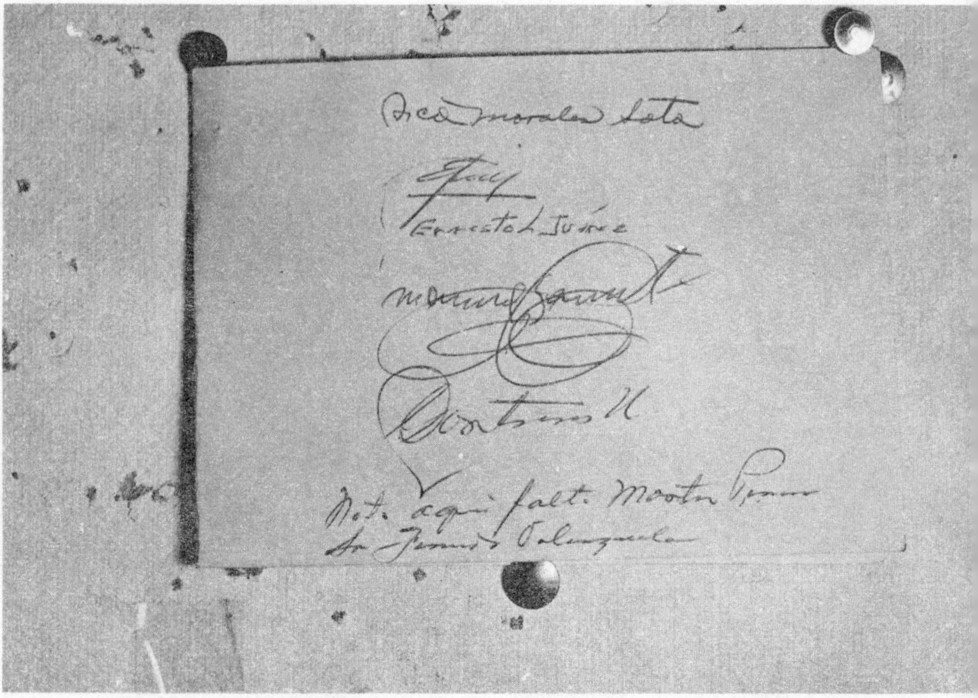

COMMISSION EXHIBIT No. 2571—Continued

In Reply, Please Refer to
File No.

UNITED STATES DEPARTMENT OF JUSTICE
Oswald, Lee H. Post-Russian Period 3-1
FEDERAL BUREAU OF INVESTIGATION
Other Individuals and Organizations
Involved or Interviewed
WASHINGTON 25, D. C.

July 31, 1964

Valenzuela, Fernando

LEE HARVEY OSWALD

BASIS FOR INQUIRY

As has been previously reported, on September 27, 1963, OSWALD registered at the Hotel del Comercio, Calle Bernardino de Sahagun No. 19, Mexico City, under the name of LEE, HARVEY OSWALD. His name was contained in the guest records of the hotel through October 1, 1963. He occupied room No. 18.

According to the guest records of the hotel, FERNANDO VALENZUELA, Chihuahua, State of Chihuahua, Mexico, occupied room No. 6 from September 26 through October 1, 1963.

INTERVIEW OF FERNANDO VALENZUELA

On July 10, 1964, FERNANDO VALENZUELA, Calle 33 No. 2213, Chihuahua, State of Chihuahua, Mexico, furnished the following information to a confidential source, who has furnished reliable information in the past.

VALENZUELA stated he resided at the Hotel del Comercio during the last week of September, 1963, and the first part of October, 1963, but could not recall the exact dates.

VALENZUELA viewed a series of photographs of LEE HARVEY OSWALD and stated he knew who this individual was as a result of the publicity concerning him following the

COMMISSION EXHIBIT No. 2572

assassination of President JOHN F. KENNEDY. VALENZUELA said he did not recall ever having seen the subject.

VALENZUELA said he did recall that there were a few Americans, or at least persons who spoke English, at the hotel during the period of time he was there. VALENZUELA also recalled that a Cuban family and possibly one or two young Cuban men were also there, but he could not recall the names or descriptions of these individuals, other than the Cuban family.

VALENZUELA recalled that a political dispute arose between a tie salesman of unknown origin and the Cuban, who was awaiting passage for Miami, Florida, with his family. VALENZUELA recalled that this discussion led to some comments concerning communism and vaguely recalled that the tie salesman was trying to convince the Cuban concerning a point about communism. VALENZUELA did not recall any of the details of the discussion, but it was his impression that the Cuban who was planning to travel to Miami, Florida, apparently opposed any communist ideas.

VALENZUELA stated he could not furnish any additional identifying information regarding any of the other guests at the hotel or any of the activities at the hotel which may have concerned OSWALD, during the period of time that VALENZUELA was a guest at the hotel.

COMMISSION EXHIBIT No. 2572—Continued

Commission Exhibit No. 2573

UNITED STATES DEPARTMENT OF JUSTICE

FEDERAL BUREAU OF INVESTIGATION

In Reply, Please Refer to File No.

WASHINGTON 25, D. C.

August 4, 1964

LEE HARVEY OSWALD

BASIS FOR INQUIRY

As has been previously reported, OSWALD was registered from September 27, 1963, through October 1, 1963, in Room No. 18 of the Hotel del Comercio, located at Calle Bernardino de Sahagun No. 19, Mexico, D. F., Mexico.

The records of the hotel reflect that ERNESTO LIMA JUAREZ, Reynosa, Tamaulipas, Mexico, was registered in Room No. 8 on September 26, 1963, and FRANCISCO MORALES, also of Reynosa, was registered in Room No. 8 from September 27, 1963, through October 1, 1963.

On interview in Reynosa on June 16, 1964, ERNESTO LIMA JUAREZ, a masonry contractor, advised he was in Mexico, D. F., Mexico, where he stayed in Room No. 8, Hotel del Comercio, for a few days in the latter part of September, 1963, and possibly the first day or two in October, 1963. He was in Mexico, D. F., on business and was accompanied by FRANCISCO MORALES, whom he was attempting to aid in securing employment.

While at the hotel, LIMA JUAREZ noticed an American, whom he later recognized from news media photographs as LEE HARVEY OSWALD. He did not associate with OSWALD, and as far as he knows, MORALES did not associate with OSWALD. He pointed out that at that time he had no reason to pay any particular attention to OSWALD.

LIMA JUAREZ also saw four Cubans at the hotel and saw OSWALD associating with these Cubans on one or two occasions, but these meetings appeared to be social in nature. He did not associate with the Cubans and did not learn their names or addresses; however, MORALES had some

COMMISSION EXHIBIT No. 2573

drinks with them on one or two occasions and might possibly have their names or other information pertaining to them.

GUILLERMO GARCIA LUNA, owner and manager, Hotel del Comercio, Calle Bernardino de Sahagun No. 19, Mexico, D. F., Mexico, and SEBASTIAN PEREZ HERNANDEZ, the desk clerk at this hotel, advised on July 15, 1964, that ANTONIO OLIVA, described as a tall, slender, male Negro, about 29 years of age, had resided at the Hotel del Comercio during late September and early October, 1963. Mr. GARCIA said that OLIVA was sometimes referred to as a Cuban, apparently due to his appearance, but claimed to be a Mexican from Veracruz, Veracruz, Mexico.

RESULTS OF INVESTIGATION CONDUCTED TO LOCATE AND INTERVIEW ANTONIO OLIVA

A confidential source abroad furnished the following information on July 31, 1964, concerning the efforts that had been made to locate and identify ANTONIO OLIVA at Mexico, D. F., Mexico.

The records of various agencies of the Mexican Government including the Immigration Department, the four Mexico City Police Departments, tax records, voters' registration records, and Mexico City Drivers' License Bureau were checked without locating any information identifiable with ANTONIO OLIVA. Source also checked the records of musicians' and waiters' unions with negative results. The confidential source explained that such searches were difficult in Mexico City when the second Spanish surname is not available.

Investigation at Calle Sullivan 23, Mexico, D. F., Mexico, disclosed that a gasoline station is located at this address, and inquiry in the area failed to locate anyone acquainted with an ANTONIO OLIVA.

However, on July 21, 1964, Mr. RODRIGUEZ-NAVARRO, owner of a night club named LOS PERICOS, located at Calle Sullivan 13, stated that ANTONIO OLIVA was

- 2 -

COMMISSION EXHIBIT No. 2573—Continued

formerly employed as a waiter at this night club. According to Mr. RODRIGUEZ, OLIVA is from Honduras and is probably in Mexicó illegally. He recalled that OLIVA possessed a waiter's credential that was issued by a labor union in Veracruz, Veracruz, Mexico.

Mr. RODRIGUEZ advised that the night club was raided by the police in January, 1964, and OLIVA was taken into custody. He stated that OLIVA has not returned to the night club since that time, and, since OLIVA owes money to Mr. RODRIGUEZ, Mr. RODRIGUEZ also is trying to locate OLIVA.

- 3 -

COMMISSION EXHIBIT No. 2573—Continued

UNITED STATES DEPARTMENT OF JUSTICE
FEDERAL BUREAU OF INVESTIGATION

In Reply, Please Refer to
File No.

WASHINGTON 25, D. C.

August 7, 1964

LEE HARVEY OSWALD

Commission Exhibit No. 2574

BASIS FOR INQUIRY

As has been previously reported, OSWALD was registered from September 27, 1963, through October 1, 1963, in Room No. 18 of the Hotel del Comercio, located at Calle Bernardino de Sahagun No. 19, Mexico, D. F., Mexico.

The records of the hotel disclosed that GABRIEL CONTRERAS, Ciudad Juarez, Chihuahua, Mexico, was registered at the hotel during the pertinent period.

INTERVIEW OF GABRIEL CONTRERAS UVINA

GABRIEL CONTRERAS UVINA, who was residing temporarily at the Fermont Hotel, Chihuahua, Chihuahua, Mexico, furnished the following information to a confidential source abroad on July 29, 1964:

CONTRERAS recalled that he had resided at the Hotel del Comercio, Calle Bernardino de Sahagun No. 19, Mexico, D. F., Mexico, in late September and early October, 1963. CONTRERAS was in Mexico City on business, as well as to make an appointment to undergo eye surgery at the Hospital Colonia, operated by the Mexican National Railroad in Mexico City. CONTRERAS stated that he had cataracts on both eyes, which had reduced his vision to approximately thirty per cent of normal, according to his doctors.

CONTRERAS said that he had been unable to undergo this surgery at that time and returned to Mexico City in late November, 1963, for the operation.

COMMISSION EXHIBIT No. 2574

CONTRERAS stated that his normal residence is Ciudad Camargo, Chihuahua, Mexico. He stated that he owns and operates a small store called "El Sol" (The Sun), selling small electrical appliances and new and used electrical parts. He said he is a retired employee of the Mexican National Railroad and is occasionally called upon by the firm known as "Aceites de Algodon" (Cotton Oil Company) to serve as an expediter of tank cars. He added that he spots and moves cars for loading and transfer on all of the company's sidings throughout Mexico. As a result, he is usually in Mexico City at least once a month.

During his stay at the Hotel del Comercio in late September and early October, 1963, he was in the habit of having his meals at a restaurant next to the Hotel del Comercio, which is operated by a woman named LOLA. CONTRERAS said that it was very possible he had seated himself at the same table as LEE HARVEY OSWALD during one of his visits to the restaurant, since the restaurant is often crowded during mealtimes. CONTRERAS pointed out that he could not see very well at the time and did not know LEE HARVEY OSWALD, did not remember ever seeing OSWALD during his stay at the hotel, and if he spoke to OSWALD, it would have been no more than a courtesy greeting.

After viewing a number of photographs that were exhibited to him, CONTRERAS had no trouble in selecting photographs of OSWALD. CONTRERAS pointed out that he became aware of OSWALD and his background as a result of the world-wide publicity which occurred as a result of the death of President KENNEDY. CONTRERAS said that he did not recall ever having seen OSWALD before or after his visit to the Hotel del Comercio in late September or early October, 1963.

CONTRERAS said that LOLA had advised Agents of the Mexican Ministry of Government, who had conducted investigation in regard to OSWALD's stay at the Hotel del Comercio, that CONTRERAS had been at the same table with OSWALD. CONTRERAS said that this was possible, but, because of his bad vision, he did not recall this incident.

CONTRERAS said that he was not aware of any Americans residing at the hotel during the period he was there. He associated with three of the guests, to the best of his recollection, and remembered a man named LIMA JUAREZ, who was at the hotel with another individual. CONTRERAS believed that both of these men came from Monterrey, Nuevo Leon, Mexico, and were in Mexico City to seek employment. CONTRERAS could not recall the first name of LIMA JUAREZ and could not recall the name of the friend of LIMA JUAREZ.

CONTRERAS stated that the third man with whom he spoke on two or three occasions was a Cuban, who was residing at the hotel while waiting for a visa to enter the United States, en route to the State of Florida. CONTRERAS could not think of the name of this individual, but when the name of JULIAN FRANCISCO HUERTA was mentioned, he immediately acknowledged that this was the person he had in mind. CONTRERAS recalled going to an office of the Mexican Ministry of Government with HUERTA on one occasion to obtain some papers that HUERTA needed. CONTRERAS was not certain of the name or location of the office and could not identify the person to whom HUERTA spoke.

CONTRERAS said that he knew HUERTA was acquainted with LIMA JUAREZ and the friend of LIMA JUAREZ, but he did not know if HUERTA visited with other persons in the hotel.

CONTRERAS said that he had not known LIMA JUAREZ prior to his visit to the hotel during the pertinent period. CONTRERAS ascertained that LIMA JUAREZ was a member of some labor union and that the friend of LIMA JUAREZ apparently was an electrician.

CONTRERAS said that the best description he could furnish of LIMA JUAREZ, due to his limited vision, was that LIMA JUAREZ was a white, male, Mexican, about 55 years old, 5 feet 7 inches tall, weighing 165 pounds, with grey hair and wearing glasses. The friend of LIMA JUAREZ was a white, male, Mexican, about 5 feet 7 inches tall, weighing about 160 pounds, with black hair.

CONTRERAS recalled going out with LIMA JUAREZ, the friend of LIMA JUAREZ, JULIAN FRANCISCO HUERTA, and another man, whose name he could not recall. This unknown individual is a huge man, who is a rancher from Zacatecas, Zacatecas, Mexico, or from Saltillo, Coahuila, Mexico, and CONTRERAS thought that his name might be MACIAS. CONTRERAS recalled that this man occupied Room No. 12 in the hotel and was in Mexico City to conduct some business with the Confederacion Nacional Campesina (National Federation of Farmers) and the Mexican Department of Farm and Colonization Matters in Mexico City. CONTRERAS and the other four individuals left the hotel together and visited the Tijuana Bar, located on the corner of Plaza Buenavista and Calle Heroes Ferrocarrilleros, Mexico City. While at this bar, a sidewalk photographer took two pictures of the group. The photographer developed the pictures on the spot. CONTRERAS bought one of the pictures and HUERTA also bought one. CONTRERAS did not recall whether or not everyone signed the photographs but did say that some of the group signed the photographs.

CONTRERAS said that he looked at the photograph in the hotel the next day and decided that he would not want his wife to see the photograph since she might object to his drinking and being photographed while drinking. He then tore up the photograph and threw the pieces away.

CONTRERAS stated that he usually does not drink and the above-mentioned incident was the only time he went out with anyone to visit a bar.

CONTRERAS said that he did not know if the other men who went with him to the Tijuana Bar were regular customers there. He did not know if they went to other nearby bars. He could not recall that any of these persons had engaged in conversations with any Americans or with any other persons who were not Mexicans.

CONTRERAS was certain that he had not seen LEE HARVEY OSWALD, regardless of the statement by LOLA indicating that CONTRERAS and OSWALD had shared a table in the restaurant. CONTRERAS said that the only reason he could identify a photograph of OSWALD was the fact he had seen photographs of OSWALD frequently in newspapers and other news media.

- 4 -

COMMISSION EXHIBIT No. 2574—Continued

UNITED STATES DEPARTMENT OF JUSTICE

FEDERAL BUREAU OF INVESTIGATION

In Reply, Please Refer to File No.

WASHINGTON 25, D. C.
August 10, 1964

LEE HARVEY OSWALD

As has been previously reported, OSWALD was registered from September 27, 1963, through October 1, 1963, in Room No. 18 of the Hotel del Comercio, located at Calle Bernardino de Sahagun No. 19, Mexico, D. F., Mexico.

ERNESTO LIMA JUAREZ from Reynosa, Tamaulipas, was a guest of the Hotel del Comercio on September 26, 1963. LIMA JUAREZ previously advised that a photograph had been taken of a group of the guests of the hotel.

JULIAN HUERTA OLIVA, a Cuban who was residing at the Hotel del Comercio shortly prior to the arrival of OSWALD in September, 1963, furnished a copy of a photograph of a group of the guests at the Hotel del Comercio in September, 1963.

ERNESTO LIMA JUAREZ also advised that he believed that he had seen OSWALD conversing with two Cuban Negroes who were residing at the Hotel del Comercio

Employees of the Hotel del Comercio stated that ANTONIO OLIVA, a young Negro, possibly a Cuban, had resided in Room No. 4 at the Hotel del Comercio during the period of time that OSWALD was a guest at the hotel. A housemaid at the hotel advised that OLIVA was visited frequently by another young Spanish speaking Negro who may have been a Cuban.

COMMISSION EXHIBIT No. 2575

EXHIBITION OF PHOTOGRAPH
TO EMPLOYEES OF HOTEL DEL COMERCIO

The photograph furnished by JULIAN HUERTA OLIVA was exhibited by a confidential source abroad to SEBASTIAN PEREZ, desk clerk, Hotel del Comercio, Mexico, D. F., Mexico, on August 7, 1964. PEREZ advised that he was personally acquainted with all of the individuals in this photograph as being former guests at the hotel. PEREZ identified them as being, left to right:

FRANCISCO MORALES, the friend of ERNESTO LIMA JUAREZ.

GABRIEL CONTRERAS, from Chihuahua, Chihuahua, Mexico.

JULIAN HUERTA, the Cuban who was waiting for a visa to enter the United States.

MANUEL SANTOS, the representative of an agricultural workers union from Saltillo, Coahuila, Mexico.

ERNESTO LIMA JUAREZ, from Reynosa, Tamaulipas, Mexico.

The confidential source abroad exhibited this photograph to DOLORES RAMIREZ DE BARREIRO, proprietor of "Loncheria Esperanza," a restaurant located at Calle Bernardino de Sahagun No. 18, Mexico, D. F., Mexico, and she identified GABRIEL CONTRERAS as the man who sat at the same table as OSWALD on at least one occasion.

INTERVIEWS OF ANTONIO OLIVA ALVAREZ,
JUSTINO RODRIGUEZ HERNANDEZ, and
IRMA CANSECO ORTIZ

The records of the Visa Section, United States Embassy, Mexico, D. F., Mexico, disclosed that JUSTINO RODRIGUEZ HERNANDEZ, born August 5, 1919, Quemados de Guines, Cuba, bearing Cuban passport No. 01596, issued

January 17, 1956, at Havana, Cuba, was issued a visa to travel to New York City in April, 1961. RODRIGUEZ was described as being 5 feet 6 inches tall, weighing 142 pounds, black hair, brown eyes, and employed as a musician.

The confidential source abroad mentioned above obtained the following information on August 6, 1964:

A photograph of JUSTINO RODRIGUEZ HERNANDEZ was exhibited to MATILDE GARNICA, the housemaid at the Hotel del Comercio, and she advised that it could be a photograph of the individual who visited OLIVA at the Hotel del Comercio.

JUSTINO RODRIGUEZ HERNANDEZ, Salado Alvarez 17-10, Mexico, D. F., Mexico, advised on August 6, 1964, that he vaguely recalled ANTONIO OLIVA as a former employee of the night club called "Los Pericos," Mexico, D. F., Mexico, where RODRIGUEZ was employed as an entertainer. RODRIGUEZ claimed that he was not a close friend of OLIVA and did not know his present whereabouts. RODRIGUEZ claimed that he had never heard of the Hotel del Comercio and had never visited OLIVA there.

When photographs of OSWALD were exhibited to RODRIGUEZ, he said that he recognized OSWALD only as the result of seeing his photograph in the newspapers.

It is noted that RODRIGUEZ was barely coherent during this interview and appeared to be under the influence of alcohol or drugs.

A confidential source, who has furnished reliable information in the past, obtained the following information on August 6, 1964:

ANTONIO OLIVA ALVAREZ was encountered by chance at Salado Alvarez 17, Mexico, D. F., Mexico, on August 6, 1964. OLIVA stated that he was born in La Ceiba, Honduras, and entered Mexico in August, 1961, at Chetumal, Quintana Roo, Mexico.

OLIVA stated that he was formerly employed as a cook at the night club called "Los Pericos," Sullivan 13, Mexico, D. F., Mexico, but is presently unemployed. OLIVA stated that he was visiting JUSTINO RODRIGUEZ, a Cuban, residing at Salado Alvarez 17, Apartment 10, Mexico, D. F., Mexico.

The confidential source abroad mentioned above obtained the following information on August 7, 1964:

ANTONIO OLIVA ALVAREZ was interviewed at his present residence in the Hotel Fornos, Revillagigedo 92, Room 17, Mexico, D. F., Mexico. OLIVA stated that he was formerly a waiter at the "Los Pericos" night club and is currently unemployed. He stated that he was born on June 13, 1933, at La Ceiba, Honduras.

OLIVA said that he resided at the Hotel del Comercio from about June, 1963, until January, 1964, in Room No. 4, located on the roof of the hotel, with his common-law wife, IRMA CANSECO.

OLIVA stated that he does not recall ever having seen any Americans residing at that hotel during the time that he was a guest.

OLIVA said that he had read about OSWALD in the newspapers but had never seen OSWALD in person and did not possess any information concerning OSWALD, other than that gained from newspapers.

OLIVA stated that he did not associate with any of the guests at the Hotel del Comercio and did not know any of them by name. OLIVA pointed out that he worked late hours and he and his wife limited their personal contacts with the hotel staff to those contacts that were absolutely necessary.

OLIVA was not acquainted with any Cubans residing at the Hotel del Comercio, nor was he acquainted with any Negroes residing in the hotel. OLIVA stated that he is often mistakenly identified as a Cuban, perhaps because

- 4 -

COMMISSION EXHIBIT No. 2575—Continued

he is a Negro and a Spanish speaking foreigner. OLIVA stated that he had a Negro friend, who was in the habit of visiting him at the Hotel del Comercio, but OLIVA could not recall this person's name and did not know his present whereabouts. OLIVA stated that he would locate this individual and make him available for interview.

IRMA CANSECO ORTIZ was interviewed at the Hotel Fornos where she is residing with ANTONIO OLIVA in Room No. 17. She stated that she was born on August 15, 1944, in Oaxaca, Oaxaca, Mexico.

CANSECO confirmed that she had resided with OLIVA at the Hotel del Comercio from approximately June, 1963, to January, 1964. She stated that the housemaid was the only person at the hotel with whom she had any contact.

CANSECO stated that she had never seen an American at the Hotel del Comercio and the only information she possessed concerning OSWALD was obtained through newspaper reports.

- 5 -

COMMISSION EXHIBIT No. 2575—Continued

UNITED STATES DEPARTMENT OF JUSTICE
FEDERAL BUREAU OF INVESTIGATION

In Reply, Please Refer to
File No.

WASHINGTON 25, D. C.

May 18, 1964

LEE HARVEY OSWALD

BASIS FOR INQUIRY

The inquiries recorded hereinunder were conducted on the basis of information received from a confidential source abroad to the effect that LEE HARVEY OSWALD was alleged to have visited "some museums" during the time he was in Mexico City from September 27 to October 2, 1963.

INQUIRIES AT PRINCIPAL AND MOST ACCESSIBLE MUSEUMS

The information which follows was provided by a confidential source, who has furnished reliable information in the past and who explained that, while he had made a thorough survey of personnel at the various museums mentioned, all located in Mexico City, he had not always been able to obtain the names and in some instances the complete names of individuals interviewed, because of their sensitivity to questions concerning their identities and insistence upon receiving an explanation as to the manner in which their names would be utilized prior to furnishing same. He explained that he had desisted from inquiring further concerning their full names when he encountered resistance in connection therewith.

MUSEUM OF NATIONAL HISTORY
(MUSEO NACIONAL DE HISTORIA)

Photographs of OSWALD were displayed to the following persons at the Museum of National History located near the Chapultepec Castle, Chapultepec Park, without locating anyone who could recall his having visited the museum at any time:

COMMISSION EXHIBIT No. 2576

AGUSTIN ZARATE, ticket salesman and collector mornings
RAYMUNDO ESPINOSA, ticket salesman and collector afternoons
LUIS BANDA, guide
SALVADOR BRAVO, guide
JOSE BRITO, guide
LUIS ESTRADA, caretaker
JESUS BLANCAS, caretaker
LUIS ARELLANO, caretaker
JUAN MARTINEZ, caretaker
NICOLAS JIMENEZ, caretaker
RAMON AVILA, caretaker
ALBINO TEPUJE, caretaker
JOAQUIN M. OCAMPO, caretaker
ANTONIO MUNGUIA, caretaker
ARTURO LANGLE, Assistant Director
BERTOLDO TORRES ALDANA, caretaker of parking area
BARTOLOME CASTILLO, elevator operator
Eight other individuals who have business concessions in the area of the museum and whose complete names were not obtained.

NATIONAL MUSEUM OF ANTHROPOLOGY AND HISTORY
(MUSEO NACIONAL DE ANTROPOLOGIA Y HISTORIA)

The foregoing museum is located in the heart of Mexico City near the Government Square (Zocalo) at Calle de la Moneda No. 13. Photographs of LEE HARVEY OSWALD were shown to the following personnel thereof without locating anyone who could recall his having been a visitor at that establishment:

Mr. FLORES, guide
Mr. AVILA, guide
Mr. GUZMAN, ticket seller
Mr. HAYDES, ticket seller
Mr. POMPA, librarian
JUAN BALTAZAR, caretaker and security
Mr. VARELA, caretaker
AGUSTIN MIJARES, caretaker
FRANCISCO CARDENAS, caretaker

- 2 -

COMMISSION EXHIBIT No. 2576—Continued

MARCIAL ROJAS HERNANDEZ, caretaker
Miss SOFIA GOMEZ, director of Office of Public Relations, sale of post cards, booklets, official publications, etc.

Most of the persons interviewed were able to recognize the photographs of OSWALD from having seen them in the newspapers, but they were unable to remember his having visited the museum.

BENITO JUAREZ MUSEUM
(MUSEO RECINTO DE JUAREZ)

This museum is at the National Palace (Government Offices). It was determined that there are few employees, as no charge is made for admission. A review of the museum registration book failed to develop any information identifiable with OSWALD. The following employees were shown photographs of OSWALD and stated that they did not remember his having visited the museum:

Mr. BETANCOURT, caretaker of the registration book
Mr. MUNOZ, librarian
Miss AURITA, assistant librarian
Mr. MANZANILLA, caretaker
ANDRES ROMO, caretaker
ENRIQUE ROMO, caretaker

THE INTERAMERICAN INDIGENOUS INSTITUTE
(INSTITUTO INDIGENISTA INTERAMERICANO)

The foregoing establishment is at Calle Ninos Heroes 139. Photographs of OSWALD were displayed to the following persons connected therewith without locating anyone who could recall him as a visitor to the Institute:

Mr. SODI, office employee
Mr. CANTU, office employee
Mrs. HOLEY, office employee
Mrs. DERBES, office employee
Mrs. AGUILAR, office employee

- 3 -

COMMISSION EXHIBIT No. 2576—Continued

Miss OBREGON, librarian
JULIAN RUIZ, caretaker
FELIPE RUIZ, policeman at entrance
ROGELIO CALERO, car watchman
BALDOMERO CASTRO, car watchman
MARCELINO NOGUEDA, car watchman
LINO HERNANDEZ, car watchman
Six or seven other persons who operate concessions or commercial establishments in the vicinity of the entrance to the museum.

THE ETHNOGRAPHIC MUSEUM
(MUSEO ETNOGRAFICO - Ruins of an Aztec Temple)

This museum is located at the corner of Guatemala and Seminario Streets.

It was determined that only two employees are present on a regular basis, IGNACIO SENDRERO, ticket vendor on duty at the entrance, and EDULIO JUAREZ, caretaker, both of whom viewed photographs of OSWALD without being able to remember him as anyone who had visited the establishment.

THE WAX MUSEUM
(MUSEO DE CERA)

The foregoing is located at Calle Argentina (no number) and there are only two employees on duty who function as ticket vendors and caretakers. GUSTAVO HERNANDEZ and CONSUELO HERNANDEZ, after viewing photographs of OSWALD, advised they could not recall him as having been a visitor at the Wax Museum.

NATIONAL MUSEUM OF NATURAL HISTORY
(MUSEO NACIONAL DE LA HISTORIA NATURAL)

The following information was obtained by a confidential source abroad:

The Museum of Natural History is located at Calle Dr. Enrique Gonzalez Martinez No. 10 and on April 16, 1964,

- 4 -

COMMISSION EXHIBIT No. 2576—Continued

ALFONSO MANCILLA GOMEZ advised that he is the caretaker at that museum, a position which he has occupied for the past twenty-five years. He related that few American tourists visit the museum and that he follows the practice of spending some time assisting and explaining the interesting exhibits of the institution to those tourists who do appear there. He stated that he believed he would remember most American visitors, and upon viewing a photograph of OSWALD, advised that he could not recall him as a visitor at the museum and did not believe he had ever seen him at the Museum of Natural History.

- 5 -

COMMISSION EXHIBIT No. 2576—Continued

How You Can Help Greyhound Handle Your Baggage

We want you to have the best baggage service. Please read this panel and give consideration to:

WHAT IS BAGGAGE?

Baggage is wearing apparel, non-liquid toilet articles and personal effects necessary for YOUR comfort or convenience during the journey. This definition excludes such items carried for persons other than yourself—or any items intended for sale.
Radios, firearms, money, negotiable papers, jewelry, perishables, liquids and household effects are NOT baggage. Loss or damage to such articles is the sole responsibility of the owner.

MARK BAGGAGE CLEARLY

Make sure each piece of baggage carries your name and home address—preferably an identification card placed inside each bag. Otherwise an outside tag will do. If you forgot to do either, ask the ticket or baggage agent for an identification tag now.

DECLARE BAGGAGE VALUE

On checked baggage you have protection (in most states) for $25.00 on each adult ticket—$12.50 on each half-fare ticket. If further protection is needed, advise the baggage agent at the time baggage is checked. Protection can be increased to $125.00 by paying 10 cents or to $225.00 for just twenty cents.

BAGGAGE WEIGHT ALLOWANCE

Up to 150 lbs. of baggage may (in most states) be checked on each adult ticket—75 lbs. on each half-fare ticket at no extra cost. Baggage weighing more than described above will be handled at a small additional charge depending on amount it weighs.

SAVE STORAGE CHARGES

Claim your baggage as soon as you arrive at your destination. Baggage left over 24 hours will be stored at 15c a day or $3.00 for each month. Trunks and other large containers will be stored at 25c a day or $5.00 for each month.

CARE OF BELONGINGS

Coats, wraps, umbrellas, books, magazines, etc., cannot be checked and must be carried in the bus. Please be careful with your personal belongings as we cannot assume responsibility for loss, damage or theft inside the bus.

REPORT LOST ARTICLES

If you forgot articles when you left the bus, report them to the agent immediately. Also tell the agent if your checked baggage is missing upon arrival at your destination. He will make every effort to recover your missing items promptly.

FINALLY

We hope this information has been helpful to you. We desire to give you the best possible service, and your cooperation by following these rules will be appreciated.

Now, relax . . . enjoy your trip . . . and leave the driving to us!

GREYHOUND

Printed in U.S.A. by Russell's Guides

MEMPHIS—DALLAS—EL PASO
FT. WORTH—HOUSTON—NEW ORLEANS
SAN ANTONIO—LAREDO

3

BUS TIME TABLES

GREYHOUND

Commission Exhibit No. 2577

JANUARY 8, 1964

These schedules subject to change

COMMISSION EXHIBIT No. 2577

Refer to Station Column or Table Heading For the Time System Used.

DALLAS—FT. WORTH—ABILENE—EL PASO

READ DOWN

Run Numbers → 270 (1-8-64)		603 AtLA	637 MiLA	619 M-LA	693 D-SF	621 M-LA	647 NO-SF	695 D-SF	611 M-SD	641 NO-LA	601 AtLA	920 NO-Dn	617 D-LA	649 MiSF	629 D-Lu	615 M-LA
St. Louis, Mo.......(CST) (261) (CGL)	Lv	9 45		9 45	2 15	2 15			5 00		10 15					3 15
Dallas, Tex.......(CST) (263)	Ar	2 05		3 00	6 20	6 20			9 45		4 15					9 55
Atlanta, Ga.......(EST) (356) (SGL)	Lv	1 45		3 50	8 45	8 45			10 45		3 00					10 30
Birmingham, Ala....(CST) (354)	Lv	5 00		7 35	12 15	12 15			3 00		7 00					1 45
Memphis, Tenn.....(CST)	Ar	11 45		2 35	6 30	6 30			10 00		1 00					7 15
Memphis, Tenn.....(CST) (264) (CGL)	Lv	12 30		3 15	7 30	7 30		↶	11 15		3 30				↶	8 00
Dallas, Tex.	Ar	1 05		4 10	6 45	6 45			11 40		4 15					9 45
▲**Dallas, Tex.**..(CST) (GPH)	Lv	▫t2 15		5 55	t 7 10	t 8 45		t 1 30	t 1 30		t 5 00		t 7 20		t11 00	t11 00
▲**Ft. Worth, Tex.**....(GPH)	Ar	▫t2 55		6 50	t 7 50	t 9 30		t 2 10	t 2 10		t 5 40		t 8 00		t11 40	t11 40
New Orleans, La.........(363) (SGL)	Lv	6 30	2 45	10 45	10 45		8 45	7 30		12 45	12 45	12 45	12 45	7 00		3 30
Houston, Tex...........(277) (CGL)	Ar	6 45	12 05	10 05	10 05		5 15	6 40		9 35	9 35	11 25	11 25	3 55		3 25
Houston, Tex...........(272)	Lv	7 30	1 30	12 30	12 30		6 30	7 10	↷	10 10	9 55	12 10	12 10	5 00	↶	4 15
Ft. Worth, Tex.	Ar	2 20		6 40	6 40			2 05			5 00	7 10	7 10			11 30
▲**Ft. Worth, Tex.**	Lv	3 00	Thru Service Miami-Los Angeles via Kerrville	7 00	7 55	9 40	Thru Service New Orleans-San Francisco via Kerrville	2 20	2 20	Thru Service New Orleans-Los Angeles via Kerrville	5 50	8 15	8 15	Thru Service Miami-San Francisco via Kerrville	11 50	11 50
▲Weatherford		■		7 42	8 40	10 25		3 05	3 05		6 35	9 00	9 00		ss	ss
Camp Wolters Gate					f				f		f	f			f	f
▲**Mineral Wells**	Ar				9#06				3#31		7#01	9#26			12 54	12 54
▲**Mineral Wells**	Lv				9 17				3 42		7 15	9 37			12 54	12 54
Palo Pinto					f				f		- - -	f			f	- - -
Cantey					f				f		- - -	f			f	- - -
Caddo					■				■							
▲**Breckenridge**					10 20				4 45		8 18	10 40			1 56	
▲Albany					10 50				5 15		8 48	11 10			2 25	
δStrawn																f
▲Gordon Jct. (3 mi.)		f		f				f					f			
▲**Ranger**	Ar	D		8 47		11 30		4 12					10 07		Thru Bus Dallas-Lubbock Ar Lubbock 6 35 a.m.	D
▲**Ranger**	Lv	D		8 47		11 30		4 12					10 07			D
Olden				■				■								D
▲Eastland		f		9 00		11 43		4 27					10 21			D
▲Cisco		f		9 13		11 56		4 41					10 35			D
▲Putnam		f		9 29		12 13		4 58					f			- - -
▲Baird		f		9 43		12 28		5 16					ss			
▲Clyde		■		f		f		f								
▲**Abilene**..........(GPH) (CGL)	Ar	6‖10		10#15	11‖35	1‖00		5‖50	6‖00		9#33	11#55	11#40			3#15
Abilene..........(3990) (SsS)	Lv	8 15				1 30		6 40	6 40							
San Angelo	Ar	10 50				4 00		9 10	9 10							
▲**Abilene**..........(CGL)	Lv	6 40		10 30	12 01	1 50		6 30	6 30		9 50	12 10	12 10			3 30
▲Merkel		7 04			ss	ss		D	ss			D				D
δTrent		f			D	f			D			D				
▲**Sweetwater**..........(LB)	Ar	7 34		11 19	12 55	2 44		7 25	7 26		10 40	1 04	1 04			4 19
▲**Sweetwater**	Lv	7 35		11 19	Thru Service Dallas-San Francisco	2 45		Thru Service Dallas-San Francisco	7 26		10 40	New Orleans-Denver See Table 259	1 04			4 19
▲Roscoe		7 45				ss			ss							
▲Loraine		8 00				ss			ss				■			
▲Colorado City		8 14		ss		3 25			8 06		ss		ss			- - -
δWestbrook		f				f			f							
δCoahoma		f				f			f							
▲**Big Spring**..........(LB)	Ar	9#02		12‖39		4#15			8#55		11 59		2 26			5 33
▲**Big Spring**	Lv	9 15		1 05		4 30			9 06		12 01		2 26			5 33
▲Stanton		9 44		ss		5 00			ss		ss		ss			6 02
▲Midland..........(LB)		10 10		1 57		5 29			▫10 01		12 53		3 18			6 29
▲**Odessa**	Ar	10 40		2 25		6 00			10 31		1#21		3#46			6#57
▲**Odessa**	Lv	10 45		2 25		6 05			▫10 36		1 32		4 01			7 08
▲Monahans		11 30		ss		6 50			ss		ss		- - -			7 52
▲Pyote		ss		- - -		ss			- - -		- - -		- - -			ss
δBarstow		f		- - -		f			- - -		- - -		- - -			f
▲**Pecos**..........(GPH)	Ar	12‖20		3#50		7‖34			12#04		3#00		5#30			8‖35
Pecos, Tex...........(832) (NMT)	Lv			4 00									5 50			9 15
Roswell, N.M.	Ar			6 40									8 50			12 15
Albuquerque, N.M.	Ar			11 00	10 55			6 00					1 20			5 55
San Antonio, Tex...........(784) (KBC)	Lv		7 30				12 01			4 30				10 30		
Pecos	Ar		3#35				8#10			12#45				6‖15		
▲**Pecos**	Lv	12 50	3 50	4 05		8 05	8 25		12 30	1 00	3 15		5 50	6 45		9 05
δToyah		f	f	- - -		f	- - -		f	- - -	- - -		f	- - -		f
▲Kent		ss	ss			ss	- - -		ss	- - -	- - -		ss	- - -		ss
▲**Van Horn**	Ar	2#29	5‖29	5‖42		9#39	- - -		2#09	2#39	4 52		7‖29	- - -		10#44
▲**Van Horn**..........(CST)	Lv	2 40	6 00	6 15		9 50	- - -		2 25	2 50	5 00		8 00	- - -		10 55
▲Sierra Blanca..........(MST)		2 19	ss	- - -		ss			- - -	- - -	ss		7 39			ss
▲McNary		2 54	ss								f		8 14			f
▲Ft. Hancock		3 00	ss								f		8 20			f
▲Fabens		3 30	ss								ss		8 48			ss
▲Ysleta		3 50	ss								ss		9 08			f
▲**El Paso, Tex.**..........(CGL)	Ar	4‖20	7#30	7#30		11#10	11#15		3#45	4#05	6‖20		9#35	9#40		12‖25
El Paso, Tex...........(667) (WGL)	Lv	5 15	8 40	8 25		12 01	12 01		4 50	4 55	7 15		10 50	10 40		1 30
Tucson, Ariz.	Ar	11 50	3 05			6 30			11 45		1 50		6 10	5 25		
Phoenix, Ariz...........(MST)	Ar	2 35		5 00		9 30	9 22			2 37	4 50		8 15	8 30		10 45
San Diego, Calif...........(PST)	Ar		1 10	1 10		4 50			8 45				3 40			
Los Angeles, Calif.	Ar	10 25	1 20	1 05		5 05				11 00	1 25		3 50			6 30
San Francisco, Calif......(PST) (667-9)	Ar				12 50		2 50	7 10						1 20		

Index numbers adjacent to towns refer to local tables in Russell's Guide.

#—Rest stop.
‖—Meal stop.
■—Highway stop.
▫—Mail run.
D—Will go into town to discharge passengers.
All trips operate daily unless otherwise noted.

Times shown in ITALICS indicate service via connecting trip or trips.
f—Flag stop.
ss—Station stop.
t—Schedules operate via Turnpike between Ft. Worth and Dallas.

▲—Agency stations to which baggage may be checked and interline express consigned.
δ—Express agency only. No tickets or checked baggage.
δ—Station having drop off service for prepaid express only.
(*LB*)—Lock box for deposit of express during station's closed hours.

COMMISSION EXHIBIT No. 2577—Continued

Refer to Station Column or Table Heading For the Time System Used.

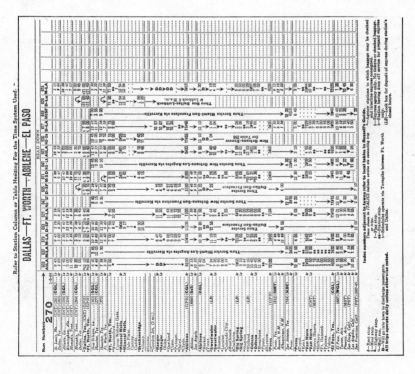

EL PASO—ABILENE—FT. WORTH- -DALLAS

READ DOWN

Run Numbers → 270 (1-8-64)		624 SD-M	698 SF-D	650 SF-Mi	612 LA-M	608 SD-At	919 Dn-NO	638 LA-Mi	618 LA-M	694 SF-D	648 SF-NO	622 LA-D	716 LA-M	628 Va-D	606 LA-At	636 LA-NO
San Francisco, Cal. (PST) (667-9) (WGL)	Lv		6 15	6 45						6 15	8 00			11 45		
Los Angeles, Calif...........(667)	Lv	2 30	Thru Bus San Francisco-Dallas		8 15			11 45	1 15			5 30	7 15		8 45	10 15
San Diego, Calif...........(PST)	Lv	6 15			9 00	2 00					6 15				10 15	10 15
Phoenix, Ariz...........(MST)	Lv			2 05	6 15			9 50	11 40		3 00	3 05	4 30			8 45
Tucson, Ariz.	Lv	5 25		4 55		12 01			3 05		5 50		7 30		11 30	
El Paso, Tex.	Ar	11#45		11#40	3#20	6‖15		6‖35	9‖25		12‖45	12‖45	2#15		6‖05	6‖20
▲**El Paso, Tex.**..........(CGL)	Lv	12 30		12 30	4 00	7 00		7 20	10 15		1 45	1 45	3 15		7 30	7 30
▲Ysleta				ss	f			7 42	10 37			ss				ss
▲Fabens				ss	ss			8 02	10 57			2 27				8 12
▲Ft. Hancock				ss	f			8 30	11 25			ss				ss
▲McNary				ss	f			8 36	11 31			ss				ss
▲Sierra Blanca..........(MST)		- - -		ss	f	f		9 11	12 06		- - -	3 36	- - -		- - -	9 21
▲**Van Horn**..........(CST)	Ar	3#45		4#00	7‖25	10#15		10#50	1‖45		5#05	5#15	6‖35		10#50	11#00
▲**Van Horn**	Lv	3 58		4 11	7 55	10 30		11 01	2 15		5 20	5 30	7 15		11 05	11 15
▲Kent		- - -		ss	ss	- - -		ss	ss		- - -	ss	- - -		- - -	ss
δToyah		- - -		f	f	- - -		f	f		- - -	f	- - -		- - -	f
▲**Pecos**..........(GPH)	Ar	5‖35		5‖50	9#34	12‖07		12‖40	3#54		6‖58	7‖09	8#52		12#44	12#54
Pecos..........(784) (KBC)	Lv			6 25				1 00			7 30					1 30
San Antonio, Tex.	Ar			3 25				9 35			3 40					11 00
Albuquerque, N.M...........(832) (NMT)	Lv		10 45						6 20	9 30			11 50	4 00	4 00	
Roswell, N.M.	Ar								10 40				4 10		8 25	
Pecos, Tex.	Ar								3 40				9 00		1 05	
▲**Pecos**	Lv	6 05		Thru Service San Francisco-Miami, via Kerrville	9 47	12 40	Thru Service Denver-New Orleans See Table 259	Thru Service Los Angeles-Miami, via Kerrville	4 10	Thru Service San Francisco-Dallas	Thru Service San Francisco-New Orleans, via Kerrville	7 45	9 05	Thru Service Vaughn-Dallas	1 10	Thru Service Los Angeles-New Orleans, via Kerrville
δBarstow		f			f	f			f			f	- - -		- - -	
▲Pyote		f			ss	ss			ss			ss	- - -		- - -	
▲Monahans		6 50			10 31	1 25			4 54			8 29	D		ss	
▲**Odessa**	Ar	7 35			11 15	2 10			5 38			9 13	10#30		2#37	
▲**Odessa**	Lv	7 39			11 15	2 15			5 43			9 18	10 41		2 52	
▲Midland..........(LB)		8 09			11 45	2 45			6 13			9 48	11 09		3 20	
▲Stanton		8 36			12 12	3 12			6 40			10 15	- - -		ss	
▲**Big Spring**..........(LB)	Ar	9#05			12‖41	3#42			7‖10			10#44	12 01		4 12	
▲**Big Spring**	Lv	9 20			1 10	3 59			7 55			11 00	12 01		4 15	
δCoahoma		f			f	■			f			■				
δWestbrook		f			f	■						■				
▲Colorado City		10 09			1 57	4 47			8 44			ss	- - -		ss	
▲Loraine		10 23			2 11	■			ss							
▲Roscoe		D			D	ss									ss	
▲**Sweetwater**..........(LB)	Ar	10 50			2 37	5 25			9 25			12 22			5 35	
▲**Sweetwater**	Lv	10 50	10 36		2 37	5 25	5 25		9 25	9 25		12 22			5 37	
δTrent		D	f		f	D	■								f	
Merkel		D	ss		ss	D	ss		ss						ss	
▲**Abilene**..........(GPH)	Ar	11‖45	11‖32		3#31	6‖20	6‖20		10#20	10#19		1#15	2#05		6‖35	
San Angelo..........(3990) (SsS)	Lv				11 10				6 35			10 40				
Abilene	Ar				1 40				9 10			12 45				
▲**Abilene**	Lv	12 15	12 15		3 46	6 55	6 55		10 35	10 35		1 30	2 20		7 15	
▲Clyde					f										f	
▲Baird		12 43			4 17	ss			- - -				D		7 47	
▲Putnam		12 58			ss	ss			- - -				- - -		8 02	
▲Cisco		1 15			4 49	7 55			f				D		8 19	
▲Eastland		1 28			5 03	8 08			f				D		8 32	
Olden		D			■								D		D	
▲**Ranger**	Ar	1 41			5 16	8 21			D				D		8 45	
▲**Ranger**	Lv	1 41			5 16	8 21			D				D		8 45	
▲Gordon Jct. (3 mi.)		f				f			- - -				- - -			
δStrawn					f										f	
▲Albany			1 00				7 40			11 18		2 13		5 18		
▲**Breckenridge**			1 30				8 10			11 47		2 42		5 47		
Caddo			■				f								f	
Cantey			f		- - -		f			- - -		- - -		- - -	f	
Palo Pinto			f		- - -		f			- - -		- - -		- - -	f	
▲**Mineral Wells**	Ar		2#34		6#13		9 13			12 50		3 45		6 50	9#42	
▲**Mineral Wells**	Lv		2 45		6 24		9 15			12 50		3 45		6 53	9 55	
Camp Wolters Gate			f		f		- - -			- - -		- - -		f	f	
▲Weatherford		2 45	3 15		6 51	9 25	ss		f	ss		ss	ss	7 19	10 21	
▲**Ft. Worth, Tex.**....(GPH)	Ar	3#30	4 00		7 36	10 10	10#20		1 45	1 55		4#50	5#30	8#05	11 06	
Ft. Worth, Tex...........(272)	Lv	5 00	↶		7 45	↷	10 50		3 45	↶				8 25	12 15	
Houston, Tex.	Ar	11 59		8 55	2 40		5 20	3 25	11 05		9 00			3 45	7 30	4 55
Houston, Tex...........(277) (CGL)	Lv	12 55		10 20	4 15		7 30	4 15	12 01		10 15			5 00	8 30	5 45
New Orleans, La...........(363) (SGL)	Ar	11 30		7 15	1 45		7 20	1 45	11 25		7 30			4 30	7 50	2 20
▲**Ft. Worth, Tex.**..........(CGL)	Lv	t3 40	t4 05		t7 36	t10 20	10 20		t1 45	t 1 55		t5 00	t5 40	t8 15	t11 15	
▲**Dallas, Tex.**........(GPH)	Ar	t4‖25	t4 45		t8‖15	t11#00	11 00		t2‖25	t2 35		t5 40	t6‖20	t8 55	t11‖55	
Dallas, Tex...........(264)	Lv	5 45	↶		9 15	12 05			3 45	↶		↷	7 30		1 00	
Memphis, Tenn.	Ar	6 00			9 10	11 50			4 45				8 45		1 55	
Memphis, Tenn...........(354) (SGL)	Lv	7 30			10 30	12 45			6 30				9 30		3 00	
Birmingham, Ala.........(CST)	Ar	2 00			5 35	7 10			1 00				3 45		9 30	
Atlanta, Ga...........(EST) (356)	Ar	7 30			11 55	1 15			6 15				9 55		4 10	
Dallas, Tex.......(CST) (263) (CGL)	Lv	5 30			8 30	12 01			4 50				7 45	9 45	2 45	
St. Louis, Mo.......(CST) (261)	Ar	10 35			2 20	5 25			11 15				12 35	5 00	9 20	

(CGL)—Central Greyhound Lines.
(SGL)—Southern Greyhound Lines.
(SsS)—Sunset Stages.
(WGL)—Western Greyhound Lines.
▸—Texas Motor Coach.
AM—Light Face. **PM—Bold Face.**
(CDT)—Central Daylight Time.
(CST)—Central Standard Time.
(EST)—Eastern Standard Time.

(MST)—Mountain Standard Time.
(PST)—Pacific Standard Time.
(PDT)—Pacific Daylight Time.
(GPH)—Greyhound Post House.
At-LA or **LA-At**—Thru bus Atlanta-Los Angeles.
D-LA or **LA-D**—Thru bus Dallas-Los Angeles.
D-SF or **SF-D**—Thru bus Dallas-San Francisco.
D-Va or **Va-D**—Thru bus Dallas-Vaughn.
LA-M or **M-LA**—Thru bus Los Angeles-Memphis.

LA-Mi or **Mi-LA**—Thru bus Los Angeles-Miami.
Lu-D or **D-Lu**—Thru bus Lubbock-Dallas.
NO-Dn or **Dn-NO**—Thru bus New Orleans-Denver.
NO-LA or **LA-NO**—Thru bus New Orleans-Los Angeles.
NO-SF or **SF-NO**—Thru bus New Orleans-San Francisco.
SD-At or **At-SD**—Thru bus San Diego-Atlanta.
SD-M or **M-SD**—Thru bus San Diego-Memphis.
SF-Mi or **Mi-SF**—Thru bus San Francisco-Miami.

COMMISSION EXHIBIT No. 2577—Continued

Refer to Station Column or Table Heading For the Time System Used.

MEMPHIS—PINE BLUFF—TEXARKANA—DALLAS

264
1-8-64

M-SD	M-LA	M-LA	AtLA	M-LA	AtLA	READ DOWN / READ UP	SDAt	LA-M	LA-M	LAAt	SD-M	LA-M
4 30	10 30	12 01	......	8 45	7 00	Lv New York, N.Y....(EST) (65) (EGL)..Ar	10 10	6 55	8 30	......	12 05	7 35
5 30	10 45	12 30	......	11 30	6 30	Lv Philadelphia, Pa..........(66)..........Ar	9 20	4 05	7 55	......	11 50	7 35
8 35	2 10	3 40	......	1 55	10 25	Lv Baltimore, Md.......(65a-66) (EGL)..Ar	6 25	1 40	4 25	......	8 25	3 55
10 00	3 40	5 15	......	3 30	12 01	Lv Washington, D.C..(EST) (303) (SGL)..Ar	4 45	12 20	3 00	......	7 00	2 33
6 30	2 00	2 00	8 15	1 15	11 00	Lv Norfolk, Va.......(EST) (69) (EGL)..Ar	9 15	1 30	5 30	......	↑	4 00
10 30	5 50	5 50	7 00	5 30	2 30	Lv Richmond, Va....(EST) (306a) (SGL)..Ar	4 30	9 56	2 05	......	↑	11 45
3 45	11 45	11 45	......	11 30	7 30	Lv Roanoke, Va......(EST) (303)..........Ar	10 00	4 10	8 25	......	1 10	6 15
7 45	3 40	3 15	......	4 25	12 40	Lv Bristol, Va..............................Ar	5 45	10 37	3 25	......	9 30	2 15
11 30	7 30	6 30	......	8 15	4 45	Lv Knoxville, Tenn..........(353)..........Ar	2 15	6 45	11 15	......	6 05	11 10
3 00	↓	6 30	......	11 59	↓	Lv Chattanooga......(EST) (353a)..........Ar	11 15	3 00	↑	......	5 00	↑
5 00	12 30	10 00	6 15	1 30	10 30	Lv Nashville........(CST) (353)..........Ar	7 00	10 52	3 10	8 50	12 15	3 45
10 15	6 05	2 30	11 55	6 45	3 15	Ar Memphis, Tenn..............................Lv	1 15	5 30	9 45	2 15	7 00	9 45
10 45	8 45	3 50	1 45	10 30	3 30	Lv Atlanta, Ga.......(EST) (356)..........Ar	1 15	6 15	9 55	4 10	7 30	11 55
3 00	12 15	7 35	5 00	1 45	7 30	Lv Birmingham, Ala...(CST) (354)..........Ar	7 10	1 00	3 45	9 30	2 00	5 35
10 00	6 30	2 35	11 45	7 15	1 30	Ar Memphis, Tenn................(SGL)..Lv	12 45	6 30	9 30	3 00	7 30	10 30
611	621	619	603	615	601	←—— Run Numbers ——→	603	618	616	605	624	612
11 15	7 30	3 15	12 30	8 00	3 30	Lv*Memphis, Tenn....(CST) (CGL)..Ar	11‖50	4 45	8 45	1#55	6 00	9 10
11 35	7 50	3 35	12 50	8 20	ss	*West Memphis, Ark.	↑	ss	8 25	D	D	ss
- - -	ss	ss	ss	ss	- - -	*Hicks Station	- - -	D	ss	- - -	- - -	ss
- - -	ss	ss	ss	ss	- - -	*Madison Jct. (½ mi.)	- - -	D	ss	- - -	- - -	ss
12 20	8 35	4 30	1 45	9 10	ss	*Forest City..........(LB)	(1)	3 30	7 37	12 50	ss	7 58
- - -	ss	ss	ss	ss	- - -	*Wheatley	- - -	D	ss	f	- - -	ss
12 50	9 05	5 00	2 15	9 40	ss	*Brinkley	10 20	3 00	7 07	12 20	4 25	7 28
- - -	ss	5 28	2 40	10 10	D	*Clarendon	D	D	6 40	ss	- - -	ss
- - -	f	f	ss	ss	- - -	*Roe	D	D	ss	f	- - -	f
1 39	9 55	5 58	3 08	10 40	D	*Stuttgart..........(LB)	9 30	2 09	6 15	11 30	3 35	6 40
- - -	f	6 15	3 25	10 57	- - -	*Humphrey	f	1 52	ss	f	- - -	ss
- - -	f	f	f	11 07	- - -	Wabbaseka	f	1 42	ss	f	- - -	ss
- - -	f	6 30	3 40	11 13	- - -	*Altheimer	f	1 36	ss	f	- - -	f
2#29	10#45	6‖55	4‖05	11‖40	6‖40	Ar*Pine Bluff..........(GPH)..........Lv	8 40	1 15	5 20	10 40	2 45	5 50
↓	↓	6 25	2 45	11 20	↓	Lv Little Rock..........(284)..........Ar	10 05	2 30	6 20	↑	↑	↑
↓	↓	7 45	4 05	12 40	↓	Ar Pine Bluff..............................Lv	8 45	1 10	5 00	↑	↑	↑
2 45	11 05	7 50	4 40	12 40	7 10	Lv*Pine Bluff..........(GPH)..........Ar	8#20	12‖40	□4‖50	10#15	2#28	5‖18
↓	↓	■	ss	1 15	7 45	*Rison	■	12 06	□4 15	■	↑	■
- - -	- - -	f	f	f	f	δKingsland	f	f	□ f	f	- - -	- - -
ss	D	8 45	5 40	1 40	8 10	*Fordyce	7 25	11 41	3 50	ss	ss	ss
- - -	- - -	f	f	f	f	*Thornton	- - -	f	f	f	- - -	f
- - -	- - -	ss	6 00	2 00	8 30	*Bearden	- - -	ss	3 28	ss	- - -	f
4 23	D	9 28	6 23	2 23	8 53	*Camden	6 42	10 54	□3 03	8 34	12 50	3 40
- - -	- - -	- - -	ss	ss	ss	Buena Vista Jct. (1/3 mi.)	- - -	ss	ss	ss	- - -	- - -
- - -	- - -	- - -	ss	ss	ss	Ogemaw Jct. (½ mi.)	- - -	ss	ss	ss	- - -	- - -
f	- - -	ss	6 47	2 47	9 17	*Stephens	- - -	ss	2 36	ss	f	f
- - -	- - -	- - -	ss	ss	ss	*McNiel	- - -	ss	ss	ss	- - -	- - -
- - -	- - -	- - -	f	f	f	Southern State College	- - -	f	f	f	- - -	- - -
5#10	↓	10 14	7#10	3#10	9#40	Ar*Magnolia..........(LB)..........Lv	5 56	10 01	2 10	7 45	12 01	↑
5 21	↓	10 14	7 21	□3 25	9 51	Lv*Magnolia..........(LB)..........Ar	□5‖31	9#50	1 44	7‖14	12 01	↑
f	- - -	f	ss	3 35	ss	Waldo	- - -	9 39	ss	ss	- - -	- - -
f	- - -	f	f	f	f	*Buckner	- - -	f	f	f	- - -	- - -
f	- - -	f	ss	□3 54	10 20	*Stamps	f	9 20	1 15	6 45	f	f
ss	- - -	f	ss	4 01	10 27	*Lewisville	ss	9 12	1 07	6 37	ss	ss
f	- - -	f	f	f	f	*Garland City, Ark.	- - -	f	f	f	- - -	- - -
6 32	2#20	11#32	8 38	4 43	11 10	Ar*Texarkana, Tex..........Lv	□4 20	8 30	12 25	5 55	10 50	1 55
12 45	9 20	↓	(3)	(3)	4 30	Lv Little Rock, Ark..(8186) (8353) (CTS)..Ar	↑	(3)	(3)	(3)	4 40	6 45
2 10	10 55	↓	4 25	12 30	↓	Lv Hot Springs, Ark..........Ar	↑	12 50	4 50	10 10	3 10	5 20
5 05	1 35	↓	7 30	3 10	8 25	Ar Texarkana, Tex..........Lv	↑	10 00	2 15	7 30	12 30	2 30
6 37	2 35	11 50	8 45	4 50	11 15	Lv*Texarkana, Tex..........(CGL)..Ar	4 15	8 25	12 21	5 50	□10#30	1#41
ss	- - -	- - -	ss	5 20	11 45	*Maud	- - -	ss	ss	ss	ss	- - -
ss	- - -	- - -	ss	5 54	12 19	*Naples	- - -	ss	ss	4 46	ss	- - -
7 37	- - -	- - -	ss	6 00	12 25	*Omaha	- - -	ss	11 11	4 40	ss	- - -
7‖57	D	1 10	10 05	6‖20	12‖45	Ar*Mt. Pleasant..........Lv	2 56	7 00	10 51	4 20	□9 10	12 21
8 25	D	1 10	□10 05	6 50	1 10	Lv*Mt. Pleasant..........Ar	2 56	6‖35	□10#40	4#09	9 10	12 21
ss	- - -	- - -	ss	7 10	1 30	*Mt. Vernon	- - -	6 15	□10 19	3 49	ss	- - -
ss	- - -	- - -	ss	ss	ss	*Saltillo	- - -	ss	□ ss	ss	ss	- - -
f	- - -	- - -	f	f	f	Weaver	- - -	f	f	f	f	- - -
9 15	D	D	10 55	7 40	2 00	*Sulphur Springs	↑	5 45	□9 48	3 18	8 20	11 31
■	↓	↓	↓	↓	■	Brashear	↑	↑	D	D	D	↑
f	↓	↓	↓	↓	↓	Cumby	↑	↑	↑	↑	D	↑
↓	- - -	- - -	- - -	- - -	f	Cumby Jct.	- - -	- - -	f	f	- - -	- - -
f	↓	↓	↓	↓	↓	Campbell	↑	↑	↑	↑	D	↑
10 05	5#02	2#35	11#35	8 22	2 42	Ar*Greenville..........Lv	1 36	5 05	□9 05	2 35	7 31	10 51
10 05	5 15	2 50	11 46	8 25	2 45	Lv*Greenville..........Ar	1#25	5 05	9 05	2 35	7#20	10#40
10 28	5 36	↓	↓	↓	3 08	*Farmersville	↑	↑	8 42	2 10	6 57	↑
ss	ss	- - -	f	ss	ss	*Copeville	- - -	f	ss	ss	ss	- - -
f	f	- - -	f	f	f	Lavon	- - -	f	f	f	f	- - -
ss	ss	- - -	ss	ss	3 32	*Wylie	- - -	ss	8 18	1 45	ss	- - -
ss	ss	↓	↓	ss	3 45	*Garland	ss	↑	8 05	1 30	6 20	ss
11‖40	6‖45	4‖10	□1#05	9#45	4‖15	Ar*Dallas, Tex.......(GPH)..........Lv	12 05	3 45	7 30	1 00	5 45	9 15
1 30	8 45	5 55	2 15	11 00	5 00	Lv Dallas, Tex..........(270)..........Ar	11 00	2 25	6 20	11 55	4 25	8 15
2 10	9 30	6 50	2 55	11 40	5 40	Ar Ft. Worth..............................Lv	10 20	1 45	5 40	11 15	3 40	7 36
6 00	1 00	10 15	6 10	3 15	9 33	Ar Abilene..........(CST)..........Lv	6 55	10 35	2 20	7 15	12 15	3 46
3 45	11 10	7 30	4 20	12 25	6 20	Ar El Paso, Tex..........(MST)..........Lv	7 00	10 15	3 15	7 30	12 30	4 00
4 50	12 01	8 25	5 15	1 30	7 15	Lv El Paso, Tex.....(MST) (667) (WGL)..Ar	6 15	9 25	2 15	6 05	11 45	3 20
8 45	4 50	1 10	↓	↓	↓	Ar San Diego, Cal.....(PST)..........Lv	2 00	↑	6 15	10 15	6 15	9 00
11 00	5 05	1 05	10 25	6 30	1 25	Ar Los Angeles, Cal..(PST) (667) (WGL)..Lv	11 45	1 15	7 15	8 45	2 30	8 15
12 15	[illegible]	7 30	3 35	10 30	5 15	Lv Dallas, Tex.......(CST) (271) (CGL)..Ar	11 25	3 30	7 10	12 30	5 10	7 20
2 35	[illegible]	9 49	5 50	12 55	7 20	Ar Waco..............................Lv	9 24	1 30	4 48	10 10	3 00	5 00
5 20	12 50	12 50	9 00	3 37	9 49	Ar Austin..............................Lv	7 09	11 05	2 05	7 25	12 05	2 11
7 45	2 55	3 15	11 15	5 45	11 45	Ar San Antonio..............................Lv	5 05	9 00	12 10	5 00	9 30	12 01
12 20	6 50	6 50	3 45	12 20	5 30	Ar Laredo..........(280)..........Lv	11 15	4 40	......	......	3 00	7 15
......	7 50	7 50	4 15	12 25	5 45	Ar Corpus Christi, Tex......(279)..........Lv	10 30	5 00	......	......	......	7 10

AM—Light Face. PM—Bold Face.
Times shown in ITALICS indicate service via connecting trip or trips.
(EDT)—Eastern Daylight Time.
(EST)—Eastern Standard Time.
(CDT)—Central Daylight Time.
(CST)—Central Standard Time.
(MST)—Mountain Standard Time.
(PDT)—Pacific Daylight Time.
(PST)—Pacific Standard Time.
(EGL)—Eastern Greyhound Lines.
(CGL)—Central Greyhound Lines.
(CTS)—Continental Trailways System.
(SGL)—Southern Greyhound Lines.
(WGL)—Western Greyhound Lines.
- - -—Indicates Route. No local service performed.
□—Handles U.S. Mail Sundays only.
□—Handles U.S. Mail.
AtLA or **LAAt**—Thru bus Atlanta-Los Angeles.
LA-M or **M-LA**—Thru bus Los Angeles-Memphis.
SDAt—Thru bus San Diego-Atlanta.
SD-M or **M-SD**—Thru bus San Diego-Memphis.
D—Stops to discharge passengers only.
*—Agency stations to which baggage may be checked and to which interline express may be consigned.
(GPH)—Greyhound Post House.
‖—Meal stop. f—Flag stop. #—Rest stop.
(1)—Will stop to discharge passengers originating in Memphis or points East, or to pick up passengers destined to points beyond Brinkley.
(1)—Will stop to discharge passengers originating West of Brinkley, or to pick up passengers destined to Memphis or beyond.
(3)—Connection for Little Rock made in Pine Bluff.
ss—Station stop. ■—Highway stop.
(LB)—Lock box for deposit of express during station closing hours.
All trips operate daily unless otherwise noted.

Refer to Station Column or Table Heading For the Time System Used.

SAN FRANCISCO—AMARILLO—OKLAHOMA CITY—FT. SMITH
LITTLE ROCK—MEMPHIS
BIRMINGHAM—ATLANTA

265
1-8-64

OCAt	SFAt	OCM	OCM	OCAt	READ DOWN / READ UP	MOC	AtSF	MOC	AtOC	AtOC
......	11 45	6 15	......	6 15	Lv San Francisco, Cal...PST (WGL) Ar	7 10	12 50	......	......	12 50
7 15	7 15	1 30	10 15	1 15	Lv Los Angeles, Cal.....(PST) (669) Ar	12 10	b 5 20	9 45	11 20	5 15
↓	3 15	9 45	7 15	11 00	Lv Albuquerque, N.M.(MST) (CGL) Ar	6 05	11 10	2 45	5 35	10 15
↓	11 30	5 45	3 00	7 00	Lv Amarillo, Tex.........(CST) (262) Ar	12 55	5 10	9 10	11 55	4 05
8 30	5 45	1 00	10 30	4 00	Lv Oklahoma City, Okla..(4017) (OT) Ar	6 45	11 05	2 55	5 30	9 45
12 30	9 20	4 20	1 45	7 50	Lv McAlester, Okla..........Ar	3 25	7 40	11 59	2 25	5 50
2 50	11 50	6 40	4 00	10 15	Ar Ft. Smith, Ark..........Lv	1 00	5 15	9 40	12 01	3 30
3 30	12 20	7 20	4 15	10 55	Lv Ft. Smith, Ark.......(763) (CCo) Ar	11 50	4 15	8 50	11 20	3 05
5 10	2 04	9 06	5 58	12 38	Ar Danville..........Lv	10 07	2 40	7 10	9 34	1 29
7 25	4 10	11 20	8 00	2 40	Ar Little Rock, Ark..........Lv	8 10	12 45	5 10	7 40	11 30
710	696	688	690	708	←——Run Numbers——→	689	697	691	705	707
8 00	5 00	12 15	8 25	2 50	Lv*Little Rock, Ark.(CST)......Ar	7‖35	11‖45	4 30	7‖10	11#10
8 05	5 05	12 20	8 30	2 55	North Little Rock	ss	ss	ss	ss	ss
f	f	f	f	f	Scott	f	f	f	f	f
f	f	f	f	f	Toltec	f	f	f	f	f
f	f	f	f	f	Keo	f	f	f	f	f
8 37	5 40	12 52	9 00	3 25	*England	6 55	11 08	3 50	6 33	10 35
f	f	f	f	f	Coy Jct..........(½ mi.)	f	f	f	f	f
f	f	f	f	f	Ryan	f	f	f	f	f
ss	ss	ss	ss	f	*Humnoke	ss	ss	ss	ss	ss
f	f	f	f	f	Brummitt	f	f	f	f	f
9 12	6 15	1 29	9 35	4 00	*Stuttgart..........(LB)	6 20	10 33	3 13	5 58	10 00
f	f	f	f	f	Ulm	f	f	f	f	f
f	ss	ss	ss	f	*Roe	f	ss	ss	ss	f
9 37	6 40	1 55	10 02	4 25	*Clarendon	5 55	10 07	2 44	5 28	9 33
10 05	7 07	2 25	10 30	4 48	*Brinkley	5 30	9 40	2 15	5 00	9 05
ss	ss	ss	ss	- - -	*Wheatley	- - -	ss	ss	ss	ss
f	f	f	f	- - -	Goodwin	- - -	f	f	f	f
10 35	7 37	2 57	11 00	- - -	*Forrest City..........(LB)	ss	9 10	1 45	4 30	8 35
ss	ss	ss	ss	- - -	*Madison Jct..........(½ mi.)	- - -	ss	ss	ss	ss
ss	ss	ss	ss	- - -	*Hicks Station	- - -	ss	ss	ss	ss
11 25	8 25	3 50	11 50	↓	*West Memphis, Ark.	4 20	8 20	12 50	3 35	7 50
11#45	8#45	4 10	12 10	6‖30	Ar*Memphis, Tenn..........Lv	4 00	8 00	12 30	3 15	7 30
1 00	9 30	6 30	12 45	7 30	Lv Memphis, Tenn.......(354) (SGL) Ar	3 45	7‖15	11 45	2#35	6‖30
7 00	3 45	1 00	7 10	2 00	Ar Birmingham, Ala...(CST)..........Lv	9 30	1 45	5 00	7 35	12 15
12 30	9 55	6 15	1 15	7 30	Ar Atlanta, Ga..........(EST) (356) Lv	5 30	10 30	1 45	3 50	8 45

SAN ANTONIO—HOUSTON

267
1-8-64

LA-M		SF-M	LA-N		SF-N	READ DOWN / READ UP	M-LA	N-SF	N-LA		M-SF	
4 40	2 00	11 15	7 15	3 00	9 15	Lv Laredo, Tex.......(CST) (CGL) Ar	12 20	3 45	6 50	10 10	......	5 30
8 15	5 45	3 00	11 05	6 20	1 00	Ar San Antonio, Tex..........(280)..Lv	8 30	12 05	3 30	6 30	......	2 10
638	6744	650	636	6742	648	←——Run Numbers——→	637	647	641	6741	649	6743
10 45	6 25	4 00	11 30	7 15	4 05	Lv*San Antonio, Tex.(GPH)....Ar	6 15	11 30	3 20	5 45	10 10	12 25
↓	f	↓	↓	f	↓	New Schirmerville	↑	f	↑	f	↑	↑
11 35	7 15	4 49	12 22	8 05	4 50	*Seguin	5 30	10 40	2 30	4 56	9 18	11 30
	↓	f	f	↓	f	Kingsbury	f	- - -	f	f	↑	
12 02	↓	◆5 15	12 52	↓	5 17	*Luling	5 00	10 10	2 00	4 29	↑	11 05
- - -	↓	◆ f	f	↓	f	Harwood	f	- - -	f	f	f	- - -
↓	f	↓	↓	f	↓	Oil Pool	↑	↑	↑	↑	f	↑
↓	f	↓	↓	f	↓	Belmont	↑	↑	↑	↑	f	↑
↓	f	↓	↓	f	↓	Oak Forest	↑	↑	↑	↑	f	↑
↓	7 59	↓	↓	8 49	↓	*Gonzales	↑	↑	↑	↑	8 39	↑
↓	f	↓	↓	f	↓	Saturn	↑	↑	↑	↑	f	↑
- - -	8 24	- - -	1 25	9 14	ss	*Waelder	- - -	ss	ss	4 00	8 14	ss
- - -	8 40	- - -	ss	9 30	ss	*Flatonia	- - -	ss	ss	3 46	7 59	ss
- - -	f	- - -	f	f	f	Engle	- - -	- - -	f	f	f	- - -
12#50	8#56	6‖10	2#00	9#41	6#13	Ar*Schulenburg..........Lv	4 00	9 13	1 05	3 30	7 44	10 15
1 10	9 11	6 40	2 11	9 56	6 30	Lv*Schulenburg..........Ar	3#45	9#02	12‖40	3#15	7#33	10#00
- - -	9 22	- - -	ss	10 06	ss	*Weimar	- - -	ss	12 29	3 06	7 23	ss
- - -	f	- - -	f	f	f	Glidden	- - -	- - -	f	f	f	- - -
- - -	9 43	- - -	2 48	10 28	7 00	*Columbus	ss	8 32	12 08	2 46	7 03	9 30
- - -	f	- - -	f	f	f	Alleyton	- - -	- - -	f	f	f	- - -
- - -	10 07	- - -	3 09	10 52	7 24	*Eagle Lake	ss	8 08	11 47	2 23	6 40	9 10
- - -	10 27	- - -	ss	11 12	ss	*East Bernard	- - -	ss	11 26	1 59	6 16	ss
- - -	10 45	- - -	3 51	11 32	8 05	*Rosenberg	ss	7 26	11 05	1 38	5 55	8 35
- - -	10 51	- - -	3 58	11 45	ss	*Richmond	ss	ss	10 59	1 31	ss	ss
- - -	f	- - -	f	f	f	Harlem	- - -	- - -	f	f	f	f
- - -	11 01	- - -	4 11	11 58	ss	Sugarland	ss	ss	10 47	1 19	ss	ss
↓	↓	↓	4 18	12 05	ss	*Stafford	↑	ss	↑	1 13	ss	↑
			f	f	f	Missouri City		f		f	f	
3 25	11 35	8 55	4 55	12 40	9 00	Ar*Houston, Tex...(GPH)..........Lv	1 30	6 30	10 10	12 40	5 00	7 40
5 45	12 10	10 00	5 15	1 35	9 05	Lv Houston, Tex..........(TxB) Ar	11 35	↑	9 40	12 30	3 45	6 45
7 30	1 35	11 35	6 50	3 10	10 55	Ar Galveston, Tex..........(4159) Lv	10 15	↑	8 00	11 10	2 30	5 15
4 15	12 55	10 20	5 45	1 40	10 15	Lv Houston, Tex..........(CGL) Ar	12 05	5 15	9 35	11 25	3 55	6 45
7 50	4 30	2 00	9 25	5 30	1 55	Ar Lake Charles, La..........(277)..Lv	8 25	1 45	5 50	7 45	12 30	2 30
8 30	4 45	2 25	9 45	6 00	2 30	Lv Lake Charles, La..........(SGL) Ar	7 50	1 30	5 25	7 15	12 00	2 15
1 45	11 30	7 15	2 20	1 00	7 30	Ar New Orleans, La..........(363)..Lv	2 45	8 45	12 45	12 45	7 00	6 30

MT. PLEASANT—TYLER—LUFKIN
BEAUMONT—PORT ARTHUR

263
(CST) 1-8-64

MP-Lu		DOWN / READ UP		Lu-MP
3 10	11 15	Lv Memphis, Tenn.264 (CGL) Ar	1 55	6 00
10 55	6 37	Lv Texarkana, Tex..........Ar	5 50	10 30
12 25	7 57	Ar Mt. Pleasant..........Lv	4 20	9 10
1283	1281	←—— Run Numbers ——→	6352	1284
3 15	8 40	Lv*Mt. Pleasant..........Ar	3 10	8 05
3 35	9 00	*Pittsburg	2 50	7 50
4 00	9 25	*Gilmer	[illegible]	7 25
4 20	9 45	*Gladewater	2 05	7 05
↓	f	Winona	↑	f
↓	f	Camp Fannin	↑	f
5 00	10#30	Ar*Tyler..........Lv	1 30	6 25
1283	1281	←—— Run Numbers ——→	6842	1284
5 55	11 00	Lv*Tyler..........Ar	11#45	5‖55
f	f	Bullard	↑	f
f	f	Mt. Selman	f	f
6 45	11 50	Ar*Jacksonville..........Lv	11 10	5 10
6 45	11 50	Lv*Jacksonville..........Ar	11 10	5 10
7 05	12 10	*Rusk	10 50	4 50
7 20	12 25	*Alto	10 35	4 35
f	f	Forest Jct.	f	f
7 40	12 45	*Wells	10 15	4 15
8 10	1 15	Ar*Lufkin, Tex..........Lv	9 55	3 55
8 45	1 40	Lv Lufkin, Tex...(3850) (LfB) Ar	9 45	......
11 30	4 25	Ar Beaumont..........Lv	6 50	......
12 30	5 10	Lv Beaumont.....(278) (CGL) Ar	6 45	......
1 05	6 10	Ar Port Arthur..........Lv	5 45	......
8 45	1 45	Lv Lufkin.......(8196) (CBS) Ar	9 45	3 00
11 25	4 40	Ar Houston, Tex..........Lv	6 45	12 30

TYLER—WACO

268
9-1-63

DOWN			READ UP	
3 10	11 15	Lv Memphis, Tenn.264 (CGL) Ar	1 55	......
10 55	6 37	Lv Texarkana, Tex..........Ar	5 50	......
12 25	7 57	Ar Mt. Pleasant..........Lv	4 20	......
3 15	8 40	Lv Mt Pleasant.........(266)..Ar	3 10	......
5 00	10 30	Ar Tyler..........Lv	1 30	......
6799	6795	←—— Run Numbers ——→	6794	6798
6 00	11 55	Lv*Tyler, Tex..........Ar	10 20	8 20
f	f	Chandler	f	f
f	f	*Brownsboro	f	f
f	f	Murchinson	f	f
6 55	12 45	Ar*Athens..........Lv	9 25	7 30
6 55	12 45	Lv*Athens..........Ar	9#13	7#22
7 05	12 55	*Malakoff	9 00	7 09
f	f	δTrinidad	f	f
7 20	1 10	Kerens	8 40	6 50
7 40	1 30	Ar*Corsicanna..........Lv	8 20	6 30
7 40	1 30	Lv*Corsicanna..........Ar	8 15	□6 30
8 05	1 55	*Dawson	7 45	□6 00
8 15	2 05	*Hubbard	7 35	□5 50
■	■	Mt. Calm	■	□5 38
8 50	2 45	Ar*Waco, Tex...(GPH)..........Lv	6 50	5 05
9 40	2 50	Lv Waco, Tex.....(271)..........Ar	6 21	4 40
12 02	5 20	Ar Austin..........Lv	3 45	2 11
1 55	7 45	Ar San Antonio, Tex..........Lv	1 45	12 01

#—Rest stop. ‖—Meal stop. f—Flag stop.
ss—Station stop. □—Handles U.S. Mail.
- - -—Indicates Route. No local service performed.
(CBS)—Continental Bus System.
(CCo)—Crown Coach Co. (TxB)—Texas Bus Lines.
(LfB)—Mack's Lufkin-Beaumont Motor Coaches.
(OT)—Oklahoma Transp. Co.
(CGL)—Central Greyhound Lines.
(SGL)—Southern Greyhound Lines.
*—Agency stations to which baggage may be checked.
δ—Express Agency only. No tickets or checked baggage.
◆—Stops anywhere to discharge passengers picked up at these points. *—Change Buses.
(GPH)—Greyhound Post House.
(CST)—Central Standard Time.
(MST)—Mountain Standard Time.
(PST)—Pacific Standard Time.
AtOC or **OCAt**—Thru bus Oklahoma City-Atlanta.
AtSF or **SFAt**—Thru bus San Francisco-Atlanta.
OCM or **MOC**—Thru bus Memphis-Oklahoma City.
Lu-MP or **MP-Lu**—Thru bus Mt. Pleasant-Lufkin.
LA-M or **M-LA**—Thru bus Miami-Los Angeles.
SF-M or **M-SF**—Thru bus Miami-San Francisco.
LA-N or **N-LA**—Thru bus New Orleans-Los Angeles.
SF-N or **N-SF**—Thru bus New Orleans-San Francisco.
Index numbers adjacent to towns refer to local tables in Russell's Guides.
AM—Light Face. **PM—Bold Face.**
All trips operate daily unless otherwise noted.

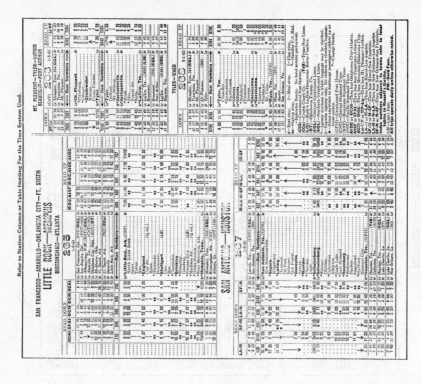

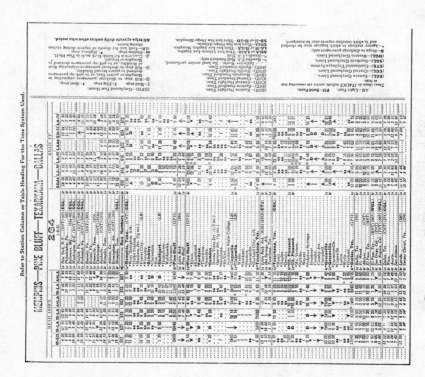

Refer to Station Column or Table Heading For the Time System Used.

DALLAS—FT. WORTH—WACO—AUSTIN—SAN ANTONIO

READ DOWN — 271 — 1-8-64 — READ UP

	C-L	DCC			SL-SA	C-L	DL	C-L		DL		Station		L-C	SA-T	L D	CCD			CCD	L-C		L-C
10 45	5 00		1 15		10 45	8 45		4 15			1 15	Lv New York, N.Y. EST-EGL Ar		2 40	11 30	8 25		6 45			2 30	4 10	6 55
7 00	2 30		11 00		6 35	↓		1 45			11 00	Lv Pittsburgh, Pa...(EST) (76) Ar		4 00	↑	1015		1035			4 35	7 20	11 00
⊙	5 15		2 20		9 15	6 45		4 15			1 25	Ar St. Louis, Mo....(CST) Lv		10 00	11 30	5 00		5 45			12 15	1 30	6 30
12 15	10 45		8 00			1155		9 45			5 15	Lv Chicago, Ill....(141) (EGL) Ar		4 10	6 45	1020		1 15			6 00	8 45	12 50
6 00	5 00		2 25			7 25		3 55			11 30	Ar St. Louis, Mo. Lv		9 45	11 15	3 15		7 00			12 15	1 20	6 00
7 45	6 15		3 15		10 15	7 45		5 00			2 15	Lv St. Louis, Mo..(CST) CGL Ar		9 20	10 35	2 05		5 25			11 15	12 35	5 00
2 05	12 05		9 00		3 00	1 15		10 40			7 50	Lv Springfield, Mo. Ar		3 20	4 55	7 35		1125			5 45	8 30	11 30
4 10	1 51		10 55		4 40	3 05		12 20			9 35	Lv Joplin, Mo. Ar		1 35	3 20	5 50		9 50			4 05	6 30	9 45
7 25	5 30		1 00		7 20	5 15		2 05			11 40	Ar Tulsa, Okla.....(261) Lv		11 25	1 15	3 40		7 45			2 00	4 25	6 45
8 30	7 00		2 00		8 00	6 05		3 00			12 05	Lv Tulsa, Okla.....(263) Ar		10 30	1 03	3 23		7 00			12 30	3 00	5 40
10 30	↓		↓		↓	↓		↓			↓	Ar Oklahoma City		↑	↑	↑		↑			↑	12 55	↑
10 45												Lv Oklahoma City.....(281) Ar										12 15	
OC	10 00		6 15		11 50	9 30						Lv McAlester Ar		7 30	10 05	1231		4 05			9 13	↑	2 25
↓	11 06		6 40		12 55	1100		6 25			3 17	Lv Atoka, Okla. Ar		6 05	8 56	1125		2 59			7 54	OC	1 01
3 00	2 05		9 55		4 15	2 25		9 45			6 20	Ar Dallas, Tex.....(263) Lv	↱	2 45	5 30	8 30		1201			4 50	7 45	9 45
↓	12 30		8 00		3 30		11 15				7 15	Lv Memphis, Tenn....(264) Ar	1 55		6 00	9 10	11 50	1150			4 45	8 45	↑
	8 45		4 50		11 10		6 37				2 35	Lv Texarkana, Tex. Ar	5 50		10 30	1 41	4 15	4 15			8 25	12 21	
	1 05		9 45		4 15		11 40				6 45	Ar Dallas, Tex. Lv	1 00	↱	5 45	9 15	12 05	1205		↱	3 45	7 30	
	581	1145	6443	6439	1101	585	1169	579		1167	6431	← Run Numbers →	6440	578	1104	1166	1144	6442		1148	582	6432	580
↳	ᵅ3 35	1210	ᵅ10 30	ᵅ7 00	5 15	3 15	12 15	10 15		8 25	7 30	Lv *Dallas, Tex.....(CST) Ar	12 30	2‖20	5‖10	7 20	10 45	1125		2 30	3#30	7‖10	9#20
	f		f	f		↓	f				f	Pleasant Run	f							f		↑	f
	↓	↓	↓	↓		f	↓	↓			↓	Lisbon	↑	↑	↑	↑	↑	↑		↑	↑	f	↑
						f						Lancaster										f	
	f	f	f	f		f	f				f	Sterrett	f		f					f		f	f
	4 17	1253	11 13	7 43		4 02	12 57	10 57			8 13	*Waxahachie	11 45	1 35	ss	6 35	10 03	D		1 45		6 17	8 37
		f	f	f		f	f				f	Forreston	f		f		f			f		f	f
		ss	ss	ss		4 23	1 18				ss	*Italy	ss		4 11	f	ss			ss		5 56	8 16
		1 22	11 41	8 11		4 29	1 26				8 41	*Milford	ss		4 05	f	ss			1 20		5 50	8 10
		1 43	12 02	8 32		4 49	1 47	11 42			9 02	Ar *Hillsboro Lv	11 00	12 51	3 45	5 52	9 18			1 00	D	5 30	7 50
652			919	6775	658		656		654			← Run Numbers →		6772	6774	920			669	657		659	
3 45	↓	↓	10 50	7 45	5 00	↓	12 15	↓	8 25		↓	Lv *Fort Worth Ar	↑	2 05	5 00	7 10	↑	↑	1130	2 20	↑	6 40	↑
f			f	f	f		f		f			Burleson		f	f	f			f	f			
D			ss	ss	5 40		12 56		9 03			*Alvardo		1 28	D	6 30			1052	D		↑	
ss			ss	ss	5 53		1 09		9 17			*Grandveiw		1 14	4 10	6 16			1038	ss			
ss			ss	ss	6 03		1 19		9 27			*Itasca		1 04	4 00	6 06			1028	ss			
4 54			11 59	D	6 17		1 37		9 41			Ar *Hillsboro Lv		12 50	3 46	5 52			1014	1 07		D	
4 54		1 43	12 02	8 32		4 49	1 47	11 42	9 41		9 02	Lv *Hillsboro Ar	11 00	12 51	3 45	5 52	9 18		1014	1 00	D	5 30	7 50
■	↓	■	■	■		■	■	↓	■		■	Abbott (HS-¼ mi.)	■	↑	■	↑	↑	↑	↑	■	↑	■	■
↓	↓	2 05	12 23	D		5 09	2 08	↓	D		9 23	*West	10 35	↑	3 25	↑	ss	↑	↑	12 40	↑	■	7 25
f		f	f	f		f	f		f		f	Elm Mott	f		f					f		f	f
↓	↓	↓	D	↓		f	↓	↓	↓		↓	*Connally AFB	↑	↑	↑	f	↑	↑	↑	③	↑	↑	f
5 40	ᵅ5‖50	2#30	ᵅ12#56	9#20	7#20	5‖40	2#35	12‖25	10 25	10#30	9#49	Ar *Waco.....(GPH) Lv	10 10	12 10	3 00	5 00	8 30	9 24	9 30	12 15	1 30	4 48	6 55
↳	581	1145	6443	6439	1101	585	1169	579	↳	1167	6431	← Run Numbers →	6440	578	1104	1166	1144	6442	↑	1148	582	6432	580
	6 25	2 50	1 15	ᵅ9 40	ᵅ7 35	6 05	2 50	12 55		10 41	10 15	Lv *Waco.....(GPH) Ar	9#56	11‖30	2#45	4#40	8#19	9 19	⤴	11#50	1#19	4#28	6‖21
	ss	■	■	■		ss	ss				ss	δLorena	ss		ss		ss			■		■	ss
	ss	■	■	■		ss	ss				ss	*Bruceville	ss		ss		ss			■		■	ss
	6 57	D	D	D		6 36	3 21	↓			10 47	*Eddy	9 24	↑	2 12		7 46	↑		D	↑	↑	5 50
	ss	■	■	■		ss	ss				ss	*Troy	ss		ss		ss			ss			ss
	7 19	3 44	2 04	10 30	8 20	7 00	3 43	1 40		11 30	11 10	*Temple	9 02	10 45	1 50	3 49	7 24	8 29		10 57	12 34	3 43	5 27
	7 34	4 00	2 20	10 45		7 25	3 58	1 56			11 26	*Belton	8 46	10 30	1 30	3 32	7 07			10 40	12 18	3 26	5 08
	f	f	f	■		f	f				f	Salado	f		f		f			f		f	f
	ss	ss	ss	ss		ss	ss				ss	*Jarrell	ss		ss		ss			ss		ss	ss
	8 16	4 45	3 00	ss		8 10	4 40	2 39		D	ᵅ1208	*Georgetown	6 04	9 50	12 49	2 48	6 25			9 58		2 44	4 24
	8 30	4 59	D			8 24	4 54				12 22	*Round Rock	7 50		12 34		6 11			9 42		2 30	4 10
	9#00	5#24	3#37	12#02	9#49	8#51	5‖20	3#19		12‖50	ᵅ1250	Ar *Austin Lv	7 25	9 15	12 05	2 11	5 44	7 09		9 15	11 05	2 05	3 45
	9 11	5 40	3 48	ᵅ1215	10 00	9 06	5 50	3 30		1 20	1 20	Lv *Austin Ar	7‖00	9#00	11‖35	2#00	5‖14	6#58		9#04	10#52	2#00	ᵅ3#34
	↓	↓	↓	↓		↓	6 12	↓			1 42	*Buda	6 34	↑	11 09	↑	↑	↑		↑	↑	↑	↑
	9 44	ss	■			9 39	6 23				1 53	*Kyle	6 23		10 58					ss			
	9 58	6 25	4 32	ss	D	9 53	6 35	4 12			2 07	*San Marcos.....(LB)	6 09	8 18	10 44	1 16	4 27	6 08		8 19	10 10	1 18	2 52
	10 22	6 51	4 57		↓	1017	7 01	4 36		↓	2 34	*New Braunfels	5 43	7 53	10 18	1250	4 00	5 42		7 51	9 42	12 52	2 27
	11‖15	7‖40	5 45	ᵅ1 55	ᵅ1145	1105	7#45	5‖25		2#55	3 15	Ar *San Antonio.....GPH Lv	5 00	7 10	9 30	1201	3 10	5 05		7 00	9 00	12 10	ᵅ1#45
	12 20	8 30		↳	2 05	↲		6 30		↳	4 00	Lv San Antonio, Tex.....(279) Ar		↑		1100	2#20			5#40	8 45		12 30
	4 15	1225			5 45			10 15			7 50	Ar Corpus Christi, Tex. Lv				7 10	10 30			1 45	5 00		8 40
	5 30	2 45			8 40						9 30	Lv Corpus Christi, Tex. 8301 UB Ar				4 30				11 15	2 45		6 45
	11 20	6 10		↓	12 10	↓	↓			↓	12 55	Ar Harlingen Lv				1115				7 50	11 15		3 15
	12 05	6 55			12 55						1 40	Ar Brownsville, Tex. Lv				1030				7 05	10 30		2 30
	12 05	8 30		2 10	2 10	2 10	9 00	6 30		3 30	↲	Lv San Antonio, Tex. (280) CGL Ar		6 20		1105	3 00			5 45	8 15		1 00
	3 45	1220		5 30	5 30	5 30	12 20	10 10		6 50		Ar Laredo, Tex. Lv		3 00		7 15	11 15			2 00	4 40		9 15
	4 30	1 00		6 00	6 00		1 00	10 45		7 15		Lv Laredo, Tex. (4100) (TDN) Ar		2 00			10 30			12 30	3 15		8 45
	9 15	5 45		10 45	10 45		5 45	3 30		12 01		Ar Monterrey, Mex. Lv		9 30			6 15			8 30	11 30		4 20
	11 30						7 30					Ar Mexico City, Mex. Lv		8 30							9 00		8 00

(CGL)—Central Greyhound Lines.
(EGL)—Eastern Greyhound Lines.
(TDN)—Transportes del Norte.
(UB)—Continental Union Trailways.
(GPH)—Greyhound Post House.
OC—Via Oklahoma City.
(CDT)—Central Daylight Time.
(CST)—Central Standard Time.
(EDT)—Eastern Daylight Time.
(EST)—Eastern Standard Time.
*—Agency station to which baggage may be checked and prepaid or collect express may be consigned.
δ—Express Agency only. No tickets or checked baggage.

AM—Light Face. **PM—Bold Face.**
#—Rest stop.
‖—Meal stop.
■—Highway stop.
ᵅ—Handles U.S. Mail.
⊙—Connection made in Tulsa.
①—Ft. Worth bus will serve West when there are passengers on the bus destined for West.
②—Transfer passengers for Connally AFB at Hillsboro
③—Transfer passengers for Connally AFB at Waco.
(LB)—Lock box for deposit of express during station's closed hours.
All trips operate daily unless otherwise noted.

D—Will go into town only to discharge passengers.
- - -—Indicates route. No local service performed.
f—Flag stop.
ss—Station stop.
CCD or **DCC**—Thru bus between Corpus Christi and Dallas.
DL or **LD**—Thru bus between Dallas and Laredo.
C-L or **L-C**—Thru bus Chicago-Laredo.
T-SA or **SA-T**—Thru bus San Antonio-Tulsa.
SL-SA or **SA-SL**—Thru bus St. Louis-San Antonio.
LNY—Thru bus Laredo-New York.
KSA or **SAK**—Thru Bus Knoxville-San Antonio.

COMMISSION EXHIBIT No. 2577—Continued

Refer to Station Column or Table Heading For the Time System Used.

LOS ANGELES—EL PASO—FT. WORTH—DALLAS—WACO—HOUSTON—NEW ORLEANS

READ DOWN — 272 — 1-8-64 — READ UP

DnNO		FWNO	FWNO	FWNO	FWNO	Station	NOFW			NODn	NOFW	NOFW
		6 15		11 45	6 15	Lv San Francisco, (PST) (667-9) (WGL) Ar	12 50	7 10		1 20		
11 45	8 15	2 30	10 15	7 15	1 15	Lv Los Angeles, Cal.....(PST) (667) Ar	1 05	11 00	1 25	3 50	6 30	10 25
2 00	9 00	6 15	10 15	↓	↓	Lv San Diego.....(PST) Ar	1 10	8 45	↑	3 40	↑	↑
9 50	6 15	2 05	8 45	4 30	11 40	Lv Phoenix, Ariz.....(MST) (667) Ar	5 00	2 37	4 50	8 15	10 45	2 35
12 01	↓	5 25	11 30	7 30	3 05	Lv Tucson, Ariz. Ar	3 05	11 45	1 50	6 10	↑	11 50
6 15	3 20	11 45	6 20	2 15	9 25	Ar El Paso, Tex. Lv	8 25	4 50	7 15	10 50	1 30	5 15
7 00	4 00	12 30	7 30	3 15	10 15	Lv El Paso, Tex.....(270) (CGL) Ar	7 30	3 45	6 20	9 35	12 25	4 20
12 40	9 47	6 05	1 10	9 05	4 10	Lv Pecos.....(CST) Ar	3 50	12 04	3 00	5 30	8 35	12 20
2 15	11 15	7 39	2 52	10 41	5 43	Lv Odessa Ar	2 25	10 31	1 21	3 46	6 57	10 40
3 59	1 10	9 20	4 15	12 01	7 55	Lv Big Spring Ar	12 39	8 55	11 59	2 26	5 33	9 02
6 55	3 46	12 15	7 15	2 20	10 35	Lv Abilene Ar	10 15	5 50	9 33	11 55	3 15	6 10
8 21	5 16	1 41	8 45	D	D	Lv Ranger Ar	8 47	4 12	↑	10 07	D	D
9 15	6 24	2 45	9 55	6 53	12 50	Lv Mineral Wells Ar	9 06	3 31	7 01	9 26	12 54	↑
10 20	7 36	3 30	11 06	8 05	1 45	Ar Ft. Worth, Tex.....(270) Lv	7 00	2 20	5 50	8 15	11 50	3 00
919	6775	658	656	654	652	← Run Numbers →	659	6772	6774	920	669	657
10 50	7 45	5 00	12 15	ᵅ8 25	3 45	Lv *Ft. Worth, Tex. Ar	6 40	2 05	5 00	7 10	11 30	2 20
f	f	f	f	f	f	Burleson	- - -	f	f	f	f	f
D	ss	5 40	12 56	9 03	D	*Alvarado	↑	1 28	D	6 30	10 52	D
ss	ss	5 53	1 09	9 17	ss	*Grandview	- - -	1 14	4 10	6 16	10 38	ss
ss	ss	6 03	1 19	9 27	ss	*Itasca	- - -	1 04	4 00	6 06	10 28	ss
11 59	D	6 17	1 37	9 41	4 54	*Hillsboro	D	12 50	3 46	5 52	10 14	1 07
■	■	■	■	■	■	Abbott	↑	■	↑	■	↑	■
①	①	D	①	D	↓	*West		12 30		f		②
④	↓	↓	↓	↓		*Connally AFB		↑		③		D
12#45	9#40	7 00	2#25	ᵅ10#25	5‖40	Ar *Waco Lv	4 50	12 05	3 05	5 00	9 30	12 20
10 30	7 00	5 15	12 15	8 25	3 35	Lv Dallas.....(271) Ar	7 10	2 20	5 10	7 20	11 25	2 30
12 02	8 32	↓	1 47	↓	- - -	Lv Hillsboro Ar	5 30	12 51	3 45	5 52	↑	1 00
12 55	9 20	7 20	2 35	10 30	5 50	Ar Waco Lv	4 48	12 10	3 00	5 00	9 24	12 15
1 10	10 15	7 35	2 50	10 45	6 25	Lv *Waco Ar	4#35	11 35	2#50	4#40	ᵅ9#07	12#03
f	f	f	f	f	f	Harrison	- - -	f	f	- - -	f	f
f	f	f	f	f	f	Riesel	- - -	f	f	f	f	f
f	f	f	f	f	f	Perry	- - -	f	f	- - -	f	f
1 45	10 53	8 15	3 30	11 28	7 03	*Marlin	f	10 56	2 07	3 59	ᵅ8 29	11 25
f	f	f	f	f	f	Reagan	- - -	f	f	f	f	f
ss	ss	8 38	3 53	11 53	7 26	*Bremond	- - -	10 34	1 46	f	8 07	ss
f	f	f	f	f	f	Hammond	- - -	f	f	- - -	f	f
ss	ss	8 56	4 11	12 11	7 44	*Calvert	- - -	10 16	1 26	f	7 48	ss
f	f	f	f	f	f	Segar	- - -	f	f	- - -	f	f
2 35	11 45	9 07	4 23	12 22	7 55	Ar *Hearne Lv	ss	10 05	1 15	3 05	7 38	10 34
↓	↓	↓	11 40		↓	Lv Fort Hood.....(4089) (AC) Ar	8 35	↑	↑		↑	↑
			12 40	9 45		Lv Killeen Ar	8 25			6 30		
			3 15	12 20		Ar Hearne Lv	6 00			3 45		
2 35	11 45	ᵅ9 07	4 23	12 22	7 55	Lv *Hearne Ar	ss	10 05	1 15	3 05	7 38	10 34
f	f	f	f	f	f	Sutton	- - -	f	f	- - -	f	f
f	f	f	f	f	f	Benchley	- - -	f	f	- - -	f	f
3#02	12#12	9#34	4#50	12 50	8#24	Ar *Bryan Lv	2 46	9 36	12 45	2 36	7 10	10 05
3 15	12 25	ᵅ9 45	5 05	1 15	8 40	Lv *Bryan Ar	2#35	9#25	12‖18	2#25	6‖38	9#52
f	f	f	f	f	f	College Station	- - -	f	f	f	f	f
3 45	1 01	10 21	5 41	1 51	9 20	*Navasota	ss	8 50	11 43	1 49	6 03	9 17
f	f	f	f	f	f	Chaille	- - -	f	f	- - -	f	f
f	f	f	f	f	f	Courtney	- - -	f	f	- - -	f	f
f	f	f	f	f	f	Howth	- - -	f	f	- - -	f	f
4 11	1 27	10 47	6 09	2 19	9 48	*Hempstead	ss	8 23	11 15	1 20	5 35	8 49
ss	f	ss	6 17	2 27	9 56	*Prairie View Rd.	D	8 16	ss	ss	5 26	8 41
ss	f	ss	6 23	2 33	10 02	*Waller	- - -	8 10	f	f	5 20	8 35
f	f	f	f	f	f	Hockley	- - -	f	f	- - -	f	f
f	f	f	f	f	f	Cypress	- - -	f	f	- - -	f	f
f	f	f	f	f	f	Satsuma	- - -	f	f	- - -	f	f
f	f	f	f	f	f	Carverdale	- - -	f	f	- - -	f	f
f	f	f	f	f	f	Fairbanks	- - -	f	f	- - -	f	f
5‖20	2 40	ᵅ11#59	7‖30	3‖45	11‖05	Ar *Houston, Tex. Lv	12 30	7 10	9 55	12 10	4 15	7 30
7 30	4 15	12 55	8 30	5 00	12 01	Lv Houston, Tex.....(277) Ar	10 05	6 40	9 35	11 25	3 25	6 45
9 47	6 05	2 55	10 40	7 11	2 03	Ar Beaumont Lv	8 01	4 45	7 31	↑	1 16	4 26
10 40	6 51	3 35	11 26	8 00	3 00	Ar Orange, Tex. Lv	7 15	4 10	6 45	8 45	12 28	3 30
11 40	7 50	4 30	12 20	8 55	3 55	Ar Lake Charles, La.....(CGL) Lv	6 15	3 15	5 50	7 45	11 30	2 30
5 05	11 35	9 20	5 20	2 20	9 10	Ar Baton Rouge.....(363) (SGL) Lv	12 55	8 20	2 35	↑	↑	8 55
7 20	1 45	11 30	7 50	4 30	11 25	Ar New Orleans, La. Lv	10 45	7 30	12 45	12 45	3 30	6 30

f—Flag stop.
#—Rest stop.
(WGL)—Western Greyhound Lines.
(SGL)—Southern Greyhound Lines.
(CGL)—Central Greyhound Lines.
(AC)—Arrow Coach Lines.
D—Will go into town to discharge passengers.
*—Agency station to which baggage may be checked.
NOTE: *Times shown in ITALICS indicate service via connecting trip or trips.*

■—Highway stop.
‖—Meal stop.

①—Transfer passengers for West at Hillsboro.
②—Transfer passengers for West at Waco.
③—Transfer passengers for Connally AFB at Waco.
④—Transfer passengers for Connally AFB at Hillsboro.
- - -—Indicates Route. No local service performed.
(PST)—Pacific Standard Time.
(PDT)—Pacific Daylight Time.
(MST)—Mountain Standard Time.
(CST)—Central Standard Time.

Index numbers adjacent to towns refer to local tables in Russell's Guide.
ss—Station stop. ᵅ—Handles U.S. Mail.
Light Figures A.M. Time.
Bold Figures P.M. Time.
NOFW or **FWNO**—Thru bus New Orleans-Ft. Worth.
DnNO or **NODn**—Thru bus Denver-New Orleans.
All trips operate daily unless otherwise noted.

COMMISSION EXHIBIT No. 2577—Continued

Refer to Station Column or Table Heading For the Time System Used.

LOS ANGELES—HOUSTON—LAKE CHARLES—NEW ORLEANS

277 1-8-64 — READ DOWN

Station	FWNO	LA-M	DnNO	SFNO	FWNO		FWNO	LANO	FWNO	SF-M
San Francisco, Cal. (PST) (667-9) (WGL) Lv	.....	.....	.....	8 00	.....	.....	11 45	.....	.....	6 45
Los Angeles, Cal. (667) Lv	2 30	11 45	11 45	5 30	1 15	.....	7 15	10 15	8 45	2 30
San Diego, Cal. Lv	6 15	2 00	2 00	6 15	↓	.....	↓	10 15	10 15	6 15
El Paso, Tex. (MST) Ar	11 40	6 35	6 15	12 45	9 25	.....	2 15	6 20	6 05	11 40
El Paso, Tex. (270) (CGL) Lv	12 30	7 20	7 00	1 45	10 15	.....	3 15	7 30	7 30	12 30
Ft. Worth, Tex. (CST) Ar	3 30	K	10 10	↓	1 45	.....	5 30	↓	11 06	↓
Ft. Worth, Tex. (272) Lv	5 00	7 45	10 50	K	3 45	.....	8 25	K	12 15	K
Dallas, Tex. Lv	5 15	7 00	10 30	↓	3 35	.....	8 25	↓	12 15	↓
Houston, Tex. Ar	11 59	3 25	5 20	9 00	11 05	.....	3 45	4 55	7 30	8 55
Mexico City, Mex. (4100) (TDN) Lv	.....	9 00	│	8 00	│	8 30	│	.....	│	.....
Monterrey, Mex. Lv	8 30	11 30	│	4 30	│	9 30	│	.....	│	6 15
Laredo, Tex. Ar	12 30	3 15	│	8 45	│	2 00	│	.....	│	10 30
Laredo, Tex. (280) (CGL) Lv	2 00	4 40	│	9 15	│	3 00	│	7 15	│	11 15
San Antonio, Tex. (267) Lv	6 25	10 45	│	4 05	│	7 15	│	11 30	│	4 00
Houston, Tex. Ar	11 35	3 25	↓	9 00	↓	12 40	↓	4 55	↓	8 55
Run Numbers	658	638	919	648	652	676	654	636	656	650
*Houston, Tex. (GPH) (CST) Lv	12 55	4 15	7 30	10 15	12 01	1 40	5 00	5 45	□8 30	◆10 20
Dawes	f	f	f	│	f	f	f	│	f	...
Sheldon	f	f	f	│	f	f	f	│	f	...
*Crosby	↓	↓	8 11	│	↓	2 22	5 42	│	9 12	↓
Stilson	f	f	f	│	f	f	f	│	f	...
*Dayton	ss	ss	8 33	│	12 55	2 42	6 02	│	ss	ss
*Liberty (LB)	1 55	ss	8 43	│	1 05	2 52	6 12	│	9 42	11 20
Ames	f	f	f	│	f	f	f	│	f	...
Raywood	f	f	f	│	f	f	f	│	f	...
*Devers	ss	ss	9 00	Via Hiway 73	ss	3 09	6 29	Via Hiway 73	ss	...
Felicia	f	f	f	│	f	f	f	│	f	...
*Nome	ss	ss	9 15	│	ss	3 21	6 41	│	ss	...
China	f	f	f	│	f	f	f	│	f	...
Pine Island	f	f	f	│	f	f	f	│	f	...
Amelia	f	f	f	│	f	f	f	│	f	...
*Beaumont (GPH) Ar	2 55	6#05	9#47	│	2#03	3#50	7#11	│	10#40	12#20
Beaumont (278) Lv	│	7 30	10 15	│	2 10	5 10	8 00	│	↪	12 30
Port Arthur Ar	│	8 30	11 15	│	3 10	6 10	9 00	│	.....	1 05
Galveston (4161a) (TxB) Lv	│	.....	7 45	│	11 00	.....	4 20	│	7 40	.....
Beaumont Ar	↓	.....	10 00	│	1 15	.....	6 40	│	9 55	.....
*Beaumont Lv	3 00	6 16	10 00	│	2 25	4 01	□7 22	│	10 51	12 31
Vidor	■	■	f	│	■	f	■	│	■	↓
Terry	f	│	...	↓	f	f	f	↓	f	...
*Port Arthur (LB) Ar	↓	↓	↓	12#05	↓	↓	↓	7#35	↓	↓
*Port Arthur (LB) Lv				12 16				7 46		
*Orange, Tex. (LB)	3 35	6 51	10 40	1 00	3 00	4 36	□8 00	8 30	11 26	1 06
Toomey, La.	f	f	f	f	f	f	f	f	f	...
*Vinton	ss	7 10	10 58	1 19	3 19	4 54	8 18	8 48	11 44	...
*Sulphur	ss	7 30	11 16	1 35	3 35	5 12	8 36	9 06	12 02	...
West Lake Road	f	f	f	f	f	f	f	f	f	...
*Lake Charles, La. (GPH) Ar	4#30	7‖50	11‖40	1‖55	3#55	5‖30	□8#55	9#25	□12#20	2#00
Lake Charles, La. (363) (SGL) Lv	4 45	8 30	12 15	2 30	4 20	6 00	9 45	9 45	12 45	2 25
Jennings Ar	5 33	│	1 05	│	5 15	6 55	10 40	│	1 35	│
Crowley Ar	5 58	│	1 35	│	5 45	7 25	11 10	│	2 05	│
Lafayette Ar	6 35	│	2 30	│	6 35	8 10	11 55	│	2 50	│
New Iberia Ar	↓	│	↓	│	↓	9 00	↓	│	3 38	│
Houma Ar		↓		↓		11 25		│	6 00	↓
Opelousas Ar	7 45	10 15	3 30	4 15	7 40	↓	12 50	↓	↓	4 00
Baton Rouge Ar	9 20	11 35	5 05	5 35	9 10	│	2 20	12 35	│	5 20
New Orleans, La. Ar	11 30	1 45	7 20	7 30	11 25	1 00	4 30	2 20	7 50	7 15

10 THRU Schedules Between HOUSTON and NEW ORLEANS

○ No Change of Bus ○

BEAUMONT—PORT ARTHUR READ DOWN — Run Numbers **278** 1-8-64

Station	6819	6827	6831	6835	6837	6839	
*Beaumont, Tex. Lv	7 30	10 15	2 10	5 10	8 00	12 30	.....
*Nederland	7 50	10 35	2 30	5 30	8 20	↓	.....
*Port Neches	7 55	10 40	2 35	5 35	8 25	↓	.....
*Port Arthur, Tex. Ar	8 30	11 15	3 10	6 10	9 00	1 05	.....

All trips operate daily unless otherwise noted.

No Change of Bus VIA THE "OLD SPANISH ROUTE"

Refer to Station Column or Table Heading For the Time System Used.

NEW ORLEANS—LAKE CHARLES—HOUSTON—LOS ANGELES

277 1-8-64 — READ DOWN

Station	NOSF		NOLA	NODn	NOFW	M-SF	NOFW	NOFW	M-LA		
New Orleans, La. (363) (SGL) Lv	8 45	7 30	12 45	12 45	3 30	7 00	6 30	10 45	2 45	1 45	.....
Baton Rouge Lv	10 40	↓	2 35	│	↓	8 55	↓	12 55	4 45	↓	.....
Opelousas Lv	11 55	↓	3 50	↓	↓	10 15	↓	2 30	6 05	↓	.....
Houma Lv	│	9 45	│	↓	5 10	│	8 15	│	│	3 35	.....
New Iberia Lv	│	12 08	│	4 16	7 42	│	10 47	↓	│	6 07	.....
Lafayette Lv	│	12 55	│	5 10	8 50	│	11 59	3 30	│	7 15	.....
Crowley Lv	│	1 35	│	5 45	9 35	│	12 45	4 15	│	7 55	.....
Jennings Lv	↓	2 00	↓	6 10	10 05	↓	1 15	4 45	↓	8 20	.....
Lake Charles, La. Ar	1#30	3#00	5‖25	7‖15	11‖05	12‖00	2#15	5‖45	7‖50	9#20	.....
Run Numbers	647	675	641	920	669	649	657	659	637	673	
*Lake Charles, La. (GPH) (CGL) Lv	1 45	3 15	5 50	7 45	11 30	12 30	2 30	6 15	8 25	9 35	.....
West Lake Road	f	f	f	f	f	│	f	f	...	f	.....
*Sulphur	2 05	ss	ss	8 05	11 50	│	2 50	6 35	◆	9 55	.....
*Vinton	2 20	ss	ss	8 25	12 08	│	3 10	6 55	◆	10 10	.....
Toomey, La.	f	f	f	f	f	↓	f	f	...	f	.....
*Orange, Tex. (LB)	2 40	4 10	6 45	8 45	12 28	1 20	3 30	7 15	□9 20	10 30	
*Port Arthur Ar	↓	↓	↓	9#30	↓	2 05	↓	↓	↓	11 15	↷
*Port Arthur (LB) Lv				9 41		2 05				11 15	11 20
Terry	f	f	f	│	f	│	...	f	f	│	↓
Vidor	■	■	■	│	■	│	↓	■	■	│	↓
*Beaumont (GPH) Ar	3#15	4 45	7#20	│	1#05	│	4#15	7#50	9#55	│	12 10
Beaumont (4161e) (TxB) Lv	.....	│	7 20	│	│	│	4 30	7 50	│	│	.....
Galveston Ar	.....	│	9 35	│	│	│	6 55	10 05	│	│	.....
Port Arthur (278) (CGL) Lv	11 20	│	5 45	│	│	│	3 20	6 20	│	│	.....
Beaumont Ar	12 10	↓	6 45	│	↓	│	4 20	7 20	↓	│	.....
*Beaumont Lv	3 26	4 45	7 31	│	1 16	│	4 26	8 01	10 06	│	.....
Amelia	Via Hiway 124 & 73	f	f	Via Hiway 73	f	Via Hiway 73	f	f	◆	Via Hiway 73	.....
Pine Island	│	f	f	│	f	│	f	f	...	│	.....
China	│	f	f	│	f	│	f	f	◆	│	.....
*Nome	│	f	ss	│	f	│	ss	ss	ss	│	.....
Felicia	│	f	f	│	f	│	f	f	...	│	.....
*Devers	│	f	ss	│	f	│	ss	ss	◆	│	.....
Raywood	│	f	f	│	f	│	f	f	◆	│	.....
Ames	│	f	f	│	f	│	f	f	...	│	.....
*Liberty (LB)	│	ss	8 30	│	2 16	│	5 30	9 00	11 05	│	.....
*Dayton	│	f	ss	│	ss	│	5 40	ss	ss	│	.....
Stilson	│	f	f	│	f	│	...	f	...	│	.....
*Crosby	│	↓	ss	│	ss	│	ss	↓	↓	│	.....
Sheldon	│	f	f	│	f	│	...	f	f	│	.....
Dawes	↓	f	f	↓	f	↓	...	f	...	↓	.....
*Houston, Tex. (GPH) Ar	5‖15	6 40	9#35	11‖25	3#25	3‖55	6‖45	10#05	12 05	1 00	.....
Houston, Tex. (267) Lv	6 30	.....	10 10	12 40	│	5 00	7 40	│	1 30	↩	.....
San Antonio (267) Ar	11 30	.....	3 20	5 45	│	10 10	12 25	│	6 15	.....	.....
Laredo, Tex. (280) Ar	3 45	.....	6 50	10 10	│	5 30	5 30	│	12 20	.....	.....
Laredo, Tex. (4123) (TDN) Lv	4 30	.....	7 15	10 45	│	6 00	6 00	│	1 00	.....	.....
Monterrey, Mex. Ar	9 15	.....	12 01	3 30	│	10 45	10 45	│	5 45	.....	.....
Mexico City, Mex. Ar	11 30	.....	.....	.....	↓	.....	.....	↓	.....	.....	.....
Houston, Tex. (272) (CGL) Lv	6 30	7 10	9 55	12 10	4 15	5 00	7 30	12 30	1 30	.....	.....
Dallas, Tex. Ar	↓	2 20	5 10	7 20	11 25	↓	2 30	7 10	↓	.....	.....
Ft. Worth, Tex. Ar	K	2 05	5 00	7 10	11 30	K	2 20	6 40	K	.....	.....
Ft. Worth, Tex. (270) Lv	↓	2 20	K	8 15	11 50	↓	3 00	7 00	↓	.....	.....
El Paso, Tex. (MST) Ar	11 15	3 45	4 05	9 35	12 25	9 40	4 20	7 30	7 30	.....	.....
El Paso, Tex. (667) (WGL) Lv	12 01	4 50	4 55	10 50	1 30	10 40	5 15	8 25	8 40	.....	.....
San Diego, Cal. (PST) Ar	4 50	8 45	↓	3 40	↓	3 40	↓	1 10	1 10	.....	.....
Los Angeles, Cal. Ar	5 05	11 00	11 00	3 50	6 30	3 50	10 25	1 05	1 20	.....	.....
San Francisco, Cal. (667-9) Ar	2 50	7 10	.....	1 20	.....	1 20	.....	12 50	.....	.....	.....

AM—Light Face. **PM—Bold Face.**
(**CGL**)—Central Greyhound Lines.
(**SGL**)—Southern Greyhound Lines.
(**TDN**)—Transportes del Norte.
(**TxB**)—Texas Bus Lines.
(**WGL**)—Western Greyhound Lines.
(GPH)—Greyhound Post House.
Index numbers adjacent to towns refer to local tables in Russell's Guide.
M-SF or **SF-M**—Thru bus Miami-San Francisco.
M-LA or **LA-M**—Thru bus Miami-Los Angeles.
(CST)—Central Standard Time.
(MST)—Mountain Standard Time.
(PDT)—Pacific Daylight Time.
(PST)—Pacific Standard Time.
#—Rest stop.
‖—Meal stop.
■—Highway stop.
◆—Stops anywhere to discharge passengers picked up at scheduled stops.
□—Mail run.
NOSF or **SFNO**—Thru bus New Orleans-San Francisco.
NOFW or **FWNO**—Thru bus New Orleans-Ft. Worth.
^—Handles U.S. Mail Sundays only.
*—Agency stations to which baggage may be checked and interline express consigned.
. . .—Indicates Route. No local service performed.
f—Flag stop.
K—Via Kerrville and Pecos.
ss—Station stop.
(*LB*)—Lock box for deposit of express during station closing hours.
NOSA or **SANO**—Thru bus New Orleans-San Antonio.
NOLA or **LANO**—Thru bus New Orleans-Los Angeles.
NOSD or **SDNO**—Thru bus New Orleans-San Diego.
NODn or **DnNO**—Thru bus New Orleans-Denver.

All trips operate daily unless otherwise noted.

PORT ARTHUR—BEAUMONT 1-8-64 READ DOWN — Run Numbers **278**

Station	6816	6818	6824	6826	6830	6834	
*Port Arthur, Tex. Lv	5 45	8 40	1 00	3 20	6 20	11 20	.....
*Port Neches	6 10	9 05	1 25	3 45	6 45	↓	.....
*Nederland	6 15	9 10	1 30	3 50	6 50	11 45	.....
*Beaumont, Tex. Ar	6 45	9 40	2 00	4 20	7 20	12 10	.....

No Change of Bus VIA THE "OLD SPANISH ROUTE"

ALL TRIPS OPERATE DAILY UNLESS OTHERWISE NOTED.

Refer to Station Column or Table Heading For the Time System Used.

SAN ANTONIO—BEEVILLE—CORPUS CHRISTI—BROWNSVILLE

279 1-7-64

Read Down				DCC		Read Up	CCD	CCD		
10 15	5 00	2 15	9 45	3 15	Lv St. Louis, Mo. (CST) Ar	2 05	5 25	11 15	11 15	5 00
3 00	10 40	7 50	3 00	9 00	Lv Springfield Ar	7 35	11 25	5 45	5 45	11 20
4 40	12 15	9 35	4 30	10 55	Lv Joplin, Mo. (261) Ar	5 50	9 50	4 05	4 05	9 45
8 00	3 00	12 05	7 00	2 00	Lv Tulsa, Okla. (263) Ar	3 23	7 00	12 30	12 30	5 40
11 50	↓	↓	10 00	5 15	Lv McAlester, Okla. Ar	12 31	4 05	9 13	9 13	2 25
7 00	10 15	8 25	3 35	12 10	Lv Dallas, Tex. (271) Ar	7 20	10 45	2 30	3 30	9 20
7 45	↓	8 25	3 45	↓	Lv Fort Worth Ar	7 10	11 30	2 20	6 40	↑
9 40	12 55	10 41	6 25	2 50	Lv Waco Ar	4 40	8 19	11 50	1 19	6 21
12 15	3 30	1 20	9 11	5 40	Lv Austin Ar	2 00	5 14	9 04	10 54	3 34
1 55	5 25	2 55	11 15	7‖40	Ar San Antonio Lv	12 01	3 10	7 00	9 00	1 45
6463	6473	6469	6465	1145	←Run Numbers→	6464	1144	1148	6466	6468
□2 05	6 30	4 00	12 20	□8 30	Lv*San Antonio Ar	11 00	2#20	5‖40	8 45	12 30
2 50	7 20	4 50	1 09	□9 20	*Floresville	10 09	1 31	4 50	7 56	11 42
2 59	7 29	4 59	1 18	□9 30	*Poth	10 00	1 22	4 40	7 47	11 34
3 10	7 40	5 09	1 29	□9 42	*Fall City	9 49	1 12	4 28	7 37	11 24
f	f	f	f	f	Hobson	f	f	f	f	f
3 24	7 54	5 22	1 41	□9 55	*Karnes City	9 35	12 58	4 14	7 23	11 11
3 33	8 02	5 30	1 50	□10 04	*Kenedy (LB)	9 26	12 49	4 04	7 14	11 02
↓	↓	■	↓	↓	Green	■	↑	↑	↑	↑
f	f	f	f	f	Burnell	f	f	f	f	f
f	f	f	f	f	Tulsa	f	f	f	f	f
3 55	8 22	5 52	2 11	□10 27	Pettus	9 07	12 29	3 45	6 54	10 43
f	f	f	f	f	Tuleta	f	f	f	f	f
f	f	f	f	f	Normanna	f	f	f	f	f
4 17	8#41	6#14	2#31	□10#50	Ar*Beeville (LB) Lv	8 48	12 08	3 25	6 33	10 23
4 17	8 52	6 25	2 46	11 01	Lv*Beeville Ar	8#33	11#53	3#10	6#22	10#08
4 33	9 08	6 41	3 02	□11 17	*Skidmore	8 15	11 37	2 54	6 06	9 50
f	f	f	f	f	Papalote	f	f	f	f	f
f	f	f	f	f	St. Paul	f	f	f	f	f
4 58	9 33	□7 06	3 28	□11 42	*Sinton	7 51	11 12	2 28	5 41	9 25
5 10	9 45	□7 11	3 41	□11 54	*Taft	7 39	11 00	2 18	5 29	9 13
5 22	9 56	7 30	3 52	12 05	*Gregory	7 28	10 49	2 06	5 17	9 01
5 29	10 02	7 37	4 00	12 12	Portland	7 23	10 43	2 00	5 13	8 55
□5 45	10 15	□7 50	4 15	□12 25	Ar*Corpus Christi Lv	7 10	10 30	1 45	5 00	8 40
8 40	2 00	9 30	-----	2 45	Lv Corpus Christi (UB) Ar	-----	-----	11 15	2 45	6 45
11 35	4 50	12 20	-----	5 35	Ar Raymondville (8301) Lv	-----	-----	8 17	11 50	3 50
12 10	5 25	12 55	-----	6 10	Ar Harlingen Lv	-----	-----	7 50	11 15	3 15
12 55	6 15	1 40	-----	6 55	Ar Brownsville Lv	-----	-----	7 05	10 30	2 30
8 50	1 50	9 25	5 40	2 45	Lv Corpus Christi (8308) Ar	4 30	-----	11 30	2 30	8 20
12 45	5 45	1 30	9 15	6 35	Ar Edinburg Lv	12 55	-----	7 45	10 50	3 56
1 30	6 05	1 50	9 35	6 55	Ar McAllen Lv	12 25	-----	7 25	10 30	3 35
-----	-----	-----	11 20	-----	Ar Harlingen Lv	11 15	-----	-----	-----	-----
-----	-----	-----	12 05	-----	Ar Brownsville Lv	10 30	-----	-----	-----	-----

OKLAHOMA CITY—DALLAS

281 4-23-63

DN SL-D		UP D-SL
7 45	Lv St. Louis (CST) (CGL Ar	12 35
2 05	Lv Springfield (261) Ar	8 30
4 10	Lv Joplin, Mo. Ar	6 30
8 30	Lv Tulsa, Okla. Ar	3 00
1030	Ar Oklahoma City Lv	12 55
583	← Run Numbers →	584
10 45	Lv*Oklahoma City Ar	12‖15
f	*Norman	f
- - -	Purcell	f
f	Pauls Valley	f
- - -	Wynnewood	- - -
- - -	Davis	f
12#50	Ar*Ardmore Lv	10 00
12 55	Lv*Ardmore Ar	9#50
D	Marietta, Okla.	D
D	Gainesville, Tex.	D
- - -	Sanger	- - -
- - -	Denton	f
3 00	Ar*Dallas, Tex. (GPII) Lv	7 45
3 35	Lv Dallas, Tex. (271) Ar	7 10
11 15	Ar San Antonio, Tex. Lv	12 10

DN FT. LEONARD WOOD—ST. LOUIS UP

282 10-27-63

Sat. 6284	← Run Numbers →	Sun 6285
12 01	Lv Waynesville, Mo. Ar	11 00
12 20	Ar Ft. Leonard Wood Lv	10 40
12 30	Lv Ft. Leonard Wood Ar	10 40
↓	Ar Rolla Lv	9 50
	Lv Rolla Ar	9 40
2 55	Ar The Diamonds Lv	↑
3 05	Lv The Diamonds Ar	
4 20	Ar St. Louis, Mo. (CST) Lv	7 00

FT. LEONARD WOOD—SPRINGFIELD

283 6-16-61

Sat. 6283	← Run Numbers →	Sun 6289
12 30	Lv Ft. Leonard Wood Ar	8 05
12 50	Ar Waynesville Lv	7 45
12 50	Lv Waynesville Ar	7 45
2 35	Ar Springfield, Mo. Lv	6 00

LITTLE ROCK—PINE BLUFF

284 12-15-63

DOWN 6609	6607	6605	LRN 941		UP 6604	6606	LRN 942	6608
6 25	2 45	□1120	7 00	Lv*Little Rock, Ark. (CGL) CST Ar	10 05	2 30	□6 20	1130
6 30	2 50	11 25	7 05	North Little Rock	f	f	f	f
f	f	□f	f	Scott	f	f	□f	f
f	f	f	f	Toltec	f	f	f	f
f	f	f	f	Keo	f	f	f	f
7 05	3 25	□1159	7 40	*England	9 25	1 50	□5 40	1055
f	f	f	f	Ferda	f	f	f	f
7 18	3 38	□1213	7 53	*Tucker	9 12	1 37	□5 27	1042
7 23	3 43	□1218	7 58	Sherrill	9 07	1 32	□5 22	1037
f	f	f	f	Wigal Store	f	f	f	f
7 45	4 05	□1240	8#20	Ar*Pine Bluff, Ark. Lv	8 45	1 10	□5 00	1015
----	----	----	8 45	Lv Pine Bluff, Ark. (ACA) (3818) Ar	----	----	4#55	----
----	----	----	2 40	Ar Tallulah, La. Lv	----	----	1 05	----
----	----	----	5 20	Ar Natchez, Miss. Lv	----	----	10 40	----
----	----	----	5 30	Lv Natchez, Miss. (SGL) Ar	----	----	10 20	----
----	----	----	7 45	Ar Baton Rouge, La. (360) Lv	----	----	8 00	----
----	----	----	10 05	Ar New Orleans, La. Lv	----	----	5 35	----

SAN ANTONIO—EAGLE PASS—LAREDO

280 9-11-63

Read Down		C-L	DL	C-L	DL	C-L			Read Up DL			L-C	L-C	L-C	
----	10 15	7 45	-----	5 00	2 15	6 15	3 15	Lv St. Louis, Mo. (CST) Ar	2 05	5 25	-----	11 15	5 00	9 20	-----
----	3 00	1 15	-----	10 40	7 50	12 05	9 00	Lv Springfield (261) Ar	7 35	11 25	-----	5 45	11 30	3 20	-----
----	4 40	3 05	-----	12 15	9 35	1 51	10 55	Lv Joplin, Mo. Ar	5 50	9 50	-----	4 05	9 45	1 35	-----
----	8 00	6 05	-----	3 00	12 05	7 00	2 00	Lv Tulsa, Okla. (263) Ar	3 23	7 00	-----	12 30	5 40	10 30	-----
----	11 50	9 30	-----	↓	↓	10 00	5 15	Lv McAlester, Okla. Ar	12 31	4 05	↷	9 13	2 25	7 30	-----
----	7 00	3 15	12 15	10 15	8 25	3 35	12 10	Lv Dallas, Tex. (271) Ar	7 20	10 45	2 30	3 30	9 20	2 20	-----
----	7 45	↓	12 15	↓	8 25	3 45	↓	Lv Fort Worth Ar	7 10	11 30	2 20	6 40	↑	2 05	-----
----	9 40	6 05	2 50	12 55	10 41	6 25	2 50	Lv Waco Ar	4 40	8 19	11 50	1 19	6 21	11 30	-----
----	12 15	9 06	5 50	3 30	1 20	9 11	5 40	Lv Austin Ar	2 00	5 14	9 04	10 54	3 34	9 00	-----
----	1 55	11 05	7 45	5 25	2 55	11 15	7 40	Ar San Antonio, Tex. Lv	12 01	3 10	7 00	9 00	1 45	7 10	-----
----	↓	6 30	↓	12 45	12 45	8 45	2 45	Lv New Orleans, La. (SGL) Ar	4 30	7 15	11 30	1 45	7 30	1 00	-----
----		2 30		7 45	5 50	1 45	8 25	Lv Lake Charles, La. CGL Ar	9 25	2 00	4 30	7 50	1 55	5 30	-----
----		4 26		↓	7 31	3 26	10 06	Lv Beaumont, Tex. Ar	7 11	12 20	2 55	6 05	↑	3 50	-----
----		6 45		11 25	9 35	5 15	12 05	Ar Houston, Tex. (277) Lv	5 45	10 20	12 55	4 15	10 15	1 40	-----
----		7 40		12 40	10 10	6 30	1 30	Lv Houston, Tex. (CGL) Ar	4 55	8 55	11 35	3 25	9 00	12 40	-----
----	↓	12 25	↓	5 45	3 20	11 30	6 15	Ar San Antonio, Tex. (267) Lv	11 30	4 00	6 25	10 45	4 05	7 15	-----
		585	1169	579	1167	581	6489	← Run Numbers →	1166	6488	6492	582	580	578	
----	→	□2 10	9 00	6 30	3 30	12 05	8 30	Lv*San Antonio Ar	11‖05	3 00	5 45	8#15	□1#00	6‖20	-----
----	-----	ss	9 37	7 10	4 07	12 45	9 10	*Lytle	10 20	2 18	5 05	- - -	12 17	ss	-----
----	-----	ss	9 44	7 18	4 14	12 52	9 18	*Natalia	10 13	2 10	4 57	- - -	12 10	ss	-----
----	-----	ss	9 50	7 24	4 20	12 58	9 25	*Devine	10 07	2 02	4 50	f	12 04	ss	-----
----	-----	f	f	7 37	f	f	9 38	Moore	9 55	1 49	4 38	- - -	11 52	f	-----
----	-----	ss	10 15	7 54	4 45	1 27	9 57	*Pearsall	9 38	1 32	4 21	ss	11 34	5 03	-----
----	-----	f	f	f	f	f	f	Melon	f	f	f	- - -	f	f	-----
----	-----	f	f	f	f	f	f	Derby	f	f	f	- - -	f	f	-----
----	-----	3 44	10 35	8#15	5 05	1#48	10#20	Ar*Dilley Lv	9 16	1 12	4 01	6 40	11 13	4 43	-----
----	-----	↓	↓	8 25	↓	↓	10 30	Lv Dilley (3822) (WGB) Ar	9 00	↑	↑	6 25	↑	↑	-----
----	-----			8 55			11 00	Ar Big Wells Lv	8 25			5 50			-----
----	-----			9 25			11 30	Ar Carrizo Springs Lv	7 55			5 25			-----
----	-----			10 30			12 30	Ar Eagle Pass Lv	7 00			4 30			-----
----	-----	3 44	10 35	8 26	5 05	1 58	10 31	Lv*Dilley Ar	9#05	1#01	3#50	6#29	11#02	4 43	-----
----	-----	f	f	f	f	f	f	Millett	f	f	f	- - -	f	f	-----
----	-----	f	f	f	f	f	f	Gardendale	f	f	f	- - -	f	f	-----
----	-----	4 04	10 55	8 47	5 25	2 19	10 53	*Cotulla	8 43	12 40	3 25	ss	□1041	ss	-----
----	-----	f	f	f	f	f	f	Artesia Wells	f	f	f	- - -	f	f	-----
----	-----	4 41	11 30	9 22	6 00	2 56	11 30	*Encinal	8 05	12 04	2 50	f	10 05	ss	-----
----	-----	f	f	f	f	f	f	Webb	f	f	f	- - -	f	f	-----
----	-----	□5 30	12 20	10 10	6 50	3 45	12 20	Ar*Laredo, Tex. Lv	7 15	11 15	2 00	4 40	□9 15	3 00	-----
----	-----	6 00	1 00	10 45	7 15	4 30	1 00	Lv Laredo (4100) (TDN) Ar	-----	10 30	12 30	3 15	8 45	2 00	-----
----	-----	10 45	5 45	3 30	12 01	9 15	5 45	Ar Monterrey Lv	-----	6 15	8 30	11 30	4 30	9 30	-----
----	-----	-----	7 30	7 30	-----	11 30	-----	Ar Mexico City Lv	-----	-----	-----	9 00	8 00	8 30	-----

AM—Light Face. **PM—Bold Face.**
(**ACA**)—Arrow Coach Lines of Arkansas.
(**CGL**)—Central Greyhound Lines.
(**SGL**)—Southern Greyhound Lines.
TxB—Texas Bus Lines.
(**TDN**)—Transportes del Norte.
(**UB**)—Union Bus Lines, Inc.
(**WGB**)—Winter Garden Bus Line.
C-L or **L-C**—Thru bus Chicago-Laredo.
CCD—Thru bus Corpus Christi-Dallas.
DL—Thru bus Laredo and Dallas.
D-SL or SL-D—Thru bus St. Louis-Dallas.
LH or **HL**—Thru bus Laredo and Houston.
LR-N—Thru bus Little Rock-Natchez.
(CST)—Central Standard Time.
(CDT)—Central Daylight Time.
□—Mail run. f—Flag stop. ■—Highway stop.
#—Rest stop. ‖—Meal stop. ss—Station Stop.
- - -—Indicates Route. No local service performed.
*—Agency stations to which baggage may be checked.
(*LB*)—Lock box for deposit of express during station closing hours.

Commission Exhibit No. 2577—Continued

Refer to Station Column or Table Heading For the Time System Used.

"Old Hickory Route"

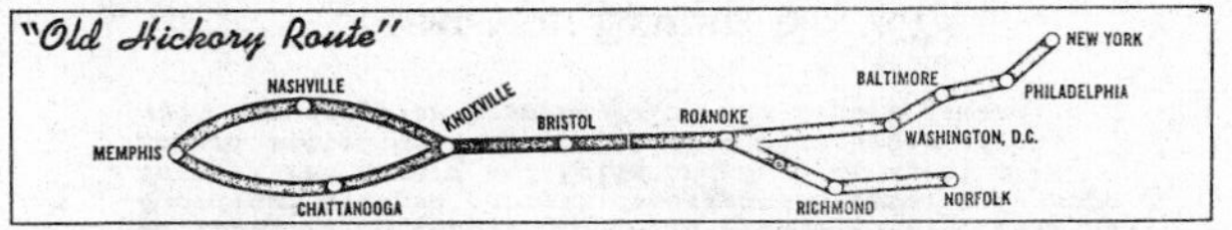

NEW YORK WASHINGTON KNOXVILLE MEMPHIS

THRU BUSES NEW YORK, PHILADELPHIA AND NORFOLK TO AND FROM DALLAS

10 1-7-64

READ DOWN 167	177	165	131	171	163	173	169		READ UP 174	172	168	178	164	170	166	182
8 45	7 00	4 30	1 30	12 01	10 30	7 30	2 20	Lv New York, N.Y. (65) (EST) Port Authority Terminal Ar	10 10	2 00	6 55	11 50	12 30	12 05	4 40	7 35
9 55	5 55	↓	12 55	■	↓	↓	↓	Lv Jersey City, N.J. Ar	1 35	1 35	6 30	11 25	2 50	↑	5 50	↑
9 20	6 35	4 35	1 15	12 35	10 35	6 35		Lv Newark, N.J. Ar	10 55	1 00	6 50	10 00	11 55		5 00	
11 30	6 30	4 45	1 30	■	10 45	7 45		Lv Philadelphia, Pa. (66) Ar	9 20	12 55	4 05	7 55	10 30		3 05	7 35
11 30	8 25	6 00	2 35		11 50	8 50	↓	Lv Wilmington, Del. Ar	8 30	↑	5 00	6 50	9 30		4 00	6 10
1 55	10 25	8 35	5 00		2 10	10 55	6 45	Lv Baltimore, Md. Ar	6 25	9 25	1 40	4 25	7 25	8 25	12 25	3 55
2 50	11 10	9 30	5 55	4 35	3 05	11 50	7 40	Ar Washington, D.C. (65) EGL Lv	5 30	8 30	12 45	3 30	6 30	7 30	11 30	3 00
3 30	11 45	10 00	6 30	5 15	3 30	12 30	8 15	Lv Washington, D.C. (303) SGL Ar	4 45	8 03	12 20	3 00	5 50	7 00	11 00	2#33
f	f	↓	6 53		↓		8 38	Lv Alexandria, Va. Ar	↑	7 40	12 02	↑	f			2 10
5 30	1 45		8 48		5 45		10 38	Ar Winchester Lv		5 45	10 15		3 55		↑	12 15
5 35	1 45		9 00		6 15		10 53	Lv Winchester Ar		5 05	10 00		3 40			11 45
7 02	f	f	10 22	7 50	D	3 05	12 16	Lv New Market Ar	2 05	3 43	8 46	f	↑		8 30	10 24
7 50	3 45	ss	10 50	8 45	8 00	3 45	1 15	Lv Harrisonburg Ar	1 20	3 02	8 20	11 50	2 00		7 10	9 56
8 27	4 20		11 25		8 35	4 22	1 52	Lv Staunton Ar	12 40	2 22	7 24	11 07	1 23		6 26	9 14
9 30	5 10		12 20		9 30	5 20	2 50	Ar Lexington Lv	11 50	1 30	6 32	10 20	12 35		5 40	8 22
9 30	5 35		12 35		9 45	5 40	2 50	Lv Lexington Ar	11 50	1 25	6 27	10 20	12 20		5 30	8 12
9 52	5 50	↓	1 00		10 10	6 00	3 12	Lv Natural Bridge Ar	11 30	1 05	6 05	10 00	↑		↑	7 50
10 53	6 50	3 30	2 00	11 15	11 10	7 05	4 15	Ar Roanoke (303) SGL Lv	10 30	12 00	5 00	9 00	10 59	1 30	4 15	6 45
1 15	11 00	6 30	6 30	1 30	1 30	10 45	9 00	Lv Norfolk, Va. (69) EGL Ar	9 15	9 15	1 30	5 30	8 00		↑	4 00
3 55	2 05	10 10	10 10	5 15	5 15	1 30	11 15	Ar Richmond (69) EGL Lv	5 30	5 30	10 30	2 30	4 45			12 30
5 30	2 30	10 30	10 30	5 50	5 50	2 10	11 45	Lv Richmond (306a) SGL Ar	4 30	4 30	9 56	2 05	3 55			11 45
10 27	6 50	2 45	2 45	10 25	10 25	7 05	4 45	Ar Roanoke, Va. (306a) SGL Lv	11 35	11 35	5 10	9 45	10 59			6 45
11 30	7 30	3 45	3 00	11 45	11 45	7 45	5 15	Lv Roanoke, Va. (303) SGL Ar	10 00	11 20	4 10	8 25	10 20	1 10	3 50	6 15
1 45	9 45	5 35	4 45	1 30	1 40	9 40	7 35	Ar Wytheville Lv	8 05	9 05	1 40	6 10	8 15	11 20	1 55	4 15
2 00	9 55	5 55	4 45	1 45	2 00	9 40	8 00	Lv Wytheville Ar	7#35	8 51	1 10	5 37	8 00	11 20	1 45	3 50
4 15	12 05	7 40	6 25	3 15	3 40	11 20	9 50	Ar Bristol Lv	5 55	6 50	11 00	3 35	6 15	9 45	12 10	2 15
4 25	12 40	7 45	7 10	3 15	3 40	11 35	10 05	Lv Bristol, Va. Ar	5 45	↶	10 40	3 25	5 50	9 30	12 10	2 15
5 05	1 15	8 20	7 55	■	4 20	12 10	10 40	Lv Kingsport, Tenn. Ar	f		10 02	2 47	5 10	8 55	11 30	f
6 02	2 15	9 05	8 52		5 06	f	11 25	Lv Rogersville Ar	f	-----	9 05	1 50	4 15	ss	10 45	f
7 30	3 50	10 35	10 30	5 50	6 40	2 25	12 55	Ar Knoxville, Tenn. (303) SGL Lv	3 00	-----	7 30	12 15	2 45	6 45	9 15	11 30
								VIA CHATTANOOGA								
8 15	5 00	11 10	Run No. 713	EXPRESS	7 30	3 00	-----	Lv Knoxville, Tenn. (344) SGL Ar	2 40	-----	6 45	11 35	↑	EXPRESS	8 30	Run No. 720
8 55	↓	11 45			8 10	↓	-----	Ar Oak Ridge Lv	↑	-----	6 05	10 55			↑	
9 58	6 25	12 50			9 10	4 15	-----	Ar Rockwood Lv	1 20	-----	5 00	9 50				
11 40	8 10	2 35			10 45	5 45	-----	Ar Chattanooga, Tenn. Lv	11 45	-----	3 20	8 05			5 45	
1 15	8 45	3 15			11 15	6 40	-----	Lv Chattanooga, Tenn. (355) Ar	11 25	-----	↑	7 15			4 26	
4 00	11 45	6 45			2 45	10 00	-----	Ar Birmingham, Ala. Lv	6 10	-----		3 20			10 45	
4 10	9 50	4 40			-----	10 20	-----	Ar New Orleans, La. (347) Lv	5 30	-----		3 55			-----	
11 59	-----	3 00			-----	6 30	-----	Lv Chattanooga, Tenn. (EST) Ar	11 15	-----	3 00	-----			5 00	
12 15	-----	3 15			-----	6 40	-----	Ar Monteagle (CST) Lv	9 00	-----	12 50	-----			2 45	
12 30	-----	3 30			-----	6 55	-----	Lv Monteagle Ar	8 45	-----	12 30	-----			2 45	
2 40	-----	6 05			-----	9 30	-----	Ar Lawrenceburg Lv	6 15	-----	10 05	-----			12 10	
2 40	-----	6 25			-----	9 50	-----	Lv Lawrenceburg Ar	5 45	-----	9 50	-----			11 40	
4 30	-----	8 16			-----	11 55	-----	Ar Selmer Lv	3 40	-----	7 55	-----			9 35	
6 45	-----	10 30	↓		-----	2 20	-----	Ar Memphis, Tenn. (353a) SGL Lv	1 15	-----	5 45	-----			7 15	
	175							**VIA NASHVILLE**				176				
9 00	4 45	↓	11 30	6 30	7 30	3 00	-----	Lv Knoxville, Tenn. (353) SGL Ar	2 15	-----	7 00	11 15	1 30	6 05	7 20	11 10
↓	5 25		↓	■	↓	↓	-----	Ar Oak Ridge Lv	↑	-----	↑	↑	↑	■	↑	10 30
10 13	6 25		12 50	ss	8 49	ss	-----	Ar Rockwood (EST) Lv	1 06	-----	5 40	9 50	12 26	ss	6 05	9 35
10 30	6 40		1 10	7 40	9 10	4 10	-----	Ar Sparta (CST) Lv	10 45	-----	3 20	7 30	10 05	2 55	3 50	7 25
10 45	7 00		1 30	7 40	9 25	4 30	-----	Lv Sparta Ar	10 26	-----	3 05	7 12	9 50	2 55	3 35	7 10
11 25	7 45		2 11	■	10 06	5 10	-----	Ar McMinnville Lv	9 46	-----	2 25	6 31	9 10	■	2 50	6 25
12 23	8 48		3 16		11 05	6 10	-----	Ar Murfreesboro Lv	8 48	-----	1 30	5 33	8 10		1 50	5 25
1 10	9 35		4 10	9 35	11 50	7 00	-----	Ar Nashville Lv	8 00	-----	1245	4 45	7 15	1 00	1 00	4 30
1 30	10 15		5 00	10 00	12 30	8 00	-----	Lv Nashville Ar	7 00	-----	1052	3 10	6 15	12 15	↶	3 45
↓	↓		6 50		ss	↓	-----	Ar Linden Lv	5 03	-----	9 03	↑	↑			↑
2 55	11 40		↓		2 08	9 40	-----	Ar Waverly Lv	↑	-----	↑	1 51	4 41			2 04
4 30	1 13		8 10		3 30	12 01	-----	Ar Jackson Lv	3 45	-----	7 47	11 52	2 50	9 20	-----	12 15
4 45	1 30		8 25	↓	3 45	12 20	-----	Lv Jackson Ar	3 28	-----	7 36	11 42	2 35	9 05	-----	11 50
6 45	3 20	↓	10 15	2 30	6 45	2 33	-----	Ar Memphis, Tenn. (353) SGL Lv	1 15	-----	5 30	9 45	12 30	7 00	-----	9 45
8 00	3 30	→	11 15	3 15	7 30	3 15	-----	Lv Memphis, Tenn. (264) CGL Ar	11 50	-----	4 45	8 45	-----	6 00	-----	9 10
11 50	6 40	-----	2 29	6 55	10 45	6 55	-----	Ar Pine Bluff, Ark. Lv	8 40	-----	1 15	5 15	-----	2 45	-----	5 50
4 43	11 10	-----	6 32	11 32	2 20	11 32	-----	Ar Texarkana, Tex. Lv	4 20	-----	8 30	12 40	-----	10 50	-----	1 55
9 45	4 15	-----	11 40	4 10	6 45	4 10	-----	Ar Dallas, Tex. (264) CGL Lv	12 05	-----	3 45	7 30	-----	5 45	-----	9 15
11 00	5 00	-----	1 30	5 53	8 45	5 53	-----	Lv Dallas (CST) (270) Ar	11 00	-----	2 25	6 20	-----	4 25	-----	8 15
12 25	6 20	-----	3 45	7 30	11 10	7 30	-----	Ar El Paso, Tex. (MST) (270) CGL Lv	7 00	-----	10 15	3 15	-----	12 30	-----	4 00
↓	↓	-----	8 45	1 10	↓	1 10	-----	Ar San Diego, Cal. (PST) (667) WGL Lv	2 00	-----	↑	6 15	-----	6 15	-----	9 00
6 30	1 25	-----	11 00	1 05	5 05	1 05	-----	Ar Los Angeles, Cal. (667) WGL Lv	11 45	-----	1 15	7 15	-----	2 30	-----	8 15

Column notes (printed vertically): 167—Thru Scenicruiser Service New York to Memphis; 177—Thru Scenicruiser Service New York to New Orleans; 165—Thru Scenicruiser Service New York to Memphis; 131—Thru Bus; Thru Scenicruiser Service Norfolk to Memphis; 171—Thru Scenicruiser Service New York to Memphis; EXPRESS; 163—Thru Scenicruiser Service New York to Memphis; 173—Thru Scenicruiser Service Philadelphia to Memphis; 174—Thru Scenicruiser Service Memphis to Philadelphia; 168—Thru Scenicruiser Service Memphis to New York; 178—Thru Scenicruiser Service New Orleans to New York; 164—Thru Scenicruiser Service Memphis to New York; 170—Thru Scenicruiser Service Memphis to New York; EXPRESS; 166—Thru Scenicruiser Service Memphis to Norfolk; 182—Thru Bus; Thru Scenicruiser Service Memphis to New York.

REFERENCE MARKS:
*—Change buses.
L—Connects at Lexington, Va.
O—Will stop to discharge passengers whose origin is north of Winchester.
Index numbers in ITALICS refer to detailed tables in Russell's Guide.

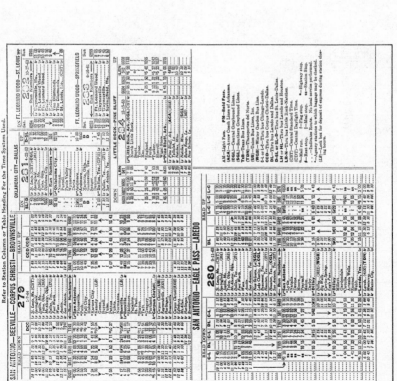

Commission Exhibit No. 2577—Continued

SHIPPING PROBLEM?
GREYHOUND PACKAGE EXPRESS
IT'S THERE IN HOURS... AND COSTS YOU LESS!
Faster delivery to more areas, including many not reached by other public transportation. Round-the-clock service, seven days a week, with no delays by weekends or holidays.
Arrival time can usually be determined in advance, saving time, money and confusion.
GREYHOUND PACKAGE EXPRESS

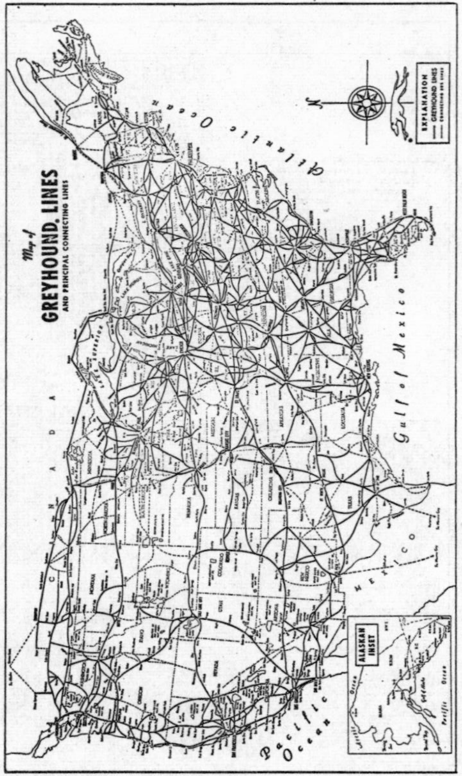

COMMISSION EXHIBIT No. 2577—Continued

UNITED STATES DEPARTMENT OF JUSTICE
FEDERAL BUREAU OF INVESTIGATION
Other Individuals and Organizations
...d or Interviewed
WASHINGTON 25, D. C.

In Reply, Please Refer to
File No.

May 28, 1964

LEE HARVEY OSWALD

On May 27, 1964, Special Agent James M. (Mike) Howard, United States Secret Service, was interviewed in the presence of Inspector Thomas J. Kelley, Secret Service, by a representative of the Federal Bureau of Investigation with regard to an article which appeared in the May 9, 1964, issue of the "National Guardian", a weekly newspaper published in New York City. The article under discussion bore the caption, "Oswald Case: A New Angle", and information set out therein was attributed to Attorney Mark Lane.

Special Agent Howard explained that on Sunday morning, February 9, 1964, he, along with his brother, Pat C. Howard, Deputy Sheriff of the Tarrant County, Texas, Sheriff's Office, was assigned to transport Mrs. Marguerite Oswald from her residence at 2220 Thomas Place, Fort Worth, Texas, to Love Field, Dallas, Texas, where Mrs. Oswald was to take a plane to Washington, D. C., for purposes of her appearance before the President's Commission. Special Agent Howard further stated that at the insistence of Mrs. Oswald, he and his brother also were accompanied by Theyer Waldo, who, Mrs. Oswald explained, was making the trip with her from Fort Worth to Dallas at the suggestion of her attorney, Mark Lane. Howard related that after Mrs. Oswald was placed aboard the plane, he and his brother, along with Special Agent in Charge Forrest V. Sorrels of the Dallas office of Secret Service, went into the airport restaurant or coffee shop, also accompanied by Waldo. The news column in the "National Guardian" alleged certain conversation between Deputy Sheriff Pat Howard and Waldo and Special Agent Mike Howard stated he had no knowledge whatsoever of any such conversation between Waldo and Deputy Howard.

COMMISSION EXHIBIT No. 2578

Agent Howard related at the airport Waldo asked if Agent Howard would give him a ride back to Fort Worth from Love Field and Agent Howard acquiesced inasmuch as he was driving his personally-owned vehicle. En route to Fort Worth, Agent Howard drove the car with his brother, Pat Howard, riding in the front seat and Waldo was riding in the rear seat alone. During the ride Agent Howard, in discussion with his brother, related to his brother Pat a story which Agent Howard had been told on January 1, 1964, while on a special detail accompanied by two detectives of the Dallas Police Department. On that occasion Detective Jack Bryan had told Agent Howard about an incident involving a Negro man who was questioned by the Dallas police in connection with his being in the Texas Book Depository Building on the day of the assassination of President Kennedy and that the Negro man had left the building hurriedly after the shooting. When later questioned by Dallas police why he had left the building in a hurry, the Negro man stated that because he had a police record, he feared he would be suspected of having been involved in the shooting.

Special Agent Howard stated while relating this incident to his brother Pat, he did not know Waldo, in the back seat of the car, could have overheard the conversation; however, Waldo leaned forward over the rear of the front seat and asked Agent Howard if this person, the Negro man who was the topic of conversation, would be called to testify before the Warren Commission. Agent Howard stated that in jest he replied to Waldo, "Why yes, I'm sure he will be". In response to a question by Waldo as to where this man was, Deputy Pat Howard replied jokingly, "They probably have him hidden out someplace."

Agent Howard stated neither he nor his brother, Pat Howard, realized Waldo was a newspaper reporter and later that night, after having returned to Fort Worth, he learned television and radio coverage had been given to a story attributed to Waldo that a witness who was to

testify before the Warren Commission was being hidden by police officers. Special Agent Howard stated the Fort Worth newspaper "Star-Telegram" carried a story by Waldo in the same vein and he immediately called Waldo telephonically to make inquiry where Waldo had gotten such a story. In reply Waldo told Agent Howard he (Waldo) had talked to his attorney and that Waldo did not have to divulge the source of his information and said Agent Howard had nothing to worry about. Agent Howard stated his brother, Pat Howard, also contacted Waldo telephonically and received a similar assurance.

Agent Howard stated that during the ride from Dallas back to Fort Worth with Waldo in the car, Agent Howard did not make any statements such as were attributed to him concerning, "Wait until that old black boy gets in front of the Warren Commission . . ." Agent Howard stated he did not make any statement to the effect that the Negro janitor was a witness to the shooting of the President. Agent Howard stated these alleged quotes attributed to him were entirely a fabrication.

With regard to the article in the "Nationa Guardian", Agent Howard prepared a memorandum dated May 27, 1964, and a copy of this memorandum furnished by Inspector Thomas J. Kelley is attached hereto. Inspector Kelley furnished the copy on May 28, 1964.

1

DL 100-10461
RPG/ds

In the May 9, 1964, issue of the "National Guardian", there appears an article captioned "OSWALD CASE: A NEW ANGLE".

According to this article, MARK LANE claims that the United States Secret Service deliberately planted a false story in the press to cast further guilt on OSWALD. This article names a U. S. Secret Service Agent MIKE (MICHAEL) HOWARD; PAT HOWARD, a Deputy Sheriff of Tarrant County, Texas, and a brother of the U. S. Secret Service Agent, MIKE HOWARD; and, THAYER WALDO, a reporter for the "Fort Worth Star Telegram". This article alleges that MIKE HOWARD, PAT HOWARD and THAYER WALDO engaged in conversations on or about February 9, 1964, in Fort Worth and Dallas, Texas, concerning the existence of a Negro witness who saw OSWALD shoot at President KENNEDY.

171

COMMISSION EXHIBIT No. 2579

FD-302 (Rev. 3-3-59)

FEDERAL BUREAU OF INVESTIGATION

1

Date 6/2/64

THAYER WALDO, news reporter, "Fort Worth Star Telegram", dictated the following signed statement to "Star Telegram" stenographer BETTY JOHNSON in the conference room at the "Fort Worth Star Telegram" in the presence of Special Agents B. TOM CARTER and JOSEPH L. SCHOTT. After dictating the statement, WALDO said he intended to read it over after it was typed, make any corrections which he deemed necessary in his own handwriting, maintain one copy for himself and another copy in the files of the "Fort Worth Star Telegram".

Special Agents SCHOTT and CARTER returned to the "Fort Worth Star Telegram" approximately five hours after this statement was dictated and WALDO handed over the original. He said that he had signed his name on each individual page and that all corrections in ink on the statement were made in his own handwriting, and for that reason did not consider it necessary to initial each correction.

The statement is as follows:

"Fort Worth, Texas
May 28, 1964

"I, Thayer Waldo, make the following voluntary statement to B. Tom Carter and Joseph L. Schott, Special Agents of the Federal Bureau of Investigation.

"On the morning of February 9, 1964, attorney Mark Lane called me from San Francisco and asked if I would accompany Mrs. Marguerite Oswald and a secret service man on the drive from Fort Worth to Dallas Love Field. Lane said Mrs. Oswald was to take a plane to Washington_ D. C. to appear before the Warren Commission and wanted 'someone she knew and could trust to make the ride with her.'

172

on 5/28/64 at Fort Worth, Texas File # DL 100-10461
by Special Agent B. TOM CARTER and JOSEPH L. SCHOTT/ds Date dictated 6/2/64

This document contains neither recommendations nor conclusions of the FBI. It is the property of the FBI and is loaned to your agency; it and its contents are not to be distributed outside your agency.

COMMISSION EXHIBIT No. 2579—Continued

"I went to Mrs. Oswald's house shortly after noon. Two men were standing by a car in the driveway and one of them greeted me by name, saying, 'I'm Mike Howard.' The other one introduced himself as Pat Howard.

"We drove to Love Field; Mrs. Oswald and I were in the back seat, Mike Howard driving and Pat Howard by him. At the airport Forrest V. Sorrels, Chief of the Secret Service Office in Dallas and another agent who was to accompany Mrs. Oswald on the flight, met us.

"After Mrs. Oswald's plane took off, Sorrels invited all of us to have a cup of coffee with him. We sat at the counter in the coffee shop; Sorrels and Mike Howard conversed between themselves and I was talking to Pat Howard on my left. (Pat Howard at that time identified himself as a deputy in the Tarrant County Sheriff's Department, and as a brother of Mike Howard).

"We were discussing various angles of the assassination of President Kennedy, of the subsequent killing of Oswald when Pat put his hand on my knee and said; 'Waldo, if it hasn't already come out of the Warren Commission by then, after this Ruby trial is over I'm going to come up and give you a story that will blow everybody's head off.'

"I tried to get him to give me more details, but he refused. However, when we left the coffee shop--Sorrels and Mike Howard walking some distance ahead of us--Pat took me by the arm and added:

"'I'll tell you just this much right now. It has to do with a witness who saw the shooting of the

"'President and can positively identify Oswald as the killer. Is that good enough?'

"In the car on the return trip, I sat alone in the back seat. Mike was driving and began talking, a rather long monologue about various aspects of the two killings. Then, very casually, he said:

"'Well, when that old black boy gets up before the Warren Commission and tells what he knows, that will stop them all talking.'

"Pat turned half around in his seat and gave me an elaborate wink, with raised eyebrows, as if to say, 'so here is what I was telling you about.'

"Then he leaned close to Mike and said something inaudible to me. But Mike appeared to pay no attention and continued telling his story.

"He stated that a Negro employee of the Texas School Book Depository had been on the sixth floor of that building at mid-day on November 22, 1963; that he was looking out the window at the passing presidential motorcade when he heard a shot close beside him; then he looked and saw Oswald kneeling at the next window with a rifle aimed into the street.

"Mike Howard said the Negro later told Dallas Police officers to whom he surrendered, 'I was scared to death, I thought he would kill me too. I just turned and ran way over to the far side of that room and squeezed me down behind some empty crates. While I was running, I heard another shot, maybe two. When Oswald dropped his gun and ran out down the stairway, he almost stepped on me as he went by.'

"Mike said the unnamed Negro waited a few minutes, then left the building, and went straight to Dallas Police Headquarters, where he turned himself in to Special Services.

"'He said he knew about that branch because they handle gambling cases and he had been picked up a few times for shooting craps,' Mike Howard explained.

"Howard said he had seen this Negro witness once, while the latter was still in the Dallas City Jail.

"'They slapped a vagrancy charge on him so they could hold him,' Mike said. 'He was still just about the scaredest Negro I ever saw--nothing but whites to his eyes.

"'They have now transferred him somewhere else, I understand. I don't know where.'

"During this recital, Pat Howard kept giving me significant grins and broad winks. Nothing was said at anytime by either of them about not repeating this story, that it was off the record or in anyway confidential. There was no request to omit use of names.

"Mike and Pat dropped me off at the Star-Telegram. This was not a normal working day for me, but I felt that the editors should know at once about what I had been told.

"The city editor naturally saw it as a sensationally good story. He called the managing editor and a decision was made to make it a copyright story in the first edition for Monday. It was then about 5:45 P.M.

"I wrote the story at once and it appeared under an eight column, double bank banner in the one star edition, which hit the streets shortly after 8 P.M. Within minutes the story was being broadcast on radio and TV.

"At about 8:25, I received a call from Pat Howard, who said:

"'Hey, boy, that's quite a story! You aren't using anybody's name on it, are you?'

"I assured him I was not, and he said, 'Good stuff.'

Less than ten minutes later, Mike Howard called me. He seemed considerably upset and agitated, but conceded that no request to withhold the story had been made.

"'Well, for God's sake at least don't use my name,' he said.

"I told him I had not and would not.

"Except for the Star-Telegram's editors and the local Associated Press correspondent, I did not mention Mike Howard's name to anyone--including the F.B.I., to whom I talked by telephone on Tuesday, February 11--until about one month ago.

"At that time, Mark Lane called me from Dallas, said he was on his way to give a talk at the University of Texas in Austin and asked if I could see him in Dallas.

"I explained that I was too busy to leave the newspaper, so he took a rent car and came to Fort Worth to see me.

"He said he was conducting an investigation on 'four or five important angles' of the Kennedy-Oswald-Ruby case and was particularly interested to know further details about my February 9th story.

"His manner of speaking gave me to understand that anything I told or showed him would be held in confidence. I took him to the reference room, where he read the Star-Telegram for the morning of February 10th. Then he asked if I would mind telling him my source. Believing this to be a lawyer's request with normal legal discretion, I told him the complete story.

"I heard nothing more from Mr. Lane. About two weeks later Mrs. Marguerite Oswald called and asked me if I could come to her home, 'as I have several important things to show you.'

"One of the items she showed me was a copy of the National Guardian for May 9th, 1964. In a front page article, Mark Lane was quoted, revealing all the details I had given him on the story.

"As regards identity of the Negro referred to by Mike Howard, Howard said he didn't know the name, 'or if I did, I've forgotten it now.'

"I dictated the above statement containing 7 pages to Star-Telegram stenographer, Betty Johnson, and it is true and correct.

"/s/ Thayer Waldo
"Thayer Waldo

"/s/ Joseph L. Schott, Special Agent, FBI, Dallas, Texas, 5/28/64.
"/s/ B. Tom Carter, Special Agent, F.B.I., Dallas, Texas, 5/28/64."

Date 6/2/64

PAT CLYDE HOWARD, Patrolman, Hurst Police Department, advised he would make the following free and voluntary oral statement to Special Agents B. TOM CARTER and JOSEPH L. SCHOTT of the Federal Bureau of Investigation.

HOWARD stated he presently resides at 508 Norwood, Hurst, Texas. He said he had come to work at the Hurst Police Department during the first part of May 1964 and for approximately one year prior to that had been employed as a Deputy Sheriff at the Tarrant County Sheriff's Office, Fort Worth, Texas.

HOWARD stated that his brother, MIKE HOWARD, had been employed for the past two or three years as a Special Agent of the U. S. Secret Service.

HOWARD said that about three or four months ago, probably during the month of February 1964, his brother, MIKE, called him on the telephone and asked him to go along when MIKE drove Mrs. MARGUERITE OSWALD from her residence in Fort Worth, Texas, to Love Field in Dallas, at which place she was to take an airplane to Washington, D. C., and testify before the President's Commission. PAT HOWARD said he accompanied his brother in MIKE's car to the residence of Mrs. MARGUERITE OSWALD and, while waiting for her to finish packing, she informed them that a friend of her attorney, MARK LANE, was going to accompany them on the ride from Fort Worth to Love Field in Dallas. Mrs. OSWALD identified this individual who was to accompany them as THAYER WALDO, a reporter for the "Fort Worth Star Telegram".

PAT HOWARD said that THAYER WALDO arrived at Mrs. OSWALD's residence by taxi, to the best of his recollection. He accompanied them to Dallas. During the ride, MIKE HOWARD drove the car, PAT HOWARD sat in the front seat with his brother, and WALDO and Mrs. OSWALD sat in the back seat.

178

on 6/1/64 at Hurst, Texas File # DL 100-10461

by Special Agent B. TOM CARTER and JOSEPH L. SCHOTT/ds Date dictated 6/2/64

2

DL 100-10461

At Love Field in Dallas they met FORREST SORRELS, the Special Agent in Charge of the Secret Service in Dallas, and also another Secret Service Agent, whose name was not recalled by PAT HOWARD at this time. This Agent who accompanied SORRELS got on the plane for Washington with Mrs. OSWALD to accompany her on the trip.

After the plane departed, SORRELS, MIKE HOWARD, PAT HOWARD and THAYER WALDO went into the coffee shop at Love Field Terminal to have a cup of coffee. In the coffee shop, the four seated themselves in such a way that FORREST SORRELS and MIKE HOWARD could engage in a private conversation out of earshot of the other two, and PAT HOWARD and WALDO could converse privately. PAT HOWARD said this situation arose because of the way they were seated at either the counter or a long table.

In conversation with WALDO, PAT HOWARD said he had some interesting highlights on the events immediately following the Presidential assassination that he might tell WALDO sometime.

PAT HOWARD said what he had in mind when he made the statement was that he had accompanied Sheriff LON EVANS of Fort Worth and several Secret Service Agents to Dallas on November 22, 1963, after the news of the Presidential assassination was broadcast. They arrived at Parkland Hospital just about the time the news of the President's death was announced. When the news was announced, PAT HOWARD observed the reactions of many of the individuals in the hall and outside the hospital and referred to these reactions as "interesting human drama". He said that he thought these little incidents of human drama would make good newspaper stories, and these incidents were what he referred to when he told WALDO he would sometime like to give him some interesting sidelights on the events immediately after the assassination.

On the return trip to Fort Worth from Love Field, Dallas, MIKE HOWARD drove and PAT HOWARD sat in the front seat

3

DL 100-10461

with him. THAYER WALDO sat in the back. On the return trip, MIKE HOWARD mentioned that there had been a Negro male in the Texas School Book Depository at the time the assassination had occurred. After the shooting, the Negro left the building hastily because he was afraid he might be implicated in some way as he had several minor arrests against him for gambling or vagrancy. PAT HOWARD said MIKE HOWARD told this as an amusing incident and never at any time did he indicate that this Negro male had actually been a witness to anyone shooting at the President.

PAT HOWARD recalled that MIKE HOWARD's source of information about the Negro male was a detective on the Dallas Police Department, whose name was not recalled by PAT HOWARD. PAT HOWARD said it was his recollection that this Negro male had been identified shortly after the assassination and had been checked out by the Dallas Police Department and the Secret Service.

PAT HOWARD said that the next morning after the story came out in the "Fort Worth Star Telegram" that a Negro witness had observed LEE HARVEY OSWALD shooting the President, he called THAYER WALDO at the "Star Telegram" and protested, but had not received any sort of satisfactory answer from WALDO regarding his reasons for having written the story.

At the conclusion of the interview, PAT HOWARD reinterated that neither he nor his brother, MIKE, had told WALDO that the Negro male MIKE talked about had been a witness who had observed LEE HARVEY OSWALD shoot at the President in the Texas School Book Depository at Dallas, Texas, on November 22, 1963.

4. CLAIM: Oswald was treated at Parkland Memorial Hospital, Dallas, Texas, at the age of seven after an automobile accident. Pages 124 and 199.

INVESTIGATION: Records of the hospital do not substantiate Gun's claim. Those records do show, however, that Oswald, at age five, was treated as an emergency case on April 18, 1945, for an injury sustained when hit in the left eye by a rock. He was treated with ice packs and discharged on April 19, 1945.

5. CLAIM: A doctor examining President Kennedy at Parkland Memorial Hospital found on his stretcher a bullet that, without doubt, had fallen from one of the President's wounds in the course of surgical measures. Page 133.

INVESTIGATION: The Secret Service has advised this Bureau that the intact bullet found in the hospital in connection with the assassination was reportedly found as it fell from a stretcher used in the handling and treatment of Texas Governor John B. Connally. This bullet was examined by the FBI Laboratory and was found to have been fired from the rifle owned by Oswald.

6. CLAIM: A "Buddy Walthers" of the Dallas County Sheriff's Office affirms that the shots, or at least one of the shots, fired in the assassination had come from the overpass in front of the Presidential motorcade. In addition, Walthers ran in that direction and with a Secret Service Agent found a bullet, "the fourth bullet," in the grass near the overpass. Pages 152 and 211.

INVESTIGATION: Walthers is undoubtedly Eddie Raymond Walthers of the Dallas County Sheriff's Office who has denied making the above statement regarding the origin of the bullet, has denied looking for a bullet with any Secret Service Agent, and has denied finding "the fourth bullet." In addition, the Secret Service has advised that it has no knowledge of any of its Agents finding a "fourth bullet."

7. CLAIM: The number of employees in the Texas School Book Depository Building is referred to as 91 and more than 250. Pages 153 and 206.

INVESTIGATION: In connection with this Bureau's inquiry, signed statements were taken from 72 individuals reportedly working in this building on the day of the assassination and it was determined that two individuals in the building on the day in question were on sick leave on the day when the signed statements were taken.

COMMISSION EXHIBIT No. 2580

8. CLAIM: Captain Will Fritz, Chief of Detectives of the municipal police of Dallas, had the description of Oswald broadcast over the police radio system after he had been advised by Roy S. Truly, Superintendent of the Texas School Book Depository, that Oswald was missing from the building. Pages 153 and 154.

INVESTIGATION: Captain J. W. Fritz, Dallas Police Department, has advised that he did not have a description of Oswald broadcast for fear that Oswald might learn he was wanted. Captain Fritz has also stated that he did not advise anyone else at the Dallas Police Department of Oswald's description. The description broadcast by the Dallas Police Department at 12:43 p.m. on November 22, 1963, was obtained from an unidentified individual who furnished the information to a police official at the scene of the Texas School Book Depository Building. It is noted that at the time of the above broadcast Captain Fritz had not yet been advised by Mr. Truly that Oswald was missing from the building.

9. CLAIM: According to police, Marina Oswald is said to have recognized the weapon of the crime as belonging to her husband. Page 157.

INVESTIGATION: Marina Oswald advised an Agent of this Bureau on November 22, 1963, that she had been shown a rifle at the Dallas Police Department on that date that had been reportedly found in the Texas School Book Depository Building. She advised that she was unable to identify it positively as the same rifle kept in the garage at Mrs. Ruth Paine's residence by Oswald.

10. CLAIM: Following Oswald's arrest, a paper found in his wallet had his Beckley Street address. Page 157.

INVESTIGATION: After Oswald's arrest, he admitted to Dallas Police Department interrogators and FBI Agents that he had been living at 1026 North Beckley Street, in Dallas, Texas. However, no such paper was found among photographs of the articles in Oswald's wallet shown an FBI Agent on November 24, 1963.

11. CLAIM: In a certain photograph taken by an amateur at the passing of the President's procession, Oswald can clearly be seen brandishing the rifle of the crime and the pistol which served to kill Dallas Police Officer Tippit. Page 165.

INVESTIGATION: Investigation by this Bureau has failed to develop any information regarding the existence of such a photograph.

COMMISSION EXHIBIT No. 2580—Continued

"THE RED ROSES OF DALLAS"

12. CLAIM: The Dallas Police Department found on Oswald after his arrest the Post Office Box number to which the alleged assassination rifle had been shipped. Page 166.

INVESTIGATION: No such item was observed by Agents of this Bureau among photographs of things taken from Oswald when he was arrested.

13. CLAIM: Oswald affirmed to Pauline Bates, public stenographer of Fort Worth, Texas, in June, 1962, that he had become a "secret agent" of the United States Government and that he was soon going to return to Russia "for Washington." Page 172.

INVESTIGATION: Miss Bates has denied a newspaper report that Oswald told her he was working for the United States Department of State. She has advised that when Oswald first told her that the State Department had advised him he would be on his own while in Russia she assumed that he was working with the Department of State. However, she realized later that her assumption was false.

14. CLAIM: One Lucio Lopez, employed by the Mexican bus line, Transportes Frontera, recognized Oswald on television as a passenger who had asked him to indicate a cheap hotel and then to obtain a reduction in the Federal tax on the ticket. Gun claims that Lopez showed him Oswald's name on a list of travelers crossing the border into Mexico. In addition, Lopez stated that Oswald confided in him an intention to go to Cuba and asked him if a secret route existed. Pages 173 and 174.

INVESTIGATION: Our inquiry has shown that a Lucio Lopez Medina, baggage and freight handler for Transportes Frontera in Mexico City, believes he wrote "Oswld" on an October 2, 1963, manifest of the bus line. However, Medina has stated he had no personal recollection of Oswald, could not recognize Oswald in a photograph as anyone who had been at the bus terminal, and did not believe Oswald embarked on the bus noted in the manifest.

15. CLAIM: At the time of Oswald's trip to Mexico he was under surveillance by the FBI. Page 176.

INVESTIGATION: Oswald was not under day-by-day surveillance by this Bureau and was not "wanted" in the sense of a fugitive. This Bureau was, of course, alert to any information which would indicate that a Soviet intelligence service had an interest in Oswald and was in contact with him.

- 4 -

COMMISSION EXHIBIT No. 2580—Continued

2

DL 100-10461

After typing the 10 pages, she told him she had typed $10 worth of material and would be glad to type the remainder of his notes on credit. He was not agreeable to this and picked up his notes and typed pages, paid her with a $10 bill and left. He never returned.

After typing the notes, she mentioned this to her friend, CAROLINE HAMILTON, who is a reporter for The Fort Worth Press. Later, CAROLINE HAMILTON told her her people had tried unsuccessfully to contact LEE OSWALD regarding his diary.

After President KENNEDY was assassinated, she was contacted by CAROLINE HAMILTON. This was the first time she had tied up LEE OSWALD with the assassination.

On the afternoon of November 29, 1963, she had a recorded interview with the television network in her office. She pointed out the story by CAROLINE HAMILTON which appeared in the Fort Worth Press on November 29, 1963 is currect in every detail with the one exception that LEE OSWALD never stated he was working for the United States State Department. She explained LEE OSWALD stated the State Department was reluctant to give him a visa and told him he would be on his own while in Russia. From this statement she at first assumed he was working with the State Department but later realized her assumption was false.

About 3:30 PM, November 29, 1963, she received a phone call at her office from a woman who stated she was Mrs. OSWALD, mother of LEE OSWALD. Mrs. OSWALD stated "I cannot tell you where I am because I am under tight security. I heard an interview of your on the radio regarding typing LEE's diary. I remember him saying he had a public stenographer type some of his notes. I wish you wouldn't talk with anyone about this until I can talk with you. Otherwise you may hurt his widow and the children."

BATES stated she explained to Mrs. OSWALD she had originally been intervewed by a television network and had received almost 100 telephone calls from the news media from all over the United States. She also pointed out there was nothing of a derogatory nature in any of her statements to the press and television people. Mrs. OSWALD never mentioned if she knew where

538

COMMISSION EXHIBIT No. 2581

OFFICE OF THE DIRECTOR

UNITED STATES DEPARTMENT OF JUSTICE

FEDERAL BUREAU OF INVESTIGATION

WASHINGTON 25, D.C.

April 2, 1964

BY COURIER SERVICE

Honorable J. Lee Rankin
General Counsel
The President's Commission
200 Maryland Avenue, Northeast
Washington, D. C.

Dear Mr. Rankin:

Your attention is directed to the report of Special Agent Robert P. Gemberling dated November 30, 1963, page 35, which sets forth the results of an interview with Jean Hill who was present with Mary Ann Moorman in Dallas, Texas, on November 22, 1963, when President Kennedy was assassinated.

Subsequent to this interview Mr. Mark Lane, a New York attorney, at a meeting sponsored by the "National Guardian" in New York City on February 18, 1964, entitled "An Inquiry Into The Oswald Case," played a tape recording of a telephone conversation with one Miss Hill who claimed to have heard four to six shots at the time of the assassination of President Kennedy.

Enclosed for your information are four copies of a memorandum dated March 18, 1964, captioned, "Lee Harvey Oswald," which contains the results of a reinterview with Mrs. Jean Lollis Hill who resides at 9402 Bluffcreek, Dallas, Texas.

This Bureau is currently conducting additional investigation endeavoring to identify an individual observed by Mrs. Hill running west away from the Texas School Book Depository Building following the shooting.

When the results of this investigation are received, they will be furnished to you.

Sincerely yours,

J. Edgar Hoover

Enclosures (4)

COMMISSION EXHIBIT No. 2582

UNITED STATES DEPARTMENT OF JUSTICE

FEDERAL BUREAU OF INVESTIGATION

In Reply, Please Refer to
File No.

Dallas, Texas
March 18, 1964

LEE HARVEY OSWALD

In an effort to identify the "Miss Hill," a Dallas woman who heard four to six shots at the time of the assassination of John Fitzgerald Kennedy at Dallas, Texas, on November 22, 1963, with whom Mark Lane, a New York attorney, had a taped telephone conversation made on February 18, 1964, the following interview was conducted by Special Agents of the Federal Bureau of Investigation on March 13, 1964:

Mrs. Jean Lollis Hill, 9402 Bluffcreek, telephone EV 1-7419, advised she and a friend, Mary Ann Moorman of 2832 Ripplewood, were in the vicinity of Main and Houston Streets on November 22, 1963, for approximately one and one-half hours before the arrival of President John Fitzgerald Kennedy and his party. While waiting for the motorcade to arrive at this location, Mrs. Hill and Mary Ann walked around the parkway area near the Texas School Book Depository Building in attempts to determine the best vantage spot for taking photographs of the President. Mrs. Hill said she recalls talking to a uniformed policeman of the Dallas Police Department on the sidewalk near the main entrance to the Texas School Book Depository Building. While conversing with the policeman, Mrs. Hill noticed an automobile circling the area. The windows of the vehicle were covered with cardboard and the name "Honest Joe's Pawn Shop" was painted on the side of the car. Mrs. Hill made a remark about the automobile and the policeman told her the driver had permission to drive in the area.

Just before the motorcade appeared, Mary Ann Moorman and Mrs. Hill were standing on the lawn in the area between Main and Elm Streets opposite the main entrance of the Texas School Book Depository Building. Mrs. Moorman was taking photographs of the motorcade as it came into view and when the car occupied by President Kennedy was passing Mrs. Hill, she recalls shouting, "Hey!" She stated President Kennedy was looking down when she shouted, and when he turned to look

COMMISSION EXHIBIT No. 2582—Continued

at her a shot rang out and he slumped toward Mrs. Kennedy. Mrs. Hill heard more shots ring out and saw the hair on the back of President Kennedy's head fly up. She stated she thought Mrs. Kennedy cried out, "Oh, my God, he's been shot!" As the President fell forward in his seat Mrs. Hill knew he had been hit by a bullet. Mrs. Hill stated she heard from four to six shots in all and believes they came from a spot just west of the Texas School Book Depository Building. She thought there was a slight time interval between the first three shots and the remaining shots.

When the firing stopped, Mrs. Hill noticed that everyone in the vicinity seemed to be in a trance wondering what had happened. Mrs. Hill recalled it was then she noticed a white man wearing a brown raincoat and a hat running west away from the Texas School Book Depository Building in the direction of the railroad tracks. She said she does not know why but she started across the street in an effort "to see who he was." In so doing, she ran in front of the motorcycle escort following the President's car and was nearly hit by one of the policemen. Mrs. Hill said she lost the man from view when she looked down at what she first thought was a blood spot but later determined to be a red snow cone. She did not get a good look at this man, does not know who he was, and never saw him again. She thought the man was of average height and of heavy build.

Mrs. Hill then rejoined Mrs. Moorman where she had left her, and they started to leave the area. They were stopped by Mr. Featherstone, a Dallas newspaper man, who took them to the press room at the Dallas County Sheriff's Office.

Mrs. Hill stated she and Mary Ann Moorman were at the Sheriff's Office for about two hours and were questioned repeatedly by representatives of the press and various Federal and local law enforcement officers. She said the Sheriff's Office was a scene of extreme confusion and it was impossible to remember what questions were asked of her by the Secret Service Agents and Federal Bureau of Investigation Agents. She recalled that a man identifying himself as

either a Secret Service Agent or Federal Bureau of Investigation Agent asked her what she thought when a bullet hit near her feet raising the dust. Mrs. Hill told him she had no recollection of a bullet hitting near her feet. Mrs. Hill told the Agents she heard from four to six shots and heard one of the Agents make the remark, "There were three shots, three bullets, that's enough for now." She advised that at no time did any Federal Agent or other law enforcement officer attempt to tell her what she should say in regard to the number of shots fired or to force any other opinions upon her.

Mrs. Hill advised that about a month ago she received a long distance telephone call from Mark Lane, a New York attorney, who questioned her regarding the assassination of President Kennedy. Mrs. Hill stated that from reading some of Lane's statements regarding this conversation she determined that Lane had taken some of her remarks out of context, thus changing the meaning of her replies, had not used her full answers to some of the questions, and had misquoted her in this conversation. Mrs. Hill stated Lane asked her occupation and she replied she was a housewife. This point was pressed by Lane and Mrs. Hill told him she did some substitute teaching. Lane told her this was great because teachers made very good witnesses.

OFFICE OF THE DIRECTOR

UNITED STATES DEPARTMENT OF JUSTICE

FEDERAL BUREAU OF INVESTIGATION

WASHINGTON 25, D. C.

August 5, 1964

BY COURIER SERVICE

Honorable J. Lee Rankin
General Counsel
The President's Commission
200 Maryland Avenue, Northeast
Washington, D. C.

Dear Mr. Rankin:

Reference is made to your letter dated July 24, 1964, requesting the investigation of four allegations made since the assassination of President Kennedy.

Enclosed for your information are two copies of a self-explanatory communication from our Dallas Office dated July 29, 1964, containing the results of our investigation of the latter three allegations contained in your letter.

With regard to the first allegation set out in your letter, I would like to point out that this Bureau has been charged by Presidential Directive with the responsibility of coordinating the investigation of espionage, sabotage, subversive activities and related matters. Information developed along these lines is furnished to other Federal agencies within the Executive Branch of the U. S. Government and the armed forces. Any subversive information developed concerning a civilian employee of a contractor or subcontractor for the armed forces would be furnished to the interested military service. I would like to specifically point out that this Bureau does not disseminate internal security information to anyone outside the Executive Branch of the U. S. Government.

Sincerely yours,

J. Edgar Hoover

Enclosures (2)

COMMISSION EXHIBIT No. 2583

UNITED STATES DEPARTMENT OF JUSTICE

FEDERAL BUREAU OF INVESTIGATION

In Reply, Please Refer to
File No.

Dallas, Texas
July 29, 1964

LEE HARVEY OSWALD

The President's Commission, by letter dated July 24, 1964, requested investigation concerning the following allegations:

> Dallas Police Officer J. D. TIPPIT violated radio procedures in failing to notify his headquarters that he was stopping to question a suspect.
>
> Prior to the assassination, Dallas Police Officers searched other buildings in the vicinity of the Texas School Book Depository but not the Texas School Book Depository itself.
>
> Precautions taken by the Dallas Police Department on November 22, 1963, prior to the assassination included surveillance of many people, including some who did no more than speak in favor of school integration.

On July 28, 1964, JESSE E. CURRY, Chief of Police, Dallas Police Department, Dallas, Texas, advised there is no requirement or regulation of the Dallas Police Department that any police officer notify headquarters when such officer is stopping to question a suspect. He stated that if the officer is going to be away from his radio, he is required to check out with the radio dispatcher at the Dallas Police Department. He also stated that if an officer is alone and is stopping an automobile to question the occupant or occupants, the officer is required to contact the radio dispatcher at the

COMMISSION EXHIBIT No. 2583—Continued

Re: LEE HARVEY OSWALD

Dallas Police Department and give the model, the license number and the location of the automobile stopped. He stated Officer J. D. TIPPIT did not violate radio procedure in not notifying the radio dispatcher at the Dallas Police Department that he was stopping the then suspect LEE HARVEY OSWALD to question him.

Chief CURRY advised that prior to the assassination of President KENNEDY, the Dallas Police Department did not search any buildings in the vicinity of the Texas School Book Depository Building, the Texas School Book Depository Building itself, or any other buildings.

Chief CURRY advised that prior to President KENNEDY's visit to Dallas on November 22, 1963, he was advised of this proposed visit by Secret Service. Chief CURRY stated the Criminal Intelligence Division of the Dallas Police Department conducted a diligent investigation of organizations comprised of members whose political views are considered extreme, both right and left. He said the Dallas Police Department had infiltrated these organizations and had informant coverage regarding their activities. He said this investigation disclosed that only two of these organizations planned demonstrations during President KENNEDY's visit to Dallas. Chief CURRY advised that Chief of Police ANDY ANDERSON, Denton, Texas, notified the Dallas Police Department that the Young People's Republican Club at North Texas State University, Denton, Texas, planned to meet with General EDWIN WALKER's group and organize a demonstration somewhere along the route of President KENNEDY's motorcade in Dallas. Chief CURRY stated a representative of the Criminal Intelligence Division of the Dallas Police Department contacted the Young People's Republican Club at North Texas State University regarding the proposed demonstration and, as a result, the demonstration did not materialize. Further, CURRY stated, the Criminal Intelligence Division of the Dallas Police Department learned that General WALKER departed Dallas on November 21, 1963, en route to another state for a speaking engagement and his group did not make an appearance.

COMMISSION EXHIBIT No. 2583—Continued

Re: LEE HARVEY OSWALD

In addition, Chief CURRY stated, he was informed by Chief of Police ANDERSON, Denton, Texas, several weeks prior to President KENNEDY's visit of November 22, 1963, that NORMAN LEE ELKINS, 1115 West Crawford Street, Denison, Texas, had made comments that he intended to do something to embarrass President KENNEDY. He stated Detective H. M. HART and Lieutenant JACK REVILL of the Dallas Police Department, and JOE HOWLETT of Secret Service, contacted ELKINS and he advised he was not going to be in Dallas, Texas, on November 22, 1963.

Chief CURRY advised the Criminal Intelligence Division of the Dallas Police Department learned that the Indignant White Citizens Council had prepared some signs and placards which were designed to embarrass President KENNEDY. He stated the Indignant White Citizens Council planned to picket the Dallas Trade Mart and were the only demonstrators observed at the Dallas Trade Mart. CURRY advised that shortly after the assassination of President KENNEDY, six of these individuals were taken into custody by the Dallas Police Department to prevent their assault by spectators at the scene.

Chief CURRY stated the Dallas Police Department had no one under surveillance on November 22, 1963, as a precaution taken during President KENNEDY's visit to Dallas.

COMMISSION EXHIBIT No. 2583—Continued

1-E DIRECTOR

UNITED STATES DEPARTMENT OF JUSTICE

FEDERAL BUREAU OF INVESTIGATION

WASHINGTON, D.C. 20535

July 27, 1964

Honorable J. Lee Rankin
General Counsel
The President's Commission
200 Maryland Avenue, Northeast
Washington, D. C.

Dear Mr. Rankin:

I have received your letter of July 23, 1964. As you know, the Dallas Police Department lifted a latent impression off the underside of the gun barrel near the end of the foregrip of the rifle recovered on the sixth floor of the Texas School Book Depository Building. The Identification Division of the FBI determined this was a palm print which was identical with the right palm of Lee Harvey Oswald.

With respect to your specific question, no representative of this Bureau has made statements of any type to the press concerning the existence or nonexistence of this print.

Sincerely yours,

J. Edgar Hoover

COMMISSION EXHIBIT No. 2584

UNITED STATES DEPARTMENT OF JUSTICE

FEDERAL BUREAU OF INVESTIGATION

In Reply, Please Refer to
File No.

WASHINGTON 25, D.C.

June 3, 1964

"WHO KILLED KENNEDY?"
By Thomas G. Buchanan

CLAIMS AND RESULTS OF INVESTIGATION

1. CLAIM: The railway overpass toward which the President's motorcade was heading when the assassination shots were fired was left unguarded on November 22, 1963, "contrary to the most elementary security provisions." Page 81.

INVESTIGATION: Our inquiry shows that the railway overpass was guarded by a patrolman of the Dallas Police Department on November 22, 1963, at the time the President's motorcade approached that point. In addition, there were several individuals who were on the overpass at the time the President was killed. None of the above individuals has furnished any evidence that an assassin fired at the President from the overpass.

2. CLAIM: The doctors who attended President Kennedy at Parkland Memorial Hospital, Dallas, reportedly told reporters that the first shot struck the President in the throat from the front and that the second shot struck the right side of his head, apparently coming from behind the President's car. According to Buchanan, several weeks after the assassination doctors at Parkland Memorial Hospital, following a visit by Secret Service Agents showing them a document described as the autopsy report at Bethesda Naval Hospital, retracted their original statement concerning the nature of the throat wound. These doctors also stated that a new wound discovered at the autopsy had not been noticed in Dallas inasmuch as President Kennedy was lying on his back during efforts made to sustain his life and a back wound consequently would have been hidden from them. Pages 82-86.

INVESTIGATION: Doctors at Parkland Memorial Hospital did not retract previous statements made by them but did state that their efforts had been directed at keeping the President alive and not at performing an autopsy. The autopsy report prepared at

COMMISSION EXHIBIT No. 2585

the Bethesda Naval Hospital concludes that the throat wound was an exit-type wound and that all the bullets striking President Kennedy were fired from a point behind him.

3. CLAIM: Oswald was one of the worst shots in the Marines or for that matter in any other military service. Page 81.

INVESTIGATION: Buchanan himself has stated that Oswald was in the "sharpshooter" class in his shooting in the Marine Corps. In addition, Buchanan has admitted that the "sharpshooter" class is an intermediate class between "expert" on the top and "marksman" on the bottom.

4. CLAIM: The FBI denied reports that Oswald had been seen repeatedly driving a car into a Dallas rifle range for target practice. Page 91.

INVESTIGATION: The FBI has made no such public denial. However, our investigation has shown that Oswald was lacking in ability to drive a car.

5. CLAIM: The FBI in an off-the-record briefing denied that palmprints were found on the rifle associated with the assassination of President Kennedy. Page 93.

INVESTIGATION: The FBI made no such denial. As a matter of fact, the FBI Identification Division identified a latent impression taken by the Dallas Police Department from the barrel of the rifle as the right palmprint of Oswald. It is noted that Mark Lane, in the "National Guardian" of December 19, 1963, alleged that the FBI in off-the-record briefings had announced that "no palm prints were found on the rifle."

6. CLAIM: The paraffin test made of Oswald's hands and right cheek following his arrest by the Dallas Police Department showed a residue of gunpowder on his hands but none on his cheek. Therefore, according to Buchanan, the test proves that Oswald could not have fired a rifle inasmuch as the rifle would have deposited residue of gunpowder on his right cheek. Pages 93-96.

INVESTIGATION: The paraffin test has been found by the FBI Laboratory to be extremely unreliable and inconclusive as to whether or not a person has fired a weapon.

7. CLAIM: A photographer filmed the sixth-floor window of the Texas School Book Depository building at 12:30 the day of the assassination. This photograph shows two silhouettes in the stockroom and a clock on top of the building indicating the time as 12:30. Pages 96-97.

INVESTIGATION: Such a photograph is not known to the FBI. However, the FBI has a copy of a photographic print made from a movie film reportedly taken at the assassination scene. In the print an object appears in the window from which the assassination shots were fired. This photograph has been examined by the FBI Laboratory and the U.S. Navy Photographic Interpretation Center, Suitland, Maryland, and the conclusion was reached that the image seen in the window does not depict the form of a person or persons and is probably a stack of boxes later determined to have been in the room. No clock on top of the building appears in this photograph.

8. CLAIM: No employee who had access to the lunchroom at the Texas School Book Depository would have eaten his lunch on the sixth floor - "especially not Oswald, since it risked additional incrimination." However, an "outsider," hiding for a period of time prior to the assassination in the room on the sixth floor, would have required food. Pages 96-98.

INVESTIGATION: An employee of the Texas School Book Depository has advised that he ate lunch near the third double window on the southeast corner of the building on the sixth floor, sometime between 11:30 a.m. and 12 noon on November 22, 1963. The employee has stated that he left the remnants of his lunch, includ ng bones of fried chicken, near the window after he had finished eating. He has also stated that he left the sixth floor a few minutes after noon to join two fellow employees who were eating their lunch on the fifth floor of the building. He has stated that he did not see Oswald or anyone else at the windows on the south side of the building during the time he was on the sixth floor for lunch.

9. CLAIM: Oswald would have had to have been "the fastest runner since the great Olympic title holder, Jesse Owens," to have fired the assassination shots, hidden the rifle on the sixth floor, descended to the second floor lunchroom, and obtained a soft drink from a dispensing machine before the building superintendent, Roy S. Truly, and a Dallas policeman confronted Oswald at the second floor lunchroom. Pages 98-100.

INVESTIGATION: A survey was conducted by FBI Agents to determine the time taken by various routes and speeds to follow Oswald's actions immediately after the assassination shots. It is noted that the survey was conducted at a fast walk except in areas where an individual would have walked at a normal pace so as not to arouse suspicion. The survey showed that, walking from the window on the sixth floor via stairways, it would have taken Oswald about one minute and forty-five seconds to reach the front door of the Texas School Book Depository. The longest period of time to make the same journey, allowing 30 seconds in the lunchroom and involving the use of a passenger elevator for part of the descent to the second floor, was found to be three minutes and forty-nine seconds. It is noted that Truly has advised that he and the police officer arrived at the lunchroom on the second floor of the building in about two or three minutes after the assassination took place.

10. CLAIM: The assassin who fired at President Kennedy from the railway overpass fled the scene and left the murder weapon on that bridge behind him. Page 107.

INVESTIGATION: Our investigation has failed to develop any indication that a second rifle used in the assassination was found near the railway overpass and that a second assassin was involved in the killing of President Kennedy.

11. CLAIM: The name of the rifle used in the assassination appeared on the rifle. Page 108.

INVESTIGATION: Examination of the rifle used in the assassination does not reveal the name of the manufacturer of the weapon. However, it is noted that there is an inscription thereon that the rifle was made in Italy.

12. CLAIM: The Post Office Box in Dallas to which Oswald had the rifle mailed was kept under both his name and that of "A. Hidell." Page 111.

INVESTIGATION: Our investigation has revealed that Oswald did not indicate on his application that others, including an "A. Hidell," would receive mail through the box in question, which was Post Office Box 2915 in Dallas. This box was obtained by Oswald on October 9, 1962, and relinquished by him on May 14, 1963.

13. CLAIM: A detailed and "remarkably correct description" of Oswald was sent out over the police radio in Dallas at 12:36 p.m., November 22, 1963. Pages 114-116.

INVESTIGATION: The radio logs of the Dallas Police Department and the Dallas County Sheriff's Office show that no description of Oswald or any suspect in the assassination was broadcast at 12:36 p.m., November 22, 1963. Beginning at 12:43 p.m. and 12:49 p.m., respectively, and continuing until Oswald was taken into custody, the Dallas Police Department and the Dallas County Sheriff's Office broadcast descriptions of an unnamed suspect described as a slender white male, 30 years old, five feet ten inches tall, 155 or 165 pounds, who was possibly carrying a rifle. This suspect was reportedly seen running from the Texas School Book Depository after the assassination. A description of Oswald taken from background information and the autopsy report on him indicates he was 24 years old, five feet nine inches tall, weighed an estimated 150 pounds and had brown hair and blue-gray eyes. Although the descriptions broadcast approximated Oswald's height and weight, those descriptions were not accurate as to his age and lacked specific details regarding the colors of his hair and eyes. No broadcasts were made before Oswald's arrest that named Oswald as a suspect or gave a description of him. It is also noted that inquiry has shown that Oswald did not become a suspect until he was reported missing from the book building at approximately 12:50 p.m.

14. CLAIM: Police knew Oswald's boardinghouse address, 1026 North Beckley Street. The sources of his address were the records of the Texas School Book Depository, the "Red Squad" of the Dallas Police Department, and the FBI, which had been given that address by Mrs. Ruth Paine, with whom Oswald's wife was living at the time. Page 119.

INVESTIGATION: The records of the Texas School Book Depository did not show his address as 1026 North Beckley Street, but did contain Mrs. Paine's residence in Irving, Texas, as his address. The Dallas Police Department has denied that it had any record of Oswald prior to the time of the assassination. Also, Mrs. Paine had not advised the FBI of Oswald's boardinghouse address prior to the assassination.

15. CLAIM: Dallas Police Officer J. D. Tippit was not in favor with his superiors in the Dallas Police Department and had gone ten years without a promotion. Page 120.

INVESTIGATION: A copy of the Dallas Police Department file on Police Officer J. D. Tippit furnished by that Department has been reviewed by this Bureau. While the file shows that disciplinary action was taken against Tippit on several occasions, it contains no information that he was "out of favor." The file, however, shows that Tippit had received several commendations for his performance of duty both from civilian sources and from the Dallas Police Department. Superiors and associates have advised that he was an average officer who was well liked and was not overly ambitious. Several associates have stated that Tippit had taken promotional examinations but they had no information as to the results. A review of the file fails to disclose any reference to promotional examinations offered or taken by Tippit. While he was not promoted to a grade higher than patrolman, Tippit did receive so-called "service" raises in salary on a periodic basis.

16. CLAIM: Police Officer Tippit, Jack Ruby and Oswald all lived within a few blocks of each other. Page 121.

INVESTIGATION: A survey by the Dallas Office of this Bureau has indicated that by the most direct routes available, Tippit's residence was seven miles from Ruby's residence and from Oswald's boardinghouse and that the distance between Ruby's residence and Oswald's boardinghouse was one and three-tenths miles.

17. CLAIM: Jack Ruby and Dallas Police Officer Tippit were described by Ruby's sister, Mrs. Eva Grant, to reporters as "like two brothers." Page 121.

INVESTIGATION: Mrs. Grant has stated that at no time before or after the assassination has she made such a statement to any reporter or group of reporters. She has also advised that she would not make such a statement under any circumstances, since it would be completely untrue and without foundation.

18. CLAIM: There are standing orders for police in Dallas as in other cities that radio cars of the type Tippit was driving must have two policemen in them. Page 121.

INVESTIGATION: It is true that Tippit was alone in his police car; however, it has been determined from officials of the Dallas Police Department that their policy requires about 80 percent of the patrolmen working the day shift, 7 a.m. to 3 p.m., as Tippit was on the day of the assassination, to work alone and that Tippit was one of the patrolmen assigned to work alone on that day.

19. CLAIM: Tippit was violating another order not to drive out of the sector of the city to which he had been assigned. Tippit was meant to be in downtown Dallas at the time he intercepted Oswald, shortly after Oswald had left his boardinghouse at 1026 North Beckley Street. Page 122.

INVESTIGATION: A review of Tippit's file in the Dallas Police Department and the radio log of that Department does not show that Tippit should have been in downtown Dallas at the time he confronted Oswald. The radio log shows that at 12:54 p.m. he advised the police radio dispatcher he was in the Oak Cliff area and that he was told to remain available for any emergency coming in. The Dallas Police file on Tippit shows that Tippit was moved from his regular area to cover an area closer to the assassination scene.

20. CLAIM: There are witnesses - "anonymous, it seems" - who saw Oswald run into a vacant lot, eject the spent shells from his revolver after shooting, and reload that revolver. Page 126.

INVESTIGATION: Our inquiry has developed witnesses and these witnesses, not anonymous as claimed by Buchanan, have advised that they saw Oswald apparently trying to unload his revolver near the location where Tippit was shot.

21. CLAIM: Oswald was arrested in the Texas Theater at 1:36 p.m. on November 22, 1963. Page 126.

INVESTIGATION: The radio log of the Dallas Police Department shows that Oswald was reported in the Texas Theater at 1:45 p.m., by a squad car. The same radio log shows that shortly after 1:51 p.m., the radio dispatcher received a report of the arrest of Oswald. The radio log of the Dallas County Sheriff's Office shows that at 1:53 p.m., the report was given that Oswald had been taken into custody.

22. CLAIM: The Dallas Police officers who arrested Oswald "beat him up" after they had disarmed him. Page 126.

INVESTIGATION: A Special Agent of this Bureau on the scene at the time of the arrest of Oswald has advised that Oswald was not mistreated and that no force was used to subdue him other than that necessary to overcome his armed resistance.

23. CLAIM: Oswald was first questioned "exclusively about the Tippit murder." Police, as long as they were able to maintain the prisoner in isolation, permitted him to think that he was just a suspect in that murder. Page 127.

INVESTIGATION: Special Agents of this Bureau were present during the early hours of questioning of Oswald at Dallas Police Headquarters, at which time Oswald vigorously denied having shot President Kennedy and Tippit.

24. CLAIM: Oswald insisted on his right to see a lawyer, making this demand before reporters, yet for two days of "persistent questioning" this right was "relentlessly denied him." Page 127.

INVESTIGATION: Oswald was advised following his arrest of his right to counsel by both a Dallas police officer and by FBI Agents present during the early interrogation of Oswald. Oswald, when arraigned at about 7 p.m., November 22, 1963, was advised by Justice of the Peace David Johnston of his right to an attorney's services. Late that night representatives of the Dallas Civil Liberties Union went to the Dallas Police Department and later departed satisfied that Oswald had been advised of this right. There is no indication Oswald made any attempt to contact an attorney on November 22, 1963. Again on November 23, 1963, Oswald was advised by a Dallas police official of his right to have an attorney. At that time Oswald indicated he wished to call attorney John J. Abt of New York City. He was taken from his ceil on three separate occasions on that date to place collect calls via public telephones in the Dallas Police Headquarters, but on each occasion he was unable to make contact with Abt in New York City. Abt is an attorney who has represented the Communist Party, USA, in its litigation on several occasions with the Government of the U. S.

25. CLAIM: The Texas School Book Depository is owned and operated by the city government of Dallas and, therefore, Oswald was a municipal employee. Pages 131, 143, 151 and 155.

INVESTIGATION: The Texas School Book Depository is not a government agency of any municipality, county, state or Federal jurisdiction. It is a private concern which receives and distributes books to its various customers, including educational institutions. Therefore, Oswald, in his employment at the Texas School Book Depository, was not a municipal employee.

26. CLAIM: Among the papers found on Oswald by the Dallas Police Department was the name of Joseph Hosty of the Dallas Office of the FBI. In addition, information on papers found on Oswald recorded Hosty's home telephone number, office telephone number and car license number. This information appeared in the "Houston Post" and the source was reported to be Assistant District Attorney William Alexander. Page 149.

INVESTIGATION: The Hosty referred to by Buchanan is undoubtedly Special Agent James P. Hosty, Jr., of our Dallas Office. Oswald's address directory, which was found by the Dallas Police Department in Oswald's boardinghouse room, did not contain Special Agent Hosty's home telephone number. The directory did contain, however, his correct name, the telephone number and street address of the Dallas FBI Office, and the entry "MU 8605" or "MV 8605." Special Agent Hosty gave his name and the Dallas Office telephone number and street address to Mrs. Ruth Paine in contacting her on November 1, 1963, regarding Oswald's residence. Mrs. Paine has stated that she gave that data to Oswald. Marina Oswald has stated that she recorded Special Agent Hosty's license number on an occasion when he was at the Paine residence and gave it to Oswald. The 1962 license number of the automobile assigned to Special Agent Hosty on November 1, 1963, was MU 8605.

27. CLAIM: The"Philadelphia Inquirer" of December 8, 1963, contained an article stating that Hosty had seen Oswald shortly after he had left New Orleans in September, 1963. Page 149.

INVESTIGATION: Special Agent Hosty has furnished an affidavit stating that at no time prior to the assassination of President Kennedy had he ever seen or talked to Oswald. In addition, Hosty stated that he had never made any attempt to develop him as an informant or source of information.

28. CLAIM: Oswald was a double agent. Page 149.

INVESTIGATION: The Director of the FBI, John Edgar Hoover, has furnished the Commission with an affidavit categorically denying that Oswald was ever an informant of the FBI, was ever assigned a symbol number in that capacity, and was ever paid any amount of money by the FBI in any regard. It is noted that the Central Intelligence Agency has denied that Oswald was ever associated with it in any capacity.

29. CLAIM: The Walter-McCarran Act specifically calls for anyone who has attempted to renounce his U.S. citizenship to file an affidavit stating why he believes he should receive a U.S. passport. Page 151.

"WHO KILLED KENNEDY?"

INVESTIGATION: The Internal Security Act of 1950 (Walter-McCarran Act) contains no reference to an affidavit required by a U.S. citizen who has attempted to expatriate himself.

30. CLAIM: It appears that the FBI knew Oswald possessed the alleged assassination rifle prior to the assassination of President Kennedy because it would seem unlikely that within one day the FBI could trace the rifle as coming from a mail order house in Chicago. Page 153.

INVESTIGATION: The FBI had no knowledge that Oswald possessed the assassination rifle prior to the assassination of President Kennedy. The tracing of the rifle purchased by Oswald under an assumed name from the mail order house in Chicago was completed by the FBI on November 23, 1963, regardless of Buchanan's claim.

31. CLAIM: Oswald's rifle was not taken away from him even though on April 10, 1963, there was good reason to suspect he had already used it to attempt to kill General Edwin A. Walker. Page 153.

INVESTIGATION: The FBI did not investigate the attempted assassination of General Walker on April 10, 1963, and had no reason to regard Oswald as a suspect in that attempted murder until December 3, 1963, when Marina Oswald furnished information that Oswald had, on the night in question, attempted to kill General Walker. The Dallas Police Department has also indicated that it had no record of Oswald prior to the assassination and had never developed or considered Oswald as a suspect in the attempted shooting of General Walker.

32. CLAIM: It can be inferred from the fact that General Walker's name and telephone number were in Oswald's notebook that Oswald and General Walker were known to each other. Page 154.

INVESTIGATION: Our investigation has developed no indication that Oswald and General Walker were known to each other. General Walker has been publicly quoted as saying he did not know anything about Oswald until Oswald was arrested for the assassination of the President.

COMMISSION EXHIBIT No. 2585—Continued

17/smn
22 MAY 1958

FIFTH ENDORSEMENT on 1stLt MILLER's ltr JRM/rdd A17-6 of 31Mar58

From: Commanding General, Fleet Marine Force, Pacific
To: Judge Advocate General, Navy Department, Washington 25, D. C.

Subj: Investigation into the circumstances surrounding the death of Private Martin D. SCHRAND 1639694/6711 USMC at about 1900 hours on 5 January 1958

1. Forwarded.

Reviewed
AJK

2. The proceedings, findings, opinions and recommendations of the investigation, as approved by the convening and reviewing authorities, are approved.

OLIN W. JONES
By direction

JUN 1958
RECEIVED
OFFICE OF JUDGE ADVOCATE GENERAL
LAW

5 Jan 58
gunshot wound

Bnd #
5919-58

2

COMMISSION EXHIBIT No. 2586

FF13-5
7:arc
A17-6
15 MAY 1958

FOURTH ENDORSEMENT on 1stLt MILLER's ltr JRM/rdd A17-6 of 31Mar58

From: Commanding General, Aircraft, Fleet Marine Force, Pacific
To: Judge Advocate General, Navy Department, Washington 25, D.C.
Via: Commanding General, Fleet Marine Force, Pacific

Subj: Investigation into the circumstances surrounding the death of Private Martin D. SCHRAND 1639694/6711 USMC at about 1900 hours on 5 January 1958

1. Forwarded.

2. The proceedings, findings of fact, opinions and recommendations of the investigating officer and the action of the appointing and reviewing authorities thereon are approved.

CLAYTON C. JEROME

3

COMMISSION EXHIBIT No. 2586—Continued

257/drf
A17-6

THIRD ENDORSEMENT on 1STLT MILLER's ltr JRM/rdd A17-6 of 31 Mar 1958

From: Commanding General, 1st Marine Aircraft Wing, Aircraft, FMF, Pacific
To: Judge Advocate General of the Navy
Via: (1) Commanding General, Aircraft, Fleet Marine Force, Pacific
(2) Commanding General, Fleet Marine Force, Pacific

Subj: Investigation into the circumstances surrounding the death of Private Martin D. SCHRAND 1639694/6711 USMC at about 1900 hours on 5 January 1958

1. Forwarded.

2. The proceedings, findings of fact, opinions, and recommendations are approved.

C. H. HAYES

4

COMMISSION EXHIBIT No. 2586—Continued

LEG:WWC:err
A17-6/2
APR 15 1958

SECOND ENDORSEMENT on 1stLt MILLER's ltr JRM/rdd A17-6 of 31 March 1958

From: Commanding Officer, Marine Aircraft Group 11
To: Judge Advocate General, Navy Department, Washington 25, D. C.
Via: (1) Commanding General, First Marine Aircraft Wing
(2) Commanding General, Aircraft, Fleet Marine Force, Pacific
(3) Commanding General, Fleet Marine Force, Pacific

Subj: SCHRAND, Martin D., Private, 1639694/6711 USMC, Investigation Report of death of

1. Forwarded.

2. The findings are approved, and opinions and recommendations concurred in.

J. L. MUELLER

5

COMMISSION EXHIBIT No. 2586—Continued

FIRST ENDORSEMENT on 1stLt. MILLER's ltr JRM/rdd A17-6 of 31 March 1958

From: Commanding Officer, Marine Air Control Squadron 1
To: Judge Advocate General, Navy Department, Washington 25, D. C.
Via: (1) Commanding Officer, Marine Aircraft Group 11
(2) Commanding General, First Marine Aircraft Wing
(3) Commanding General, Aircraft Fleet Marine Force Pacific
(4) Commanding General, Fleet Marine Force Pacific

Subj: SCHRAND, Martin D., Private, 1639694/6711 USMC, Investigation report of death of

1. Forwarded.

2. The finding of facts and opinions are concurred in. Death of subject man was not the result of misconduct and was in line of duty.

3. Reference (b) of the basic letter returned the original Report of Investigation submitted 18 January to MACS-1 for further inquiry.

N. D. GLENN

Copy to:
H&HS, MWHG, 1stMAW
COMNAVPHIL
NAS Cubi Pt
FASRON 113

6

COMMISSION EXHIBIT No. 2586—Continued

MARINE AIR CONTROL SQUADRON 1
MARINE AIRCRAFT GROUP 11
1ST MARINE AIRCRAFT WING, AIRCRAFT, FMF, PACIFIC
C/O FLEET POST OFFICE, SAN FRANCISCO, CALIFORNIA

JRM/rdd
A17-6
31 Mar 1958

From: First Lieutenant James R. MILLER 066552/7302 USMCR
To: Commanding Officer, Marine Air Control Squadron 1

Subj: Investigation into the circumstances surrounding the death of Private MARTIN D. SCHRAND 1639694/6711 USMC at about 1900 hours on 5 January 1958

Ref: (a) Chapter II, III, IV, and V, 1955 Naval Supplement to the Manual for Courts-Martial, 1951
(b) Letter from Staff Legal Officer to CO, MAG-11 196/ty A17-5/1 of 30 January 1958

Encl: (1) CO, MACS-1 appointing order of 6 January 1958
(2) Statement of LCDR C. D. WALBRIDGE USN
(3) Statement of 1stLt. H. B. CHERRIE II USMCR SDO MACS-1
(4) Statement of Cpl R. L. ROWE USMC Cpl. of the Guard
(5) Statement of HM3 R. A. HOLT USN
(6) Copy Certificate of Death
(7) Statement of W2 F. H. MATTIESEN USN
(8) Photographs taken at scene of shooting
(9) Statement of Sergeant H. R. GODFREY 1453334/1371 USMC (Sgt. of the Guard)
(10) Statement of the Medical Officer of the Day, Station Hospital, Navy #3002

1. Preliminary Statement.

a. In accordance with enclosure (1), and in accordance with reference (a), an investigation was started on 6 January 1958 to inquire into the facts and circumstances surrounding the death of Private Martin D. SCHRAND.

b. The investigation was conducted in the following manner:

(1) The interviewing and/or procuring of written statements from available witnesses and such other persons whose testimony appeared to yield information as to the death or related events.

(2) The interviewing and/or procuring of written statements from organizations involved after the death.

c. No persons were designated as interested parties to the investigation.

d. In accordance with reference (b) this investigation was received by MACS-1 in the field on the island of Corregidor, P. I. on or about 13 February 1958.

e. Due to the frequent redeployment of this unit in the field prior to and during Operation STRONGBACK, the clerical processes and correspondence with this investigation having been slow and of limited availability resulted in unavoidable delay in the collection of evidence, drafting and submission of the report.

2. Finding of Fact.

a. That on or about 1900 hours on 5 January 1958 in the area of the carrier pier, Naval Air Station, Cubi, Point, Philippine Islands, Private Martin D. SCHRAND 1639694/6711 USMC was fatally wounded with a discharge from a riot-type shotgun, under the circumstances listed below.

b. At the above time and place the sentry on post at the crypto van, a Private First Class PERSONS, heard a shot from the area containing the parked motor vehicles and informed the Squadron Duty Officer 2ndLt. Hubert B. CHERRIE II USMCR and the Corporal of the Guard, Corporal Ronald L. ROWE USMC, by whom he had been inspected a minute or so before, in their inspection of the Area and Guard. (Encl 3&4).

c. Upon checking, the SDO and Cpl. of the Guard discovered Pvt. SCHRAND lying on his back in a manner similar to the Photograph (Encl 8) except the weapon was underneath him. Pvt. SCHRAND was lying in a pool of blood and wounded as set forth in (Encl 6).

d. The SDO notified Sick Bay from a telephone in the Crash Crew area and returned to the scene. (Encl 3)

e. At 1920 an ambulance driven by Robert A. HOLT, HM3 USN arrived at the scene and removed Pvt. SCHRAND to the Station Hospital. (Encl 5)

f. Death occured between 1920 and 1930 hours in the ambulence (Encl 5&6).

g. It is medical opinion of the Medical Officer of the Day that Pvt. SCHRAND was beyond aid from the moment of the shooting. (Encl 10) By interview of all persons involved, the investigator established that no definite form of first aid was applied due to the extreme nature of the wound.

h. Pvt. SCHRAND had been fully instructed in his duties and the Model 12 riot gun, having been on guard duty and attended guard school for at least two days previous. (Encl 4)

8

i. The MACS-1 guard was operating under verbal appointments at this time having recently debarked from an LST. There was no guard book or log that this investigation could find (Encl 4).

j. It was and is an established squadron policy that sentries on post carry their weapons with chambers empty, the safety on, and five (5) rounds in the cylinder. Under no circumstances were rounds to be injected unto the chamber unless the weapon was to be fired or under supervised instruction. In the interests of safety, permission had been extended for some sentries to carry the rounds in their pocket. (Encl 9)

k. The weapon at the scene was a Winchester Model 12 riot type shotgun No 982244 containing one spent round. This weapon does not have a sling and is illustrated in Encl (8).

l. Under extensive examination by Fred H. MATTHIESEN CHAVORD Tech W2 USN no discrepency in the weapon was revealed. (Encl 7).

m. There was no evidence discovered of criminal activity in this case. There was no evidence discovered of suicide. (Encl 2)

3. Opinions.

a. In the absence of any evidence of gross neglegence or intended self-inflection it is my opinion that Private Martin D. SCHRAND 1639694/6711 USMC died in the line of duty and not as a result of his own misconduct.

b. Pvt. SCHRAND was completely familiar with his duties and with the operation of the Model 12 riot type shotgun, and was in sound physical condition.

c. The wound was inflicted by the Winchester Model 12 riot type shotgun No. 982244 found at the scene.

d. The discharge of the riot gun was not due to malfunction.

e. Attempts to reconstruct the act of the shooting resulted in no opinion being formed as to the manner in which the weapon was fired.

f. No definite form of first aid treatment could have been employed nor was by the people present due to the nature of the wound.

4. Recommendation.

a. That continuing emphasis be exerted to acquaint all personnel with the instructions for standing guard duty and in handling the Model 12 riot gun.

COMMISSION EXHIBIT No. 2586—Continued

b. While it had no effect on the death occurring in this case knowledge of the location of accessible telephones in the Guard area should be had by all persons concerned. (Encl 3)

c. That proper guard log and records be kept whenever possibile by the Sgt. and Cpl. of the Guard.

James R. Miller
JAMES R. MILLER
1stLt. USMCR

COMMISSION EXHIBIT No. 2586—Continued

MARINE AIR CONTROL SQUADRON 1
MARINE AIRCRAFT GROUP 11
1ST MARINE AIRCRAFT WING, AIRCRAFT, FMF, PACIFIC
C/O FLEET POST OFFICE, SAN FRANCISCO, CALIFORNIA

NCW/gjw
[illegible]
6 Jan 1958

From: Commanding Officer
To: First Lieutenant James R. MILLER 066552/7302 USMCR

Subj: Investigation to inquire into the circumstances surrounding the death of Private Martin D. SCHRAND 1639694/6711 USMC at about 1900 hours on 5 January 1957.

Ref: (a) Chapter II, III, IV, and V, 1955 Naval Supplement to the Manual for Courts-Martials, 1951

1. You are hereby appointed as investigating officer to inquire into the facts and circumstances surrounding the death of Private Martin D. SCHRAND 1639694/6711 USMC at 1900 on 5 January 1958 on board the U.S. Naval Air Station, Cubi Point, Philippines.

2. You will make a thorough investigation into all of the circumstances connected with his death. You will include in your report findings of fact and opinions as to the causes and responsibility for the death, including any recommended action.

3. If at any time during the investigation there is any suggestion that misconduct on the part of any personnel is involved in the accident, you are further directed to notify subject personnel of the time and place of the meeting of the investigation and that he will be a party to the investigation, and accorded his rights as such pursuant to the Naval Supplement to the Manual for Courts-Martial. As to the duty of the investigating officer to designate individuals as parties to the investigation during the proceedings when appropriate, attention is particularly invited to Section 0304, Naval Supplement to the Manual for Courts-Martial.

N. C. Wiley
N. C. WILEY
Acting

ENCLOSURE (1)

ORIGINAL ORDERS

COMMISSION EXHIBIT No. 2586—Continued

U. S. NAVAL AIR STATION
CUBI POINT, PHILIPPINES

NA/09:tnw
A17-6

9 January 1958

From: Security Officer
To: Commanding Officer, MACS-1

Subj: Statement of LCDR C. B. WALDRIDGE, USN, 351009/1300, Security Officer, U. S. Naval Air Station, Cubi Point, concerning the incident occurring on 5 January 1958 involving SCHRAND, Martin E., 1639694, Private, U. S. Marine Corps

1. This statement incorporates entries from the Naval Air Station, Cubi Point Security Department Log and opinions derived from the investigation conducted by the Security Officer and the Criminal Investigator of the Naval Air Station, Cubi Point.

2. The incident was reported to the Naval Air Station Security Patrol office at 1940H, 5 January 1958, by Mr. Edmund L. CARBONEAU, Crash Fire Captain, Naval Air Station, Cubi Point Operations Department. The incident reported was the shooting of a Marine sentry on the west perimeter of the carrier aircraft parking area aboard the Naval Air Station, Cubi Point. The identity of the victim was established as SCHRAND, Martin T., 1639694, Pvt, USMC by his identification card removed from the body and by the Corporal of the Guard of MACS-1 on duty at the time of the occurrence of the incident. At 2005H, the victim was removed from the scene to the Cubi Ridge Naval Hospital via Navy ambulance. The victim was pronounced dead on arrival by the Medical Officer of the Day.

3. The Naval Air Station Security Officer was notified at 1943H and, accompanied by the Criminal Investigator, Mr. Kenneth V. DAVIS, arrived at the scene of the shooting at 2016H. Photographs of the surrounding scene and of a mock-up of the victim's body were made. The Corporal of the Guard was used to represent the victim since he was the first individual on the scene.

4. The Naval Air Station Security Officer and his Criminal Investigator conducted an onsight investigation to determine if another person or persons were involved in the incident. The initial inspection of the area was conducted during hours of darkness; therefore, the area was placed under security guard and re-inspected the following morning after sunrise. This second investigation disclosed beyond doubt that no other person or persons were involved in the incident. This being the case, the Naval Air Station Security Officer released all information, personal belongings of the victim, and the weapon to the Commanding Officer, MACS-1, so that he might conduct his investigation. This delay

ENCLOSURE (2)

COMMISSION EXHIBIT No. 2586—Continued

MA/09:tnw
A17-6
9 January 1958

was considered proper and necessary so as to absolve the Naval Air Station Cubi Point and the local authorities of any connection with the incident.

5. Inspection of the weapon involved in the incident and viewing of the body of the victim at the Cubi Ridge Naval Hospital prompts the Security Officer to make the following statements of opinion:

a. The weapon involved was in good and satisfactory operating condition. One round of ammunition was located in the chamber of the gun and was in the battery position. The trigger guard safety device was NOT on "safe".

b. Discharge of the weapon took place within eight inches of the left armpit.

c. The trajectory of the charge from underneath the left armpit, the path through the body of the schrapnel, and the exit of the schrapnel, at the top of the shoulder blade, leads the investigator to believe that suicide was not committed by the victim. This reasoning is offered by some of these factors:

(1) The length of the barrel of the weapon from its point to the trigger guard was twenty=seven and one-half inches. (27½")

(2) The man's arm measurement from armpit to the heel of either arm was twenty-two and three-quarters inches. (22 3/4")

(3) The man had heavy field shoes on.

Under the above conditions, to have fired the weapon and caused the charge to enter and leave the body, it would have been necessary to use a foreign object to discharge the weapon. No such object was found in the area. Pathologically, suicide victims will either discharge the weapon in the head, through the mouth, or in the heart. No such vital position was penetrated. Nothing in the man's personal property on his body at the time of the incident indicated that he might be in a depressed frame of mind. The man had on his person twenty-eight dollars and thirty-five cents ($28.35) in MPCs.

6. Statements of the victim's friends indicated to the investigator that the victim was not prone to exercise his weapon as a drill piece. It is felt that this accident may have been caused by using the riot gun to conduct Manual of Arms evolutions, and, in so doing, the gun was accidentally discharged causing the victim's death.

7. No further investigation is anticipated by the Security Department but its services and facilities will be made available at your request.

C. B. WALBRIDGE

COMMISSION EXHIBIT No. 2586—Continued

UNITED STATES DEPARTMENT OF JUSTICE
FEDERAL BUREAU OF INVESTIGATION

In Reply, Please Refer to
File No.

Dallas, Texas
July 9, 1964

LEE HARVEY OSWALD

By letter dated June 30, 1964, the President's Commission called attention to page 269 of the report of Special Agent ROBERT P. GEMBERLING dated March 10, 1964, at Dallas, Texas, which sets forth the details of an interview with WARREN REYNOLDS, who has been the subject of a newspaper article written by BOB CONSIDINE.

The President's Commission pointed out that in this interview of REYNOLDS, he states that General EDWIN A. WALKER attempted to contact him and that in the event such contact was made, REYNOLDS would report the results of such contact to the Federal Bureau of Investigation.

The President's Commission letter requested that REYNOLDS be interviewed to determine whether General WALKER has been in touch with REYNOLDS and, if so, the nature of any conversations or communications between REYNOLDS and WALKER.

On July 7, 1964, WARREN A. REYNOLDS, 8707 Mosswood, Dallas, Texas, telephone EVergreen 8-1314, was telephonically contacted at his residence for the purpose of making an appointment for interview. REYNOLDS stated he was not feeling too well and suggested that he be interviewed at that time over the telephone.

REYNOLDS was asked if he had had any recent contact with General EDWIN A. WALKER. REYNOLDS informed he was contacted telephonically by General WALKER on March 2, 1964, and at that time WALKER read an article to him from some newspaper, which article had been written by BOB CONSIDINE, a reporter,

COMMISSION EXHIBIT No. 2587

Re: LEE HARVEY OSWALD

and which stated, in substance, that it was unusual that REYNOLDS had been shot because he had "fingered" OSWALD. REYNOLDS stated that actually he did not "finger" OSWALD. He stated that on January 23, 1964, he was shot in the head by a bullet from a .22 caliber rifle in the basement of the Reynolds Motor Company, 500 East Jefferson Boulevard, Dallas, Texas, where he had gone to turn out the lights at the close of business.

Following this telephone call by General WALKER, REYNOLDS stated he went to the residence of General WALKER in Dallas, Texas, and discussed the newspaper article written by BOB CONSIDINE with General WALKER. He stated he and General WALKER believed that, although the article was "fiction-like," it was nevertheless true. REYNOLDS stated both he and General WALKER believe that the shooting of REYNOLDS has some relation to the part REYNOLDS played in the apprehension of LEE HARVEY OSWALD. REYNOLDS stated they concluded this because the prime suspect picked up by the Dallas Police Department for the shooting of REYNOLDS was DARRELL WAYNE GARNER, also known as "DAGO." REYNOLDS stated that "DAGO" is the bragging type of person. He stated further that after "DAGO" was picked up by the Dallas Police Department he was released after he, "DAGO," and three other individuals had been afforded a polygraph examination by the Dallas Police Department and were judged to be telling the truth. REYNOLDS said that, since he has no enemies he knows of and since "DAGO" was released by the Dallas Police Department, he can only reason that he was shot because of the part he played in the apprehension of LEE HARVEY OSWALD. REYNOLDS stated he has no other reason other than the above for reaching this conclusion. He said it was during this March 1964, visit at General WALKER's house that General WALKER agreed with him.

REYNOLDS advised that approximately two weeks ago he telephonically contacted General EDWIN A. WALKER and requested an appointment to see WALKER, which was granted. REYNOLDS said he sought this interview with WALKER because he had been "scared" as a result of having been shot through the head after the

COMMISSION EXHIBIT No. 2587—Continued

Re: LEE HARVEY OSWALD

assassination of President KENNEDY, which shooting he states he feels is connected with the fact that he had witnessed LEE HARVEY OSWALD running with a gun from the scene of the shooting of Dallas Police Officer J. D. TIPPIT. REYNOLDS said he wanted General WALKER's advice as to what he should do.

REYNOLDS advised that on June 24, 1964, he went to the residence of General WALKER in Dallas, Texas, and discussed the above with him. He said that, following his discussions with General WALKER, General WALKER prepared a telegram addressed to the President's Commission, Washington, D. C., and sent it with his permission. He read the telegram which General WALKER sent and it is as follows:

> "Testimony of WARREN REYNOLDS, victim of attempted assassination by a shot in the temple, cannot be ignored in a complete investigation. I respectfully request his appearance before your Commission.
>
> "/s/ General EDWIN A. WALKER"

REYNOLDS stated he has only seen General WALKER on two occasions as set out above.

REYNOLDS stated that in March 1964, his daughter, TERRI, aged 9, at that time, informed him that on her way home a man stopped his automobile and offered her money to get in the car with him. REYNOLDS said his daughter ran away and volunteered that she is not the type of child that would make up a story. He said this also has made him apprehensive and feels that the troubles he has had since the assassination of President KENNEDY are in some way connected to the part he played in the apprehension of LEE HARVEY OSWALD. He said he has no actual facts to substantiate his beliefs, but has made his beliefs known to the Dallas Police Department.

REYNOLDS was advised that in the event he felt his life was in danger he should make any information of this nature available to the Dallas Police Department.

COMMISSION EXHIBIT No. 2587—Continued

Re: <u>LEE HARVEY OSWALD</u>

On July 7, 1964, WARREN A. REYNOLDS, 8707 Mosswood, Dallas, Texas, telephone EVergreen 8-1314, telephonically contacted the Dallas Office of the Federal Bureau of Investigation and spoke with a Special Agent.

REYNOLDS stated that since his interview earlier that day he had been wondering if there was some reason he should not contact General EDWIN A. WALKER. He also inquired if there was anything wrong with someone contacting General WALKER.

REYNOLDS was informed it was not the function of the Federal Bureau of Investigation to advise anyone whom they could or could not contact. He was also informed that no comment would be made as to whether there was or was not anything wrong with a person contacting General EDWIN A. WALKER.

On July 8, 1964, WARREN A. REYNOLDS, 8707 Mosswood, Dallas, Texas, telephone EVergreen 8-1314, telephonically contacted the Dallas Office of the Federal Bureau of Investigation and spoke with a Special Agent.

REYNOLDS stated he was calling to inquire if this office had any information that he was going to be called to appear before the President's Commission in Washington, D. C.

REYNOLDS was informed that this office had no information that he was going to be called by the President's Commission. He was also informed the President's Commission functions on its own and that this office had no information as to whom they would or would not call.

REYNOLDS then asked if it would be all right for him to make plans or if he should wait for a call from the President's Commission.

REYNOLDS was informed that, as mentioned above, this office does not know whom the President's Commission is going to call or not call, and he should use his own judgment on any future plans.

- 4 -

COMMISSION EXHIBIT No. 2587—Continued

FD-302 (Rev. 3-3-59) FEDERAL BUREAU OF Commission Exhibit No. 2588

Date 6/15/64

1

Mr. WARREN A. REYNOLDS, 8707 Mosswood, telephone Evergreen 8-1314, who operates the Reynolds Motor Company, 500 East Jefferson Boulevard, telephone WH. 2-9422, personally appeared at the Dallas Office of the Federal Bureau of Investigation.

Mr. REYNOLDS advised that he is scared as a result of his having been shot through the head after the assassination of President KENNEDY which shooting, he states, he feels is connected with the fact that he had witnessed LEE HARVEY OSWALD running with a gun from the scene of the shooting of Dallas Police Officer J. D. TIPPIT.

Mr. REYNOLDS stated he has no actual facts to substantiate his feelings in this regard and has made his feelings known to the Forgery Bureau of the Dallas Police Department, who he stated investigated the shooting.

Mr. REYNOLDS was advised that, in the event he received any information to substantiate his beliefs, he should immediately advise the Dallas Office of the FBI. He was further advised that, in the event he felt his life was in danger, he should make any information of this nature available to the Dallas Police Department. He was further advised that the FBI did not have jurisdiction with respect to investigating his shooting.

168

on 6/15/64 at Dallas, Texas File # DL 100-10461

by Special Agent ROBERT P. GEMBERLING/eah Date dictated 6/15/64

COMMISSION EXHIBIT No. 2588

3.

UNITED STATES DEPARTMENT OF JUSTICE
FEDERAL BUREAU OF INVESTIGATION

Other Individuals and Organizations Involved of Interest

Tippit, J. D. 2

In Reply, Please Refer to
File No.

Dallas, Texas
March 23, 1964

ASSASSINATION OF PRESIDENT JOHN
FITZGERALD KENNEDY, NOVEMBER 22,
1963, DALLAS, TEXAS

WARREN A. REYNOLDS, Johnny Reynolds Motor Company, 500 East Jefferson Street, Dallas, Texas, was a witness to the flight of the murderer of Dallas Police Officer J. D. TIPPIT on November 22, 1963. On January 23, 1964, WARREN A. REYNOLDS was shot in the head by a bullet from a .22 caliber rifle and the prime suspect was DARRELL WAYNE GARNER.

On February 23, 1964, there appeared in the "New York Journal-American" an article by Mr. BOB CONSIDINE which indicated that GARNER had been released based in part on the testimony of BETTY (MOONEY) MAC DONALD, who had allegedly worked as a stripper at the Carousel Club and that MAC DONALD subsequently hung herself.

On March 17, 1964, Captain O. A. JONES, Forgery Bureau, Dallas Police Department, furnished the following information from the results of the investigation by the Dallas Police Department into the shooting of WARREN A. REYNOLDS:

On January 23, 1964, at approximately 9:15 P.M., WARREN A. REYNOLDS, employee, Johnny Reynolds Motor Company, 500 East Jefferson, Dallas, Texas, after pulling the keys out of all the cars and locking them, walked down to the office basement to turn out all the lights. He flipped the light switch at the door of the basement; however, the basement remained dark. Thinking the light was burned out, he proceeded downstairs to the basement fuse box and, as he reached for the fuse box, was shot in the head with a .22 caliber weapon.

COMMISSION EXHIBIT No. 2589

Re: ASSASSINATION OF PRESIDENT JOHN
FITZGERALD KENNEDY, NOVEMBER 22,
1963, DALLAS, TEXAS

REYNOLDS, not knowing if he had received an electrical shock or had been shot, started up the stairway. At this point an unknown, small white male carrying a rifle raced past him on the stairs.

REYNOLDS proceeded out of the building, fell over the hood of a vehicle near the office door, then entered the office, tried to use the telephone, and fell over on a couch.

SONNY CARTY, 425 East Jefferson, Room 5, was watching television when he heard a shot coming from the direction of the Reynolds Motor Company. He ran down the hall to the balcony and observed in the bright light of the motor company car lot a white male, 5'5", wearing brown khaki trousers, a blue flowered shirt, carrying a rifle, run out the rear of the car lot and then south in the 200 block of South Patton.

CARTY then saw REYNOLDS staggering up to the office and then observed a white compact car, believed to be a Valiant, containing two men and a woman in the front seat in front of the car lot. CARTY raced down the hall and down the stairs, by which time the vehicle was gone. He ran over to assist REYNOLDS, who advised CARTY he did not know what had happened.

Mrs. CHRISTENE JEFFERIES, Apartment 101, 429 East 12th, advised she had just walked out to her car parked on Patton and she observed a small male, race unknown, about 5'6", running down the street towards her from the direction of the Reynolds Motor Company car lot waving a rifle. The man ran down an alley and disappeared from her sight.

Investigating police officers located REYNOLDS' broken glasses and a .22 rifle bullet on the floor of the Reynolds Motor Company basement and a blood trail leading over the route traveled by REYNOLDS to the couch. Also, it was determined REYNOLDS was not robbed of anything.

L. J. LEWIS, 7616 Hume, salesman at Reynolds Motor Company, advised the light bulb had been screwed out the night before the shooting.

- 2 -

COMMISSION EXHIBIT No. 2589—Continued

Re: ASSASSINATION OF PRESIDENT JOHN FITZGERALD KENNEDY, NOVEMBER 22, 1963, DALLAS, TEXAS

On January 23, 1964, JOHNNY REYNOLDS, 622 West Five Mile Parkway, brother of WARREN, advised he was at home at the time of the shooting and that WARREN usually closed the lot at night.

On January 24, 1964, DARRELL WAYNE GARNER, also known as "DAGO", 1006 North Bishop, white male, age 24, born January 1, 1940, 5'8½", was arrested at Topper's Cafe, 315 East Jefferson, and charged with investigation, assault to murder and "drunk and disorderly." GARNER had been talking about how sorry the REYNOLDS brothers were and that WARREN REYNOLDS had received what he deserved. GARNER had been at the Reynolds Motor Company car lot on Monday, January 20, 1964, attempting to sell a 1957 Oldsmobile for which he did not have a title and became extremely upset when REYNOLDS would not purchase the vehicle.

The day after the shooting, January 24, 1964, an anonymous telephone caller advised JOHNNY REYNOLDS to go see "DAGO" and hung up.

It was determined GARNER owned a 1961 white Ford Falcon, License Number RM 1299, which he was in the process of purchasing from WELDON MC COWEN, 619 North Winnetka.

Mrs. DAHLIA GARNER, 1006 North Bishop, mother of DARRELL WAYNE GARNER, advised DARRELL does not generally reside at 1006 North Bishop and is presently living in his car. Mrs. GARNER stated DARRELL was a mentally unstable person whom she did not desire to have hanging around influencing her other boys, RICKEY, age 16, and EARNEST, age 19.

A .22 caliber rifle, Marlin Model 80-DL, was obtained in a search of 1006 North Bishop, which rifle was found not to be the one which fired the bullet removed from WARREN REYNOLDS.

DARRELL WAYNE GARNER advised that on the night of January 23, 1964, he was driving around in his car with AUDIE ANDERSON, white male, age 18, 728 Melba, and they picked up

- 3 -

COMMISSION EXHIBIT No. 2589—Continued

Re: ASSASSINATION OF PRESIDENT JOHN FITZGERALD KENNEDY, NOVEMBER 22, 1963, DALLAS, TEXAS

NANCY JANE MOONEY, also known as BETTY MC DONALD, white female, age 24, 319 North Windomere, and HELEN WOALSCHLAGER, white female, age 24, 319 North Windomere, in front of the Poodle Salon on Jefferson Avenue between Beckley and Zangs about 9:00 P.M. The four drove across the river and obtained some beer. When coming back from across the river they heard from the radio about a shooting on East Jefferson. NANCY MOONEY wanted to go see what happened so they drove around near the Reynolds Motor Company car lot for about five minutes and then left. They drove around town for awhile and took HELEN home about 10:30 P.M. DARRELL and AUDIE dropped NANCY at her place at 3:30 A.M., January 24, 1964.

A Polygraph examination on January 27, 1964, was afforded DARRELL WAYNE GARNER, RICKEY GARNER, EARNEST GARNER and AUDIE ANDERSON, and all were judged to be telling the truth and were released.

On February 3, 1964, DARRELL WAYNE GARNER made a long distance telephone call to Mrs. BILLIE BLAYLOCK, Las Vegas, Nevada, his sister-in-law, and advised her he had shot WARREN REYNOLDS.

On February 3, 1964, DARRELL GARNER was arrested on charge of investigation, assault to murder. GARNER admitted calling his sister-in-law in Las Vegas but would not state what he said. He was drunk and belligerent at this time. On February 4, 1964, GARNER stated he had been bragging to his sister-in-law so she would think he was a big shot. He also stated he frequently made statements like this when he was drunk.

On February 5, 1964, NANCY JANE MOONEY gave an affidavit substantiating GARNER's alibi for the night of January 23, 1964, when the shooting occurred. She was afforded a Polygraph examination which indicated she was telling the truth.

On February 13, 1964, at 2:45 A.M., NANCY JANE MOONEY was arrested and charged with disturbing the peace after engaging

- 4 -

COMMISSION EXHIBIT No. 2589—Continued

in a fight with PATSY SWOPE MOORE over the affections of one JIMMY WALTER KIRKPATRICK.

After being placed in a cell at the Dallas City Jail, NANCY JANE MOONEY hung herself with her toreador trousers, causing death by asphyxiation.

On February 13, 1964, WILLIAM GRADY GOODE, 1618 Lebanon, furnished an affidavit in which he stated he had known NANCY JANE MOONEY for about six weeks, during which time she had attempted suicide on two occasions. The first attempt was by gas in her bathroom at 319 Windomere, but GOODE arrived in time to revive her. The second attempt at suicide was made by cutting her wrists. MOONEY also exhibited previous scars on her wrists and stomach and advised GOODE she had done that to herself.

NANCY MOONEY, on February 5, 1964, advised Detective RAMSEY, Dallas Police Department, she had worked as a stripper at JACK RUBY's place when she was very young.

PATSY SWOPE MOORE had known NANCY MOONEY about six weeks prior to their fight over KIRKPATRICK and had shared Apartment 4 at 5400 Live Oak, Dallas, with MOONEY. Both were employed at Mickey's Bar, 1402 Greenville Avenue.

NANCY advised PATSY she had four children who resided with NANCY's mother in Paris, Texas. PATSY understood these children had been taken away from NANCY, causing her to be very despondent at times. NANCY also stated to PATSY that she had been a former striptease girl working at various bars of that type in Dallas, but the only one PATSY can specifically recall is JACK RUBY's Carousel Club.

Interviews with GEORGE SENATOR, RUBY's former roommate, and with present employees of the Carousel Club failed to identify NANCY MOONEY as a former stripper at the club.

Captain O. A. JONES received a telephone call, date unrecalled, from BOB CONSIDINE prior to CONSIDINE's article in

the "New York Journal-American", at which time CONSIDINE related substantially the material contained in his article and requested Captain JONES to comment on it. Captain JONES declined to comment on the material.

During the course of the investigation into the shooting of LEE HARVEY OSWALD by JACK L. RUBY under the caption "JACK L. RUBY; LEE HARVEY OSWALD, (Deceased) - VICTIM; CR", no information was received to the effect that NANCY JANE MOONEY, also known as BETTY MAC DONALD, had ever been employed at the Carousel Club in Dallas, Texas, for JACK L. RUBY.

1

DL 100-10461
RPG/ds

Previous investigation has reflected information concerning WARREN REYNOLDS of Johnny Reynolds Motor Company, 500 East Jefferson Street, Dallas, Texas, who witnessed the flight of the murderer of Dallas Police Officer J. D. TIPPIT on November 22, 1963. On January 23, 1964, REYNOLDS was shot in the head by a bullet from a .22 caliber rifle and the prime suspect in this matter was DARRELL WAYNE GARNER. On February 23, 1964, there appeared an article in the "New York Journal American" by Mr. BOB CONSIDINE which stated in substance that GARNER had been released, based in part on an alibi provided by BETTY (MOONEY) MAC DONALD, who had allegedly worked as a stripper at the Carousel Club and who had subsequently hanged herself.

416

COMMISSION EXHIBIT No. 2590

FD-302 (Rev. 3-3-59)

FEDERAL BUREAU OF INVESTIGATION

Date November 30, 1963

1

MR. ROBERT J. E. HUGHES, Apartment 3, 6615 Hursey, telephone EMerson 8-2751, made available one 50 ft. roll of 8 millimeter Kodachrome colored movie film. MR. HUGHES personally delivered this film to the Dallas FBI Office stating it contained some footage of the presidential motorcade November 22, 1963 just prior to the assassination of President JOHN FITZGERALD KENNEDY.

HUGHES stated he took the pictures while standing on the southwest corner of Main and Houston Streets. The presidential motorcade passed in front of him, turned right on Houston Street, one block to Elm Street, then turned left. This left turn is directly in front of the Texas School Book Depository Building which is shown in full in the photographs. From the photographs there appears to be a person in the sixth floor window of the Texas School Book Depository Building which is the most distant window to the right.

MR. HUGHES requested that when the film had served its purpose it should be returned to him.

on 11/26/63 at Dallas, Texas File # DL 100-10461

by Special Agent ROBERT M. BARRETT/tjd 6 Date dictated 11/27/63

This document contains neither recommendations nor conclusions of the FBI. It is the property of the FBI and is loaned to your agency; it and its contents are not to be distributed outside your agency.

COMMISSION EXHIBIT No. 2591

UNITED STATES SECRET SERVICE
TREASURY DEPARTMENT

ORIGIN Field	OFFICE Dallas, Texas	FILE NO. CO-2-34,030
TYPE OF CASE: Protective Research	STATUS: Continued	TITLE OR CAPTION: Assassination of President Kennedy
INVESTIGATION MADE AT: Dallas, Texas	PERIOD COVERED: Aug. 4, 1964	
INVESTIGATION MADE BY: SA John Joe Howlett		

DETAILS

SYNOPSIS

Mileage of routes believed to have been walked by Lee Harvey Oswald on 11-22-63.

DETAILS OF INVESTIGATION

Investigation was requested by Inspector Kelley via phone on 8-4-64.

Other Investigations

Mileage from cab stand, Greyhound Bus Station, on Lamar between Jackson and Commerce to the intersection of Beckley and Neeley Streets is 2.5 miles. The following route was used for measurement: Lamar south to Jackson, west on Jackson to Austin, south on Austin to Wood, west on Wood to Houston, south and southwest on Houston to Beckley, south on Beckley to Neeley.

Mileage from 1026 North Beckley to 404 East 10th Street is .9 miles. The following route was used for measurement: South on Beckley from 1026 North Beckley to Davis, east on Davis to Crawford, south on Crawford to 10th Street, east on 10th Street to 404 East 10th.

Mileage from 404 East 10th Street to the Texas Theatre, 231 West Jefferson, is .7 miles. The following route was used for measurement: West on 10th St. to Patton, south on Patton to Jefferson, west on Jefferson to the Texas Theatre, 231 West Jefferson. The above measurements were made by using the Odometer in a 1964 Plymouth, Secret Service car number 466.

DISPOSITION

This phase of the investigation is considered closed.

JJH:VS

DISTRIBUTION	COPIES	REPORT MADE BY	DATE
Chief ✓	Orig.& 1 cc	[signature] SPECIAL AGENT	8-5-64
Dallas	2 cc's	APPROVED [signature] SPECIAL AGENT IN CHARGE	8-5-64

(CONTINUE ON PLAIN PAPER)

COMMISSION EXHIBIT No. 2592

OFFICE OF THE DIRECTOR

UNITED STATES DEPARTMENT OF JUSTICE
FEDERAL BUREAU OF INVESTIGATION
WASHINGTON, D.C. 20535

August 21, 1964

BY COURIER SERVICE

Honorable J. Lee Rankin
General Counsel
The President's Commission
200 Maryland Avenue, Northeast
Washington, D. C.

Dear Mr. Rankin:

Reference is made to your undated letter received on July 29, 1964, concerning the appearance of Mr. Mark Lane on the Barry Gray radio program over Station WMCA in New York City.

Enclosed are two copies of a communication from our Dallas Office dated August 7, 1964, pertaining to our investigation of the allegation made by Mr. Lane alleging the existence of another female eyewitness to the murder of Officer J. D. Tippit. The files of this Bureau fail to disclose that Mr. Lane or anyone associated with him has ever furnished any information to the FBI indicating the existence of a second female eyewitness to the Tippit murder. No such individual has been identified or interviewed by this Bureau and had we knowledge of such a witness you would have been promptly notified.

Also enclosed are the two original recording tapes furnished with referenced letter and two copies of a verbatim transcription of the program prepared by this Bureau. A copy of each recording tape has been made and both will be maintained for future reference.

COMMISSION EXHIBIT No. 2593

Honorable J. Lee Rankin

The alleged announcements made by representatives of this Bureau, which are discussed on pages three and four of the enclosed transcription, are completely without foundation as no such announcements were made.

No further action is being taken in this matter.

Sincerely yours,

J. Edgar Hoover

Enclosures (6)

-2-

COMMISSION EXHIBIT No. 2593—Continued

OFFICE OF THE DIRECTOR

UNITED STATES DEPARTMENT OF JUSTICE

FEDERAL BUREAU OF INVESTIGATION

WASHINGTON 25, D. C.

May 6, 1964

BY COURIER SERVICE

Honorable J. Lee Rankin
General Counsel
The President's Commission
200 Maryland Avenue, Northeast
Washington, D. C.

Dear Mr. Rankin:

Reference is made to my letter dated April 2, 1964, which enclosed copies of a memorandum revealing the results of a reinterview with Mrs. Jean Lollis Hill. Mrs. Hill commented she observed a white man, wearing a brown raincoat and a hat, running west away from the Texas School Book Depository Building following the shooting. Mrs. Hill did not closely observe this individual; did not know who he was; and never saw him again. Mrs. Hill described this man as "average height and heavy build."

Additional investigation has been conducted by this Bureau endeavoring to identify this individual. This investigation included a review of all available film taken near the Texas School Book Depository Building following the shooting; a re-examination of the results of all interviews with individuals who were in the vicinity of the shooting; a review of an additional film taken by Mr. Thomas P. Alyea, WFAA-TV newsman; and interviews with Dallas Police Department and Dallas County Sheriff's Office personnel, none of which revealed the identity of the man described by Mrs. Hill.

Investigative results appear on pages 43 through 49 in the report of Special Agent Robert P. Gemberling dated April 15, 1964. This report was furnished to you by letter dated May 4, 1964, and no further action is being taken in this matter.

Sincerely yours,

J. Edgar Hoover

COMMISSION EXHIBIT No. 2594

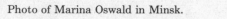

Photo of Marina Oswald in Minsk.

Commission Exhibit No. 2595

From left, Uncle Vasily, Aunt Lubova, and Marina Oswald.

Commission Exhibit No. 2596

From left, Uncle Vasily, Aunt Lubova.

COMMISSION EXHIBIT No. 2597

Uncle Vasily, Marina Oswald, Aunt Lubova.

COMMISSION EXHIBIT No. 2598

Marina Oswald on train leaving Russia.

COMMISSION EXHIBIT No. 2599

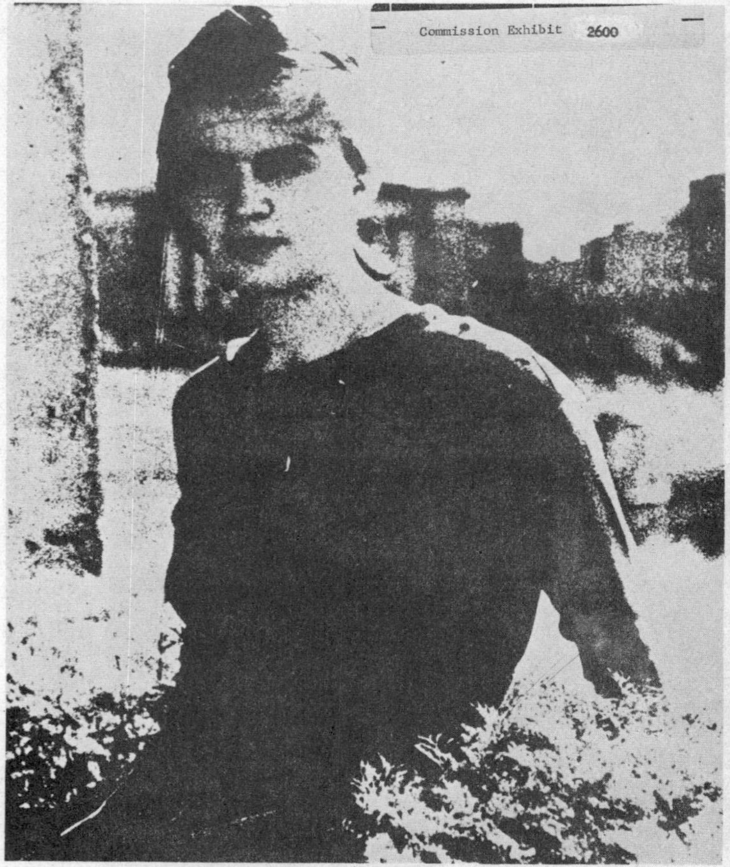

Marina Oswald in Minsk.

COMMISSION EXHIBIT No. 2600

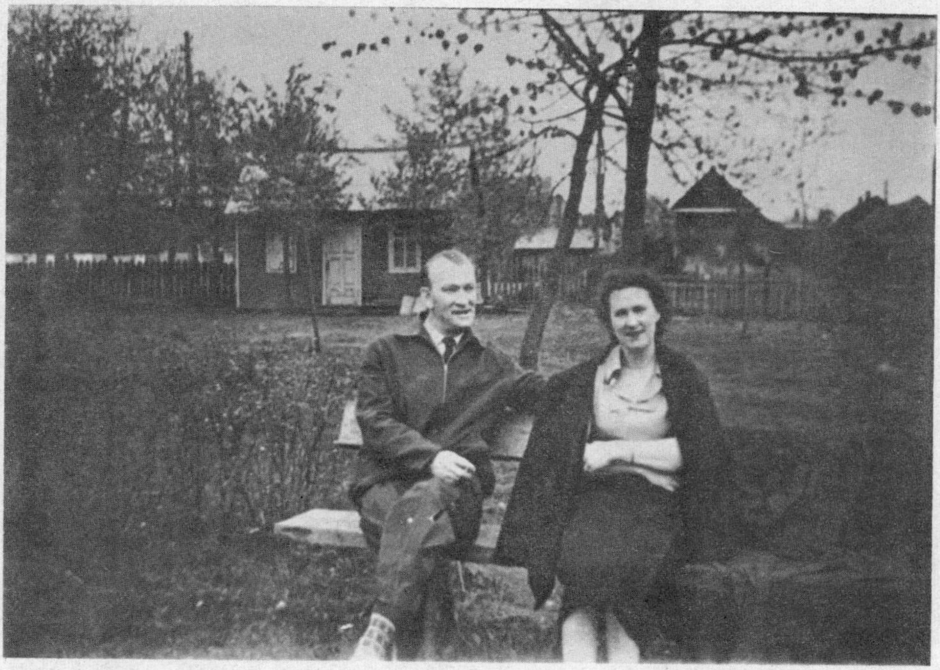

Uncle Vasily, Aunt Lubova.

COMMISSION EXHIBIT No. 2601

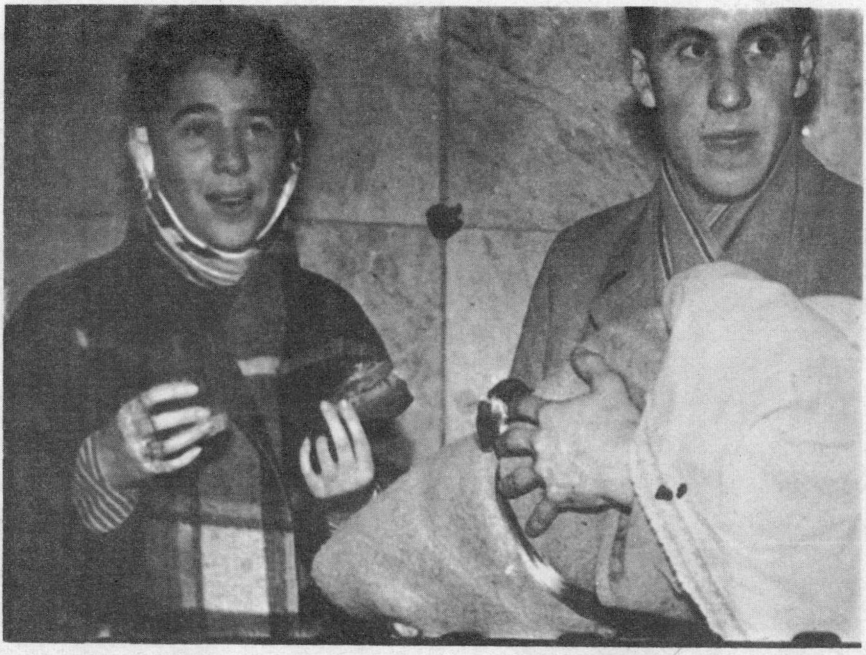

From left, Eleanor Zieger (daughter of Alexander Romanovich Zieger and Anna Zieger) and Anatole who is holding June Oswald.

COMMISSION EXHIBIT No. 2602

Uncle Vasily, Aunt Lubova, and Marina Oswald.

COMMISSION EXHIBIT No. 2603

From right, Larissa Petrovana Petrusevich and her cousin, believed named VALENTIN (last name unknown).

COMMISSION EXHIBIT No. 2604

From left, Petrusevich and Marina Oswald.

COMMISSION EXHIBIT NO. 2605

River scene at Minsk taken from Oswalds' apartment.

COMMISSION EXHIBIT NO. 2606

River scene at Minsk taken from Oswalds' apartment.

COMMISSION EXHIBIT No. 2607

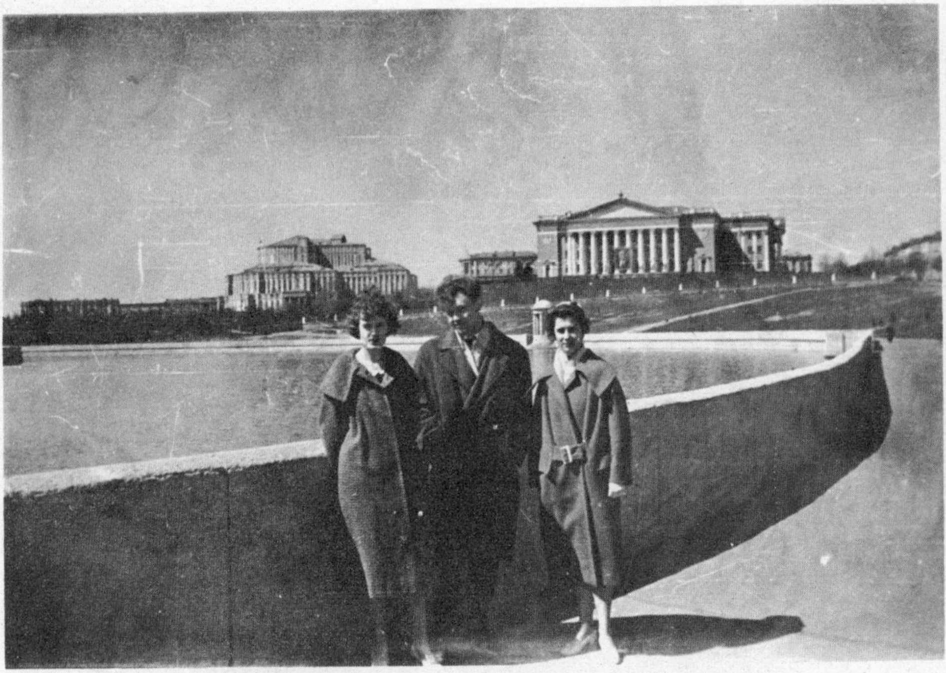

From left, Marina Oswald, Valentin (last name unknown cousin of Petrusevich) and Petrusevich.

COMMISSION EXHIBIT No. 2608

In front from left, Lee Harvey Oswald and Pavel Golovachev. At rear from left, Rosa (last name unknown) (Intourist guide in Minsk and friend of Lee Harvey Oswald) and Ella German, friend of Lee Harvey Oswald in Minsk.

COMMISSION EXHIBIT No. 2609

Lee Harvey and Marina Oswald and Aunt Lubova.

COMMISSION EXHIBIT No. 2610

From left, Lee Harvey Oswald, Anita Zieger, and Mrs. Zieger. Person standing is believed to be a Hungarian resident of Minsk, Alfred (last name unknown).

COMMISSION EXHIBIT No. 2611

Lee Harvey Oswald and Alfred (last name unknown).

COMMISSION EXHIBIT No. 2612

The Palace of Culture where Lee Harvey and Marina Oswald met.

COMMISSION EXHIBIT No. 2613

From left, Lee Harvey Oswald, person with back to camera unidentified by Marina, Mrs. Zieger, standing, and Anita Zieger (lying on ground).

COMMISSION EXHIBIT No. 2614

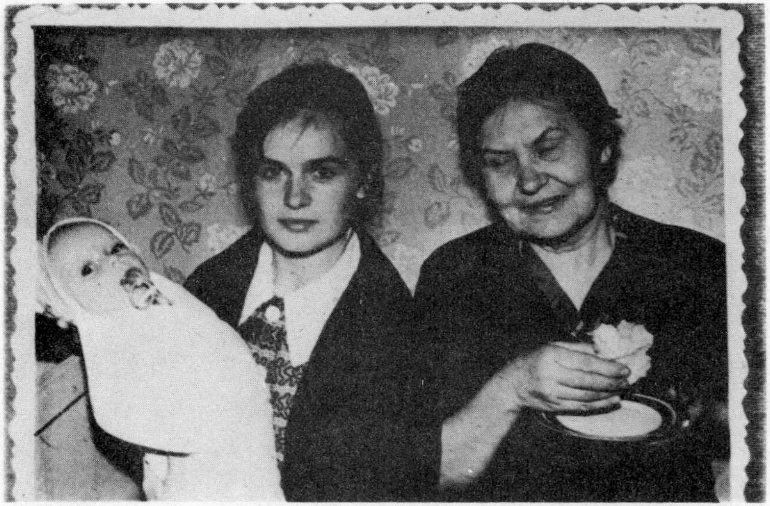

June Oswald, Marina Oswald, and Mrs. Zieger, in Oswalds' apartment in Minsk.

COMMISSION EXHIBIT No. 2615

Anita Zieger and Lee Harvey Oswald in Minsk.

Lee Harvey Oswald in Minsk.

COMMISSION EXHIBIT No. 2617

Pavel Golovachev in Minsk.

COMMISSION EXHIBIT No. 2618

Pavel Golovachev in Minsk.

COMMISSION EXHIBIT NO. 2619

Lee Harvey Oswald and Pavel Golovachev in the Oswalds' apartment in Minsk.

COMMISSION EXHIBIT NO. 2620

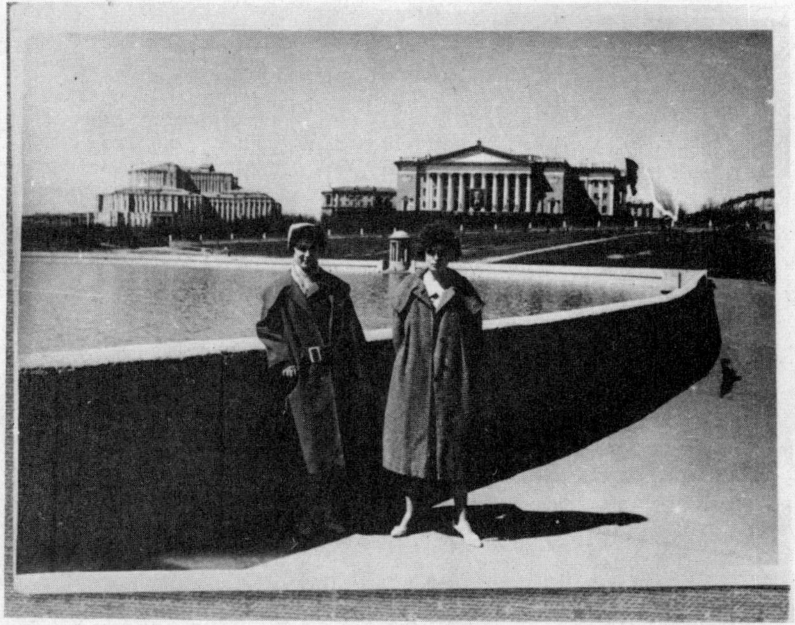

Larissa Petrovana Petrusevich and Marina Oswald.

COMMISSION EXHIBIT No. 2621

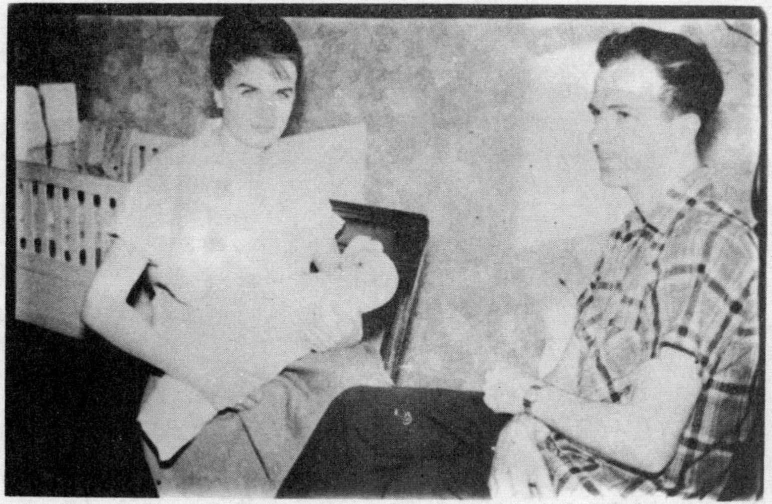

From left, Marina, June, and Lee Harvey Oswald in Minsk.

COMMISSION EXHIBIT No. 2622

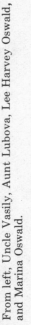

From left, Uncle Vasily, Aunt Lubova, Lee Harvey Oswald, and Marina Oswald.

COMMISSION EXHIBIT No. 2623

From left, Lee Harvey Oswald, Anatole (last name unknown) (a boy friend of Larissa Petrovana Petrusevich, a girl friend of Marina in Russia) and Mr. Alexander Romanovich Zieger.

COMMISSION EXHIBIT No. 2624

Lee Harvey Oswald (in dark glasses) and fellow workers at the radio-TV factory where Oswald was employed in Minsk.

COMMISSION EXHIBIT NO. 2625

Lee Harvey Oswald and the Intourist guide Rosa (last name unknown).

COMMISSION EXHIBIT NO. 2626

A close-up of the Palace of Culture in Minsk.

COMMISSION EXHIBIT No. 2627

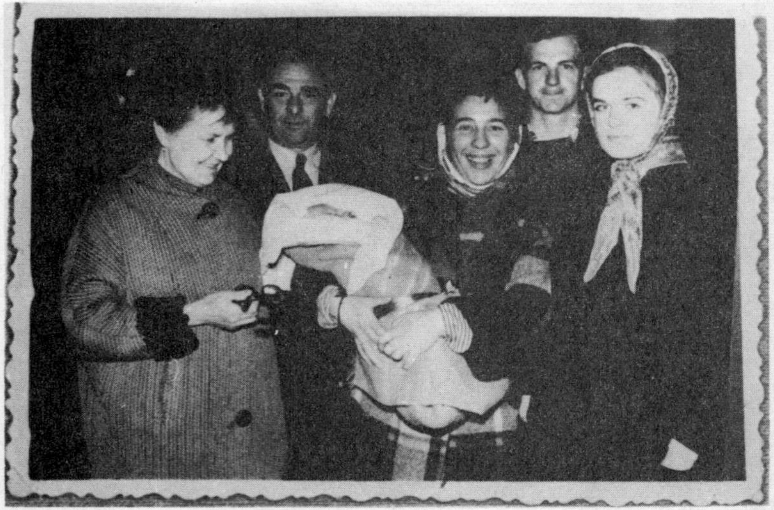

From left, Mrs. Zieger, Mr. Zieger, June Oswald, Eleanor Zieger, Lee Harvey and Marina Oswald in Minsk.

COMMISSION EXHIBIT No. 2628

Lee Harvey and Marina Oswald on train leaving Russia.

COMMISSION EXHIBIT No. 2629

Apartment in which Oswalds resided—Minsk.

COMMISSION EXHIBIT No. 2630

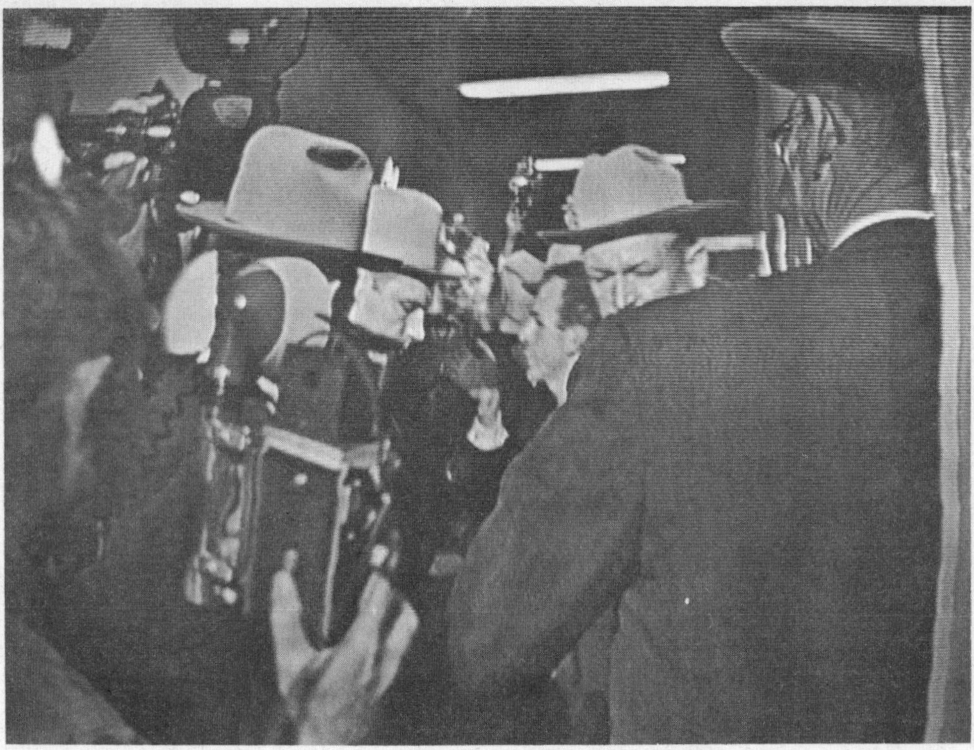

Commission Exhibit No. 2631

Commission Exhibit No. 2632

COMMISSION EXHIBIT No. 2633

COMMISSION EXHIBIT No. 2634

Commission Exhibit No. 2635

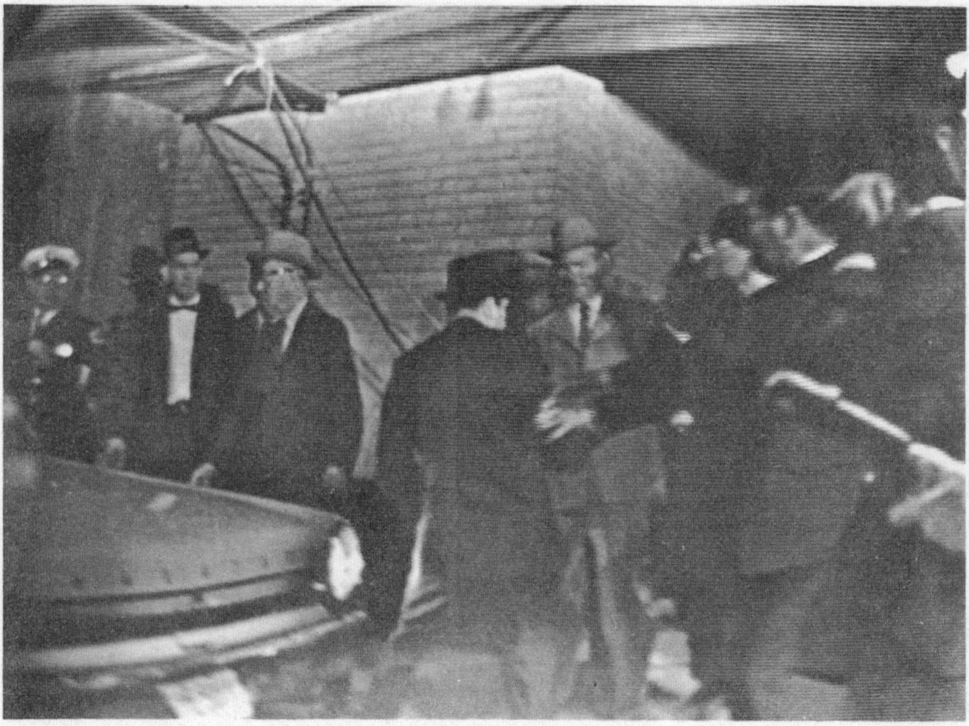

Commission Exhibit No. 2636

OFFICE OF THE DIRECTOR

UNITED STATES DEPARTMENT OF JUSTICE

FEDERAL BUREAU OF INVESTIGATION

WASHINGTON, D.C. 20535

September 4, 1964

By Courier Service

Honorable J. Lee Rankin
General Counsel
The President's Commission
200 Maryland Avenue, Northeast
Washington, D. C.

Dear Mr. Rankin:

Reference is made to your letter dated September 1, 1964, concerning a palm print which Lieutenant J. C. Day of the Dallas Police Department testified he lifted from the barrel of the assassination weapon, Commission Number 139.

This palm print lift has been compared with the assassination rifle in the FBI Laboratory. The Laboratory examiners were able to positively identify this lift as having come from the assassination rifle in the area of the wooden foregrip. This conclusion is based on a comparison of irregularities in the surface of the metal of the barrel with the impressions of these irregularities as shown in the lift.

A photograph marked to show several of the irregularities referred to is attached.

The results of the other investigation requested in your letter will be subsequently furnished.

Sincerely yours,

J. Edgar Hoover

Enclosure

COMMISSION EXHIBIT No. 2637

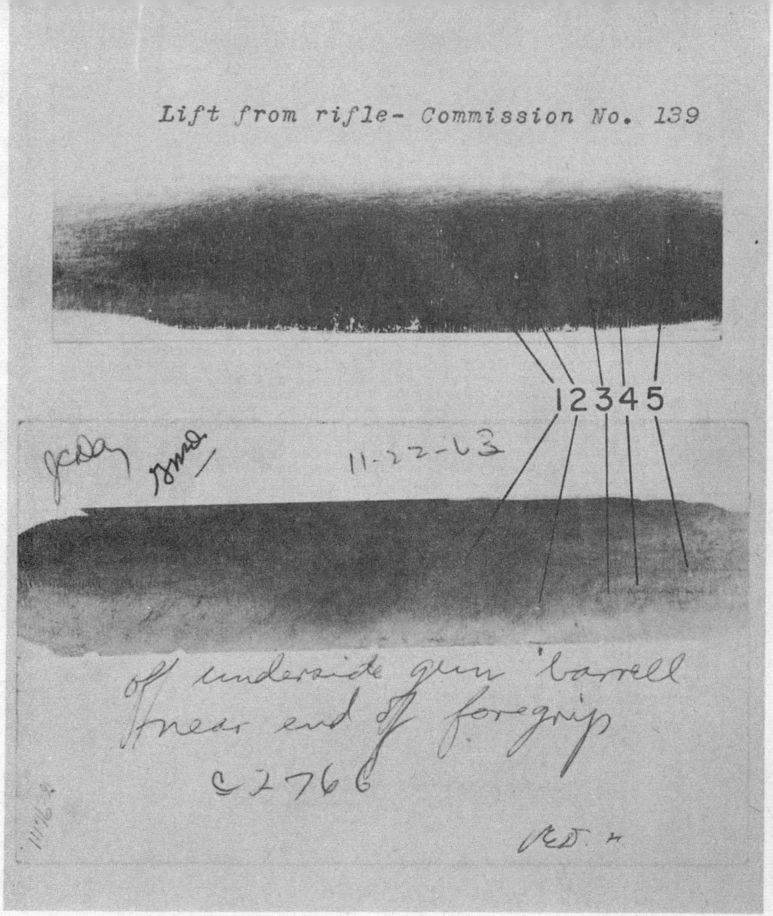

COMMISSION EXHIBIT No. 2637—Continued

UNITED STATES DEPARTMENT OF JUSTICE
FEDERAL BUREAU OF INVESTIGATION

In Reply, Please Refer to
File No.

WASHINGTON, D.C. 20535

September 4, 1964

LEE HARVEY OSWALD

Concerning the markings on the large and small maps depicted in Exhibit D-240, a confidential source abroad has advised that the central markings in the J-7 and the H-3 areas of these maps define Lee Harvey Oswald's place of residence at the Hotel del Comercio at Bernardin de Sahagun Street, Number 19, Mexico, D.F., Mexico.

Examination by the FBI Laboratory of Exhibit D-237, the portion of the Transportes del Norte bus ticket obtained from Mrs. Oswald, established that D-237 was originally connected to the two ticket stubs depicted in Exhibit D-202. The examination further established that the D-202 ticket stubs were originally connected.

According to a confidential source abroad, Mr. Ricardo Medina, Mexico City manager of the Transportes del Norte line, explained that tickets issued by his company for travel from Mexico City, Mexico, to Laredo, Texas, consist of three sections which are delivered to the purchaser. Each of these sections bears the same number. According to Mr. Medina, one section is for travel from Mexico City to Monterrey and the second is for the travel between Monterrey and Laredo, Texas. The third section, recording the total travel from Mexico City to Laredo Texas, is retained by the passenger. This section (Exhibit D-237) records the price of the ticket to be ninety-three pesos and seventy-five centavos. The tickets of the Del Norte line are pink in color and are torn from a bound, numbered book of tickets in which a stub remains to record the sale thereof.

COMMISSION EXHIBIT No. 2638

UNITED STATES DEPARTMENT OF JUSTICE
FEDERAL BUREAU OF INVESTIGATION

In Reply, Please Refer to
File No.

WASHINGTON, D.C. 20535

September 4, 1964

LEE HARVEY OSWALD

The following was received from a confidential source abroad:

Mr. Roland Barrios, former employee of the Chihuahuenses Travel Agency, Mexico, D.F., Mexico, when shown Photostats of the exchange order (Exhibit D-202) issued in connection with the travel of H. O. Lee from Mexico, D.F., Mexico, to Laredo, Texas, via the Transportes del Norte bus line on October 2-3, 1963, stated that the handprinting and signature on this document were his and that undoubtedly he handled the transaction represented by the document. A photograph of the tourist card (Exhibit J-3) of Lee Harvey Oswald was also displayed to Mr. Barrios. He stated that he would interpret the comma following the name "Lee" on the tourist card to indicate surname of the traveler to be "Lee" and, in order to avoid unnecessary writing on the exchange order, he would have used the initials of the first and middle names appearing on the tourist card which he considered to be "Harvey Oswald."

Mr. Barrios stated he could not recall Lee Harvey Oswald or his dealings with him. On viewing the above-described document , he affirmed that he would have written the name of the traveler as "H. O. Lee" had he copied this name from Oswald's tourist card.

Mr. Barrios stated that he would attempt to reconstruct the events following issuance of the exchange order in question. However, he subsequently advised that he was unable to recall his contact with the traveler for whom he issued the exchange order in the name "H. O. Lee."

COMMISSION EXHIBIT No. 2639

UNITED STATES DEPARTMENT OF JUSTICE

FEDERAL BUREAU OF INVESTIGATION

In Reply, Please Refer to File No.

Dallas, Texas
September 2, 1964

ASSASSINATION OF PRESIDENT JOHN FITZGERALD KENNEDY, NOVEMBER 22, 1963, DALLAS, TEXAS

By letter dated August 31, 1964, the President's Commission requested that Roy S. Truly, Warehouse Superintendent, Texas School Book Depository, Dallas, Texas, (TSBD) be interviewed to determine if he knows of any curtain rods having been found in the TSBD building after November 22, 1963. It was also requested that it be established through interview of Truly whether it would be customary for such discovery of curtain rods to be called to his attention.

On September 1, 1964, Mr. Roy S. Truly, Warehouse Superintendent, TSBD, advised that he is certain no curtain rods were found in the TSBD building following the assassination of President John Fitzgerald Kennedy on November 22, 1963. He stated that it would be customary for any discovery of curtain rods to immediately be called to his attention and that he has received no information to the effect that any curtain rods were found subsequent to the assassination of President Kennedy.

COMMISSION EXHIBIT No. 2640

UNITED STATES DEPARTMENT OF JUSTICE

FEDERAL BUREAU OF INVESTIGATION

In Reply, Please Refer to File No.

Dallas, Texas

April 3, 1964

LEE HARVEY OSWALD

On March 26, 1964, the President's Commission advised that CECIL J. MC WATTERS, a bus driver for the Dallas Transit Company, had testified before the President's Commission on March 12, 1964, and had stated that on November 23, 1963, he identified the number "2" man in a line-up as a man who had been on his bus on November 22, 1963. MC WATTERS advised the President's Commission that he was mistaken and that the young man who was the subject of his testimony is a "teen-ager" named MILTON JONES.

The President's Commission advised that MC WATTERS had seen this boy on a Marsalis bus several times since the assassination, and informed that this boy allegedly gets off the south-bound bus in the vicinity of Brownlee Street and lives about two blocks from the bus line, attends school half days, and has a part-time job.

On March 30, 1964, ROY MILTON JONES, 512 East Brownlee Street, Dallas, Texas, advised he is an 11th grade student attending half-day sessions at the N. R. Crozier Technical High School, Live Oak and Bryan Streets, Dallas, and is employed part time as a clerk at Buddies Supermarket, 10th and Jefferson Streets, Dallas, Texas. JONES stated that he uses the name MILTON JONES rather than his full name and is better known by this name at school and at work.

He said that on November 22, 1963, he attended the usual morning session of classes at high school and got out of school at about 11:45 AM. He said he walked to Elm Street near the Capri Theatre, where he waited for the Marsalis bus, which arrived at approximately 12:10 or 12:15 PM. He said that, upon boarding the bus, he sat in the first seat facing forward on the curb side of the bus and was alone. He recognized the driver by sight as one who frequently drove the bus at this time of day, but stated he

COMMISSION EXHIBIT No. 2641

RE: LEE HARVEY OSWALD

did not know him by name. JONES advised that the bus proceeded in the direction of Houston Street and, approximately four blocks before Houston Street, was completely stopped by traffic which was backed up in this area. He recalled that at this time a policeman notified the driver the President had been shot and he told the driver no one was to leave the bus until police officers had talked to each passenger. JONES estimated that there were about fifteen people on the bus at this time and two police officers boarded the bus and checked each passenger to see if any were carrying firearms.

JONES advised that before the bus was stopped the driver made his last passenger pickup approximately six blocks before Houston Street, that one was a blonde-haired woman and the other was a dark-haired man. He said the man sat in the seat directly behind him and the woman occupied the seat further to the rear of the bus. JONES advised that when the bus was stopped by traffic, and prior to the appearance of the police officers, the woman left the bus by the rear door and the man who was sitting behind him left the bus by the front door while it was held up in the middle of the block. JONES stated he did not observe this man closely since he sat behind him in the bus, but, on the following Monday when he caught the same bus going home from school with the same driver, the driver told him he thought this man might have been LEE HARVEY OSWALD.

JONES said that after the driver mentioned this, and from his recollection of OSWALD's picture as it appeared on television and in the newspapers, he thought it was possible it could have been OSWALD. He emphasized, however, that he did not have a good view of this man at any time and could not positively identify him as being identical with LEE HARVEY OSWALD. He said he was inclined to think it might have been OSWALD only because the bus driver told him so.

With regard to this man who sat behind him, JONES stated he did not notice anything unusual about the man when he boarded

RE: LEE HARVEY OSWALD

the bus or when he left it. He said the man was not carrying any packages and he certainly did not see a gun in his possession at any time. He said the man did not seem to appear nervous or excited and seemed to him to be an ordinary passenger.

He described this man as follows:

Race:	White
Sex:	Male
Age:	30-35
Height:	5'11"
Weight:	150
Build:	Medium
Remarks:	Wore no glasses and no hat
Hair:	Dark brown, receding at temples
Dress:	Light blue jacket and gray khaki trousers

He said he did not notice the shirt or shoes this man was wearing.

JONES stated the blonde woman who boarded the bus at the same time was definitely not traveling with this man, and that she occupied a separate seat, although they both left the bus at the same time.

JONES stated that subsequent to the shooting of the President they had seen photographs of LEE HARVEY OSWALD's wife in the newspapers, and he is positive this woman was not Mrs. OSWALD.

JONES estimated the bus was held up by the police officers for about one hour and, after they were permitted to resume, they crossed the Marsalis Bridge, where a woman, about forty to forty-five years of age, boarded the bus. She sat in the side seat immediately in front of him near the door and the bus driver asked her whether she had heard that the President had been shot. She replied that she had not heard anything in this regard, and stated

RE: LEE HARVEY OSWALD

she did not believe it was true. The driver then pointed to JONES and said, "Ask him, he saw it." JONES said the driver was smiling at this time and the woman turned to him and he told her, "I don't know anything about it. I just heard some others say that the President had been shot." He said that because of the expression on the woman's face both he and the driver were smiling at the time, and she then said, "You are both smiling, so I don't believe it."

JONES advised he could not recall any conversation between the bus driver and himself or any other person on the bus about the President being shot in the temple. He said he did not hear any person make this remark on the bus. JONES advised he believes he left this bus at Brownlee and Marsalis Streets at about 1:45 PM and went straight home. He said that, in conversation with this same bus driver on the following Monday, the driver told him the Dallas Police Department had him up until one o'clock on Saturday or Sunday morning questioning him about the passenger on his bus who looked like LEE HARVEY OSWALD.

JONES advised he is 17 years old, born December 21, 1946, at Dallas, Texas, is a white male, 5'2", 145 pounds, dark-brown hair, and brown eyes.

-4-

COMMISSION EXHIBIT No. 2641—Continued

FD-302 (Rev. 3-3-59)

FEDERAL BUREAU OF

Commission Exhibit No. 2642

1

Date 2/25/64

Mrs. LILLIAN BRADSHAW, Director, Dallas Public Library, 1954 Commerce Street, Dallas, Texas, furnished the following information:

A file of membership is not retained by the Dallas Public Library System; therefore, she has no records pertaining to LEE HARVEY OSWALD.

She further advised that the only records maintained by the Library are keyed to delinquencies; therefore, it would not be possible to determine a listing of the books read by OSWALD. In this connection, microfilmed records are maintained on books charged out. It would take a detailed review of over 2,600,000 such microfilmed records in order to establish the identity of the books charged out by OSWALD.

Mrs. BRADSHAW made available two copies of a Dallas Public Library delinquency notice which reflects LEE HARVEY OSWALD, 602 Elsbeth, Dallas, was delinquent on a book entitled, "The Shark and The Sardines", by JUAN JOSE AREVALO. The book was due on November 13, 1963, and, according to Mrs. BRADSHAW, it would have been charged out on November 6, 1963. The delinquency notice was never mailed. According to library records, the book was never returned.

Mrs. BRADSHAW indicated her records contained no other delinquencies for OSWALD.

She made available a copy of the above-described book which was authored by a former President of Guatemala, JUAN JOSE AREVALO, translated from the Spanish by JUNE COBB and Dr. RAUL OSEGUEDA and published by LYLE STUART, 225 Lafayette Street, New York 12, New York.

The Introduction to the American Reader by the Author, in part, reads as follows: "In your hands you hold a controversial book -- a book that speaks out against your

902

on 2/19/64 at Dallas, Texas File # DL 100-10461

by Special Agent RAYMOND P. YELCHAK/ds Date dictated 2/22/64

COMMISSION EXHIBIT No. 2642

2

DL 100-10461

State Department's dealing with the peoples of Latin America during the Twentieth Century. In it there is intended no insult to, nor offense to, the United States as a nation. The future of your country is identified with the future of contemporary democracy. Neither does this book seek to cast blame on the North American people --who, like us, are victims of an imperialist policy of promoting business, multiplying markets and hoarding money."

The two copies of the Dallas Public Library delinquency notice are being retained as part of this file, the copy of "The Shark and The Sardines" being returned.

403

COMMISSION EXHIBIT No. 2642—Continued

DT+

Demo Ranks Split On JFK Luncheon

The Dallas Times Herald

City News

Friday, Nov. 15, 1963

**A—23

A liberal-loyalist Democratic leader fired off an irate telegram to President Kennedy Friday protesting the ticket allotments for the Nov. 22 luncheon in Dallas in the President's honor.

Barefoot Bryant said he sent the telegram because "from the invitation list so far in Dallas, one would think Nixon won and was coming to Dallas to greet his dedicated workers."

Bryant said there was a move on the part of the liberal-labor-loyalists Democratic faction to boycott the luncheon unless more tickets are given to the people "who stand up for the President and his program day in and day out."

A spokesman for the sponsoring luncheon group quickly commented that the luncheon was not a political affair; that the President was appearing in his capacity as President of all the people and that his remarks would not be political in nature.

The Democrats will stage their party banquet in Austin Friday night. The Dallas luncheon is expected to focus on higher education or subjects entirely unrelated to party policies, the spokesman said.

Talk of a boycott could not be confirmed from other sources, however.

Charles King, president of the Dallas AFL-CIO Council, said, "I am unable to comment at this time."

Oscar Mauzy, a leader of the loyalist Democratic precinct chairmen, said he is still trying to find out who exactly has and hasn't been invited.

"I think it would be a serious mistake to exclude the people who have worked so hard for the Democratic Party," Mauzy said, but added that he had no information yet they have been excluded.

He plans to meet with the liberal-loyalist precinct chairman Tuesday night, he said, to determine exactly what the situation is.

Meanwhile, a group of Dallas business and civic leaders were to meet Friday afternoon to make some of the final arrangements for the Presidents' visit to Dallas.

Officials were still waiting shortly before noon for the official word on exactly where the luncheon will be held.

The new Trade Mart on Stemmons Freeway is expected to be the site if Secret Service agents approve it.

Another prospect is the Women's Building at Fair Park.

Bryant, in commenting on the

See SPLIT on Page 28

★ SPLIT

11-15-63 A-28

Continued From Page 23

committee which is forming the plans for the non-political, invitation-only affair, said it was made up 85 per cent of Republicans.

The complete text of his telegram to the President is as follows:

"From the invitation list so far in Dallas one would think Nixon won and was coming to greet his dedicated workers. Better not to have come if visit is used to reject supporters and reward opposition. Please do something. We can't win the John Birchers, but we can fire up our own workers in '64."

COMMISSION EXHIBIT No. 2643

FD-302 (Rev. 3-3-59)

FEDERAL BUREAU OF INVESTIGATION

Date 3/25/64

1

Mr. JOHN R. LIGON, Assistant Principal, W. H. Adamson High School, 9th and Beckley Streets, Dallas, Texas, furnished the following information:

Mr. LIGON stated that a review of High School Pupil's Permanent Record, Dallas Independent School District, reflects that ARNOLD LOUIS ROWLAND was last residing at 1604 Carson Street, Dallas, Texas, and was born at Corpus Christi, Texas, on April 29, 1945. He entered the Dallas Independent School District from Salem, Oregon. These records further reflect that ARNOLD's father was ARNOLD PATRICK ROWLAND; his mother's maiden name was BERTIE M. BROWN, and her last known name was Mrs. CLYDE TIDMORE.

These records reflect that ROWLAND was given an IQ Test in 1959 and scored 109 on this test. In addition to the IQ Test, ROWLAND was given the National Merit Scholarship Qualifying Test in the spring of 1963 and scored 127 on this test. Mr. LIGON stated this test was given in two parts throughout the United States and those scoring sufficiently high grades on the first examination were subsequently given a second examination. He stated ROWLAND did not score sufficiently high on the first examination to qualify him to take the second examination. A third test, Iowa Test of Educational Development, was administered to ROWLAND while at Adamson High School, and he scored in the 94 percentile group of this examination.

Mr. LIGON stated that Dallas Independent School District does not use a numerical system of rating students. He furnished the following ratings given by this school district:

A - Excellent
B - Good
C - Fair
D - Poor
E - Poor Passing
F - Failure
G - Bad Failure

on 3/23/64 at Dallas, Texas 65 File # DL 100-10461

by Special Agent E. J. ROBERTSON:vmseah Date dictated 3/24/64

This document contains neither recommendations nor conclusions of the FBI. It is the property of the FBI and is loaned to your agency; it and its contents are not to be distributed outside your agency.

Commission Exhibit No. 2644

COMMISSION EXHIBIT No. 2644

2
100-10461

Mr. LIGON advised the records of this school district reflect the following grades for ARNOLD LOUIS ROWLAND:

School Adamson

Session 1959 Term Fall

Subject	Class	1st	2nd Report	3rd	Examination	Average	Credit	TEACHER
English	1				E	E	1/2	ROCHETT
Elementary Civics		B	B	B	B	B	1/2	REEVES
Algebra	1			C	C	C	1/2	WAITS
General Science	1				C	C	1/2	HEAD

Date of Entrance 1-18-60

School Crozier Tech

Session 1960 Term Spring

Subject	Class	1st	2nd Report	3rd	Examination	Average	Credit	TEACHER
English	2	C	B	B	C	B	1/2	EWING
Algebra	2	E	E	C	A	D	1/2	DENSON
Spanish	1	F	E	F	F	F	no	MALLOW
General Science	2	E	F	E	C	E	1/2	FOSTER
Radio	1	E	A	C	D	C	1/2	CANNON
High School Information						D	1/4	MOSES
Military Absent		9	8	8				

Date of Entrance 2-1-60

66

COMMISSION EXHIBIT No. 2644—Continued

3
DL 100-10461

School Crozier Tech

Session 1960 Term Fall

Subject	Class	1st	2nd Report	3rd	Examination	Average	Credit	TEACHER
English	3	C	B	B	B	B	1/2	COLE
Geometry	1	B	A	A	A	A	1/2	COWGILL
Mechanical Drawing	2	A	A	A	A	A	1/2	J. MURRAY
Radio	2	A	A	A	B	A	1/2	CANNON
Typewriting	1	B	A	B	B	B	1/2	YOAKUM
Physical Education						A	1/8	QUESENBERRY
Absent		3	2	1				

Date of Entrance 9-7-60

School Crozier Tech

Session 1961 Term Spring

Subject	Class	1st	2nd Report	3rd	Examination	Average	Credit	TEACHER
English	4	B	D	A	B	B	1/2	EWING
History (World)	1	A	B	C	A	B	1/2	BROWN
Geometry	2	A	B	A	A	A	1/2	DEWSON
Radio	3	B	A	A	C	B	1/2	CANNON
Typewriting	2	B	C	B	B	B	1/2	YOAKUM
Physical Education						B	1/8	QUESENBERRY
Absent		5	7	7				

Date of Entrance 1-30-61

COMMISSION EXHIBIT No. 2644—Continued

4
DL 100-10461

School Adamson

Session 1961 Term Fall

Subject	Class	1st	2nd Report	3rd	Examination	Average	Credit	TEACHER
English	5	C	C	D	E	C	1/2	CHAPPELL
History	7	C	C	E	C	D	1/2	ROBBINS
Algebra	3			A	C	B	1/2	JENKINS
Chemistry	1			D	F	E	1/2	TILLEY
Physical Education						B	1/8	HALLMARK
Absent				5				

Date of Entrance 12-11-61

Mr. LIGON advised that ROWLAND had enrolled for the spring session of the 1962 class, but was dropped on March 19, 1962, for non-attendance of classes. He also enrolled for the fall term of the 1962 session, but was dropped on December 8, 1962, for non-attendance. No grades or credits for any classes were given ROWLAND during these two terms because of the lack of attendance.

School Crozier Tech

Session 1963 Term Spring

COMMISSION EXHIBIT No. 2644—Continued

Subject	Class	1st	2nd Report	3rd	Examination	Average	Credit	TEACHER
English	8	D	C					RAYNES
World History	2	B	A					REGELSKY
Geometry	3	F	A					COWGILL
Photography	1	C	C					MURRAY
Physics	2	F	F					FOSTER
Physical Education								QUESENBERRY
					Dropped 3-18-63			
Absent		13		3				

School Crozier Tech

Session 1963 Term Fall

Subject	Class	1st	2nd Report	3rd	Examination	Average	Credit	TEACHER
English	7	C					No credit	
Civics	3	B					No credit	
Algebra	4	F					No credit	
Public Speaking	5	A					No credit	
					Dropped 11-21-63			

Mr. LIGON advised that his records reflect ROWLAND attended Topeka High School, Topeka, Kansas, during an unknown period of time, probably during the spring or fall term of the 1962 school year. Topeka High School transferred 1/2 credit for History 8 and 1/8 credit for Phys. Ed., to the Dallas Independent School District for ROWLAND.

Mr. LIGON stated that ARNOLD LOUIS ROWLAND was refused admittance into the Adamson High School for the spring session of 1963 because of his past record at this school. ROWLAND applied for admission at N. R. Crozier Technical High School for this session after being refused admission at Adamson High School and attended Crozier Tech for a short time during 1963.

Mr. LIGON stated that Adamson High School offered no special sound courses and to his knowledge neither did Crozier Tech. He stated he could not imagine any course of study in any of the high schools of the Dallas Independent School District doing research or special work in sound and study of echo effects.

Mr. LIGON stated he had two students accepted by Rice Institute out of the entire class graduating in 1963. These students learned they had been accepted by Rice about two weeks prior to graduation from high school and both students were outstanding in citizenship and scholastic accomplishments. He stated he seriously doubted that Southern Methodist University, Texas A & M, or Rice Institute had accepted ARNOLD LOUIS ROWLAND for admission into the respective institutes inasmuch as he has not graduated from an accredited high school in the state of Texas.

Mr. LIGON advised he had counseled ROWLAND while he was attending Adamson High School on various occasions because of his absenteeism from this school. He stated he learned from contact with ROWLAND that he (ROWLAND) would not hesitate to fabricate a story if it was of any benefit for ROWLAND to do so. Mr. LIGON gave as an example an incident that occurred while ROWLAND was attending Adamson High School. ROWLAND drove a Volkswagen automobile to school and on occasions parked in the teachers' parking area. This Volkswagen automobile was repossessed by a finance company one afternoon during school hours and after school ROWLAND reported to Mr. LIGON that his car had been stolen. He asked Mr. LIGON what action he was going to take regarding the theft and Mr. LIGON advised him that since it was his (ROWLAND's) car he should report it to the police and that he was welcome to use the school telephone to make this report. ROWLAND used the telephone briefly and then left Mr. LIGON's office. Mr. LIGON stated he thought the conversation was very short for such an incident and therefore he (Mr. LIGON) called the Dallas Police Department Auto Theft Bureau and asked if they had received a report from anyone at Adamson High School reporting the theft of a vehicle. Mr. LIGON stated he was advised that the Police Department was aware that a finance company in Dallas was repossessing a Volkswagen from this school's parking lot but that there was no theft and they had received no calls from ARNOLD LOUIS ROWLAND or anyone else at the school concerning the Volkswagen.

Mr. LIGON stated ROWLAND was not a problem student in that he caused trouble or agitated other students, but he did request almost on a daily basis special privileges and seemed to have the attitude that he was superior to most of the teachers and all other students. Mr. LIGON stated he advised the Secret Service Agents attempting to locate ARNOLD LOUIS ROWLAND just prior to his appearance before the President's Commission that anything ROWLAND might tell the President's Commission would be questionable. He stated he so informed the Secret Service Agents based on his past experience with ROWLAND.

FD-302 (Rev. 3-3-59)

FEDERAL BUREAU OF INVESTIGATION

1

Date 3/25/64

Dr. WALTER J. E. SCHIEBEL, Principal, N. R. Crozier Technical High School, Bryan and Live Oak Streets, Dallas, advised this school had no records concerning ARNOLD LOUIS ROWLAND although he did attend this school. Mr. SCHIEBEL advised that all records pertaining to ROWLAND had been transferred to the W. H. Adamson High School, 9th and Beckley Streets, Dallas. He stated Mrs. EDITH McKISSOCK, Dean, Crozier Tech, had counseled ROWLAND and she would be able to furnish firsthand information concerning his veracity and reputation.

72

on 3/23/64 at Dallas, Texas File # DL 100-10461

by Special Agent E. J. ROBERTSON:vm Date dictated 3/24/64

FD-302 (Rev. 3-3-59)

FEDERAL BUREAU OF INVESTIGATION

Date 3/25/64

1

Mrs. EDITH McKISSOCK, Dean, N. R. Crozier Technical High School, Bryan and Live Oak Streets, Dallas, advised she had counseled ARNOLD LOUIS ROWLAND while he was attending Crozier Tech during the fall term of 1960, spring term of 1961, and the spring term of 1963. Mrs. McKISSOCK stated ROWLAND entered Crozier Tech during th spring term of 1963 after being refused admittance at Adamson High School in Dallas. She stated he had few friends at Crozier Tech and was generally regarded as a "lone wolf." She stated from her dealings with him she determined he could not be trusted and would not tell the truth regarding any matter. She stated he was a conniver and prevaricated whenever it was to his advantage to do so. She described ROWLAND as a smooth talker who dressed above his apparent means.

Mrs. McKISSOCK stated that ARNOLD LOUIS ROWLAND took no special courses in sound and study of echo effects at Crozier Tech while attending this school.

on 3/23/64 at Dallas, Texas File # DL 100-10461

by Special Agent E. J. ROBERTSON:vm 13 Date dictated 3/24/64

This document contains neither recommendations nor conclusions of the FBI. It is the property of the FBI and is loaned to your agency; it and its contents are not to be distributed outside your agency.

COMMISSION EXHIBIT No. 2644—Continued

FD-302 (Rev. 1-25-60)

FEDERAL BUREAU OF INVESTIGATION

Date 3/26/64

1

Mr. SAM FOSTER, 2729 Overcrest, Dallas, was interviewed at the Parkland Memorial Hospital in Dallas and furnished the following information:

Mr. FOSTER stated he was a teacher of physics at Crozier Technical High School in Dallas and had so been employed for over 20 years. He stated he remembers that ARNOLD LOUIS ROWLAND was a student at Crozier Technical High School having transferred to this school from Adamson High School in Dallas. Mr. FOSTER stated that ROWLAND attended the spring session of his physics class as a regular student during the 1963 term. He advised that this was the regular classic physics class taught in regular high schools throughout the State of Texas and was not any special course or class. Mr. FOSTER stated that part of the subject matter covered in this class was a section on sound, but this was very basic study and in no way consisted of special study of sound and echo effects. Mr. FOSTER stated that ARNOLD LOUIS ROWLAND took no special course from him nor was he enrolled in any special class studying sound and echo effects. He stated that ROWLAND did not pass the regular physics course at Crozier Technical High School.

On 3/24/64 at DALLAS, TEXAS File # DL 100-10461

by SA E. J. ROBERTSON/les 14 Date dictated 3/25/64

This document contains neither recommendations nor conclusions of the FBI. It is the property of the FBI and is loaned to your agency; it and its contents are not to be distributed outside your agency.

COMMISSION EXHIBIT No. 2644—Continued

FD-302 (Rev. 1-25-60)

FEDERAL BUREAU OF INVESTIGATION

Date 3/26/64

1

Mrs. POLLY REDFEARN, Chief Clerk, Registrar's Office, Southern Methodist University, advised that a check of the records of this institution failed to disclose any information pertaining to ARNOLD LOUIS ROWLAND. She advised that if ROWLAND had applied for admission to this institution, she would have a record of the application and a file concerning ROWLAND. She further advised that ROWLAND could not have been accepted by Southern Methodist University without first having graduated from an accredited high school in the State of Texas or from a high school outside the state and completing Southern Methodist University examinations for admittance. She stated that in no event could ROWLAND have gained admittance to this University without a high school transcript which had not been filed with this University.

On 3/24/64 at DALLAS, TEXAS File # DL 100-10461

by SA E. J. ROBERTSON/les 75 Date dictated 3/25/64

This document contains neither recommendations nor conclusions of the FBI. It is the property of the FBI and is loaned to your agency; it and its contents are not to be distributed outside your agency.

COMMISSION EXHIBIT No. 2644—Continued

FD-302 (Rev. 1-25-60)

FEDERAL BUREAU OF INVESTIGATION

Date 3/26/64

1

Dr. JOHN E. FINN, partner, Finn and Finn-Optometrists, Fidelity Union Tower Building, 1507 Pacific, Dallas, Texas, advised that a check of the records of this firm covering the past 15 years fails to reflect any information indicating that ARNOLD LOUIS ROWLAND had ever been examined by this firm. Mr. FINN advised that a record is kept on each patient examined and had ROWLAND been examined, his name would be in the files of this firm.

Dr. FINN stated he was at a loss to explain how his firm's name had been obtained by ARNOLD LOUIS ROWLAND, but stated that his firm was housed in a central location in Dallas and was generally known by most residents of this city.

On 3/24/64 at DALLAS, TEXAS File # DL 100-10461

by SA E. J. ROBERTSON/les 76 Date dictated 3/25/64

This document contains neither recommendations nor conclusions of the FBI. It is the property of the FBI and is loaned to your agency; it and its contents are not to be distributed outside your agency.

COMMISSION EXHIBIT No. 2644—Continued

UNITED STATES DEPARTMENT OF JUSTICE

FEDERAL BUREAU OF INVESTIGATION

In Reply, Please Refer to
File No.

Dallas, Texas
June 15, 1964

LEE HARVEY OSWALD

The President's Commission, by letter dated May 19, 1964, advised that Mrs. EARLENE ROBERTS, the housekeeper at 1026 North Beckley Street, Dallas, Texas, during the period that OSWALD resided there in October-November 1963, had stated that at about 1:00 P.M. on November 22, 1963, a Dallas Police car drove slowly by the front of the premises at 1026 North Beckley Street and honked the horn several times. Mrs. ROBERTS stated that the occupants of the car were not known to her, even though she did have some acquaintances on the Dallas Police force who called upon her at the above premises. She had previously stated that the Dallas Police car was number 207.

Mrs. ROBERTS, when interviewed on November 29, 1963, advised that she recalled the number of the police car as being 207 because she had worked for two policemen who drove squad car number 170, and she looked at the car to see if the two officers she knew were the ones occupying car 207. Results of this interview are reflected on page 356 of the report of Special Agent ROBERT P. GEMBERLING, dated November 30, 1963, at Dallas, Texas.

CHARLES E. BATCHELOR, Assistant Chief of Police, Dallas Police Department, advised on May 27, 1964, that his department is divided primarily into three divisions; Uniformed Traffic Division, Uniformed Squad Patrol Division, and Investigative Division composed of plain-clothes detective personnel. He advised that, of this group, only the Traffic Division and Squad Patrol Division are uniformed and have occasion to operate numbered and marked police patrol cars.

COMMISSION EXHIBIT No. 2645

Re: LEE HARVEY OSWALD

BATCHELOR advised that on Friday, November 22, 1963, the entire Traffic Division was assigned the traffic control of the intended route of the Presidential motorcade from the Love Field area to the Trade Mart on Stemmons Expressway, and that a portion of the squad patrol was assigned to assist the Traffic Division in the protection of the President. He advised the remainder of the squad patrol was assigned regular patrol duties throughout the city, as is its usual assignment. He advised the only squad cars in service that day not specifically assigned to the Presidential motorcade were manned by uniformed officers of the squad patrol.

BATCHELOR advised that on November 22, 1963, Platoon Number 2, under the command of Captain CHARLES E. TALBERT, was on duty on the 7:00 A.M. to 3:00 P.M. shift, and that units of this platoon were the only marked units which would have occasion to be in the Oak Cliff area of Dallas. BATCHELOR explained that the city area within the Dallas City limits is divided into seventy-six distinct districts to allow for population expansion; however, as many as two to three districts are frequently patrolled by one squad car.

BATCHELOR advised that the address 1026 North Beckley in the Oak Cliff section of Dallas falls within District Number 91 and that the Daily Detail Sheet for Platoon Number 2 on November 22, 1963, revealed the following cars and officers had been assigned on the 7:00 A.M. to 3:00 P.M. shift in District Number 91 and all adjacent surrounding districts:

Officer W. D. MENTZEL, assigned Districts 91 and 92, Car Number 84;
H. M. ASHCRAFT, assigned Districts 93 and 94, Car Number 24;
O. H. LUDWIG, assigned Districts 108 and 109, Car Number 242;
Officer DAVID L. PATE, assigned Districts 24 and 25, Car Number 32.

BATCHELOR advised further that each group of squad cars is under the supervision of a sergeant, who coordinates assignments of his units throughout the city. BATCHELOR advised that

- 2 -

COMMISSION EXHIBIT No. 2645—Continued

Re: LEE HARVEY OSWALD

these officers might be more cognizant of the location of their cars at any particular time and that each of these officers frequently makes a log on the activities of his squad. BATCHELOR advised that Sergeant H. F. DAVIS was in charge of the "90" series cars during the 7:00 A.M. to 3:00 P.M. shift, November 22, 1963, and that Sergeant W. G. JENNINGS was in charge of the "100" series cars during that period.

BATCHELOR advised that Squad Car Number 170 was not in operation in the City of Dallas during November 1963. He advised his records indicate Car Number 170 was a 1961 Ford four-door sedan, which was sold by his department in April 1963, and that the number "170" was not reassigned until February 1964, at which time the number was given to one of the new Ford squad cars purchased during that month. BATCHELOR advised his records further indicate that Patrolman J. M. VALENTINE was the sole occupant of Car Number 207 on November 22, 1963.

In an effort to determine whether or not any officers of his department were acquainted with any of the occupants of 1026 North Beckley, Oak Cliff, which would explain squad car officers blowing a horn at or near that address, Assistant Chief BATCHELOR checked all complaint calls for the year 1963 of complaints answered by officers of his department. BATCHELOR advised his records indicate that on February 14, 1963, Officer R. W. HIGH answered a "Drunk" complaint at 1026 North Beckley from 2:03 P.M. to 2:16 P.M. On July 28, 1963, Officer Q. M. NORMAN answered a call of "Disturbing the Peace" from 1:26 A.M. to 1:58 A.M. On September 23, 1963, Officer BOB E. CONNOR answered a call emanating from 1026 North Beckley with regard to "Auto Theft" from 5:47 P.M. to 6:15 P.M. Officer's report on this call indicates the call was in relation to a suspicious Renault automobile parked at the rear of the Gulf Service Station across the street from 1026 North Beckley.

BATCHELOR advised his records indicated that Officer R. W. HIGH had the day off on November 22, 1963, and that officers CONNOR and NORMAN were assigned to Platoon Number 3 and assigned to work the 3:00 P.M. to 11:00 P.M. shift on November 22, 1963, and, therefore, would not have been in the vicinity of 1026 North Beckley.

- 3 -

COMMISSION EXHIBIT No. 2645—Continued

Re: LEE HARVEY OSWALD

On May 27, 1964, Captain CHARLES E. TALBERT, Dallas, Texas, Police Department, advised that he is the Platoon Commander for Platoon Number 2 and that his records reflect that on November 22, 1963, his platoon was on the day schedule from 7:00 A.M. to 3:00 P.M. TALBERT advised that, following the assassination of President JOHN F. KENNEDY at approximately 12:30 P.M. on that day, he took personal charge of all assignments of his platoon and all officers were told to report to him at the Texas School Book Depository, where he was making the individual assignments.

Captain TALBERT advised that, from a review of the Daily Detail Sheets reflecting district and car assignments of each officer on duty that day and comparing same with a transcript from the dispatcher's records on the afternoon following the assassination of the President, he has been able to ascertain, with a reasonable degree of certainty, the area and assignments of each officer under his command. He advised that units from his platoon were the only marked and numbered squad cars in operation that afternoon, with the exception of three or four units, which had been specifically assigned to assist the Traffic Division in the protection of the President.

Captain TALBERT advised the following officers were on special assignment to the Traffic Division to aid in the protection of the President:

NAME	CAR
C. EDINGTON	75
F. S. WILLIAMS	119
A. R. BROCK	215
M. L. WISE	59
T. L. COX	33
E. G. SEBASTIAN	151
J. G. POLLARD	100
C. R. ORSBURN	102
G. D. BENNINGFIELD	152
R. J. ROSS	162

- 4 -

COMMISSION EXHIBIT No. 2645—Continued

NAME	CAR
R. B. COUNTS	225
B. L. BASS	232
C. F. GOODSON	125
J. T. SMITH	101
T. R. BURTON	49
B. W. ANGLIN	76

Captain TALBERT advised that the following officers were on special assignment at specified locations during this shift, and were required to remain at those posts throughout the day on November 22, 1963:

S. B. DANIEL, Headquarters Special Patrol;
Sergeant J. A. PUTNAM, Garage Sergeant;
J. F. BUTCHER, Love Field;
C. W. COMER, Love Field;
Sergeant R. C. CHILDERS, Area Commander, Northwest Substation;
C. H. WESSON, Love Field Terminal;
J. R. MORROW, Station 636 Northeast;
M. E. FERRIS, Parkland Memorial Hospital Guard (Room 229);
Lieutenant W. R. FULGHUM, Special Assignment School.

Captain TALBERT advised that Lieutenant W. R. FULGHUM was attending a traffic school at Northwestern University, Evanston, Illinois, on November 22, 1963, and not available for assignment.

Captain TALBERT advised the following officers were assigned to specific districts and squad cars up to and including the time of the assassination of the President. He advised his records reflect the following subsequent assignments of these officers:

G. W. TEMPLE and R. E. VAUGHN, assigned District 61, Car 53. This unit dispatched to Texas School Book Depository, corner Elm and Houston Streets, for guard duty where it remained until 3:30 P.M.

COMMISSION EXHIBIT No. 2645—Continued

D. A. STAFFORD and E. HILL, assigned District 62, Car 62. Both of these individuals are Negro officers and were assigned guard duty at the Texas School Book Depository until approximately 4:00 P.M.

B. L. JONES and M. D. HALL, District 102, Car 106. Car 106 dispatched from corner Pearl and Jackson Streets, 12:35 P.M., to Texas School Book Depository, until 1:20 P.M.; 105 then dispatched to vicinity 400 block East 10th Street, Oak Cliff, to answer officer shooting.

J. M. POE and L. E. JEZ, District 105, Car 96. This unit dispatched to Texas School Book Depository, 12:35 P.M., and then to 400 block East 10th Street, Oak Cliff, to answer officer shooting.

Sergeant S. W. BURKHART, District 20, unmarked car. Remained at Texas School Book Depository all afternoon following assassination.

D. P. TUCKER and C. R. GRAHAM, assigned District 21, Car 44: This unit dispatched to Texas School Book Depository following assassination where it remained until 4:00 P.M.

L. L. HILL, assigned District 22, Car 3. Dispatched to Texas School Book Depository following assassination and then to rear of Texas Theatre, Oak Cliff, following officer shooting.

B. E. BARNES, assigned District 23, Car 15. Dispatched to Parkland Memorial Hospital following assassination.

D. L. PATE, Districts 24 and 25, Car 32. Remained at Texas School Book Depository following assassination and answered calls on police radio at that station.

COMMISSION EXHIBIT No. 2645—Continued

Re: LEE HARVEY OSWALD

G. W. HAMMER, assigned Districts 26 and 27, Car 27. Dispatched to Texas School Book Depository following assassination and then dispatched to 400 block East 10th Street, Oak Cliff, following officer shooting and brought witness back to station.

J. E. CHISM, District 31, Car 126. Conducting theft investigation, Northwest Dallas, at time of assassination call. Dispatched to Parkland Memorial Hospital where remained.

J. M. LEWIS, Districts 35 and 36, Car 193. Dispatched to Texas School Book Depository and then to 400 block East 10th Street, Oak Cliff, following officer shooting, and then to Texas Theatre to assist in apprehension of LEE HARVEY OSWALD.

F. G. WOODROW, Districts 37 and 38, Car 112, was driving south on Stemmons Expressway at time of assassination. Saw motorcade coming through triple underpass en route north on Stemmons Expressway. Dispatched to Texas School Book Depository where remained rest of afternoon.

Sergeant R. D. SHIPLEY, Area Commander, Northeast Substation. Dispatched to Texas School Book Depository and remained rest of afternoon.

Sergeant D. F. FLUSCHE, dispatched to Texas School Book Depository where remained rest of the day.

P. K. WILKINS, Districts 43 and 44, Car 192. At time of assassination, was at County Jail with prisoner with Officer G. L. TOLBERT. Dispatched to Texas School Book Depository

Re: LEE HARVEY OSWALD

and assisted in search of building. WILKINS located rifle on sixth floor and remained at building rest of the day.

G. L. TOLBERT, Districts 53 and 55, Car 132. Assisted Officer P. K. WILKINS with prisoner and then dispatched to Texas School Book Depository where remained rest of the day.

N. L. STANGLIN, Districts 45 and 46, Car 67. Ordered to answer calls in respective district. Did not enter Oak Cliff area during shift.

W. F. MORRIS, District 47, Car 158, located at Valley View and Central, Northeast Dallas, at time of assassination call. Assigned to remain in area to answer calls and look for suspect.

A. D. DUNCAN, District 48, Car 70, located Northwest Highway and Central Expressway at time of assassination call. Assigned to set up roadblock at that intersection in effort to locate suspect. Did not enter Oak Cliff Section.

C. R. GILBREATH, District 49, Car 91, located intersection of Walnut Hill and Central Expressway at time of assassination call. Dispatched to Texas School Book Depository where remained until 4:00 P.M.

G. A. KELLEY, Districts 51, 52 and 54, Car 122, located intersection of Gaston and Abrams at time of assassination call. Dispatched to Texas School Book Depository where remained rest of shift.

W. P. PARKER, Districts 56 and 58, Car 77, located East Dallas, Garland Road area, at time of assassination call. Set up roadblocks in that area remainder of afternoon.

J. C. WALLACE, Districts 57 and 59, Car 131 located North Dallas at time of assassination. Assigned to set up roadblocks in that area rest of afternoon.

W. A. EVERITT, Districts 65 and 67, Car 171. Assigned to set up roadblocks at intersection Pleasant Grove and Samuels in Northeast Dallas. Did not enter Oak Cliff area.

V. G. WOODS, assigned District 68, Car 113. Remained in Northeast Dallas on call all afternoon.

Sergeant C. B. OWENS, Area Commander, Southwest Substation, dispatched to Texas School Book Depository. Interviewed witnesses on railroad tracks at rear of Texas School Book Depository following assassination, then dispatched to Oak Cliff following officer shooting. Driving unmarked car.

Sergeant H. F. DAVIS, Supervisor assigned Districts 80 and 90, Car 179. Dispatched to Texas School Book Depository where remained until 3:45 P.M.

H. H. HORN, assigned District 76, Car 57. Dispatched to Texas School Book Depository and assigned guard duty on railroad tracks at rear of building where remained rest of day.

W. E. SMITH, District 77, Car 9. Assigned to guard southeast corner, Texas School Book

Depository, where remained until after 3:00 P.M.

J. L. ANGELL, Districts 81 and 82, Car 20. Assigned to lower floor of Texas School Book Depository where remained until 3:45 P.M.

R. W. WALKER, Districts 85 and 86, Car 127. Assigned to remain in district to answer calls in regard to suspects.

R. C. NELSON, District 87, Car 156. Dispatched to Texas School Book Depository where stationed in front of building remainder of afternoon.

W. D. MENTZEL, Districts 91 and 92, Car 84. Was eating lunch at 430 West Jefferson at time of assassination. Left restaurant to answer shooting call in 400 block East 10th Street, Oak Cliff. Did not pass intersection of Zangs and Beckley.

H. M. ASHCRAFT, Districts 93 and 94, Car 24. Dispatched to Inwood Road and Stemmons Expressway to cut traffic at time of assassination call; then to Texas School Book Depository where remained rest of day.

M. N. MC DONALD and T. R. GREGORY, Districts 95 and 96, Car 130. Dispatched to Texas School Book Depository following assassination report. Approximately 1:20 P.M., Officer MC DONALD sent to vicinity 400 East 10th Street, Oak Cliff, to assist other officers in investigation of reported shooting of police officer.

Re: LEE HARVEY OSWALD

On May 27, 1964, HUGH F. DAVIS, Sergeant, Dallas, Texas, Police Department, advised that on November 22, 1963, he was the supervising sergeant assigned to Districts 80 and 90, of Platoon 2, which was working the 7:00 A.M. to 3:00 P.M. shift that month.

Sergeant DAVIS advised he recalled at the time of the assassination call he was driving Unit Number 179, an unmarked car, and was dispatched thereafter to the Texas School Book Depository at Elm and Houston Streets, where he remained until 3:45 P.M. that afternoon.

Sergeant DAVIS advised that the course of his travels took him nowhere near 1026 North Beckley in the Oak Cliff section of Dallas, Texas, on November 22, 1963.

On May 27, 1964, Sergeant WILLIAM G. JENNINGS, Dallas, Texas, Police Department, advised that on November 22, 1963, he was assigned to Car 168 to supervise the downtown area of Dallas on patrol, and that at the time of the assassination he had just left his residence at 3147 Casino Drive, in Oak Cliff, after having eaten lunch.

Sergeant JENNINGS advised that en route to town he drove down Hampton Road to Fort Worth Avenue and into town and was not, at any time, near 1026 North Beckley in Oak Cliff. He advised he was dispatched to the Texas School Book Depository where he was assigned to "shake down" passenger freight trains to the rear of the Depository. He advised he stayed there until approximately 4:00 P.M. that afternoon.

On May 28, 1964, Patrolman JIMMY M. VALENTINE, Dallas Police Department, Dallas, Texas, advised that on November 22, 1963, he was assigned to District 104 and was driving police car number 207. VALENTINE said he was patrolling the downtown area of Dallas and, shortly after noon, received a call on the radio to go to H. L. Green Department Store and pick up a fourteen-year-old shoplifter. VALENTINE said he did this and returned with the youth to the Juvenile Bureau of the Dallas Police Department. He said it was about 12:45 P.M. when he received

- 11 -

COMMISSION EXHIBIT No. 2645—Continued

Re: LEE HARVEY OSWALD

word of the assassination. VALENTINE stated he left the Juvenile Bureau immediately and went to the Texas School Book Depository building, 411 Elm Street, Dallas, Texas. He said he parked his car at the curb, entered the Texas School Book Depository building, and was assigned to the fifth floor. He said he left the building when all of the officers were dismissed, which was around 4:00 or 4:30 P.M.

VALENTINE stated his car was not driven during the time he was in the Texas School Book Depository building on November 22, 1963. He further stated that it definitely was not in use at 1:00 P.M., and, further, that he did not drive to the Oak Cliff area on November 22, 1963, in which area is located 1026 North Beckley Street. VALENTINE also advised he was not acquainted with EARLENE ROBERTS or with anyone else at 1026 North Beckley Street.

On June 1, 1964, WILLIAM DUANE MENTZEL, Officer, Dallas, Texas, Police Department, advised that on November 22, 1963, he was assigned to patrol alone Districts 91 and 92 in Car 84.

Officer MENTZEL stated at approximately 12:30 P.M. he stopped for lunch at Luby's Cafeteria, 430 West Jefferson, Oak Cliff. He advised he tried on several occasions to call the station by telephone, but did not get through to the operator until about 1:00 P.M., at which time he was told the President had just been shot. He stated he left the remainder of his lunch and went into service by car radio, and was immediately dispatched to the 800 block of West Davis on an accident call, Code 7, where he remained about ten minutes handling that call. He advised he then traveled west on Davis to Tyler when he heard the call involving a shooting of a police officer in the 400 block of East 10th Street. He stated he was dispatched to the intersection of Beckley and Jefferson to look for a reported individual running away from that intersection, but was unable to locate the suspect. He stated that he, in company with other officers, entered the library at that intersection, and then was dispatched to the Texas Theatre, where the suspect was reportedly hiding.

Officer MENTZEL advised he did not go north on Beckley to Zangs Boulevard at any time on that day, and could not recall being within six or eight blocks of that location.

- 12 -

COMMISSION EXHIBIT No. 2645—Continued

Officer MENTZEL advised he knows no one residing at 1026 North Beckley and would have no reason to stop at that address or to blow his automobile horn in passing.

On May 27, 1964, HOLLEY M. ASHCRAFT, Officer, Dallas, Texas, Police Department, advised that on November 22, 1963, he was assigned to Districts 93 and 94, Car 24, on the 7:00 A.M. to 3:00 P.M. shift, and recalls that at the time the assassination call came over the radio he was located at the intersection of Fort Worth and Sylvan Avenues. He advised he was dispatched to Inwood Road and Stemmons Expressway to cut traffic. He advised that at about 1:00 P.M. he was dispatched to the Texas School Book Depository Building, and at about 1:45 P.M. was sent to the 300 block on East Jefferson to interview witnesses regarding the shooting of Officer J. D. TIPPIT.

ASHCRAFT advised that, en route to the East Jefferson address, he did not have occasion to pass 1026 North Beckley in the Oak Cliff section of Dallas, and recalled that he was operating alone in Car 24 on that day.

On June 1, 1964, OWEN HERBERT LUDWIG, Officer, Dallas, Texas, Police Department, advised that on November 22, 1963, he was assigned to Districts 108 and 109, which was his regular beat at that time, and drove Car 242. He stated he was, on that day, assigned to Platoon Number 2, which was working the 7:00 A.M. to 3:00 P.M. shift November 22, 1963, and he was further given a special assignment to guard the front door of the Sheraton-Dallas Hotel, because of the President's expected arrival in Dallas.

Officer LUDWIG stated that he patrolled his regular beat in Districts 108 and 109 until approximately 10:45 A.M., when he took up his special assignment duties at the Sheraton-Dallas Hotel and continued in that capacity until about 6:00 P.M. the same evening. He advised he did not leave the hotel at any time, with the exception of one trip to Parkland Memorial Hospital, at approximately 1:00 P.M. that afternoon, to transport several plain-clothes agents whom he took to be either military

or Secret Service men. He advised the entire trip took about twenty minutes and, upon returning to the hotel, remained there until 6:00 P.M.

Officer LUDWIG advised he does not know any of the residents of 1026 North Beckley in the Oak Cliff section of Dallas, and did not pass that area at any time on the day of November 22, 1963.

On May 27, 1964, DAVID L. PATE, Officer, Dallas, Texas, Police Department, advised that on November 22, 1963, he was assigned alone in Car 32 to patrol Districts 24 and 25. He advised at the time of the assassination he was on Denton Drive in North Dallas and was dispatched to the intersection of Stemmons Expressway and Inwood Road, where he was instructed to cut off all traffic and keep the intersection open for emergency vehicles. He advised he stayed at that location about ten to fifteen minutes, when he was dispatched to the Texas School Book Depository, where he remained until approximately 4:00 P.M.

Officer PATE advised he definitely did not pass the intersection of Beckley and Zangs Boulevard in the Oak Cliff Section of Dallas at any time that day; did not drive by 1026 North Beckley Street; and, did not know EARLENE ROBERTS or anyone else at that address.

JFK S TEXAS TOUR

Demo Factions To Be Pacified, Salinger Says

By BOB HOLLINGSWORTH
Washington Correspondent

WASHINGTON — The White House Wednesday stuck to its "strictly nonpolitical" label for President Kennedy's tour of Texas but said every ... the state's Democrats now quarreling over tickets will be accommodated.

Press Secretary Pierre Salinger released a detailed presidential itinerary that includes a three-hour stay in Dallas and said the National Democratic Committee will pick up the tab for any excess costs necessitated by Friday night's political speech in Austin.

The non-political label was even applied to an appreciation dinner scheduled in Houston Thursday night for Rep. Albert Thomas, an ardent Democrat and one of the administration's most powerful supporters in the House.

"That is a bipartisan appreciation dinner," Salinger maintained.

Details of the President's trip closely followed previously announced schedules with stops in San Antonio, Houston, Fort Worth, Dallas and Austin. The presidential party will spend Thursday night in Fort Worth and Friday night at Vice President Lyndon Johnson's ranch near Austin.

FIRST FOR JACKIE

Mrs. Kennedy will make her first trip to Texas as First Lady.

"Mrs. Kennedy will participate in most of the activities," the White House announced, but said there would be no special functions scheduled for her.

Vice President Johnson will be also along at every stop, as will most of the state's Democratic contingent in Congress.

The White House, however, declined to identify those who will be traveling with the President until after his departure from Washington Thursday morning. No invitation list has been made public.

Salinger acknowledged the running quarrel among Texas Democrats over tickets to the various presidential appearances and said: "Every faction of the Democratic party will be taken care of."

Feuding has been under way between supporters of Gov. John Connally and Vice President Johnson on the one hand and supporters of Sen. Ralph Yarborough on the other.

ONLY POLITICAL

The White House insisted that the Friday night fund-raising dinner in Austin will be the only political appearance of the tour and said the national party will defray any costs incurred.

"The Democratic National Committee will pay for any mileage (flying time) required to get to Austin—over and above the normal requirements for the non-political appearances," Salinger said.

He admitted this would not amount to much but declined to name a figure. The President would have to fly to Austin anyway to get to the Johnson ranch.

As of now, newsmen will be barred from the ranch while the Kennedys are guests.

The President will depart Washington Thursday morning and arrive in San Antonio at 1:30 p.m. to dedicate the Aerospace Medical Health Center at Brooks Air Force Base. A motorcade will take the President from San Antonio International Airport to the air base.

OFF TO HOUSTON

He will leave San Antonio at 3:30 p.m. for Houston, where another motorcade will whisk him from the airport to the Rice Hotel. He will speak at the appreciation dinner for Rep. Thomas, then leave for Fort Worth where he arrives at Carswell Air Force Base at 10:45 p.m. Another motorcade will take him to the Texas Hotel.

The President will address a breakfast sponsored by the Fort Worth Chamber of Commerce, then fly to Dallas for a luncheon sponsored by the Dallas Citizens Council, the Dallas Assembly and the Graduate Research Center of the Southwest.

Still another motorcade—55 minutes long—will take President Kennedy from Love Field to the luncheon site at the Trade Mart.

AUSTIN SCHEDULE

The President will leave Love Field at 2:35 p.m. to journey to Austin, where he doffs his nonpolitical hat and puts on the one labeled party leader. There he will attend one reception sponsored by the State Democratic Executive Committee and another sponsored by Gov. Connally before making the big speech at the party rally in Austin's Municipal Auditorium.

President and Mrs. Kennedy will return to Washington Saturday after an overnight stay at the Johnson ranch.

In what may be a disappointment to many loyalist Democrats unable to get tickets to the nonpartisan meetings set up for the President, the White House said no airport speeches are planned at any of the cities.

The nonpolitical schedule, while billed as nonpolitical, will nevertheless allow the President maximum exposure in Texas. He is not only hitting the state's major population centers but is following an unusual custom in allowing the use of motorcades in each city.

In many cases of the President's travels, helicopters are used in place of motorcade to trim travel time. The only helicopter trip on his Texas schedule will be one from Austin to the LBJ ranch.

JFK Timetable

WASHINGTON BUREAU

WASHINGTON—Following is the schedule for the visit of President Kennedy's party to Texas Thursday, Friday and Saturday.

THURSDAY

11:00 A.M.—President departs Washington.
1:30 P.M.—Arrives San Antonio airport.
1:40 P.M.—Departs airport in motorcade to Aero-Space Center at Brooks Air Force Base.
2:25 P.M.—Arrives Brooks AFB for dedication.
3:05 P.M.—Departs Brooks for Kelly Field.
3:30 P.M.—Departs Kelly Field for Houston.
4:15 P.M.—Arrives Houston airport.
4:25 P.M.—Leaves airport via motorcade for Rice Hotel.
5:00 P.M.—Arrives Rice Hotel.
8:35 P.M.—Departs hotel for Coliseum for Thomas dinner.
8:45 P.M.—Arrives Coliseum.
9:30 P.M.—Leaves Coliseum for airport.
10:00 P.M.—Departs airport for Fort Worth.
10:45 P.M.—Arrives Carswell, motorcade to Texas Hotel.
11:00 P.M.—Arrives hotel.

FRIDAY

8:45 A.M.—Breakfast, Fort Worth Chamber of Commerce.
10:30 A.M.—Leaves hotel for Carswell.
11:15 A.M.—Departs Carswell for Love Field.
11:35 A.M.—Arrives Love Field, leaves in motorcade.
12:30 P.M.—Arrives Trade Mart.
2:00 P.M.—Leaves Trade Mart for Love Field.
2:35 P.M.—Departs Love Field for Bergstrom AFB Austin.
3:15 P.M.—Arrives Bergstrom, motorcade to Commodore Perry Hotel.
3:55 P.M.—Arrives hotel.
4:15 P.M.—Reception in Commodore Perry sponsored by State Democratic Executive Committee.
6:00 P.M.—Leaves for reception at Governor's mansion.
6:45 P.M.—Leaves mansion for hotel.
8:15 P.M.—Leaves hotel for Municipal Auditorium.
8:20 P.M.—Arrives auditorium for fund-raising dinner.
9:30 P.M.—Leaves auditorium for Bergstrom.
9:45 P.M.—Leaves Bergstrom by helicopter for LBJ Ranch.
10:20 P.M.—Arrives LBJ Ranch.

No schedule available for Saturday. Tentatively plans to leave Austin at midday for Washington.

The Gombe Stream Game Reserve is 60 square miles of forested valleys and treeless ridges in Tanganyika.

COMMISSION EXHIBIT No. 2646

A-1

LIBERALS ANGRY

DTH 11-21-63

New Fuss Erupts Over JFK Tickets

By JIM LEHRER
Staff Writer

A new controversy flared Thursday over luncheon tickets for President Kennedy's visit here Friday.

Oscar Mauzy, a liberal-loyalist Democratic leader, charged that "elected Democratic officials are being systematically excluded" from the invitation-only affair at the Trade Mart.

His charge followed the information that an invitation to the wife of Democratic precinct chairman had been withdrawn.

"The only conclusion I can draw is that her name has been withdrawn and substituted with that of a Republican," he said.

SEATING PROBLEM

A spokesman for the organizations sponsoring the affair said it had never been intended that the precinct chairman be allowed to bring guests because of the limited seating capacity at the Trade Mart.

Mr. Mauzy, however, said this was not the case. He said all precinct chairmen were told earlier in the week they would be able to bring a guest.

In other developments Thursday, it was announced that the President will ride in his own car through the streets of Dallas.

Officials revealed that the specially built limousine is being flown down in advance of the presidential party's arrival.

The car, a blue Lincoln Continental, is an open convertible but a plexiglass bubble top is a part of its equipment so the Kennedys can still see and be seen in case of inclement weather.

SPACE FOR CROWD

There also was official confirmation that the presidential 707 jet—Air Force 1—will unload at Love Field's Gate 28 at the end c[illegible]ourse.

This area was selected, authorities said, because a nearby grassy area would provide the most space for people to gather and see the President on his arrival.

There is room for approximately 10,000 people at the site where Mexicana Airlines flights normally load and unload.

The presidential plane, preceded by the vice president's and the White House presidential press corps', is scheduled to arrive in Dallas at 11:35 a.m. and depart at 2:35 p.m. following the luncheon.

Officials said it still seemed unlikely that the President would make an impromptu speech at the

See JFK on Page 18

standards," he added. "It is instead a working partner and coproducer of these resources."

The President, underlining the "nonpolitical" tag the White House has put on his trip, described his administration's scientific program as a bipartisan approach to the future that will benefit all mankind.

For a nonpolitical tour, all the stops are being pulled. Accompanying the President are Mrs. Kennedy, making her first trip to Texas as First Lady, and the bulk of Texas' Democratic contingent in Congress.

Waiting to join the entourage in Texas were Vice President Lyndon Johnson, Gov. John Connally, the State Democratic Executive Committee and every major Democratic office holder in the state.

The presidential plane, which departed Andrews Air Force Base at at 11:04 a.m. (EST), was taking the Chief Executive headlong into a nest of quarreling Democrats who have marred advance arrange-

See TRIP on Page 18

w/ attached

GET TICKETS NOW FOR 'MESSIAH'

Get your tickets for a special performance of Handel's Messiah. See page 19-A today for ticket order form.

Showers Possible For JFK

The weatherman placed a big maybe Thursday on the question of whether Dallas will have rain Friday when President Kennedy comes to town.

Early morning forecasts here Thursday made no mention of precipitation during President Kennedy's visit, but the U.S. Weather Bureau warned that showers may be added to later forecasts.

M. C. Harrison, chief forecaster at the bureau's Love Field facility, said that an eastward-moving Pacific cold front might arrive in Texas early enough to produce some scattered thundershowers in the local area during the day Friday.

WARM, WINDY WEATHER

"Our preliminary forecast just calls for mostly cloudy skies and warm and windy weather with the high Friday afternoon in the upper 70s," Mr. Harrison added, "but don't be surprised if we put showers in the forecast later."

A light drizzle Thursday morning between 8:40 and 10:35 a.m. left a trace of precipitation in the Weather Bureau's gauge at Love Field.

The Pacific cold front was moving through New Mexico Thursday and was due to arrive in extreme West Texas Thursday night.

See RAIN on Page 18

DTH 11-21-63 A-18

★ JFK

Continued From Page 1

airport before starting for town in his 55-minute 10-mile motorcade.

Meanwhile, police were investigating the first hint of any protest demonstration against the Kennedy visit. Several circulars bearing the President's picture and the words, "Wanted For Treason," were recovered by police in the downtown area.

The circulars listed seven specific complaints against the President, but made no mention of his visit to Dallas.

They were found loose in the street at Wood and Ervay, at Griffin and Pacific and in some North Dallas and White Rock areas.

FBI INVESTIGATING

Deputy Police Chief Charles Batchelor said as far as he knew there was nothing illegal in the handbills, but added there might be some civil action that could be taken.

Asked if a federal violation might possibly be involved, U.S. Atty. Barefoot Sanders acknowledged, "We have the matter under consideration." He did not elaborate.

Agents of the Federal Bureau of Investigation were known to be checking on the circulars Thursday morning.

Officials at Love Field said the air traffic situation during the arrival and departures of the presidential party is still indefinite.

SECURITY MEASURES

At present, plans call for the three planes to be given priority over all other traffic, but there will be no "sealing off" the airport as such.

Under the guidance of the Secret Service, the 350 local law enforcement officers — including Dallas police, sheriff's deputies and highway patrolmen—who will be involved in establishing security during the President's three-hour visit were receiving briefings Thursday.

The 5,000 yellow roses that will be used to decorate the Trade Mart were being installed and arranged.

Workers from the City Sanitation Department were also out with their brooms and brushes Thursday morning cleaning up Lemmon and the other streets on the official motorcade route.

DTH 11-21-63 A-18

★ RAIN

Continued From Page 1

The front is being accompanied and preceded by scattered thundershowers and followed by cooler temperatures.

If the Pacific front arrives on schedule, it would be Friday night before it reaches Central Texas.

When President Kennedy travels from Dallas to San Antonio and Austin Friday, he may encounter scattered thundershowers, according to the state forecast.

Ground fog here Thursday night reduced visibility at Love Field to 3-16s of a mile at 7 a.m., but by 7:30 the visibility was back up to a mile and a half.

Assistant forecaster John Zimmerman explained that the ground fog was due to the result of a combination of three factors: dampness from the rain Tuesday, cool night-time temperatures and southeasterly winds bringing in moisture at low levels.

Mr. Zimmerman said that there is a good chance of more ground fog again Friday morning, but he added that it probably won't be as dense.

COMMISSION EXHIBIT NO. 2647

guns, with ...... self.

DTH 11-21-63 A-18

★ TRIP

Continued From Page 1

ments by squabbles over who gets tickets to what.

Nestled in the spare seats of the President's plane are prime parties to the bickering — Sen. Ralph Yarborough, acknowledged leader of Texas' liberals, and more conservative-minded congressmen who prefer the Johnson-Connally wing of the party.

Technically, the President was to dedicate an aerospace medical center in San Antonio, join in a "bipartisan" appreciation dinner for Rep. Albert Thomas in Houston, address the Chamber of Commerce in Fort Worth, speak to a bipartisan civic gathering in staunchly Republican Dallas and save his political fireworks for a gathering of the faithful in Austin Friday night.

In his San Antonio speech the President said too many Americans assumed that space research was without value here on earth.

In his prepared speech he pointed out that wartime development of radar gave the world the transistor and that "research in space medicine holds the promise of substantial benefits for those of us who are earthbound."

Shortly before President Kennedy left Washington the Senate went along with the House in cutting space agency funds for next year to $5.1 billion from the $5.7 billion requested by the administration.

While urging that the present space effort be maintained, the President cautioned against expecting too much too soon.

"Let us not be carried away with the grandeur of our vision," he said. "Many weeks and months and years of long, hard, tedious work lie ahead.

"There will be set-backs and frustrations and disappointments. There will be pressures for our country to do less and temptations to do something else. But this research must and will go on. The conquest of space must and will go ahead."

Although the tour is officially nonpolitical, where the President goes, politics goes with him.

In San Antonio, he will be on friendly ground. The city gave him its backing in 1960. In Houston, he will bask in the glow of Rep. Thomas, a hometown favorite whose congressional district gave Kennedy more than 56 per cent of its vote three years ago.

The other half of Houston went violently for Richard Nixon.

President Kennedy's hardest tasks come Friday when he runs into Fort Worth — which favored Richard Nixon in 1960 — and Dallas, one of the most rock-ribbed Republican strongholds in the nation.

While his Dallas speech will be before an invitation—only gathering of the city's business leaders, the President's schedule was rearranged to allow a 55-minute motorcade through the heart of the city.

Austin, site of the frankly political pow-wow, is also friendly ground — or was in 1960.

KENNEDY FORMAT

In pursuing the Texas vote a year ahead of time, the President is following a format outlined earlier in an 11-state tour of the West and a foray earlier this week into Florida.

His audiences are not supposed to be confirmed followers — but rather voters he might be able to sway.

The faithful who won't get the chance to see and hear the President before he returns to Washington Saturday need only be patient — he will be back in 1964.

COMMISSION EXHIBIT No. 2647—Continued

JESUIT HOUSE OF STUDIES
3959 LOYOLA LANE
MOBILE, ALABAMA

August 22, 1963

Dear Lee:

This morning I was speaking with one of our professors who heard the talk you gave to us. He thought that you made a number of good points. One of these was your criticism of speculation in the capitalistic system. He equated stock speculation with gambling. It seems to be another form of it. Another point was your criticism of exploitation which occurs in capitalism. On both these points, speculation and exploitation, the Popes have spoken strongly against them in the past 70 years.

On the other hand, the professor to whom I am referring thought that you hadn't made sufficient application. Applying the criticism of speculation and exploitation in our country, it seems that these things are regulated. In the instances where certain individuals do overstep their bounds, it seems that such occurrences are practically inevitable in a free society. If we are going to have freedom rather than strict regimentation, then the government will naturally find it very difficult to curb all abuses. The difficulty with communism is that it suppresses freedom, as you indicated, in order to obtain efficiency.

You mentioned that there are good and bad points in each system and that possibly the best system would be a fusion of the good points of both capitalism and communism, something approaching socialism. It seems that socialism might work in a small society but again, when we apply this to our own country, it appears that we are very complex and that it would be very difficult for the government sufficiently to control such a complex society as ours along the lines of socialism. Also here again, socialism means the sacrifice of freedom in practice if it is going to work. Freedom seems to be a fundamental human value precious to every man. I think that freedom can be retained and yet we can still have a just economic, political and social system. Of course this requires that each man live up to the obligations and responsibilities of respecting the freedom of other men and exercising his own freedom in a just way. Perhaps it is more difficult to achieve a just social order by relying on individuals to show initiative and responsibility in respecting rights and living up to duties, but it seems that a society based on respect for justice and individual worth is much more lasting and solidly founded and more in accord with man's nature.

The Popes beginning with Leo XIII in 1891 and continuing up to the present day have given considerable thought and energy in trying to think through to a solution of economic and social and political abuses. You might get some ideas from the enclosed article as to how the Popes have been trying to work out the problem as well as some stimulation to your own thinking on the matter.

That's about it for now. Give my regards to Marina.

Sincerely,
Gene

COMMISSION EXHIBIT No. 2648

"TRUE COPY"

JESUIT HOUSE OF STUDIES
3959 Loyola Lane
Mobile, Alabama

July 6, 1963

Dear Lee and Moreno:

Here at the House of Studies during the summer months we have a series of lectures on various subjects given by different persons from the neighboring areas. These subjects usually deal with art, literature, economics, religion, politics, etc. We usually have a speaker every one or two weeks on a Saturday or Sunday night. Since we are studying philosophy, most of us are interested in the various phases of Communism, as this is a very timely and practical subject.

We were hoping that you might come over to talk to us about contemporary Russia and the practice of Communism there. A number of speakers have already been contacted and have definite dates on which they will speak. The best time for us to have you speak, if you are willing, is on Saturday night, July 27. The talk usually begins at 7:00 and lasts for about an hour. Then there is a five minute intermission and the speaker returns for a question period which may last a half-hour or so. When I say that we would like to have you speak on contemporary Russia and the practice of Communism there, this is only a general idea of mine. Of course we want you to chose whatever topic you like concerning your travels in Russia and to present the talk and its material in whatever way you like. It can be as informal as you like and a narration of your own observations. In other words, don't feel that it ought to be very formal and theoretical. Also, when I say that the talks usually last for an hour, I don't mean that it has to be that long. This is rather by way of a time limit. You may use whatever notes you may wish to prepare. In short, do it the way you feel you want to do it and be assured that we want you to feel at home in talking to us.

We have about 90 men who are studying philosophy in the House. Usually about 25 or so will attend these talks. We hope that you will accept our invitation and I think you will find it a good experience, as I'm sure we will too. Most of us are about your age.

I wrote my family today telling them that I planned to invite you for this occasion. They had already told me on their last visit that they hoped to invite you to come over with them when they came here sometime. I asked them if they wouldn't mind arranging to make a visit here for the same occasion so that you could come together. I told them that I would ask you to call them to make plans about this or else for them to call you. Of course we hope Moreno will come too.

You can let me know what you think about the matter and ask any further questions you may want to know about the situation. Drop me a line when you get a chance.

Sincerely,
/s/ Gene

"TRUE COPY"

COMMISSION EXHIBIT No. 2648—Continued

FD-204 (Rev. 3-3-59)

UNITED STATES DEPARTMENT OF JUSTICE
FEDERAL BUREAU OF INVESTIGATION

Copy to:

Report of: SA JOHN J. SWEENEY   Office: MOBILE
Date: 12/1/63

Field Office File No.: 89-25   Bureau File No.: 62-109060

Title: LEE HARVEY OSWALD

Character: INTERNAL SECURITY - RUSSIA

Synopsis:

EUGENE JOHN MURRETT, Scholastic in Jesuit Training at Spring Hill College, Mobile, Ala., a cousin of LEE HARVEY OSWALD, advised OSWALD, at his invitation, spoke to a number of fellow scholastics and several of his superiors at Spring Hill College, Mobile, on 7/27/63. Stated OSWALD and his wife were brought to Mobile by his parents, Mr. and Mrs. CHARLES MURRETT, from New Orleans, La., where OSWALD was then residing. MURRETT said knows little concerning OSWALD's background and stated speech consisted primarily of his life for three years in Russia. Two Priests who attended speech state OSWALD made no mention of Cuba or any statements indicating to them he had potential for violence. ROBERT J. FITZPATRICK, a scholastic at Spring Hill College, had conversation with Mrs. LEE OSWALD during time OSWALD was making speech. FITZPATRICK made available a five page summary of points discussed by OSWALD, which was composed after the President's assassination, from impressions of scholastics in attendance at OSWALD's speech 7/27/63. Records of Palms Motel, Mobile, Ala., reflect an "OSWALD" Magazine Street, New Orleans, La., was a guest at that motel on 7/27/63 and apparently checked out 7/28/63. No record of any phone calls made from OSWALD's room. BRUCE KEAHEY, Rt. 2, Ariton, Ala., who claimed to have witnessed the slaying of President KENNEDY, reported as mentally unsound and as positively being in Ariton, Ala., and not Dallas, Texas, on 11/22/63.

\- P -

Commission Exhibit No. 2649

COMMISSION EXHIBIT No. 2649

FD-302 (Rev. 1-25-60)

FEDERAL BUREAU OF INVESTIGATION

Date 12/1/63

1

Mr. EUGENE JOHN MURRETT, S. J., Scholastic, Jesuit House of Studies, Spring Hill College, Mobile, Alabama, advised that his mother and the mother of LEE HARVEY OSWALD are sisters. He advised he is 31 years of age and is approximately seven years older than OSWALD. He recalled that OSWALD lived with the MURRETT family for approximately one year shortly after OSWALD's father passed away when OSWALD was a very young boy.

MURRETT recalled that OSWALD's mother was a saleslady and that she worked in various clothing and department stores in various cities throughout the United States. He said he recalled OSWALD resided at various times, which times he could not recall, in New Orleans, Louisiana, New York City and Dallas and Fort Worth, Texas, and possibly other places.

MURRETT stated he and OSWALD were never very close because of the difference in their ages and because they never resided together for any length of time, and as a result, he did not know too much concerning OSWALD's background. He recalled that OSWALD completed approximately two years of high school and then enrolled in the U. S. Marine Corps, but he was unable to recall when this occurred. He said the last time he saw OSWALD was when OSWALD visited with the MURRETT family in New Orleans, Louisiana. He said OSWALD was on leave at this time just prior to being shipped overseas. He said this was sometime before 1959 when he entered the Society of Jesus.

MURRETT stated that sometime after 1959 he received information from his parents that OSWALD again visited them in their home in New Orleans. He said he did not recall if OSWALD told his parents he was going to Russia at this time; however, it subsequently developed this was just prior to the time OSWALD left the United States for Russia.

On 11/29/63 at Mobile, Alabama File # MO 89-25

by SA JOHN J. SWEENEY :egp Date dictated 12/1/63

2

COMMISSION EXHIBIT No. 2649—Continued

MURRETT said that sometime in the latter part of 1962 he heard from his family that OSWALD had returned to the United States after being in Russia for some three years. He said his family told him at this time that OSWALD and his Russian wife were then residing in New Orleans, Louisiana. MURRETT said that he then discussed his relationship with OSWALD and OSWALD's trip to Russia with his fellow students and superiors and with his superiors' permission, wrote OSWALD a letter inviting him to come and address the students at the Jesuit Seminary in Mobile. He recalled he addressed the letter to OSWALD at 4907 Magazine Street, New Orleans. He recalled this letter was written to OSWALD about two weeks prior to the time OSWALD actually came to Mobile, which was on July 27, 28 or 29, 1963. He said arrangements were made for OSWALD to travel with the MURRETT family to Mobile to save expenses. MURRETT said OSWALD received no remuneration for his talk at the Jesuit Seminary.

MURRETT said OSWALD spoke to approximately 20 students, who were scholastics studying to be Jesuit Priests, and to two priests at the seminary in Mobile on one of the above evenings in July 1963. He said OSWALD told of his travelling to Russia; however, was unable to recall how OSWALD said he reached there. He said that upon OSWALD's arrival in Moscow OSWALD applied for employment and also for permission to remain in Russia. He said OSWALD was then sent to Minsk where he was assigned to work in a factory doing assembly line type of work. He said he did not recall if OSWALD indicated what this factory manufactured.

MURRETT stated OSWALD further stated that while in Minsk he joined a hunting club and that he made regular week end trips into the country where he stayed overnight in the homes of the peasants. He said that on subsequent questioning by students OSWALD indicated that this hunting club was sponsored by the factory in which he worked. He also stated OSWALD said he met his wife in Minsk at a factory dance and later married her. He said apparently OSWALD and his wife had no difficulty obtaining permission from the Russian authorities for this marriage.

MURRETT recalled OSWALD discussed his living and working conditions, but did not recall exactly what OSWALD said. He said OSWALD mentioned that his work and social life was very closely connected. He advised OSWALD did not mention attending any schools there, but stated that numerous speeches were given by various Russian officials to the workers of the

factory regularly. He said OSWALD indicated he became disillusioned with life in Russia and explained communism was too oppressive to the people there and apparently the people were "dominated by roughnecks." He said he received the impression from OSWALD that it was a type of police state existence without OSWALD actually using those words. MURRETT said further that OSWALD was very vague about his leaving Russia to return to the United States. He said OSWALD mentioned that the Russians apparently had no objection to Mrs. OSWALD leaving, and apparently at the same time the U. S. Government indicated that OSWALD had not legally lost his United States citizenship by renouncing it previously. He said OSWALD evaded the subject of religion and whenever he was asked a question concerning religion OSWALD would pass over it. He said OSWALD definitely left the impression of not believing in God or a Supreme Being and of being an atheist.

MURRETT further stated OSWALD, OSWALD's wife, and the MURRETT family stayed in Mobile only one night on this occasion in July 1963. He said that to the best of his recollection they all stayed at the Palms Motel at the corner of Azalea Road and U. S. Highway 90, west.

MURRETT said the OSWALDS did not appear to be prosperous and OSWALD did not mention where cr if he were employed. He recalled OSWALD was wearing a short-sleeved sports shirt and slacks during this visit.

MURRETT said that after OSWALD left Mobile he wrote to OSWALD at the Magazine Street address in New Orleans. He recalled that during OSWALD's speech OSWALD mentioned he did not approve of speculation or the operations of the stock market inasmuch as he considered it gambling. He also said OSWALD also claimed that the working class was oppressed and no one was concerned with them. MURRETT said that in his letter he pointed out to OSWALD that the Catholic Church was definitely concerned with the welfare of the working people and enclosed a copy of the Encyclical of Pope JOHN XXIII, captioned "Mater Et Magistra." He advised he later received a letter from OSWALD, but OSWALD did not indicate he received this Enclyclical or read it. He said this was the last time he heard from OSWALD. MURRETT said he no longer has the letter in his possession, having destroyed it.

MURRETT said he did not know any of OSWALD's friends or associates and OSWALD never mentioned them to him. He

4
MO 89-25

also recalled OSWALD never mentioned the country of Cuba or any organizations to which he belonged. He said that to the best of his recollection OSWALD never made any revolutionary statements, nor did he appear prone to violence.

FD-302 (Rev. 1-25-60)

FEDERAL BUREAU OF INVESTIGATION

Date 12/1/63

1

Father MALCOLM P. MULLEN, S. J., Professor of Philosophy, Jesuit House of Studies, Spring Hill College, Mobile, Alabama, advised he attended the talk given at the Jesuit Seminary by LEE HARVEY OSWALD during the summer of 1963. He stated this talk was given for the benefit of the scholastics attending Jesuit Seminary. He recalled OSWALD was a cousin of EUGENE MURRETT and said MURRETT was a Jesuit Scholastic there. He said MURRETT arranged to have OSWALD come to the seminary.

MULLEN stated OSWALD apparently went to Russia after having read the works of KARL MARX and deciding he wanted to see how the people actually lived in Russia.

MULLEN said OSWALD claimed that upon his arrival in Moscow he applied for work and was assigned to Minsk where he worked in a factory. He said OSWALD claimed he joined a hunting club while in Minsk and spent week ends hunting. He claimed OSWALD stated he got to know the Russian peasants on these hunting expeditions as he lived in their homes. He said OSWALD further claimed he liked the Russian people very well and said he was treated well by them, even though the "U-2 incident" occurred during this time and was widely publicized there. He said apparently OSWALD became disillusioned after having been there for three to five years and said that the doors of the factories would be locked and the workers would be forced to listen to speeches by Russian authorities. He said OSWALD also complained of "regimentation" and gave the impression that a police state was in existence, although he never actually used that particular term.

He said that OSWALD further complained that the tourists were only shown the collective farms near Moscow and Leningrad, which actually were show places. He said the other farms of Russia were definitely far inferior to those which were shown to visitors.

MULLEN further advised that OSWALD in his speech also indicated he was opposed to speculation and the operation of the

On 11/30/63 at Mobile, Alabama File # M O 89-25

by SA HARRY J. DEGNAN and SA JOHN J. SWEENEY :egp Date dictated 11/30/63

2
MO 89-25

stock market. He said OSWALD considered this to be gambling and advocated the total abolition of the stock exchange. He said he did not recall where OSWALD lived while in Russia, but said it was a beautiful city, however everything was controled by the government.

Father MULLEN said that OSWALD conducted himself very well in giving the speech. He said OSWALD spoke very well and he, at the time, thought he was a college graduate.

He further recalled that whenever the subject of religion came up OSWALD passed it off and would not comment on it. He said he definitely received the impression OSWALD was an atheist.

He further advised he did not recall if OSWALD said what type of work he was presently pursuing. He said OSWALD indicated he was glad to be back in the United States, but said he was not completely happy here. He said, however, OSWALD indicated living in the United States was better than living in Russia.

Father MULLEN advised OSWALD was neatly dressed in sports attire; however, did not give the impression of being prosperous.

He further added he could not recall OSWALD making any statement that could be considered revolutionary and did not receive the impression OSWALD was a violent person by nature.

Father MULLEN advised OSWALD spoke for approximately 30 minutes and he understood he had a question period for approximately another 30 minutes. He said he did not attend this question period and left immediately after the speech.

7

COMMISSION EXHIBIT No. 2649—Continued

FD-302 (Rev. 1-25-60)

FEDERAL BUREAU OF INVESTIGATION

Date 12/1/63

1

Father JOHN F. MOORE, S.J., Professor of Logic and Epistomology, Jesuit House of Studies, Spring Hill College, Mobile, Alabama, advised that during the summer of 1963 he learned LEE HARVEY OSWALD was coming to give a talk to the Jesuit Seminarians there. He advised EUGENE MURRETT, a Jesuit Scholastic, was a first cousin of OSWALD and had invited OSWALD to give a talk concerning his stay for approximately three years in Russia.

Father MOORE stated he attended this talk by OSWALD; however missed the first part of his talk, which evidently included mostly the introductions. He said apparently OSWALD had done a great deal of reading in the United States and had become interested in the writings of KARL MARX. He said OSWALD claimed he then decided to go to Russia to observe the actual living conditions of the Russian people. He said OSWALD claimed he made application to the Russian authorities to permanently stay there and indicated he desired to renounce his United States citizenship. He recalled that OSWALD stated he was sent to Minsk and was assigned to work in some sort of factory there.

Father MOORE said OSWALD also told of belonging to a hunting club in Minsk and said that he went out hunting practically every week end. He further stated he got to know the peasants during these hunting excursions since he slept in their homes.

Father MOORE further informed OSWALD indicated he became dissatisfied in Russia after two or three years and that he felt communism had not helped the peasant people in any way whatsoever. He said OSWALD mentioned returning to the United States; however, did not recall if OSWALD said how he managed to get back to the United States with his wife.

He further recalled that he definitely received the impression OSWALD had no religion and was an atheist. He said OSWALD did not actually say he was an atheist, but

On 11/30/63 at Mobile, Alabama File # MO 89-25

by SA HARRY J. DEGNAN and SA JOHN J. SWEENEY :egp Date dictated 12/1/63

This document contains neither recommendations nor conclusions of the FBI. It is the property of the FBI and is loaned to your agency; it and its contents are not to be distributed outside your agency.

8

COMMISSION EXHIBIT No. 2649—Continued

2
MO 89-25

stated he did not care to discuss anything whatsoever concerning religion.

He estimated the entire speech by OSWALD lasted about 30 minutes and was followed by about 30 minutes of a question period.

Father MOORE advised that OSWALD was not an outstanding speaker, but in his opinion was just fair. He said OSWALD used no notes whatsoever during his talk, but handled himself very well. He said he definitely received the impression OSWALD had at least a college education. He also said OSWALD did not appear to be prosperous, but was casually dressed in sports clothing. He further informed that to the best of his recollection OSWALD made no statements indicating he was in favor of a revolution and he did not receive the impression OSWALD was a violent individual.

FD-302 (Rev. 1-25-60) FEDERAL BUREAU OF INVESTIGATION

Date 12/1/63

1

Mr. ROBERT J. FITZPATRICK, S.J., Scholastic, Jesuit House of Studies, Spring Hill College, Mobile, Alabama, advised he recalled LEE HARVEY OSWALD very well. FITZPATRICK said he was studying the Russian language and learned EUGENE MURRETT, another Jesuit Scholastic, was a cousin of OSWALD and that OSWALD spent three years in Russia. He said that arrangements were then made to have OSWALD speak to a group of the Jesuit Scholastics at the seminary there. He explained that the seminary had invited various speakers to address the Jesuit Scholastics previously and this was in connection with the same series of lectures. He recalled previous speakers had included a Protestant Minister and a Jewish Rabbi. He said it was believed OSWALD would have some information which would be extremely interesting to them.

FITZPATRICK recalled OSWALD, OSWALD's wife, who was named MARINA, and their two year old daughter named JUNE, came to Mobile, Alabama, on Saturday, July 27, 1963. He said that the OSWALDs were accompanied by the parents of EUGENE MURRETT. He also said they were accompanied also by MURRETT's brother and sister and their respective spouses and several children. FITZPATRICK said he did not attend OSWALD's talk, but stayed with the MURRETTs and OSWALD's wife. He further informed that Mrs. MURRETT was very anxious to talk with Mrs. OSWALD without LEE OSWALD being present. He explained Mrs. MURRETT told him she never had the opportunity to communicate at any great length with Mrs. OSWALD inasmuch as OSWALD had to translate for her. He said that as a result of this, he and Mrs. MURRETT and Mrs. OSWALD walked throughout the seminary grounds for approximately an hour.

FITZPATRICK stated that apparently MARINA OSWALD could not speak English except for a few words such as yes and no. He said, however, she appeared to be a very fine woman in his opinion. He said that Mrs. OSWALD told him she had been raised in the Russian Orthodox faith until she was approximately ten years of age, when her relations died. He said Mrs. OSWALD had about the equivalent of what could be considered a high school

On 11/30/63 at Mobile, Alabama File # MO 89-25

by SA HARRY J. DEGNAN and SA JOHN J. SWEENEY: egp Date dictated 12/1/63

education in the United States.

He said Mrs. OSWALD stated she was not a communist and loved Russia and the Russian people. He explained that Mrs. OSWALD's love for Russia was not the same type as that he had heard expressed by Nazis for the German fatherland. He further informed Mrs. OSWALD stated there were many inconveniences in Russia; however, people had no difficulty making a living there. He recalled Mrs. OSWALD stated she had no living relatives in Russia and said she met OSWALD at a factory dance in Minsk and that they were subsequently married.

FITZPATRICK said Mrs. OSWALD told him she liked the United States very much and there appeared to be no conflict with this and her love for Russia. He said she stated she had no opportunity to learn English inasmuch as OSWALD kept her completely away from other people. He said Mrs. OSWALD appeared to be very happy with OSWALD; however, OSWALD was definitely the head of the family. He further informed Mrs. OSWALD indicated her husband did a great deal of reading, but that it appeared scattered and apparently had no direction or planning.

FITZPATRICK stated Mrs. OSWALD only mentioned residing in the city of New Orleans, Louisiana; however, in talking to her he received the impression the OSWALDs had lived in other cities of the United States. He stated Mrs. OSWALD said her husband was presently out of work and they were having a difficult time financially. He said she told him OSWALD is away from home a great deal and she did not know any of his associates or any of his activities. He further recalled that Mrs. OSWALD stated she and her husband had a difficult time getting out of Russia, but she did not explain this remark further.

He said Mrs. OSWALD was very neatly dressed, but her clothes did not appear to be expensive. He said OSWALD, although not shabbily attired, did not appear to know how to wear clothes properly.

FITZPATRICK also recalled that Mrs. MURRETT had him ask Mrs. OSWALD if she would care to go to Mass with her the following morning, which was Sunday. He said Mrs. OSWALD stated she would like to do this very much, but could not because of her husband. He further added that on at least two occasions in his talk with Mrs. OSWALD she said a Russian word which indicated OSWALD was "without God."

FITZPATRICK also recalled Mrs. OSWALD indicated that neither she nor her husband had been to Mobile previously.

FITZPATRICK said he later talked with OSWALD for about 20 minutes after his speech at the Jesuit Seminary. He said this talk with OSWALD was in the presence of Mrs. OSWALD and the MURRETT family and a great deal of it was in the Russian language. He said OSWALD appeared to be a very tense and high-strung person. He said OSWALD never smiled and did not appear to be at all friendly. He recalled OSWALD spoke fairly good Russian; however, it definitely was not as smooth or correct grammatically as Mrs. OSWALD's.

He further stated OSWALD did not mention politics to him and evaded several questions he asked OSWALD as to how he managed to leave Russia with his wife.

FITZPATRICK also stated that he asked Mrs. OSWALD if she would care to correspond with him in Russian and she told him she would be very happy to do so. He said Mrs. OSWALD told him she would answer his letters, and also would correct his writing, and return his letters to him. He said he wrote Mrs. OSWALD a letter in Russian, which he mailed about August 8, 1963, and addressed it to 4907 Magazine Street, New Orelans, Louisiana. He advised he placed his return address on this letter; however, he has never received an answer from Mrs. OSWALD and his letter was never returned to him. FITZPATRICK said that he learned later from EUGENE MURRETT that the OSWALDs had moved from New Orleans about the time he mailed this letter.

He said he last saw OSWALD about noon, Sunday, July 28, 1963, when the OSWALDS and the MURRETT family had stopped by to say goodbye to EUGENE MURRETT before returning to New Orleans. On this occasion he did not have any conversation with either OSWALD or the MURRETT family, but merely waved at them as they drove away from Spring Hill College.

FITZPATRICK said that as soon as he heard OSWALD had been arrested as a suspect in the assassination of President JOHN F. KENNEDY, he immediately contacted several of the Jesuit Scholastics who had attended OSWALD's speech. He said he obtained the impressions of these individuals of OSWALD and some of the remarks OSWALD made during his talk. FITZPATRICK said he immediately typed up a summary of these impressions and then recontacted the same individuals to determine if this summary were correct. FITZPATRICK said he then made several additions and deletions and subsequently typed up a five page summary of OSWALD's speech and several questions which were asked him by those in attendance.

FITZPATRICK made available the following five page summary mentioned above:

"On Saturday, July 27, 1963, a relative of Lee Oswald, a member of the community at the Jesuit House of Studies, asked Mr. Oswald if he would address the scholastics on his experiences in Russia. The request was not unusual, for the scholastics try from time to time to have either prominent persons or others who have something interesting to relate speak to the scholastics on their experiences. Because Mr. Oswald was an American who had gone to live in Russia and who had returned, obviously for a reason, it was thought that he might be able to communicate the nature of the Russian people themselves better than any official reports might. Those who went to listen to him expected to hear a man who had been disillusioned with Soviet communism and had chosen America to it. What they heard was only partially this.

"The major points of Mr. Oswald's address and details from it are given below, probably never in verbatim form, but always true to his intent, at least as he was heard by a number of people.

"He worked in a factory in Minsk. When he applied for permission to live in the Soviet Union, the Russian authorities had assigned him to a fairly well advanced area, the Minsk area. He said that this was a common practice: showing foreigners those places of which Russians can be proudest.

"The factory life impressed him with the care it provided for the workers. Dances, social gatherings, sports were all benefits for the factory workers. Mr. Oswald belonged to a factory-sponsored hunting club. He and a group of workers would go into the farm regions around Minsk for hunting trips. They would spend the night in the outlying villages, and thus he

came to know Russian peasant life too. In general, the peasants were very poor, often close to starvation. When the hunting party was returning to Minsk, it would often leave what it had shot with the village people because of their lack of food. He spoke of having even left the food he had brought with him from town. In connection with the hunting party, he mentioned that they had only shotguns, for pistols and rifles are prohibited by Russian law.

"Some details of village life: in each hut there was a radio speaker, even in huts where there was no running water or electricity. The speaker was attached to a cord that ran back to a common receiver. Thus, the inhabitants of the hut could never change stations or turn off the radio. They had to listen to everything that came through it, day or night. In connection with radios, he said that there was a very large radio-jamming tower that was larger than anything else in Minsk.

"More about the factories: factory meetings were held which all had to attend. Everyone attended willingly and in a good frame of mind. Things came up for discussion and voting, but no one ever voted no. The meetings were, in a sense, formalities. If anyone did not attend, he would lose his job.

"Mr. Oswald said that he had met his wife at a factory social.

"The workers, he said, were not against him because he was an American. When the U-2 incident was announced over the factory radio system, the workers were very angry with the United States, but not with him, even though he was an American.

"He made the point: that he disliked capitalism because its foundation was the exploitation of the poor. He implied, but did not state directly, that he was disappointed in Russia because the full principles of Marxism were not lived up to and the gap between Marxist theory and the Russian practice disillusioned him with Russian communism. He said, 'Capitalism doesn't work, communism doesn't work. In the middle is socialism, and that doesn't work either.'

"After his talk a question and answer period followed. Some questions and his answers:

"Q: How did you come to be interested in Marxism? To go to Russia?

"A: He had studied Marxism, became convinced of it and wanted to see if it had worked for the Russian people.

"Q: What does atheism do to morality? How can you have morality without God?

"A: No matter whether people believe in God or not, they will do what they want to. The Russian people don't need God for morality; they are naturally very moral, honest, faithful in marriage.

"Q: What is the sexual morality in comparison with the United States?

"A: It is better in Russia than in the United States. Its foundation there is the good of the state.

"Q: What impressed you most about Russia? What did you like most?

"A: The care that the state provides for everyone. If a man gets sick, no matter what his status is, how poor he is, the state will take care of him.

"Q: What impresses you most about the United States?

"A: The material prosperity. In Russia it is very hard to buy even a suit or a pair of shoes, and even when you can get them, they are very expensive.

"Q: What do the Russian people think of Khrushchev? Do they like him better than Stalin?

"A: They like Khrushchev much better. He is a working man, a peasant. An example of the kind of things he does: Once at a party broadcast over the radio, he had had a little too much to drink and he began to swear over the radio. That's the kind of thing he does.

"Q: What about religion among the young people in Russia?

"A: Religion is dead among the youth of Russia.

"Q: Why did you return to the United States?(The question was not asked in exactly this way, but this is its content.)

"A: When he saw that Russia was lacking, he wanted to come back to the United States, which is so much better off materially. (He still held the ideals of the Soviets, was still a Marxist, but did not like the widespread lack of material goods that the Russians had to endure.)

"More points that were contained in the main part of the talk:

"He lived in Russia from 1959 to 1962. He only implied that the practice in Russia differed from the theory, never stated it directly. The policy of Russia was important:

"1) After death of Stalin, a peace reaction.

"2) Then an anti-Stalin reaction.

"3) A peace movement, leading up to the Paris conference.

"4) The U-2 incident and its aftermath.

"At the factory he had trouble at first meeting the men. They did not accept him at first. He joined a hunting club. He belonged to two or three discussion groups. He praised the Soviets for rebuilding so much and for concentrating on heavy industry. He said at one point that if the Negroes in the United States knew that it was so good in Russia, they'd want to go there.

"Another question:

"Q: Why don't the Russians see that they are being

7
MO 89-25

indoctrinated and that they are being denied the truth by these jamming stations?

"A: They are convinced that such contact would harm them and would be dangerous. They are convinced that the state is doing them a favor by denying them access to Western radio broadcasts."

17

COMMISSION EXHIBIT No. 2649—Continued

Commission Exhibit No. 2650

Form No. 1587 (Revised)
MEMORANDUM REPORT
(7-1-60)

UNITED STATES SECRET SERVICE
TREASURY DEPARTMENT

ORIGIN Dallas | OFFICE New Orleans, La. | FILE NO. CO-2-34,030

TYPE OF CASE	STATUS	TITLE OR CAPTION
Protective Research	Continued	Lee Harvey Oswald
INVESTIGATION MADE AT: New Orleans, Louisiana	PERIOD COVERED: 11-29-63 12-4-63	Assassination of President John F. Kennedy
INVESTIGATION MADE BY: SA Roger D. Counts		

DETAILS

SYNOPSIS

This report covers investigations made at the branches of the public library at New Orleans. Attached is a list of the books obtained by Lee Harvey Oswald.

DETAILS OF INVESTIGATION

Reference is made to the M/R of SA Steuart, Dallas, dated 11-27-63, in which it was mentioned that Lee Harvey Oswald had among his belongings a New Orleans Public Library card No. 8460, and also to a telephone call from SAIC Bouck to SAIC Rice requesting that inquiries be made to determine if Lee Harvey Oswald had checked out any books pertaining to the U. S. Secret Service.

On 11-29-63 Jerome Cushman, Head Librarian, New Orleans Public Library, was interviewed. Mr. Cushman advised that the library card of Lee Harvey Oswald had been issued by the Napoleon Branch library, 913 Napoleon Avenue, New Orleans, and that the original of this card had been picked up by the FBI along with all available books which had been checked out by Oswald. He further stated that it would be extremely difficult to determine if Oswald had obtained books from the Main Library, as this would require examination of the microfilms of all transactions since Oswald obtained his card. He said that it would also be quite possible that Oswald could have any number of cards issued to him. These cards are filed numerically and, without knowing the exact card number, all cards would have to be checked to determine if this was the case.

On 12-2-63 Geraldine Vaucresson, Librarian, was interviewed by SAIC Rice and the writer at the Napoleon Branch library. She stated that the correct number for the library card issued to Lee Harvey Oswald was N8640 and not 8460. This card had an expiration date of May 27, 1966, indicating that it had been issued on May 27, 1963. Mrs. Vaucresson said that the original card had been given to Mr. Cushman, Head Librarian, who had in turn given it to the FBI. She also said that a number of books which

DISTRIBUTION	COPIES	REPORT MADE BY	DATE
Chief	Orig. & 2 co's	SPECIAL AGENT Roger D. Counts	12-10-63
New Orleans	2 co's	APPROVED John W. Rice 564 SPECIAL AGENT IN CHARGE John W. Rice	12-10-63
Dallas	2 co's		

DEC 10 1963

(CONTINUE ON PLAIN PAPER)

U. S. GOVERNMENT PRINTING OFFICE 16—61300-1

COMMISSION EXHIBIT No. 2650

Oswald had checked out had been turned over to the FBI and that she had not retained a list of these.

On 12-3-63 SA Steve Callender, FBI, was interviewed and a list of the books checked out by Oswald was obtained (see attachment). This consisted of 34 books of which 27 are being held by the FBI. The 7 remaining books are in the possession of private citizens as they were checked out at the time of the investigation by the FBI.

Also on 12-3-63 a call was received from SAIC Bouck requesting that an inquiry be made to determine if Oswald had obtained any of the four books written by the following authors: U. E. Baughman, Harry Neal, Edward Starling, or Michael Reilly. On 12-4-63 a visit was made to the Napoleon Branch library where it was determined that none of the aforementioned books had been checked out by Oswald.

The difficulty in examining the records of the Main Library has been explained above. Of the nine remaining branch libraries, five have a record system similar to the Main Library. As this is the case, no effort will be made to examine these records as well as those of the other four branches unless specifically directed.

UNDEVELOPED LEADS

Investigation continued.

ATTACHMENTS - Chief and Dallas

List of books obtained by Lee Harvey Oswald from New Orleans Public Library.

RDC/mjl

CARD SHOWS RETURN DATE	TITLE	AUTHOR	DATE WOULD HAVE BEEN CHECKED OUT
10/3/63	"Goldfinger"	IAN FLEMING	9/19/63
7/3/63	"Thunderball"	"	6/24/63
10/3/63	"Moonraker"	"	9/19/63
9/5/63	"From Russia With Love"	"	8/22/63
10/3/63	"Ape And Essence"	ALDOUS HUXLEY	9/19/63
10/3/63	"Brave New World"	"	9/19/63
9/5/63	"The Sixth Galaxy Reader"	H. L. GOLD	8/22/63
9/5/63	"Portals of Tomorrow"	AUGUST DERLETH	8/22/63
8/13/63	"Mind Partner"	Edited by H. L. GOLD	7/30/63
8/1/63	"Five Spy Novels"	Selected by HOWARD HAYCRAFT	7/18/63
9/23/63	"Big Book of Science Fiction"	GROFF CONKLIN	9/9/63
7/24/63	"The Hugo Winners"	Edited by ISAAC ASIMOV	7/10/63
8/22/63	"The Worlds of Clifford Simak"	CLIFFORD SIMAK	8/8/63
8/19/63	"The Expert Dreamers"	Edited by FREDERIK POHL	8/5/63
8/14/63	"Nine Tomorrows"	ISAAC ASIMOV	7/31/63
8/26/63	"The Treasury of Science Fiction Classics"	Edited by HAROLD KUEBLER	8/12/63
8/14/63	"Everyday Life in Ancient Rome"	F. R. COWELL	7/31/63

CARD SHOWS RETURN DATE	TITLE	AUTHOR	DATE WOULD HAVE BEEN CHECKED OUT
7/1/63	"Soviet Potentials"	GEORGE B. CRESSEY	6/17/63
7/1/63	"What We Must Know About Communism"	HARRY and BONARO OVERSTREET	6/17/63
7/24/63	"Russia Under Khrushchev"	ALEXANDER WERTH	7/10/63
7/15/63	"Portrait of A President"	~~JOHN F. KENNEDY~~ WILLIAM MANCHESTER	7/1/63
6/15/63	"The Huey Long Murder Case"	HERMANN B. DEUTSCH	6/1/63
6/5/63	"Portrait of A Revolutionary: Mao Tse-Tung"	ROBERT PAYNE	5/22/63
6/15/63	"The Berlin Wall"	DEAN and DAVID HELLER	6/1/63
7/1/63	"This Is My Philosophy"	Edited by WHIT BURNETT	6/17/63
9/23/63	"The Bridge Over the River Kwai"	PIERRE BOULLE	9/9/63
8/13/63	"The Hittite"	NOEL B. GERSON	7/30/63
7/29/63	"The Blue Nile"	ALAN MOOREHEAD	7/15/63
7/20/63	"One Day In The Life of Ivan Denisovich"	ALEXANDER SOLZHENITSYN	7/6/63
9/23/63	"Ben-Hur"	LEWIS WALLACE	9/9/63
7/29/63	"Profiles In Courage"	JOHN F. KENNEDY	7/15/63
7/12/63	"A Fall of Moondust"	A. C. CLARKE	6/28/63
7/20/63	"Hornblower and The Hotspur"	C. S. FORESTER	7/6/63
6/26/63	"Conflict"	ROBERT LECKIE	6/12/63

* * *

The first 27 books are in the possession of the FBI. The remaining 7 are in the possession of private citizens who checked out these books after they were returned by Lee Harvey Oswald.

COMMISSION EXHIBIT No. 2650—Continued

FD-302 (Rev. 3-3-59) FEDERAL BUREAU OF

1

Date 2/25/64

Mrs. LILLIAN BRADSHAW, Director, Dallas Public Library, 1954 Commerce Street, Dallas, Texas, furnished the following information:

A file of membership is not retained by the Dallas Public Library System; therefore, she has no records pertaining to LEE HARVEY OSWALD.

She further advised that the only records maintained by the Library are keyed to delinquencies; therefore, it would not be possible to determine a listing of the books read by OSWALD. In this connection, microfilmed records are maintained on books charged out. It would take a detailed review of over 2,600,000 such microfilmed records in order to establish the identity of the books charged out by OSWALD.

Mrs. BRADSHAW made available two copies of a Dallas Public Library delinquency notice which reflects LEE HARVEY OSWALD, 602 Elsbeth, Dallas, was delinquent on a book entitled, "The Shark and The Sardines", by JUAN JOSE AREVALO. The book was due on November 13, 1963, and, according to Mrs. BRADSHAW, it would have been charged out on November 6, 1963. The delinquency notice was never mailed. According to library records, the book was never returned.

Mrs. BRADSHAW indicated her records contained no other delinquencies for OSWALD.

She made available a copy of the above-described book which was authored by a former President of Guatemala, JUAN JOSE AREVALO, translated from the Spanish by JUNE COBB and Dr. RAUL OSEGUEDA and published by LYLE STUART, 225 Lafayette Street, New York 12, New York.

The Introduction to the American Reader by the Author, in part, reads as follows: "In your hands you hold a controversial book -- a book that speaks out against your

802

on 2/19/64 at Dallas, Texas File # DL 100-10461

by Special Agent RAYMOND P. YELCHAK/ds Date dictated 2/22/64

COMMISSION EXHIBIT No. 2650—Continued

2

DL 100-10461

State Department's dealing with the peoples of Latin America during the Twentieth Century. In it there is intended no insult to, nor offense to, the United States as a nation. The future of your country is identified with the future of contemporary democracy. Neither does this book seek to cast blame on the North American people -- who, like us, are victims of an imperialist policy of promoting business, multiplying markets and hoarding money."

The two copies of the Dallas Public Library delinquency notice are being retained as part of this file, the copy of "The Shark and The Sardines" being returned.

203

COMMISSION EXHIBIT No. 2650—Continued

OFFICE OF THE DIRECTOR

UNITED STATES DEPARTMENT OF JUSTICE

FEDERAL BUREAU OF INVESTIGATION

WASHINGTON 25, D. C.

July 28, 1964

By Courier Service

Honorable J. Lee Rankin
General Counsel
The President's Commission
200 Maryland Avenue, Northeast
Washington, D. C.

Dear Mr. Rankin:

In accordance with arrangements made by Mr. Arlen Specter of your staff, Jack L. Ruby was afforded a polygraph examination at the Dallas County Jail, Dallas, Texas, Saturday, July 18, 1964. The polygraph examination was conducted by Special Agent Bell P. Herndon, FBI Laboratory, Washington, D. C.

It should be pointed out that the polygraph, often referred to as "lie detector" is not in fact such a device. The instrument is designed to record under proper stimuli emotional responses in the form of physiological variations which may indicate and accompany deception. The FBI feels that the polygraph technique is not sufficiently precise to permit absolute judgements of deception or truth without qualifications. The polygraph technique has a number of limitations, one of which relates to the mental fitness and condition of the examinee to be tested.

During the proceedings at Dallas, Texas, on July 18, 1964, Dr. William R. Beavers, a psychiatrist, testified that he would generally describe Jack Ruby as a "psychotic depressive." In view of the serious question raised as to Ruby's mental condition, no significance should be placed on the polygraph examination and it should be considered nonconclusive as the charts cannot be relied upon.

Sincerely yours,

J. Edgar Hoover

COMMISSION EXHIBIT No. 2651